2023 University of Illinois Federal Tax Workbook

Authors & Editors

Kelly Golish
Assistant Director, Tax Materials
University of Illinois at Urbana-Champaign

John Richmann
Tax Materials Specialist
University of Illinois at Urbana-Champaign

Chris Korban
Tax Materials Specialist
University of Illinois at Urbana-Champaign

Production Supervision

Dan Harding
Publications Manager
University of Illinois at Urbana-Champaign

Additional Content Contributors

Georgine Kryda, Colorado
Gina Marsh, Illinois
Roger McEowen, Iowa
Peg Phillips, Illinois
Dwight Roberts, Illinois
Rachel Szeklinski, Wisconsin
Shane Smith, Colorado
Kenneth Wright, Missouri

Chapter Peer Review

Keith Baum, Illinois
Diane Beers, Illinois
Linda Beers, Illinois
Jerard Brune, Illinois
Paul Bumgarner, North Carolina
Jeanne Campion, Illinois
Randy Carlson, Kansas
Fran Coet, Alabama
Curt Davis, Arkansas
Gabrielle Douglas, Illinois
Kyle Gateley, Illinois
Larry Gray, Missouri
Deborah Held, Illinois
Nancy Kukulski, Illinois
Les Marti, Illinois
Mary Olsen, Illinois
Sam Phillips, Illinois
Ronald Powell, North Carolina
Robert Rehkamp, Minnesota
Robert Rhea, Illinois
Catherine Riddick, Illinois
Karen Stevenson, Illinois
Greg Tissier, Illinois
Sue Voth, Illinois
Lori Walden, Illinois
Richard Walden, Illinois
Brenda Williams, Illinois

ILLINOIS

The University of Illinois Tax School is part of the
Department of Agricultural and Consumer Economics in the
College of Agricultural, Consumer and Environmental Sciences.

2023 Federal Tax Workbook

Published by:

University of Illinois Tax School
412 Mumford Hall, MC-710
1301 West Gregory Drive
Urbana, IL 61801

ISBN-13: 978-1-7331272-9-5

Printed in the United States of America.

It should be recognized that tax law continually changes, and includes many issues yet unresolved, awaiting guidance or precedent. The content of this book reflects current law at the time of publication. Corrections are posted on the University of Illinois Tax School website at **taxschool.illinois.edu.**

The IRS website is not considered substantial authority. Any citations thereto are for informational or contextual purposes only. It is up to the individual practitioner to perform due diligence with respect to any arguments before the IRS. See IRM 4.10.7 for more information at **uofi.tax/authority** [www.irs.gov/irm/part4/irm_04-010-007].

Portions of this workbook may have been adapted from previous editions of the *University of Illinois Federal Tax Workbook.*

2023 Tax Seminar Programs

Arkansas
Kim Magee .... Community, Professional and Economic Development, Cooperative Extension Service
University of Arkansas, Little Rock
Division of Agriculture

Florida
Brenda Robinson .... Northwest Florida State College, Niceville

Florida, Illinois, Nevada, New York, North Carolina, Oregon, Pennsylvania, South Carolina, Texas, Washington
Jeremy Rigseby .... GlobalCPE

Alabama, Colorado, Florida, Georgia, Hawaii, Kansas, Louisiana, North Carolina, Ohio, Pennsylvania, South Carolina, Tennessee, Washington, West Virginia
Randall R. Carlson .... Professional Tax Institutes, Inc.

Illinois
Gina Marsh .... Department of Agricultural and Consumer Economics, University of Illinois at Urbana-Champaign

Indiana
Maddie Brumley .... Indiana University Conferences

Kansas
Richard Llewelyn .... K-State Research and Extension, Department of Agricultural Economics, Kansas State University, Manhattan

Maine
Larry LaPlante .... SCORE Maine's Tax Workshop Committee

Missouri
Leslie Colegg .... Missouri Society of CPAs

Montana
Amy Saltzman .... School of Extended & Lifelong Learning
University of Montana, Missoula

North Dakota
Patricia Young .... Office of Extended Learning, University of North Dakota, Grand Forks

Pennsylvania
Robert Henkels, CPA, CGMA .... Professional Tax & Accounting Seminars, Inc.

Tax Workbook Topics from Past 10 Years

Year:	2023	2022	2021	2020	2019	2018	2017	2016	2015	2014
Accountable Plans					19B					
Accounting Methods					19B					14B
Agricultural Issues	23	22A	21A	20A	19A	18A	17A	16A	15A	14A
Amending Returns			21B					16A		
AMT						18A		16A, 16B		
Basis	23	22B			19A		17B	16A	15A	
C Corporations						18B			15B	
Capital Gains and Losses						18A				14C
Capitalization vs. Repair	23							16A	15A	14A
Charitable Contributions			21A	20A		18A				
Child Tax Credit			21A			18A				
Clergy					19B					
Compensation Issues			21B				17A			
Construction Workers	23									
COVID-19 Tax Issues	23		21A, 21B	20A						
Crowdfunding							17B			
Dependency Issues		22A				18A				
Depreciation	23			20A		18B	17B		15B	
Digital Assets/Cryptocurrency	23	22A	21B			18A				
Disaster Relief			21A	20A			17A			
Divorce						18A				
Earned Income Credit			21A							
Easements	23									
Education Provisions/Credits	23				19A				15A	14B
Employee Tax Issues							17A			
Energy Credits	23									
Entity Issues/Comparison			21B			18B				14B
Estate/Gift/Succession Planning	23	22B					17B			
Estimated Taxes	23									
Exempt Organizations		22A								
Fantasy Sports/Gambling							17B			
Fiduciary Tax Issues/Trusts	23		21B	20B				16B	15B	
Filing Status			21B							
Financial Distress; Bankruptcy			21A							
Flexible Spending Arrangement			21A							
Form 1099-K	23									
Form 4797		22B								
Form 7203	23	22A								
Franchises										14B
Gig Economy	23		21B							
Healthcare										14A
Health Reimbursement					19B		17A, 17B		15B	
Hobby Losses			21B	20B						
Home Office	23			20B					15B	
House Flipping		22B								
Household Employees	23						17A			14B
Identity Theft			21B			18A	17A	16A	15B	
In-Home Care Providers		22B								
Independent Contractor	23						17A			
Individual Tax Credits			21B							
Inherited IRAs	23									
Installment Sales							17B			
International Taxation		22A			19B				15B	
Investments/Wealth	23						17A	16B	15B	

xxA = 20xx Vol. A **xxB** = 20xx Vol. B **xxC** = 20xx Vol. C

Year:	2023	2022	2021	2020	2019	2018	2017	2016	2015	2014
IRS Update						18A	17A	16A	15A	
Itemized Deductions						18A				
Like-Kind Exchange					19A, 19B	18B	17B		15B	
Loss Limitation		22A		20B	19A		17B	16A		14B
Marijuana/Hemp					19B				15A	
Marriage										14A
Meals & Entertainment			21A			18B				
Military										14C
NIIT				20B	19A		17B	16A, 16B		14A
NOL/EBL			21A	20A	19B	18A, 18B				14C
Oil & Gas									15A	
Partners/Partnerships/LLCs	23	22B	21B				17B			
Passive Activities				20B						14B
Pass-through Entity Tax	23	22A, 22B								
Premium Tax Credit			21A						15A	14A
QBID			21B		19A, 19B	18A, 18B				
QCD					19A	18A				
Qualified Opportunity Zone				20A	19A					
Railroad Employment									15A	
Real Estate			21A	20B	19B					
Representation Before the IRS			21A							14A
Research & Development Credit	23	22A				18A				
Retirement/Elder Issues	23	22B		20A		18B		16A		14C
Roth IRA	23			20A						
S Corporations		22B			19B			16A, 16B		
Schedule C			21B							
Schedule E				20B						
Schedule H	23									
Schedule K-1		22A			19A					
Schedule K-2/K-3		22A								
Self-Directed IRAs							17B			
Self-Employment Taxes							17B			
Small Business Tax Credits			21B							
Soil Fertility	23									
Student Loan Forgiveness			21A							
Terminating a Business		22B								
Truck Drivers	23								15A	
Trust Taxation			21B	20B			17B	16B	15B	
Unemployment Compensation			21A							
Worker Classification	23									
Written Information Security Plan	23									

xxA = 20xx Vol. A **xxB** = 20xx Vol. B **xxC** = 20xx Vol. C

Chapter 1: Written Information Security Plans and Protecting Client Data

Note. Corrections for all of the chapters are available at **TaxSchool.illinois.edu.** For clarification about terms used throughout this chapter, see the **Acronyms and Abbreviations** section following the index.

For your convenience, in-text website links are also provided as short URLs. Anywhere you see **uofi.tax/xxx**, the link points to the address immediately following in brackets.

About the Author

John W. Richmann, EA, is a Tax Materials Specialist at the University of Illinois Tax School. Prior to joining Tax School in 2021, he owned a tax practice in St. Charles, Illinois, and held positions in private industry and consulting firms. John earned a Masters Degree in Business Administration from the University of Texas and an electrical engineering degree from the Massachusetts Institute of Technology.

Other chapter contributors and reviewers are listed at the front of this book.

INTRODUCTION

The consequences of a client data breach threaten the potential loss of a business, a life's work and calling, and much more. IBM Security estimated that the average total cost of a data breach in 2022 was $4.65 million.[1] This estimate includes notification, responses after the breach occurs, detection and escalation costs including forensic and other investigations, and lost business. The magnitude of these costs is a keen motivator for a tax practice to prepare a written information security plan (WISP).

When it compromises client data, a data breach can fracture client relationships, friendships, and even family relationships. A plan to protect a tax practice's data is, therefore, a plan to protect the network of relationships that constitute the practice.

This chapter focuses on creating a WISP that is useful for managing a tax practice's security. Although the IRS has provided a standard template, the management of each tax practice needs to assess the unique risks it faces. The firm must implement its own WISP to address those risks.

LEGISLATIVE MANDATES

The requirement for tax practitioners to have a WISP originates in the Gramm-Leach-Bliley Act (GLBA). Tax practitioners are considered **financial institutions** under 16 CFR §314.2(h)(2)(viii), which reads,

> *An accountant or other tax preparation service that is in the business of completing income tax returns is a financial institution because tax preparation services is a financial activity listed in 12 CFR 225.28(b)(6)(vi) and referenced in section 4(k)(4)(G) of the Bank Holding Company Act, 12 USC 1843(k)(4)(G).*

Therefore, the Federal Trade Commission (FTC) requires all tax preparation services to have a WISP at all times from the inception of their firms to present.[2] The required elements for a WISP are described in 16 CFR §314.4 and are listed in Appendix B at the end of this chapter.

Because this portion of federal regulations brings tax preparation services under FTC control, tax practitioners are subject to the requirements within the GLBA. Following the GLBA's Safeguards Rule,[3] they must implement safeguards protecting their tax clients' **nonpublic** personal information. A small tax practice has the same obligation to plan its data security as a large money center bank. Large firms commonly have established written plans for dealing with different contingencies. Numerous employees typically assemble these documents, with each employee's work reflecting their responsibilities or their respective departments' responsibilities.

In contrast, a single individual likely fills multiple roles in a small tax practice. Aware of this burden on such businesses, the IRS developed a template for a small-scale WISP, contained in IRS Pub. 5708, *Creating a Written Information Security Plan for your Tax & Accounting Practice*. While this WISP template may be insufficient for larger firms having personnel with more distributed responsibilities, it provides small tax practices with a start for complying with the law.

NEW REGULATIONS

In October 2021, the FTC updated the Safeguards Rule after a 2-year process of proposed rulemaking, public commentary, and evaluation by the FTC's five commissioners.[4] The proposed changes stipulated the inclusion of more detailed information in the information security plans, that tax practices encrypt all customer data, and that they implement controls to prevent unauthorized users from accessing customer information.

---

1. *Cost of a Data Breach Report 2022,* p. 5. Aug. 1, 2022. IBM Security®. [www.ibm.com/downloads/cas/3R8N1DZJ] Accessed on Mar. 24, 2023.
2. 16 CFR §§314.3 and 314.5.
3. 16 CFR §314.
4. *FTC Strengthens Security Safeguards for Consumer Financial Information Following Widespread Data Breaches*. Lincicum, David. Oct. 27, 2021. Federal Trade Commission. [www.ftc.gov/news-events/news/press-releases/2021/10/ftc-strengthens-security-safeguards-consumer-financial-information-following-widespread-data] Accessed on Feb. 15, 2023.

After the GLBA amended requirements, the FTC proposed two additional regulations implementing GLBA amendments that are effective June 9, 2023.[5] These two changes require financial institutions, including tax return preparers, to report to the FTC any data breaches in which the information of at least 1,000 consumers is "reasonably likely" to occur or has occurred. The tax return preparer must report the event to the FTC as soon as possible and no more than **30 days after its discovery.**[6] The preparer report must make the filing on the FTC's website, **www.ftc.gov**, and it must include the following.[7]

- Name and contact information of the reporting financial institution
- Description of the types of information involved in the security event
- Date or date range of the security event, if ascertainable
- General description of the security event

PENALTIES FOR VIOLATING IRC §7216

Unauthorized disclosure of taxpayer information under IRC §7216 carries substantial penalties, including criminal penalties for disclosures by tax return preparers of tax information. Violations of this Code section can trigger penalties of up to **$100,000 plus** prosecution costs. A violation may also result in up to a year of **prison time.** The law attaches severe penalties for the improper disclosure of taxpayer information, providing a solid incentive to protect this information from any threats that could result in its release.

Practitioner Planning Tip

A data breach will be considered a violation of §7216 if a proper WISP was not implemented. It is imperative for even sole practitioners to develop a WISP. Ignoring the requirement to maintain a WISP could be considered willful and reckless, subjecting the practitioner to the fines and penalties mentioned previously.

Note. A proper disclosure includes a formal consent in writing by the party whose data the tax practitioner is disclosing. Although a **§7216 disclosure consent** is normally done with a signature on paper, they may also sign electronically in some circumstances. IRC §7216 stipulates the required language in the consent form and even the minimum size of the type.

5. See 16 CFR §§314.4 and 314.5.

6. 86 Fed. Reg. 70,062 (Dec. 9, 2021).

7. 86 Fed. Reg. 70,062–70,067 (Dec. 9, 2021); *Compliance deadline for certain revised FTC Safeguards Rule provisions extended to June 2023.* Fair, Leslie. Nov. 15, 2022. Federal Trade Commission. [www.ftc.gov/business-guidance/blog/2022/11/compliance-deadline-certain-revised-ftc-safeguards-rule-provisions-extended-june-2023] Accessed on Mar. 21, 2023.

CREATING A WISP[8]

A WISP contains training requirements, evaluations of information systems, how to detect and manage system failures, as well as other items to help protect tax professionals and their clients from their personal information being compromised. The FTC sets and enforces data safeguard regulations for tax practitioners. Tax practitioners who fail to create and enact a WISP may be subjected to an FTC investigation.

A tax practice should adapt its WISP to the company's size, the type of activities in which the company engages, how complex the company is, and the sensitivity of the customer data it maintains. The FTC requires each entity to do the following in its WISP.[9]

- Designate one or more employees to coordinate its information security program
- Identify and assess the risks to customer information in each relevant area of the company's operation, and evaluate the effectiveness of the current safeguards for controlling these risks
- Design and implement a safeguards program, and regularly monitor and test it
- Select service providers that can maintain appropriate safeguards by ensuring that their contract requires them to maintain safeguards and oversee their handling of customer information
- Evaluate and adjust the program considering relevant circumstances, including changes in the firm's business or operations, or the results of security testing and monitoring

> **Note.** Tax practitioners must acknowledge the requirement for data security plans annually when they renew their practitioner tax identification number (PTIN). The tax practitioner cannot renew their PTIN unless they select the checkbox acknowledging their awareness of the need for a data security plan to provide data and system security protections for all taxpayer information.

The IRS intends the WISP to serve three important functions for tax practices.

1. The WISP is a tool to ensure the security and confidentiality of the personally identifiable information (PII) that a tax firm receives.
2. The WISP helps tax practices protect PII against threats to its integrity.[10] Not only does the FTC require financial institutions, including tax practitioners, to plan for the security of the data clients give them, but they must also ensure that its content is not available to unintended persons. In addition, tax practitioners must ensure that the PII is not corrupted while in the custody of the tax practice.
3. The WISP guides the tax practice in protecting PII from access or use that would create a substantial risk of identity theft or some other use that would harm the person identified in the PII.

---

8. IRS Pub. 5708, *Creating a Written Information Security Plan for your Tax & Accounting Practice*; IRS Pub. 4557, *Safeguarding Taxpayer Data.*
9. IRS Pub. 5708, *Creating a Written Information Security Plan for your Tax & Accounting Practice.*
10. *Gramm-Leach-Bliley Act*, PL 106-102, §501(b).

WISP TEMPLATE[11]

IRS Pub. 5708 lays out the requirements for a WISP, and includes a sample template, as well as samples of important attachments to the plan. A WISP should focus on the following.

- Employee management and training
- Information systems
- Detection and management of system failures

The WISP template recommends that tax practices provide each employee a copy and that after examining the WISP, each employee acknowledge their training and understanding of it in writing. The IRS anticipates that some employees may negligently violate either the letter or the spirit of the plan, suggesting that these steps may provide a mechanism for enforcing accountability. This sign-off process is not a "one-and-done" experience. The IRS anticipates that firms conduct this sign-off process regularly as they review and update their WISP. The IRS suggests that tax practitioners store a copy offsite in a physical location or on the Internet.

The IRS suggests that practitioners distribute documents in PDF or Word format for readability, with no mention of a hand-written WISP.

The template identifies the individuals responsible for data security, the risks the firm faces, and the assets the firm owns. A WISP includes the following seven sections.

1. Define the WISP's objectives, purpose, and scope, collectively constituting a preamble for the document
2. Identify responsible individuals
3. Assess risks
4. Inventory hardware
5. Document safety measures in place
6. Draft an implementation clause
7. Attach any ancillary procedures, including a record retention policy, rules of behavior and conduct safeguarding client PII, and security breach policy

The purpose of the WISP is to accomplish the following goals.

- Protect client data from threats to its security
- Maintain the confidentiality of clients' PII
- Secure the PII from any unauthorized access that results in a substantial risk of identity theft, fraudulent use, or harmful use of this data

> **Caution.** There is obvious judgment involved in discerning substantial risk. However, the level at which the tax practitioner sets the bar here could have legal consequences if a data breach occurs and a federal agency finds the practitioner did not comply with their own standards set forth in the WISP.

11. IRS Pub. 5708, *Creating a Written Information Security Plan for your Tax & Accounting Practice.*

Practitioner Planning Tip

It is probably wise to state in the WISP's preamble that its purpose is to fulfill requirements imposed on the firm by the GLBA. It should also state that it sets a standard for evaluating the effectiveness of measures taken to safeguard data held in the firm's custody.

PERSONALLY IDENTIFIABLE INFORMATION

In the WISP template, the objective section identifies five specific types of data elements that become PII when combined with a taxpayer's first name and last name (or first initial and last name). These data elements are classified as follows.

1. Information that fundamentally identifies an individual who is a U.S. person, including their social security number (SSN), date of birth, and employment data
2. State-issued identification information, including driver's license information or other state-issued IDs
3. Income data, data from tax returns, data from retirement plans, data about assets that the taxpayer owns, and data about investments that a tax client owns
4. Information of **item 3** extended one more level by including the following
    a. Account numbers
    b. Credit and debit card numbers, possibly with security codes
    c. Access codes
    d. Personal identification numbers
    e. Passwords associated with a tax client's financial accounts
5. Taxpayer's contact information, such as a phone number and email address

Practitioner Planning Tip

Practitioners may wish to avoid storing specific credit card and debit card data to limit the potential compromise of client information.

What is Not PII

It is also important to recognize which data is not considered PII. It does not include information from public sources, such as the following.

- Mailing address
- Phone directory listing
- Data available from government records lawfully available to the general public

Example 1. As an enrolled agent, Gregory has operated his tax practice as a sole practitioner for many years. About 10 years ago, he started scanning all records that a client brings so that he could reconstruct how he had prepared a tax return if needed.

Two of Gregory's clients, Herb and Wendy, are a married couple with two children under the age of 17. They own their home and are registered to vote in a state that discloses home ownership and sales prices. Gregory scans the following information.

- Drivers' licenses
- Home and cell phone numbers
- Birth certificates of children
- School and medical records for children, establishing their addresses
- Marriage license
- Forms W-2, *Wage and Tax Statement*
- Forms 1099
- Evidence of contributions to §529 accounts for each child

Their income is considered PII, as this information is not available from publicly available sources. The other information in the documents above is also considered PII, with the likely exception of Herb and Wendy's home address, because this information is available from public sources due to their owning their home and being registered voters.

Access to PII

Access to PII should be restricted to people that require access for their direct responsibilities. Within the tax practice, only individuals with responsibility for a particular client should be able to view that client's data. Outside of the tax practice, clients should be able to view their own data but not that of other clients.

Example 2. Stan owns a tax practice in Illinois. On June 15, one of his employees, Stacey, leaves the firm for a better opportunity. Stan's WISP states that employee access to client PII is to be removed immediately upon leaving employment, but Stan forgets to remove Stacey from the document management system until the time of his normally scheduled monthly review on June 25.

One of Stacey's new clients, Chuck, is divorced and races against his ex-wife Mary (a client of Stan) every year to file first to claim their children. On June 20, Stacey logs on to Stan's tax software (to which she still has access), and checks Mary's e-file status. Stacey notices that Mary's return has not yet been filed, so she quickly claims the dependents on Chuck's return and e-files it.

When Stan subsequently goes to file Mary's return, the IRS rejects it. Stan has to track down why it was rejected and discuss alternatives with Mary.

This situation could possibly have been avoided if Stan had followed his own WISP and immediately terminated Stacey's access to the firm's systems when she quit.

Security Management by Group. Providing each employee in a tax practice with their own security and permissions may seem like a lot of work. Indeed, it is, but that is not the only problem. It is easy to leave a security gap when each employee is treated separately, possibly weakening the entire WISP. Fortunately, most secure software streamlines this process by allowing the creation of security groups that can limit user account permissions to those necessary to perform their jobs, but no more.[12]

The tax practice's data security coordinator (explained in detail later) can place employees with similar needs to access PII in their own security group. In turn, the security permissions are set at the group level, giving all group members the same access privileges to data and the same window during which they can log in to the local network. Even in a small practice, management can anticipate the need for at least three security groups.

- Employees, having limited access to PII based on their client responsibilities
- Management, having unlimited access to PII
- Network administrators, having broad access to the functions of the network, but possibly limited access to PII

Example 3. Use the same facts as in **Example 2,** except that Stan's network administrator sets up the following four security groups on the network.

- Office Administration
- Tax Professional
- Management
- Network Administration

The network administrator provides Stan with two logins, one of which is in the management group, which he uses to review tax returns and financial statements. Because Stan has basic network administration skills, the network administrator also gives him a login to the network administration group, which Stan can use to administer the network on an emergency basis if the network administrator is unavailable. Stan's management login is deliberately not given these capabilities, preventing Stan from inadvertently making changes to the network.

On June 18, Stan notices that Stacey's user ID is still enabled, even though she left the firm several days earlier. Stan removes Stacey from the Tax Professional security group and then disables her user ID after verifying that she did not use her user ID to access the system since leaving the firm.

---

12. *Recommended Best Practices for Administrators: Identity and Access Management*, p. 8. Feb. 27, 2023. National Security Agency and Cybersecurity & Infrastructure Security Agency. [media.defense.gov/2023/Mar/21/2003183448/-1/-1/0/ESF IDENTITY AND ACCESS MANAGEMENT RECOMMENDED BEST PRACTICES FOR ADMINISTRATORS PP-23-0248_508C.PDF] Accessed on Mar. 24, 2023.

RESPONSIBLE INDIVIDUALS AND SPECIFIC POLICIES

The WISP template identifies two individuals with specific responsibilities, a data security coordinator and a public information officer.

Data Security Coordinator[13]

The data security coordinator is responsible for the overall implementation of the WISP, ranging from daily operating procedures to periodic training, even requiring third-party service providers to adhere to security measures in the WISP. Perhaps most importantly, the data security coordinator identifies where data is stored.

The IRS suggests the following responsibilities for the data security coordinator.

- Implementing the WISP, including daily operational protocols
- Identifying all data repositories that are subject to the WISP protocols, designating them as secured assets, and ensuring access to this data is restricted
- Verifying that every employee has completed recurring information security training
- Monitoring and testing employee compliance with the WISP's policies and procedures
- Evaluating the ability of third-party service providers to comply with appropriate security measures within the WISP
- Reviewing the scope of the security measures in the WISP at least annually or when a significant change in business practices occurs, particularly if the change potentially affects PII integrity
- Conducting an **annual** training session for all owners, managers, and independent contractors, at which all are required to certify their attendance and their familiarity with the requirements for protecting PII

Public Information Officer

The public information officer is responsible for disseminating information about a data breach to a wide range of outside entities, from law enforcement agencies to clients to news media. The public information officer role becomes prominent if the company's data is compromised. This individual is the firm's designated spokesperson in the event of an adverse event that possibly involves a compromise of PII.

The public information officer oversees the following.

- All client communications, whether by phone conversation or by writing
- All communication with law enforcement agencies

> **Caution.** The tax practice owner may want to consult an attorney for guidance regarding communication with law enforcement agencies.

- All releases to news media
- All information released to business associates, nearby businesses, and trade associations

> **Note.** The role of public information officer is not mentioned in the FTC's amended regulations.[14] The notes following the WISP indicate that the IRS expects that the data security coordinator and the public information officer are separate individuals. However, in many small tax practices, this segregation of duties is not feasible.

---

13. The FTC's regulations refer to the data security coordinator as a "qualified individual." These regulations appear in Appendix B at the end of this chapter.

14. *Standards for Safeguarding Customer Information*. Dec. 9, 2021. Federal Trade Commission. [www.federalregister.gov/documents/2021/12/09/2021-25736/standards-for-safeguarding-customer-information] Accessed on Feb. 15, 2023.

RISK ASSESSMENT[15]

The WISP template contains two sections on risk mitigation. The first covers **inside-the-firm risks**, such as collecting PII and holding employees accountable for complying with the firm's implementation of the WISP. The WISP also covers **outside-the-firm risks.**

INSIDE-THE-FIRM RISKS

The WISP template addresses policies and procedures a tax firm can implement to reduce risks to PII records being compromised from within the firm.

Record Retention Policy

A **record retention policy** documents a tax practice's policy covering how long the firm should retain client records before destroying them. The longer a tax practice retains PII, the greater the risk of that data being compromised. Documents should be expunged upon reaching the end of their retention period. To expunge paper documents, the firm can either shred them or return them to the taxpayers who provided them. Electronic documents can be "electronically shredded" (a more permanent and secure form of destruction than simple file deletion).

Caution. Document destruction practices have legal consequences that may sometimes require a tax professional to consult with their legal counsel.

Note. Deleting paper documents can be time-consuming. A tax practice's staff can readily delete electronic data, provided operators can see its expiration, or its document management system can delete it automatically.[16] Some document management systems enable operators to set lifetimes for a particular document type.[17]

Example 4. Joseph owns a small tax practice that employs a few seasonal tax preparers and a year-round office manager. He distributes his firm's record retention policy with the annual engagement letter and organizer in early January.

Following the firm's record retention policy, the office manager ensures that the scanned documents in the document management system are labeled with an expiration date seven years after the due date of each year's returns. Consequently, they can delete or destroy information used to prepare 2021 tax returns after April 18, 2029. Their tax practice likely filed these individual returns on or before April 18, 2022.

---

15. IRS Pub. 5708, *Creating a Written Information Security Plan for your Tax & Accounting Practice.*

16. *How to delete old documents from a site using retention policies.* Zelfond, Gregory. Aug. 25, 2020. Sharepoint Maven. [sharepointmaven.com/how-to-delete-old-documents-from-a-site-using-retention-policies/] Accessed on Feb. 15, 2023.

17. *IBM Content Manager, Version 8.5.0.3.* 2015. IBM Corporation. [www.ibm.com/docs/ko/content-manager/8.5.0?topic=policies-retention-expiration] Accessed on Feb. 15, 2023.

Example 5. Patrick owns a tax practice, employing only Kennedy, a seasonal office manager, during tax season. Kennedy has worked for Patrick for five years, starting when the digital document management system was implemented. The firm has a written policy of retaining documents for five years, and some documents that Kennedy scanned when first working for Patrick have reached expiration. She receives alerts to destroy those documents electronically.

While giving the documents one last review, Kennedy notices that some expired paper documents pertain to pending litigation. Kennedy alerts Patrick to the significance of the expired documents. He contacts the firm's attorney, who instructs Patrick to retain the documents because of the likelihood of a court order pertaining to them.

Caution. Keeping client information longer than required can create a legal problem if a client's information is used to incriminate them. An exception to this point may be a practitioner's permanent files for each client.

PII Disclosure Policy

The **PII disclosure policy** imposes several important restrictions on a tax practice's maintenance of client PII. According to the WISP template, nonemployees may not be present in an office area where client information is physically stored unless an employee accompanies them. As one example, this provision has the practical effect of requiring an employee to be present when the midnight cleaning crew does its work.

Practitioner Planning Tip

To satisfy the requirement that visitors are never unattended, tax practitioners employing an outside cleaning service may consider reviewing the contract with the cleaning service for the hours the service works to ensure that an employee can monitor them.

PII should not be present on an employee's desk when the employee is not working. The WISP template addresses this by stipulating that "employees are trained to keep all paper and electronic records containing PII securely on premises at all times." The tax practitioner preparing the WISP may decide to make this more explicit.

Employees working remotely check out the records containing PII, which may be stored on "solid state drives, and removable or swappable drives, and USB storage media." Only the minimum data necessary for remote work should be removed from the business premises. This is a challenging requirement in the new era of remote work. A tax practitioner often accesses client data through the public Internet, probably through a cloud-based document management application. The PII disclosure policy in the WISP template stipulates that no media, either paper or electronic, should be present in an unattended car, in a home, or in some other location that may not be secure.

Practitioner Planning Tip

Practitioners may consider changing the language from the template to allow an employee who is driving a long distance with client information to stop at a rest area to stretch their legs. Driving a long distance without a break is unreasonable if the reason for denying a break is the presence of PII in the employee's vehicle.

The template provides for sharing information with outside tax authorities and other tax and legal advisors who may assist the tax practice in the normal course of work. It acknowledges that information technology (IT) firms may occasionally see PII while performing their work. It also permits sharing of PII with the following outside entities who encounter PII in the normal course of business.

- IT support firms
- Tax software vendors
- Bookkeeping services
- Payroll services
- CPA/EA firms
- Legal counsel
- Business advisors
- Law enforcement agencies
- Other governmental agencies

The WISP limits the permitted disclosure of information to the minimum necessary to meet the business need. These individuals must comply with the standards of the WISP, at the very least. Although the WISP template provides exclusions from this requirement for tax software vendors and governmental agencies, it does so with the expectation that they comply with even stricter regulations.

The PII disclosure policy includes document safety measures that seek to secure PII pertaining to the tax practice's clients, employees, and contractors. The policy describes principles for data collection and retention, such as the following.

- Making sure that the person to whom PII is being disclosed is really the person intended by the client
- Restricting access to places where PII is stored
- Reviewing the security measures contained in the WISP

The policy also requires the tax practice's managers to define the minimum amount of PII it requires and identify who in the practice should have access to it. Thus, a tension exists between minimizing data collection to minimize data risks, even while the IRS periodically enlarges due diligence requirements, which necessarily increases the volume of data required.

The first item of business for a tax practitioner whose client has asked them to disclose their PII to a third party is to verify the third party's identity.

Example 6. While refinancing his principal residence, Mark asks his tax practitioner, George, to send Mark's mortgage broker a copy of his last two tax returns. George sends Mark a §7216 disclosure consent, which Mark promptly signs and returns. George also asks Mark to verify that he is providing the information to the correct party.

Mark provides George with the broker's work phone number and email address. Soon George's receptionist receives a phone call from an individual claiming to be a mortgage broker working with Mark. George does not accept the call. Instead, George calls the number Mark provided to ensure that he speaks with the correct person. Before calling, George performs an Internet search to verify the phone number Mark provided is associated with the broker. George then calls the mortgage broker, speaks directly with the individual whose name Mark provided, and sets up a means to securely provide the tax returns.

Personnel Accountability Policy

Without compelling the activities of individuals, a WISP would be without consequences and, therefore, without effect. The **personnel accountability policy** requires individual employees and contractors to acknowledge receipt of the WISP and their ongoing compliance with it. Not only are all employees required to be trained on the WISP, but they are also subject to periodic reviews by the data security coordinator to verify their compliance. The WISP template encourages employees to report security risks:

- To the data security coordinator, or
- To the firm's principals or owners if the data security coordinator is the source of the security risk.

The tax practice is responsible for the following.

- Creating general rules of behavior and conduct regarding the security of PII
- Screening of procedures before granting existing employees access to PII
- Conducting background checks on new employees

Additionally, the firm should consider requiring employees who have PII access to execute nondisclosure agreements. This policy ensures employees know their responsibilities to secure PII by applying the following.

- Removing files containing PII from their desks when they are not present at the desk and requiring the electronic storage of PII to be either secured by password or encryption, if not both ("clear desk policy")
- Locking computers when employees are not present at their desks ("clear screen policy")
- Removing paper files and other PII sources to locked storage, either in a file cabinet or their locked desks

As noted previously, tax practitioners must encrypt all customer data per the Safeguards Rule. The requirement to encrypt data can be waived if a qualified individual, presumably the tax practice's data security coordinator, permits an "alternative means to protect customer information."[18] With a notice dated November 15, 2022, the FTC announced the delayed effectiveness of this rule until June 9, 2023.[19] This notice cited a "reported shortage of qualified personnel" capable of implementing the security upgrades required by the new rule. FTC Commissioner Wilson stated her agreement with the delay. Still, her opinion is that the requirements impose "new onerous, misguided, and complex obligations" with neither a significant reduction in data security risks nor consumer benefits.[20]

---

18. 86 Fed. Reg. 70,286.

19. *Compliance deadline for certain revised FTC Safeguards Rule provisions extended to June 2023.* Fair, Lesley. Nov. 15, 2022. Federal Trade Commission. [www.ftc.gov/business-guidance/blog/2022/11/compliance-deadline-certain-revised-ftc-safeguards-rule-provisions-extended-june-2023] Accessed on Nov. 17, 2022; *Standards for Safeguarding Customer Information.* Nov. 18, 2022. Federal Trade Commission. [www.ftc.gov/system/files/ftc_gov/pdf/Final-Effective-Date-Notice.pdf] Accessed on Nov. 18, 2022.

20. *Concurring Statement of Commissioner Christine S. Wilson.* Wilson, Christine S. Nov. 14, 2022. Federal Trade Commission. [www.ftc.gov/system/files/ftc_gov/pdf/Concurring Statement of Commissioner Wilson SG Rule.pdf] Accessed on Nov. 18, 2022.

The personnel accountability policy provides for discipline or termination of employees who deliberately disclose PII to unauthorized parties. It also requires the revocation of computer system access when employees terminate, either willfully or otherwise. This requirement includes the termination of externally hosted computer systems in the cloud and voicemail, which may require significant time if there are many disconnected systems. They must also surrender their keys, badges, and other means of physical access to the tax practice's office.

Security. The data security coordinator must maintain lists of all lock combinations, passwords, and keys. The WISP may restrict the data security coordinator to only having custody of passwords required to manage the network. The data security coordinator should not possess passwords that individual employees use, which would be a security breach because employees should not share their passwords with anyone.

A WISP should specify that file cabinets be locked when not actively used. This protects against any unplanned visits from persons not on tax practice staff.

Note. This policy may lead to an office **closing procedure** to ensure that PII is secure and the office itself is physically secure each time tax practice personnel vacate it. A closing procedure is a systematic means of ensuring that file cabinets and computers are locked, as well as the office's external doors. This procedure could take the form of a daily checklist.

Note. The password requirement effectively mandates that the data security coordinator use a password manager. An analysis and comparison of various password managers is beyond the scope of this chapter. More information about password managers, including reviews of features, is available on various tech websites.

Example 7. Thad owns a tax practice and rents an office on the second floor of an office building. Thad's office has several file cabinets containing clients' PII, and the office closing procedure includes verification that all file cabinets are locked.

Thad is at home on a hot Sunday afternoon in July, enjoying a televised baseball game. He is interrupted by a message from his office landlord, who occupies a first-floor office in the same building. Already an hour old, the message informs Thad that water is leaking into the landlord's office from Thad's office above it. Because structural damage to the building is a possible result, the message states that the landlord must immediately enter Thad's office to determine the source of the leak.

As Thad listens to the message, he receives a phone call from the landlord, who wants to discuss condensation from the air conditioning that cannot drain. The condensation has formed a pool of water in Thad's office. Because the last person to leave Thad's office locked the file cabinets as they left, Thad did not have to disclose the breach to clients or to regulatory authorities.

Reportable Event Policy

The purpose of the **reportable event policy** is to establish a communication plan for the tax practice's response to adverse data security events. Before any event happens, this policy recommends the data security coordinator maintains all prudent and necessary insurance and legal counsel on retainer for the firm, including the following.

- Data theft insurance
- Cyber theft insurance riders
- Retention of legal counsel

The reportable event policy requires the data security coordinator to review any security incident and analyze the nature of the event and the firm's response to it. As a result of the review, the firm must record any changes to its WISP.

IRS protocols require the tax practice to notify the following agencies following a data breach.

- IRS stakeholder liaison
- State law enforcement authorities
- Local law enforcement authorities

Although the WISP template explicitly charges the data security coordinator with this responsibility in the reportable event policy, this activity aligns with the responsibilities delegated to the firm's public information officer.

The notes following the WISP template state the need for the tax practice to construct an inventory of all data containing PII. This inventory might include the following devices.

- Computers
- Servers
- Network devices
- Cell phones
- Printers, scanners, and copy machines
- Modems
- Routers

As shown in Appendix A at the end of this chapter, Attachment E to the WISP template provides a 5-column spreadsheet for a tax practitioner to maintain inventory information, including hardware item, location, principal user, in-service date, and when last inventoried.

Cyber Insurance.[21] The FTC recommends cyber insurance coverage that protects against the following threats.

- Data breaches (e.g., incidents involving theft of personal information)
- Cyberattacks on tax practice data held by third parties, including vendors
- Cyberattacks on the tax practice's network
- Cyberattacks occurring anywhere in the world, not just in the United States
- Terrorist acts

Additionally, tax practitioners should consider the following policy endorsements or features.

- Defending the tax practice in a lawsuit or regulatory investigation
- Umbrella coverage
- Provision of a 24/7 breach hotline

---

21. *Cybersecurity for Small Business*. Federal Trade Commission. [www.ftc.gov/system/files/attachments/cybersecurity-small-business/cybersecuirty_sb_factsheets_all.pdf] Accessed on Nov. 10, 2022.

First-party coverage should provide the following.

- Legal counsel to determine tax practice notification and regulatory obligations
- Customer notification and call center services
- Crisis management and public relations
- Forensic investigation services
- Recovery and replacement of lost or stolen data
- Business interruption coverage
- Cyber extortion and fraud coverage
- Coverage for fees, fines, and penalties related to the security breach

Third-party coverage protects a tax practitioner against claims by a third party following a data breach. The coverage typically protects against the following.

- Payments to customers suffering loss
- Claims and settlement expenses relating to disputes
- Losses related to defamation and intellectual property infringement
- Litigation costs
- Costs for responding to regulatory inquiries
- Accounting costs
- Other settlements, damages, and judgments

OUTSIDE-THE-FIRM RISKS

The IRS addresses risks from external sources to PII by recommending a variety of policies and procedures.

Network Protection Policy

A network protection policy incorporates six levels of security that collectively protect the tax practice's network from external threats.

1. Firewall protection, operating system security patches, and all software products should be patched and up to date on any computer accessing the firm's network.
2. System security software, such as antivirus and Internet security software, should be patched with up-to-date modifications and installed on any computer accessing the firm's network.
3. User authentication protocols should require two-factor authentication (2FA), and strong, complex passwords that are changed at least every 90 days. Tax-practice passwords should not be the same as personal passwords.
4. The WISP template requires continuous monitoring of computer systems, enabling prompt detection of unauthorized access to PII data. This activity requires **event logging** on all computers attached to the network. Event logging is a method that computer operating systems use to record everything that takes place on a computer. This record enables system administrators to track events that may have led to a security breach or a system failure.[22]

---

22. See *Spotting the Adversary with Windows Event Log Monitoring*. Feb. 28, 2013. National Security Agency/Central Security Service. [cryptome.org/2014/01/nsa-windows-event.pdf] Accessed on Mar. 23, 2023; See also *Event Log*. Rouse, Margaret. May 11, 2015. Techopedia Inc. [www.techopedia.com/definition/25410/event-log-networking] Accessed on Mar. 22, 2023.

5. A tax practice's firewall should "be secured and maintained by the practice's IT services provider" and updated as the vendor indicates. As a practical matter, this rules out consumer router/firewall products commonly available at retail stores. This element mandates the implementation of a firewall on each computer, typically a software-based one.
6. The WISP template requires continuous review and installation of operating system patches. Additionally, the data security coordinator should "conduct a top-down security review at least every 30 days."

Note. In terms of employee time, conducting a complete security review every 30 days is a costly requirement for a small tax practice to implement, especially during tax season.

Practitioner Planning Tip

A tax practice should consider adding to its network protection policy a requirement that all removable storage devices, such as USB drives, be tested for viruses or malware on a computer that is **not** connected to the tax practice's network and has updated antivirus software.

User Access Control Policy

This policy requires user passwords to be changed no less frequently than every 90 days. Additionally, users must have unique passwords and not share passwords or accounts on any computer system, Internet access, or product downloads.

Electronic Exchange of PII Policy

The policy for exchanging PII with outside parties requires that a tax practice not send data by an unsecured medium, such as an unencrypted text message. Some email systems can safely send PII because they use **symmetric encryption.** This method requires the sender and receiver to exchange a password, which they must share through a different medium, such as a phone call or a text message. Banks often use an asymmetric encryption method to send PII through email. **Asymmetric encryption** does not require the parties to exchange a password. Instead, they exchange information using pairs of related digital keys.[23]

While email has greatly facilitated convenient communication between businesses and their customers, it has not been great at facilitating **secure** communication. Secure communication generally requires the exchange of certificates or digital IDs between parties without the use of email. A **digital certificate** authenticates the sender of a message and can be used to encrypt communication between the two parties.[24]

Note. Tax practices may wish to perform a web search for "secure email services" to find services that facilitate the exchange of certificates in providing secure email communication. These services are likely to still require the use of a password known to both parties. Because some of these services are located in other countries, tax practitioners should understand the issues arising from storing data in a country other than the United States, as well as the privacy laws in that country.

---

23. *Public-key cryptography*. Feb. 25, 2023. Wikipedia. [en.wikipedia.org/wiki/Public-key_cryptography] Accessed on Feb. 27, 2023.

24. *Digital Certificate.* Shacklett, Mary and Loshin, Peter. Sep. 2021. TechTarget.com. [www.techtarget.com/searchsecurity/definition/digital-certificate] Accessed on Apr. 12, 2023.

Practitioner Planning Tip

A firm's WISP should grant the tax practice permission to share PII with external firms when necessary to complete tax returns. The disclosures must be done in compliance with Circular 230 and other laws and regulations. This includes court-ordered demands to disclose information.[25]

Secure Portals.[26] A tax practice should communicate a preference for exchanging PII through a secure portal with clients. With a portal, electronic documents are uploaded to a secure storage facility online rather than sent directly through email. Because portals can readily have hefty security, often with 2FA, tax practices can have increased confidence that PII exchanged through this mechanism is secure. Tax practice management should consider a secure portal as a trusted network and protect it with its firewall.

Practitioner Planning Tip

Tax practitioners should consider selecting a portal that integrates with the firm's phones, emails, website, etc.[27] This makes it easier for clients to upload a variety of documents to the secure portal. Additionally, the portal should be integrated with the firm's document management system.

Additional features to consider are cloud-based portals, mobile applications, ability to pay invoices through the portal, custom website address to conform to the firm's brand, and support for multiple and/or large files. Most importantly, the portal should have robust security and encryption.

USB Drives.[28] Although less common than a few years ago, taxpayers may provide data to their tax practitioners on USB drives. While this is a convenient way of exchanging information at an in-person meeting, it is not necessarily secure.

There is a risk of infecting the tax practice's network system, but another risk is present with this exchange of information. A USB drive can hold a large amount of PII. For example, an employee of the tax practice may take home the USB drive to work on a tax return but stops at the grocery store where they lose the USB drive. In this unfortunate circumstance, the tax practice should assume it has disclosed all unencrypted PII on the USB drive. The WISP template requires all USB drives containing PII to have some form of encryption.

---

25. IRC §6103(i).

26. *Protecting Federal Tax Information (FTI) in Web Portals.* Apr. 5, 2023. IRS. [www.irs.gov/privacy-disclosure/protecting-federal-tax-information-fti-in-web-portals] Accessed on Apr. 6, 2023; *Client Portals: A Secure Alternative to E-Mail.* Defelice, Alexandra. Feb. 2020. Journal of Accountancy. [www.journalofaccountancy.com/issues/2010/feb/20092359.html] Accessed on Mar. 22, 2023.

27. *2021 Reviews of Client Portals for Accounting Firms.* Wagner, Garrett, CPA. Feb. 22, 2021. CPA PracticeAdvisor. [www.cpapracticeadvisor.com/2021/02/22/2021-reviews-of-client-portals-for-accounting-firms/40620/] Accessed on Mar. 10, 2023.

28. *Using Caution with USB Drives.* Feb. 1, 2021. Cybersecurity & Infrastructure Security Agency. [www.cisa.gov/news-events/news/using-caution-usb-drives] Accessed on Mar. 22, 2023; *The Risks of Using Portable Devices*, p. 1. Walters, Pennie. 2012. Cybersecurity & Infrastructure Security Agency. [www.cisa.gov/sites/default/files/publications/RisksOfPortableDevices.pdf] Accessed on Mar. 22, 2023.

Wi-Fi Access Policy

The WISP template requires strong encryption on the firm's internal Wi-Fi network. If the firm provides Wi-Fi to guests, they must connect to an entirely separate network. This separation prevents guests from intercepting information on a firm's internal work network.

The policy acknowledges that the tax practice may have devices with wireless network interfaces. These networks commonly connect printers but might also include refrigerators or fax machines. The policy asserts the responsibility of the tax practice to change factory passwords to passwords that the firm assigns.

> **Note.** While changing the factory password may be good practice for protecting the appliance, it does not necessarily protect the tax practice. Tax practices may decide that connecting specific devices is not worth the security risk they present.

Remote Access Policy

The WISP template requires remote access software to encrypt Internet traffic between the remote user and the office and provide 2FA. The WISP template cautions that, "Remote access is dangerous if not configured correctly and is the preferred tool of many hackers."

Despite remote access becoming an industry standard, this is a reasonable warning for even small tax practices to heed. If they do not carefully implement remote access policies, they make their own and their clients' data vulnerable to hostile actors.

> *Organizations should carefully consider the balance between the benefits of providing remote access to additional resources and the potential impact of a compromise of those resources. Organizations should ensure that any internal resources they choose to make available through remote access are hardened appropriately against external threats and that access to resources is limited to the minimum necessary through firewalling and other access control mechanisms.*[29]

Additionally, the remote access policy should include a "no after-business-hours remote access policy." Hackers often capitalize on the network not being monitored by employees during the off-hours to hack the local network.

> **Example 8.** Based on input from his cyber insurance provider, Frank restricts the hours that all staff other than he can log into the firm's computer network. The administrator sets up a schedule that allows all employees to log in to the network between 7:30 AM and 7:00 PM from January 15 until April 1 and from 7:30 AM until 10:00 PM from April 2 until April 18. Frank is permitted to log in at all hours throughout the year.

> **Note.** If a tax practice permits remote work, it may consider providing employees with company-owned computers to ensure they have appropriate security software.[30] These devices should have a secure virtual private network (VPN), antivirus, and other security software installed to protect the computers and the practice's network. Because employees may use mobile devices in less-controlled environments, the practice may consider a special agreement for employees to whom mobile equipment is assigned. These agreements could include the following employee requirements to prevent data theft.
>
> - Prevent use by nonemployees
> - Lock the device when not using it
> - Report loss immediately if the device is misplaced or stolen

29. *Guide to Enterprise Telework, Remote Access, and Bring Your Own Device (BYOD) Security*, p. 4. Souppaya, Murugiah and Scarfone, Karen. Jul. 2016. National Institute of Standards and Technology. [nvlpubs.nist.gov/nistpubs/specialpublications/nist.sp.800-46r2.pdf] Accessed on Mar. 23, 2023.

30. IRS Pub. 4557, *Safeguarding Taxpayer Data,* p. 7 (2021).

Remote Access Options.[31] Tax practice owners and managers can choose from multiple remote access options. **Remote desktop protocol** (RDP) allows a remote user to take over a physical computer in the office of the tax practice.

Because RDP effectively takes over one of the computers on the network, employees in the office can generally observe actions that the remote user is taking. It permits remote employee access to applications that may only be authorized to run on the computer which they have set up for remote access. This access also makes the WISP requirement to restrict remote login hours more reasonable. RDP services generally encrypt traffic, but a tax practice should vary the existence and strength of any encryption used. However, there is a risk with RDP that the wrong employees observe the legitimate actions of an authorized remote user.

An alternative to RDP is to set up **VPN access** to the tax practice's network. This allows the remote computer to function as a computer on the local network, although it may be thousands of miles away. Persons working in the office may not be able to directly monitor remote activity by looking at a computer on a desk. The VPN encryption allows the remote user to access the tax practice's private network through the public Internet. Once connected, it accesses the tax practice's network through a VPN server, which is a gate to restrict traffic and only allows permitted users access to the network. Organizations implementing a VPN have additional factors to consider, such as the following.[32]

- Employees working remotely may receive a greater number of phishing emails.
- If the tax practice does not use 2FA, it is more vulnerable to phishing attacks.
- VPNs are more likely to be used around the clock, making it more difficult to apply security updates, perhaps increasing the likelihood they will not be installed.

A VPN can protect remote computers, even though it adds a level of complexity to the management of the computer. A VPN protects remote computers by encrypting information the user transmits over the Internet and also by disguising the user's location.[33] Thus, if employees use their company computer outside the office but do not need to access the employer's network, they may still wish to use a VPN connection to access the Internet to protect themselves from hostile parties.

Note. This discussion only introduces the importance of including remote access policies in a WISP, not to advise the implementation of a specific remote access mechanism. The leadership of a tax practice should consult a knowledgeable IT services firm with demonstrable experience implementing remote access for advice specific to their requirements. They may wish to review Internet articles from both remote desktop protocol providers and VPN providers, as well as other alternatives for securing remote network access.

Example 9. Cindy is a CPA who often works remotely from her home for a small tax practice. On March 25, she goes to a local coffee house to meet a friend but arrives an hour early to finish some work. After accessing the coffeehouse's network, she immediately connects to her employer's VPN to encrypt all traffic. This precaution complies with the company's remote access policy, which requires using a secure VPN while working remotely, either from home or on a public network. By using the company-supplied VPN, Cindy complies with the requirement in the WISP template to use remote access only with encryption.

Caution. Coffee shops often have unsecured public Wi-Fi networks, but they are also present in airports, hotels, restaurants, and many other public accommodations.

---

31. VPN *vs. RDP: what's the difference?* Markuson, Daniel. Jun. 11, 2022. Nord VPN. [nordvpn.com/blog/vpn-vs-rdp/] Accessed on Nov. 14, 2022.

32. *Enterprise VPN Security*. Apr. 15, 2020. Cybersecurity & Infrastructure Security Agency. [www.cisa.gov/news-events/cybersecurity-advisories/aa20-073a] Accessed on Mar. 23, 2023.

33. *A VPN can protect your online privacy. But there's a catch.* Hautala, Laura. Mar. 29, 2019. CNET. [www.cnet.com/tech/services-and-software/vpn-protect-online-privacy-its-complicated] Accessed on Apr. 6, 2023.

Even mobile device charging stations can be insecure if a user connects their equipment in a manner that allows data connectivity in addition to power charging. Hostile actors may place charging stations in airports that permit them to grab data from connected phones. This practice is sometimes known as "juice-jacking."[34] While traveling, it is recommended to use "power-only USB cables" that do not transfer data, or plug the phone's charger into a dedicated AC power outlet (if available) rather than a charging station. There are also USB data blockers that prevent the exchange of data.[35]

Example 10. Lucy, CPA, takes a vacation on April 20, closing out a tumultuous tax season. Without charging her phone, Lucy leaves for the airport, confident she can find a public charger. She plugs her phone into a public charging station in the airport terminal. The plane bound for Florida arrives late, allowing the phone to charge for two hours.

Unknown to Lucy, the plug not only fills her phone's battery but also installs malware, compromising client information that she had not removed following tax season. Lucy must file a claim with her insurance company on a $300,000 cybersecurity loss.

Example 11. A large national pipeline company, Colonial Pipeline, implemented a VPN after already establishing a complex password policy.[36] However, a group of cybercriminals found an employee's unencrypted password on the server, giving them access to the network through a VPN connection. The company had not implemented 2FA on the specific application. Before 5:55 AM one morning, an employee found a $5 million ransom note. By 6:10 that morning, the company had shut down its entire pipeline system, stretching 5,500 miles, thereby threatening fuel to millions of Americans.

Note. These examples make it clear that a WISP should include provisions for protecting data with a 2FA, a VPN or remote data connection, and even an inexpensive data blocker. Although implementing these tools requires some preparation and expense, they are essential in protecting a company's data. In adopting the WISP template to their practices, the tax practice may wish to consider the costs and benefits of protecting their company's systems.

Caution. Although using a VPN in the United States is legal, some countries, such as the People's Republic of China, prohibit their use.[37] For this reason, a tax practitioner traveling in China, even for vacation, may wish to leave at home all electronic equipment that could be used to connect to any network.[38]

Connected Devices Policy

The WISP template requires all new devices to undergo a thorough security review before connecting to the tax practice's network. This thorough review should check for security patches and password protocols.

---

34. *Do you need a USB data blocker? You do if you use public USB charging stations.* Betts, Anne. Dec. 6, 2021. Packing Light Travel. [packinglighttravel.com/travel-tech/do-you-need-a-usb-data-blocker/] Accessed on Nov. 14, 2022.

35. *How to Safely Use Airport Charging Stations*. Wilton, Thomas James. Oct. 27, 2022. Lifewire: Tech for Humans. [www.lifewire.com/safely-use-airport-charging-stations-4690583] Accessed on Nov. 3, 2022.

36. *Colonial Pipeline paid $5 million ransom one day after cyberattack, CEO tells Senate*. Wilkie, Christina. Jun. 9, 2021. CNBC. [www.cnbc.com/2021/06/08/colonial-pipeline-ceo-testifies-on-first-hours-of-ransomware-attack.html] Accessed on Nov. 14, 2022; *One password allowed hackers to disrupt Colonial Pipeline, CEO tells senators*. Kelly, Stephanie and Resnick, Jessica. Jun. 8, 2021. Reuters. [www.reuters.com/business/colonial-pipeline-ceo-tells-senate-cyber-defenses-were-compromised-ahead-hack-2021-06-08/] Accessed on Nov. 14, 2022.

37. *Is Using a VPN Legal?* Vigderman, Aliza and Turner, Gabe. Nov. 14, 2022. Security.org. [www.security.org/vpn/legality/] Accessed on Dec. 6, 2022.

38. *Bring a burner to the Olympics, and other mobile device travel safety tips*. Vigliarolo, Brandon. Feb. 3, 2022. Tech Republic. [www.techrepublic.com/article/bring-a-burner-to-the-olympics-and-other-mobile-device-travel-safety-tips/] Accessed on May 25, 2023.

Many AutoRun or AutoPlay features facilitate software installation from a CD-ROM or USB device or to play music from a CD.[39] Unfortunately, this also makes it easy for malware to install itself on a computer. The WISP template attempts to minimize this possibility by requiring AutoRun or AutoPlay to be disabled. Tax practitioners must still check any USB device a client brings for malware.

Example 12. Every year Nancy, the partnership representative of CSQ Partnership, provides Carla, EA with a USB drive containing all records necessary to prepare Form 1065, *U.S. Return of Partnership Income,* and the associated state tax returns. In 2022, Carla implemented a WISP that prohibits USB drives from being connected to its internal network.

When Carla sends out her organizer at the beginning of 2023, she includes a note about her new policy of not allowing USB drives. She provides information on how to set up an account on her secure portal. Before their February meeting, Nancy successfully sets up CSQ's account and uploads all the relevant documents. Nancy and Carla feel secure knowing the information is encrypted and protected on the portal.

Old storage devices, such as disk drives, present a problem when they become obsolete. The WISP template mandates erasure of these devices where possible, or otherwise prevent their ability to connect to other devices.

The WISP template mentions the need for **antivirus software** to be running and licensed. The tax practice's computers must update the virus signatures regularly, and the network must be "tested weekly to ensure the protection is current and up to date" to prevent connected devices from introducing viruses or malware.

Caution. Tax practitioners may also wish to consider how devices themselves may collect data. Because portable devices are so powerful, their owners may unwittingly release information to firms that should not have this data in their possession. This capability also makes the tax practices' policies concerning cell phones and tablet computers particularly important because these devices are likely to have speech recognition software (e.g., Apple's Siri or Google Assistant). The broad availability of artificial intelligence magnifies the risk of data compromise.

Information Security Training Policy

Training personnel is arguably the most important portion of a WISP. If a tax practice's employees do not understand the WISP, they cannot fulfill their responsibilities, making it hard to hold them accountable for appropriately controlling access to data. When a tax practice's management makes regular data security training available, it emphasizes the value it places on the security of customer PII.

Annual training sessions have been the standard for training tax practice employees. Tax professionals may consider holding sessions more frequently.

Credit Card Processing Policy

Although not part of the WISP template, a tax practice should consider how it complies with credit card laws and regulations. The payment card industry (PCI) maintains standards covering the security of credit card information.[40] Some rules restrict credit card processing to a single computer within the firm and prohibit the storage of credit card information. In 2021, the IRS recommended using Transport Layer Security Level 1.3 as a faster and more secure alternative to secure sockets layer (SSL) transmission of any credit card information.[41] Principals of tax practices may wish to review these rules to ensure that their firms are compliant and can access credit card processing networks.

---

39. *AutoRun.* Oct. 13, 2020. Wikipedia. [en.wikipedia.org/wiki/AutoRun] Accessed on Nov. 14, 2022; *The Risks of Using Portable Devices*, p. 3. Walters, Pennie. 2012. Cybersecurity & Infrastructure Security Agency. [www.cisa.gov/sites/default/files/publications/RisksOfPortableDevices.pdf] Accessed on Mar. 22, 2023.

40. *The Prioritized Approach to Pursue PCI DSS Compliance.* Aug. 2022. PCI Security Standards Council. [docs-prv.pcisecuritystandards.org/PCI%20DSS/Supporting%20Document/Prioritized-Approach-For-PCI-DSS-v4-0.pdf] Accessed on Nov. 15, 2022.

41. IRS Pub. 4557, *Safeguarding Taxpayer Data,* p. 16 (2021); *An Overview of TLS 1.3 — Faster and More Secure.* 2023. Kinsta, Inc. [kinsta.com/blog/tls-1-3/] Accessed on Feb. 21, 2023.

ANNUAL CHECKLIST[42]

Each year, a tax practice should review its WISP template, making changes as needed to reflect changes in regulations and in the practice itself. IRS Pub. 4557, *Safeguarding Taxpayer Data,* contains the following checklist that practitioners can use to evaluate and monitor the WISP for their tax practices.

ONGOING	DONE	N/A	Employee Management and Training
☐	☐	☐	The success of your information security plan depends largely on the employees who implement it. Consider these steps:
☐	☐	☐	The success of your information security plan depends largely on the employees who implement it. Consider these steps:
☐	☐	☐	Check references or doing background checks before hiring employees who will have access to customer information.
☐	☐	☐	Ask every new employee to sign an agreement to follow your company's confidentiality and security standards for handling customer information.
☐	☐	☐	Limit access to customer information to employees who have a business reason to see it. For example, give employees who respond to customer inquiries access to customer files, but only to the extent they need it to do their jobs.
☐	☐	☐	Control access to sensitive information by requiring employees to use "strong" passwords that must be changed on a regular basis. (Tough-to-crack passwords require the use of at least six characters, upper- and lower-case letters, and a combination of letters, numbers, and symbols.) (**IRS suggestion**: passwords should be a minimum of eight characters, the NIST standard. Prevent password sharing; ensure each employee with access to taxpayer accounts uses a unique password.)
☐	☐	☐	Use password-activated screen savers to lock employee computers after a period of inactivity.
☐	☐	☐	Develop policies for appropriate use and protection of laptops, PDAs, cell phones, or other mobile devices. For example, make sure employees store these devices in a secure place when not in use. Also, consider that customer information in encrypted files will be better protected in case of theft of such a device.

42. IRS Pub. 4557, *Safeguarding Taxpayer Data.*

ONGOING	DONE	N/A	
☐	☐	☐	Train employees to take basic steps to maintain the security, confidentiality, and integrity of customer information, including:
☐	☐	☐	• Locking rooms and file cabinets where records are kept;
☐	☐	☐	• Not sharing or openly posting employee passwords in work areas;
☐	☐	☐	• Encrypting sensitive customer information when it is transmitted electronically via public networks;
☐	☐	☐	• Referring calls or other requests for customer information to designated individuals who have been trained in how your company safeguards personal data; and
☐	☐	☐	• Reporting suspicious attempts to obtain customer information to designated personnel.
☐	☐	☐	Regularly remind all employees of your company's policy — and the legal requirement — to keep customer information secure and confidential. For example, consider posting reminders about their responsibility for security in areas where customer information is stored, like file rooms.
☐	☐	☐	Develop policies for employees who telecommute. For example, consider whether or how employees should be allowed to keep or access customer data at home. Also, require employees who use personal computers to store or access customer data to use protections against viruses, spyware, and other unauthorized intrusions.
☐	☐	☐	Impose disciplinary measures for security policy violations.
☐	☐	☐	Prevent terminated employees from accessing customer information by immediately deactivating their passwords and user names and taking other appropriate measures. (**IRS Suggestion**: Deactivate access prior to termination.)
☐	☐	☐	(**IRS Suggestion:** Add labels to documents to signify importance, such as "Sensitive" or "For Official Business" to further secure paper documents.)

Information Systems

Information systems include network and software design, and information processing, storage, transmission, retrieval, and disposal. Here are some FTC suggestions on maintaining security throughout the life cycle of customer information, from data entry to data disposal:

ONGOING	DONE	N/A	
☐	☐	☐	Know where sensitive customer information is stored and store it securely. Make sure only authorized employees have access. For example:
☐	☐	☐	• Ensure that storage areas are protected against destruction or damage from physical hazards, like fire or floods.

ONGOING	DONE	N/A	
☐	☐	☐	• Store records in a room or cabinet that is locked when unattended.
☐	☐	☐	• When customer information is stored on a server or other computer, ensure that the computer is accessible only with a "strong" password and is kept in a physically secure area. (**IRS Suggestion:** If using a cloud storage service, use a strong password, multi-factor authentication options and beware of thieves posing as providers.)
☐	☐	☐	• Where possible, avoid storing sensitive customer data on a computer with an Internet connection.
☐	☐	☐	• Maintain secure backup records and keep archived data secure by storing it off-line and in a physically-secure area.
☐	☐	☐	• Maintain a careful inventory of your company's computers and any other equipment on which customer information may be stored.
☐	☐	☐	Take steps to ensure the secure transmission of customer information. For example:
☐	☐	☐	• When you transmit credit card information or other sensitive financial data, use a Secure Sockets Layer (SSL) or other secure connection, so that the information is protected in transit. (**IRS Suggestion:** Transport Layer Security 1.3 is newer and more secure.)
☐	☐	☐	• If you collect information online directly from customers, make secure transmission automatic. Caution customers against transmitting sensitive data, like account numbers, via email or in response to an unsolicited email or pop-up message.
☐	☐	☐	• If you must transmit sensitive data by email over the Internet, be sure to encrypt the data. (**IRS Suggestion:** Rather than using email, transmit files via Secure File Transfer Protocol (SFTP), successor to File Transfer Protocol (FTP)).
☐	☐	☐	Dispose of customer information in a secure way and, where applicable, consistent with the FTC's Disposal Rule. For example:
☐	☐	☐	• Consider designating or hiring a records retention manager to supervise the disposal of records containing customer information. If you hire an outside disposal company, conduct due diligence beforehand by checking references or requiring that the company be certified by a recognized industry group.
☐	☐	☐	• Burn, pulverize, or shred papers containing customer information so that the information cannot be read or reconstructed.
☐	☐	☐	• Destroy or erase data when disposing of computers, disks, CDs, magnetic tapes, hard drives, laptops, PDAs, cell phones, or any other electronic media or hardware containing customer information.

ONGOING	DONE	N/A	
			## Detecting and Managing System Failures
			Effective security management requires your company to deter, detect, and defend against security breaches. That means taking reasonable steps to prevent attacks, quickly diagnosing a security incident, and having a plan in place for responding effectively. Consider implementing the following procedures:
☐	☐	☐	Monitor the websites of your software vendors and read relevant industry publications for news about emerging threats and available defenses.
☐	☐	☐	Maintain up-to-date and appropriate programs and controls to prevent unauthorized access to customer information. Be sure to:
☐	☐	☐	• check with software vendors regularly to get and install patches that resolve software vulnerabilities;
☐	☐	☐	• use anti-virus and anti-spyware software that updates automatically;
☐	☐	☐	• maintain up-to-date firewalls, particularly if you use a broadband Internet connection or allow employees to connect to your network from home or other off-site locations;
☐	☐	☐	• regularly ensure that ports not used for your business are closed; and
☐	☐	☐	• promptly pass along information and instructions to employees regarding any new security risks or possible breaches.
			Use appropriate oversight or audit procedures to detect the improper disclosure or theft of customer information. It's wise to:
☐	☐	☐	• keep logs of activity on your network and monitor them for signs of unauthorized access to customer information;
☐	☐	☐	• use an up-to-date intrusion detection system to alert you of attacks;
☐	☐	☐	• monitor both in- and out-bound transfers of information for indications of a compromise, such as unexpectedly large amounts of data being transmitted from your system to an unknown user; and
☐	☐	☐	• insert a dummy account into each of your customer lists and monitor the account to detect any unauthorized contacts or charges.
			Take steps to preserve the security, confidentiality, and integrity of customer information in the event of a breach. If a breach occurs:
☐	☐	☐	• take immediate action to secure any information that has or may have been compromised. For example, if a computer connected to the Internet is compromised, disconnect the computer from the Internet;
☐	☐	☐	• preserve and review files or programs that may reveal how the breach occurred; and

ONGOING	DONE	N/A	
☐	☐	☐	• if feasible and appropriate, bring in security professionals to help assess the breach as soon as possible.
			Consider notifying consumers, law enforcement, and/or businesses in the event of a security breach. For example:
☐	☐	☐	• notify consumers if their personal information is subject to a breach that poses a significant risk of identity theft or related harm;
☐	☐	☐	• notify law enforcement if the breach may involve criminal activity or there is evidence that the breach has resulted in identity theft or related harm;
☐	☐	☐	• notify the credit bureaus and other businesses that may be affected by the breach. See Information Compromise and the Risk of Identity Theft: Guidance for Your Business; and
☐	☐	☐	• check to see if breach notification is required under applicable state law.
☐	☐	☐	• (**IRS suggestions:** Practitioners who experience a data loss should contact the IRS and the states. Also, consider having a technical support contract in place, so that hardware events can be fixed within a reasonable time and with minimal disruption to business availability.)

EMPLOYEE CODE OF CONDUCT

The WISP template includes a sample written employee code of conduct that provides specific guidelines for protecting clients' PII. The Rules of Behavior and Conduct Safeguarding Client PII as provided by the IRS is included as Attachment B in Appendix A at the end of this chapter.

Email Usage

Employees cannot depend on poor grammar to detect phishing attempts. Instead, employees should call the sender to verify the legitimacy of any links in messages purporting to come from them. Employees can also inspect the web address of the destination link by hovering the computer cursor over a hyperlink in an email. The employee should consider destroying the message if the destination link does not contain a domain related to a trusted source.

Example 13. Cameron expects blank Forms 1099-NEC, *Nonemployee Compensation*, to arrive any day, and he knows the vendor uses WPS to ship them by next-day services. He receives an email from WPS containing the WPS logos and other graphical elements that strongly resemble other emails from the shipper. Because he is anxious to receive the package, he clicks on the link without checking the embedded destination web address. As the link is opening, he notices that the browser window points to the tinyurl.com domain.

Cameron immediately shuts down the browser and informs his firm's data security coordinator of the possible threat per the employee code of conduct in place. Cameron is known to be vigilant regarding email and phishing attempts and is current with the firm's security training. Cameron's managers thank him for reporting the incident and proactively shutting down his computer. They note that his alertness prevented what could have been a virus infection of his computer and potentially the entire company's network.

Note. A tax practice's principals may consider stating in their WISP that an employee reporting a security breach will not be disciplined if the breach is reported promptly. Fear of retribution because an employee mistakenly clicked on a link in an email may result in the employee not reporting security events and, therefore, the threat is not neutralized before it can cause harm.

Internet Usage

The code of employee conduct mandates the segregation of devices for business and personal use. Hence, it would require employees to use personal devices during lunch to check personal email or social media accounts.

Note. If a tax practice maintains a separate network for clients and vendors, it should decide whether it wants employees' personal devices to use it for Internet connections. If a firm's principals decide to permit this, the WISP should provide rules governing the content accessed through its Internet connection.

Personal or Untrusted Storage Devices

Employees should not comingle external storage devices between personal and business devices to avoid introducing malware. As discussed previously, employees should disable any AutoRun or AutoPlay features as well.

Software Copyright and Licensing Integrity

The employee code of conduct instructs employees to avoid downloading software from websites that are unknown. It prudently cautions against freeware or shareware, even though some publishers distribute legitimate software in this manner.

Note. Software required for an employee's responsibilities should be vetted by the data security coordinator, preferably in conjunction with the tax practice's IT staff or IT consultant.

Providing Personal or Business Information

Individuals must use caution when providing personal or business information. A **social engineer** attempts to acquire physical or electronic access to data by manipulating people often by using a person, website, or email. The target receives an email or call with believable information that includes names, titles, responsibilities, and other personal or business information to convince them the request is credible.

The employee code of conduct should remind employees to never respond to unsolicited calls or emails or disclose sensitive business or personal information. Additionally, employees should never provide usernames or passwords and the company should never request that information. Hackers can also use information on the type of operating system, brand of firewall, Internet browser, or which applications are installed to break into the system; employees should beware of providing that information.

Pop-Up Windows

An employee code of conduct should remind employees to watch out for pop-up windows when they are connected to the Internet. Employees should not click on pop-up windows and should use a pop-up blocker that only allows pop-up windows on trusted websites.

Password Management

An employee code of conduct should include password management for using strong passwords. Strong passwords should abide by the following protocols.

- Passwords should consist of a random sequence of at least 12 upper and lowercase letters, numbers, and special characters.
- Employees should use 2FA for systems or applications with important information.
- After acquiring new devices, employees should immediately change default administration passwords.
- Passwords should be changed at least every three months.
- Passwords protecting business information should not be reused.

Conducting Business Online Securely

Employees conducting online business, commerce, or banking should do so only on a secure browser connection. A secure browser connection is generally indicated by a small lock icon in the lower right corner or the upper left of the browser window. The code of conduct recommends employees regularly erase the web browser cache, cookies, temporary Internet files, and history, especially after using a public computer or following any online commerce or banking activities. Clearing the Internet activity prevents hackers from stealing important information if the system is compromised. Employees should look in the web browser's privacy or security menu or review the web browser's help manual for assistance.

SECURITY BREACH PROCEDURES

Despite the best intentions of a tax practice, it may still become a victim of a data breach. A compromised practice should have a response plan ready that identifies the necessary parties who should be alerted. Attachment C in Appendix A at the end of this chapter identifies the following parties that a victim should notify.

- IRS Stakeholder Liaison
- State Attorney General
- FBI, if the breach is a cybercrime that involves electronic data theft
- FTC
- Local law enforcement

- Tax software vendor
- Insurance carrier or agency

Note. If a compromised tax practice has an insurance policy under which a claim may be made, the tax practitioner should contact the agency as soon as possible. Not only is this important to establish coverage, but the insurance company may also be able to deploy a team of its employees to assist with complying with federal and state laws in notifying clients, notifying government agencies, in protecting the practice from further intrusions, and undertaking forensic investigations to determine the extent of the breach.

- Attorney
- Clients[43]

Note. Firms may also consider informing credit bureaus and any state revenue agency. Many states require businesses that collect certain data to notify affected clients and possibly the attorney general in the event of a data loss.[44] For example, under state law in Illinois, the attorney general must be notified if more than 500 Illinois residents are affected by a data breach. Tax practitioners with clients who are Illinois residents wishing to make this report or to discuss it with the attorney general's office should email **datasecurity@ilag.gov** or call 1-800-243-0618.[45] The law is relevant even for tax practitioners residing in states other than Illinois if they have more than 500 affected clients living in Illinois.

Note. The following pages on the IRS website may contain valuable information in the event of a data breach.

- **uofi.tax/23x1x1** [www.irs.gov/identitytheft]
- **uofi.tax/23x1x2** [www.irs.gov/identity-theft-fraud-scams/identity-theft-information-for-tax-professionals]
- **uofi.tax/23x1x3** [www.irs.gov/newsroom/identity-theft-information-for-businesses]

The WISP template also provides the following procedures for a firm to follow after suffering a data breach.

- Visit IRS e-Services and check an electronic filing identification number (EFIN) activity report to verify any returns filed on the practitioner's EFIN.
- Check if any questionable returns were submitted at odd hours outside normal business hours, such as overnight or on weekends.
- Scrutinize any returns transmitted on a Monday or Tuesday morning as often a thief will remotely steal the client data over the weekend when no one is in the office to notice, then rework the returns over the weekend and transmit them on a business workday after the weekend.

Note. Practitioners can find more information on security breach procedures at **uofi.tax/21x1x4** [www.irs.gov/newsroom/tax-security-101-security-summit-outlines-data-theft-reporting-process-for-tax-professionals-speed-helps-protect-taxpayers].

---

43. For guidance on notifying victims, see *Data Breach Response: A Guide for Business*. Feb. 2021. Federal Trade Commission. [www.ftc.gov/business-guidance/resources/data-breach-response-guide-business] Accessed on Dec. 9, 2022.

44. 815 ILCS 530/10(e)(2).

45. *Data Breach Reporting for Businesses and State Government Agencies.* Office of the Illinois Attorney General. [illinoisattorneygeneral.gov/consumer-protection/for-businesses/data-breach] Accessed on Sep. 6, 2023.

DATA ATTACKS

Client information is at a constant risk of attack, both from a cyberattack and physical compromise of data. Practitioners need to be aware of the different types of attacks to develop effective counterattacks to protect personal data.

Tax practices are vulnerable to attempted data theft because they maintain PII. To accurately prepare tax returns, tax practitioners maintain documents that verify clients' identities and their income, deductions, and credits. For a data thief, the following information is probably as valuable as the money in a bank.

- **Tax practitioner's name and contact information.**[46] A tax practitioner's name, contact information, and EFIN constitute valuable information when possessed by the wrong persons. Cybercriminals can use this information to file fraudulent tax returns. Using tools on the IRS website, a tax practitioner can monitor the use of their EFIN and PTIN. If the number of returns filed with a tax practitioner's PTIN is significantly greater than those they know they have prepared and filed, it likely indicates fraudulent use of the PTIN. [46]
- **Client personal information.** With possession of a client's personal information, criminals could file a fraudulent tax return and possibly steal money from the federal treasury.
- **Financial and employment information.** Information about a taxpayer's bank accounts, investment accounts, and employment aids a criminal in making their fraudulent attempt to impersonate a taxpayer more realistic, enabling them to pilfer the taxpayer's money, take out loans that the taxpayer is obligated to repay, or obtain a large refund by filing a fraudulent tax return in the taxpayer's name.
- **Powers of attorney.** Attorneys, EAs, and CPAs can communicate directly with the IRS regarding a client's status, provided that the IRS has on file a power of attorney (POA) or tax information authorization (TIA). Unfortunately, on rare occasions, criminals have been able to impersonate enrolled tax practitioners, enabling them to acquire taxpayers' confidential information. Aware of this threat, the IRS now validates enrolled practitioners' identities by asking callers to confirm their SSNs and dates of birth.

Practitioner Planning Tip

Tax practitioners can confirm that POAs are on file only for current clients. They may find that they still have access to former clients' records, necessitating their withdrawal from the representation of those clients.

This confirmation aims to ensure that the tax practitioner is only authorized to access records for current clients. It requires submitting a Centralized Authorization File (CAF) Client Listing Request, described on the IRS website: **uofi.tax/23x1x5** [www.irs.gov/privacy-disclosure/freedom-of-information-act-foia-guidelines]. This request is the eighth item in the list on this page, and provides a sample letter to request a listing of POAs and TIAs on file with the CAF unit of the IRS. Tax practitioners can file this request on the webpage for **FOIA.gov**, but they can also mail it to an address provided on the webpage.

46. *IRS, Summit Partners Issue Urgent EFIN Scam Alert to Tax Professionals.* Feb. 10, 2021. IRS. [www.irs.gov/newsroom/irs-summit-partners-issue-urgent-efin-scam-alert-to-tax-professionals] Accessed on Mar. 16, 2023; See *How to Maintain, Monitor and Protect Your EFIN*. Jun. 16, 2022. IRS. [www.irs.gov/tax-professionals/how-to-maintain-monitor-and-protect-your-efin] Accessed on Mar. 24, 2023.

The report showing POAs and TIAs may prove even more valuable if it includes a fraudulently filed POA, possibly indicating an individual has sought to impersonate a tax practitioner. To determine this, the tax practitioner needs to review the entire list of POAs and TIAs, looking for individuals having unfamiliar names because they have never been clients. The presence of an unfamiliar name implies someone could fraudulently impersonate the tax practitioner to obtain information on the individual with the unfamiliar name.

PHISHING ATTACKS[47]

Phishing attacks attempt to steal PII by enticing the recipient of an email into surrendering information. These attacks generally use email to initiate communication with an unsuspecting victim. The volume of emails is such that an individual message may not receive the scrutiny it needs for its recipient to discern it as fraudulent. In other cases, the fraudulent message may appear on social media or arrive by text or phone. Individuals with fraudulent intent may use phone calls in conjunction with phishing attacks to gain the confidence of unsuspecting employees, resulting in them providing passwords over the phone or surrendering other valuable information.

Example 14. In 2018, the City of Batavia, Illinois, fell victim to a phishing attack that led to employee PII being released to an unknown fraudster.[48] It started when a city employee received an emailed request for Form W-2 information. The email appeared to come from the city administrator on the day that Forms W-2 had to be filed, January 31. The employee replied with the names, addresses, SSNs, and earnings of 240 city employees and city council members. Only after sending the information did the employee question the message's authenticity.

The city administrator met with employees to discuss the release of PII after immediately notifying them. The city notified the local police, who investigated the incident, as well as their insurance carrier. The city provided employees with one year of credit monitoring and identity theft protection at no cost to them.

The objective of phishing attacks is not always the direct theft of PII. Phishing attacks can also attempt to install malware on computers, later subjecting them to a less detectable form of data theft.[49] The malware could be ransomware, which renders the computer inoperable.

A barrage of email messages may attempt to contact as many individuals as possible at once in the hope that one recipient, who is not careful, triggers the mechanism that installs malware or releases PII. One estimate holds that 3.4 billion phishing messages are sent **each day.**[50] Another strategy is to closely emulate an expected email message so that even a relatively cautious recipient mistakes the fraud for a legitimate email message. Because the fraudulent sender of this type of message usually is directed at specific individuals, it has earned the dubious distinction of its own name, specifically "spear phishing."[51]

---

47. *Report Phishing and Online Scams.* Jan. 20, 2023. IRS. [www.irs.gov/privacy-disclosure/report-phishing] Accessed on Mar. 16, 2023.

48. *Confidential information of Batavia city employees, elected officials stolen in phishing scam.* Girardi, Linda. Feb. 2, 2018. Aurora Beacon-News. [www.chicagotribune.com/suburbs/aurora-beacon-news/ct-abn-batavia-phishing-st-0204-20180202-story.html] Accessed on Nov. 17, 2022; *Phishing attacks: defending your organisation.* Jan. 7, 2022. National Cyber Security Centre. [www.ncsc.gov.uk/guidance/phishing] Accessed on Nov. 17, 2022.

49. *How to Recognize, Remove, and Avoid Malware.* May 2021. Federal Trade Commission. [consumer.ftc.gov/articles/how-recognize-remove-avoid-malware] Accessed on Mar. 24, 2023.

50. *How Many Phishing Emails Are Sent Daily in 2023? (New Stats).* Campbell, Stefan. Dec. 3, 2022. The Small Business Blog. [thesmallbusinessblog.net/how-many-phishing-emails-are-sent-daily] Accessed on Mar. 24, 2023.

51. *Spear phishing targets tax pros and other businesses.* Jun. 30, 2022. IRS. [www.irs.gov/newsroom/spear-phishing-targets-tax-pros-and-other-businesses] Accessed on Mar. 24, 2023.

Tax practitioners who receive messages that they believe may be phishing attempts should follow these steps.[52]

- If the message claims to be from the IRS, tax practitioners should verify it actually originated at the IRS before replying to it.
- Emails requesting information from Forms W-2 should be reported to the Internet Crime Complaint Center at **www.ic3.com**.
- If a tax practitioner falls victim to a request for PII, especially Form W-2 information, they should report this to **dataloss@irs.gov**.
- Tax practitioners should report unsolicited email messages referencing the IRS or tax matters to **phishing@irs.gov**.
- Tax practitioners should report unsolicited **fax** messages referencing the IRS both to the Treasury Inspector General for Tax Administration at **www.tigta.gov/hotline** and to the IRS at **phishing@irs.gov**.
- Suspicious phishing email messages that do not claim to be from the IRS can be forwarded to **reportphishing@antiphishing.org**.
- An individual may receive a suspicious email message which they suspect carries malware or other malicious code, but which does not claim to be from the IRS. If they have clicked on a link in the message or downloaded an attachment, they should visit **OnGuardOnline.gov**, where they can get up-to-date information from the FTC on action to be taken.

Note. The IRS takes attacks on small businesses, including tax practices, very seriously. As such, it listed phishing attacks on the Dirty Dozen list of top tax scams during 2023.[53]

SMISHING ATTACKS[54]

Some enterprising hackers have turned text messages into devices for pilfering PII, using the same strategy as phishing emails. The name smishing is a combination of "SMS" (short message service) and "phishing." Because text messages generally come from individuals one already knows, and smishing attacks are new, they receive more credibility. The IRS requests that individuals report tax-related smishing attacks to the agency via email. Individuals should send the email to **phishing@irs.gov**, including the caller ID number and email address from the incoming message, the date and time of the message, and the recipient's phone number. Although they can send it as a screenshot, the IRS prefers text information.

---

52. *Report Phishing and Online Scams.* Jan. 20, 2023. IRS. [www.irs.gov/privacy-disclosure/report-phishing] Accessed on Mar. 24, 2023.

53. *Dirty Dozen.* Apr. 5, 2023. IRS. [www.irs.gov/newsroom/dirty-dozen] Accessed on Jun. 1, 2023.

54. *Dirty Dozen: IRS urges tax pros and other businesses to beware of spearphishing; offers tips to avoid dangerous common scams.* Mar. 29, 2023. IRS. [www.irs.gov/newsroom/dirty-dozen-irs-urges-tax-pros-and-other-businesses-to-beware-of-spearphishing-offers-tips-to-avoid-dangerous-common-scams] Accessed on Apr. 10, 2023.

KEYLOGGERS[55]

Keyloggers intercept messages or passwords as computer users enter them on a keyboard. Modern keystroke logging is often a form of software that collects keystrokes. Sometimes this software is used in a legitimate sense, for example, when an IT department attempts to resolve issues. Other keystroke loggers are also available, which could be among the following.

- USB devices innocuously plugged into the back of a computer
- Software running on the low-level firmware of a computer or even on a nearby smartphone
- Sensors receiving electromagnetic emissions that are triggered when a typist presses specific keys on a keyboard

RANSOMWARE[56]

Ransomware removes an employee's ability to access their firm's data by covertly encrypting it and offering to decrypt it after their firm pays a ransom. Thus, users still have their proprietary data but cannot see it, interact with it, or use it because it is encrypted. This attack devastates a tax practice because it removes the firm's ability to prepare tax returns for its clients. The hackers do not have access to the firm's data but instead request untraceable funds transfers as ransom. The Treasury Department announced that the losses associated with 2021 ransomware attacks exceeded $1 billion.[57]

The federal Cybersecurity and Infrastructure Security Agency (CISA) publishes a list of Ransomware Prevention Best Practices, which may assist tax practitioners in preventing ransomware attacks on their businesses. They suggest the following actions.[58]

- Backup data, system images and configurations, keeping the backups offline
- Update and patch systems
- Ensure that security solutions are up to date
- Review and exercise (or practice) the business's incident response plan
- Pay attention to other ransomware events, applying lessons learned

Local Copy vs. Cloud Copy[59]

In the past, most small businesses used local backups, as slow Internet connection speeds did not make storing PII on the cloud practical. While this was useful, storing PII on a detachable storage device in a practitioner's possession did not protect data from a regional disaster.

---

55. *Tax Security 2.0 — A "Taxes-Security-Together" Checklist – Step* 3. Jan. 31, 2023. IRS. [www.irs.gov/newsroom/tax-security-2-0-a-taxes-security-together-checklist-step-3] Accessed on Mar. 24, 2023; *Keystroke Logging*. Oct. 13, 2022. Wikipedia. [en.wikipedia.org/wiki/Keystroke_logging] Accessed on Nov. 17, 2022.

56. IRS Pub. 4557, *Safeguarding Taxpayer Data; Ransomware Guide*. Sep. 2020. Cybersecurity & Infrastructure Security Agency. [www.cisa.gov/stopransomware/ransomware-guide] Accessed on Nov. 17, 2022.

57. *Reported Ransomware Incidents, Costs Soared in 2021, Treasury Says*. Rundle, James. Nov. 4, 2022. Wall Street Journal. [www.wsj.com/articles/reported-ransomware-incidents-costs-soared-in-2021-treasury-says-11667513649?mod=Searchresults_pos2&page=1] Accessed on Nov. 17, 2022.

58. *CISA INSIGHTS: Ransomware Outbreak*. Aug. 21, 2019. Cybersecurity & Infrastructure Security Agency. [www.cisa.gov/uscert/sites/default/files/2019-08/CISA_Insights-Ransomware_Outbreak_S508C.pdf] Accessed on Feb. 22, 2023.

59. *What is Cloud Backup? Cloud vs Local Backup Comparison*. Jan. 20, 2023. Acronis International GmbH. [acronis.com/en-us/blog/posts/cloud-vs-local-backup] Accessed on Mar. 26, 2023; See *Disaster Recovery*. Jan. 14, 2023. Wikipedia. [en.wikipedia.org/wiki/Disaster_recovery] Accessed on Mar. 26, 2023.

The preference for Internet-based (cloud) backups changed when Internet connection speed increased. It became practical to store data on remote storage in another part of the country, far removed from the same threat of regional disaster as the tax practice might face. Thus, it is now common for small tax practices to store backups of their data securely on remote devices.

However, there may be circumstances when **local** data is still preferred. If a tax practice receives a ransomware attack during tax season, it may be possible to restore data from the Internet without paying a ransom, but it potentially takes a long time. Data restoration from a local device may be the only practical means of restoring the data during tax season. Thus, tax practices may consider a network-attached storage device for local data backup. Fraudsters may encrypt PII possessed by the tax practice in a ransomware attack. In that case, restoration from a network-attached storage device stored in the server room may enable recovery from a ransomware attack within a few hours and without paying a ransom.

BRUTE FORCE ENTRY[60]

With a brute force entry attack, a hostile individual attempts to access a computer system with repeated guesses at passwords. For this reason, many systems disable logging in after a certain number of failed attempts. The hostile individual may start with simple passwords, which are subsequently modified. The user generally attempts to access the computer remotely, which enables them to use software that enters password guesses repeatedly.

The following are some characteristics of a typical victim's technical environments.

- Lacks 2FA
- Allows easy-to-guess passwords (e.g., "Taxhelp123")
- Uses inbox synchronization, which downloads email from the Internet to remote devices
- Permits users to set up email forwarding
- Limits logging, which in turn limits the investigations of any event
- Uses federated authentication, which enables access to multiple systems from a single sign-on

PHYSICAL REMOVAL[61]

Physical theft of a computer is sometimes a threat. Generally, tax practitioners can prevent physical theft of the computer system by securing the room in which the computer is stored or by securing the computer with a cable lock.

Mobile devices present a special challenge, as the very reason users carry them also makes them susceptible to physical theft. Thus, the case for encrypted hard disks is strong for laptop computers, much more than servers or other devices used only in locked locations.

INVOLVEMENT OF OUTSIDE IT SERVICES FIRMS

The WISP template and the FTC impose requirements for technical sophistication on every tax practice. Tax practitioners have all they can handle with tax law changes, let alone the rapid evolution of security threats and the computer technology they use to prepare tax returns. Thus, the involvement of outside IT specialists strengthens the long-term viability of a tax practice.

---

60. *Brute Force Attacks Conducted by Cyber Actors.* May 6, 2020. Cybersecurity & Infrastructure Security Agency. [www.cisa.gov/uscert/ncas/alerts/TA18-086A] Accessed on Nov. 17, 2022.

61. *Protecting Portable Devices: Physical Security.* McDowell, Mindi. Sep. 27, 2019. Cybersecurity & Infrastructure Security Agency. [www.cisa.gov/news-events/news/protecting-portable-devices-physical-security] Accessed on Apr. 10, 2023.

ETHICAL HACKERS[62]

An ethical hacker is an outside consultant hired by a business to probe its security weaknesses. They may attempt to access the firm's network remotely, either through a VPN or another remote access mechanism. They may test the complexity of the password attached to the firm's router. An ethical hacker helps a firm find weaknesses in its data protection.

Because many security breaches result from office personnel voluntarily providing access information or passwords, ethical hackers may use phone calls to test the resistance that office personnel offer to requests for PII. For example, an ethical hacker may call the tax practice and request that the receptionist urgently provide copies of Forms W-2 or tax returns.

NETWORK MONITORING[63]

Any server controlling a local network generates a large volume of statistics reflecting the health of the network and potential security issues. During tax season, when a tax practice is most dependent on the productivity of its employees, it may well be unreasonable to expect an employee to recognize potential issues affecting the health or even the viability of the firm. Outsourcing this function to an organization that specializes in it may prove to be the most cost-effective approach to maintaining employees' productivity and possibly averting a data breach.

INTERNET CONNECTION MONITORING[64]

In almost all cases, a router connects the tax practice's internal network to the outside world, receiving and sending data on these networks. As previously indicated, the WISP template requires that a router be "secured and maintained by the firm's IT services provider." In effect, this mandates that an outside IT firm protect PII in the tax practice's possession. Because its manufacturer must refresh a router periodically with new software and firmware, a contract with the router's manufacturer should be anticipated and perhaps budgeted.

WEBSITE FIREWALL MANAGEMENT[65]

A website for any firm is typically on an external network not directly controlled by the firm's internal network or its outside IT consultants. Nevertheless, a website can be hacked, infected with malware, or fall victim to other adverse consequences. Although some website hosting services specializing in websites for tax practices may provide management and protective functions, a website constructed by an independent designer may need its own firewall to protect the site from being taken over by malicious parties. Although it is unlikely that a tax practice would store PII on a website, tax practitioners should periodically check to ensure that no PII is accessible on the practice's website.

> **Note**. Tax practitioners can identify vendors by searching on the Internet for "website endpoint firewall" or "web application firewall."

TRAINING

An IT services firm may be able to provide training for tax practice employees on security-related matters. This training could be incorporated into the required annual training, so that employees are confident in their abilities to detect phishing messages that are probably harmful.

---

62. Baysden, Chris (Host). How to protect your CPA practice from hackers. [Audio podcast episode] In *Journal of Accountancy Podcast.* [www.journalofaccountancy.com/podcast/protect-cpa-practice-from-hackers.html] Accessed on Apr. 10, 2023.

63. *Monitoring Active Directory for Signs of Compromise*. Jun. 6, 2022. Microsoft Corp. [learn.microsoft.com/en-us/windows-server/identity/ad-ds/plan/security-best-practices/monitoring-active-directory-for-signs-of-compromise] Accessed on Dec. 7, 2022.

64. *What is a Router?* 2022. Cisco Systems, Inc. [www.cisco.com/c/en/us/solutions/small-business/resource-center/networking/what-is-a-router.html#~how-to-choose-small-business-routers] Accessed on Dec. 7, 2022.

65. *What is a Web Application Firewall?* 2022. Cloudflare, Inc. [www.cloudflare.com/learning/ddos/glossary/web-application-firewall-waf/] Accessed on Dec. 7, 2022.

DISCUSSION SCENARIOS

The following scenarios are offered to encourage tax practitioners to consider applications of the principles addressed previously.

DISCUSSION SCENARIO 1

Ken owns a small tax practice, employing two full-time, year-round tax professionals and three staff who work on a seasonal basis. Ken owns a central computer server on which his firm has loaded its network-based tax software for the past 10 years. Ken also owns document management software that stores the 1,500 tax returns the practice prepares and files annually. Ken is not considering changing tax preparation software but moving to an externally-hosted platform so that he does not have to manage the server.

What are the security considerations? ______________________________

____

____

____

Should the firm move the tax software to an externally hosted server? ______________________________

____

____

____

How should the firm implement the requirement that passwords be changed every three months? ______________

____

____

____

What other actions should the firm undertake to protect PII? ______________________________

____

____

____

DISCUSSION SCENARIO 2

TNY, CPA, is a small tax practice trying to wean its clients from using unsecured email to submit documents. However, the clients are not responding and continue to send PII through email, including Forms W-2.

Does TNY have liability for documents it receives from clients that the clients do not send securely? ______________

____

____

____

Should TNY invest in a secure email system, and if so, at what price is it no longer worth it? ____________________

____

____

____

Are there other actions that TNY should undertake, possibly in its engagement letter or its organizer? ____________

____

____

____

Are there services that tax practices could use to collect clients' tax information more securely with less effort? ____

____

____

____

DISCUSSION SCENARIO 3

Garcia-Jones, a medium-sized tax practice preparing 2,200 tax returns for businesses and individuals, completed its WISP in November, concluding a 6-month process that had started in May, shortly after the previous filing season ended. Although the document was completed before filing season started, the firm's management realized in early December that employees had not been trained to follow its provisions for protecting client PII.

What should the practice do with its freshly printed WISP in December?______________________________

____

____

____

What should it do with the WISP in March? Are there training activities that the tax practice could reasonably undertake during filing season? ____

____

____

____

What should it do in May? Should revisions to the WISP be discussed at the tax practice's post-filing season meetings?_

____

____

____

DISCUSSION SCENARIO 4

Use the same facts as **Discussion Scenario 3.** The following July, Garcia-Jones plans to complete 600 more returns during the upcoming filing season but cannot hire competent tax professionals locally. It is confident it can hire at least three licensed tax professionals, but all live in other states, and will work remotely.

What should the firm do? ____

____

____

____

What changes might be required in its WISP? ____

____

____

____

What data security implications does this have? ____

____

____

____

Table of Contents

1

WISP - Outline

The bare essentials of a Written Information Security Plan are outlined below. Be sure you incorporate all the required elements in your plan, but scale the comprehensiveness to your firm's size and type of operation. The elements in the outline are there to provide your firm a narrower scope of purpose and define the limitations the document is meant to cover. Therefore, many elements also provide your firm with a level of basic legal protections in the event of a data breach incident. For a detailed explanation of each section, please review the detailed outline provided in this document.

I. **Define the WISP objectives, purpose, and scope**

II. **Identify responsible individuals**

   a. List individuals who will coordinate the security programs as well as responsible persons.
   b. List authorized users at your firm, their data access levels, and responsibilities.

III. **Assess Risks**

   a. Identify Risks
      - List types of information your office handles
      - List potential areas for data loss (internal and external)
      - Outline procedures to monitor and test risks

IV. **Inventory Hardware**

   a. List description and physical location of each item
   b. Record types of information stored or processed by each item

V. **Document Safety Measures in place**

   a. Suggested policies to include in your WISP:
      - Data collection and retention
      - Data disclosure
      - Network protection
      - User access
      - Electronic data exchange
      - Wi-Fi access
      - Remote access
      - Connected devices
      - Reportable Incidents
   b. Draft Employee Code of Conduct

VI. **Draft an implementation clause**

VII. **Attachments**

Written Information Security Plan (WISP)

For

[Your Firm Name Here]

This Document is for general distribution and is available to all employees.
This Document is available to Clients by request and with consent of the Firm's Data Security Coordinator.

Last Modified/Reviewed **[Last Modified Date]**
[Should review and update at least annually]

I. OBJECTIVE

Our objective, in the development and implementation of this comprehensive **Written Information Security Plan (WISP)**, is to create effective administrative, technical, and physical safeguards for the protection of the **Personally Identifiable Information (PII)** retained by **[Your Firm Name],** (hereinafter known as **the Firm**). This WISP is to comply with obligations under the Gramm-Leach-Bliley Act and Federal Trade Commission Financial Privacy and Safeguards Rules to which the Firm is subject. The WISP sets forth our procedure for evaluating our electronic and physical methods of accessing, collecting, storing, using, transmitting, and protecting PII retained by the Firm. For purposes of this WISP, PII means information containing the first name and last name or first initial and last name of a Taxpayer, Spouse, Dependent, or Legal Guardianship person in combination with any of the following data elements retained by the Firm that relate to Clients, Business Entities, or Firm Employees:

A. Social Security number, Date of Birth, or Employment data

B. Driver's license number or state-issued identification card number

C. Income data, Tax Filing data, Retirement Plan data, Asset Ownership data, Investment data

D. Financial account number, credit or debit card number, with or without security code, access code, personal identification number; or password(s) that permit access to a client's financial accounts

E. E-mail addresses, non-listed phone numbers, residential or mobile or contact information

PII shall not include information that is obtained from publicly available sources such as a Mailing Address or Phone Directory listing; or from federal, state or local government records lawfully made available to the general public.

II. PURPOSE

The purpose of the WISP is to:

A. Ensure the Security and Confidentiality of all PII retained by the Firm.

B. Protect PII against anticipated threats or hazards to the security or integrity of such information.

C. Protect against any unauthorized access to or use of PII in a manner that creates a substantial risk of Identity Theft or Fraudulent or Harmful use.

III. SCOPE

The Scope of the WISP related to the Firm shall be limited to the following protocols:

A. Identify reasonably foreseeable internal and external risks to the security, confidentiality, and/or integrity of any electronic, paper, or other records containing PII.

B. Assess the potential damage of these threats, taking into consideration the sensitivity of the PII.

C. Evaluate the sufficiency of existing policies, procedures, customer information systems, and other safeguards in place to control identified risks.

D. Design and implement this WISP to place safeguards to minimize those risks, consistent with the requirements of the Gramm-Leach-Bliley Act, the Federal Trade Commission Financial Privacy and Safeguards Rule, and National Institute of Standards recommendations.

E. Regular monitoring and assessment of the effectiveness of aforementioned safeguards.

IV. IDENTIFIED RESPONSIBLE OFFICIALS

[The Firm] has designated [Employee's Name] to be the Data Security Coordinator (hereinafter the DSC). The DSC is the responsible official for the Firm data security processes and will implement, supervise, and maintain the WISP. Accordingly, the DSC will be responsible for the following:

- Implementing the WISP including all daily operational protocols
- Identifying all the Firm's repositories of data subject to the WISP protocols and designating them as Secured Assets with Restricted Access
- Verifying all employees have completed recurring Information Security Plan Training
- Monitoring and testing employee compliance with the plan's policies and procedures
- Evaluating the ability of any third-party service providers not directly involved with tax preparation and electronic transmission of tax returns to implement and maintain appropriate security measures for the PII to which we have permitted them access, and
- Requiring third-party service providers to implement and maintain appropriate security measures that comply with this WISP
- Reviewing the scope of the security measures in the WISP at least annually or whenever there is a material change in our business practices that affect the security or integrity of records containing PII
- Conducting an annual training session for all owners, managers, employees, and independent contractors, including temporary and contract employees who have access to PII enumerated in the elements of the WISP. All attendees at such training sessions are required to certify their attendance at the training and their familiarity with our requirements for ensuring the protection of PII. See Employee/Contractor Acknowledgement of Understanding at the end of this document

[The Firm] has designated [Employee's Name] to be the Public Information Officer (hereinafter PIO). The PIO will be the firm's designated public statement spokesperson. To prevent misunderstandings and hearsay, all outward-facing communications should be approved through this person who shall be in charge of the following:

- All client communications by phone conversation or in writing
- All statements to law enforcement agencies
- All releases to news media
- All information released to business associates, neighboring businesses, and trade associations to which the firm belongs

V. INSIDE THE FIRM RISK MITIGATION

To reduce internal risks to the security, confidentiality, and/or integrity of any retained electronic, paper, or other records containing PII, the Firm has implemented mandatory policies and procedures as follows:

PII Collection and Retention Policy

A. We will only collect the PII of clients, customers, or employees that is necessary to accomplish our legitimate business needs, while maintaining compliance with all federal, state, or local regulations.

B. Access to records containing PII is limited to employees whose duties, relevant to their job descriptions, constitute a legitimate need to access said records, and only for job-related purposes.

C. The DSC will identify and document the locations where PII may be stored on the Company premises:

- **a.** Servers, disk drives, solid-state drives, USB memory devices, removable media
- **b.** Filing cabinets, securable desk drawers, contracted document retention and storage firms
- **c.** PC Workstations, Laptop Computers, client portals, electronic Document Management
- **d.** Online (Web-based) applications, portals, and cloud software applications such as Box
- **e.** Database applications, such as Bookkeeping and Tax Software Programs
- **f.** Solid-state drives, and removable or swappable drives, and USB storage media

D. Designated written and electronic records containing PII shall be destroyed or deleted at the earliest opportunity consistent with business needs or legal retention requirements.

- **a.** Paper-based records shall be securely destroyed by shredding or incineration at the end of their service life.
- **b.** Electronic records shall be securely destroyed by deleting and overwriting the file directory or by reformatting the drive on which they were housed.
- **c.** Specific business record retention policies and secure data destruction policies are in an attachment to this WISP.

Personnel Accountability Policy

A. A copy of the WISP will be distributed to all current employees and to new employees on the beginning dates of their employment. It will be the employee's responsibility to acknowledge in writing, by signing the attached sheet, that he/she received a copy of the WISP and will abide by its provisions. Employees are actively encouraged to advise the DSC of any activity or operation that poses risk to the secure retention of PII. If the DSC is the source of these risks, employees should advise any other Principal or the Business Owner.

- **a.** The Firm will create and establish general Rules of Behavior and Conduct regarding policies safeguarding PII according to IRS Pub. 4557 Guidelines. **[complete and attach after reviewing supporting NISTIR 7621, NIST SP-800 18, and Pub 4557 requirements]**
- **b.** The Firm will screen the procedures prior to granting new access to PII for existing employees.
- **c.** The Firm will conduct Background Checks on new employees who will have access to retained PII.
- **d.** The Firm may require non-disclosure agreements for employees who have access to the PII of any designated client determined to have highly sensitive data or security concerns related to their account.

B. The DSC or designated authorized representative will immediately train all existing employees on the detailed provisions of the Plan. All employees will be subject to periodic reviews by the DSC to ensure compliance.

C. All employees are responsible for maintaining the privacy and integrity of the Firm's retained PII. Any paper records containing PII are to be secured appropriately when not in use. Employees may not keep files containing PII open on their desks when they are not at their desks. Any computer file stored on the company network containing PII will be password-protected and/or encrypted. Computers must be locked from access when employees are not at their desks. At the end of the workday, all files and other records containing PII will be secured by employees in a manner that is consistent with the Plan's rules for protecting the security of PII.

D. Any employee who willfully discloses PII or fails to comply with these policies will face immediate disciplinary action that includes a verbal or written warning plus other actions up to and including termination of employment.

E. Terminated employees' computer access logins and passwords will be disabled at the time of termination. Physical access to any documents or resources containing PII will be immediately discontinued. Terminated employees will be required to surrender all keys, IDs or access codes or badges, and business cards that permit access to the firm's premises or information. Terminated employees' remote electronic access to personal information will be disabled; voicemail access, e-mail access, Internet access, Tax Software download/update access, accounts and passwords will be inactivated. The DSC or designee shall maintain a highly secured master list of all lock combinations, passwords, and keys, and will determine the need for changes to be made relevant to the terminated employee's access rights.

PII Disclosure Policy

A. No PII will be disclosed without authenticating the receiving party and without securing written authorization from the individual whose PII is contained in such disclosure. Access is restricted for areas in which personal information is stored, including file rooms, filing cabinets, desks, and computers with access to retained PII. An escort will accompany all visitors while within any restricted area of stored PII data.

B. The Firm will take all possible measures to ensure that employees are trained to keep all paper and electronic records containing PII securely on premises at all times. When there is a need to bring records containing PII offsite, only the minimum information necessary will be checked out. Records taken offsite will be returned to the secure storage location as soon as possible. Under no circumstances will documents, electronic devices, or digital media containing PII be left unattended in an employee's car, home, or in any other potentially insecure location.

C. All security measures included in this WISP shall be reviewed annually, beginning **[annual calendar review date]** to ensure that the policies contained in the WISP are adequate and meet all applicable federal and state regulations. Changes may be made to the WISP at any time they are warranted. When the WISP is amended, employees will be informed in writing. The DSC and principal owners of the firm will be responsible for the review and modification of the WISP, including any security improvement recommendations from employees, security consultants, IT contractors, and regulatory sources.

D. **[The Firm]** shares Employee PII in the form of employment records, pension and insurance information, and other information required of any employer. The Firm may share the PII of our clients with the state and federal tax authorities, Tax Software Vendor, a bookkeeping service, a payroll service, a CPA firm, an

Enrolled Agent, legal counsel, and/or business advisors in the normal course of business for any Tax Preparation firm. Law enforcement and governmental agencies may also have customer PII shared with them in order to protect our clients or in the event of a lawfully executed subpoena. An IT support company may occasionally see PII in the course of contracted services. Access to PII by these third-party organizations will be the minimum required to conduct business. Any third-party service provider that does require access to information must be compliant with the standards contained in this WISP at a minimum. The exceptions are tax software vendors and e-Filing transmitters; and the state and federal tax authorities, which are already compliant with laws that are stricter than this WISP requires. These additional requirements are outlined in IRS Publication 1345.

Reportable Event Policy

A. If there is a Data Security Incident that requires notifications under the provisions of regulatory laws such as The Gramm-Leach-Bliley Act, there will be a mandatory post-incident review by the DSC of the events and actions taken. The DSC will determine if any changes in operations are required to improve the security of retained PII for which the Firm is responsible. Records of and changes or amendments to the Information Security Plan will be tracked and kept on file as an addendum to this WISP.

B. The DSC is responsible for maintaining any Data Theft Liability Insurance, Cyber Theft Insurance Riders, or Legal Counsel on retainer as deemed prudent and necessary by the principal ownership of the Firm.

C. The DSC will also notify the IRS Stakeholder Liaison, and state and local Law Enforcement Authorities in the event of a Data Security Incident, coordinating all actions and responses taken by the Firm. The DSC or person designated by the coordinator shall be the sole point of contact with any outside organization not related to Law Enforcement, such as news media, non-client inquiries by other local firms or businesses and other inquirers.

VI. OUTSIDE THE FIRM RISK MITIGATION

To combat external risks from outside the firm network to the security, confidentiality, and/or integrity of electronic, paper, or other records containing PII, and improving - where necessary - the effectiveness of the current safeguards for limiting such risks, the Firm has implemented the following policies and procedures.

Network Protection Policy

A. Firewall protection, operating system security patches, and all software products shall be up to date and installed on any computer that accesses, stores, or processes PII data on the Firms network. This includes any Third-Party Devices connected to the network.

B. All system security software, including anti-virus, anti-malware, and internet security, shall be up to date and installed on any computer that stores or processes PII data or the Firms network.

C. Secure user authentication protocols will be in place to:

- **a.** Control username ID, passwords and Two-Factor Authentication processes
- **b.** Restrict access to currently active user accounts
- **c.** Require strong passwords in a manner that conforms to accepted security standards (using upper- and lower-case letters, numbers, and special characters, eight or more characters in length)
- **d.** Change all passwords at least every 90 days, or more often if conditions warrant
- **e.** Unique firm related passwords must not be used on other sites; or personal passwords used for firm business. Firm passwords will be for access to Firm resources only and not mixed with personal passwords

D. All computer systems will be continually monitored for unauthorized access or unauthorized use of PII data. Event Logging will remain enabled on all systems containing PII. Review of event logs by the DSC or IT partner will be scheduled at random intervals not to exceed 90 days.

E. The Firm will maintain a firewall between the internet and the internal private network. This firewall will be secured and maintained by the Firm's IT Service Provider. The Firewall will follow firmware/software updates per vendor recommendations for security patches. Workstations will also have a software-based firewall enabled.

F. Operating System (OS) patches and security updates will be reviewed and installed continuously. The DSC will conduct a top-down security review at least every 30 days.

Firm User Access Control Policy

A. The Firm will use 2-Factor Authentication (2FA) for remote login authentication via a cell phone text message, or an app, such as Google Authenticator or Duo, to ensure only authorized devices can gain remote access to the Firm's systems.

B. All users will have unique passwords to the computer network. The firm will not have any shared passwords or accounts to our computer systems, internet access, software vendor for product downloads, and so on. The passwords can be changed by the individual without disclosure of the password(s) to the DSC or any other Firm employee at any time.

C. Passwords will be refreshed every 90 days at a minimum and more often if conditions warrant. The DSC will notify employees when accelerated password reset is necessary.

D. If a Password Utility program, such as LastPass or Password Safe, is utilized, the DSC will first confirm that:

a. Username and password information is stored on a secure encrypted site.

b. 2-factor authentication of the user is enabled to authenticate new devices.

Electronic Exchange of PII Policy

A. It is Firm policy that PII will not be in any unprotected format, such as e-mailed in plain text, rich text, html, or other e-mail formats unless encryption or password protection is present. Passwords MUST be communicated to the receiving party via a method other than what is used to send the data; such as by phone call or SMS text message (out of stream from the data sent).

B. The Firm may use a Password Protected Portal to exchange documents containing PII upon approval of data security protocols by the DSC.

C. MS BitLocker or similar encryption will be used on interface drives, such as a USB drive, for files containing PII.

Wi-Fi Access Policy

A. Wireless access (Wi-Fi) points or nodes, if available, will use strong encryption. Firm Wi-Fi will require a password for access. If open Wi-Fi for clients is made available (guest Wi-Fi), it will be on a different network and Wi-Fi node from the Firm's Private work-related Wi-Fi.

B. All devices with wireless capability such as printers, all-in-one copiers and printers, fax machines, and smart devices such as TVs, refrigerators, and any other devices with Smart Technology will have default factory passwords changed to Firm-assigned passwords. All default passwords will be reset or the device will be disabled from wireless capability or the device will be replaced with a non-wireless capable device.

Remote Access Policy

The DSC and the Firm's IT contractor will approve use of Remote Access utilities for the entire Firm. **Remote access is dangerous if not configured correctly and is the preferred tool of many hackers.** Remote access using tools that encrypt both the traffic and the authentication requests (ID and Password) used will be the standard. Remote Access will not be available unless the Office is staffed and systems are monitored. **Nights and Weekends are high threat periods for Remote Access Takeover data theft.** Remote access will only be allowed using 2 Factor Authentication (2FA) in addition to username and password authentication.

Connected Devices Policy

A. Any new devices that connect to the Internal Network will undergo a thorough security review before they are added to the network. The Firm will ensure the devices meet all security patch standards and login and password protocols before they are connected to the network.

B. "AutoRun" features for USB ports and optical drives like CD and DVD drives on network computers and connected devices will be disabled to prevent malicious programs from self-installing on the Firm's systems.

C. The Firm or a certified third-party vendor will erase the hard drives or memory storage devices the Firm removes from the network at the end of their respective service lives. If any memory device is unable to be erased, it will be destroyed by removing its ability to be connected to any device, or circuitry will be shorted, or it will be physically rendered unable to produce any residual data still on the storage device.

D. The firm runs approved and licensed anti-virus software, which is updated on all servers continuously. Virus and malware definition updates are also updated as they are made available. The system is tested weekly to ensure the protection is current and up to date.

Information Security Training Policy

All employees will be trained on maintaining the privacy and confidentiality of the Firm's PII. The DSC will conduct training regarding the specifics of paper record handling, electronic record handling, and Firm security procedures at least annually. All new employees will be trained before PII access is granted, and periodic reviews or refreshers will be scheduled until all employees are of the same mindset regarding Information Security. Disciplinary action may be recommended for any employee who disregards these policies.

VII. IMPLEMENTATION

Effective **[date of implementation]**, [The Firm] has created this Written Information Security Plan (WISP) in compliance with regulatory rulings regarding implementation of a written data security plan found in the Gramm-Leach-Bliley Act and the Federal Trade Commission Financial Privacy and Safeguards Rules.

Signed: ______________________________ **Date:** ______________

Title: [Principal Operating Officer/Owner Title]

Signed: ______________________________ **Date:** ______________

Title: Data Security Coordinator

SAMPLE WISP ATTACHMENTS

Attachment A: Record Retention Policies

Designated retained written and electronic records containing PII will be destroyed or deleted at the earliest opportunity consistent with business needs or legal retention requirements.

It is Firm policy to retain no PII records longer than required by current regulations, practices, or standards.

I. In no case shall paper or electronic retained records containing PII be kept longer than ____ Years.

II. Paper-based records shall be securely destroyed by cross-cut shredding or incineration at the end of their service life.

III. Electronic records shall be securely destroyed by deleting and overwriting the file directory or by reformatting the drive where they were housed or destroying the drive disks rendering them inoperable if they have reached the end of their service life.

Attachment B: Rules of Behavior and Conduct Safe-guarding Client PII

Create and distribute rules of behavior that describe responsibilities and expected behavior regarding computer information systems as well as paper records and usage of taxpayer data. Have all information system users complete, sign, and comply with the rules of behavior. **NISTIR 7621, Small Business Information Security: The Fundamentals, Section 4**, has information regarding general rules of Behavior, such as:

- **Be careful of email attachments and web links**
  - Do not click on a link or open an attachment that you were not expecting. If it appears important, call the sender to verify they sent the email and ask them to describe what the attachment or link is. Before you click a link (in an email or on social media, instant messages, other webpages), hover over that link to see the actual web address it will take you to. Train employees to recognize phishing attempts and who to notify when one occurs.
- **Use separate personal and business computers, mobile devices, and email accounts**
  - This is especially important if other people, such as children, use personal devices. Do not conduct business or any sensitive activities (like online business banking) on a personal computer or device and do not engage in activities such as web surfing, gaming, downloading videos, etc., on business computers or devices. Do not send sensitive business information to personal email addresses.
- **Do not connect personal or untrusted storage devices or hardware into computers, mobile devices, or networks.**
  - Do not share USB drives or external hard drives between personal and business computers or devices. Do not connect any unknown/untrusted hardware into the system or network, and do not insert any unknown CD, DVD, or USB drive. Disable the "AutoRun" feature for the USB ports and optical drives like CD and DVD drives on business computers to help prevent such malicious programs from installing on the systems.
- **Be careful downloading software**
  - Do not download software from an unknown web page. Be very careful with freeware or shareware.
- **Watch out when providing personal or business information**
  - Social engineering is an attempt to obtain physical or electronic access to information by manipulating people. A very common type of attack involves a person, website, or email that pretends to be something it's not. A social engineer will research a business to learn names, titles, responsibilities, and any personal information they can find; calls or sends an email with a believable but made-up story designed to convince you to give certain information.
  - Never respond to unsolicited phone calls that ask for sensitive personal or business information. Employees should notify their management whenever there is an attempt or request for sensitive business information.
  - Never give out usernames or passwords. No company should ask for this information for any reason. Also, beware of people asking what kind of operating system, brand of firewall, internet browser, or what applications are installed. This is information that can make it easier for a hacker to break into the system.

- **Watch for harmful pop-ups**
  - When connected to and using the Internet, do not respond to popup windows requesting that users click "OK." Use a popup blocker and only allow popups on trusted websites.
- **Use strong passwords**
  - Good passwords consist of a random sequence of letters (upper- and lower-case), numbers, and special characters. The NIST recommends passwords be at least 12 characters long. For systems or applications that have important information, use multiple forms of identification (called "multi-factor" or "dual factor" authentication).
  - Many devices come with default administration passwords – these should be changed immediately when installing and regularly thereafter. Default passwords are easily found or known by hackers and can be used to access the device. The product manual or those who install the system should be able to show you how to change them.
  - Passwords should be changed at least every three months.
  - Passwords to devices and applications that deal with business information should not be re-used.
  - You may want to consider using a password management application to store your passwords for you.
- **Conduct online business more securely**
  - Online business/commerce/banking should only be done using a secure browser connection. This will normally be indicated by a small lock visible in the lower right corner or upper left of the web browser window.
  - Erase the web browser cache, temporary internet files, cookies, and history regularly. Ensure to erase this data after using any public computer and after any online commerce or banking session. This prevents important information from being stolen if the system is compromised. This will also help the system run faster. Typically, this is done in the web browser's "privacy" or "security" menu. Review the web browser's help manual for guidance.

Attachment C: Security Breach Procedures and Notifications

I. Notifications

If the Data Security Coordinator determines that PII has been stolen or lost, the Firm will notify the following entities, describing the theft or loss in detail, and work with authorities to investigate the issue and to protect the victim's identity and credit.

- The **IRS Stakeholder Liaison** who coordinates IRS divisions and other agencies regarding a Tax Professional Office data breach.
- The state Attorney General's Office
- The FBI if it is a cyber-crime involving electronic data theft
- The Federal Trade Commission, in accordance with GLB Act provisions as outlined in the Safeguards Rule.
- Local law enforcement
- Tax software vendor (can assist with next steps after a data breach incident)
- Liability insurance carrier who may provide forensic IT services
- Legal counsel
- To the extent required by regulatory laws and good business practices, the Firm will also notify the victims of the theft so that they can protect their credit and identity. The FTC provides guidance for identity theft notifications in: **Information Compromise and the Risk of Identity Theft: Guidance for Your Business**

II. Procedures

Read this **IRS Newswire Alert** for more information

Examples:

- Go to IRS e-Services and check your EFIN activity report to see if more returns have been filed on your EFIN than you transmitted.
- Check to see if you can tell if the returns in question were submitted at odd hours that are not during normal hours of operation, such as overnight or on weekends.
- Were the returns transmitted on a Monday or Tuesday morning?
    - Typically, a thief will remotely steal the client data over the weekend when no one is in the office to notice. They then rework the returns over the weekend and transmit them on a normal business workday just after the weekend.

Attachment D: Employee/Contractor Acknowledgement of Understanding

I, **[Employee Name]**, do hereby acknowledge that I have been informed of the Written Information Security Plan used by [The Firm]. I have undergone training conducted by the Data Security Coordinator. I have also been able to have all questions regarding procedures answered to my satisfaction so that I fully understand the importance of maintaining strict compliance with the purpose and intent of this WISP.

I also understand that there will be periodic updates and training if these policies and procedures change for any reason. It has been explained to me that non-compliance with the WISP policies may result in disciplinary actions up to and including termination of employment.

I understand the importance of protecting the Personally Identifiable Information of our clients, employees, and contacts, and will diligently monitor my actions, as well as the actions of others, so that [The Firm] is a safe repository for all personally sensitive data necessary for business needs.

Signed,

[Employee Name] Date: **[Date of Initial/Last Training]**

Title: **[Employee Title Description]**

Attachment E: Firm Hardware Inventory containing PII Data

Below is the enumerated list of hardware and software containing client or employee PII that will be periodically audited for compliance with this WISP.

Hardware Item	Location	Principal User	In-Service Date	Last Inventoried

Attachment F: Firm Employees Authorized to Access PII

Name	Role	Job Duties	Access Level	Date access Granted	Date Access Terminated
John Doe	DSC	Office Manager	Full access to all PII	01/01/2015	

APPENDIX B — FULL TEXT OF 16 CFR §314.4

In order to develop, implement, and maintain your information security program, you shall:

- **a.** Designate a qualified individual responsible for overseeing and implementing your information security program and enforcing your information security program (for purposes of this part, "Qualified Individual"). The Qualified Individual may be employed by you, an affiliate, or a service provider. To the extent the requirement in this paragraph (a) is met using a service provider or an affiliate, you shall:
  - **1.** Retain responsibility for compliance with this part;
  - **2.** Designate a senior member of your personnel responsible for direction and oversight of the Qualified Individual; and
  - **3.** Require the service provider or affiliate to maintain an information security program that protects you in accordance with the requirements of this part.
- **b.** Base your information security program on a risk assessment that identifies reasonably foreseeable internal and external risks to the security, confidentiality, and integrity of customer information that could result in the unauthorized disclosure, misuse, alteration, destruction, or other compromise of such information, and assesses the sufficiency of any safeguards in place to control these risks.
  - **1.** The risk assessment shall be written and shall include:
    - **i.** Criteria for the evaluation and categorization of identified security risks or threats you face;
    - **ii.** Criteria for the assessment of the confidentiality, integrity, and availability of your information systems and customer information, including the adequacy of the existing controls in the context of the identified risks or threats you face; and
    - **iii.** Requirements describing how identified risks will be mitigated or accepted based on the risk assessment and how the information security program will address the risks.
  - **2.** You shall periodically perform additional risk assessments that reexamine the reasonably foreseeable internal and external risks to the security, confidentiality, and integrity of customer information that could result in the unauthorized disclosure, misuse, alteration, destruction, or other compromise of such information, and reassess the sufficiency of any safeguards in place to control these risks.

c. Design and implement safeguards to control the risks you identity through risk assessment, including by:

1. Implementing and periodically reviewing access controls, including technical and, as appropriate, physical controls to:

    i. Authenticate and permit access only to authorized users to protect against the unauthorized acquisition of customer information; and

    ii. Limit authorized users' access only to customer information that they need to perform their duties and functions, or, in the case of customers, to access their own information;

2. Identify and manage the data, personnel, devices, systems, and facilities that enable you to achieve business purposes in accordance with their relative importance to business objectives and your risk strategy;

3. Protect by encryption all customer information held or transmitted by you both in transit over external networks and at rest. To the extent you determine that encryption of customer information, either in transit over external networks or at rest, is infeasible, you may instead secure such customer information using effective alternative compensating controls reviewed and approved by your Qualified Individual;

4. Adopt secure development practices for in-house developed applications utilized by you for transmitting, accessing, or storing customer information and procedures for evaluating, assessing, or testing the security of externally developed applications you utilize to transmit, access, or store customer information;

5. Implement multi-factor authentication for any individual accessing any information system, unless your Qualified Individual has approved in writing the use of reasonably equivalent or more secure access controls;

6.

    i. Develop, implement, and maintain procedures for the secure disposal of customer information in any format no later than two years after the last date the information is used in connection with the provision of a product or service to the customer to which it relates, unless such information is necessary for business operations or for other legitimate business purposes, is otherwise required to be retained by law or regulation, or where targeted disposal is not reasonably feasible due to the manner in which the information is maintained; and

    ii. Periodically review your data retention policy to minimize the unnecessary retention of data;

7. Adopt procedures for change management; and

8. Implement policies, procedures, and controls designed to monitor and log the activity of authorized users and detect unauthorized access or use of, or tampering with, customer information by such users.

d.

1. Regularly test or otherwise monitor the effectiveness of the safeguards' key controls, systems, and procedures, including those to detect actual and attempted attacks on, or intrusions into, information systems.

2. For information systems, the monitoring and testing shall include continuous monitoring or periodic penetration testing and vulnerability assessments. Absent effective continuous monitoring or other systems to detect, on an ongoing basis, changes in information systems that may create vulnerabilities, you shall conduct:

i. Annual penetration testing of your information systems determined each given year based on relevant identified risks in accordance with the risk assessment; and

ii. Vulnerability assessments, including any systemic scans or reviews of information systems reasonably designed to identify publicly known security vulnerabilities in your information systems based on the risk assessment, at least every six months; and whenever there are material changes to your operations or business arrangements; and whenever there are circumstances you know or have reason to know may have a material impact on your information security program.

e. Implement policies and procedures to ensure that personnel are able to enact your information security program by:

1. Providing your personnel with security awareness training that is updated as necessary to reflect risks identified by the risk assessment;
2. Utilizing qualified information security personnel employed by you or an affiliate or service provider sufficient to manage your information security risks and to perform or oversee the information security program;
3. Providing information security personnel with security updates and training sufficient to address relevant security risks; and
4. Verifying that key information security personnel take steps to maintain current knowledge of changing information security threats and countermeasures.

f. Oversee service providers, by:

1. Taking reasonable steps to select and retain service providers that are capable of maintaining appropriate safeguards for the customer information at issue;
2. Requiring your service providers by contract to implement and maintain such safeguards; and
3. Periodically assessing your service providers based on the risk they present and the continued adequacy of their safeguards.

g. Evaluate and adjust your information security program in light of the results of the testing and monitoring required by paragraph (d) of this section; any material changes to your operations or business arrangements; the results of risk assessments performed under paragraph (b)(2) of this section; or any other circumstances that you know or have reason to know may have a material impact on your information security program.

h. Establish a written incident response plan designed to promptly respond to, and recover from, any security event materially affecting the confidentiality, integrity, or availability of customer information in your control. Such incident response plan shall address the following areas:

1. The goals of the incident response plan;
2. The internal processes for responding to a security event;
3. The definition of clear roles, responsibilities, and levels of decision-making authority;
4. External and internal communications and information sharing;
5. Identification of requirements for the remediation of any identified weaknesses in information systems and associated controls;
6. Documentation and reporting regarding security events and related incident response activities; and
7. The evaluation and revision as necessary of the incident response plan following a security event.

i. Require your Qualified Individual to report in writing, regularly and at least annually, to your board of directors or equivalent governing body. If no such board of directors or equivalent governing body exists, such report shall be timely presented to a senior officer responsible for your information security program. The report shall include the following information:

   1. The overall status of the information security program and your compliance with this part; and

   2. Material matters related to the information security program, addressing issues such as risk assessment, risk management and control decisions, service provider arrangements, results of testing, security events or violations and management's responses thereto, and recommendations for changes in the information security program.

Chapter 2: Capitalization vs. Repair Review

Note. Corrections for all of the chapters are available at **TaxSchool.illinois.edu.** For clarification about terms used throughout this chapter, see the **Acronyms and Abbreviations** section following the index.

For your convenience, in-text website links are also provided as short URLs. Anywhere you see **uofi.tax/xxx**, the link points to the address immediately following in brackets.

About the Author

Chris Korban, CPA, is a Tax Materials Specialist at the University of Illinois Tax School. He joined Tax School in 2023 with nine years of experience in public accounting. Chris earned both his Bachelor's Degree in Accounting and Master of Accounting Science from the University of Illinois.

Other chapter contributors and reviewers are listed at the front of this book.

INTRODUCTION

One of the more complex areas of accounting and taxation is knowing whether to expense a purchase immediately or to recognize the expense over time through depreciation or amortization. Whether to write off certain business expenses or depreciate them requires critically analyzing facts and circumstances. IRC §162(a) allows taxpayers engaged in a trade or business to deduct "ordinary and necessary" business expenses. At the same time, IRC §263(a) disallows deductions for buildings and most tangible property improvements (i.e., betterments, adaptations, and restorations). Instead of deducting these costs immediately, taxpayers must capitalize §263(a) enhancements and recover these investments through depreciation.

Distinguishing between "ordinary and necessary" expenses and property improvements often proves challenging for accountants and tax professionals. For example, one could argue that replacing a window in a rental unit would constitute an ordinary and necessary business expense. Others, however, may consider that same expense an improvement to that rental unit.

The IRS attempted to provide guidance on the distinction between §§162(a) and 263(a) by consolidating case law and other administrative rulings.[1] To remove some of the ambiguity in the Code, the IRS also created certain safe harbors for taxpayers as part of these tangible property regulations.

The tangible property regulations went into effect for tax years beginning on or after January 1, 2014. Nearly 10 years after its adoption, the application of Treasury Decision (TD) 9636 is still a perplexing and laborious task. While these regulations provide more guidance and insight, they do not clarify every position. Facts-and-circumstances tests still require a reasonable application of the Code and the regulations to analyze a taxpayer's unique situation.

Everyone who files a Schedule C, *Profit or Loss From Business*; Schedule F, *Profit or Loss From Farming;* or Schedule E, *Supplemental Income and Loss*, is subject to TD 9636. Consequently, the tangible property regulations have a far-reaching impact, necessitating taxpayers with businesses and farms to familiarize themselves with the concepts contained therein.

The tangible property regulations take the approach that taxpayers must capitalize all noninventory tangible property (i.e., depreciated on the taxpayer's return) unless an exception applies. Exceptions include qualifying materials and supplies[2], as well as repairs and maintenance.[3] These exceptions are not subject to depreciation and can be deducted on the taxpayer's return. The deduction's timing varies by item type and how the taxpayer treats the item for business purposes. In addition to exceptions, the final regulations allow taxpayers to deduct certain items that otherwise must be capitalized and to capitalize certain items that otherwise could be deducted through special elections and safe harbors.

1. TD 9636, 2013-43 IRB 331.
2. Treas. Reg. §1.162-3.
3. Treas. Reg. §1.162-4.

SCOPE OF TD 9636

The tangible property regulations focus on expense recognition, which is a broad area that involves numerous aspects of accounting concepts. There are 13 separate regulations in TD 9636 that encompass the following subjects.

- Materials and supplies (Treas. Reg. §1.162-3)
- Repairs (Treas. Reg. §1.162-4)
- Rentals (Treas. Reg. §1.162-11)
- Obsolescence of non-depreciable property (Treas. Reg. §1.165-2)
- Leased property (Treas. Reg. §1.167(a)-4)
- Accounting for depreciable property (applicability note modifying Treas. Reg. §1.167(a)-7)
- Retirements (applicability note modifying Treas. Reg. §1.167(a)-8)
- Accounting for modified accelerated cost recovery system (MACRS) property (Treas. Reg. §1.168(i)-7)
- Capital expenditures, in general (Treas. Reg. §1.263(a)-1)
- Amounts paid to acquire or produce tangible property (Treas. Reg. §1.263(a)-2)
- Amounts paid to improve tangible property (Treas. Reg. §1.263(a)-3)
- Election to deduct or capitalize certain expenses (Treas. Reg. §1.263(a)-6)

WARRANT FOR REVISITATION

While the tangible property regulations took effect nearly a decade ago, it may behoove taxpayers and practitioners to revisit the rules, nuances, and application of these regulations. Since the introduction of these regulations, the enactment of new tax laws and procedures have occurred, particularly the Tax Cuts and Jobs Act (TCJA). Among its changes, TCJA included the change to IRC §168(k) allowing taxpayers to expense purchased capital assets using 100% bonus depreciation instead of the prior 50%.[4] Starting in 2023, this provision begins to phase-out, where taxpayers may only immediately expense 80% bonus depreciation. This change will result in taxpayers needing to more carefully assess whether capitalization of new purchases or expensing them provides the most benefit, as these will no longer result in the same amount of immediate deduction as it had before. Consequently, taxpayers and practitioners must familiarize themselves with the tangible property regulations to determine which methods apply to them and how to implement any necessary changes.

Additionally, a taxpayer's tax situation and business can change over time. Income from a business could change from year to year, prompting owners to evaluate whether expense recognition should be accelerated. One area that provides such flexibility is in the capitalization of expenditures. Tax planning around these expenses can help in adjusting the amount of expenses a taxpayer reports on their tax return. However, taxpayers and practitioners need to be aware of the rules and concepts behind this strategy, especially implementing a change in their method of accounting to coordinate these efforts, described in detail later in this chapter. As taxpayers' businesses change, or if practitioners obtain new clients, one should familiarize themselves with the tangible property regulations regularly to stay compliant in implementing new and different strategies.

4. *Tax Cuts and Jobs Act*, PL 115-97, §13201.

FUNDAMENTAL CONCEPTS

Examining fundamental principles in tangible property regulations is required to discuss the concepts of capitalization and repair. These regulations introduced new concepts into the theory of the U.S. tax system and are vital to understanding the nature of the changes contained therein for systematized and compliant tax return preparation.

UNIT OF PROPERTY[5]

Unit of property (UOP) is a critical concept in the tangible property regulations that clarifies whether a taxpayer may deduct an item or is required to capitalize it. The regulations define UOP as consisting of all the components of property that are **functionally interdependent.** Functional interdependence is achieved when the placing in service of one component is dependent on the placing in service of another component. For example, a vehicle engine is not in and of itself a UOP because it cannot function without a vehicle, and vice versa. On the other hand, a computer and printer can function independently from each other, so they are considered separate UOPs. The regulations distinguish between building property and tangible nonbuilding property (i.e., personal property and nonbuilding real property) in determining the UOP.

Building Property

An entire building structure (roof, walls, windows, floors, and ceiling) is one UOP. Each building system is a separate UOP. The regulations identify the following building systems considered separate UOPs from the building structure.

- Heating, ventilating, and cooling (HVAC) system
- Plumbing system
- Electrical system
- Escalator system
- Elevator system
- Fire protection and alarm system
- Security system
- Gas distribution system
- Other structural components identified in published guidance in the Federal Register or the Internal Revenue Bulletin

Property Other Than Buildings

Generally, all components of real or personal property that are functionally interdependent comprise a single UOP. Unlike an asset-by-asset determination for class life and recovery period, functional interdependence depends on **the taxpayer's use of the asset.**

Special rules apply to plant property, network assets, leased property other than buildings, and components placed in service in taxable years beginning before January 1, 2014.

5. TD 9636, 2013-43 IRB 331.

Plant Property.[6] Plant property is functionally interdependent machinery or equipment, other than network assets (described later), used to perform an industrial process, such as manufacturing, generation, warehousing, distribution, automated materials handling in service industries, or similar activities. For plant property specifically used to perform an industrial process, the UOP is further divisible into smaller units comprised of each component or group of components that perform a discrete and major function or operation within the functionally interdependent machinery or equipment.

2

Network Assets.[7] Network assets generally include assets that form an interconnected grid or web system. This category includes pipelines, railroad tracks, water and sewage lines, power transmission lines, and cable lines. The particular facts and circumstances or industry guidance from the Treasury Department and the IRS determine the UOP and the application of the improvement analysis.

Leased Property.[8] For determination of the UOP, when a taxpayer is the lessee of leased property other than buildings, the same general rule, plant property rule, and network asset rule apply as they would otherwise. For taxpayers who lease buildings or portions of buildings, the UOP comprises the following.

- Each building and its structural components and systems
- The portion of each building subject to the taxpayer's lease and the portion of the structural components and systems that are part of the leased building

Example 1. Alice leases space for her consulting business on the third floor of an office building. The UOP for Alice's consulting business is the portion of the building she leases, including the structural components of her leased space.

Components Placed in Service in a Tax Year Beginning Before 2014.[9] Consider situations where a taxpayer placed a component (or group of components) in service before 2014. Suppose those component(s) are now considered a UOP under the regulations and that the taxpayer properly treated the component(s) as being in a different MACRS class than the UOP. In that case, the taxpayer must treat those component(s) as a separate UOP. This practice also applies when the taxpayer properly depreciated the component using a different method than the UOP.

Special Rules Applicable to All Properties

Although there are certain exceptions, **a taxpayer generally must capitalize all related amounts paid to improve a UOP owned by the taxpayer.**[10] This extends to amounts paid for more than one taxable year. Whether amounts are related to the same improvement depends on the facts and circumstances of the performed activities.[11]

Certain Spare Parts. If the costs of rotable spare parts, temporary spare parts, or standby emergency spare parts (discussed later) were capitalized and used as an improvement to a UOP, then for purposes of applying the preceding requirement to capitalize improvements to the UOP, the part is not a UOP separate from the UOP improved.[12]

---

6. Treas. Reg. §1.263(a)-3(e)(3)(ii).
7. Treas. Reg. §1.263(a)-3(e)(3)(iii).
8. Treas. Reg. §1.263(a)-3(e)(2)(v).
9. Treas. Reg. §1.263(a)-3(e)(5)(i).
10. Treas. Reg. §1.263(a)-3(d).
11. Treas. Reg. §1.263(a)-3(g)(3).
12. Treas. Reg. §1.263(a)-3(e)(4).

Changes in Subsequent Year. There may be instances where depreciation of a UOP occurred under these regulations, but in later years either the taxpayer or the IRS determines that a portion of that UOP belongs in a different MACRS class or requires a different depreciation method. Treas. Reg. §1.263(a)-3(e)(5)(ii) provides clarity on these scenarios. If the taxpayer or the IRS changes the treatment of a UOP (or any portion thereof) that the taxpayer placed in service in a prior taxable year to a proper MACRS class or depreciation method, then the taxpayer must change the UOP determination for consistency with the change in treatment for depreciation purposes. Such a change could result from a cost segregation study or a change in the property's use.

Thus, if a taxpayer properly reclassifies a portion of a UOP to a different MACRS class, then the taxpayer should treat the reclassified portion of the property as a separate UOP. If, on the other hand, a taxpayer finds properties previously depreciated in different classes to be part of the same UOP, then the taxpayer must treat them uniformly as the same UOP.

Example 2. Todd purchased a building for his photography business in 2020 for $240,000. He capitalized the $40,000 costs of the electrical wiring for the building separately as 7-year property. After performing a cost segregation study of the building in 2023, Todd's accountant appropriately determined that the wiring in Todd's building was a structural component and needs to be depreciated as 39-year nonresidential real property. Consequently, Todd changes his method of accounting to address this difference in treatment. Todd needs to consider the wiring as part of the building's UOP.

Todd files Form 3115, *Application for Change in Accounting Method,* and computes the excess depreciation he claimed in 2020 and 2021 using the 7-year life instead of the correct 39-year life. Todd's original depreciation schedule showing the wiring of the building having a 7-year depreciable life follows.

Asset	Date in Service	Cost	Life	Convention [a]	Prior Depreciation	2022 Depreciation
Building	1/01/2020	$200,000	39	MM S/L	$10,043	$ 5,128
Wiring	1/01/2020	40,000	7	HY 200DB	15,510	6,997
Total		$240,000			$25,553	$12,125

[a] MM S/L = midmonth straight-line, HY 200DB = half-yeardouble-declining balance.

Todd's corrected depreciation schedule with the wiring having a 39-year depreciable life is as follows.

Asset	Date in Service	Cost	Life	Convention	Prior Depreciation	2022 Depreciation
Building	1/01/2020	$200,000	39	MM S/L	$10,043	$5,128
Wiring	1/01/2020	40,000	39	MM S/L	2,009	1,026
Total		$240,000			$12,052	$6,154

Todd must add this excess depreciation of $13,501 ($15,510 of prior 7-year depreciation – $2,009 of corrected 39-year accumulated depreciation) to his income.

Note. For more information on depreciation methods and conventions, see the 2023 *University of Illinois Tax Workbook,* Chapter 7: Depreciation.

MATERIALS AND SUPPLIES

Treas. Reg. §1.162-3 clarifies what are considered materials and supplies that taxpayers may expense. Materials and supplies are any tangible property a taxpayer uses or consumes in their operations, are not inventory, and **meet at least one of the following criteria.**[13]

2

1. Is a component a taxpayer acquires to maintain, repair, or improve a unit of tangible property they own, lease, or service and **that they do not acquire as part of any single UOP**
2. Consists of fuel, lubricants, water, and similar items, reasonably expected for a taxpayer to consume in 12 months or less, beginning when used in their operations
3. Is a UOP that has an **economic useful life** of 12 months or less, beginning when a taxpayer uses or consumes the property in their operations
4. Is a UOP that has an acquisition cost or production cost (determined under IRC §263A) of $200 or less or an amount provided in further guidance in the Federal Register or the Internal Revenue Bulletin
5. Is otherwise identified in published guidance in the Federal Register or the Internal Revenue Bulletin as materials and supplies for purposes of this regulation

Materials and Supplies Categories[14]

The regulations classify materials and supplies into the following three categories.

1. Incidental
2. Nonincidental
3. Rotable, temporary, or standby emergency spare parts

These categories determine when taxpayers can deduct the cost of materials and supplies on their returns.

Incidental Materials and Supplies. Incidental materials and supplies are items a taxpayer carries on hand that they exclude from inventory and do not keep records regarding their consumption. Examples of incidental supplies include pens, calculators, coffee pots, and paper towels. Amounts the taxpayer pays to purchase or produce incidental materials and supplies are deductible in the tax year paid (or the year incurred for accrual-basis taxpayers).

> **Example 3.** Sam owns and operates a grocery store and purchases hand sanitizer for customer and employee use. Sam does not keep records of its consumption. Therefore, the hand sanitizer is incidental in Sam's case. Sam is a cash-basis taxpayer, so he deducts the cost of hand sanitizer in the year he purchases it.

Nonincidental Materials and Supplies. Nonincidental materials and supplies (NIMS) are materials and supplies that do not fall into the incidental category. Examples of NIMS include disposable cups at a coffee shop where the owner counts cups monthly to eliminate shrinkage, and shaving cream at a barber shop where the barber keeps track of the amount of product used weekly. A taxpayer generally deducts the cost of NIMS when they place these items in service for business use or when consumed in operations.

> **Example 4.** Molly uses catering trays to transport food to customers of her catering business. She regularly keeps track of how many trays she has on hand to ensure she has enough for customer orders throughout a given month. The catering trays are nonincidental because Molly keeps track of the number of trays that she has. Molly is permitted to deduct the cost of the trays in the year she places them in service.

---

13. Treas. Reg. §1.162-3(c)(1).

14. Treas. Reg. §1.162-3.

Small Business Taxpayer Exemption.[15] Taxpayers with gross receipts less than $10 million are not required to maintain an inventory when the production, purchase, or sale of merchandise is an income-producing factor. Small business taxpayers can either treat inventory as a NIMS, follow the inventory rules stated in the taxpayer's applicable financial statement (AFS) (discussed later), or use their books and records prepared in accordance with their accounting procedures if they do not have an AFS.

Taxpayers who treat inventory as NIMS still treat the items as inventory. The costs are recovered through cost of goods sold in the later of either the year the inventory was provided to the customer or when the costs are paid or incurred. **The costs cannot be immediately written off.**

> **Example 5.** Larry has a retail furniture store whose average annual gross receipts are $5 million. His inventory purchases each year vary between $2 million and $3 million. Although Larry is a qualifying small business and is not required to use IRC §471 to track his inventory, he chooses to use the NIMS method to deduct his cost of goods sold.

Rotable, Temporary, or Standby Emergency Spare Parts. Rotable and temporary parts are components used to improve, repair, or maintain a UOP owned, leased, or serviced by a taxpayer. A taxpayer cannot acquire these components as part of the UOP purchase (e.g., an engine salvaged from another vehicle a taxpayer owns is not a spare part because the other vehicle was the UOP).

To qualify as a **rotable** spare part, the item must be:

- Acquired for installation on a UOP,
- Removable from that UOP,
- Repairable or improvable, and
- Either reinstalled on a UOP or stored for later installation.

Temporary spare parts are parts for use only until a new or repaired part is available for installation. Such parts are subsequently removed and stored for later use.

A taxpayer generally acquires **standby emergency** spare parts to prepare for crisis situations when a key piece of equipment malfunctions. Standby emergency spare parts are materials and supplies if they **meet all the following criteria.**

1. Acquired when a particular piece of machinery or equipment is acquired
2. Set aside to minimize operational downtime due to equipment failure or emergency
3. Readily available for use (located at or near the equipment site)
4. Directly related to the machinery or the equipment intended for repair
5. Normally expensive
6. Must be special ordered (otherwise not readily available)
7. Not subject to periodic replacement
8. Not interchangeable in another piece of machinery or equipment
9. Not acquired in large quantity
10. Not repaired and reused

---

15. IRC §471; Treas. Reg. §1.471-1.

Unless an exception applies, the regulations deem that a taxpayer first uses a rotable or temporary spare part in the tax year in which the taxpayer **disposes** of the part. This practice may delay the expense deduction of these parts for quite some time. Applicable exceptions to this rule include the following.

- An election to capitalize the expense for the qualified parts
- Using an optional method of accounting for **all** rotable and temporary spare parts
- An election to use a de minimis safe harbor

Optional Method.[16] When using the optional method of accounting for rotable and temporary spare parts, a taxpayer must deduct the cost of these parts when first installed. However, upon removal of the part, the taxpayer must add the fair market value (FMV) of the part to gross income. The taxpayer would then include the FMV and the removal costs in the part's basis. The basis would also include any subsequent repairs, maintenance, or improvement costs for the part. The taxpayer cannot deduct these amounts until they dispose of or reinstall the part.

Election to Capitalize Cost of Qualified Parts.[17] Taxpayers may elect to capitalize and depreciate costs for rotable, temporary, or standby emergency spare parts used to repair, maintain, or improve a UOP owned, leased, or serviced by the taxpayer. This election changes the tax treatment of these parts to capital assets; therefore, they are no longer considered materials or supplies. By electing to capitalize these costs, the taxpayer may be able to start recovering the expenses of acquiring spare parts sooner than waiting for the part's disposition.

Ineligible Costs. Taxpayers **cannot elect** to capitalize the cost of rotable, temporary, or standby emergency spare parts under the following circumstances.

1. The part is intended for use as a component of a UOP that:
   - Has an economic useful life of 12 months or less, beginning with the taxpayer's use or consumption,
   - The part costs $200 or less, or
   - The part is identified in published guidance in the Federal Register or the Internal Revenue Bulletin.
2. The taxpayer cannot or has not elected to capitalize the property that the part would fix.
3. The taxpayer uses the optional method of accounting for rotable and temporary spare parts.

Manner of Election. The taxpayer must make the election to capitalize rotable, temporary, or standby emergency spare parts on a timely filed original federal tax return (including extensions) for the tax year the asset is placed in service for determining depreciation. To make the election, the taxpayer capitalizes the cost of the part in the year of acquisition. However, the taxpayer does not begin to recover the costs through depreciation until they place the part in service. **No separate election statement is necessary.** The election is entity-level for S corporations and partnerships; partners or shareholders do not make the election individually. Taxpayers can make the election for each part. Revocation of the election requires the IRS's consent.

> **Example 6.** Terry Stevens' printing and copier services business uses multiple printing machines. One of the high-end printers uses a laser that must be special-ordered and can sometimes take weeks to ship out. To ensure that the printer is not down for long periods of time if its laser requires replacement, Terry purchases a spare laser in 2022. The spare laser qualifies as a temporary spare part. Because the spare laser is a material or supply cost, Terry does not capitalize it. However, Terry must wait to deduct the cost of the spare part until he **disposes** of it.
>
> Because the part is relatively expensive, and he does not know when he will need to use it and how long it will take until he ultimately disposes of it, Terry elects to capitalize the expense. He lists the asset on his 2022 depreciation schedule but delays recovery of his costs through depreciation until the year he places the part in service.

---

16. Treas. Reg. §1.162-3(e)(2).
17. Treas. Reg. §1.162-3(d).

Application to Farmers[18]

A farmer who operates a farm for profit is entitled to deduct from gross income as necessary expenses all amounts actually expended in conducting the farming business. The expenditure **(not the consumption)** of materials and supplies serves as the basis for the deduction and remains available to all farmers.

> **Observation.** Treas. Reg. §1.162-12(a) specifically applies to farmers. It is an exception from the more general provisions of Treas. Reg. §1.162-3(a), which otherwise defers the deductibility of NIMS until the year consumed. For this reason, cash-method farmers may report their financial position and results of operations using generally accepted accounting principles (GAAP) based financial statements without the requirement of deferring tax deductions for prepaid expenses if the expenses are deferred on the financial statement.

Tires[19]

Non-Agricultural Tires. For non-agricultural trucks and tractors, the IRS provides a safe harbor method of accounting for the cost of original and replacement tires for qualifying vehicles. The tangible property regulations did not change the safe harbor. Under the safe harbor, a qualifying vehicle's tires are treated as part of the vehicle and not as separate assets. A qualifying vehicle is one for which §168 determines depreciation and includes converter dollies and vehicles described in asset class 00.241 (light general-purpose trucks), 00.242 (heavy general-purpose trucks), 00.26 (tractor units for over-the-road use) and 00.27 (trailers and trailer-mounted containers) of Rev. Proc. 87-56.[20]

Under the safe harbor, a taxpayer must capitalize the cost of the original tires of a qualifying vehicle and depreciate them under §168 using the same depreciation method, recovery period, and convention applicable to the vehicle on which the taxpayer first installed the tires. The taxpayer must also treat the qualifying vehicle's original tires as disposed of when disposing of the vehicle on which the taxpayer first installed the tires. Additionally, the taxpayer must deduct the cost of the replacement tires of the qualifying vehicle as an expense in the tax year the taxpayer installs the replacement tires on the vehicle.

Example 7. Jack placed a light truck in service in 2018 and replaced the tires in 2020 and 2022. Under the safe harbor, Jack depreciates the original tires as part of the truck over the truck's 5-year MACRS recovery period (even though he replaced them in 2020) but can expense the cost of the replacement tires in 2020 and 2022.

Agricultural Tires. Rev. Proc. 2002-27 applies to "qualifying vehicles," which includes those in asset classes 00.241, 00.242, 00.26 and 00.27. As mentioned previously, these are light general-purpose trucks (i.e., pickups), heavy general-purpose trucks, truck tractors, and truck trailers. These asset classes do not include farm tractors.

Example 8. Ricky bought a used tractor in 2019 and depreciated the tractor's cost (including the tires) over seven years using the 200% declining balance method for farm equipment. In 2022, Ricky paid $20,000 to replace all the tires on his tractor. Because Ricky's tractor is property other than a building, the general rule in Treas. Reg. §1.263(a)-3(e)(3)(i) determines the initial UOP for the tractor. It is composed of all the functionally interdependent components. Under this rule, Ricky must treat the tractor, including its tires, as a single UOP. This treatment results from the tractor and tires having functional interdependence (that is, the placing in service of the tires depends upon the placing in service of the tractor).[21] The replacement tires do not improve the tractor (they do not adapt the tractor to a new or different use, are not a betterment, and are not a restoration). Therefore, Ricky can deduct the cost of the tires as a business expense under §162 on his 2022 income tax return.

---

18. Treas. Reg. §1.162-12(a).

19. Rev. Proc. 2002-27, 2002-1 CB 802.

20. Rev. Proc. 87-56, 1987-2 CB 674.

21. Treas. Reg. §1.263(a)-3(e)(6), example 16.

Further bolstering the point that the treatment of farm tires is not as separate components of a UOP, Treas. Reg. §1.263(a)-3(e)(5) states:

> *Notwithstanding the unit of property determination under paragraph (e)(3) of this section, a component (or a group of components) of a unit property must be treated as a separate unit of property* ***if,*** [emphasis added] *at the time the unit of property is initially placed in service by the taxpayer, the taxpayer has properly treated the component as being within a different class of property under section 168(e) (MACRS classes) than the class of the unit of property of which the component is a part, or the taxpayer has properly depreciated the component using a different depreciation method than the depreciation method of the unit of property of which the component is a part.*

The key word of that regulation is "if." The concept of the regulation does not apply in agriculture to farm tractor (or combine, etc.) tires. Farm tractor tires do not wear out in one year, and the easier approach is to treat them as part of the asset's cost. Because taxpayers do not depreciate farm tractor tires separately, the component rule of the regulation does not apply.

Summary. The standard still holds that if the asset wears out (because truck tires are viewed as separate assets) within 12 months, the taxpayer would expense them. This standard is beneficial to the trucking industry because it allows the benefit of separately handling tires. Additionally, only over-the-road trucks and trailers are eligible equipment for purposes of the safe harbor of Rev. Proc. 2002-27. Rev. Proc. 2002-27 does not apply to all tires used in any business; it does not apply to farm tractor tires.

Tractor tires are always deductible when a taxpayer purchases them to replace tires on an existing tractor. Therefore, the taxpayer does not separately identify and depreciate the tires, instead treating them as part of the UOP — the tractor. The taxpayer treats the replaced tires as repairs. However, these costs are not deductible when the taxpayer buys a tractor. Although heavy trucks also see use in agriculture, they are commonly depreciable as a unit (including their tires). Taxpayers do not treat agricultural heavy truck tires separately as a 7-year farm equipment asset.

APPLICABLE FINANCIAL STATEMENT[22]

Taxpayers with an AFS are subject to different qualification requirements than non-AFS taxpayers regarding certain tangible property classifications and thresholds described later in this chapter. AFS fall into the following three categories (listed in the order of priority from highest to lowest).

1. A financial statement having a filing requirement with the Securities and Exchange Commission (SEC) (the 10-K or the Annual Statement to Shareholders)
2. A certified audited financial statement that is accompanied by the report of an independent CPA (or, in the case of a foreign entity, by the report of a similarly qualified independent professional) for the use of one of the following:
   - Credit purposes
   - Reporting to shareholders, partners, or similar persons
   - Any other substantial **nontax** purpose
3. A financial statement (other than a tax return) required by the federal or a state government/agency, excluding the SEC or the IRS

Note. Whether a taxpayer has an AFS is important because it determines the taxpayer's economic useful life of an asset and affects the taxpayer's de minimis threshold. However, acceptance of (and reliance on) the taxpayer's financial statement by an outside party or agency (such as a bank or government agency) is necessary for a valid AFS.

22. Treas. Regs. §§1.162-3(c)(4)(iii)(A)-(C).

ECONOMIC USEFUL LIFE

The regulations define economic useful life as "the period over which the property may reasonably be expected to be useful to the taxpayer in its trade or business or for the production of income, as applicable."[23]

A taxpayer should reference previous experience with similar assets to determine the expected useful life of an asset, considering any unique facts and circumstances related to the property but disregarding salvage value. Factors of consideration include the item's wear and tear or natural decay or decline, industry-specific developments or technological changes, the taxpayer's business climate, and the taxpayer's repair or replacement policy.[24]

When taxpayers do not have sufficient experience with an asset to determine its economic useful life, they can use the industry's general experience until their own experience allows more informed judgment. A taxpayer can adjust an asset's estimated remaining useful life if the asset's condition causes a significant change in such life, but there must be a "clear and convincing" basis for any redetermination.[25]

A taxpayer determines an asset's economic useful life differently depending on whether they have an AFS. Taxpayers with an AFS retain the useful life initially used to depreciate the item on the AFS. If a taxpayer expensed an item on the AFS that would otherwise be subject to depreciation, the taxpayer determines that asset's useful life as described in the preceding paragraphs.[26]

Example 9. As the owner-manager of a small restaurant, Wilma Kendricks uses the camera feature on her smart phone to take photos of her lunch specials, which she posts daily on social media. Due to the ever-increasing number of social media apps, she often runs out of storage space on her phone. She generally replaces her phone with the latest model every 18 months at a cost of approximately $300 after trade-in. Wilma does not have an AFS.

Wilma's phone would not fall into the material or supply category because its economic useful life is greater than 12 months in Wilma's hands. The phone costs more than $200, and it is not a consumable item. Furthermore, Wilma does not use the phone to improve, repair, or maintain her property. Wilma must capitalize the expense for her replacement phone and recover its cost over time.

Example 10. Mike Anders also uses a smart phone in his insurance business to take pictures of claims and to communicate with his clients. Because he has a personal history of dropping his phone and cracking its screen, he has a policy of replacing his phone annually at a cost of approximately $375. Mike's phone is not a material or supply because the phone's economic useful life in Mike's hands is 12 months or less. He can deduct the expense for a new phone.

SAFE HARBOR ELECTIONS

Instead of analyzing expenditures to determine whether a taxpayer must capitalize a given cost or can expense it, the regulations allow the following alternatives.

1. Routine maintenance safe harbor
2. Safe harbor for buildings for small taxpayers
3. De minimis safe harbor

---

23. Treas. Reg. §1.162-3(c)(4)(i).

24. Treas. Reg. §1.167(a)-1(b).

25. Ibid.

26. Treas. Reg. §1.162-3(c)(4)(ii).

Routine Maintenance Safe Harbor[27]

While Treas. Reg. §1.263(a)-3 provides numerous examples for illustration, it often is still difficult to discern a repair from an improvement. The regulations guide taxpayers through these gray areas by introducing the routine maintenance safe harbor.

2

The routine maintenance safe harbor allows taxpayers to deduct work performed that meets **all** the following parameters.

1. The taxpayer uses the property in a trade or business.
2. As a result of the business use of the property, the taxpayer expects to perform maintenance on a **recurring** basis.
3. The recurring maintenance will keep the property in its **ordinarily efficient operating condition.**
4. At the time the property is placed in service, the taxpayer **reasonably expects** to perform the recurring maintenance:
    - More than once over the next 10 years for building property and building systems, or
    - More than once during the alternative depreciation system class life of the nonbuilding property.

If a taxpayer does not actually perform the maintenance work more than once in the prescribed time allotments, it does not invalidate this safe harbor. The taxpayer can rely on the following factors in making a reasoned prediction.

- The recurring nature of the activity
- Industry practice
- Manufacturer recommendations
- The taxpayer's experience with similar or identical property

Routine maintenance performed on rotable and temporary parts generally qualifies for this safe harbor unless the taxpayer uses the optional method of accounting for these parts.

Routine maintenance does not include the following amounts.

1. Betterment to a UOP
2. Replacement of a UOP's component for which a taxpayer properly deducted (other than a casualty loss)
3. Replacement of a UOP's component that a taxpayer properly adjusted basis in realizing gain or loss resulting from the sale or exchange of the component
4. Restoration of damage to a UOP requiring a taxpayer to take a basis adjustment resulting from a casualty loss or relating to a casualty event subject to the limits identified in Treas. Reg. §1.263(a)-3(k)(4)
5. Return of a UOP to its ordinarily efficient operating condition, if the property has deteriorated to a state of disrepair and is no longer functional for its intended use
6. Adaptation of a UOP to a new or different use
7. Repairs, maintenance, or improvement of network assets
8. Repairs, maintenance, or improvement of rotable and temporary spare parts to which a taxpayer applies the optional method of accounting for rotable and temporary spare parts

---

[27] Treas. Reg. §1.263(a)-3(i).

Example 11. Use the same facts as **Example 6.** Terry Stevens purchased a used copier machine for his copier and printing services business in 2022. While Terry prefers to purchase new machinery and equipment, this particular copier is specialized and expensive. Terry hired a service company to perform annual preventative maintenance on the copier machine to ensure it stays in efficient working condition. Shortly after the first time the company serviced the machine, it went out of business. Terry has yet to find a replacement service company and is concerned about finding one in his area. Because he reasonably expects to perform annual maintenance on the copier to keep it in its ordinarily efficient operating condition, Terry can still use the routine maintenance safe harbor for his service costs in 2022.

The safe harbor for routine maintenance is **not an election.** The IRS intended prior law to serve as the basis for these regulations.[28] A taxpayer who complied with the previous regulations is not required to take any action to be protected by this safe harbor. However, a taxpayer who was not compliant or who wants to change their accounting method to use this safe harbor should file Form 3115. A common scenario for applying the safe harbor includes situations in which the taxpayer changes to the routine maintenance safe harbor or already applies it in the regular course of business.

Safe Harbor Election for Buildings for Small Taxpayers[29]

The final regulations provide another safe harbor that allows qualified small taxpayers to deduct certain costs for **eligible building property.** Under the small taxpayer safe harbor, taxpayers may deduct eligible expenditures in the year paid. Qualified small taxpayers must have **average annual gross receipts of $10 million or less for the three preceding tax years.**

The term "eligible building property" applies to each unit of building property with an **unadjusted basis of $1 million or less.** A taxpayer who leases building property determines the unadjusted basis of the leased property by multiplying the undiscounted rent paid or expected to be paid by the taxpayer for the entire lease term. This term should include renewal periods if the taxpayer reasonably expects renewal.

Qualified Expenditures. Qualified expenditures under this safe harbor include repairs, maintenance, improvements, and similar activities performed on each eligible building, limited to the **lesser** of:

- 2% of the building's unadjusted basis, or
- $10,000.

Qualified expenditures otherwise would not be capitalized under the de minimis safe harbor election or the routine maintenance safe harbor for buildings.

The limitation on expenditures applies individually to buildings (i.e., if a taxpayer owns multiple buildings, the limits apply separately to each building). If the expenses for a particular building exceed the limitation threshold, the taxpayer cannot use the small taxpayer safe harbor for that building. The taxpayer then must determine the UOP and apply the betterment, adaptation, or restoration (BAR) tests (discussed later) to the expenditures. The taxpayer may use the safe harbor for routine maintenance and the de minimis safe harbor election for expenses that do not qualify for the small taxpayer safe harbor.

28. *Tangible Property Regulations — Frequently Asked Questions.* Nov. 10, 2022. IRS. [www.irs.gov/businesses/small-businesses-self-employed/tangible-property-final-regulations] Accessed on Feb. 8, 2023.

29. Treas. Reg. §1.263(a)-3(h).

De Minimis Safe Harbor Election[30]

Under the tangible property regulations, a taxpayer may elect to apply a **de minimis safe harbor** to amounts **paid to acquire or produce tangible property, including materials and supplies.** This safe harbor allows the taxpayer to deduct small-dollar expenditures without analyzing each purchase to determine whether to capitalize them.

Materials and Supplies

	Election	Who May Elect
Parts used in repairs and maintenance	None	
Useful life of (or consumed in) less than 12 months	None	
Individual items costing less than $200	None	
Individual items costing less than $2,500	Annual de minimis safe harbor election	All taxpayers
Individual items costing less than $5,000	Annual de minimis safe harbor election	Only taxpayers issuing an AFS

The choice to use the de minimis safe harbor is an **annual election** which does not constitute a change in accounting method. Therefore, when the taxpayer decides to use (or not use) the de minimis safe harbor for any tax year, they are not required to file Form 3115.

Generally, the tangible property regulations do **not** change the rules for deducting materials and supplies. The general rules define materials and supplies as tangible, noninventory property used and consumed in the taxpayer's operations. These regulations indicate that costs relating to property in any of the following categories qualify as materials or supplies.

Category	Description of Costs
Acquired components	Costs of components acquired to maintain, repair, or improve tangible property owned, leased, or serviced by the taxpayer that are not acquired as part of a larger item of tangible property
Consumables	Costs of fuel, lubricants, water, and similar items that are reasonably expected to be consumed in 12 months or less, beginning when used in operations
12-month property	Costs of tangible property that has an economic useful life of 12 months or less, beginning when the property is used or consumed in operations
$200 property	Costs of tangible property that has an acquisition cost or production cost of $200 or less

30. *Tangible Property Regulations — Frequently Asked Questions.* Nov. 10, 2022. IRS. [www.irs.gov/businesses/small-businesses-self-employed/tangible-property-final-regulations] Accessed on Feb. 8, 2023.

The de minimis safe harbor election is an administrative convenience that permits taxpayers to elect the deduction of small-dollar expenditures that otherwise require capitalization under the general rules. Under the tangible property regulations, a taxpayer may elect to apply the de minimis safe harbor to these expenditures if they qualify. The qualifications depend on whether the taxpayer has an applicable AFS. The following table summarizes these qualifications for taxpayers with and without an AFS.

AFS Taxpayers[31]	Non-AFS Taxpayers[32]
The taxpayer must have **written** accounting procedures at the beginning of the tax year that, for nontax purposes, treat as an expense: • Amounts costing less than a specified amount, or • Amounts paid for property with an economic useful life of 12 months or less.	The taxpayer must have accounting procedures at the beginning of the tax year that, for nontax purposes, treat as an expense: • Amounts costing less than a specified amount, or • Amounts paid for property with an economic useful life of 12 months or less.
The AFS must reflect the deduction of costs as outlined in the **written** accounting procedures.	Books and records must reflect the deduction of costs as outlined in the accounting procedures.
The amounts of the items expensed under the written accounting policy do not exceed **$5,000** per invoice (or per item as substantiated by an invoice).	The amounts of the items expensed under the accounting policy do not exceed **$2,500** per invoice (or per item as substantiated by an invoice).

Note. Non-AFS taxpayers are not required to have their accounting procedures **written.** However, to deduct the costs of materials and supplies under this safe harbor, treating the costs as current expenses must be part of a consistent accounting policy or procedure that exists at the beginning of the tax year.[33] Even if an expenditure meets the conditions allowing immediate expense under these rules, the cost might be subject to capitalization under the §263A uniform capitalization rules.[34]

The intention behind the $5,000 and $2,500 threshold amounts **does not represent ceilings on the amounts taxpayers can deduct as ordinary business expenses.** Using the de minimis election does not mean that the taxpayer must capitalize all expenditures over the threshold amount that applies to them.

31. Treas. Reg. §1.263(a)-1(f)(1)(i).

32. Treas. Reg. §1.263(a)-1(f)(1)(ii).

33. *Tangible Property Regulations — Frequently Asked Questions.* Nov. 10, 2022. IRS. [www.irs.gov/businesses/small-businesses-self-employed/tangible-property-final-regulations] Accessed on Feb. 8, 2023.

34. Treas. Reg. §1.263(a)-1(f)(1).

Eligibility Requirements for De Minimis Safe Harbor. Taxpayers electing the de minimis safe harbor must apply the threshold amount to all tangible property placed in service during the tax year and to material and supply costs for which an exception does not apply.

2

Although a written policy is not required, an example of a financial accounting policy follows.

[Company Name] Financial Accounting Policy: Capitalization

The purpose of this policy is to create an accurate assessment of the company's financial position. The following capitalization policy will be followed in accounting for asset acquisitions.

Assets that meet both of the following requirements will be deemed "capital assets" and must be capitalized and depreciated for bookkeeping purposes:

1. A unit of property that has an economic useful life to the company in excess of 12 months, and
2. A unit of property that was acquired or produced for $___ or more.

All assets acquired for a cost less than $____ must be expensed for bookkeeping purposes.

All assets with an economic useful life to the company of 12 months or less must be expensed for bookkeeping purposes, regardless of cost.

This policy is intended to satisfy the provisions of the de minimis safe harbor election of Treasury Regulation §1.263(a)-1(f).

Setting the dollar threshold at the $2,500 maximum amount may sound tempting. However, examining the taxpayer's unique facts and circumstances before setting the threshold limit is prudent. The taxpayer's nontax books and records **must reflect the same treatment** that the taxpayer elects on their tax return.

Example 12. Joe Donaldson plans to sell his used book store and retire soon. Accordingly, he opens his financials to prospective buyers. To show as much income as possible, Joe adopts a $500 threshold for capitalization for 2022. This way, he is protected from a challenge when deducting low-cost improvements, but his books reflect more income and make his business appear more attractive to prospective buyers.

Electing the De Minimis Safe Harbor. To use the safe harbor, the taxpayer attaches a statement titled "Section 1.263(a)-1(f) De Minimis Safe Harbor Election" to the timely filed original federal tax return (including extensions) for the tax year in which they paid de minimis amounts. The statement includes the taxpayer's name, address, and taxpayer identification number (TIN), as well as a declaratory statement that the taxpayer is making the de minimis safe harbor election.

Example 13. Use the same facts as **Example 6.** Terry Stevens operates his printing and copying services business as a sole proprietorship. In 2022, he purchases a printer for $360. Terry does not have an AFS. The printer does not meet the definition of a material or supply under the general rules. Therefore, Terry must capitalize and depreciate the printer unless he makes the de minimis safe harbor election for 2022 or makes an election under IRC §179. Terry attaches the following statement to his 2022 return.

Terry Stevens **TIN: 123-45-6789**

Address: 23 Main St., Boston, MA 02108

Section 1.263(a)-1(f) De Minimis Safe Harbor Election

The taxpayer elects to make the de minimis safe harbor election under Regulation 1.263(a)-1(f).

Example 14. Use the same facts as **Example 13,** except the printer costs $150. Terry does not need to make the safe harbor election because the printer costs under $200. Therefore, it qualifies as a material or supply under the general rules.

The intention of the safe harbor is not to prevent taxpayers from reaching an agreement with IRS examiners to use a larger amount. It may be prudent to elect the $500 amount even if the taxpayer uses a larger amount. The taxpayer does not capitalize amounts they deduct under the de minimis rule and does not treat them as a material or supply. Instead, the taxpayer treats these amounts as "small equipment" and tracks them separately on their books and records.

Note. The sale of items for which a taxpayer elected the de minimis safe harbor is covered later in this chapter.

Safe Harbor Election to Capitalize Maintenance Costs[35]

The tangible property regulations allow taxpayers to elect the capitalization and depreciation of repair and maintenance costs as qualified improvements if both the following occur.

1. The taxpayer incurs the costs in carrying on a trade or business.
2. The taxpayer treats the amounts as capital expenditures on their books and records regularly used for computing income.

This election reduces administrative burdens on taxpayers by permitting their tax treatments to match the capitalization policies they use for books and records. Taxpayers and their practitioners can also use the election as a tax planning tool.

Taxpayers electing to capitalize repair and maintenance costs may still apply the safe harbors (de minimis, small taxpayers, and routine maintenance) to repair and maintenance costs that taxpayers do not treat as capital expenditures on their books and records.

Taxpayers making this election must apply the election to **all** repair and maintenance amounts that they treat as capital expenditures on their books and records for that tax year. Depreciation on these costs begins when the taxpayer places the deemed improvements in service.

The cost of repairing or maintaining rotable or temporary spare parts is **not** eligible for this election if the taxpayer uses the optional method of accounting for these parts.

To make this annual, irrevocable election, the taxpayer must attach a statement to their timely filed original federal tax return (including extensions) for the tax year in which they placed the improvement in service. The statement must include the following information.

- Title: "Section 1.263(a)-3(n) Election"
- Taxpayer's name
- Taxpayer's address
- TIN
- A statement that the election to capitalize repairs and maintenance costs is being made under §1.263(a)-3(n)

Elections for S corporations and partnerships are made at the entity level, not by individual shareholders or partners.

35. Treas. Reg. §1.263(a)-3(n).

Partial Disposition Election

Generally, if a taxpayer replaces a portion of an asset with a capitalized improvement, the improvement cost is added to the depreciation schedule. Moreover, **any remaining basis allocable to the portion of the replaced asset** remains on the depreciation schedule.

Example 15. Susan owns a commercial building, which she purchased in 2017. In 2022, she replaced one of two air conditioners. Under the facts and circumstances analysis, replacing the air conditioner is considered a restoration of a major portion of a building system. Susan must capitalize the expenditure.

Susan adds the cost of the new air conditioner to her depreciable building property. Any remaining basis attributable to the replaced air conditioner continues to be included in the basis of the building. Susan does not adjust the basis or accumulated depreciation of the building after the air conditioner replacement.

Under the regulations,[36] certain events automatically qualify as partial dispositions based on the nature of the events. In other situations, the taxpayer may **elect** to treat a portion of an asset as having been disposed of when a taxpayer capitalizes the replacement for that portion under the same asset class. The taxpayer must make the election on a **timely filed (including extensions) original return** for the year of the disposition. **Generally, a taxpayer makes the election by reporting the gain, loss, or other deduction related to the disposition and properly capitalizing the improvement.**

> **Note.** This election may be particularly beneficial for owners of real estate. Such owners may not expense replacement costs incurred because the tangible property regulations may require capitalization of those costs. However, this partial disposition election may allow owners to deduct the amount of the adjusted basis remaining in a replaced asset.

Example 16. Use the same facts as **Example 15.** Susan identified the portion of the original purchase price of the building that applied to the replaced air conditioner. She separates that cost and the accumulated depreciation allocable to that cost from her adjusted basis in the building. Susan takes the adjusted basis of the old air conditioner as a loss on her original 2022 return.

Susan adds the cost of the new unit to her depreciable assets using the same class life as the original unit. By treating the disposition and replacement consistently with the election, Susan has effectively made the partial disposition election for that asset for 2022.

Mandatory Imposition of Partial Disposition Rule.[37] A taxpayer generally may elect to claim a disposition of a portion of any type of MACRS property. However, there are cases when the partial disposition rule is **mandatory,** as in the following situations.

- A partial disposition resulting from a casualty event
- A partial disposition of an asset for which gain (determined without regard to depreciation recapture) is not recognized in whole or in part under a like-kind exchange or eminent domain process
- The transfer of a portion of an asset in a "step-in-the-shoes" transaction
- The sale of a portion of an asset

36. Treas. Reg. §1.168(i)-8.

37. Ibid.

Planning Considerations Regarding the Partial Disposition Election. Making the partial disposition election provides an immediate tax deduction for the portion of the basis allocable to the retired asset. However, practitioners should consider the possible effects of the election if the sale of the retired asset occurs in a subsequent year.

1. The gain from the sale can be higher than it would have been without the election. However, the portion of the gain attributable to depreciation will be lower. Thus, a portion of the gain **might** shift from higher ordinary rates to lower capital gain rates.

2. The entire capital gain may be subject to the net investment income tax, depending on the taxpayer's income level.

3. The gain may increase the taxpayer's adjusted gross income (AGI) to levels that subject the taxpayer to phase-outs of various deductions and credits. Common tax provisions subject to phase-outs include education incentives, personal exemptions, itemized deductions, and individual retirement arrangement (IRA) deductions.

4. Although the tax rate for capital gains is the same for alternative minimum tax (AMT) and regular tax purposes, the tax rate for ordinary income is not. Both the ordinary income portion of the gain and the taxpayer's other income may be subject to the AMT rates and phase-outs.

5. The loss on the disposition is subject to recapture under IRC §1231 for five tax years after the election of the partial disposition treatment. The term **recapture** for this purpose refers to the recharacterization of §1231 gains as ordinary income rather than long-term capital gains.

Gain or Loss on Partial Dispositions.[38] Except in situations involving the demolition of a structure,[39] the following rules apply when a taxpayer disposes of an asset during a tax year. These general rules also apply to partial dispositions.

1. If a taxpayer disposes of an asset by sale, exchange, or involuntary conversion, the taxpayer must recognize the gain or loss.

2. If a taxpayer disposes of an asset by physical abandonment, the taxpayer must recognize the loss. The amount of loss is the adjusted depreciable basis[40] of the asset at the time of the abandonment (accounting for the applicable convention). However, if the abandoned asset is subject to **nonrecourse** indebtedness, it may be necessary to recognize a gain on the disposition. For a taxpayer to recognize a loss from physical abandonment, they must intend to discard the asset **irrevocably** (so that the taxpayer will neither use the asset again nor retrieve it for sale, exchange, or other disposition).

3. A limit to the amount of loss may exist if a taxpayer disposes of an asset other than by sale, exchange, involuntary conversion, physical abandonment, or conversion to personal use. Examples of this type of disposition include transferring the asset to a supplies or scrap account. In this situation, the taxpayer recognizes no gain. The allowed loss is limited to the amount, if any, by which the adjusted depreciable basis exceeds the asset's FMV at the time of the disposition.

Basis of the Disposed Portion of the Asset.[41] In calculating gain or loss on a partial disposition, the adjusted basis of the asset's disposed portion is its adjusted depreciable basis at the time of its disposal, as determined under the applicable convention for the asset. If determining the unadjusted depreciable basis[42] of the disposed portion of the asset is impracticable based on the taxpayer's records, the taxpayer may use any reasonable method to determine the unadjusted depreciable basis of the disposed portion of the asset.

---

38. Treas. Reg. §1.168(i)-8(e).
39. See IRC §280B and Treas. Reg. §1.280B-1.
40. As defined in Treas. Reg. §1.168(b)-1(a)(4).
41. Treas. Reg. §1.168(i)-8(f).
42. As defined in Treas. Reg. §1.168(b)-1(a)(3).

Suppose a taxpayer disposes of more than one portion of the same asset. In that case, **the reasonable method used by the taxpayer must consistently apply** to all portions of the same asset to determine the unadjusted depreciable basis of each disposed-of portion.

Identification of the Disposed Portion of the Asset.[43] Generally, the taxpayer must identify the specific asset disposed and the tax year in which they placed the asset in service. A taxpayer may account for the asset in a multiple-asset account (or pool), but it may be impracticable to determine the tax year in which they placed the asset in service based on the taxpayer's records. In that event, the taxpayer must identify the asset using any applicable method listed in the following table.

Method	Description
First-in, first-out (FIFO) method	The taxpayer identifies the multiple-asset account with the earliest placed-in-service year that has the same recovery period as the asset disposed of and that has assets at the beginning of the tax year of the disposition. The taxpayer treats the portion of the disposed asset as being from that asset.
Modified FIFO method	The taxpayer identifies the multiple-asset account with the earliest placed-in-service year that has the same recovery period as the asset disposed of and that has assets at the beginning of the tax year of the disposition with the same unadjusted depreciable basis as the disposed asset. The taxpayer treats the portion of the asset disposed of as being from that multiple-asset account.
Mortality dispersion table	The taxpayer uses this method if the disposed asset is part of a mass asset. The taxpayer must base the mortality dispersion table on an acceptable sampling of their actual disposition experience for mass assets or other acceptable statistical or engineering techniques. To use a mortality dispersion table, the taxpayer must adopt recordkeeping practices consistent with the taxpayer's prior practices and in accordance with good accounting and engineering practices.

Note. A **mass asset account** generally includes numerous small-value items. Each item has a nominal value relative to the value of the overall group of mass assets in the account. Identifying any particular item in a mass asset account is generally impractical, and the taxpayer does not typically account for each item individually. Instead, the taxpayer accounts for the total dollar value. See Treas. Reg. §1.168(i)-8 for further details.

In addition to the preceding three methods, the IRS has the authorization to provide other acceptable methods by publishing them in the Federal Register or the Internal Revenue Bulletin.

Note. A last-in, first-out (LIFO) method of accounting **is not permissible.** For information about disposed assets in multiple-asset accounts, see Treas. Reg. §1.168(i)-8.

43. Treas. Reg. §1.168(i)-8(g).

DISTINGUISHING BETWEEN REPAIRS AND IMPROVEMENTS[44]

Qualifying repairs and maintenance costs are not subject to capitalization unless the taxpayer makes an election to capitalize these costs. The taxpayer generally must capitalize improvements unless they elect a safe harbor.

Analyzing specific facts and circumstances is critical in determining whether an expense is a deductible repair or a capitalized improvement. However, establishing the UOP is necessary before this analysis can take place. Upon determination of the UOP, the application of the following tests should proceed in identifying if incurring an expense was to better, adapt, or restore the UOP.

BAR Tests: Betterment, Adaptation, or Restoration

If an expense falls into one of the three "BAR" categories — betterment, adaptation, or restoration — it is considered an improvement to a UOP. Therefore, taxpayers must capitalize those costs unless they claim a safe harbor election. The BAR tests are as follows.

1. **Betterment.**[45] An amount is paid for a betterment to a UOP if it:

   a. Ameliorates a material condition or defect that was present before the taxpayer acquired the UOP or that occurred during production;

   b. Is for a material addition — including a physical enlargement, expansion, extension, or addition of a major component to a UOP — or a material increase in a UOP's capacity; or

   c. Is reasonable to expect to materially increase the productivity, efficiency, strength, quality, or output of a UOP.

> **Note.** Upgrading a UOP due to the unavailability of the same size replacement part is not a betterment.[46] Additionally, an amount incurred to satisfy a regulatory requirement is also not treated as a betterment.[47]

A taxpayer's expenditure for a UOP may be necessary due to normal wear and tear or damage that occurred during the use of the UOP. In that case, the taxpayer must determine whether the expenditure constitutes a betterment to the UOP. **This determination consists of comparing the property's condition immediately after the expense with its condition immediately before the circumstances necessitating the expenditure,** using the following guidance.

- In the case of normal wear and tear to a UOP, the condition of the property immediately before the circumstances necessitating the expenditure is the condition of the property after the last time the taxpayer corrected the effects of normal wear and tear (whether the amounts paid were for maintenance or improvements). Or, if the taxpayer has not previously corrected the effects of normal wear and tear, the condition of the property immediately before the circumstances necessitating the expenditure is the condition of the property when placed in service by the taxpayer.
- In the case of damage to a UOP, the condition of the property immediately before the circumstances necessitating the expenditure is the condition of the property immediately before the damage.

---

44. *Tangible Property Regulations — Frequently Asked Questions.* Nov. 10, 2022. IRS. [www.irs.gov/businesses/small-businesses-self-employed/tangible-property-final-regulations] Accessed on Feb. 8, 2023.

45. Treas. Reg. §1.263(a)-3(j).

46. Treas. Reg. §1.263(a)-3(j)(2)(iii).

47. Treas. Reg. §1.263(a)-3(j)(3), example 12.

2. **Adaptation.**[48] An adaptation prepares a UOP for a new or different use inconsistent with its ordinary use when the taxpayer placed it in service.

3. **Restoration.**[49] A restoration replaces, returns, or rebuilds a UOP or reinstates a UOP's basis after an adjustment. A restoration includes amounts paid for any of the following purposes.

   a. Replace a major component of a UOP that the taxpayer properly deducted a loss for that component, other than a casualty loss

   b. Replace a component of a UOP that the taxpayer properly accounted for the adjusted basis of the component in realizing gain or loss resulting from the sale or exchange of the component

   c. Restore a UOP that required the taxpayer to take a basis adjustment as a result of a casualty loss

   d. Return a UOP to its ordinarily efficient operating condition if the UOP deteriorated to a state of disrepair and no longer functions for its intended use

   e. Rebuild a UOP to a like-new condition after the end of its class life

   f. Replace the part or combination of parts that comprise a major component or a substantial structural part of a UOP

      - A major component is a part or combination of parts that perform a discrete and critical function in the operation of the UOP.[50]

      - A substantial structural part is a part or combination of parts that comprise a large portion of the physical structure of the UOP.[51]

COST SEGREGATION STUDY[52]

Cost segregation studies can be an effective part of a property owner's annual tax-saving strategy. From its beginnings as an IRS legal memorandum, the practice of employing cost segregation studies in the accounting community has grown and evolved considerably.

Cost segregation is separating a single purchase into multiple depreciation classes. This process allows the taxpayer to maximize shorter depreciation periods instead of keeping the entire purchase cost lumped into one asset with a longer depreciation period. It is important to distinguish between the components and systems of the building and assets that are IRC §1245 (generally, tangible personal property) and those that are IRC §1250 (such as land improvements). Depending on the code section type they fall under, components and systems may be subject to shorter depreciation recovery periods and may qualify for bonus depreciation (when available).

48. Treas. Reg. §1.263(a)-3(l).

49. Treas. Reg. §1.263(a)-3(k).

50. Treas. Reg. §1.263(a)-3(k)(6)(i)(A).

51. Treas. Reg. §1.263(a)-3(k)(6)(i)(B).

52. See *Cost Segregation Audit Technique Guide.* Jun. 1, 2022. IRS. [www.irs.gov/pub/irs-pdf/p5653.pdf] Accessed on Apr. 18, 2023.

Example 17. Phoenix, Inc. owns a building that it uses in its retail business. The building contains two elevator banks, which consist of three elevators each. Phoenix, Inc. replaces one of the cars to increase the weight capacity rating of one of the elevators. Together, the six elevators comprise a building system. The amount paid by Phoenix, Inc. for a replacement car is a betterment to the building.

Phoenix, Inc. must therefore capitalize and depreciate the cost of the new car over 39 years. However, if Phoenix, Inc. used a cost segregation study to allocate the basis of the building to the various costs of the building structure, it would be able to deduct the remaining basis of the replaced old car.[53]

> **Note.** Useful information about cost segregation is contained in the IRS Audit Technique Guide found at **uofi.tax/23x2x1** [www.irs.gov/pub/irs-pdf/p5653.pdf]. The document provides industry-specific guidelines for casinos, restaurants, retail industries, the biotech and pharmaceutical industries, and auto dealerships. Additionally, the guide contains issue-specific guidelines for electrical distribution systems.

Practitioner Planning Tip

Cost segregation studies are a valuable service for practitioners to encourage clients to utilize. With bonus depreciation sunsetting by the end of 2026 and decreasing by 20% each year beginning in 2023, there is an extra incentive for taxpayers to utilize cost segregation studies sooner rather than later while the bonus depreciation option is still available and results in smaller expense recognition as time passes.[54]

IS A CHANGE IN ACCOUNTING METHOD NECESSARY OR ADVISABLE?

Every business taxpayer has a method of accounting for tax purposes. The taxpayer may adopt this approach through written procedures or by filing a tax return. Practitioners may consider the following questions to determine if their clients should change their accounting methods and, if so, what procedures their clients should follow.

1. What accounting methods does the taxpayer currently use?
2. Are methods the taxpayer currently uses permissible?
    - A taxpayer whose method of accounting complies with the tax rules for capitalization and repairs does **not need** to make a change in accounting method to continue being in compliance. Therefore, they are **not required** to file Form 3115.
    - A taxpayer who chooses to make **elections** or forgoes making elections is not changing their method of accounting. They are **not required** to file Form 3115.[55]
    - Once a taxpayer adopts a proper method of accounting by filing a return using that method, they may **not** adopt a different method of accounting by filing an amended return. To change the method of accounting, the taxpayer must file Form 3115 even if they used the previous method on only one return.[56]

---

53. Adapted from Treas. Reg. §1.263(a)-3(e)(6), Example 2.

54. *Tax Cuts and Jobs Act*, PL 115-97, §13201.

55. *Tangible Property Regulations — Frequently Asked Questions.* Nov. 10, 2022. IRS. [www.irs.gov/businesses/small-businesses-self-employed/tangible-property-final-regulations] Accessed on Feb. 8, 2023.

56. IRM 4.11.6.3 (2005).

3. Is the taxpayer using impermissible methods that result in a significant misstatement of their tax liabilities? If a mistake affects only one tax return, the taxpayer can amend the affected return without filing Form 3115.[57] Filing the amended return must precede the filing of next year's return.[58]
4. If the accounting methods used by the taxpayer are not compliant with the tangible property regulations, the taxpayer has the following options to become compliant.
   - The taxpayer can change the method by filing Form 3115 and making an IRC §481(a) adjustment on the current return using the standard calculating method. The §481(a) adjustment will include all transactions treated improperly in all prior tax years.
   - If the taxpayer used the improper method on two consecutive returns, they have established a method of accounting. Therefore, amended returns are not an avenue to change the method of accounting. Form 3115 is required to institute a change to a permissible method.

Even taxpayers in compliance may wish to adopt one or more of the methods approved under the current rules instead of continuing to use their existing accounting procedures. Such a change may produce a more favorable tax result or make tracking assets more practical than the current method.

The best tax result varies based on the taxpayer's circumstances and tax year. Accordingly, the taxpayer should consider the options available for changing to the preferred method and the costs and benefits of each option.

CHANGING AN ACCOUNTING METHOD

TYPES OF ACCOUNTING CHANGES FOR REPAIR REGULATION

Some changes in accounting methods under the tangible property regulations are automatic, while others are not automatic and require IRS review and approval. This section examines the different types of changes that fall into these categories.

Automatic Consent Procedures[59]

The automatic consent procedures allow only the changes listed in Rev. Proc. 2022-14 (or its successors). If the taxpayer meets the conditions and follows the procedures in Rev. Proc. 2022-14, the IRS is automatically deemed to consent for the taxpayer to make the change. **There is no required fee for applications filed under the automatic consent procedures.** The IRS does not acknowledge its approval of applications filed under these procedures.

Generally, a taxpayer may receive automatic consent to change an accounting method by completing and filing Form 3115 and **including it with the timely filed original federal tax return** for the year of change. A taxpayer must also file a signed copy of Form 3115 with the appropriate office.

A taxpayer generally may **not** use automatic consent procedures under the following circumstances. (However, there are exceptions, and the taxpayer should consult Rev. Proc. 2015-13 if they appear to fall under one of these prohibitions.)

1. Within the requested year of change, the taxpayer engages in a liquidation or reorganization transaction to which IRC §381(a) applies.
2. The requested year of change is the final year of the trade or business.
3. The taxpayer made or requested an overall method change during any of the five tax years ending with the year of change.
4. The taxpayer made or requested a change for the same item during any of the five tax years ending with the year of change.

---

57. Rev. Rul. 72-491, 1972-2 CB 104 and Rev. Rul. 90-38, 1990-1 CB 57.

58. IRM 4.11.6.3 (2005).

59. Rev. Proc. 2015-13, 2015-5 IRB 419 and Rev. Proc. 2022-14, 2022-7 IRB 502.

If the IRS requires more information after reviewing the requested change, it notifies the taxpayer. In general, the taxpayer must furnish additional information in writing within 30 calendar days from the date of the request. The IRS may grant the applicant an additional 30 calendar days to provide the information if the applicant requests an extension and the IRS deems it appropriate.[60]

A qualifying taxpayer complying with an automatic change request procedure may assume that the IRS granted consent. However, this is true only if:[61]

- The affected item(s) are clearly and expressly identified on the taxpayer's Form 3115, and
- The taxpayer complies with all the applicable provisions and implements the change on their federal income tax return for the requested year of change.

Note. In addition to changes related to the tangible property regulations, Rev. Proc. 2022-14 covers the procedures for all other accounting method changes allowed under the automatic consent procedures. Practitioners might be interested in §9 regarding computer software expenditures, §15 regarding changes in overall methods of accounting, or §6.12 relating to changes from impermissible to permissible methods of accounting for depreciation or amortization for disposed depreciable or amortizable property. This last change is a powerful tool to offset the allowed or allowable rule when less than the allowable amount of depreciation was taken.

Nonautomatic Change Requests[62]

A taxpayer who does not qualify for automatic consent procedures or who requests a change not included in the list of automatic changes may request IRS approval for a nonautomatic change (previously known as advance consent procedures). Form 3115 requesting a nonautomatic change generally must be filed **during the year of the requested change.**

User fees apply to most changes requested under the nonautomatic change procedures. Rev. Proc. 2022-1 (or its successor) provides a list of the applicable fees.

If the IRS requires more information after reviewing the requested change, it notifies the taxpayer. In general, additional information must be furnished in writing within **21 calendar days** from the date of the request. The IRS may grant the applicant an additional 15 calendar days to provide the information if the applicant requests an extension and the IRS deems it appropriate.

The IRS has the right to decline to process any nonautomatic changes requested on Form 3115 in situations in which it would not be in the best interest of sound tax administration to permit the requested change. In this regard, the IRS considers whether the change in method of accounting clearly and directly frustrates compliance efforts of the IRS in administering the income tax laws.

SPECIFICS OF ACCOUNTING CHANGE ADJUSTMENTS UNDER §481(a)[63]

The Code allows a taxpayer to change their method of accounting from one tax year to another only with the IRS's approval. If said change causes the duplication or omission of income, the Code requires the calculation of an adjustment under §481(a). The taxpayer must make this adjustment for the year of change to prevent such duplication or omission.

The taxpayer calculates the §481(a) adjustment as of the beginning of the tax year of the changed method. The adjustment represents the cumulative difference without regard to the statute of limitations between the present and proposed methods.

---

60. Rev. Proc. 2023-1, 2023-1 IRB 1.

61. Rev. Proc. 2015-13, 2015-5 IRB 419.

62. Rev. Proc. 2023-1, 2023-1 IRB 1.

63. IRM 4.11.6 (2021).

A net positive §481(a) adjustment increases income, resulting in a taxpayer-unfavorable adjustment. A net negative §481(a) adjustment decreases income, resulting in a taxpayer-favorable adjustment.

When a taxpayer uses a voluntary-method change procedure or a regulation provision, a net negative §481(a) adjustment generally takes effect in the year of change. A taxpayer making a voluntary net positive §481(a) adjustment recognizes it over four years starting with the year of change. A taxpayer can also elect under §481(a) to recognize the entire adjustment, if less than $50,000, as income in the year of change.[64]

Note. When the IRS imposes a method change (an involuntary-method change) resulting from an examination, the taxpayer accounts for the entire net positive or negative §481(a) adjustment in the year of change.

The IRS may determine that certain changes in accounting method require using a **cut-off method** instead of a §481 adjustment.[65] Under a cut-off method, only the items arising on or after the beginning of the year of change are accounted for under the new method of accounting. The taxpayer continues to account for any items arising before the year of change under the former method of accounting. Because there is no duplication or omission of income when using a cut-off method, no §481(a) adjustment is necessary. The taxpayer may use the cut-off method if they initiated a change specifically allowed or required by a statute or regulation or by the IRS in published guidance.

The IRS grants most automatic accounting method changes with **audit protection.** Consequently, the IRS will not require the taxpayer to change their accounting method for the same item for a tax year prior to the year of change.[66]

Example 18. Gus Industries has been using an impermissible method of accounting for certain items for several years. In 2022, Gus files Form 3115 to change to a proper method of accounting for these items. If Gus makes the change with audit protection, the IRS cannot propose an adjustment for the improper method of accounting for these items in an examination of a tax year prior to 2022.

Observation. This incentive encourages the taxpayer to voluntarily change from an impermissible method to a permissible one when the change results in a positive §481(a) adjustment. If the IRS were to discover the error during an audit, the taxpayer would not be subject to interest or penalties on understatement of tax related to that error because the taxpayer already used an IRS-approved method to correct it.

Example 19. Weston Principles has improperly treated the office equipment it uses as leased assets. Review of the lease agreement shows that Weston actually purchased the office equipment under a 2020 purchasing agreement.

In 2022, Weston purchases additional equipment using the same agreement and wants to account for the new equipment properly. With its 2022 return, Weston files Form 3115 using the automatic consent procedures provided in §6.03 of Rev. Proc. 2022-14. Weston makes this change of accounting method using a cut-off method, and it applies only to transactions occurring on or after the beginning of the year of change.[67] However, by filing Form 3115, Weston receives audit protection for the 2020 equipment, as it falls under the same item that is subject to the filed Form 3115, and Weston is not under examination. Consequently, the IRS would not require Weston to change its method of accounting for tax years between the year Weston filed Form 3115 and 2020 when Weston purchased the equipment.

64. Rev. Proc. 2015-13, 2015-5 IRB 419.

65. IRM 4.11.6.5.5 (2017) and Treas. Reg. §1.446-1(e)(3)(ii).

66. IRM 4.11.6.6.4 (2021).

67. Rev. Proc. 2022-14, 2022-7 IRB 502.

FILING FORM 3115

General Procedures

Generally, a taxpayer must obtain IRS consent to change from a current accounting method to a new one.[68] Rev. Proc. 2015-13[69] provides the general procedures for obtaining IRS consent to change accounting methods. This supersedes the previous guidance provided under Rev. Proc. 97-27 as amplified, clarified, and modified by subsequent revenue procedures.

Rev. Proc. 2022-14[70] provides the **entire list of automatic changes allowed as of the date it was issued (January 31, 2022)** and specific procedures for each automatic change. This procedure is effective for a Form 3115 filed on or after January 31, 2022, for a year of change ending on or after May 31, 2021. It supersedes Rev. Proc. 2019-43 and Rev. Proc. 2019-48.

The address of the appropriate IRS center to mail a copy of Form 3115 varies depending on the changes made and the type of entity making the changes. The instructions provide a list of those addresses.

When and Where To File.[71] Except as otherwise specifically provided, Form 3115 is filed in duplicate as follows.

1. The taxpayer attaches the original Form 3115 to their timely filed (including extensions) federal income tax return for the year of change.
2. The taxpayer files a copy of Form 3115 with the IRS national office unless Rev. Proc. 2022-14 or other published guidance requires filing the copy with the IRS office in Ogden, Utah. The taxpayer must file the copy no earlier than the first day of the year of change and no later than the date of filing of the original with the federal income tax return for the year of change.

Name and Signature.[72] In general, the taxpayer is the filer and applicant of Form 3115. The applicant and the filer may not be the same entity in some instances involving consolidated groups and other multiple taxpayers. These situations require obtaining multiple signatures.

For changes requested under the automatic consent procedures, the filer must attach a copy of Form 3115 to the return for the year of change. In addition, the filer must send a signed and dated copy of Form 3115 to the IRS national office or the office in Ogden, Utah. If the individual preparing Form 3115 is not the applicant, the preparer must sign the application. However, the copy of Form 3115 attached to the income tax return does not need to be signed.

In every case, someone signing for the applicant must have personal knowledge of the facts and the authority to bind the filer regarding the matter.

Individuals. Form 3115 requires the name of both spouses on the first line of the application for taxpayers filing a joint income tax return. Both spouses must sign on the signature line.

Partnerships. One of the general partners or limited liability company members must sign on behalf of a partnership.

Corporations. For a nonconsolidated corporation, personal service corporation, S corporation, cooperative, or insurance company, an officer of the entity must sign Form 3115.

Estates and Trusts. The fiduciary, personal representative, executor, administrator, or person acting in one of these capacities must sign Form 3115 for an estate or trust.

---

68. IRC §446(e); *Hawse v. Comm'r*, TC Memo 2015-99 (May 28, 2015).

69. Rev. Proc. 2015-13, 2015-5 IRB 419.

70. Rev. Proc. 2022-14, 2022-7 IRB 502.

71. Instructions for Form 3115.

72. Ibid.

Exempt Organizations. For an exempt organization, a principal officer or person with a similar role must sign Form 3115.

2

Form 2848.[73] A tax practitioner may want to communicate directly with the IRS about the request for a change in accounting method. In such cases, the IRS must have Form 2848, *Power of Attorney and Declaration of Representative,* on file. The taxpayer must sign Form 2848. A person with the authority to appoint a representative must sign for an entity.

Form 2848 must specifically authorize the practitioner to represent the filer before the IRS regarding the requested change in accounting method. A copy of the signed Form 2848 must accompany the copy of Form 3115 mailed to the IRS national office or the office in Ogden, Utah. Without a signed Form 2848, the IRS will not discuss the application with the taxpayer's representative, even if that representative prepared or signed the Form 3115.

> **Note**. The IRS now allows electronic submissions of Form 2848 via e-services and ID.me. The form may also be mailed or faxed. For more information, see the instructions for Form 2848.

Option to Receive Correspondence by Fax.[74] An applicant may request that the IRS correspond with them by fax instead of by mail regarding Form 3115. The applicant makes this request by attaching a statement to Form 3115. The statement must list the names and fax numbers of the persons who are to receive the fax. The listed persons must have authorization to sign Form 3115 or a representative who has authorization on Form 2848.

Additional Information.[75] The IRS may request additional information when it processes the request for a change in accounting method. The applicant must respond within a certain time frame, depending on whether the request is under automatic or nonautomatic change procedures as discussed previously. The IRS may impose shorter reply periods for subsequent requests for additional information.

The IRS may grant an extension of time to furnish information. The taxpayer must submit in writing any request for an extension of time. Additionally, the taxpayer must submit these requests before the end of the original deadline. Unusual circumstances may make issuing a written request impractical. In that event, the taxpayer should notify the IRS before the deadline explaining that there is a problem and that they will soon provide the written request for an extension.

The IRS representative reviewing the application has the authority to grant or deny the extension. If the taxpayer should have included the additional information with Form 3115 according to the instructions, the IRS usually denies the extension. Accordingly, the taxpayer should receive prompt notification of the approval or denial of the requested extension. If the IRS denies the extension request, there is no right of appeal.

If the taxpayer does not furnish the required information to the IRS within the reply period, the IRS notifies the taxpayer that the request to change the accounting method has been denied. If the taxpayer wants to submit the additional information at a later date, they must submit it with a new Form 3115 (plus user fee, if applicable). If the deadline for the timely filing of Form 3115 has passed, the change will be effective for the year the new form is timely filed.

Penalties of Perjury Statement for Additional Information. The following declaration must accompany additional information submitted to the IRS.

> *Under penalties of perjury, I declare that I have examined this information, including accompanying documents, and, to the best of my knowledge and belief, the information contains all the relevant facts relating to the request for the information, and such facts are true, correct, and complete.*

The taxpayer or a duly authorized person acting on behalf of the entity must sign this declaration.

---

73. Ibid.

74. Ibid.

75. Rev. Proc. 2023-1, 2023-1 IRB 1.

Requesting a Conference.[76] As a matter of right, a taxpayer is entitled to one conference with the IRS regarding the application if the IRS indicates that it will reject or disallow the change in accounting method. However, once the IRS denies the request for change, the taxpayer does **not** have the right to appeal to any IRS official.

The applicant may request a conference by checking the box in part II on line 18 of the original Form 3115.[77] Alternatively, the applicant may make the request in writing after the IRS has indicated that it plans to deny the application.

Depending on the circumstances, a telephone conference may be an option. The taxpayer may request a telephone conference for various reasons. For example, the taxpayer may believe that the issue involved does not warrant the expense of traveling to Washington, DC, or Ogden, Utah. The IRS has the authority to decide if a telephone conference is appropriate in any particular situation. If the IRS approves the request, they will advise the taxpayer when to call the IRS.

After the conference, the taxpayer should furnish the IRS with any additional data, reasoning, precedents, and so on that they proposed and discussed but did not previously or adequately present in writing. The taxpayer must furnish the additional information within **21 calendar days** from the conference date.

Reliance on IRS Consent.[78] If the national office determines that the consent to a change in accounting method was issued in error or is not in accordance with the IRS's current views, it may revoke or modify its consent by issuing a notice of revocation or modification to the taxpayer. In rare and unusual circumstances, a taxpayer may change their accounting method and is subsequently required to change or modify it. In those cases, the required change or modification will not receive retroactive application if meeting **all** the following conditions.

1. The taxpayer complied with all the applicable provisions.
2. The taxpayer neither misstated nor omitted any material facts.
3. The material facts serving as the basis for the consent have not changed.
4. The applicable law has not changed.
5. The taxpayer, with granted consent, acted in good faith in relying on the consent, and applying the change in accounting method or modification retroactively would be to the taxpayer's detriment.

Procedures Related to the Tangible Property Regulations

The following sections of Rev. Proc. 2022-14 include instructions for automatic changes in accounting methods under the tangible property regulations.

- §6.12: Permissible to permissible method of accounting for depreciation of MACRS property for property in pooled or general asset accounts (GAAs)
- §6.13: Disposition of buildings or structural components
- §6.14: Dispositions of §1245 property and depreciable land improvements
- §6.15: Dispositions of tangible depreciable assets in GAAs[79]
- §11.08: Certain tangible property changes

76. Ibid.

77. Rev. Proc. 2023-1, 2023-1 IRB 1; Instructions for Form 3115.

78. Rev. Proc. 2015-13, 2015-5 IRB 419.

79. IRC §168(i)(4) and Treas. Reg. §1.168(i)-1.

These automatic changes in accounting methods for tangible property have several procedures in common and only minor differences. The following two procedures apply to all five sections listed previously.

1. A single Form 3115 may be used for more than one accounting method change. Practitioners using Form 3115 for multiple changes should review Rev. Procs. 2015-13 and 2022-14 for additional guidance.

2. A taxpayer may use statistical sampling to determine the §481(a) adjustment amount. Rev. Proc. 2011-42 provides specific guidance on statistical sampling for this purpose.

These changes qualify for the "short" Form 3115 for small business taxpayers. For this purpose, small business taxpayers are those with average annual gross receipts of $10 million or less. The following table summarizes the specific instructions for each section, identifying which portions of Form 3115 small business taxpayers must complete.

Revised Form 3115 Requirements for Small Taxpayers

Change Section	§6.12	§6.13	§6.14	§6.15	§11.08
The identification section of page 1 (above Part I)	X	X	X	X	X
The signature section at the bottom of page 1	X	X	X	X	X
Part I	X	X	X	X	line 1(a) only
Part II					
Lines 4–12, 14, 15a, and 18	X	X	X	X	X
Lines 16a and 16b, if the change is made due to impracticability of calculating basis	X	X	X	X	
Line 15 if the change involves depreciating property					X
Part IV					
Line 25	X				
Lines 26–28	X	X	X	X	X
Line 29	X	X	X	X	
Schedule E					
Line 3	X	X	X	X	If applicable
Additional information required in attachment[a]		X	X	X	X
Statistical sampling may be used to calculate §481(a) adj.		X	X		X
Designated automatic change number	200	205	206	207	[b]

[a] See the detailed explanations for each section later in the chapter for a list of the additional information that is required.

[b] See table later in the chapter under §11.08, Certain Tangible Property Changes.

Note. Special rules apply to public utility property[80] under all these sections. This chapter does not cover these rules.

The instructions for each section specify which changes combine into one net §481(a) adjustment and which separate into two categories — positive adjustments and negative adjustments — if §481(a) is applicable. If the changes result in two categories of §481(a) adjustments, the taxpayer treats the net negative adjustments under the provisions for immediate recognition. The taxpayer recognizes the net positive adjustments over four years.

80. IRC §168(i)(10).

§6.12 Permissible to Permissible Method for Depreciation for Pooled Assets or GAAs. As mentioned, the automatic change procedures include this set of changes. Because the original accounting method was permissible, a taxpayer can make this change by filing Form 3115. The designated automatic accounting method change number for a change to a method of accounting under this section is **200.**

Section 6.12 of Rev. Proc. 2022-14 applies only to the changes in accounting methods for the depreciation of MACRS property in multiple-asset (i.e., pooled) accounts or GAAs.

To make it easier to calculate MACRS depreciation, a taxpayer may group separate properties into one or more GAAs.[81] The taxpayer depreciates all the assets in a given GAA as a single item of property. The taxpayer makes the election on a timely filed tax return (including extensions) by completing line 18 of Form 4562, *Depreciation and Amortization*, for the year the taxpayer places the property in service.

The changes under this section are grouped into three categories as follows.

1. Changes related to assets that are **not** subject to the GAA election that **qualify** for the simplified procedures for small business taxpayers
2. Changes related to assets that are **not** subject to the GAA election that **do not qualify** for the simplified procedures for small business taxpayers
3. Changes related to assets that are subject to a GAA election. (None of these changes qualify for the simplified procedures.)

A complete list of the changes that may be made under this procedure is provided in the appendix to this chapter. The appendix also specifies the method of making the adjustment for each change. Some changes require a §481(a) adjustment (explained earlier in the chapter), some require making the change using the cut-off method, and others require the taxpayer to use a modified cut-off method.

Definition of the Cut-Off Method. As mentioned previously, under the cut-off method, a taxpayer accounts for only the items arising on or after the beginning of the year of change under the new method of accounting. The taxpayer continues to account for any items arising before the year of change under the former method of accounting. Because there is no duplication or omission of items from income when a taxpayer uses a cut-off method, no §481(a) adjustment is necessary.

Definition of the Modified Cut-Off Method. Under the modified cut-off method, a taxpayer accounts for the unadjusted depreciable basis and the asset's depreciation reserve as of the beginning of the year of change using the proposed method of accounting. See Rev. Proc. 2022-14, §6.12(4)(a), for specific instructions for each change made using this method.

§6.13 Disposition of Buildings or Structural Components. As mentioned, the automatic change procedures include this set of changes. The taxpayer may make all these changes using the simplified procedures under Rev. Proc. 2022-14. The designated automatic accounting method change number for a change to a method of accounting under this section is **205.**

Rev. Proc. 2022-14 §6.13 covers the applicable rules for a change in the accounting method related to the following.

- Disposing of a building or a structural component
- Disposing of a portion of a building (including its structural components) to which the **partial disposition rule** applies

> **Note.** Changes relating to partial dispositions may only be of the type that does **not require an election** on the original return.[82] See the exceptions in the section "Partial Disposition Election," earlier in this chapter.

81. IRS Pub. 946, *How To Depreciate Property*.

82. Rev. Proc. 2015-14, 2015-5 IRB 450.

A change of accounting method for dispositions affects the determination of the gain or loss from disposing of these assets. It may also affect whether the taxpayer must capitalize amounts paid to restore a unit of property.

2

A taxpayer should make a change under this set of procedures if they want to change their method of identifying which assets or portions of assets they disposed of or if they need to correct a partial disposition occurring in a prior year. A taxpayer should also use this set of procedures if they need to remove an asset from the depreciation schedule to claim a gain or loss that occurred in a prior year. Finally, a taxpayer should use this set of procedures to change how they determine the unadjusted basis of assets that they disposed of. The appendix of this chapter provides a complete list of the changes a taxpayer can make under this procedure.

These change procedures do **not apply** to the following.

1. Any multiple buildings, condominium units, or cooperative units that the taxpayer treats as a **single building** under their present method of accounting or that they will treat as a single building under their proposed method of accounting[83]

2. Any disposition of a portion of an asset requiring a partial disposition election[84] but for which the taxpayer **did not make such an election**

3. Any demolition of a structure to which IRC §280B and Treas. Reg. §1.280B-1 apply

Information Required with Form 3115. Taxpayers making changes under §6.13 must attach a description of the assets with the applied change to their Form 3115. Depending on the change, the taxpayer must also include the following.

1. If the taxpayer changes how assets are determined, a description of the assets for disposition purposes under the taxpayer's present and proposed accounting methods must accompany Form 3115.

2. If the taxpayer makes a change that involves identifying assets in a multiple-asset account, a description of the methods of identifying which assets have been disposed of under the taxpayer's present and proposed accounting methods must accompany Form 3115.

3. If the taxpayer makes a change that involves assets in the same multiple-asset account, the taxpayer must include a description of the methods of determining the unadjusted depreciable basis of the disposed asset or disposed portion of the asset, as applicable, under the taxpayer's present and proposed accounting methods.

4. If the taxpayer makes a change that involves determining the unadjusted depreciable basis of an asset's **disposed portion**[85] from an unreasonable method to a reasonable one, they must include a description of the methods of determining the unadjusted depreciable basis of the disposed portion of the asset, as applicable, under the taxpayer's present and proposed accounting methods.

IRC §481(a) Adjustment Period. The following taxpayers must consider the entire amount of the §481(a) adjustment in computing taxable income for the year of change, even if the adjustment is a positive amount.

- A taxpayer making a change in the method of determining which asset (or portion of an asset) has been disposed of if a gain or loss under Temp. Treas. Reg. §1.168(i)-8T has been recognized in a tax year before the year of change

- A taxpayer making a change from recognizing gain or loss under Temp. Treas. Reg. §1.168(i)-8T upon the disposition of an asset[86] included in a GAA to recognizing gain or loss upon the disposition of the same asset under the final Treas. Reg. §1.168(i)-8

---

83. Treas. Reg. §1.1250-1(a)(2)(ii).

84. Treas. Reg. §1.168(i)-8(d)(2).

85. Treas. Reg. §1.168(i)-8(f)(3).

86. Treas. Reg. §1.168(i)-8(c)(4)(ii)(A), (B), or (D), as applicable.

All other taxpayers may claim a negative §481(a) adjustment in the year of change and spread a positive adjustment over four years.[87]

§6.14 Dispositions of Certain Tangible Depreciable Assets. As mentioned, the automatic change procedures includes this set of changes. All these changes qualify for the simplified procedures under Rev. Proc. 2022-14. The designated automatic accounting method change number under this section is **206.**

Section 6.14 of Rev. Proc. 2022-14 covers the applicable rules to change the accounting method related to dispositions of the following assets.

- §1245 property
- Depreciable land improvements
- A portion of §1245 property or depreciable land improvements to which the partial disposition rule applies (Changes under this section may be made only by a taxpayer whose partial disposition was of the type not requiring an election on the original return.)

> **Note.** For further details regarding partial dispositions that do not require an election, see the section "Partial Dispositions Election" earlier in this chapter.

Changes under §6.14 affect the determination of gain or loss from disposing of these assets. It may also affect whether the taxpayer must capitalize amounts paid to restore a UOP.

A taxpayer should make a change under this set of procedures if they want to change their method of identifying which assets or portions of assets they disposed of or if they need to correct a partial disposition occurring in a prior year. A taxpayer should also use this set of procedures if they need to remove an asset from the depreciation schedule to claim a gain or loss that occurred in a prior year. Finally, a taxpayer should use this set of procedures to change how they determine the unadjusted basis of assets of which they disposed. The appendix to this chapter provides a complete list of changes that a taxpayer may make under this procedure.

This section does **not** apply to the following.

1. Any asset[88] the taxpayer does not depreciate under MACRS under the present method of accounting and, if applicable, under the proposed method of accounting
2. Any building, condominium unit, or cooperative unit or any improvement or addition to such an asset, including any structural component (See §6.13 for changes related to buildings.)
3. Any asset subject to a GAA election[89] (See §6.12 for changes related to assets subject to the GAA election and §6.15 for changes related to disposing of assets subject to the GAA election.)
4. Any disposition of a portion of an asset requiring a partial disposition election[90] but for which the taxpayer **did not make such an election**

---

87. Rev. Proc. 2022-14, 2022-7 IRB 502, referencing Rev. Proc. 2015-13, 2015-5 IRB 419.

88. Treas. Reg. §1.168(i)-8(c)(4).

89. IRC §168(i)(4) and the related regulations.

90. Treas. Reg. §1.168(i)-8(d)(2).

2

Information Required with Form 3115. A taxpayer making a change under §6.14 of Rev. Proc. 2022-14 must attach a description of the assets to which the change applies to their Form 3115. Depending on the change, the taxpayer must also include the following.

1. If a taxpayer makes a change in how assets are determined, they must include a description of the assets for disposition purposes under the taxpayer's present and proposed accounting methods.
2. If a taxpayer makes a change that involves identifying assets in a multiple-asset account, a description of the methods of identifying which assets have been disposed of under the taxpayer's present and proposed accounting methods must accompany Form 3115.
3. If a taxpayer makes a change that involves assets in the same multiple-asset account, the taxpayer must include a description of the methods of determining the unadjusted depreciable basis of the disposed asset or disposed portion of the asset, as applicable, under the taxpayer's present and proposed accounting methods.
4. A taxpayer makes a change that involves determining the unadjusted depreciable basis of an asset's **disposed portion**[91] from an unreasonable method to a reasonable one. The taxpayer must include a description of the methods of determining the unadjusted depreciable basis of the disposed portion of the asset, as applicable, under the taxpayer's present and proposed accounting methods.

IRC §481(a) Adjustment Period for Changes. The following taxpayers must consider the entire amount of the §481(a) adjustment in computing taxable income for the year of change, even if the adjustment is a positive amount.

- A taxpayer making a change in the method of determining which asset (or portion of an asset) has been disposed if a gain or loss under Temp. Treas. Reg. §1.168(i)-8T has been recognized in a tax year before the year of change
- A taxpayer making a change from recognizing gain or loss under Temp. Treas. Reg. §1.168(i)-8T upon the disposition of an asset included in a GAA to recognizing gain or loss upon the disposition of the same asset under the final Treas. Reg. §1.168(i)-8

All other taxpayers may claim a negative §481(a) adjustment in the year of change and spread a positive adjustment over four years.

§6.15 Dispositions of Tangible Depreciable Assets in GAA. As mentioned, the automatic change procedures include this set of changes. All these changes qualify for the simplified procedures under Rev. Proc. 2022-14. The designated automatic accounting method change number under this section is **207.**

Section 6.15 covers changes related to **disposing** an asset subject to the GAA election.[92] Changes in these procedures may also affect the determination of gain or loss from the asset's disposal and may affect whether the taxpayer must capitalize amounts paid to restore a UOP.[93]

A taxpayer should use the procedures in this section if they want to change how they determine which assets they disposed of and the unadjusted depreciable basis of the assets. The appendix to this chapter includes a complete list of covered changes.

91. Treas. Reg. §1.168(i)-8(f)(3).

92. IRC §168(i)(4) and the related regulations.

93. Treas. Regs. §§1.263(a)-3(e) or (f); or Treas. Reg. §1.263(a)-3(k), as applicable.

This section does **not** apply to the following.

1. Any asset[94] that the taxpayer is **not** depreciating using MACRS under the present method of accounting and, if applicable, proposed method of accounting

2. Any asset **not** subject to a GAA election

Information Required with Form 3115. A taxpayer making a change under §6.15 must attach a description of the assets to which the change applies to their Form 3115. Depending on the change being made, a taxpayer must also include the following.

1. If a taxpayer makes a change in how assets are determined, they must include a description of the assets for disposition purposes under the taxpayer's present and proposed accounting methods.

2. If a taxpayer makes a change involving identifying assets in a GAA, they must include a description of the methods of identifying which assets they disposed of under the present and proposed accounting methods.

3. A taxpayer makes a change that involves determining the unadjusted depreciable basis of an asset's **disposed portion**[95] from an unreasonable method to a reasonable one. The taxpayer must include a description of the methods of determining the unadjusted depreciable basis of the disposed portion of the asset, as applicable, under the taxpayer's present and proposed accounting methods.

IRC §481(a) Adjustment Period. When making a change listed in §6.15, taxpayers may claim a negative §481(a) adjustment in the year of change and spread a positive adjustment over four years. However, the calculation of taxable income for the year of change includes the entire amount of a positive §481(a) adjustment if **both** the following conditions are true.

- The taxpayer makes a change in the method of determining which asset or portion of an asset they disposed.
- The taxpayer previously filed Form 3115 and recognized a gain or loss under Temp. Treas. Regs. §1.168(i)-1T or §1.168(i)-8T on the disposition of the asset.

---

94. Treas. Reg. §1.168(i)-1(e)(2)(viii).

95. Treas. Reg. §1.168(i)-8(f)(3).

§11.08 Certain Tangible Property Changes. As mentioned, the automatic change procedures include this set of changes. All these changes qualify for the simplified procedures under Rev. Proc. 2022-14. In essence, §11.08 covers changes under the final tangible property regulations[96] that are not included elsewhere. The automatic accounting method designated change numbers (DCNs) are different for all the types of changes listed, as shown in the following table.[97]

2

Description of Change	DCN	Treas. Reg. Citations
Change to deducting amounts paid or incurred for repair and maintenance or a change to capitalizing amounts paid or incurred for improvements to tangible property and, if depreciable, to depreciating such property under IRC §§167 or 168. Includes a change, if any, in the **method of identifying the unit of property, or in the case of a building, identifying the building structure or building systems** for the purpose of making this change	184	§§1.162-4, 1.263(a)-3
Change to the regulatory accounting method	185	§1.263(a)-3(m)
Change to deducting NIMS when used or consumed	186	§§1.162-3(a)(1), (c)(1)
Change to deducting incidental materials and supplies when paid or incurred	187	§§1.162-3(a)(2), (c)(1)
Change to deducting nonincidental rotable and temporary spare parts when disposed of	188	§§1.162-3(a)(3), (c)(2)
Change to the optional method for rotable and temporary spare parts	189	§1.162-3(e)
Change by a dealer in property to deduct commissions and other costs that facilitate the sale of property	190	§1.263(a)-1(e)(2)
Change by a nondealer in property to capitalize commissions and other costs that facilitate the sale of property	191	§1.263(a)-1(e)(1)
Change to capitalize acquisition or production costs and, if depreciable, to depreciate such property under §§167 or 168	192	§1.263(a)-2
Change to deduct certain costs for investigating or pursuing the acquisition of real property	193	§1.263(a)-2(f)(2)(iii)

96. Treas. Regs. §§1.162-3, 1.162-4, 1.263(a)-1, 1.263(a)-2, or 1.263(a)-3.

97. Rev. Proc. 2022-14, 2022-7 IRB 502.

Section 11.08 does **not** apply to the following.

1. A taxpayer wanting to change their accounting method for dispositions of depreciable property, including a change in the asset disposed of (These are covered under §§6.10, 6.13, 6.14, and 6.15.)
2. Amounts paid or incurred for certain materials and supplies the taxpayer has elected[98] to capitalize and depreciate
3. Amounts paid or incurred to which the taxpayer has elected[99] to apply the de minimis safe harbor
4. Amounts paid or incurred for employee compensation or overhead that the taxpayer has elected[100] to capitalize
5. Amounts paid or incurred to which the taxpayer has elected[101] to apply the safe harbor for small taxpayers
6. Amounts paid or incurred for repair and maintenance costs that the taxpayer has elected[102] to capitalize
7. Amounts paid or incurred to facilitate the acquisition or disposition of assets that constitute a trade or business[103]
8. Amounts paid or incurred for repair and maintenance costs that the taxpayer is changing from capitalizing to deducting and for which the taxpayer has:
   a. Claimed a federal income tax credit,
   b. Elected to apply §168(k)(4) (as in effect on the day before the date of enactment of TCJA), or
   c. Received a payment for specified energy property in lieu of tax credits under section 1603 of the American Recovery and Reinvestment Tax Act of 2009, Div. B of Pub. L. No. 111-5, 123 Stat. 115 (February 17, 2009), as amended by section 707 of the Tax Relief, Unemployment Insurance Reauthorization, and Job Creation Act of 2010, Pub. L. No. 111-312, 124 Stat. 3296 (December 17, 2010).

Information Required with Form 3115. In addition to the other information required on line 14 of Form 3115, the taxpayer must include the following.

1. The taxpayer must include a citation to the paragraph of the regulations that provides for the proposed method(s) of accounting to which the taxpayer is changing.
2. If the taxpayer changes any UOP[104] or the identification of any building structure(s) or building system(s)[105] for purposes of determining whether amounts are deducted as repair and maintenance costs[106] or capitalized as improvement costs,[107] they must include:
   a. A detailed description of the UOP, building structure(s), or building system(s) used under its present method of accounting;
   b. A detailed description of the UOP, building structure(s), or building system(s) under its proposed method of accounting; and
   c. A citation to the paragraph of the final regulation or temporary regulation under which the change in identifying the UOP, building structure, or building system is permitted.
3. A taxpayer changing their method of accounting to capitalize amounts paid or incurred and to depreciate assets must complete Schedule E, *Change in Depreciation or Amortization,* of Form 3115.

---

98. Treas. Reg. §1.162-3(d).
99. Treas. Reg. §1.263(a)-1(f).
100. Treas. Reg. §1.263(a)-2(f)(2)(iv)(B).
101. Treas. Reg. §1.263(a)-3(h).
102. Treas. Reg. §1.263(a)-3(n).
103. See Rev. Proc. 2022-14, 2022-7 IRB 502, for procedures to make changes related to these transactions.
104. Treas. Reg. §1.263(a)-3(e) (or Temp. Treas. Reg. §1.263(a)-3T(e)).
105. Treas. Reg. §1.263-3(e)(2) (or Temp. Treas. Reg. §1.263-3T(e)(2)).
106. Treas. Reg. §1.162-4 (or Temp. Treas. Reg. §1.162-4T).
107. Treas. Reg. §1.263(a)-3 (or Temp. Treas. Reg. §1.263(a)-3T).

IRC §481(a) Adjustment Period. Most taxpayers changing to a method of accounting under §11.08 of Rev. Proc. 2022-14 may claim a negative §481(a) adjustment in the year of change and spread a positive adjustment over four years.[108] However, the adjustment is limited for certain changes.

For changes to a method of accounting under the following regulations, the §481(a) adjustment **includes only amounts paid or incurred in tax years beginning on or after January 1, 2014.** (Alternatively, a taxpayer may consider amounts paid or incurred in tax years beginning on or after January 1, 2012.)

- Treas. Reg. §1.162-3 (not including §1.162-3(e)) for accounting procedures regarding materials and supplies except the optional method of accounting for rotable and temporary spare parts
- Treas. Reg. §1.263(a)-2(f)(2)(iii) regarding costs to facilitate the acquisition of real property and allocating those costs to personal property acquired at the same time
- Treas. Reg. §1.263(a)-2(f)(3)(ii) relating to inherently facilitative amounts allocable to the purchase of real or personal property when the property is ultimately not purchased
- Treas. Reg. §1.263(a)-3(m) for adopting the optional regulatory accounting method to determine whether amounts paid to repair, maintain, or improve tangible property are treated as deductible expenses or capital expenditures
- Treas. Reg. §1.263A-1(e)(2)(i)(A) requiring manufacturers to capitalize direct material costs that become an integral part of specific property produced when those materials are consumed in the ordinary course of production and the materials can be identified or associated with particular units or groups of UOP produced
- Treas. Reg. §1.263A-1(e)(3)(ii)(E) requiring manufacturers to capitalize indirect materials costs when those materials are consumed in the ordinary course of production and cannot be identified or associated with particular units or groups of UOP produced

If a taxpayer previously elected to use the repair allowance under Treas. Reg. §1.167(a)-11(d)(2) (which has been repealed), the amount included in the election cannot be included in the §481(a) adjustment. This applies when the taxpayer changes to a method of accounting provided by Treas. Reg. §1.263(a)-3 for improvements to tangible property.

Example 20. Halle's Beauty (Halle) is a calendar-year taxpayer. Halle acquired and placed in service a building and its structural components on July 1, 2008. This property's basis was $150,000, with $15,000 (10% of the total cost) attributable to the land and the remaining $135,000 attributable to the building. The building was capitalized as one asset for depreciation purposes.

In 2019, Halle replaced the building's roof at a cost of $40,000. It claimed this $40,000 as a repair on its 2019 tax return. The company did **not** recognize a loss on the retirement of the original roof and continued to depreciate the original roof.

The IRS examined Halle's 2019 return. Upon examination, the IRS disallowed the $40,000 repair deduction and required that it be capitalized instead.

Halle's CPA, Patience, recommends that the company file Form 3115 with its 2022 corporate income tax return. Filing this form facilitates a deduction of the remaining loss from the roof that was replaced. Because the IRS capitalized the $40,000 repair cost, a change by the company from depreciating the original roof to recognizing a loss upon its retirement is covered under Rev. Proc. 2022-14, §6.13.

The original building and its components were not accounted for separately for depreciation purposes. Accordingly, the cost of the original roof must be separated from the cost of the entire building using any reasonable method.[109]

---

108. Rev. Proc. 2022-14, 2022-7 IRB 502, referencing Rev. Proc. 2015-13, 2015-5 IRB 419.

109. Treas. Reg. §1.168(i)-8(f).

Patience notes that the FMV of the real estate at the time the roof was replaced in 2019 was $300,000. Because 10% of the original property's purchase price in 2008 was allocated to the land, Patience allocates 10% of the 2019 FMV of the entire property to the land. Therefore, of the $300,000 FMV, $30,000 is allocated to the land. The remaining $270,000 is the FMV attributable to the building and components.

Patience consults an insurance adjuster who tells her that in their area of the country, the replacement cost is usually 150% of the FMV. Patience uses that estimate to determine that the replacement cost of the entire building would have been $405,000 ($270,000 × 150%). Because it cost $40,000 to replace the roof, Patience determines that 9.88% ($40,000 ÷ $405,000) of the original cost of the building was attributable to the original roof.

As of December 31, 2021, the basis of the building and the accumulated depreciation were $135,000 and $46,587, respectively. Patience allocates these amounts as follows.

	Building		Accumulated Depreciation		Adjusted Basis	
Balance on Dec. 31, 2021	$135,000	$135,000	$46,587	$46,587	$88,413	$88,413
Percent allocated to roof	× 9.88%		× 9.88%		× 9.88%	
Amount attributed to roof	$ 13,338	(13,338)	$ 4,603	(4,603)	$ 8,735	(8,735)
Amount attributed to remaining building		$121,662		$41,984		$79,678

Next, Patience determines whether Halle's average annual gross receipts exceed $10 million. Based on her review of Halle's 2019–2021 tax returns, Patience determines that Halle's average annual gross receipts are $2 million. Accordingly, Halle qualifies to complete only selected sections of Form 3115 to request a change in accounting procedures under Rev. Proc. 2022-14, §6.13. Patience completes only the required parts and lines of Form 3115. (See the table earlier in this section for the required parts and lines under Rev. Proc. 2022-14.)

For Example 20

2

Form **3115** (Rev. December 2022) Department of the Treasury Internal Revenue Service

Application for Change in Accounting Method

Go to *www.irs.gov/Form3115* for instructions and the latest information.

OMB No. 1545-2070

Attachment Sequence No. **315**

Name of filer (name of parent corporation if a consolidated group) (see instructions) **Halle's Beauty, Inc.**	**Identification number** (see instructions) **12-3456789** Principal business activity code number (see instructions) **456120 (Cosmetics Store)**
Number, street, and room or suite no. If a P.O. box, see the instructions. **1 Gotham Lane**	Tax year of change begins (MM/DD/YYYY) **01/01/2022** Tax year of change ends (MM/DD/YYYY) **12/31/2022**
City or town, state, and ZIP code **New York, NY 10009**	Name of contact person (see instructions) **Patience Philips**
Name of applicant(s) (if different than filer) and identification number(s) (see instructions)	Contact person's telephone number **(315) 555-3265**

Does the filer want to receive a copy of the change in method of accounting letter ruling or other correspondence related to this Form 3115 by fax or encrypted email attachment? If "Yes," see instructions . . . . ☐ Yes ☒ No

If the applicant is a member of a consolidated group, check this box . . . . ☐

If **Form 2848**, Power of Attorney and Declaration of Representative, is attached (see instructions for when Form 2848 is required), check this box . . . . ☒

Check the box to indicate the type of applicant.

- ☐ Individual
- ☒ Corporation
- ☐ Controlled foreign corporation (Sec. 957)
- ☐ 10/50 corporation (Sec. 904(d)(2)(E))
- ☐ Qualified personal service corporation (Sec. 448(d)(2))
- ☐ Exempt organization. Enter Code section:
- ☐ Cooperative (Sec. 1381)
- ☐ Partnership
- ☐ S corporation
- ☐ Insurance co. (Sec. 816(a))
- ☐ Insurance co. (Sec. 831)
- ☐ Other (specify):

Check the appropriate box to indicate the type of accounting method change being requested. See instructions.

- ☐ Depreciation or Amortization
- ☐ Financial Products and/or Financial Activities of Financial Institutions
- ☐ Other (specify):

Caution: To be eligible for approval of the requested change in method of accounting, the taxpayer must provide all information that is relevant to the taxpayer or to the taxpayer's requested change in method of accounting. This includes (**1**) all relevant information requested on this Form 3115 (including its instructions), and (**2**) any other relevant information, even if not specifically requested on Form 3115.

The taxpayer must attach all applicable statements requested throughout this form.

Part I Information for Automatic Change Request

		Yes	No
1	Enter the applicable designated automatic accounting method change number ("DCN") for the requested automatic change. Enter only one DCN, except as provided for in guidance published by the IRS. If the requested change has no DCN, check "Other," and provide both a description of the change and a citation of the IRS guidance providing the automatic change. See instructions.		
a	(1) DCN: 205 (2) DCN: ___ (3) DCN: ___ (4) DCN: ___ (5) DCN: ___ (6) DCN: ___ (7) DCN: ___ (8) DCN: ___ (9) DCN: ___ (10) DCN: ___ (11) DCN: ___ (12) DCN: ___		
b	Other ☐ Description:		
2	Do any of the eligibility rules restrict the applicant from filing the requested change using the automatic change procedures (see instructions)? If "Yes," attach an explanation		×
3	Has the filer provided all the information and statements required (**a**) on this form and (**b**) by the List of Automatic Changes under which the applicant is requesting a change? See instructions	×	
	Note: Complete Part II and Part IV of this form, and, Schedules A through E, if applicable.		

Part II Information for All Requests

		Yes	No
4	During the tax year of change, did or will the applicant (**a**) cease to engage in the trade or business to which the requested change relates, or (**b**) terminate its existence? See instructions		×
5	Is the applicant requesting to change to the principal method in the tax year of change under Regulations section 1.381(c)(4)-1(d)(1) or 1.381(c)(5)-1(d)(1)?		×
	If "No," go to line 6a. If "Yes," the applicant cannot file a Form 3115 for this change. See instructions.		

Sign Here

Under penalties of perjury, I declare that I have examined this application, including accompanying schedules and statements, and to the best of my knowledge and belief, the application contains all the relevant facts relating to the application, and it is true, correct, and complete. Declaration of preparer (other than applicant) is based on all information of which preparer has any knowledge.

Signature of filer (and spouse, if joint return)	Date	Name and title (print or type)
		Laurel Hadare, President

Preparer (other than filer/applicant)

Print/Type preparer's name	Preparer's signature	Date
Patience Philips		
Firm's name **Philips CPA**		

For Privacy Act and Paperwork Reduction Act Notice, see the instructions. Cat. No. 19280E Form **3115** (Rev. 12-2022)

For Example 20

Form 3115 (Rev. 12-2022) Page **2**

Part II **Information for All Requests** *(continued)*		Yes	No
6a	Does the applicant (or any present or former consolidated group in which the applicant was a member during the applicable tax year(s)) have any federal income tax return(s) under examination (see instructions)? If "No," go to line 7a.		×
b	Is the method of accounting the applicant is requesting to change an issue under consideration (with respect to either the applicant or any present or former consolidated group in which the applicant was a member during the applicable tax year(s))? See instructions		
c	Enter the name and telephone number of the examining agent and the tax year(s) under examination. Name ____ Telephone number ____ Tax year(s) ____		
d	Has a copy of this Form 3115 been provided to the examining agent identified on line 6c?		
7a	Does audit protection apply to the applicant's requested change in method of accounting? See instructions. If "No," attach an explanation.	×	
b	If "Yes," check the applicable box and attach the required statement. ☒ Not under exam ☐ 3-month window ☐ 120 day: Date examination ended ____ ☐ Method not before director ☐ Negative adjustment ☐ CAP: Date member joined group ____ ☐ Audit protection at end of exam ☐ Other		
8a	Does the applicant (or any present or former consolidated group in which the applicant was a member during the applicable tax year(s)) have any federal income tax return(s) before Appeals and/or a federal court? If "No," go to line 9.		×
b	Is the method of accounting the applicant is requesting to change an issue under consideration by Appeals and/or a federal court (for either the applicant or any present or former consolidated group in which the applicant was a member for the tax year(s) the applicant was a member)? See instructions. If "Yes," attach an explanation.		
c	If "Yes," enter the name of the (check the box) ☐ Appeals officer and/or ☐ counsel for the government, telephone number, and the tax year(s) before Appeals and/or a federal court. Name ____ Telephone number ____ Tax year(s) ____		
d	Has a copy of this Form 3115 been provided to the Appeals officer and/or counsel for the government identified on line 8c?		
9	If the applicant answered "Yes" to line 6a and/or 8a with respect to any present or former consolidated group, attach a statement that provides each parent corporation's (**a**) name, (**b**) identification number, (**c**) address, and (**d**) tax year(s) during which the applicant was a member that is under examination, before an Appeals office, and/or before a federal court.		
10	If for federal income tax purposes, the applicant is either an entity (including a limited liability company) treated as a partnership or an S corporation, is it requesting a change from a method of accounting that is an issue under consideration in an examination, before Appeals, or before a federal court, with respect to a federal income tax return of a partner, member, or shareholder of that entity?		×
11a	Has the applicant, its predecessor, or a related party requested or made (under either an automatic or non-automatic change procedure) a change in method of accounting within any of the 5 tax years ending with the tax year of change? If "No," go to line 12.		×
b	If "Yes," for each trade or business, attach a description of each requested change in method of accounting (including the tax year of change) and state whether the applicant received consent.		
c	If any application was withdrawn, not perfected, or denied, or if a Consent Agreement granting a change was not signed and returned to the IRS, or the change was not made or not made in the requested year of change, attach an explanation.		
12	Does the applicant, its predecessor, or a related party currently have pending any request (including any concurrently filed request) for a private letter ruling, change in method of accounting, or technical advice? If "Yes," for each request attach a statement providing (**a**) the name(s) of the taxpayer, (**b**) identification number(s), (**c**) the type of request (private letter ruling, change in method of accounting, or technical advice), and (**d**) the specific issue(s) in the request(s).		×
13	Is the applicant requesting to change its **overall** method of accounting? If "Yes," complete Schedule A on page 4 of the form.		×

Form **3115** (Rev. 12-2022)

For Example 20

Form 3115 (Rev. 12-2022) Page 3

Part II Information for All Requests *(continued)*	Yes	No
14 If the applicant is either **(i) not** changing its overall method of accounting, or **(ii)** changing its overall method of accounting **and** changing to a special method of accounting for one or more items, attach a detailed and complete description for each of the following (see instructions):		
a The item(s) being changed.		
b The applicant's present method for the item(s) being changed.		
c The applicant's proposed method for the item(s) being changed.		
d The applicant's present overall method of accounting (cash, accrual, or hybrid).		
15a Attach a detailed and complete description of the applicant's trade(s) or business(es). See section 446(d).		
b If the applicant has more than one trade or business, as defined in Regulations section 1.446-1(d), describe **(i)** whether each trade or business is accounted for separately; **(ii)** the goods and services provided by each trade or business and any other types of activities engaged in that generate gross income; **(iii)** the overall method of accounting for each trade or business; and **(iv)** which trade or business is requesting to change its accounting method as part of this application or a separate application.		
Note: If you are requesting an automatic method change, see the instructions to see if you are required to complete lines 16a–16c.		
16a Attach a full explanation of the legal basis supporting the proposed method for the item being changed. Include a detailed and complete description of the facts that explains how the law specifically applies to the applicant's situation and that demonstrates that the applicant is authorized to use the proposed method.		
b Include all authority (statutes, regulations, published rulings, court cases, etc.) supporting the proposed method.		
c Include either a discussion of the contrary authorities or a statement that no contrary authority exists.		
17 Will the proposed method of accounting be used for the applicant's books and records and financial statements? For insurance companies, see the instructions		
If "No," attach an explanation.		
18 Does the applicant request a conference with the IRS National Office if the IRS National Office proposes an adverse response?		×
19a If the applicant is changing to either the overall cash method, an overall accrual method, or is changing its method of accounting for any property subject to section 263A, any long-term contract subject to section 460 (see 19b), or inventories subject to section 471 or 474, enter the applicant's gross receipts for the 3 tax years preceding the tax year of change.		

1st preceding year ended: mo. yr.	2nd preceding year ended: mo. yr.	3rd preceding year ended: mo. yr.
$	$	$

b If the applicant is changing its method of accounting for any long-term contract subject to section 460, in addition to completing 19a, enter the applicant's gross receipts for the 4th tax year preceding the tax year of change:
4th preceding year ended: mo. ____________ yr. ______ $ ______________

Part III Information for Non-Automatic Change Request	Yes	No
20 Is the applicant's requested change described in any revenue procedure, revenue ruling, notice, regulation, or other published guidance as an automatic change request?		
If "Yes," attach an explanation describing why the applicant is submitting its request under the non-automatic change procedures.		
21 Attach a copy of all documents related to the proposed change (see instructions).		
22 Attach a statement of the applicant's reasons for the proposed change.		
23 If the applicant is a member of a consolidated group for the year of change, do all other members of the consolidated group use the proposed method of accounting for the item being changed?		
If "No," attach an explanation.		
24a Enter the amount of **user fee** attached to this application (see instructions) . . . . . . $ ______________		
b If the applicant qualifies for a reduced user fee, attach the required information or certification (see instructions).		

Form **3115** (Rev. 12-2022)

For Example 20

Form 3115 (Rev. 12-2022) Page **4**

Part IV **Section 481(a) Adjustment**	Yes	No
25 Does published guidance require the applicant (or permit the applicant and the applicant is electing) to implement the requested change in method of accounting on a cut-off basis? . . . . If "Yes," attach an explanation and do not complete lines 26, 27, 28, and 29 below.		
26 Enter the section 481(a) adjustment. Indicate whether the adjustment is an increase (+) or a decrease (-) in income. $ **(8,735)** Attach a summary of the computation and an explanation of the methodology used to determine the section 481(a) adjustment. If it is based on more than one component, show the computation for each component. If the applicant waived any deductions with respect to the method of accounting pursuant to Regulations section 1.59A-3(c)(6)(i), include a summary of the waived deductions. If more than one applicant is applying for the method change on the application, attach a list of the (**a**) name, (**b**) identification number, and (**c**) the amount of the section 481(a) adjustment attributable to each applicant.		
27 Is the applicant required to take into account in the year of change any remaining portion of a section 481(a) adjustment from a prior change (see instructions)? If "Yes," enter the amount. $ ______		×
28 Is the applicant making an election to take the entire amount of the adjustment into account in the tax year of change? If "Yes," check the box for the applicable elective provision used to make the election (see instructions). ☐ $50,000 de minimis election ☐ Eligible acquisition transaction election		×
29 Is any part of the section 481(a) adjustment attributable to transactions between members of an affiliated group, a consolidated group, a controlled group, or other related parties? . . . . If "Yes," attach an explanation.		×

...ange in Overall Method of Accounti... ...ule A applies, Pa... ...ted.)

11 Oth... cost...

Schedule E—Change in Depreciation or Amortization (see instructions)

Applicants requesting approval to change their method of accounting for depreciation or amortization complete this section. Applicants ***must*** provide this information for each item or class of property for which a change is requested.

Note: See the ***Summary of the List of Automatic Accounting Method Changes*** in the instructions for information regarding automatic changes under sections 56, 167, 168, or 197, or former sections 168, 1400I, or 1400L. **Do not** file Form 3115 with respect to certain late elections and election revocations. See instructions.

1 Is depreciation for the property determined under Regulations section 1.167(a)-11 (CLADR)? . . . . ☐ **Yes** ☐ **No**
If "Yes," the only changes permitted are under Regulations section 1.167(a)-11(c)(1)(iii).

2 Is any of the depreciation or amortization required to be capitalized under any Code section, such as section 263A? . . . . ☐ **Yes** ☐ **No**
If "Yes," enter the applicable section ______

3 Has a depreciation, amortization, expense, or disposition election been made for the property, such as the election under sections 168(f)(1), 168(i)(4), 179, 179C, or Regulations section 1.168(i)-8(d)? . . . . ☐ **Yes** ☒ **No**
If "Yes," state the election made ______

4a Attach a statement describing the property subject to the change. Include the property's description, type, placed-in-service year, and use in the applicant's trade or business or income-producing activity. Also include the type and amount of any federal tax credit claimed or grant received, along with any necessary adjustments to basis required under the Internal Revenue Code, with respect to the property.

b If the property is residential rental property, did the applicant live in the property before renting it? . . ☐ **Yes** ☐ **No**

c Is the property public utility property? . . . . ☐ **Yes** ☐ **No**

5 To the extent not already provided in the applicant's description of its present method, attach a statement explaining how the ...

For Example 20

Halle's Beauty, Inc. FEIN: 12-3456789

Form 3115 Attachment

Information required by Rev. Proc. 2022-14

The taxpayer is changing its method of identifying property disposed of in a prior year. Under the prior method, the roof was capitalized as part of the building and was not separately stated. The IRS has examined the 2019 income tax return of the taxpayer and determined that the roof was replaced in that year. The IRS examination resulted in the capitalization of the roof replacement.

Under the proposed method of accounting, the taxpayer is separating the original cost basis of the replaced roof and claiming a loss on its disposition. For the proposed change, the unadjusted basis of the roof at the time the building was purchased has been determined using the cost to replace the roof as a percentage of the estimated replacement cost of the entire building.

Part II, line 14

a. The taxpayer claims a loss on the remaining adjusted basis of the roof component of the building as of December 31, 2021, for the roof that was replaced in 2019.

b. Depreciation of the replaced roof was continued after it was disposed of.

c. The remaining adjusted basis will be claimed as a loss using the §481(a) adjustment.

d. The taxpayer uses the cash method of accounting.

Part IV, line 25

The total §481(a) adjustment for this change is –$8,735. This represents the remaining basis of the disposed roof as of December 31, 2021.

The original unadjusted basis of the commercial building and its components was $135,000 when the building was placed into service on July 1, 2008. The building has been depreciated using the midmonth convention on the straight-line basis with a 39-year life.

As of December 31, 2021, the basis of the building and the accumulated depreciation were $135,000 and $46,587, respectively. These were allocated based on the assumption that the original cost of the roof was 9.88% of the cost of the building as a whole. This percentage was calculated based on a replacement cost of $40,000 for the roof and an estimated replacement cost for the entire building of $405,000 at the time the roof was replaced in 2019.

	Building	Accumulated Depreciation	Adjusted Basis
Balance on Dec. 31, 2021	$135,000	$46,587	$88,413
Percent allocated to roof	× 9.88%	× 9.88%	× 9.88%
Amount attributed to roof	$ 13,338	$ 4,603	$ 8,735

Halle reports the disposition of the old roof on Form 4797, *Sale of Business Property*.

Form **4797**

Department of the Treasury
Internal Revenue Service

Sales of Business Property

(Also Involuntary Conversions and Recapture Amounts Under Sections 179 and 280F(b)(2))

Attach to your tax return.

Go to *www.irs.gov/Form4797* for instructions and the latest information.

OMB No. 1545-0184

2022

Attachment Sequence No. **27**

Name(s) shown on return: **Halle's Beauty**

Identifying number: 12-3456789

1a	Enter the gross proceeds from sales or exchanges reported to you for 2022 on Form(s) 1099-B or 1099-S (or substitute statement) that you are including on line 2, 10, or 20. See instructions	**1a**	
b	Enter the total amount of gain that you are including on lines 2, 10, and 24 due to the partial dispositions of MACRS assets	**1b**	
c	Enter the total amount of loss that you are including on lines 2 and 10 due to the partial dispositions of MACRS assets	**1c**	

Part I **Sales or Exchanges of Property Used in a Trade or Business and Involuntary Conversions From Other Than Casualty or Theft—Most Property Held More Than 1 Year** (see instructions)

2 (a) Description of property	(b) Date acquired (mo., day, yr.)	(c) Date sold (mo., day, yr.)	(d) Gross sales price	(e) Depreciation allowed or allowable since acquisition	(f) Cost or other basis, plus improvements and expense of sale	(g) Gain or (loss) Subtract (f) from the sum of (d) and (e)
Roof	**07/01/2008**	**01/01/2022**		**4,603**	**13,338**	**(8,735)**

3	Gain, if any, from Form 4684, line 39	3	
4	Section 1231 gain from installment sales from Form 6252, line 26 or 37	4	
5	Section 1231 gain or (loss) from like-kind exchanges from Form 8824	5	
6	Gain, if any, from line 32, from other than casualty or theft	6	
7	Combine lines 2 through 6. Enter the gain or (loss) here and on the appropriate line as follows	7	**(8,735)**
	Partnerships and S corporations. Report the gain or (loss) following the instructions for Form 1065, Schedule K, line 10, or Form 1120-S, Schedule K, line 9. Skip lines 8, 9, 11, and 12 below.		
	Individuals, partners, S corporation shareholders, and all others. If line 7 is zero or a loss, enter the amount from line 7 on line 11 below and skip lines 8 and 9. If line 7 is a gain and you didn't have any prior year section 1231 losses, or they were recaptured in an earlier year, enter the gain from line 7 as a long-term capital gain on the Schedule D filed with your return and skip lines 8, 9, 11, and 12 below.		
8	Nonrecaptured net section 1231 losses from prior years. See instructions	8	
9	Subtract line 8 from line 7. If zero or less, enter -0-. If line 9 is zero, enter the gain from line 7 on line 12 below. If line 9 is more than zero, enter the amount from line 8 on line 12 below and enter the gain from line 9 as a long-term capital gain on the Schedule D filed with your return. See instructions	9	

Part II **Ordinary Gains and Losses** (see instructions)

10 Ordinary gains and losses not included on lines 11 through 16 (include property held 1 year or less):

11	Loss, if any, from line 7	11	(**8,735**)
12	Gain, if any, from line 7 or amount from line 8, if applicable	12	
13	Gain, if any, from line 31	13	
14	Net gain or (loss) from Form 4684, lines 31 and 38a	14	
15	Ordinary gain from installment sales from Form 6252, line 25 or 36	15	
16	Ordinary gain or (loss) from like-kind exchanges from Form 8824	16	
17	Combine lines 10 through 16	17	**(8,735)**
18	For all except individual returns, enter the amount from line 17 on the appropriate line of your return and skip lines a and b below. For individual returns, complete lines a and b below.		
a	If the loss on line 11 includes a loss from Form 4684, line 35, column (b)(ii), enter that part of the loss here. Enter the loss from income-producing property on Schedule A (Form 1040), line 16. (Do not include any loss on property used as an employee.) Identify as from "Form 4797, line 18a." See instructions	18a	
b	Redetermine the gain or (loss) on line 17 excluding the loss, if any, on line 18a. Enter here and on Schedule 1 (Form 1040), Part I, line 4	18b	

For Paperwork Reduction Act Notice, see separate instructions. Cat. No. 13086I Form **4797** (2022)

Halle's depreciation schedule before capitalizing the $40,000 repair cost is as follows.

Asset	Date in Service	Cost	Life	Convention	Prior Depreciation	Current Depreciation
Building	7/01/2008	$135,000	39	MM S/L	$46,587	$3,461
Land	7/01/2008	15,000		Land	0	0
Total		$150,000			$46,587	$3,461

Halle's depreciation schedule after capitalizing the $40,000 repair cost and separating the original roof's depreciable cost from the building cost is as follows.

Asset	Date in Service	Cost	Life	Convention	Prior Depreciation	Current Depreciation
Building	7/01/2008	$121,662	39	MM S/L	$41,984	$3,119
Roof (original)	7/01/2008	13,338	39	MM S/L	4,603	0
Roof (new)	7/01/2019	40,000	39	MM S/L	2,521	1,026
Land	7/01/2008	15,000		Land	0	0
Total		$190,000			$49,108	$4,145

Failure to File Form 3115

In the event that a taxpayer changes their accounting method to comply with tangible property regulations but fails to file Form 3115, if required, the effects are as follows.

1. This constitutes **an unauthorized change of accounting method.**[110]
2. On examination, the IRS can change the taxpayer's method of accounting to one that it believes most clearly reflects income. In so doing, the IRS may impose a §481(a) adjustment encompassing prior years without regard to a statute of limitations.[111]
3. Any §481(a) adjustment is imposed in one year rather than over a 4-year period as allowed for a voluntary positive §481(a) adjustment.[112]
4. If the examination results in an increase in tax, the failure-to-pay penalty may apply to the earlier understatement of tax. The taxpayer may also be subject to accuracy-related and other penalties.[113]

SIMPLIFIED PROCEDURE FOR SMALL TAXPAYERS

The IRS did not intend to make complying with the new tangible property regulations burdensome for taxpayers — especially small business taxpayers. The IRS designed the simplified procedure under Rev. Proc. 2015-20[114] to make it easier for small business taxpayers to adopt accounting procedures consistent with the new regulations.

110. See Treas. Reg. §1.446-1(e)(2)(i).

111. IRC §§481, 1311–1314; *Graff Chevrolet Co. v. Campbell*, 343 F.2d 568 (5th Cir. 1965).

112. Rev. Proc. 2002-18, 2002-13 IRB 678.

113. Ibid.

114. Rev. Proc. 2015-20, 2015-9 IRB 694.

Small Business Taxpayer Defined[115]

To qualify for these simplified procedures, a small business taxpayer must meet **one** of the following conditions.

1. Be a taxpayer with total **assets of less than $10 million** as of the first day of the tax year for which a change in accounting method is effective
2. Have a separate and distinct trade or business with average annual gross receipts of $10 million or less for the prior three tax years (The calculation of average annual gross receipts for this purpose uses the same method as the small business safe harbor election.[116])

The taxpayer applies the simplified procedure to each separate and distinct trade or business they own. A taxpayer may have more than one separate and distinct trade or business. In that case, they can choose the simplified procedure only for the trades or businesses that meet at least one of the preceding criteria. Therefore, the taxpayer may be able to apply the simplified procedure to some of their businesses but not others.

Simplified Procedure for Changes in Accounting Methods

Rev. Proc. 2015-20[117] was issued specifically to address the burden of retroactively changing accounting procedures to comply with the new tangible property regulations. It provides two procedures for the small business taxpayer to change their accounting method for certain depreciable items, as discussed in this chapter.

Under the **first simplified procedure,** the taxpayer **does not file Form 3115.** The taxpayer simply adopts the method with the tax return filed for the **first tax year beginning on or after January 1, 2014.** The taxpayer does not make an adjustment for different methods used prior to January 1, 2014.

The **second simplified procedure** applies to taxpayers who did not change their method of accounting in 2014 for items affected by the new tangible property regulations. Under this procedure, **the taxpayer files Form 3115** but only adjusts for transactions occurring **on or after** January 1, 2014. This cut-off date is in contrast to the usual procedure, which requires that the adjustment include all prior-year transactions affected by the change in accounting procedure.

The following table summarizes the **only types of changes in accounting methods allowable using the simplified procedure.**

115. Ibid.

116. See Treas. Reg. §1.263(a)-3(h)(3).

117. Rev. Proc. 2015-20, 2015-9 IRB 694.

Type of Change in Accounting Method	Section of Rev. Proc. 2022-14	Description of Change in Accounting Method
Certain changes from one permissible method to another permissible method for assets in multiple accounts	§§6.12(3)(a)(iv), (v), (vii), (viii)	This change involves the methods used to identify which assets (or which portion of assets) in multiple-asset accounts have been disposed of as permitted under Treas. Reg. §1.168(i)-8(g).
Changes related to the disposition of buildings or structural components of buildings	§6.13	These rules apply to a taxpayer who wants to make a change in the method of accounting for: • Disposing of a building or a structural component thereof, or • Disposing of a portion of a building (including its structural components) to which the partial disposition rule applies. This change does not apply to any disposition of a portion of an asset for which a partial disposition election[118] is required but for which the taxpayer did not make such an election. This change also affects the determination of gain or loss from disposing of the building, the structural component, or the portion of the building (including its structural components). It may also affect whether the taxpayer must capitalize the amounts paid to restore a UOP.
Certain dispositions of tangible depreciable assets (**other than** a building or its structural components)	§6.14	This change applies to dispositions of the following types of property. • §1245 property • Depreciable land improvements • Portions of §1245 property or depreciable land improvements This change does not apply to any disposition of a portion of an asset for which a partial disposition election[119] is required but for which the taxpayer did not make such an election. This change also affects the determination of gain or loss from disposing of these types of property. It may also affect whether the taxpayer must capitalize the amounts paid to restore a UOP.
Certain disposition of tangible depreciable assets in a GAA	§6.15	This section applies to a change in disposing of an asset subject to a GAA election.[120] This change also affects the determination of gain or loss from disposing of these types of property. It may also affect whether the taxpayer must capitalize the amounts paid to restore a UOP.
Certain tangible property changes	§11.08	This section applies to a change **to deducting** amounts paid or incurred for repair and maintenance or a change **to capitalize** amounts paid or incurred for improvements to tangible property and depreciating qualifying property. This change may also involve a change in the method of identifying the UOP, or in the case of a building, identifying the building structure or building systems for the purpose of making this change. Many additional changes are included in this section.

118. Per Treas. Reg. §1.168(i)-8(d)(2).

119. Ibid.

120. IRC §168(i)(4) and Treas. Reg. §1.168(i)-1.

DISPOSITIONS UNDER THE TANGIBLE PROPERTY REGULATIONS

The tangible property regulations deem the following situations to be dispositions.

- Transfer of ownership interest in an asset
- Permanent withdrawal of an asset from a taxpayer's trade or business or the production of income
- The sale or exchange of an asset
- The retirement of an asset
- The physical abandonment of an asset
- The destruction of an asset
- The retirement of a structural component (or a portion thereof) of a building (if the partial disposition rule applies)

SALE OF TANGIBLE PROPERTY EXPENSED UNDER DE MINIMIS SAFE HARBOR

When a taxpayer sells or otherwise disposes of property to which they applied the de minimis safe harbor, identifying the treatment of the property is critical. The taxpayer cannot treat that property as a capital asset under IRC §1221 nor as depreciable property used in a trade or business under §1231.[121] It is important to review the basics of §§1221 and 1231.

Review of IRC §§1221 and 1231

IRC §1221 describes a capital asset by stating what it is not. Among other things, a capital asset is not inventory or depreciable business property used in a trade or business. The latter type of property falls under §1231.

A capital asset qualifies for preferential tax treatment when sold, notably in the form of reduced tax rates.[122] For the 2023 tax year, the capital gain tax rate is as follows.[123]

Capital Gain Tax Rate	Income Threshold: Single	Income Threshold: Married Filing Jointly
0%	$0 to $44,625	$0 to $89,250
15%	$44,626 to $492,300	$89,251 to $553,850
20%	More than $492,300	More than $553,850

Note. Higher maximum capital gains tax rates apply to some sales, such as depreciable real estate, some small business stock, and collectibles. In addition, the net investment income tax may apply.

121. Treas. Reg. §1.263(a)-1(f)(3)(iii).

122. IRC §1(h).

123. IRS Pub. 505, *Tax Withholding and Estimated Tax*, p. 34 (2023).

IRC §1231 property must be used in a trade or business and held for over one year. It generally includes all depreciable assets and real property, regardless of whether it is depreciable. Amortizable intangibles, such as acquired goodwill, also are §1231 assets. (Self-created intangibles, such as goodwill generated by a business, are considered capital assets under §1221 and not §1231.) IRC §1231 does not include property held in inventory.

IRC §1231 property receives the best of both worlds regarding tax treatment. Losses are deducted as ordinary income, while gains exceeding the depreciation component qualify for the preferential capital gains tax rates.[124]

Ordinary Income Treatment of Gains[125]

Taxpayers deducting items under the de minimis safe harbor election do not characterize the expenses as capital expenditures under §1231. Instead, **taxpayers treat these expenses as regular business expenses,** provided they qualify as ordinary and necessary expenses incurred in carrying on a trade or business.

Because tangible property deducted under the de minimis safe harbor election cannot be considered capital assets or §1231 property, the income derived from dispositions of such property is **ordinary income**. Consequently, the proceeds of these dispositions do not qualify for preferential capital gain tax treatment.

> **Example 21.** At a bankruptcy auction, Terry Stevens from **Example 11** bought another copier machine for $800 on January 31, 2021. He used the machine in his business until October 31, 2022, when he sold the equipment for $1,200.
>
> In 2021, Terry's tax preparer deducted the cost of the copier machine using the de minimis safe harbor election. On his 2022 return, Terry must report the entire $1,200 sales price as ordinary income. Because Terry is in the 24% tax bracket, he pays $288 ($1,200 × 24%) of income tax on the sale of the machine.
>
> **Example 22.** Use the same facts as **Example 21,** except in 2021, Terry's tax preparer deducted the $800 cost of the machine using the §179 election. Terry reports the entire $1,200 as a gain on his 2022 tax return. However, only the $800 depreciation component is taxable as ordinary income. The remaining $400 gain ($1,200 – $800) is subject to capital gain tax rates. Because Terry is in the 24% income tax bracket, he pays $252 ($800 × 24% + $400 × 15%) of income tax on the sale of the machine.

BUILDING PROPERTY DISPOSITIONS[126]

If a taxpayer claims deductions for building property improvements under the de minimis safe harbor election, the improvements generally are not sold separately from the rest of the building. Therefore, the improvements are part of the building sale.

The building and corresponding building system components and improvements are reported on the taxpayer's Form 4797. Consequently, **the disposition of building property improvements deducted under the de minimis safe harbor does not trigger self-employment tax or depreciation recapture under §1250.**

---

124. IRS Pub. 544, *Sales and Other Dispositions of Assets.*

125. Treas. Regs. §§1.263(a)-1(f)(3)(iii) - (iv).

126. Treas. Reg. §1.263(a)-1(f)(3); IRC §1402(a)(3)(A).

APPENDIX

AUTOMATIC CHANGES FOR DISPOSITIONS OF TANGIBLE PROPERTY[127]

The following table summarizes the changes in accounting methods that a taxpayer may make under Rev. Proc. 2022-14.

Final Regulation Section	Section in Rev. Proc. 2022-14	DCN
§1.167(a)-4, Depreciation of leasehold improvements	6.11	199
GAAs		
§1.168(i)-1(c), Change in grouping assets	6.12	200
§1.168(i)-1(e)(2)(viii), Change in determining asset disposed of	6.15	207
§1.168(i)-1(j)(2), Change in method of identifying which assets or portions of assets have been disposed of from one method to another method specified in §1.168(i)-1(j)(2)	6.12	200
§1.168(i)-1(j)(2), Change in method of identifying which assets or portions of assets have been disposed of from a method not specified in §1.168(i)-1(j)(2) to a method specified in §1.168(i)-1(j)(2)	6.15	207
§1.168(i)-1(j)(3), Change in determining unadjusted depreciable basis of disposed asset or disposed portion of an asset from one reasonable method to another reasonable method when it is impracticable from the taxpayer's records to determine the unadjusted depreciable basis of disposed asset or disposed portion of asset	6.12	200
§1.168(i)-1(j)(3), Change in determining unadjusted depreciable basis of disposed asset or disposed portion of an asset from not using to using the taxpayer's records when it is practicable from the taxpayer's records to determine the unadjusted depreciable basis of disposed asset or disposed portion of asset	6.15	207
§1.168(i)-1(j)(3), Change in determining unadjusted depreciable basis of disposed asset or disposed portion of an asset from an unreasonable method to a reasonable method when it is impracticable from the taxpayer's records to determine the unadjusted depreciable basis of disposed asset or disposed portion of asset	6.15	207
Single-Asset Accounts or Multiple-Asset Accounts for MACRS Property		
§1.168(i)-7, Change from single-asset accounts to multiple-asset accounts, or vice versa	6.12	200
§1.168(i)-7(c), Change in grouping assets in multiple-asset accounts	6.12	200

127. Rev. Proc. 2022-14, 2022-7 IRB 502.

Final Regulation Section	Section in Rev. Proc. 2022-14	DCN
Dispositions of MACRS Property (not in GAAs)		
§1.168(i)-8(c)(4), Change in determining asset disposed of	6.13 (Building or structural component)	205
	6.14 (Property other than a building or structural component)	206
§1.168(i)-8(f)(2) or (3), Change in determining unadjusted depreciable basis of disposed asset in a multiple-asset account or disposed portion of an asset from one reasonable method to another reasonable method when it is impracticable from the taxpayer's records to determine the unadjusted depreciable basis of disposed asset or disposed portion of asset	6.12	200
§1.168(i)-8(f)(2) or (3), Change in determining unadjusted depreciable basis of disposed asset in a multiple-asset account or disposed portion of an asset from not using to using the taxpayer's records when it is practicable from the taxpayer's records to determine the unadjusted depreciable basis of disposed asset or disposed portion of asset	6.13 (Building or structural component)	205
	6.14 (Property other than a building or structural component)	206
§1.168(i)-8(f)(2) or (3), Change in determining unadjusted depreciable basis of disposed asset in a multiple-asset account or disposed portion of an asset from an unreasonable method to a reasonable method when it is impracticable from the taxpayer's records to determine the unadjusted depreciable basis of disposed asset or disposed portion of asset	6.13 (Building or structural component)	205
	6.14 (Property other than a building or structural component)	206
§1.168(i)-8(g), Change in method of identifying which assets in a multiple-asset account or portions of assets have been disposed of from one method to another method specified in §1.168(i)-8(g)(1) or (2)	6.12	200
§1.168(i)-8(g), Change in method of identifying which assets in a multiple-asset account or portions of assets have been disposed of from a method not specified in §1.168(i)-8(g)(1) or (2) to a method specified in §1.168(i)-8(g)(1) or (2)	6.13 (Building or structural component)	205
	6.14 (Property other than a building or structural component)	206
§1.168(i)-8(h)(1), Change from depreciating a disposed asset or disposed portion of an asset to recognizing gain or loss upon disposition when a taxpayer continues to depreciate the asset or portion that they disposed of prior to the year of change	6.13 (Building or structural component)	205
	6.14 (Property other than a building or structural component)	206
§1.168(i)-8(d)(2)(iii), Partial disposition election for the disposition of a portion of an asset to which the IRS's adjustment pertains	6.10	198

§6.12: Permissible to Permissible Method for Depreciation of Pooled Assets or GAAs

The following changes allowed under §6.12 are for items of MACRS property that are **not** subject to a GAA election and that qualify under the simplified procedures for small business taxpayers.[128]

1. A change in the method of identifying which assets in multiple-asset accounts or which portions of assets have been disposed of by the taxpayer from the FIFO method of accounting[129] or the modified FIFO method of accounting[130] to the specific identification method[131] (using a §481(a) adjustment)
2. A change in the method of identifying which assets in multiple-asset accounts or which portions of assets have been disposed of by the taxpayer from the FIFO method of accounting[132] to the modified FIFO method of accounting[133] or vice versa (using a §481(a) adjustment)
3. A change in the method of identifying which mass assets[134] in multiple-asset accounts or which portions of mass assets have been disposed of by the taxpayer from the FIFO method of accounting[135] or the modified FIFO method of accounting[136] to a mortality dispersion table[137] (using a §481(a) adjustment)
4. A change in the method of identifying which mass assets[138] in multiple-asset accounts or which portions of mass assets have been disposed of by the taxpayer from a mortality dispersion table[139] to the specific identification method,[140] the FIFO method of accounting,[141] or the modified FIFO method of accounting[142] (using a §481(a) adjustment)

The following changes allowed under §6.12 are for items of MACRS property that are **not** subject to a GAA election but **do not** qualify under the simplified procedures.

1. A change[143] from single-asset accounts (or item accounts) for specific items of MACRS property to multiple-asset accounts (or pools) for the same assets or vice versa (using the modified cut-off method, defined later)
2. A change[144] from grouping specific items of MACRS property in multiple-asset accounts to a different grouping of the same assets in multiple-asset accounts (using the modified cut-off method, defined later)

---

128. See IRC §168(i)(4) and related regulations.
129. Under Treas. Reg. §1.168(i)-8(g)(2)(i).
130. Under Treas. Reg. §1.168(i)-8(g)(2)(ii).
131. Under Treas. Reg. §1.168(i)-8(g)(1).
132. Under Treas. Reg. §1.168(i)-8(g)(2)(i).
133. Under Treas. Reg. §1.168(i)-8(g)(2)(ii).
134. As defined in Treas. Reg. §1.168(i)-8(b)(3).
135. Under Treas. Reg. §1.168(i)-8(g)(2)(i).
136. Under Treas. Reg. §1.168(i)-8(g)(2)(ii).
137. In accordance with Treas. Reg. §1.168(i)-8(g)(2)(iii).
138. As defined in Treas. Reg. §1.168(i)-8(b)(3).
139. In accordance with Treas. Reg. §1.168(i)-8(g)(2)(iii).
140. Under Treas. Reg. §1.168(i)-8(g)(1).
141. Under Treas. Reg. §1.168(i)-8(g)(2)(i).
142. Under Treas. Reg. §1.168(i)-8(g)(2)(ii).
143. Under Treas. Reg. §1.168(i)-7.
144. Under Treas. Reg. §1.168(i)-7(c).

3. A change in the method of identifying which assets in multiple-asset accounts or which portions of assets have been disposed of by the taxpayer from the specific identification method[145] to the FIFO method[146] or the modified FIFO method[147] (using a cut-off method and applying to dispositions occurring on or after the beginning of the year of change). A change in the method of identifying which mass assets[148] in multiple-asset accounts or which portions of mass assets have been disposed of by the taxpayer from the specific identification method[149] to a mortality dispersion table[150] (using a cut-off method and applying to dispositions occurring on or after the beginning of the year of change). For disposition of an asset in a multiple-asset account[151] when it is impracticable from the taxpayer's records to determine the unadjusted depreciable basis of the asset disposed of, a change in the method of determining the unadjusted depreciable basis of all assets in the same multiple-asset account from one reasonable method to another reasonable method (using a cut-off method and applying to dispositions occurring on or after the beginning of the year of change)

4. For disposition of a portion of an asset[152] when it is impracticable from the taxpayer's records to determine the unadjusted depreciable basis of the disposed portion of the asset, a change in the method of determining the unadjusted depreciable basis of all disposed portions of the asset from one reasonable method to another reasonable method (using a cut-off method and applying to dispositions occurring on or after the beginning of the year of change)

The following changes allowed under this provision are for the items of MACRS property that **are subject** to a GAA election.[153]

1. A change from grouping specific items of MACRS property in GAAs to a different grouping of the same assets in GAAs[154] (using the modified cut-off method, defined earlier)

2. A change in the method of identifying which assets or which portions of assets have been disposed of by the taxpayer from the specific identification method[155] to the FIFO method[156] or the modified FIFO method[157] (using a cut-off method and applying to dispositions occurring on or after the beginning of the year of change)

3. A change in the method of identifying which assets or which portions of assets have been disposed of by the taxpayer from the FIFO method of accounting[158] or the modified FIFO method of accounting[159] to the specific identification method[160] (using a §481(a) adjustment, but the §481(a) adjustment should be zero unless the special rules for terminating GAAs[161] apply to the asset subject to the change (See IRS Pub. 946, *How to Depreciate Property*, for more information about terminating a GAA election.)

---

145. Under Treas. Reg. §1.168(i)-8(g)(1).
146. Under Treas. Reg. §1.168(i)-8(g)(2)(i).
147. Under Treas. Reg. §1.168(i)-8(g)(2)(ii).
148. As defined in Treas. Reg. §1.168(i)-8(b)(3).
149. Under Treas. Reg. §1.168(i)-8(g)(1).
150. In accordance with Treas. Reg. §1.168(i)-8(g)(2)(iii).
151. Under Treas. Reg. §1.168(i)-8(f)(2).
152. Under Treas. Reg. §1.168(i)-8(f)(3).
153. See IRC §168(i)(4) and related regulations.
154. In accordance with Treas. Reg. §1.168(i)-1(c).
155. Under Treas. Reg. §1.168(i)-1(j)(2)(i)(A).
156. Under Treas. Reg. §1.168(i)-1(j)(2)(i)(B).
157. Under Treas. Reg. §1.168(i)-1(j)(2)(i)(C).
158. Under Treas. Reg. §1.168(i)-1(j)(2)(i)(B).
159. Under Treas. Reg. §1.168(i)-1(j)(2)(i)(C).
160. Under Treas. Reg. §1.168(i)-1(j)(2)(i)(A).
161. See Treas. Reg. §1.168(i)-1(e)(3).

4. A change in the method of identifying which assets or which portions of assets have been disposed of by the taxpayer from the FIFO method[162] to the modified FIFO[163] or vice versa (using a §481(a) adjustment, but the §481(a) adjustment should be zero unless the special rules for terminating GAAs[164] apply to the asset subject to the change)
5. A change in the method of identifying which mass assets[165] or which portions of mass assets that are in a separate GAA[166] have been disposed of by the taxpayer from the specific identification method[167] to a mortality dispersion table[168] (using a cut-off method and applying to dispositions occurring on or after the beginning of the year of change)
6. A change in the method of identifying which mass assets[169] or which portions of mass assets that are in a separate GAA[170] have been disposed of by the taxpayer from the FIFO method[171] or the modified FIFO method[172] to a mortality dispersion table[173] (using a §481(a) adjustment, but the §481(a) adjustment should be zero unless the special rules for terminating GAAs[174] apply to the asset subject to the change)
7. A change in the method of identifying which mass assets[175] or which portions of mass assets that are in a separate GAA[176] have been disposed of by the taxpayer from a mortality dispersion table[177] to the specific identification method,[178] the FIFO method,[179] or the modified FIFO method[180] (using a §481(a) adjustment, but the §481(a) adjustment should be zero unless the special rules for terminating GAAs[181] apply to the asset subject to the change)
8. A change in the method of determining the unadjusted depreciable basis of all assets in the same GAA from one reasonable method to another reasonable method (using a cut-off method and applying to dispositions occurring on or after the beginning of the year of change) (This change applies[182] if the basis of a disposed asset or a disposed portion of an asset is included in a GAA and it is impracticable from the taxpayer's records to determine the unadjusted depreciable basis of the disposed asset or the disposed portion of the asset.)

---

162. Under Treas. Reg. §1.168(i)-1(j)(2)(i)(B).
163. Under Treas. Reg. §1.168(i)-1(j)(2)(i)(C).
164. See Treas. Reg. §1.168(i)-1(e)(3).
165. As defined in Treas. Reg. §1.168(i)-1(b)(6).
166. In accordance with Treas. Reg. §1.168(i)-1(c)(2)(ii)(H).
167. Under Treas. Reg. §1.168(i)-1(j)(2)(i)(A).
168. In accordance with Treas. Reg. §1.168(i)-1(j)(2)(i)(D).
169. As defined in Treas. Reg. §1.168(i)-1(b)(6).
170. In accordance with Treas. Reg. §1.168-1(c)(2)(ii)(H).
171. Under Treas. Reg. §1.168(i)-1(j)(2)(i)(B).
172. Under Treas. Reg. §1.168(i)-1(j)(2)(i)(C).
173. In accordance with Treas. Reg. §1.168(i)-1(j)(2)(i)(D).
174. See Treas. Reg. §1.168(i)-1(e)(3).
175. As defined in Treas. Reg. §1.168(i)-1(b)(6).
176. In accordance with Treas. Reg. §1.168(i)-1(c)(2)(ii)(H).
177. In accordance with Treas. Reg. §1.168(i)-1(j)(2)(i)(D).
178. Under Treas. Reg. §1.168(i)-1(j)(2)(i)(A).
179. Under Treas. Reg. §1.168(i)-1(j)(2)(i)(B).
180. Under Treas. Reg. §1.168(i)-1(j)(2)(i)(C).
181. See Treas. Reg. §1.168(i)-1(e)(3).
182. Under Treas. Reg. §1.168(i)-1(j)(3).

§6.13 Disposition of Buildings or Structural Components

Covered changes include the following.

2

1. A change to the appropriate asset[183] for purposes of determining which asset or portion of an asset has been disposed of[184]
2. A change in how assets are determined, a change from depreciating a disposed asset to recognizing a gain or loss on its disposition, and a change from depreciating such disposed asset to capitalizing the loss sustained in the case of a demolition of a structure[185]
3. A change in how assets are determined, a change from depreciating a disposed portion of an asset to recognizing a gain or loss on its disposition, and a change from depreciating such disposed portion of an asset to capitalizing the loss sustained in the case of a demolition of a structure[186]
4. A change from depreciating a disposed asset to recognizing a gain or loss upon disposition for dispositions that occurred in a prior tax year (This change applies if the taxpayer's present method of accounting for structural components and buildings, condominium units, and cooperative units, as well as improvements or additions to such assets, is in accordance with the applicable regulations.)[187] and a change from depreciating such disposed asset to capitalizing the loss sustained in the case of a demolition of a structure[188]
5. A change from depreciating a disposed portion of an asset to recognizing a gain or loss upon disposition for dispositions that occurred in a prior tax year (This change applies if the taxpayer's present method of accounting for structural components and buildings, condominium units, and cooperative units, as well as improvements or additions to such assets, is in accordance with the applicable regulations.)[189] and a change from depreciating such disposed portion of an asset to capitalizing the loss sustained in the case of a demolition of a structure[190]
6. A change in the method of identifying which assets in multiple-asset accounts or which portions of assets have been disposed of from an improper method (e.g., the LIFO method) to an accounting method specified in the regulation[191]
7. A change in the method of determining the unadjusted depreciable basis of a disposed asset in a multiple-asset account[192] from a method of not using the taxpayer's records to a method of using the taxpayer's records (This change applies when it is practicable from the taxpayer's records to determine the unadjusted depreciable basis of the disposed asset.)

---

183. As determined under Treas. Regs. §§1.168(i)-8(c)(4)(ii)(A), (B), or (D), as applicable.

184. Based on Treas. Reg. §1.168(i)-8(c)(4).

185. As defined in Treas. Reg. §1.280B-1.

186. Ibid.

187. In accordance with Treas. Regs. §§1.168(i)-8(c)(4)(ii)(A), (B), and (D).

188. As defined in Treas. Reg. §1.280B-1.

189. In accordance with Treas. Regs. §§1.168(i)-8(c)(4)(ii)(A), (B), and (D).

190. As defined in Treas. Reg. §1.280B-1.

191. In accordance with Treas. Regs. §§1.168(i)-8(g)(1) or (2)(i), (ii), or (iii), as applicable.

192. Under Treas. Reg. §1.168(i)-8(f)(2).

8. A change in the method of determining the unadjusted depreciable basis of all assets in the same multiple-asset account[193] from an unreasonable method to a reasonable method (This change applies when it is impracticable from the taxpayer's records to determine the unadjusted depreciable basis of the disposed asset. An example of an unreasonable method is discounting the cost of the replacement asset to its placed-in-service year cost using the Consumer Price Index.)

9. A change in the method of determining the unadjusted depreciable basis of the **disposed portion**[194] of an asset from a method of not using the taxpayer's records to a method of using the taxpayer's records (This change applies when it is practicable from the taxpayer's records to determine the unadjusted depreciable basis of the disposed portion of the asset.)

10. A change in the method of determining the unadjusted depreciable basis of the **disposed portion**[195] of an asset from an unreasonable method to a reasonable method (This change applies when it is impracticable from the taxpayer's records to determine the unadjusted depreciable basis of the disposed portion of the asset.)

11. A change from recognizing gain or loss under Temp. Treas. Reg. §1.168(i)-8T upon the disposition of an asset[196] included in a GAA to recognizing gain or loss upon the disposition of the same asset under Treas. Reg. §1.168(i)-8

§6.14 Dispositions of Certain Tangible Depreciable Assets

Instructions for the following types of changes in accounting method are included in this section.

1. For purposes of determining the asset disposed of, a change to the appropriate asset[197]

2. A change in how assets are determined **and** a change from depreciating a disposed asset to recognizing a gain or loss on a disposition that occurred in a prior tax year

3. A change in how assets are determined **and** a change from depreciating a disposed portion of an asset to recognizing a gain or loss on a partial disposition that occurred in a prior tax year

4. A change from depreciating a disposed asset to recognizing a gain or loss upon disposition for dispositions that occurred in a prior tax year (This change applies if the taxpayer's present method of accounting for the covered assets is in accordance with the applicable regulations.)[198]

5. A change from depreciating a disposed portion of an asset to recognizing a gain or loss upon disposition for dispositions that occurred in a prior tax year (This change applies if the taxpayer's present method of accounting for the covered assets is in accordance with the applicable regulations.)[199]

6. A change in the method of identifying which assets in multiple-asset accounts or which portions of assets have been disposed of from using an improper method (e.g., the LIFO method) to a method of accounting specified in the regulations[200]

---

193. Under Treas. Reg. §1.168(i)-8(f)(2).

194. Under Treas. Reg. §1.168(i)-8(f)(3).

195. Ibid.

196. As determined under Treas. Regs. §§1.168(i)-8(c)(4)(ii)(A), (B), or (D), as applicable.

197. As determined under Treas. Regs. §§1.168(i)-8(c)(4)(i), (ii)(C), or (ii)(D), as applicable.

198. In accordance with Treas. Regs. §§1.168(i)-8(c)(4)(i) or (ii).

199. Ibid.

200. As determined under Treas. Regs. §§1.168(i)-8(g)(1) or (2)(i), (ii), or (iii), as applicable.

7. A change in the method of determining the unadjusted depreciable basis of a disposed asset in a multiple-asset account[201] from a method of not using the taxpayer's records to a method of using the taxpayer's records (This change applies when it is practicable from the taxpayer's records to determine the unadjusted depreciable basis of the disposed asset.)
8. A change in the method of determining the unadjusted depreciable basis of all assets in the same multiple-asset account[202] from an unreasonable method to a reasonable method (This change applies when it is impracticable from the taxpayer's records to determine the unadjusted depreciable basis of the disposed asset. An example of an unreasonable method is discounting the cost of the replacement asset to its placed-in-service year cost using the Consumer Price Index.)
9. A change in the method of determining the unadjusted depreciable basis of the **disposed portion**[203] of an asset from a method of not using the taxpayer's records to a method of using the taxpayer's records (This change applies when it is practicable from the taxpayer's records to determine the unadjusted depreciable basis of the disposed portion of the asset.)
10. A change in the method of determining the unadjusted depreciable basis of the **disposed portion**[204] of an asset from an unreasonable method to a reasonable method (This change applies when it is impracticable from the taxpayer's records to determine the unadjusted depreciable basis of the disposed portion of the asset.)
11. A change from recognizing gain or loss under Temp. Treas. Reg. §1.168(i)-8T upon the disposition of an asset covered in this section that was included in a GAA to recognizing gain or loss upon the disposition of the same asset under Treas. Reg. §1.168(i)-8

§6.15 Dispositions of Tangible Depreciable Assets in a GAA

Instructions for the following types of changes in accounting method are included in this section.

This section applies only to the following changes in methods of accounting for an asset subject to a GAA election.

1. For purposes of determining the asset disposed of,[205] a change to the appropriate asset[206]
2. A change in the method of identifying which assets or which portion of assets have been disposed of from an accounting method not specified in the regulations[207] (e.g., the LIFO method) to an accounting method specified in these regulations
3. A change in the method of determining the unadjusted depreciable basis of a disposed asset[208] (or portion of an asset) from a method of not using the taxpayer's records to a method of using the taxpayer's records (This change applies when it is practicable from the taxpayer's records to determine the unadjusted depreciable basis of the disposed asset.)
4. A change in the method of determining the unadjusted depreciable basis[209] of all assets in the same GAA from an unreasonable method to a reasonable method (This change applies when it is impracticable from the taxpayer's records to determine the unadjusted depreciable basis of the disposed asset. An example of an unreasonable method is discounting the cost of the replacement asset to its placed-in-service year cost using the Consumer Price Index.)

---

201. Under Treas. Reg. §1.168(i)-8(f)(2).

202. Ibid.

203. Under Treas. Reg. §1.168(i)-8(f)(3).

204. Ibid.

205. Under Treas. Reg. §1.168(i)-1(e)(2)(viii).

206. As determined under Treas. Regs. §§1.168(i)-1(e)(2)(viii)(A) or (B), as applicable.

207. Treas. Regs. §§1.168(i)-1(j)(2)(i)(A), (B), (C), or (D).

208. Under Treas. Reg. §1.168(i)-1(j)(3).

209. Ibid.

Chapter 3: Independent Contractors

3

Note. Corrections for all of the chapters are available at **TaxSchool.illinois.edu.** For clarification about terms used throughout this chapter, see the **Acronyms and Abbreviations** section following the index.

For your convenience, in-text website links are also provided as short URLs. Anywhere you see **uofi.tax/xxx**, the link points to the address immediately following in brackets.

About the Authors

Kelly Golish, CPA, is the Assistant Director, Tax Materials, at the University of Illinois Tax School. She was previously a manager at Crowder, CPAs in Danville, IL and worked for both public and private accounting firms in Decatur, IL, Cleveland, OH, and San Jose, CA. Kelly earned a Masters in Accounting with an emphasis in Taxation and a Bachelors in Accounting at the University of Notre Dame.

Chris Korban, CPA, is a Tax Materials Specialist at the University of Illinois Tax School. He joined Tax School in 2023 with nine years of experience in public accounting. Chris earned both his Bachelor's Degree in Accounting and Master of Accounting Science from the University of Illinois.

John W. Richmann, EA, is a Tax Materials Specialist at the University of Illinois Tax School. Prior to joining Tax School in 2021, he owned a tax practice in St. Charles, Illinois, and held positions in private industry and consulting firms. John earned a Masters Degree in Business Administration from the University of Texas and an electrical engineering degree from the Massachusetts Institute of Technology.

Other chapter contributors and reviewers are listed at the front of this book.

One of the most misunderstood issues facing tax preparers is the ongoing struggle with how business owners classify their hired laborers. Technically, there is no choice to make. Rather, there is a determination, and a knowledgeable preparer should be able to explain the determination rules to their client and assist them with proper employee classification. This chapter discusses the proper classification rules and how to apply them, along with other unique areas of interest specific to independent contractors in general. This chapter also addresses rules that apply to construction workers, gig economy workers, and truck drivers where applicable.

Small businesses may struggle to classify an individual working for them without a bright-line test (i.e., a straightforward, objective rule that prevents subjective interpretation). In October 2022, the U.S. Department of Labor proposed a change in regulations supporting the Fair Labor Standards Act (FLSA).[1] Although this proposed regulation focuses on the FLSA rather than tax law, its language aligns with IRS pronouncements on the employee-independent contractor status issue.[2]

> *It is fundamental to the [Labor] Department's obligation to administer and enforce the FLSA, however, that workers who should be covered under the Act are able to receive its protections, as the misclassification of employees as independent contractors remains one of the most serious problems facing workers, businesses, and the broader economy.*

DETERMINING WORKER CLASSIFICATION

Some businesses attempt to classify workers as independent contractors rather than employees. This choice may appear to result in financial savings (employment taxes, benefits, etc.) and administrative savings.

> **Caution.** In addition to tax issues, there may be insurance, liability, and other issues about which other professionals should advise. Tax preparers may want to refer clients to these other professionals for specific advice.

COMMON LAW RULES OF CONTROL

The most fundamental concept to determining whether an individual is an employee or an independent contractor is the issue of **control**. A worker is generally an employee if the business or individual paying the worker controls the circumstances of the service being performed. Conversely, if the worker controls the circumstances of their work, they are typically independent contractors. However, the final determination may depend on other considerations.

A worker is an employee for federal employment tax purposes if the worker qualifies as an employee under common law. Under common law, an employer-employee relationship exists when the firm or person for whom the worker performs the services has the right to control and direct the worker in how the worker performs the services. **Right to control** refers to the degree of control over the means and details of the worker's tasks. Such control is the litmus test of an employer-employee relationship. The employer does not need to exercise this control. Merely having the right to control the worker is sufficient to conclude that the worker is an employee and not an independent contractor.[3]

1. 87 Fed. Reg. 62,218 (Oct. 13, 2022).
2. 87 Fed. Reg. 62,225 (Oct. 13, 2022).
3. Rev. Rul. 87-41, 1987-1 CB 296.

Tax practitioners should review with the business owner the following general common law rules to determine whether the worker is an employee or an independent contractor.[4]

1. **Behavioral** – whether the business owner or the worker controls what the worker does and how the worker does their tasks

2. **Financial** – whether the business owner or the worker controls the business aspects of the worker's job, such as how the worker is paid, if they are entitled to reimbursement, and which party provides the tools and supplies

3. **Relationship** – whether there are written agreements; whether the business provides employee benefits; whether the work performed is a key aspect of the business

20 FACTORS[5]

The IRS uses 20 factors to determine whether a worker is an employee or an independent contractor. The IRS notes that these factors are only a **guide;** each factor's importance depends on each case's circumstances. The following factors indicate the various aspects of a typical work relationship.

1. **Instructions.** An employer instructing the worker about when, where, and how the worker performs work indicates an employer-employee relationship. Independent contractors have more control over their work.

2. **Training and meetings.** Providing worker training and requiring the worker to attend meetings indicates the existence of an employer-employee relationship.

3. **Integration of work performed into firm operations.** Strong integration of the worker's services into the operations of the person who hired the worker indicates an employer-employee relationship.

4. **Personal performance of services.** Employees must personally perform services. The same requirement might not be expected of an independent contractor, although exceptions exist. This factor alone is often not determinative.

5. **Personnel control.** A firm's control over the hiring, supervision, and payment of a worker's assistants suggests an employer-employee relationship. Independent contractors typically maintain and control their staff.

6. **Length of the working relationship.** A continual, long-term work relationship implies an employer-employee relationship. Such a long-term relationship may also exist with an independent contractor. Therefore, this factor alone is not determinative.

7. **Work schedule.** An established work schedule for the worker indicates that an employer-employee relationship exists. Independent contractors generally retain more freedom in scheduling the performance of their services to a firm.

8. **Hours of service required.** Requiring substantially full-time work from the worker in the firm's service indicates an employer-employee relationship. Conversely, part-time hours worked for one firm or person while simultaneously providing services to other firms or persons suggests that the worker may be an independent contractor.

9. **Location of services.** Requiring the worker to perform services at the firm's or person's location suggests an employer-employee relationship. However, this factor alone is not determinative because employees can only perform some types of work at the firm's or person's worksite.

---

4. *Independent Contractor (Self-Employed) or Employee?* Apr. 5, 2023. IRS. [www.irs.gov/businesses/small-businesses-self-employed/independent-contractor-self-employed-or-employee] Accessed on May 23, 2023.

5. Ibid.

10. **Control over work technique.** Control by the firm or person over the worker's technique or order of tasks indicates that an employer-employee relationship exists. A worker who has control over the technique or task order in the performance of services suggests that the worker may be an independent contractor.

11. **Periodic reporting.** Requiring regular written or verbal reports from the worker to other firm personnel or persons associated with the firm indicates an employer-employee relationship. However, requiring progress reports by an independent contractor is also common. Therefore, this factor alone is not determinative.

12. **Payment method.** Payment at regular intervals (hourly, weekly, or monthly) suggests an employer-employee relationship. Alternatively, payment to the worker based on the job or project or invoices the worker issues suggests an independent contractor relationship.

13. **Work-related expenses.** Payment of the worker's business and travel expenses suggests an employer-employee relationship. However, this arrangement may also exist between a firm or person and an independent contractor. Therefore, this factor alone is not determinative.

14. **Provision of tools.** Tools furnished by the worker indicate that the worker is an independent contractor. If the firm or person provides the worker with tools, this suggests the existence of an employer-employee relationship.

15. **Work facilities.** A worker who invests in and provides work facilities is likely to be an independent contractor, particularly if the facilities are of a type not generally maintained by employees. The lack of investment in facilities indicates the worker's dependence on the firm or person to provide such facilities, suggesting an employer-employee relationship.

16. **Profit potential and risk of loss.** Workers who profit from the success of a business and bear the risk of loss from failure are more likely to be independent contractors than employees. Employers typically pay employees a fixed amount without regard to profits or losses.

17. **Providing services to multiple firms.** An employee tends to provide services to a single firm or person. In contrast, an independent contractor frequently services several firms or persons.

18. **Providing service to the general public.** Workers who regularly and consistently offer their services to the public are more likely to be independent contractors.

19. **Right of discharge.** The firm's right to terminate the worker suggests an employer-employee relationship. If the firm is liable for penalties upon a worker's termination without cause, this indicates a higher degree of worker independence, suggesting the worker is an independent contractor.

20. **Worker's right of termination.** If the worker can terminate the relationship with the firm or person at will without penalty, this indicates an employer-employee relationship.

Note. The IRS's voluntary classification settlement program (VCSP) provides payroll tax relief to employers who are currently treating their workers (or a group of workers) as independent contractors and want to prospectively treat the workers as employees. This amnesty program offers the employer a low-cost way to reclassify their workers.

For more information on the VCSP, its eligibility requirements, and misclassification penalties, see the 2017 *University of Illinois Federal Tax Workbook,* Volume A, Chapter 2: Employment Issues. This can be found at **uofi.tax/arc** [taxschool.illinois.edu/taxbookarchive].

Additionally, the IRS answers some frequently asked questions on the VCSP at **uofi.tax/23x3x1** [www.irs.gov/businesses/small-businesses-self-employed/voluntary-classification-settlement-program-vcsp-frequently-asked-questions].

TAX COURT TEST

The IRS outlined its "20-factor" test in Rev. Rul. 87-41. However, the Tax Court is not bound by pronouncements in revenue rulings. The weight the Tax Court gives to a revenue ruling in a case depends upon "the persuasiveness and consistency" of the IRS position over time.[6]

To determine whether a worker is an employee or an independent contractor, the Tax Court considers the following seven factors.[7]

3

1. The degree of the firm's (or person's) control over the worker
2. The worker's investment in work facilities
3. Profit or loss potential for the worker
4. The degree of ease with which the firm or person can discharge the worker
5. The degree of integration of the worker's services to the firm's (or person's) principal function
6. The temporary or permanent nature of the relationship
7. The parties' understanding of the nature of their relationship

> **Note.** A worker who is properly classified as an independent contractor must pay the full Federal Insurance Contributions Act (FICA) tax, must acquire insurance on their own, may have income eligible for the qualified business income deduction, may have deductible business expenses, might be eligible for certain retirement plans, and may be able to deduct 50% of their health insurance premiums among other impactful items.

FORM 1099-NEC

Business owners who pay independent contractors $600 or more[8] in a calendar year for their services are required to issue a Form 1099-NEC, *Nonemployee Compensation.*[9] The Code excludes the following forms of compensation normally reported in Form 1099-NEC, box 1.[10]

- Payments reported on a 1099-K, *Payment Card and Third-Party Network Transactions,*[11] such as payments via credit card, Venmo, or PayPal

> **Caution.** Unlike Venmo and PayPal, Zelle does not report any transactions to the IRS, even if the total is $600 or more. Therefore, it is the taxpayer's responsibility to report any Zelle payments they receive to the IRS.[12]

- Generally, payments to a corporation or a limited liability company (LLC) treated as a corporation, although exceptions exist
- Payments for merchandise, telephone, freight, storage, and similar items

---

6. *Taproot Administrative Services, Inc. v. Comm'r*, 133 TC 202 (2009), *aff'd* 679 F.3d 1109 (9th Cir. 2012).
7. *Herman v. Comm'r*, TC Memo 1986-590 (Dec. 18,1986).
8. IRC §6041(a).
9. Instructions for Forms 1099-MISC and 1099-NEC.
10. Treas. Reg. §1.6041-3; Instructions for Forms 1099-MISC and 1099-NEC.
11. Instructions for Forms 1099-MISC and 1099-NEC.
12. *Does Zelle report how much money I receive to the IRS?* Zelle. [www.zellepay.com/faq/does-zelle-report-how-much-money-i-receive-irs] Accessed on May 23, 2023.

- Payments of rent to real estate agents or property managers
- Wages, including wages paid as bonuses, prizes, or awards to employees, which should be reported on Form W-2, *Wage and Tax Statement*
- Military differential wage payments made to employees during active military duty, as Form W-2 should report these items
- Business travel allowances paid to employees, as Form W-2 typically reports these items
- Cost of an employee's life insurance protection, as this should be reported on Form W-2
- Payments to tax-exempt organizations, including individual retirement arrangements (IRAs), the United States, any state, possession, territory, a foreign government, or a foreign central bank
- Payments made to or for homeowners from the Housing Finance Agency Hardest Hit Fund or equivalent state program, which should be reported on Form 1098-MA, *Mortgage Assistance Payments*
- Compensation as a public safety officer for injuries, sickness, or death of a public safety officer, paid by the U.S. Department of Justice, or received as a survivor's benefit arising from the death of a public safety officer under a state program providing benefits to beneficiaries of public safety officers if they died of injuries sustained in the line of duty
- Compensation paid for wrongful incarceration
- Fees paid to informants about criminal activity if paid by a government entity

Note. All businesses or persons involved in a trade must provide Form 1099-NEC to the provider of the services by January 31 of the year following **payment.**[13]

Example 1. Osage Petroleum Company engages organist Buzz Cantrell to liven up its December holiday party with some organ music. As an independent contractor, Buzz receives an $800 check dated January 4, 2023, one week after his performance. In January 2024, Osage issues Buzz a 2023 Form 1099-NEC.

Note. If the status of the worker is unclear, the worker or the firm can obtain an IRS determination letter resolving this issue. The worker or firm makes a request by filing Form SS-8, *Determination of Worker Status for Purposes of Federal Employment Taxes and Income Tax Withholding.* A firm can request a determination for the status of a single worker or an entire class of workers.

For more information on requesting IRS classification and the Form SS-8, see the 2017 *University of Illinois Federal Tax Workbook,* Volume A, Chapter 2: Employment Issues. This can be found at **uofi.tax/arc** [taxschool.illinois.edu/taxbookarchive].

13. IRC §6041(d).

SELECTED TRADES OR BUSINESSES

Without a bright-line test, special rules guide employment status determination in specific trades or businesses. The nuances for determining the employment status for three types of trades or businesses are described next.

Construction Workers[14]

3

A 1970 IRS Revenue Ruling revised existing IRS procedures regarding whether a construction worker was considered an employee. Often, construction workers function independently at construction sites, with managers stopping by only occasionally to inspect their work. The following factors may indicate an individual construction worker is an employee.

- The worker does not keep an office or other place of business.
- The worker has a written contract with a construction company, in which the construction worker provides construction labor to build houses, along with all required tools.
- Under the contract, the construction company pays the cost of labor, materials, supplies, building permits, and insurance.
- The contract entitles the worker to pay at a set hourly rate.
- A construction company regularly visits the site to inspect the work, even though they may not work there full-time.
- The worker must act as a superintendent of construction and foreman. They may hire other individuals to assist, although the construction company retains the right to "select, approve, or discharge" any individuals hired by the worker.
- The construction company is responsible for any faults or "defects of construction or wasteful operations," not the construction worker.
- When the construction is complete, the worker is entitled to a bonus equal to a specified percentage of the total construction costs of the project.
- The worker provides a weekly accounting of what they pay workers and other amounts, although the construction worker is not responsible for their wages.

Under these circumstances, the IRS considers the construction worker an **employee** of the construction company, even though the company may not dictate specific work hours, and the worker provides their tools. Although this differs from some of the 20 factors, it reflects the IRS's framework for interpreting construction work agreements. Rev. Rul. 70-618 specifically subjects this construction worker to FICA, the Federal Unemployment Tax Act (FUTA), and the Collection of Income Tax at Source of Wages Act.

---

14. Rev. Rul. 70-618, 1970-2 CB 227.

Gig Economy Workers[15]

The **gig economy** includes activities where people earn income by providing on-demand work, services, or goods. Some examples of gig economy work include the following.

- Drive a car for booked rides or deliveries
- Rent out all or part of their property
- Run errands or complete tasks
- Sell goods online
- Rent personal equipment
- Provide creative or professional services
- Provide other temporary, on-demand, or freelance work

Often, taxpayers find the work through a **digital platform.** Digital platforms are businesses that match workers' services or goods with customers via apps or websites. This includes businesses that provide access to the following nonexclusive services.

- Ridesharing services
- Delivery services
- Crafts and handmade item marketplaces
- On-demand labor and repair services
- Property and space rentals

Taxpayers engaged in the gig economy must understand whether they are considered an employee or an independent contractor. Employers should withhold tax from paychecks associated with gig work performed as an employee. Independent contractors report their activity on Schedule C, *Profit or Loss From Business* (assuming their activity is undertaken with a profit motive), are responsible for self-employment (SE) taxes, and may need to pay estimated taxes.

> **Note.** For more information on the gig economy, profit motive, and reporting requirements, see the 2021 *University of Illinois Federal Tax Workbook,* Volume B, Chapter 3: Schedule C. This can be found at **uofi.tax/arc** [taxschool.illinois.edu/taxbookarchive].

Truck Drivers

Transportation industry workers must abide by specific rules. For someone to be considered a transportation industry worker for tax purposes, their job must meet the following requirements.[16]

- Directly involves moving people or goods by airplane, barge, bus, ship, train, or truck
- Regularly requires traveling away from home and, during any single trip, usually involves traveling to an area or areas eligible for different standard meal allowance rates (explained in detail later). A truck driver is a classic example of a transportation industry worker.

---

15. *Gig Economy Tax Center.* Oct. 4, 2022. IRS. [www.irs.gov/businesses/gig-economy-tax-center] Accessed on Mar. 14, 2023; *Manage Taxes for Your Gig Work.* May 19, 2022. IRS. [www.irs.gov/businesses/small-businesses-self-employed/manage-taxes-for-your-gig-work] Accessed on Mar. 14, 2023.

16. IRS Pub. 463, *Travel, Entertainment, Gift, and Car Expenses.*

Worker Classification.[17] A truck driver is either an employee who receives a Form W-2 or an independent contractor who receives a Form 1099-NEC. A truck driver engaged in business as an **owner-operator** is an independent contractor and, therefore, self-employed.

Determining whether a truck driver is an employee or an independent contractor is essential for tax purposes. Referring to the 20 factors discussed previously, the IRS noted that these factors serve only as a guide and that each factor's importance depends on each case's circumstances. The 20 factors consider a firm's degree of control over a truck driver across various aspects of a typical work relationship.[18]

3

> **Note.** For further details on how these factors should be applied, see Rev. Rul. 87-41. These factors are not unique to truck drivers; they apply to all payment-for-work relationships. Accordingly, if a truck driver hires someone to work for them, these factors may apply in determining whether that person is an employee or an independent contractor of the truck driver.

The *Peno Trucking, Inc. v. Comm'r* case illustrates the application of these factors in a case involving a trucking company whose workers had contracts specifically stating they were independent contractors.[19] Peno Trucking (PT) owned 15 trucks and leased them to OTC Transport. PT used these trucks to provide OTC with hauling services. PT agreed to provide drivers and to ensure that their work was performed in accordance with the leases. PT hired, fired, disciplined, and supervised the drivers. PT also determined the days the drivers could work and required them to maintain commercial driving licenses, driving logs, and other documents. PT negotiated the rate of pay with each driver. In addition, PT's contract with each driver indicated that it was not possible for the driver to become indebted to PT in any way. PT provided the drivers with necessary equipment, although drivers were free to provide extra equipment at their own cost. PT paid for all fuel, tolls, and truck maintenance and repairs.

To provide the hauling services required by the OTC agreement, PT offered drivers the opportunity to accept hauls each day. A driver was free to decline any haul that was offered. However, if the driver accepted, PT provided directions to the driver regarding pick-up and delivery locations and times. PT provided drivers with beepers to keep in contact with them on the road.

In each driver's contract, PT designated them as an independent contractor. Each year, PT issued each driver a Form 1099-MISC, *Miscellaneous Income,* that reported the driver's annual pay. PT did not withhold federal taxes, social security, or Medicare taxes from any driver's pay.

The Tax Court focused on seven of the 20 factors to conclude that Peno Trucking's drivers were employees, not independent contractors, as the contract provided. The Tax Court concluded the drivers were employees, regardless of language in the drivers' contracts, because of the control that Peno had over them.

> **Note.** For more details on the 20-factor test as it applies to the *Peno Trucking* case, see the 2015 *University of Illinois Federal Tax Workbook,* Volume A, Chapter 6: Special Taxpayers. This can be found at **uofi.tax/arc** [taxschool.illinois.edu/taxbookarchive].

---

17. Rev. Rul. 87-41, 1987-1 CB 296.

18. Ibid.

19. *Peno Trucking, Inc. v. Comm'r*, TC Memo 2007-66 (Mar. 21, 2007), *rev'd* 296 Fed.Appx. 449 (6th Cir. 2008).

STATUTORY EMPLOYMENT RELATIONSHIPS[20]

Although the 20 factors guide the common law determination of tax status for most workers, explicit provisions in the Code establish a bright-line test for a relatively narrow set of workers. The Code defines the following four types of workers as employees, regardless of their status under common law tests.

1. Corporate officers
2. Agent-drivers or commission-drivers
3. Full-time life insurance salespersons
4. Home workers

Corporate Officers

The Code states that corporate officers are employees without qualification. The supporting regulations leave a small exception if the officers perform only insignificant services for which they receive no compensation.[21]

Agent-Drivers or Commission-Drivers

Drivers who distribute meat, vegetable, fruit, or bakery products are considered employees by explicit Code provision. Although this provision generally includes persons who distribute beverages, it excludes those who distribute **milk**. Drivers distributing laundry or dry-cleaned clothing are specifically designated as employees.

Full-Time Life Insurance Salespersons

The Code stipulates an individual selling life insurance full-time is an employee.[22] The regulations also apply this provision to individuals who sell annuities.[23] However, these regulations exclude individuals who sell other insurance products under their service contracts. In this event, the insurance salesperson is not necessarily a statutory employee but may still be a common law employee under different subsections of IRC §3121. Life insurance salespersons are statutory employees under §3121(d)(3).

Home Workers

Home workers generally perform tasks in their homes for employers who do not have them work on-premises.[24] They work with materials or goods furnished by their employer. Their employers typically provide specifications for the work, and when complete, home workers return the products to the employer or a person whom the employer nominates. Such individuals may manufacture clothing in their homes for merchant tailors.[25] Home workers are statutory employees according to §3121(d)(3)(C).

Home workers perform very different tasks from home **care** workers, who typically perform personal care services for elderly or infirm individuals.

---

20. IRC §3121(d).
21. Treas. Reg. §31.3121(d)-1(b).
22. IRC §3121(d)(3)(B).
23. Treas. Reg. §31.3121(d)-1(d)(3)(ii).
24. IRC §3121(d)(3)(C).
25. Rev. Rul. 72-88, 72-1 CB 319.

Other Statutory Workers

Traveling or City Salesperson. An individual soliciting orders from potential customers on their employer's behalf is also an employee by statute.[26] Other parts of the Code and regulations supporting §3121(d) define other workers as nonemployees.

Real Estate Agents. The Code does not regard real estate agents as employees if they satisfy the following criteria.[27]

3

1. The person is a licensed real estate agent.
2. Substantially all their total compensation, in whatever form received, is based on real estate sales amounts rather than their work hours.
3. The person performs sales services under a **written** contract, which explicitly states the person is not an employee under federal tax law.

This treatment extends to **individuals in the office who recruit, train, and supervise** individuals who make sales.[28] This person may be the owner of the brokerage, but they must satisfy all three requirements to qualify for the employee exclusion. This regulation also clarifies that real estate sales do not include real property management.[29]

> **Example 2.** Sue is the managing broker at which Sam sells real estate. The real estate brokerage primarily sells single-family homes and condominiums. It does not manage properties for investors who have purchased properties through them. Because Sue is also a licensed real estate agent, receives compensation based on Sam's sales, and works under a written contract, she is considered a nonemployee under Prop. Treas. Reg. §31.3508-1(b).

Corporate Directors. Provided that they are also not employees of the same corporation, corporate directors are statutory **nonemployees** under Treas. Reg. §31.3121(d)-1(b), the same regulation that requires the classification of corporate officers as employees. A corporate director represents the interests of the corporation's shareholders, who commonly are not present at corporate board meetings except for very small corporations. This concept underlies the different statutory treatments of corporate officers and corporate directors.

A director of a corporation should receive Form 1099-NEC if they receive $600 or more in a single calendar year. They should report this income on Schedule C attached to their Form 1040, *U.S. Individual Income Tax Return*, where it is subject to SE tax.[30]

> **Example 3.** Henry was elected to the board of directors of the Bedford Falls Savings and Loan Company in January 2022. He attended all four board meetings that year and is not an officer of the corporation. Each director is paid $2,000 for their services at each board meeting. In January 2023, Henry receives a Form 1099-NEC, which reports $8,000 in box 1.

---

26. IRC §3121(d)(3)(D).
27. IRC §3508(b)(1).
28. Prop. Treas. Reg. §31.3508-1(b).
29. Ibid.
30. IRS Pub. 17, *Your Federal Income Tax*, p. 72 (2022).

TAX HOME ISSUES

An independent contractor's **tax home** governs the treatment of many expenses on their tax returns, including the deductibility of travel, lodging, and meal expenses. IRC §162 permits a deduction for these expenses based on the logic that a taxpayer incurs duplicated expenses because of the "exigencies [requirements] of business,"[31] but only while away from one's tax home.

HOW TAX HOME IS DETERMINED

A taxpayer's home for business purposes in §162(a)(2) is usually not their residence. Instead, it is "the vicinity of a taxpayer's principal place of business."[32] In some cases, a taxpayer can generally treat their residence as their tax home if their principal place of business is temporary, as distinguished from indefinite.

Although not explicitly mentioned in the Code, the IRS determines the taxpayer's tax home according to the following three classifications.[33]

1. The taxpayer's principal place of business if they have more than a single place of business.
2. If the taxpayer has no regular place of business, then their tax home is their "regular place of abode in a real and substantial sense."
3. If neither 1 nor 2 apply, the IRS considers the taxpayer an itinerant worker having a home wherever they work.

Principal Place of Business

A principal place of business is the location from which a taxpayer plies their trade.[34] They may work for employers or clients at that location or travel to another site designated by the employer or client.[35]

The question of tax home arose from the 1939 Code's allowance of an income tax deduction for "traveling expenses … while away from home in pursuit of a trade or business."[36] In the 1946 *Flowers* case, the U.S. Supreme Court determined that this reference to "home" did not refer to a taxpayer's abode but their "place of business."[37] The Court mentioned that the Tax Court and treasury regulations for the 1939 Code consistently interpret "home" as referring to the taxpayer's "business headquarters" or principal place of business, not their abode or legal residence.

Thus, a tax home is the general vicinity of a taxpayer's principal place of employment. The Code allows an exception if a taxpayer's place of employment temporarily changes for a limited time.[38] In this circumstance, a taxpayer's tax home does not change if the change of employment location is temporary and **not indefinite.**

Sometimes independent contractors must travel directly from their residence to a temporary work location, even if they have a regular or main job.[39] If the taxpayer travels to a temporary location for work expected to last less than a year, their tax home does not change.[40]

---

31. *Comm'r v. Flowers*, 326 U.S. 465 (1946).
32. *Geiman v. Comm'r*, TC Memo 2021-80 (Jun. 30, 2021).
33. Rev. Rul. 93-86, 1993-2 CB 71.
34. IRC §280A(c)(1); Rev. Rul. 94-24, 1994-1 CB 87.
35. IRC §162(a)(2).
36. IRC §23(a)(1) (1939).
37. *Comm'r v. Flowers*, 326 U.S. 465 (1946).
38. *Mark R. Pedersen v. Comm'r*, TC Summ. Op. 2022-11 (Jun. 28, 2022), citing *James E. Peurifoy, et al., v. Comm'r*, 27 TC 149 (1956), *aff'd* 254 F.2d 483 (4th Cir. 1957).
39. *James E. Peurifoy, et al., v. Comm'r*, 27 TC 149 (1956), *aff'd* 254 F.2d 483 (4th Cir. 1957).
40. Rev. Rul. 93-86, 1993-2 CB 71.

Example 4. Joe, an independent union plumber, travels between his small office next to the union hall in Savoy, Illinois, to a customer's place of business in Mahomet, approximately 18 miles away. The project is expected to last three months, according to a contract from the general contractor. Joe's small office in Savoy continues to be his tax home because the Mahomet project lasts less than one year. He has a signed contract to substantiate the expected length of his project. In addition, Joe's principal residence and office are in the general vicinity of the project in Mahomet.

Example 5. Use the same facts as **Example 4,** except that Joe takes on a job in Danville, Illinois, which is 39 miles away from his office. Because Joe expects this project to last two weeks, he does not go to the office next to the union hall, and Joe's office in Savoy continues to be his tax home.

Distinguishing Temporary and Indefinite Employment. A tax home changes if the work lasts longer than one year or is indefinite.[41] In these circumstances, the taxpayer's tax home changes to the location where they perform the work. Even if the work unexpectedly lasts less than one year, the taxpayer's tax home changes because they initially expected the work to last one year or longer.[42] The client's ability to terminate the work on very short notice does not alter its indefinite duration or nullify the change in tax home.[43]

Example 6. Use the same facts as **Example 4,** except that Joe's project is in Fort Wayne, Indiana, and is of uncertain length. Because it involves remodeling a large commercial building, Joe can reasonably expect to work on this project for longer than one year. Under these circumstances, Joe's tax home changes to Fort Wayne because his Savoy, Illinois, office is no longer near his work.

Significantly, Joe loses the ability to deduct travel costs, discussed later, from his home in Urbana to the project in Fort Wayne. Even if the client prematurely cancels the remodeling project, Joe's tax home remains in Fort Wayne for the project's duration.

No Separate Principal Place of Business[44]

Sometimes a taxpayer may not have a principal place of business distinct from their residence. In this case, the taxpayer's tax home sometimes is their residence. This arrangement may often be the case for professionals working from their residences or those engaged in the gig economy.

Example 7. Use the same facts as **Example 4,** except that Joe works from his principal residence in Urbana, as he does not have a separate office. Joe uses a small area of his residence regularly and exclusively for managing his business. Joe's principal residence is his tax home.

However, the taxpayer must have a **business** connection with their residence's location. In a 1981 case, the U.S. Court of Appeals for the First Circuit decided that a married law student with a husband and a home in Boston did **not** have a tax home there.[45] While a student at Harvard Law School outside of Boston, she worked a summer job as a law clerk in New York City. Although she had a clear personal tie to Boston, her business tie was to New York City, making that location her tax home, if only for her summer work. The court rejected the argument that her short tenure for summer employment exempted her from the requirement to have a business tie to the place she called home.

---

41. IRC §162(a).

42. Rev. Rul. 1993-86, 1993-2 CB 71. See situation 2.

43. Ibid.

44. Rev. Rul. 93-86, 1993-2 CB 71; IRS Pub. 463, *Travel, Gift, and Car Expenses*, p. 3 (2022).

45. *Hantzis v. Comm'r*, 638 F.2d (1st Cir. 1981).

No Tax Home[46]

In other circumstances, a taxpayer may not maintain a permanent residence because their work requires full-time travel. If a taxpayer travels full-time and does not maintain a permanent residence, the IRS may consider them **itinerant** workers, having their tax home wherever they may be working. Even if they tend to stay with the same family members in the same location when not working, the IRS and the courts view these individuals as having no home absent a written agreement for paying rent or a share of expenses.

In these circumstances, the taxpayer's tax home is wherever they happen to work, eliminating the possibility of tax deductions for travel expenses. In a dissenting opinion to *Henderson v. Comm'r*,[47] Judge Kozinski coined the term "tax turtle" to describe Mr. Henderson's lack of a fixed residence, even though he generally returned to his parents' home in Idaho when not on the road working as a stagehand. Because he did not incur duplicated living costs, the courts affirmed the IRS's denial of travel costs. Consequently, to establish a tax home and deductible travel costs, taxpayers must incur living costs associated with one's principal residence.

SELECTED TRADES OR BUSINESSES

Tax home concepts affect construction workers, gig economy workers, and truck drivers because their work locations frequently change. This section will focus on the application of tax home to these three respective industries.

Construction Workers

By their very nature, independent contractors work on-site at different locations. Although an independent contractor working in construction may perform bookkeeping work from a single site, they perform very little actual construction work from a fixed location. A construction worker's tax home can readily change if unexpected delays prolong a project beyond the 1-year limit for temporary work.

> **Example 8.** Corey is an electrician and a sole proprietor living in Peoria, Illinois, normally working in the Peoria area. In early 2022, he signs a contract for a project in Bloomington, which is 43 miles from his residence.
>
> When the Bloomington project starts on March 11, 2022, the general contractor tells Corey it will last approximately eight months. However, on November 20, 2022, the general contractor asks him to remain on the project for another five months. Corey does so, completing the project on April 16, 2023.
>
> Corey's assignment in Bloomington starts as temporary but assumes an indefinite status when the general contractor extends it another five months. Because Corey realistically expected the job to last only eight months at its start, it was temporary from March 11 through November 20, 2022. However, due to changed circumstances, Corey could no longer expect the Bloomington project to last for one year or less after November 20, 2022. Therefore, the job has an indefinite duration from November 21, 2022, through the completion date on April 16, 2023.

A recent Tax Court case suggests that the IRS may attempt to undermine construction workers' tacit assertions that their tax homes have not changed and that they are eligible for deduction of travel expenses.[48] In *Pedersen v. Comm'r*, the court sustained the IRS's disallowance of a construction worker's deductions because he did not maintain a copy of an employment agreement or a work schedule that listed his principal place of employment and the job sites to which he was assigned.

---

46. IRS Pub. 463, *Travel, Gift, and Car Expenses*, p. 3 (2023).

47. *Henderson v. Comm'r*, 143 F.3d 497 (9th Cir. 1998).

48. *Mark R. Pedersen v. Comm'r*, TC Summ. Op. 2022-11 (Jun. 28, 2022). That Mr. Pedersen was a common law employee does not affect the application of case law to independent contractors in this case.

Practitioner Planning Tip

Tax practitioners may consider advising their clients who are construction workers to insist on receiving **written** assignments with the expected duration for their work. This document, combined with a work schedule and a mileage log, may strengthen the taxpayer's position that the construction worker's tax home changed because their project was expected to be longer than a year or had an indeterminate length.

3

Gig Economy Workers[49]

A gig is "a job usually for a specified period of time"[50] or "any job, especially one of short or uncertain duration."[51] Most gigs are short-term endeavors, perhaps lasting even less than a day in some cases, such as ride-sharing drivers. In other cases, a gig worker may be engaged to work on a project for several months. As mentioned previously, if a project's expected duration is shorter than one year, the gig worker's tax home does not change from their regular work location. On the other hand, if the duration of the work is unknown, indeterminate, or expected to last 12 months or longer, the gig worker's tax home changes to the location of the work.

Truck Drivers

Generally, a truck driver's tax home is either:

- The principal place of business, such as a terminal, or
- The regular abode (if there is no principal place of business because of the nature of the truck driver's work).[52]

Note. These tax-home rules apply to truck drivers who work as employees or self-employed owner-operators (independent contractors). An employed truck driver's principal place of business is the employer's principal place of business.

If the truck driver performs work at a principal place of business, such as their home terminal, that place of business is their tax home.[53] This concept applies even if the truck driver's principal place of business is also their residence.[54] However, some truck drivers have no identifiable principal place of business but maintain a residence from which employers send them on temporary assignments. This residence is their tax home.[55]

Note. The location of the truck driver's tax home is always subject to a facts and circumstances analysis.[56] Some general rules applied in this analysis are discussed later in this chapter. No clear definition of the term tax home applies to all taxpayers, and the application of the following general rules has been the subject of significant litigation.

49. Rev. Rul. 93-86, 1993-2 CB 71.
50. *Gig*. Merriam-Webster. [www.merriam-webster.com/dictionary/gig] Accessed on Mar. 8, 2023.
51. *Gig*. Dictionary.com. [www.dictionary.com/browse/gig] Accessed on Mar. 8, 2023.
52. Rev. Rul. 75-432, 1975-2 CB 60.
53. Rev. Rul. 55-236, 1955-1 CB 274.
54. IRS Pub. 463, *Travel, Gift, and Car Expenses*.
55. Rev. Rul. 75-432, 1975-2 CB 60.
56. Ibid.

A truck driver's tax home includes the entire city or general area in which they work.[57] Accordingly, the truck driver must be outside this tax-home area to meet the away-from-home requirement.

Note. The extent of the surrounding territory included in the taxpayer's tax home is unclear. For example, various courts have held that the tax-home area includes the entire city or town,[58] the greater metropolitan area of a major city,[59] a county,[60] and even a port area.[61]

Work Assignments. Generally, their main terminal is the tax home for a truck driver who works from there as a principal business location.[62] However, a truck driver may receive an assignment to another post of duty instead of their principal place of business. Such a work assignment may be either temporary or indefinite.

Example 9. Samantha is an independent truck driver who normally drives for Monrovia Transport, LLC (MT). She works each day from MT headquarters near downtown Chicago hauling farm produce to major grocery stores. To facilitate the loading of trucks with goods from ships, MT is headquartered about six miles south of downtown Chicago near piers on Lake Michigan. Samantha lives a few miles away and uses her home office when invoicing MT for her services.

During 2023, Samantha works from MT's Chicago headquarters from January through September. In October 2023, her contact at the company informs her that she would be at the Schaumburg office "for two or three months" because of the increased demand for trucked goods west of Chicago. (Chicago and Schaumburg are both located in Cook County.)

When Samantha's contact informs her of the Schaumburg assignment, she believes that the assignment's end in December 2023 is realistic and that she can expect to resume working in MT's Chicago headquarters in January 2024. However, Samantha resumes working from MT's Chicago headquarters on March 1, 2024. She also incurs additional travel expenses because of her assignment to the Schaumburg terminal, such as mileage and meal costs.

For the first nine months of 2023, Samantha's tax home is MT's headquarters because this is the principal place of business from which she works. MT's headquarters continues to be Samantha's tax home during her assignment to the Schaumburg terminal.

Example 10. Use the same facts as **Example 9,** except MT assigns Samantha to work from its terminal in Champaign, Illinois. (Champaign is approximately 135 miles away from MT's Chicago headquarters.) In addition, before making the assignment, Samantha's supervisor tells her to plan on working from the Champaign location "until the expansion of the Chicago terminal at headquarters is complete, which should take several years."

Champaign is not within the same general area as Chicago for tax home purposes. In addition, the supervisor's statement to Samantha indicates that her Champaign work assignment lasts more than one year. Therefore, Samantha realistically expects the work assignment to be indefinite.

Because Samantha is an independent contractor and not an employee of MT, the facts and circumstances of her engagement with MT and her home office in Chicago likely govern the determination of her tax home. If, instead, Samantha were a common law employee, it is clear that her tax home would shift to Champaign.

---

57. Rev. Rul. 60-189,1960-1 CB 60; See *Harry F. Schurer v. Comm'r*, 3 TC 544 (1944); IRS Pub. 463, *Travel, Entertainment, Gift, and Car Expenses*.

58. *Smith v. Comm'r*, 21 TC 991 (1954); *Podems v. Comm'r*, 24 TC 21 (1955).

59. *Amoroso v. Comm'r*, 193 F.2d 583 (1st Cir. 1952), *cert. denied*, 343 U.S. 926 (1952).

60. *J. Summerour v. M. H. Allen*, 99 F.Supp. 318 (M.D. Ga. 1951).

61. *Steinhort v. Comm'r*, 335 F.2d 496 (5th Cir. 1964).

62. Rev. Rul. 55-236, 1955-1 CB 274.

Caution. In this hypothetical example, the IRS has multiple incentives to determine that Samantha is an employee of MT, not an independent contractor. This determination would make Champaign her tax home, eliminating traveling expense deductions (discussed later). The IRS could attempt to collect social security and Medicare on Samantha's **gross** pay, not just the **net** income shown on her Schedule C.

3

Example 11. Use the same facts as **Example 10,** except Samantha's contact at MT tells her she has been assigned to work from Champaign for the next two months, filling in for another employee on leave. Samantha's Champaign assignment lasts for the anticipated 2-month duration. The assignment is therefore considered temporary. Samantha had a realistic belief in the temporary nature of her assignment, which lasted for one year or less. While Samantha works from Champaign, her tax home continues to be Chicago, potentially permitting the deduction of travel expenses associated with working from the Champaign location if she maintains the required records.

Observation. Realistically believing that a work assignment has a duration shorter than one year is an element of a temporary work assignment. It may be prudent for a truck driver to document reasons for having a belief because that element may become an issue if their travel expenses are subject to an IRS examination. Obtaining a letter from the client or employer or making appropriate notations in a log or journal may provide adequate documentation.

Example 12. Use the same facts as **Example 11.** Samantha works from Champaign for the 2-month temporary assignment during October and November 2023. However, before the end of November, her MT contact extends her Champaign assignment for three months.

Samantha continues working from Champaign during December 2023 and January and February 2024. MT contacts her on February 15, 2024, commending her work and again extending her assignment, this time for the rest of 2024.

MT's communication to Samantha on February 15, 2024, eliminates her realistic belief that her assignment is temporary. **On that date, her assignment becomes indefinite.** However, her work from Champaign before February 15, 2024, is characterized as temporary. Samantha can deduct her travel expenses from October 2021 through February 15, 2024, if she meets the other requirements for deducting travel expenses.

Multiple Work Locations. Some truck drivers work from two or more business or employment locations. Such an individual must determine which location constitutes their tax home to determine if and when they meet the away-from-home requirement for deducting certain travel expenses.

For transportation workers, their tax home is typically the terminal at which they usually begin and end trips. The IRS has deemed that the home terminal and its vicinity comprise the tax home for a long-haul truck driver.[63]

A secondary terminal or location does not constitute a tax home, even if the transportation worker has a personal residence near the secondary location.[64] In this situation, the IRS considers the truck driver away from home even if they maintain a residence at or near the minor business location.

Example 13. Georgina lives in Arlington, Virginia, where Anywhere Logistics, Inc. (AL) employs her as a truck driver. Georgina's job duties consist primarily of completing short-haul assignments directly from AL's warehouse in Washington, DC. However, each Wednesday and Friday at noon, she travels approximately 60 miles round trip between AL's warehouse in Washington, DC, and AL's satellite logistics office in Bethesda, Maryland. While at the satellite office, she performs administrative duties.

The AL warehouse in Washington, D.C., is Georgina's tax home, and she should consider the satellite office within its surrounding general area for tax purposes.

63. Ibid.

64. Rev. Rul. 55-604, 1955-2 CB 49.

SUMMARY

The concept of tax home arises from Congress including a simple and commonly understood word in the Code: "home."[65] The courts and the IRS discerned in Congress's choice of this word the intention to allow a deduction for personal costs duplicated only because of the demands of a taxpayer's business. For this reason, understanding an independent contractor's tax home is the key to understanding what travel expenses are deductible. This understanding also indicates the importance of project duration and the taxpayer's connection to their home.

The expected duration of the employment affects tax home issues, as summarized in the following table.[66]

Projected Length	Tax Home Issue
The project is expected to be completed in less than one year, but it takes longer than one year[67]	Tax home changes to location of the project when expected project duration changes: travel expenses of contractor **not** deductible
The project is expected to last longer than one year[68]	Tax home changes to location of the project: travel expenses of contractor **not** deductible
The project is expected to be completed in less than one year[69]	Tax home does **not** change: travel expenses deductible

GROSS INCOME ISSUES

The IRS defines gross income very broadly.[70]

> *Except as provided in the Internal Revenue Code, gross income includes income from whatever source derived.*

Independent contractors should, therefore, include all gross income.

SELECTED TRADES OR BUSINESSES

Construction Workers

IRS Pub. 5522, *Construction Industry Audit Technique Guide,* provides a framework to understand the nuances of tax accounting for the industry and to familiarize agents undertaking examinations with the industry's practices. This guide reflects the variety of contracts and the different circumstances for recognizing income that the construction industry faces. The length of a construction contract influences the method of accounting for a specific contract. Beyond that, contracts that span multiple tax years raise a plethora of issues affecting how much revenue the taxpayer recognizes in each tax year.

65. IRC §162(a).
66. IRS Pub. 463, *Travel, Gift, and Car Expenses*, p. 3 (2022); Treas. Reg. §1.162-17.
67. IRC §162(a); Rev. Rul. 93-86, 1993-2 CB 71. See situation 3.
68. Ibid. See situation 2; *Norwood v. Comm'r*, 66 TC 467 (1976).
69. Rev. Rul. 93-86, 1993-2 CB 71. See situation 1.
70. Instructions for Schedule C.

Short-Term Contracts.[71] A short-term contract is one that the construction contractor completes within the same tax year that the contract is signed. If the construction contractor uses the cash method, they deduct costs in the year in which they paid them. If the construction contractor uses another method of accounting, such as the accrual method, then they deduct costs in the year of construction, regardless of when paid. The construction contractor treats the related construction costs as current period costs, other than nonincidental materials and supplies, if the construction contractor did not make the de minimis safe harbor election under all accounting methods.

3

It is common for independent contractors to use the cash method of accounting, particularly if most of their contracts are short-term endeavors. A discussion of the cash method follows the discussion of long-term contracts.

Long-Term Contracts. A contract is long-term when its completion does not fall within the taxpayer's taxable year, such as a contract that a calendar-year taxpayer started in November 2022 and finished in January 2023.[72] Even though the contract lasted less than three months, it is a long-term contract for tax purposes. Treas. Regs. §§1.460-1 through 5 defines the accounting methods permissible for long-term contracts.

The Code requires long-term contracts to use the percentage-of-completion method (PCM), except when the construction worker qualifies as a small contractor or a home builder.[73] Qualifying small contractors (3-year average gross receipts of $29 million for tax years beginning after December 31, 2023)[74] and home builders may use any allowable accounting method, provided they apply it consistently.[75]

Treas. Reg. §1.460-3 adds important commentary and criteria for construction contracts exempt from the PCM mandate. The construction contract must pertain to real estate or property permanently connected to real estate. Thus, a contract for installing an elevator is long-term if the associated work is connected to a building and extends into the following year. The regulations do not provide the same benefit if the construction worker installs the elevator on a ship, which does not qualify as real estate.[76]

The same regulation also excludes small-scale residential construction projects. If a construction company undertakes a project at a single-family home that extends into the next fiscal year, it is not required to use a long-term construction accounting method. The regulation applies not only to single-family homes but also to buildings having fewer than five dwelling units.

Cash Method of Accounting. Construction industry taxpayers are allowed to use the cash method of accounting if they meet the criteria for small businesses and home builders discussed earlier in this section.

Accrual Methods of Accounting. By its nature, the construction industry involves contracts that last from one tax year into the next, enabling a variety of options for recognizing revenue before a contract is completed. PCM is the most common method, in addition to the completed-contract method (CCM) and the exempt-contract percentage-of-completion method (EPCM). All three methods are discussed next.

PCM. Generally, construction contractors must use the PCM to account for long-term revenue.[77] The amount of revenue earned each year by a contract is determined by multiplying the estimated total contract price times the percentage of completion at the end of the tax year, less any income recognized in the prior tax years of the contract. Firms may elect to defer both revenue and costs until the contract has incurred 10% of the total estimated allocable costs.[78]

---

71. IRS Pub. 5522, *Construction Industry Audit Technique Guide.*

72. Ibid.

73. Treas. Reg. §1.460-3(b)(1).

74. Treas. Reg. §1.460-3(b)(3). The threshold stated is for $27 million in 2022 and $29 million in 2023, adjusted for inflation from $25 million in 2018; IRC §448(c)(1); Rev. Proc. 2022-38, 2022-45 IRB 445.

75. Treas. Reg. §1.460-4(c).

76. Treas. Reg. §1.460-3(a).

77. IRC §460(a).

78. IRC §460(b)(5); IRS Pub. 5522, *Construction Industry Audit Technique Guide,* pp. 81-82 (2021).

Although the PCM recognizes revenue based on a construction project's **degree of completion**, there are two methods of computing this percentage.

1. **Cost-to-Cost Method.**[79] Large contractors must use the cost-to-cost PCM to determine the degree of completion.[80] They may not use engineering estimates or other approaches to determine the degree of completion.

   Construction contractors compute the percentage of completion under the cost-to-cost method by dividing the total cumulative costs incurred by the estimated total contract costs.[81]

$$\textbf{Percentage of completion} = \frac{\textbf{Total cumulative costs incurred to date}}{\textbf{Estimated total contract costs}}$$

   The costs incurred to measure the percentage of completion must include specially ordered materials and supplies for a project. Total costs cannot include contingency reserves.

   Because the calculation of **revenue** under PCM depends on the allocation of costs, tax practitioners must consider the following costs when a construction worker uses the PCM, either by choice or requirement.

   - **Direct Material Costs.**[82] All direct material costs which become an integral part of the finished project and all materials consumed in the ordinary course of completing the project must be allocated to the contract.

     Direct material costs include the invoice price for the materials minus any discounts taken plus transportation or other necessary charges incurred to acquire possession of the goods.[83] They also include materials provided by subcontractors.

     The costs of direct materials and supplies purchased specifically for a particular long-term contract are allocable to the contract in the taxable year in which such costs are incurred.[84] The costs of other direct materials and supplies (such as those previously held by the taxpayer) are allocable to the contract in the taxable year in which such materials and supplies are dedicated to the contract.[85]

   - **Direct Labor Costs.**[86] All direct labor costs identified or associated with a long-term contract must be allocated to the contract. The elements of direct labor costs include basic compensation, overtime pay, vacation and holiday pay, sick leave pay, shift differential, payroll taxes, and payments to a supplemental unemployment benefit plan paid or incurred on behalf of employees engaged in direct labor. The cost of labor supplied by subcontractors is also a direct labor cost.

   - **Cost-Plus and Federal Contracts.**[87] All costs specifically identified by the terms of a **cost-plus contract** (agreement for reimbursement of a project's expenses plus an additional fee) and by federal, state, or local laws and regulations must also be allocated to cost-plus and federal contracts, respectively. These costs can include the time value of money if the contract includes an associated charge.

---

79. IRS Pub. 5522, *Construction Industry Audit Technique Guide*, pp. 72–78 (2021).

80. IRC §460(b)(1)(A); Treas. Reg. §1.460-4(b).

81. IRC §460(b); Treas. Reg. §1.460-4(b).

82. Treas. Reg. §1.460-5(b)(2).

83. Treas. Reg. §1.263(a)-2(d)(1).

84. IRC §460(c)(1).

85. Treas. Reg. §1.460-5(b)(2)(i).

86. Treas. Regs. §§1.263A-1(e)(2)(i)(B) and 1.263A-1(e)(3)(ii)(D).

87. IRC §460(c)(2); Treas. Reg. §1.460-5(b)(2)(iv); IRS Pub. 5522, *Construction Industry Audit Technique Guide*, p. 80 (2021).

- **Indirect Costs.**[88] Indirect costs include all costs other than direct material and labor costs. Some indirect costs may benefit both the long-term contract activity of the taxpayer and other business activities of the taxpayer.[89] Accordingly, these costs require a reasonable allocation between the portion attributable to each long-term contract and the portion attributable to the other business activities of the taxpayer.

  Indirect costs must be allocated to a long-term contract by either the specific identification method or using burden rates such as ratios based on direct cost or hours.

3

The **indirect** costs **requiring allocation to long-term contracts of large contractors** include the following.[90]

a. Indirect supervisory wages, including basic compensation, overtime pay, vacation and holiday pay, sick leave pay, shift differential, payroll taxes, and contributions to a supplemental unemployment benefit plan

b. Officers' compensation

c. Stock bonus, pension, profit-sharing, or annuity plan contributions or other plans deferring the receipt of compensation

d. Employee benefit expenses paid or accrued on behalf of labor

e. Indirect materials and supplies

f. Purchasing and handling costs

g. Storage costs

h. Depreciation and amortization on equipment and facilities

i. Depletion, whether or not in excess of cost

j. Rent

k. Taxes attributable to labor, materials, supplies, equipment, or facilities

l. Insurance on equipment, facilities, materials, and so forth

m. Utilities

n. Repairs and maintenance of equipment or facilities

o. Engineering and design costs, including preproduction costs, excluding experimental costs

p. Experimental expenses directly attributable to a long-term contract in existence at the incurrence of the expenses[91]

q. Rework labor, scrap, and spoilage

r. Tools and equipment not capitalized

s. Cost of quality control and inspection

---

88. Treas. Reg. §1.263A-1(e)(3).

89. IRS Pub. 5522, *Construction Industry Audit Technique Guide*, p. 74 (2021).

90. Treas. Reg. §1.263A-1(e)(3); IRS Pub. 5522, *Construction Industry Audit Technique Guide*, pp. 73–74 (2021).

91. Treas. Reg. §§1.263A-1(e)(3)(ii)(P) and 1.263A-1(e)(3)(iii)(B).

- **t.** Bidding expenses incurred in soliciting a long-term contract awarded to the taxpayer.[92] If the taxpayer does not win the contract, bidding costs are deductible when there is hard evidence that the taxpayer's bid is not accepted.[93]
- **u.** Licensing and franchise costs
- **v.** Administrative costs directly attributable to the long-term contract
- **w.** Direct and indirect costs incurred by any service, administrative, or support function to the extent such costs are allocable to a long-term contract

Costs not requiring allocation to long-term contracts include the following.[94]

- **a.** Marketing, selling, and advertising expenses
- **b.** Research and experimental expenses that are not directly attributable to an agreement in existence at the time the expenses are incurred
- **c.** The cost of assets deducted under IRC §179
- **d.** Casualty, theft, and capital losses[95]
- **e.** Depreciation and amortization on temporarily idle equipment and facilities. An asset used in construction is idle when it is not en route to or located at a job site.
- **f.** Income taxes
- **g.** Costs attributable to strikes
- **h.** Warranty and product liability costs
- **i.** Bidding expenses incurred in the solicitation of contracts not awarded to the taxpayer

There is a table of these costs later in this section, summarizing the treatment of them under different accounting methods.

2. **Simplified Cost-to-Cost Method.**[96] Construction workers who are independent contractors using the PCM for all long-term contracts may use a simplified cost-to-cost method. However, they cannot use the simplified method if they elect not to report contracts less than 10% complete. A further restriction applies to those using the percentage-of-completion/capitalized-cost method (PCCM) for residential construction contracts, discussed later.

   Under the simplified cost-to-cost method, the determination of the percentage of completion consists of only the following costs.

   - Direct material costs and direct labor costs (including subcontractors)
   - Depreciation and amortization on equipment and facilities directly related to the construction project

   A taxpayer using the simplified cost-to-cost method must use the same costs in determining the costs allocated to the contract, the costs incurred before the close of the taxable year, and the estimated total contract cost.

---

92. Treas. Reg. §1.263A-1(e)(3)(ii)(T).

93. Treas. Reg. §1.263A-1(e)(3)(iii)(J).

94. Treas. Reg. §1.263A-1(e)(3)(iii).

95. Treas. Reg. §1.263A-1(e)(3)(iii)(D).

96. Treas. Reg. §1.460-5(c).

Practitioner Planning Tip

Once a taxpayer elects this method, they must use it for all subsequent long-term contracts.[97] They must also use it for subsequent alternative minimum tax (AMT) and look-back method calculations.

3

CCM.[98] The CCM is an alternative to the PCM for long-term contracts, as it enables eligible construction workers to defer recognition of income and expenses until they have completed the contracts. It is available to construction contractors who qualify for the small contractor exception, which applies if the contractor's annual average revenue in 2023 is under $29 million (indexed for inflation) for the last three years combined.[99]

Example 14. Franklin is an independent contractor in the construction industry with gross receipts for the 2020–2022 tax years equaling $22 million, $28 million, and $13 million, respectively. Franklin's annual average revenue for the last three years is $21 million (($22 million + $28 million + $13 million) ÷ 3 = $21 million). Franklin can use the CCM per the gross receipts test.

When the contract is complete, the construction worker recognizes income. The Code gives the word "complete" a special meaning, being the **earlier** of the following two dates.[100]

1. Final completion and acceptance of the subject of the contract; or
2. The construction worker's customer has used the subject of the contract for its intended purpose, **and** the construction worker has incurred at least 95% of the contract costs associated with the contract.

Example 15. Use the same facts as **Example 14,** except that Franklin signs a contract to build a small office building for a consulting engineer on January 15, 2022. The contract amounts to $500,000, and Franklin plans for $420,000 in costs, including cost allocations. The consulting engineer occupies the building on December 15, 2022, even though some uncompleted items were on the punch list. The costs associated with the incomplete items are only $6,300, or 1.5% of the total costs associated with the contract. Franklin completes these items in January 2023, and the consulting engineer accepts the project and arranges with their mortgagee to pay Franklin on January 15.

Because the customer of the contract had occupied the building for its intended use and the construction contractor has incurred at least 95% of the allocable contract costs, the contractor must recognize the revenue for the project in 2022, even though the consulting engineer did not pay him until January 15 of the following year.

The costs that Franklin must include in the allocation of construction costs are identified in the second column from the right in the *Allocation of Costs to Contracts* table, as shown later. The costs incurred govern the amount of revenue to recognize.

---

97. Ibid.

98. Treas. Reg. §1.460-4(d).

99. Treas. Reg. §1.460-3(b)(3). The threshold stated is for $27 million in 2022 and $29 million in 2023, adjusted for inflation from $25 million in 2018; IRC §448(c)(1); Rev. Proc. 2022-38, 2022-45 IRB 445.

100. Treas. Reg. §1.460-1(c)(3)(i).

EPCM.[101] The Code exempts certain taxpayers from the requirement to use the PCM for recognizing revenue. Under the EPCM, construction contractors report expenses in the year incurred and revenues in proportion to the amount of the contract completed. Taxpayers can apply EPCM to any of the following exempt construction contracts.[102]

- Exempt construction contracts as defined in Treas. Reg. §1.460-3(b) for post-completion-year income
- The non-PCM portion of a qualified ship contract, as defined in Treas. Reg. §1.460-2(d)
- The non-PCM portion of a residential construction contract, as defined in Treas. Reg. §1.460-3(c)

These contractors calculate the current year revenue by multiplying the estimated total contract price times the percentage of completion at the end of the tax year and subtracting any recognized revenue in the prior tax years of the contract.

Current year revenue = Estimated total contract price × Percentage of completion − Prior year revenue

The EPCM gives the construction contractor flexibility in choosing how to calculate the percentage of completion, provided the method clearly reflects income. They can determine the percentage of completion **at the end of the tax year** by either of the following methods.[103]

- **Cost Comparison Method.** The cost comparison method uses the ratio of the costs incurred at the end of the tax year to the estimated total contract costs for each contract. A taxpayer can use any cost comparison, provided they use the method consistently for that contract. The three most common types of cost comparisons include:
    1. Contract costs compared to total estimated contract costs
    2. Direct labor costs compared to total estimated direct labor costs
    3. Direct labor hours compared to total estimated direct labor hours
- **Work Comparison Method.** The work comparison method compares, as of the end of the taxable year, the work the taxpayer performs on the contract with the estimated total work the taxpayer expects to perform. Examples of this method include measuring output based on units produced, units delivered, phases completed, and value added.

Practitioner Planning Tip

Practitioners should include change orders in the EPCM calculation and exclude nondeductible expenses and allowances for contingencies.[104]

101. Treas. Reg. §1.460-4(c)(2).
102. Treas. Reg. §1.460-4(c)(1).
103. Treas. Reg. §1.460-4(c)(2)(i).
104. Treas. Reg. §1.460-4(b)(5)(iii).

AMT.[105] Many small construction independent contractors, other than those involved in home construction, must compute alternative minimum taxable income (AMTI) using the PCM. This adjustment for AMT is also subject to look-back rules (defined under large contractors) for long-term contracts, which a taxpayer reports on line 2p of part I, Form 6251, *Alternative Minimum Tax*.

Residential Construction Contractors.[106] A residential construction contract is a home construction contract where the buildings contain more than four dwelling units each. A taxpayer may report income for this type of long-term contract using either the PCM or the PCCM. Under the PCCM, the calculation of 70% of the reportable income uses PCM, and the remaining 30% uses any other permissible method.[107]

3

> **Note.** For more discussion on construction industry issues, see the 2003 *University of Illinois Federal Tax Workbook,* Chapter 2: Small Business Issues. This can be found at **uofi.tax/arc** [taxschool.illinois.edu/taxbookarchive].

Land Contracts. Construction contracts are exempt from the long-term contract revenue recognition rules if the contractor sells land and the construction costs constitute less than 10% of the contract's value.[108] The calculation of construction costs includes a portion of the construction cost of a "common improvement." This requirement applies regardless of whether the contractor's obligation to construct the common improvement arises from the contract or a legal requirement.

Allocation of Costs to Contracts. The following table compares the allocation of costs to contracts for revenue purposes across various methods of accounting for long-term contracts.

---

105. IRC §56(a)(3); Treas. Reg. §§1.56-1(c)(1) and 1.460-4(f).

106. IRC §460(e)(4); Treas. Regs. §§1.460-1(a)(2)(ii) and 1.460-3(c).

107. Treas. Reg. §1.460-4(e).

108. Treas. Reg. §1.460-1(b)(2)(ii).

Allocation of Costs to Contracts for Revenue Purposes Under Different Methods of Accounting for Long-Term Contracts

	PCM	PCM Simplified	CCM	EPCM
Authority	Treas. Reg. §1.460-5	Treas. Reg §1.460-5	Treas. Reg §1.460-5	Treas. Reg §1.460-4
Who may use	Anyone	[a]	[b]	[b]
Direct costs				
Materials	Yes	Yes	Yes	Electable
Labor	Yes	Yes	Yes	Electable
Subcontracts	Yes	Yes	Yes	Electable
Indirect Costs				
1. Indirect supervisory wages (and related costs)	Yes	No	Yes	Electable
2. Officers' compensation	Yes	No	Yes	Electable
3. Deferred compensation plans	Yes	No	No	Electable
4. Employee benefits	Yes	No	No	Electable
5. Indirect materials and supplies	Yes	No	No	Electable
6. Purchasing and handling	Yes	No	No	Electable
7. Storage	Yes	No	No	Electable
8. Depreciation and amortization on production assets	Tax	Tax	Financial	Electable
9. Depletion (whether or not in excess of cost)	Yes	No	Cost only	Electable
10. Rent	Yes	No	Yes	Electable
11. Taxes	Yes	No	Yes	Electable
12. Insurance	Yes	No	Yes	Electable
13. Utilities	Yes	No	Yes	Electable
14. Repairs and maintenance of production assets	Yes	No	Yes	Electable
15. Engineering and design	Yes	No	No	Electable
16. Contract-related research	Yes	No	No	Electable
17. Rework labor, scrap, and spoilage	Yes	No	No	Electable
18. Tools and equipment (not capitalized)	Yes	No	Yes	Electable
19. Quality control and inspection	Yes	No	Yes	Electable
20. Successful bidding	Yes	No	No	Electable
21. Unsuccessful bidding	No	No	No	Electable
22. Licensing and franchising	Yes	No	No	Electable
23. Administrative costs (attributable to long-term contracts)	Yes	No	No	Electable
24. Marketing, selling, and advertising expenses	No	No	No	Electable
25. Research (not contract related)	No	No	No	Electable
26. Cost of assets deducted under IRC §179	No	No	No	Electable
27. Casualty, theft, and capital losses	No	No	No	Electable
28. Depreciation and amortization on idle assets	No	No	No	Electable
29. Income taxes	No	No	No	Electable
30. Costs attributable to strikes	No	No	No	Electable
31. Warranty and product liability costs	No	No	No	Electable
32. Interest	[c]	[c]	[c]	[c]
33. Costs identified in contract or in law	Yes	No	No	Electable

[a] Anyone who uses PCM for all long-term contracts and who has not elected to defer contracts less than 10% complete. Excludes residential developers using PCCM, under which 70% of revenue is calculated using PCM and 30% another method.

[b] Small contractors: contract shorter than 24 months and contractors having average annual gross receipts under $29 million (2023).

[c] Depends on the length and total cost of the contract.

Gig Economy Workers[109]

Gig workers perform a variety of unconventional services and may receive income in a variety of unconventional forms. Taxpayers must report gig income regardless of whether the income arises from part-time or temporary work and regardless of whether customers pay taxpayers in currency, property, or digital assets. Even in situations where the taxpayer does not receive a Form W-2 or 1099 for this income, they must report it as income on their tax return unless one of the few statutory exceptions applies.[110]

3

> **Example 16.** In December 2022, Maggie signs a contract to provide a website for her landlord, Waterford Apartments, LLC. Waterford's managing member is familiar with her work at a local advertising firm. Maggie's work must start in January 2023 and be complete by June 30, 2023. The landlord agrees that Maggie does not need to pay rent during this time. This rent forgiveness is barter income. Maggie is responsible for reporting the value of six months' rent on her 2023 tax return.

There are no specific rules and guidelines for whether a gig worker must use either the cash or accrual method of accounting. The facts and circumstances of the situation should guide the taxpayer in making their choice. The circumstances include prevalent practices in the taxpayer's industry.

Truck Drivers

Method of Accounting. As with all businesses, truckers with their own businesses must decide whether they should use the cash method of accounting or the accrual method. The cash method provides an indication of a business's cash flow. Although it has additional complexities, the accrual method may provide greater insight into the company's financial operations.

Lumper Fees. Laborers who receive payment to load and unload containers are referred to as lumpers. Lumpers often work independently of trucking companies, although employee drivers can perform loading and unloading services for additional compensation.

---

109. *IRS Tax Tip 2023-42: All income is taxable, including gig economy and tip income*. Mar. 30, 2023. IRS. [www.irs.gov/newsroom/all-income-is-taxable-including-gig-economy-and-tip-income] Accessed on Apr. 10, 2023.

110. IRC §61(a).

TREATMENT OF EQUIPMENT

The way independent contractors treat equipment for tax purposes is a key issue because ownership of equipment is one of the indices of their status as an employee or a contractor. Independent contractors tend to own the equipment they use because they make their own investments and have a profit motive and have risk of loss. In this section, the assumption is that the equipment is either personal property (as opposed to real property) or intangible property, such as software.

CAPITALIZATION OF EQUIPMENT AND DEPRECIATION

In general, taxpayers must capitalize equipment they purchase for use in their trade or business and depreciate it.[111] The cost would normally not be deductible in the year the asset is placed in service unless it is available for bonus depreciation[112] or §179 expense.

> **Note.** Depreciation is covered in greater detail in the 2023 *University of Illinois Federal Tax Workbook,* Chapter 7: Depreciation. For more information on capitalization issues, including the safe harbor election under Treas. Reg. §1.263(a)-1(f), see the 2023 *University of Illinois Federal Tax Workbook,* Chapter 2: Capitalization vs. Repair Review.

Regular Depreciation

A taxpayer can recover the equipment's cost through regular depreciation before the property's disposition. The Code subjects independent contractors to the same depreciation rules as all other taxpayers. An independent contractor reports their depreciation expense on line 13 of Schedule C, unless a portion is attributable to the cost of goods sold.[113]

Regular depreciation is not used unless the taxpayer chooses not to use bonus depreciation for the class of the asset under consideration[114] or §179 expense. If bonus depreciation is available for the asset class, it must be used to recover the newly acquired asset's cost unless the taxpayer elects to forgo it.

Bonus Depreciation

A taxpayer may use bonus depreciation to recover the equipment's cost. This choice is not an election; instead, it is the default option. For equipment placed in service before January 1, 2023, a taxpayer could deduct 100% of the amount for the tax year the property was placed in service.[115] Starting with that date, the rate declines 20% per year. As a result, the maximum bonus depreciation available for assets placed in service during 2023 is **80%.** After January 1, 2027, bonus depreciation is no longer available, except for property with longer production periods.[116]

> **Caution.** The decision to opt out of bonus depreciation is made on a class-by-class basis, not for an individual asset. A tax practitioner should review other units of property in the same class to determine if the election to forgo bonus depreciation is in the client's best interests.

111. IRC §167(a).

112. IRC §168(k).

113. Treas. Reg. §1.263A-1(e)(3)(ii)(I); See Instructions for Schedule C.

114. IRC §168(k)(7).

115. IRC §168(k)(6)(A)(i).

116. IRC §§168(k)(2)(B), (2)(C), and (7)(B).

IRC §179 Expense

IRC §179 provides an alternative method of cost recovery available. Similar to bonus depreciation mentioned previously, taxpayers can generally elect to recover the cost of the equipment with §179 expense deduction in the tax year they place the equipment in service.[117] There are some caveats, however.

- The property must be either tangible property under IRC §168 or computer software and treated as IRC §1245 property.[118]
- Special limits apply to passenger vehicles.[119]
- The deduction is limited to net income from a trade or business.[120]

3

The annual limit for the deduction is indexed for inflation. For assets placed in service during 2023, §179 expensing is available if the total cost of elected §179 expense does not exceed $1,160,000.[121] Additionally, when assets placed in service during 2023 exceed $2,890,000, the limit under §179(b)(1) is reduced from $1,160,000 dollar for dollar.[122] If business use of a §179 asset decreases to 50% or less of total usage, the taxpayer must recapture some amount of the prior §179 depreciation.[123]

> **Note.** For more information on §179 expense, see the 2023 *University of Illinois Federal Tax Workbook,* Chapter 7: Depreciation.

Example 17. Laura has two businesses, one that purchased §179 qualified property of $100,000 and another that purchased §179 qualified property of $1,050,000 in 2023. These transactions do not limit the amount of the potential §179 expense because the total ($1,150,000) is less than the annual limit.

Qualifying and Eligible Property. **Eligible** property is either tangible personal property, subject to §168, or computer software, defined in IRC §197(e)(3)(B). The property must also qualify as §1245 property or meet tests in §§1245(a)(3)(B) – (E).

Once a property is determined to be eligible, it must also be **qualifying.** The property can fail this test in either of two ways.

- Less than 50% is used in trade or business[124]
- It was acquired from a related person, where "related" is defined broadly by IRC §§267(b) or 707(b)[125]

---

117. IRC §179(a).
118. IRC §179(d)(1).
119. IRC §179(b)(5).
120. IRC §179(b)(3).
121. Rev. Proc. 2022-38, 2022-45 IRB 445, providing the annual limit for §179 expense under IRC §179(b)(1).
122. Rev. Proc. 2022-38, 2022-45 IRB 445, providing the annual limit for §179 expense under IRC §179(b)(2).
123. Treas. Reg. §1.791-1(e).
124. Ibid.
125. IRC §179(d)(2)(A).

Thus, not only is property acquired from a relative ineligible for §179 treatment, but so also are the following.

- Inherited property[126]
- Property acquired from a trustee when a taxpayer is a beneficiary of that trust[127]
- Property exchanged between an executor of an estate and a beneficiary unless the property is part of a pecuniary bequest[128]
- Property distributed from a partnership or an S corporation in which a taxpayer owns an interest[129]

Advantages of Using §179 Expense. Independent contractors usually can choose between using §179 expensing and bonus depreciation. As mentioned previously, starting January 1, 2023, bonus depreciation can only be taken for 80% of an asset's adjusted basis, while the full basis can be deducted for §179 purposes. An independent contractor may realize a few other benefits.

- For an independent contractor with significant fourth-quarter purchases, §179 expensing may prevent triggering the mid-quarter convention.[130]
- The §179 expense deduction permits a taxpayer to select some assets to be chosen for the deduction while excluding others.[131] In contrast, bonus depreciation requires that all assets acquired during a tax year be subject to bonus depreciation.[132] By electing the §179 expense deduction for specific assets, instead of including an entire class, it facilitates taxpayers determining more precisely their deductions, and, consequently, their taxable income.
- It may increase the maximum Roth IRA contribution for which a taxpayer having income just over the phase-out range is eligible.[133]

EQUIPMENT LEASING

Leasing may be an attractive alternative to some businesses. With an **operating lease,** the asset owner, or lessor, transfers only the right to use the property to the lessee. The lessor retains ownership of the leased property, and possession of the property reverts to them at the conclusion of the lease. Payments under an operating lease are deductible to the lessee.[134]

Alternately, a **capital lease** is one in which the lessor's sole task is to finance the "leased" asset, and all other rights of ownership transfer to the lessee.[135] As a result, if the leasing transaction constitutes a capital lease, the asset is the lessee's property and, for accounting purposes, is recorded as a fixed asset in the lessee's general ledger. For tax purposes, the lessee deducts the interest portion of the capital lease payment, not the entire lease payment as with an operating lease.[136] Some portion may also be eligible for depreciation, provided that the lease conveys incidents of ownership to the lessee.[137]

---

126. IRC §179(d)(2)(C)(ii).
127. IRC §267(b)(6).
128. IRC §267(b)(13).
129. IRC §§267(b)(10) and 707(b).
130. Treas. Reg. §1.168(d)-1(b)(4)(i).
131. IRC §179(c)(1).
132. IRC §168(k)(7).
133. IRC §408A(c)(3).
134. IRC §162(a)(3); Treas. Reg. §1.162-11(a); Rev. Rul. 55-540, 1955-2 CB 39.
135. Rev. Rul. 55-540, 1955-2 CB 39.
136. Ibid. See §4.01(f).
137. IRS Pub. 946, *How to Depreciate Property*, p. 4 (2022); *Cargill Inc. v. Comm'r*, 91 F.Supp.2d 1293 (D. Minn. Mar. 29, 2000).

According to the Financial Accounting Standards Board (FASB),[138] a transaction is a capital lease if it meets any of the following conditions.

- Ownership of the asset shifts to the lessee by the end of the lease period.
- The lease contains a bargain purchase option, allowing the lessee to buy the property from the lessor for a below-market price.
- The lease term is equal to 75% or more of the estimated economic life of the leased property and the lease cannot be canceled during that time.
- The present value of the minimum lease payments required under the leases is at least 90% of the fair value of the asset at the lease's inception.

If none of these conditions is satisfied, the transaction is considered an operating lease. In that event, the lessee can deduct each lease payment as a business expense. The lessee does not treat the leased property as an asset.

Potential Tax Benefits

The distinction between operating and capital leases carries significance. With a capital lease, the lessee deducts depreciation expense in addition to the interest expense.[139] Thus, the early years of a capital lease may yield larger deductions than an operating lease, although the bookkeeping is more involved because these expenses decrease over time, even as the lease payments are constant. However, the effect of FASB Accounting Standards Codification (ASC) 842, *Leases,* moves additional leases onto the balance sheets of business entities by removing bright-line tests.[140] In contrast, an operating lease enables a constant deduction for the lease payment over its term.

DISPOSITION OF EQUIPMENT[141]

Equipment does not last forever, and independent contractors may wish to dispose of it even before it is no longer fit for use. Before the Tax Cuts and Jobs Act (TCJA), trading in equipment for similar equipment generally resulted in an IRC §1031 like-kind exchange. This legislation disallowed like-kind treatment to the disposition of personal property for transactions occurring after December 31, 2017.[142]

Outright Sale of Equipment

When taxpayers sell equipment, they realize a gain if the amount realized is greater than the equipment's adjusted basis. Conversely, they realize a loss if the amount realized is less than the adjusted basis. The amount realized includes the money received and the fair market value of any property received. Furthermore, the amount realized also includes any liabilities associated with the equipment they transfer to the new owner, such as a mortgage or tax liability.

Trade-In Exchange for New Equipment

When an independent contractor trades in one item of equipment for another, the transaction is reported as a sale for the fair market value of the trade-in property plus a purchase of the full purchase price of the new property. The trade difference amount is no longer reported.

---

138. *Original Pronouncements as Amended: Statement of Financial Accounting Standards No. 13*. Nov. 1976. FASB. [www.fasb.org/Page/ShowPdf?path=aop_FAS13.pdf&title=FAS+13+%28AS+AMENDED%29] Accessed on May 1, 2023.

139. IRS Pub. 946, *How to Depreciate Property*, p. 4 (2022); *Cargill Inc. v. Comm'r*, 91 F.Supp.2d 1293 (D. Minn. Mar. 29, 2000).

140. *Review Engagements: Implementation of the New Lease Standard*, p. 2. Jan. 18, 2023. AICPA Center for Plain English Accounting. [us.aicpa.org/content/dam/aicpa/interestareas/centerforplainenglishaccounting/resources/2023/cpea-january-2023-report-review-engagements-implementation-of-the-new-lease-standard.pdf] Accessed on May 5, 2023.

141. IRS Pub. 544, *Sales and Other Dispositions of Assets*.

142. *Tax Cuts and Jobs Act*, PL 115-97, §13303.

Example 18. Bosworth operates a vegetable distributorship as a sole proprietorship. On June 1, 2023, Bosworth trades in a used tomato packing machine with a fair market value of $50,000 and a tax basis of $0 and acquires a new tomato packing machine with a full purchase price of $90,000. Bosworth reports the disposition of the used property on Form 4797, *Sales of Business Property,* resulting in a gain of $50,000. The full purchase price of $90,000 must be capitalized under bonus or regular depreciation or expensed under §179. The depreciation amount is reported on Bosworth's Form 4562, *Depreciation and Amortization,* and Schedule C.

Abandonment of Equipment

When a taxpayer abandons equipment, they relinquish ownership without transferring it to a new owner. The taxpayer must intend to "discard the asset irrevocably."[143]

Gain or Loss.[144] Abandoning old equipment results in a loss under IRC §165 usually, but not necessarily. If a taxpayer transfers a liability to a new owner with the abandonment, a gain could result if the remaining basis was less than the relinquished liability. Otherwise, the loss on an abandonment is equal to the asset's adjusted basis, less any **recourse** indebtedness. If **nonrecourse** debt is attached to an abandoned asset, its sale or exchange is controlled by Treas. Reg. §1.168(i)-8(e)(1). Either gain or loss, the transaction is reported in the year of abandonment on Form 4797 part II, *Ordinary Gains and Losses*, Line 10.[145]

Casualty Losses.[146] A casualty is the damage, destruction, or loss of property resulting from an unforeseen event that is sudden, unexpected, or unusual. Fires, theft, storms, floods, tornadoes, vandalism, earthquakes, and other accidents are examples of casualties. Although an uninsured casualty loss may result in abandonment, an insurance recovery may result in a taxable gain, particularly if the taxpayer had substantially depreciated the property.

PERSONAL USE OF EQUIPMENT[147]

Changing an asset from business to personal use is treated as a disposition in the year of conversion, provided it was being treated as modified accelerated cost recovery system (MACRS) property. If the property is used partially for personal use and partially for business use, special provisions may change how the owner recovers its cost.

Depreciation Recapture[148]

If an independent contractor elected §179 expense deduction for property where business use decreases to 50% or less, they are required to recapture of a portion of the expense already taken.

But the amount recaptured is not simply the entire amount of §179 expense taken, rather it is the **benefit** derived from the §179 expense deduction over what the depreciation under §168 would have been if the §179 election had not been taken.

---

143. Treas. Reg. §1.168(i)-8(e)(2).

144. Ibid; IRS Pub. 5712, *Capitalization of Tangible Property Audit Technique Guide*, p. 143 (2022).

145. 2022 Instructions for Form 4797.

146. Treas. Reg. §1.165-7.

147. Treas. Reg. §1.168(i)-4.

148. Treas. Reg. §1.179-1(e)(1); Treas. Reg. §1.168(i)(c); IRC §280F(b)(2) and (d)(4).

Example 19. On April 15, 2021, Hank purchased a small desk for business use, electing to expense its $5,000 purchase price under §179. Assume that in 2021, Hank elected out of bonus depreciation for other 7-year assets. In 2023, Hank's business use drops to 40%.

In 2023, Hank must recapture $2,710, determined as follows.

§179 deduction claimed in 2021		$5,000
Allowable deduction (MACRS 7-year property) instead of §179 deduction		
2021 depreciation ($5,000 × 14.29%)	$ 715	
2022 depreciation ($5,000 × 24.49%)	1,225	
2023 depreciation ($5,000 × 17.49% × 40% business use)	350	
Total allowable depreciation	$2,290	(2,290)
Recapture amount		$2,710

The recapture amount on Hank's Form 4797, line 35, is reduced by almost half because the recaptured amount is the excess benefit, not the total benefit. The recapture amount is reported back on the Schedule C on which it was originally claimed. Hank needs to increase his basis in the property by the recapture amount. If Hank had retained the business use of the desk for seven years, no recapture would have been required.

Note. The recapture is triggered when business use drops to 50% or less, not when the asset is sold.

Depreciation is recaptured in the year the taxpayer personally disposes of it, following the provisions of either IRC §§1245 or 1250. If the property is converted to personal use in the year it was placed in service, it is not eligible for depreciation.

If the business use of listed property falls to 50% or less, the taxpayer must recapture excess depreciation in the year the use falls below that threshold. The taxpayer must also use the alternative depreciation system (ADS) under §168(g).[149] As a result, the taxpayer must use straight-line depreciation to recover the balance of the equipment's cost. If the business use is greater than 50% but less than 100%, the depreciation is limited to that associated with business use.

Note. The possibility of either recapture or a reduced depreciation deduction highlights the importance of maintaining records, particularly if the taxpayer may elect §179 expensing for the property or the property is listed property.

This change of use can have unfortunate economic consequences. For example, a taxpayer who purchases a luxury vehicle can benefit from substantial first-year depreciation, up to $20,200 for vehicles placed in service during 2023.[150] The change to personal use can affect the depreciation normally allowable for the vehicle.

Allocating Equipment Use Expenses Between Personal and Business

The method of allocation varies according to the nature of the property. It makes sense to allocate a vehicle's use between business and personal use based on the mileage for each use.

149. IRC §280F(b)(2)(A).

150. Rev. Proc. 2023-14, 2023-06 IRB 466.

SELECTED TRADES OR BUSINESSES

Construction Workers

Generally, independent contractors working in construction can expense any tool costing less than $200.[151] With the appropriate accounting policy in place, these construction workers can treat more expensive tools as an immediate expense.[152]

However, it may be preferable to depreciate equipment over time. For a lengthy construction project, a deduction in a future year may be more valuable because the income generated by the equipment may be recognized in a future year. Generally, small tools can be expensed. In some cases, large equipment must be capitalized.

Most people assume that casualty losses result in tax losses. However, unexpected results may occur if an insurance recovery exceeds the adjusted basis in the lost property.

> **Example 20.** Fred, a 70-year-old carpenter who works as an independent contractor, lost his tools when they were stolen from his shop on July 4, 2023. He acquired these tools between 2009 and 2012, and they were either fully depreciated or Fred had elected §179 expensing for them. He received a settlement from his insurance company of $18,000 in September 2023. Their total original cost exceeded $25,000.
>
> Disheartened by the loss, Fred decides to retire and does not replace the tools. As a result, he recognizes a 2023 gain of $18,000 from the casualty.

Gig Economy Workers

Gig workers use a wide variety of equipment to which these principles apply. Most gig-related income-producing activities require a computer to manage, making it a depreciable asset.

For a gig worker who provides ride-sharing services, their vehicle becomes property held for the production of income and is thus eligible for depreciation.[153] However, eligibility for depreciation is accompanied by strict documentation standards under IRC §274(d) and the possibility of depreciation recapture if the business use declines to less than 50%.

> **Example 21.** In early January 2019, Jim purchased a $30,000 luxury vehicle to provide ride-sharing services. During that year, he put 32,161 miles on the car, documented by a December 31, 2019, receipt for the oil change at the dealership. Using an app on his cell phone, Jim determined that he had put 27,595 miles on the car with his ride-sharing services. This resulted in 85.8% business use of the vehicle (27,595 business miles ÷ 32,161 total miles). Because Jim provided such good documentation, his tax practitioner had no trouble determining that Jim qualified for the $18,100 bonus depreciation deduction for 2019, although this amount was reduced to $15,530 ($18,100 full bonus depreciation × 85.8% business use).
>
> The next year started briskly, but Jim provided few rides after mid-March because of COVID-19. For 2020, his mileage app showed 8,796 miles, of which only 4,230 miles or 48% were for his ride-sharing business. As a result, the ride-sharing business was no longer the dominant use of the vehicle.
>
> This change forced a difficult decision on Jim's tax practitioner. He was required to recapture the excess depreciation expense on the previous year's tax return, causing an increase in Jim's taxable income even though the cash generated by his business was down significantly. In addition, Jim's tax return could no longer use an accelerated depreciation method. Any future depreciation would be subject to the ADS requirement for straight-line depreciation.

---

151. Treas. Reg. §1.162-3(c)(1)(iv).

152. Ibid.

153. IRC §167(a)(2).

Short-Term Rental of Residence.[154] Some gig workers are landlords, renting out their homes or other property on a short-term basis. In some cases, the individual does not need to recognize income from the short-term rental of a residence, provided they do not deduct any expense associated with the rental, but only if the period rented is 14 or fewer days during the tax year.

Note. For more information on rental use of personal property, see the 2020 *University of Illinois Federal Tax Workbook,* Volume B, Chapter 6: Schedule E. This can be found at **uofi.tax/arc** [taxschool.illinois.edu/taxbookarchive].

3

Truck Drivers

Independent trucker drivers generally own or lease equipment, making depreciation alternatives important considerations. The largest expenditures are for equipment, such as tractors, trucks, and trailers.

A **tractor** is a highway vehicle designed to tow another vehicle, such as a trailer or a semitrailer. It does not carry cargo on the same chassis as the engine.[155] A tractor is depreciated over three years.[156]

A **truck** is a highway vehicle designed to transport a load on the same chassis as the engine, even if it is also equipped to tow a vehicle, such as a trailer or a semitrailer.[157] A truck is depreciated over five years.[158]

A **trailer** or **semitrailer** is customarily used in connection with a vehicle that is equipped to tow it.[159] A trailer is a vehicle pulled by a tractor in hauling freight. A trailer or trailer-mounted container is depreciated over five years.[160]

Trucks, tractors, trailers, and semitrailers are eligible for expensing under §179 or for bonus depreciation under §168(k).

Note. Ownership of a heavy vehicle normally subjects owner of the truck, tractor, or trailer to an excise tax defined in IRC §4051. These owners must file Form 2290, *Heavy Highway Vehicle Use Tax Return*, if they register a qualifying vehicle in a state or Washington D.C. They must also file Form 720, *Quarterly Federal Excise Tax Return*, to report fuel consumption tax.

Truckers may also need tools in their businesses, which are eligible for the safe harbor election treating them as current expenses.

TRAVEL EXPENSES

Independent contractors are likely to incur expenses for traveling to operate their trade and generate income. While this type of expenditure may be common, the rules and regulations surrounding the deductibility of expenses can be nuanced and specific. This section identifies what types of expenditures qualify as travel expenses and discusses the various rules and restrictions for deducting them.

---

154. Prop. Treas. Reg. §1.280A-3(b).

155. Treas. Reg. §145.4051-1(e)(1).

156. IRS Pub. 946, *How to Depreciate Property*.

157. Treas. Reg. §145.4051-1(e)(2).

158. IRS Pub. 946, *How to Depreciate Property*.

159. Instructions for Form 2290; IRS Pub. 946, *How to Depreciate Property*.

160. IRS Pub. 946 *How to Depreciate Property*.

GENERAL RULES

Independent contractors can deduct travel expenses they incur in the operation of their business and employment.[161] The enactment of TCJA resulted in employees no longer being able to deduct unreimbursed business expenses, such as travel, as a miscellaneous itemized deduction subject to the 2% floor.[162] For independent contractors filing a Schedule C, the TCJA did not alter their ability to deduct business expenses. Consequently, independent contractors who incur travel expenses may generally deduct them if they meet the following criteria.[163]

1. The taxpayer incurs the expense in pursuit of a trade or business.
2. The taxpayer incurs the expense while away from home.
3. The expense is ordinary and necessary.

Pursuit of a Trade or Business[164]

The Code and regulations specify that a taxpayer may deduct transportation costs for trips made primarily for business purposes. Therefore, transportation costs for trips made primarily for personal purposes are not deductible, even when they incur qualifying business expenses that are deductible. The distinction between business and personal purposes of a trip and the associated transportation costs depends on the facts and circumstances surrounding the nature of the taxpayer's business and the trip itself. The taxpayer must distinguish between business and personal activities they perform on the trip and the duration of those activities in relation to the length of the trip as a whole.

Example 22. Ned is a marketing consultant who resides in Illinois and takes a 5-week trip to Orlando, Florida, in 2023. While on this trip, Ned spends two weeks meeting with his business clients and attending conferences for marketing professionals. Ned spends the remaining three weeks of his trip as a vacation, golfing alone and relaxing in a resort. Because Ned spends three out of the five weeks of the trip vacationing, Ned's trip is considered primarily for personal purposes, and he **cannot deduct** any of the transportation costs incurred traveling to and from Florida. However, Ned can deduct other qualifying business expenses (including transportation costs) he incurs during the two weeks he performs business activities in Florida.

Example 23. Assume the same facts as **Example 22,** except Ned stays an additional three weeks on the same trip to Orlando, Florida. Ned spends those additional three weeks engaging in business activities. Looking at his trip, Ned spends five out of the eight weeks of the trip for business. Therefore, the majority of the trip is for business purposes, and Ned **can deduct** the transportation costs to and from Florida.

Away from Home[165]

A taxpayer may deduct travel expenses they incur for trips where the taxpayer is traveling away from home. In the context of §162(a)(2), home refers to the taxpayer's tax home.[166] Because of this requirement, determining a taxpayer's tax home is essential in evaluating the deductibility of travel expenses. The determination of a taxpayer's tax home is described in detail earlier in this chapter.

---

161. Treas. Reg. §1.162-2.

162. IRC §67; *Tax Cuts and Jobs Act*, PL 115-97, §11045.

163. IRC §162(a).

164. Treas. Reg. §1.162-2(b).

165. IRC §162(a)(2).

166. *Daly v. Comm'r*, 72 TC 190 (1979), *aff'd* 662 F.2d 253 (4th Cir. 1981).

An additional criterion that the IRS imposes on a taxpayer for their travel to be considered away from home is the need for the taxpayer to sleep or rest as part of the travel.[167] The IRS clarifies that the respite from work only fulfills the rest requirement if it is long enough to provide adequate time for reasonable sleep or rest. Therefore, the taxpayer does not need to be away from home from sunup to sundown on a given day to meet this requirement. However, a 1-hour break or nap in one's car would not fulfill the rest requirement, and the IRS would not deem the travel away from home.

3

Example 24. Use the same facts as **Example 23.** Ned's tax home is in Illinois, where he is a resident and maintains his principal office. Because the trip to Florida was eight weeks, Ned stayed at a hotel for the duration of the trip. Ned's trip to Florida meets the requirements for being away from home in that he was physically away from his tax home in Illinois while in Florida, and he slept and rested during the trip to meet the demands of his work.

Ordinary and Necessary Expenses[168]

Along with other business expenses, travel expenses must be ordinary and necessary for a taxpayer to deduct them. Due to the subjectivity of this criteria, the ability to deduct travel expenses depends on the facts and circumstances surrounding the taxpayer's business and trip. The IRS provides a listing of potential expenses that a taxpayer may deduct while incurred during travel.[169]

- Transportation, including airfare, train or bus tickets, and automobile expenses
- Fares for taxis and buses
- Baggage and shipping costs
- Automobile expenses, including actual expenses or standard mileage rates, or car rental expenses
- Lodging and meals, provided neither is lavish or extravagant
- Cleaning services, such as dry cleaning and laundry
- Telephone and other communication expenses for business calls and correspondence
- Tips associated with any of the expenses listed above
- Other expenses associated with traveling that would be reasonably ordinary and necessary

Note. The IRS and legislative courts do not provide a bright-line test to determine whether expenses are ordinary and necessary, instead stating that the facts and circumstances surrounding the expenses dictate whether they would fit those criteria.[170] As such, the determination of whether an expense is ordinary and necessary is subjective, and the IRS could challenge it with relative ease. Because the burden of proof is on the taxpayer to substantiate their position on this matter, it may be highly beneficial for taxpayers to maintain records of their travel expenses with detailed information as to where they were traveling to, who they were meeting with, and what activities they performed during the trip. This information, along with documented reasons and justification for the expenses, can help taxpayers defend their position if the IRS challenges them.

167. IRS Pub. 463, *Travel, Gift, and Car Expenses.*

168. IRC §162(a).

169. IRS Pub. 463, *Travel, Gift, and Car Expenses.*

170. IRC §162(a).

When assessing whether an expense is necessary or ordinary, a taxpayer should consider the function of the expense and how it pertains to their business. To illustrate this concept, the regulations draw specific attention to travel expenses for a taxpayer's spouse.[171] Generally, travel expenses that the taxpayer incurs for their spouse, family member, or other individuals to accompany them are not deductible unless there is a bona fide business purpose. If the individual is an employee or performs substantive work for the business, their travel expenses would be ordinary and necessary, and therefore deducible. Otherwise, if the spouse or individual has no business purpose or only provides incidental menial tasks or services, the expenses for their travel would not qualify as necessary or ordinary from a business perspective.

DOMESTIC VS. FOREIGN TRAVEL

While identifying the costs and their business purpose is critical in determining the deductibility of travel expenses, other factors also warrant review. One such factor is whether the taxpayer's travel is abroad or within the United States. While travel within the United States follows the general rules specified earlier in this section, traveling abroad has different rules and nuances for deducting travel expenses.

Travel Within the United States[172]

Independent contractors traveling within the United States, which includes all 50 states and the District of Columbia, follow the general rules described earlier in this section. The criteria of the expenses required to pursue a trade or business are of key importance when comparing domestic to foreign travel. For travel costs within the United States, a taxpayer may deduct the entirety of travel costs provided that the purpose of the trip was primarily for business. Travel costs outside of the United States have different rules, which this section describes later.

For trips where part of the travel is outside of the United States, taxpayers must account for the travel costs associated with the portion within the United States separately from those outside the United States. The portion of the trip within the United States follows the general rules, while the portion outside of the United States follows the rules for foreign travel.

Travel Outside the United States

Similar to travel inside the United States, deducting the expense of traveling outside the United States depends on how much of the trip was for business purposes. However, additional criteria and nuances are associated with travel outside the United States compared to within.

Entirely For Business Purposes.[173] Taxpayers can deduct all travel costs for trips where the purpose is entirely for business. This concept may sound similar to trips within the United States that are entirely for business purposes. However, travel outside the United States adds four exceptions to trips where the purpose is not entirely for business purposes. If **any of the four exceptions are met,** the IRS considers the trip entirely for business purposes, and all travel costs are deductible. The four exceptions follow.

1. The taxpayer does not have substantial control over the travel arrangements of the trip. This lack of control does not apply specifically to the timing of the trip but rather to other factors that include the following.
    - The taxpayer is reimbursed by their employer for the cost of the trip or receives an allowance for travel expenses, **and**
    - There is no familial (including half-siblings and spouses) or fiduciary relationship between the employer and taxpayer, and the taxpayer does not own more than 10% of outstanding stock in the employed company, **or**
    - The taxpayer is not a managing executive with the authority of necessitating business travel not subject to veto.

---

171. Treas. Reg. §1.162-2(c).

172. IRS Pub. 463, *Travel, Gift, and Car Expenses*.

173. Treas. Reg. §1.274-4.

> **Note.** The IRS generally considers self-employed taxpayers as having substantial control over their travel arrangements. Consequently, self-employed taxpayers are unlikely to meet this exception.

3

2. The taxpayer was outside of the United States for no more than a week during the trip. While this exception may seem simple in concept, the regulations specify how a taxpayer can meet this exception, which is as follows.
   - The taxpayer must factor in both business and nonbusiness activities in assessing the number of days of the trip.
   - The IRS states that one week means seven consecutive days in this context.
   - The taxpayer does not include the day they left the United States in counting the number of days the trip was outside the United States.
   - The taxpayer includes the day they return to the United States in counting the number of days the trip was outside the United States.
3. The taxpayer's personal activities account for less than 25% of all activities during the trip. Additionally, the taxpayer must travel outside the United States for more than one week. Unlike the second exception, the taxpayer counts **both** the days for traveling from and returning to the United States in this assessment.
4. A personal vacation was not a major consideration in arranging the trip.

> **Note.** The fourth exception is fairly subjective, and taxpayers should consider the facts and circumstances surrounding the trip and the personal vacation in determining whether the exception applies. For example, bringing family members who are not involved in the business may indicate that a vacation was a major consideration for the trip.

Primarily For Business Purposes.[174] For travel outside of the United States that is primarily for business purposes but also has personal purposes, the taxpayer is generally not able to deduct all the travel expenses. This rule differs from travel in the United States primarily for business purposes, where all travel expenses are deductible. Instead, the taxpayer must use an allocation formula to determine the deductible portion of travel expenses. The allocation is based on the percentage of time the taxpayer spent for business purposes for the entire trip. The formula is as follows.

$$\textbf{Deductible percentage of travel costs} = \frac{\textbf{Total \# of business days outside the U.S.}}{\textbf{Total \# of business and nonbusiness days outside the U.S.}}$$

174. Treas. Reg. §1.274-4(d).

For calculating the deductible percentage of travel costs, the regulations stipulate that a day is a full business day, even if it consists of both business and personal activities, if the day meets any of the following criteria.

- Transportation days are business days when the taxpayer travels to and from a destination for business purposes. However, if the taxpayer takes a non-direct route for a destination for personal activities, only the days that a taxpayer would travel if using a direct route between destinations for business purposes can count as business days.
- Days on which the taxpayer's presence is required for business activities are full business days, even if the taxpayer spends most of that day on personal activities.
- Days on which the taxpayer's primary activity during working hours is for business purposes are business days. If there are circumstances beyond the taxpayer's control that prevent them from working on a given day, then those days are also business days.
- Weekends and holidays are business days if they fall between days for business purposes. If a taxpayer remains at a destination after the conclusion of their business for personal reasons, the weekends and holidays that occur during that time do not constitute business days.

Example 25. Ned, the marketing consultant from **Example 22,** travels to Bermuda for 20 days, including both the departure and return dates. For the first six days, Ned attends a conference and spends most of his time on business activities during those days. Ned did not work the following two days due to a hurricane but resumed his work by meeting with a customer and working on a marketing campaign with them for four days. Ned took the following four days off to sightsee and relax on the beach. None of those four days took place over a weekend. Ned spent the remaining three days attending a different marketing conference and flew back to Illinois on the last day.

Ned spent 14 days performing business activities by attending two conferences, traveling to and from the United States, and meeting with a client (6+3+4+1). The two days that Ned could not work because of the hurricane are included as business days, as Ned was unable to work due to circumstances beyond his control. Therefore, the total number of business days for Ned's trip was 16 (14+2). The remaining four days that Ned spent as a vacation were personal. Ned can deduct 80% of his travel expenses for his trip to Bermuda (16 business days ÷ 20 total days).

Primarily For Personal Purposes. Similar to travel within the United States, expenses for travel outside the United States for trips primarily for personal purposes are not deductible. However, nontravel expenses incurred for business purposes on those trips are deductible.

TRANSPORTATION FOR TRAVEL NOT AWAY FROM TAX HOME[175]

While taxpayers can deduct expenses for trips away from their tax home as travel expenses, they can also deduct certain costs within their tax home as transportation expenses. Such costs can include car, air, rail, bus, and taxi transportation. The deductibility of these costs primarily depends on the point of departure and destination of the travel. The following diagram from IRS Pub. 463, *Travel, Gift, and Car Expenses,* illustrates these principles.

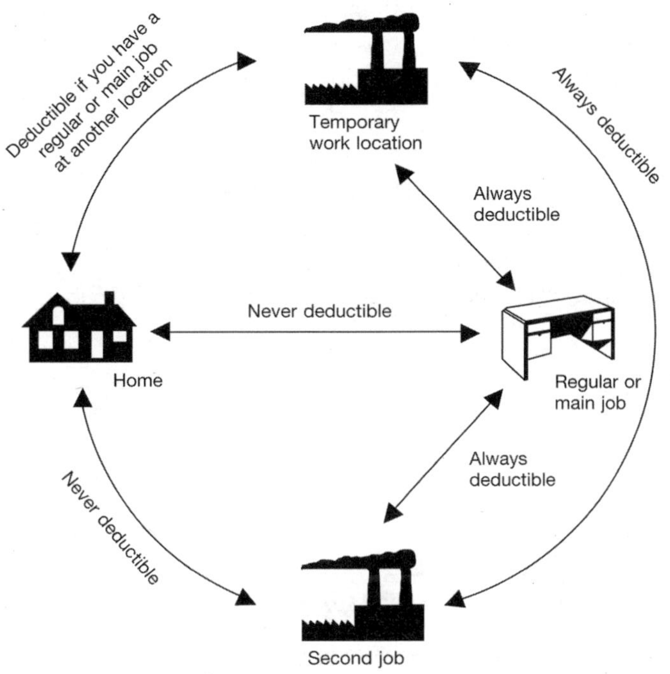

Home: The place where you reside. Transportation expenses between your home and your main or regular place of work are personal commuting expenses.

Regular or main job: Your principal place of business. If you have more than one job, you must determine which one is your regular or main job. Consider the time you spend at each, the activity you have at each, and the income you earn at each.

Temporary work location: A place where your work assignment is realistically expected to last (and does in fact last) one year or less. Unless you have a regular place of business, you can only deduct your transportation expenses to a temporary work location outside your metropolitan area.

Second job: If you regularly work at two or more places in one day, whether or not for the same employer, you can deduct your transportation expenses of getting from one workplace to another. If you don't go directly from your first job to your second job, you can only deduct the transportation expenses of going directly from your first job to your second job. You can't deduct your transportation expenses between your home and a second job on a day off from your main job.

175. IRS Pub. 463, *Travel, Gift, and Car Expenses.*

Personal Residence

Generally, travel from a taxpayer's residence to their workplace is not deductible. The IRS considers this travel a regular commute and does not qualify for a deduction. However, a notable exception to this rule involves a taxpayer having a temporary work location.

Temporary Work Location

Taxpayers may have more than one work location for a given business. Similar to temporary and indefinite employment rules for determining one's tax home, a taxpayer may consider a work location as temporary if they reasonably expect their employment at that location to last for no more than one year. Taxpayers can deduct expenses for travel from their residence to a temporary work location, provided the taxpayer has a different location as their principal place of business. This chapter defines a taxpayer's principal place of business and its criteria earlier in the tax home section.

Second Job

Travel expenses to and from a second job are deductible when the taxpayer travels from or to their principal place of business or temporary work location. Travel expenses to and from the second job and the taxpayer's residence are commuting and are not deductible.

SELECTED TRADES OR BUSINESSES

Construction Workers

Taxpayers in the construction industry have an added consideration for travel expenses regarding when to capitalize them as part of a construction project. The regulations stipulate that taxpayers must capitalize all direct costs and certain indirect costs allocable to real property.[176] Therefore, construction workers must identify whether the travel costs they incur are direct or indirect costs requiring capitalization.

Direct costs include direct material and labor costs, while indirect costs are all other costs.[177] Travel costs typically fall under indirect costs. Construction workers would then need to determine whether the travel costs directly benefitted the construction project or were incurred because of performing the construction itself. This assessment is subjective, and the facts and circumstances surrounding the nature of the project and travel expenses drive the assessment. The construction worker should include the travel expenses as indirect costs for capitalization if they determine that the travel costs in question directly benefitted or were necessary for the construction project.

> **Note.** For a more in-depth analysis of capitalization rules, exceptions, and de minimis alternatives available to taxpayers, see the 2023 *University of Illinois Federal Tax Workbook,* Chapter 2: Capitalization vs. Repair Review.

Gig Economy Workers

While gig workers must adhere to the general rules for deducting travel expenses, they should be mindful of the locations to which and from which they travel, particularly if they have a home office. A gig worker can deduct transportation costs from their residence to another work location if the office in their home serves as their principal place of business.[178] These deductible expenses include travel for meeting with customers or attending business meetings.

---

176. Treas. Reg. §1.263A-1(a)(3)(i).

177. Ibid.

178. IRS Pub. 463, *Travel, Gift, and Car Expenses.*

Truck Drivers[179]

As discussed earlier in this chapter, truck drivers, in particular, are likely to have unconventional tax homes due to the nature of the business requiring frequent mobility. Consequently, truck drivers may find themselves where an entire city or general area is their tax home, making local travel expenses nondeductible under the general rules for travel expenses.

However, truck drivers can deduct certain expenses for transportation and travel through their trucks. Semi-trucks are qualified nonpersonal use vehicles, indicating that the majority of use for the vehicle by design is nonpersonal.[180] Truck drivers, therefore, must use actual expenses incurred in using and maintaining their trucks instead of a standard mileage rate for any deductions.

Truck drivers cannot deduct any fines for traffic violations. As with other business deductions, truck drivers should maintain records of the costs associated with these truck expenses to substantiate their deductibility if the IRS challenges them.

MEALS AND ENTERTAINMENT EXPENSES

An independent contractor will likely incur meals and entertainment expenses. Depending on the facts and circumstances, these costs can significantly impact a contract's or project's profitability and are subject to more scrutiny than other expenses because of the unique and varied rules for deductibility applicable to them. This section covers the general regulations surrounding meals and entertainment and highlights aspects of these expenses unique to independent contractors in specific industries.

BASIC PRINCIPLES FOR ENTERTAINMENT DEDUCTION

Entertainment expenses are costs associated with activities that constitute recreation or amusement.[181] These expenses include attending sporting events, social events such as parties, stage shows, and other similar costs.[182] Historically, the deductibility of entertainment expenses was not straightforward and subject to specific criteria. After the enactment of the TCJA, entertainment expenses are subject to more simplified and encompassing restrictions for deductibility. However, some aspects of entertainment expenses still exist that taxpayers should be aware of and consider.

Generally Nondeductible[183]

The TCJA generally made entertainment expenses nondeductible since its enactment in 2017.[184] This change eliminates various costs qualifying as entertainment activities that taxpayers could previously deduct. Entertainment events that taxpayers host or attend with clients or other business affiliates for purposes of business are no longer deductible. Additionally, costs for using facilities for entertainment, including rent, depreciation, lease payments, etc., are also nondeductible.[185] Notably, membership dues for clubs fall under nondeductible entertainment expenses, regardless of whether the club is for business, entertainment, or other social purposes.[186]

179. Ibid.

180. Treas. Reg. §1.274-5(k)(2).

181. IRC §274(a).

182. Treas. Reg. §1.274-2(b)(1).

183. IRC §274(a).

184. *Tax Cuts and Jobs Act,* PL 115-97, §13304(a).

185. IRS Pub. 463, *Travel, Gift, and Car Expenses.*

186. IRC §274(a)(3).

Example 26. Pamela is a floral designer whose business specializes in making floral arrangements for various customer needs. In 2023, Pamela hosted a customer-appreciation party costing $1,200. She also spent $130 for an annual membership to a local horticulture club which functions primarily as a social organization. Under the TCJA rules, Pamela cannot deduct either the costs of hosting her party or her annual club membership expense. Both expenditures fall under nondeductible entertainment expenses.

Deductible Entertainment Expenses

Entertainment expenses taxpayers incur that are ordinary and necessary for the type of business in **which** they engage may be deductible.[187]

Example 27. Use the same facts as **Example 26,** except that Pamela hosts a floral show, renting space at a local venue to display a showcase of her floral arrangements for the upcoming season. While hosting this event would generally constitute nondeductible entertainment expenses for most business industries, Pamela's business relies on these events to promote and sell her floral arrangements. Therefore, Pamela could deduct the costs of hosting the floral show.

In addition to business-specific considerations, there are exceptions to the general nondeductible rule for entertainment expenses that taxpayers may deduct.[188]

- The cost of **food and beverages for their employees,** provided the taxpayer furnishes them on their business premises
- Entertainment expenses that taxpayers included as **compensation** for their employees as wages
- **Reimbursed entertainment expenses** from an employer (provided the employer did not include them in the taxpayer's wages as compensation) or other individuals (if the taxpayer can substantiate them)
- **Recreational expenses** for a taxpayer's employees, such as holiday parties or other social gatherings
- Entertainment expenses directly related to **business meetings** for employees, stockholders, agents, or directors
- Entertainment expenses for attending business meetings for IRC §§501(c)(3) and 501(a) **exempt organizations**
- Entertainment expenses for goods or services that the taxpayer makes **available to the general public,** which would not include employees or an exclusive list of guests.
- Entertainment expenses for goods or services that the taxpayer **sells to customers**
- Entertainment expenses a taxpayer pays a **non-employee as compensation,** except for expenses that are required to be included (or would be required except that the amount is less than $600) in any information return filed by such taxpayer

Example 28. Use the same facts as **Example 26.** Pamela hosts a customer appreciation event at a local venue, inviting 50 customers as guests. Because the event is not open to the public and is restricted only to the customers she invited, Pamela cannot deduct the cost of renting the space from the venue as an entertainment expense. If she opened the event to the public in addition to the customers she specifically invited, she could deduct the expense.

---

187. Treas. Reg. §1.274-2(d).

188. IRC §274(e).

BASIC PRINCIPLES FOR MEALS DEDUCTION

Taxpayers can deduct meals that are not lavish or extravagant for which they or their employees are present at the furnishing, subject to some limitations covered in this section.[189] Unlike the deductibility of entertainment expenses, the deductibility of meals has remained consistent and unchanged by the provisions of the TCJA. However, Congress temporarily allowed taxpayers to deduct 100% of business meals purchased from a qualified restaurant for the 2021 and 2022 tax years to provide relief to the restaurant industry during the COVID-19 pandemic.[190] For the 2023 tax year, this provision is no longer in effect. Taxpayers must adhere to the general rules as follows.

3

50% Limit[191]

Taxpayers are generally subject to a 50% deduction limit for business meals. Such meals include those for business meetings and while traveling for business. As with other business expenses, meals are deductible only if they are ordinary and necessary. The IRS clarifies that meals are ordinary if the expenditure is common in the trade or business in which the taxpayer engages. Furthermore, the IRS distinguishes meals as necessary when appropriate for the business.

Note. This clarification is helpful, as some might interpret the term **necessary** to be synonymous with required. The IRS explicitly states that a meal does not necessarily have to be a requirement for it to be a necessary expense to qualify for the deduction.[192]

The meal costs subject to the 50% limit include food and beverage and any tax or tips the taxpayer incurs on said purchase. Conversely, the cost of traveling to and from the meal location is not included in the meal cost subject to the 50% limit.

Example 29. Buddy is an independent contractor who repairs and refurbishes condiment dispensing machines. He meets with one of his clients for lunch to discuss future projects. Buddy paid a $22 cab fare to arrive at the restaurant, $50 for his meal and his client's, which included sales tax, and $10 for a tip. Buddy's meal costs include the food, beverage, sales tax, and tip, totaling $60 ($50 + $10). Therefore, Buddy can deduct $30 as a meal expense ($60 × 50%). The $22 cab fare is deductible as a transportation cost.

Business entertainment may include food and beverage at an event. The meal is only deductible if separately stated on the invoice or is otherwise billed independently from the rest of the entertainment expense.

Example 30. Use the same facts as from **Example 29.** Buddy hosts two customer appreciation parties during 2023. He only invites specific customers to both parties, and the events do not meet an exception to the general nondeductible rule for entertainment expenses. The invoice for the first party is $500 for the entire event, of which $100 is **estimated** to be the portion for food and beverage. The vendor does not itemize the invoice, as the pricing for their events is all-inclusive. The invoice for the second party is $650, which includes an itemized $120 for food and beverage. While Buddy is not able to deduct any amount as entertainment expenses for the two parties, he can deduct $60 in meal expenses for the second party ($120 × 50%). If the $100 of food and beverage for the first party had been itemized or billed separately, Buddy could deduct an additional $50 ($100 × 50%) in meals for 2023.

---

189. IRC §274(k).

190. *Consolidated Appropriations Act of 2021,* PL 116-260, §210.

191. IRS Pub. 463, *Travel, Gift, and Car Expenses.*

192. Ibid.

Practitioner Planning Tip

Because the deductibility of meals during entertainment relies on the explicit statement or separation of the cost of food and beverages from the other entertainment costs, practitioners should relay the importance of maintaining records and documentation to their clients to support such deductions. Taxpayers with copies of invoices or itemized receipts can better defend their positions if challenged by the IRS regarding these expenditures.

Exceptions to the 50% Limit[193]

The meal cost is fully deductible if the taxpayer meets any of the following criteria.

- The cost of meals that taxpayers included as **compensation** for their employees as wages
- **Reimbursed meal expenses** from an employer (provided the employer did not include them in the taxpayer's wages as compensation) or other individuals (if the taxpayer can substantiate them)
- **Meals a taxpayer provides for their employees** during events such as holiday parties or other social gatherings
- Meals at functions that the taxpayer makes **available to the general public,** which would not include employees or an exclusive list of guests
- Meals that the taxpayer **sells to customers**
- Meals a taxpayer pays a **non-employee as compensation,** except for expenses that were or would be reported on an information return under Chapter 61, subchapter A part III of the tax code
- Meals that the taxpayer **pays or reimburses for an employee as part of their moving expenses** provided the taxpayer included them in the employee's taxable wages
- Meals that the taxpayer provides to specific **commercial crew members** or on particular **oil or gas platforms or drilling rigs** (see §274(n)(2)(C) for further details)

Example 31. Nicole is an IT consultant with an office in Omaha, Nebraska. In 2023, Nicole hires Stanley as a new administrative assistant to work in her office in Omaha. Stanley was living in Idaho at the time, so Nicole agrees to reimburse his moving expenses from Idaho to Nebraska, including $50 for meals during the move. Nicole includes the $50 reimbursement for the meals in Stanley's wages and reports them on his 2023 Form W-2. Nicole deducts the full $50 reimbursement for the meals as wage expense on her 2023 tax return and does not reduce the amount by 50% per the general meals deduction rule.

193. IRC §274(n)(2).

SELECTED TRADES OR BUSINESSES

For independent contractors working in the construction and gig economy industries, taxpayers adhere to the general rules, limitations, and exceptions to those limitations. However, independent contractors in the trucking industry have unique rules compared to the aforementioned industries.

Truck Drivers

3

Truck drivers are subject to federal hours of service by the Department of Transportation per Title 49 of the Code of Federal Regulations (CFR) Part 395. This includes certain air transportation workers, interstate truck operators and bus drivers, certain railroad employees, and certain merchant mariners under Coast Guard regulations.[194] For truck drivers and motor carriers subject to federal hours of service, the Code does not subject the taxpayers to a 50% limitation on meal expenses. Instead, truck drivers deduct **80% of their meal expenses.**[195] However, for the meals to be deductible, the truck driver must consume the food or beverage while away from their tax home while working.

The 80% deductibility provision only pertains to the general limitation, where the Code only changes the language to the amount that a taxpayer can deduct for meal expenses in general.[196]

> **Example 32.** Lindsey is a truck driver whose tax home is the city of Louisville, Kentucky. While traveling outside Louisville in March 2023, Lindsey paid $440 for meals. Lindsey can deduct $352 ($440 x 80%) because she is subject to federal hours of service by the Department of Transportation and can deduct 80% of her meal expenses compared to the standard 50%.

Special Standard Meal Allowance.[197] Truck drivers and other taxpayers working in the transportation industry can use a special standard meal allowance to deduct meal costs during travel. Instead of calculating their meal deduction using actual expenses, taxpayers use a standard travel allowance rate per day. For 2023, the allowance rate is $69 per day of travel within and $74 per day of travel outside the continental United States.[198] To take the special standard meal allowance for travel, taxpayers must meet the following conditions.

- The taxpayer has direct involvement in transporting people or goods by plane, bus, ship, train, or truck.
- The taxpayer regularly travels away from home in their line of work, with trips typically consisting of travel to locations subject to different standard meal allowance rates.

Taxpayers must use the special standard meal allowance for **all** trips they take in a tax year if they choose to use this method for **any** trip they take during the year. Consequently, truck drivers cannot pick and choose which trips to use the special standard meal allowance in one year. An additional restriction to consider concerns the departure and return travel days. Taxpayers must calculate a reduced allowance for those days, where they can either use a standard 75% portion or another reasonable proration method they apply consistently for all departure and return travel days.

> **Example 33.** Use the same facts as **Example 32.** Lindsey's travel outside her home in March 2023 consisted of an 8-day trip, including departure and return days. If Lindsey used the special standard meal allowance, she would deduct $52 for each departure and return day ($69 × 75%) and $414 for the six days in between ($69 × 6 days). Lindsey's total deduction for the trip is $518 ($52 + $52 + $414).

> **Note.** While taxpayers do not need to substantiate the cost of their meals if they use the special standard meal allowance in calculating their meals deduction, they must maintain adequate travel logs and supporting records to substantiate the number of travel days away from their homes.

---

194. IRS Pub. 463, *Travel, Gift, and Car Expenses.*

195. IRC §274(n)(3).

196. Ibid.

197. IRS Pub. 463, *Travel, Gift, and Car Expenses.*

198. IRS Notice 2022-44, 2022-41 IRB 277.

OTHER EXPENSE ISSUES

While pursuing their vocations, independent contractors may encounter various expenses, some of which may be specific to their industries. These expenses may be tax-deductible,[199] unlike those incurred by Form W-2 employees.[200]

SELECTED TRADES OR BUSINESSES

Construction Workers

Among the variety of other expenses incurred by construction workers, the treatment of interest expense provides some of the greatest challenges, yet some opportunities. This discussion of other expenses incurred by independent contractors in construction focuses on two interest expense issues, capitalization of production period interest and interest tracing rules.

Capitalization of Production Period Interest.[201] Independent contractors in the construction industry often incur debt to purchase materials or meet payroll. With the debt comes interest, for which construction workers and firms record interest expense as they pay it. However, under certain circumstances, the Code requires taxpayers to capitalize interest associated with debt in producing the following property.

- Real property
- Non-inventory tangible personal property with a 20-year or more class life
- Tangible personal property that the taxpayer estimates to have a production period exceeding two years
- Tangible personal property that the taxpayer estimates to have a production period exceeding one year **and** a production cost exceeding $1 million

Several factors can trigger the requirement to capitalize interest expenses. The **production period** starts on the day the taxpayer begins production of that property and ends when the property is ready for placement in service or to hold for sale. Additionally, the production period is pivotal in determining what interest expense may be subject to capitalization in producing real or tangible personal property. Only the interest expense the taxpayer incurs or pays during the production period is subject to the interest capitalization rules under IRC §263A(f).

The use of the debt's proceeds also influences whether a taxpayer must capitalize interest expense. For a given project or contract, interest on the direct indebtedness for **production expenditures** could be subject to capitalization. Production expenditures include the direct costs of a unit of property (UOP) and its share of allocable indirect costs.[202] Additionally, interest on indebtedness for purchasing property used to produce the UOP must be capitalized, and the taxpayer would allocate that interest to the UOP.

> **Note.** For details on the UOP concept and its associated rules, see the 2023 *University of Illinois Federal Tax Workbook,* Chapter 2: Capitalization vs. Repair Review.

199. IRC §62(a)(1).

200. IRC §67(g).

201. IRC §263A(f).

202. IRC §263A(a).

However, interest from other indebtedness not directly related to the production of a UOP may also be subject to capitalization. Such indebtedness may be known as **avoided cost,** the interest cost a taxpayer could have avoided or reduced if they had not incurred the production expenditures for a UOP.[203] This requirement is complex and requires using the avoided cost method to calculate and allocate this cost. The source of other indebtedness would not include the acquisition of a taxpayer's residence or a home equity loan on the taxpayer's residence.[204]

3

Example 34. Darren is an independent contractor who works on the construction of nonresidential buildings. In early 2023, Darren entered a contract to work on constructing a new building for a dentistry practice. Construction began on May 1 of that year and is expected to end on October 31, 2024, when Darren anticipates that the building will be ready to be placed in service.

In anticipation of the project, on February 3, 2023, Darren obtained a 2-year loan from Third Mid National Bank of $250,000 for the construction of the building, primarily for Darren to purchase materials and hire labor. Darren made monthly payments on the loan beginning on March 1.

A portion of Darren's interest expense in 2023 on the Third Mid National Bank loan must be capitalized because Darren incurred the debt to produce nonresidential real property. Darren used the loan proceeds for production expenditures that constituted direct costs. Darren must capitalize the interest he paid starting on May 1, when the production period started. Therefore, Darren would not capitalize the interest he paid in March or April.

Interest Tracing.[205] Interest tracing involves associating the use of the debt proceeds with the associated interest expense. As such, the deductibility of interest is traced to the **use of the proceeds**, not their source or how they are secured. Taxpayers must continuously monitor where they spend the debt proceeds, as they may spend them for different purposes on a given loan over time.

Note. Interest tracing is not specific only to individuals within the construction industry, but is included in this section for comparison purposes.

If a taxpayer uses debt proceeds for business purposes, they can deduct the associated interest expense from their business income. Even if the loan is secured by a nonbusiness asset, such as a personal residence via a refinanced mortgage or home equity loan, the taxpayer may deduct the interest expense from their business income if they use the proceeds for business purposes.[206] Consequently, mortgage refinancing or a home equity loan may be useful strategies for construction workers if they use the proceeds for business purposes. The result may be a beneficial interest expense deduction.

203. Treas. Reg. §1.263A-9.

204. IRC §163(h)(3)(A).

205. Temp. Treas. Reg. §1.163-8T.

206. IRS Pub. 936, *Home Mortgage Interest Deduction,* p. 8 (2022).

Example 35. Alex is a carpenter, working as an independent contractor for several larger construction firms in the metropolitan area. While scrutinizing the repair bills for his diesel truck in his home office one evening, Alex notices that maintenance costs are up significantly, even though he has not driven any more than in previous years.

Alex decides to replace his truck but has no ready sources of cash for a significant purchase. He inquires about a home equity loan while visiting the bank on March 11, 2023, and the banker informs Alex that this is possible. Still, the interest is generally not deductible, given the provisions of the TCJA.[207]

Because the mortgage balance on his home is so small, Alex and his wife decide this is the best course of action. He opens a new bank account for the business specifically to hold funds for the purchase of the truck. Because he sometimes carries loads of bricks with his tools, the truck has a loaded gross vehicle weight of 15,000 pounds and is a qualified nonpersonal use vehicle. Alex has never used his business truck for personal purposes.

Alex draws $50,000 on the line of credit on March 22, 2023. Two days later, on March 24, Alex takes possession of the truck, paying for it with the $50,000 proceeds from the home equity loan. During 2023, Alex pays $2,500 of interest on the home equity loan, as attested by Form 1098, *Mortgage Interest Statement*, which he receives the next January.

At a February 2024 meeting with Joan, his tax practitioner, Alex provides Form 1098 from his bank, even though he does not believe it has value on the tax return. Because she had not received a Form 1098 with this account number previously, Joan asks Alex how he and his wife used the loan.

Alex informs Joan that the proceeds were used to buy the large truck in her parking lot. Joan responds that Temp. Treas. Reg. §1.163-8T permits this interest to be placed on Schedule C for Alex's carpentry business. Even though his principal residence secures the loan, using the loan's proceeds to purchase a vehicle used entirely in Alex's business enables the interest to be treated as a business expense.

In setting up the loan, Alex has done several things right. Under Treas. Reg. §1.163-15, he has a 60-day window during which he is presumed to have used the proceeds to purchase his new truck with the proceeds. This window starts 30 days before the loan proceeds are received and ends 30 days after their receipt. Alex used the proceeds within two days. Also, he used a specific bank account to receive the proceeds, removing any doubt that funds were used to buy the truck used for his business.

Although Alex was not required to set up a special bank account to hold the proceeds of the loan, having one makes it easy for Joan to see that the loan's proceeds were used to acquire the truck.

Note. The concept of interest tracing relies on the **use** of the debt proceeds. Because a taxpayer may use the debt proceeds for different purposes or change how they use the proceeds over time, taxpayers should continue to keep track of how they use debt proceeds to determine whether the associated interest expense may be traced to a source of income eligible for deduction. For example, if Alex does not repay the loan when he sells his truck and uses the proceeds to go on vacation, the interest expenses cease to be associated with his business.

207. *Tax Cuts and Jobs Act*, PL 115-97, §11043, amending IRC §163(h)(3).

Gig Economy Workers

Home Office Expenses.[208] In recent years, there has been a substantial rise in the number of people working from home, with the U.S. Census Bureau finding that number tripled between 2019 and 2021.[209] Consequently, gig workers may not have a separate physical office or work primarily from home. The Code allows taxpayers to deduct specific expenses they incur in maintaining and working from a home office, subject to limitations and qualifying criteria.

3

Generally, a gig worker's expenses for their residence are nondeductible due to being primarily for personal use by nature.[210] However, taxpayers may deduct some of these expenses if they have a home office by meeting one or more of the following criteria.[211]

- The taxpayer uses part of their residence as their **principal place of business** exclusively and regularly.
- The taxpayer uses part of their residence exclusively and regularly to **meet with customers** to conduct business.
- The taxpayer uses a **separate structure** from their home exclusively and regularly for business purposes.
- The taxpayer uses part of their residence for **storing inventory regularly.**
- The taxpayer **rents** out part of their residence.
- The taxpayer uses part of their residence as a **daycare facility.**

Exclusive Use.[212] One criterion the Code imposes on taxpayers to deduct home office expenses is restricting the space **exclusively** for business purposes. As the term indicates, the taxpayer must use the part of their home as a home office only for business purposes and cannot partially use it for nonbusiness purposes.

> **Example 36.** Darla is a graphic designer who develops visual aspects of various media on demand. She uses a spare bedroom in her house as a home office, where she has a desk with a computer on it to create project designs. Darla does not use the spare bedroom for any other purpose or spend any time for personal reasons in that space. Her home office would therefore meet the criteria of being used exclusively for business.

The space in a taxpayer's home they use for business does not need to be separated by walls or other partitions to meet the definition of exclusive use.[213] However, taxpayers must exercise caution in using that space only for business purposes; otherwise, the home office expenses would not be deductible.[214]

> **Example 37.** Use the same facts as **Example 36** except that Darla has a bookshelf with fiction books that she likes to read for pleasure in the chair sitting next to it. Even though she uses the space for business purposes, Darla's partial use of the home office for personal reasons makes her expenses nondeductible.

---

208. IRC §280A.

209. *The Number of People Primarily Working From Home Tripled Between 2019 and 2021*. Sep. 15, 2022. United States Census Bureau. [www.census.gov/newsroom/press-releases/2022/people-working-from-home.html] Accessed on May 5, 2023.

210. IRC §280A(a).

211. IRC §280A(c).

212. Ibid.

213. IRS Pub. 587, *Business Use of Your Home*, p. 3 (2022).

214. *Rayden v. Comm'r*, TC Memo 2011-1 (Jan. 3, 2011).

Gig workers who are daycare providers or use their space to store inventory are exempt from the exclusive use rules. However, for storing inventory, taxpayers must meet an additional set of criteria to deduct home office expenses which include the following.[215]

- The taxpayer's business is selling the inventory at wholesale or retail.
- The taxpayer's home is the only location where they store their inventory.
- The taxpayer uses the space to store inventory regularly.
- The taxpayer uses a separately identifiable space to store their inventory that is appropriate for such use.

Regular Use.[216] Along with exclusive use, a taxpayer must also use a space regularly for business to deduct home office expenses. For a taxpayer to use the space regularly, they must use it for business on a continual, ongoing, or recurring basis.[217] In other words, the basis for use cannot be occasional or incidental. The facts and circumstances surrounding the nature of the business and the taxpayer's use of their home office will determine whether they meet the criteria for regular use.

Principal Place of Business.[218] If taxpayers exclusively and regularly use part of their residence as their principal place of business, they can take a home office deduction. A principal place of business is where a taxpayer performs substantial administrative or management activities for their business and uses no other location for such purpose.[219] These administrative or management activities include billing, ordering supplies, scheduling appointments, and maintaining books and records.

Having other business locations does not prevent a taxpayer's home office from being a principal place of business. The IRS identifies that taxpayers performing activities other than substantially administrative or managing at other locations would not disqualify a home office as the principal place of business. Or, if a taxpayer conducts administrative or managing activities in a nonfixed location such as a vehicle or hotel room, the principal place of business for the home office does not fail. Additionally, having personnel perform such activities at different locations would not result in the home office failing the principal place of business test. As with other aspects of the home office deduction, facts and circumstances will drive the basis for a taxpayer being able to consider their home office as their principal place of business for a given business activity.

> **Example 38.** Use the same facts as **Example 36.** Darla uses her home office as a space to create graphic designs for hired projects. She also manages her calendar with the computer in her office to schedule customer meetings. Darla uses that same computer for her accounting program to keep track of her revenue and expenses. While away from home, she sometimes takes phone calls from customers on her cell phone and brings a laptop with her on trips to work while staying at hotels. Darla's principal place of business is her home office.

A taxpayer's home office can be the principal place of business for multiple businesses in which the taxpayer engages. The taxpayer needs to assess each business separately and apply the criteria discussed previously to determine whether their home office is the principal place of business for each activity.

---

215. IRC §280A(c)(2).

216. IRS Pub. 587, *Business Use of Your Home*, p. 3 (2022).

217. *Donald T. and Marlene B. Robinson v. Comm'r*, TC Memo 2011-99 (May 5, 2011).

218. IRS Pub. 587, *Business Use of Your Home*.

219. IRC §280A(c)(1).

Location for Meeting Customers.[220] To claim the home office deduction under the meeting with customers criteria, taxpayers must adhere to the following considerations.

1. The taxpayer physically meets with customers at their home office.
2. The customer's home office use is substantial and integral in conducting the business activity.

3

Substantiality and frequency come into play again in assessing whether a taxpayer meets the criteria for the deduction. The proposed regulations clarify that a taxpayer making phone calls to customers does not fulfill the above criteria and that occasional meetings are insufficient to identify a home office as a primary location for meeting with customers.

Separate Structure as a Home Office.[221] Independent contractors sometimes use a structure separate from their residences for business purposes. In this circumstance, they may deduct associated costs as home office expenses. To qualify for the deduction, the taxpayer must use the space exclusively and regularly for business.

Methods for Deducting Home Office Expenses. Once taxpayers have determined they can deduct home office expenses from their business income on their tax return, they must calculate their deduction using one of two methods. The first method utilizes a taxpayer's **actual expenditures.** In contrast, the other, **simplified method** assigns an estimated deduction based on the percentage of a taxpayer's space they use as a home office compared to their total residence. This section analyzes both methods for deducting home office expenses.

- **Actual Expense Method.**[222] Taxpayers electing to use actual expenses they incurred for the home office deduction must separate their home office expenses into two categories, direct and indirect expenses. An expense is **direct** when the taxpayer only incurs it for the business portion of their home. Direct expenses could include repairs to the home office space or installing carpeting for the office. Taxpayers can deduct direct expenses in full. An expense is **indirect** when the taxpayer incurs it for maintaining their overall residence. Property taxes, homeowners' insurance, mortgage interest, depreciation, and utilities are generally indirect expenses as the expense is for the total home space for both personal and business use. Consequently, taxpayers may not fully deduct indirect expenses. Instead, they must determine the business portion of the expense they can deduct.

  Taxpayers determine the business portion of an indirect home office expense by applying a business percentage to the indirect cost. The business percentage is equal to the space of the home used for business divided by the total space of the home. Generally, taxpayers use square footage to measure the space of their home in calculating the business percentage, although the IRS allows any reasonable method in calculating the area of the home and office space, such as the number of rooms of equal size.[223]

  > **Example 39.** Use the same facts as **Example 36,** except Darla measures the spare bedroom she uses as a home office at 280 square feet. The square footage of her home is 1,400. If Darla uses the actual expense method, the business percentage that she applies to any indirect costs would be 20% (280 ÷ 1,400).

220. Prop. Treas. Reg. §1.280A-2(c).

221. Ibid.

222. IRS Pub. 587, *Business Use of Your Home*, p. 6 (2022).

223. Ibid.

The amount of home office expense that taxpayers can deduct using the actual expense method is subject to limitation. Specifically, the business portion of home office expenses that a taxpayer would not otherwise be able to deduct on their return is subject to this limitation. These expenses may include insurance, utilities, and depreciation. They would not include mortgage interest, real estate taxes, and any casualty losses, as these expenses may be taken as itemized deductions on a taxpayer's Schedule A, *Itemized Deductions*. The business portion of otherwise nondeductible home office expenses is limited to the business's gross income, less the business portion of home expenses that is otherwise deductible and nonhome business expenses. However, a taxpayer may carry over the unused business portion of home expenses to a future tax year in which the taxpayer uses the actual expense method. These expenses are again subject to limitations for that tax year. A taxpayer may carry over these expenses even if they use a different space for a home office in the future tax year.

> **Example 40.** Assume the same facts as **Example 39.** In 2023, Darla incurs $10,000 in real estate taxes, $7,500 in mortgage interest, $2,000 in utility expenses, $700 in homeowner's insurance, and $500 to repair carpet damage in her home office. Darla's accountant calculated $3,200 of depreciation expense for Darla's home in 2023. Darla has gross receipts from her graphic design business of $50,000 and has other non-home business expenses totaling $12,000.
>
> Darla uses the actual expense method to calculate her home office deduction in 2023. She first identifies her direct costs for the home office as the $500 repair to carpeting because the expense is solely for the space of Darla's home used for business. All other home costs are indirect, requiring Darla to multiply them by the business percentage of 20% that she calculated in **Example 39.** The resulting indirect costs are $2,000 in real estate taxes ($10,000 × 20%), $1,500 in mortgage interest ($7,500 × 20%), $400 in utilities ($2,000 × 20%), $140 in insurance ($700 × 20%), and $640 of depreciation ($3,200 × 20%). The total home office expense, including direct and indirect costs, is $5,180 ($2,000 + $1,500 + $400 + $140 + $640 + $500).
>
> To determine whether her home office expenses are subject to limitation and need to be carried over, Darla identifies that her gross income of $50,000 exceeds her total business expenses of $17,180 ($12,000 non-home business expense + $5,180 home office expense). Therefore, Darla could deduct the entire $5,180 of home office expenses that she calculated.

When using the actual expenses method, taxpayers calculate and report the home office expenses on Form 8829, *Expenses for Business Use of Your Home*.

Taxpayers must consider depreciation recapture when selling their home with a home office where they used the actual expense method for deducting home office expenses. Usually, when a taxpayer sells a primary residence, they can offset a sizable amount of capital gain with an exclusion provided under IRC §121, provided they meet the requirements therein. However, when using the actual expense method for deducting home office expenses, any amount of depreciation that the taxpayer recognized or could have recognized is not exempt under §121 and is subject to §1250 depreciation recapture when the taxpayer sells the property.[224] The taxpayer must report the unrecaptured §1250 gain on Form 8949, *Sales and Other Dispositions of Capital Assets*, and subsequently on Schedule D, *Capital Gains and Losses*. Unrecaptured §1250 gain is subject to a maximum 25% tax rate.[225]

---

224. Treas. Reg. §1.121-1(d)(1).

225. *Topic Number 409 — Capital Gains and Losses*. Apr. 4, 2023. IRS. [www.irs.gov/taxtopics/tc409] Accessed on May 10, 2023.

- **Simplified Method.**[226] A taxpayer can use an alternative method for calculating and deducting home office expenses. This method is known as the simplified method, primarily due to the relative ease of calculating the expense and not requiring a taxpayer to allocate or substantiate actual expenses that they incur. Consequently, taxpayers may opt to use this method over the actual expense method when they do not incur significant property expenses or have difficulty maintaining appropriate documentation to support those expenditures.

  Taxpayers make the election using the simplified method by filing their tax returns on a timely basis. This election is made on a per-year basis, meaning that a taxpayer may switch from using the simplified method to the actual expense method or vice versa without it constituting a change in accounting method, possibly requiring approval from the Commissioner. Calculating the deductible home office expense under the simplified method requires multiplying the square footage of a taxpayer's home used for business by the prescribed rate of $5 per square foot. While taxpayers who use the simplified method for a business may not deduct any home office expenses to reduce their income from that business, they can still itemize property taxes and mortgage interest, as well as deduct casualty losses on their returns.

  The deduction for home office expenses under the simplified method is limited to the business's gross income, less the taxpayer's nonhome business expenses. The taxpayer's use of the simplified method is limited to 300 square feet. A taxpayer may not generate a business loss from the home office deduction. Unlike the actual expense method, the taxpayer may not carry over any amount of unused home office deduction when they use the simplified method.

  As the simplified method does not include recognizing depreciation expense, a taxpayer does not need to consider §1250 depreciation recapture when selling their residence with a home office, where they only used the simplified method to calculate home office expenses. However, because taxpayers may switch methods annually, they must still recognize a §1250 gain for any year they used the actual expense method. This consideration is why a taxpayer may favor using the simplified method over the actual expense method to avoid the administrative inconvenience of calculating and tracking depreciation expenses on their home office.

  Example 41. Assume the same facts as **Example 40.** If Darla uses the simplified method, her home office deduction is $1,400 (280 square footage of home office × $5 standard rate). Considering only her business income and expenses, the actual expense method in Darla's situation would yield a larger home office deduction than the simplified method.

Note. When comparing **Example 40** and **Example 41,** it may be tempting to recommend that Darla use the actual expense method over the simplified method. However, practitioners should also consider other factors when recommending one method for deducting home office expenses over the other. For example, depreciation recapture may come into play for taxpayers who sell their homes for which they used the actual expense method for deducting home office expenses. Depreciation recapture is not relevant when a taxpayer uses the simplified method.

Additionally, practitioners should consider whether taxpayers can itemize their property taxes or mortgage interest. If they can itemize those expenses, it may be beneficial for the taxpayer to recognize a portion of the expense to offset their business income to reduce any SE tax or result in having a lower adjusted gross income (AGI).

Note. For a home office refresher, see the 2020 *University of Illinois Federal Tax Workbook,* Volume B, Chapter 5: Small Business Issues. This can be found at **uofi.tax/arc** [taxschool.illinois.edu/taxbookarchive].

226. Rev. Proc. 2013-13, 2013-06 IRB 478.

Truck Drivers

Specialized Clothing. Deducting clothing as a business expense largely depends on the facts and circumstances surrounding a taxpayer's business. Given that this decision involves a judgment call, the IRS has an incentive to challenge clothing deductions, prompting taxpayers to provide bona fide reasons for the clothing when performing their duties.

Truck drivers should be aware that some of their clothing, depending on the circumstances, may be a deductible business expense. For example, in *Henke v Comm'r*, the taxpayer was a truck driver who purchased safety shoes and gloves. The court found the deduction was reasonable because the taxpayer worked with blacktop material that was very hot, and therefore safety clothing was necessary to perform the taxpayer's job.[227]

Truck drivers may deduct specialized clothing and safety equipment for their jobs if they can establish the following criteria.[228]

1. The clothing is required or essential in the taxpayer's employment.
2. The clothing is not suitable for general or personal wear.
3. The taxpayer does not wear the clothing for general or personal wear.

As with other business expenses, the taxpayer must be able to substantiate their expenses with supporting documentation. In addition to documentation supporting the existence of the expense, truck drivers should also document why the clothing they are trying to deduct is required or essential to their profession. Finally, they should state that they could not and did not use it for personal purposes.

SE TAX

In addition to income tax, a tax of 15.3% is imposed on SE income. **SE income** is defined as net earnings from self-employment activities.[229] **Net earnings from self-employment** are defined as gross income derived by an individual from a trade or business that the individual conducts less deductions allowed.[230]

A taxpayer generally pays SE tax if they have SE net earnings of $400 or more.[231] The amount subject to SE tax is 92.35% of a taxpayer's SE net earnings. The maximum net earnings subject to the social security tax in 2023 are $160,200.[232] All net earnings are subject to the Medicare tax.

A taxpayer is in business for SE tax purposes if they meet the following 2-prong test:[233]

- Continuity and regularity and
- Profit motive.

227. *Henke v. Comm'r*, TC Memo 1973-186 (Aug. 21, 1973).
228. *Nolder v. Comm'r*, TC Summ. Op. 2012-50 (May 29, 2012).
229. IRC §1402(b).
230. IRC §1402(a).
231. *Topic No. 544, Self-Employment Tax.* Apr. 6, 2023. IRS. [www.irs.gov/taxtopics/tc554] Accessed on Apr. 19, 2023.
232. *Fact Sheet.* Social Security Administration. [www.ssa.gov/news/press/factsheets/colafacts2023.pdf] Accessed on Apr. 20, 2023.
233. Rev. Rul. 58-112, 1958-1 CB 323. See also *Comm'r v. Groetzinger,* 480 U.S. 23 (1987) and *Batok v. Comm'r,* TC Memo 1992-727 (Dec. 28, 1992).

For the purpose of deducting losses, a taxpayer is in business if the facts and circumstances show that the taxpayer operated the venture like a business instead of like an activity **not engaged in for profit.** The IRS looks at nine primary factors, which, when viewed together, paint a picture of the taxpayer's intent.[234] In looking at these factors, courts evaluate the taxpayer's intent to earn a profit.

1. The **manner** in which the taxpayer carried on the activity
2. The **expertise** of the taxpayer or their advisors
3. The **time and effort** expended by the taxpayer in carrying on the activity
4. The taxpayer's **expectation** that the **value** of the assets used in the business will increase
5. The **previous success** of the taxpayer in carrying on similar or dissimilar activities
6. The **history of income and losses** with respect to the activity
7. The amount of **occasional profits**, if any, which are earned
8. The **financial status** of the taxpayer
9. Any elements of **personal pleasure** or recreation in the activity

No one factor is determinative, and other factors may also be considered. The IRS and the courts place greater weight on objective facts than on taxpayers' assertions of intent. Accordingly, taxpayers who maintain proper contemporaneous documentation are more likely to be able to prove their intent.

Note. For an in-depth discussion of these factors, see the 2021 *University of Illinois Federal Tax Workbook,* Volume B, Chapter 3: Schedule C. This can be found at **uofi.tax/arc** [taxschool.illinois.edu/taxbookarchive].

Practitioner Planning Tip

Taxpayers with a loss or a small amount of SE income may benefit from using an optional method to compute net earnings from SE activities. For taxpayers engaged in farming activities, the **farm optional method** is available for any number of years if gross farm income is $9,060 or less or net farm profits are less than $6,540 (2022).[235] The **nonfarm optional method** is available only five years in a taxpayer's lifetime if net nonfarm profits are less than $6,540 (2022) and also less than 72.189% of gross nonfarm income. The instructions for Schedule SE, *Self-Employment Tax,* contain additional rules. The optional methods benefit self-employed taxpayers by providing credit toward social security coverage or increasing earned income for the earned income credit or the child and dependent care credit.[236]

234. Treas. Reg. §1.183-2; IRC §183.

235. 2022 Instructions for Schedule SE.

236. *Topic No. 544, Self-Employment Tax.* Apr. 6, 2023. IRS. [www.irs.gov/taxtopics/tc554] Accessed on Apr. 19, 2023.

Taxpayers calculate their SE tax on Schedule SE of Form 1040. Self-employed taxpayers are allowed to deduct one-half of the SE tax to arrive at AGI.[237]

Example 42. Jackson is a self-employed truck driver who files single. His total gross income from trucking for the tax year 2022 was $75,000. Jackson incurred the following expenses related to his trucking business.

Fuel	$15,000
Repairs and maintenance	5,000
Insurance	3,000
Licensing fees	1,500
Meals and entertainment (50% deductible)	2,000
Other miscellaneous expenses	1,500
Total expenses	$28,000

Jackson's net SE income is $43,405 (($75,000 – $28,000) × 92.35%). The SE tax rate for 2022 is 15.3%. Because Jackson is self-employed, he is responsible for the full portion of the tax, resulting in a total SE tax of $6,641 (15.3% × $43,405). Jackson reports his SE tax of $6,641 on Schedule SE, which is attached to his Form 1040 when filing his income tax return.

Jackson deducts half of his SE tax as an adjustment to his income on his Form 1040, which reduces his overall tax liability.

STATE INCOME TAX ISSUES

Because there are 41 states that levy income taxes, plus the District of Columbia, there are 42 ways that states can complicate the tax lives of independent contractors, especially if they travel between states with income taxes. The construction worker who only undertakes projects in South Dakota and Wyoming is very fortunate because those are the only two contiguous states that do not tax incomes. For most independent contractors working in multiple states, their tax practitioners must consider a series of facts and circumstances to determine whether their clients are responsible for filing in the state that is not their tax home.

GENERAL PRINCIPLES FOR STATE INCOME TAX LIABILITY

The general principle is that if an independent contractor performs work in a state, then the work performed there is taxable. For example, a gig worker in Indiana may incur an Illinois income tax liability if they travel into Illinois and perform work for a client. In contrast, a construction worker who works as an independent contractor in Indiana for an Illinois firm but never enters Illinois would not be considered to have earned Illinois income.[238] Other states have different rules, as shown in the following matrix of reciprocity agreements.[239]

237. Ibid.

238. *IT 13-0009-GIL 98/26/2013 Compensation,* p. 3. Stocker, Brian L. Illinois Department of Revenue. [tax.illinois.gov/content/dam/soi/en/web/tax/research/legalinformation/letterrulings/it/documents/2013/it-13-0009.pdf] Accessed on Apr. 24, 2023.

239. *Do Unto Others: The Case for State Income Tax Reciprocity*. Walczak, Jared. Nov. 16, 2022. Tax Foundation. [taxfoundation.org/state-reciprocity-agreements] Accessed on Apr. 27, 2023. Used with permission.

	IL	IN	IA	KY	MD	MI	MN	MT	NJ	ND	OH	PA	VA	WV	WI	DC	Count
IL			✓	✓		✓									✓		4
IN				✓		✓					✓	✓			✓		5
IA	✓																1
KY	✓	✓				✓					✓		✓	✓	✓		7
MD												✓	✓	✓		✓	4
MI	✓	✓		✓			✓				✓				✓		6
MN						✓				✓							2
MT										✓							1
NJ												✓					1
ND							✓	✓									2
OH		✓		✓		✓						✓		✓			5
PA		✓			✓				✓		✓		✓	✓			6
VA				✓	✓							✓		✓		✓	5
WV				✓	✓						✓	✓	✓				5
WI	✓	✓		✓		✓											4
DC					✓								✓				2

Sources: State statutes and regulations; Bloomberg Tax; Tax Foundation research.

This matrix shows that residents of some states do not need to file a return for another state in which they earn wages if the two states have a reciprocity agreement. More specifically, residents of one state are not required to file a tax return in the other state if they have only earnings from wages, salaries, tips and commissions from working in the other state. For example, the Illinois reciprocal agreement does not include SE income.[240] Thus, even though employees living in Michigan, but working in Illinois, are not required to file Illinois income tax returns, independent contractors living in Michigan and working in Illinois are required to file tax returns with **both** states.

Example 43. Tom and Jerry are twin brothers, both of whom are engaged in the same business. However, Tom is an employee of XYZ Corp. based in Illinois. Tom is a resident of Michigan and works in Michigan 90% of the time. For the balance of his time, he works in the Illinois headquarters. Because Tom has no other source of Illinois income, he is not required to file an Illinois income tax return.

Even though he performs the same type of work, Jerry is an independent contractor residing in Michigan. Jerry works 90% of the time in Michigan and 10% in Illinois. Jerry must file an Illinois Form IL-1040, *Individual Income Tax Return.*

240. *What if I live or work in the state that has a reciprocal agreement with Illinois?* Illinois Department of Revenue. [tax.illinois.gov/questionsandanswers/12.html] Accessed on Apr. 24, 2023; 35 ILCS §5/502(a)(1)–(2).

Practitioner Planning Tip

Tax professionals should research details of reciprocity agreements if a client may benefit from applying the agreement. Each state implements reciprocity in its own way.

Generally, independent contractors must file income tax returns for each state from which they derive income. Reciprocity agreements providing an exemption from filing requirements generally cover wages, but not SE income. Sixteen states have reciprocal agreements.[241]

Based on this, the question of nexus for **income tax** purposes arises, which may be distinct from nexus for sales tax purposes. In some cases, even a simple connection, such as driving through the state with cargo, may be sufficient to establish an income tax filing requirement. Some states have clearly defined rules that establish when a filing requirement exists, as summarized in the following table.

State	Statute	Nonresident Filing Requirement
California	Cal. Rev. and Tax. Code §§17041 and 17951	An independent contractor must file a tax return if any California-source income is earned
Connecticut	Conn. Gen. Stat. §12-711	An independent contractor must file a Connecticut tax return if they have any sources of income from within the state. The amount of income recognized is the net amount of income, gain, loss, and deduction considered for Connecticut AGI.
Georgia	Ga. Code Ann. §48-7-50	Nonresident independent contractors must file a Georgia income tax return if they have federal gross income from sources within Georgia.
Illinois	35 ILCS 5/304(a) and (h)	Nonresident independent contractors must file an Illinois income tax return if they have enough income from Illinois sources to have a tax liability. In this case, the business income is apportioned to Illinois based on the proportion of Illinois sales to total sales.[243]
Massachusetts	Mass. Gen. Laws, chap. 62, §5A	A business is engaged in business within the commonwealth if it has "Any trade or business" in the state. Nonresident independent contractors must file if they have state-sourced income exceeding $8,000 or state-source income exceeding the state exemption amount multiplied by the ratio of state-sourced income to total income.[244]

241. *Do Unto Others: The Case for State Income Tax Reciprocity*. Walczak, Jared. Nov. 16, 2022. Tax Foundation. [taxfoundation.org/state-reciprocity-agreements] Accessed on Apr. 27, 2023.

242. See 2022 Instructions for Schedule NR, Form IL-1040, particularly the Business or Farm Income Apportionment Formula (IAF) Worksheet.

243. *2022 Massachusetts Nonresident or Part-Year Resident Income Tax*, p. 3. Dec. 2022. Department of Revenue, Commonwealth of Massachusetts. [www.mass.gov/doc/2022-form-1-nrpy-instructions/download] Accessed on Apr. 27, 2023.

3

State	Statute	Nonresident Filing Requirement
Michigan	Mich. Comp. Laws §206.621	A taxpayer has "substantial nexus" in the state if (a) they have had a physical presence for more than 1 day during the tax year; (b) if they have actively solicited sales in the state and have gross receipts exceeding $349,999; or (c) has an interest in a pass-through entity having a substantial nexus in the state. Nonresident independent contractors must pay income tax on all income earned or attributable to Michigan.[245]
New Jersey	N.J. Stat. Ann. §54A:2-1.1	The independent contractor must file a New Jersey tax return if they have state-sourced income and meet the threshold for filing based on gross income from all sources. Spending more than 30 days in the state makes the independent contractor a part-year resident.[246]
New York	N.Y. Tax Law §§209, 631[247]	Nonresident independent contractors are taxed on New York state income from all sources. They must file if their New York AGI exceeds the New York standard deduction.[248]
Ohio	Ohio Rev. Code Ann. §§5747.01, 5747.24(A)(D)[249]	If a nonresident independent contractor earns any Ohio-sourced income, they have an Ohio filing requirement, even if they are not Ohio residents. They may wish to file Ohio Form IT NRS, *Ohio Nonresident Statement,* to establish their nonresidency.
Pennsylvania	61 Pa. Code §§101.8(2), 109.4[250]	An independent contractor is subject to Pennsylvania tax for any income earned in Pennsylvania. The cited code section states that a "business, trade, profession or occupation ... is carried on partly within and partly without [the state] if one or more of the activities" is carried on in the state.
Virginia	Va. Code Ann. §§58.1-302, 58.1-325	Nonresident independent contractors are subject to Virginia income tax based on a percentage of their Virginia taxable income. The percentage is the ratio of the **net** amount of income, gain, loss, and deductions from Virginia sources to the **net** amount of all income gain, loss, and deductions from all sources. However, Virginia nonresidents must file if their **Virginia** AGI is above a filing threshold and they derive any income from Virginia sources.
Wisconsin	Wis. Stat. §§71.02(2), 71.03(2)(a)(2)	Nonresident persons, including independent contractors, must file if their **gross** income is $2,000 or more if they transact business within the state.

244. 2022 Instructions for [Michigan] Schedule NR, *Nonresident and Part-Year Resident Schedule.*

245. 2022 Instructions for Form NJ-1040NR, p. 2.

246. See *Instructions for Form IT-203, Nonresident and Part-Year Resident Income Tax Return,* Mar. 30, 2023. New York State Department of Taxation and Finance. [www.tax.ny.gov/forms/current-forms/it/it203i.htm] Accessed on Apr. 25, 2023.

247. *Filing information for New York State nonresidents.* Dec. 6, 2022. Department of Taxation and Finance, New York State. [www.tax.ny.gov/pit/file/nonresidents.htm] Accessed on Apr. 27, 2023.

248. See *Ohio 2022: Instructions for Filing Original and Amended Individual Income Tax (IT 1040).* pp. 11, 49. Ohio Department of Taxation. [tax.ohio.gov/static/forms/ohio_individual/individual/2022/it1040-sd100-instruction-booklet.pdf] Accessed on Apr. 25, 2023.

249. *§109.4. Business carried on partly within and partly without this Commonwealth.* Commonwealth of Pennsylvania. [www.pacodeandbulletin.gov/Display/pacode?file=/secure/pacode/data/061/chapter109/s109.4.html&d=reduce] Accessed on Apr. 25, 2023; *Instructions for Nonresidents and Part-Year Residents.* Pennsylvania Department of Revenue. [www.revenue.pa.gov/TaxTypes/PIT/Pages/Nonresident%20and%20Part-Year%20Resident%20Instructions.aspx] Accessed on Apr. 25, 2023.

Caution. Each state has its own complex set of laws, and the summaries in the previous table should not be considered authoritative. Each of the state's laws is subject to change at the discretion of its elected or regulatory officials. Furthermore, this summary only includes states having a bright-line test, which is admittedly subjective.

SELECTED TRADES OR BUSINESSES

Construction Workers

Construction contractors may encounter adverse tax issues when they cross state boundaries to work. In addition to potential state rules that establish nexus in the state where they work, they may encounter other state laws affecting their status as independent contractors, unemployment insurance, and industry regulation. The construction company may even acquire nexus in a state by hiring an independent contractor to work in another state.

This result may be the case in California, where having an independent contractor could result in a construction firm located in another state becoming subject to California's requirement for a tax return, even though none of the firm's employees ever entered the state. The California Franchise Tax Board presumes a firm is doing business in the state if the business's sales exceed the lesser of the following.[250]

- $500,000
- 25% of total sales

For example, a Nevada construction company could engage the services of an independent contractor to perform work in California, for which the Nevada company bills $100,000. Suppose the Nevada company's total annual revenue is less than $400,000. In that case, the California statute indicates that the Nevada company is doing business in California, even though its employees never entered that state, and it has no property in California. The ownership of real or tangible personal property may also establish that a taxpayer is doing business in that state.[251]

Sales and Use Tax. State sales and use tax laws may impose sales tax on the materials that construction firms, including sole proprietors in the construction industry, provide to their customers. In general, California contractors are liable for sales tax.[252]

Illinois treats the matter differently. This state assumes that construction firms that affix any type of personal property to a building or other element of real property incur a **use** tax liability.[253] If the construction firm sells the building material directly to a customer, it incurs sales tax liability.[254]

Income Tax. Many independent contractors in the construction industry work in states other than their state of residence. If the other state imposes an income tax, filing a return for that state is almost certainly required.

---

250. Cal. Rev. & Tax. Code §§23101(a) and (b)(2).

251. Cal. Rev. & Tax. Code §§23101(a) and (b)(3).

252. *Construction and Building Contractors*, p. 27. Apr. 2022. California Department of Tax and Fee Administration. [www.cdtfa.ca.gov/formspubs/pub9.pdf] Accessed on Apr. 26, 2023.

253. Ill. Admin. Code title 86 §§130.1940 (2000) and 130.2075 (2001); See *ST-21-0047*. Nov. 23, 2021. Wolters, Richard S. IDOR. [tax.illinois.gov/content/dam/soi/en/web/tax/research/legalinformation/letterrulings/st/documents/2021/st21-0047-gil.pdf] Accessed on Apr. 26, 2023.

254. Ill. Admin. Code title 86 §130.1940(b) (2000), where the term "retailers' occupation tax" is used to denote sales tax.

Practitioner Planning Tip

Reviewing a construction contractor's bank and credit card records may be tedious, but these documents may suggest questions about out-of-state travel that could be related to a project in another state, resulting in a filing requirement in that state. These records should reflect travel noted in mileage logs.

3

Gig Economy Workers

Generally, gig workers must follow regular state tax rules for nexus and filing requirements, as indicated earlier. Gig workers who travel in multiple states do not usually have the protections afforded by state reciprocity agreements, which normally only apply to common law employees, their state tax liabilities and filing requirements depend on the diligence with which the taxpayer completes their mileage logs, meal records, and similar documents.

Truck Drivers

Because of the mobile nature of a trucker's business, their travels naturally raise the issue of state taxation whenever they cross a state line. However, 49 USC §14503 limits the ability of states, other than their state of residence, to tax truck drivers.

> *No part of the compensation paid by a motor carrier providing transportation subject to jurisdiction under subchapter I of chapter 135 or by a motor private carrier to an employee who performs regularly assigned duties in 2 or more States as such an employee with respect to a motor vehicle shall be subject to the income tax laws of any State or subdivision of that State, other than the State or subdivision thereof of the employee's residence.*

Appearing in Title 49 of the US Code, rather than Title 26 where the IRC exists, this provision has significant implications for truck drivers. Furthermore, the next sentence refers to 49 USC §31132 to define "employee" to include independent contractors working as truckers.

> *"[E]mployee" means an operator of a commercial motor vehicle (including an* ***independent contractor*** *[emphasis added] when operating a commercial motor vehicle, a mechanic, a freight handler or an individual not an employer, who —*
>
> ***a.*** *Directly affects commercial motor vehicle safety in the course of employment...*

Thus, independent contractors may be exempt from state income taxation because of a provision in federal law.

A 2020 general information letter from the Illinois Department of Revenue (IDOR) illustrates the importance of carefully analyzing truckers' activities, whether they are employees or independent contractors.[255] In this letter, IDOR concedes the supremacy of federal law but parses its text to ensure that the transportation worker, in this case, an Arizona-based common law employee of an Illinois-based trucking firm, falls within the federal exemption from state income taxation. The letter indicates that the Arizona employee would be exempt if they comply with the requirements of the Illinois Administrative Code.[256]

- The employee is paid compensation by a motor carrier or a motor private carrier.
- The employee performs regularly assigned duties in two or more states.

---

255. *IT-20-0006-GIL*, p. 3. Mankowski, Michael D. Mar. 5, 2020. IDOR. [tax.illinois.gov/content/dam/soi/en/web/tax/research/legalinformation/letterrulings/it/documents/2020/it20-0006-gil.pdf] Accessed on Apr. 26, 2023.

256. 86 Ill. Admin. Code §100.2590(a)(2).

Other states have similar provisions.[257] In a 2001 case, the Oregon Tax Court decided a case in favor of a Washington state-based truck driver who occasionally earned income in Oregon, exempting him from that state's income tax because of 49 USC §14503.[258] In her opinion, Magistrate Sally L. Kimsey referred to Senator Slade Gorton's statement made during the debate on the Amtrak Act.

> *The court finds further support in the purpose of the Amtrak Act. The Amtrak Act was passed so that "rail and motor carrier transportation workers will only have to pay State Taxes to their State of residence."*

The Magistrate's decision follows.[259]

> *IT IS THE DECISION OF THIS COURT that Plaintiffs' income, although earned in Oregon, is exempt from state income tax under the Amtrak Act.*

> **Example 44.** David is an independent trucker who typically drives for Prairie Trucklines, Inc., which is based in Danville, Illinois. This firm regularly pays David, and it qualifies under 49 USC §14503 as a motor private carrier. Because David's normal base of operations is at the firm's Indianapolis terminal, a few miles from his residence, his tax home and his residence are in Indiana. David carries loads on a regular basis into Michigan and Ohio but never into Illinois and performs no incidental service in Illinois. Consequently, he has no Illinois nexus, even though the company for which he performs most work is based there. Furthermore, 49 USC §14503 exempts David from Ohio and Michigan taxation.

The issue of whether truckers can even be independent contractors is under contention. A California law tests whether a worker is an employee or an independent contractor. Companies employing truckers as independent contractors must prove their status based on the following three conditions.[260]

1. The trucker has the freedom to control how they perform their service.
2. The trucker provides service that is outside the company's usual scope of service or business.
3. The trucker acts in an independently established trade, occupation, or business.

Independent truckers can readily satisfy the first and third conditions, but they are unlikely to perform their work outside of the normal scope of business for the company's engaging their services. Although this law pertains solely to California, other states and the federal government should be expected to adopt, either in whole or in some part. This adoption would have implications for the deductibility of truckers' expenses, as employee-paid expenses are not tax deductible until 2026.[261]

Practitioner Planning Tip

Tax practitioners may consider ways of carefully determining whether clients who are independent truck drivers fit within the exemption provided by 49 USC §14503. This exemption is contingent on the facts and circumstances of the truck driver's work fitting this section of the U.S. Code.

---

257. See, for example, Or. Admin. R. 150-316-0173 (2016).
258. *Roe v. Department of Revenue*, Or. Tax TC-MD 000905F (2001).
259. Ibid.
260. Cal. Labor Code §2750.3(a)(1) (2019).
261. *Tax Cuts and Jobs Act*, PL 115-97, §11045, amending IRC §67 through Dec. 31, 2025.

Chapter 4: Select Topics for Partnership Operations

4

Note. Corrections for all of the chapters are available at **TaxSchool.illinois.edu.** For clarification about terms used throughout this chapter, see the **Acronyms and Abbreviations** section following the index.

For your convenience, in-text website links are also provided as short URLs. Anywhere you see **uofi.tax/xxx**, the link points to the address immediately following in brackets.

About the Authors

Kelly Golish, CPA, is the Assistant Director, Tax Materials, at the University of Illinois Tax School. She was previously a manager at Crowder, CPAs in Danville, IL and worked for both public and private accounting firms in Decatur, IL, Cleveland, OH, and San Jose, CA. Kelly earned a Masters in Accounting with an emphasis in Taxation and a Bachelors in Accounting at the University of Notre Dame.

Georgine Kryda, Ph.D., Esq., LLM (Taxation), is an attorney with over a decade of experience in the areas of trust and estate planning and administration, probate litigation, and tax matters. She is also a CPA, a CFE, a mediator-arbitrator, and based in Golden, Colorado.

Kenneth Wright has a law degree and a Master of Laws in Taxation from the University of Florida. He has been in private practice and has taught continuing education courses for the University of Missouri, the IRS, the AICPA, and the American Bar Association among others. Ken has served as Vice Chair of the Taxpayer Advocacy Panel, a Federal Advisory Group to the IRS, and was the first non-IRS recipient of the National Taxpayer Advocate Award for his work with the IRS on cancellation of indebtedness income and individual bankruptcy tax issues.

Other chapter contributors and reviewers are listed at the front of this book.

This chapter builds upon the "Partnership Basics" chapter in the 2022 *University of Illinois Federal Tax Workbook* by examining certain specialized aspects of partnerships. This chapter intentionally omits any discussion of the termination or winding up of partnerships, which will be the subject of a future chapter.

Note. For purposes of this chapter, assume a limited liability company (LLC) is a multi-member LLC (MMLLC) being taxed as a partnership. An MMLLC may elect to be taxed as a C corporation or an S corporation. For more information on these "check the box" rules, see the 2022 *University of Illinois Federal Tax Workbook,* Volume B, Chapter 3: Partnership Basics.

Note. In the partnership taxation realm, there are three types of capital accounts.

1. **Tax basis,** which reflects the partners' adjusted inside tax basis in the entity
2. **Book basis** (IRC §704(b)), which reflects fair market value (FMV) of assets and related adjustments
3. **Generally accepted accounting principles (GAAP) or other financial reporting basis,** which reflects the partnership's activity as reported in its financial statements

For purposes of this chapter, references to capital accounts represent book basis. Tax basis is distinguished with "tax" preceding capital accounts, which generally reflects adjusted basis. Unless explicitly identified, GAAP or other financial reporting basis is not discussed in this chapter.

PARTNERSHIP AGREEMENT

A partnership is governed by the statutes of the state in which the partnership is organized. The partnership's operating agreement,[1] if such an agreement exists, allows the partners to contract among themselves — for example, allowing guaranteed payments to one or more partners in addition to year-end distributions. A partnership agreement includes the original agreement and any modifications agreed to by all the partners or adopted in any other manner provided by the partnership agreement.[2] The agreement can be written or oral, depending on the applicable state law.[3] State or local law governs in any matters where the partnership agreement is silent.[4]

Note. A tax return preparer should review the partnership agreement each year because the agreement is the contract between the partners that affects their respective capital accounts and interests through the classification of expenses, the allocation of income and expenses, and other agreed upon provisions. It is important to ensure that the partners are continuing to operate in accordance with their partnership agreement.

In particular, a preparer should examine the partnership agreement for the following items.

- Members and their interests
- Types of contributions made by each partner
- Partners' distributive shares, special allocations, any guaranteed payments, health or other benefits
- Consistency of the partnership agreement with the partners' understanding of the entity and their expectations
- Provisions of applicable state law for tax matters, such as its provisions for allocations, distributions, liquidations, etc., which become significant if the partnership agreement does not exist or is silent

1. A partnership's operating agreement may also be referred to as a partnership agreement.
2. IRC §761(c).
3. Treas. Reg. §1.761-1(c).
4. Ibid.

Practitioner Planning Tip

During a review of partnership agreements, a tax practitioner may become aware of deficiencies in the partnership agreement. Rather than attempt to fix the agreement themselves, they should build relationships with local attorneys who are knowledgeable about partnership law. Unless the tax practitioner is a licensed attorney with partnership law expertise, involving a competent attorney to guide the client in partnership legal and tax matters serves the client's interests better.

CAPITAL ACCOUNTING

For income tax purposes, partnerships have a dual personality: for some purposes they are treated as separate entities from their partners under the **entity theory** of partnership taxation.[5] For other purposes, they are treated as individual taxpayers engaging in a common activity.[6] This is referred to as the **aggregate theory** of partnership taxation.[7] This increases the complexity of partnership tax rules, which must reconcile the interests of partners with those of the partnership. These interests sometimes conflict. A good example of this is the IRC §754 election that allows inside basis adjustments of partnership assets with respect to outside occurrences affecting individual partners.

It is, therefore, necessary to have some benchmark by which the interactions of partner and partnership transactions can be measured to promote uniformity in the application of subchapter K to partnerships and their partners. One of these benchmarks is the capital account of each partner.

For purposes of Schedule K-1 (Form 1065), *Partner's Share of Income, Deductions, Credits, etc.,* reporting, the IRS now mandates **tax basis capital accounts.**[8] The capital account analysis is reported in box L of Schedule K-1 (Form 1065) as follows.

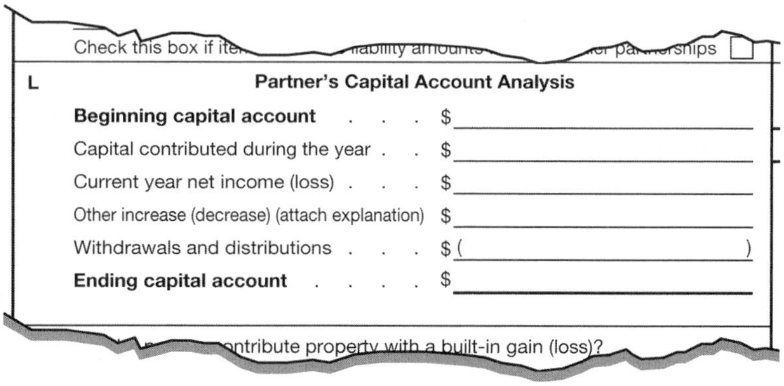

L **Partner's Capital Account Analysis**

Beginning capital account	$
Capital contributed during the year	$
Current year net income (loss)	$
Other increase (decrease) (attach explanation)	$
Withdrawals and distributions	$ ( )
Ending capital account	$

---

5. See the 1954 *Conference Report on Section 707:* H.R. Conf. Rep. No. 2543, 83d Cong., 2d Sess. 59 (1954).

6. IRC §701.

7. See, e.g., *Holiday Village Shopping Center, Inc. v. U.S.,* 773 F.2d 276 (Fed. Cir. 1985).

8. IRC §722; IRS Notice 2019-66, 2019-52 IRB 1509; IRS Notice 2020-43, 2020-27 IRB 1; IRS Notice 2021-13, 2021-06 IRB 832.

This replaces optional methods of determining capital accounts on Schedules K-1 because their lack of uniformity frustrated the IRS's efforts to use them for compliance purposes. However, nothing prevents a partnership from simultaneously employing a separate capital accounting using traditional §704(b) rules or GAAP. In fact, the §704(b) rules are very relevant for partnerships with partners who have contributed property with book-tax disparities or partnerships that have special allocations, as discussed later. The following materials, therefore, discuss both tax basis capital accounting and §704(b) capital accounting.

TAX BASIS CAPITAL ACCOUNTS

The IRS has never explained why it requires tax basis capital account reporting. The consensus, however, is that the information provided by the capital account analysis did not permit the IRS to determine such things as partners not recognizing gain when disposing of partnership interests with negative capital accounts. Real estate limited partnerships that have nonrecourse financing are prone to this issue. Limited partners can use qualified nonrecourse financing as basis that enables them to take deductions — especially depreciation or equity-based distributions — in excess of their economic investments, resulting in negative capital accounts. Yet, if an individual disposes of a partnership interest, the IRS is concerned that the income tax consequences of those negative capital accounts too often go unreported.[9] Requiring uniformity in capital accounts reporting is potentially a tool enabling the IRS to better identify failures to report tax consequences of such things as negative capital accounts and distributions in excess of basis.[10]

Partners' tax basis capital accounts must be prepared using the **transactional method** as described in the instructions for Form 1065, *U.S. Return of Partnership Income*. The use of any other method is prohibited.[11] There is, however, a "small" partnership exception. Under this, if a partnership satisfies all four of the following conditions, it is exempt from completing the balance sheet at Schedule L, *Balance Sheets per Books,* Schedules M-1, *Reconciliation of Income (Loss) per Books with Analysis of Net Income (Loss) per Return,* and M-2, *Analysis of Partners' Capital Accounts*. The partnership is not required to report negative tax basis capital account information.[12]

1. The partnership's total receipts for the tax year were less than $250,000.
2. The partnership's total assets at the end of the tax year were less than $1 million.
3. Schedules K-1 are filed with the return and furnished to the partners on or before the due date (including extensions) for the partnership return.
4. The partnership is not filing and is not required to file Schedule M-3, *Net Income (Loss) Reconciliation for Certain Partnerships.*

---

9. Treas. Reg. §1.704-1(b)(2)(ii)(b)(3).

10. *Partnerships: Audit Technique Guide,* p. 7-5. Sep. 2002. IRS. [www.unclefed.com/SurviveIRS/MSSP/partnershipsatg12-16.pdf] Accessed on Apr. 11, 2023.

11. IRS Notice 2021-13, 2021-06 IRB 832.

12. See Form 1065, Schedule B, *Other Information,* question 4.

Schedules M-1 and M-2 for Form 1065 are shown below.

22 Total liabilit

Schedule M-1 **Reconciliation of Income (Loss) per Books With Analysis of Net Income (Loss) per Return**
Note: The partnership may be required to file Schedule M-3. See instructions.

1	Net income (loss) per books		6	Income recorded on books this year not included on Schedule K, lines 1 through 11 (itemize):	
2	Income included on Schedule K, lines 1, 2, 3c, 5, 6a, 7, 8, 9a, 10, and 11, not recorded on books this year (itemize):		a	Tax-exempt interest $	
3	Guaranteed payments (other than health insurance)		7	Deductions included on Schedule K, lines 1 through 13d, and 21, not charged against book income this year (itemize):	
4	Expenses recorded on books this year not included on Schedule K, lines 1 through 13d, and 21 (itemize):		a	Depreciation $	
a	Depreciation $		8	Add lines 6 and 7	
b	Travel and entertainment $		9	Income (loss) (Analysis of Net Income (Loss), line 1). Subtract line 8 from line 5	
5	Add lines 1 through 4				

Schedule M-2 **Analysis of Partners' Capital Accounts**

1	Balance at beginning of year . . .		6	Distributions: **a** Cash	
2	Capital contributed: **a** Cash . . .			**b** Property	
	b Property . .		7	Other decreases (itemize):	
3	Net income (loss) (see instructions) .				
4	Other increases (itemize):		8	Add lines 6 and 7	
5	Add lines 1 through 4		9	Balance at end of year. Subtract line 8 from line 5	

Form **1065** (2022)

Practitioner Planning Tip

Although the partnership is not required to complete Schedules L, M-1, and M-2 under these conditions, the information contained in these schedules may be necessary in the future to properly prepare returns.

Reporting Transactions

Tax basis capital accounts are determined each year using the following adjustments.[13]

	Tax Basis Capital
Beginning capital account	$
Capital contributed during the year	$
Current year net income (loss)	$
Other increase (decrease) (attach explanation)	$
Withdrawals and distributions	$( )
Ending capital account	$

13. Instructions for Form 1065.

Capital Contributions.[14] For tax basis capital account purposes, capital contributed includes the amount of cash plus the **adjusted tax basis** of all property contributed by the partner to the partnership during the year. The amount entered on this line must be reduced by any liabilities assumed by the partnership in connection with the contribution or liabilities to which the property is subject immediately before the contribution. This amount might be negative, such as a transfer of property subject to liabilities in excess of the contributing partner's basis in the property.

Current Year Income or Loss. This line is the partner's distributive share of partnership income and gain (including tax-exempt income) for the year as determined for tax purposes, minus the partner's distributive share of partnership loss and deductions (including nondeductible, noncapital expenditures) as determined for tax purposes.

Other Increases and Decreases.[15] This line is the sum of all other increases or decreases that affected the partner's capital account for tax purposes during the year. A statement must be attached to Form 1065 explaining each adjustment. The 2022 Form 1065 instructions give the following examples of increases and decreases that should be reported on this line.

Increases	Decreases
The partner's distributive share of the excess of the tax deductions for depletion (other than oil and gas depletion) over the adjusted tax basis of the property subject to depletion.	The partner's distributive share of tax deductions for depletion of any partnership oil and gas property, but not exceeding the partner's share of the adjusted tax basis of that property.
The partner's share of any increase to the adjusted tax basis of partnership property under IRC §734(b).	The partner's share of any decrease to the adjusted tax basis of partnership property under §734(b).

In the event of uncertainty on how to report a partnership event or transaction, the instructions say to account for it in a manner generally consistent with determining the partner's adjusted tax basis in its partnership interest (without regard to partnership liabilities), taking into account the following rules and principles.

IRC §705. This section deals generally with how annual basis adjustments are made to a partner's basis in its partnership interest and will also affect the tax basis capital account. Basis is increased by:[16]

1. Additional contributions of cash and basis of property contributed to the partnership and allocation of partnership liabilities;
2. The partner's distributive share of non-separately computed and separately stated income;
3. The partner's distributive share of partnership tax-exempt income; and
4. The partner's distributive share of the excess of the deductions for depletion in excess of the partnership's basis for the depletable property.

Basis is decreased, but not below zero, by:[17]

1. The amount of money and the adjusted basis of property distributed to the partner by the partnership, including money attributable to a partner's reduction in partnership liabilities allocated to the partner;
2. The partner's distributive share of separately and non-separately stated partnership losses, including capital losses;
3. The partner's distributive share of nondeductible partnership expenses that are not capital expenditures; and
4. The amount of the partner's deduction for depletion for any partnership oil and gas wells, up to the proportionate share of the partnership's adjusted basis for its depletable properties.

14. IRS Notice 2020-43, 2020-27 IRB 1.

15. 2022 Instructions for Form 1065.

16. IRC §705(a); Treas. Regs. §§1.705-1 and 1.705-2.

17. IRC §§705(a)(2) and (3).

IRC §722. This section states that the basis of a partner's interest in the partnership is the amount of money and adjusted basis of property contributed by the partner, increased by any gain required to be recognized under IRC §721(b) if the partnership is treated as an investment company.

IRC §733. This section deals with the effect of nonliquidating distributions on a partner's basis of its partnership interest. It requires that the partner's basis be reduced (but not below zero) by the sum of any money distributed and the partnership's adjusted basis of any property distributed (but not in excess of the partner's adjusted basis in its partnership interest after reduction by any money distributed).

IRC §742. Under this section, the basis of a partner's partnership interest acquired other than by contribution to the partnership is to be determined under the usual basis rules beginning at IRC §1011. This includes, for example, such things as FMV inherited basis under IRC §1014 and carryover gift basis under IRC §1015.

4

Withdrawals and Distributions. This line should have the amount of cash plus the adjusted tax basis of all property distributed by the partnership to the partner during the year. The amount entered must be reduced by any liabilities assumed by the partner in connection with the distribution or liabilities to which the property was subject immediately before the distribution. This amount may be negative.

Ending Capital Account. The sum of the amounts previously discussed from the chart constitute the partner's ending capital account, which may be negative if the sum of a partner's losses and distributions exceeds the sum of the partner's contributions and share of income.

Observation. Prohibiting the use of liabilities in determining tax basis **capital** accounts tends to portray a more realistic picture of a partner's actual economic relationship with the partnership. This is especially true with respect to real estate partnerships where deductions and distributions attributable to nonrecourse debt can easily exceed a partner's economic investment.

IRC §704(b) CAPITAL ACCOUNTS

Traditional capital accounting under §704(b) is used to measure a partner's **economic investment** in a partnership as opposed to its **tax investment. Capital accounts are commonly referred to as "book" accounts** to distinguish them from tax capital accounts. The principal difference between the two is that book capital accounts are based on the FMV of contributed assets,[18] while tax capital accounts use the adjusted tax basis of contributed assets.[19] In this section, the term "capital account" refers to "book" unless stated otherwise. Tax basis capital accounts are discussed previously.

Although the maintenance of capital accounts is intended to track the partners' economic interests in a partnership, these accounts are generally adjusted with respect to tax items, rather than through the use of normal financial accounting rules. This is because the fundamental rule of partnership allocations is that tax allocations must follow book allocations.[20] In this context "following book" establishes the standard by which special allocations are measured: an allocation that has a tax effect without also affecting the economic circumstances of a partner may be disregarded.

Note. In addition, special rules are provided under §704(c) (described in the section titled "IRC §704(c) Allocations") for contributions of property with a book value that differs from its tax basis (referred to as **book-tax disparities)** because, in these instances, tax allocations and book allocations necessarily differ. Information concerning contributions to a partnership of §704(c) assets by a partner and mandatory allocations of items with respect to such property are reportable on partners' Schedules K-1.

---

18. See Treas. Regs. §§1.704-1(b)(2)(iv)(b) and 1.704-1(b)(2)(iv)(g).

19. IRC §722.

20. Treas. Reg. §1.704-1(b)(2)(ii).

Each partner's book capital account begins at zero and, in general, is **increased** by the following items.[21]

- The amount of money contributed by the partner to the partnership
- The FMV of property contributed by the partner to the partnership, net of liabilities secured by such contributed property that the partnership is considered to assume or take under IRC §752
- Allocations to the partner of partnership income and gain, including tax-exempt income and certain special allocations required by the regulations

The following items **decrease** book capital accounts.[22]

- The amount of money distributed to a partner by the partnership
- The FMV of property distributed to the partner net of liabilities secured by the distributed property that the partner is considered to assume or take under §752
- Allocations to the partner of nondeductible, noncapital expenditures of the partnership
- Allocations of partnership loss and deductions

A partner who has more than one interest in a partnership is required to have a single book capital account that combines all interests of the partner in the partnership.[23]

Many rules must be followed in maintaining book capital accounts. These are generally found in Treas. Regs. §§1.704-1(b)(2)(iv)(c)–(q). The rules are briefly described in the following material (noncompensatory options are omitted).

Liabilities[24]

For book purposes, money contributed by a partner to a partnership includes the amount of any partnership liabilities assumed by the partner other than liabilities assumed by a distributee-partner in connection with distributed property. Money distributed to a partner by a partnership includes the amount of the partner's individual liabilities that are assumed by the partnership other than liabilities secured by contributed property. Liabilities are considered assumed only to the extent:

- The assuming party is subjected to personal liability,
- The benefitting party is aware of the assumption and can directly enforce the assuming party's obligation, and
- The assuming party is ultimately liable (rather than the party from whom the liability is assumed).

Liabilities do not include constructive cash distributions and partner contributions resulting from liability shifts occurring as a result of contributions and distributions of encumbered property.

FMV[25]

The FMV assigned to property by the partners is generally accepted for book purposes if the value is reasonably agreed to among the partners in arm's-length negotiations and the partners have sufficiently adverse interests. If these conditions are not satisfied and the property values are overstated or understated by more than an insignificant amount, the partners' capital accounts are not considered to satisfy the economic effect requirement (other than economic equivalence).[26] FMV is determined without taking into account the IRC §7701(g) requirement that the FMV of property securing a nonrecourse liability is not treated as less than the amount of the nonrecourse liability.

---

21. Treas. Reg. §1.704-1(b)(2)(iv)(b).
22. Ibid.
23. Ibid.
24. Treas. Reg. §1.704-1(b)(2)(iv)(c).
25. Treas. Reg. §1.704-1(b)(2)(iv)(h)(1).
26. Ibid.

Promissory Notes

A partner's contribution of a promissory note does not result in any increase in the partner's book account unless the partnership disposes of the note in a taxable transaction or payments are actually made against the note principal by the contributing partner.[27] If the note is readily tradable on an established securities market, however, this limitation is not applicable.[28] Similarly, a partner's capital account is not decreased for distribution of a partnership's note to a partner unless there is a taxable disposition of the note by the partner or the partnership makes principal payments.[29]

IRC §704(c) Considerations

4

The partnership agreement must require that the partners' capital accounts be adjusted to reflect differences between book value and tax basis with respect to contributed property subject to a §704(c) special allocation for precontribution gain or loss.[30] The capital accounts **are not adjusted,** however, to reflect the actual tax allocations required under §704(c).[31]

> **Note.** A partner's share of net unrecognized §704(c) gain or loss can be reported on their Schedule K-1 in Part II, item N.[32]

Distributed Property

A partner's capital account is decreased by the FMV of property distributed to the partner. In doing so, the capital accounts of all the partners first must be adjusted to reflect the manner in which the unrealized income, gain, loss, and deduction inherent in the property that has not previously been reflected in capital accounts would be allocated among the partners if there were a taxable disposition of the property for its FMV.[33] For this purpose, the excess of nonrecourse liabilities over FMV is taken into account.[34]

Revaluations of Partnership Property

A partnership agreement may increase or decrease the capital accounts of the partners to reflect a revaluation of partnership property on the partnership's books, including intangible assets such as goodwill.[35] For revaluations to be acceptable, they must be made principally for a substantial nontax business purpose such as any of the following.[36]

- Admission of a new partner
- Contributions by existing partners
- Liquidation of the partnership or a distribution of money or other property to a retiring or continuing partner as consideration for an interest in the partnership
- Issuance of a partnership interest to an existing or new partner in exchange for services performed to the partnership
- Issuance by the partnership of a noncompensatory option
- Under generally accepted industry accounting practices, if substantially all the partnership's property is readily tradable stock, securities, etc.

---

27. Treas. Reg. §1.704-1(b)(2)(iv)(d)(2).
28. Ibid.
29. Treas. Reg. §1.704-1(b)(2)(iv)(e)(2).
30. Treas. Reg. §1.704-1(b)(2)(iv)(d)(3).
31. Ibid.
32. 2022 Instructions for Form 1065; See IRS Notice 2019-66, 2019-52 IRB 1510.
33. Treas. Reg. §1.704-1(b)(2)(iv)(e)(1).
34. Ibid.
35. Treas. Reg. §1.704-1(b)(2)(iv)(f).
36. Treas. Regs. §§1.704-1(b)(2)(iv)(f)(5)(i)–(v).

In addition, the partnership agreement must generally require that the capital accounts be adjusted to reflect the manner in which the unrealized income, gain, loss, and deduction inherent in the property would be allocated among the partners under §704(c) special allocation principles if there were a taxable disposition of the property for FMV on the date of distribution.[37]

Special Adjustments to Reflect Book Values

One of the goals of the **substantial economic effect test** (discussed later) is to apply economic rules to a partnership's bookkeeping that, over time, eliminate the differences between the partnership's tax values (basis) and its book values (FMV). This is also a purpose of the mandatory §704(c) special allocations with respect to precontribution gain or loss. Allocations to the partners of depreciation, depletion, amortization, and gain or loss for book purposes must, therefore, be made for the book value of the property using the same ratio as the corresponding tax item over the tax basis of the property.[38] For depreciation and other amortization purposes, if the property has a zero tax basis, the corresponding book deduction may be determined under any reasonable method selected by the partnership.[39]

Example 1. A partner contributes property with an FMV of $90 and an adjusted basis of $60 to a partnership. The depreciation deduction for the first year following the contribution is $20, which is one-third of the adjusted basis of the property. For purposes of book accounting, the partnership is therefore required to depreciate one-third of the $90 book value, or $30.

Nondeductible Expenditures[40]

Nondeductible, noncapital expenditures of the partnership (e.g., the 50% disallowance of meal and entertainment expenses) reduce a partner's book account. Unless an election is made under IRC §709(b) to amortize organizational expenditures, they are treated as nondeductible, noncapital expenses. Losses that are disallowed under IRC §§267 or 707(b) for sales or exchanges of partnership property to related parties are also treated as such expenditures.

Depletion

Depletion deductions are separately stated items for income tax purposes. For book accounting, however, the regulations require that "simulated" depletion be determined at the partnership level and be used to adjust book value without regard to the tax limitations that apply at the individual partner level. Alternatively, each partner's actual depletion deduction can be used.[41]

Transfers of Partnership Interest

Upon the transfer of all or a part of an interest in the partnership, the capital account of the transferor that is attributable to the transferred interest must carry over to the transferee-partner.[42] Prior to the Tax Cuts and Jobs Act (TCJA), the provisions of IRC §708 could cause technical terminations of partnerships. The TCJA nullified these provisions, enabling partnerships to continue even if more than 50% of the capital interests changed within a 12-month period.

Under current law, if two partnerships merge, the book capital accounts of the two entities are combined. The Code considers the resulting partnership to be the continuation of the partnership whose partners held more than 50% of the capital in the new, combined partnership. The book capital accounts of the successor entity consist of the merged book capital accounts of each merged partnership.[43] Conversely, if a partnership divides into multiple partnerships, the Code considers each a continuation of the prior partnership.[44]

---

37. Treas. Regs. §§1.704-1(b)(2)(iv)(f)(1)–(4).
38. Treas. Regs. §§1.704-1(b)(2)(iv)(g)(1) and (3).
39. Treas. Reg. §1.704-1(b)(2)(iv)(g)(3).
40. Treas. Reg. §1.704-1(b)(2)(iv)(i).
41. Treas. Reg. §1.704-1(b)(2)(iv)(k).
42. Treas. Reg. §1.704-1(b)(2)(iv)(l).
43. IRC §708(b)(2)(A).
44. IRC §708(b)(2)(B).

Optional Basis Adjustments

A partnership that has a §754 election in effect is generally not permitted to adjust the book account of a transferee-partner or of the partnership in the case of an IRC §743 adjustment under which a transferee-partner adjusts the partner's share of inside tax basis to reflect the outside tax basis.[45] This does not apply, however, to the extent the basis adjustment is allocated to the common basis of partnership property.[46] IRC §732(d) adjustments for partnerships that do not have a §754 election in effect are treated in the same manner.[47]

If there is an adjustment under §734 (discussed later) as a result of gain or loss being recognized by a distributee-partner upon distribution of property from the partnership, the partner receiving the distribution giving rise to the adjustment is required to have a corresponding adjustment made to their book account.[48] If the distribution is made other than in liquidation of the partner's interest, however, the capital accounts of all partners are adjusted. The adjustment should be made in the manner in which the unrealized income and gain that is displaced by the adjustment would have been shared if the property whose basis is adjusted were sold immediately prior to the adjustment for its recomputed adjusted tax basis.[49]

A partner's capital account may be adjusted for §§732, 734, and 743 basis adjustments to partnership property but only to the extent that such basis adjustments are permitted to partnership property under IRC §755 and result in a change in the amount for such property on the partnership's balance sheet for book purposes.[50]

Partnership Level Characterization

Except as otherwise required for depletion, the book capital accounts of partners must be determined by applying federal tax rules at the partnership level without regard to how items would be required to be treated at the individual partner level. In other words, book accounting treats the partnership as an entity rather than as an aggregate.[51]

Capital Accounts and Guaranteed Payments

Guaranteed payments to a partner under §707(c) cause the capital account of the recipient partner to be adjusted only to the extent of the partner's distributive share of any partnership deduction, loss, or other downward capital account adjustment resulting from such payment.[52]

Minor Discrepancies

Minor discrepancies between the actual balances in the capital accounts of the partners and the balances that would have existed had the book accounting rules been properly followed are not treated as violating the substantial economic effect requirement as long as they are attributable to good faith error by the partnership.[53]

45. Treas. Reg. §1.704-1(b)(2)(iv)(m)(2).
46. Ibid.
47. Treas. Reg. §1.704-1(b)(2)(iv)(m)(3).
48. Treas. Reg. §1.704-1(b)(2)(iv)(m)(4).
49. Ibid.
50. Treas. Reg. §1.704-1(b)(2)(iv)(m)(5).
51. Treas. Reg. §1.704-1(b)(2)(iv)(n).
52. Treas. Reg. §1.704-1(b)(2)(iv)(o).
53. Treas. Reg. §1.704-1(b)(2)(iv)(p).

Adjustments When Guidance Is Lacking

If the regulations fail to provide guidance on how adjustments to capital accounts should be made with respect to particular items, then adjustments must be made in a manner that:[54]

1. Maintains equality between the aggregate governing capital accounts of the partners and the amount of partnership capital reflected on the partnership's balance sheet, as computed for book purposes;
2. Is consistent with the underlying economic arrangement of the partners; and
3. Is based, whenever practicable, on federal tax accounting principles.

IRC §704(c) ALLOCATIONS

The purpose of §704(c) is to prevent the shifting of tax consequences among partners with respect to precontribution gain, loss, income, or deductions. Under §704(c), therefore, a partnership **must** allocate back to the contributing partner any precontribution income, gain, loss, and deductions with respect to property contributed by the partner to the partnership to the extent of any difference between the adjusted tax basis of the property and its FMV at the time of contribution. This is commonly referred to as **book-tax disparity** because the contributing partner's capital account is credited with the FMV of the property, while the partner's partnership basis attributable to the contributed property uses the property's adjusted basis. Such special allocations must be made using a reasonable method that is consistent with the purpose of §704(c). These allocations are **mandatory,** whether contained in the partnership agreement or not.

Built-in gain on §704(c) property (more common than built-in loss) is the excess of the property's book (fair market) value over the contributing partner's tax basis in their partnership interest upon contribution. The built-in gain is thereafter reduced by decreases in the gap between the property's book value and adjusted tax basis. Built-in loss on §704(c) property is the excess of the contributing partner's basis over the property's book value upon contribution. The built-in loss is thereafter reduced by decreases in the gap between the property's adjusted tax basis and book value.[55] If the property is sold, the built-in gain or loss as of the sale date must be specially allocated back to the contributing partner and only gain or loss in excess of that is divisible among all partners.

> **Note**. Allocation of built-in gain or loss to a partner will increase or decrease their **basis** in their partnership interest, but there will be **no adjustment to their capital account** because the built-in gain or loss for capital account purposes is already reflected in determining the initial capital account value of the contributed property.

54. Treas. Reg. §1.704-1(b)(2)(iv)(q).
55. Treas. Reg. §1.704-3(a)(3)(ii).

Example 2. In exchange for a 50% interest in a new partnership, Amos contributes fully depreciated property with a FMV of $100 and an adjusted basis of $0. The property, therefore, has $100 of §704(c) built-in gain because Amos' capital account is $100, the property's FMV, but his partnership basis is zero, the contributed property's adjusted basis. There are five years remaining in the depreciable period. Beatrice, the other partner, contributes $100 of cash and therefore has no book-tax disparity because both her capital account and her partnership basis are $100. The partnership agreement provides that all allocations are 50-50.

Under the simplest approach to §704(c), if the property is sold for $150, Amos is allocated the first $100 of gain. This eliminates the book-tax disparity because his partnership basis increases to $100. His capital account, however, is not increased by the $100 of gain (normally it would be) because that $100 is already represented by the $100 FMV of the property based on its precontribution gain. The remaining $50 of gain is then allocated equally between the two partners under §704(b) (the usual partnership allocation rules). Therefore, Amos is allocated a total of $125 of the $150 of gain, and Beatrice is allocated $25, which is her 50% share of the $50 of post-contribution gain in excess of the §704(c) $100 of built-in gain allocated to Amos.

Thus, in the end, each partner will have a capital account of $125 and a partnership basis of $125. The partnership will have $250 cash. If the cash is distributed to the partners in the liquidation of the partnership, each will receive $125 of cash against their $125 of basis so that liquidating distributions are nontaxable.

Failure to account for and properly apply the §704(c) rules is not just a violation of rules and regulations, it can actually have an economic impact on partners, as demonstrated by the following example.

Example 3. Use the same facts as in **Example 2,** except that, when the property is sold, §704(c) is not taken into account. As a result, the entire $150 of gain is divided equally between Amos and Beatrice, with each reporting $75 of gain. Each partner's capital account increases by $75, so that each has a $175 capital account. Similarly, their respective partnership bases increases by $75, so that Amos will have $75 of basis and Beatrice $175.

If the partnership then distributes its assets 50-50 in liquidation, each partner receives $125 of cash. Amos has $50 of capital gain because the $125 of cash distributed exceeds his $75 of partnership basis. Beatrice has a $50 capital loss because the $125 of cash distributed to her is less than her $175 basis.

Amos's $50 capital gain represents half of the $100 built-in gain he should have recognized under §704(c). The $50 of capital loss for Beatrice represents the other $50 of built-in gain, the tax on which should have been paid by Amos but was instead paid by Beatrice. Thus, on a present value basis, Amos has a tax windfall by deferring paying tax on $50 (half the built-in gain) until the liquidation of the partnership. Beatrice suffers a tax detriment because she has paid income tax on $50 of gain that is actually not her income and does not recover that prepayment until liquidation of the partnership. This distortion would be even worse if the $100 were ordinary income, such as depreciation recapture. In that case, Amos would effectively convert $50 of ordinary income to long-term capital gain, and Beatrice would convert $50 of ordinary income to a long-term capital loss.

Caution. Beatrice is likely to be very unhappy with her tax returns. A situation like this could be considered preparer malpractice.

The problem is more complicated, however, than simply waiting until the property is disposed of to allocate the built-in gain. Instead, the §704(c) regulations **mandate** that the book-tax disparity be eliminated as quickly as possible. "Elimination" means that adjustments must be made that will, over time, cause all partners' income tax bases to equal their capital accounts. This can be done through any reasonable method. Although no particular method is required by the Code or regulations, the regulations set out three methods that generally are considered reasonable (traditional method, traditional method with curative allocation, and remedial method).[56] The following is a very simplistic example of one method for correcting a book-tax disparity.[57]

Example 4. Use the same facts as **Example 3.** Additionally, the $100 of cash contributed by Beatrice is used to purchase depreciable property. Assume that the property is depreciated for both book and tax purposes at the rate of $20 per year over five years (ignoring conventions). The two partners' initial capital accounts and tax bases in the partnership are as follows.

Partner	Capital Account	Tax Basis
Amos	$100	$ 0
Beatrice	100	100

Amos has a book-tax disparity of $100 because his capital account exceeds his partnership basis by that amount. Beatrice has no book-tax disparity, but in eliminating Amos's disparity, adjustments are also made to Beatrice's capital account and bases. In this case, that will be accomplished through special allocations of depreciation deductions for income tax purposes (**but not for capital account purposes)** that will, as soon and as much as possible, cause both partners to have capital accounts that equal their partnership tax bases. Thus, over the five years the property is depreciated, capital accounts and tax bases are adjusted as follows.

Year	Capital Account	Book Depreciation	Tax Basis	Tax Depreciation
Amos				
1	$100	$10	$ 0	$ 0
2	80	10	0	0
3	60	10	0	0
4	40	10	0	0
5	20	10	0	0
6	0	0	0	0
Beatrice				
1	$100	$10	$100	$20
2	80	10	80	20
3	60	10	60	20
4	40	10	40	20
5	20	10	20	20
6	0	0	0	0

Beginning in year six, the book-tax disparity has been eliminated. There is also no remaining depreciation to be allocated between the partners.

56. Treas. Regs. §§1.704-3(b)–(d).

57. This is the traditional method at Treas. Reg. §1.704-3(b).

> **Observation.** It is important to be able to recognize circumstances involving §704(c) assets because the existence of book-tax disparities has a significant effect on the proper maintenance of capital accounts and allocations of minimum gain under the nonrecourse debt rules. In addition, the 2022 Schedule K-1 (Form 1065), part II, item M, asks whether the partner contributed property with a built-in gain or loss. If so, the partnership must attach a statement showing the property contributed, the date of the contribution, and the amount of any built-in gain or loss. Subsequent special allocations under §704(c) must also be reported to the partner at line 20, "other information," with a code AA. In any year that a partner is allocated any §704(c) gain or loss, the partnership must also show the net unrecognized §704(c) gain or loss at the beginning at the end of that year in item N.[58]

4

GUARANTEED PAYMENTS

Partners who are working full time for the partnership generally cannot wait until after the end of the partnership's tax year to receive their distributive share of partnership income. As a result, partners generally receive payments during the year. It is therefore necessary to determine the character of such payments and their income and employment tax effects. The IRS has ruled that partners are not employees of a partnership for employment tax purposes and that remuneration received by a partner from the partnership is not wages, a position it maintains today.[59] Under existing guidance, therefore, it is virtually impossible for a partner working in the partnership's business to be treated as an employee of the partnership for either withholding or fringe benefit purposes except when the latter are expressly permitted in the Code, such as for certain pension purposes.

CHARACTERIZATION

In the partnership context, therefore, payments received by a partner during the year and before their distributive share for that year is determined can be one of three types: an advance draw, an interim distribution, or a guaranteed payment. With an **advance draw**, the partner is essentially borrowing against their end of the year distributive share. The draws are therefore not taxable when received because they are simply part of the partner's distributive share determined as of the close of the partnership's tax year.[60] If the payment is an **interim distribution,** it is taxable only to the extent it exceeds the partner's basis in the partnership as of the distribution date.[61] Finally, if the payment is a **guaranteed payment,** it is treated as self-employment (SE) income (if paid for services) to the recipient partner and is an expense of the partnership.[62]

General partners must include guaranteed payments as SE net earnings. However, a limited partner must include in net earnings only those guaranteed payments for services rendered to, or on behalf of, the partnership.[63] If the purpose of the guaranteed payment is to provide a minimum return on capital, though, then the SE tax is not imposed.[64] SE tax arising from partnership activities is discussed later.

Determining which type of payment a partner has received may not be readily apparent, especially if not specifically addressed in the partnership agreement. Even then, however, the actual conduct of the parties may differ from the terms of the partnership agreement. In such cases, the determination becomes based on the facts and circumstances surrounding what the parties did and how that was done. However, in this regard there are a few rules of thumb based on the characteristics of each type of payment.[65]

---

58. Partner's Instructions for Schedule K-1 (Form 1065).

59. Rev. Rul. 69-184, 1969-1 CB 256.

60. IRC §704(b).

61. IRC §731.

62. IRC §707(c).

63. IRC §1402; *Question: Are partners considered employees of a partnership or are they considered self-employed?* Sep. 6, 2022. IRS. [www.irs.gov/faqs/small-business-self-employed-other-business/entities/entities-1#] Accessed on Apr. 13, 2023.

64. IRC §1402(a)(2).

65. *Mangham v. Comm'r,* TC Memo 1980-280 (Jul. 29, 1980).

ADVANCE

An advance against a partner's distributive share is effectively a loan. Therefore, if the partner's distributive share for the year is less than the sum of the advances, there must be an obligation for the partner to repay the excess.

Distributions are made from a partner's capital account and are nontaxable returns of capital only to the extent of the partner's basis. It may be somewhat more difficult to distinguish between distributions and guaranteed payments so that facts and circumstances must be more closely examined. In general, if the payments are made even though the partnership has a loss for the year and there is no proper capital accounting by the partnership, such payments may be found to be guaranteed payments.[66]

Guaranteed payments are those made to a partner who is acting in a capacity other than as a partner.[67] There is no specific definition of what acting as "other than a partner" means; rather it is based on the parties' conduct. So long as it appears that a partner is entitled to particular payments (even if the amounts vary) without regard to the partnership's profit or loss and the partner's distributive share, it is likely to be a guaranteed payment.[68]

Generally, the IRS has been willing to consider all facts and circumstances in differentiating between payments based directly on partnership income versus those based on a formula that references partnership income. However, the courts have been more stringent in finding that any payment linked to partnership income does not qualify as a guaranteed payment.[69] Thus, it may be easier to think of guaranteed payments as akin to arm's-length transactions with non-members of the partnership.

TAX IMPACTS

From the partnership perspective, guaranteed payments may be either:

- Deductible under IRC §162(a) as ordinary or necessary business expenses, or
- Capitalized under IRC §263.

"[A] partner who receives guaranteed payments is not regarded as an employee of the partnership for the purposes of withholding of tax at source, deferred compensation plans, etc."[70] Thus, the partnership is not responsible for withholding employment taxes from guaranteed payments.[71]

From the recipient's perspective, the guaranteed payment is ordinary income solely for purposes of IRC §61 and is not a distributive share of partnership profits or payment to an employee that would entitle the recipient partner to employee benefits.[72] The income should also be reported in the same taxable year as the partnership deducts the payment.[73]

---

66. *Clark v. Comm'r,* TC Memo 1982-401 (Jul. 19, 1982).

67. IRC §707(a).

68. Ibid.

69. See *Pratt v. Comm'r,* 64 TC. 203, 210-211 (1975), finding that a partnership agreement guaranteeing each partner a management fee calculated as a fixed percentage of gross rental income did not meet the requirements of §707.

70. Treas. Reg. §1.707-1(c).

71. Rev. Rul. 56-326, 1956-2 CB 501.

72. Treas. Reg. §1.707-1(c).

73. Ibid.

Example 5. ABC Partnership has three partners. All partnership items are allocated in accordance with the partners' percentage interests. The partners have the following ownership interests, tax bases, and capital accounts.

Partner	Percentage	Tax Basis	Capital Account
Avery	80	$80,000	$80,000
Basil	15	15,000	15,000
Carlita	5	5,000	5,000

Carlita receives a $10,000 guaranteed payment. Each partner is allocated their respective share of deduction for the guaranteed payment, which reduces their capital accounts accordingly.

Partner	Percentage	Deduction	Capital Account
Avery	80	$8,000	$72,000
Basil	15	1,500	13,500
Carlita	5	500	4,500

Thus, Carlita receives $10,000, but her capital account is reduced by only her $500 share of the partnership's deduction for the payment.

Example 6. Use the same facts as **Example 5,** except pursuant to the partnership agreement, Avery receives $5,000 annually for her services, without regard to partnership income, plus 20% of the partnership's taxable gain or loss. The other 80% of partnership gain or loss is allocated between Basil and Carlita. Carlita receives no guaranteed payment. If the partnership has $40,000 income after deducting the $5,000 guaranteed payment to her, Avery reports $13,000 of ordinary income comprised of the $5,000 guaranteed payment and $8,000 share of ABC's income (20% × $40,000).[74]

Guaranteed Payment	Allocated Partnership Gain/Loss	Reported Ordinary Income
$5,000	20% × $40,000 = $8,000	$13,000

Example 7. Use the same facts as **Example 5,** except pursuant to the partnership agreement, Basil receives 25% of the partnership's taxable gain or loss before taking into account any guaranteed payments, with a guaranteed minimum of $20,000. Carlita receives no guaranteed payment. If the partnership's income is $90,000, then Basil receives $22,500 (25% × $90,000) as his distributive share and no guaranteed payment.

(A) Guaranteed Minimum	(B) Allocated Partnership Gain/Loss	(A − B) Guaranteed Payment (Limited to $0)	Distributive Share
$20,000	$90,000 × 25% = $22,500	$0	$22,500

If the partnership's income is only $60,000, then Basil receives $15,000 (25% × $60,000) as his distributive share and $5,000 ($20,000 − $15,000) as a guaranteed payment.[75]

(A) Guaranteed Minimum	(B) Allocated Partnership Gain/Loss	(A − B) Guaranteed Payment (Limited to $0)	Distributive Share
$20,000	$60,000 × 25% = $15,000	$5,000	$15,000

74. Treas. Reg. §1.707-1(c). See example 1.

75. Treas. Reg. §1.707-1(c). See example 2.

Example 8. Use the same facts as **Example 5,** except pursuant to the partnership agreement, Carlita receives 30% of the partnership's taxable gain or loss, and a guaranteed payment of $15,000 for services. If the partnership has a loss of $6,000 after deducting the $15,000 guaranteed payment, then Carlita reports the $15,000 as ordinary income, and $1,800 (30% × $6,000) as a loss under §704(d).[76]

Percentage	Guaranteed Payment	Allocated Partnership Loss	Reported Ordinary Income
30	$15,000	30% × $6,000 = $1,800	$15,000

Example 9. Use the same facts as **Example 5,** except pursuant to the partnership agreement, Carlita receives 30% of the partnership's taxable gain or loss, and a guaranteed payment of $15,000 for services. If the partnership has only capital gains of $30,000 prior to deducting the $15,000 guaranteed payment, then Carlita reports the $15,000 as ordinary income, $4,500 (30% × $15,000) of ordinary loss, and $9,000 (30% × $30,000) as a capital gain – all segregated per IRC §702(a).[77]

Percentage	Guaranteed Payment	Allocated Partnership Loss (Ordinary)	Reported Ordinary Income	Reported Capital Gain
30	$15,000	30% × $15,000 = $4,500	$15,000	30% × $30,000 = $9,000

PROPERTY TRANSACTIONS

If a partner makes or receives a transfer of money or property with a partnership, and the transaction may be characterized as a sale or exchange of property (that is, not a contribution or distribution), then, under §707(a), the partner is treated as acting in a capacity other than as a member of the partnership.

If the partner directly or indirectly owns more than 50% of the capital interest or profits interest in the partnership, then the entity is considered a controlled entity.[78] The Code disallows losses between the partnership and the partner, even if the transaction is conducted through a second partnership in which the partner owns more than a 50% interest. However, if the transferee subsequently sells or exchanges the property for a gain, then the previously disallowed loss is allowed.[79]

Example 10. Partners Dana, Edward, and Felicity own 30%, 30%, and 40%, respectively, of partnership DEF. Dana and Edward are related under §267(c). Dana sells property with $8,000 market value and $12,000 basis to DEF for $8,000. Dana cannot recognize any of the $4,000 loss.

Example 11. Use the same facts as **Example 10,** except DEF, as transferee, sells the property for $15,000. DEF's realized gain of $7,000 ($15,000 – $8,000) less Dana's disallowed deferred loss of $4,000 ($8,000 – $12,000) equals a $3,000 gain that DEF must recognize.

If the property being sold or exchanged is not a capital asset under IRC §1221 (that is, the property is a trade accounts receivable, inventory, stock in trade, depreciable property used in a trade or business, or real property used in a trade or business), and the partner directly or indirectly owns more than 80% of the capital interest or profits interest in one or both partnerships involved in the transaction, then gains are treated as ordinary income.[80]

---

76. Treas. Reg. §1.707-1(c). See example 3.

77. Treas. Reg. §1.707-1(c). See example 4.

78. IRC §707(b)(1).

79. IRC §267(d).

80. Treas. Reg. §1.707-1(b)(2).

Example 12. Partner Gary has an 85% interest in GH partnership and a 90% interest in the GJ partnership. Gary sells a delivery van that had been used in GJ and depreciated to an adjusted basis of $8,000 to GH for $10,000. GH plans to use the van in its business. Gary recognizes $2,000 **ordinary** gain from GH.

QUALIFIED BUSINESS INCOME DOES NOT INCLUDE GUARANTEED PAYMENTS

TCJA[81] added IRC §199A — at least for tax years after December 31, 2017, through December 31, 2025 — to provide pass-through entities such as partnerships with a benefit similar to the reduced corporate tax rate. IRC §199A(a) allows a taxpayer who is not a corporation to deduct the lesser of:

- The taxpayer's combined qualified business income (QBI), or
- 20% of the excess of the taxpayer's taxable income over net capital gain.

4

IRC §199A(c)(4) excludes guaranteed payments from the definition of QBI. Guaranteed payments reduce the amount of QBI, and guaranteed payments do not qualify as Form W-2, *Wage and Tax Statement,* payments. Thus, reliance on guaranteed payments reduces the potential QBI deduction.

Note. For more information on specific QBI rules, see the 2018 *University of Illinois Federal Tax Workbook,* Volume B, Chapter 2: Small Business Issues, and the 2019 *University of Illinois Federal Tax Workbook,* Volume B, Chapter 1: QBID Update. These can be found at **uofi.tax/arc** [taxschool.illinois.edu/taxbookarchive].

See also the 2023 *University of Illinois Federal Tax Workbook,* Chapter 10: Small Business Issues.

ALLOCATIONS

The general rule of partnership taxation under subchapter K is that a partner's distributive share of income, gain, loss, deduction, or credit is determined by the partnership agreement.[82] Partners are usually able to allocate these items under the partnership agreement in any manner they choose unless allocations lack substantial economic effect.[83] The most basic form of allocation is simply to allocate all items among the partners in proportion to their partnership ownership interest.

Whenever allocations depart from this standard, they are generally referred to as **special allocations.** The classic example of special allocations is to allocate initial limited partnership losses to the limited partners. The fact that there is a special allocation does not necessarily mean it is abusive. The attractive feature of special allocations is that they give the partners the ability to change various aspects of allocations to more accurately reflect the economic relationship they have or to enhance that relationship through the addition of tax benefits.

The downside of special allocations is that they significantly increase the complexity of partnership tax rules. The IRS published extensive regulations under §704(b) intended to permit partnerships to make special allocations while simultaneously attempting to control the potential for abuse. These regulations are some of the most complex provisions of partnership tax under subchapter K.

81. *Tax Cuts and Jobs Act*, PL 115-97.

82. IRC §704(a).

83. IRC §704(b)(2).

SUBSTANTIAL ECONOMIC EFFECT REQUIREMENT[84]

A special allocation is an allocation of a partnership item that is disproportionate to the partners' capital contributions or to their ratio for sharing other partnership items. For special allocations to be respected, the regulations require that they have **substantial economic effect.** This means the income tax consequences of an allocation must be assigned to the partner who receives the benefit or bears the burden of the economic consequences.[85] For example, a partner who is allocated a disproportionately large share of depreciation must also be assigned the same disproportionately large reduction in the economic value of the partner's partnership interest. Thus, tax allocations **must be matched** by economic allocations — or, as commonly stated, taxes must follow the money.

If an allocation is found not to have substantial economic effect, the offending allocation is required to be reallocated among the partners in proportion to their **interests in the partnership.**[86] This is based on the manner in which the partners have agreed to share the economic benefit (income) or burden (deduction), if any, corresponding to the item that is specially allocated. It is a facts-and-circumstances determination, with no set rules. In determining a partner's interest in the partnership, the regulations list the following factors as being among those that are considered.[87]

- The partners' relative contributions to the partnership
- The interests of the partners in economic profits and losses if different from their interests in taxable income or loss
- The interests of the partners in cash flow and other nonliquidating distributions
- The rights of the partners to distributions of capital upon liquidation

The determination of whether an allocation has substantial economic effect involves a 2-part analysis that is made at the end of the partnership tax year to which the allocation relates.[88]

1. The allocation must have **economic effect.**
2. The economic effect of the allocation must be **substantial.**

ECONOMIC EFFECT[89]

To ensure allocations have the necessary economic effect, the regulations require that, throughout the full term of the partnership, the partnership agreement contain the following provisions.[90]

- The partners' capital accounts, discussed previously, are determined and maintained throughout the full term of the partnership in accordance with the capital (book) accounting rules of Treas. Reg. §1.704-1(b)(2)(iv).
- Liquidation proceeds are required (after certain capital account adjustments) to be distributed only in accordance with positive capital account balances by the later of the end of the tax year or 90 days after the date of liquidation.
- There is a **deficit restoration obligation (DRO)** in the partnership agreement or under applicable state law. This is an unconditional obligation requiring a partner to restore to the partnership any negative balance in the partner's capital account by the later of the end of the tax year or 90 days after the date of liquidation. This can also be satisfied by the partner giving a promissory note to the partnership.

---

84. Treas. Reg. §1.704-1(b)(2).
85. Treas. Reg. §1.704-1(b)(2)(ii)(a).
86. Treas. Reg. §1.704-1(b)(1)(i).
87. Treas. Reg. §1.704-1(b)(3)(ii).
88. Treas. Reg. §1.704-1(b)(2)(i).
89. Treas. Reg. §1.704-1(b)(2).
90. Treas. Reg. §1.704-1(b)(2)(ii)(b).

Example 13. Satisfaction of Economic Effect Test. Giselle and Marcus form an LLC with cash contributions of $40,000 each. This is used to purchase depreciable property for $80,000. The operating agreement provides that the members share income and losses equally except that all depreciation deductions are allocated to Giselle. The operating agreement further complies with the economic effect requirements, including a DRO.

In the LLC's first tax year, income and expenses are equal, and there is a depreciation deduction of $20,000 allocated entirely to Giselle. The LLC liquidates at the end of its first tax year and distributes assets in proportion to the members' capital accounts.

	Giselle		Marcus	
	Tax Basis	Book Basis	Tax Basis	Book Basis
Initial capital account	$40,000	$40,000	$40,000	$40,000
Depreciation	(20,000)	(20,000)	0	0
Capital account end of Year 1	$20,000	$20,000	$40,000	$40,000

Upon liquidation of the LLC, Giselle is entitled to a distribution of only $20,000, reflecting the $20,000 of depreciation allocated to her. Marcus, who had no depreciation allocation and whose capital account remains unchanged, is entitled to a distribution of $40,000.

Although the LLC does not have a DRO under state law, the operating agreement in the preceding example is presumed to have one for purposes of simplicity. In fact, an LLC will probably use the alternate economic effect test (qualified income offset, which is discussed later).

In the preceding example, the value of the asset is deemed to decline to the extent of the tax depreciation.[91] Furthermore, the capital accounting rules do not permit revaluation of the asset to determine its true market value on the presumed liquidation date.[92] This is in keeping with the requirement that value equals basis, which ensures that tax allocations have a dollar-for-dollar impact on a partner's economic investment in the partnership.

The following examples illustrate the effects of a **failure to comply** with the capital account distribution rules.

Example 14. Failure of Liquidating Test. Use the same facts as **Example 13,** except that, upon liquidation, distributions are made equally between Giselle and Marcus without regard to capital accounts. Each member is therefore entitled to a distribution of $30,000. This fails to satisfy the economic effect test because Marcus's cumulative economic investment in the LLC is $40,000, yet he receives only $30,000 in liquidation. Giselle, on the other hand, has a cumulative economic investment of only $20,000, but she receives a $30,000 distribution.

In effect, Marcus pays for half of the depreciation deduction without being allocated any of it.[93] This fails the economic effect test, and the depreciation deduction must be reallocated in accordance with the members' equal interests in the LLC.

91. Treas. Reg. §1.704-1(b)(2)(iv)(g)(1).

92. Treas. Reg. §1.704-1(b)(2)(iv)(f).

93. Treas. Reg. §1.704-1(b)(2)(ii)(b)(2).

Example 15. Failure of DRO. Mitch and Rita form an LLC with contributions of $75,000 and $25,000, respectively. The operating agreement divides all items of income and loss equally between the two members and otherwise satisfies the requirements of the regulations except that there is no DRO and the alternate test is not satisfied. Therefore, the agreement does not satisfy the economic effect test, and the allocations will not be respected.

The LLC has a total of $60,000 in losses from its first three years of operation. Therefore, each partner, has $30,000 of losses allocated to their capital accounts. If the allocations in the operating agreement were honored and the partnership liquidated at the end of Year 3, the capital accounts would be as follows.

	Mitch		Rita	
	Tax Basis	**Book Basis**	**Tax Basis**	**Book Basis**
Initial capital account	$75,000	$75,000	$25,000	$25,000
Losses years 1, 2, 3	(30,000)	(30,000)	(30,000)	(30,000)
Capital account end of Year 3	$45,000	$45,000	($ 5,000)	($ 5,000)

The value of the LLC's assets was reduced from $100,000 to $40,000. In a liquidating distribution, Mitch should receive $45,000, but only receives $40,000. Thus, Mitch is suffering $5,000 of economic loss attributable to Rita's deficit capital account.

If the operating agreement contained a DRO (or satisfied the alternate test, discussed later), the allocation would have been respected. With a DRO, Rita would be obligated to contribute $5,000 to the LLC to restore her deficit capital account to zero. The $5,000 would be distributable to Mitch, who would then have received the entire $45,000 to which he was entitled.

The economic effect test is satisfied to the extent a partner has a DRO. Alternatively, a partner may provide a **limited DRO,** which satisfies the economic effect test to that extent. This may be accomplished by including a provision for a limited DRO in the operating agreement.

If there is no express obligation for a DRO in the operating agreement, the partner can contribute a **promissory note** to the LLC. A promissory note constitutes a DRO to the extent of its outstanding principal balance as long as the partner is the maker of the note and meets the following requirements.[94]

1. The note is required to be satisfied no later than the end of the partnership year in which the partner's interest is liquidated or, if later, within 90 days after the date of such liquidation.
2. If the promissory note is negotiable, the partnership agreement can provide that satisfaction under **item 1** is not required, but the partnership will retain the note. The partner must contribute the excess of the outstanding principal of the note over its FMV at the time of liquidation.

Example 16. Curative DRO. Use the same facts as **Example 15,** except Rita contributed a promissory note to the LLC with a face amount of $5,000. If the note satisfies the requirements of the regulations, Rita is treated as having a $5,000 limited DRO, and the allocation of the additional $5,000 loss to Mitch will be respected.

A partner is permitted to reduce or eliminate an existing DRO as long as the reduction or elimination operates only prospectively and does not affect a DRO the partner may have for an existing deficit capital account.[95]

94. Treas. Reg. §1.704-1(b)(2)(ii)(c).

95. Treas. Reg. §1.704-1(b)(2)(ii)(f).

A member's **guarantee of an LLC's debt** owed to a third party is **not** the same thing as a DRO. A DRO is essentially a debt owed to another partner in the partnership, not to third parties. The existence of guarantees by LLC members relates to whether the LLC's debt is classified as recourse or nonrecourse for purposes of allocating basis among partners.[96]

Example 17. Guarantee of Third-Party Debt. Viola and Tom contribute $7,500 and $2,500, respectively, to an LLC taxed as a partnership. The LLC borrows $90,000, with each partner signing a full guarantee of the entire $90,000. Other income and expenses are equal and the depreciation deduction is in excess of those items. All tax items are divided between the partners based on their ownership percentages except depreciation, which is allocated equally between them. The operating agreement satisfies the requirements for the economic effect test except that there is no DRO (nor compliance with the alternate test).

4

Because of the guarantees, the $90,000 of debt is treated as recourse. Viola is allocated $67,500 (75%) of the debt and Tom is allocated $22,500 (25%), based on their ownership percentages.

The partnership buys a depreciable asset for $100,000. Each year, $10,000 of depreciation is allocated equally: $5,000 each to Viola and Tom. Based on this fact, the partnership agreement fails the economic effect test in the first year.

At the end of year 2, the partnership liquidates. No principal payments were made on the loan. The property is sold for $80,000, which is equal to its basis, and the proceeds of the sale are used for loan repayment. Under their guarantees, Viola pays $7,500 to the lender and Tom pays $2,500. This is treated as a constructive contribution to the partnership, increasing their bases by the same amount. The following accounting shows why the economic effect test is not satisfied.

	Viola		Tom	
	Tax Basis	**Book Basis**	**Tax Basis**	**Book Basis**
Initial capital account	$ 7,500	$ 7,500	$ 2,500	$ 2,500
Allocated debt	67,500		22,500	
Depreciation Years 1, 2	(10,000)	(10,000)	(10,000)	(10,000)
Interim capital account end of Year 2	$65,000	($ 2,500)	$15,000	($ 7,500)
Relief from partnership debt (constructive cash distribution)	(67,500)	0	(22,500)	0
Constructive cash contribution for guarantee loan payments	7,500	7,500	2,500	2,500
Additional liability relief	(7,500)	(7,500)	(2,500)	(2,500)
Ending capital accounts	($ 2,500)	($ 2,500)	($ 7,500)	($ 7,500)

The capital accounting rules do not take into account a partner's allocated share of partnership-level liabilities. In addition, while the guaranteed payments on the loan may be treated as constructive contributions, use of those funds to make actual debt payments does not reduce book capital accounts. Finally, liability relief is treated as a cash distribution, reducing tax capital accounts and resulting in a constructive cash distribution to the partners in excess of basis (represented by the negative ending tax bases).

Under the economic effect test, Viola is entitled to receive $2,500, but there are no partnership assets left with which to make distributions. Because the guarantees were only to the third-party lender and no DRO exists, the lender is paid but Viola cannot obtain the $2,500 owed her, and Tom has an extra $2,500 deduction. The economic effect test is not satisfied through the guarantees.

96. Treas. Reg. §1.752-1(a)(1).

Example 18. Curative Allocation. Because the depreciation allocations in **Example 17** do not satisfy the economic effect test, they must be reallocated in accordance with the partners' interests in the LLC. This requires a curative allocation of $5,000 of depreciation in Years 1 and 2 to be reallocated to Viola (again ignoring the failure to satisfy the economic effect test in Year 1). This results in negative capital account balances for both partners and matching income tax losses in proportion to their interests in the LLC.

	Viola		Tom	
	Tax Basis	**Book Basis**	**Tax Basis**	**Book Basis**
Initial capital account	$ 7,500	$ 7,500	$ 2,500	$ 2,500
Allocated debt	67,500		22,500	
Depreciation Years 1, 2 (curative allocation)	(15,000)	(15,000)	(5,000)	(5,000)
Interim capital account end of Year 2	$60,000	($ 7,500)	$20,000	($ 2,500)
Liability relief	(67,500)	0	(22,500)	0
Constructive cash contribution for guarantee payments	7,500	7,500	2,500	2,500
Additional liability relief	(7,500)	(7,500)	(2,500)	(2,500)
Ending capital accounts	($ 7,500)	($ 7,500)	($ 2,500)	($ 2,500)

Alternate Economic Effect Test.[97] The alternate economic effect test is classically used by limited partnerships and generally appears to be used for LLCs. The first two requirements for economic effect (maintenance of capital accounts and positive account liquidating distributions) must be satisfied.[98] Instead of a DRO, however, the partnership agreement can provide for a **qualified income offset (QIO).**[99] This is a provision in the partnership agreement that satisfies the following requirements.

- No allocation can be made to a partner with a QIO that causes or increases a deficit balance in that partner's capital account as of the end of the partnership tax year to which the allocation relates.[100]
- The partnership agreement must provide that a partner who unexpectedly receives allocations or distributions resulting in a deficit capital account is allocated pro rata items of partnership income and gain in an amount and manner sufficient to eliminate the deficit balance as quickly as possible.[101]

97. Treas. Reg. §1.704-1(b)(2)(ii)(d).

98. Treas. Regs. §§1.704-1(b)(2)(ii)(d)(1) and (2).

99. Treas. Reg. §1.704-1(b)(2)(ii)(d)(3).

100. Ibid.

101. Treas. Reg. §1.704-1(b)(2)(ii)(d).

In determining the capital account of a partner with a QIO at the end of a tax year for allocation purposes, the regulations require the capital account to be reduced first to reflect the following adjustments that are reasonably expected at the end of the year to be made in subsequent years.[102]

- Oil and gas depletion
- Losses and deductions allocated to the partner under the family partnership rules,[103] the rules governing retroactive allocations,[104] and the rules governing disproportionate distributions of unrealized receivables and substantially appreciated inventory[105]
- Distributions the partner anticipates receiving that exceed reasonably expected increases in the partner's capital account in the same year as the subsequent distribution

4

Observation. The income allocations are for both tax and capital account purposes, but distributions based on that income are still in accordance with the partnership agreement.[106] This is because a partner with a deficit capital account has essentially borrowed from the other partners and is therefore required to pay them back.

The reason depletion and the other listed allocations are considered "unexpected" is that they are governed by rules that allocate them independently of the partnership agreement. Thus, the application of any one of these allocations for a partnership year creates unique, special allocations that are separate from or that override normal allocations for that year. Because these allocations occur without regard to their economic effect, special allocations are necessary to eliminate the deficits as quickly as possible.

Caution. It is important to understand that "unexpected" does not include such events as an unforeseen loss from the normal business operations of the partnership. However, a partner subject to the alternate economic effect test and who has a zero or deficit capital account for any year is prevented from being allocated any of the "usual" partnership deductions and losses attributable to its normal operations, even if they are unexpected in an economic or business sense.[107]

The alternate economic effect test is **applied on an annual basis.**[108] The test may therefore be satisfied in some years but not in others or may be only partially satisfied in a year. To the extent the test is not satisfied in any year, special allocations are prohibited unless they satisfy the economic effect requirement in some other manner, such as economic effect equivalence (discussed later).[109]

---

102. Ibid.

103. Treas. Reg. §1.704-1(b)(2)(ii)(d)(5); IRC §704(e).

104. Treas. Reg. §1.704-1(b)(2)(ii)(d)(5); IRC §706(d)(1).

105. Treas. Reg. §1.704-1(b)(2)(ii)(d)(5); IRC §751.

106. Treas. Regs. §§1.704-1(b)(2)(ii)(d)(3)–(6).

107. Ibid.

108. Ibid.

109. Ibid.

The following examples illustrate the alternate economic effect test.

Example 19. Alternate Economic Effect Allocation. Waldo and Amy form an LLC organized as a partnership with cash contributions of $40,000 each. The LLC uses these funds to buy depreciable personal property for $80,000. All tax items are to be divided equally between Waldo and Amy except depreciation, which is allocated entirely to Waldo. Other income and expenses are equal and the depreciation deduction is in excess of those items. Assume the operating agreement satisfies the alternate economic effect test.

Depreciation for the first year is $20,000 and the entire amount is allocated to Waldo. The allocation has economic effect.

	Waldo		Amy	
	Tax Basis	**Book Basis**	**Tax Basis**	**Book Basis**
Initial capital account	$40,000	$40,000	$40,000	$40,000
Depreciation	(20,000)	(20,000)	0	0
Capital account end of Year 1	$20,000	$20,000	$40,000	$40,000

Example 20. Partial Alternate Economic Effect Allocation. Use the same facts as **Example 19.** The LLC has a $25,000 depreciation deduction in Year 2 allocated entirely to Waldo. Because this causes Waldo's capital account to have a deficit of $5,000 ($20,000 capital account end of Year 1 – $25,000 depreciation), the allocation is valid only to the extent of $20,000. The remaining $5,000 of depreciation must be reallocated in accordance with the partners' interests in the partnership.

The regulations determine the partners' interests in the partnership by assuming the property is sold at the end of Year 2 for $35,000, its adjusted basis (this conforms to the value equals basis rule discussed previously). The entire $35,000 is distributed to Amy, who has a $40,000 capital account, and none to Waldo, who would have a $5,000 deficit capital account if the entire amount of depreciation were allocated to him. Amy, not Waldo, would then bear the economic burden of $5,000 of the depreciation. This $5,000 depreciation is reallocated from Waldo to Amy. Waldo is allocated the remaining $20,000 of depreciation, bringing his capital account at the end of Year 2 to zero. If the LLC's net income in Year 3 before depreciation is zero, no depreciation is allocated to Waldo in Year 3.

	Waldo		Amy	
	Tax Basis	**Book Basis**	**Tax Basis**	**Book Basis**
Initial capital account	$40,000	$40,000	$40,000	$40,000
Depreciation Years 1 and 2	(40,000)	(40,000)	(5,000)	(5,000)
Capital account end of Year 2	$ 0	$ 0	$35,000	$35,000

Example 21. Invalid Allocation under Alternate Economic Effect. Use the same facts as **Example 20,** except that the depreciation deduction for Year 2 is $20,000 instead of $25,000. In addition, the property is sold for $35,000 at the beginning of Year 3, which results in a $5,000 tax loss ($35,000 sales price – ($80,000 cost of property – $40,000 total depreciation for Years 1 and 2)), and the partnership is liquidated. Allocations in accordance with the partnership agreement result in the following capital accounts after the sale.

	Waldo		Amy	
	Tax Basis	**Book Basis**	**Tax Basis**	**Book Basis**
Capital account beginning of Year 2	$20,000	$20,000	$40,000	$40,000
Depreciation Year 2	(20,000)	(20,000)	0	0
Capital account end of Year 2	$ 0	$ 0	$40,000	$40,000
Loss on sale in Year 3	(2,500)	(2,500)	(2,500)	(2,500)
Interim capital account before liquidation	($ 2,500)	($ 2,500)	$37,500	$37,500

The $35,000 of sale proceeds are distributable entirely to Amy because only she has a positive capital account. However, Amy is entitled to $37,500. The $2,500 loss allocated to Waldo is improper because it is Amy, not Waldo, who bears the economic loss attributable to that deduction. Therefore, the entire $5,000 loss must be allocated to Amy. In addition, Waldo is unable to use the deduction because he has zero basis. The revised capital accounts are as follows.

	Waldo		Amy	
	Tax Basis	**Book Basis**	**Tax Basis**	**Book Basis**
Capital account beginning of Year 2	$20,000	$20,000	$40,000	$40,000
Depreciation Year 2	(20,000)	(20,000)	0	0
Capital account end of Year 2	$ 0	$ 0	$40,000	$40,000
Loss on sale in Year 3	0	0	(5,000)	(5,000)
Interim capital account before liquidation	$ 0	$ 0	$35,000	$35,000

Example 22. Qualified Income Offset. Use the same facts as **Example 21,** except that the property is not sold at the beginning of Year 3. At the end of Year 2, Waldo's capital account is zero and Amy's is $40,000. In Year 3, the partnership borrows $20,000 (which is unforeseen at the end of Year 2) and distributes $10,000 each to Waldo and Amy. In addition, in Year 3, the partnership has income of $50,000, expenses (exclusive of depreciation) of $50,000, and depreciation of $20,000.

Waldo's capital account has unexpectedly become negative because of the $10,000 distribution. The QIO therefore requires that $10,000 of partnership gross income be allocated to Waldo to restore the deficit to zero. This allocation reduces the partnership's gross income from $50,000 to $40,000, giving the partnership a $10,000 loss before the $20,000 depreciation deduction.

The $10,000 gross income allocation restores Waldo's deficit capital account to zero. However, no losses can be allocated to him because of the zero capital account. The $10,000 loss and $20,000 of depreciation must therefore be allocated entirely to Amy, who has a $30,000 capital account after the $10,000 distribution. After the $10,000 loss and $20,000 depreciation are allocated to Amy, her capital account is also zero at the end of Year 3.

Example 23. Allocation in Accordance with Partners' Interests in Partnership. Use the same facts as **Example 22,** except the partnership had $40,000 of gross income instead of $50,000 and $10,000 of the $40,000 is specially allocated to Waldo. Losses and deductions of the partnership for the year total $40,000. The first $30,000 is allocated entirely to Amy, reducing her capital account to zero. Because both partners now have zero capital accounts, the remaining $10,000 of the loss must be allocated in accordance with the partners' interests in the partnership. Based on their equal capital contributions and share of items other than depreciation, the $10,000 excess is allocated $5,000 to each partner. This leaves each partner with a $5,000 deficit capital account at the end of Year 3.

Economic Effect Equivalence.[110] **Economic effect equivalence** is sometimes referred to as "dumb but lucky." It applies to allocations that fail the economic effect or alternate economic effect tests. As long as the partners can demonstrate that the economic effect of the allocation is equivalent to the results that would have occurred under either of the two tests, however, the allocation is accepted. This requires the partners to show that a liquidation of the partnership in the current or any future year would have the same economic effect as if the partnership agreement contained a requirement for capital accounts, liquidating distributions with respect to positive capital accounts, and a DRO.

Substantial Effect

To satisfy the substantial economic effect requirement, not only must special allocations have economic effect, but the **economic effect must be substantial.**[111] This is a **separate requirement.** An allocation that has economic effect may not have a substantial economic effect. An economic effect is substantial only if it has a **substantial impact on the dollar amounts** the partners will receive independently of tax consequences.[112]

For purposes of determining substantial effect, **value generally equals basis.** This means the FMV of assets is presumed to be equal to their adjusted bases. If book value differs from adjusted basis, however, book value is used instead.[113] This rule is intended to prevent partnerships from attempting to justify special allocations based on anticipated increases in the value of partnership assets.[114]

The regulations describe three different types of allocations that **lack substantial economic effect.**

1. **After-tax economic consequences.** The allocation is not substantial if, at the time the allocation becomes part of the partnership agreement:

   - The after-tax economic consequences of at least one partner may, in present value terms, be enhanced compared to the consequences if the allocation was not contained in the partnership agreement; and

   - There is a strong likelihood that the after-tax economic consequences of no partner will, in present value terms, be substantially diminished.[115]

2. **Shifting allocations.** These are special allocations that occur within a tax year that have the same effect on partners' capital accounts as if the special allocations had not been made, but that result in a lower overall income tax liability for the partners than would have occurred without the allocations.[116]

3. **Transitory allocations.** These are special allocations that occur over more than one tax year. At the end of this period, the partners' capital accounts are substantially the same as they would have been without the special allocations, but the partners' overall tax liability is less than it would have been without the allocations.[117]

---

110. Treas. Reg. §1.704-1(b)(2)(ii)(i).

111. Treas. Reg. §1.704-1(b)(2)(i).

112. Treas. Reg. §1.704-1(b)(2)(iii)(a).

113. Ibid.

114. Ibid.

115. Ibid.

116. Treas. Reg. §1.704-1(b)(2)(iii)(b).

117. Treas. Reg. §1.704-1(b)(2)(iii)(c).

In applying the substantial effect rules, the "nonpartner" individual tax attributes of a partner that are unrelated to their status as a partner must be taken into account.[118] This includes such factors as whether a partner is subject to tax or is tax-exempt, is insolvent or in bankruptcy, or has a net operating loss carryover from an activity other than the partnership.

> **Note.** There appears to be no legal means under the Code, however, for a partnership to force an individual partner to disclose such information.

Shifting Allocations.[119] Shifting allocations are special allocations of tax items within a single tax year that have no different effect on the partners' year-end capital accounts. This means that the partners' capital accounts would have been the same without the special allocations. If this is the case, there is a strong presumption that the special allocations lack substantial economic effect. However, the partners can rebut the presumption by showing that facts and circumstances indicate that a strong likelihood of a shifting allocation did not exist at the time the provision for the allocation became part of the partnership agreement.

4

To apply the shifting allocation test, the partners' year-end capital accounts with the special allocation must be compared to what their capital accounts would have been without the allocation. If there is no substantial difference, the partners' tax liabilities with and without the allocation must then be compared, taking into account each partner's nonpartnership tax attributes.[120]

Example 24. Shifting Allocation. James and Sharon form a partnership and contribute equal amounts to its capital. The partnership agreement satisfies the requirements of the general economic effect test. The partnership agreement also provides that James and Sharon share equally in all items of partnership income and loss.

The partnership invests equally in tax-exempt bonds and corporate stock. For its first year, James expects to be in a substantially higher marginal tax bracket than Sharon. The partnership agreement is modified for the first year to allocate the first $100,000 of tax-exempt interest for that year 90% to James and 10% to Sharon and to allocate the first $100,000 of corporate dividends 10% to James and 90% to Sharon. All other items are shared equally between the two.

At the beginning of the tax year when the agreement was modified, there was a strong likelihood there would be at least $100,000 each of tax-exempt interest and corporate dividends. Although these allocations would have economic effect, the economic effect is not substantial because there was a strong likelihood that the amendment would not alter the before-tax economic arrangements of the partners. However, the allocation would result in a lower total tax liability. Because the offsetting allocations occur in the same tax year, they are shifting allocations.

Transitory Allocations. Transitory allocations occur over more than one tax year. Otherwise, they are analyzed in essentially the same manner as shifting allocations. There are two exceptions to the transitory allocation rules.[121]

1. An allocation is not considered transitory if there is a strong likelihood it will not be largely offset within five years (determined on a first-in, first-out basis).
2. An allocation is not considered transitory if the partnership activity is of a sufficiently risky nature that there is not a strong likelihood that there will be a future offsetting allocation.

118. Treas. Reg. §1.704-1(b)(2)(iii)(a).

119. Treas. Reg. §1.704-1(b)(2)(iii)(b).

120. Ibid.

121. Treas. Regs. §§1.704-1(b)(2)(iii)(c) and 1.704-1(b)(5), Example 3.

Example 25. Transitory Allocation. Use the same facts as **Example 24,** except the partnership owns depreciable real property generating $50,000 in annual depreciation deductions. Because James expects to be in a substantially higher marginal tax bracket than Sharon during the partnership's first tax year, they agree to allocate the first year of depreciation deductions to James and the second year of depreciation deductions to Sharon. All other items are shared equally, and this allocation has economic effect.

At the time the provision for the allocations of depreciation deductions was added to the agreement, there is a strong likelihood that the capital accounts of James and Sharon, after reflecting these allocations, would not differ substantially from what would have happened if the allocations were not made. Moreover, the overall tax liability of the two partners is reduced by such allocations. The allocations are therefore transitory because the offsetting allocations occur over a period of more than one tax year.

EFFECT OF IRC §§734(b) AND 743(b) ADJUSTMENTS

Observation. Adjustments under §§734(b) and 743(b) are only made if the partnership has made a §754 election. This election is irrevocable without the consent of the IRS.[122] Practitioners making a §754 elections must consult the appropriate regulations.[123]

IRC §754 ELECTION

Inside and outside bases can become unequal when events such as the following occur.

- A taxpayer buys a partnership interest for an amount that differs from the selling partner's basis in the interest.
- A partner dies and the §1014 FMV basis is different from the deceased partner's partnership basis.
- A partnership distributes cash or property with a basis in excess of the recipient partner's basis in the partnership interest.

If there is a change to an individual partner's outside basis through purchase or inheritance, there is no effect on the partnership's inside basis in its assets. The effect is therefore to delay the acquiring partner's ability to recover the higher outside basis until termination of the partnership interest or of the partnership.

Differences between inside and outside bases can be eliminated if the partnership made or makes an election under §754 for the tax year in which the difference arises. This election permits the inside bases of partnership assets to be adjusted in accordance with the following Code sections.

- IRC §743(b) and its regulations[124] for transfers of partnership interests
- IRC §734(b) and its regulations[125] for distributions in a manner that restores equality between inside and outside basis

In addition, guidance is provided under the following Code sections.

- IRC §755 and its regulations[126] provide the actual manner in which allocations are made.
- IRC §754 and its regulations[127] provide the manner in which the election is made.

---

122. Treas. Reg. §1.754-1(c)(1).

123. Treas. Reg. §§1.734-1 and 1.734-2 (adjustments to partnership's inside basis based on distributions to partners); Treas. Reg. §1.743-1 (adjustments to partner's outside basis and share of partnership's inside basis); Treas. Reg. §1.755-1 (allocation of bases among partnership assets for adjustments under §§734 and 743).

124. Treas. Reg. §1.743-1.

125. Treas. Regs. §§1.734-1 and 1.734-2.

126. Treas. Reg. §1.755-1.

127. Treas. Reg. §1.754-1.

Making the Election

The §754 election must be made by the partnership before the due date of the partnership income tax return (including extensions) for the year in which the distribution or transfer occurs.[128] No particular form is required for the election, but the election must include the name and address of the electing partnership, a declaration that the partnership elects, under §754, to apply the provisions of §§734(b) and 743(b), and the signature of any partner.[129] The election must be made in a written statement filed with the partnership return for a tax year not later than the year in which the distribution occurs.

Example 26. During 2012, Alicia, Barry, Charles, and Deidre formed Happy Valley Farm Partnership. They each contributed $500,000 to the partnership. With the $2 million of contributed cash, the partnership bought land for $1.2 million and other nondepreciable assets for $800,000. As a result, after formation and purchase of assets, the partnership's balance sheet is as follows.

	Book/Tax Basis
Land	$1,200,000
Other nondepreciable assets	800,000
Total assets	$2,000,000
Capital account: Alicia	$ 500,000
Capital account: Barry	500,000
Capital account: Charles	500,000
Capital account: Deidre	500,000
Total equity	$2,000,000

Each partner has a capital account equal to the amount of cash that particular partner contributed to the partnership. The total of the partners' capital accounts equals the total basis the partnership has in its assets. Thus, the partnership has an inside basis in its partnership assets of $2 million, and each partner's share of that inside basis is $500,000.

In early 2022, the value of the land held by the partnership was appraised at $1.8 million and the other assets were valued at $800,000. Assuming there were no other changes, the partnership's balance sheet in 2022 is as follows.

	Book/Tax Basis	FMV
Land	$1,200,000	$1,800,000
Other nondepreciable assets	800,000	800,000
Total assets	$2,000,000	$2,600,000
Capital account: Alicia	$ 500,000	$ 650,000
Capital account: Barry	500,000	650,000
Capital account: Charles	500,000	650,000
Capital account: Deidre	500,000	650,000
Total equity	$2,000,000	$2,600,000

128. An automatic 12-month extension is possible if certain procedural requirements are followed. Treas. Reg. §301.9100-2.

129. Treas. Reg. §1.754-1(b). The IRS proposed regulations in 2017 that would eliminate the signature requirement for a §754 election. This amendment is final when published as a final regulation, but taxpayers may rely upon it for tax years preceding the proposed effective date. The IRS will apparently no longer take the position that the lack of a signature on the election form invalidates the election. See, e.g., *DTDV, LLC v. Comm'r,* TC Memo 2018-32 (Mar. 20, 2018).

In mid-2022, Alicia sells her interest to Edwin for $650,000. Alicia recognizes gain of $150,000 on the sale[130] ($650,000 – $500,000 basis). Edwin's basis in the partnership interest (outside basis) is the purchase price of $650,000.[131] However, Edwin's share of the inside basis the partnership holds in its assets is $500,000. With respect to inside basis, Edwin merely "steps into the shoes" of Alicia's previous capital account of $500,000. Thus, after the transaction, Edwin's capital account differs from his tax basis, as shown in the following table.

	Capital Account Inside Basis	Tax Basis Outside Basis
Barry	$ 500,000	$ 500,000
Charles	500,000	500,000
Deidre	500,000	500,000
Edwin	500,000	650,000
Total equity	$2,000,000	$2,150,000

The partnership made a §754 election for the year in which Edwin purchased Alicia's interest. Accordingly, the partnership increased the basis of its land by the amount that Edwin's outside basis in the acquired interest ($650,000) exceeded his share of the inside basis ($500,000). Thus, the partnership increased the basis of its land by $150,000, which is the same amount as the gain that Alicia recognized on the sale.

The §754 election was identified on Happy Valley Farm Partnership's Form 1065, Schedule B, *Other Information,* line 10a. The optional basis adjustment was marked on Form 1065, Schedule B, line 10b, and a statement showing the computation and allocation of the basis adjustment was attached to the return. In addition, the §754 election statement was attached.

		Yes	No
10a	Is the partnership making, or had it previously made (and not revoked), a section 754 election? See instructions for details regarding a section 754 election.	X	
b	Did the partnership make for this tax year an optional basis adjustment under section 743(b) or 734(b)? If "Yes," attach a statement showing the computation and allocation of the basis adjustment. See instructions	X	
c	Is the partnership required to adjust the basis of partnership assets under section 743(b) or 734(b) because of a substantial built-in loss (as defined under section 743(d)) or substantial basis reduction (as defined under section 734(d))? If "Yes," attach a statement showing the computation and allocation of the basis adjustment. See instructions		

Form **1065** (2022)

Sample IRC §754 election statement

Election to Adjust the Basis of Partnership Property of Happy Valley Farm Partnership, Farm Avenue, Farm Town

Pursuant to Treas. Reg. §1.754-1(b)(1), the partnership hereby elects to adjust the basis of the partnership property for the tax year ended 12/31/22. Under the provisions of the Internal Revenue Code, this partnership will elect to apply IRC §§734(b) and 743(b).

Statement 1
Form 1065, Schedule B, Line 10b
Optional Basis Adjustment Supporting Detail

Land basis adjustment: $150,000

Allocated to partner Edwin

130. IRC §741.

131. IRC §1012.

Form 1065 instructions take into account partnership basis adjustments under §734(b) on the line for "other increases and decreases." However, adjustments to partnership basis under §743(b) that pertain only to a particular partner are disregarded. Therefore, if the beginning tax basis capital account included any positive or negative §743(b) adjustments for a partner, they should have been removed by reducing positive adjustments and increasing negative adjustments by the §743(b) portion. The following sections examine these adjustments and the distinction between the two.

IRC §734 ADJUSTMENTS

IRC §734 special basis adjustments prevent distortions from occurring inside the partnership with respect to other partners because of gain or loss reported by a partner receiving a distribution or in the event a distributee partner's basis in an asset differs from the partnership's basis in that asset.

4

Example 27. Ann, Bernard, and Cora are equal partners in a partnership. The partnership's balance sheet follows.

	Tax Basis	FMV
Assets		
Cash	$2,000	$2,000
Capital asset	1,000	4,000
Total	$3,000	$6,000
Capital		
Ann	$1,000	$2,000
Bernard	1,000	2,000
Cora	1,000	2,000
Total	$3,000	$6,000

Ann receives a liquidating distribution of $2,000 in cash and therefore recognizes $1,000 of gain ($2,000 cash – $1,000 basis). With no §754 election in effect, the partnership's balance sheet following the distribution is as follows.

	Tax Basis	FMV
Assets		
Capital asset	$1,000	$4,000
Total	$1,000	$4,000
Capital		
Bernard	$1,000	$2,000
Cora	1,000	2,000
Total	$2,000	$4,000

If the partnership sells the asset for its $4,000 value, the partnership has a $3,000 gain, half of which is reported by each of the remaining partners. Thus, $4,000 of gain has been reported between the distributee partner (Ann) and the remaining partners, when there was only $3,000 of appreciation in the partnership assets. However, partners Bernard and Cora receive increases in their tax bases of $1,500 each with respect to the gain they have reported. Thus, they have $2,500 of tax basis each following the sale of the asset.

Each of them is entitled to a tax-free liquidating distribution of $2,000, resulting in a $500 capital loss to each. Thus, the net taxable amount among all concerned is only $3,000, but the lack of a §754 election results in a distortion. With the election in effect, the partnership's basis in the asset would have been increased by the $1,000 of gain recognized by Ann, resulting in only $2,000 of gain on a sale of the asset. Thus, the distortion would have been avoided.

If a §754 election is in effect, §734 uses the amount of gain or loss to the distributee partner or the basis differential between the partnership's basis and the distributee's basis to make the adjustment to the bases of inside assets to prevent the distortion. Assets are divided into capital gain and ordinary income groups as with §743 adjustments. If the adjustment is a result of the recognition of gain or loss by the distributee, it is applied only to the capital gain group. If it is a result of a basis differential, it is applied to partnership assets of the same category to which the distributed property belonged.

IRC §743 ADJUSTMENTS

Under §743, the partnership adjusts its basis of inside assets to reflect the outside increase or decrease of basis for a transfer of a partnership interest. The total amount of adjustment is the difference between the acquiring partner's basis in the partnership interest and that partner's share of the partnership's basis for its assets, including liabilities but excluding cash.

Example 28. Derek and Erin own a 40% and 60% interest in partnership DE, respectively, with an FMV of $100 and an adjusted basis of $50. Derek sells his interest to Farrell for $100. The partnership has a depreciable asset with an FMV of $200 and an adjusted basis of $100, of which Derek's share of inside basis is $40.

After the sale, Farrell has a partnership interest with an outside basis of $100 based on the purchase price. Under the entity approach, however, Farrell continues to have the same $40 inside basis share that Derek had.

DE partnership made a §754 election. Farrell can increase the inside basis he has in the asset by $60, the excess of his outside basis ($100) over his share of the partnership's inside basis ($40).

Farrell now has a $100 inside basis in the partnership asset to equal his $100 outside basis. When the asset with an adjusted basis of $100 is fully depreciated, Erin will have taken $60 of depreciation and reduced her outside basis to zero. Farrell will have taken $100 of depreciation because depreciation on the $60 increase in basis he receives under §743 will be specially allocated to him. His basis will therefore also be zero.

If the asset is sold for $200, the partnership will have $200 of gain ($200 amount realized – $0 adjusted basis). Farrell will be allocated $80 of the gain and Erin will be allocated $120 of the gain. Erin's outside basis will increase by her $120 of gain and Farrell's basis will increase by his $80 of gain. A distribution to each of their shares of the proceeds will be nontaxable

DEBT-FINANCED ACQUISITIONS AND DISTRIBUTIONS

The Tax Reform Act of 1986 made significant changes to interest expense deductions. In general, it created five different categories of interest expenses, each with different rules of deductibility.[132] These are the most common categories and are applicable to both partnerships (as well as S corporations) and individuals.

1. **Personal interest**, which is not deductible
2. **Trade or business interest**, which is generally fully deductible (ignoring such things as capitalization rules or limits on losses)
3. **Investment interest**, deductible to the extent of net investment income
4. **Passive activity interest**, deductible to the extent of passive activity income
5. **Qualified residence interest**, deductible in accordance with the Code and regulations[133]

The issue is how to determine which type of interest a taxpayer has paid. To address this, the IRS issued temporary regulations that are still in effect. These are referred to in the materials as **interest tracing**.

132. IRC §163(h)(2).

133. Temp. Treas. Reg. §1.163-10T (not updated to reflect certain post-1986 statutory changes).

INTEREST TRACING RULES

The interest tracing rules are actually **debt tracing** rules, and are found in the temporary regulations at Temp. Treas. Reg. §1.163-8T. In general, the interest tracing rules work in the following manner.

If an individual borrows money, the type of interest that accrues on the borrowed money is determined by the **use** to which the taxpayer puts the debt.[134] The use of the debt is determined by tracing expenditures of the debt by the taxpayer to see what the taxpayer actually uses it for.[135] Thus, if a taxpayer receives $100,000 of loan proceeds in cash and uses the cash to buy a building, the $100,000 debt is traced directly to that building. Similarly, if $100,000 of debt proceeds are deposited to a taxpayer's checking account and the taxpayer writes a check using the $100,000 of debt to buy a building (or the check is issued at closing by a closing agent), that debt will be traced to the building.

4

When an expenditure of debt by a taxpayer has been traced to an asset or use, the debt is attached to the asset or use (hereafter referred to as asset). The taxpayer must then determine how the taxpayer uses the asset to which the debt has attached, taking into account the passive activity rules. The use of the asset characterizes the use of the debt proceeds that are attached to it and the use of the debt proceeds characterizes the type of interest that accrues on the debt.[136]

> **Example 29.** A taxpayer borrows $100,000 and uses it to purchase a building. The debt is attached to the building. The building is used the entire year in a trade or business in which the taxpayer materially participates. The debt is therefore trade or business debt and the interest that accrues during that period of time is trade or business interest.

If the use of an asset changes, the regulations require the attached debt to be **reallocated** to the new use.[137] Any interest that accrues after a reallocation of debt proceeds will be characterized by the new use of the debt brought about by the changing use of the asset to which the debt attaches.

> **Example 30.** Use the same facts as **Example 29** except that the taxpayer stops using the building in the business and begins to rent it. Because rental is a passive activity, the use of the asset has changed and the attached debt must therefore be reallocated to the new use. Thus, the debt becomes passive activity debt and the interest that accrues from the point of reallocation forward will be treated as passive activity interest and subject to those limitations.

If an asset having debt attached to it is disposed, any proceeds are traced back to the taxpayer. If the proceeds are used to repay the debt, interest tracing stops. If, however, the debt is not repaid, the proceeds will continue to be treated as debt and will be traced (reallocated) to new assets as expenditures of the proceeds are made.

Except in the case of a qualified residence indebtedness, the interest tracing rules apply **without regard** to what property secures a debt.[138] Thus, if a taxpayer has a certificate of deposit (CD) in a bank that the bank uses as collateral for a loan used for business purposes, the debt is still treated as business debt and the interest as business interest because it is traced to the business and not to the CD.

The regulations provide that any time **a deposit of debt** proceed is held in any kind of banking account, regardless of whether the account pays interest, the debt is treated for that time as used for investment purposes. Thus, a taxpayer who deposits borrowed funds into a checking account and who does not immediately write a check carrying the debt out of that account will technically have investment interest for some period of time.[139]

---

134. Temp. Treas. Reg. §1.163-8T(c)(1).

135. Temp. Treas. Reg. §1.163-8T(a)(3).

136. Temp. Treas. Reg. §1.163-8T(c)(2)(ii)(A).

137. Temp. Treas. Reg. §1.163-8T(j)(1).

138. Temp. Treas. Reg. §1.163-8T(c)(1).

139. Temp. Treas. Reg. §1.163-8T(c)(4).

If loan proceeds are paid directly from the lender to a third party, debt is automatically allocated to that disbursement.[140] If a taxpayer receives debt in cash or is deposited to the taxpayer's account, the general rule is that debt proceeds are treated as paid out by the taxpayer on a first-in, first-out basis. This means that if the proceeds from more than one loan have been deposited in a checking account, the money from the loans is treated as being paid out chronologically in the same order the loans were received. Unborrowed money is treated as being paid out of the account after all loan money has been paid out.

There is a 30-day exception to the general rule, however, which should apply to most taxpayers.[141] Under this rule, any payments made within 30 days before or after debt proceeds have been received can be designated by the taxpayer as being expenditures of debt proceeds without regard to any ordering rules.

PASSTHROUGH ENTITIES

Prior to the Tax Reform Act of 1986, a taxpayer incurring debt to buy an interest in a corporation or partnership was treated as purchasing an investment interest. This applied in the case of corporation stock without regard to whether the corporation was a C corporation or an S corporation. Any interest paid would therefore have been investment interest and deductible only to the extent of net investment income.

The IRS became concerned that individuals would try to use passthrough entities to circumvent the prohibition against deducting personal interest. It therefore issued a series of notices which, until regulations are issued in this area, govern how taxpayers who use debt to acquire an interest in a passthrough entity must determine their interest deductions and how the entities are to determine interest on debt-financed distributions.

The first of these was IRS Notice 88-20,[142] which provided the original allocation rules. The second was IRS Notice 88-37,[143] which set out how taxpayers report interest determined under IRS Notice 88-20. Both notices have been modified. IRS Notice 88-20 is largely superseded by IRS Notice 89-35,[144] which restates and elaborates the rules of IRS Notice 88-20 and, to some extent, those of IRS Notice 88-37. Anyone who has clients with interests in partnerships, LLCs classified as partnerships, or S corporations should be familiar with these notices.

DEBT-FINANCED ACQUISITIONS[145]

If a taxpayer incurs debt to purchase an interest in a partnership, it is treated not as the purchase of an interest in the partnership itself, but as if the debt had been used instead to purchase an interest directly in the assets of the partnership. The debt is allocated among the assets of the partnership in accordance with the rules in IRS Notice 89-35. Once the debt has been allocated among assets, a taxpayer must determine how each asset is used by the partnership to classify properly the debt attached to those assets. The use of assets — trade or business, passive activity, investment, or personal — is determined on the basis of the partnership's use of the assets. This determines the nature of the interest accruing on the allocated debt and thereby determines how partners report the interest on their returns.

---

140. Temp. Treas. Reg. §1.163-8T(c)(3).

141. Prop. Treas. Reg. §1.163-15(a); IRS Notice 89-35, 1989-1 CB 675.

142. IRS Notice 88-20, 1988-1 CB 487.

143. IRS Notice 88-37, 1988-1 CB 522.

144. IRS Notice 89-35, 1989-1 CB 675.

145. Ibid.

Types of Debt-Financed Acquisitions

Partners determine how debt is allocated among assets of the partnership based on whether the purchase is treated as a **debt-financed acquisition that is not a contribution to capital** or as a **debt-financed acquisition that is a contribution to capital**. The difference between these two is simply where the money goes. If the partnership winds up with the borrowed money, the partners treat the debt as a debt-financed acquisition that **is** a contribution to capital. If a partner or anyone other than the partnership gets the money, it is a debt-financed acquisition that **is not** a contribution to capital.[146]

4

Practitioner Planning Tip

To determine whether there is a debt-financed acquisition of an interest in a passthrough entity, practitioners should look to see whether (1) debt was incurred at either the partner or the partnership level and (2) as a result of that, someone's equity ownership interest in the partnership was directly or indirectly increased.

Example 31. Alice borrows $100,000 from a bank to buy an interest in an LLC. If Alice contributes the money to the LLC in exchange for an interest in the LLC, this is a debt-financed acquisition that is a contribution to capital. If Alice buys the LLC interest from another member, it is a debt-financed acquisition that is not a contribution to capital. Thus, in the first scenario the LLC winds up with the money, while in the second someone else does. In either case, however, Alice's equity interest in the partnership is increased.

Example 32. An LLC borrows money from a bank to redeem a member's interest. Because the member winds up with the money and the equity interests of the remaining members is increased by the departure of the redeemed member, this is a debt-financed acquisition by the remaining members that is not a contribution to capital. This is true even though it was the LLC that borrowed the money and pays the interest, and even if there is no loan guarantee by the members. Each member's share of the LLC's interest will therefore have to be specially allocated to the members for them to apply the principles discussed in these materials for determining their interest expense deduction on their proportionate share.

Note. The following examples from private letter rulings applying IRS Notice 89-35 illustrate various transactions and how they are classified under the Notice. With one exception, the rulings deal with S corporations. They are included here because the principles illustrated by these rulings are generally applicable to partners and partnerships, too.

146. IRS Notice 88-20, 1988-1 CB 487.

Not a Contribution to Capital

In the following letter rulings, transactions were treated as debt-financed interests that were not a contribution to capital.

- **Stock purchase from shareholder.** Two employees purchased 100% of the shares of an S corporation from the owner. The buyers gave the seller a promissory note for the purchase price. This is a debt-financed acquisition that is not a contribution to capital because the selling shareholder received the proceeds and, as a result of the debt-financed purchase, the buyers increased their equity interests in the S corporation. If the buyers instead borrowed the money from a bank and paid the seller cash, the result would have been the same.[147] This is equally applicable to borrowing money to buy a partner's interest in a partnership.

- **Trust distribution to beneficiaries.** Two electing small business trusts (ESBTs) held all the stock of an S corporation. The ESBTs had current income beneficiaries who were entitled to all income for life, following which distribution of the shares would be made to the remainder beneficiaries. To resolve family feuding, the S corporation would make loans to the two ESBTs on arm's-length terms, using as part of the loan proceeds money the corporation would borrow from an unrelated third party. The ESBTs would use the loans to buy out the interests of the life income beneficiaries and some of the remainder beneficiaries to whom the shares would ultimately have been distributed on termination of the trust. The trusts would then be terminated and the shares distributed to the remainder beneficiaries whose interests had not been bought out.

  The beneficiaries would take distribution of their shares subject to a security interest the corporation had in those shares for repayment of the loan, and they would assume and agree to pay back to the corporation the ESBT's loan. The IRS ruled that the remainder beneficiaries should treat the debt as if it were incurred for purposes of their purchasing the stock, making this a debt-financed acquisition, not a contribution to capital.[148] This is because other shareholders wound up with the money, not the corporation and as a result of the transaction, the equity interests of the remaining shareholders increased.

- **Corporate split-off.** To resolve irreconcilable differences between two 50-50 shareholders who owned an S corporation, the shareholders undertook a corporate split-off. To do so, the existing corporation formed a subsidiary to which it transferred assets in exchange for all the subsidiary's stock. To help equalize values, the parent corporation also borrowed money and distributed the borrowed money to the subsidiary. The shares in the parent corporation owned by the departing shareholder were then redeemed by the parent in exchange for all its shares in the newly formed subsidiary. The result was two separate corporations, each owned individually by one of the shareholders. The IRS treated the debt the parent incurred for equalization purposes as a debt-financed acquisition of an interest in an S corporation, not as a contribution to capital, but did not explain their reasoning.[149]

  The proper explanation, however, is that the subsidiary corporation wound up with the money borrowed by the parent. To be treated as a contribution to capital, IRS Notice 89-35 requires that the corporation that borrows the money also be the corporation which winds up with the money. In addition, the result of the transaction was to increase the ownership interest of the remaining shareholder in the parent corporation from 50% to 100%.

- **Redemption of shares.** An S corporation redeemed all the shares of some of the shareholders for cash and the corporation's promissory note. Because the effect of the redemption was to increase the ownership interests of the remaining shareholders and it was the redeemed shareholders who were getting the cash, the redemption was treated as debt-financed acquisition that was not a contribution to capital.[150]

---

147. Ltr. Rul. 9037027 (Jun. 18, 1990).

148. Ltr. Rul. 9804026 (Oct. 23, 1997).

149. Ltr. Rul. 9441025 (Jul. 11, 1994).

150. Ltr. Rul. 9116008 (Jan. 10, 1991).

- **Partnership.** Nearly all letter rulings concerning IRS Notice 89-35 involve S corporations. In one letter ruling, however, the IRS addressed the issue of the deductibility of interest payments by the transferor spouse where there was an installment purchase of the transferee spouse's interest in a partnership that was community property.[151] The purchase itself was not a taxable transaction because it was subject to the gift treatment rule of IRC §1041. The transferor spouse therefore received a carryover basis from the transferee spouse, the latter of whom recognized neither gain nor loss. The ruling set out the facts as follows.

  - *P1* is a California limited partnership formed in 1982. The husband, *H*, owned a 5% general partnership interest in *P1's* profits, losses, and capital. In 1988, *H* transferred this interest in *P1* to trust *T*. *H* is the settlor, trustee, and current beneficiary of *T*. The agreement governing *T* provides that the settlor has the power to alter, amend, or revoke *T* in whole or in part by one or more written instruments, other than will, executed and delivered to the trustee from time to time during settlor's lifetime. *H's* spouse (*W*) owns a 95% limited partnership interest in *P1's* profits, losses, and capital.
  - *P1* owns a limited partnership interest in *P2*, another California limited partnership, and an interest in a receivable. *P2* owns an interest in a receivable, cash, and certain rental buildings and their improvements.
  - During their divorce, the couple negotiated a written settlement agreement providing that *H* purchase *W's* interest in *P1*.
  - In 1987, *H* previously borrowed an amount and invested all the loan proceeds in certain securities. *H* will dispose of some of the securities and use all the proceeds from the disposition to pay *W* the purchase price for *W's* interest in *P1*. *H* will then transfer this interest in *P1* to *T*.

  The facts are visually represented by the following diagram.

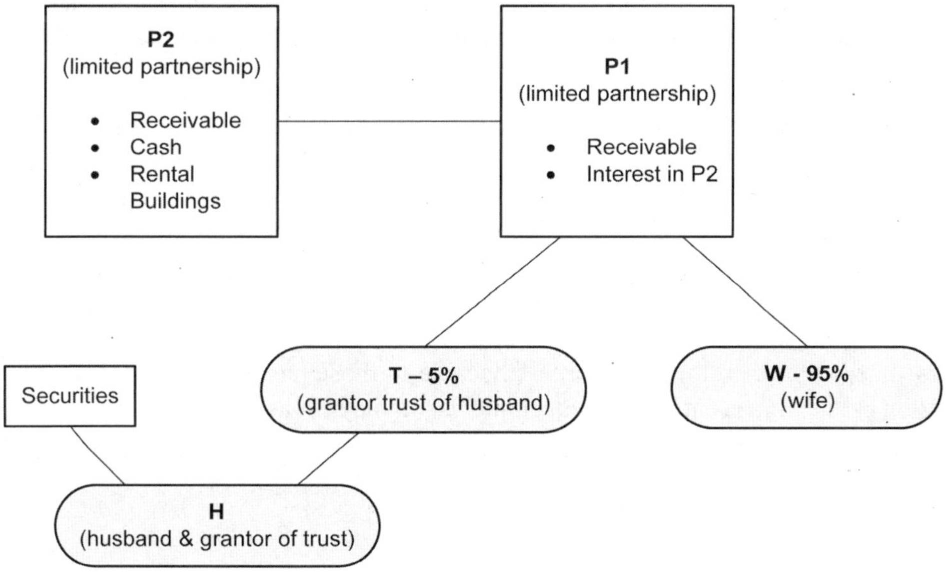

  In the ruling, the IRS concluded that the original debt proceeds, having been used to purchase portfolio property, would result in *H* having investment interest expenses up until the date of the disposition of the securities. When part of the securities were disposed, that portion of the debt proceeds attached to those securities was deemed reacquired by *H* and were thereupon subject to reallocation.

151. Ltr. Rul. 9031022 (May 7, 1990).

Because the reacquired debt proceeds were used to acquire an interest in a partnership, the passthrough entity tracing rules of IRS Notice 89-35 applied. *H* was therefore required to reallocate the debt proceeds among the assets of *P1* and *P2* using any reasonable method of allocation. The interest would then be deductible in accordance with the nature of the partnership assets to which the debt proceeds attached. For example, to the extent debt proceeds attach to assets producing portfolio income, interest paid by *H* would be investment interest. Similarly, to the extent debt proceeds attached to assets used in the rental activity, interest paid on such debt would be passive. The IRS concluded its analysis by saying that the mere fact that debt is incurred in connection with a transfer incident to a divorce does not operate automatically to make it personal interest.[152]

Contributions to Capital

There appears to be only one ruling involving contributions to capital of a partnership.[153] That may be because the purchase of an interest from the entity itself using borrowed money is clearly a contribution to capital. Thus, if an individual borrows money to purchase from the partnership itself an interest in a limited partnership, (1) there is an increase in the individual's equity interest in the partnership, and (2) it is the partnership that winds up with the money.

In the ruling, a nongrantor trust holds assets consisting primarily of real estate located in several states. The real estate apparently had debt associated with it. Upon termination of the trust, the assets are to be distributed among the beneficiaries, but disproportionate distributions are permitted, which the trust intended to do. Under the termination plan, the trust formed a single-member LLC of which it was the sole member. The LLC was a disregarded entity, so the LLC's activities remained taxable to the trust.

The trust transferred assets to the LLC, which also became a co-debtor with the trust on debt encumbering the transferred assets. The trust also borrowed money against trust assets, but none of the borrowed money was transferred to the LLC. In termination, some beneficiaries received a mixture of cash and property; some a mixture of cash and interests in the LLC; and a few received only cash. The ruling requested was that the beneficiary-partners of the LLC be permitted to deduct interest paid by the LLC as investment interest.

The IRS began by saying that the distribution of the LLC interest from the trust to the beneficiaries resulted in the disregarded entity becoming a partnership. Citing a revenue ruling,[154] the IRS said that the beneficiaries would therefore be treated upon distribution of the membership interests as having received proportionate shares of the LLC's assets subject to proportionate shares of its liabilities, and then immediately thereafter contributing those debt-encumbered assets to a new partnership in exchange for interests in the new partnership. Because the partnership receives property subject to debt, but receives no cash distributions of that debt, the partnership is treated as constructively borrowing the remaining debt on the property and investing that same amount in the property.[155] The assumed debt, therefore, is entirely allocable to those partnership assets. Because the assets are investment assets, the partnership is entitled to deduct interest on the debt as investment interest in accordance with the rules governing investment interest.

---

152. See *Seymour v. Comm'r*, 109 TC 279 (1997). The Tax Court rejected the IRS's argument that interest paid on debt to buy out wife's interest in assets as a result of their divorce was nondeductible personal interest, but was instead deductible or not in accordance with the tracing rules.

153. Ltr. Rul. 200613025 (Dec. 14, 2005).

154. Rev. Rul. 99-5, 1999-1 CB 434.

155. Citing Temp. Treas. Reg. §1.163-8T(c)(3)(ii).

The ruling requested was whether it would be reasonable to allocate the debt among the investment assets using ratios of their FMVs. Citing IRS Notice 85-35, the IRS stated that, in the case of debt proceeds treated as a contribution to capital, the debt is to be allocated among the entity's assets using any reasonable method. The IRS concluded that the proposed method was reasonable.[156]

> **Observation.** Contrast this ruling with the ruling involving distribution of S corporation stock from an ESBT. In that ruling, the entity (the S corporation) was already in existence. The debt assumed by the shareholders was therefore for purposes of acquiring the shares. As a result of the debt, the redeemed beneficiaries received the money, not the S corporation, and the beneficiaries who became shareholders thereby increased their equity interests in the S corporation. The partnership ruling, however, involves the creation of a new entity that acquired assets that were purchased in part with borrowed money. Because the debt remained with the assets and the assets were transferred to the entity, no person other than the partnership could be said to have received any of the debt proceeds, which makes it a contribution to capital.

4

This ruling involved the formation of a new partnership using encumbered assets. An existing partnership that incurs debt to acquire assets simply uses the tracing rules to allocate debt to the acquired assets. Furthermore, the ruling focused on allocation of that debt rather than the type of debt-financed transaction that was involved. Another letter ruling dealing with S corporations may help to add light to this issue.

In the ruling, an S corporation borrowed money and used the debt to build a building used in its business.[157] The debt was secured by a mortgage on the building. To increase their debt basis, the shareholders personally assumed the corporation's loan and mortgage. (Presumably this meant they were assuming the corporation's loan from the bank and the corporation was becoming indebted to them — in other words, a back-to-back loan.) Because the corporation had been the recipient of the original debt proceeds and the use of those debt proceeds was not going to change, the IRS ruled that the assumption of the loan by the shareholders would be treated as a debt-financed acquisition of an interest that was a contribution to capital. The debt would therefore remain allocated to the building.

ALLOCATION OF DEBT AMONG ASSETS

For debt-financed acquisitions that are not contributions to capital, the debt proceeds are to be allocated among all the assets of the entity using any reasonable method. According to IRS Notice 89-35, reasonable methods ordinarily include a pro rata allocation based on the FMV, book value, or adjusted bases of the assets. In determining the ratios, appropriate reductions must be made for any debt of either the entity or the owners that has already been allocated to any assets.

Examples of how the debt allocation rules actually work in the case of acquisitions that are not capital contributions are illustrated by two letter rulings. In the first one, involving a stock redemption, the IRS ruled that the following proposed allocation method represented a reasonable method under IRS Notice 89-35.[158]

1. At the end of each month, the book value of the corporation's assets will be segregated into classes identified as business assets, passive activity assets, investment assets, and personal assets.
2. A ratio equal to the total book value of assets in each class identified in step 1 to the total book value of all assets will be compared each month.
3. Finally, an average ratio for the entire year will be computed based on the number of months in the taxable year of the taxpayer.

---

156. Ltr. Rul. 200613025 (Dec. 14, 2005).

157. Ltr. Rul. 8949091 (Sep. 14, 1989).

158. Ltr. Rul. 9116008 (Jan. 10, 1991).

Allocations for debt-financed acquisitions that are contributions to capital may apparently be done in the same manner as acquisitions that are not contributions. In addition, IRS Notice 89-35 permits such debt to be allocated using the normal tracing rules of the temporary regulations. Normally, one would want to choose the allocation method providing the most favorable benefit to the partners, assuming that switching between methods would not be interpreted as being unreasonable. There are no letter rulings on this type of allocation. The following is a simple example to show the significance of the method chosen.

Example 33. The partners of a partnership borrow $100 from an unrelated bank and lend it to the partnership to be used for the construction of a building that will be used in the partnership's active trade or business. In addition, the partnership has $100 worth of investment assets.

If the proportionate allocation rules are used, half the debt must be allocated to the building and half to the investment assets. If the tracing method is used, all the debt can be allocated to the building.

IRS Notice 89-35 requires debt to be allocated among **all** assets of the partnership unless the tracing approach is properly being used. Although there is no direct authority, it would seem that this approach should therefore include not only the physical assets of the partnership, but also its intangible assets. However, equipment depreciated under modified accelerated cost recovery system (MACRS) may have little or no basis. As a **general rule,** therefore, one would want to use FMV for allocations of debt in a partnership or S corporation conducting an active trade or business, as this will usually result in a larger business interest deduction and minimize that portion of debt allocable to investment or other non-business assets.

In classifying assets, bank accounts are always treated as investment assets regardless of whether they are interest bearing or are working capital. Accounts receivable generated by a partnership as a normal part of its trade or business are treated as business assets, however.[159]

If a debt-financed acquisition is treated as a contribution to the capital of the partnership and the debt is allocated using the tracing rules rather than proportionately among all the partnership assets, applying the reallocation rule should be relatively easy. Because the debt is allocated to assets that were created by the debt, only those assets need to be tracked and there is no requirement to determine the FMV, book value, or adjusted basis of assets.

Determining when there should be a reallocation of debt that has been allocated under the pro rata rule is more difficult. All IRS Notice 89-35 says is that such proceeds shall be reallocated among the assets of the entity as the assets of such entity, or the use of such assets, changes. Taken literally this would be a nightmare, as the values of assets to which debt has been allocated could change daily, such as inventory or balances in bank accounts. There should therefore be some threshold, below which changes would not be deemed significant enough to require reallocation, commonly referred to as a **de minimis rule.**

There does appear to be some authority for a de minimis rule in one letter ruling.[160] In this ruling, which involved a corporate split-off, the S corporation to be divided conducted a commercial real estate business consisting of three commercial buildings and an apartment building. The ruling does not say how many of those buildings the parent corporation (the subject of the ruling) retained following the split-off but it appears to be more than one.

The corporation's proposal to allocate its debt using a ratio based on FMVs of assets determined at the end of each taxable year was acceptable to the IRS. The IRS stated, however, that the debt would have to be reallocated during the taxable year anytime there was a significant change in the assets of the corporation. The ruling defined "significant change" to mean a sale or other disposition of any of the corporation's commercial buildings or if there was otherwise a 15% change in the corporation's assets, determined on the basis of FMV.

---

159. TAM 200010004 (Sep. 21, 1999).

160. Ltr. Rul. 9441025 (Jul. 11, 1994).

Because the corporation possessed only a few commercial buildings, a disposition of any of them would certainly seem to be a significant change. But, what if one of the buildings made up only 10% of the total FMV of values? Under the 15% rule this would seem not to be significant. It does not seem unreasonable, therefore, to use the following rules for determining when a significant change in FMV has occurred requiring a reallocation calculation.

1. If a single asset has a FMV that is 15% or more of the value of total assets, its sale or other disposition or a 15% or more change in its FMV is a significant change.

2. Assets individually having a FMV less than 15% of the FMV of total assets are grouped by activity (trade or business, passive activity, etc.). If there is a 15% or more change in FMV of the **group** in any class, it is a significant change.

4

> **Note.** Although the ruling focused on allocating interest expense based on the values of assets owned by two S corporations, nothing in the opinion prevents its application to partnerships, apart from the limitation imposed by IRC §6110(k)(3) to parties addressed in the ruling.

The next question is how one keeps track of the values of all assets and how often grouped assets must be revalued to see if there has been a significant change. It is probable the IRS would say it is dependent on facts and circumstances. For example, if a corporation has grouped assets that tend not to be disposed of and the values of which tend to be relatively stable, it might be enough to revalue only once a year or even as necessitated by facts and circumstances, such as an expected increase or decrease in values of assets of that kind in that area. Except in the case of individual assets that are 15% or more of the value of all assets, it would seem unreasonable to require revaluations more than once a month.

If a taxpayer is using ratios of book value or adjusted basis for allocating debt, the determination of whether there has been a significant change could probably be made on the basis of book value or adjusted basis, though exactly how this would be done and whether 15% would be a reasonable de minimis amount are open to question. It certainly would be easier to track changes, because original book value and basis are more objective numbers than FMV.

REPORTING

> **Note**. The following reporting rules were promulgated prior to the TCJA and may be affected by that act as well as any sunsetting provisions. References to lines and columns on forms are based on 2022 forms. Return preparation software should handle proper reporting on forms if the practitioners input data properly.

Individuals should report interest expense paid or incurred in connection with debt-financed acquisitions on either Schedule E, *Supplemental Income and Loss*, or Schedule A, *Itemized Deductions*, of Form 1040, *U.S. Individual Income Tax Return*, depending on the type of expenditure to which the interest expense is allocated. An interest expense is considered allocated to a particular expenditure of a passthrough entity if the interest expense is allocated to such expenditure under the tracing rules of Temp. Treas. Reg. §1.163-8T and IRS Notice 89-35. In addition, any interest expense allocated under the rules of IRS Notice 89-35 to assets used in an activity must be treated for reporting by individuals in the same manner as interest expense allocated to an expenditure for such assets would be treated.

Trade or Business Expenditures[161]

Interest expense allocated to a trade or business expenditure of a passthrough entity should be reported in part II of Schedule E. This interest expense should be identified on a separate line in column (a) as business interest, followed by the name of the passthrough entity to which the interest expense relates. The amount of such interest expense should be entered in column (i). This interest expense is generally deductible and should not be entered on Form 8582, *Passive Activity Loss Limitations*, or Form 4952, *Investment Interest Expense Deduction*.

> **Note**. Listing interest as a trade or business expenditure necessarily assumes there is material participation. If there is not, the interest should be treated as a passive activity expenditure.

Passive Activity Expenditures

Interest expense allocated to a passive activity expenditure of a passthrough entity should be entered on Form 8582 as a deduction from the activity in which such expenditure was made. The deductible amount of such interest expense, if any, as determined under the passive activity regulations, should be reported in part II of Schedule E.[162] This interest expense should be identified on a separate line in column (a) as passive interest, followed by the name of the passthrough entity to which the interest expense relates, and the amount of such interest expense should be entered in column (g).

Investment Expenditures

Interest expense allocated to an investment expenditure of a passthrough entity should be entered on Form 4952.[163] Any deductible amount allocated to **royalties** should be entered on a separate line of Schedule E, part II. Practitioners should enter "investment interest" and the name of the entity in column (a) and the amount in column (i).[164] The deductible amount (if any) of such interest expense should be reported on line 9 of Schedule A or on Schedule E in accordance with the instructions for Form 4952 or, if appropriate, on Schedule A without being entered on Form 4952. The balance of the deductible amount is reported on Schedule A, line 9.

Personal Expenditures

Interest expense allocated to a personal expenditure made by a passthrough entity for or on behalf of the owner is not deductible.

Debt-Financed Distributions

Unless the optional allocation rule is used, debt of passthrough entities and the associated interest expense must be allocated under the rules of Temp. Treas. Reg. §1.163-8T. In general, when debt proceeds of a passthrough entity are allocated to distributions to owners of the entity, the debt proceeds distributed to any owner and the associated interest expense are to be allocated under Temp. Treas. Reg. §1.163-8T in accordance with the **owner's** use of the debt proceeds. For example, if the owner uses distributed debt proceeds to purchase an interest in a passive activity, the owner's share of the interest expense on the debt proceeds is allocated to a passive activity.

---

161. Instructions for Schedule E.

162. Ibid.

163. Instructions for Form 4952.

164. Instructions for Schedule E.

An owner's share of a passthrough entity's interest expense on debt proceeds allocated to distributions to owners may exceed the entity's interest expense on the portion of the debt proceeds distributed to that particular owner.[165] In such cases, the entity must allocate the owner's excess interest expense using any reasonable method. The determination of whether a particular method of allocating such excess interest expense is reasonable depends on the facts and circumstances, including whether the entity consistently applies the method from year to year.

Under the **optional allocation rule,** a passthrough entity may allocate distributed debt proceeds and the associated interest expense to one or more expenditures (other than distributions) of the entity that are made during the same tax year of the entity as the distribution to the extent that debt proceeds (including other distributed debt proceeds) are not otherwise allocated to such expenditures.[166] However, distributed debt proceeds must be allocated under the general allocation rule to distributions to owners of the entity to the extent that they exceed the entity's expenditures (other than distributions) for the taxable year. Once debt proceeds are allocated under the optional rule, the debt proceeds must be reallocated, when necessary, under the general reallocation rule of Temp. Treas. Reg. §1.163-8T.

Any repayment of debt of a passthrough entity allocated to distributions to owners of the entity and to one or more other expenditures may, at the option of the passthrough entity, be treated first as a repayment of the portion of the debt allocated to such distributions.[167]

To the extent debt proceeds of a passthrough entity are allocated to distributions to owners of the entity, the portion of an owner's share of the entity's interest expense on debt proceeds allocated to the owner that does not exceed the entity's interest expense on the portion of the debt proceeds distributed to such owner should be included with code W in box 13 on Schedule K-1 for other deductions. This interest expense should be identified on an attached schedule as interest expense allocated to debt-financed distributions.

The manner in which the owner should report such interest expense depends on the types of expenditures that the owner makes with the distributed debt proceeds. For example, if the owner uses the debt proceeds to make a personal expenditure, the debt is personal debt and the owner cannot deduct the interest.

To the extent an owner's share of a passthrough entity's interest expense on debt proceeds allocated to distributions to owners exceeds the entity's interest expense on the portion of the debt proceeds distributed to such owner, the excess interest expense should be reported on Schedule K-1 in a manner consistent with the allocation of such interest expense by the entity. For example, if the passthrough entity allocates the excess interest expense to a rental activity, the expense should be taken into account by the entity in computing the income or loss from the rental activity that is reported to the owner on Schedule K-1.

If the passthrough entity uses the optional rule to allocate distributed debt proceeds and associated interest expense, the entity's interest expense on debt proceeds allocated to the other expenditures should be reported on Schedule K-1 in a manner consistent with the allocation of the debt proceeds. For example, if the passthrough entity allocates distributed debt and the associated interest expense to an expenditure in connection with a rental activity, the entity should take the interest expense on the debt into account in computing the income or loss from the rental activity that is reported to the owner on Schedule K-1.

165. Prop. Treas. Reg. §1.163-14(d)(1)(ii); IRS Notice 88-37, 1988-1 CB 522.

166. IRS Notice 89-35, 1989-1 CB 675.

167. Ibid.

CASE STUDY

There is an interesting Tax Court opinion involving both debt-financed distributions and debt-financed acquisitions of interests in partnerships.[168] This is a reviewed opinion and provides an excellent illustration of the application of IRS Notice 89-35 to partnerships.

Maurice was a partner in three rental real estate partnerships for many years. In 2009, the three partnerships borrowed millions of dollars through loans secured by their properties. They then distributed significant portions of the debt proceeds to the two partners, including Maurice. The partnerships paid interest on the loans and allocated to each partner's Schedule K-1 that partner's share of the interest expense. This was a debt-financed distribution. Maurice used his share of the debt to purchase investment assets and correctly reported his share of partnership interest as investment interest on his Schedule A in accordance with the rules governing debt-financed distributions and the tracing rules. Maurice had sufficient net investment income to deduct all of the investment interest.

In 2011, Maurice gifted part of his three real estate partnership interests to his son, William, who agreed to be bound by the partnership agreements. William did not assume personal liability for any of the partnerships' debts. As a result of gifting the partnership interests to William, Maurice was relieved of related shares of the nonrecourse partnership liabilities. On his 2011 income tax return, Maurice treated this as a sale of those partnership interests and paid income tax on millions of dollars of capital gains.

Maurice also held directly small general and limited partnership interests in a fourth real estate partnership as well as a separate interest held indirectly through a family limited partnership. The real estate partnership, like the others, incurred a nonrecourse loan and used it to make debt-financed distributions to its partners, including direct and indirect distributions to Maurice. Maurice used these distributions to acquire investment assets, which he held until his death. As with the other partnerships, Maurice received a Schedule K-1 with his share of the partnership's interest on the loan and treated it as investment interest on his individual return.

Maurice died in 2013. William inherited Maurice's general and limited partnership interests in the fourth real estate partnership and part of his interest in the family limited partnership. William did not assume personal responsibility for any of the partnership's debt.

Once William was a partner in these partnerships, he began receiving Schedules K-1 with his share of interest on the still outstanding loans. However, William had no investment assets and had never received any of the loan proceeds upon which interest was being paid by the partnerships. He treated the interest as having been paid on indebtedness properly allocable to the partnerships' rental real estate assets and deducted the interest expense against his distributive shares of the partnerships' real estate income. He did this on Schedule E by netting against the income for each partnership the corresponding amount of interest expense, reporting only the net income on his Form 1040.

The IRS audited William and recharacterized his distributive share of partnership interest as investment interest deductible only to the extent of net investment income, of which William had none. The matter then went to Tax Court.

In court, the IRS argued that William stepped into his father's shoes so that his share of the interest remained investment interest as long as the partnerships had the loans. The Tax Court said it could find no support for this theory in the statute, regulations, or decided cases. It noted that Maurice had treated the interest correctly in accordance with the interest tracing regulations and IRS Notice 89-35. Furthermore, William had not received, directly or indirectly, any portion of the debt-financed distributions that went to Maurice. Nor did he use distributions from the partnerships to make investment expenditures. Thus, the facts that caused the interest to be investment interest in Maurice's hands did not apply to William.

---

168. *Lipnick v. Comm'r*, 153 TC 1 (2019).

The court quoted the following from the regulations that explain how debt should be allocated where no proceeds are dispersed to a taxpayer.

> *If a taxpayer incurs or assumes a debt in consideration for the sale or use of property . . . or takes property subject to a debt, and no debt proceeds are disbursed to the taxpayer, the debt is treated for purposes of this section as if the taxpayer used an amount of the debt proceeds equal to the balance of the debt outstanding at such time to make an expenditure for such property.*[169]

The court found that William had acquired his interests from Maurice while those interests were subject to existing indebtedness. He was treated as using his allocated share of that debt to make an expenditure for such property — his partnership interests. This constituted a debt-financed **acquisition** of an interest in a partnership in accordance with IRS Notice 89-35 rather than a debt-financed distribution. He was thus required to allocate the debt among the assets of the partnerships, which were actively managed rental real estate properties constituting trades or businesses.

4

The IRS also argued that the tracing rules were not applicable to this situation because William, when acquiring the partnership interests from his father, did not become personally liable on the partnerships' nonrecourse loans. The court found no support for that position. It cited a previous case[170] that considered whether a corporation should be considered to have assumed a liability for purposes of IRC §357(c)[171] where a shareholder contributed to it an interest in a partnership whose assets were encumbered by nonrecourse debt. The court ruled that if the partnership interests transferred are in substance encumbered by a right of foreclosure on the partnership's real property, the corporation acquires such interests subject to those encumbrances. The court also noted that the IRS had previously taken the same position in a revenue ruling.[172]

The court concluded that both the tracing rules and IRS Notice 89-35 applied to William's acquisitions of his partnership interests and sustained William's treatment of the interest expenses as correct in all respects.

Observation. The return preparers for the two taxpayers in this case did everything right. IRS Notice 89-35 is a more sophisticated and complex notice than initially meets the eye. As was demonstrated in this case, things may not always be as they appear.

---

169. Temp. Treas. Reg. §1.163-8T(c)(3)(ii).

170. *Smith v. Comm'r,* 84 TC 889 (1985), *aff'd*, 805 F.2d 1073 (D.C. Cir. 1986).

171. With certain exceptions, §357(c) requires recognition of gain on an otherwise nontaxable transfer under IRC §351 of assets to a corporation in exchange for stock to the extent aggregate liabilities on transferred assets exceeds aggregate bases in those assets.

172. Rev. Rul. 80-323, 1980-2 CB 124.

PARTNERSHIPS AND SE TAX

IRS Large Business and International division currently has an active campaign targeting partners who may be misusing the limited partnership exception from the Self-Employment Contributions Act (SECA) tax to avoid payment of that tax.[173] The issue has become especially pronounced following the advent of LLCs. Unfortunately, the waters surrounding this issue remain very muddied.

IRC §1402(a) defines SE income as including a general partner's distributive share of business income from a partnership and guaranteed payments to a partner for performance of services in the partnership's trade or business. General partners are liable for SE tax on their distributive shares of the partnership's business income based solely on their status as general partners and without regard to the extent or whether they actually participate in the partnership's business.[174] Thus, if an LLC's members are general partners for federal tax purposes, their distributive shares of the LLC's business income are SE income unless an exclusion applies.

The partnership reports SE income to a partner on their Schedule K-1 in box 14.

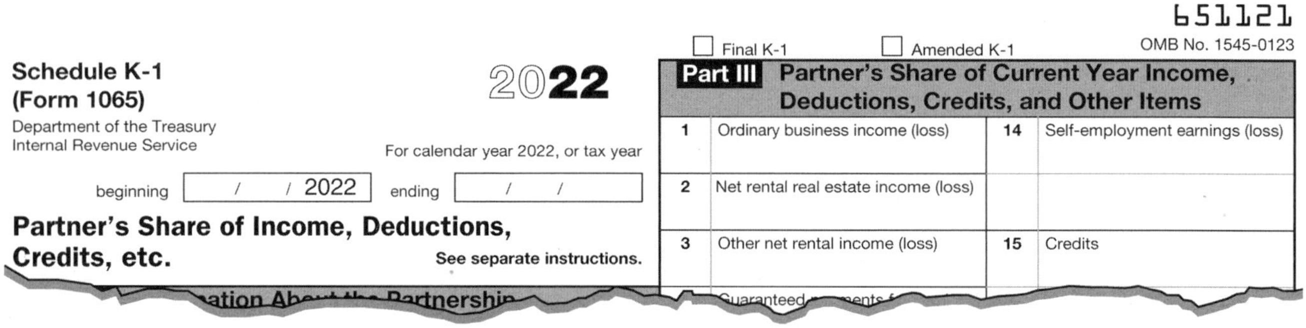
651121

☐ Final K-1 ☐ Amended K-1 OMB No. 1545-0123

Schedule K-1 (Form 1065) **2022**

Department of the Treasury
Internal Revenue Service

For calendar year 2022, or tax year

beginning / / 2022 ending / /

Partner's Share of Income, Deductions, Credits, etc. See separate instructions.

Part III Partner's Share of Current Year Income, Deductions, Credits, and Other Items

1	Ordinary business income (loss)	14	Self-employment earnings (loss)
2	Net rental real estate income (loss)		
3	Other net rental income (loss)	15	Credits

The partner calculates their SE tax on Schedule SE, *Self-Employment Tax,* based on the income they report on page 2 of Schedule E. These forms are reproduced on the following pages.

[173]. *Large Business and International Active Campaigns*. Mar. 21, 2023. IRS. [www.irs.gov/businesses/corporations/lbi-active-campaigns] Accessed on Mar. 28, 2023.

[174]. See *Cokes v. Comm'r,* 91 TC 222 (1988).

SCHEDULE SE (Form 1040)	Self-Employment Tax	OMB No. 1545-0074
Department of the Treasury Internal Revenue Service	Go to *www.irs.gov/ScheduleSE* for instructions and the latest information. **Attach to Form 1040, 1040-SR, or 1040-NR.**	**2022** Attachment Sequence No. **17**

Name of person with self-employment income (as shown on Form 1040, 1040-SR, or 1040-NR) | Social security number of person with **self-employment** income

4

Part I Self-Employment Tax

Note: If your only income subject to self-employment tax is **church employee income**, see instructions for how to report your income and the definition of church employee income.

A If you are a minister, member of a religious order, or Christian Science practitioner **and** you filed Form 4361, but you had $400 or more of **other** net earnings from self-employment, check here and continue with Part I . . . ☐

Skip lines 1a and 1b if you use the farm optional method in Part II. See instructions.

Line	Description	Box	Amount
1a	Net farm profit or (loss) from Schedule F, line 34, and farm partnerships, Schedule K-1 (Form 1065), box 14, code A	1a	
b	If you received social security retirement or disability benefits, enter the amount of Conservation Reserve Program payments included on Schedule F, line 4b, or listed on Schedule K-1 (Form 1065), box 20, code AH	1b	( )
	Skip line 2 if you use the nonfarm optional method in Part II. See instructions.		
2	Net profit or (loss) from Schedule C, line 31; and Schedule K-1 (Form 1065), box 14, code A (other than farming). See instructions for other income to report or if you are a minister or member of a religious order	2	
3	Combine lines 1a, 1b, and 2	3	
4a	If line 3 is more than zero, multiply line 3 by 92.35% (0.9235). Otherwise, enter amount from line 3	4a	
	Note: If line 4a is less than $400 due to Conservation Reserve Program payments on line 1b, see instructions.		
b	If you elect one or both of the optional methods, enter the total of lines 15 and 17 here	4b	
c	Combine lines 4a and 4b. If less than $400, **stop**; you don't owe self-employment tax. **Exception:** If less than $400 and you had **church employee income**, enter -0- and continue	4c	
5a	Enter your **church employee income** from Form W-2. See instructions for definition of church employee income — 5a		
b	Multiply line 5a by 92.35% (0.9235). If less than $100, enter -0-	5b	
6	Add lines 4c and 5b	6	
7	Maximum amount of combined wages and self-employment earnings subject to social security tax or the 6.2% portion of the 7.65% railroad retirement (tier 1) tax for 2022	7	147,000
8a	Total social security wages and tips (total of boxes 3 and 7 on Form(s) W-2) and railroad retirement (tier 1) compensation. If $147,000 or more, skip lines 8b through 10, and go to line 11 — 8a		
b	Unreported tips subject to social security tax from Form 4137, line 10 — 8b		
c	Wages subject to social security tax from Form 8919, line 10 — 8c		
d	Add lines 8a, 8b, and 8c	8d	
9	Subtract line 8d from line 7. If zero or less, enter -0- here and on line 10 and go to line 11	9	
10	Multiply the **smaller** of line 6 or line 9 by 12.4% (0.124)	10	
11	Multiply line 6 by 2.9% (0.029)	11	
12	**Self-employment tax.** Add lines 10 and 11. Enter here and on **Schedule 2 (Form 1040), line 4**	12	
13	**Deduction for one-half of self-employment tax.** Multiply line 12 by 50% (0.50). Enter here and on **Schedule 1 (Form 1040), line 15** — 13		

Part II Optional Methods To Figure Net Earnings (see instructions)

Farm Optional Method. You may use this method **only** if **(a)** your gross farm income[1] wasn't more than $9,060, **or (b)** your net farm profits[2] were less than $6,540.

Line	Description	Box	Amount
14	Maximum income for optional methods	14	6,040
15	Enter the **smaller** of: two-thirds (2/3) of gross farm income[1] (not less than zero) **or** $6,040. Also, include this amount on line 4b above	15	

Nonfarm Optional Method. You may use this method **only** if **(a)** your net nonfarm profits[3] were less than $6,540 and also less than 72.189% of your gross nonfarm income,[4] **and (b)** you had net earnings from self-employment of at least $400 in 2 of the prior 3 years. **Caution:** You may use this method no more than five times.

Line	Description	Box	Amount
16	Subtract line 15 from line 14	16	
17	Enter the **smaller** of: two-thirds (2/3) of gross nonfarm income[4] (not less than zero) **or** the amount on line 16. Also, include this amount on line 4b above	17	

[1] From Sch. F, line 9; and Sch. K-1 (Form 1065), box 14, code B.
[2] From Sch. F, line 34; and Sch. K-1 (Form 1065), box 14, code A—minus the amount you would have entered on line 1b had you not used the optional method.
[3] From Sch. C, line 31; and Sch. K-1 (Form 1065), box 14, code A.
[4] From Sch. C, line 7; and Sch. K-1 (Form 1065), box 14, code C.

For Paperwork Reduction Act Notice, see your tax return instructions. Cat. No. 11358Z **Schedule SE (Form 1040) 2022**

Name(s) shown on return. Do not enter name and social security number if shown on other side. | **Your social security number**

Caution: The IRS compares amounts reported on your tax return with amounts shown on Schedule(s) K-1.

Part II Income or Loss From Partnerships and S Corporations

Note: If you report a loss, receive a distribution, dispose of stock, or receive a loan repayment from an S corporation, you **must** check the box in column **(e)** on line 28 and attach the required basis computation. If you report a loss from an at-risk activity for which **any** amount is **not** at risk, you **must** check the box in column **(f)** on line 28 and attach **Form 6198**. See instructions.

27 Are you reporting any loss not allowed in a prior year due to the at-risk or basis limitations, a prior year unallowed loss from a passive activity (if that loss was not reported on Form 8582), or unreimbursed partnership expenses? If you answered "Yes," see instructions before completing this section . . . ☐ **Yes** ☐ **No**

28	**(a)** Name	**(b)** Enter **P** for partnership; **S** for S corporation	**(c)** Check if foreign partnership	**(d)** Employer identification number	**(e)** Check if basis computation is required	**(f)** Check if any amount is not at risk
A			☐		☐	☐
B			☐		☐	☐
C			☐		☐	☐
D			☐		☐	☐

	Passive Income and Loss		Nonpassive Income and Loss		
	(g) Passive loss allowed (attach **Form 8582** if required)	**(h)** Passive income from **Schedule K-1**	**(i)** Nonpassive loss allowed (see **Schedule K-1**)	**(j)** Section 179 expense deduction from **Form 4562**	**(k)** Nonpassive income from **Schedule K-1**
A					
B					
C					
D					
29a Totals					
b Totals					

30	Add columns (h) and (k) of line 29a . . .	30	
31	Add columns (g), (i), and (j) of line 29b . . .	31	( )
32	**Total partnership and S corporation income or (loss).** Combine lines 30 and 31 . . .	32	

Part III Income or Loss From Estates and Trusts

33	**(a)** Name	**(b)** Employer identification number
A		
B		

	Passive Income and Loss		Nonpassive Income and Loss	
	(c) Passive deduction or loss allowed (attach **Form 8582** if required)	**(d)** Passive income from **Schedule K-1**	**(e)** Deduction or loss from **Schedule K-1**	**(f)** Other income from **Schedule K-1**
A				
B				
34a Totals				
b Totals				

35	Add columns (d) and (f) of line 34a . . .	35	
36	Add columns (c) and (e) of line 34b . . .	36	( )
37	**Total estate and trust income or (loss).** Combine lines 35 and 36 . . .	37	

Part IV Income or Loss From Real Estate Mortgage Investment Conduits (REMICs)—Residual Holder

38 (a) Name	**(b)** Employer identification number	**(c)** Excess inclusion from **Schedules Q**, line 2c (see instructions)	**(d)** Taxable income (net loss) from **Schedules Q**, line 1b	**(e)** Income from **Schedules Q**, line 3b

39	Combine columns (d) and (e) only. Enter the result here and include in the total on line 41 below .	39	

Part V Summary

40	Net farm rental income or (loss) from **Form 4835**. Also, complete line 42 below . . .	40	
41	**Total income or (loss).** Combine lines 26, 32, 37, 39, and 40. Enter the result here and on Schedule 1 (Form 1040), line 5 . . .	41	
42	**Reconciliation of farming and fishing income.** Enter your **gross** farming and fishing income reported on Form 4835, line 7; Schedule K-1 (Form 1065), box 14, code B; Schedule K-1 (Form 1120-S), box 17, code AD; and Schedule K-1 (Form 1041), box 14, code F. See instructions .	42	
43	**Reconciliation for real estate professionals.** If you were a real estate professional (see instructions), enter the net income or (loss) you reported anywhere on Form 1040, Form 1040-SR, or Form 1040-NR from all rental real estate activities in which you materially participated under the passive activity loss rules . . .	43	

Schedule E (Form 1040) 2022

IRC §1402(a)(13) excludes from SE income a limited partner's distributive share of a partnership's business income. Because the SE laws and regulations governing partners' distributive shares of partnership business income were enacted long before LLCs existed in the United States, there is presently no formal IRS guidance for determining whether a member of an LLC should, for SECA, be treated as the equivalent of a general partner or limited partner. As a result, there is a wide array of opinions concerning the extent to which LLC members should be considered general or limited partners. There is a developing body of court cases and IRS rulings addressing the issue. (Although the IRS in 1997 issued proposed regulations[175] on this issue, the regulations have never been finalized and have been disregarded in cases and rulings.)

The general approach taken by courts has been to examine cases in light of Congress' reason for enacting the limited partner exception from SECA and how the characteristics of limited partners under state law can best be analogized to members of LLCs. The seminal case in this regard is *Renkemeyer, Campbell & Weaver, LLP v. Comm'r*,[176] in which lawyers in a law firm limited liability partnership (LLP) treated themselves as limited partners not subject to SECA on their distributive shares. The Tax Court ruled against them, noting that all the firm's income was derived from personal services performed by the partners. In determining whether they should be treated as limited partners, the court quoted from the legislative history of §1402(a)(13):

> *Under present law each partner's share of partnership income is includable in his net earnings from self-employment for social security purposes, irrespective of the nature of his membership in the partnership. The bill would exclude from social security coverage, the distributive share of income or loss received by a limited partner from the trade or business of a limited partnership. This is to exclude for coverage purposes certain earnings which are basically of an investment nature. However, the exclusion from coverage would not extend to guaranteed payments (as described in 707(c) of the Internal Revenue Code), such as salary and professional fees, received for services actually performed by the limited partner for the partnership.*[177]

The court then went on to say the following.

> *[T]he intent of section 1402(a)(13) was to ensure that individuals who merely invested in a partnership and who were not actively participating in the partnership's business operations (which was the archetype of limited partners at the time) would not receive credits toward Social Security coverage. The legislative history of section 1402(a)(13) does not support a holding that Congress contemplated excluding partners who performed services for a partnership in their capacity as partners (i.e., acting in the manner of self-employed persons), from liability for self-employment taxes.*[178]

The Tax Court also said that, in the absence of statutory guidance on the definition of "limited partner," the term would be given its ordinary meaning. This may have led to a tendency to compare LLCs to state law definitions of limited partners.[179] Courts have noted such things as limited partnership laws requiring both a general and a limited partner, the requirement that a limited partnership be formally created as such, limited partners' limited liability for debts of the partnership, and a prohibition against their participation in management of the partnership on pain of reclassification as general partners (the last item no longer an issue under more recent limited partnership statutes). In those cases, however, the members of the LLCs had rights to participate in management and performed services for the LLC, both of which were the most significant factors.

---

175. REG-209824-96 (Jan. 13, 1997) amending Treas. Reg. §1.1402(a)-2.

176. *Renkemeyer, Campbell & Weaver, LLP v. Comm'r*, 136 TC 137 (2011).

177. *Renkemeyer, Campbell & Weaver, LLP v. Comm'r*, 136 TC 137 (2011), quoting H. Rept. 95-702 (Part 1), at 11 (1977) (original emphasis added by court).

178. *Renkemeyer, Campbell & Weaver, LLP v. Comm'r*, 136 TC 137 (2011).

179. See *Castigliola, et al. v. Comm'r*, TC Memo 2017-62 (Apr. 12, 2017).

The IRS has addressed the SECA issue in two Chief Counsel Advices (CCAs). In the first, a management company organized as an LLC successor to an S corporation managed a number of investment limited partnerships for which the LLC was paid management fees.[180] The members of the LLC performed extensive services in managing and carrying out the trading activities of the limited partnerships as well as operational services for the LLC itself. The LLC had both voting and nonvoting membership interests, but distributive shares were allocated on the basis of total units owned without regard to class. The management company treated all its members as limited partners not subject to SE tax on their distributive shares. The only amounts reported as SE income were guaranteed payments representing health insurance premiums and parking benefits paid on behalf of the members by the LLC. However, each partner also received a Form W-2 each year, although the amounts were redacted in the CCA.

The LLC was under examination on the issue of whether their distributive shares were subject to SECA. The LLC argued that the Form W-2 wages constituted reasonable compensation for services and that each partner was therefore a limited partner with respect to their distributive shares of partnership income and not subject to SECA on those amounts.

The IRS utilized an approach similar to that in *Renkemeyer*. It noted that limited partners traditionally are passive investors who perform no role in the management or operations of the partnership. Instead, it is the general partners who do so. In this case, all the LLC members worked extensively in the LLC's business. That being the case, there was no basis for characterizing their distributive shares as a return on capital. Furthermore, relying on Rev. Rul. 69-184,[181] holding that partners who perform services for the partnership cannot be treated as employees, and a District Court case in which members of an LLC improperly paid themselves Form W-2 wages and treated distributive shares as a non-SE return on investment,[182] the IRS stated that such things as reasonable compensation for services and return on capital have no application to general partners in a partnership.

In the second CCA, an individual was a partner in an LLC that operated a number of franchise restaurants.[183] He was involved in the management and operations of the LLC on a full-time basis. The LLC had a large number of employees, many of whom had management or supervisory responsibilities. There was also an executive management team consisting of financial and operations executive employees who were not members of the LLC. The individual was paid guaranteed payments from the LLC (amounts redacted). He treated the guaranteed payments as SE income but not his distributive shares of partnership income. An IRS examiner was recommending that the distributive share be subject to SE tax.

Although admitting that the individual, as a member of the LLC, was not the equivalent of a limited partner, the LLC argued that the traditional limited partnership analysis should not apply to LLCs that derive their income from the sale of products, have made substantial capital investments, and have delegated significant management responsibility to executive-level employees. Instead, they should be treated more like corporations and permitted in cases like this to a non-SECA return on investment.

The IRS rejected the LLC's argument that an LLC classified as a partnership could combine elements of return on capital with reasonable compensation for services. Relying on the legislative history of §1402(a)(13) and *Renkemeyer,* it said that:

> *Section 1402(a)(13) provides an exclusion for limited partners, not for a reasonable return on capital, and does not indicate that a partner's status as a limited partner depends on the presence of a guaranteed payment or the capital-intensive nature of the partnership's business.*[184]

The IRS concluded that the SE exclusion was intended by Congress to apply only to those who merely invested and not to those who actively participated and performed services for a partnership in their capacity as partners.

---

180. CCA 201436049 (May 20, 2014).

181. Rev. Rul. 69-184, 1969-1 CB 256.

182. *Riether v. Comm'r,* 919 F.2d 1140 (D. N.M. 2012).

183. Ltr. Rul. 201640014 (Jun. 15, 2016).

184. Ibid.

The Tax Court again addressed the issue of a law firm organized as an LLC where the lawyer-members failed to pay SE tax on their distributive shares of partnership income in *Castigliola, et al. v. Comm'r*.[185] The three members of the firm met with their long-time, experienced CPA to discuss reporting payments from their newly formed member-managed LLC. The CPA advised them that they could make guaranteed payments that would be subject to SE tax, but that distributive shares in excess of that would not be. As a result, the lawyers made guaranteed payments to themselves that the court found were comparable to local legal salaries in the area determined on the basis of a survey. The IRS treated the distributive shares in excess of the guaranteed payments as SE income and assessed an SE tax deficiency.

4

In Tax Court, the taxpayers contended that the limited partner exclusion at §1402(a)(13) applied to their distributive shares in excess of the guaranteed payments. Because the term "limited partner" is nowhere defined in the Code or regulations, the court employed what it termed a "well-established rule of construction" that, if a statute does not define a term, it is to be given its ordinary meaning at the time of enactment.

The court noted that its prior opinion in *Renkemeyer* had indicated that the meaning of limited partner is not necessarily confined solely to the limited partnership context. Following that approach, the court determined its first inquiry was whether a person claiming the limited partner exception held a position in a partnership entity that is functionally equivalent to that of a limited partner in a limited partnership. It then reviewed the history of limited partnership statutes in Mississippi (whose law governed) and noted that, although the limited partners under the law in effect during the years at issue permitted limited partners to have a few rights with respect to participation — such as voting on dissolution of the partnership or a sale of substantially all of its assets — nevertheless, a limited partner would lose limited liability protection if, in addition to exercising those rights, the individual participated in the control of the business. Thus, the primary characteristics of a limited partner were limited liability and lack of control of the business.

In this case, because the LLC was member-managed, each of the members had management power over the business of the LLC. There was no written operating agreement or any other evidence showing that a member's management power was limited in any way. Furthermore, all of them actually participated in management decisions, such as collectively making decisions regarding their distributive shares, control of employees, and supervision of associates. Consequently, they would not have been treated as limited partners under the state's limited partnership act.

Another case demonstrates how a member of an LLC actually can be treated as a limited partner. In *Hardy v. Comm'r*,[186] Dr. Hardy, a plastic surgeon, performed some procedures in his office, but any procedures requiring anesthesia had to be performed outside the office and employ the services of an anesthesiologist. Dr. Hardy had been performing these procedures in local hospitals, but often had difficulty getting space. Surgical procedures generally had three fee components: a fee for Dr. Hardy's surgical services; a fee for the anesthesiologist; and a fee for the use of a surgical facility and its accompanying services. Patients paid the facility fee directly to the facility separately from Dr. Hardy's fee for services.

To more conveniently perform day-surgery, Dr. Hardy purchased a 12.5% minority interest in an LLC that operated an outpatient surgical center. Although Dr. Hardy was a member of the LLC, he never managed it and had no day-to-day responsibilities. He did meet quarterly with other members, but had no input into management decisions. The LLC was professionally managed and directly billed patients for facility fees. The opinion did not indicate whether the LLC was member or manager managed, though given the discussion of Dr. Hardy's role, one has the impression that the result would have been the same either way. Dr. Hardy received a distribution from the LLC regardless of whether he performed any surgeries at the surgery center. His distribution was not dependent on how many surgeries he performed and the LLC had no minimum surgery requirement in order for a member to receive a distribution.

185. *Castigliola, et al. v. Comm'r*, TC Memo 2017-62 (Apr. 12, 2017).

186. *Hardy v. Comm'r*, TC Memo 2017-16 (Jan. 17, 2017).

In court, the IRS argued that Dr. Hardy was liable for SECA on his distributive share from the LLC because he performed surgeries at the surgery center and was not acting as a limited partner. The Tax Court disagreed. Unlike the lawyers in *Renkemeyer,* Dr. Hardy performed no services in the operations of the LLC itself. His distributions were based on the fees patients paid to use the facility and had no relationship to his services, for which he was separately paid by patients. His distributive share of the LLC's business income was therefore received by him in his capacity as an investor and not subject to SECA. It is notable that in *Hardy* the court did not mention state limited partnership laws, relying entirely on Dr. Hardy's lack of involvement in the LLC.

In another case involving a doctor who performed surgeries for an LLC, the Tax Court stated that it had been concluded "in Renkemeyer that an interest other than a limited partner interest could be treated as such for purposes of that section only if the holder is merely a passive investor in the entity who does not actively participate in the entity's business operations."[187]

IRS PROPOSED REGULATIONS[188]

The 1997 proposed regulations (which have never been finalized or withdrawn) apply to all entities classified as partnerships for federal tax purposes, regardless of what the entity is called under state law. To do this, the proposed regulations attempt to adopt an approach based on the relationship among the partner, the partnership, and the partnership's business. State law characterizations of whether an individual is a limited partner or otherwise do not matter.

An individual generally is treated as a limited partner under the proposed regulations unless the individual:

- Has personal liability for the debts of or claims against the partnership solely by reason of being a partner,
- Has authority to contract on behalf of the partnership under the law of the jurisdiction in which the partnership is organized, or
- Participates in the partnership's trade or business for more than 500 hours during the tax year.

If, however, substantially all of the activities of a partnership involve the performance of services in the fields of health, law, engineering, architecture, accounting, actuarial science, or consulting, any individual who provides services as part of that trade or business will not be considered a limited partner, meaning the individual will always be subject to SECA on their entire distributive share from all interests the individual has in the service partnership. A partner is not considered to be a service partner, however, if that partner only performs a small amount of services to or on behalf of the partnership. A small amount is not defined in the proposed regulations. The IRS refers to these as **functional tests.**

Although an individual may not be treated as a limited partner under the general rule of the proposed regulations, two special rules permit some partners to exclude all or a portion of their distributive shares from SE net earnings. The first exception permits an exclusion from SECA for an interest held by an individual who has more than one class of interest in the partnership to the extent a class of interest held by the individual would, immediately after it is acquired, qualify as a limited partnership interest under the substantial interest test. This is comparable to an individual who holds both general and limited partnership interests in the same partnership.

The second exception deals with the payment for services rule and permits an individual who participates in the partnership's trade or business for more than 500 hours still to be treated as a limited partner if the individual owns only one class of interest in a class of interests that are treated as being limited partnership interests. In such a case, the partner would have SE income in the form of a guaranteed payment to the extent necessary to compensate the partner for services to the LLC, similar to the rule applied to limited partners under existing law.

---

187. *Joseph v. Comm'r,* TC Memo 2020-65 (May 19, 2020).

188. REG-209824-96, 1997-11 IRB 19, amending Treas. Reg. §1.1402(a)-2.

Whether a class of interest is treated as a limited partnership interest is determined in the same manner for both exceptions under a **substantial interest test.**[189] This regulation imposes the following requirements on the particular class of interest.[190]

- The class of interest has limited partners within the meaning of the general rule who own a substantial, continuing interest in that specific class of partnership interest; and
- Individual's rights and obligations with respect to that specific class of interest are identical to the rights and obligations of that class held by similarly situated partners owning that same class of interest.

A **substantial interest** in a class is determined on the basis of facts and circumstances, but ownership of 20% or more of a specific class of interest is deemed substantial.

4

A **class of interests** is an interest that grants the holder specific rights and obligations. If a holder's rights and obligations from an interest are different from another holder's rights and obligations, each holder's interest belongs to a separate class of interest. An individual may hold more than one class of interest in the same partnership provided that each class grants the individual different rights or obligations. The existence of a guaranteed payment made to an individual for services rendered to or on behalf of a partnership is not a factor in determining the rights and obligations of a class of interest.

Example 34. Anthony, Betsy, and Carl form Blackacre, LLC under the laws of their state to engage in a business that is not a service partnership. Blackacre, classified as a partnership for federal tax purposes, allocates all items of income, deduction, and credit of the LLC to Anthony, Betsy, and Carl in proportion to their ownership of LLC. Anthony and Carl each contribute $10,000 for one LLC unit. Betsy contributes $20,000 for two LLC units. Each LLC unit entitles its holder to receive 25% of LLC's tax items, including profits. Anthony does not perform services for Blackacre. Each year, however, Betsy receives a guaranteed payment of $60,000 for 600 hours of services rendered to the LLC, and Carl receives a guaranteed payment of $100,000 for 1,000 hours of services rendered to Blackacre. Carl also is elected LLC's manager [meaning, presumably, that the LLC is a manager-managed LLC]. Under the state's law, he has the authority to contract on behalf of LLC.[191]

Anthony is treated as a limited partner in the LLC because he is not personally liable for debts of or claims against LLC. Anthony does not have authority to contract for Blackacre, LLC under state law, and he does not participate in Blackacre's trade or business for more than 500 hours during the tax year. Therefore, Anthony's distributive share attributable to his LLC unit is excluded from his SE net earnings under §1402(a)(13).

Betsy's guaranteed payment of $60,000 is included in her SE net earnings under §1402(a)(13). Betsy is not treated as a limited partner because, although she is not liable for debts of or claims against Blackacre and does not have authority to contract for the LLC under state law, Betsy does participate in its trade or business for more than 500 hours during the tax year. Furthermore, Betsy is not treated as a limited partner because she does not hold more than one class of interest in the LLC. Nevertheless, although she worked more than 500 hours during the year, Betsy qualifies for the exception for members holding only one class of interest for two reasons. First, she qualifies for the exception because she owns a substantial and continuing interest in Blackacre. Secondly, she has the same rights and obligations provided by the **same** class of interest that Anthony, as a limited partner, owned. In this example, Betsy's distributive share is deemed to be a return on her investment in LLC and not payment for her service to LLC. Thus, Betsy's distributive share attributable to her two LLC units is **not** SE net earnings under §1402(a)(13).

---

189. Ibid.

190. Ibid. See paragraph (6)(i).

191. Based on an example in the Proposed Regulations.

Carl's guaranteed payment of $100,000 is included in his SE net earnings under §1402(a). In addition, Carl's distributive share attributable to his Blackacre, LLC unit also is SE net earnings under §1402(a) because he is not a limited partner under any of the rules of the proposed regulations. Carl is not treated as a limited partner under the general rule because he has the authority under the state's law to enter into a binding contract on behalf of the LLC and because he participates in LLC's trade or business for more than 500 hours during the tax year. Carl is also not treated as a limited partner under the exception for holders of more than one class of interests because Carl does not hold more than one class of interest in LLC. Finally, Carl is not treated as a limited partner under the exception for holders of one class because he has the power to bind LLC. Thus, Carl's guaranteed payment and distributive share both are included in his SE net earnings under §1402(a).

Note. Although the regulations are proposed, the IRS has said that the regulations cannot be enforced against taxpayers. Instead, the applicable analysis is the statutory language, legislative history, and case law. Taxpayers, however, may rely on the 1997 proposed regulations. In other words, the IRS will respect a partner's status as a limited partner if the partner qualifies as a limited partner under the 1997 proposed regulations.[192]

APPROACHES TO SE TAX AS APPLIED TO LLC MEMBERS

General Partner Model

If an LLC is manager-managed, it should be treated as a general partnership for tax purposes. That is because it will fail the second test: authority to contract on behalf of the partnership under the law of the jurisdiction in which the partnership is organized. Therefore, all members of a member-managed LLC should be subject to SE tax on their distributive shares of the partnership's trade or business income, regardless of their degree of participation.

Limited Partner Model

In a manager-managed LLC, only the managing members have the right to conduct the affairs of the LLC and to bind the LLC to contracts. Nonmanaging members have no such rights. An arrangement such as this is analogous to a limited partnership under state law. The managing member serves the same function as the general partner and the nonmanaging members fill the roles of limited partners. This model is also, with the exception of service partnerships, effectively treated by the proposed regulations as a limited partnership.

If one wanted to create an LLC with the greatest chance of having some distributive shares exempt from SE tax, the limited partnership model probably has the best chance. In fact, this was essentially the approach taken by the 1997 proposed regulations. To make it resemble a limited partnership as much as possible, the LLC could be structured with two classes of members, such as class A and class B. The managing members would be class A members and would hold their management positions by virtue of the type of membership interest owned and not as a result of election. Nonmanaging members would be class B members and would have no right to participate in the selection of management members except under circumstances, such as death or withdrawal of a class A member, as would traditionally permit limited partners to choose a new general partner under limited partnership law. The managers should have small membership interests, such as 1%, and be paid guaranteed payments for their services. In addition, the managers should own nonmanaging membership interests. This would be the equivalent of a general partner who is also a limited partner.

---

192. *Self-Employment Tax and Partners*, p. 19. Feb. 13, 2019. IRS. [www.irs.gov/pub/irs-utl/pst_c_366_01_01_01.pdf] Accessed Mar, 29, 2023.

Although the proposed regulations require members of a service partnership to treat all distributive shares as SE income without the possibility of limited partnership treatment, this is an unreasonable approach. This is apparently based on an IRS view that personal service businesses are not permitted to operate in limited partnership form under state law and therefore should not be permitted to be treated as such for purposes of SECA. They cite nothing in support of this contention, however. A professional service provider will always have personal liability under state law for their own malfeasance no matter what the form of entity is. S corporations already give such individuals the ability to have the equivalent of limited partner protection (to the extent it can be had in such circumstances) plus the ability to pay non-SECA distributions in addition to the payment of FICA wages for services.

The assumption really appears to be that all distributive income is the result of the personal services of the members, and that there can be no return on capital. This might arguably be the case if all services of the LLC are furnished only by its members, such as was the case in *Renkemeyer*.[193] This is not always the case, however. Instead, income is also derived from employees, who are as much capital as any fixed asset for purposes of generation of income and return on capital investment.

4

DISCUSSION

Much of the discussion of the *Renkemeyer* case concerns the extent to which the limited partnership interest exception remains available. William O'Shea, director of the pass-through group at Deloitte Tax LLP's National Tax Office and former IRS associate chief counsel for passthroughs and special industries was quoted in an article in *Tax Notes Today* (subscription service) as saying that, under *Renkemeyer*, even limited partners under state law are not safe in that they may not meet the limited partner exception under §1402(a)(13).[194] In fact, *Renkemeyer* may be as much an application of an extreme case. None of the partners paid SE tax, inviting the IRS and the Tax Court to recharacterize everything.

One of the problems with drawing limited partner conclusions from *Renkemeyer* is that it was an LLP, not a limited LLP. In other words, it was a Kansas general partnership which had made a limited liability election. That did not make it a limited partnership under Kansas law; it remained a general partnership. The Tax Court pointed this out in its opinion, but commentators seem to have ignored that.

IRC §1402(a) includes as an individual's SE net earnings, plus

> *[H]is distributive share (whether or not distributed) of income or loss described in section 702(a)(8) from any trade or business carried on by a partnership of which he is a member.*[195]

Both the regulations and cases have said that the lack of a partner's participation in the business is irrelevant in determining whether a distributive share of partnership profit should be treated as SE net earnings. It is the status as a general partner that matters, not the extent of participation.

The *Renkemeyer* court could simply have held that the partners' statuses as general partners under Kansas law was also binding for federal income tax purposes and left it at that. The court's analysis of the limited partner exception appeared to have more to do with rebutting the appropriateness of the partnership's limited partnership exception argument. In that respect, the court appears to have done a commendable job.

In the *Riether* case, although not actually discussed, it appears the LLC there was also member-managed.[196] If so, the court was correct: all of the distributive share of business income should have been subject to SE tax because the two members should have been treated as general partners.

---

193. *Renkemeyer, Campbell & Weaver, LLP v. Comm'r*, 136 TC 137 (2011).

194. *Renkemeyer Rationale Consistent With Statute, IRS Official Says*. May 26, 2011. Ellliott, Amy S. Tax Analysts. [www.taxnotes.com/tax-notes-today-federal/partnership-taxation/renkemeyer-rationale-consistent-statute-irs-official-says/2011/05/26/vx0n?highlight=Doc%20 2011-11386] Accessed on Apr. 20, 2023.

195. IRC §1402(a).

196. *Riether v. Comm'r*, 919 F.2d 1140 (D. N.M. 2012).

The original point of the limited partner exception was to prevent individuals from making passive investments in partnerships to earn social security retirement credit without working for it. This was contrary to the underlying philosophy of social security retirement being earned by the performance of work. For a similar reason, net earnings from rental real estate, although trade or business income for income tax purposes, is excluded from qualifying for social security retirement credit.

The cases and IRS CCAs seem to be situations of bad facts making bad law. It has been clearly recognized in S corporation cases that, even if there is a personal service activity, an S corporation shareholder is entitled to a non-compensatory distributive share of S corporation business income as a return on capital when capital is a material income-producing factor and the shareholder otherwise receives reasonable compensation for services. This was true in *David E. Watson, P.C. v. U.S.*[197]

In this case, a CPA firm had four CPAs whose partnership interests in the practice were held through individual S corporations. The firm had more than 25 associates who billed time. Watson's S corporation paid him $24,000 in salary each year and $204,000 and $175,000 in distributions in each of the two years under examination. The court accepted the IRS's expert witness testimony that reasonable compensation for Watson's services — independent of any return on capital — was $91,000 each year. The District Court sustained an IRS recharacterization of a portion of the distributions as wages. However, that still left $137,000 and $108,000 each year as distributions.

A similar fact pattern has not yet emerged in the LLC context, although the court in *Castigliola* noted that the partners supervised associates. Yet, even §1402(a)(13) and its legislative history seem to acknowledge that, for limited partners, there can be a bifurcation between a portion of a distributive share representing return on investment and SE income. Outside of personal service activities it might be much easier to persuade the IRS that a limited partnership type membership interest represents an investment interest without — as in *Hardy* — having to be totally passive, but instead permitting a reasonable return on investment.

Based on the analyses in the authorities, it is becoming clear that members of LLCs who participate in management or the LLC's business can expect to be treated by the IRS as the equivalent of general partners whose distributive shares of the LLC's business income is subject to SE tax. This is especially true for personal service LLCs. Regardless of whether the LLC's business is personal services, however, it is equally clear that neither the IRS nor the courts are to this point accepting arguments that any portion of the distributive share of an LLC member who is found to be more than a passive investor can be excluded from SE tax on the basis of return of capital or investment. For the time being, the only way to achieve that may be by using S corporations or structuring a non-personal service LLC as the equivalent of a limited partnership.

197. *David E. Watson, P.C. v. U.S.*, 668 F.3d 1008 (8th Cir. 2012), *cert denied*, 133 S.Ct. 364 (2012), *aff'g* 757 F.Supp.2d 877 (S.D. Ia. 2010).

Chapter 5: Agricultural Issues and Rural Investments

5

Note. Corrections for all of the chapters are available at **TaxSchool.illinois.edu.** For clarification about terms used throughout this chapter, see the **Acronyms and Abbreviations** section following the index.

For your convenience, in-text website links are also provided as short URLs. Anywhere you see **uofi.tax/xxx**, the link points to the address immediately following in brackets.

About the Author

Roger McEowen, JD, is the Kansas Farm Bureau Professor of Agricultural Law and Taxation at Washburn University School of Law in Topeka, Kansas. He is a published author and prominent speaker, conducting more than 80 seminars annually across the United States for farmers, agricultural business professionals, lawyers, and tax professionals. He can also be heard on WIBW radio and RFD-TV. His writing can be found in national agriculture publications, a monthly publication, *Kansas Farm and Estate Law,* his two books, *Principles of Agricultural Law* and *Agricultural Law in a Nutshell,* as well as on **www.washburnlaw.edu/waltr.** He received a B.S. with distinction from Purdue University in Management in 1986, an M.S. in Agricultural Economics from Iowa State University in 1990, and a J.D. from the Drake University School of Law in 1991. He is a member of the Iowa and Kansas Bar Associations and is admitted to practice in Nebraska. He is also a past President of the American Agricultural Law Association.

Other chapter contributors and reviewers are listed at the front of this book.

DEDUCTING RESIDUAL (EXCESS) SOIL FERTILITY

While the practice of deducting residual soil fertility costs has been utilized for some time, the recent increase in farmland values and fertilizer prices has encouraged some farmland buyers to allocate part of the total purchase price of the farmland to fertilizer that the seller applied before the purchase. The same practice may also occur when the owner dies with part of the fair market value (FMV) of the land at the date of death being allocated to fertilizer that was applied before death. Such an allocation (either upon purchase or upon death) will allow a deduction for the value of the fertilizer rather than the full acquisition value being solely attributed to the land's basis. The concept is known as deducting "residual soil fertility." If the taxpayer can show that fertilizer or nutrients applied to the land are a separate asset that can be distinguished from the soil, and can establish their FMV, part of the purchase price of the land can be allocated to the fertilizer or nutrients and recovered through depreciation deductions.

Caution. Calculations for this deduction should be performed by an agronomist. Tax preparers must consider the reasonableness of the information provided in preparing the return.

RULES FOR ALLOCATION

When a group of assets that constitute a trade or business is purchased, the buyer must use a residual method to allocate the purchase price among the assets.[1] The seller must follow the same allocation rules to report gain or loss.[2] Depreciation can be claimed on depreciable assets associated with the farmland starting with the first tax year in which possession of the land is taken or the assets are placed in service. Under IRC §1060, the amount claimed is tied to the portion of the total cost of the farmland that can be allocated to any depreciable asset, such as fencing, field drainage tile, grain storage facilities, farm buildings, and irrigation equipment, just to name a few of the more common depreciable items.

Note. The seller must use the same allocation rules as the buyer to report gain or loss on the sale of a group of assets that constitute a trade or business as defined by Treas. Reg. §1.1060-1(b)(2)(i).

1. IRC §1060.
2. Ibid.

Note. The IRS implements allocations under §1060 via Form 8594, *Asset Acquisition Statement Under Section 1060.* Form 8594 sets forth the allocations to seven classes of assets. Form 8594 is used by both the seller and buyer of a trade or business group of assets to report such a sale if goodwill or a going concern value applies or could apply to the assets being sold.

Most farmland sales are **not** subject to the allocation rules of §1060 unless the land is purchased with a group of assets constituting a trade or business. Thus, while the parties to the sale transaction do not need to file Form 8594 to report the purchase price allocation, the buyer must allocate the purchase price to determine the income tax basis in the land and each depreciable improvement on the land.[3] Likewise, the seller must allocate the purchase price for purposes of gain allocation between the land and any improvements on the land based on the ratio of the FMV of each item purchased (land and improvements) to the total combined FMV of the assets.[4]

5

Note. Even if taxpayers do not need to file Form 8594, many states require buyers and sellers of real estate to report the transaction and identify the parties to the transaction. If the parties made the same allocations, they are less likely to be challenged.

If the parties to the transaction have adverse interests and the transaction is a bona fide arm's length transaction, a court will generally honor the manner in which the parties allocate the purchase price among the assets purchased in a group.[5] Likewise, if those conditions are met, the IRS will also honor the allocation.[6] Other than for related party sales, most farmland sales involve parties with adverse interests. **The buyer wants to allocate as much of the purchase price to depreciable assets and the seller wants to allocate as little as possible to those assets to avoid ordinary gain recognition. Conversely, the buyer wants to allocate as little as possible to land because it is non-depreciable, but the seller wants to allocate as much as possible to land to trigger capital gain rather than ordinary gain recognition.**

Deduction

IRC §180 allows a taxpayer engaged in the trade or business of farming to annually elect (by deducting the expense on the return) to deduct the cost of fertilizer, lime, potash, or other materials which enrich, neutralize, or condition land used in farming that has been either purchased or acquired during the tax year.[7] Under the definition, a "farmer" is one who cultivates, operates, or manages a farm for gain or profit, either as owner or tenant. For a landlord, if the rent is based on production, the landlord meets the definition of a "farmer" for this purpose. A landlord receiving a fixed amount of rent will not satisfy the definition unless the landlord participates to a material extent in the operation or management of the farm.

Note. The §180 election is effective for one year, and once it is made it may only be revoked with the IRS's consent.[8]

3. Treas. Reg. §1.167(a)-5.

4. Treas. Reg. §1.61-6(a).

5. See, e.g., *Black Industries, Inc. v. Comm'r,* TC Memo 1979-61 (Feb. 22, 1979).

6. See IRS Pub. 225, *Farmer's Tax Guide* (2022), p. 33 for a further discussion of allocating the basis of acquired assets.

7. For this purpose, the definition of a "farmer" is set forth in Treas. Reg. §1.180-1(b) which cross references Treas. Reg. §1.175-3.

8. Treas. Reg. §1.180-2.

If fertilization costs are not expensed, they are required to be capitalized (similar to field drainage tile or fencing expense deductions being amortized over a presumed useful life). This means residual soil fertility is a **capital asset** in the hands of an operating farmer, crop-share landlord, or cash rent landlord when farmland is acquired, with the cost amortized over the useful life of the asset. That useful life is typically three to four years. The general 15-year amortization rules do not apply because this is an acquisition of tangible, not intangible, property. Instead, the IRS position is that fertilizer costs should be amortized based on the percentage of use or benefit each year. That likely means that straight-line depreciation does not apply. An agronomist or other soil scientist may be able to provide sufficient information so that the property annual expense allocation can be determined.[9]

Note. A tax practitioner should follow the agronomist's report, when available.[10] Usually, about 60% is deducted in the first year, with 30% deducted in the second year and the last 10% deducted in the third year. Using straight-line depreciation would result in recognizing deductions in a slower manner. Given the potential difficulties of measuring costs utilized annually, straight-line depreciation may be an acceptable alternative.

For farmland inherited from a decedent, the date of the decedent's death is the measurement date for determining whether residual soil fertility exists.[11] If it does, the FMV of the fertility can be depreciated by the decedent's estate or the beneficiaries of the estate that receive the farmland.

Practitioner Planning Tip

There is no IRS guidance on **how** to amortize fertility. Logically, the amount for excess fertility would be reported on Form 4562, *Depreciation and Amortization,* because that is where capitalization and amortization are typically reported. An appropriate approach would be to deduct the excess fertilizer supply on Schedule F, *Profit or Loss From Farming,* or Form 4835, *Farm Rental Income and Expenses,* as part of the overall deduction for fertilizer. This requires the tax practitioner to separately track the deduction. IRC §180 is the only election but it applies only to the deduction for **purchased** fertilizer. The deduction is actually more similar to IRC §611 dealing with depletion, for which there is no form.

9. See, e.g., IRS Pub. 225, *Farmer's Tax Guide* (2022), Chapter 4.

10. Ibid.

11. IRC §180(a).

IRS GUIDANCE

The IRS issued Technical Advice Memorandum (TAM) 9211007[12] providing guidance on the deductibility of residual fertilizer supply and emphasizing that the taxpayer claiming the deduction must have beneficial ownership of the fertilizer. Under the facts involved, a corporation was owned by shareholders A and B. The corporation bought buildings, irrigators, pumps, wells, grain bins, and "residual fertilizer supply" on land that the shareholders purchased in their individual names. The shareholders leased the land to the corporation through a 1-year lease that automatically renewed unless notice of termination was given. The corporation amortized the value allocated to the residual fertilizer supply over seven years. The IRS determined that the corporation could not claim any amortization deduction because it was not the beneficial owner of the fertilizer.[13]

> **Note.** The TAM does not discuss claiming a deduction for the residual supply under §180 because the residual supply was amortized over seven years.

5

In addition to beneficial ownership of the residual fertilizer supply, the IRS also specified in the TAM that the taxpayer must do the following.

1. Establish the presence and the extent of the fertilizer
2. Show the level of soil fertility attributable to the fertilizer applied by the prior owner
3. Provide a basis upon which to measure the increase in fertility in the land
4. Provide evidence indicating the period over which the fertility attributable to the residual fertilizer will be exhausted

In 1995, the IRS published a Market Segment Specialization Program (MSSP) addressing residual soil fertility.[14] In the MSSP, the IRS notes that a deduction for residual fertilizer supply will be denied unless the taxpayer can establish the following.

1. Beneficial ownership of the residual fertilizer supply
2. The presence and extent of the residual fertilizer
3. That the residual fertilizer supply is actually being exhausted

In addition, the MSSP instructs IRS examining agents to make sure that the values assigned to depreciable farm assets are reasonable.

> **Note.** If a deduction for residual fertilizer supply is taken under §180, the taxpayer does not need to provide evidence of the period over which the fertility of the fertilizer will be exhausted. This requirement applies to amortization. IRC §180 does not require the taxpayer to establish that the fertilizer (or other soil conditioner) is being exhausted.

12. TAM 9211007 (Dec. 3, 1991).

13. See also *Helvering v. F. & R. Lazarus & Co.*, 308 U.S. 252 (1939).

14. IRS MSSP, *Guideline on Grain Farmers* (Training 3149-133, Jul. 1995).

Points on the Requirements

Some additional points about the requirements set forth in the TAM and the MSSP can be made.

- **Beneficial ownership.** Where the fertilizer and the land are purchased by the same taxpayer as the farm operator (e.g., farm tenant buys the farmland), a showing of beneficial ownership of the fertilizer will not be an issue.
- **Presence and extent of fertilizer.** A taxpayer claiming a deduction for residual fertilizer supply should hire an agronomist to conduct soil tests and document the presence and extent of soil nutrients. Documenting the soil sampling procedure is critical, and the sampling should occur before the taxpayer applies any additional fertilizer. If possible, soil samples should be taken at the time of purchase. For farmland that is inherited, the sampling should occur before any new fertilization is applied.

Note. If farmland has an actual **excess** soil fertility base, it will normally bring a price premium upon sale.[15] That is the same rationale that applies when farmland with fences, field drainage tile, and grain storage facilities is purchased — a price premium applies to factor in the existence of those assets. As for residual fertilizer supply, the excess amount can be measured by **grid sampling.** A buyer can anticipate that grid sampling will likely cost $15–$30 per acre. Agronomists and agricultural soil testing labs follow certain guidelines and procedures to determine average (base) soil fertility for various soil types. Once grid soil samples are obtained, the fertility levels of those samples are compared to the base fertility guideline levels for particular soil types to establish the amount of "excess" fertility on a tract of acquired farm real estate.

- **Level of fertility attributable to prior owner.** Having the soil tested at the time of purchase will distinguish the fertilizer level in the soil at the time of purchase.
- **Basis to measure increase in fertility.** This is difficult to establish because of the variability of soil fertility in general. The key is to obtain data for the established base soil fertility for the type of soil on the purchased farmland from comparable tracts and comparable soil types. By establishing the base soil fertility, the actual sampling on the purchased property will reveal whether excess residual fertilizer is present. But a taxpayer should be prepared for the IRS to counter with its own soil analysis showing a different base fertility level.

Note. There is little IRS guidance on what an acceptable baseline is for measuring residual fertilizer supply or excess available nutrients.

- **Period of exhaustion.** This depends on the types of nutrients, soil, crop rotations, etc. A professional agronomic report will be needed to establish the exhaustion period.

AMOUNT OF DEDUCTION

The actual deduction might be less than the agronomist's value of the excess amount. If the land's value combined with the value of the excess fertility exceeds the purchase price of the land, an allocation must be done for each one based on their respective FMVs.[16]

Example 1. Bill buys farmland for $8,000 per acre. An agronomist values the excess fertility at $4,000 per acre. Comparable land in the area without excess fertility sells for $7,000 per acre. When the $4,000 per acre for excess fertility is added to the land value without excess fertility, the total is $11,000. Thus, the land is 63.6% ($7,000 sale price without excess fertility ÷ $11,000 total cost) of the total value, and the excess fertility is 36.4% ($4,000 excess fertility ÷ $11,000 total cost). A reasonable deduction would be $2,912 per acre (36.4% × $8,000 purchase price) as the deduction for excess fertilizer supply, not the $4,000 per acre that the agronomist determined.

---

15. IRS MSSP, *Guideline on Grain Farmers* (Training 3149-133, p. 12-1, Jul. 1995).

16. Ibid.

DOCUMENTATION

While the IRS does not require it, perhaps the best way to document the deduction for excess soil fertility is to provide for the allocation of value to the amount of above average soil fertility in the purchase contract for the farmland. In addition, a written summary of how the computation was made and the time period over which it would deplete due to crop production should be obtained from the agronomist or other expert involved. This will be beneficial for establishing the proper amortization period for the excess soil fertility and will provide substantiation of the deduction upon any subsequent IRS (or state) audit.

> **Example 2.** Farmer buys 80 acres of land at a January auction for $16,000 per acre. Farmer hires an agronomist to analyze fertility values resulting in a fertility valuation of $1,500 per acre. For this soil type, the baseline fertility value is deemed to be $300 per acre. The excess fertility amount is $1,200 per acre ($1,500 – $300) and is expected to be utilized equally over three years. For the year of purchase and each of the next two years, Farmer will have an excess fertility deduction of $32,000 (80 acres × $1,200 = $96,000 total fertility ÷ 3 years).
>
> The total fertility deduction is 7.5% of the purchase price ($1,200 excess fertility ÷ $16,000 purchase price).

5

RECAPTURE

If a deduction for excess fertilizer supply is claimed and the land is later sold, the amount of the selling price **attributable to the excess fertility** will be recaptured as ordinary income similar to all other depreciable property. It does not qualify for capital gain treatment. Any remaining gain will be taxed at capital gain rates. If the taxpayer continues to own the land until death, recapture is avoided.[17]

APPLICATION TO PASTURE/RANGELAND

The IRS has not specifically addressed the application of §180 to pasture or rangeland. The only IRS guidance on the excess soil fertility issue is the 1991 TAM and the MSSP referenced previously. But, §180 does indicate that "land used in farming" for purposes of the provision includes "land used…for the sustenance of livestock." So, in theory, the same concepts that apply to cropland apply to land used for grazing. However, the makeup and value of the minerals differs. With pasture and rangeland, the value of potassium and phosphorous contained in the soil is much less than the value of the same minerals in soil used to raise row crops.[18] The value per unit is not the same such that the owner of the grazing land would not apply fertilizer (especially at the current high prices) to enhance the land's value — the economics disincentivize such activity.

Native Pasture

The nutrient balance on a native pasture is very tight and there is no "excess" nutrient in a native pasture system.[19] These systems are rarely, if ever, fertilized with commercial fertilizer or external manure applications, with the exception being (perhaps) for a native field that is hayed. Nitrogen can increase production and allow increased stocking rates, but is not profitable to do so. Native hay meadows are sometimes fertilized with 30-40# nitrogen and 10# phosphorous. Fertilizing native grass usually increases any cool-season grasses in the stand (e.g., Kentucky bluegrass and annual bromes) and increases broadleafs. Prescribed burning in the late spring is then recommended to set those unwanted species back the next year.

---

17. IRC §1250(d)(2).

18. *Livestock Production: Nutritional Value of Range Forage.* Frost, Rachel & Mosley, Jeff. The Rangelands Partnership. [rangelandsgateway.org/topics/uses-range-pastureland/nutritional-value-range-forage] Accessed on Jul. 27, 2023.

19. *Management Strategies for Rangeland and Introduced Pastures.* Bidwell, T.G. & Woods, Bob. Mar. 2017. Oklahoma State University Extension. [extension.okstate.edu/fact-sheets/management-strategies-for-rangeland-and-introduced-pastures.html] Accessed on Jul. 27, 2023.

Native rangeland is very efficient at using nitrogen and obtains it from lightning/rainfall and non-symbiotic fixation (e.g., Clostridium and Azotobacter). There may be some symbiotic nitrogen fixation by native legumes. The year after a drought, biomass on rangeland may increase because of unused nitrogen in the soil, if rainfall is normal or above. This increase in production not only relies on moisture, but on how the pasture was managed during the year of drought.

Application

While §180 applies to grazing land, pasture grass is not the same as cropland when it comes to nutrients.[20] While the **concept** applies equally, the **application** does not. Given that rangeland has a lower per acre FMV than cropland, and the excess soil fertility (even if it is present and can be measured) would be less than what is present on cropland, any associated §180 deduction would likely be insufficient to justify the cost.

Caution. Some states may not follow IRS guidance on deducting excess soil fertility. Practitioners should familiarize themselves with applicable state rules.

COST SEGREGATION — AN ALTERNATIVE

As an alternative to the approach laid out previously for obtaining a deduction for residual fertilizer supply, cost segregation can identify the "available nutrients" in the soil. With a cost segregation approach, the buyer allocates part of the land's purchase price to the land's components on the basis of FMV.[21]

Authority exists for allocating part of the land's purchase price to the assets acquired with the land.

- **Timber.** Treas. Reg. §1.611-3(f) allows taxpayers to use scientific methodology to allocate part of the purchase price of land to standing timber acquired with the land. Procedurally, a forester would estimate the value of the trees on the land at the time of purchase by conducting a timber "cruise."[22] The purchase price would then be allocated to the basis of the land and the basis of the timber using the FMV for each asset respectively.
- **Water rights.** The sale of land with vested water rights allows for the allocation of the purchase price between the taxpayer's basis in the land and the water rights.[23] The allocation is allowed on the theory that a premium was paid for the land to acquire the water rights. In *Gladden*, the court remanded the case to the Tax Court for a determination of the premium that was paid. The court held that if, on remand, the Tax Court found it "impracticable or impossible" to determine the premium, the taxpayers could use the full cost basis in the land to reduce their gain on the sale of the water rights.[24]

Note. The basis of water rights for land overlying the Ogallala formation (located in the central High Plains region) is the difference in value of land with a supply of ground water and land without a supply of ground water.[25]

- **Sod.** Sod is a natural deposit that is depletable under §611.[26] Likewise, soil and loam are natural deposits.[27] Thus, taxpayers can claim a cost depletion allowance attributable to the sale of topsoil as a partial offset to gain realized on the transaction.

---

20. Ibid.
21. See *Hospital Corporation of America v. Comm'r,* 109 TC 21 (1997); AOD 1999-008 (Aug. 30, 1999).
22. See, e.g., *Planning a timber cruise and using it.* Jun. 2011. Oregon State University. [extension.oregonstate.edu/forests/health-managment/planning-timber-cruise-using-it] Accessed on Jul. 5, 2023.
23. Treas. Reg. §1.61-6(a). See also *Gladden v. Comm'r,* 262 F.3d 851 (9th Cir. 2001).
24. Ibid, citing *Inaja Land Co., Ltd. v. Comm'r,* 9 TC 727 (1947).
25. Rev. Proc. 66-11, 1966-1 CB 624.
26. See, e.g., *Meyers v. Comm'r,* 66 TC 235 (1976).
27. Rev. Rul. 79-411, 1979-2 CB 246.

When a farm is purchased, the cost segregation approach allows the purchase price to be allocated among the land, buildings, fences, tile lines, timber, mineral rights, and other assets purchased with the land. Then the amount allocated to the land is further allocated to the soil and the nutrients in the soil, the cost of which could then be amortized over the anticipated period of exhaustion.[28] In the *Hospital Corporation of America* case, the court held that taxpayers can allocate part of the cost of a building to components of the building, and depreciate the components over their respective (shorter) recovery periods.

Example 3. Kelly Ghoulish paid $1,225,000 ($1.2 million purchase price and $25,000 transaction costs) for 140 acres of farmland. The land was pattern tiled and contained an old machine shed. A soil test revealed that the land had high levels of soil nutrients due to the seller spreading excess hog manure. Kelly and the seller did not enter into an agreement concerning the allocation of the purchase/selling price to the nutrients or improvements, and neither of them filed Form 8594.

Shortly after the purchase, Kelly met with her tax preparer, Gina Bogg, who told Kelly that she could allocate part of the purchase price to the tile and soil nutrients if she could establish their value. Based on that advice, Kelly located the map of the tile lines (obtained from the county National Resources Conservation Service (NRCS) office) that showed the tiling was five years old. She took the map to a tiling contractor (who was on an NRCS-approved list) who provided a written estimate that the tiling had another 50 years of usefulness and would cost (presently) $40,000 to replace.

Kelly estimated that the FMV of the tile was $36,364, calculated as follows.

$$\textbf{Tile FMV} = \left(\frac{\textbf{Replacement cost}}{\textbf{Full tile lifespan}}\right) \times \textbf{Remaining tile lifespan}$$

$$= \left(\frac{\$40{,}000}{\text{50 years remaining usefulness} + \text{5 years of past use}}\right) \times \text{50 years}$$

$$= \left(\frac{\$40{,}000}{55}\right) \times 50$$

$$= \$36{,}364$$

Kelly did not allocate any value to the machine shed because it was in poor shape and either needed substantial repairs to be useful or to be demolished. The tile has a 15-year class life and is eligible property for IRC §179 expensing, bonus depreciation, or modified accelerated cost recovery system (MACRS) regular depreciation.

Kelly paid $4,000 to an agronomist to analyze the soil. The agronomist took the results of soil samples and compared them with what the state land grant university recommended as optimal for the various soil types of the land that Kelly purchased. The agronomist valued the available nutrients in excess of the suggested optimal amount by multiplying that excess by what it would cost Kelly to buy and apply that amount of excess. The agronomist then determined the period of time it would take Kelly to use up the excess amount based on the crops she would plant in a normal crop rotation for the area if she did not add any additional nutrients to the soil. Kelly took the agronomist's report and estimated the FMV of the various soil nutrients on a per acre basis to be $450, or $63,000 for the 140 acres. Lastly, Kelly hired an appraiser to provide her with an estimate of the FMV of comparable farmland without pattern tiling and without excess nutrients. The appraisal came in at $1.1 million.

28. *Hospital Corporation of America v. Comm'r*, 109 TC 21 (1997).

Kelly gave this information to Gina. Gina allocated the $1,225,000 purchase price as follows.

Land (including transaction costs)	$1,125,636
Field tile	36,364
Excess fertility	63,000
Total purchase price	$1,225,000

The excess fertility was further defined by each soil nutrient based on the FMV of each. The allocated purchase price to each particular soil nutrient identified by the agronomist was depreciated based on the exhaustion period the agronomist specified.

Kelly's potential tax savings to help pay for the farmland investment from this allocation process amount to $270 per acre, calculated as follows.

FMV of nutrients ($450 × 140 acres)	$63,000
FMV of tile	36,364
Depreciable costs	$99,364
Tax rate [a]	38%
Potential tax savings	$37,758
	÷ 140
Potential savings per acre	$ 270

[a] 22% federal rate × 80% qualified business income deduction (QBID) + 15.3% self-employment tax rate + 5.1% state tax.

BUY-SELL AGREEMENTS

A buy-sell agreement is a frequently used mechanism by a closely held farming or ranching business (as well as many non-farm businesses) to integrate the needs and capabilities of the business with the succession planning and transition objectives of the owners. A well-drafted buy-sell agreement can be a very useful document to assist in transitioning a family business from one generation to the next. It can also be a useful device for balancing out inheritances among heirs by ensuring the heirs interested in running the family business end up with control of the business and other heirs end up with non-control interests.

Common events that trigger buy-sell agreements are death, divorce, or bankruptcy. A buy-sell agreement can effectively provide a market for the ownership interests, limit transferability of those interests outside the immediate family, and establish a procedure for buying a deceased owner's interests which, in turn, can aid in establishing certainty as to the value of the shares for federal estate tax purposes. Likewise, when utilized properly, a buy-sell agreement may also provide estate tax valuation discounts.

Note. A buy-sell agreement is typically a separate document, although some (or all) of its provisions may be incorporated in its bylaws, the partnership agreement, the limited liability company (LLC) operating agreement and, on occasion, in an employment agreement with owner-employees. For many small businesses, a well-drafted buy-sell agreement is perhaps just as important as a will or trust. It can be the key to passing on the business to the next generation successfully.

VALUATION

While very few farming and ranching operations (and small businesses in general) are subject to the federal estate tax because of the current level of the exemption, some are.[29] For those that are, in addition to providing a market for closely held shares at a determinable price, the buy-sell agreement can serve as a mechanism for establishing the value of the interest for estate tax purposes — or otherwise establish the value of the decedent's interest at death.

General Rule[30]

In general, the value of a closely held business (or other property) is determined without regard to any option, agreement, or other right to acquire or use the property at a price less than the FMV of the property, or any restriction on the right to sell or use the property.

Exception. A buy-sell agreement can establish the value of a deceased owner's interest if six basic requirements are satisfied. Three of the requirements are statutory[31] and three have been judicially created. The statutory requirements specify that the buy-sell agreement must:

5

1. Be a bona fide business arrangement;[32]
2. Not be a device to transfer property to members of the decedent's family for less than full and adequate consideration in money or money's worth;[33] and
3. Contain terms that are comparable to other arrangements entered into by persons in an arm's length transaction.[34]

A buy-sell agreement must satisfy each of the three statutory requirements if family members own 50% or more of the property subject to the restriction. An agreement is deemed to satisfy all three of the statutory requirements if more than 50% percent of the value of the property subject to the restriction is owned directly or indirectly by individuals who are **not** members of the transferor's family. The interests owned by the nonfamily members must be subject to the same restrictions as the property owned by the transferor.[35]

Judicial opinions have created three additional requirements that a buy-sell agreement must satisfy to be effective to establish the value of a decedent's interest.[36] The agreement must also meet the following requirements.

- Contain a purchase price that is fixed and determinable under the agreement
- Be legally binding during life and after death
- Be entered into for a bona fide business reason and not be a substitute for a testamentary disposition for full and adequate consideration

To establish the purchase price with certainty, an appropriate valuation method must be established. An independent party valuation will not only satisfy the requirements of IRC §2703 but also provide an estimate of the potential funding obligation and the liquidity expectations of the seller/estate.[37]

---

29. IRC §2010.
30. IRC §2703(a).
31. IRC §2703(b).
32. IRC §2703(b)(1).
33. IRC §2703(b)(2).
34. IRC §2703(b)(3).
35. Treas. Reg. §25.2703-1(b)(3).
36. See e.g., *Estate of True v. Comm'r,* 390 F.3d 1210 (10th Cir. 2004); *St. Louis County Bank v. U.S.,* 674 F.2d 1207 (8th Cir. 1982).
37. See Rev. Rul. 59-60, 1959-1 CB 237, as amplified by Rev. Rul. 83-120,1983-2 CB 170.

Business Purpose. The courts have indicated that preserving a business with family control for purposes of continuity and management can serve as a bona fide business arrangement.[38] This includes planning for the future liquidity needs of the decedent's estate.[39] But an entity that consists only of marketable securities is not a bona fide business arrangement.[40] The long-established position of the IRS is that:

> *It is always necessary to consider the relationship of the parties, the relative number of shares held by the decedent, and other material facts to determine whether the agreement represents a bona fide business arrangement or a device to pass the decedent's shares to the natural objects of his bounty for less than an adequate and full consideration in money or money's worth.*[41]

Note. The business reasons for executing the buy-sell agreement should be documented.

Nondevice. The buy-sell agreement must not simply be a device to reduce estate tax value. This requires more than expressing a desire to maintain family control of the business.[42]

Comparable Terms. This requirement is satisfied if the agreement is one that unrelated parties in the same line of business could have reached in an arm's length transaction.[43] This fair bargain standard is typically based on expert opinion testimony.

TYPES OF AGREEMENTS

There are three basic types of buy-sell agreement:

1. Redemption
2. Cross-purchase
3. Hybrid

Redemption Agreement

A redemption agreement is also known as an "entity purchase" agreement. It is a contract between the owners of the business and the business whereby each owner agrees to sell their interest to the business upon the occurrence of certain events. For redemption agreements, if the requirements of IRC §§302(b) and 303 are not satisfied, the redemption is taxed as a dividend distribution (ordinary income without recovery of basis) to the extent of the stockholder's allocable portion of current and accumulated earnings and profits, without regard to the stockholder's basis in their shares. This can be a significant problem for post-mortem redemptions. The estate of a deceased shareholder would normally receive a basis in the shares equal to their value on the date of death or the alternate valuation date. Thus, dividend treatment can result in the recognition of the entire purchase price as ordinary income to a redeemed estate, whereas sale or exchange treatment results in recognition of no taxable gain whatsoever.

---

38. See *St. Louis County Bank v. U.S.*, 674 F.2d 1207 (8th Cir. 1982); *Estate of Lauder v. Comm'r,* TC Memo 1992-736; *Estate of Gloeckner v. Comm'r,* 152 F.3d 208 (2nd Cir. 1998).

39. *Estate of Amlie v. Comm'r,* TC Memo 2006-76 (Apr. 17, 2006).

40. *Holman v. Comm'r,* 601 F.3d 763 (8th Cir. 2010).

41. Rev. Rul 59-60, 1959-1 CB 137. See also *Estate of True v. Comm'r,* TC Memo 2001-167, *aff'd.*, 390 F.3d 1210 (2004); *Estate of Blount v. Comm'r,* TC Memo 2004-116 (Oct. 31, 2005).

42. See, e.g., *Estate of True v. Comm'r,* 390 F.3d 1210 (10th Cir. 2004); *Estate of Lauder v. Comm'r*, TC Memo 1992-736 (1992).

43. Treas. Reg. §25.2703-1(b)(4).

Cross-Purchase Agreement

This type of agreement is a contract between or among the owners (the business is not necessarily a party to the agreement) whereby each owner agrees to sell their shares to the other owners on the occurrence of specified events. With a cross-purchase agreement, unless the shareholder is a dealer in stock, any gain on the sale is a capital gain regardless of the character of the corporation's underlying assets.[44] For an estate that sells the stock shortly after the shareholder's death, no gain is recognized if the agreement sets the sale price at the date of death value.[45] The purchasing shareholders increase their basis in their total holdings of corporate stock by the price paid for the shares purchased under the agreement, even if the shares are paid for with tax-free life insurance proceeds.

Hybrid Agreement

Sometimes businesses use a hybrid agreement. This type of agreement is a contract between the business and the owners whereby the owners agree to offer their shares first to the corporation and then to the other owners on the occurrence of certain events. Under a "wait and see" type of buy-sell agreement, the identity of the purchaser is not disclosed until the actual time of purchase as triggered in the agreement. The corporation will have the first opportunity to purchase shares, followed by the remaining shareholders. Finally, the corporation may be obligated to buy any remaining shares.

5

If an S corporation election is in place, the corporate income is taxed to the shareholders and can be withdrawn from the corporation to fund a cross-purchase agreement without triggering additional tax. If the triggering event is something other than death, a cross-purchase agreement is required to achieve an increased cost basis to the purchasing shareholder(s). A hybrid agreement requires the corporation to redeem only as much stock as will qualify for a sale or exchange treatment under §303, and then requires the other shareholders to buy the balance of the available stock. This permits the corporation to finance part of the purchase price to the extent required to pay estate taxes and expenses, and assures the sale or exchange treatment on the entire transaction.[46]

A buy-sell agreement that imposes employment-related restrictions may create ordinary compensation income (without recovery of basis).[47] However, an agreement containing transfer restrictions that are sufficient to render the stock substantially non-vested (substantial risk of forfeiture) may prevent the current recognition of ordinary income.

FUNDING APPROACHES

To be operational, the parties to the agreement must have funds available to buy the stock at the time the agreement is triggered. It is possible to use the business's accumulated earnings to fund a redemption. Such a strategy may not be treated as a "reasonable need of the business," with the result that the business (if it is a C corporation) could be subject to the **accumulated earnings tax.**[48] However, corporate accumulations used to pay off a note given to a stockholder for a redemption is a reasonable need of the business as a debt retirement cost.[49]

Life Insurance

Typically, life insurance is purchased for each business owner to cover the total purchase price (or at least the down payment of coverage). However, the premiums on such policies are not deductible[50] and can create a substantial ongoing expense.

---

44. IRC §1221.

45. IRC §§1014 and 2032.

46. IRC §303(b)(3).

47. IRC §83.

48. IRC §531.

49. See *Smoot Sand & Gravel Corp. v. Comm'r,* 274 F.2d 495 (4th Cir. 1960), cert. denied, 362 U.S. 976 (1960).

50. See IRC §264.

Corporate-Owned Policy. One approach is for the corporation to buy a life insurance policy on the life of each stockholder, with the corporation as the policy owner, premium payor, and beneficiary of these policies. The corporation would then use the life insurance to finance the purchase if, at the end of the first option period, the corporation buys the deceased stockholder's interest. Alternatively, the corporation could lend the insurance proceeds to the stockholders if, at the end of the corporate option period, it is decided that the surviving stockholders should be the buyers (or to the extent stock remained to be purchased after the corporation's option expires). Investment payments would be deductible to the stockholders and considered income to the corporation.

Shareholder-Owned Policy. An alternative approach is for each shareholder to buy, pay for, own, and be the beneficiary of a life insurance policy for each of the other shareholders. The surviving shareholders would then receive the proceeds when one shareholder dies, and, if a cross-purchase is indicated and appropriate, use the proceeds as the necessary funds to carry out the buy-sell agreement. The surviving shareholders could also lend the proceeds to the corporation if a redemption agreement is utilized to enable the corporation to buy additional shares. Alternatively, the surviving shareholders could make capital contributions, which would have the effect of increasing each shareholder's stock basis.

Observation. Generally, the cash value of a permanent life insurance policy may be withdrawn by a loan or surrender of the policy, but the value may be a very small percentage of the death benefit, making it inadequate to finance the buy-out. Disability insurance may be used to finance a purchase occasioned by an owner's disability, but it can be quite expensive. Furthermore, it cannot be applied toward the purchase of an interest of an owner who is retiring, or be used to prevent the sale of an interest in the business to a buyer outside the family unit.

Other Approaches. A combination of the above approaches could also be used for funding the wait-and-see buy-sell agreement. For example, the corporation could own cash value life insurance, and the owners could own term insurance. Also, the parties could have a split-dollar arrangement whereby the corporation pays for the cash value portion of the premiums and the shareholders own the policy and pay for the term portion of the premiums, with the proceeds split between them.

Potential Problem. One potential problem of a corporation being the beneficiary of a life insurance policy designed to fund the buy-out of the shares of a deceased shareholder is that the IRS could argue the policy proceeds are included in the corporate value. In *Estate of Blount v. Comm'r,*[51] the issue was whether the insurance proceeds were contractually tied to the redemption of corporate shares treated as corporate property for valuation purposes. The decedent owned 83% of the stock in a corporation at death. There was a life insurance policy owned by the company that provided some $3.1 million to pay off the mandated buyout of the shares under a buy-sell agreement, providing for a fixed value of the decedent's shares. The buy-sell agreement value was held not to be controlling for estate tax purposes, mainly because the deceased owned 83% of the stock and could have changed the agreement at any time. Furthermore, the court determined that the buy-sell agreement was not similar to those involved in arm's length transactions.

The 11th Circuit reversed on the basis that the redemption obligation of the buy-sell agreement was a liability offsetting the value of the death benefits used to fund the redemption.[52] Thus, even if the death benefits were included in the corporate value, there was a corresponding offsetting liability that would be accounted for by a "reasonably competent businessperson interested in acquiring the company."[53]

Note. In the *Cartwright* decision preceding the Tax Court's decision in *Blount*, the Ninth Circuit court deducted the insurance proceeds from the value of the organization when they were offset by an obligation to pay those proceeds to the estate in a stock buyout.[54]

---

51. *Estate of Blount v. Comm'r,* TC Memo 2004-116 (May 12, 2004).

52. *Estate of Blount v. Comm'r,* 428 F.3d 1338 (11th Cir., 2005).

53. Ibid.

54. *Cartwright v. Comm'r,* 183 F.3d 1034 (9th Cir., 1999).

The issue in *Blount* and *Cartwright* resurfaced in *Connelly v. U.S.*[55] In *Connelly,* two brothers were the only shareholders of a closely held family roofing and siding materials business. They entered into a stock purchase agreement that required the company to buy back shares of the first brother to die. The company then purchased about $3.5 million in life insurance coverage to ensure it had enough cash to redeem the stock. The brother holding the majority of the company's shares (77.18%) died on October 1, 2013. The company received $3.5 million in insurance proceeds. The surviving brother chose not to buy his shares, so the company used a portion of the proceeds to buy the deceased brother's shares from his estate for $3 million pursuant to a sale and purchase agreement. Under the agreement, the estate received $3 million, and the decedent's son received a 3-year option to buy company stock from the surviving brother. If the surviving brother sold the company within 10 years, the brother and decedent's son would split evenly any gain from the sale.

The estate valued the decedent's stock at $3 million and included that amount in the taxable estate. Upon audit, the IRS asserted that the FMV of the decedent's corporate stock should have factored in the $3 million in life insurance proceeds used to redeem the shares. This would have resulted in a higher value of the decedent's stock than was reported. The IRS assessed over $1 million in additional estate tax. The estate paid the deficiency and filed a refund claim in federal district court.

5

The district court noted that a stock-purchase agreement is respected when determining the FMV of stock for estate tax purposes upon satisfying the requirements of §2703(b) (as noted previously) and the additional judicially created requirements (also noted previously). The IRS expert claimed that the insurance proceeds should be included in the company's value as a nonoperating asset. Allowing the redemption obligation to offset the insurance proceeds undervalued the company's equity and the decedent's equity interest in the company, and would create a windfall for a potential buyer that a willing seller would not accept. The IRS expert concluded that the FMV of the company was $6.86 million rather than $3.86 million. The IRS also claimed that the stock purchase agreement failed to control the value of the company. The estate claimed that the company sold the decedent's shares at FMV and that the shares had been properly valued. Thus, according to the estate, the $3 million in life insurance proceeds were properly excluded from the decedent's estate based on the appellate opinion in *Blount*. The estate claimed that the stock purchase agreement provided a sufficient basis for the court to accept the estate's valuation as the proper estate-tax value of the decedent's shares. On that point, the IRS claimed that the stock purchase agreement was not a bona fide business arrangement and, as such, did not control the value of the decedent's stock. The IRS's position was that the stated estate planning objectives of the stock purchase of continued family ownership of the company were insufficient to make it a bona fide business arrangement, particularly because the brothers did not follow it by disregarding the agreement's pricing mechanisms.

The district court did not rule on the bona fide business arrangement issue because it determined that the estate had failed to show that the stock purchase agreement was not a device to transfer wealth to the decedent's family members for less than full-and-adequate consideration. The process that the surviving brother and the estate used in selecting the redemption price bolstered the court's conclusion that the stock purchase agreement was a testamentary device. They also did not obtain an outside appraisal or professional advice on setting the redemption price, thereby disregarding the appraisal requirement set forth in the agreement. The district court also noted that the agreement did not provide for a minority interest discount for the surviving brother's shares or a lack of control premium for the decedent's shares, with the result that the decedent's shares were undervalued. According to the district court, this also demonstrated that the stock purchase agreement was a testamentary device to transfer wealth to the decedent's family members for less than full-and-adequate consideration and was not comparable to similar agreements negotiated at arm's length.

55. *Connelly v. U.S.,* No. 4:19-cv-01410-SRC, 2021 U.S. Dist. LEXIS 179745 (E.D. Mo. Sep. 21, 2021).

On the issue of whether the life insurance proceeds should be included in the corporate value, the court rejected the appellate court's approach in *Blount*, finding it to be analytically flawed. The court concluded that the appellate court in *Blount* misread Treas. Reg. §20.2031-2(f)(2), and that the regulation specifically requires consideration to be given to nonoperating assets, including life insurance proceeds, "to the extent such nonoperating assets have not been taken into account in the determination of net worth." The district court concluded that the text of the regulation does not indicate that the presence of an offsetting liability means that the life insurance proceeds have already been "taken into account in the determination of a company's net worth." The court also concluded that, "by its plain terms, the regulation means that the proceeds should be considered in the same manner as any other nonoperating asset in the calculation of the FMV of a company's stock… and… a redemption obligation is not the same as an ordinary corporate liability."

There is a difference, the court noted, between a redemption obligation that simply buys shares of stock, and one that also compensates for a shareholder's past work. One that only buys stock is not an ordinary corporate liability — it does not change the value of the corporation as a whole before the shares are redeemed. It involves a change in the ownership structure with a shareholder essentially "cashing out." The court noted that the parties had stipulated that the decedent's shares were worth $3.1 million, aside from the life insurance proceeds. The insurance proceeds were not offset by the company's redemption obligation and, accordingly, the company's FMV and the decedent's shares included all of the insurance proceeds. The IRS position was upheld.

On appeal, the U.S Court of Appeals for the 8th Circuit affirmed.[56] The appellate court held that the stock purchase agreement requiring the redemption of a deceased shareholder's shares did not affect the value of the shares for estate tax purposes under §2703 because it did not provide for a fixed price or a formula for arriving at one. Instead, the agreement merely laid out two mechanisms by which the brothers might agree on a price - mutual agreement or appraisal. As for the appraisal approach, there was nothing in the agreement that fixed or prescribed a formula or measure for determining the price that the appraisers would reach. Thus, neither mechanism constituted a fixed or determinable price for valuation purposes. The appellate court determined that the $3 million that the corporation actually paid for the deceased brother's shares constituted an amount determined after death that was derived by an agreement between the brothers and not by any formula in the buy-sell agreement.

As for the value of the corporation (and, hence, the deceased brother's interest in the corporation), the appellate court determined that the life insurance proceeds were an asset that increased the shareholders' equity, and that an obligation to redeem shares is **not** a liability in the ordinary business sense. Thus, the proper valuation of the corporation in accordance with IRC §§2042 and 2031 must include the life insurance proceeds without treating the obligation to redeem shares as an offsetting liability. The court reasoned, that for a willing buyer at the time of the brother's death to own the stock outright, a willing buyer would account for control of the life insurance proceeds. The buyer would therefore pay up to $6.86 million for the corporation, "taking into account" the life insurance proceeds and then either extinguishing the agreement or redeeming the shares. Conversely, the appellate court determined that a hypothetical willing seller of the corporation would not find acceptable a price of $3.86 million with the knowledge that the company would be receiving $3 million in life insurance proceeds.

To illustrate its rationale, the appellate court explained that if it valued the corporation without accounting for the life insurance proceeds intended for redemption, then upon the brother's death, each share was worth $7,720 before redemption. After redemption, the deceased brother's interest is extinguished, with the surviving brother having full control of the corporation's $3.86 million value. The appellate court noted that this would essentially quadruple the value of the surviving brother's shares, but that treating the life insurance as an offsetting liability would leave the stock value undisturbed (which was the estate's position). The economic reality of the situation, the appellate court concluded, was that the life insurance proceeds were an asset that increased shareholders' equity. The buy-sell agreement thus had nothing to do with being a corporate liability.

Note. There is now a split on this issue between the 8th Circuit on one side, and the 9th and 11th Circuits on the other.

56. *Connelly v. U.S.*, No. 21-3683, 2023 U.S. App. LEXIS 13629 (8th Cir. 2023).

IMPROPER USAGE OF CHARITABLE REMAINDER ANNUITY TRUSTS

A **charitable remainder trust** is an irrevocable trust to which cash or other property is transferred.[57] The trust takes a carryover income tax basis in the transferred asset(s). The trust then sells the transferred assets (the sale is not taxable because the seller is a charity) and uses the income from the sale to pay the donor or other designated person(s). The payments continue for a specific term of up to 20 years or the life of one or more beneficiaries (typically the transferor). At the end of the term, the remainder of the trust passes to at least one designated charity. The remainder donated to the charity must be at least 10% of the initial net FMV of all the property placed in the trust.

There are two types of charitable remainder trusts. The type of trust is tied to how payment from the trust is made. A **charitable remainder unitrust (CRUT) pays a percentage** of the trust value annually to noncharitable beneficiaries.[58] The payments must be at least 5% and not exceed 50% of the FMV of the trust's assets, valued annually. A **charitable remainder annuity trust (CRAT) pays a specific dollar** amount each year.[59] The amount is at least 5% and no more than 50% of the value of the trust's property, valued as of the date the trust was established.

5

Payments from a charitable remainder trust are taxed to the non-charitable beneficiaries.[60] The non-charitable beneficiaries report the income on Schedule K-1 (Form 1041), *Beneficiary's Share of Income, Deductions, Credits, etc.*, as distributions of the trust's income and gains.

The distributions are reported in a particular order.[61]

Tier 1. Payments are considered ordinary income first to the extent the trust had ordinary income for the year and undistributed ordinary income from prior years. This means that if the trust had enough ordinary income to cover all the payments, the payments would be are taxed as ordinary income.

> **Observation.** It is not advisable to transfer ordinary income property to the trust — especially not ordinary income property with low or no income tax basis.

Tier 2. Once the trust's ordinary income is exhausted, payments are taxed as capital gains based on the sale or disposition of the trust's capital assets. The payments are taxed as capital gains to the extent of the trust's capital gain for the current year and any undistributed capital gain income from prior years.

Tier 3. After all the trust's ordinary income and capital gain have been distributed, any additional payments are then characterized as other income to the extent of the trust's current year and accumulated other income.

Tier 4. Finally, after the first three tiers of distributions have been made, any further payments are considered to be from the principal of the trust and are not taxable.

The contribution to a charitable remainder trust will qualify for a partial charitable deduction. The deduction is limited to the present value of the charitable organization's remainder interest, calculated as the value of the donated property minus the **present value** of the annuity that the trust pays to the non-charitable beneficiary (or beneficiaries).[62] The deduction is also subject to adjusted gross income (AGI) and other limits set forth in IRC §170(e).

A charitable remainder trust must file Form 5227, *Split-Interest Trust Information Return*, every year. A beneficiary must report any income received from the trust as reported on Schedule K-1 of Form 1041.

57. IRC §664.

58. IRC §664(d)(2).

59. IRC §664(d)(1).

60. Treas. Reg. §1.664-1(d)(ii)(a).

61. Ibid.

62. Treas. Reg. §1.664-2(c).

IRS CONCERNS

The IRS closely monitors the use of charitable trusts. The following are some of the issues that draw the IRS's attention.

- Inflating the basis of assets transferred to the trust and failure to account for the transfer of any assets to the trust
- Mischaracterizing distributions of ordinary or capital gain income as distributions of corpus
- Not closely following the ordering rules
- Self-dealing, making an upfront cash payment to a charitable beneficiary in lieu of the remainder interest, or a transfer of the trust's remainder interest to a non-qualified organization
- Paying personal expenses with trust funds, or borrowing funds from the trust
- Using loans or forward sales of assets or other financial schemes to hide capital gains or income in the trust

Furrer Case

In *Furrer,*[63] the Tax Court began its opinion by noting that the Furrers formed a CRAT, "after seeing an advertisement in a farm magazine." The Furrers raised corn and soybeans on their Indiana farm. In July 2015, they formed the first of two CRATs, naming their son as trustee. The Furrers were the life beneficiaries, and they designated three qualified charities as remaindermen. They transferred 100,000 bushels of corn and 10,000 bushels of soybeans from their farm to the first CRAT, which then sold the grain for $469,003. The CRAT distributed $47,000 to the charities and used the balance to purchase a single premium immediate annuity (SPIA), which made annual payments to the Furrers of $84,369 in 2015, 2016, and 2017. The SPIA issued a Form 1099-R, *Distributions From Pensions, Annuities, Retirement or Profit-Sharing Plans, IRAs, Insurance Contracts, etc.,* to the trustee listing the annuity payments as "gross distributions" and showed a small amount of interest as the "taxable amount." The Furrers claimed a $47,000 charitable deduction.

The Furrers created a second CRAT in 2016, naming themselves as the life beneficiaries and seven qualified charities as the remainder beneficiaries. They also funded that trust with grain that they raised. The CRAT sold the grain for $691,827 and distributed $69,294 to the charities. The annuity from this trust was payable over 2016 and 2017 in the amount of $124,921 each year. The SPIA also issued a Form 1099-R to the trustee listing the annuity payments as "gross distributions" and showing a small amount of interest as the "taxable amount." They claimed a charitable deduction of $69,294.

On their 2015 and 2016 returns, the Furrers did not claim charitable deductions for their transfers to the CRATs, but reported only the interest income from the SPIA, which was reported to them by the life insurance company providing the annuity. They treated the balance of the annuity distributions that they received as a nontaxable return of corpus under IRC §664(b)(4). They also reported their transfers of crops to the CRATS on Forms 709, *United States Gift (and Generation-Skipping Transfer) Tax Return,* for 2015 and 2016, which reflected the FMV of the crops with a cost basis of zero. The CRATs reported the sales of crops as sales of business property on Form 4797, *Sales of Business Property,* treating the crops as having substantial basis (derived from the purported purchase of the grain at FMV) that generated a small loss for 2015 and a small gain for 2016. Their son (as trustee) prepared the CRATs' returns.

On audit, the Furrers claimed they should be entitled to charitable deductions for the in-kind transfers of the crops that were ultimately destined for the charitable remaindermen, which were not claimed on their return. They made this claim even though they had no income tax basis in the grain that was transferred to the CRATs. The IRS Revenue Agent allowed the charitable deductions, but the IRS still issued a notice of deficiency for each year because of the omitted income from the annuity, and increased the Furrer's Schedule F income by $83,440 in 2015, and $206,967 in 2016 and 2017. This resulted in tax deficiencies of $55,040 for 2015, $56,904 for 2016, and $95,907 for 2017. The IRS also added an accuracy-related penalty for each year.

---

63. *Furrer v. Comm'r,* TC Memo 2022-100 (Sep. 28, 2022).

Note. A transfer of crops to a CRAT can be a good tax strategy if a charitable deduction is not desired or needed. The transfer is not a sale and avoids inclusion on Schedule F, where it also avoids self-employment (SE) tax.

At no time did the Furrers secure an appraisal (qualified or otherwise) of the crops they transferred to the CRATs. They also did not attach to their 2015 or 2016 return a completed Form 8283, *Noncash Charitable Contributions,* substantiating the gifts, and they did not maintain the written records that the regulations required. But, even had they done so, they would not have been entitled to any charitable deduction because of the lack of an income tax basis in the grain transferred to the trusts.

Note. For gifts of property (other than publicly traded securities) valued in excess of $5,000, the taxpayer generally must obtain a qualified appraisal of the property and attach a fully completed appraisal summary on Form 8283 to the return on which the deduction is claimed.[64] A "qualified appraisal" must be prepared by a "qualified appraiser" no later than the due date of the return, including extensions.[65] The taxpayer must also maintain records substantiating the deduction.[66]

5

After the Furrers filed the Tax Court petition, the IRS conceded the accuracy-related penalties due to lack of the immediate supervisor's approval. But, the IRS attorneys also requested leave to amend its answer to disallow the charitable deductions that the revenue agent allowed. The Tax Court held that the IRS carried its burden of proof on the charitable deduction disallowance issue — the Furrers did not substantiate the in-kind donations and they had no income tax basis in the crops. Thus, any charitable deduction was limited to zero, regardless of whether they would have satisfied the substantiation requirements.

The IRS also maintained that the annuity distributions were fully taxable as ordinary income on the basis that the grain was inventory that the Furrers held for sale to customers in the ordinary course of their farming business. The Tax Court agreed and noted that the Furrers violated the ordering rules for income tax treatment of distributions from the CRATs. The trusts' sale of the grain involved a sale of ordinary income property (raised grain). As a result, the annuity was purchased with the proceeds of ordinary income property, and any distributions from the trust to the Furrers retained that same ordinary income character. While the Furrers tried to apply the income exclusion rules of IRC §72 to the annuity distributions, the Tax Court noted that §664 provides a special rule for annuity distributions from CRATS that was not in their favor. In addition, even if §72 applied, the Tax Court noted that the Furrers would not have been able to use the exclusion rule because they had no "investment in the contract" – the funds used to purchase the contract had never been taxable. Among the biting comments by the Tax Court in the opinion was: "This argument does not pass the straight-face test."

Note. Many aspects of the set-up of the CRATs were wrong, and by not accepting the adjustment made by the IRS revenue agent and filing a Tax Court petition, the Furrers ended up **losing** the charitable deductions that the revenue agent had (mistakenly) allowed. Granted, the Furrers got the accuracy-related penalty to go away, but that was achieved at the price of losing substantial charitable deductions. Whether the IRS should have conceded on the penalty issue is an open question. The Tax Court's approach to IRS supervisory approval as a prerequisite to applying penalties has been disregarded by two Circuit Courts of Appeal. According to the 11th and 9th Circuits, supervisor approval at any time before assessment is enough to satisfy the statute.[67]

64. IRC §170(f)(11)(C).

65. IRC §170(f)(11)(E); Treas. Reg. §1.170A-13(c)(3).

66. Treas. Reg. §1.170A-13(b)(2)(ii)(D).

67. See, e.g., *Kroner v. Comm'r,* 48 F.4th 1272 (11th Cir. 2022) and *Laidlaw's Harley Davidson Sales, Inc. v. Comm'r,* 29 F.4th 1066 (9th Cir. 2022).

Gerhardt, et al. Case

The *Gerhardt, et al.*[68] case involved facts substantially similar to that of Furrer. Indeed, the case involved the same promoters of the CRAT and SPIA that were involved in Furrer. The case involved family members in different states that contributed appreciated property, including farmland and hog buildings, to CRATs. The CRATs then sold the properties and bought 5-year SPIAs with most of the proceeds. Like the Furrers, the Gerhardts did not report the annuity payments as income except for small amounts of interest. One branch of the family exchanged their Iowa farm property including farmland, hog buildings, and equipment (plus cash) with another family member in a transaction intended to qualify as a like-kind exchange under IRC §1031.

The Tax Court held that the annuity payments were distributions taxable as ordinary income under §664, and that IRC §1245 precluded the deferral of gain realized on the disposition of the Iowa farm property. The Tax Court also noted that IRC §1015 governs transfers in trust (other than in trust by gift) and that under **either** §1015(a) or (b), the basis in the property transferred to the CRAT is what it otherwise would be in the donor's hands. Thus, like the result in *Furrer,* the Tax Court rejected the Gerhardts' view that the basis of assets donated to the CRAT was its FMV.

Note. The Tax Court noted that it had considered facts and arguments nearly identical in *Furrer* and had reached the same conclusion. The court also invited the Gerhardts to distinguish themselves from *Furrer,* but their briefs did not even mention *Furrer,* even though their legal counsel was the same person that represented the Furrers. The Tax Court also noted that the Gerhardts failed to cite even a single case in support of their position.

The Tax Court also held that §1245 property was involved in the §1031 exchange, and that §1245 precluded deferral of the gain realized. The Tax Court noted that the gain from the disposition of §1245 property is recognized as ordinary income as limited under §§1245(a) and (b). The Tax Court also noted that if both §1245 property and non-§1245 property are disposed of in the same transaction, then gain is allocated between the §1245 property and the non-§1245 property in proportion to their respective FMVs.[69] The Tax Court rejected the Gerhardt's argument that §1031 trumps §1245 as to the timing of gain recognition.

Note. IRC §1245 property includes "property which is or has been property of a character subject to the allowance for depreciation provided in section 167" that is either personal property or a single-purpose agricultural or horticultural structure.[70]

Observation. In early 2022, the U.S. Department of Justice filed a complaint seeking to bar the professionals involved in selling the CRATs and SPIAs involved in the *Furrer* and *Gerhardt* cases from continuing to do so. The government allegations detail the defendants' involvement with at least 70 CRATs in a scheme estimated to result in $40 million of unreported income and $8 million in lost tax revenue. In May 2023, a court permanently barred five defendants from promoting this CRAT tax scheme and ordered multiple parties to disgorge $1.5 million in alleged ill-gotten gains.[71]

---

68. *Gerhardt, et al. v. Comm'r,* 160 T.C. (2023).

69. Treas. Reg. §1.1245-1(a)(5).

70. IRC §§1245(a)(3)(A) and (D).

71. *Court Permanently Bars Five Defendants From Promoting Charitable Remainder Annuity Trust Tax Scheme.* May 31, 2023. U.S. Department of Justice. [www.justice.gov/opa/pr/court-permanently-bars-five-defendants-promoting-charitable-remainder-annuity-trust-tax] Accessed on Jul. 4, 2023.

FORM 1041 FOR FARM ESTATES AND TRUSTS

There are two kinds of taxes owed by an estate — the federal estate tax on the **transfer of assets** from the decedent to beneficiaries and heirs reported on Form 706, *United States Estate (and Generation-Skipping Transfer) Tax Return* and on the **income generated by assets** of the decedent's estate reported on Form 1041, *U.S. Income Tax Return for Estates and Trusts*.

Note. Form 706 can be thought of as the final "balance sheet" of the decedent, and Form 1041 can be thought of as the first "income statement" of the estate. This topic is also covered in detail in the Settling a Taxpayer's Estate section of the 2023 *University of Illinois Federal Tax Workbook,* Chapter 9: Individual Taxpayer Issues.

Observation. Most estates do not have a federal estate tax obligation because the estate does not exceed the level of the exemption equivalent of the unified credit at death ($12,920,000 for deaths in 2023). However, Form 706 may be filed for portability purposes if there is a surviving spouse. Even if no Form 706 is filed (either for tax or portability purposes), there may be a state-level tax associated with death which will necessitate the completion of a final inventory of the decedent's assets. States that presently have either a state estate tax or state inheritance tax are as follows: CT; HI; IL; IA (through 2024); KY; ME; MD; MA; MN; NE; NJ; NY; OR; PA; RI; VT; and WA. The District of Columbia also has an estate tax.

5

When someone dies, their assets become property of their estate. Any income those assets generate is also part of the estate and may trigger the requirement to file an estate income tax return. Examples of assets that would generate income to the decedent's estate include savings accounts, certificates of deposit (CDs), stocks, bonds, mutual funds, farmland, business, and rental property.

Estates and non-grantor trusts must file income tax returns just as individuals do, but with some important differences. Income is taxed at either the entity or beneficiary level depending on whether it is allocated to principal or allocated to distributable income, and whether it is distributed to the beneficiaries.

For decedents that held an interest in a partnership at death, IRC §706(a) provides a general rule:

> *Except in the case of a termination of a partnership and except as provided in paragraph (2) of this subsection, the taxable year of a partnership shall not close as the result of the death of a partner, the entry of a new partner, the liquidation of a partner's interest in the partnership, or the sale or exchange of a partner's interest in the partnership.*[72]

The tax year of a partnership closes with respect to a partner whose entire interest in the partnership terminates (whether by reason of death or otherwise).[73] Although death may cause a dissolution of a partnership under state law principles in some states,[74] for federal tax purposes, termination occurs only when specified conditions occur. These conditions include when "no part of any business, financial operation, or venture of the partnership continues to be carried on by any of its partners in a partnership."[75]

Note. Many farm partnerships are 2-member partnerships. In such situations, Rev. Rul. 99-6 is critical.[76] The ruling provides the applicable tax treatment when a partnership (or LLC) goes from being taxed as a partnership to becoming a disregarded entity. This occurs, for example, when a surviving partner buys out a deceased partner (or a living partner who wants to retire) and continues the partnership business.

72. IRC §706(c)(1).

73. IRC §706(c)(2).

74. See, e.g., Uniform Partnership Act §31.

75. IRC §708(b)(1).

76. Rev. Rul. 99-6, 1999-6 IRB 6.

Ultimately, the decedent's interest in partnership income determined for the portion of the partnership tax year before death is included on the final Schedule K-1 (Form 1065), *Partner's Share of Income, Deductions, Credits, etc.*, for the decedent and reported on the decedent's final return.[77] The post-death share of income associated with the partnership interest is reported by the transferee.[78] This results in more than one Schedule K-1 issued for the partnership interest in that year.

FORM 1041

The decedent and the decedent's estate are separate taxable entities. An **estate** is required to file Form 1041 if it has gross income of $600 or more for the tax year (the personal exemption amount for an estate), or a beneficiary who is a non-resident alien.[79] Form 1041 is also required for a domestic trust that has any taxable income for the tax year, gross income of $600 or more for the tax year, or a beneficiary who is a non-resident alien.

Form 1041 is used by the fiduciary of a domestic decedent's estate, trust, or bankruptcy estate to report the following.[80]

- Income, deductions, gains, losses, etc. of the estate or trust
- Income that is either accumulated or held for future distribution or distributed currently to the beneficiaries
- Income tax liability of the estate or trust
- Employment tax on wages paid to household employees

The Form 1041 exemption amounts are as follows.

- Estate: $600
- Simple trust: $300
- All other trusts: $100

Note. Form 1041 cannot be properly prepared without first reading the governing document(s) for provisions regarding taxation.

Computation of Gross Income

A decedent's estate figures its gross income in much the same manner as an individual. Most deductions and credits allowed to individuals are also allowed to estates and trusts. However, a trust or decedent's estate is also allowed an income distribution deduction for distributions to beneficiaries. There are generally two types of beneficiaries — income beneficiaries and remainder beneficiaries. Income distributions are reported to beneficiaries and the IRS on Schedules K-1 (Form 1041).

77. See, e.g., Treas. Reg. §1.706-4.

78. Ibid.

79. IRC §1041; Instructions for Form 1041.

80. Instructions for Form 1041.

Beneficiaries and State Tax

A determination must be made to identify which state(s) has **nexus (jurisdiction)** to tax the estate or trust. Although a will or trust may express which state's laws govern administration of the estate or trust, nexus for purposes of state taxation is usually based on the location of any real property held in the estate or trust, the principal place of the administration of the estate or trust, and transactions and other income flows involving the estate, trust, and beneficiaries. In essence, if the beneficiaries have a **present right to income or other distributions,** there may be nexus for tax purposes on the share of their interest even though the administration is in another state.[81]

> **Note.** Form 56, *Notice Concerning Fiduciary Relationships*, should be filed with the IRS to ensure notices with respect to the decedent will be sent to the appropriate fiduciary. If necessary, Form 2848, *Power of Attorney and Declaration of Representative,* should also be filed under the signature of the fiduciary designated on Form 56. Care should be taken to ensure that powers of attorney for more than one person, such as an attorney and a CPA, do not supersede prior powers.

5

Filing Deadline

For **calendar-year estates and trusts,** Form 1041 and Schedule(s) K-1 must be filed on or before April 15 of the following year.[82] For **fiscal-year estates and trusts,** Form 1041 must be filed by the 15th day of the 4th month following the close of the tax year. An automatic 5½ -month extension can be applied for if more time is needed to file the estate income tax return (Form 1041) via Form 7004, *Application for Automatic Extension of Time to File Certain Business Income Tax, Information, and Other Returns*.

Estimated Tax

In general, an estate or trust must pay quarterly estimated income tax in the same manner as individuals.[83] Form 1041-ES, *Estimated Income Tax for Estates and Trusts,* is used to compute and pay estimated tax. However, trusts and estates are exempt from the estimated tax requirement during the first two taxable years following the grantor's death.

> **Note.** Shortly after death, the executor or administrator should obtain an employer identification number (EIN) for the estate. The EIN is in the format 12-345678X and can be applied for online or by fax or mail.

POSSIBLE INCOME-GENERATING ITEMS FOR AN ESTATE

Income of estates and non-grantor trusts is taxed at either the entity or the beneficiary level, depending on the answer to the following two questions.

- Is each income, loss, or deduction item part of the trust's or estate's distributable income, or is it part of a change in the principal?
- Is the income, loss, or deduction item distributed to the beneficiaries, or does the entity retain it?

Form 1041 identifies the types of income that must be included and calculated on an estate's income tax return. The instructions to Form 1041 provide detailed advice on filling out and completing Form 1041 with examples of income-generating assets. Selected types of such assets are described next.

> **Note.** IRS Pub. 559, *Survivors, Executors, and Administrators,* provides guidance for survivors, executors, and administrators of estates, and provides discussion about income that needs to be included on Form 1041.

81. See *North Carolina Department of Revenue v. Kimberley Rice Kaestner 1992 Family Trust*, 139 S. Ct. 2213 (2019).

82. Instructions for Form 1041.

83. Ibid.

Interest Income[84]

Any type of property owned by the estate that generates interest will generally be considered an income-generating asset. Examples of assets that generate interest income include the following.

- Accounts with banks and credit unions (including CDs and money market accounts)
- Notes, loans, and mortgages
- U.S. Treasury bills, notes, and bonds
- U.S. savings bonds
- Interest earned from other assets that show up on the decedent's Form 1099-INT, *Interest Income*
- Other assets described in IRS examples

Dividends

Dividends are distributions from corporations and mutual funds paid to the decedent or estate when they own stock.[85] Ordinary dividends, typically stock, are taxable as income (i.e., not capital gains). In general, any dividend received from common or preferred stock is an ordinary dividend.

If the decedent or estate receives a Form 1099-DIV, *Dividends and Distributions,* ordinary dividends are shown in box 1a.[86] A Form 1099-DIV is issued by every payor (i.e., corporation) that provides dividends of at least $10 in a given year.

Business Income

Business income is any income the decedent or their estate receives from their business.[87] If there is any connection between the income received and the business, it is business income. A connection exists if the income payment would not have been made if the decedent did not have the business. Business income is usually received in the form of cash, checks, and credit card charges.

Examples of business income include the following.[88]

- Bartering for property or services (e.g., a lawyer who provides legal services for a fee, an artist who sells a painting)
- Real estate rents (e.g., the owner of a hotel)
- Personal property rents (e.g., the rental of vehicles, tuxedos, televisions)

Observation. If the decedent was a farmer or the decedent's estate operates a farm, the income generated from the farm must usually be reported on the estate's income tax return. The asset that generates the income is clear — it is the farm. In general, farm income usually comes from the sale of farm products (e.g., livestock and crops).

84. Ibid.

85. Ibid.

86. Form 1099-DIV, *Dividends and Distributions.*

87. Instructions for Form 1041.

88. Ibid.

Capital Gain (or Loss)

Capital gain (or loss) is the difference in the value of an asset from when it was bought to when it was sold.[89] The net gain or loss from sales and exchanges of capital assets made by the trust or estate is reported on Schedule D (Form 1041), *Capital Gains and Losses,* and attached to Form 1041. Any net **gain** is reported on Form 1041 line 4, which flows from part III, line 19, column (3) of Schedule D. Any net **loss** is reported on line 4, which flows from part IV, line 20 of Schedule D.

> **Note.** Schedule D, *Capital Gains and Losses* (Form 1040), *U.S. Individual Income Tax Return,* **cannot** be substituted for Schedule D, *Capital Gains and Losses* (Form 1041), *U.S. Income Tax Return for Estates and Trusts.*

Capital gains are assessed on any asset the estate or decedent owned and used for personal or investment purposes.[90] If the decedent or estate has capital gains, they will usually be taxed at a lower rate than ordinary income.

5

Examples of possible capital assets include the following.[91]

- Stocks and bonds
- Timber
- Household furnishings
- Car used for pleasure or commuting
- Coin and stamp collections
- Gems and jewelry
- Gold, silver, and other metals

> **Note.** If an estate has a home that was recently sold, the difference in value between when it was acquired and when it was sold might be considered a capital gain reported on Schedule D (Form 1041).

Ordinary Gain

Ordinary gain is income earned from the sale of an asset that is not a capital asset.[92] The sale of non-capital assets will result in ordinary gains or losses. Common examples of non-capital assets that can generate income include stock held mainly for sale to customers, accounts receivable acquired in the ordinary course of business, certain copyrights, harvested crops of a farmer, and supplies normally used or consumed during the normal course of business.

---

89. IRC §1221.
90. Instructions for Form 1041.
91. Ibid.
92. IRC §1221.

Suggested Steps to Completing Form 1041

To complete Form 1041, it is imperative to identify each estate asset that is generating income, define the income correctly, and obtain the proper tax forms to fill out. From a procedural standpoint, the following is a suggested approach.

1. Start with interest income and work through the various income types to compute the amount of income the estate has generated in the past year.
2. Aside from using Form 1041 to see what other forms are needed, do not complete Form 1041 until later. A Schedule C, *Profit or Loss From Business* or Schedule F, for instance, may be necessary.
3. If the estate has business income reported on Schedule C (Form 1040), calculate the business's gross receipts and total expenses. Then, subtract total expenses from the gross receipts to calculate net profit to be entered on Form 1041.
4. Transfer the appropriate numbers from the schedules to the appropriate lines on Form 1041.
5. To calculate the estate's total income, add the numbers on lines 1 through 8 and enter the result on line 9 of Form 1041.

WHERE TO REPORT INCOME

Taxable income received by a cash-basis taxpayer prior to death is reported on Form 1040.[93] Depending on the titling of the assets in the decedent's estate, any income received after death may be reported by one of the following.

- A trust on Form 1041
- An estate on Form 1041
- The beneficiaries on their income tax returns
- The decedent's final Form 1040 if an election is made to report accrued interest on U.S. savings bonds under the IRC §454(a) election

The following table summarizes the reporting locations for the various types of post-death income.

Type of Holding	Income After Death Reported by...
Accounts with designated beneficiaries (including payable-on-death and transfer-on-death)	Beneficiaries directly
Assets owned by trusts	Trusts on Form 1041
Assets passing through probate estates	Estates on Form 1041
Assets owned jointly with the right of survivorship	Survivors directly
Assets owned under tenancy by the entirety	Surviving spouse
Assets owned by the deceased as tenants in common with another person	Estates on Form 1041
Assets owned by trusts and held as tenants in common with another person or entity	Trusts on Form 1041
Assets titled to the deceased alone with no beneficiaries or joint tenancy	Estates on Form 1041

93. Instructions for Form 1040.

METHOD OF ACCOUNTING AND TAX YEAR

Taxable income for an estate is computed using the method of accounting regularly used in keeping the estate's books and records.[94] The method used must clearly reflect income. The accounting method may only be changed with IRS consent via Form 3115, *Application for Change in Accounting Method,* and filing Form 1128, *Application to Adopt, Change or Retain a Tax Year*.

The moment of death determines the end of the decedent's tax year.[95] The fiduciary selects the estate's tax period upon filing the first income tax return. The estate's first tax year may be any period of 12 months or less that ends on the last day of the month. If the last day of any month other than December is selected, a fiscal tax year is adopted.

> **Note.** A distinguishing factor applicable to an estate is that it can elect a fiscal year other than a calendar year. Making the election might give the estate or beneficiaries a tax-deferral opportunity and provide the executor with additional time to organize the estate's affairs. This can be advantageous when the decedent dies late in the calendar year.

5

DEDUCTIONS

A decedent's estate is allowed the following deductions (not miscellaneous itemized deductions) in arriving at AGI.[96]

- Costs paid or incurred in connection with the administration of the estate or trust that would not have been incurred if the property were not held in such estate or trust
- Deductions allowable under IRC §642(b) (concerning the personal exemption of an estate or non-grantor trust)
- Distribution deduction under IRC §651 (the deduction for simple trusts required to distribute current income)
- Distribution deduction under IRC §661 (the deduction for complex trusts)

A cost is subject to the 2% floor on itemized deductions if all the following apply.[97]

- It is included in the definition of miscellaneous itemized deductions under IRC §67(b);
- It is incurred by an estate or non-grantor trust; and
- It commonly or customarily would be incurred by a hypothetical individual holding the same property.

These requirements can provide uncertainty as to how to handle some common expenses of a trust or an estate. Common areas of concern include the following.

- Ownership costs
- Tax preparation fees
- Investment advisory fees
- Appraisal fees
- Certain fiduciary expenses

---

94. IRS Pub. 559, *Survivors, Executors, and Administrators.*

95. Ibid.

96. Ibid.

97. Treas. Reg. §1.67-4(a)(2).

Charitable Deduction

An estate is allowed an unlimited charitable deduction for amounts paid or treated as paid during the year for charitable purposes.[98] To be deductible, the bequest must be pursuant to the terms of the governing instrument that gives specific authority for the fiduciary to make the contribution, be from gross income, and be for a qualifying charitable purpose.

> **Note.** The payment from gross income includes all forms of gross income (capital gain, income in respect of a decedent (IRD), etc.).

Miscellaneous Itemized Deductions

The Tax Cuts and Jobs Act (TCJA) eliminates miscellaneous itemized deductions that would have otherwise been subject to the 2% floor for tax years beginning after 2017 and before 2026.[99] However, above-the-line trust and estate administration expenses, such as fiduciary fees, are not miscellaneous itemized deductions. These amounts are reported as excess deductions on Form 1041, Schedule K-1, box 11, code A.[100]

IRC §67(e) carves out an exception for estates and non-grantor trusts. Under the exception, certain deductions are allowable at arriving at AGI and are not subject to the 2% floor if the amount of the claimed deduction is paid or incurred in connection with the administration of the estate or trust and would not have been incurred if the property were not held in the trust or estate (e.g., a fiduciary fee, tax preparation fee for estates and non-grantor trusts). For grantor trusts, items of income and expense pass through to the grantor, and the trust is disregarded as a separate taxable entity. Thus, administration expenses for a grantor trust are attributed to the grantor/owner and are disallowed.

> **Note.** Only the portion of a bundled fiduciary fee allocable to trust administration is considered an allowable deduction in arriving at AGI.

Non-Miscellaneous Itemized Deductions

For the final return of a trust, if there are excess deductions (i.e., total deductions, excluding the charitable deduction and the exemption, exceeding gross income) on termination that are non-miscellaneous itemized deductions, a beneficiary's share of the excess deductions should be entered in box 11, using Code B, on Schedule K-1 (Form 1041).[101] The fiduciary should provide a descriptive statement and amount for each of the allowable non-miscellaneous deductions. The beneficiary may deduct the excess deduction on Schedule A, *Itemized Deductions,* of Form 1040. If the beneficiary does not have sufficient income in that year to absorb the entire deduction, the balance may not be carried over to a succeeding year. The amount of excess deductions in the final year is determined as follows.

- Each deduction directly attributable to a class of income is allocated in accordance with Treas. Reg. §1.652(b)-3(a);[102]
- To the extent of any remaining income after application of the allocation rules under Treas. Reg. §1.652(b)-3(a), deductions are allocated in accordance with the provisions in Treas. Reg. §1.652(b)-3(b);[103] and
- Deductions remaining after the application of the first two steps comprise the excess deductions on termination of the estate and are allocated to the beneficiaries under Treas. Reg. §1.642(h)-4.[104]

---

98. IRS Pub. 559, *Survivors, Executors, and Administrators.*

99. *Tax Cuts and Jobs Act,* PL 115-97, Title I, §11045(a), creating IRC §67(g).

100. Instructions for Schedule K-1 (Form 1041).

101. Treas. Regs. §§1.642(h)-2(a)(1), (a)(2), and (b)(1).

102. Treas. Reg. §1.642(h)-2(b)(2)(i).

103. Treas. Reg. §1.642(h)-2(b)(2)(ii).

104. Treas. Reg. §1.642(h)-2(b)(2)(iii).

Distributable Net Income

An estate or trust's distributable net income (DNI) is computed using a formula: gross income less deductible expenses, less personal exemption.[105] The trust or estate distributes (or is required to distribute) the income to a beneficiary and generally deducts that amount. The beneficiary includes that amount in its gross income. A **distributions deduction** prevents the double taxation of the income of the trust or estate. The deduction is the lesser of DNI or the sum of the income required to be distributed and other amounts "properly paid or credited or required to be distributed" to the beneficiaries.[106]

> **Note.** There is no distribution deduction for "amounts paid, permanently set aside, or to be used for charitable, etc., purposes" even if the charitable contribution deduction itself is not allowed.[107]

5

DNI allows the fiduciary to determine how much income is subject to tax and how much is taxed to the beneficiaries.[108] DNI helps to characterize the income distributed to beneficiaries for the distribution deduction, as well as measuring the amount of the income that is distributed to the beneficiaries, creating an amount of deductible income for the estate or trust.

The DNI of a trust or estate is equal to the taxable net income of the trust or estate after subtracting the income distribution deduction itself, the personal exemption, and most capital gains and losses (but special rules apply).[109] In other words, DNI is calculated based on accounting income less any tax-exempt income net of allocable expenses.

> **Note.** The accounting method and period of the estate determine when the deduction may be claimed.[110] The beneficiary's tax year is not relevant.

The reason the distribution deduction is not included in the calculation of DNI is because the distribution to beneficiaries is a function of DNI.[111] Additionally, the personal exemption is not used because it is not a component of DNI. Instead, it offsets income and is not allocated to beneficiaries through DNI. Finally, capital gains and losses are generally allocated to the principal and thus not typically included in the DNI calculation.

Generally, capital gains are excluded from DNI and, thus, are taxed to the estate or trust. If the governing instrument allocates capital gains to income, they are included in DNI and are taxed to the beneficiary. Capital gains are excluded from DNI to the extent that such gains are allocated to corpus and are not: paid, credited, or required to be distributed to any beneficiary during the tax year, or paid, permanently set aside, or to be used for charitable purposes.[112]

The distribution deduction is unique to trusts and estates and is not available to individuals.[113] A trust or estate is not allowed a deduction for the distribution of principal to beneficiaries. A deduction against a trust's or estate's taxable income is only allowed for the distribution of trust or estate income to beneficiaries.

---

105. IRC §643(a).

106. IRC §661(a).

107. *Mott v. U.S.*, 462 F.2d 512 (Ct. Cl. 1972).

108. IRS Pub. 559, *Survivors, Executors, and Administrators.*

109. Ibid.

110. Ibid.

111. Ibid.

112. IRC §643(a)(3).

113. IRS Pub. 559, *Survivors, Executors, and Administrators.*

The amount of the income distribution deduction is subject to a DNI limitation.[114] The amount of the DNI limitation is equal to the DNI of the trust or estate less certain tax-exempt interest of the trust or estate.

Generally, an income distribution deduction is allowed if a trust or estate is required to distribute income to beneficiaries.[115] To determine this deduction, it is necessary to calculate the DNI, as well as the fiduciary accounting income (FAI) and the distributions that are required to be made to the beneficiaries. Typically, this distribution is equal to the lesser of the total amount of income distribution (required to be) made to the beneficiaries or the DNI of the trust or estate.

Deduction In Respect of a Decedent

Expenses otherwise deductible do not cease to be deductible because of a person's death.[116] Thus, a deduction in respect of a decedent (DRD) must be identified when preparing a Form 1041. Deductions relating to interest, taxes, depletion, and expenses relating to business property or property used for the production of income may be items of DRD, as well as the foreign tax credit.

> **Note.** There is no definition of DRD, and thus it is not always clear when a deduction within one of these deduction categories is an item of DRD.[117]

For an item to be DRD, the decedent, or a prior decedent, must have been liable for such expenses.[118] Examples of deductions attributable to a decedent include unreimbursed employee expenses, hobby losses, and expenses attributable to the decedent's business.

RATE BRACKETS

The rate brackets applicable to trusts and estates (2023) are set forth in the following table.[119] The rate structure for the taxation of accumulated income of estates and trusts is substantially compressed to reduce the benefits of retaining income inside an estate or a trust.

Trusts and Estates

If Taxable Income Is			
Over	But Not Over	The Tax Is	Of the Amount Over
$ 0	$2,900	10%	$ 0
2,900	10,550	290.00 + 24%	2,900
10,550	14,450	2,126.00 + 35%	10,550
14,450		3,491.00 + 37%	14,450

114. IRC §651.

115. IRC §661(c).

116. Instructions for Form 1041.

117. IRC §691(b).

118. Ibid.

119. IRC §1(e).

DEATH OF REVOCABLE TRUST GRANTOR

The purpose of many revocable grantor trusts is to handle the disposition of the taxpayer's assets upon the grantor's death without subjecting the decedent's assets to probate. Assets held by a trust are not required to be probated; this can save court costs and keep the assets' disposition private. When the grantor dies, the trust becomes irrevocable and requires a separate income tax return (Form 1041) to report trust income earned after death. The assets held by the trust are gathered, maintained, and/or distributed according to the trust's terms by the successor trustee.

Obtaining a Taxpayer Identification Number

After the grantor dies, the trust must obtain a taxpayer identification number (TIN). This is the case even if the trust obtained a separate TIN during the grantor's life.[120]

Example 4. P.J. established the P.J. Revocable Family Trust on January 2, 2015. Under the trust's terms, P.J. retained control over all assets and rights of the trust. P.J. obtained a TIN and opened a bank account at 1st Hometown Bank in the trust's name. Upon P.J.'s death on July 1, 2023, the trust was required to obtain a new TIN.

5

Caution. Care must be exercised in the trust's transition year when reporting the amount of income, gains, losses, deductions, and credits allocable to the grantor and the trust in the pre-death and post-death periods. For instance, if the trust provided the grantor's social security number (SSN), a TIN will need to be provided to third-party payors because the grantor's SSN dies with the grantor. Upon receipt of a TIN, banks and brokers, for example, may require the trust to establish new accounts. This could present timing and logistical challenges for the trustee.

Income Follows Title

One of the most difficult aspects of preparing the trust return after the grantor's death is identifying the assets and related income that belong to the trust. Intentionally or not, many individuals do not title all their assets in the trust's name. The practitioner must understand the flow of the assets from the deceased person to the ultimate beneficiaries to properly report the taxable events.

Note. For a farmer or rancher, many assets do not have a title. These assets include crops, livestock, machinery, equipment, all-terrain vehicles, and vehicles used solely on the farm. Transferring these assets to a trust before death can make the estate administration easier.

It is not uncommon for some of the decedent's assets to fail being retitled into the name of the trustee of the trust before death. This could result in a probate of those assets requiring the probate estate to file a separate income tax return (Form 1041) to report the income earned by the estate post-death.[121] To "catch" the assets not titled to the trust, many individuals also include a **pour-over** or **spill-over** provision in their wills stating that any assets not already in the trust will be transferred to the trust after their deaths.

Example 5. Use the same facts as **Example 4.** P.J. owned a home but failed to have the house titled in the name of her trust. P.J.'s will includes the following pour-over provision.

I give the rest and residue of my property to the successor trustee of The P.J. Revocable Family Trust dated January 2, 2015.

P.J.'s executor hired an attorney to probate her will. Because of the pour-over will provision, the house was transferred to the trust through probate administration.

120. Treas. Reg. §301.6109-1(a)(3)(i)(A).

121. An estate may use a fiscal year ending at the end of a month not to exceed a 1-year period after death.

Even though a taxpayer has a pour-over will, not all assets are subject to estate administration. Assets that do not pass upon death through the estate or trust include the following.

- Assets held jointly with rights of survivorship — these assets and the related income pass directly to the other owner(s).
- Accounts with designated beneficiaries — these assets are distributed directly to the designated beneficiaries.

Example 6. Use the same facts as **Example 5.** P.J. had three other accounts at the bank where the trust savings account was maintained.

1. P.J.'s primary checking account was in her name alone with no other owners or beneficiaries specified. This account did not receive any interest income. This account became part of her estate because there were no other owners and no designated beneficiaries. Under the terms of her will, the balance of the checking account was distributed to the trust.
2. Her interest-bearing checking account was held jointly with rights of survivorship with her niece, K.M. This account did not become part of the estate or the trust. The balance of this account went directly to K.M.
3. P.J. had a money market account with her husband listed as the beneficiary. This account did not become part of either the estate or the trust. The account's balance passed directly to her husband.

Note. The savings account under the trust's original EIN belonged to the trust and stayed with the trust.

IRC §645 Election

Most revocable living trusts meet the definition of a **qualified revocable trust** under §645 because of the grantor's retained right to revoke the trust.[122] This is particularly important if the decedent's estate also has assets not in a revocable trust at death that must be probated. IRC §645 allows the trust and the estate to be combined on one tax return by means of an election via filing Form 8855, *Election to Treat a Qualified Revocable Trust as Part of an Estate,* made by the trustee and the executor to treat the trust as part of the estate.[123]

Note. The §645 election is valid for two years after the decedent's date of death, where the electing trust is taxed as part of the applicable estate. The duration of the election starts on the day of the decedent's death and ends on the day both the trust and estate distributed all their assets or the day before the applicable date, whichever is **earlier.** The applicable date depends on whether a Form 706 is required to be filed. For estates where Form 706 **is not required** to be filed, the applicable date is two years after the decedent's date of death. For estates where Form 706 **is required** to be filed, the applicable date is two years after the decedent's date of death, or six months after the date of the final determination of estate tax liability, whichever is **later.**[124]

122. IRC §645(b)(1). The election is made no later than the time for filing the return for the first tax year of the estate, including extensions. Once made, the election is irrevocable.

123. IRC §645(a). Even if there is no separate probate estate, the election can be used to file the trust return (or several separate qualified revocable trusts as though the trust were an estate.

124. Treas. Reg. §1.645-1(f).

There are various income tax advantages associated with making a §645 election that would not otherwise be available with a separate trust filing. These advantages include the following.

- The use of a fiscal year end for the trust[125]
- A larger exemption amount ($600 rather than $300 for a simple trust compared to $100 for all other trusts)
- The ability to deduct medical expenses paid by the trust on the decedent's final income tax return
- A potentially longer timeframe for owning S corporation stock (period of administration rather than a 2-year period)
- The ability to claim a charitable deduction for amounts permanently set aside for charitable purposes but not yet paid[126]
- The ability to deduct losses for in-kind pecuniary bequests otherwise nondeductible under the related-party rules for trusts
- A 2-year waiver of the material participation requirement under the passive loss rules[127]

Note. During the election period, income and deductions are reported on a combined basis (in terms of reporting income and expenses on Form 1041), but the DNI deduction must be computed separately for the estate and trust.[128] Thus, it is possible that distributions from the estate and trust will result in different allocations to beneficiaries as well as different income tax liabilities for the estate and trust.

When the election terminates, the electing trust component is deemed to have been distributed to a new trust. The new trust will be required to report on a calendar year, which may cause beneficiaries to receive two Schedule K-1s in the same tax year where the co-electing estate files on a fiscal year basis.

REPORTING INCOME EARNED FROM THE DECEDENT'S ASSETS

Nominee Forms[129]

The Forms 1099 issued to a deceased person often report income that was paid after death. The deceased person in this case is treated as a **nominee.** The IRS requires that a nominee file the appropriate Forms 1099 to report the income attributable to the actual recipients.

Copy A of the applicable Form 1099 must be filed with a Form 1096, *Annual Summary and Transmittal of U.S. Information Returns*, to the appropriate IRS service center by the last day of February following the calendar year for which the income is reported (the due date is March 31 if the nominee form is filed electronically).

The income recipient(s) must be given Copy B of the Form 1099 by the last day of January following the calendar year for which the income is reported. On the Form 1099, the nominee should be listed as the "payer." The actual recipients are listed as the "recipient" on each Form 1099 issued by the nominee.

---

125. This might allow income to be deferred to a future tax year. It may also allow sufficient time to file only one tax return and finalize estate matters more efficiently.

126. IRC §642(c).

127. IRC §469(i)(4). Participation is treated as active.

128. Treas. Reg. §1.645-1(e)(2)(iii).

129. Instructions for Form 1040.

Decedent's Final 1040

On the decedent's final Form 1040, all income reported under the decedent's SSN should be shown on the return.[130] Adjustments for amounts actually received by other people should be subtracted on the appropriate form.

FAI[131]

There are several ways that FAI can be determined under state law and, therefore, for federal income tax purposes. Generally, FAI (often called trust or estate accounting income or simply net income) is the amount of money the fiduciary calculates to be on-hand and available to currently distribute to the income beneficiaries of a trust or an estate. FAI is calculated by the fiduciary based on the terms of the governing instrument and the local laws of the estate's situs.

INCOME TAX BASIS

The decedent's estate includes all property owned by the decedent at death to the extent of the decedent's ownership interest. In general, the income tax basis of property in the hands of a person acquiring the property from a decedent or to whom the property passed from a decedent is the FMV of the property as of the date of the decedent's death.[132]

Note. The IRC §1014 basis step-up rule for appreciated property acquired from a decedent can sometimes also be leveraged with the gain exclusion under IRC §121. Farm business owners sometimes retire to a place in town, acquiring a residence separate from the farm or ranch that the surviving spouse or family may be willing to sell. As a result, this provision can provide liquidity without tax consequences.[133]

Income in Respect of a Decedent

IRC §1014(c) carves out property that constitutes the right to receive IRD from the scope of the basis adjustment rules of §1014.

Note. IRC §691(a) describes the IRD concept and its scope. Conceptually, IRD is aimed at equalizing the treatment of cash and accrual-basis taxpayers with regard to items of income that is earned and thus accrues (economically) before a realization event has occurred to cause that income item to be taken into account for tax purposes. Common examples of IRD include compensation earned but not yet paid, accounts receivable from a cash-basis taxpayer, U.S. savings bond interest, and unearned gains on installment contracts.

Basis adjustments are also specifically required for IRD in the case of S corporation stock inherited from a decedent.[134] Similar adjustments are likewise required in partnerships, but rules within subchapter K permit different outcomes at death as compared with an S corporation. Rather than the rigid per-share, per-day allocation method of Subchapter S, Subchapter K allows partnerships to vary allocations by agreement.[135] Allocations pursuant to those agreements must satisfy the requirement of substantial economic effect.[136] Those agreements may also be overridden by other provisions of the Code.[137]

---

130. Ibid.

131. Ibid.

132. IRC §1014(a). Exceptions to the fair market rule exist for property subject to a special use valuation election under IRC §§2032 or §2032A; property representing IRD as defined under IRC §691; certain domestic international sales corporation (DISC) stock as defined in IRC §992(a); and appreciated property that the decedent acquired within a year of death as defined by §1014(e).

133. If an installment contract is used to finance the sale of the principal residence, *Debough v. Shulman,* 799 F.3d 1210 (8th Cir. 2015), holds that under IRC §1038(e), a taxpayer loses the benefit of the IRC §121 exclusion if the residence is repossessed and not resold within one year thereafter.

134. See IRC §1367(b)(4) (requiring basis of inherited stock to be reduced by the value attributed to IRD).

135. IRC §704(a).

136. See IRC §704(b).

137. See, e.g., IRC §704(c).

Pre-Paid Farm Expenses. Many farmers pre-pay and deduct farm production inputs (feed, seed, fertilizer) in the tax year of purchase rather than the year in which the inputs are used in the farming business. That can raise questions of the tax treatment if the farmer dies after pre-paying for the inputs in one tax year but before using them in crop/livestock production in the following tax year. This issue was addressed in *Estate of Backemeyer v. Comm'r*,[138] involving a farm couple in Nebraska. In *Backemeyer,* the husband incurred expenses for the purchase of seed, chemicals, fertilizer, and fuel during 2010, which he planned to use for the 2011 crop production cycle. Unfortunately, he died on March 13, 2011, before he was able to use these inputs. His estate reported these items as "inventory" with an FMV equal to the purchase price. The couple deducted the inputs as expenses on their joint 2010 income tax return.

The husband's estate plan directed that the inputs were to be transferred to his family trust, in which his wife was the trustee. After his death, his surviving widow became actively involved in farming, using those inputs to grow crops in 2011. She sold a portion of those crops in 2011 and a portion in 2012, reporting the full value of the crops sold as gross income. She then prepared two Schedules F for their joint return for 2011. One of them claimed income from crop sales during her husband's life. The other reported the income from her own farming operations, which claimed the input costs as deductions that were also claimed as deductions on the husband's Schedule F in 2010.

The IRS audited and asserted a deficiency associated with the deduction of the prepaid expenses in the 2011 tax year, arguing that there was no evidence that expenses were incurred in excess of cash expenses the wife paid in connection with 2011 crop production. The wife challenged the IRS by filing a Tax Court petition. At the Tax Court, the IRS changed its position, arguing that the deduction was appropriate in 2011, but the **tax benefit rule** required the value of the 2010 deductions to be recaptured.

The Tax Court disagreed with the IRS position and upheld the 2010 deductions, ruling that the tax benefit rule did not require those amounts to be taken into income when they were not used in production for the husband on account of his death. The surviving wife also acquired these inputs at FMV (which was deemed to be their purchase price) at the time of death under §1014. The inputs were includable assets on the husband's Form 706 and were deemed to be taxed there.

Note. If not for the basis step-up rule of §1014, the surviving wife would have acquired the inputs at zero basis. Normally, double deductions are not allowed, but §1014 is a policy choice that Congress made allowing for nonrecognition on account of death. However, the Tax Court in *Backemeyer* also noted that the depreciation recapture rules under IRC §§1245 and 1250 do **not** extend to transfers at death.

---

138. *Estate of Backemeyer v. Comm'r,* 147 TC 17 (Dec. 8, 2016).

Crops and Livestock. Farm crops (whether harvested or still growing) and livestock (whether raised or purchased) by a cash method farmer[139] are also treated as inventory and subject to basis adjustment under §1014, rather than IRD. In Rev. Rul. 58-436,[140] the IRS ruled that livestock and farm crops, whether raised or received from tenants for rent, by a cash method farmer was not IRD, but inventory or property subject to the rules of §1014.[141] The ruling follows *Estate of Burnett v. Comm'r,*[142] which distinguished these items from rights to receive income that would otherwise fall in the category of IRD. Also, the ruling treats the value of feed on hand at the date of death, which would be consumed by cattle before their sale, as includable in the estate and then treated as a deductible administration expense for estate tax purposes.[143]

Note. Treas. Reg. §1.61-4 addresses gross income of farmers and allows crop shares to be included as gross income in the year they are reduced to money. Owning such property is not, therefore, ownership of a right to income. Stepped-up basis rules do not apply to property owned by a crop share landlord.

Contract Grain and Livestock Deliveries. If a farmer delivers grain to satisfy a contract which is not paid until after their death, the contract right is a right to receive income that is within the scope of IRD.[144] According to the court, if the decedent lived to receive these amounts due to them under the cooperative contracts, they would have been reportable and taxable in the decedent's hands as income. The court distinguished *Burnett* on the grounds that the taxpayer had no realization event at death because there was no contract. The IRS later agreed in a private letter ruling that *Linde* should not be extended to the farmer who died owning crops, thereby resulting in the crops being treated as IRD.[145]

In *Estate of Peterson v. Comm'r,*[146] the decedent contracted to sell calves raised on Nebraska ranches to a feeder in Sioux City, Iowa. The terms required him to wean and weigh the calves, then tender those calves to a delivery point. The total number was an estimate, with the buyer having an opportunity to reject those that did not meet his standards. The parties agreed to defer the date for delivery as some of the calves were not ready to wean. The decedent bore the risk of loss and was required to feed the calves until the buyer accepted the calves. Several hundred calves were culled from the herd because the decedent thought that the buyer would not like them.

---

139. The term "farmer" as used here means an individual that bears the risk of production or risk of price change associated with the production of an agricultural commodity. The term does not include a non-material participation crop share landlord that is not bearing the risk of production or risk of price change.

140. Rev. Rul. 58-436, 1958-2 CB 366. The ruling also extends to livestock and crops when the executor elects the alternative valuation date under IRC §2032. Any change in value between the date of death and the date of disposition is ignored for this purpose, meaning that the executor who sells the property before the alternative valuation date does not realize income. Instead, the full value of the property is included in the decedent's estate.

141. Compare against *Willging v. U.S.*, 474 F.2d 12 (9th Cir. 1973), where the court held that an accrual basis farmer using the farm price method in a community property state was not eligible to apply §1014 to step up the basis of crop inventories produced during the year in which he died. Taxpayer Husband died on November 15, at which time his farm inventories had increased from $1,195 at the beginning of the year to $37,953 at the time of his death.

142. *Estate of Burnett v. Comm'r,* 2 TC 897 (1943).

143. *Estate of Backemeyer v. Comm'r,* 147 TC 17 (2016) supports claiming deductions for income tax purposes associated with these items, even though the Tax Court's ruling does not specifically address the issue.

144. See, e.g., *Comm'r v. Linde*, 213 F.2d 1 (9th Cir. 1954) (contract rights associated with grapes delivered to cooperatives that were comingled with grapes from other producers for further processing into wine, brandy, and other products, of which the taxpayer would receive a share after expenses, were IRD in the hands of the taxpayer's surviving spouse).

145. See PLR 5612115440A (Dec. 11, 1956).

146. *Estate of Peterson v. Comm'r,* 74 TC 630 (1980), 667 F.2d 675 (8th Cir. 1981).

The decedent died before delivering the calves. His estate fed and cared for them, ultimately delivering the calves, and receiving the balance of payment. At issue was whether the entire proceeds received were IRD or whether only the proceeds representing the incremental value of the calves compared with their value as of the date of death. The key factor for the court was whether the decedent had a contractual right to payment at the date of his death. The court noted that the issue was not whether the decedent "closed" the sale or transferred title and possession of an asset before death, but whether his successor acquired a right to receive proceeds from an asset's disposition on the one hand or acquired the asset itself on the other. The court focused on the following four elements.

1. A contract regarding the disposition of the underlying assets
2. Performance of the substantive, non-ministerial acts required as preconditions for sale, such that the right to the proceeds derives from death and not efforts on behalf of the estate
3. No economically material contingencies that might have disrupted the sale
4. The decedent would have actually or constructively received the sales proceeds had he lived

5

The court determined that three of these four elements were satisfied (items 1, 3, and 4), but the fact that only about 2/3 of the calves were old enough to wean meant that the performance of the contract required additional work to complete the delivery. The right to receive the proceeds thus stemmed from further efforts to satisfy the contract. These were not perfunctory or ministerial acts, but essential and substantial ones. Thus, the proceeds from the sale of the calves were not IRD because a significant number of the calves were not in a deliverable state on the date of the decedent's death, and the activities the estate performed were substantial and essential acts that the decedent had not performed before death.

Farm Landlord as Decedent. The outcome is different for a cash-basis landlord operating under a non-material participation share lease.[147] Treas. Reg. §1.61-4 generally provides that crop shares are included in gross income in the year when they are sold. In Rev. Rul. 64-289,[148] the IRS took the position that crop shares or livestock held by the decedent at the time of death, along with crop shares the taxpayer had a right to receive at the time of death for economic activities occurring before death, are IRD taken into account in the year the crops or livestock are sold. In the ruling, the IRS used a pro-rata method that treats the portion of rent as IRD based on the number of days in the rental period up through the day of death and the portion of rent treated as income for the estate running from the day after death to the end of the rental period.

> **Example 7.** Larry Landlord entered into a crop share lease with Thomas Tennent effective January 1, 2023, for the 2023 calendar year. Larry died on August 28, 2023. Thus, 240 days of the rental period occurred during his life. Larry's share of his corn crop was delivered to his estate on December 6, 2023. The estate sold half the corn in 2023, and the balance in 2024. According to the IRS, 65.75% (240 ÷ 365) of the proceeds of each sale are treated as IRD, while 34.25% (125 ÷ 365) are treated as income for the estate.

> **Note.** Larry as a **crop share landlord** did not receive any stepped-up basis for the growing crop value on August 28, 2023. If Larry had been an **operating farmer** and Schedule F filer, a stepped-up basis would have applied.

147. See Rev. Rul. 64-289, 1964-2 CB 173.

148. Ibid.

Intentionally Defective Grantor Trust

An estate planning technique that is largely restricted in usage to higher wealth individuals is that of an intentionally defective grantor trust (IDGT).[149] With an IDGT, the grantor sells assets to a grantor trust, and the trust pays for the assets by issuing a note to the grantor. There is no gain because the seller (grantor) is treated as still owning the assets. Because the note bears a fixed rate of interest that freezes the value of the assets in the grantor's estate, over time an enormous amount of property can be leveraged out of the estate. Under IRC §7872, if credit is extended to a family member or to a trust for the benefit of a family member, the note should bear the applicable federal rate (AFR).

A significant question involves whether the trust assets receive an FMV basis at the time of the grantor's death. Rev. Rul. 85-13[150] states that a grantor trust is ignored for income tax purposes but not for estate tax purposes. As a result, the assets transferred to the trust are not included the transferor's estate. In a typical IDGT transaction, the basis of the assets in the grantor's hands is lower than what the basis in the assets will be at death. The trust takes the grantor's (low) basis. The amount for which the grantor sells the assets to the IDGT does not matter in this regard. It is a gift, not a sale.

The answer to the question of what the basis of the trust's assets are upon the grantor's death has not been entirely clear. The question is whether a stepped-up basis is achieved without the assets being included in the grantor's estate. Up until the time the grantor dies, the grantor is treated as owning the assets.[151] At death, the assets are treated for income tax purposes as being transferred to the trust — acquired from a decedent (basis step-up).[152] In Chief Counsel Advice (CCA) 200923024,[153] the IRS took the position that there is no gain recognition when assets leave a grantor trust at death — there is no deemed sale at death. But the IRS followed that up with CCA 200937028[154] saying that a step-up in basis is not achieved for assets in a grantor trust when the grantor dies. Later, in 2012, the IRS issued a private letter ruling[155] saying that there is a stepped-up basis on assets in a grantor trust when the grantor dies. Ultimately, in 2015, the IRS said it would not issue any more rulings while it "studied the matter."[156]

In early 2023, the IRS concluded its study of the issue and with the issuance of Rev. Rul. 2023-2,[157] took the position that there is no step up in basis because the property was not a bequest, devise, or inheritance from the decedent and did not fall within one of the six other types of property listed in §1014(b) that qualify for a basis adjustment at death.

IMPACT OF DEATH ON TAX ATTRIBUTES

Some Code provisions expressly deal with the matter of a surviving spouse's entitlement to tax attributes connected with a joint return, but others leave room for ambiguity.[158] Outside of marriage, tax attributes are generally not transferable.[159] Within marriage, joint filing "generally does not permit either spouse to inherit or otherwise retain after the marriage ends a tax benefit that was originally conferred upon the other spouse."[160]

> **Note.** Although the surviving spouse is entitled to file a joint return in the year the spouse dies, the income reported on the joint return only includes the deceased spouse's income (and deductions) preceding death and the surviving spouse's income (and deductions) for the entire taxable year.[161]

149. *Helping a client benefit from an intentionally defective grantor trust.* Bryniarski, Barbara. Nov. 2021. AICPA. [www.thetaxadviser.com/newsletters/2021/nov/helping-client-benefit-intentionally-defective-grantor-trust.html] Accessed on Aug. 15, 2023.

150. Rev. Rul. 85-13, 1985-1 CB 184.

151. IRC §671.

152. IRC §§671 and 1014.

153. CCA 200923024 (Jun. 5, 2009).

154. CCA 200937028 (Sep. 11, 2009).

155. Ltr. Rul. 201245006 (Nov. 9, 2012).

156. Rev. Proc. 2015-37, 2015-26 IRB 1196.

157. Rev. Rul. 2023-2, 2023-16 IRB 658.

158. See, e.g., *Vichich v. Comm'r*, 146 TC 12 (2016), where the Tax Court explained that despite the ability to file a joint tax return, some tax attributes are personal and subject to defeasance at death.

159. Ibid.

160. Ibid.

161. IRC §6013(a)(3); Treas. Reg. §1.6013-1(d)(1).

Net Operating Losses

Net operating losses (NOLs) attributed to one spouse may be used to offset the income of the other spouse to the full extent of their combined income.[162] An NOL attributed to one spouse before marriage may not be used to offset income attributed to another spouse after marriage.[163] Likewise, a surviving spouse who incurred an NOL after her husband's death was not permitted to carry them back to the joint returns during their marriage in which all income belonged to her husband.[164]

When both spouses are engaged in farming and share the risk of the farming operation as equal "partners," the surviving spouse may carry forward half of the NOL reflected on a joint return to offset the surviving spouse's own income after the first spouse dies.[165]

In the year of death, operating losses and any NOL from business operations can be deductible only on the decedent's final return filed on their behalf. Unused amounts are not deductible by the decedent's estate.[166] The same is true of capital losses, including unused carryforwards.[167]

5

Capital Loss Carryovers

Capital loss carryovers expire at death to the extent they are not utilized on the final return.[168] When a deceased spouse has a capital loss during the final year or a capital loss carryforward, the surviving spouse may be able to utilize that tax attribute by filing a joint return and attempting to create gains to offset the loss by selling their separate property, but only during the year of the deceased spouse's death.

> **Example 8.** Victor has a capital loss carryforward of $100,000 during 2023. Under IRC §1211(b), the couple could only use $3,000 of that loss to offset ordinary income in the final return, leaving $97,000 to expire. However, if Victor and his wife held property in joint tenancy in which the surviving wife now has a basis of, for instance, $300,000 and the property has a FMV of $400,000, upon the surviving wife's sale of the property, she may be able to utilize the carryforward to avoid tax on the gain, but only on a joint return filed for the year of Victor's death.

Passive Activity Losses

If a taxpayer with an interest in a passive activity experiences losses, those losses may be suspended (deferred) under IRC §469(a) and carried forward to future tax years to reduce passive activity income in those years. Rental activities (other than engaged in by a qualified real estate professional) are presumptively covered.[169] A limited exception is also available for up to $25,000 of deductions attributable to rental activities in which an individual actively participated, subject to a phase-out beginning at $100,000 of AGI.[170]

---

162. Ibid., citing Treas. Regs. §§1.172-7(c) and 1.175-3(d).

163. Ibid., citing *Calvin v. U.S.,* 354 F.2d 202 (10th Cir. 1965).

164. Ibid., citing *Zeeman v. U.S.*, 395 F.2d 861 (2nd Cir. 1968).

165. See *Rose v. Comm'r*, TC Memo 1973-207 (Sep. 19, 1973) and Rev. Rul. 74-175, 1974-1 CB 52. While *Rose* and the Revenue Ruling do not involve a farming set of facts, they do provide guidance on the treatment of an NOL when both spouses are informally operating the farming business as equal "partners." The case and ruling should not be read to likewise apply to USDA farm program payments, self-employment tax, or other Code provisions.

166. See Rev. Rul. 74-175, 1974-1 CB 52.

167. Ibid.

168. Ibid.

169. See IRC §469(c)(2).

170. See IRC §469(i).

If a taxpayer disposes of an entire interest in a passive activity in a fully taxable transaction that does not involve a related party, suspended losses are treated as a loss which is not from a passive activity to the extent those losses exceed other passive gains.[171]

A disposition by death is subject to a special rule that coordinates with the adjusted basis rules in §1014. Any suspended loss in the year of disposition is reduced by the step-up in basis that occurs in the hands of the transferee.[172] This reduction in the suspended loss is disallowed and may not be deducted by anyone.[173] If any suspended loss remains after this reduction, then the loss may be taken as a deduction on the decedent's final return and may be used to offset nonpassive income.[174]

Note. A qualified business loss (QBL) also expires upon the taxpayer's death and is not deductible by the decedent's estate.[175]

Charitable Deduction

Charitable contributions are subject to limitations based on gross income, with excess contributions carried forward for up to five future tax years.[176] Excess charitable contributions are personal to the taxpayer who made the contributions.[177]

For a deceased spouse, the regulations provide in part:

> *In case of the death of one spouse, any unused portion of an excess charitable contribution which is allocable in accordance with subdivision (i) of this subparagraph to such spouse shall not be treated as paid in the taxable year in which such death occurs or in any subsequent taxable year except on a separate return made for the deceased spouse by a fiduciary for the taxable year which ends with the date of death or on a joint return for the taxable year in which such death occurs.*[178]

Practitioner Planning Tip

Filing a joint return to expand the contribution base, using as much of the carryforward as possible, is advisable not only in the final year, but in all years affected by an excess contribution carryover.

Observation. Married couples filing joint returns and making contributions to charity should also carefully consider how their contributions are documented. The regulations presuppose that contributions are tracked specifically for each spouse, along with income earned by each spouse, for purposes of computing a separate limitation for each spouse.[179]

---

171. See IRC §§469(g)(1)(A) and (B).

172. See IRC §469(g)(2)(A).

173. See IRC §469(g)(2)(B).

174. See FSA 200106018 (Feb. 9, 2001).

175. IRS Pub. 559, *Deduction of Losses,* referencing IRS Pub. 536, *Net Operating Losses (NOLs) for Individuals, Estates, and Trusts.*

176. See IRC §170(d)(1).

177. *Vichich v. Comm'r,* 146 TC 12 (2016).

178. Treas. Reg. §1.170A-10(d)(4)(iii) (containing an example that the deceased spouse's allocable share of the unused contribution carryforward is extinguished).

179. Different considerations are involved for taxpayers in community property states; Treas. Regs. §§1.170A-8(a) and (d)(2)(ii).

Soil and Water Conservation Expenses

IRC §175 provides for a deduction attributable to soil and water conservation expenditures. There is a limitation on deductibility that requires otherwise deductible expenditures to be limited to 25% of the gross income derived from farming during the taxable year, with the excess carried forward to succeeding taxable years.[180] However, the provision says nothing about the consequences of death before all the expenditures have been deducted. Presumably, the excess is a tax attribute that dies with the taxpayer if it cannot be used in the taxpayer's final return.[181]

In contrast, if an assessment from a soil or water conservation or drainage district is assessed on farmland, a portion of that assessment is potentially deferred over a 9-year period.[182] The deferred amount can be treated as paid or incurred during the taxable year when the taxpayer dies.[183]

E-FILING AND ELECTRONIC SIGNATURES

Form 1041 was added to the Modernized e-File (MeF) platform on January 2014. MeF can accept the current and prior two tax years.[184] Thus, in processing year 2023, MeF will accept Form 1041 tax years 2020, 2021, and 2022. In addition to prior tax years, MeF offers the ability to file amended 1041 returns and attach any supporting documents as a PDF.

5

> **Note**. Documents can no longer be mailed to the IRS if Form 1041 is filed electronically.[185]

Qualified fiduciaries or transmitters may be able to file Form 1041 and related schedules electronically. For an electronically filed Form 1041, it may be signed by using a personal identification number (PIN).[186] Form 1041 may also be e-filed using Form 8453-FE, *U.S. Estate or Trust Declaration for an IRS e-file Return*. If Form 1041 is e-filed and there is a balance due, the fiduciary may authorize an electronic funds withdrawal with the return. If there are joint fiduciaries, only one is required to sign the return.

TAX ISSUES ASSOCIATED WITH EASEMENT PAYMENTS

Rural landowners often receive payment from utility companies, oil pipeline companies, wind energy companies, solar energy companies, and others for rights-of-way or easements over their property. The rights acquired might include the right to install pipeline, aerogenerators and associated access roads, electric lines, and similar access rights. Payments may also be received for the placement of a negative easement on the property such that the landowner is restricted from utilizing their property in a manner that might decrease an adjacent landowner's property value.

The receipt of easement payments raises several tax issues. The payments may trigger income realization and recognition, or could be offset partially or completely by the recipient's income tax basis in the land that the easement impacts.[187] A sale of only part of the land could be involved, or a separate payment for crop damage could be made.

---

180. IRC §175(b).

181. Note that the FMV basis of the farmland under §1014 principles would presumably incorporate the value of any such conservation expenditures, negating the impact of IRC §1252, which otherwise requires a recovery of tax benefits under §175 if the connected farmland is disposed of within 10 years of the date of acquisition. This approach would be similar to that recognized in depreciation recapture provisions, such as §§1245 and 1250, where death trumps recapture rules.

182. IRC §175(f).

183. IRC §175(f)(3).

184. *E-file for Estates and Trusts.* May 30, 2023. IRS. [www.irs.gov/e-file-providers/estates-and-trusts] Accessed on Aug. 15, 2023.

185. Ibid.

186. See Form 8879-F, *IRS e-file Signature Authorization for Form 1041.*

187. For a general and brief discussion of the issue, see IRS Pub. 225, *Farmer's Tax Guide*, p. 18 (2022).

NATURE OF THE TRANSACTION

The grant of a right-of-way often involves a **perpetual easement** that "runs with the land" and is recorded with the title to the land. This binds the current and subsequent property owners subject to the grant. If a perpetual easement is conveyed and the grantor **does not** retain beneficial rights, the transaction involves a **sale** of the underlying tract.[188] However, in many situations, the landowner retains beneficial rights to use the easement property. For example, a landowner may grant an easement to a pipeline company to bury a pipe but retains the right to plant crops on the surface of the easement property if the use does not interfere with the easement. In a situation involving retained rights, the transaction involves the sale of an easement rather than a sale of the underlying tract.

Caution. Sometimes the parties to a transaction may believe that a sale of an easement is involved, and the transaction may be described in that manner. However, the transaction, in reality, may be structured as a lease. If the transaction is a lease, sale treatment is not possible, and ordinary income results without an ability to offset the income by the affected property's basis. If not a sale, the favored provisions of IRC §§1031 (like-kind exchange) and 1033 (involuntary conversion rules) are not available.

EASEMENT PAYMENTS

Permanent Easements

The grant of a limited easement is treated as the sale of a **portion** of the rights in the land impacted by the easement, with the proceeds first applied to reduce the affected land's basis.[189]

Note. Generally, if the grant of an easement deprives the taxpayer of practically all the beneficial interest in the land except for the retention of mere legal title, the transaction is considered a sale of the land that the easement covers. In such cases, gain or loss is computed in the same manner as a sale of the land itself under IRC §§1221 or 1231.[190]

When an easement is granted over a **specific portion** of the landowner's property, only the land's basis that is allocable to that portion is reduced by the amount received for the grant of the easement.[191] Any excess amount received is treated as a capital gain.[192]

Treas. Reg. §1.61-6(a) follows this principle.

> *When a part of a larger property is sold, the cost or other basis of the entire property shall be equitably apportioned among the several parts, and the gain realized or loss sustained on the part of the entire property sold is the difference between the selling price and the cost or other basis allocated to such part. The sale of each part is treated as a separate transaction and gain or loss shall be computed separately on each part. Thus, gain or loss shall be determined at the time of sale of each part and not deferred until the entire property has been disposed of.*[193]

---

188. Rev. Rul. 72-255, 1972-1 CB 221; *Fasken v. Comm'r,* 71 TC 650 (1979); *Wickersham v. Comm'r,* TC Memo 2011-78 (Jul. 28, 2011).

189. See Rev. Rul. 54-575, 1954-2 CB 145; Rev. Rul. 59-121, 1959-1 CB 212.

190. Ibid.

191. See, e.g., Rev. Rul. 59-121, 1959-1 CB 212.

192. Ibid.

193. See also Rev. Rul. 72-255, 1972-1 CB 221.

The regulation presents two tax issues associated with allocating the landowner's income tax basis in the property.

1. The allocation of basis between the portion of the property that is subject to the easement and the balance of the property that is not subject to the easement[194]
2. The allocation of basis between the rights created by the easement and the balance of the rights in the property

Note. Under the regulation, allocation of basis does **not** require proration based on acreage of the entire tract. Instead, basis allocation is "equitably apportioned." For example, if the land subject to the easement is adjacent to a road, it is possible to allocate a greater portion of the basis per acre to the property subject to the easement.[195] Allocation is most often based on FMV but can also be based on assessed value at the time of the acquisition.[196]

Based on the regulation, a taxpayer cannot compare the entire basis in the property from which an easement is acquired with the sale price of the easement unless the entire property is truly impacted by the easement. For example, in *Iske v. Comm'r,*[197] the taxpayer sold easements during condemnation proceedings initiated by a utility to acquire right-of-way easements across land the taxpayer owned. The taxpayer did not include the condemnation award in gross income on the tax return for that year because, as the taxpayer argued, he did not receive a taxable gain on the sale of the easements. However, the court disagreed with the taxpayer's position. The court reasoned that Treas. Reg. §1.61-6(a) required the taxpayer to apportion his basis in the property between the land sold and the land retained. The taxpayer could not use his entire basis in the two parcels involved to offset the amount he received for the easements. **The court found it crucial that the taxpayer did not provide any evidence that a portion of his basis could not be allocated to the property that the easement affected.**

5

Example 9. Garrulous Energy Company paid $4,000 for an easement along the eastern boundary of Marcia Megawatt's farm. The easement is for the construction of an access road to the location on Marcia's farm where an aerogenerator will be erected. The easement covers approximately five acres of Marcia's 160-acre farm.

Marcia has an income tax basis of $750 per acre in her farmland. For purposes of reporting gain from the $4,000 easement payment, Marcia can offset the $4,000 payment by the $3,750 income tax basis that is allocable to the five acres that the easement impacts ($750 per acre basis × 5 acres). Thus, Marcia must only report $250 of gain ($4,000 – $3,750) from the sale of the easement.[198]

Note. Easement contracts usually describe the exact area of the property affected by the easement. From the legal description, the square footage of that area can be determined. Basis can then be computed per acre. One acre equals 43,560 square feet.

If the easement impacts the taxpayer's entire property (which is uncommon), the amount received for the easement can be offset by the taxpayer's basis in the entire property for purposes of computing taxable gain.

Observation. A taxpayer who takes the position that the grant of an easement impacts their entire property bears the burden of proving that position. The IRS will likely challenge it. The ultimate outcome is heavily fact dependent.

194. If the easement affects only a specific portion of the tract, only the basis allocable to the affected portion is reduced by the price received from the easement. Rev. Rul. 68-291, 1968-1 CB 351.

195. See, e.g., *Vaira v. Comm'r,* 52 TC 986 (1969); Treas. Reg. §1.61-6(a).

196. *Medlin v. Comm'r,* TC Memo 2003-224 (Jul. 29, 2003).

197. *Iske v. Comm'r,* TC Memo 1980-61 (Mar. 5, 1980).

198. The gain is IRC §1231 gain. For further guidance on the calculation technique utilized in the example, see Rev. Rul. 68-291, 1968-1 CB 351.

Example 10. Vern sells multiple easements to a wind energy company for access to a major aerogenerator project on his ranch. The easements cover 550 acres (out of 640 total acres that Vern owns) and bisect Vern's property. The wind energy company constructed fences on each side of every easement and installed gates in the fences so that Vern could move his livestock through the easements. Because of these particular facts, Vern might successfully argue for an offset of basis in his entire 640 acres. Vern must establish that the easements affect his use of the entire 640 acres rather than just the 550 acres covered by the easements.[199]

Caution. If it is not possible to allocate the basis of the entire property between the interest that is sold and the interest that is retained, then the easement proceeds can be used to reduce the basis in the entire property affected.[200] However, the IRS is likely to challenge an allocation of basis across the entire property. A favorable IRS letter ruling or court decision in which the court finds it impracticable or impossible to determine the specific portion of the property impacted by the easement may be necessary.[201]

Income tax basis must also be allocated between the rights that the taxpayer retains and the easement rights that are sold. For purposes of this basis allocation, the general rule is that the allocation of basis in the property must be allocated between the interest sold and the interest retained in the proportions that their respective FMVs bear to the FMV of the entire property.[202]

It may be possible to determine the actual portion of a client's property that is impacted by an easement project by examining the terms of the particular easement. Many easement agreements prohibit the landowner from building anything on the property that would interfere with the maintenance or operation of the easement holder's property. That could give the landowner a reasonable argument that the easement affects **all** the landowner's property. If there is sufficient basis in the land to absorb the easement payment, the landowner will not have any gain to report.

Example 11. Tom owns an 80-acre tract of farmland that he bought in 1983 for $40,000. It is entirely pastureland and no improvements were made to it. Tom was approached by a wind energy company to construct three aerogenerators on his property. The company is willing to pay Tom $25,000 for an easement. The easement terms prevent Tom from building anything on the property that would obstruct the company's access to the aerogenerators or that would block the wind. Tom should be able to reduce the basis in his entire tract by the amount of the easement payment. This reduces his basis to $15,000 ($40,000 – $25,000) and no gain to report.

Note. If the wind energy company were to pay Tom for the right to construct additional aerogenerators on his property in a future year, Tom would again reduce his remaining basis in his tract by the amount of the additional payment. To the extent the payment exceeds Tom's basis in his property, Tom would have a taxable gain reportable on part 1 of Form 4797 (where it is netted with other §1231 gains and losses).

---

199. This example is based on the facts in *Bledsoe v. U.S.*, 67-2 TC 9581 (1967). See also *Conway v. U.S.*, 73-1 TC 9318 (1973).

200. Rev. Rul. 77-414, 1977-2 CB 299.

201. See, e.g., *Gilbertz v. U.S.*, 808 F.2d 1374 (10th Cir. 1987). Also see *Fasken v. Comm'r*, 71 TC 650 (1979). Taxpayer was granted four easements for utility lines. The court required the consideration received for the easements applied against the portion of the adjusted basis for the ranch allocable to the acreage affected by each particular easement instead of applying the consideration against the ranch's entire basis. The taxpayer was unable to show that usefulness of the ranch was affected by easements or that it was not possible to allocate basis to the area actually affected by each easement.

202. Rev. Rul. 77-413, 1977-2 CB 298 (the amount realized from the sale of real property did not include the value of a 20-year possessory interest retained in part of the property). See also, Ltr. Rul. 8025116 (Mar. 28, 1980).

Caution. Tom's logic in **Example 11** may be challenged by the IRS. Many commercial aerogenerators are placed on 300–350 foot towers. If this is the case, the tips of the blades might reach as high as 525 feet. In that scenario, it might be illogical for Tom to argue that his future construction of a machine shed, for example, could possibly block the wind to the three aerogenerators.

If Tom wants to erect a structure on his farm, he should ask the wind energy company if the structure violates the standard "no interference" clause. In most scenarios, permission is granted to erect the structure.

The following case law supports the argument that an easement can affect **all** of a taxpayer's property and, hence, allows the taxpayer's entire basis in the property to be applied against the easement payment.

- *Bledsoe v. U.S.*[203] — The landowner sold nine perpetual easements to the U.S. Army Corps of Engineers to allow road access to a dam. The easements covered only 47.3 acres, but the court allowed the landowner to reduce the basis of the entire 454.54 acres because the easements restricted his use of the property. The easements varied in width from 100 to 400 feet and bisected his ranch. The easement holder then constructed a fence along the road on both sides and built gates in the fences so that the taxpayer could move his cattle across the easements. **Contrary** to the general rule, the court held that the easements were not sales, and that the taxpayer was entitled to apply the easement proceeds against the property's basis.
- *Conway v. U.S.*[204] — The landowner sold a right-of-way across his farm to a coal company, retaining ingress and egress rights and a reversion of the right-of-way upon abandonment. The court allowed the landowner to offset the payment received for the grant by the landowner's basis in the entire property.
- *Inaja Land Co., Ltd. v. Comm'r*[205] — The City of Los Angeles paid the landowner $50,000 for a perpetual easement that allowed the city to flood the land when it diverted water into a river that flowed through the land. The easement did not cover the entire tract, but because it affected the use of the entire tract, the court allowed the payment for the easement to reduce the basis of the entire tract. The court specifically noted that apportionment was impossible.

Severance Damage Payments

An easement can bisect a landowner's property in such a manner that the property not subject to the easement can no longer be put to its highest and best use. This is more likely with commercial property and agricultural land that has the potential to be developed. Severance damages may be paid to compensate the landowner for the resulting lower value of the unaffected property. For example, in *Foster, et al. v. Comm'r*,[206] the amount received from a utility company for a right-of-way easement for high voltage lines was applied against the taxpayer's basis in the entire property as severance damages. The court determined that an additional amount paid for a "sway" easement also reduced the basis in the entire property. The court found that both easements were integrally related and impacted the entire property.

203. *Bledsoe v. U.S.*, 67-2 TC 9581 (1967).

204. *Conway v. U.S.*, 73-1 TC 9318 (1973).

205. *Inaja Land Co., Ltd. v. Comm'r*, 9 TC 727 (1947).

206. *Foster, et al. v. Comm'r*, 80 TC 34 (1983), *aff'd and vacated*, 756 F.2d 1430 (9th Cir. 1985).

If severance damages exceed the landowner's basis in the property not subject to the easement, gain is recognized.[207]

> **Note.** Under §1033, the landowner may be able to defer gain resulting from the payment of severance damages by using the severance damages to restore the property affected by the easement or by investing the damages in a timely manner in other qualified property.[208] The landowner is not required to apply the severance damages to the portion of the property subject to the easement. Additionally, if the easement affects the remainder of the property such that the pre-easement use of the property is not possible, the sale of the remainder of the property and use of the sale proceeds (plus the severance damages) to acquire other qualified property can be structured as a deferral transaction under §1033.[209]

Temporary Easement Payments

Some easements may involve an additional temporary easement to allow the holder to have space for access, equipment, and material storage while conducting construction activities on the easement property. A separate designation for a **temporary easement** for these purposes generates **rental income** for allocated amounts. As one alternative, it may be advisable to include the temporary space in the perpetual easement, which is then reduced after an established period. Under this approach, the payment attributable to the temporary easement can be applied to reduce the basis in the tract subject to the permanent easement.[210] A second alternative, classifying any payments for a temporary easement as damage payments, may be possible, depending on the facts.

Damage Payments

Upfront payments to a landowner for actual, current damage to the property caused by easement construction activities may be offset by basis in the affected property.[211] Payments for property damage caused by environmental contamination and/or soil compaction are examples of this type of payment. A payment for damage to growing crops, however, is treated as a sale of the crop, which is reported by an operating farmer on line 2 of Schedule F. If the landowner is a crop share landlord, the payments are reported on line 1 of Form 4835.

Any payment for **future** property damage is generally treated as rent.

> **Note.** Most easements contain release language covering loss of rents, damage to the surface, damage to fences, water impoundments, vegetation, and crops. The release language generally applies to future damages. In the IRS's view, any associated payment constitutes rent that cannot be offset by basis. Clearly, careful drafting of the easement that distinguishes between upfront damage payments and covenants to compensate for future damages is essential. It is unclear whether courts would assume that construction activities necessarily result in damages. In any event, maintaining relevant documentation is key.

207. Rev. Rul. 68-37, 1968-1 CB 359.

208. Rev. Rul. 83-49, 1983-1 CB 191.

209. Rev. Rul. 59-361, 1959-2 CB 183.

210. Rev. Rul. 73-161, 1973-1 CB 366.

211. See, e.g., FSA 200228005 (Mar. 29, 2002). Settlement proceeds received for land contamination and impact on water rights are treated as a nontaxable return of capital to the extent of basis.

Lease Payments

A right of use that is not an easement generates ordinary income to the landowner and is, potentially, net investment income subject to the 3.8% net investment income tax.[212] Thus, transactions that are a lease or a license generate rental income with no basis offset. For example, when a landowner grants surface rights for oil and gas exploration, the transaction is most likely a lease. Easements for pipelines, roads, surface sites, and similar interests that are for a definite term of years are leases.[213] Likewise, if the easement is for "as long as oil and gas is produced in paying quantities," it is a lease.[214]

Note. When a landowner retains reversionary rights, sale treatment may not result unless the retained rights are contingent. However, a transaction involving a contingent reversion in case the easement is not used or abandoned constitutes a sale of an easement.[215] Likewise, if reversion is triggered, for example, on the failure to maintain insurance coverage, the filing of bankruptcy, assignments for the benefit of creditors, or an unauthorized assignment or like events, the easement status is maintained.

5

A lease is characterized by periodic payments. A lease is indicated when failure to make a payment triggers default procedures and potential forfeiture.

Lease payments are not subject to SE tax in the hands of the recipient, regardless of the landowner's participation in the activity.[216] Accordingly, the annual lease payment income is reported on Schedule E, *Supplemental Income and Loss,* with the landowner likely having few or no deductible rental expenses.

Practitioner Planning Tip

Tax preparers should review Forms 1099 received by the landowner and properly report and document upon which forms the income is reported.

Note. Lease transactions are most likely to be found with respect to oil and gas exploration and development, and solar energy production agreements. The lease payment structure for solar energy development is similar to that of an oil and gas transaction, except that solar royalty payments are not as common as solar rental payments. This is because there are many variables involved when attempting to calculate revenues and expenses associated with solar farm production, making annual rental payments more efficient.

212. IRC §1411.

213. *Gilbertz v. U.S.*, 808 F.2d 1374 (10th Cir. 1987).

214. *Vest v. Comm'r*, 481 F.2d 238 (5th Cir. 1973); *Estate of Reinke v. Comm'r*, TC Memo 1993-197 (May 4, 1993); *Wineberg v. Comm'r*, TC Memo 1961-336 (Dec. 14, 1961), *aff'd*, 326 F.2d 157 (9th Cir. 1963).

215. Ibid.

216. IRC §1402(a)(1).

Negative Easement Payments

A landowner may make a payment to an adjacent or nearby landowner to acquire a **negative easement** over the other landowner's tract. A negative easement is a restriction placed on the tract to prevent the owner from specified uses of the tract that might diminish the value of the payor's land. For instance, a landowner may fear that their property would lose market value if a pipeline, high-power transmission line, or aerogenerator were placed on adjacent property. Thus, the landowner might seek a negative easement over the adjacent property to prevent that landowner from granting an easement to a utility company for that type of activity on the adjacent property.

In a field service advice (FSA) memorandum,[217] the IRS decided that a negative easement payment is rental income in the hands of the recipient. It is not income derived from the taxpayer's trade or business. The facts of the ruling involved a C corporation that owned property adjacent to a plant owned by another corporation. The adjacent corporation wanted to protect itself from potential liability as a result of activities on the C corporation's property. Accordingly, it paid the C corporation for a negative easement over a strip of land closest to its border to act as a buffer. The agreement between the parties for the recorded negative easement called for annual payments for a term of years. The C corporation wanted to characterize the payments as business income to avoid triggering an additional 20% tax under the personal holding company (PHC) rules of IRC §§541-547.

Note. A C corporation is a PHC under IRC §542(a)(1) if more than 50% of the corporate stock is held, either directly or indirectly, by five or fewer individuals, **and** the corporation derives at least 60% of its adjusted ordinary gross income (AOGI) from passive investment sources. Rental income is included in AOGI unless adjusted rental income:

- Is at least 50% of AOGI, and
- Dividends for the tax year equal or exceed the amount (if any) by which the corporation's nonrent PHC income for that year exceeds 10% of its ordinary gross income.

In other words, if the mixture of rental income and other passive income sources exceed the 10% threshold and the rental income exceeds the 50% threshold, the PHC tax could be triggered.

The IRS noted that there was no direct authority as to how to treat negative easement payments for PHC purposes. However, the IRS did find cases involving conservation reserve program (CRP) payments to landowners and the SE tax treatment of those payments to be relevant. In *Morehouse v. Comm'r*,[218] the 8th Circuit reversed the Tax Court and held that CRP payments were rental payments (for SE tax purposes) because they were compensation to the landowner for the government's possession and use of the landowner's property. The court determined that the CRP payments were synonymous with easement payments and were not subject to SE tax in the hands of a nonfarmer.

In the FSA, the IRS defined rent as "amounts received for the use of, or right to use, property of the corporation." The IRS cited *Morehouse* for the proposition that CRP payments are "rents" that are paid to the landowner for the government's **use** of the property. In the FSA, the IRS determined that the negative easement payments were made to prevent the C corporation from using its property in a way that would diminish the value of the other corporation's property. This, the IRS found, was a "use" of the C corporation's property.[219] The IRS believed that *Morehouse* supported its FSA position because Mr. Morehouse was a nonfarmer and the government was using his property for the government's own purposes.

Note. Although the FSA was not the result that the taxpayer desired (because of the complications with the PHC), the FSA does hold that negative easement payments are "rents" that are not subject to SE tax. However, the rents would be treated similarly to other passive sources of income and could be subjected to the 3.8% net investment income tax under IRC §1411. In addition, the IRS's position taken in the FSA could be applied to situations involving the government's use of a taxpayer's property to enhance wildlife and conservation.

---

217. FSA 20152102F (Feb. 25, 2015).

218. *Morehouse v. Comm'r*, 769 F.3d 616 (8th Cir. 2014), *rev'g* 140 TC 350 (2013).

219. The IRS stated, "We believe this is using/employing the property for the accomplishment of a business purpose, i.e., to avoid/limit liability."

Reporting the Transaction

The party that acquires the easement must report the transaction using Form 1099-S, *Proceeds From Real Estate Transactions.*[220] Rental payments and damage payments are reported on Form 1099-MISC, *Miscellaneous Income.*[221]

EMINENT DOMAIN

Proposed easement acquisitions can be contentious for many landowners. Often, landowners may not willingly grant a pipeline company or a wind energy company the right to use the landowners' property. In those situations, eminent domain procedures under state law may be invoked. These procedures involve a property's condemnation. The power of eminent domain is the right of the state government (called the "taking power" for the federal government) to acquire private property for public use, subject to the constitutional requirement that "just compensation" be paid. Although eminent domain is a power of the government, developers of pipelines and certain other types of energy companies are often delegated the authority to condemn private property. The condemnation award (the constitutionally required "just compensation") paid is treated as a sale for tax purposes.[222]

5

> **Note.** The condemnation award is tied to the "taken" property's FMV. As is the case with negotiated easements, the landowner may also recover amounts for a temporary easement, severance damages, crop damage payments, and for the relocation of fixtures and personal property. Interest on these amounts may also be recovered. These additional amounts must be authorized by state law. Payments to relocate fixtures and personal property are typically set at the lesser of the property's FMV or the actual cost to relocate the property. If any amount paid is allocated to §§1245 or 1250 property, recapture could be triggered.

The IRS's view is that a condemnation award represents the sales price of the property taken, and the Tax Court generally agrees.[223] However, if the condemnation award clearly exceeds the FMV of the property taken, a court may entertain arguments about the various components of the award.[224] Thus, it is important for a landowner to preserve any evidence that might support allocating the award to various types of damages.

> **Observation.** If a personal residence is part of the condemnation, the taxable amount of the award is decreased by the gain excluded under §121(d)(5)(B).

Deferral of Gain

Although a condemnation award is treated as a sale for tax purposes, §1033 (involuntary conversion rules) allows a recipient to elect to defer gain realized from a condemnation (and sales made under threat of condemnation) by reinvesting the proceeds in qualifying property.

> **Note.** A sale made under threat of condemnation can occur, for example, when a landowner sells easements over their property to a company that is threatening to condemn the easement unless the landowner grants it.[225]

---

220. Instructions for Form 1099-S.

221. Instructions for Form 1099-MISC.

222. See, e.g., *Hawaiian Gas Products, Ltd., v. Comm'r*, 126 F.2d 4 (9th Cir. 1942).

223. Rev. Rul. 59-173, 1959-1 CB 201; *Asjes v. Comm'r*, 74 TC 1005 (1980).

224. See, e.g., *Conran v. U.S.*, 322 F.Supp. 1055 (E.D. Mo. 1971).

225. In these situations, one issue is whether the company actually has the power of condemnation. See, e.g., *Texas Rice Land Partners, Ltd. v. Denbury Green Pipeline-Texas, LLC,* 363 S.W.3d 192 (Tex. 2012). An operator of a carbon dioxide pipeline secured easements under the threat of condemnation when the operator was not a common carrier having such power at the time of the acquisitions. See also Rev. Rul. 74-8, 1974-1 CB 200. A sale made under the threat of condemnation was an involuntary conversion when the utility at issue did not actually possess the power of eminent domain, even though the utility could acquire it.

The election to defer gain under §1033 is made by simply not reporting the condemnation gain realized on the return for the tax year the award is received.[226] However, in the year in which the gain is realized, the regulations require the taxpayer to disclose the details concerning the replacement property.[227]

Example 12. Ole McDonald received a $200,000 condemnation award on a tract of farmland from Earth, Wind, & Fire Inc. on December 1, 2022. A Form 1099-S is issued to Mr. McDonald. He plans to purchase qualifying replacement property within three years. The transaction is reported on Form 4797 as follows.

Form **4797**

Department of the Treasury
Internal Revenue Service

Sales of Business Property
(Also Involuntary Conversions and Recapture Amounts Under Sections 179 and 280F(b)(2))
Attach to your tax return.
Go to *www.irs.gov/Form4797* for instructions and the latest information.

OMB No. 1545-0184
2022
Attachment Sequence No. **27**

Name(s) shown on return	Identifying number
Ole McDonald	*****-**-6789**

1a	Enter the gross proceeds from sales or exchanges reported to you for 2022 on Form(s) 1099-B or 1099-S (or substitute statement) that you are including on line 2, 10, or 20. See instructions	1a	**200,000**
b	Enter the total amount of gain that you are including on lines 2, 10, and 24 due to the partial dispositions of MACRS assets	1b	
c	Enter the total amount of loss that you are including on lines 2 and 10 due to the partial dispositions of MACRS assets	1c	

Part I **Sales or Exchanges of Property Used in a Trade or Business and Involuntary Conversions From Other Than Casualty or Theft—Most Property Held More Than 1 Year** (see instructions)

2 (**a**) Description of property	(**b**) Date acquired (mo., day, yr.)	(**c**) Date sold (mo., day, yr.)	(**d**) Gross sales price	(**e**) Depreciation allowed or allowable since acquisition	(**f**) Cost or other basis, plus improvements and expense of sale	(**g**) Gain or (loss) Subtract (f) from the sum of (d) and (e)
Land Condemnation	**07/01/99**	**12/01/22**	**200,000**		**200,000**	**0**

Mr. McDonald attaches the following election to his return:

An election is made under IRC § 1033 to defer gain on condemnation award received. The taxpayer intends to replace the property within the replacement period.

Note. The purpose of showing the receipt of the funds on Form 4797 is to reduce the likelihood of receiving a CP-2000 (underreported income) notice and to begin the documentation of the need for acquiring replacement property within the prescribed time. The basis reported is equal to the gross sales price to accomplish the deferral of income.

226. A partnership makes the election at the partnership level. *Demirjian v. Comm'r,* 457 F.2d 1 (1972).

227. Treas. Reg. §1.1033(a)-2(c)(2). If the replacement property has not been acquired at the time the return is due and, thus, the details concerning the replacement property are not available to disclose, the election to defer the gain is deemed to have been made if no gain is reported.

For real property acquired by condemnation or threat of condemnation, the gain realized can be deferred if the proceeds are reinvested in like-kind property[228] **within three years after the close of the first tax year in which the taxpayer realizes any part of the gain** (i.e., in the first year in which the proceeds exceed the taxpayer's basis in the affected property) on the involuntary conversion.[229] More specifically, the replacement period begins on the earlier of the date of disposition or the date that condemnation is threatened, and ends three years after the close of the first tax year in which any part of the gain is realized.[230]

Note. Detailed information concerning the condemnation should be disclosed with the return for any year in which gain from the transaction is realized. Likewise, information concerning the replacement property should be disclosed for the tax year (or years) in which the replacement property is acquired. Form 4797 is used to report an involuntary conversion of property used in the taxpayer's trade or business (or capital assets held for business or profit). Form 8949, *Sales and Other Dispositions of Capital Assets,* is used to report gain from capital assets not held for business or profit.

If the landowner uses severance damages to restore property that is retained or to reinvest in the replacement property, the severance damages may also qualify for deferral under §1033. Likewise, if the condemnation makes the use of the remainder of the landowner's land impractical such that the landowner sells the remaining property, the sale proceeds may also qualify for deferral under §1033.

If the amount realized from the condemnation is less than the cost of the replacement property, the taxpayer's basis in the replacement property is the cost of the replacement property less any unrecognized gain. If the amount realized from the condemnation exceeds the cost of the replacement property, the landowner has gain recognition to the extent of the excess of the amount of the gain realized over cost, and the basis in the replacement property is the cost less any unrecognized gain.[231]

The IRS ruled that basis is allocated between land and improvements,[232] even if the condemnation award was only for land. IRC §1223 establishes the holding period for the replacement property, and the IRS ruled that the holding period of the condemned property is attributed proportionally to the property acquired.[233]

Note. Deferral under §1033 may not result in the deferral of recapture income under §§1245 or 1250. This is particularly the case if multiple classes of property are condemned because the regulations require the amount realized from the condemnation to be allocated between the various classes. In situations when the sale proceeds would be treated as a capital gain, and the replacement property would reduce ordinary income, reporting both the sale and expense may be preferable to income deferral.

---

228. Like-kind property is property that is similar or related in service or use. IRC §1033(a). But, the "like-kind" rules for real property set forth in IRC §1031 apply. IRC §1033(g); Treas. Reg. §1.1031(a)-1(b). This is a more relaxed standard than applies for personal property trades.

229. The replacement period is three years if the condemned property is held for productive use in the taxpayer's trade or business or for investment. When a §1033 election is made, the IRS has three years from the date it receives notification of replacement or failure to replace in which to assess a deficiency.

230. Constructive receipt rules apply. Also, it is important to ensure that the transaction for the replacement property is finalized within the replacement period. See, e.g., *Fort Hamilton Manor v. Comm'r,* 445 F.2d 879 (2d Cir. 1971). Upon request, the IRS may extend the replacement period for good cause.

231. IRC §1033(b)(2).

232. Rev. Rul. 79-402, 1979-2 CB 297.

233. Rev. Rul. 81-285, 1981-1 CB 173.

Expenses

Expenses that the landowner incurs during the condemnation process are treated as capital expenditures. Thus, they are added to the landowner's basis in the property subject to the easement. This has the effect of reducing the gain (or increasing the loss) upon condemnation. Expenses that are made to substantiate and recover severance damages are capitalized as part of the basis of the property that is not condemned.

ESTATE TAX IMPLICATIONS

Long-term leases (known as a "leased-fee interest")[234] can also impact the federal estate value of the land subject to the lease. Property is valued for estate tax purposes at its FMV as of the date of the decedent's death. FMV is determined under a willing-buyer, willing-seller test.[235] The Tax Court has held that leased-fee interests must be taken into account for their impact on the value of the real estate for estate tax purposes.[236] In *Estate of Mitchell v. Comm'r,*[237] the decedent's estate included various residential rental properties with one of the properties having an unexpired lease at the time of the decedent's death. Under the terms of the lease, the tenant could renew the lease for about 20 years after the date of the decedent's death. The Tax Court valued the property subject to the lease by adding the value of the landlord's reversionary interest in the property to the adjusted value of the lease payments that were owed to the decedent. The result was an enhancement to the property's value for estate tax purposes.

Observation. A long-term agreement signed shortly before death likely has little impact on the subject property's estate tax value, because the agreement (particularly for mineral and wind energy development) has an initial development/prospecting phase that runs for several years before the primary phase of the easement. Thus, if the decedent dies during the prospecting phase, uncertainty remains as to whether production will ever occur on the premises. Consequently, there should be no valuation enhancement. However, if death occurs after the development phase and activity commenced on the leased premises, the IRS could argue for a valuation enhancement.

A related estate tax concern involves special-use valuation.[238] One court held that grant of an easement was a disposition of a property interest under federal law resulting in recapture tax being triggered under IRC §2032A(c)(1).[239]

SOLAR ENERGY PRODUCTION

As noted previously, the transactions that farm, ranch, and rural landowners enter into with solar energy companies are most likely to be lease agreements. The tax principles applicable to lease agreements with wind energy companies, oil and gas companies, and others are likewise applicable to solar energy leases. However, there are some unique aspects of solar energy leases, such as the following.

- Easement and allocation of basis issues are likely not present. A lease will be for a certain amount of acres and the solar arrays will take up that amount of the land.
- Under many state laws, solar farms are exempt from personal property tax and instead pay an annual nameplate capacity tax on a per megawatt of electricity generation basis.
- State law often continues to classify and value the land under the solar arrays as if the arrays did not exist.[240] Thus, land that is classified as agricultural before arrays are placed on the land under a solar energy lease will continue to be classified as agricultural land.

---

234. In *Marks v. Comm'r,* TC Memo 1985-179 (Apr. 10, 1985), the court said that a leased-fee interest exists when the "owner of commercial or income-producing property has the right to receive the actual contract rent that the property is generating over the remaining terms of the outstanding leases on the property…"

235. Rev. Rul. 59-60, 1959-1 CB 237; Treas. Reg. §20.2031-1(b).

236. *Estate of Mitchell v. Comm'r,* TC Memo 2011-94 (Apr. 28, 2011).

237. Ibid.

238. IRC §2032A.

239. *Estate of Gibbs v. U.S.,* 161 F.3d 242 (3d Cir. 1998). At issue was the grant of an agriculture preservation easement that ensured the land subject to the easement would not be developed.

240. See, e.g., Neb. Rev. Stat. §77-6203(4).

Another approach involving solar energy production involves a landowner's investment in solar equipment and the related rights and responsibilities. In these situations, questions can arise concerning the taxpayer's income tax basis in the solar equipment, bonus depreciation, the at-risk rules of IRC §465, and the passive activity rules of §469. In 2018, the Tax Court dealt with these issues.

Golan Case[241]

In 2010, the Golans (a married couple) bought an investment in solar equipment and its related rights and obligations from a solar contractor formed as an LLC. The LLC installed solar panels and related solar equipment on three of the Golans's properties. The parties engaged in a **power purchase agreement (PPA),** providing that the Golans would buy the electricity generated at a discount and the LLC would retain ownership of the equipment and the right to tax benefits for a short period of time. During that time, the LLC retained the burdens and benefits of ownership.

In 2011, the LLC sold the equipment to the Golans, and the equipment was installed on the roofs of three of their properties. The purchase was subject to the PPA. The Golans paid $300,000 consisting of a down payment of $90,000, a credit for certain rebates of $57,750, and a $125,000 promissory note (maturity date of 2041) with no fixed payment amount and interest at 2% (which the Golans personally guaranteed). The note required all monthly revenue generated by the panels to be paid to the LLC. The Golans granted the LLC an option to buy the solar equipment for the outstanding balance of the promissory note after the 5-year tax credit recapture period. The panels were not connected to the grid until after the Golans bought them.

After an audit, the IRS asserted that the Golans could not claim the IRC §46 rehabilitation credit and could not claim IRC §179 depreciation. The IRS did not make any claim that the Golans could not claim the energy credit of IRC §48 or bonus depreciation under IRC §168(k). The IRS did, however, reduce the Golan's basis in the solar equipment from $300,000 to $152,500 on the grounds that they had not paid anything toward the down payment during 2011. The IRS asserted that the Golans were not at risk under §465 because the LLC had a continuing interest in the projects and could not claim basis in $57,750 of utility rebates that were assigned to the LLC. The IRS also claimed that the Golans were engaged in a passive activity under §469.

Basis. The court noted that the $90,000 down payment was not paid in 2011; therefore, under Treas. Reg. §1.1012-1(a), the Golans could not add it to their basis for that year. As for the $57,750 of utility rebates, the court noted that the Golans neither received them nor reported them as income. Instead, the Golans had assigned the rebates to the LLC. Accordingly, the rebates could not be added to the Golans's basis in the solar equipment. But, the promissory note was a recourse obligation issued in exchange for the solar equipment. Thus, the principal amount of the note counted as basis.

Caution. The court (and IRS) appeared to be unconcerned that the promissory note was serving as a means of providing cash flow for the investment. Because the Golans did not make any payment on the note in 2011 and the cash flow limitation in the note, the IRS could have claimed that the LLC was the owner of the solar equipment in 2011 at the time the panels were placed in service.

Bonus Depreciation. The court held that the Golans could claim bonus depreciation because they were the original users of the panels. The IRS claimed that the panels were placed in service under the contract before the Golans owned them. But, the court noted that the panels were not connected to the grid until after the Golans had purchased them. As such, the panels were not ready and available for use until the time of the grid connection.

Note. The IRS did not argue that the Golans were not entitled to the energy credit of §48, which also requires that the "original use of such property commences with the taxpayer."[242]

---

241. *Golan v. Comm'r,* TC Memo 2018-76 (Jun. 5, 2018).

242. IRC §48(a)(3)(B)(ii). An exception to this rule exists for sale-leasebacks within 3-months of the placed in-service date per IRC §50(d)(4).

At-Risk. The court determined that the Golans were at-risk with respect to the promissory note for the purpose of depreciation. The court held that the LLC did not have a prohibited continuing interest in the panels because the LLC was not entitled to any assets of the projects upon a liquidation. Instead, the LLC only had a gross receipts interest (monthly revenue) rather than a prohibited net profits interest. The fact that a loan in a transaction is made by a promoter of the transaction does not necessarily mean that the promoter has a prohibited continuing interest in the transaction.[243]

Passive Activity. The court held that the Golans were not subject to the passive loss rules of §469. The court, based on what it determined was the Golans's credible testimony, held that they spent more than 100 hours on the projects at the three properties during the year in question and no one else spent more time than they did.[244]

Penalties. The court determined that the Golans relied in good faith on the advice of a tax preparer who had sufficient expertise to justify their reliance and to whom they provided all necessary accurate information. The court also acknowledged that the Golans met with the tax professional four times to discuss the solar venture. The court found that the couple made a good-faith effort to establish their proper tax liability and reasonably relied on the advice of their return preparer; therefore, they were not liable for the accuracy-related penalties.

TAX TREATMENT OF R&E AND R&D EXPENSES

Before a recent change in the law (explained next), a taxpayer could elect to currently deduct the amount of certain reasonable research and experimentation (R&E) expenses paid or incurred in connection with a trade or business.[245] The research and development (R&D) credit, computed based upon qualified research expenditures, is a general business tax credit which reduces tax liability (rather than reducing taxable income), if allowed.[246]

Expenses associated with innovative activities that develop a new business product are deductible R&E expenditures, even though the innovations provide future benefits.[247] That can also apply to activities that develop a new chemical that can be applied to seed or crops that enhances productivity. In short, due to the R&E expenditures, the farmer does not need to determine if the expense provides only a current benefit or a benefit that may last into the future. However, the TCJA limited the tax benefit for tax years beginning after 2021.[248]

Note. Agriculture-related businesses deduct R&E expenditures every year as their customer-farmers experiment with different chemicals and fertilizers. The benefit of the credit depends upon weather, soil types, and hardiness of the plants. Expenses associated with product development activities can count, and they may also generate an R&D credit under IRC §41.

---

243. See, e.g., *Krause* v. Comm'r, 92 TC 1003 (1989).

244. See Treas. Reg. §1.469-5T(a). A good case for the detailed evidence that is required to document 100 hours of work in a taxable year is *Leland v. Comm'r,* TC Memo 2015-240 (Dec. 14, 2015).

245. IRC §174.

246. IRC §41.

247. IRC §174.

248. *Tax Cuts and Jobs Act,* PL 115-97, §13206 part 3 subpart A.

DEDUCTIONS FOR R&E EXPENSES

As mentioned previously, through 2021, taxpayers could elect to currently deduct the amount of certain reasonable R&E expenditures in the year paid or incurred in connection with a trade or business.[249] Instead of making the election, a taxpayer could forgo a current deduction, capitalize the expenses, and recover them ratably over the useful life of the research for up to five years. Alternatively, an election could be made to recover them over a period of 10 years. By doing so, the taxpayer would avoid alternative minimum tax (AMT) preferences and adjustments.

> **Note.** Software development costs could be deducted immediately, amortized over five years from the date of completion, or amortized over three years from the date the software was placed in service.[250]

Generally, no current deduction is allowable for expenditures for the acquisition or improvement of land, or of depreciable or depletable property used in connection with any research or experimentation.[251] In addition, no current deduction is allowed for research expenses incurred for the purpose of ascertaining the existence, location, extent, or quality of any deposit of ore or other mineral, including oil and gas.[252]

5

Qualified research is related to developing a product that can be used in the taxpayer's trade or business.[253] It is an activity or project that a taxpayer undertakes to create a new or improved component of the taxpayer's business using a systemic experimentation process that relies on principles of physical or biological sciences, engineering, or computer science designed to evaluate one or more alternatives to achieve a result that was uncertain when the research activity began.[254]

R&E Expenses under the TCJA

The TCJA specifies that for amounts paid or incurred in tax years beginning **after** Dec. 31, 2021, "specified R&E expenses" incurred in the United States **must be capitalized** and amortized ratably over a 5-year period beginning with the midpoint of the tax year in which the specified R&E expenses were paid or incurred.[255]

> **Note.** The provision is one of the permanent provisions of the TCJA that does **not** sunset and return to its pre-2018 version.

The R&E expenses cannot be currently deducted. Amortization continues even if the underlying property is disposed of, retired, or abandoned during that period, with the amortization period beginning at the midpoint of the tax year in which the expenditures are incurred or paid. This effectively limits the first-year deduction to 10% of the IRC §174 expenditures in years one through five, with the remaining 50% deducted in year six.

Example 13. For tax year 2021, Widget Corp., had taxable income of $2 million. Widget's total R&E expenses (domestic) were $400,000. The full $400,000 was deductible in 2021, resulting in a taxable income of $1.6 million. At a 21% corporate rate, the federal income tax due is $336,000.

Assume that Widget Corp. had the same tax situation for 2022. The deduction is 50% of one-fifth of $400,000, which is $40,000. Taxable income is $1.96 million and the resulting federal income tax due would be $411,600 ($1.96 million × 21% federal rate). This is an increase of $75,600 ($411,600 – $336,000) or 22.5% ($75,600 ÷ $336,000).

> **Note.** Software development costs are to be treated as §174 expenses.

---

249. IRC §174.

250. Rev. Proc. 2000-50, 2000-52 IRB 601.

251. IRC §174(c)(1).

252. IRC §174(c)(2).

253. Treas. Reg. §1.174-2(a).

254. Ibid.

255. *Tax Cuts and Jobs Act,* PL 115-97, §13206, amending IRC §174.

The TCJA amendment also specifies that adherence to the new capitalization rules represents a change in the taxpayer's accounting method under IRC §481 that was initiated by the taxpayer and made with IRS's consent. The IRS has added the §174 change to the list of automatic accounting method changes to be made on Form 3115.[256] Instead of filing Form 3115, a taxpayer can file a statement with their return for the first year of adoption only.[257] The statement must include the following information for each applicant.

- Name and EIN
- Year of change
- Designated change number (DCN 265)
- Description of the type of R&E expenditures
- Amount of R&E expenditures paid or incurred
- Declaration that the applicant is changing its method of accounting to amortize R&E expenditures over the applicable 5-year or 15-year period and the change is being made on a cut-off basis

If the expenses are incurred in tax years beginning after December 31, 2025, the provision is applied on **a cut-off basis.** That means there is no adjustment under §481(a) for expenses paid or incurred in tax years that begin before 2026.

> **Note.** For taxpayers engaged in the trade or business of farming, if §174 is not applicable, the expenses incurred are likely to be ordinary and necessary expenses incurred in the ordinary course of the trade or business of farming and, therefore, deductible in the year paid under IRC §162.

R&D TAX CREDIT

The Economic Recovery Tax Act of 1981[258] introduced the credit for increasing research activities. The credit is better known as the research and development credit, or simply the R&D credit. It is a general business credit for R&D costs that a taxpayer either incurs directly or that a third party performs for the taxpayer. A qualified taxpayer is one with under $50 million in average annual gross receipts.[259] The credit offsets both regular tax and AMT.[260] The purpose of the credit as enacted is still the same today — to incentivize research and experimentation by providing a tax credit for activities that develop a new component of a taxpayer's business or improve an existing component's performance, functionality, reliability, or quality.[261]

> **Note.** For more information on the R&D credit, see the 2023 *University of Illinois Federal Tax Workbook,* Chapter 11: New Developments.

256. Rev. Proc. 2023-11, 2023-3 IRB 417.
257. Ibid.
258. *Economic Recovery Tax Act of 1981,* PL 97-34.
259. IRC §38(c)(5)(A)(iii).
260. IRC §38(c)(1).
261. IRC §41(d)(3)(A).

For certain defined smaller businesses, the credit can offset the employer portion of social security taxes up to $500,000 (with some limitations).[262] Smaller businesses for purposes of the R&D credit are those with less than $5 million in gross receipts for the applicable taxable year and no gross receipts for any of the five preceding taxable years.[263]

Observation. Claiming the R&D credit can partially offset the higher tax liability (post-2021) from the TCJA change to §174. For the year in which the R&D credit is claimed, the wages, supplies, and 65% of contract research expenses need not be amortized based on the §174 rules when calculating the R&D credit.

Note. While R&D expenses qualify as R&E expenses under §174, not all R&E expenses qualify for the R&D credit. Costs for facilities and depreciation, among others, must still be amortized.

While the R&D credit is available to a wide array of businesses, including farming businesses, primary questions surround the provision's scope of application.

5

Definitions

As noted previously, the R&D credit applies to activities (including research and software development) that develop a new business component or improve an existing component's performance, functionality, reliability, or quality.[264] A **business component** is "any product, process, computer software, technique, formula, or invention which is to be held for sale, lease, or license," or which is used by the taxpayer in the taxpayer's trade or business. The credit equals a percentage of the taxpayer's current year **qualified research expenses (QREs)** that exceed a base amount. Expenses that are incurred with respect to a qualified activity are used to compute the R&D credit and are QREs. A QRE can result from in-house activity as well as expenses incurred via contracts. For in-house activity, a QRE includes wages on Form W-2, *Wage and Tax Statement,* paid to employees that are either directly involved in an activity (including research) that develops, supervises, or supports a new business, as well as the cost of supplies and payments for qualified services (e.g., consultants and engineers).[265]

Under certain federal farm programs, especially those programs designed to provide environmental benefits, the U.S. Department of Agriculture (USDA) shares part of the expense associated with complying with the program.[266] While the expense associated with establishing a conservation/environmental structure/program on the farm might otherwise qualify as a QRE, the portion that the government subsidizes (via IRC §126) would not be a QRE because the taxpayer did not incur the cost. In addition, as explained next, qualified expenses would be limited to a test plot rather than those incurred for an entire field (e.g., research expenses associated with an entire field compared to another field that used different sprays, etc.). For farm taxpayers, this is a key point of understanding. The taxpayer must determine to what extent expenses are merely operating expenses (not QREs) or valid expenses toward the R&D credit.

---

262. *The Inflation Reduction Act of 2022,* PL 117-169, increased the credit amount from $250,000 to $500,000 for qualified small businesses for tax years beginning after December 31, 2022. See IRC §41(h)(4)(B)(i)(II).

263. IRC §41(h)(3)(A).

264. Treas. Reg. §1.41-4(a).

265. IRC §41(b); see also *Suder v. Comm'r*, TC Memo 2014-201 (Oct. 1, 2014).

266. See, e.g., IRC §126.

An expense is a QRE if it satisfies the following 4-part test.

1. **Qualified purpose test.** The research activity must be intended to discover information that is applied to develop or improve the functionality, quality, etc., of a business component. A business component is any product, process, computer software, technique, formula, or invention which is to be held for lease, sale, license, or use in the taxpayer's trade or business.[267]
2. **Technological nature test.** The process of experimentation used to discover information must fundamentally rely on principles of the physical or biological sciences, engineering, or computer science.[268]
3. **Experimentation test.** Substantially all (80% or more) of the activities must employ a process of experimentation.[269] A process of experimentation is a process that is designed to evaluate one or more alternatives (through, for example, modeling, simulation, or a systematic trial and error methodology) to achieve a desired result where the capability or the method of achieving that result, or the appropriate design of that result, is uncertain as of the beginning of the taxpayer's research activities.[270]
4. **Uncertainty test.** The process of experimentation/research must be designed to eliminate uncertainty (regarding the company's capability, methodology, or appropriateness of design of a business component).[271]

Note. Each of the four tests applies separately to each business component a taxpayer uses as the factual basis for the research credit claim.[272] In addition, the application of the four tests under §41(d)(1) to business components and requirements related to the four tests does not change if a taxpayer uses a statistical sample under Rev. Proc. 2011-42[273] to substantiate a research credit claim. This does not change when the IRS uses a statistical sample to audit a research credit claim.

Note. Treas. Reg. §1.41-4A(d) provides a general exclusion for funded research. It states that research funded by any grant, contract, or otherwise by another person, including any governmental entity, does not constitute qualified research for purposes of the research credit. In addition, all agreements entered into between the taxpayer performing the research and other persons must be considered in determining the extent to which the research is funded — not only research contracts.

267. IRC §41(d)(1)(B)(ii); Treas. Reg. §1.41-4(a)(2)(i).
268. IRC §41(d)(1)(B)(i); Treas. Reg. §1.41-4(a)(4).
269. IRC §41(d)(1)(C).
270. Treas. Reg. §1.41-4(a)(2)(iii).
271. IRC §41(d)(1)(A); Treas Reg. §1.41-4(a)(2).
272. FAA 20212501F (May 10, 2021).
273. Rev. Proc. 2011-42, 2011-37 IRB 318.

Illustrative Cases

- In *Max v. Comm'r,*[274] a fashion designer's multistep process of designing garments failed three tests of the 4-part test and, therefore, did not constitute qualified research. The Tax Court determined that the petitioner failed the "uncertainty" test because its activities were not "investigative" in nature as it already had the requisite information to solve problems as they arose. The petitioner's employees had already faced the uncertainties in prior years — how to align prints, alter standard patterns for the plus-size line, fit garments, and cut fabrics along the proper grain. Thus, these issues were not uncertainties as contemplated by §174. The Tax Court also found that the petitioner failed the technological nature test because the taxpayer's fit testing was not engineering, draping fabric was not materials science, and shrinkage tests were not chemistry. The petitioner failed the experimentation test because the petitioner's "method of simple trial and error" was not akin to the scientific method or a systematic trial and error methodology. In addition, the Tax Court held that the petitioner did not prove that substantially all the garments underwent a process of experimentation.

- In *Little Sandy Coal Co. v. Comm'r,*[275] the Tax Court held that the petitioner failed to show that "substantially all" the activities in developing vessels satisfied the experimentation test. The petitioner claimed that because the vast majority of the vessel, including every major system on the vessel, was re-engineered and redesigned, the "substantially all" requirement was met. Alternatively, the petitioner claimed that 87% of employee development time involved elements of the vessel that differed from the previous model. The Tax Court disagreed, concluding that the "substantially all" requirement applies in reference to activities and not the physical elements of the business component being developed or improved. The Tax Court also pointed out that direct support does not constitute qualified research and is not included in the numerator in determining whether substantially all the taxpayer's activities constitute elements of a process of experimentation.

- In *Harper v. Comm'r,*[276] the Tax Court held that the IRS failed to show a military structures builder was not entitled to $825,300 in tax credits for R&E expenses. The petitioner specialized in military design-build projects, including over 30 military housing projects. The IRS claimed that the designs were not tangible "products" under §41. The Tax Court rejected the IRS position on the basis that the designs could still potentially constitute "processes, techniques, or inventions" which would qualify under §41. This is a significant taxpayer win.

Example 14. In 2023, Acme Co. incurs the following employee hours and wage expense in developing a new product.

- **Qualified research.** 600 engineering hours ($72,000 of wage expense) in developing and testing the new product
- **Direct supervision.** 60 manager hours ($9,000 of wage expense) directly supervising the engineering team developing and testing the new product
- **Direct support.** 120 production hours ($9,600 of wage expense) for machining prototypes of the new product used in qualified research

The total number of employee hours incurred is 780 at a cumulative wage expense of $90,600.

Acme Co.'s development activities do not satisfy the "substantially all" requirement of the process of experimentation test at the product level because the qualified research constitutes only 77% (600 ÷ 780) of employee hours and only 79.5% ($72,000 ÷ $90,600) of the wage expense relate to the performance of qualified research. Thus, Acme Co. can either not claim the R&D credit, apply the "shrinking back" rule to find discreet elements of the new product that satisfy the "substantially all" requirement, or review the manager or production hours to see whether some of those hours constitute qualified research.

---

274. *Max v. Comm'r,* TC Memo 2021-37 (Mar. 29, 2021).

275. *Little Sandy Coal Co. v. Comm'r,* TC Memo 2021-15 (Feb. 11, 2021).

276. *Harper v. Comm'r,* TC Memo 2023-57 (May 10, 2023).

Mechanics of the R&D Tax Credit

Once the qualified activities and QREs are determined, the R&D tax credit is 6% of eligible expenses for each of the first three years that qualified research activities are conducted.[277] After that, the alternative simplified method sets the R&D credit at 14% of the excess of QREs for the tax year over 50% of the average QREs for the three preceding tax years multiplied by 79% (factoring in a reduction via IRC §280C).[278] The reduction factor is 1 minus the highest corporate tax rate and increased from 65% to 79% upon enactment of the TCJA.

Example 15. Bucky is trying to determine his R&D credit for 2023. Because this is his 4th year of incurring research activity expenses, Bucky applies the alternative simplified credit computation. Assume that Bucky incurs QREs of $50,000 in 2020, $62,500 in 2021, and $75,000 in 2022. The average over those three years is $62,500. For 2023, Bucky incurs $75,000 of QREs. From that amount, Bucky subtracts 50% of the average QREs for the prior three years, or $31,250 ($62,500 × 50%) resulting in $43,750 eligible costs ($75,000 QRE − $31,250). That amount is then multiplied by 14%, resulting in a preliminary credit of $6,125. Bucky elects the reduced credit under §280C to avoid reducing his deductible expenses by the amount of the R&D credit. The $6,125 amount is then multiplied by 79% (the §280C credit reduction), which yields an R&D credit of $4,839. The instructions for Form 6765, *Credit for Increasing Research Activities,* are instrumental in properly computing the credit and accurately completing Form 6765. Bucky claims the credit in Section B as shown on the following Form 6765.

Section B—Alternative Simplified Credit. Skip this section if you are completing Section A.

18	Certain amounts paid or incurred to energy consortia (see the line 1 instructions)			18	0
19	Basic research payments to qualified organizations (see the line 2 instructions)	19	0		
20	Qualified organization base period amount (see the line 3 instructions)	20	0		
21	Subtract line 20 from line 19. If zero or less, enter -0-			21	0
22	Add lines 18 and 21			22	0
23	Multiply line 22 by 20% (0.20)			23	0
24	Wages for qualified services (do not include wages used in figuring the work opportunity credit)	24	75,000		
25	Cost of supplies	25			
26	Rental or lease costs of computers (see the line 7 instructions)	26			
27	Enter the applicable percentage of contract research expenses. See the line 8 instructions	27			
28	Total qualified research expenses. Add lines 24 through 27	28	75,000		
29	Enter your total qualified research expenses for the prior 3 tax years. If you had no qualified research expenses in any one of those years, skip lines 30 and 31	29	187,500		
30	Divide line 29 by 6.0	30	31,250		
31	Subtract line 30 from line 28. If zero or less, enter -0-	31	43,750		
32	Multiply line 31 by 14% (0.14). If you skipped lines 30 and 31, multiply line 28 by 6% (0.06)			32	6,125
33	Add lines 23 and 32			33	6,125
34	Are you electing the reduced credit under section 280C? ▶ Yes ☒ No ☐ If "Yes," multiply line 33 by 79% (0.79). If "No," enter the amount from line 33 and see the line 17 instructions for the statement that must be attached. Members of controlled groups or businesses under common control, see instructions for the statement that must be attached			34	4,839

For Paperwork Reduction Act Notice, see separate instructions. Cat. No. 13700H Form **6765** (Rev. 12-2020)

Note. If a taxpayer does not incur at least the level of QREs that Bucky did in the preceding example, it may not be worth the extra recordkeeping and tax preparation cost of claiming the credit.

277. IRC §41(c)(5)(B)(ii).

278. IRC §§41(c)(5) and (h).

Privately held businesses having $50 million or less in average gross receipts for the three preceding tax years can use the R&D credit to offset the AMT.[279] Additionally, start-up companies, or those with less than $5 million in gross receipts for the current tax year and no gross receipts for the five preceding years, may use R&D credits against their payroll tax liability.[280]

Recordkeeping

A taxpayer claiming the R&D credit must retain records in a sufficiently usable form and detail to substantiate that the expenditures claimed are eligible for the credit.[281]

Research Credit Refund Claims

A refund will be disallowed unless the taxpayer files a valid claim for refund before the expiration of the limitations period under IRC §6511.[282] A valid claim for refund must set forth in detail each ground upon which the refund is claimed and facts sufficient to establish the exact basis of the refund claim.[283]

The IRS requires a taxpayer to include minimum facts in a refund claim for it to be valid under the specificity requirement for research credit refund claims filed on or after January 10, 2022.[284] At a minimum, a research credit refund claim must:[285]

1. Identify all the business components to which the research credit refund claim relates for the tax year;
2. For each business component, identify all research activities performed, all individuals who performed each research activity, and all the information each individual sought to discover; and
3. Provide the total qualified employee wage expenses, total qualified supply expenses, and total qualified contract research expenses for the claim year, which may be done on Form 6765.

The IRS requires taxpayers provide the facts in a written statement rather than the production of supporting documents, such as a research credit study, unless the taxpayer specifies the exact pages in the documents a specific fact. The taxpayer must verify the accuracy of the facts provided by signed declaration under the penalty of perjury. In most cases, the signature on the amended return will satisfy this requirement. Instead of specific names of each individual who performed each research activity, taxpayers may identify the individuals by listing their titles or positions. Information may be aggregated but must identify the specific number of individuals and each individual's title or position.[286]

Note. For additional information about the required documentation and the particulars of a refund claim, see **uofi.tax/23x5x1** [www.irs.gov/businesses/corporations/research-credit-claims-section-41-on-amended-returns-frequently-asked-questions].

279. IRC §38(c)(5)(A)(iii).
280. IRC §§41(h)(3)(A)(i) and (4)(B)(i).
281. Treas. Reg. §1.41-4(d).
282. Treas. Reg. §301.6402-2(a)(1).
283. Treas. Reg. §301.6402-2(b)(1).
284. FAA 20214101F (Sep. 17, 2021).
285. Ibid.
286. Ibid.

Transition Period[287]

A transition period exists through January 10, 2024, during which taxpayers have 45 days to perfect an R&D credit refund claim before the IRS's final determination on the claim. If during the transition period an R&D credit refund claim is determined to be deficient, the taxpayer will be mailed a letter providing 45 days to perfect the claim. If the IRS does not receive the information or the missing information is insufficient, the entire claim for refund will be rejected.

Application to Agriculture

As noted previously, the R&D credit applies to costs incurred associated with research to develop new products or improve existing ones. It is important that the research involves technological information or some sort of application that is intended to develop new or improved business products or processes. It is also important that the research activities have a process of experimentation that relates to a new or improved function, performance, reliability, efficiency, or quality.

The kind of research activities on a farm that generates qualified expenses for the R&D credit are those that are new to the farm and involve testing of something before it can be used on a larger scale. For farmers, the credit could potentially have a wide application – farmers often are tinkering or investigating ways to improve productivity or efficiency of crop or livestock production. Common examples might include:

- Testing new fungicides and seed treatment in an attempt to control insect disease;
- Testing precision planting equipment in an effort to find ways to increase efficiency and/or yield;
- Experimenting with organic fertilizer or a cover crop to determine the impact on soil fertility and/or soil erosion;
- Trying new cultivation techniques such as strip tillage;
- Experimenting with irrigation and drainage and determining the impact on soil productivity and/or erosion;
- Coming up with new weed/pest management techniques;
- Experimenting with crop genetics;
- Testing various planting dates, plant population, and row spacing to determine the impact on plant growth and development;
- Testing combines and other harvesting equipment to minimize crop waste and/or decrease harvest time;
- Working on customized animal feed formulations;
- Developing customized software; and
- Researching and designing new grain bins.

Observation. The R&D credit can have a broad application to many activities that occur on a farm or ranch. But, the IRS is unlikely to allow the R&D credit to be applied to the whole farm. The credit is for R&D — in other words, something that would occur in a laboratory. The entire farm is not a laboratory, but a test plot is. It is likely that the IRS will argue that the qualified research activities (which give rise to QREs) would have to occur in a test plot or similar research focused area, with expenses (including qualified wages, and the cost of chemicals, fertilizer, seed, etc.) allocated to the specific area of the test plot. That will result in a small number for most farmers, especially in the Midwest. Higher value crops, such as potatoes, onions, and fruits, might have bigger numbers, but the point remains that the QREs (and, hence, the R&D credit) must be associated with a test plot or similar research focused area and not the entire farm.

---

287. *Research Credit Claims (Section 41) on Amended Returns Frequently Asked Questions.* Oct. 4, 2022. IRS. [www.irs.gov/businesses/corporations/research-credit-claims-section-41-on-amended-returns-frequently-asked-questions] Accessed on Jul. 6, 2023.

Caution. The IRS has been focused on abuses with the R&D credit for the past few years. In situations where the IRS has suspected abuses, it has threatened to turn CPA firms over to the IRS Office of Professional Responsibility.[288] On May 20, 2022, the IRS Criminal Investigation Division raided the Houston headquarters of R&D tax consulting firm, Alliantgroup. Related to that raid, the IRS subpoenaed various CPA firms that referred clients to Alliantgroup and sought client tax returns as part of the investigation. The government's demand references R&D tax credits, cost segregation, and IRC §179D (commercial buildings energy efficiency deduction) and any related information from as far back as January 1, 2011.

AGRICULTURE-RELATED RULINGS AND CASES

5

EXCISE TAX

Excise Tax Expense Rather Than Gross Excise Tax Liability Used in Computing Cost of Goods Sold for Fuel Blender

***Growmark, Inc. v. Comm'r,* 160 TC 11 (May 16, 2023)**

Growmark, Inc., an agricultural supply cooperative that also blends fuel (including ethanol and biodiesel), serves the supply needs of its member-patrons that are primarily independent farmers. Growmark incurred an IRC §4801 fuel excise tax liability when it removed a taxable fuel that it owned as a position holder (holding inventory in a fuel distribution facility) from a rack at a distribution facility. Growmark also incurred the §4801 tax regarding gallons of ethanol and biodiesel that Growmark removed and sold as part of an alcohol fuel mixture or biodiesel mixture. During the tax years at issue, the excise tax reflected Growmark's fuel mixtures for sale to third parties for use as a fuel. The ethanol that Growmark produced and then blended with taxable fuel was eligible for either the alcohol fuel mixture excise tax credit[289] or the alcohol mixture income tax credit.[290] However, Growmark only claimed the alcohol fuel and biodiesel mixture excise tax credits under IRC §6426 for all the alcohol fuel and biodiesel mixtures it produced and sold during 2009 and 2010.

Growmark filed Form 720, *Quarterly Excise Tax Credit Tax Return*, for each of the quarters beginning or ending within its tax years 2009-2010 and claimed the credit. As a fuel blender, Growmark could reduce its taxable income from fuel mixture sales by subtracting its cost of goods sold (COGS), including certain federal excise taxes. For each year in issue, Growmark filed Form 1120-C, *U.S. Income Tax Return for Cooperative Associations,* on which it included in its COGS its actual excise tax expense (excise tax liability less the amount of tax credits allowed under §6426). That caused Growmark's COGS to be lower and its taxable income higher than it would have been had its excise tax liability not been reduced by the tax credits it received. Growmark later claimed that it could claim its gross excise tax liability unreduced by the tax credits it received as part of its COGS. The IRS disagreed. Thus, the issue was whether Growmark had to reduce deductions based on fuel tax liability or include the refundable fuel tax credits in income.

---

288. *Galleria High Rise Offices Target of IRS Criminal Investigators Friday [UPDATED].* Downing, Margaret. May 20, 2022. Houston Press. [www.houstonpress.com/news/irs-raids-galleria-offices-13421664] Accessed on Aug. 18, 2023.

289. IRC §§6426(a)(1) and (b).

290. IRC §40(a)(1).

The IRS had previously taken the position that when there is no actual excise tax liability, a purely refundable fuel tax credit does not reduce any deduction for fuel or create any addition to income.[291] When there is actual fuel tax liability, the IRS's position is that the credits must first offset this liability and reduce the deduction for tax expense (or COGS) or be included in income.[292] The IRS has also won several court cases on the issue.[293] The Tax Court agreed with the IRS, noting that the legislative history and the statutory construction support the conclusion that the tax credits must first be used to offset tax liability — actual excise expense rather than gross excise tax liability — must be used to calculate COGS.

> **Note.** The facts of the case did not allow the Tax Court to address the situation where the entity generating the fuel tax credit is separate from the activity generating the excise tax liability. Potentially, it could be possible to achieve the result the petitioner sought by structuring the taxpayer's business differently.

HOBBY LOSS

IRS Focuses on Wrong Issues — Loses Hobby Loss Argument and Misses Reallocation Argument

***Carson v. Comm'r*, No. 23086-21S (U.S. Tax Ct. Mar. 22, 2023)**

The Oklahoma ranch at issue was originally owned by Leslyn Jo Carson's grandmother and then inherited by Leslyn Jo's mother. In 2009, as part of a family succession plan, Leslyn Jo's mother transferred the ranch to a revocable trust. Under the trust's terms, if Leslyn Jo's mother died and was predeceased by Leslyn Jo's stepfather, the ranch would pass equally to Leslyn Jo and her brother. If Leslyn Jo's stepfather was alive at the time of Leslyn Jo's mother's death, the ranch would remain in trust for his life and then be distributed equally to Leslyn Jo and her brother upon their stepfather's death. Leslyn Jo and her mother executed two separate agreements in 2013 and 2016, whereby Leslyn Jo agreed to contribute financially to the ranch and that Leslyn Jo and her mother would jointly agree about the amount, if any, of cash distributions from ranch earnings that would be made to Leslyn Jo.

From 2014 to 2019, Leslyn Jo paid the ranch expenses, but her mother reported on her return the income from cattle sales. Leslyn Jo did not receive any cash distributions from ranching activities and did not report ranch income. Leslyn Jo's children participated in rodeos, and the income from the rodeo activities was reported on Leslyn Jo's Schedule F under "livestock activities." For 2017, the Carson's Schedule F reported gross income of $2,741 and deductions of $128,990 from the ranching activity. For 2018, the Carson's Schedule F reported gross income of $8,063, including $1,867 of compensation for labor services performed by the children for local ranches and $6,196 for the children's rodeo competition winnings. Expense deductions claimed on Schedule F were $133,929. From 2014-2019, the Carsons reported cumulative losses of $502,742 on Schedule F which far exceeded the cumulative Schedule F gross income and largely offset the Carson's ordinary income (primarily wage income). The IRS audited the couple and determined that the Schedule F activity was rodeo and not ranching, ignoring the fact that the Schedule F expenses were predominantly from the ranching activity. As a result, the IRS determined that the rodeo activity was not engaged in with the requisite profit motive and disallowed all Schedule F deductions for 2017 and 2018.

---

291. CCA 201342010 (Aug. 29, 2013).

292. See IRS Notice 2015-65, 2015-35 IRB 235; CCA 201406001 (Jan. 13, 2014).

293. See *Sunoco, Inc. v. U.S.*, 908 F.3d 710 (Fed. Cir. 2018), *cert. denied*, 140 S. Ct. 46 (2019); *Delek US Holdings, Inc. v. U.S.*, 32 F.4th 495 (6th Cir. 2022); *Exxon Mobil Corporation v. U.S.*, 43 F. 4th 424 (5th Cir. 2022).

The Tax Court determined that the IRS had focused improperly on the rodeo activity rather than the ranching activity. The Tax Court further noted that the Carsons credibly testified that the Schedule F activities primarily related to the ranch and not to rodeos. As such, the losses related to the ranching activity and not the rodeo activity, and the IRS failed to challenge the profit motive of the ranching activity. The Tax Court refused to allow the IRS to refocus its challenge to the Schedule F deductions on the ranching activity, holding that the IRS had waived its right to do so. **Thus, the activity reported on Schedule F for 2017 and 2018 was deemed to be engaged in for profit.**

Observation. It could be expected that the IRS would question the arrangement between Leslyn Jo and her mother. It was not anticipated that the IRS would focus solely on the Schedule F income that resulted solely from the rodeo activity of the Carson children. The arrangement between Leslyn Jo and her mother was more akin to that of a partnership, and the fact that the ranch was in a revocable trust meant that the mother could revoke the trust at any time. This possibly led to an IRS argument that there really was not a trade or business activity being conducted. Indeed, the expenses Leslyn Jo paid were really the trust's expenses. It was the trust that was conducting the trade or business activity. Clearly, the arrangement was designed to prevent Leslyn Jo from recognizing any income. But, the IRS made the mistaken assertion that the primary purpose of the business was to fund the rodeo activities of the children, and failed to acquire and analyze relevant information about the nature of the ranching activity.

In *Carson*, because the IRS did not focus on a partnership arrangement between Leslyn Jo and her mother, it also did not press a reallocation argument. The IRS has broad powers to reallocate income, deductions, credits, or allowances as necessary to reflect economic reality or prevent tax evasion.[294]

In a 2010 case, the U.S. Tax Court again used the assignment of income doctrine in another farm case involving a "midstream" incorporation. In *Slota v. Comm'r,*[295] a farm couple operated a sole proprietorship farming operation. Income from the operation consisted of proceeds from the sale of crops and the receipt of federal farm program payments. The crop income and the farm program income was deposited into the couple's personal farm account. In September of 2005, the couple formed a corporation and named themselves as the sole shareholders and directors. They did not execute a deed, sales contract, or any written agreement that transferred or leased the couple's farmland to the corporation. They did transfer to the corporation $10,000 from their personal bank account to establish the corporate account. After incorporation, in October 2005, Mr. Slota deposited the 2005 government payments (except one) into their personal account. That one government payment was deposited into the corporate account. Later in October, Mr. Slota transferred the balance of the USDA payments and the crop sale proceeds to the corporate account. For 2005, the Slotas reported $195,938 from crop sales and $61,416 in farm program payments on Schedule F. They claimed an expense deduction for $44,165 of USDA payments and $20,532 of crop sale proceeds that they had put in the corporate account. They reported $481 of SE tax liability. For the fiscal year ending September 30, 2006, the corporation reported $370,647 of income, but completely offset it by expenses.

The IRS disagreed with the Slota's reporting, attributing to the couple all the funds that were deposited into or transferred to the corporate account in 2005 (except the one government payment). The IRS increased the Slotas' tax liability to $28,445 under the assignment of income doctrine. While the Slotas argued that they transferred their crops to the corporation, the IRS did not agree. The IRS noted that the Slotas had already reduced the crops to income before transferring the crop income (proceeds) to the corporation. Consequently, the couple earned the income before transferring it to the corporation. Likewise, because the USDA payments were issued in the couple's names, those payments were not corporate income.

---

294. IRC §482; see, e.g., *Rooney v. U.S.,* 305 F.2d 681 (9th Cir. 1962). The IRS was upheld in reallocating production expenses incurred by the individual taxpayer to a newly formed corporation. The case involved a July 31 transfer of a growing hop crop (which had been sold under contract the prior January 22) to a new corporation with the crop harvested in late August and early September.

295. *Slota v. Comm'r,* TC Summ. Op. 2010-152 (Oct. 12, 2010).

The court agreed with the IRS, applying the assignment of income doctrine. The court specifically noted that the Slotas had no documents indicating that they had actually transferred the land or the crops to the corporation. All they transferred was the proceeds of the crops and the government payments that had been paid to them personally.

LODGING AND MEALS

Value of Employer-Provided Housing Not Excludable from Income

***Smith v. Comm'r*, TC Memo 2023-6 (Jan. 12, 2023)**

The value of meals and lodging furnished on the business premises for the employer's convenience and as a condition of employment are not taxable income to the employee (and the employee's spouse and dependents) and are deductible by the employer if they are provided in-kind.[296] Likewise, the value of meals and lodging furnished on the business premises for the convenience of the employer are not wages for Federal Insurance Contributions Act (FICA) and Federal Unemployment Tax Act (FUTA) purposes.

Note. As an employer-provided fringe benefit, the meals and lodging arrangement is available only to an individual who is an employee of a C corporation. Owners of other entities cannot take advantage of this fringe benefit. For instance, sole proprietors and partners in a partnership do not have the necessary employee status to qualify for the fringe benefit. Also, IRC §1372 bars S corporation employees who own, directly or indirectly, more than 2% of the outstanding stock from receiving tax-free fringe benefits, including the IRC §119 meals and lodging fringe benefit. In addition, with respect to S corporations, the IRC §318 attribution rules apply in determining who is considered an S corporation shareholder.[297]

Cory Smith was an Air Force veteran and engineer who accepted an offer of employment with a defense contractor to work as an engineer in Australia. He was given options for housing: a furnished house for which he would have to report the fair rental value on his return, or a payment to compensate him for the cost of owning or renting housing. He accepted company-provided housing approximately 11 miles from his work location. After eight years of living in the company-provided housing, the company ceased providing housing and he had to find housing on his own.

For 2016 and 2017, Cory reported the value of the housing provided to him on his return, but then filed amended returns claiming an offsetting deduction for "employee benefit programs." On his 2018 return, he reported the value of the housing but also claimed a deduction for "employee benefit programs." The IRS disallowed the deductions.

The Tax Court noted that certain conditions must be satisfied to exclude the value of employer-provided lodging from income under §119. For example, the lodging must be furnished for the convenience of the employer, furnished on the business premises, and the employee must be required to accept the lodging as a condition of employment. The Tax Court determined that the lodging was not furnished on the business premises. Cory's occasional business activities at the home were not sufficient to establish the housing was integral to his business activities and the housing was not necessary for the performance of his duties.

Note. The phrase "on the business premises" has been the subject of extensive judicial interpretation. But the principles have been applied relatively uniformly. A key case on the matter is *Benninghoff v. Comm'r,*[298] where the court noted that the "touchstone" of the business premises test is the lodging's relationship to the business activity of the employer. In other words, the lodging must bear an integral relationship to the business activity of the employer.

296. IRC §119. This tax treatment is available only for meals and lodging furnished to *employees*, not *tenants*. See *Weeldreyer v. Comm'r,* TC Memo 2003-324 (Nov. 25, 2003); *Schmidt v. Comm'r,* TC Memo 2003-325 (Nov. 25, 2003); *Tschetter v. Comm'r,* TC Memo 2003-326 (Nov. 25, 2003); *Waterfall Farms, Inc. v. Comm'r,* TC Memo 2003-327 (Nov. 25, 2003).

297. The IRS will not issue rulings on whether the value of meals or lodging is excludable from gross income by an employee who is a controlling shareholder of the corporate employer. Rev. Proc. 2013-3, 2013-1 IRB 113.

298. *Benninghoff v. Comm'r*, 71 TC 216 (1978).

Meals that are provided to employees during working hours without the furnishing of lodging must be furnished for substantial non-compensatory business reasons of the employer. Examples include emergency call situations, employer business activity that permits a short meal break, and insufficient eating facilities in the vicinity of the employer's premises.[299]

A significant question is whether the value of groceries furnished to an employee that the employee then prepares into meals is eligible for the exclusion. The IRS claims that it is not.[300] However, the courts have ruled that either the employer or the employee may prepare the groceries into meals if the arrangement otherwise meets the requirements of §119.[301] The issue is not settled. Some courts have held that groceries are included under the definition of meals, but other courts and the IRS have ruled that the value of groceries is not meals and is includable in an employee's gross income.

For the value of lodging to be excluded, the employee must be required to accept the lodging on the premises as a condition of employment (such as for security reasons, livestock observation, or periodic chores). The lodging must be provided in-kind. Cash allowances for lodging (and meals) are includable in gross income to the extent the allowance constitutes compensation.[302]

5

The litigated cases on this issue date back to the 1930s. The first pair of cases involved individuals working for the Dole Corporation in Hawaii. These individuals were plantation managers in pineapple fields, and they argued that they were required to remain on the premises and, as such, the value of meals and lodging provided to them by the corporation should not be included in their income. They prevailed in court.

In a 1948 case, the rental value of a corporate-owned farmhouse occupied by the sole shareholder of the farm corporation was included in the shareholder's taxable income. In a 1966 Wyoming case, *Wilhelm v. U.S.*,[303] the taxpayers owned a ranch in a remote location several miles from the nearest town. The taxpayers transferred the ranch, ranch house, and all the equipment to the corporation and attempted to live in the house tax-free. The corporation also bought the food and treated it as a deductible expense. The IRS challenged the practice. The Federal District Court for the District of Wyoming ruled against the IRS and noted that the ranch was a grass ranch that put up very little hay and required constant attention by persons experienced in grass ranch requirements to keep cattle alive. The court also noted that during snowstorms, the cattle needed to be fed daily, needed to be moved, waterholes had to be kept open, and the cattle had to be protected against the hazards of being trapped or falling into ravines. The court felt that the employees had no other choice but to accept the facilities furnished by the corporate employer, and that the food and lodging were furnished to the employees not only for the convenience of the employer, but were indispensable to have the employees on the job at all times.

---

299. Treas. Reg. §1.119-1(a)(2).

300. Rev. Rul. 77-80, 1977-1 CB 36.

301. *Jacobs v. Comm'r,* 493 F.2d 1294 (3d Cir. 1974) (the definition of groceries included non-food items such as napkins, toilet tissue, and soap, because these items were an integral part of furnishing meals and lodging); *Harrison v. Comm'r,* TC Memo 1981-211 (Apr. 28, 1981) (corporate employees (farm wives) bought the groceries and converted them into meals which were then furnished to the corporate employees and their families on the farm premises; farm wives were paid a small annual salary with their duties defined as including the preparation of meals for corporate employees).

302. See, e.g., Ltr. Rul. 9801023 (Sep. 30, 1997).

303. *Wilhelm v. U.S.* 257 F. Supp 16 (D. Wyo. 1966).

The *Wilhelm* case was a very important decision, but it also raised the question of how a court would view the situation if the corporation were located in a less remote area. In 1971, the U.S. Court of Appeals for the 9th Circuit addressed this issue in the context of a grape and crop farming operation in *Caratan v. Comm'r.*[304] In *Caratan*, the corporation was located within a 10-minute drive from a residential area of a nearby town. Company policy required supervisory and management personnel to reside on the farm. Company-owned lodging was supplied free of charge for this purpose. The court, in ruling against the IRS, held that the issue was not the remoteness of the corporation, but whether there was a good business reason to require the employees to remain on the premises. The court indicated that the nature of the farming enterprise would determine the reasonableness of requiring employees to reside on the premises rather than the location of the corporation from the nearest town. Whether corporate business required around the clock work such as the case with a grain drying operation, a farrow-to-finish operation, a dairy, or a cattle ranch with characteristics similar to the ranch involved in the *Wilhelm* case was the real issue.

Historically, cash grain operations have had the greatest difficulty in successfully excluding the cost of lodging and meals provided by the corporation to employees. The IRS has difficulty in accepting the fact that grain farmers simply cannot lock up their machinery after the fall harvest, return the next spring and expect it to still be there. The IRS does not put much weight on security, and thinks there is no reason why a grain farmer cannot live in town if all that occurs is the planting, cultivating, and harvesting of a crop. On the other hand, livestock ventures or those that are irrigating or drying grain typically have had better success against an IRS challenge. For example, taxpayers were successful in one case involving only a grain operation with the emphasis on grain drying as a reason to be on the premises on a continuing basis.[305]

Note. For farming and ranching corporations attempting to exclude the cost of meals and lodging from employees' income, there should be a resolution by the board of directors clearly setting forth the requirement that employees are required to live on the premises.[306] Sometimes this resolution is questioned because the same people who make the decision as members of the board of directors are the same people who are also employees living in the corporation's house and eating the corporation's food. Thus, while it is not necessarily an arm's length determination, such a resolution should be adopted.

A 1994 decision from the same court (but a different judge) that decided *Wilhelm* in 1966 declared that the reasoning in *Wilhelm* "is no longer persuasive." In *Dilts v. U.S.*,[307] the court disallowed the deductibility of the value of the shareholder's food and lodging from their taxable income. The case involved an unusual set of facts where the taxpayers, to get around the limits applicable to S corporations, argued that the operation was really a partnership and cited a 1968 case treating partners as employees (one of the few cases to do so). The court in *Dilts* rejected that argument. Although not part of the holding, the court then proceeded to criticize the tax code provision allowing meals and lodging to be excluded from shareholders' incomes. The court cited public policy concerns and congressional intent to treat similarly situated people as similar for tax purposes to achieve "horizontal equity." The court reasoned that it would be inequitable to allow corporate shareholders to receive benefits in the form of exclusions that are unavailable to sole proprietors.

Observation. The *Dilts* case is out of step with the IRS, Tax Court, and the Circuit Courts of Appeal that have decided cases in this area.

---

304. *Caratan v. Comm'r,* 442 F.2d 606 (9th Cir. 1971).

305. *Johnson v. Comm'r,* TC Memo 1985-175 (Apr. 8, 1985); compare with *J. Grant Farms, Inc. v. Comm'r,* TC Memo 1985-174 (Apr. 8, 1985) (swine raising and grain drying operation).

306. Corporate resolutions that authorized the construction of a residence on the farm business premises for the controlling shareholder that focused on the need to entertain business visitors at the corporate location to justify the construction of the residence, rather than the need for ongoing poultry breeding activities, weakened the corporation's argument that the controlling shareholder was required to live in the corporate residence as a condition of employment, resulting in a loss of the exclusion. *Peterson v. Comm'r,* TC Memo 1966-196 (Sep. 2, 1966) (controlling shareholder had also resided in a nearby community for about the prior 10 years while managing the farming business).

307. *Dilts v. U.S.*, 845 F. Supp. 1505 (D. Wyo. 1994).

CONSERVATION EASEMENTS

Penalties Imposed on Donated Conservation Easement Transaction

***Plateau Holdings, LLC, Waterfall Development Manager, LLC, Tax Matters Partner v. Comm'r,* TC Memo 2021-133 (Nov. 30, 2021).**

Plateau donated a conservation easement to a qualified charity and claimed a $25.5 million charitable donation deduction. The IRS challenged the valuation of the easement and its validity in an earlier decision. The Tax Court agreed, disallowed the deduction, and imposed a 40% penalty for gross overvaluation of the easements. The deduction was disallowed because the easements were not protected in perpetuity. This was due to a provision in the deeds granting the easements to the charity that reduced the charity's proportionate share of the sale proceeds by an impermissible carve-out for donor improvements upon a judicial extinguishment of the easements. In the present case, the IRS sought an additional 20% penalty for negligence due to Plateau's substantial understatement of tax under IRC §§6662(a) and (b)(1)-(2). The 20% penalty would apply to the portion of the underpayment resulting from the Tax Court's decision in the prior case that Plateau was not entitled to a charitable deduction. The Tax Court did not allow the 20% accuracy-related penalty because Plateau had reasonable cause and acted in good faith with respect to the claimed charitable deduction corresponding to the correct valuation of the easements.

5

Safe Harbor Language Provided for Conservation Easement Deeds

IRS Notice 2023-30, 2023-17 IRB 766

Under the SECURE 2.0 Act, §605(d)(1), which was enacted as part of the Consolidated Appropriations Act of 2023,[308] the IRS was required to provide safe harbor language for extinguishment and boundary line adjustment clauses in conservation easement deeds by April 28, 2023. The IRS issued this notice on April 24, 2023, providing the safe harbor language and triggering a 90-day period for a donor to amend an easement deed to substitute the safe harbor language for the corresponding language in the original deed. Thus, under §605(d)(2) of the SECURE 2.0 Act, donors are allowed, but not required, to amend their deeds to include this language. Donors wanting to make the change must do so by July 24, 2023. Any amendment will be treated as effective as of the date of the recording of the original easement deed. The IRS points out in the notice that an amendment cannot be made for any easement deed relating to any contribution that was part of a reportable transaction or was a transaction that was not treated as a qualified conservation contribution by reason of §170(h)(7).This includes a transaction for which a charitable deduction contribution had been disallowed by the IRS and the donor was contesting the disallowance in federal court before the amended deed was recorded, or a transaction for which a claimed charitable deduction for the contribution resulted in an underpayment and a penalty under IRC §§6662 or 6663 had been finally determined.

308. *Consolidated Appropriations Act of 2023,* PL 117-328.

Easement Donation Case Heads to Trial

***Morgan Run Partners, LLC v. Comm'r*, TC Memo 2022-61 (Jun. 14, 2022)**

Morgan Run Partners sought a readjustment of partnership items after the IRS disallowed Morgan's $26 million deduction for the donation of a syndicated conservation easement and assessed penalties. The IRS claimed that the deed granting the easement on 232 acres of farmland near Birmingham, Alabama, failed to protect the easement in perpetuity as §170(h)(5)(A) requires. The IRS moved for summary judgment.

The Tax Court analyzed the language of the deed granting the easement and first noted that it did not specify when the FMV of the donee's property right in the farmland was to be calculated. Also, the Tax Court noted that the deed language did not address the possibility that the easement might be extinguished in a future judicial proceeding. The deed stated that the parties intended there would not be future events that would result in the extinguishment of the easement and that nothing would cause the easement donation to fail as a qualified contribution under §170(h). The deed also stated the easement could be terminated by the exercise of eminent domain, but it did not clearly specify how any proceeds were to be allocated. The Tax Court noted that Treas. Reg. §170A-14(g)(6)(i) establishes a formula for determining the allocation of proceeds between the donor and donee upon the extinguishment of the easement. However, the Tax Court reasoned the deed's general language that §170(h) would not be violated gave Morgan a reasonable argument that it had not violated the requirement that the easement be protected in perpetuity or the "extinguishment" regulation.

Accordingly, summary judgment for the IRS on the "protected in perpetuity" requirement was denied. However, the Tax Court granted summary judgment to the IRS on the penalty issue finding Morgan's claim that the Revenue Agent may have communicated information regarding an assessment to Morgan failed to introduce a fact issue.

Retained Ownership of Minable Surface Negates Conservation Easement Deduction

CCA 202236010 (Sep. 9, 2022)

The Chief Counsel's office of the IRS has taken the position that a conservation easement donation is invalid under the requirements of §170(h) if:

- The donor of the easement retains a qualified mineral interest,
- The ownership of the surface estate and mineral interest has never been separated, and
- Under the terms of the deed, the donor can use a surface-mining method to extract the subsurface minerals with the donee's approval.

The IRS said the result would be the same even if the donee would have to approve the surface-mining method because the donated easement would not be donated exclusively for conservation purposes in accordance with §170(h)(5). The IRS pointed out that Treas. Reg. §1.170A-14(g)(4) states that a donated easement does not protect conservation purposes in perpetuity if any method of mining that is inconsistent with the particular conservation purposes of the contribution is permitted at any time.

But the IRS pointed out that a deduction is allowed if the mining method at issue has a limited, localized impact on the real estate and does not destroy significant conservation interests in a manner that cannot be remedied. Surface mining, however, is specifically prohibited where the ownership of the surface estate and the mineral interest has never been separated. On the specific facts involved, the IRS determined that the donated easement would not be treated as being made exclusively for conservation purposes, because the donee could approve surface mining of the donor's subsurface minerals.

FARMING DEDUCTIONS

IRS Questions Farming Practices, But Tax Court Allows Most Deductions

***Hoakison v. Comm'r*, TC Memo 2022-117 (Dec. 5, 2022)**

Steven and Judy Hoakison, a married couple, farmed in southwest Iowa. Judy worked off-farm at a veterinary clinic, and Steven was a full-time delivery driver for United Parcel Service (UPS). He purchased his first farm in 1975, four years after graduating high school, and started a cow-calf operation. The Hoakisons lived frugally and always avoided incurring debt, when possible, by purchasing used equipment with cash and Steven doing his own repairs and maintenance. The Hoakisons were able to weather the farm crises of the early-mid 1980s by farming in this manner. Ultimately, the couple owned five tracts totaling 482 acres. The tracts were noncontiguous and ranged anywhere from six to 14 miles apart. On the tracts, the Hoakisons conducted a row-crop and cow-calf operation. Steven worked on the farms early in the mornings before his UPS shift and after his shift ended until late into the night. Over the years, the couple acquired approximately 40 tractors with 17 in use during the years in issue (2013-2015). The tractors had specific features or used a variety of mounted implements to perform the various tasks needed to operate the noncontiguous farms. Certain tractors were dedicated to a particular tract and attached to implements to save time and effort in taking the implements off and reattaching them. The Hoakisons also had several used pickup trucks and a machine shed that they used to store farm equipment.

The Hoakisons's tax returns for 2013-2015 showed farm losses each year, primarily due to depreciation and other farm expenses. The IRS disallowed significant amounts of depreciation and other farm expense deductions, largely on its claim that the Hoakisons were not engaged in a farming business, but rather were engaged in a "nostalgic" activity with an excessive and unnecessary amount of old tractors. The IRS imposed a substantial understatement penalty of over $25,000 for the years combined. The IRS took the position that the couple's pickups and other vehicles were subject to the listed property strict substantiation requirements of IRC §274(d).

The Tax Court disagreed about the trucks that had been modified for use on the farm and were only driven a de minimis amount for personal purposes, but agreed regarding one pickup the Hoakisons used to travel from farm to farm and to the UPS office. As to the disallowed depreciation on certain tractors, the IRS asserted that the tractors were not used in the Hoakisons's farming business because, according to the IRS, Steven was a collector of antique tractors and the acquisition and maintenance of 40 tractors, most of them more than 40 years old, served no business purpose and involved an element of "nostalgia." The Tax Court disagreed, noting that Steven had sufficiently detailed his farming practices – avoidance of debt and personally repairing and maintaining the tractors and other farm equipment to avoid hiring mechanic work – and that this was an approach that worked well for them. The Tax Court also noted that the IRS failed to account for the Hoakisons's noncontiguous tracts, which meant that it was necessary to have various tractors and implements located at each farm to save time moving tractors from farm to farm and assembling and disassembling various attachments. As such, the Tax Court concluded that the items of farm machinery and tractors were used in the couple's farming business and, thus, it was immaterial whether the purchase of the various farm tractors and implements constituted ordinary and necessary expenses. The Tax Court also determined that the machine shed was a depreciable farm building.

As to various other farming expenses, the Tax Court allowed the Hoakisons's claimed deductions for utilities, insurance, gasoline, fuel, oil, and repair/maintenance expenses. The Tax Court upheld the accuracy-related penalty with respect to the underpayment of tax related to depreciation claimed on assets that had been previously depreciated, but otherwise denied the penalty.

ENTITY ISSUE

Corporation Separate Entity from Shareholders

***Vorreyer, et al. v. Comm'r,* TC Memo 2022-97 (Sep. 21, 2022)**

John and Chris Dowson operated a farm individually and through several related entities, including an S corporation and a partnership. The Dowsons were shareholders of an S corporation, and they paid property taxes and utility expenses on behalf of the S corporation in proportion to their respective ownership interests. They then deducted the amounts on their personal returns. The IRS denied the deductions and the Tax Court agreed.

The Tax Court noted that a taxpayer cannot deduct expenses paid on behalf of another taxpayer.[309] That rule extends to corporations and their shareholders.[310] A shareholder cannot deduct, as a personal expense, an expense that furthers the corporation's business.[311] While there is a limited exception allowing a deduction by a shareholder on behalf of a corporate taxpayer for an expenditure the corporation is financially unable to pay to "protect or promote" the business,[312] the exception did not apply in this case. The Tax Court pointed out that although S corporation income or loss eventually flows through to the shareholders, a corporation "remains a separate taxable entity [from its shareholders] regardless of whether it is a subchapter S corporation or a subchapter C corporation."[313] Thus, the business expenses of the S corporation could not be disregarded at the corporate level for purposes of §162. The income of the S corporation had to be matched at the corporate level against the S corporation's expenses that were incurred to produce that income before the net income or loss amount can flow through to the shareholders.[314] The partnership bought two semi-trucks with a cost of $70,126 and included the expense as part of its claimed repairs and maintenance expense deduction on Schedule F of its Form 1065, *U.S. Return of Partnership Income,* which the IRS disallowed. The Tax Court upheld the IRS determination, noting that the partnership had not made a §179 election on its return for the truck purchases.

---

309. See *Deputy v. du Pont,* 308 U.S. 488 (1940).

310. See *Westerman v. Comm'r,* 55 TC 478 (1970).

311. See *Kahn v. Comm'r,* 26 TC 273 (1956).

312. See, e.g., *Lohrke v. Comm'r,* 48 TC 679 (1967).

313. *Russell v. Comm'r,* TC Memo 1989-207 (May 1, 1989).

314. IRC §1366(a)(2).

REAL ESTATE

Loss on Sale of Real Estate was Capital Loss
***Musselwhite v Comm'r*, TC Memo 2022-57 (Jun. 8, 2022)**

William Musselwhite had been involved in real estate ventures since the mid-1980's. In 2005, William and his business partner formed an LLC. In 2006, the LLC bought four unimproved lots for $1 million and re-platted them into nine lots. The terms of the sale agreement included certain guarantees-of-resale-within-one-year and allocation of ownership of the nine lots between the parties, with the seller allocated five lots. The sales agreement also included buy-back provisions and other conditions related to development and sale of the lots. The seller was to complete improvements on some of the lots. William financed the purchase of the lots via a loan from a bank. In 2007, the real estate market collapsed, and due to no improvements and lack of sales, the LLC sued the seller. To settle the suit, the seller transferred his partially improved lots to William. The LLC made no further improvement to those lots. The bank's later appraisals indicated that the lots were not known to be for sale. The LLC divided up the lots and the existing debt and distributed four of the lots to William. Within four months, William sold the lots at a loss of $1,022,726 and reported a Schedule C deduction of $1,022,726 as COGS. The IRS disagreed, characterizing the loss as a capital loss because the lots were, in the IRS's view, capital assets.

5

The Tax Court agreed with the IRS that the lots were capital assets and did not meet the definition of stock in trade under §1221(a)(1) that would either be held in inventory or held primarily for sale to customers in the ordinary course of business. The Tax Court noted that the distinction between a capital asset and one held for sale to customers in the ordinary course of business is a fact question. Those factors in the 4th Circuit (the Circuit to which the case would be appealable) include the following.

1. The purpose for which the property was acquired
2. The purpose for which the property was held
3. Improvements, and their extent, that the taxpayer made to the property
4. The frequency, number, and continuity of sales
5. The extent and substantiality of the transaction
6. The nature and extent of the taxpayer's business
7. The extent of advertising or lack thereof
8. The listing of the property for sale directly through a broker

The Tax Court noted while no single factor is determinative, the factors overwhelmingly favor the IRS. The Tax Court also noted that the reason a taxpayer holds real estate can change by the taxpayer developing investment property to prepare it for sale, and that IRC §735(a)(2) provides that gain or loss on the sale or exchange by a distributive partner of inventory items distributed by a partnership is ordinary income/loss if the items are sold or exchanged within five years from the date of distribution.

SHAREHOLDER COMPENSATION

Deduction for Full Amount of C Corporate Shareholder Compensation Not Deductible

***Clary Hood, Inc. v. Comm'r*, TC Memo 2022-15 (Mar. 2, 2022), *aff'd in part, vac'd in part and remanded*, No. 2022-1573, 2023 U.S. App. LEXIS 13385 (4th Cir. May 31, 2023)**

The Hoods, a married couple, were the sole shareholders of Clary Hood, Inc., a corporation engaged in the construction business that excavated, graded, and prepared land for development. The petitioner's growth was irregular from 2000 on. Clary Hood took a relatively modest salary between 2000 and 2012, but took a big increase in the years 2013 to 2016, ostensibly to compensate for earlier years. The company had an outside consulting firm perform an analysis to determine what Clary's compensation should be. While the IRS conceded that Clary had been underpaid, the IRS challenged the amount in 2015 and 2016 as excessive.

The Tax Court examined the usual factors considered in such a case, including the following.

- The employee's qualifications
- The nature, extent, and scope of the employee's work
- The size and complexities of the business
- A comparison of salaries paid with gross income and net income
- The prevailing general economic conditions
- A comparison of salaries with distributions to stockholders
- The prevailing rates of compensation for comparable positions in comparable concerns
- The salary policy of the taxpayer as to all employees

The Tax Court denied a deduction for the full amount of the compensation. In addition, the IRS assessed an accuracy-related penalty for both years. Clary was able to show that he relied in good faith on the advice of the accounting firm and the Tax Court did not sustain the penalty. However, for the second year, Clary could not substantiate its reliance on the outside adviser.

On appeal, the appellate court affirmed the Tax Court's denial of deductions stemming from $10 million in total bonuses paid to Clary, concluding that they were more like non-deductible dividends based on the multi-factor approach required by the Treasury Regulations. **However, the appellate court vacated the $282,000 penalty for 2016 because Clary had relied on a professional's advice in paying out the bonus for that year that was based on a "consistent methodology."**

Chapter 6: Ethics

6

Note. Corrections for all of the chapters are available at **TaxSchool.illinois.edu.** For clarification about terms used throughout this chapter, see the **Acronyms and Abbreviations** section following the index.

For your convenience, in-text website links are also provided as short URLs. Anywhere you see **uofi.tax/xxx**, the link points to the address immediately following in brackets.

About the Authors

Kelly Golish, CPA, is the Assistant Director, Tax Materials, at the University of Illinois Tax School. She was previously a manager at Crowder, CPAs in Danville, IL and worked for both public and private accounting firms in Decatur, IL, Cleveland, OH, and San Jose, CA. Kelly earned a Masters in Accounting with an emphasis in Taxation and a Bachelors in Accounting at the University of Notre Dame.

Gina Marsh, EdM, has been with the University of Illinois Tax School since 2014 and program director since 2021. She has edited and reviewed content for the *University of Illinois Federal Tax Workbook* and other publications throughout her time with Tax School.

Other chapter contributors and reviewers are listed at the front of this book.

CONFLICTS OF INTEREST

Conflicts of interest can arise at any time and are not always apparent. Relationships with others may cause a person or firm to lack objectivity in dealing with one client versus another. A practitioner's failure to be impartial to any and all engaged parties can lead to potential conflicts of interest. This does not mean a tax professional cannot provide services if the service can be provided impartially and objectively. If a potential conflict does exist, the practitioner must disclose it to the potential client.

Circular 230, §10.29, lists the following situations it deems conflicts of interest.

1. The representation of one client is directly adverse to another client.
2. There is a significant risk that the representation of one client will be limited by the practitioner's responsibilities to another client, a former client or a third person, or by the personal interest of the practitioner.

Section 10.29(b) provides that, even when a conflict exists, the practitioner may still represent the client if:

1. The practitioner reasonably believes they will be able to diligently represent each affected client competently;
2. There is no law preventing the practitioner from representing the client; and
3. Each client affected by a potential conflict of interest has been informed of the conflict and gives **written** consent to proceed, acknowledging the potential conflict of interest.

> **Note.** Circular 230, §10.29(b)(3), allows the written confirmation of a waiver of the conflict of interest to be made within a reasonable time after the informed consent, but not later than 30 days.

Section 10.29(c) requires practitioners to retain the written consents for at least 36 months from the date the affected client's representation ended. The written representations must be provided to the IRS upon request.

Discussion Scenario 1

Jack and Jill are a married couple. They have been Carrie's tax clients for 15 years. Jill comes to Carrie's office during the 2023 tax preparation season and announces she is divorcing Jack. She also lets Carrie know that Jack is not yet aware that she is going to file for divorce and that Carrie should refrain from mentioning it to him when she prepares their 2023 tax returns. Jill predicts that they will split their assets and asks Carrie for advice on which particular assets she should request in the divorce.

Carrie's continued representation of both Jill and Jack has implications under §10.29. Representation of either client would arguably be directly adverse to the other client and/or limited by Carrie's responsibilities to the other client, even for the tax advice associated with preparing their tax returns. For example, if Carrie advises them to file as married filing jointly (MFJ), each divorcing spouse is jointly and severally liable for any tax owed for that tax year. If Carrie advises them to file as married filing separately (MFS), this may result in a higher tax liability for one or both spouses.

What are some issues that would cause Carrie to consider withdrawing from the engagement?__________________

____

____

____

____

> **Note.** Withdrawing representation may require revocation of Form 2848, *Power of Attorney and Declaration of Representative.* For further details on how a tax practitioner revokes Form 2848, see IRS Pub. 947, *Practice Before the IRS and Power of Attorney.* Failure to properly revoke this form may result in continued obligations to a former client under Circular 230.

Under what circumstances can Carrie continue representing one or both spouses? ______________________

What advice can Carrie give Jill on which assets to pursue during the divorce proceedings? ______________

> **Observation.** Many states have statutes specifically prohibiting the practice of law by nonattorneys. Generally, the practice of law is defined as the giving of advice when that advice requires the use of any degree of legal knowledge or skill.

Discussion Scenario 2

Maria, EA, is the accountant for Hokey Partnership. She is also the accountant for the two partners — Homer, who owns 70% of the partnership, and Keysha, who owns 30%. Homer asks Maria if she will advise him because he is having financial difficulties. He would like to creatively refinance some of the large debts he has accumulated. He asks that she not discuss his problems with Keysha.

What are the major issues that Maria faces if she continues to represent both the partners individually as well as the partnership? ______________________

What are the Circular 230 issues with this request? ______________________

6

Is Maria obligated to disclose Homer's situation with Keysha because it could be pertinent to the success of the partnership? ____

____

____

____

How would the situation be different if Homer and Keysha were not both general partners with joint and several liability?

____

____

____

Is Maria absolved of her responsibilities if she has both Homer and Keysha sign a conflict-of-interest statement? Why or why not? ____

____

____

____

CONFIDENTIALITY AND PRIVILEGE

There is sparse information in Circular 230 concerning practitioner/client communications. Section 10.37 states practitioners may give written advice (including by means of electronic communication) concerning federal tax matters. Such advice must adhere to the facts and relate applicable law to these facts. Circular 230 contains no requirements pertaining to the confidentiality and security of communications between practitioners and their clients. For statutory requirements in this regard, practitioners should look to IRC §7216 and the Gramm-Leach-Bliley Act (GLBA). The former contains rules regarding disclosure and use of clients' tax return data and the latter contains safeguards and privacy rules that concern storage and communication of client data. For purposes of communicating with clients, a tax practitioner must take the necessary steps to prevent client data from falling into the hands of an unauthorized party.

> **Note.** For more information on practitioners' obligations to secure client data, see the 2023 *University of Illinois Federal Tax Workbook,* Chapter 1: Written Information Security Plans and Protecting Client Data.

In addition to Circular 230, §7216, and the GLBA, there are other matters tax practitioners should consider when communicating with their clients. For example, practitioners should recognize the extent to which practitioner-client communications are privileged by law. They should also consider legal disclaimers and record retention policies.

PRIVILEGES RELATING TO TAXPAYER COMMUNICATIONS[1]

Under the Code, communications between any **federally authorized practitioner** and a taxpayer have the same common law protection of confidentiality that applies between an attorney and a taxpayer. However, this protection is limited to **tax advice** and only to the extent that the communication would be a privileged communication if it took place between a taxpayer and an attorney. Furthermore, this privileged communication protection can only be asserted for:

1. Any noncriminal tax matter before the IRS, and
2. Any noncriminal tax proceeding in federal court brought by or against the United States.

A federally authorized practitioner, for this purpose, is any individual who is authorized under federal law to practice before the IRS if such practice is subject to federal regulation under 31 USC §330. This includes attorneys, CPAs, and EAs.[2]

Tax advice refers to any advice a practitioner gives concerning a matter that is within the scope of the practitioner's authority to practice except for advice that concerns tax shelter promotion. A key point is that tax advice does not include **tax return information.** Because tax return information is intended to be disclosed to the IRS, related client-practitioner communications **are not privileged communications** subject to protection. This is the case even when the communication serves a dual purpose (e.g., tax return preparation and litigation).[3] Therefore, in practice, many client-practitioner communications are not privileged communications subject to protection.

6

FURNISHING INFORMATION TO THE IRS

Circular 230, §10.20, addresses a practitioner's duty to furnish information to the IRS. This provision has a "production of information" component and a "cooperation with IRS" component.

Production of Information

When the IRS properly and lawfully requests information, the practitioner:

- Must promptly submit the information to the IRS, and
- Must not interfere with IRS efforts to obtain the information, unless the practitioner has a good faith belief based upon reasonable grounds that the information is privileged.

Attorney-Client Privilege and Tax Return Preparation. Most case law indicates that communications in connection with the preparation of a tax return are not covered by the attorney-client privilege. The U.S. 9th Circuit Court of Appeals accepted the argument that communication pertinent merely to the preparation of a tax return does not involve giving or receiving legal advice.[4] Therefore, information given to the attorney by the client did not fall under the attorney-client privilege. The U.S. 8th Circuit Court of Appeals held that a tax return itself is not privileged because its purpose is disclosure to a third party (the IRS). Therefore, an expectation of confidentiality cannot exist.[5] There are contrary cases that have held that the attorney-client privilege might apply to a communication about what to claim on a return[6] or that tax return communications should be considered legal advice.[7] However, the overall weight of authority indicates that the attorney-client privilege does not apply in connection with communications regarding tax return preparation.

---

1. IRC §7525.
2. Circular 230, §10.3.
3. *U.S. v. Frederick,* 182 F.3d 496 (7th Cir. 1999) and *U.S. v. BDO Seidman,* 337 F.3d 802 (7th Cir. 2003).
4. *U.S. v. Gurtner,* 474 F.2d 297 (9th Cir. 1973).
5. *U.S. v. Cote,* 456 F.2d 142 (8th Cir. 1972).
6. *U.S. v. Abrahams,* 905 F.2d 1276, 1283 (9th Cir. 1990).
7. *Colton v. U.S.,* 306 F.2d 633 (2nd Cir. 1962).

Accountant-Client Privilege. Like the attorney-client privilege, the accountant-client privilege also involves confidentiality. Many states[8] have laws that provide an accountant-client privilege. In some states, the accountant-client privilege is evidentiary. It can be used to bar the admission of evidence in court just like the attorney-client privilege. In other states, the accountant-client privilege is more limited.

In connection with federal income tax issues, federal law does **not** recognize any accountant-client privilege.[9] Accordingly, this privilege cannot be successfully asserted in matters involving the IRS or federal tax law.

Cooperation with IRS

If the IRS requests information that the practitioner or client does not have, the practitioner must:

- Make reasonable inquiry of the client about who may have the information, and
- Provide the IRS with any known information about any person who the practitioner believes may have the information.

AICPA Code of Professional Conduct. The American Institute of Certified Public Accountants (AICPA) Code of Professional Conduct Rule 301, "Confidential Client Information," states that a CPA "shall not disclose any confidential client information without the specific consent of the client." In certain circumstances, the CPA might find a conflict situation between the Circular 230, §10.20 provision of automatic disclosure to the IRS and the AICPA Rule 301, particularly when the client cannot be reached for further inquiry or when the client does not consent to provide information on the location of records to the IRS.

> **Note.** There are many professional associations, such as the National Association of Enrolled Agents (NAEA), and National Association of Tax Professionals (NATP). Each has their own codes of conduct. NAEA rules of professional conduct include rules that govern professional independence, advertising, and soliciting.[10]

THIRD-PARTY DISCLOSURE UNDER IRC §6103

A taxpayer may authorize the IRS to disclose their return or return information to a third party as long as doing so does not prevent the IRS from effectively administering the federal tax laws.[11]

The Taxpayer First Act (TFA)[12] adds the requirements that anyone designated by the taxpayer to receive their return information cannot use the information for anything other than the designated purpose and may not disclose the information to anyone else without the taxpayer's permission.[13] These conditions are effective for disclosures made after December 28, 2019.

> **Caution.** When sharing stories about a client's situation, the best course of action to follow is to change circumstances **sufficiently** to avoid any potential unauthorized disclosures. It may be wiser not to share client stories at all.

---

8. The Illinois Public Accounting Act provides an accountant-client privilege. It is codified at 225 ILCS 450/27. It is evidentiary but cannot be used in an investigation or hearing pursuant to the Public Accounting Act.

9. *Couch v. U.S.*, 409 U.S. 322 (1973).

10. *Code of Ethics and Rules of Professional Conduct.* Nov. 2010. NAEA. [www.naea.org/wp-content/uploads/2020/05/Proposed-Revised-Code-of-Ethics-and-Rules-of-Professional-Conduct2019-25oct19-GSM-review-FINAL.pdf] Accessed on Aug. 8, 2023.

11. IRC §6103(c) before amendment by the *Taxpayer First Act,* PL 116-25.

12. *Taxpayer First Act,* PL 116-25.

13. IRC §6103(c).

Unwittingly disclosing a client's confidential information can happen more easily than one may think. Chatting with friends outside of business or using business networking sites can potentially lead to the unauthorized disclosure of client information and violations of Circular 230, §10.51(a)(15), §7216 (criminal penalties), and IRC §6713 (civil penalties). Discretion must be exercised when describing a client's situation, regardless of the outcome. A client's confidential information should not be disclosed without the client's permission.[14]

Examples of prohibited disclosures include the following.

- Publicly (or in writing) stating the client's name without consent
- Giving enough information about the taxpayer that could allow someone to ascertain to whom the practitioner is referring

If client information is disclosed, a practitioner could be in violation of Circular 230, §10.51(a)(15), for an unauthorized disclosure of tax return information.

Consent of the Client

A **knowing and voluntary** written consent of the client can be obtained as authorization to disclose or use the client's tax information for purposes other than tax preparation.[15] For the client consent to be valid, it must generally contain the following information.

6

- Names of the taxpayer and tax return preparer
- The intended purpose of any disclosure and the intended recipients of the information
- The nature of any uses of the tax information authorized
- A description of the tax return information to be used
- The signature of the taxpayer and the date[16]

Generally, if the tax return preparer tells the client that tax services will **only** be offered if the client consents to disclose their information for other purposes, the consent is deemed **involuntary** and will not be valid. However, there is an exception to this rule for tax return preparers who may need to rely on the expertise of another tax return preparer to complete the client's return. In this case, the tax return preparer may make the client's disclosure consent a prerequisite to the provision of tax preparation services.[17]

The duration of the consent may be specified. However, if no duration is specified, the consent is deemed valid for one year from the date of the client's signature.[18] Consent can **never** be retroactive and therefore must be obtained before the disclosure or use of client information that requires the consent.[19]

If the tax return preparer intends to use the client's tax information for the solicitation of products or services other than tax preparation services, the consent must identify the specific products or services being solicited (such as mutual funds, individual retirement arrangement (IRA) accounts, life insurance, portfolio management, or other products or services).[20]

---

14. Circular 230, §10.51(a)(15).
15. Treas. Reg. §301.7216-3(a)(1).
16. Treas. Reg. §301.7216-3(a)(3)(i).
17. Treas. Reg. §301.7216-3(a)(1).
18. Treas. Reg. §301.7216-3(b)(5).
19. Treas. Reg. §301.7216-3(b)(1).
20. Treas. Reg. §301.7216-3(a)(3)(i)(B).

The regulations under §7216 regarding disclosure and use of client tax information are lengthy and complex. Among situations that have special use or disclosure rules are the following.

- Tax return preparer disclosure of client tax information to obtain legal advice
- Disclosure of tax information by fiduciaries, such as by trustees to other parties
- Disclosure or use of a client's tax information in connection with a state or local tax audit
- Use of tax information lists to solicit tax preparation business
- Disclosure of tax information due to the death of a taxpayer

Improper use of a client's tax return information in a manner that violates §7216 constitutes **disreputable conduct** even without the conviction of the tax return preparer. Circular 230, §10.51, lists several items that constitute disreputable conduct. This list of items includes conviction of any criminal offense under the federal tax laws[21] or conviction of any criminal offense involving dishonesty or breach of trust.[22] Therefore, a tax return preparer violation of §7216 will constitute disreputable conduct under Circular 230.[23]

Permitted Disclosures[24]

Sanctions (civil or criminal) do **not** apply to **permitted** disclosures or use of tax return information. For this purpose, the following **disclosures** and **uses** of tax return information are permitted.

- **Disclosure** pursuant to any other Code section or Treasury regulation
- **Disclosure** to the IRS
- **Disclosure** pursuant to a court order
- **Use** of a client's tax return information when updating tax preparation/filing software
- **Use** of and **disclosure** to tax return preparers located within the same firm **inside** the United States for tax preparation or auxiliary services for that client
- **Use** of and **disclosure** to tax return preparers located within the same firm **outside** the United States for tax preparation or auxiliary services for that client (with the client's consent)
- **Use** of and **disclosure** between tax return preparers located within the same firm **outside** the United States if the information was originally provided to the firm by the taxpayer
- **Disclosure** to tax return preparation software/equipment contractors **only to the extent necessary** to provide contracted services
- **Disclosure** and **use** for certain related taxpayers
- **Disclosure** when securing legal advice, or during Treasury investigations or court proceedings concerning the preparer
- **Use** and **disclosure** to other members of the preparer firm for other tax, legal, or accounting services to the client

---

21. Circular 230, §10.51(a)(1).

22. Circular 230, §10.51(a)(2).

23. Circular 230, §10.51(a)(15).

24. Treas. Reg. §301.7216-2.

- **Use** and **disclosure** to other members of the preparer firm for other tax, legal, or accounting services for work on **another** client to the extent relevant to that work
- Certain **disclosure** and **use** by a preparer who also serves as a corporate fiduciary to the same client
- **Disclosure** to the taxpayer's fiduciary when the taxpayer dies or becomes incompetent, insolvent, or bankrupt
- **Disclosure** or **use** in preparation for an audit of state or local tax returns or assisting a taxpayer with foreign country tax obligations
- **Disclose** or **use** to the extent necessary to process or collect payment for tax preparation services
- **Use** in preparation of other tax returns of the taxpayer or in connection with an IRS examination of any tax return or subsequent tax litigation relating to the tax return
- **Use** of certain tax return information in compiling client lists for solicitation of tax return preparation business
- **Use** and **disclosure** of certain tax return information in producing statistical information in connection with tax return preparation business
- **Disclosure** or **use** of information for quality, peer, or conflict reviews to a reviewer who is eligible to practice before the IRS
- **Disclosure** to a federal, state, or local official when reporting the commission of a crime or suspected crime
- **Disclosure** to the legal representative of an incapacitated or deceased tax return preparer for the purpose of assisting the representative in operating the business

6

Preparers may also use tax return information for preparation of the client's state and local tax returns and declarations of estimated tax.

Unless **disclosure** or **use** of tax return information is specifically authorized, as previously described, a tax return preparer may not disclose or use a client's tax return information prior to obtaining a written consent from the client.[25]

IRC §7216 PENALTIES FOR IMPROPER DISCLOSURE

Under §7216, a tax return preparer generally may not use or provide a taxpayer's **return information** to another party, unless:[26]

- The **use** or **disclosure** is specifically permitted by §7216 or Treas. Reg. §301.7216-2, or
- The tax return preparer obtains valid consent from the taxpayer.

The TFA increases the civil penalty for unauthorized or improper disclosure or use of information by tax return preparers.[27] The penalty, which was $250, increased to $1,000 effective July 1, 2019. The penalty applies when the disclosure or use is made in connection with a crime relating to the misuse of another person's identity.

The TFA increases the calendar-year limit on such civil penalties from $10,000 to $50,000.[28] The calendar-year limit is applied separately with respect to disclosures or uses made in connection with taxpayer identity theft.

The TFA also increases the criminal penalty for knowing or reckless conduct to $100,000 for disclosures or uses in connection with taxpayer identity theft.[29]

---

25. Treas. Reg. §301.7216-3(a)(1).
26. IRC §7216(a)(1); Treas. Reg. §301.7216-3.
27. PL 116-25, §2009.
28. Ibid.
29. Ibid.

Discussion Scenario 3

Kennedy is a seasoned tax professional. Over lunch, she starts complaining to her best friend about one of her clients, who is really bugging her. She shares that the client runs a small local pest control company and "even though he has done work for just about every house in town, he can't tell me how many clients he worked with last year or provide me with any records. He just jots notes down in this little notebook in his truck and expects me to make sense of it!" Kennedy's friend asks if this is the company over on Main Street and Kennedy replies, "yes, that's the one."

Which types of violations are present in this scenario? ______________________________

What civil and criminal penalties could Kennedy be subject to? ______________________________

How would this situation be different if Kennedy was selling her practice and her friend was a prospective buyer of the business? ______________________________

Discussion Scenario 4

Talia is a CPA and a member of her state-sponsored CPA society. She attends one of their networking events over the holiday season. While enjoying cocktail hour, she asks another attendee for advice on a client situation. She mentions that her client, who operates a small Italian restaurant in her town, is currently being audited by the Small Business Administration (SBA) for inappropriate use of Paycheck Protection Program (PPP) funds. Talia asks the other CPA if she has ever successfully defended a client in a similar situation.

Has Talia violated her client's confidentiality in this situation? Would the result be different if Talia provided the other CPA with her business card that reflects the name of the small town in which Talia and her client reside? __________

What is the likely penalty that Talia would face for making this inadvertent disclosure? ______________________________

How could Talia solicit assistance without violating nondisclosure rules? ______________________________

____

____

____

INDUSTRY-FOCUS AND COMPETENCE

Based on a 2022 Client Advisory Services survey, 77% of practices specialize in one or more industries rather than being a generalized practice.[30] Examples of a specialized **practice focus** include financial planning, client advisory services, sales and use tax, foreign taxation, technology consulting, cybersecurity services, and human resources consulting. Examples of a specialized **industry focus** include restaurant/hospitality, construction, real estate, agriculture, financial institutions, healthcare, and technology industry.[31]

Some benefits of specialization include increased efficiencies (such as understanding industry trends), improved quality by having a deeper understanding of the industry, and a greater value to a firm's clients.

6

Firms that are focusing on a specialization should consider the following areas of Circular 230 in their practices if they are going to prepare income tax returns.

COMPETENCE

Section 10.35 of Circular 230 requires practitioners to have a minimum level of competency and understanding to address the issues presented to them by clients. Tax professionals can never use ignorance of the law as a defense. Competent representation can be achieved by seeking the assistance of persons with greater knowledge of a given topic than the practitioner possesses.[32]

Practitioner Planning Tip

It might appear difficult to comply with the provisions of §10.35, especially for newer practitioners or for practitioners engaging a client with an activity with which the tax practitioner has little familiarity. While tax professionals should seek to continually expand their knowledge, lack of knowledge in a given area of tax law does not preclude the practitioner from learning about the activity concerned. Circular 230, §10.35(a) provides that practitioners may become competent in a given issue by consulting experts or by studying the laws relating to the issue. The intent of the provision is to be competent, to seek knowledge, never claim ignorance, or to refer an unfamiliar situation to another professional. This is where a tax practitioner who specializes in a particular industry or practice can charge a premium and serve as a reference to firms who perform more generalized tasks.

30. *CAS Benchmark Survey.* 2022. CPA.com. [www.cpa.com/sites/cpa/files/2022-12/cas-benchmark-survey-22-cpacom.pdf] Accessed on Jun. 30, 2023.

31. *Why specialization is the key to firm growth.* Merhib, Kalil. Mar. 21, 2023. CPA.com. [www.cpa.com/blog/2023/03/21/why-specialization-key-firm-growth] Accessed on Jun. 30, 2023.

32. Circular 230, §10.35(a).

Discussion Scenario 5

Floyd is an EA with five years of experience preparing individual tax returns. Last year, he took a course on preparing trust tax returns and has very limited exposure to the preparation of Form 1041, *U.S. Income Tax Return for Estates and Trusts.*

During the summer, a local bank's trust department contacts Floyd and asks him if he would be willing to prepare Forms 1041 for their bank. The bank has several trusts that they serve as trustees for and their current tax preparer has retired and they are looking for a new tax preparer.

What are some things Floyd should do to ensure that he has the necessary knowledge, skill, thoroughness, and preparation required for taking on this task? ______________________________

____

____

____

Should Floyd turn down this business opportunity because of Circular 230, §10.35? If not, what can he do to prepare himself for this task? ______________________________

____

____

____

If Floyd consults with an experienced colleague in preparing the returns, has he met his obligation under Circular 230, §10.35? Why or why not?______________________________

____

____

____

Discussion Scenario 6

Rhonda is a CPA who passed the CPA exam two years ago. She now operates her own accounting and tax preparation firm as a sole practitioner. For the past two years, she completed Forms 1040, *U.S. Individual Income Tax Return,* 1120, *U.S. Corporation Income Tax Return,* and 1065, *U.S. Return of Partnership Income,* and related forms and schedules for her small but growing number of clients.

In June 2021, Rhonda met with Bob and Barbara. They are married and moved to the United States from Canada to work for a U.S. company. They told Rhonda that they would receive Forms W-2, *Wage and Tax Statement,* after the end of the year showing their respective salaries for 2021. They also mentioned that they would have some Canadian wage and investment income in the form of interest and dividends. They received this income in early 2021 before moving to the United States.

Bob and Barbara asked Rhonda to complete their 2021 tax return, which was the first U.S. tax return they filed. Rhonda had never prepared an initial tax return for a new U.S. resident. However, she thought that Bob and Barbara's 2021 U.S. tax return would not be materially different from other MFJ returns she had prepared.

Bob and Barbara furnished Rhonda with their Forms W-2, the amounts of Canadian wage and investment income they received, and income taxes they paid in Canada. The next day, Rhonda researched how to report the Canadian wage and investment income on Form 1040. She also researched how to convert the Canadian dollar amounts to the U.S. dollar equivalents that must be shown on Form 1040. Rhonda completed their Form 1040 and met with Bob and Barbara to review the return. After all three of them signed the return, it was filed.

In June 2023, Bob and Barbara contacted Rhonda about letters they had received from the IRS and the Financial Crimes Enforcement Network (FinCEN). They furnished copies of the letters to her. The letters identified the following issues with Bob and Barbara's 2021 tax return.

- Bob and Barbara failed to report their Canadian retirement and investment accounts on FinCEN Form 114, *Report of Foreign Bank and Financial Accounts,* as required under the Bank Secrecy Act.
- Bob and Barbara failed to attach Form 8938, *Statement of Specified Foreign Financial Assets,* with their return to disclose their Canadian retirement and investment accounts.

Was Rhonda's preparation and research adequate to provide the level of competence necessary to complete Bob and Barbara's tax return? Why or why not?____

What other research or actions should Rhonda have taken to exercise adequate due diligence under Circular 230, §10.22?

Does it make Rhonda's actions worse if she worked in a large firm that had an international tax department and did not consult with them?____

COMPLIANCE WITH PRACTICE PROCEDURES

Per Circular 230, §10.36, the person in a firm assigned the responsibility for determining compliance with the firm's practice procedures must take all reasonable steps to make certain there are processes in place to apply these standards. This applies not just to persons working for the firm but also to those who provide services and are therefore considered to be associated with the firm.

Businesses often need to hire persons to provide services the company cannot provide without assistance. However, the firm still has a responsibility to understand what the contractor is providing and cannot merely rely on what the contractor may say and ignore potential issues.

Discussion Scenario 7

Sarah is a CPA with Jones & Smith, CPAs. She specializes in providing tax services to clients in the construction industry. One of her longstanding clients, XYZ Construction, is a medium-sized company that has been experiencing financial difficulties due to the economic downturn in the industry. As a result, they are exploring various strategies to minimize their liabilities and improve their financial position.

During a routine tax consultation with XYZ Construction, the company's owner, John, confides that they may have misclassified workers as independent contractors to avoid payroll taxes. He emphasized that other construction companies commonly engage in these practices and that it is necessary for XYZ Construction to do the same to remain competitive.

Jones & Smith's policies include having an initial discussion with all clients on the difference between wage employees and independent contractors, including the consequences of misclassifying workers. Another policy states that when an employee is uncertain on a particular matter, the company has other specialists who may be contacted to obtain further expertise within an industry and may rely on their expertise.

Upon reviewing her files on XYZ, Sarah sees a document where the independent contractor requirements were reviewed with John when XYZ first became a client. Sarah discusses XYZ's case with another CPA, Marcus, who is employed outside of her firm. Marcus agrees with John that is common within the construction industry to classify workers as independent contractors. However, Marcus is not privy to the specific details of XYZ's workers because Sarah does not want to inadvertently disclose client information.

Can Sarah rely on the opinion of Marcus in accordance with Jones & Smith's policies? ______________________

____

____

____

____

What are Sarah's ethical requirements regarding the potential misclassification of independent contractors? _______

____

____

____

____

How should Sarah approach her ongoing relationship with XYZ Construction in the light of the ethical concerns raised? What steps can she take to ensure that her practice remains compliant with Circular 230 while still providing valuable tax services to her clients? ____

____

____

____

____

Discussion Scenario 8

Use the same facts and circumstances as **Scenario 7,** except that Jones & Smith also has a policy stating that once a client has been informed of the difference between wage employees and independent contractors, there are two options concerning the engagement.

1. The engagement continues if the client agrees to be compliant with court rulings and IRS regulations going forward.
2. Disengage the client if they refuse to be compliant.

Based on this company policy, how should Sarah proceed with XYZ Construction?____________________________

____

____

____

____

If Sarah can document that XYZ's determination of independent contractors is within the "industry standard" as Marcus states, may she continue the engagement without concerns of company policy and Circular 230?__________

____

____

____

____

INCOMPETENCE AND DISREPUTABLE CONDUCT

Circular 230, §10.51, enumerates various courses of conduct that constitute incompetence and are considered disreputable. This provision carries forward from §10.50, which addresses sanctions such as the ability of the Office of Professional Responsibility (OPR) to censure, suspend, or disbar a practitioner.[33] Circular 230, §10.51(a) illustrates a series of potentially actionable offenses that constitute incompetence and disreputable conduct.[34]

There are several circumstances that constitute disreputable conduct on the part of the practitioner. These provisions can be summarized by the following actions.

- Criminal convictions
- Felony convictions resulting in the practitioner being unfit to represent taxpayers before the IRS
- Giving false or misleading testimony or helping others to give false or misleading testimony to IRS or Treasury employees
- False, misleading, or deceptive advertising practices
- Practitioners not filing their own returns or paying the tax they owe
- Assisting or suggesting ways a taxpayer may violate the law
- Taking funds from a taxpayer intended to pay tax obligations and using them personally

33. Circular 230, §10.50(a).

34. Circular 230, §§10.51(a)(1)–(18).

- Attempting to bribe Treasury officials
- Disbarment from practice by their state governing authority
- Assisting disbarred persons to practice before the IRS
- Rude, abusive, or threatening treatment of IRS employees
- Taking misleading positions known to be contrary to law
- Intentionally failing to sign returns prepared by the practitioner
- Unauthorized disclosure of taxpayer information
- Failing to maintain records of returns prepared
- Preparation of returns without a valid preparer tax identification number (PTIN)

Discussion Scenario 9

Carson is an EA who owns his own tax practice. He has a small staff that consists of two other preparers who are unlicensed. Carson's practice is located in a Chicago suburb where most of his clients are business-owners and various other business professionals.

One of Carson's longtime clients, Jordan, decides to leave his corporate job and buys a small farm to grow pumpkins and start a family-friendly pumpkin patch. Jordan has no experience in farming, and likewise, Carson is not experienced in taxation specific to agriculture. However, Carson assures Jordan that his research skills are topnotch, and he will acquire the necessary knowledge to competently complete Jordan's return.

Carson recommends Jordan get in touch with Guy, a businessman he knows who can facilitate Jordan donating an easement on the farm property. Guy has been in some hot water with the IRS recently, but Carson assures Jordan the odds of an audit are low. Jordan expresses some reluctance. Carson sends Jordan's preliminary return to Guy anyway so Guy can sway Jordan by calculating the tax savings.

Carson gets swamped preparing returns in April and tells one of the unlicensed preparers in his office to sign off on Jordan's return. The preparer rarely signs returns and did not renew her PTIN the preceding year. However, she signs the return anyway.

How would the situation be different if Carson worked in a firm that specialized in agriculture?__________________

____

____

____

____

Which of Carson's actions are in violation of §10.51 of Circular 230? __________________________

____

____

____

____

Can Carson be held responsible for the unlicensed preparer's actions? ______________________________

____

____

____

____

CONTINGENT FEES[35]

Contingent fees are generally disallowed for services related to any matter before the IRS.[36] These restrictions are designed to ensure independent judgment is used by practitioners while representing clients with tax issues.

Under Circular 230, tax practitioners may charge contingent fees for representations on matters **before the IRS** only in the following circumstances.

- For services rendered in connection with the IRS examination of, or challenge to, one of the following:
  - An original tax return, or
  - An amended return or claim for refund or credit filed within 120 days of the taxpayer receiving an IRS written notice challenging or examining the **original** tax return.
- For services rendered regarding a claim for credit or refund of IRS-assessed penalties and/or statutory interest
- Any judicial proceeding arising under the Code

A contingent fee is any fee that depends, wholly or partly, on whether a position taken on a tax return or other filing avoids challenge by the IRS or is sustained either by the IRS or in litigation. Such fees include those based on any of the following.

- A percentage of the refund reported on a return
- A percentage of the taxes saved, or that otherwise depends on a specific result
- An arrangement to waive fees if a position taken on a tax return or other filing is challenged by the IRS or is not sustained

For this purpose, a matter **before the IRS** includes the following.

- Tax planning and advice
- Preparing or filing, or assisting in preparing or filing, returns or claims for refund or credit
- All matters connected with a presentation to the IRS relating to a taxpayer's rights, privileges, or liabilities under laws or regulations administered by the IRS

Practitioner presentations on matters before the IRS include the following.

- Preparing and filing documents
- Corresponding and communicating with the IRS
- Rendering written advice with respect to any entity, transaction, plan, or arrangement
- Representing a client at conferences, hearings, and meetings

---

35. Circular 230, §10.27(b).

36. Circular 230, §10.27(b)(1).

In the 2014 case of *Ridgely v. Lew et al.,*[37] the court ruled that the IRS did not have the authority to regulate Gerald Ridgely in his role as a tax preparer for the contingent fee arrangement used in preparation of an ordinary refund claim. In reviewing a statute enacted in 1884, which the IRS cited as its source of regulatory authority, the court observed that this statute provides the IRS with authority to regulate "representatives," not tax return preparers.

Gerald Ridgely argued that a CPA does not engage in legal representation of a taxpayer by assisting with the preparation and filing of a refund claim. He argued that representation does not begin until the IRS subsequently responds to the claim and the CPA submits the required power of attorney form to engage in client representation. The IRS took the position that current law, consisting of the Horse Act of 1884,[38] provided the IRS with authority to regulate aspects of practice such as Gerald Ridgely's contingent fee arrangement. The IRS further argued the regulation of contingent fee arrangements was essential because of concerns about ensuring the tax advisor's professional independence, and such independence is jeopardized if the tax advisor and taxpayer have aligned their financial interests through a contingent fee arrangement.

The court reviewed the Horse Act statute that the IRS cited as its source of regulatory authority and noted that the *Loving*[39] case served as precedent. *Loving* is the case in which the previously mandated registered tax return preparer (RTRP) program was set aside. *Loving* indicated that the Horse Act definition of a "representative" that the IRS may regulate was limited to persons with the authority to bind others in the course of representation. *Loving* distinguished "representatives" from tax return preparers, noting that tax return preparers cannot be regulated by the IRS because a tax return preparer has no authority to bind the taxpayer in the course of their work. Therefore, the court concluded, the Horse Act of 1884 did not provide the IRS with the authority to regulate Gerald Ridgely in his role as a tax preparer for the contingent fee arrangement used in preparation of an ordinary refund claim. The court concluded it was compelled under the Administrative Procedure Act to hold that the attempted IRS regulation of Ridgely's contingent fee arrangement was beyond the scope of statutory IRS regulatory authority and was unlawful.

Observation. Circular 230, §10.27 represents the official position of the IRS as revised June 2014. Ridgely successfully challenged the authority of the IRS prior to the change to Circular 230 in June 2014 to enforce the provision against practitioners charging contingent fees in the mere preparation of a refund claim.

Discussion Scenario 10

Sophia is a CPA who regularly prepares payroll and income tax returns for many small businesses, including sole proprietors, corporations, and partnerships. Sophia learns about the employee retention credit (ERC) and begins reviewing the business operations of her clients to determine which, if any, of those clients might benefit from such a claim. She determines that several of her clients satisfy the required decline in gross revenues and qualify for the credit.

During late 2021 and the first half of 2022, she reaches out to the affected clients and offers her services to prepare and file the refund claims on their behalf. She has the clients execute engagement letters specific to the ERC refund claims and states that her fee to prepare the claims will be 10% of the resulting refunds. The clients all sign the engagement letters and Sophia proceeds with the preparation and filing of the Form 941-X, *Adjusted Employer's QUARTERLY Federal Tax Return or Claim for Refund,* for each of the clients and the amended income tax returns that are required.

---

37. *Ridgely v. Lew,* 44 F.Supp.3d 89 (D.C. Cir. 2014).

38. This law, in its present form, is currently codified at 31 USC 330.

39. *Loving v. IRS,* 742 F.3d 1013 (D.C. Cir. 2013).

Is Sophia's contingent fee a violation of §10.27 of Circular 230? Why or why not? ______________________________

____

____

____

____

Would the answer be different if Sophia charged the same 10% fee to represent the client after the IRS notified the client that they were auditing the amended payroll and income tax returns? ______________________________

____

____

____

____

What would happen if Sophia offered to prepare all future Forms 941 for a fee of 10% of the tax liability?________

____

____

____

____

EFFECT OF INCENTIVES

Because certain contingent fees are permitted under Circular 230, it begs the question: does the existence of contingent fees incentivize tax preparers to not comply with tax law?

POWER OF ATTORNEY

Under Circular 230, §10.2(a)(4), practice before the IRS includes "preparing documents; filing documents; corresponding and communicating with the Internal Revenue Service... and representing a client at conferences, hearings, and meetings." IRS Pub. 947 provides a list of categories of individuals who may practice before the IRS and states when a power of attorney (POA) is required. For example, a POA is required to represent a client at a meeting with the IRS and to receive a client's confidential tax information from the IRS.

WITHDRAW/REVOKE

For a qualified tax return preparer to have full authority to represent a new client before the IRS, the preparer must be authorized by the client. This is typically accomplished by using Form 2848. Only practitioners eligible to practice before the IRS can use this form to obtain full representational authority. An eligible practitioner is one who has not been disbarred or suspended from IRS practice and is one of the following.

- An attorney
- A CPA
- An EA
- An enrolled actuary
- An enrolled retirement plan agent

Filing a new Form 2848 to appoint a new practitioner automatically revokes the authorization of the previous practitioner who was engaged for the same matters and years covered by Form 2848. However, should the client want to retain a previously authorized practitioner, Form 2848 provides an option for doing so. In addition to checking the appropriate box on Form 2848, a copy of the Form 2848 that authorized the previous practitioner must be attached to the Form 2848 that authorizes the new practitioner.

6 **Retention/revocation of prior power(s) of attorney.** The filing of this power of attorney automatically revokes all earlier power(s) of attorney on file with the Internal Revenue Service for the same matters and years or periods covered by this form. If you **do not** want to revoke a prior power of attorney, check here . . . . ▶ ☐

YOU MUST ATTACH A COPY OF ANY POWER OF ATTORNEY YOU WANT TO REMAIN IN EFFECT.

A client can **revoke** the decision to authorize a particular practitioner as representative. The client that used Form 2848 or Form 8821, *Tax Information Authorization,* to assign representation can accomplish the revocation by forwarding a copy of the original Form 2848 or Form 8821 with the word "revoke" written across the top of the form. In addition, underneath the original signature, the effective date of revocation must be provided along with a current signature. The practitioner can also use this method to **withdraw** as representative if a Form 2848 or 8821 was used for the original authorization and they no longer wish to represent a particular client.[40]

Note. A Form 8821 cannot revoke a previously submitted Form 2848, and a Form 2848 cannot revoke a previously submitted Form 8821.[41]

If the client wishes to revoke and has no copy of the Form 2848 or did not use this form, it is sufficient to send the IRS a written statement that includes the following details.[42]

- An indication that the POA is revoked
- An indication that the revocation is removed for all years or periods or a specific list of particular matters, years, or periods for which selective revocation is made
- The name and address of each representative being revoked
- A signature and date

The withdrawing practitioner can also withdraw using a similar statement. The name, taxpayer identification number, and address (if known) of the client must be stated.

Practitioner Retiring or Closing a Practice

If a practitioner retires or closes a tax practice, it is essential that they withdraw from representation for each client. If the practitioner remains on record as the representative for clients, they continue to owe those clients the various duties, obligations, and responsibilities outlined in Circular 230. Withdrawing from representation keeps the IRS informed that the practitioner is no longer responsible for various duties and obligations to the taxpayer. Withdrawal from client representation does not mean revocation of qualified practitioner status under Circular 230.

40. See Form 2848 and Form 8821 instructions.

41. IRM 4.11.55.2.8 (2010).

42. See Form 2848 instructions.

Firing a Client

A practitioner may feel relief after firing a client and, after providing any necessary transition documents, they move on with their practice. However practitioners should withdraw the POA on file for that client. Failing to do so can create similar circumstances to leaving a POA in place when retiring or closing a practice, as practitioners have responsibilities and obligations to the taxpayer for as long as the POA is on file.

Discussion Scenario 11

Carol, a CPA, has had a tax practice for 35 years. She is retiring and the closing date on the sale of her entire practice is about six months away. She is selling her practice to FGH Accounting Services, LLC. Carol begins the process of withdrawing as representative for each of her clients.

What are Carol's options for withdrawing her POAs? ______________________________

____

____

____

____

Is it sufficient if Carol has each client execute a new Form 2848 that appoints FGH Accounting Services, LLC as a POA? Does she need to identify a specific individual at the new firm? ______________________

____

____

____

____

If Carol does not withdraw the POAs that she has on file, what responsibilities does she still owe her former clients?

____

____

____

____

ATTEMPTS TO BYPASS[43]

It is important that tax preparers respond to IRS requests in a timely manner. If the taxpayer's representative has a valid signed POA on file, the IRS will make all requests for documents and appointments to the representative. While an audit request may come at the most inopportune time, the revenue agent normally tries to accommodate both the taxpayer and their representative. However, the agent cannot be delayed indefinitely. If the IRS determines the practitioner is intentionally causing unreasonable delay to the audit process, it can bypass the POA and contact the taxpayer directly.[44] Continually ignoring an IRS request ultimately results in a contact from OPR.

> **Note.** The bypass procedures do not constitute a disbarment or a suspension of the practitioner.

Prior to bypassing the POA, the IRS must document any of the following.

- The practitioner impedes or delays an examination by not submitting the taxpayer's records or information as requested by the IRS agent.
- The practitioner impedes or delays an examination by missing scheduled appointments.
- The practitioner impedes or delays an examination by not returning phone calls or written correspondence.

After the trend of delays is noted and the IRS has ensured that all reasonable efforts were taken to work directly with the practitioner, the following steps are taken.

1. The taxpayer receives copies of all written correspondence to the practitioner.
2. The practitioner receives either a Letter 4020-A, *Warning for Bypass Procedures for Preparers covered under Circular 230,* or Letter 4020-B, *Warning for Bypass Procedures for Unenrolled Preparers* (blank examples of both letters are shown on the following pages). Additionally, the practitioner receives copies of prior document requests, a list of outstanding items, and a brief chronology of events. This information is not sent to the taxpayer.

In the event that both the taxpayer and the practitioner are intentionally uncooperative, the IRS must issue a summons rather than using the bypass procedures previously outlined. A summons is also required if the practitioner refuses to provide documentation because they believe the information is privileged or that the request is of doubtful legality. The summons in this instance allows the practitioner to request a court to consider the legal issues of privilege.

---

43. See IRM 4.11.55.4 (2010).

44. IRC §7521(c); IRS Pub. 947, *Practice Before the IRS and Power of Attorney.*

Department of the Treasury
Internal Revenue Service
[Operating Division / Program Name]

IRS

Date:
07/13/2023
Taxpayer ID number (last 4 digits):

Person to contact:

Employee ID number:

Contact telephone number:

Dear [enter Name]:

Our records indicate that you are the representative for in connection with the tax matters of Form(s) . We have on file a Form 2848, *Power of Attorney and Declaration of Representative,* authorizing you to receive confidential information and to perform specified acts on behalf of the taxpayer relating to the tax returns under examination.

We have requested information from you to complete our examination. Your responses to our requests have been consistently late or incomplete. A schedule of our prior requests and a list of items currently outstanding are attached. The currently outstanding items must be submitted by , days from the date of this letter. Further, any information we request in the future will be due within days from the date of the request. If you do not respond to this request, our rules permit us to bypass you and contact the taxpayer directly for the requested information. Where a recognized representative has unreasonably delayed or hindered an examination, collection, or investigation by failing to furnish, after repeated request, nonprivileged information necessary to the examination, collection, or investigation, the Internal Revenue Service employee conducting the examination, collection, or investigation may be given permission to bypass the representative and contact the taxpayer directly for such information. 26 C.F.R. § 601.506(b) (Statement of Procedural Rules).

Please be advised that failure to promptly submit records or information in response to a proper and lawful request of an Internal Revenue Service officer or employee, or unreasonable delay or hindrance of an examination, may constitute a violation of Treasury Department Circular No. 230 (31 C.F.R. Part 10), *Regulations Governing the Practice of Attorneys, Certified Public Accountants, Enrolled Agents, Enrolled Actuaries, and Appraisers Before the Internal Revenue Service.* Section 10.20(a)(1) of Circular 230 requires a practitioner, upon a proper and lawful request by a duly authorized officer or employee of the Internal Revenue Service, to promptly submit records or information in any matter before the Internal Revenue Service, unless the practitioner believes in good faith and on reasonable grounds that the records or information are privileged. Section 10.23 of Circular 230 prohibits a practitioner from unreasonably delaying the prompt disposition of any matter before the Internal Revenue Service.

Letter 4020-A (Rev. 1-2017)
Catalog Number 47377C

Department of the Treasury
Internal Revenue Service
[Operating Division / Program Name]

IRS

Date:
07/13/2023
Taxpayer ID number (last 4 digits):

Person to contact:

Employee ID number:

Contact telephone number:

Dear [enter Name]:

Our records indicate that you are the representative for   in connection with the tax matters of   Form(s)   . We have on file a Form 2848, *Power of Attorney and Declaration of Representative,* authorizing you to receive confidential information and to perform specified acts on behalf of the taxpayer relating to the tax returns under examination.

We have requested information from you to complete our examination. Your responses to our requests have been consistently late or incomplete. A schedule of our prior requests and a list of items currently outstanding are attached. The currently outstanding items must be submitted by   ,   days from the date of this letter. Further, any information we request in the future will be due within   days from the date of the request. If you do not respond to this request, our rules permit us to bypass you and contact the taxpayer directly for the requested information. Where a recognized representative has unreasonably delayed or hindered an examination, collection, or investigation by failing to furnish, after repeated request, nonprivileged information necessary to the examination, collection, or investigation, the Internal Revenue Service employee conducting the examination, collection, or investigation may be given permission to bypass the representative and contact the taxpayer directly for such information. 26 C.F.R. § 601.506(b) (Statement of Procedural Rules).

Please be advised that neglecting or refusing to submit records or information in response to a proper and lawful request of an Internal Revenue Service officer or employee, or unreasonably delaying the prompt disposition of a matter, may constitute a violation of Revenue Procedure 81-38, 1981-2 C.B. 592. Section 7.03 of the revenue procedure prohibits an unenrolled preparer, upon a proper and lawful request by a duly authorized officer or employee of the Internal Revenue Service, from neglecting or refusing to submit records or information in any matter before the Internal Revenue Service, unless the unenrolled preparer believes in good faith and on reasonable grounds that the request for such records or information is of doubtful legality. Section 7.06 of the revenue procedure prohibits an unenrolled preparer from unreasonably delaying the prompt disposition of any matter before the Internal Revenue Service. Under Section 10 of the revenue procedure, an unenrolled preparer whose conduct violates the revenue procedure may be determined ineligible to exercise the privilege of limited practice before the Internal Revenue Service.

Letter 4020-B (Rev. 1-2017)
Catalog Number 47378N

Discussion Scenario 12

Roland is a practitioner who fired a client two years ago and forgot he had a POA on file with the IRS for this client. He received a notice from collections concerning this client. Because he no longer is engaged with the client, Roland destroys the notice and does not respond. A few weeks later, Roland is contacted by the IRS by phone. The IRS states they cannot proceed to contact the taxpayer until the current POA is withdrawn or revoked.

What is Roland's responsibility under Circular 230? ____

____

____

____

____

Does he have a responsibility to respond to the client in question?________________________________

____

____

____

____

What are a preparer's options for withdrawing a POA? ____

____

____

____

____

6

REPORTING UNETHICAL PREPARERS[45]

A client who wishes to file a complaint against a practitioner or tax preparation business may do so using Form 14157, *Return Preparer Complaint.* This form may also be used by a tax practitioner who wishes to lodge a complaint against another practitioner. A copy of this form is shown on the following pages.

Form 14157 is filed directly with the return preparer office (RPO) in Atlanta, Georgia. The RPO reviews each complaint and determines whether an investigation should be initiated. Complaints with criminal issues may be referred to the U.S. Department of Justice for investigation. Some common types of return preparer misconduct that may lead to an investigation include instances in which the return preparer:

- Did not provide the client with a copy of the return they prepared and refused to provide a copy after a request;
- Did not return some or all of the client's original records (which is a violation of Circular 230, §10.28);
- Did not sign a federal tax return they prepared;
- Claimed to be an attorney, CPA, or EA, without actually having the credential claimed or without a valid credential (e.g., it expired, was suspended, or revoked);
- Indicated to the client that their return would be filed but failed to file the return;
- Charged for services that were never performed;
- Failed to remit the client's money for taxes due when their relationship with the client made them responsible for doing so;
- Filed a return or submitted other information for a client document without that client's knowledge, authorization, or consent;
- Failed to explain that a cash advance, fast refund, or instant refund was actually a refund anticipation loan borrowed against an income tax refund and/or failed to explain the related fees and interest charges;
- Was misleading or failed to ensure that the client understood financial products and related fees;
- Used a PTIN belonging to another preparer; or
- Prepared a return without a PTIN or failed to indicate their PTIN on a return they prepared.

45. Instructions for Form 14157.

Form **14157** (June 2018)	Department of the Treasury - Internal Revenue Service **Return Preparer Complaint**	OMB Number 1545-2168

Use this form to file a complaint with the IRS against a tax return preparer or tax preparation business.

CAUTION: READ THE INSTRUCTIONS BEFORE COMPLETING THIS FORM. There may be other more appropriate forms specific to your complaint. (For example, if you believe you are a victim of identity theft, please complete Form 14039, Identity Theft Affidavit).

Section A - Return Preparer Information *(complete all known information)*

1. Preparer's professional status *(check all that apply)*

☐ Attorney ☐ Certified Public Accountant ☐ Other/Unknown

☐ Enrolled Agent ☐ Payroll Service Provider

2. Preparer's name and address	3. Preparer's business name and address *(if different)*
4. Preparer's telephone number(s) *(include area code)*	5. Preparer's email address
6. Preparer's website	7. Preparer Electronic Filing Identification Number (EFIN)
8. Preparer Tax Identification Number (PTIN)	9. Employer Identification Number (EIN)

Section B - Complaint Information

10a. Tax period(s) impacted

10b. Did you pay a fee to your preparer ☐ Yes ☐ No	If "Yes", enter fee amount

How did you pay the fee *(e.g., deducted from refund, personal payment)*

11a. Review the complaints below and check all that apply

☐ Theft of Refund *(Diverted refund to unknown account; return filed does not match taxpayer's copy)*

☐ E-File *(e-filed returns using pay stub, non-commercial software or Free File without properly securing taxpayer's signature)*

☐ Preparer Misconduct *(Failed to provide copy of return, return records, sign returns or remit payments for taxes due; misrepresentation of credentials; agreed to file return but did not; filed return without authorization or consent.)*

☐ PTIN Issues *(Failed to include Preparer Tax Identification Number (PTIN) or any identification number on tax return; indicated the return was "self-prepared" when it was not.)*

☐ False Items/Documents *(False expenses, deductions, credits, exemptions or dependents; false or altered documents; false or overstated Form W-2 or 1099; incorrect filing status)*

☐ Employment Taxes *(Failed to file forms 940, 941, 943, or 945 or remit Employment Tax payment)*

☐ Return Preparer self reported event *(Compromised PTIN, data breach/security incident, return count discrepancy, someone used your identity to obtain a PTIN)*

☐ Other *(explain below)*

Attach a **copy** of any documents you received from the tax return preparer (e.g., **tax returns**, advertisements, business cards, Form 8879, IRS e-file Signature Authorization, Form 8888, Allocation of Refund (including savings bond purchases), Contract for Service Agreement, and Refund Transfer Agreement). Do not send original returns or payments with this form.

Catalog Number 55242M www.irs.gov Form **14157** (Rev. 6-2018)

6

11b. Provide facts and other information related to the complaint *(attach additional sheets if necessary).*

Section C - Taxpayer's Information **Are you the taxpayer?** ☐ Yes ☐ No

This information may be necessary to process your complaint. If you are the taxpayer complete section C only. If you are not the taxpayer, complete sections C and D.

12. Name *of individual or business*

13. Mailing address *(street, city, state, ZIP code)*

14. Telephone number(s) *(include area code)*

15. Email address

16. Taxpayer's signature

17. Date of complaint

Section D - Your Information *(do not complete if you are the taxpayer)*

This information is not required to process your complaint but is helpful if we need to contact you for additional information.

18. Name *(Last, First, MI)*

19. Date of complaint

20. Mailing address *(street, city, state, ZIP code)*

21. Telephone number(s) *(include area code)*

22. Email address

23. Your relationship to Preparer

- ☐ Client
- ☐ Return preparer working for a different firm*
- ☐ Return preparer working for the same firm*
- ☐ Return preparer self reported event
- ☐ IRS employee
- ☐ Other *(specify)* ______

* Taxpayers' information and any information relating to another professional are confidential. Please obtain your client's consent before sharing any protected tax information, even with the IRS.

The completed form along with all supporting information can be filed by fax or regular mail.

If faxing Form 14157 send to: **855-889-7957**

If mailing Form 14157 send to:

Attn: Return Preparer Office
401 W. Peachtree Street NW
Mail Stop 421-D
Atlanta, GA 30308

Privacy Act and Paperwork Reduction Act Notice

We ask for the information on this form to carry out the Internal Revenue laws of the United States. We need it to ensure that preparers are complying with these laws and to allow us to figure and collect the right amount of tax.

You are not required to provide the information requested on a form that is subject to the Paperwork Reduction Act unless the form displays a valid OMB control number. Books or records relating to a form or its instructions must be retained as long as their contents may become material in the administration of any Internal Revenue law. Generally, tax returns and return information are confidential, as required by Internal Revenue Code section 6103.

The time require to complete this form will vary depending on individual circumstances. The estimated average time is 15 minutes. The primary purpose of this form is to report potential violations of the Internal Revenue laws by tax return preparers. We are requesting this information under authority of 26 U.S.C. § 7801 and § 7803. Providing this information is voluntary, and failure to provide all or part of the information will not affect you. Providing false or fraudulent information may subject you to penalties. We may disclose this information to the Department of Justice to enforce the tax laws, both civil and criminal, and to cities, states, the District of Columbia, and U.S. commonwealths or possessions to carry out their tax laws. We may also disclose this information to other countries under a tax treaty, to federal and state agencies to enforce federal non-tax criminal laws, and to federal law enforcement and intelligence agencies to combat terrorism.

Catalog Number 55242M www.irs.gov Form **14157** (Rev. 6-2018)

Discussion Scenario 13

Chris is meeting with a new client, Leonard, who has concerns about his previous practitioner. Chris requests Leonard bring his three most recent tax returns and the associated source documents to the appointment.

When Leonard presents his 2019 and 2020 returns (his most recently filed returns), Chris notices the returns do not include a PTIN or paid preparer's information, nor were they signed. Neither tax return has the accompanying source documents. However, there is an invoice marked "paid" with each return. Leonard states he was always asked to pay the invoice in cash. Chris asks about the source documents and Leonard says the previous practitioner always kept them. Leonard also states the last two years returns have not been completed even though the previous practitioner has had the documents for over a year.

Chris asks about certain deductions for materials and office expenses on Leonard's Schedule C, *Profit or Loss From Business*. Leonard states that for his projects, the customers purchase the materials and he provides the labor. His only office expense is the occasional purchase of an invoice book for $10. The return shows a $5,000 expense in materials and $1,500 in office expenses. Chris also notes there is an American Opportunity Credit on the return for Leonard. When he asks Leonard what he is studying at East Carolina University, Leonard states that no one in his family is attending college, and asks why Chris is inquiring.

6

Chris asks who the previous practitioner was so he can contact them, with Leonard's approval, to obtain his source documents so they can move forward.

Does Chris have sufficient cause to report Leonard's previous preparer to the IRS, and if so, what issues should be addressed on the complaint? ____________________

____

____

____

What should Chris do to ensure the accuracy of the previously filed returns? ____________________

____

____

____

____

Can they proceed with preparing any unfiled or future returns? Why or why not? ____________________

____

____

____

____

Discussion Scenario 14

Use the same facts as **Scenario 13,** except Chris discovers that Leonard's previous practitioner has passed away. The previous practitioner's family does not grant access to the practitioner's office for Chris or Leonord to obtain the records.

How should Chris proceed to obtain the records? ____

____

____

____

Eventually, the family grants access to the records at the deceased practitioner's office. Chris goes with Leonard to recover his records. They discover all the practitioner's files are lined up on the floor in rows in such a way that everyone's records are visible to anyone walking in and the only verification done when walking out with records is someone checking photo identification and matching it with the name on the documents.

Does Chris have an obligation to report the practitioner or the estate to the IRS for unauthorized disclosure or anything else in Circular 230? ____

____

____

____

____

PUBLICATION OF TAX PREPARATION FEES[46]

Practitioners may publish a fee schedule and the following fee information.

- Fixed fees for specific routine services
- Hourly fee rates
- A fee range for specific services
- The fee for an initial consultation

If the fee schedule or information concerns work where out-of-pocket costs could arise, it should clarify whether clients are responsible for such costs. Once the fee schedule is published, a practitioner can charge **no more** than the published fee rates for **at least 30 calendar days** from the date of publication.

Fee information can be communicated via professional lists, telephone directories, print media, mailings, electronic mail, facsimile, hand-delivered flyers, radio, television, and any other method if it does not result in untruthful or deceptive communication of the information.

When a practitioner uses radio or television broadcasting, they must retain a recording of the actual transmission. For direct mail and e-commerce communications, the practitioner must retain a copy of the actual communication, along with a list or other description of the persons to whom the communication was distributed. The practitioner must keep the copy for at least 36 months from the date of the last transmission or use.

A practitioner must not contact prospective clients who have communicated that they do not wish to be solicited.

46. See Circular 230, §10.30.

Discussion Scenario 15

Grant is an EA in a competitive market. He purchases advertisement space in the newspaper and promotes that he has the lowest rates in town. He will prepare a Form 1040 for the low, low price of $150. The ad runs on February 1.

Gretchen sees the ad and makes an appointment with Grant for February 18. She provides all the relevant tax information for her small sewing business, as well as her husband's Form W-2. She brings her prior year return and her infant son's social security card to prove his dependency. Grant immediately starts preparing her return.

At the end of the appointment, Grant hands Gretchen her return and her bill. She is shocked to see the bill is not the $150 quoted in the paper but rather $500. Grant explains that the $150 rate was only good for the week the ad ran in the paper. Furthermore, the Schedule C he prepared for Gretchen is not considered part of the Form 1040. Grant also charged extra because Gretchen had a dependent and obviously the $150 rate implied no dependents.

Gretchen refused to pay, and Grant refused to return her documents until she paid him the full amount.

How did Grant violate the rules about publishing his fees? ______________________________

____

____

____

____

Is it reasonable that Grant charge extra for a Schedule C? Are associated schedules considered part of a Form 1040? Why or why not? ______________________________

____

____

____

____

Can Grant refuse to return Gretchen's documents if she refuses to pay? If no, what provision of Circular 230 does this violate? ______________________________

____

____

____

____

6

DEATH OF A TAX PREPARER[47]

Circular 230, §10.33, describes various best practices that a tax practitioner should implement in their practice. This can be extended to preparations a tax practitioner makes before their death to protect the practitioner, their clients, their firm, and their family to avoid violations of privacy and confidentiality.

47. See *Best Practices: How to prepare for and what to do when a tax practitioner dies.* Jun. 27, 2023. IRS. [content.govdelivery.com/accounts/USIRS/bulletins/360ff31] Accessed on Jul. 11, 2023.

Some IRS best practices during engagements with clients include the following.

- Communicate regularly and clearly with clients to manage expectations
- Discuss all significant aspects of the engagement including scope, terms, purposes or objectives, and actions to be taken during and after the engagement (ideally, this is covered in a written engagement letter)
- Provide regular updates and revise the engagement letter if necessary, during the engagement (this would assist in any transition of client matters to another tax practitioner in the event the original practitioner becomes incapacitated or dies)
- Establish clear policies for retention, disposition/destruction, and returning client files to avoid burdening the successor or estate with dealing with the files and records
- Implement a data security and privacy plan

> **Note.** For more information on implementing a data security and privacy plan, see the 2023 *University of Illinois Federal Tax Workbook,* Chapter 1: Written Information Security Plans and Protecting Client Data.

- Adopt a business continuity plan to prepare for extraordinary events such as a natural disaster, cyberattack, pandemic, or the incapacity or death of the tax practitioner

SUCCESSION PLAN

A succession plan for a tax practitioner should address how to handle the sale or termination of a practitioner's business. The succession plan should be shared with clients. Best practices for a succession plan include the following.

- Enter an agreement with an **assisting practitioner** who will be responsible for wrapping up the affairs of the deceased practitioner
- Keep a current inventory of all open client matters and contact information to facilitate an assisting practitioner to quickly determine any client needs and minimize delays in addressing them (documents should be secured with passwords and encryption to which the assisting practitioner has access)
- Ensure that the assisting practitioner can access information and funds to pay bills
- Discuss with clients if they wish to authorize additional practitioners to represent them via Forms 2848 or 8821
- Devise a plan to inform clients in the event of the practitioner's incapacity or death
- Speak with family members regarding the succession plan and any involvement they may have with it

COMMUNICATION AFTER INCAPACITATION OR DEATH

Assuming the practitioner had a succession plan in place prior to their incapacitation or death, the assisting practitioner should implement that plan and communicate with the practitioner's clients and the IRS. If the practitioner did not have a succession plan in place, the responsibilities will likely fall to an executor or administrator of the practitioner's estate.

The communication with the practitioner's clients should include the following.

- Procedures for handling any ongoing client matters or the disposition of client files
- Practitioner's firm or a preapproved successor must ensure all necessary paperwork is completed with the IRS for clients remaining with the firm/successor
- Clients not remaining with the firm/successor should receive their files in a prompt and orderly manner per Circular 230, §10.28
- If the practitioner did not have a succession plan or provide advance notice to their clients, the assisting practitioner should promptly notify each client and confirm arrangements (the assisting practitioner cannot transfer any client files without the expressed consent of the client)

In addition to communicating with clients, the assisting practitioner should consider the following best practices when implementing a succession plan.

- Ensure that no one removes any files without client consent
- Control physical access to the practitioner's premises
- Backup electronic files
- Interview employees, contractors, and vendors to ascertain all known clients and client properties beyond the practitioner's available records
- Publish a notice in local media alerting the public of the office closure and for clients to retain new representation and collect their files
- Keep copies of any necessary documents for the practitioner's estate in the event of any potential claims against the practitioner and to help determine any rights to fees and reimbursable expenses
- Track and confirm that clients received appropriate notice
- Safeguard client confidentiality

Additionally, an assisting practitioner needs to communicate with the IRS that the practitioner is incapacitated or deceased. The assisting practitioner does not need to inform the RPO if the practitioner had a PTIN. Every month, the RPO checks the National Accounts Profile and updates PTIN statuses to "deceased" as necessary. The fiduciary (guardian or trustee with Form 56, *Notice of Fiduciary Relationship,* on file with the IRS) needs to inform the RPO if the practitioner is incapacitated. This will cause the practitioner's PTIN status to be updated to "inactive." If a nonfiduciary, such as the assisting practitioner, informs the RPO regarding the incapacitation, the RPO will log the information and the PTIN will subsequently expire.

The Centralized Authorization File (CAF) unit must also be notified of the practitioner's incapacitation or death. The written request should be sent via fax or mail to the CAF unit identified in the "Where to File" chart in the instructions to Forms 2848 and 8821. The CAF unit will then mark the CAF number for the practitioner as deceased, which will nullify all CAF notifications for the practitioner.

Although a practitioner's employer identification number (EIN) cannot technically be canceled, the assisting practitioner can and should close the business account that is associated with the EIN. The business account can only be closed after all necessary returns are filed and any outstanding taxes paid. To close the account, a letter should be sent to the IRS that includes the following.

- Full legal name of the business
- EIN
- Business address
- Reason for closing the account
- Original notice from the IRS assigning the EIN if available

Discussion Scenario 16

Lon is diagnosed with terminal cancer during 2022. Because he wants the distraction of work and to make sure his family is left with as much money as possible, he continues working until his death in February 2023. Lon tells the clients that he sees about his diagnosis but does not craft a written succession plan. He does, however, identify a fellow practitioner, Margo, as the successor to his practice.

Shortly before he passes away, Lon takes Margo on a tour of his office. He shows her where he keeps the keys to the filing cabinets but assures her that they are usually unlocked. Additionally, Lon points out the sticky notes next to his computer where all his passwords are written down.

Margo is overwhelmed in February when Lon dies due to juggling both her clients and all of Lon's clients whose work he did not complete before his death. She finds it emotionally draining to tell many of Lon's clients about his passing. Margo does not notify the IRS about Lon's death until the middle of May.

What are some best practices that Lon implemented appropriately? ______________________________

____

____

____

____

What are some best practices that Lon should have implemented? ______________________________

____

____

____

____

What is a reasonable amount of time for Margo to notify the IRS of Lon's death? ______________________________

____

____

____

____

Would Lon be considered as releasing client data to Margo without their approval? What about for the clients he told he was terminally ill but did not provide a succession plan in writing? ______________________________

____

____

____

____

Paragraph 1. The authority citation for 31 CFR, part 10 continues to read as follows:
Authority: Sec. 3, 23 Stat. 258, secs. 2-12, 60 Stat. 237 et. seq.; 5 U.S.C. 301, 500, 551-559; 31 U.S.C. 321; 31 U.S.C. 330; Reorg. Plan No. 26 of 1950, 15 FR 4935, 64 Stat. 1280, 3 CFR, 1949-1953 Comp., p. 1017.

§ 10.0 Scope of part.

(a) This part contains rules governing the recognition of attorneys, certified public accountants, enrolled agents, enrolled retirement plan agents, registered tax return preparers, and other persons representing taxpayers before the Internal Revenue Service. Subpart A of this part sets forth rules relating to the authority to practice before the Internal Revenue Service; subpart B of this part prescribes the duties and restrictions relating to such practice; subpart C of this part prescribes the sanctions for violating the regulations; subpart D of this part contains the rules applicable to disciplinary proceedings; and subpart E of this part contains general provisions relating to the availability of official records.

(b) *Effective/applicability date.* This section is applicable beginning August 2, 2011.

Subpart A — Rules Governing Authority to Practice

§ 10.1 Offices.

(a) *Establishment of office(s).* The Commissioner shall establish the Office of Professional Responsibility and any other office(s) within the Internal Revenue Service necessary to administer and enforce this part. The Commissioner shall appoint the Director of the Office of Professional Responsibility and any other Internal Revenue official(s) to manage and direct any office(s) established to administer or enforce this part. Offices established under this part include, but are not limited to:

(1) The Office of Professional Responsibility, which shall generally have responsibility for matters related to practitioner conduct and shall have exclusive responsibility for discipline, including disciplinary proceedings and sanctions; and

(2) An office with responsibility for matters related to authority to practice before the Internal Revenue Service, including acting on applications for enrollment to practice before the Internal Revenue Service and administering competency testing and continuing education.

(b) Officers and employees within any office established under this part may perform acts necessary or appropriate to carry out the responsibilities of their office(s) under this part or as otherwise prescribed by the Commissioner.

(c) *Acting.* The Commissioner will designate an officer or employee of the Internal Revenue Service to perform the duties of an individual appointed under paragraph (a) of this section in the absence of that officer or employee or during a vacancy in that office.

(d) *Effective/applicability date.* This section is applicable beginning August 2, 2011, except that paragraph (a)(1) is applicable beginning June 12, 2014.

6

§ 10.2 Definitions.

(a) As used in this part, except where the text provides otherwise —

(1) *Attorney* means any person who is a member in good standing of the bar of the highest court of any state, territory, or possession of the United States, including a Commonwealth, or the District of Columbia.

(2) *Certified public accountant* means any person who is duly qualified to practice as a certified public accountant in any state, territory, or possession of the United States, including a Commonwealth, or the District of Columbia.

(3) *Commissioner* refers to the Commissioner of Internal Revenue.

(4) *Practice before the Internal Revenue Service* comprehends all matters connected with a presentation to the Internal Revenue Service or any of its officers or employees relating to a taxpayer's rights, privileges, or liabilities under laws or regulations administered by the Internal Revenue Service. Such presentations include, but are not limited to, preparing documents; filing documents; corresponding and communicating with the Internal Revenue Service; rendering written advice with respect to any entity, transaction, plan or arrangement, or other plan or arrangement having a potential for tax avoidance or evasion; and representing a client at conferences, hearings, and meetings.

(5) *Practitioner* means any individual described in paragraphs (a), (b), (c), (d), (e), or (f) of §10.3.

(6) A *tax return* includes an amended tax return and a claim for refund.

(7) *Service* means the Internal Revenue Service.

(8) *Tax return preparer* means any individual within the meaning of section 7701(a)(36) and 26 CFR 301.7701-15.

(b) *Effective/applicability date.* This section is applicable on August 2, 2011.

§ 10.3 Who may practice.

(a) *Attorneys.* Any attorney who is not currently under suspension or disbarment from practice before the Internal Revenue Service may practice before the Internal Revenue Service by filing with the Internal Revenue Service a written declaration that the attorney is currently qualified as an attorney and is authorized to represent the party or parties. Notwithstanding the preceding sentence, attorneys who are not currently under suspension or disbarment from practice before the Internal Revenue Service are not required to file a written declaration with the IRS before rendering written advice covered under §10.37, but their rendering of this advice is practice before the Internal Revenue Service.

(b) *Certified public accountants.* Any certified public accountant who is not currently under suspension or disbarment from practice before the Internal Revenue Service may practice before the Internal Revenue Service by filing with the Internal Revenue Service a written declaration that the certified public accountant is currently qualified as a certified public accountant and is authorized to represent the party or parties. Notwithstanding the preceding sentence, certified public accountants who are not currently under suspension or disbarment from practice before the Internal Revenue Service are not required to file a written declaration with the IRS before rendering written advice covered under §10.37, but their rendering of this advice is practice before the Internal Revenue Service.

(c) *Enrolled agents.* Any individual enrolled as an agent pursuant to this part who is not currently under suspension or disbarment from practice before the Internal Revenue Service may practice before the Internal Revenue Service.

(d) *Enrolled actuaries.*

(1) Any individual who is enrolled as an actuary by the Joint Board for the Enrollment of Actuaries pursuant to 29 U.S.C. 1242 who is not currently under suspension or disbarment from practice before the Internal Revenue Service may practice before the Internal Revenue Service by filing with the Internal Revenue Service a written declaration stating that he or she is currently qualified as an enrolled actuary and is authorized to represent the party or parties on whose behalf he or she acts.

(2) Practice as an enrolled actuary is limited

Page 6 — § 10.2 Treasury Department Circular No. 230

to representation with respect to issues involving the following statutory provisions in title 26 of the United States Code: sections 401 (relating to qualification of employee plans), 403(a) (relating to whether an annuity plan meets the requirements of section 404(a) (2)), 404 (relating to deductibility of employer contributions), 405 (relating to qualification of bond purchase plans), 412 (relating to funding requirements for certain employee plans), 413 (relating to application of qualification requirements to collectively bargained plans and to plans maintained by more than one employer), 414 (relating to definitions and special rules with respect to the employee plan area), 419 (relating to treatment of funded welfare benefits), 419A (relating to qualified asset accounts), 420 (relating to transfers of excess pension assets to retiree health accounts), 4971 (relating to excise taxes payable as a result of an accumulated funding deficiency under section 412), 4972 (relating to tax on nondeductible contributions to qualified employer plans), 4976 (relating to taxes with respect to funded welfare benefit plans), 4980 (relating to tax on reversion of qualified plan assets to employer), 6057 (relating to annual registration of plans), 6058 (relating to information required in connection with certain plans of deferred compensation), 6059 (relating to periodic report of actuary), 6652(e) (relating to the failure to file annual registration and other notifications by pension plan), 6652(f) (relating to the failure to file information required in connection with certain plans of deferred compensation), 6692 (relating to the failure to file actuarial report), 7805(b) (relating to the extent to which an Internal Revenue Service ruling or determination letter coming under the statutory provisions listed here will be applied without retroactive effect); and 29 U.S.C. § 1083 (relating to the waiver of funding for nonqualified plans).

(3) An individual who practices before the Internal Revenue Service pursuant to paragraph (d)(1) of this section is subject to the provisions of this part in the same manner as attorneys, certified public accountants, enrolled agents, enrolled retirement plan agents, and registered tax return preparers.

(e) *Enrolled retirement plan agents* —

(1) Any individual enrolled as a retirement plan agent pursuant to this part who is not currently under suspension or disbarment from practice before the Internal Revenue Service may practice before the Internal Revenue Service.

(2) Practice as an enrolled retirement plan agent is limited to representation with respect to issues involving the following programs: Employee Plans Determination Letter program; Employee Plans Compliance Resolution System; and Employee Plans Master and Prototype and Volume Submitter program. In addition, enrolled retirement plan agents are generally permitted to represent taxpayers with respect to IRS forms under the 5300 and 5500 series which are filed by retirement plans and plan sponsors, but not with respect to actuarial forms or schedules.

(3) An individual who practices before the Internal Revenue Service pursuant to paragraph (e)(1) of this section is subject to the provisions of this part in the same manner as attorneys, certified public accountants, enrolled agents, enrolled actuaries, and registered tax return preparers.

(f) *Registered tax return preparers.*

(1) Any individual who is designated as a registered tax return preparer pursuant to §10.4(c) of this part who is not currently under suspension or disbarment from practice before the Internal Revenue Service may practice before the Internal Revenue Service.

(2) Practice as a registered tax return preparer is limited to preparing and signing tax returns and claims for refund, and other documents for submission to the Internal Revenue Service. A registered tax return preparer may prepare all or substantially all of a tax return or claim for refund of tax. The Internal Revenue Service will prescribe by forms, instructions, or other appropriate guidance the tax returns and claims for refund that a registered tax return preparer may prepare and sign.

(3) A registered tax return preparer may represent taxpayers before revenue agents, customer service representatives, or similar officers and employees of the Internal Revenue Service (including the Taxpayer Advocate Service) during an examination if the registered tax return preparer signed the tax return

Treasury Department Circular No. 230

§ 10.3 — Page 7

or claim for refund for the taxable year or period under examination. Unless otherwise prescribed by regulation or notice, this right does not permit such individual to represent the taxpayer, regardless of the circumstances requiring representation, before appeals officers, revenue officers, Counsel or similar officers or employees of the Internal Revenue Service or the Treasury Department. A registered tax return preparer's authorization to practice under this part also does not include the authority to provide tax advice to a client or another person except as necessary to prepare a tax return, claim for refund, or other document intended to be submitted to the Internal Revenue Service.

(4) An individual who practices before the Internal Revenue Service pursuant to paragraph (f)(1) of this section is subject to the provisions of this part in the same manner as attorneys, certified public accountants, enrolled agents, enrolled retirement plan agents, and enrolled actuaries.

(g) *Others.* Any individual qualifying under paragraph §10.5(e) or §10.7 is eligible to practice before the Internal Revenue Service to the extent provided in those sections.

(h) *Government officers and employees, and others.* An individual, who is an officer or employee of the executive, legislative, or judicial branch of the United States Government; an officer or employee of the District of Columbia; a Member of Congress; or a Resident Commissioner may not practice before the Internal Revenue Service if such practice violates 18 U.S.C. §§ 203 or 205.

(i) *State officers and employees.* No officer or employee of any State, or subdivision of any State, whose duties require him or her to pass upon, investigate, or deal with tax matters for such State or subdivision, may practice before the Internal Revenue Service, if such employment may disclose facts or information applicable to Federal tax matters.

(j) *Effective/applicability date.* Paragraphs (a), (b), and (g) of this section are applicable beginning June 12, 2014. Paragraphs (c) through (f), (h), and (i) of this section are applicable beginning August 2, 2011.

§ 10.4 Eligibility to become an enrolled agent, enrolled retirement plan agent, or registered tax return preparer.

(a) *Enrollment as an enrolled agent upon examination.* The Commissioner, or delegate, will grant enrollment as an enrolled agent to an applicant eighteen years of age or older who demonstrates special competence in tax matters by written examination administered by, or administered under the oversight of, the Internal Revenue Service, who possesses a current or otherwise valid preparer tax identification number or other prescribed identifying number, and who has not engaged in any conduct that would justify the suspension or disbarment of any practitioner under the provisions of this part.

(b) *Enrollment as a retirement plan agent upon examination.* The Commissioner, or delegate, will grant enrollment as an enrolled retirement plan agent to an applicant eighteen years of age or older who demonstrates special competence in qualified retirement plan matters by written examination administered by, or administered under the oversight of, the Internal Revenue Service, who possesses a current or otherwise valid preparer tax identification number or other prescribed identifying number, and who has not engaged in any conduct that would justify the suspension or disbarment of any practitioner under the provisions of this part.

(c) *Designation as a registered tax return preparer.* The Commissioner, or delegate, may designate an individual eighteen years of age or older as a registered tax return preparer provided an applicant demonstrates competence in Federal tax return preparation matters by written examination administered by, or administered under the oversight of, the Internal Revenue Service, or otherwise meets the requisite standards prescribed by the Internal Revenue Service, possesses a current or otherwise valid preparer tax identification number or other prescribed identifying number, and has not engaged in any conduct that would justify the suspension or disbarment of any practitioner under the provisions of this part.

(d) *Enrollment of former Internal Revenue Service employees.* The Commissioner, or delegate, may grant enrollment as an enrolled agent or enrolled retirement plan agent to an applicant who, by virtue of past service and technical experience in the Internal Revenue Service, has qualified for such enrollment and who has not engaged in any conduct that would justify the suspension or disbarment of any practitioner under the provisions of this part, under the following circumstances:

(1) The former employee applies for enrollment on an Internal Revenue Service form and supplies the information requested on the form and such other information regarding the experience and training of the applicant as may be relevant.

(2) The appropriate office of the Internal Revenue Service provides a detailed report of the nature and rating of the applicant's work while employed by the Internal Revenue Service and a recommendation whether such employment qualifies the applicant technically or otherwise for the desired authorization.

(3) Enrollment as an enrolled agent based on an applicant's former employment with the Internal Revenue Service may be of unlimited scope or it may be limited to permit the presentation of matters only of the particular specialty or only before the particular unit or division of the Internal Revenue Service for which the applicant's former employment has qualified the applicant. Enrollment as an enrolled retirement plan agent based on an applicant's former employment with the Internal Revenue Service will be limited to permit the presentation of matters only with respect to qualified retirement plan matters.

(4) Application for enrollment as an enrolled agent or enrolled retirement plan agent based on an applicant's former employment with the Internal Revenue Service must be made within three years from the date of separation from such employment.

(5) An applicant for enrollment as an enrolled agent who is requesting such enrollment based on former employment with the Internal Revenue Service must have had a minimum of five years continuous employment with the Internal Revenue Service during which the applicant must have been regularly engaged in applying and interpreting the provisions of the Internal Revenue Code and the regulations relating to income, estate, gift, employment, or excise taxes.

(6) An applicant for enrollment as an enrolled retirement plan agent who is requesting such enrollment based on former employment with the Internal Revenue Service must have had a minimum of five years continuous employment with the Internal Revenue Service during which the applicant must have been regularly engaged in applying and interpreting the provisions of the Internal Revenue Code and the regulations relating to qualified retirement plan matters.

(7) For the purposes of paragraphs (d)(5) and (6) of this section, an aggregate of 10 or more years of employment in positions involving the application and interpretation of the provisions of the Internal Revenue Code, at least three of which occurred within the five years preceding the date of application, is the equivalent of five years continuous employment.

(e) *Natural persons.* Enrollment to practice may be granted only to natural persons.

(f) *Effective/applicability date.* This section is applicable beginning August 2, 2011.

§ 10.5 Application to become an enrolled agent, enrolled retirement plan agent, or registered tax return preparer.

(a) *Form; address.* An applicant to become an enrolled agent, enrolled retirement plan agent, or registered tax return preparer must apply as required by forms or procedures established and published by the Internal Revenue Service, including proper execution of required forms under oath or affirmation. The address on the application will be the address under which a successful applicant is enrolled or registered and is the address to which all correspondence concerning enrollment or registration will be sent.

(b) *Fee.* A reasonable nonrefundable fee may be charged for each application to become an enrolled agent, enrolled retirement plan agent, or registered tax return preparer. See 26 CFR part 300.

(c) *Additional information; examination.* The Internal Revenue Service may require the applicant, as a condition to consideration of an application, to file additional information and to submit to any written or oral examination under oath or otherwise. Upon the applicant's written request, the Internal Revenue Service will afford the applicant the opportunity to be heard with respect to the application.

(d) *Compliance and suitability checks.*

(1) As a condition to consideration of an application, the Internal Revenue Service may conduct a Federal tax compliance check and suitability check. The tax compliance check will be limited to an inquiry regarding whether an applicant has filed all required individual or business tax returns and whether the applicant has failed to pay, or make proper arrangements with the Internal Revenue Service for payment of, any Federal tax debts. The suitability check will be limited to an inquiry regarding whether an applicant has engaged in any conduct that would justify suspension or disbarment of any practitioner under the provisions of this part on the date the application is submitted, including whether the applicant has engaged in disreputable conduct as defined in §10.51. The application will be denied only if the results of the compliance or suitability check are sufficient to establish that the practitioner engaged in conduct subject to sanctions under §§10.51 and 10.52.

(2) If the applicant does not pass the tax compliance or suitability check, the applicant will not be issued an enrollment or registration card or certificate pursuant to §10.6(b) of this part. An applicant who is initially denied enrollment or registration for failure to pass a tax compliance check may reapply after the initial denial if the applicant becomes current with respect to the applicant's tax liabilities.

(e) *Temporary recognition.* On receipt of a properly executed application, the Commissioner, or delegate, may grant the applicant temporary recognition to practice pending a determination as to whether status as an enrolled agent, enrolled retirement plan agent, or registered tax return preparer should be granted. Temporary recognition will be granted only in unusual circumstances and it will not be granted, in any circumstance, if the application is not regular on its face, if the information stated in the application, if true, is not sufficient to warrant granting the application to practice, or the Commissioner, or delegate, has information indicating that the statements in the application are untrue or that the applicant would not otherwise qualify to become an enrolled agent, enrolled retirement plan agent, or registered tax return preparer. Issuance of temporary recognition does not constitute either a designation or a finding of eligibility as an enrolled agent, enrolled retirement plan agent, or registered tax return preparer, and the temporary recognition may be withdrawn at any time.

(f) *Protest of application denial.* The applicant will be informed in writing as to the reason(s) for any denial of an application. The applicant may, within 30 days after receipt of the notice of denial of the application, file a written protest of the denial as prescribed by the Internal Revenue Service in forms, guidance, or other appropriate guidance. A protest under this section is not governed by subpart D of this part.

(f) *Effective/applicability date.* This section is applicable to applications received on or after August 2, 2011.

§ 10.6 Term and renewal of status as an enrolled agent, enrolled retirement plan agent, or registered tax return preparer.

(a) *Term.* Each individual authorized to practice before the Internal Revenue Service as an enrolled agent, enrolled retirement plan agent, or registered tax return preparer will be accorded active enrollment or registration status subject to renewal of enrollment or registration as provided in this part.

(b) *Enrollment or registration card or certificate.* The Internal Revenue Service will issue an enrollment or registration card or certificate to each individual whose application to practice before the Internal Revenue Service is approved. Each card or certificate will be valid for the period stated on the card or certificate. An enrolled agent, enrolled retirement plan agent, or registered tax return preparer may not practice before the Internal Revenue Service if the card or certificate is not current or otherwise valid. The card or certificate is in addition to any notification that may be provided to each individual who obtains a preparer tax identification number.

(c) *Change of address.* An enrolled agent, enrolled retirement plan agent, or registered tax return preparer must send notification of any change of address to the address specified by the Internal Revenue Service within 60 days of the change of address. This notification must include the enrolled agent's, enrolled retirement plan agent's, or registered tax return preparer's name, prior address, new address, tax identification number(s) (including preparer tax identification number), and the date the change of address is effective. Unless this notification is sent, the address for purposes of any correspondence from the appropriate Internal Revenue Service office responsible for administering this part shall be the address reflected on the practitioner's most recent application for enrollment or registration, or application for renewal of enrollment or registration. A practitioner's change of address notification under this part will not constitute a change of the practitioner's last known address for purposes of section 6212 of the Internal Revenue Code and regulations thereunder.

(d) *Renewal.*

(1) *In general.* Enrolled agents, enrolled retirement plan agents, and registered tax return preparers must renew their status with the Internal Revenue Service to maintain eligibility to practice before the Internal Revenue Service. Failure to receive notification from the Internal Revenue Service of the renewal requirement will not be justification for the individual's failure to satisfy this requirement.

(2) *Renewal period for enrolled agents.*

(i) All enrolled agents must renew their preparer tax identification number as prescribed by forms, instructions, or other appropriate guidance.

(ii) Enrolled agents who have a social security number or tax identification number that ends with the numbers 0, 1, 2, or 3, except for those individuals who received their initial enrollment after November 1, 2003, must apply for renewal between November 1, 2003, and January 31, 2004. The renewal will be effective April 1, 2004.

(iii) Enrolled agents who have a social security number or tax identification number that ends with the numbers 4, 5, or 6, except for those individuals who received their initial enrollment after November 1, 2004, must apply for renewal between November 1, 2004, and January 31, 2005. The renewal will be effective April 1, 2005.

(iv) Enrolled agents who have a social security number or tax identification number that ends with the numbers 7, 8, or 9, except for those individuals who received their initial enrollment after November 1, 2005, must apply for renewal between November 1, 2005, and January 31, 2006. The renewal will be effective April 1, 2006.

(v) Thereafter, applications for renewal as an enrolled agent will be required between November 1 and January 31 of every subsequent third year as specified in paragraph (d)(2)(i), (d)(2)(ii), or (d)(2)(iii) of this section according to the last number of the individual's social security number or tax identification number. Those individuals who receive initial enrollment as an enrolled agent after November 1 and before April 2 of the applicable renewal period will not be required to renew their enrollment before the first full renewal period following the receipt of their initial enrollment.

(3) *Renewal period for enrolled retirement plan agents.*

(i) All enrolled retirement plan agents must renew their preparer tax identification number as prescribed by the Internal Revenue Service in forms, instructions, or other appropriate guidance.

(ii) Enrolled retirement plan agents will be required to renew their status as enrolled retirement plan agents between April 1 and June 30 of every third year subsequent to their initial enrollment.

(4) *Renewal period for registered tax return preparers.* Registered tax return preparers must renew their preparer tax identification number and their status as a registered tax return preparer as prescribed by the Internal Revenue Service in forms, instructions, or other appropriate guidance.

(5) *Notification of renewal.* After review and approval, the Internal Revenue Service will notify

the individual of the renewal and will issue the individual a card or certificate evidencing current status as an enrolled agent, enrolled retirement plan agent, or registered tax return preparer.

(6) *Fee*. A reasonable nonrefundable fee may be charged for each application for renewal filed. See 26 CFR part 300.

(7) *Forms*. Forms required for renewal may be obtained by sending a written request to the address specified by the Internal Revenue Service or from such other source as the Internal Revenue Service will publish in the Internal Revenue Bulletin (see 26 CFR 601.601(d)(2)(ii)(b)) and on the Internal Revenue Service webpage (www.irs.gov).

(e) *Condition for renewal*: continuing education. In order to qualify for renewal as an enrolled agent, enrolled retirement plan agent, or registered tax return preparer, an individual must certify, in the manner prescribed by the Internal Revenue Service, that the individual has satisfied the requisite number of continuing education hours.

(1) *Definitions*. For purposes of this section —

(i) *Enrollment year* means January 1 to December 31 of each year of an enrollment cycle.

(ii) *Enrollment cycle* means the three successive enrollment years preceding the effective date of renewal.

(iii) *Registration year* means each 12-month period the registered tax return preparer is authorized to practice before the Internal Revenue Service.

(iv) *The effective date of renewal* is the first day of the fourth month following the close of the period for renewal described in paragraph (d) of this section.

(2) *For renewed enrollment as an enrolled agent or enrolled retirement plan agent* —

(i) *Requirements for enrollment cycle*. A minimum of 72 hours of continuing education credit, including six hours of ethics or professional conduct, must be completed during each enrollment cycle.

(ii) *Requirements for enrollment year*. A minimum of 16 hours of continuing education credit, including two hours of ethics or professional conduct, must be completed during each enrollment year of an enrollment cycle.

(iii) *Enrollment during enrollment cycle* —

(A) *In general*. Subject to paragraph (e)(2)(iii)(B) of this section, an individual who receives initial enrollment during an enrollment cycle must complete two hours of qualifying continuing education credit for each month enrolled during the enrollment cycle. Enrollment for any part of a month is considered enrollment for the entire month.

(B) *Ethics*. An individual who receives initial enrollment during an enrollment cycle must complete two hours of ethics or professional conduct for each enrollment year during the enrollment cycle. Enrollment for any part of an enrollment year is considered enrollment for the entire year.

(3) *Requirements for renewal as a registered tax return preparer*. A minimum of 15 hours of continuing education credit, including two hours of ethics or professional conduct, three hours of Federal tax law updates, and 10 hours of Federal tax law topics, must be completed during each registration year.

(f) *Qualifying continuing education* —

(1) *General* —

(i) *Enrolled agents*. To qualify for continuing education credit for an enrolled agent, a course of learning must —

(A) Be a qualifying continuing education program designed to enhance professional knowledge in Federal taxation or Federal tax related matters (programs comprised of current subject matter in Federal taxation or Federal tax related matters, including accounting, tax return preparation software, taxation, or ethics); and

(B) Be a qualifying continuing education program consistent with the Internal Revenue Code and effective tax administration.

(ii) *Enrolled retirement plan agents*. To qualify for continuing education credit for an enrolled retirement plan agent, a course of learning must —

(A) Be a qualifying continuing education program designed to enhance professional knowledge in qualified retirement plan matters; and

(B) Be a qualifying continuing education program consistent with the Internal Revenue Code and effective tax administration.

(iii) *Registered tax return preparers*. To

qualify for continuing education credit for a registered tax return preparer, a course of learning must —

(A) Be a qualifying continuing education program designed to enhance professional knowledge in Federal taxation or Federal tax related matters (programs comprised of current subject matter in Federal taxation or Federal tax related matters, including accounting, tax return preparation software, taxation, or ethics); and

(B) Be a qualifying continuing education program consistent with the Internal Revenue Code and effective tax administration.

(2) *Qualifying programs* —

(i) *Formal programs*. A formal program qualifies as a continuing education program if it —

(A) Requires attendance and provides each attendee with a certificate of attendance;

(B) Is conducted by a qualified instructor, discussion leader, or speaker (in other words, a person whose background, training, education, and experience is appropriate for instructing or leading a discussion on the subject matter of the particular program);

(C) Provides or requires a written outline, textbook, or suitable electronic educational materials; and

(D) Satisfies the requirements established for a qualified continuing education program pursuant to §10.9.

(ii) *Correspondence or individual study programs (including taped programs)*. Qualifying continuing education programs include correspondence or individual study programs that are conducted by continuing education providers and completed on an individual basis by the enrolled individual. The allowable credit hours for such programs will be measured on a basis comparable to the measurement of a seminar or course for credit in an accredited educational institution. Such programs qualify as continuing education programs only if they —

(A) Require registration of the participants by the continuing education provider;

(B) Provide a means for measuring successful completion by the participants (for example, a written examination), including the issuance of a certificate of completion by the continuing education provider;

(C) Provide a written outline, textbook, or suitable electronic educational materials; and

(D) Satisfy the requirements established for a qualified continuing education program pursuant to §10.9.

(iii) *Serving as an instructor, discussion leader or speaker*.

(A) One hour of continuing education credit will be awarded for each contact hour completed as an instructor, discussion leader, or speaker at an educational program that meets the continuing education requirements of paragraph (f) of this section.

(B) A maximum of two hours of continuing education credit will be awarded for actual subject preparation time for each contact hour completed as an instructor, discussion leader, or speaker at such programs. It is the responsibility of the individual claiming such credit to maintain records to verify preparation time.

(C) The maximum continuing education credit for instruction and preparation may not exceed four hours annually for registered tax return preparers and six hours annually for enrolled agents and enrolled retirement plan agents.

(D) An instructor, discussion leader, or speaker who makes more than one presentation on the same subject matter during an enrollment cycle or registration year will receive continuing education credit for only one such presentation for the enrollment cycle or registration year.

(3) *Periodic examination*. Enrolled Agents and Enrolled Retirement Plan Agents may establish eligibility for renewal of enrollment for any enrollment cycle by —

(i) Achieving a passing score on each part of the Special Enrollment Examination administered under this part during the three year period prior to renewal; and

(ii) Completing a minimum of 16 hours of qualifying continuing education during the last year of an enrollment cycle.

(g) *Measurement of continuing education coursework.*

(1) All continuing education programs will be measured in terms of contact hours. The shortest recognized program will be one contact hour.

(2) A contact hour is 50 minutes of continuous participation in a program. Credit is granted only for a full contact hour, which is 50 minutes or multiples thereof. For example, a program lasting more than 50 minutes but less than 100 minutes will count as only one contact hour.

(3) Individual segments at continuous conferences, conventions and the like will be considered one total program. For example, two 90-minute segments (180 minutes) at a continuous conference will count as three contact hours.

(4) For university or college courses, each semester hour credit will equal 15 contact hours and a quarter hour credit will equal 10 contact hours.

(h) *Recordkeeping requirements.*

(1) Each individual applying for renewal must retain for a period of four years following the date of renewal the information required with regard to qualifying continuing education credit hours. Such information includes —

(i) The name of the sponsoring organization;

(ii) The location of the program;

(iii) The title of the program, qualified program number, and description of its content;

(iv) Written outlines, course syllibi, textbook, and/or electronic materials provided or required for the course;

(v) The dates attended;

(vi) The credit hours claimed;

(vii) The name(s) of the instructor(s), discussion leader(s), or speaker(s), if appropriate; and

(viii) The certificate of completion and/or signed statement of the hours of attendance obtained from the continuing education provider.

(2) To receive continuing education credit for service completed as an instructor, discussion leader, or speaker, the following information must be maintained for a period of four years following the date of renewal —

(i) The name of the sponsoring organization;

(ii) The location of the program;

(iii) The title of the program and copy of its content;

(iv) The dates of the program; and

(v) The credit hours claimed.

(i) *Waivers.*

(1) Waiver from the continuing education requirements for a given period may be granted for the following reasons —

(i) Health, which prevented compliance with the continuing education requirements;

(ii) Extended active military duty;

(iii) Absence from the United States for an extended period of time due to employment or other reasons, provided the individual does not practice before the Internal Revenue Service during such absence; and

(iv) Other compelling reasons, which will be considered on a case-by-case basis.

(2) A request for waiver must be accompanied by appropriate documentation. The individual is required to furnish any additional documentation or explanation deemed necessary. Examples of appropriate documentation could be a medical certificate or military orders.

(3) A request for waiver must be filed no later than the last day of the renewal application period.

(4) If a request for waiver is not approved, the individual will be placed in inactive status. The individual will be notified that the waiver was not approved and that the individual has been placed on a roster of inactive enrolled agents, enrolled retirement plan agents, or registered tax return preparers.

(5) If the request for waiver is not approved, the individual may file a protest as prescribed by the Internal Revenue Service in forms, instructions, or other appropriate guidance. A protest filed under this section is not governed by subpart D of this part.

(6) If a request for waiver is approved, the individual will be notified and issued a card or certificate evidencing renewal.

(7) Those who are granted waivers are required to file timely applications for renewal of enrollment or registration.

(j) *Failure to comply.*

(1) Compliance by an individual with the requirements of this part is determined by the Internal Revenue Service. The Internal Revenue Service will provide notice to any individual who fails to meet the continuing education and fee requirements of eligibility for renewal. The notice will state the basis for the determination of noncompliance and will provide the individual an opportunity to furnish the requested information in writing relating to the matter within 60 days of the date of the notice. Such information will be considered in making a final determination as to eligibility for renewal. The individual must be informed of the reason(s) for any denial of a renewal. The individual may, within 30 days after receipt of the notice of denial of renewal, file a written protest of the denial as prescribed by the Internal Revenue Service in forms, instructions, or other appropriate guidance. A protest under this section is not governed by subpart D of this part.

(2) The continuing education records of an enrolled agent, enrolled retirement plan agent, or registered tax return preparer may be reviewed to determine compliance with the requirements and standards for renewal as provided in paragraph (f) of this section. As part of this review, the enrolled agent, enrolled retirement plan agent or registered tax return preparer may be required to provide the Internal Revenue Service with copies of any continuing education records required to be maintained under this part. If the enrolled agent, enrolled retirement plan agent or registered tax return preparer fails to comply with this requirement, any continuing education hours claimed may be disallowed.

(3) An individual who has not filed a timely application for renewal, who has not made a timely response to the notice of noncompliance with the renewal requirements, or who has not satisfied the requirements of eligibility for renewal will be placed on a roster of inactive enrolled individuals or inactive registered individuals. During this time, the individual will be ineligible to practice before the Internal Revenue Service.

(4) Individuals placed in inactive status and individuals ineligible to practice before the Internal Revenue Service may not state or imply that they are eligible to practice before the Internal Revenue Service, or use the terms enrolled agent, enrolled retirement plan agent, or registered tax return preparer, the designations "EA" or "ERPA" or other form of reference to eligibility to practice before the Internal Revenue Service.

(5) An individual placed in inactive status may be reinstated to an active status by filing an application for renewal and providing evidence of the completion of all required continuing education hours for the enrollment cycle or registration year. Continuing education credit under this paragraph (j)(5) may not be used to satisfy the requirements of the enrollment cycle or registration year in which the individual has been placed back on the active roster.

(6) An individual placed in inactive status must file an application for renewal and satisfy the requirements for renewal as set forth in this section within three years of being placed in inactive status. Otherwise, the name of such individual will be removed from the inactive status roster and the individual's status as an enrolled agent, enrolled retirement plan agent, or registered tax return preparer will terminate. Future eligibility for active status must then be reestablished by the individual as provided in this section.

(7) Inactive status is not available to an individual who is the subject of a pending disciplinary matter before the Internal Revenue Service.

(k) *Inactive retirement status*. An individual who no longer practices before the Internal Revenue Service may request to be placed in an inactive retirement status at any time and such individual will be placed in an inactive retirement status. The individual will be ineligible to practice before the Internal Revenue Service. An individual who is placed in an inactive retirement status may be reinstated to an active status by filing an application for renewal and providing evidence of the completion of the required continuing education hours for the enrollment cycle or registration year. Inactive retirement status is not available to an individual who is ineligible to practice before the Internal Revenue Service or an individual who is the subject of a pending disciplinary matter under this part.

Treasury Department Circular No. 230 **§ 10.6 — Page 15**

(l) *Renewal while under suspension or disbarment.* An individual who is ineligible to practice before the Internal Revenue Service by virtue of disciplinary action under this part is required to conform to the requirements for renewal of enrollment or registration before the individual's eligibility is restored.

(m) *Enrolled actuaries.* The enrollment and renewal of enrollment of actuaries authorized to practice under paragraph (d) of §10.3 are governed by the regulations of the Joint Board for the Enrollment of Actuaries at 20 CFR 901.1 through 901.72.

(n) *Effective/applicability date.* This section is applicable to enrollment or registration effective beginning August 2, 2011.

§ 10.7 Representing oneself; participating in rulemaking; limited practice; and special appearances.

(a) *Representing oneself.* Individuals may appear on their own behalf before the Internal Revenue Service provided they present satisfactory identification.

(b) *Participating in rulemaking.* Individuals may participate in rulemaking as provided by the Administrative Procedure Act. See 5 U.S.C. § 553.

(c) *Limited practice* —

(1) *In general.* Subject to the limitations in paragraph (c)(2) of this section, an individual who is not a practitioner may represent a taxpayer before the Internal Revenue Service in the circumstances described in this paragraph (c)(1), even if the taxpayer is not present, provided the individual presents satisfactory identification and proof of his or her authority to represent the taxpayer. The circumstances described in this paragraph (c)(1) are as follows:

(i) An individual may represent a member of his or her immediate family.

(ii) A regular full-time employee of an individual employer may represent the employer.

(iii) A general partner or a regular full-time employee of a partnership may represent the partnership.

(iv) A bona fide officer or a regular full-time employee of a corporation (including a parent, subsidiary, or other affiliated corporation), association, or organized group may represent the corporation, association, or organized group.

(v) A regular full-time employee of a trust, receivership, guardianship, or estate may represent the trust, receivership, guardianship, or estate.

(vi) An officer or a regular employee of a governmental unit, agency, or authority may represent the governmental unit, agency, or authority in the course of his or her official duties.

(vii) An individual may represent any individual or entity, who is outside the United States, before personnel of the Internal Revenue Service when such representation takes place outside the United States.

(2) *Limitations.*

(i) An individual who is under suspension or disbarment from practice before the Internal Revenue Service may not engage in limited practice before the Internal Revenue Service under paragraph (c)(1) of this section.

(ii) The Commissioner, or delegate, may, after notice and opportunity for a conference, deny eligibility to engage in limited practice before the Internal Revenue Service under paragraph (c)(1) of this section to any individual who has engaged in conduct that would justify a sanction under §10.50.

(iii) An individual who represents a taxpayer under the authority of paragraph (c)(1) of this section is subject, to the extent of his or her authority, to such rules of general applicability regarding standards of conduct and other matters as prescribed by the Internal Revenue Service.

(d) *Special appearances.* The Commissioner, or delegate, may, subject to conditions deemed appropriate, authorize an individual who is not otherwise eligible to practice before the Internal Revenue Service to represent another person in a particular matter.

(e) *Fiduciaries.* For purposes of this part, a fiduciary (for example, a trustee, receiver, guardian, personal representative, administrator, or executor) is considered to be the taxpayer and not a representative of the taxpayer.

(f) *Effective/applicability date.* This section is applicable beginning August 2, 2011.

§ 10.8 Return preparation and application of rules to other individuals.

(a) *Preparing all or substantially all of a tax return.* Any individual who for compensation prepares or assists with the preparation of all or substantially all of a tax return or claim for refund must have a preparer tax identification number. Except as otherwise prescribed in forms, instructions, or other appropriate guidance, an individual must be an attorney, certified public accountant, enrolled agent, or registered tax return preparer to obtain a preparer tax identification number. Any individual who for compensation prepares or assists with the preparation of all or substantially all of a tax return or claim for refund is subject to the duties and restrictions relating to practice in subpart B, as well as subject to the sanctions for violation of the regulations in subpart C.

(b) *Preparing a tax return and furnishing information.* Any individual may for compensation prepare or assist with the preparation of a tax return or claim for refund (provided the individual prepares less than substantially all of the tax return or claim for refund), appear as a witness for the taxpayer before the Internal Revenue Service, or furnish information at the request of the Internal Revenue Service or any of its officers or employees.

(c) *Application of rules to other individuals.* Any individual who for compensation prepares, or assists in the preparation of, all or a substantial portion of a document pertaining to any taxpayer's tax liability for submission to the Internal Revenue Service is subject to the duties and restrictions relating to practice in subpart B, as well as subject to the sanctions for violation of the regulations in subpart C. Unless otherwise a practitioner, however, an individual may not for compensation prepare, or assist in the preparation of, all or substantially all of a tax return or claim for refund, or sign tax returns and claims for refund. For purposes of this paragraph, an individual described in 26 CFR 301.7701-15(f) is not treated as having prepared all or a substantial portion of the document by reason of such assistance.

(d) *Effective/applicability date.* This section is applicable beginning August 2, 2011.

§ 10.9 Continuing education providers and continuing education programs.

(a) *Continuing education providers* —

(1) *In general.* Continuing education providers are those responsible for presenting continuing education programs. A continuing education provider must —

(i) Be an accredited educational institution;

(ii) Be recognized for continuing education purposes by the licensing body of any State, territory, or possession of the United States, including a Commonwealth, or the District of Columbia;

(iii) Be recognized and approved by a qualifying organization as a provider of continuing education on subject matters within §10.6(f) of this part. The Internal Revenue Service may, at its discretion, identify a professional organization, society or business entity that maintains minimum education standards comparable to those set forth in this part as a qualifying organization for purposes of this part in appropriate forms, instructions, and other appropriate guidance; or

(iv) Be recognized by the Internal Revenue Service as a professional organization, society, or business whose programs include offering continuing professional education opportunities in subject matters within §10.6(f) of this part. The Internal Revenue Service, at its discretion, may require such professional organizations, societies, or businesses to file an agreement and/or obtain Internal Revenue Service approval of each program as a qualified continuing education program in appropriate forms, instructions or other appropriate guidance.

(2) *Continuing education provider numbers* —

(i) *In general.* A continuing education provider is required to obtain a continuing education provider number and pay any applicable user fee.

(ii) *Renewal.* A continuing education provider maintains its status as a continuing education provider during the continuing education provider cycle by renewing its continuing education provider number as prescribed by forms, instructions or other appropriate guidance and paying any applicable user fee.

(3) *Requirements for qualified continuing education programs.* A continuing education provider must ensure the qualified continuing education program complies with all the following requirements —

(i) Programs must be developed by individual(s) qualified in the subject matter;

(ii) Program subject matter must be current;

(iii) Instructors, discussion leaders, and speakers must be qualified with respect to program content;

(iv) Programs must include some means for evaluation of the technical content and presentation to be evaluated;

(v) Certificates of completion bearing a current qualified continuing education program number issued by the Internal Revenue Service must be provided to the participants who successfully complete the program; and

(vi) Records must be maintained by the continuing education provider to verify the participants who attended and completed the program for a period of four years following completion of the program. In the case of continuous conferences, conventions, and the like, records must be maintained to verify completion of the program and attendance by each participant at each segment of the program.

(4) *Program numbers* —

(i) *In general.* Every continuing education provider is required to obtain a continuing education provider program number and pay any applicable user fee for each program offered. Program numbers shall be obtained as prescribed by forms, instructions or other appropriate guidance. Although, at the discretion of the Internal Revenue Service, a continuing education provider may be required to demonstrate that the program is designed to enhance professional knowledge in Federal taxation or Federal tax related matters (programs comprised of current subject matter in Federal taxation or Federal tax related matters, including accounting, tax return preparation software, taxation, or ethics) and complies with the requirements in paragraph (a)(2)of this section before a program number is issued.

(ii) *Update programs.* Update programs may use the same number as the program subject to update. An update program is a program that instructs on a change of existing law occurring within one year of the update program offering. The qualifying education program subject to update must have been offered within the two year time period prior to the change in existing law.

(iii) *Change in existing law.* A change in existing law means the effective date of the statute or regulation, or date of entry of judicial decision, that is the subject of the update.

(b) *Failure to comply.* Compliance by a continuing education provider with the requirements of this part is determined by the Internal Revenue Service. A continuing education provider who fails to meet the requirements of this part will be notified by the Internal Revenue Service. The notice will state the basis for the determination of noncompliance and will provide the continuing education provider an opportunity to furnish the requested information in writing relating to the matter within 60 days of the date of the notice. The continuing education provider may, within 30 days after receipt of the notice of denial, file a written protest as prescribed by the Internal Revenue Service in forms, instructions, or other appropriate guidance. A protest under this section is not governed by subpart D of this part.

(c) *Effective/applicability date.* This section is applicable beginning August 2, 2011.

Subpart B — Duties and Restrictions Relating to Practice Before the Internal Revenue Service

§ 10.20 Information to be furnished.

(a) *To the Internal Revenue Service.*

(1) A practitioner must, on a proper and lawful request by a duly authorized officer or employee of the Internal Revenue Service, promptly submit records or information in any matter before the Internal Revenue Service unless the practitioner believes in good faith and on reasonable grounds that the records or information are privileged.

(2) Where the requested records or information are not in the possession of, or subject to the control of, the practitioner or the practitioner's client, the practitioner must promptly notify the requesting Internal Revenue Service officer or employee and the practitioner must provide any information that the practitioner has regarding the identity of any person who the practitioner believes may have possession or control of the requested records or information. The practitioner must make reasonable inquiry of his or her client regarding the identity of any person who may have possession or control of the requested records or information, but the practitioner is not required to make inquiry of any other person or independently verify any information provided by the practitioner's client regarding the identity of such persons.

(3) When a proper and lawful request is made by a duly authorized officer or employee of the Internal Revenue Service, concerning an inquiry into an alleged violation of the regulations in this part, a practitioner must provide any information the practitioner has concerning the alleged violation and testify regarding this information in any proceeding instituted under this part, unless the practitioner believes in good faith and on reasonable grounds that the information is privileged.

(b) *Interference with a proper and lawful request for records or information.* A practitioner may not interfere, or attempt to interfere, with any proper and lawful effort by the Internal Revenue Service, its officers or employees, to obtain any record or information unless the practitioner believes in good faith and on reasonable grounds that the record or information is privileged.

(c) *Effective/applicability date.* This section is applicable beginning August 2, 2011.

§ 10.21 Knowledge of client's omission.

A practitioner who, having been retained by a client with respect to a matter administered by the Internal Revenue Service, knows that the client has not complied with the revenue laws of the United States or has made an error in or omission from any return, document, affidavit, or other paper which the client submitted or executed under the revenue laws of the United States, must advise the client promptly of the fact of such noncompliance, error, or omission. The practitioner must advise the client of the consequences as provided under the Code and regulations of such noncompliance, error, or omission.

§ 10.22 Diligence as to accuracy.

(a) *In general.* A practitioner must exercise due diligence —

(1) In preparing or assisting in the preparation of, approving, and filing tax returns, documents, affidavits, and other papers relating to Internal Revenue Service matters;

(2) In determining the correctness of oral or written representations made by the practitioner to the Department of the Treasury; and

(3) In determining the correctness of oral or written representations made by the practitioner to clients with reference to any matter administered by the Internal Revenue Service.

(b) *Reliance on others.* Except as modified by §§10.34 and 10.37, a practitioner will be presumed to have exercised due diligence for purposes of this section if the practitioner relies on the work product of another person and the practitioner used reasonable care in engaging, supervising, training, and evaluating the person, taking proper account of the nature of the relationship between the practitioner and the person.

6

(c) *Effective/applicability date.* Paragraph (a) of this section is applicable on September 26, 2007. Paragraph (b) of this section is applicable beginning June 12, 2014.

§ 10.23 Prompt disposition of pending matters.

A practitioner may not unreasonably delay the prompt disposition of any matter before the Internal Revenue Service.

§ 10.24 Assistance from or to disbarred or suspended persons and former Internal Revenue Service employees.

A practitioner may not, knowingly and directly or indirectly:

(a) Accept assistance from or assist any person who is under disbarment or suspension from practice before the Internal Revenue Service if the assistance relates to a matter or matters constituting practice before the Internal Revenue Service.

(b) Accept assistance from any former government employee where the provisions of § 10.25 or any Federal law would be violated.

§ 10.25 Practice by former government employees, their partners and their associates.

(a) *Definitions.* For purposes of this section —

(1) *Assist* means to act in such a way as to advise, furnish information to, or otherwise aid another person, directly, or indirectly.

(2) *Government employee* is an officer or employee of the United States or any agency of the United States, including a special Government employee as defined in *18 U.S.C. 202(a)*, or of the District of Columbia, or of any State, or a member of Congress or of any State legislature.

(3) *Member of a firm* is a sole practitioner or an employee or associate thereof, or a partner, stockholder, associate, affiliate or employee of a partnership, joint venture, corporation, professional association or other affiliation of two or more practitioners who represent nongovernmental parties.

(4) *Particular matter involving specific parties* is defined at 5 CFR 2637.201(c), or superseding post-employment regulations issued by the U.S. Office of Government Ethics.

(5) *Rule* includes Treasury regulations, whether issued or under preparation for issuance as notices of proposed rulemaking or as Treasury decisions, revenue rulings, and revenue procedures published in the Internal Revenue Bulletin (see *26 CFR 601.601(d)(2)(ii)(b)*).

(b) *General rules* —

(1) No former Government employee may, subsequent to Government employment, represent anyone in any matter administered by the Internal Revenue Service if the representation would violate *18 U.S.C. 207* or any other laws of the United States.

(2) No former Government employee who personally and substantially participated in a particular matter involving specific parties may, subsequent to Government employment, represent or knowingly assist, in that particular matter, any person who is or was a specific party to that particular matter.

(3) A former Government employee who within a period of one year prior to the termination of Government employment had official responsibility for a particular matter involving specific parties may not, within two years after Government employment is ended, represent in that particular matter any person who is or was a specific party to that particular matter.

(4) No former Government employee may, within one year after Government employment is ended, communicate with or appear before, with the intent to influence, any employee of the Treasury Department in connection with the publication, withdrawal, amendment, modification, or interpretation of a rule the development of which the former Government employee participated in, or for which, within a period of one year prior to the termination of Government employment, the former government employee had official responsibility. This paragraph (b)(4) does not, however, preclude any former employee from appearing on one's own behalf or from representing a taxpayer before the Internal Revenue Service in connection with a particular matter involving specific

parties involving the application or interpretation of a rule with respect to that particular matter, provided that the representation is otherwise consistent with the other provisions of this section and the former employee does not utilize or disclose any confidential information acquired by the former employee in the development of the rule.

(c) *Firm representation* —

(1) No member of a firm of which a former Government employee is a member may represent or knowingly assist a person who was or is a specific party in any particular matter with respect to which the restrictions of paragraph (b)(2) of this section apply to the former Government employee, in that particular matter, unless the firm isolates the former Government employee in such a way to ensure that the former Government employee cannot assist in the representation.

(2) When isolation of a former Government employee is required under paragraph (c)(1) of this section, a statement affirming the fact of such isolation must be executed under oath by the former Government employee and by another member of the firm acting on behalf of the firm. The statement must clearly identify the firm, the former Government employee, and the particular matter(s) requiring isolation. The statement must be retained by the firm and, upon request, provided to the office(s) of the Internal Revenue Service administering or enforcing this part.

(d) *Pending representation.* The provisions of this regulation will govern practice by former Government employees, their partners and associates with respect to representation in particular matters involving specific parties where actual representation commenced before the effective date of this regulation.

(e) *Effective/applicability date.* This section is applicable beginning August 2, 2011.

§ 10.26 Notaries.

A practitioner may not take acknowledgments, administer oaths, certify papers, or perform any official act as a notary public with respect to any matter administered by the Internal Revenue Service and for which he or she is employed as counsel, attorney, or agent, or in which he or she may be in any way interested.

§ 10.27 Fees.

(a) *In general.* A practitioner may not charge an unconscionable fee in connection with any matter before the Internal Revenue Service.

(b) *Contingent fees* —

(1) Except as provided in paragraphs (b)(2), (3), and (4) of this section, a practitioner may not charge a contingent fee for services rendered in connection with any matter before the Internal Revenue Service.

(2) A practitioner may charge a contingent fee for services rendered in connection with the Service's examination of, or challenge to —

(i) An original tax return; or

(ii) An amended return or claim for refund or credit where the amended return or claim for refund or credit was filed within 120 days of the taxpayer receiving a written notice of the examination of, or a written challenge to the original tax return.

(3) A practitioner may charge a contingent fee for services rendered in connection with a claim for credit or refund filed solely in connection with the determination of statutory interest or penalties assessed by the Internal Revenue Service.

(4) A practitioner may charge a contingent fee for services rendered in connection with any judicial proceeding arising under the Internal Revenue Code.

(c) *Definitions.* For purposes of this section —

(1) *Contingent fee* is any fee that is based, in whole or in part, on whether or not a position taken on a tax return or other filing avoids challenge by the Internal Revenue Service or is sustained either by the Internal Revenue Service or in litigation. A contingent fee includes a fee that is based on a percentage of the refund reported on a return, that is based on a percentage of the taxes saved, or that otherwise depends on the specific result attained. A contingent fee also includes any fee arrangement in which the practitioner will reimburse the client for all or a portion of the client's fee in the event

that a position taken on a tax return or other filing is challenged by the Internal Revenue Service or is not sustained, whether pursuant to an indemnity agreement, a guarantee, rescission rights, or any other arrangement with a similar effect.

(2) *Matter before the Internal Revenue Service* includes tax planning and advice, preparing or filing or assisting in preparing or filing returns or claims for refund or credit, and all matters connected with a presentation to the Internal Revenue Service or any of its officers or employees relating to a taxpayer's rights, privileges, or liabilities under laws or regulations administered by the Internal Revenue Service. Such presentations include, but are not limited to, preparing and filing documents, corresponding and communicating with the Internal Revenue Service, rendering written advice with respect to any entity, transaction, plan or arrangement, and representing a client at conferences, hearings, and meetings.

(d) *Effective/applicability date.* This section is applicable for fee arrangements entered into after March 26, 2008.

§ 10.28 Return of client's records.

(a) In general, a practitioner must, at the request of a client, promptly return any and all records of the client that are necessary for the client to comply with his or her Federal tax obligations. The practitioner may retain copies of the records returned to a client. The existence of a dispute over fees generally does not relieve the practitioner of his or her responsibility under this section. Nevertheless, if applicable state law allows or permits the retention of a client's records by a practitioner in the case of a dispute over fees for services rendered, the practitioner need only return those records that must be attached to the taxpayer's return. The practitioner, however, must provide the client with reasonable access to review and copy any additional records of the client retained by the practitioner under state law that are necessary for the client to comply with his or her Federal tax obligations.

(b) For purposes of this section — Records of the client include all documents or written or electronic materials provided to the practitioner, or obtained by the practitioner in the course of the practitioner's representation of the client, that preexisted the retention of the practitioner by the client. The term also includes materials that were prepared by the client or a third party (not including an employee or agent of the practitioner) at any time and provided to the practitioner with respect to the subject matter of the representation. The term also includes any return, claim for refund, schedule, affidavit, appraisal or any other document prepared by the practitioner, or his or her employee or agent, that was presented to the client with respect to a prior representation if such document is necessary for the taxpayer to comply with his or her current Federal tax obligations. The term does not include any return, claim for refund, schedule, affidavit, appraisal or any other document prepared by the practitioner or the practitioner's firm, employees or agents if the practitioner is withholding such document pending the client's performance of its contractual obligation to pay fees with respect to such document.

§ 10.29 Conflicting interests.

(a) Except as provided by paragraph (b) of this section, a practitioner shall not represent a client before the Internal Revenue Service if the representation involves a conflict of interest. A conflict of interest exists if —

(1) The representation of one client will be directly adverse to another client; or

(2) There is a significant risk that the representation of one or more clients will be materially limited by the practitioner's responsibilities to another client, a former client or a third person, or by a personal interest of the practitioner.

(b) Notwithstanding the existence of a conflict of interest under paragraph (a) of this section, the practitioner may represent a client if —

(1) The practitioner reasonably believes that the practitioner will be able to provide competent and diligent representation to each affected client;

(2) The representation is not prohibited by law; and

(3) Each affected client waives the conflict of

interest and gives informed consent, confirmed in writing by each affected client, at the time the existence of the conflict of interest is known by the practitioner. The confirmation may be made within a reasonable period of time after the informed consent, but in no event later than 30 days.

(c) Copies of the written consents must be retained by the practitioner for at least 36 months from the date of the conclusion of the representation of the affected clients, and the written consents must be provided to any officer or employee of the Internal Revenue Service on request.

(d) *Effective/applicability date.* This section is applicable on September 26, 2007.

§ 10.30 Solicitation.

(a) *Advertising and solicitation restrictions.*

(1) A practitioner may not, with respect to any Internal Revenue Service matter, in any way use or participate in the use of any form of public communication or private solicitation containing a false, fraudulent, or coercive statement or claim; or a misleading or deceptive statement or claim. Enrolled agents, enrolled retirement plan agents, or registered tax return preparers, in describing their professional designation, may not utilize the term "certified" or imply an employer/employee relationship with the Internal Revenue Service. Examples of acceptable descriptions for enrolled agents are "enrolled to represent taxpayers before the Internal Revenue Service," "enrolled to practice before the Internal Revenue Service," and "admitted to practice before the Internal Revenue Service." Similarly, examples of acceptable descriptions for enrolled retirement plan agents are "enrolled to represent taxpayers before the Internal Revenue Service as a retirement plan agent" and "enrolled to practice before the Internal Revenue Service as a retirement plan agent." An example of an acceptable description for registered tax return preparers is "designated as a registered tax return preparer by the Internal Revenue Service."

(2) A practitioner may not make, directly or indirectly, an uninvited written or oral solicitation of employment in matters related to the Internal Revenue Service if the solicitation violates Federal or State law or other applicable rule, e.g., attorneys are precluded from making a solicitation that is prohibited by conduct rules applicable to all attorneys in their State(s) of licensure. Any lawful solicitation made by or on behalf of a practitioner eligible to practice before the Internal Revenue Service must, nevertheless, clearly identify the solicitation as such and, if applicable, identify the source of the information used in choosing the recipient.

(b) *Fee information.*

(1)(i) A practitioner may publish the availability of a written schedule of fees and disseminate the following fee information —

(A) Fixed fees for specific routine services.

(B) Hourly rates.

(C) Range of fees for particular services.

(D) Fee charged for an initial consultation.

(ii) Any statement of fee information concerning matters in which costs may be incurred must include a statement disclosing whether clients will be responsible for such costs.

(2) A practitioner may charge no more than the rate(s) published under paragraph (b)(1) of this section for at least 30 calendar days after the last date on which the schedule of fees was published.

(c) *Communication of fee information.* Fee information may be communicated in professional lists, telephone directories, print media, mailings, and electronic mail, facsimile, hand delivered flyers, radio, television, and any other method. The method chosen, however, must not cause the communication to become untruthful, deceptive, or otherwise in violation of this part. A practitioner may not persist in attempting to contact a prospective client if the prospective client has made it known to the practitioner that he or she does not desire to be solicited. In the case of radio and television broadcasting, the broadcast must be recorded and the practitioner must retain a recording of the actual transmission. In the case of direct mail and e-commerce communications, the practitioner must retain a copy of the actual communication, along with a list or other description of persons to whom the communication was mailed or otherwise distributed. The copy must be retained by the practitioner for a period of at least 36 months from the date of the last transmission or use.

(d) *Improper associations.* A practitioner may not, in matters related to the Internal Revenue Service, assist, or accept assistance from, any person or entity who, to the knowledge of the practitioner, obtains clients or otherwise practices in a manner forbidden under this section.

(e) *Effective/applicability date.* This section is applicable beginning August 2, 2011.

(Approved by the Office of Management and Budget under Control No. 1545-1726)

§ 10.31 Negotiation of taxpayer checks.

(a) A practitioner may not endorse or otherwise negotiate any check (including directing or accepting payment by any means, electronic or otherwise, into an account owned or controlled by the practitioner or any firm or other entity with whom the practitioner is associated) issued to a client by the government in respect of a Federal tax liability.

(b) *Effective/applicability date.* This section is applicable beginning June 12, 2014.

§ 10.32 Practice of law.

Nothing in the regulations in this part may be construed as authorizing persons not members of the bar to practice law.

§ 10.33 Best practices for tax advisors.

(a) *Best practices.* Tax advisors should provide clients with the highest quality representation concerning Federal tax issues by adhering to best practices in providing advice and in preparing or assisting in the preparation of a submission to the Internal Revenue Service. In addition to compliance with the standards of practice provided elsewhere in this part, best practices include the following:

(1) Communicating clearly with the client regarding the terms of the engagement. For example, the advisor should determine the client's expected purpose for and use of the advice and should have a clear understanding with the client regarding the form and scope of the advice or assistance to be rendered.

(2) Establishing the facts, determining which facts are relevant, evaluating the reasonableness of any assumptions or representations, relating the applicable law (including potentially applicable judicial doctrines) to the relevant facts, and arriving at a conclusion supported by the law and the facts.

(3) Advising the client regarding the import of the conclusions reached, including, for example, whether a taxpayer may avoid accuracy-related penalties under the Internal Revenue Code if a taxpayer acts in reliance on the advice.

(4) Acting fairly and with integrity in practice before the Internal Revenue Service.

(b) *Procedures to ensure best practices for tax advisors.* Tax advisors with responsibility for overseeing a firm's practice of providing advice concerning Federal tax issues or of preparing or assisting in the preparation of submissions to the Internal Revenue Service should take reasonable steps to ensure that the firm's procedures for all members, associates, and employees are consistent with the best practices set forth in paragraph (a) of this section.

(c) *Applicability date.* This section is effective after June 20, 2005.

§ 10.34 Standards with respect to tax returns and documents, affidavits and other papers.

(a) *Tax returns.*

(1) A practitioner may not willfully, recklessly, or through gross incompetence —

(i) Sign a tax return or claim for refund that the practitioner knows or reasonably should know contains a position that —

(A) Lacks a reasonable basis;

(B) Is an unreasonable position as described in section 6694(a)(2) of the Internal Revenue Code (Code) (including the related regulations and other published guidance); or

(C) Is a willful attempt by the practitioner to understate the liability for tax or a reckless or intentional disregard of rules or regulations by the practitioner as described in section 6694(b)(2) of the Code (including the related regulations and other published guidance).

(ii) Advise a client to take a position on a tax return or claim for refund, or prepare a portion of a tax return or claim for refund containing a position, that —

(A) Lacks a reasonable basis;

(B) Is an unreasonable position as described in section 6694(a)(2) of the Code (including the related regulations and other published guidance); or

(C) Is a willful attempt by the practitioner to understate the liability for tax or a reckless or intentional disregard of rules or regulations by the practitioner as described in section 6694(b)(2) of the Code (including the related regulations and other published guidance).

(2) A pattern of conduct is a factor that will be taken into account in determining whether a practitioner acted willfully, recklessly, or through gross incompetence.

(b) *Documents, affidavits and other papers* —

(1) A practitioner may not advise a client to take a position on a document, affidavit or other paper submitted to the Internal Revenue Service unless the position is not frivolous.

(2) A practitioner may not advise a client to submit a document, affidavit or other paper to the Internal Revenue Service —

(i) The purpose of which is to delay or impede the administration of the Federal tax laws;

(ii) That is frivolous; or

(iii) That contains or omits information in a manner that demonstrates an intentional disregard of a rule or regulation unless the practitioner also advises the client to submit a document that evidences a good faith challenge to the rule or regulation.

(c) *Advising clients on potential penalties* —

(1) A practitioner must inform a client of any penalties that are reasonably likely to apply to the client with respect to —

(i) A position taken on a tax return if —

(A) The practitioner advised the client with respect to the position; or

(B) The practitioner prepared or signed the tax return; and

(ii) Any document, affidavit or other paper submitted to the Internal Revenue Service.

(2) The practitioner also must inform the client of any opportunity to avoid any such penalties by disclosure, if relevant, and of the requirements for adequate disclosure.

(3) This paragraph (c) applies even if the practitioner is not subject to a penalty under the Internal Revenue Code with respect to the position or with respect to the document, affidavit or other paper submitted.

(d) *Relying on information furnished by clients.* A practitioner advising a client to take a position on a tax return, document, affidavit or other paper submitted to the Internal Revenue Service, or preparing or signing a tax return as a preparer, generally may rely in good faith without verification upon information furnished by the client. The practitioner may not, however, ignore the implications of information furnished to, or actually known by, the practitioner, and must make reasonable inquiries if the information as furnished appears to be incorrect, inconsistent with an important fact or another factual assumption, or incomplete.

(e) *Effective/applicability date.* Paragraph (a) of this section is applicable for returns or claims for refund filed, or advice provided, beginning August 2, 2011. Paragraphs (b) through (d) of this section are applicable to tax returns, documents, affidavits, and other papers filed on or after September 26, 2007.

§ 10.35 Competence.

(a) A practitioner must possess the necessary competence to engage in practice before the Internal Revenue Service. Competent practice requires the appropriate level of knowledge, skill, thoroughness, and preparation necessary for the matter for which the practitioner is engaged. A practitioner may become competent for the matter for which the practitioner has been engaged through various methods, such as consulting with experts in the relevant area or studying the relevant law.

(b) *Effective/applicability date.* This section is applicable beginning June 12, 2014.

§ 10.36 Procedures to ensure compliance.

(a) Any individual subject to the provisions of this part who has (or individuals who have or share) principal authority and responsibility for overseeing a firm's practice governed by this part, including the provision of advice concerning Federal tax matters and preparation of tax returns, claims for refund, or other documents for submission to the Internal Revenue Service, must take reasonable steps to ensure that the firm has adequate procedures in effect for all members, associates, and employees for purposes of complying with subparts A, B, and C of this part, as applicable. In the absence of a person or persons identified by the firm as having the principal authority and responsibility described in this paragraph, the Internal Revenue Service may identify one or more individuals subject to the provisions of this part responsible for compliance with the requirements of this section.

(b) Any such individual who has (or such individuals who have or share) principal authority as described in paragraph (a) of this section will be subject to discipline for failing to comply with the requirements of this section if—

(1) The individual through willfulness, recklessness, or gross incompetence does not take reasonable steps to ensure that the firm has adequate procedures to comply with this part, as applicable, and one or more individuals who are members of, associated with, or employed by, the firm are, or have, engaged in a pattern or practice, in connection with their practice with the firm, of failing to comply with this part, as applicable;

(2) The individual through willfulness, recklessness, or gross incompetence does not take reasonable steps to ensure that firm procedures in effect are properly followed, and one or more individuals who are members of, associated with, or employed by, the firm are, or have, engaged in a pattern or practice, in connection with their practice with the firm, of failing to comply with this part, as applicable; or

(3) The individual knows or should know that one or more individuals who are members of, associated with, or employed by, the firm are, or have, engaged in a pattern or practice, in connection with their practice with the firm, that does not comply with this part, as applicable, and the individual, through willfulness, recklessness, or gross incompetence fails to take prompt action to correct the noncompliance.

(c) *Effective/applicability date.* This section is applicable beginning June 12, 2014.

§ 10.37 Requirements for written advice.

(a) *Requirements.*

(1) A practitioner may give written advice (including by means of electronic communication) concerning one or more Federal tax matters subject to the requirements in paragraph (a)(2) of this section. Government submissions on matters of general policy are not considered written advice on a Federal tax matter for purposes of this section. Continuing education presentations provided to an audience solely for the purpose of enhancing practitioners' professional knowledge on Federal tax matters are not considered written advice on a Federal tax matter for purposes of this section. The preceding sentence does not apply to presentations marketing or promoting transactions.

(2) The practitioner must—

(i) Base the written advice on reasonable factual and legal assumptions (including assumptions as to future events);

(ii) Reasonably consider all relevant facts and circumstances that the practitioner knows or reasonably should know;

(iii) Use reasonable efforts to identify and ascertain the facts relevant to written advice on each Federal tax matter;

(iv) Not rely upon representations, statements, findings, or agreements (including projections, financial forecasts, or appraisals) of the taxpayer or any other person if reliance on them would be unreasonable;

(v) Relate applicable law and authorities to facts; and

(vi) Not, in evaluating a Federal tax matter, take into account the possibility that a tax return will not be audited or that a matter will not be raised on audit.

(3) Reliance on representations, statements, findings, or agreements is unreasonable if the practitioner knows or reasonably should know that one or more representations or assumptions on which any representation is based are incorrect, incomplete, or inconsistent.

(b) *Reliance on advice of others.* A practitioner may only rely on the advice of another person if the advice was reasonable and the reliance is in good faith considering all the facts and circumstances. Reliance is not reasonable when—

(1) The practitioner knows or reasonably should know that the opinion of the other person should not be relied on;

(2) The practitioner knows or reasonably should know that the other person is not competent or lacks the necessary qualifications to provide the advice; or

(3) The practitioner knows or reasonably should know that the other person has a conflict of interest in violation of the rules described in this part.

(c) *Standard of review.*

(1) In evaluating whether a practitioner giving written advice concerning one or more Federal tax matters complied with the requirements of this section, the Commissioner, or delegate, will apply a reasonable practitioner standard, considering all facts and circumstances, including, but not limited to, the scope of the engagement and the type and specificity of the advice sought by the client.

(2) In the case of an opinion the practitioner knows or has reason to know will be used or referred to by a person other than the practitioner (or a person who is a member of, associated with, or employed by the practitioner's firm) in promoting, marketing, or recommending to one or more taxpayers a partnership or other entity, investment plan or arrangement a significant purpose of which is the avoidance or evasion of any tax imposed by the Internal Revenue Code, the Commissioner, or delegate, will apply a reasonable practitioner standard, considering all facts and circumstances, with emphasis given to the additional risk caused by the practitioner's lack of knowledge of the taxpayer's particular circumstances, when determining whether a practitioner has failed to comply with this section.

(d) *Federal tax matter.* A Federal tax matter, as used in this section, is any matter concerning the application or interpretation of---

(1) A revenue provision as defined in section 6110(i)(1)(B) of the Internal Revenue Code;

(2) Any provision of law impacting a person's obligations under the internal revenue laws and regulations, including but not limited to the person's liability to pay tax or obligation to file returns; or

(3) Any other law or regulation administered by the Internal Revenue Service.

(e) *Effective/applicability date.* This section is applicable to written advice rendered after June 12, 2014.

§ 10.38 Establishment of advisory committees.

(a) *Advisory committees.* To promote and maintain the public's confidence in tax advisors, the Internal Revenue Service is authorized to establish one or more advisory committees composed of at least six individuals authorized to practice before the Internal Revenue Service. Membership of an advisory committee must be balanced among those who practice as attorneys, accountants, enrolled agents, enrolled actuaries, enrolled retirement plan agents, and registered tax return preparers. Under procedures prescribed by the Internal Revenue Service, an advisory committee may review and make general recommendations regarding the practices, procedures, and policies of the offices described in §10.1.

(b) *Effective date.* This section is applicable beginning August 2, 2011.

Subpart C — Sanctions for Violation of the Regulations

§ 10.50 Sanctions.

(a) *Authority to censure, suspend, or disbar.* The Secretary of the Treasury, or delegate, after notice and an opportunity for a proceeding, may censure, suspend, or disbar any practitioner from practice before the Internal Revenue Service if the practitioner is shown to be incompetent or disreputable (within the meaning of §10.51), fails to comply with any regulation in this part (under the prohibited conduct standards of §10.52), or with intent to defraud, willfully and knowingly misleads or threatens a client or prospective client. Censure is a public reprimand.

(b) *Authority to disqualify.* The Secretary of the Treasury, or delegate, after due notice and opportunity for hearing, may disqualify any appraiser for a violation of these rules as applicable to appraisers.

(1) If any appraiser is disqualified pursuant to this subpart C, the appraiser is barred from presenting evidence or testimony in any administrative proceeding before the Department of Treasury or the Internal Revenue Service, unless and until authorized to do so by the Internal Revenue Service pursuant to §10.81, regardless of whether the evidence or testimony would pertain to an appraisal made prior to or after the effective date of disqualification.

(2) Any appraisal made by a disqualified appraiser after the effective date of disqualification will not have any probative effect in any administrative proceeding before the Department of the Treasury or the Internal Revenue Service. An appraisal otherwise barred from admission into evidence pursuant to this section may be admitted into evidence solely for the purpose of determining the taxpayer's reliance in good faith on such appraisal.

(c) *Authority to impose monetary penalty* —

(1) *In general.*

(i) The Secretary of the Treasury, or delegate, after notice and an opportunity for a proceeding, may impose a monetary penalty on any practitioner who engages in conduct subject to sanction under paragraph (a) of this section.

(ii) If the practitioner described in paragraph (c)(1)(i) of this section was acting on behalf of an employer or any firm or other entity in connection with the conduct giving rise to the penalty, the Secretary of the Treasury, or delegate, may impose a monetary penalty on the employer, firm, or entity if it knew, or reasonably should have known of such conduct.

(2) *Amount of penalty.* The amount of the penalty shall not exceed the gross income derived (or to be derived) from the conduct giving rise to the penalty.

(3) *Coordination with other sanctions.* Subject to paragraph (c)(2) of this section —

(i) Any monetary penalty imposed on a practitioner under this paragraph (c) may be in addition to or in lieu of any suspension, disbarment or censure and may be in addition to a penalty imposed on an employer, firm or other entity under paragraph (c)(1)(ii) of this section.

(ii) Any monetary penalty imposed on an employer, firm or other entity may be in addition to or in lieu of penalties imposed under paragraph (c)(1)(i) of this section.

(d) *Authority to accept a practitioner's consent to sanction.* The Internal Revenue Service may accept a practitioner's offer of consent to be sanctioned under §10.50 in lieu of instituting or continuing a proceeding under §10.60(a).

(e) *Sanctions to be imposed.* The sanctions imposed by this section shall take into account all relevant facts and circumstances.

(f) *Effective/applicability date.* This section is applicable to conduct occurring on or after August 2, 2011, except that paragraphs (a), (b)(2), and (e) apply to conduct occurring on or after September 26, 2007, and paragraph (c) applies to prohibited conduct that occurs after October 22, 2004.

§ 10.51 Incompetence and disreputable conduct.

(a) *Incompetence and disreputable conduct.* Incompetence and disreputable conduct for which a practitioner may be sanctioned under §10.50 includes, but is not limited to —

(1) Conviction of any criminal offense under the Federal tax laws.

(2) Conviction of any criminal offense involving dishonesty or breach of trust.

(3) Conviction of any felony under Federal or State law for which the conduct involved renders the practitioner unfit to practice before the Internal Revenue Service.

(4) Giving false or misleading information, or participating in any way in the giving of false or misleading information to the Department of the Treasury or any officer or employee thereof, or to any tribunal authorized to pass upon Federal tax matters, in connection with any matter pending or likely to be pending before them, knowing the information to be false or misleading. Facts or other matters contained in testimony, Federal tax returns, financial statements, applications for enrollment, affidavits, declarations, and any other document or statement, written or oral, are included in the term "information."

(5) Solicitation of employment as prohibited under §10.30, the use of false or misleading representations with intent to deceive a client or prospective client in order to procure employment, or intimating that the practitioner is able improperly to obtain special consideration or action from the Internal Revenue Service or any officer or employee thereof.

(6) Willfully failing to make a Federal tax return in violation of the Federal tax laws, or willfully evading, attempting to evade, or participating in any way in evading or attempting to evade any assessment or payment of any Federal tax.

(7) Willfully assisting, counseling, encouraging a client or prospective client in violating, or suggesting to a client or prospective client to violate, any Federal tax law, or knowingly counseling or suggesting to a client or prospective client an illegal plan to evade Federal taxes or payment thereof.

(8) Misappropriation of, or failure properly or promptly to remit, funds received from a client for the purpose of payment of taxes or other obligations due the United States.

(9) Directly or indirectly attempting to influence, or offering or agreeing to attempt to influence, the official action of any officer or employee of the Internal Revenue Service by the use of threats, false accusations, duress or coercion, by the offer of any special inducement or promise of an advantage or by the bestowing of any gift, favor or thing of value.

(10) Disbarment or suspension from practice as an attorney, certified public accountant, public accountant, or actuary by any duly constituted authority of any State, territory, or possession of the United States, including a Commonwealth, or the District of Columbia, any Federal court of record or any Federal agency, body or board.

(11) Knowingly aiding and abetting another person to practice before the Internal Revenue Service during a period of suspension, disbarment or ineligibility of such other person.

(12) Contemptuous conduct in connection with practice before the Internal Revenue Service, including the use of abusive language, making false accusations or statements, knowing them to be false, or circulating or publishing malicious or libelous matter.

(13) Giving a false opinion, knowingly, recklessly, or through gross incompetence, including an opinion which is intentionally or recklessly misleading, or engaging in a pattern of providing incompetent opinions on questions arising under the Federal tax laws. False opinions described in this paragraph (a)(13) include those which reflect or result from a knowing misstatement of fact or law, from an assertion of a position known to be unwarranted under existing law, from counseling or assisting in conduct known to be illegal or fraudulent, from concealing matters required by law to be revealed, or from consciously disregarding information indicating that material facts expressed in the opinion or offering material are false or misleading. For purposes of this paragraph (a)(13), reckless conduct is a highly unreasonable omission or misrepresentation involving an extreme departure from the standards of ordinary care that a practitioner should observe under the circumstances. A pattern of conduct is a factor that will be taken into account in determining whether a practitioner acted knowingly, recklessly, or through gross incompetence. Gross incompetence

includes conduct that reflects gross indifference, preparation which is grossly inadequate under the circumstances, and a consistent failure to perform obligations to the client.

(14) Willfully failing to sign a tax return prepared by the practitioner when the practitioner's signature is required by Federal tax laws unless the failure is due to reasonable cause and not due to willful neglect.

(15) Willfully disclosing or otherwise using a tax return or tax return information in a manner not authorized by the Internal Revenue Code, contrary to the order of a court of competent jurisdiction, or contrary to the order of an administrative law judge in a proceeding instituted under §10.60.

(16) Willfully failing to file on magnetic or other electronic media a tax return prepared by the practitioner when the practitioner is required to do so by the Federal tax laws unless the failure is due to reasonable cause and not due to willful neglect.

(17) Willfully preparing all or substantially all of, or signing, a tax return or claim for refund when the practitioner does not possess a current or otherwise valid preparer tax identification number or other prescribed identifying number.

(18) Willfully representing a taxpayer before an officer or employee of the Internal Revenue Service unless the practitioner is authorized to do so pursuant to this part.

(b) *Effective/applicability date.* This section is applicable beginning August 2, 2011.

§ 10.52 Violations subject to sanction.

(a) A practitioner may be sanctioned under §10.50 if the practitioner —

(1) Willfully violates any of the regulations (other than §10.33) contained in this part; or

(2) Recklessly or through gross incompetence (within the meaning of §10.51(a)(13)) violates §§ 10.34, 10.35, 10.36 or 10.37.

(b) *Effective/applicability date.* This section is applicable to conduct occurring on or after September 26, 2007.

§ 10.53 Receipt of information concerning practitioner.

(a) *Officer or employee of the Internal Revenue Service.* If an officer or employee of the Internal Revenue Service has reason to believe a practitioner has violated any provision of this part, the officer or employee will promptly make a written report of the suspected violation. The report will explain the facts and reasons upon which the officer's or employee's belief rests and must be submitted to the office(s) of the Internal Revenue Service responsible for administering or enforcing this part.

(b) *Other persons.* Any person other than an officer or employee of the Internal Revenue Service having information of a violation of any provision of this part may make an oral or written report of the alleged violation to the office(s) of the Internal Revenue Service responsible for administering or enforcing this part or any officer or employee of the Internal Revenue Service. If the report is made to an officer or employee of the Internal Revenue Service, the officer or employee will make a written report of the suspected violation and submit the report to the office(s) of the Internal Revenue Service responsible for administering or enforcing this part.

(c) *Destruction of report.* No report made under paragraph (a) or (b) of this section shall be maintained unless retention of the report is permissible under the applicable records control schedule as approved by the National Archives and Records Administration and designated in the Internal Revenue Manual. Reports must be destroyed as soon as permissible under the applicable records control schedule.

(d) *Effect on proceedings under subpart D.* The destruction of any report will not bar any proceeding under subpart D of this part, but will preclude the use of a copy of the report in a proceeding under subpart D of this part.

(e) *Effective/applicability date.* This section is applicable beginning August 2, 2011.

Subpart D — Rules Applicable to Disciplinary Proceedings

§ 10.60 Institution of proceeding.

(a) Whenever it is determined that a practitioner (or employer, firm or other entity, if applicable) violated any provision of the laws governing practice before the Internal Revenue Service or the regulations in this part, the practitioner may be reprimanded or, in accordance with §10.62, subject to a proceeding for sanctions described in §10.50.

(b) Whenever a penalty has been assessed against an appraiser under the Internal Revenue Code and an appropriate officer or employee in an office established to enforce this part determines that the appraiser acted willfully, recklessly, or through gross incompetence with respect to the proscribed conduct, the appraiser may be reprimanded or, in accordance with §10.62, subject to a proceeding for disqualification. A proceeding for disqualification of an appraiser is instituted by the filing of a complaint, the contents of which are more fully described in §10.62.

(c) Except as provided in §10.82, a proceeding will not be instituted under this section unless the proposed respondent previously has been advised in writing of the law, facts and conduct warranting such action and has been accorded an opportunity to dispute facts, assert additional facts, and make arguments (including an explanation or description of mitigating circumstances).

(d) *Effective/applicability date.* This section is applicable beginning August 2, 2011.

§ 10.61 Conferences.

(a) *In general.* The Commissioner, or delegate, may confer with a practitioner, employer, firm or other entity, or an appraiser concerning allegations of misconduct irrespective of whether a proceeding has been instituted. If the conference results in a stipulation in connection with an ongoing proceeding in which the practitioner, employer, firm or other entity, or appraiser is the respondent, the stipulation may be entered in the record by either party to the proceeding.

(b) *Voluntary sanction* —

(1) *In general.* In lieu of a proceeding being instituted or continued under §10.60(a), a practitioner or appraiser (or employer, firm or other entity, if applicable) may offer a consent to be sanctioned under §10.50.

(2) *Discretion; acceptance or declination.* The Commissioner, or delegate, may accept or decline the offer described in paragraph (b)(1) of this section. When the decision is to decline the offer, the written notice of declination may state that the offer described in paragraph (b)(1) of this section would be accepted if it contained different terms. The Commissioner, or delegate, has the discretion to accept or reject a revised offer submitted in response to the declination or may counteroffer and act upon any accepted counteroffer.

(c) *Effective/applicability date.* This section is applicable beginning August 2, 2011.

§ 10.62 Contents of complaint.

(a) *Charges.* A complaint must name the respondent, provide a clear and concise description of the facts and law that constitute the basis for the proceeding, and be signed by an authorized representative of the Internal Revenue Service under §10.69(a)(1). A complaint is sufficient if it fairly informs the respondent of the charges brought so that the respondent is able to prepare a defense.

(b) *Specification of sanction.* The complaint must specify the sanction sought against the practitioner or appraiser. If the sanction sought is a suspension, the duration of the suspension sought must be specified.

(c) *Demand for answer.* The respondent must be notified in the complaint or in a separate paper attached to the complaint of the time for answering the complaint, which may not be less than 30 days from the date of service of the complaint, the name and address of the Administrative Law Judge with whom the answer must be filed, the name and address of the person representing the Internal Revenue Service to whom a copy of the answer must be served, and

Treasury Department Circular No. 230 **§ 10.62 — Page 31**

that a decision by default may be rendered against the respondent in the event an answer is not filed as required.

(d) *Effective/applicability date.* This section is applicable beginning August 2, 2011.

§ 10.63 Service of complaint; service of other papers; service of evidence in support of complaint; filing of papers.

(a) *Service of complaint.*

(1) *In general.* The complaint or a copy of the complaint must be served on the respondent by any manner described in paragraphs (a) (2) or (3) of this section.

(2) *Service by certified or first class mail.*

(i) Service of the complaint may be made on the respondent by mailing the complaint by certified mail to the last known address (as determined under section 6212 of the Internal Revenue Code and the regulations thereunder) of the respondent. Where service is by certified mail, the returned post office receipt duly signed by the respondent will be proof of service.

(ii) If the certified mail is not claimed or accepted by the respondent, or is returned undelivered, service may be made on the respondent, by mailing the complaint to the respondent by first class mail. Service by this method will be considered complete upon mailing, provided the complaint is addressed to the respondent at the respondent's last known address as determined under section 6212 of the Internal Revenue Code and the regulations thereunder.

(3) *Service by other than certified or first class mail.*

(i) Service of the complaint may be made on the respondent by delivery by a private delivery service designated pursuant to section 7502(f) of the Internal Revenue Code to the last known address (as determined under section 6212 of the Internal Revenue Code and the regulations there under) of the respondent. Service by this method will be considered complete, provided the complaint is addressed to the respondent at the respondent's last known address as determined under section 6212 of the Internal Revenue Code and the regulations thereunder.

(ii) Service of the complaint may be made in person on, or by leaving the complaint at the office or place of business of, the respondent. Service by this method will be considered complete and proof of service will be a written statement, sworn or affirmed by the person who served the complaint, identifying the manner of service, including the recipient, relationship of recipient to respondent, place, date and time of service.

(iii) Service may be made by any other means agreed to by the respondent. Proof of service will be a written statement, sworn or affirmed by the person who served the complaint, identifying the manner of service, including the recipient, relationship of recipient to respondent, place, date and time of service.

(4) For purposes of this section, *respondent* means the practitioner, employer, firm or other entity, or appraiser named in the complaint or any other person having the authority to accept mail on behalf of the practitioner, employer, firm or other entity or appraiser.

(b) *Service of papers other than complaint.* Any paper other than the complaint may be served on the respondent, or his or her authorized representative under §10.69(a)(2) by:

(1) mailing the paper by first class mail to the last known address (as determined under section 6212 of the Internal Revenue Code and the regulations thereunder) of the respondent or the respondent's authorized representative,

(2) delivery by a private delivery service designated pursuant to section 7502(f) of the Internal Revenue Code to the last known address (as determined under section 6212 of the Internal Revenue Code and the regulations thereunder) of the respondent or the respondent's authorized representative, or

(3) as provided in paragraphs (a)(3)(ii) and (a)(3)(iii) of this section.

(c) *Service of papers on the Internal Revenue Service.* Whenever a paper is required or permitted to be served on the Internal Revenue Service in connection with a proceeding under this part, the paper will be served on the Internal Revenue Service's authorized representative under §10.69(a)(1) at the address designated in the complaint, or at an address provided in a notice of appearance. If no address is designated in the complaint or provided in a notice of appearance, service will be made on the office(s) established to enforce this part under the authority of §10.1, Internal Revenue Service, 1111 Constitution Avenue, NW, Washington, DC 20224.

(d) *Service of evidence in support of complaint.* Within 10 days of serving the complaint, copies of the evidence in support of the complaint must be served on the respondent in any manner described in paragraphs (a)(2) and (3) of this section.

(e) *Filing of papers.* Whenever the filing of a paper is required or permitted in connection with a proceeding under this part, the original paper, plus one additional copy, must be filed with the Administrative Law Judge at the address specified in the complaint or at an address otherwise specified by the Administrative Law Judge. All papers filed in connection with a proceeding under this part must be served on the other party, unless the Administrative Law Judge directs otherwise. A certificate evidencing such must be attached to the original paper filed with the Administrative Law Judge.

(f) *Effective/applicability date.* This section is applicable beginning August 2, 2011.

§ 10.64 Answer; default.

(a) *Filing.* The respondent's answer must be filed with the Administrative Law Judge, and served on the Internal Revenue Service, within the time specified in the complaint unless, on request or application of the respondent, the time is extended by the Administrative Law Judge.

(b) *Contents.* The answer must be written and contain a statement of facts that constitute the respondent's grounds of defense. General denials are not permitted. The respondent must specifically admit or deny each allegation set forth in the complaint, except that the respondent may state that the respondent is without sufficient information to admit or deny a specific allegation. The respondent, nevertheless, may not deny a material allegation in the complaint that the respondent knows to be true, or state that the respondent is without sufficient information to form a belief, when the respondent possesses the required information. The respondent also must state affirmatively any special matters of defense on which he or she relies.

(c) *Failure to deny or answer allegations in the complaint.* Every allegation in the complaint that is not denied in the answer is deemed admitted and will be considered proved; no further evidence in respect of such allegation need be adduced at a hearing.

(d) *Default.* Failure to file an answer within the time prescribed (or within the time for answer as extended by the Administrative Law Judge), constitutes an admission of the allegations of the complaint and a waiver of hearing, and the Administrative Law Judge may make the decision by default without a hearing or further procedure. A decision by default constitutes a decision under §10.76.

(e) *Signature.* The answer must be signed by the respondent or the respondent's authorized representative under §10.69(a)(2) and must include a statement directly above the signature acknowledging that the statements made in the answer are true and correct and that knowing and willful false statements may be punishable under 18 U.S.C. §1001.

(f) Effective/applicability date. This section is applicable beginning August 2, 2011.

§ 10.65 Supplemental charges.

(a) *In general.* Supplemental charges may be filed against the respondent by amending the complaint with the permission of the Administrative Law Judge if, for example —

(1) It appears that the respondent, in the answer, falsely and in bad faith, denies a material allegation of fact in the complaint or states that the respondent has insufficient knowledge to form a belief, when the respondent possesses such information; or

(2) It appears that the respondent has knowingly

introduced false testimony during the proceedings against the respondent.

(b) *Hearing.* The supplemental charges may be heard with other charges in the case, provided the respondent is given due notice of the charges and is afforded a reasonable opportunity to prepare a defense to the supplemental charges.

(c) *Effective/applicability date.* This section is applicable beginning August 2, 2011.

§ 10.66 Reply to answer.

(a) The Internal Revenue Service may file a reply to the respondent's answer, but unless otherwise ordered by the Administrative Law Judge, no reply to the respondent's answer is required. If a reply is not filed, new matter in the answer is deemed denied.

(b) *Effective/applicability date.* This section is applicable beginning August 2, 2011.

§ 10.67 Proof; variance; amendment of pleadings.

In the case of a variance between the allegations in pleadings and the evidence adduced in support of the pleadings, the Administrative Law Judge, at any time before decision, may order or authorize amendment of the pleadings to conform to the evidence. The party who would otherwise be prejudiced by the amendment must be given a reasonable opportunity to address the allegations of the pleadings as amended and the Administrative Law Judge must make findings on any issue presented by the pleadings as amended.

§ 10.68 Motions and requests.

(a) *Motions* —

(1) *In general.* At any time after the filing of the complaint, any party may file a motion with the Administrative Law Judge. Unless otherwise ordered by the Administrative Law Judge, motions must be in writing and must be served on the opposing party as provided in §10.63(b). A motion must concisely specify its grounds and the relief sought, and, if appropriate, must contain a memorandum of facts and law in support.

(2) *Summary adjudication.* Either party may move for a summary adjudication upon all or any part of the legal issues in controversy. If the non-moving party opposes summary adjudication in the moving party's favor, the non-moving party must file a written response within 30 days unless ordered otherwise by the Administrative Law Judge.

(3) *Good Faith.* A party filing a motion for extension of time, a motion for postponement of a hearing, or any other non-dispositive or procedural motion must first contact the other party to determine whether there is any objection to the motion, and must state in the motion whether the other party has an objection.

(b) *Response.* Unless otherwise ordered by the Administrative Law Judge, the nonmoving party is not required to file a response to a motion. If the Administrative Law Judge does not order the nonmoving party to file a response, and the nonmoving party files no response, the nonmoving party is deemed to oppose the motion. If a nonmoving party does not respond within 30 days of the filing of a motion for decision by default for failure to file a timely answer or for failure to prosecute, the nonmoving party is deemed not to oppose the motion.

(c) *Oral motions; oral argument* —

(1) The Administrative Law Judge may, for good cause and with notice to the parties, permit oral motions and oral opposition to motions.

(2) The Administrative Law Judge may, within his or her discretion, permit oral argument on any motion.

(d) *Orders.* The Administrative Law Judge should issue written orders disposing of any motion or request and any response thereto.

(e) *Effective/applicability date.* This section is applicable on September 26, 2007.

§ 10.69 Representation; ex parte communication.

(a) *Representation.*

(1) The Internal Revenue Service may be represented in proceedings under this part by an attorney or other employee of the Internal Revenue Service. An attorney or an employee of the Internal

Revenue Service representing the Internal Revenue Service in a proceeding under this part may sign the complaint or any document required to be filed in the proceeding on behalf of the Internal Revenue Service.

(2) A respondent may appear in person, be represented by a practitioner, or be represented by an attorney who has not filed a declaration with the Internal Revenue Service pursuant to §10.3. A practitioner or an attorney representing a respondent or proposed respondent may sign the answer or any document required to be filed in the proceeding on behalf of the respondent.

(b) *Ex parte communication.* The Internal Revenue Service, the respondent, and any representatives of either party, may not attempt to initiate or participate in ex parte discussions concerning a proceeding or potential proceeding with the Administrative Law Judge (or any person who is likely to advise the Administrative Law Judge on a ruling or decision) in the proceeding before or during the pendency of the proceeding. Any memorandum, letter or other communication concerning the merits of the proceeding, addressed to the Administrative Law Judge, by or on behalf of any party shall be regarded as an argument in the proceeding and shall be served on the othe party.

(c) *Effective/applicability date.* This section is applicable beginning August 2, 2011.

§ 10.70 Administrative Law Judge.

(a) *Appointment.* Proceedings on complaints for the sanction (as described in §10.50) of a practitioner, employer, firm or other entity, or appraiser will be conducted by an Administrative Law Judge appointed as provided by *5 U.S.C. 3105*.

(b) *Powers of the Administrative Law Judge.* The Administrative Law Judge, among other powers, has the authority, in connection with any proceeding under §10.60 assigned or referred to him or her, to do the following:

(1) Administer oaths and affirmations;

(2) Make rulings on motions and requests, which rulings may not be appealed prior to the close of a hearing except in extraordinary circumstances and at the discretion of the Administrative Law Judge;

(3) Determine the time and place of hearing and regulate its course and conduct;

(4) Adopt rules of procedure and modify the same from time to time as needed for the orderly disposition of proceedings;

(5) Rule on offers of proof, receive relevant evidence, and examine witnesses;

(6) Take or authorize the taking of depositions or answers to requests for admission;

(7) Receive and consider oral or written argument on facts or law;

(8) Hold or provide for the holding of conferences for the settlement or simplification of the issues with the consent of the parties;

(9) Perform such acts and take such measures as are necessary or appropriate to the efficient conduct of any proceeding; and

(10) Make decisions.

(c) *Effective/applicability date.* This section is applicable on September 26, 2007.

§ 10.71 Discovery.

(a) *In general.* Discovery may be permitted, at the discretion of the Administrative Law Judge, only upon written motion demonstrating the relevance, materiality and reasonableness of the requested discovery and subject to the requirements of §10.72(d)(2) and (3). Within 10 days of receipt of the answer, the Administrative Law Judge will notify the parties of the right to request discovery and the timeframe for filing a request. A request for discovery, and objections, must be filed in accordance with §10.68. In response to a request for discovery, the Administrative Law Judge may order —

(1) Depositions upon oral examination; or

(2) Answers to requests for admission.

(b) *Depositions upon oral examination* —

(1) A deposition must be taken before an officer duly authorized to administer an oath for general purposes or before an officer or employee of the Internal Revenue Service who is authorized to administer an oath in Federal tax law matters.

(2) In ordering a deposition, the Administrative Law Judge will require reasonable notice to the opposing party as to the time and place of the deposition. The opposing party, if attending, will be provided the opportunity for full examination and cross-examination of any witness.

(3) Expenses in the reporting of depositions shall be borne by the party at whose instance the deposition is taken. Travel expenses of the deponent shall be borne by the party requesting the deposition, unless otherwise authorized by Federal law or regulation.

(c) *Requests for admission.* Any party may serve on any other party a written request for admission of the truth of any matters which are not privileged and are relevant to the subject matter of this proceeding. Requests for admission shall not exceed a total of 30 (including any subparts within a specific request) without the approval from the Administrative Law Judge.

(d) *Limitations.* Discovery shall not be authorized if—

(1) The request fails to meet any requirement set forth in paragraph (a) of this section;

(2) It will unduly delay the proceeding;

(3) It will place an undue burden on the party required to produce the discovery sought;

(4) It is frivolous or abusive;

(5) It is cumulative or duplicative;

(6) The material sought is privileged or otherwise protected from disclosure by law;

(7) The material sought relates to mental impressions, conclusions, of legal theories of any party, attorney, or other representative, or a party prepared in the anticipation of a proceeding; or

(8) The material sought is available generally to the public, equally to the parties, or to the party seeking the discovery through another source.

(e) *Failure to comply.* Where a party fails to comply with an order of the Administrative Law Judge under this section, the Administrative Law Judge may, among other things, infer that the information would be adverse to the party failing to provide it, exclude the information from evidence or issue a decision by default.

(f) *Other discovery.* No discovery other than that specifically provided for in this section is permitted.

(g) *Effective/applicability date.* This section is applicable to proceedings initiated on or after September 26, 2007.

§ 10.72 Hearings.

(a) *In general* —

(1) *Presiding officer.* An Administrative Law Judge will preside at the hearing on a complaint filed under §10.60 for the sanction of a practitioner, employer, firm or other entity, or appraiser.

(2) *Time for hearing.* Absent a determination by the Administrative Law Judge that, in the interest of justice, a hearing must be held at a later time, the Administrative Law Judge should, on notice sufficient to allow proper preparation, schedule the hearing to occur no later than 180 days after the time for filing the answer.

(3) *Procedural requirements.*

(i) Hearings will be stenographically recorded and transcribed and the testimony of witnesses will be taken under oath or affirmation.

(ii) Hearings will be conducted pursuant to *5 U.S.C. 556.*

(iii) A hearing in a proceeding requested under §10.82(g) will be conducted de novo.

(iv) An evidentiary hearing must be held in all proceedings prior to the issuance of a decision by the Administrative Law Judge unless —

(A) The Internal Revenue Service withdraws the complaint;

(B) A decision is issued by default pursuant to §10.64(d);

(C) A decision is issued under §10.82 (e);

(D) The respondent requests a decision on the written record without a hearing; or

(E) The Administrative Law Judge issues a decision under §10.68(d) or rules on another motion that disposes of the case prior to the hearing.

(b) *Cross-examination.* A party is entitled to present his or her case or defense by oral or documentary evidence, to submit rebuttal evidence, and to conduct cross-examination, in the presence of the Administrative Law Judge, as may be required for a full and true disclosure of the facts. This paragraph (b) does not limit a party from presenting evidence contained within a deposition when the Administrative Law Judge determines that the deposition has been obtained in compliance with the rules of this subpart D.

(c) *Prehearing memorandum.* Unless otherwise ordered by the Administrative Law Judge, each party shall file, and serve on the opposing party or the opposing party's representative, prior to any hearing, a prehearing memorandum containing —

(1) A list (together with a copy) of all proposed exhibits to be used in the party's case in chief;

(2) A list of proposed witnesses, including a synopsis of their expected testimony, or a statement that no witnesses will be called;

(3) Identification of any proposed expert witnesses, including a synopsis of their expected testimony and a copy of any report prepared by the expert or at his or her direction; and

(4) A list of undisputed facts.

(d) *Publicity* —

(1) *In general.* All reports and decisions of the Secretary of the Treasury, or delegate, including any reports and decisions of the Administrative Law Judge, under this subpart D are, subject to the protective measures in paragraph (d)(4) of this section, public and open to inspection within 30 days after the agency's decision becomes final.

(2) *Request for additional publicity.* The Administrative Law Judge may grant a request by a practitioner or appraiser that all the pleadings and evidence of the disciplinary proceeding be made available for inspection where the parties stipulate in advance to adopt the protective measures in paragraph (d)(4) of this section.

(3) *Returns and return information* —

(i) *Disclosure to practitioner or appraiser.* Pursuant to *section 6103(l)(4) of the Internal Revenue Code,* the Secretary of the Treasury, or delegate, may disclose returns and return information to any practitioner or appraiser, or to the authorized representative of the practitioner or appraiser, whose rights are or may be affected by an administrative action or proceeding under this subpart D, but solely for use in the action or proceeding and only to the extent that the Secretary of the Treasury, or delegate, determines that the returns or return information are or may be relevant and material to the action or proceeding.

(ii) *Disclosure to officers and employees of the Department of the Treasury.* Pursuant to *section 6103(l)(4)(B) of the Internal Revenue Code* the Secretary of the Treasury, or delegate, may disclose returns and return information to officers and employees of the Department of the Treasury for use in any action or proceeding under this subpart D, to the extent necessary to advance or protect the interests of the United States.

(iii) *Use of returns and return information.* Recipients of returns and return information under this paragraph (d)(3) may use the returns or return information solely in the action or proceeding, or in preparation for the action or proceeding, with respect to which the disclosure was made.

(iv) *Procedures for disclosure of returns and return information.* When providing returns or return information to the practitioner or appraiser, or authorized representative, the Secretary of the Treasury, or delegate, will —

(A) Redact identifying information of any third party taxpayers and replace it with a code;

(B) Provide a key to the coded information; and

(C) Notify the practitioner or appraiser, or authorized representative, of the restrictions on the use and disclosure of the returns and return information, the applicable damages remedy under *section 7431 of the Internal Revenue Code*, and that unauthorized disclosure of information provided by the Internal Revenue Service under this paragraph (d)(3) is also a violation of this part.

(4) *Protective measures* —

(i) *Mandatory protection order.* If redaction of names, addresses, and other identifying information of third party taxpayers may still permit indirect identification of any third party taxpayer, the Administrative Law Judge will issue a protective order to ensure that the identifying information is available to the parties and the Administrative Law Judge for purposes of the proceeding, but is not

6

disclosed to, or open to inspection by, the public.

(ii) *Authorized orders.*

(A) Upon motion by a party or any other affected person, and for good cause shown, the Administrative Law Judge may make any order which justice requires to protect any person in the event disclosure of information is prohibited by law, privileged, confidential, or sensitive in some other way, including, but not limited to, one or more of the following —

(1) That disclosure of information be made only on specified terms and conditions, including a designation of the time or place;

(2) That a trade secret or other information not be disclosed, or be disclosed only in a designated way.

(iii) *Denials.* If a motion for a protective order is denied in whole or in part, the Administrative Law Judge may, on such terms or conditions as the Administrative Law Judge deems just, order any party or person to comply with, or respond in accordance with, the procedure involved.

(iv) *Public inspection of documents.* The Secretary of the Treasury, or delegate, shall ensure that all names, addresses or other identifying details of third party taxpayers are redacted and replaced with the code assigned to the corresponding taxpayer in all documents prior to public inspection of such documents.

(e) *Location.* The location of the hearing will be determined by the agreement of the parties with the approval of the Administrative Law Judge, but, in the absence of such agreement and approval, the hearing will be held in Washington, D.C.

(f) *Failure to appear.* If either party to the proceeding fails to appear at the hearing, after notice of the proceeding has been sent to him or her, the party will be deemed to have waived the right to a hearing and the Administrative Law Judge may make his or her decision against the absent party by default.

(g) *Effective/applicability date.* This section is applicable beginning August 2, 2011.

§ 10.73 Evidence.

(a) *In general.* The rules of evidence prevailing in courts of law and equity are not controlling in hearings or proceedings conducted under this part. The Administrative Law Judge may, however, exclude evidence that is irrelevant, immaterial, or unduly repetitious.

(b) *Depositions.* The deposition of any witness taken pursuant to §10.71 may be admitted into evidence in any proceeding instituted under §10.60.

(c) *Requests for admission.* Any matter admitted in response to a request for admission under §10.71 is conclusively established unless the Administrative Law Judge on motion permits withdrawal or modification of the admission. Any admission made by a party is for the purposes of the pending action only and is not an admission by a party for any other purpose, nor may it be used against a party in any other proceeding.

(d) *Proof of documents.* Official documents, records, and papers of the Internal Revenue Service and the Office of Professional Responsibility are admissible in evidence without the production of an officer or employee to authenticate them. Any documents, records, and papers may be evidenced by a copy attested to or identified by an officer or employee of the Internal Revenue Service or the Treasury Department, as the case may be.

(e) *Withdrawal of exhibits.* If any document, record, or other paper is introduced in evidence as an exhibit, the Administrative Law Judge may authorize the withdrawal of the exhibit subject to any conditions that he or she deems proper.

(f) *Objections.* Objections to evidence are to be made in short form, stating the grounds for the objection. Except as ordered by the Administrative Law Judge, argument on objections will not be recorded or transcribed. Rulings on objections are to be a part of the record, but no exception to a ruling is necessary to preserve the rights of the parties.

(g) *Effective/applicability date.* This section is applicable on September 26, 2007.

§ 10.74 Transcript.

In cases where the hearing is stenographically reported by a Government contract reporter, copies of the transcript may be obtained from the reporter at rates not to exceed the maximum rates fixed by contract between the Government and the reporter. Where the hearing is stenographically reported by a regular employee of the Internal Revenue Service, a copy will be supplied to the respondent either without charge or upon the payment of a reasonable fee. Copies of exhibits introduced at the hearing or at the taking of depositions will be supplied to the parties upon the payment of a reasonable fee (Sec. 501, Public Law 82-137) (65 Stat. 290) (31 U.S.C. § 483a).

§ 10.75 Proposed findings and conclusions.

Except in cases where the respondent has failed to answer the complaint or where a party has failed to appear at the hearing, the parties must be afforded a reasonable opportunity to submit proposed findings and conclusions and their supporting reasons to the Administrative Law Judge.

§ 10.76 Decision of Administrative Law Judge.

(a) *In general* —

(1) *Hearings.* Within 180 days after the conclusion of a hearing and the receipt of any proposed findings and conclusions timely submitted by the parties, the Administrative Law Judge should enter a decision in the case. The decision must include a statement of findings and conclusions, as well as the reasons or basis for making such findings and conclusions, and an order of censure, suspension, disbarment, monetary penalty, disqualification, or dismissal of the complaint.

(2) *Summary adjudication.* In the event that a motion for summary adjudication is filed, the Administrative Law Judge should rule on the motion for summary adjudication within 60 days after the party in opposition files a written response, or if no written response is filed, within 90 days after the motion for summary adjudication is filed. A decision shall thereafter be rendered if the pleadings, depositions, admissions, and any other admissible evidence show that there is no genuine issue of material fact and that a decision may be rendered as a matter of law. The decision must include a statement of conclusions, as well as the reasons or basis for making such conclusions, and an order of censure, suspension, disbarment, monetary penalty, disqualification, or dismissal of the complaint.

(3) *Returns and return information.* In the decision, the Administrative Law Judge should use the code assigned to third party taxpayers (described in §10.72(d)).

(b) *Standard of proof.* If the sanction is censure or a suspension of less than six months' duration, the Administrative Law Judge, in rendering findings and conclusions, will consider an allegation of fact to be proven if it is established by the party who is alleging the fact by a preponderance of the evidence in the record. If the sanction is a monetary penalty, disbarment or a suspension of six months or longer duration, an allegation of fact that is necessary for a finding against the practitioner must be proven by clear and convincing evidence in the record. An allegation of fact that is necessary for a finding of disqualification against an appraiser must be proved by clear and convincing evidence in the record.

(c) *Copy of decision.* The Administrative Law Judge will provide the decision to the Internal Revenue Service's authorized representative, and a copy of the decision to the respondent or the respondent's authorized representative.

(d) *When final.* In the absence of an appeal to the Secretary of the Treasury or delegate, the decision of the Administrative Law Judge will, without further proceedings, become the decision of the agency 30 days after the date of the Administrative Law Judge's decision.

(e) *Effective/applicability date.* This section is applicable beginning August 2, 2011.

Treasury Department Circular No. 230 **§ 10.76 — Page 39**

§ 10.77 Appeal of decision of Administrative Law Judge.

(a) *Appeal.* Any party to the proceeding under this subpart D may appeal the decision of the Administrative Law Judge by filing a notice of appeal with the Secretary of the Treasury, or delegate deciding appeals. The notice of appeal must include a brief that states exceptions to the decision of Administrative Law Judge and supporting reasons for such exceptions.

(b) *Time and place for filing of appeal.* The notice of appeal and brief must be filed, in duplicate, with the Secretary of the Treasury, or delegate deciding appeals, at an address for appeals that is identified to the parties with the decision of the Administrative Law Judge. The notice of appeal and brief must be filed within 30 days of the date that the decision of the Administrative Law Judge is served on the parties. The appealing party must serve a copy of the notice of appeal and the brief to any non appealing party or, if the party is represented, the non-appealing party's representative.

(c) *Response.* Within 30 days of receiving the copy of the appellant's brief, the other party may file a response brief with the Secretary of the Treasury, or delegate deciding appeals, using the address identified for appeals. A copy of the response brief must be served at the same time on the opposing party or, if the party is represented, the opposing party's representative.

(d) *No other briefs, responses or motions as of right.* Other than the appeal brief and response brief, the parties are not permitted to file any other briefs, responses or motions, except on a grant of leave to do so after a motion demonstrating sufficient cause, or unless otherwise ordered by the Secretary of the Treasury, or delegate deciding appeals.

(e) *Additional time for briefs and responses.* Notwithstanding the time for filing briefs and responses provided in paragraphs (b) and (c) of this section, the Secretary of the Treasury, or delegate deciding appeals, may, for good cause, authorize additional time for filing briefs and responses upon a motion of a party or upon the initiative of the Secretary of the Treasury, or delegate deciding appeals.

(f) *Effective/applicability date.* This section is applicable beginning August 2, 2011.

§ 10.78 Decision on review.

(a) *Decision on review.* On appeal from or review of the decision of the Administrative Law Judge, the Secretary of the Treasury, or delegate, will make the agency decision. The Secretary of the Treasury, or delegate, should make the agency decision within 180 days after receipt of the appeal

(b) *Standard of review.* The decision of the Administrative Law Judge will not be reversed unless the appellant establishes that the decision is clearly erroneous in light of the evidence in the record and applicable law. Issues that are exclusively matters of law will be reviewed de novo. In the event that the Secretary of the Treasury, or delegate, determines that there are unresolved issues raised by the record, the case may be remanded to the Administrative Law Judge to elicit additional testimony or evidence.

(c) *Copy of decision on review.* The Secretary of the Treasury, or delegate, will provide copies of the agency decision to the authorized representative of the Internal Revenue Service and the respondent or the respondent's authorized representative.

(d) *Effective/applicability date.* This section is applicable beginning August 2, 2011.

§ 10.79 Effect of disbarment, suspension, or censure.

(a) *Disbarment.* When the final decision in a case is against the respondent (or the respondent has offered his or her consent and such consent has been accepted by the Internal Revenue Service) and such decision is for disbarment, the respondent will not be permitted to practice before the Internal Revenue Service unless and until authorized to do so by the Internal Revenue Service pursuant to §10.81.

(b) *Suspension.* When the final decision in a case is against the respondent (or the respondent has offered his or her consent and such consent has been accepted by the Internal Revenue Service) and such decision is for suspension, the respondent will not be permitted to practice before the Internal Revenue Service during the period of suspension. For periods after the suspension, the practitioner's future representations may be subject to conditions as authorized by paragraph (d) of this section.

(c) *Censure*. When the final decision in the case is against the respondent (or the Internal Revenue Service has accepted the respondent's offer to consent, if such offer was made) and such decision is for censure, the respondent will be permitted to practice before the Internal Revenue Service, but the respondent's future representations may be subject to conditions as authorized by paragraph (d) of this section.

(d) *Conditions*. After being subject to the sanction of either suspension or censure, the future representations of a practitioner so sanctioned shall be subject to specified conditions designed to promote high standards of conduct. These conditions can be imposed for a reasonable period in light of the gravity of the practitioner's violations. For example, where a practitioner is censured because the practitioner failed to advise the practitioner's clients about a potential conflict of interest or failed to obtain the clients' written consents, the practitioner may be required to provide the Internal Revenue Service with a copy of all consents obtained by the practitioner for an appropriate period following censure, whether or not such consents are specifically requested.

(e) *Effective/applicability date*. This section is applicable beginning August 2, 2011.

§ 10.80 Notice of disbarment, suspension, censure, or disqualification.

(a) *In general*. On the issuance of a final order censuring, suspending, or disbarring a practitioner or a final order disqualifying an appraiser, notification of the censure, suspension, disbarment or disqualification will be given to appropriate officers and employees of the Internal Revenue Service and interested departments and agencies of the Federal government. The Internal Revenue Service may determine the manner of giving notice to the proper authorities of the State by which the censured, suspended, or disbarred person was licensed to practice.

(b) *Effective/applicability date*. This section is applicable beginning August 2, 2011.

§ 10.81 Petition for reinstatement.

(a) *In general*. A practitioner disbarred or suspended under §10.60, or suspended under §10.82, or a disqualified appraiser may petition for reinstatement before the Internal Revenue Service after the expiration of 5 years following such disbarment, suspension, or disqualification (or immediately following the expiration of the suspension or disqualification period, if shorter than 5 years). Reinstatement will not be granted unless the Internal Revenue Service is satisfied that the petitioner is not likely to engage thereafter in conduct contrary to the regulations in this part, and that granting such reinstatement would not be contrary to the public interest.

(b) *Effective/applicability date*. This section is applicable beginning June 12, 2014.

§ 10.82 Expedited suspension.

(a) *When applicable*. Whenever the Commissioner, or delegate, determines that a practitioner is described in paragraph (b) of this section, the expedited procedures described in this section may be used to suspend the practitioner from practice before the Internal Revenue Service.

(b) *To whom applicable*. This section applies to any practitioner who, within 5 years prior to the date that a show cause order under this section's expedited suspension procedures is served:

(1) Has had a license to practice as an attorney, certified public accountant, or actuary suspended or revoked for cause (not including a failure to pay a professional licensing fee) by any authority or court, agency, body, or board described in §10.51(a)(10).

(2) Has, irrespective of whether an appeal has been taken, been convicted of any crime under title

Treasury Department Circular No. 230 **§ 10.82 — Page 41**

6

26 of the United States Code, any crime involving dishonesty or breach of trust, or any felony for which the conduct involved renders the practitioner unfit to practice before the Internal Revenue Service.

(3) Has violated conditions imposed on the practitioner pursuant to §10.79(d).

(4) Has been sanctioned by a court of competent jurisdiction, whether in a civil or criminal proceeding (including suits for injunctive relief), relating to any taxpayer's tax liability or relating to the practitioner's own tax liability, for —

(i) Instituting or maintaining proceedings primarily for delay;

(ii) Advancing frivolous or groundless arguments; or

(iii) Failing to pursue available administrative remedies.

(5) Has demonstrated a pattern of willful disreputable conduct by—

(i) Failing to make an annual Federal tax return, in violation of the Federal tax laws, during 4 of the 5 tax years immediately preceding the institution of a proceeding under paragraph (c) of this section and remains noncompliant with any of the practitioner's Federal tax filing obligations at the time the notice of suspension is issued under paragraph (f) of this section; or

(ii) Failing to make a return required more frequently than annually, in violation of the Federal tax laws, during 5 of the 7 tax periods immediately preceding the institution of a proceeding under paragraph (c) of this section and remains noncompliant with any of the practitioner's Federal tax filing obligations at the time the notice of suspension is issued under paragraph (f) of this section.

(c) *Expedited suspension procedures.* A suspension under this section will be proposed by a show cause order that names the respondent, is signed by an authorized representative of the Internal Revenue Service under §10.69(a)(1), and served according to the rules set forth in §10.63(a). The show cause order must give a plain and concise description of the allegations that constitute the basis for the proposed suspension. The show cause order must notify the respondent —

(1) Of the place and due date for filing a response;

(2) That an expedited suspension decision by default may be rendered if the respondent fails to file a response as required;

(3) That the respondent may request a conference to address the merits of the show cause order and that any such request must be made in the response; and

(4) That the respondent may be suspended either immediately following the expiration of the period within which a response must be filed or, if a conference is requested, immediately following the conference.

(d) *Response.* The response to the show cause order described in this section must be filed no later than 30 calendar days following the date the show cause order is served, unless the time for filing is extended. The response must be filed in accordance with the rules set forth for answers to a complaint in §10.64, except as otherwise provided in this section. The response must include a request for a conference, if a conference is desired. The respondent is entitled to the conference only if the request is made in a timely filed response.

(e) *Conference.* An authorized representative of the Internal Revenue Service will preside at a conference described in this section. The conference will be held at a place and time selected by the Internal Revenue Service, but no sooner than 14 calendar days after the date by which the response must be filed with the Internal Revenue Service, unless the respondent agrees to an earlier date. An authorized representative may represent the respondent at the conference.

(f) *Suspension*—

(1) *In general.* The Commissioner, or delegate, may suspend the respondent from practice before the Internal Revenue Service by a written notice of expedited suspension immediately following:

(i) The expiration of the period within which a response to a show cause order must be filed if the respondent does not file a response as required by paragraph (d) of this section;

(ii) The conference described in paragraph (e) of this section if the Internal Revenue Service finds that the respondent is described in paragraph (b) of this section; or

(iii) The respondent's failure to appear, either personally or through an authorized representative, at a conference scheduled by the Internal Revenue Service under paragraph (e) of this section.

(2) *Duration of suspension.* A suspension under this section will commence on the date that the written notice of expedited suspension is served on the practitioner, either personally or through an authorized representative. The suspension will remain effective until the earlier of:

(i) The date the Internal Revenue Service lifts the suspension after determining that the practitioner is no longer described in paragraph (b) of this section or for any other reason; or

(ii) The date the suspension is lifted or otherwise modified by an Administrative Law Judge or the Secretary of the Treasury, or delegate deciding appeals, in a proceeding referred to in paragraph (g) of this section and instituted under §10.60.

(g) *Practitioner demand for §10.60 proceeding.* If the Internal Revenue Service suspends a practitioner under the expedited suspension procedures described in this section, the practitioner may demand that the Internal Revenue Service institute a proceeding under §10.60 and issue the complaint described in §10.62. The demand must be in writing, specifically reference the suspension action under §10.82, and be made within 2 years from the date on which the practitioner's suspension commenced. The Internal Revenue Service must issue a complaint demanded under this paragraph (g) within 60 calendar days of receiving the demand. If the Internal Revenue Service does not issue such complaint within 60 days of receiving the demand, the suspension is lifted automatically. The preceding sentence does not, however, preclude the Commissioner, or delegate, from instituting a regular proceeding under §10.60 of this part.

(h) *Effective/applicability date.* This section is generally applicable beginning June 12, 2014, except that paragraphs (b)(1) through (4) of this section are applicable beginning August 2, 2011.

Subpart E — General Provisions

§ 10.90 Records.

(a) *Roster.* The Internal Revenue Service will maintain and make available for public inspection in the time and manner prescribed by the Secretary, or delegate, the following rosters —

(1) Individuals (and employers, firms, or other entities, if applicable) censured, suspended, or disbarred from practice before the Internal Revenue Service or upon whom a monetary penalty was imposed.

(2) Enrolled agents, including individuals —

(i) Granted active enrollment to practice;

(ii) Whose enrollment has been placed in inactive status for failure to meet the requirements for renewal of enrollment;

(iii) Whose enrollment has been placed in inactive retirement status; and

(iv) Whose offer of consent to resign from enrollment has been accepted by the Internal Revenue Service under §10.61.

(3) Enrolled retirement plan agents, including individuals —

(i) Granted active enrollment to practice;

(ii) Whose enrollment has been placed in inactive status for failure to meet the requirements for renewal of enrollment;

(iii) Whose enrollment has been placed in inactive retirement status; and

(iv) Whose offer of consent to resign from enrollment has been accepted under §10.61.

(4) Registered tax return preparers, including individuals —

(i) Authorized to prepare all or substantially all of a tax return or claim for refund;

(ii) Who have been placed in inactive status for failure to meet the requirements for renewal;

(iii) Who have been placed in inactive retirement status; and

(iv) Whose offer of consent to resign from their status as a registered tax return preparer has been accepted by the Internal Revenue Service under §10.61.

6

(5) Disqualified appraisers.

(6) Qualified continuing education providers, including providers —

(i) Who have obtained a qualifying continuing education provider number; and

(ii) Whose qualifying continuing education number has been revoked for failure to comply with the requirements of this part.

(b) *Other records.* Other records of the Director of the Office of Professional Responsibility may be disclosed upon specific request, in accordance with the applicable law.

(c) *Effective/applicability date.* This section is applicable beginning August 2, 2011.

§ 10.91 Saving provision.

Any proceeding instituted under this part prior to June 12, 2014, for which a final decision has not been reached or for which judicial review is still available is not affected by these revisions. Any proceeding under this part based on conduct engaged in prior to June 12, 2014, which is instituted after that date, will apply subpart D and E of this part as revised, but the conduct engaged in prior to the effective date of these revisions will be judged by the regulations in effect at the time the conduct occurred.

§ 10.92 Special orders.

The Secretary of the Treasury reserves the power to issue such special orders as he or she deems proper in any cases within the purview of this part.

§ 10.93 Effective date.

Except as otherwise provided in each section and Subject to §10.91, Part 10 is applicable on July 26, 2002.

John Dalrymple,
Deputy Commissioner for Services and Enforcement

Approved: June 3, 2014
Christopher J. Meade,
General Counsel

[FR Doc. 2014-13739 Filed 06/09/2014 at 4:15 pm; Publication Date: 06/12/2014]

Chapter 7: Depreciation

7

Note. Corrections for all of the chapters are available at **TaxSchool.illinois.edu.** For clarification about terms used throughout this chapter, see the **Acronyms and Abbreviations** section following the index.

For your convenience, in-text website links are also provided as short URLs. Anywhere you see **uofi.tax/xxx**, the link points to the address immediately following in brackets.

About the Author

John W. Richmann, EA, is a Tax Materials Specialist at the University of Illinois Tax School. Prior to joining Tax School in 2021, he owned a tax practice in St. Charles, Illinois, and held positions in private industry and consulting firms. John earned a Masters Degree in Business Administration from the University of Texas and an electrical engineering degree from the Massachusetts Institute of Technology.

Other chapter contributors and reviewers are listed at the front of this book.

Depreciation of income-producing property affects not only current-year returns but also future returns. When an asset is first placed in service, a tax practitioner faces a complex set of determinations and decisions. While the proper treatment is sometimes obvious, oftentimes, situations require practitioners to research available treatments to accurately report the expense.

This chapter covers the following eight steps that a taxpayer and their practitioner use to evaluate available depreciation options.

1. Determine whether the asset's cost can be recovered through depreciation
2. Calculate the asset's **basis,** including the impact of tax credits on an asset's depreciable basis
3. Determine if the asset is subject to special rules for **listed** property
4. Evaluate electing the IRC §179 deduction to expense all or part of the cost on the current return
5. Determine if **bonus depreciation applies and evaluate the option to elect out** for the class of the asset
6. Decide which depreciation system and **method** to use for any basis remaining after any §179 and bonus depreciation elections
7. Determine the proper **recovery period for any remaining basis**
8. Apply the correct **convention** for depreciating the assets placed in service in the current year

These steps represent the typical sequence of decisions a tax practitioner must make concerning depreciation of assets newly placed in service during the year. In addition, this chapter discusses two other significant depreciation issues.

- Changes in business use of assets
- Correcting prior-year depreciation errors

STEP 1 — DETERMINE WHETHER THE ASSET'S COST CAN BE RECOVERED THROUGH DEPRECIATION

The first decision faced by a taxpayer and their practitioner is whether the asset's cost can be recovered through depreciation. Property can only be depreciated if it is either:[1]

- Used in the taxpayer's trade or business, or
- Held for the production of income.

In addition, certain assets are not depreciable. For example, land is not a depreciable asset.[2] With very narrow exceptions,[3] its cost can only be recovered when the taxpayer disposes of it. Similarly, inventory cannot be depreciated,[4] even though an expenditure for inventory may seem like an investment.

> **Note.** For more information on property that may not be depreciated, see IRS Pub. 946, *How to Depreciate Property.*

---

1. IRC §167(a).
2. Treas. Reg. §1.167(a)-2.
3. For example, IRC §612 allows depletion of natural resources acquired with land.
4. Treas. Reg. §1.167(a)-2.

Only the **business portion** of property that is used for multiple purposes can be used to calculate the depreciation deduction for the property.[5]

Example 1. QRP Landscaping, LLC, is a single-member limited liability company (LLC) owned by Ed. In 2023, QRP purchases a $4,000 lawnmower. Ed uses it 85% of the time to mow the yards of commercial and residential customers. The other 15% of the time, Ed uses it to mow property owned by his church. Only $3,400 ($4,000 × 85%) of the cost qualifies to be depreciated.

PLACED-IN-SERVICE DATE

A taxpayer may not claim depreciation on an asset until the property is placed in service for use either in a trade or business or in the production of income.[6] The placed-in-service date is the date the property is **ready and available** for a specific use. This is **not necessarily** the date it is first used. If the property was held for personal use and is then converted to business use, the property becomes depreciable on the conversion date.[7]

The placed-in-service requirement is met if the property is ready to be placed in service, even though it is not actually used.[8]

Example 2. Heather is a professional speaker, working as a sole proprietor. In preparing for a January 2023 speaking engagement, she pays $2,000 for a portable sound system. She purchases and receives the system in December 2022. She may begin depreciating the system on her 2022 return even though she has not yet used the system. It is in her possession and could have been used if she had a December engagement.

STEP 2 — CALCULATE THE ASSET'S BASIS

Generally, for business property purchased during the year, the basis is the cost of the property.[9] Certain adjustments must be made to the unadjusted basis before calculating allowable depreciation. The result of these adjustments is the **adjusted basis** of the property.

Although not an exhaustive list, the following items increase the basis of the property.[10]

- Installation costs
- Legal fees paid to defend or perfect a title
- Impact fees
- Capital improvements
- Assessments for local improvements
- Restoring damaged property as a result of casualty losses
- Zoning costs
- Sales tax paid

---

5. IRC §167(a).
6. IRC §168(i)(6)(B).
7. IRS Pub. 946, *How to Depreciate Property*.
8. Treas. Reg. §1.167(a)-11(e)(1).
9. IRC §263A.
10. IRS Pub. 551, *Basis of Assets*.

BASIS REDUCED FOR CERTAIN CREDITS

When a tax credit is based on a taxpayer's investment in depreciable property, the asset's basis must be reduced by the credit before calculating any related depreciation deduction.[11] This is true even if the taxpayer cannot benefit from the full amount of the credit in the current year.

COST SEGREGATION AND RENTAL PROPERTY CONSISTENCY

Cost segregation may result in shorter depreciation recovery periods for some assets, and in most cases, better aligns the period over which assets are depreciated with their economic usefulness. For example, if a cost segregation study is not performed on a residential rental property, the entire dwelling unit with all its components is generally depreciated over 27.5 years.[12]

Although that period is accurate for the carpentry work in constructing the house, a landlord who replaces the refrigerator after 10 years and the garbage disposer after three years will not receive 27.5 years of benefit from those replacements. The capitalization and repair regulations that went into effect in 2014 can correct that disparity to some extent.

Note. For more information about the capitalization and repair regulations, see the 2023 *University of Illinois Federal Tax Workbook*, Chapter 2: Capitalization & Repair Review.

Note. If a taxpayer owns multiple properties, similar assets should be consistently placed in the same asset classes, regardless of the buildings in which they are located. For example, a refrigerator should not be classified as 5-year property when located in one building but 7-year property when located in another. There may be extenuating circumstances that create exceptions, but the reasons for those exceptions should be clearly documented.

BASIS OF REAL PROPERTY ACQUIRED THROUGH LIKE-KIND EXCHANGES

Currently, only real estate qualifies for deferred recognition of gains or losses from a like-kind exchange.[13] However, these basis rules also apply to property acquired because of casualties and other special circumstances.[14]

When qualified like-kind property is exchanged, and all other requirements are met, no gain or loss is recognized in that year.[15] The taxpayer's adjusted basis in the new property is dependent on their adjusted basis in the old property.[16]

General Rule[17]

Generally, the adjusted basis of the exchanged property is depreciated over its remaining life. Any boot or other consideration[18] given to obtain the acquired property is separately depreciated as the new asset. **Boot** is also called excess basis;[19] it is the amount of any cash or non-like-kind property given in the exchange. However, a taxpayer can elect to add the remaining basis of the exchanged property to any basis of newly acquired property and depreciate the total over the recovery period of the new asset.[20]

11. IRC §50(c)(1).
12. IRC §168(c).
13. *Tax Cuts and Jobs Act,* PL 115-97.
14. IRC §1033.
15. IRC §1031(a).
16. IRC §1031(d).
17. IRS Pub. 946, *How to Depreciate Property*; TD 9314, 2007-14 IRB 845; Treas. Reg. §1.168(i)-6(c)(3).
18. Treas. Reg. §1.168(i)-6(b)(8).
19. Ibid.
20. IRS Pub. 946, *How to Depreciate Property*; Treas. Reg. §1.168(i)-6(i).

Example 3. Willdor Partnership exchanges an office building for a warehouse in a like-kind exchange in 2023. The partnership pays $100,000 in closing costs as part of the exchange. Both properties are commercial buildings depreciated over 39 years using the straight-line method.

The office building was originally placed in service in 2016. Its adjusted basis at the time of the exchange is $3.84 million (after depreciation of $840,000). There are 32 years remaining on its depreciable life.

Under the general rule, the warehouse basis has two components placed in service.

	Cost	Recovery Life
Warehouse component 1: unrecovered basis of office building	$3,840,000	32 years
Warehouse component 2: exchange costs	100,000	39 years
Total depreciable basis	$3,940,000	

If the new property has a longer recovery period or slower method[21] than the old property, the remaining adjusted basis must be recovered over the period applicable to the new property.

Example 4. Use the same facts as **Example 3,** except the building that Willdor exchanged was previously used as a farm building (20-year property) instead of an office building. The partnership must depreciate the newly acquired warehouse over a 39-year period that began when the exchanged property, the farm building, was placed in service.

7

Practitioner Planning Tip

Tax practitioners must determine how to link the different components of the same asset after a trade in their depreciation software. It may be helpful to rename, relabel, renumber, or reorder the old asset on the depreciation schedule.

Electing Out

Taxpayers can elect not to apply the like-kind exchange rules, but this election must be made for each like-kind exchange.[22]

Example 5. Use the same facts as **Example 4,** except instead of leaving building costs in two components, Willdor combines the costs into one $3.94 million basis depreciated over 39 years beginning on the exchange date. This election reduces the annual depreciation deduction for the partnership from this building.

A taxpayer makes the election not to apply the like-kind exchange rules by attaching a statement to a timely filed return (including extensions) for the year of replacement. The statement should state, "Election made under section 1.168(i)-6(i)."[23] The election statement should indicate that the election is being made for each asset. For a partnership, S corporation, or consolidated group, the election is made at the entity level. This election is irrevocable without IRS consent, which the IRS grants only in extraordinary circumstances.[24]

21. IRS Pub. 946, *How to Depreciate Property*; Treas. Reg. §1.168(i)-6(c)(4).

22. Treas. Reg. §1.168(i)-6(j)(1).

23. Instructions for Form 4562.

24. Treas. Reg. §1.168(i)-6(j)(4).

Bonus Depreciation[25]

If a taxpayer acquires property qualified for bonus depreciationDepreciation:bonusDepreciation:bonusDepreciation:bonusDepreciation:bonusDepreciation:bonusDepreciation:bonusDepreciation:bonus in a like-kind exchange, and the qualified property is **new** property, the old basis and any new basis are eligible for bonus depreciation.

If the qualified property is **used** property, only the excess basis of the acquired property is eligible for bonus depreciation. After calculating the bonus depreciation, the taxpayer can take regular depreciation on the remaining carryover basis.

IRC §179 Election[26]

When applying the §179 election to a like-kind exchange, only the boot paid for the replacement property is eligible.

Debt Included in Like-Kind Exchange[27]

Taxpayers entering like-kind exchanges with eligible real estate must evaluate debt assumed as part of the exchange. The taxpayer is considered to have received boot to the extent of any debt reduction. The only exception is the situation where the additional cash paid on acquiring the replacement property equals or exceeds the debt reduction.

Note. Taxable boot can play a role in a well-planned exchange depending on the taxpayer's goals. For example, if the taxpayer wants to receive some cash or debt reduction and is willing to pay some tax, having taxable boot may be appropriate. Otherwise, boot should be avoided so the exchange is entirely tax-deferred.

STEP 3 — DETERMINE IF ASSET IS SUBJECT TO SPECIAL RULES FOR LISTED PROPERTY

Special depreciation rules apply to listed property. Listed property falls into one of the following classifications.[28]

1. Passenger automobiles weighing 6,000 pounds or less **unloaded** gross vehicle weight (GVW)
2. Any other property used for transportation, **unless** it is one of the following excepted vehicles[29]
    a. Clearly marked police and fire vehicles
    b. Unmarked vehicles used by law enforcement officers if the use is officially authorized
    c. Ambulances and hearses, provided they are used as such
    d. Any vehicle with a **loaded** GVW of more than 14,000 pounds that is designed to carry cargo
    e. Bucket trucks (cherry pickers), cement mixers, dump trucks (including garbage trucks), flatbed trucks, and refrigerated trucks
    f. Combines, cranes and derricks, and forklifts
    g. Delivery trucks with seating only for the driver or only for the driver plus a folding jump seat
    h. Qualified moving vans

---

25. IRS Pub. 946, *How to Depreciate Property*; Treas. Reg. §1.168(k)-2(g)(5)(iii).
26. Treas. Reg. §1.168(i)-6(g).
27. Treas. Reg. §1.1031(b)-1.
28. IRC §280F(d).
29. Treas. Reg. §1.274-5(k)(2). See also IRS Pub. 946, *How to Depreciate Property*.

i. Qualified specialized utility repair trucks

j. School buses used in transporting students and employees of schools

k. Other buses with a capacity of at least 20 passengers that are used as passenger buses

l. Tractors and other special-purpose farm vehicles

Note. Vehicles between 6,000 and 14,000 pounds GVW are **not** subject to the special rules for **passenger automobiles.**[30] However, they are "property used for transportation" subject to the rules for **listed property.** In addition, vehicles in this weight range that are classified as **sports utility vehicles (SUVs)**[31] are subject to additional §179 limitations. This limit is $28,900 for 2023.[32]

3. Property generally used for entertainment, recreation, or amusement (including photographic, phonographic, communication, and video-recording equipment)

Listed property must be used predominantly **(more than 50%)**[33] for **qualified business use**[34] to qualify for any of the following.

- §179 deduction[35]
- Bonus depreciation
- Depreciation using the general depreciation system (GDS) (discussed later)
- Declining balance method of calculating depreciation

Qualified business use of listed property is any use of the property in the taxpayer's trade or business. The following uses are **not** included.[36]

- The leasing of property to any 5% owner or related person (to the extent the property is used by a 5% owner or person related to the owner or lessee of the property)
- The use of the property as payment for the services of a 5% owner or related person
- The use of the property as payment for services of any person (other than a 5% owner or related person), unless the value of the use is included in that person's gross income and income tax is withheld on that amount when required

If the taxpayer does **not** use the property predominantly for qualified business use, the following three rules apply.

1. Any depreciation deduction under the modified accelerated cost recovery system (MACRS) must be calculated using the **straight-line method** over the alternative depreciation system (ADS) recovery period. This rule applies each year of the recovery period.

2. Excess depreciation on property previously used predominantly for qualified business use must be recaptured in the first year in which it is no longer used predominantly for qualified business use.[37]

---

30. IRS Pub. 946, *How to Depreciate Property.*

31. IRC §179(b)(5).

32. Rev. Proc. 2022-38, 2022-45 IRB 1.

33. IRC §280F(b)(3).

34. IRC §§280F(d)(6)(B) and (C).

35. IRC §179(d)(10).

36. Treas. Reg. §1.280F-6(d); IRS Pub. 946, *How to Depreciate Property.*

37. IRC §280F(b)(2)(B).

3. A lessee must add an inclusion amount to income in the first year in which the leased property is not used predominantly for qualified business purposes.[38]

PASSENGER AUTOMOBILES

The Code limits the depreciation deduction that a taxpayer can claim for a passenger automobile in any one year. This limit includes the §179 expense deduction. The limit is increased by $8,000 if the vehicle qualifies for bonus depreciation and the taxpayer does not elect out of bonus depreciation for this class of assets.[39] For vehicles placed in service during 2023, the inflation-adjusted limits by vehicle type are shown in the following chart.[40]

Vehicle Type	§179 Expense Deduction	Bonus Depreciation	Total First-Year Maximum Cost Recovery Excluding Regular Depreciation
GVW 6,000 pounds or less	$12,200	$8,000	$20,200
GVW over 6,000 pounds and 14,000 pounds or less	28,900[41]	No limit	No limit
GVW over 14,000 pounds	No limit	No limit	No limit

LISTED PROPERTY WITH BUSINESS-USE OF 50% OR LESS

When the business use of listed property declines to 50% or less after the year it was placed in service, some amount of its depreciation must be recaptured. However, the depreciation to be recovered is not the full amount but rather the amount in **excess of straight-line depreciation.** Excess depreciation is calculated as follows.[42]

1. The depreciation allowable for the property (including any §179 deduction and special depreciation allowance claimed) for years before the first year the taxpayer does not use the property predominantly for qualified business use, **less**
2. The depreciation that would have been allowable for those years if the taxpayer had not used the property predominantly for qualified business use in the year it was placed in service.

To determine the amount in item 2, depreciation must be refigured using the straight-line method and the ADS recovery period.

Example 6. Elizabeth purchased and placed in service a pickup truck for $18,000 in June 2018. She used it exclusively for her plumbing business between 2018 and 2021. Elizabeth claimed §179 deduction of $10,000 in 2018. She depreciated the truck using the double-declining method over five years. The pickup truck had a GVW in excess of 6,000 and was not subject to passenger automobile limits.

---

38. See IRS Pub. 463, *Travel, Entertainment, Gift, and Car Expenses*, and IRS Pub. 946, *How to Depreciate Property*, for calculating the inclusion amount.

39. IRC §168(k)(2)(F)(i).

40. Rev. Proc. 2023-14, 2023-6 IRB 466.

41. IRC §179(b)(5)(A); Rev. Proc. 2022-38, 2022-39 IRB 239.

42. IRS Pub. 946, *How to Depreciate Property*.

During 2022, Elizabeth used the truck 50% in her plumbing business and 50% for personal use. She includes $4,018 of excess depreciation in her 2022 gross income as shown in the following calculation. Elizabeth uses table A-8 in IRS Pub. 946, as shown next, to determine the applicable depreciation rates.

Table A-8. **Straight Line Method Half-Year Convention**

Year	Recovery periods in years												
	2.5	3	3.5	4	5	6	6.5	7	7.5	8	8.5	9	9.5
1	20.0%	16.67%	14.29%	12.5%	10.0%	8.33%	7.69%	7.14%	6.67%	6.25%	5.88%	5.56%	5.26%
2	40.0	33.33	28.57	25.0	20.0	16.67	15.39	14.29	13.33	12.50	11.77	11.11	10.53
3	40.0	33.33	28.57	25.0	20.0	16.67	15.38	14.29	13.33	12.50	11.76	11.11	10.53
4		16.67	28.57	25.0	20.0	16.67	15.39	14.28	13.33	12.50	11.77	11.11	10.53
5				12.5	20.0	16.66	15.38	14.29	13.34	12.50	11.76	11.11	10.52
6					10.0	16.67	15.39	14.28	13.33	12.50	11.77	11.11	10.53
7						8.33	15.38	14.29	13.34	12.50	11.76	11.11	10.52
8								7.14	13.33	12.50	11.77	11.11	10.53
9										6.25	11.76	11.11	10.52
10												5.56	10.53

§179 deduction	$10,000	
Depreciation claimed for 2018 through 2021	6,618	
Total depreciation claimed	$16,618	$16,618
Less: depreciation allowable		
2018 (10% × $18,000)	$ 1,800	
2019 (20% × $18,000)	3,600	
2020 (20% × $18,000)	3,600	
2021 (20% × $18,000)	3,600	
Total allowable depreciation	$12,600	(12,600)
Excess depreciation		$ 4,018

If Elizabeth's use of the truck does not change to 50% for business and 50% for personal purposes until 2024, there is no excess depreciation. Because the pickup truck is a 5-year asset, the total depreciation allowable through 2024 will be $18,000, which equals the total of the §179 deduction and depreciation Elizabeth will have claimed.

SPECIAL SUBSTANTIATION REQUIREMENTS

Business use of listed assets must be properly documented.[43] Although a taxpayer may calculate their vehicle expenses, for example, with the standard mileage rate, they are still required to document the business use of the listed property and personal use of the property, along with its date and time.[44] This information must be recorded at the time of the expenditure or near that time.[45]

The taxpayer must maintain this practice even when the asset's recovery period has ended.[46] For example, if a taxpayer acquires a vehicle in 2023, they generally depreciate it over a 5-year period ending in 2028. However, the taxpayer must continue to maintain records to support their business use of the vehicle even after the vehicle is fully depreciated.

43. IRC §274(d)(3).

44. Treas. Regs. §§1.274-5(c) and (j).

45. Ibid.

46. Temp. Treas. Reg. §1.280F-3T(d)(3).

STEP 4 — EVALUATE ELECTING §179 DEDUCTION ON ALL OR PART OF THE COST

Property eligible for the §179 expense deduction must satisfy the following three criteria.[47]

1. Tangible, depreciable property or computer software
2. Either IRC §1245 property or qualified real property
3. Used in a trade or business

IRC §1245 property is tangible and intangible personal property that can be depreciated or amortized. In simpler terms, it refers to assets that are subject to depreciation and are not classified as real property, although some buildings qualify in narrow cases. Examples of §1245 property include machinery, equipment, and furniture, but also single-purpose agricultural or horticultural buildings and other items. The tax treatment of §1245 property requires that the depreciation deductions taken over the years are recaptured as ordinary income when the property is sold.

Qualified real property must satisfy both of the following criteria.[48]

- Improvement made to the **interior** of an **existing nonresidential** building that does not enlarge it, provide for an elevator or escalator, or alter the building's internal framework[49]
- Adding a roof, heating, ventilation, air conditioning, fire protection and alarm systems, or security systems to an existing **nonresidential** building[50]

In general, businesses cannot claim a §179 expense deduction for property that they lease to other taxpayers unless the lessor is a corporation, or the lease term is shorter than half the class life of the property (class life is discussed later).[51]

Not all taxpayers can benefit from the §179 expense deduction. In fact, **estates and trusts are explicitly excluded** as eligible taxpayers for the deduction. Even if an estate or a trust operates a business having assets, it is not eligible to benefit from the §179 deduction.[52]

IRC §179 PROPERTY MUST BE PURCHASED

The §179 expense deduction is only available for property that has been **purchased** by a taxpayer. Property acquired by inheritance or gift may be depreciated, but it is ineligible for §179 expense deduction.[53]

Property acquired by purchase from a **related person** is generally not eligible for the §179 deduction. The definition of a related person for these purposes is based on IRC §§267 and 707(b). Family for these purposes only includes spouses, ancestors, and lineal descendants.[54] Thus, property purchased from one's father is not eligible for the §179 expense deduction. Under the §179 rules, siblings are **not** considered related persons.[55]

---

47. IRC §179(d)(1).
48. IRC §179(e).
49. IRC §168(e)(6). This paragraph defines qualified improvement property.
50. IRC §179(e)(2).
51. IRC §179(d)(5).
52. IRC §179(d)(4).
53. IRC §179(d)(2)(C).
54. IRC §179(d)(2)(A).
55. Ibid.

Example 7. Mary owns and manages a restaurant located in a building constructed in 1950. She wishes to replace her antiquated air conditioning with a new energy-efficient one from a major manufacturer. Her father owns a heating, ventilation, and air conditioning (HVAC) contracting firm and has offered to sell her a unit at his cost plus installation. She can acquire the same unit at the manufacturer's suggested price from another HVAC contractor but must pay an additional 25%.

If Mary buys the unit from her father's business, the unit is not eligible for the §179 expense deduction because he is a member of her family. However, the purchase of the air conditioning unit from an unrelated HVAC supplier would be eligible for §179 treatment. Mary has a choice between a lower-priced improvement with a longer cost recovery or a higher-priced air conditioning unit that she could expense when placed in service.

In addition to immediate family members, related parties are the following.[56]

- Ancestors and lineal descendants
- Corporations and partnerships in which the individual has more than half the value of the equity
- Two corporations that are both members of a controlled group
- An organization exempt under IRC §501 and a person controlling the organization
- The fiduciary of a trust of which one was a beneficiary[57]

ACTIVE TRADE OR BUSINESS

7

To qualify for the §179 expense deduction, the property must have been acquired for use in an active trade or business.[58] In addition, the taxpayer must have been actively involved in the business to claim the deduction. The regulations state directly that the purpose of the active trade or business requirement is to prevent **passive investors** from using the §179 expense deduction.[59]

To satisfy the active conduct requirement, the treasury regulations require that the taxpayer participates **meaningfully** in the management or operation of the business.[60] This may include creating or reviewing budgets and conducting financial reviews, or it may include regular involvement in the income-generating activities of the business.

Note. Neither the Code nor the underlying treasury regulations distinguish **meaningful** participation from **material** participation. The standard for meaningful participation is not defined in the Code, although it may be lower than the standard for material participation under the passive activity regulations.[61] There is no bright-line test to determine if a taxpayer's involvement is regular and continuous. Instead, the determination is based on the facts and circumstances of the taxpayer.

56. IRC §179(d)(2)(A), referencing IRC §§267 and 707(b).
57. IRC §179(d)(4).
58. IRC §179(d)(1)(C).
59. Treas. Reg. §1.179-2(c)(6).
60. Treas. Reg. §1.179-2(c)(6)(ii).
61. Temp. Treas. Reg. §1.469-5T.

Example 8. Abby owns a salon as a sole proprietorship and employs Betty to operate it.[62] Abby periodically meets with Betty to review the business's performance and discuss trends in the salon business. Abby reviews and approves the annual budget that Betty creates. Betty hires all beauticians, purchases any supplies needed, and pays bills on a weekly basis, which Abby signs. Abby does not work in the operations of the business, only in its management. Because of her involvement with the finances of the salon, Abby meets the threshold of meaningful participation in its management.

Note. The IRS created a safe harbor to determine if a rental activity qualifies as a trade or business for purposes of the qualified business income deduction (QBID).[63] Although the safe harbor applies only to QBID, a taxpayer who meets this safe harbor's requirements is likely also in a trade or business for §179 purposes.

Note. For a thorough discussion on real estate professionals, see the 2019 *University of Illinois Federal Tax Workbook,* Volume B, Chapter 4: Selected Real Estate Topics. This can be found at **uofi.tax/arc** [taxschool.illinois.edu/taxbookarchive].

Partial Business Use

When a property is used for both business and nonbusiness purposes, the taxpayer can elect the §179 deduction only if they use the property **more than 50%** for business in the year they place it in service.[64] The business cost of the property is determined by multiplying the cost of the property by the percentage of business use. The resulting business cost is used to calculate the §179 deduction.

Example 9. Jason purchases §179 property primarily used in his sole proprietor business. He pays $10,000 for the equipment in January 2023. Jason used the property in his business 80% of the time, and the rest of the time, he uses it in conjunction with an exempt §501(c)(3) organization for which he sits on the board of directors. Of the $10,000 cost, Jason may elect to deduct up to $8,000 ($10,000 × 80%) of the cost for 2023.

INCOME LIMITATION[65]

The §179 expense deduction may not exceed a taxpayer's income from their trades or businesses (i.e., may not create a loss). Taxable business income is calculated differently depending on the form of the business.[66]

For individuals, the business income limit includes the taxable income from the active conduct of all trades and businesses during the year. **Net income from a trade or business also includes all the following.**

- Wages, salaries, tips, or other pay earned as an employee
- IRC §1231 gains or losses
- Interest from working capital of trades or businesses

62. Based on example in Treas. Reg. §1.179-2(c)(6)(iii).

63. Rev. Proc. 2019-38, 2019-42 IRB 942.

64. Treas. Reg. §1.179-1(d)(1).

65. IRC §179(b); Treas. Reg. §1.179-2.

66. IRC §179(b)(3).

At the individual level, business income **does not include** any of the following.

- §179 deductions
- Self-employment (SE) tax deduction
- Net operating loss (NOL) deduction
- Unreimbursed employee business expenses

Example 10. In 2023, Clara earns $7,000 as an employee, and she operates a sole proprietorship. Her business has net profit of $20,000 before depreciation deductions. Her only depreciable asset is a piece of equipment purchased in 2023 for $25,000. Clara's trade or business income for 2023 is $27,000 ($20,000 net profit + $7,000 wages). Thus, she may deduct the entire $25,000 using the §179 election on her 2023 return.

Carryover of Disallowed Deduction[67]

Taxpayers can carry over for an unlimited number of years the cost of any §179 property they elected to expense but were unable to deduct because of the business income limit.

If the taxpayer places more than one property in service in a year, they can select the properties for which all or a part of the costs are carried forward. The selections must be shown in their books and records. For this purpose, §179 costs allocated from a partnership or an S corporation are treated as one item of §179 property. If the taxpayer does not make a selection, the total carryover is allocated equally among the properties they elected to expense for the year.

7

If costs from more than one year are carried forward to a subsequent year in which only part of the total carryover can be deducted, the taxpayer must deduct the costs being carried forward from the earliest year first.

If there is a sale or other disposition of the property (including a transfer at death) before the taxpayer can use the full amount of any outstanding carryover of the disallowed §179 deduction, neither the taxpayer nor the new owner can deduct any of the unused amount. Instead, the taxpayer must add the unused carryforward back to the property's basis.[68]

Practitioner Planning Tip

Electing §179 in excess of current year business income results in a carryover that is immediately available to offset business income in the following year. This will likely result in a faster cost recovery of the deduction than the default class life duration. Due to the complexity and various options available, this election needs to be considered on a case-by-case basis.

67. IRC §179(b)(3)(B); Treas. Reg. §1.179-3.

68. Treas. Reg. §1.179-3(f)(1).

RECAPTURE RULES UNDER §179

The §179 expense deduction must be recaptured in the tax year during which the percentage of business use drops to 50% or less during the property's recovery period.[69] These rules do not apply if the property is sold, exchanged, or otherwise disposed of.[70] Separate rules apply to listed property as described previously. A taxpayer recognizes the recapture amount as **ordinary** income in the year the business use first declines to 50% or less.[71]

> **Caution.** The recapture of §179 and bonus depreciation deductions are different types of recapture than the depreciation recapture used to determine the portion of a gain taxed as ordinary income versus qualified capital gain. Thus, if business use of property for which §179 and bonus deductions were **not** claimed drops to 50% or less, no depreciation recapture occurs until the taxpayer disposes of the property.

STEP 5 — DETERMINE IF BONUS DEPRECIATION APPLIES[72]

If a taxpayer does not make a §179 election to write off the entire basis of a specific asset, they next must decide whether to claim bonus depreciation. For eligible assets, the default position is to claim bonus depreciation;[73] however, taxpayers can elect out of bonus depreciation by specific classes of assets.[74] This election out applies to all assets in that class of property that were placed in service during the tax year. This is in contrast to the §179 election, which is made on an asset-by-asset basis.

When originally added to the Code by the Job Creation and Worker Assistance Act of 2002,[75] IRC §168(k) allowed taxpayers to claim an additional depreciation deduction equal to 30% of the adjusted basis of qualified property placed in service after September 10, 2001, and before September 11, 2004. This additional deduction is often referred to as bonus depreciation or special depreciation. Over the years, amendments to §168(k) have changed the bonus depreciation rate numerous times, extended the placed-in-service date, and made other changes.[76] The following table shows how the bonus depreciation rate has changed since the provision was revived by the Economic Stimulus Act of 2008.[77]

Placed in Service Date	Bonus Depreciation Rate
After December 31, 2007 and before September 9, 2010	50%
After September 8, 2010 and before January 1, 2011	100% or 50% [a]
After December 31, 2010 and before January 1, 2012	100%
After December 31, 2011 and before September 28, 2017	50%
After September 27, 2017 and before January 1, 2023	100%
After December 31, 2022 and before January 1, 2024	**80%** [b]
After December 31, 2023 and before January 1, 2025	60%
After December 31, 2024 and before January 1, 2026	40%
After December 31, 2025 and before January 1, 2027	20%
After December 31, 2026	0%

[a] Using the election under Rev. Proc. 2011-26.

[b] The rate shown applies to property **other than** property with longer production periods and certain aircraft.

69. Treas. Reg. §1.179-1(e).
70. Treas. Reg. §1.179-1(e)(2).
71. Treas. Reg. §1.179-1(e).
72. IRC §168(k).
73. IRC §168(k)(1).
74. IRC §168(k)(7).
75. *Job Creation and Worker Assistance Act of 2002,* PL 107-147.
76. TD 9874, 2019-41 IRB 809.
77. *Economic Stimulus Act of 2008,* PL 110-185.

The amount of bonus depreciation is calculated by multiplying the percentage shown in the previous table times the adjusted basis of the property.[78] The proper percentage is determined by the date the asset was placed in service.

Example 11. JoJo purchases a copier for $5,000 on February 1, 2023, for use in her tax preparation business. When preparing her 2023 return, she decides not to take the §179 deduction for the purchase. Instead, she claims bonus depreciation of $4,000 ($5,000 × 80%) and depreciates the remaining $1,000 cost using MACRS.

For calendar year **2023** taxpayers, the bonus depreciation deduction has **dropped to 80%** of the asset's basis for **most** assets. However, for specified types of properties, the percentages shown previously are increased by 20% the year they are placed in service.[79] Thus for specified assets placed in service in calendar year 2023, the applicable percentage is 100%.

After December 31, 2026, most assets will not qualify for bonus depreciation. However, specified assets qualify for 20% bonus depreciation if placed in service between then and January 1, 2028. The specified assets are certain aircraft and property that meet the long-production-period qualifications. To be treated as having a longer production period, the property must:[80]

1. Have a recovery period of at least 10 years (or be used to transport people or property),
2. Be subject to the capitalization and inclusion in inventory rules,[81]
3. Have an estimated production period exceeding one year,[82]
4. Have a cost exceeding $1 million,[83] **and**
5. Have a long useful life.[84]

The following types of property may qualify for bonus depreciation.[85]

- Tangible property with a MACRS recovery period of 20 years or less
- Computer software defined in and depreciated under IRC §167(f)(1)(B)
- Water utility property
- Qualified film, television, and live theatrical productions, as defined in IRC §§181(d) and (e)
- Specified plants for which the taxpayer made the election to apply §168(k)(5) for the tax year in which the plant is planted or grafted[86]

The property can be either **new property** or certain types of **used property.**

---

78. IRC §§168(k)(1)(A) and (k)(5).
79. IRC §168(k)(6)(B).
80. IRC §168(k)(2)(B)(i).
81. Under IRC §263A.
82. IRC §168(k)(2)(B)(i)(VI), referencing IRC §263A(f)(1)(B)(iii).
83. Ibid.
84. Ibid.
85. IRC §168(k)(2).
86. Under IRC §168(k)(5)(C), this election can only be revoked with IRS consent.

Used property qualifies for bonus depreciation if, in addition to the other requirements,[87] it was not used by the taxpayer **or a predecessor** at any time before acquiring it. Use is defined as having a **depreciable interest** in the property at any time during the five calendar years immediately prior to the taxpayer's current placed-in-service year.[88]

A predecessor for this purpose includes the following.[89]

- A transferor of an asset to a transferee in a carryover transaction among entities subject to corporate acquisition rules[90]
- A transferor of a gift (that is, an asset for which the transferee's basis in the asset is determined, in whole or in part, by reference to the basis of the asset in the hands of the transferor)
- A partnership that is considered as continuing under rules providing for the merger, consolidation, or division of a partnership[91]
- A decedent, in the case of an asset acquired by the estate
- A transferor of an asset to a trust

Example 12. On August 1, 2020, Anna bought a new machine for $35,000 from an unrelated party for use in her trade or business. On July 1, 2022, she sold it to Bill, another unrelated party, for its fair market value (FMV) of $20,000. Anne is not a predecessor because Bill's basis is not determined in reference to hers.

Bill puts the machine into service in his business in 2023. If all the other requirements are met, the $20,000 purchase qualifies for the bonus depreciation deduction.

The property must be used for business purposes **or** be held for the production of income.[92] Thus, unlike §179, bonus depreciation can be claimed for assets used in a rental activity even if the activity does not rise to the level of a trade or business.

> **Note. Listed property** must be used **predominately** for **business** purposes to qualify for bonus depreciation.[93] If the business use of **listed property** declines to 50% or less, some amount of the property's special depreciation must be recaptured.[94] This was discussed previously in the chapter.

A taxpayer's election not to apply the bonus depreciation rules to any class of property can only be revoked with IRS consent.[95]

87. IRC §168(k)(2)(E)(ii); Treas. Reg. §1.168(k)-2(b)(3)(iii).
88. Treas. Reg. §1.168(k)-2(b)(3)(iii).
89. Treas. Reg. §1.168(k)-2(b)(3)(iv).
90. IRC §381(a).
91. IRC §708(b)(2) and Treas. Reg. §1.708-1.
92. IRC §168(k)(1)(A) referencing IRC §167(a).
93. IRS Pub. 946, *How to Depreciate Property;* IRC §280F(b)(1).
94. IRC §280F(b)(2).
95. IRC §168(k)(7).

20 YEARS OR LESS MACRS PROPERTY

Properties that may qualify for bonus depreciation because they have recovery periods of 20 years or less currently include the following.[96]

- Vehicles
- Appliances used in residential rental activities
- Tools, machinery, equipment, and other general business assets
- Land improvements
- Farm buildings
- Qualified improvement property (QIP)
- Many others

Qualified Improvement Property

The definition of **QIP** has undergone many transformations since the concept was first introduced into the Code. Currently, there is only one type of QIP[97] for depreciation purposes. In general, the term means any qualified improvement made by the taxpayer to **nonresidential** real property.

To be qualified, the improvements must be to the **interior** portion of a building that was placed in service before the improvements were made.

7

The following are certain types of improvements that are specifically **excluded** from QIP.[98]

- Exterior building improvements
- Enlargement of the building
- Any elevator or escalator
- Changes to the internal structural framework of the building

QIP is eligible for §179,[99] bonus depreciation, or straight-line depreciation over 15 years.[100]

Example 13. GHI, LLC, is a partnership that owns a small office building, built in 1990, that it rents to commercial tenants, typically with 3-year leases. In negotiating a 5-year lease with a new tenant, GHI agrees to make $80,000 in improvements to the property.

The improvements are specifically for the new tenant and consist of interior work to create individual offices. The improvements do not enlarge the building, alter its structural framework, or modify the building's elevator. Thus, they satisfy the definition of QIP, making them eligible for bonus depreciation or straight-line depreciation over 15 years.

---

96. IRS Pub. 946, *How to Depreciate Property*.
97. IRC §168(e)(6)
98. IRC §168(e)(6)(B).
99. IRC §179(d)(1)(B).
100. IRC §§168(b)(3)(G) and (e)(3)(E)(vii).

EXCLUDED PROPERTY

Property that **does not** qualify for bonus depreciation includes property:[101]

- For which the taxpayer **elects** not to claim any bonus depreciation;
- Placed in service or planted or grafted, and disposed of during the same tax year;
- Converted from business use to personal use in the same tax year it is acquired;
- **Required** to be depreciated under the ADS;
- Primarily used in a trade or business involving furnishing or sale of certain energy sector services;[102]
- Used in a trade or business that has had floor plan financing indebtedness;[103]
- That the taxpayer acquires by gift or inheritance;
- Used by the taxpayer before purchasing it; or
- Acquired from a related person[104] or from another member of a controlled group.

IRC §179 EXPENSE VS. BONUS DEPRECIATION

Both §179 and bonus depreciation enable taxpayers to deduct the cost of newly acquired property the year they put the property into service. For assets placed in service **in 2023, §179 allows up to 100%** of the cost as a current-year deduction, while **bonus depreciation only includes 80%** of the cost of the property. Deductions for certain kinds of **leased** property are restricted under §179 but not bonus depreciation.

The following table highlights additional ways the two provisions compare.

	Bonus Depreciation	**IRC §179**
Maximum amount (2023)	Unlimited, but bonus depreciation limited to 80% of the property's basis	$1,160,000
Maximum qualifying property (2023)	Unlimited	$2,890,000
Provision end date	100% through 2022 (one year longer for certain property types), then reduced by 20% annually	None; amounts adjusted annually for inflation
Qualifying property	• Tangible property with a recovery period of 20 years or less • Water utility property • Computer software (depreciable) • Qualified film, television, and live theatrical productions • Specified plants	• Tangible personal property • Other tangible property • Single-purpose agricultural or horticultural structures • Storage facilities used for petroleum • Computer software • Qualified real property
Allowable for used property	Yes	Yes
Election required	No; can elect **out** for any class of property; otherwise, bonus depreciation is automatic	Yes; can elect specific items of property
Effect on mid-quarter convention, discussed later	Amounts depreciated do not reduce basis for purposes of determining if convention applies	Amounts expensed reduce basis for purposes of determining if convention applies

101. IRS Pub. 946, *How to Depreciate Property*.

102. IRC §168(k)(9)(A), referencing IRC §163(j)(7)(A)(iv). See also IRC §168.

103. IRC §168(k)(9)(B), referencing §163(j)(9)(B).

104. As defined by IRC §§267 or 707(b).

Phaseouts and Limitations Based on Purchases

For assets placed in service during calendar year 2023, the following provisions apply.

- The §179 deduction is limited to $1,160,000,[105] while bonus depreciation is unlimited.
- The §179 deduction is subject to phaseouts when taxpayers place too much eligible property into service during the tax year. The phaseout begins after the total cost of qualified assets exceeds $2,890,000,[106] at which point a dollar-for-dollar reduction goes into effect. Thus §179 is completely phased out after purchases exceed $4,050,000 ($2,890,000 + $1,160,000).

Example 14. Ms. McFlugelheimer purchases and places in service $1 million worth of 5-year property in 2023. The property qualifies for both §179 and bonus depreciation. **Her maximum §179 deduction is $1 million.** Her maximum deduction using only bonus depreciation and MACRS is $840,000, calculated as follows.

Cost basis	$1,000,000	$1,000,000	
	× 80%		
Bonus depreciation	$ 800,000	(800,000)	$800,000
Remaining cost basis		$ 200,000	
		× 20%	
MACRS deduction		$ 40,000	40,000
Total 2023 depreciation deduction without §179			$840,000

Example 15. Use the same facts as **Example 14,** except the cost is $5 million. At this level of investment, the §179 deduction is completely phased out. However, her MACRS depreciation deduction with bonus depreciation is $4,200,000.

Cost basis	$5,000,000	$5,000,000	
	× 80%		
Bonus depreciation	$4,000,000	(4,000,000)	$4,000,000
Remaining cost basis		$1,000,000	
		× 20%	
MACRS deduction		$ 200,000	200,000
Total 2023 depreciation deduction without §179			$4,200,000

Business Income Limitations[107]

The §179 deduction is capped by the taxpayer's business income. If the taxpayer qualifies for and elects to deduct more under §179 than the business income limit allows, the excess is carried forward to the next year. **There is no business income limitation on property qualifying for bonus depreciation** (i.e., bonus depreciation can create a loss). Thus, the bonus depreciation deduction can be used to offset income from other sources.

105. Rev. Proc. 2022-38, 2022-45 IRB 1.

106. Ibid.

107. IRC §168(k) contains no provision to limit bonus depreciation to the taxpayer's business income; Treas. Reg. §1.179-2(c).

Pass-throughs from Partnerships and S Corporations

The §179 expense deduction passes to the owners as a separately stated item subject to limitations at both the corporate and recipient levels. The amount allowed at the entity levels is shown on a separate line of the Schedule K-1 (Form 1065), *Partner's Share of Income, Deductions, Credits, etc.*, or Schedule K-1 (Form 1120-S), *Shareholder's Share of Income, Deductions, Credits, etc.*, received by the partners and shareholders.[108] The deduction is then subject to the same limitations applied at the recipient level based on their individual tax situations.

Example 16. Buzz is the 100% shareholder in an S corporation with net ordinary business income of $20,000 in **2023** before considering depreciation. He materially participates in the business and has sufficient basis and risk to recognize any losses. In 2023, the S corporation purchases an asset for $45,000, which is eligible for both §179 and bonus depreciation.

If Buzz elects the **§179** deduction for the full $45,000, the §179 deduction that passes through on his Schedule K-1 (Form 1120-S), is limited to $20,000 (§179 deductions cannot create a loss). The remaining §179 deduction of $25,000 ($45,000 – $20,000) carries forward to 2024. Thus, the net income attributable to the S corporation on his 2023 return is **$0** ($20,000 ordinary net income – $20,000 §179 deduction).

Example 17. Use the same facts as **Example 16,** except Buzz chooses not to elect §179 treatment. The asset still qualifies for 80% **bonus** depreciation. Thus, bonus depreciation of $36,000 ($45,000 × 80%) is deducted from income of $20,000 which creates a **loss of $16,000 ($20,000 – $36,000).** This loss passes through to Buzz's personal return, along with the MACRS depreciation deduction arising from the 20% portion of the asset that did not qualify for bonus depreciation in 2023.

Note. If Buzz elects out of bonus depreciation **and** does not elect the §179 deduction, the depreciation deduction for the asset is calculated using MACRS, as explained later. The ordinary income passed through to him would be $20,000 minus the MACRS deduction.

Observations

- Property acquired from a related party is not eligible for §179, but new property acquired from a related party is eligible for bonus depreciation.
- Property having a business use of 50% or less is not eligible for §179, but it is eligible for bonus depreciation for the percentage of business use.
- Property for which a §179 expense deduction has been taken is subject to the recapture requirements if the business use drops to 50% or less. However, bonus depreciation is not subject to recapture unless it is listed property.
- Both §179 and bonus depreciation can be applied to QIP.[109]
- The §179 deduction cannot create an NOL[110] but instead must be carried forward.[111] Bonus depreciation can create an NOL, which may be eligible to be carried back under IRC §172.

---

108. Treas. Reg. §§1.702-1(a)(8) and 1.1366-1(a)(2).

109. IRC §168(e)(3)(E)(vii).

110. IRC §179(b)(3)(A).

111. IRC §179(b)(3)(B).

Impact of Depreciation Elections on Other Tax Provisions

A multitude of other deductions and credits are contingent upon the net income determined after applying these provisions. Both §179 and bonus depreciation are important tools for achieving the best result for taxpayers, but they may affect other tax provisions differently. The following two common tax situations show how using these tools can have additional tax consequences.

Roth Individual Retirement Arrangement Contributions. Simply stated, a Roth individual retirement arrangement (IRA) is an individual retirement plan that taxpayers cannot deduct their contributions, but distributions are tax-free. Generally, a taxpayer can contribute to their Roth IRA if they have taxable compensation and a modified adjusted gross income (MAGI) that is less than the following thresholds for 2023.[112]

- $218,000 for married filing jointly or qualifying surviving spouse
- $138,000 for single, head of household, or married filing separately and the taxpayer did not live with their spouse at any time during the year
- $10,000 for married filing separately and the taxpayer lived with their spouse at any time during the year

> **Note.** Roth IRAs are covered in detail in the 2023 *University of Illinois Federal Tax Workbook,* Chapter 8: Retirement Plan Issues for Individuals.

7

Because both the §179 deduction and bonus depreciation reduce the income available to make contributions to retirement plans, taxpayers can use them as tools to increase their direct contributions to Roth accounts. For taxpayers wishing to contribute larger amounts to their retirement savings, both deductions generally work contrary to this objective.

Due to the order in which the two deductions are applied, the way they are applied to either individual assets or to classes, and other limitations, it may be possible to use the related elections to avoid contribution limits affected by total income.

Example 18. Use the same facts as **Example 16,** except that Buzz also has a part-time job with employee wages. In 2023, his total wages from Form W-2, *Wage and Tax Statement,* are $153,000. He has no other income or deductions. Before Buzz finalizes his S corporation return, he wants to know how the depreciation elections affect his ability to contribute directly to a Roth IRA.

If Buzz elects to write off 100% of the cost under §179, the net effect to his personal return is zero. Thus, if he chooses this option, his MAGI[113] of $153,000 is too high to contribute to a Roth IRA for the year.

If Buzz applies bonus depreciation, an ordinary loss of $16,000 passes through to Buzz's personal return. This lowers his MAGI to $137,000 ($153,000 – $16,000), which is below the phase-out amount for Roth IRA contributions.

Earned Income Credit.[114] The earned income credit (EIC) is a refundable credit for individual taxpayers meeting certain qualifications. The amount of the credit phases in and out based on the taxpayer's earned income and other income-related factors. Elections regarding depreciation deductions may have a significant effect on this credit.

---

112. IRS Pub. 590-A, *Contributions to Individual Retirement Arrangements (IRAs); Amount of Roth IRA Contributions That You Can Make For 2023.* Oct. 26, 2022. IRS. [www.irs.gov/retirement-plans/amount-of-roth-ira-contributions-that-you-can-make-for-2023] Accessed on Jul. 16, 2023.

113. IRC §408A(c)(3)(B)(i).

114. IRC §32.

The Code establishes limits for taxpayers' earned income amounts,[115] although these amounts are indexed for inflation.[116] The IRS publishes updated limits late in the previous year.[117] Taxpayers must have earned income at least as much as the **earned income amount** to receive any EIC. However, if their earned income exceeds a **threshold phaseout amount,** the credit decreases before phasing out entirely when the taxpayer's income reaches the **completed phaseout amount.** The table showing the various EIC amounts based on the taxpayer's income, filing status, and number of dependent children with valid social security numbers is published in the instructions for Form 1040.

Example 19. Samantha is self-employed, files a Schedule C, *Profit or Loss From Business (Sole Proprietorship),* and meets the qualifications for the EIC. In 2022, she realizes $50,000 in profit from her business before she considers depreciation options. She has no children and uses the single filing status.

During the summer, she purchases an asset for $60,000 that she places in service in the fall. The asset qualifies for both §179 and bonus depreciation. She does not purchase any other depreciable property this year.

She **elects to use §179** for the entire $60,000. As a result, her earned income is $0 ($50,000 profits – $50,000 §179 limited to income), and she receives no EIC.

Example 20. Use the same facts as **Example 19.** If Samantha **elects out** of bonus depreciation, she will take regular depreciation on the asset, which equals $12,000 for the year. Her business income is therefore $38,000 ($50,000 income – $12,000 depreciation). After taking a deduction for her 50% of SE tax (calculated as $2,685 for the year), Samantha has total earned income of $35,315 ($38,000 business income – $2,685 SE tax deduction).

Samantha looks up her earned income amount on the Earned Income Credit (EIC) Table, and finds that she is ineligible for the EIC.

2022 Earned Income Credit (EIC) Table
Caution. This is **not** a tax table.

1. To find your credit, read down the "At least - But less than" columns and find the line that includes the amount you were told to look up from your EIC Worksheet.

2. Then, go to the column that includes your filing status and the number of qualifying children you have who have valid SSNs as defined earlier. Enter the credit from that column on your EIC Worksheet.

Example. If your filing status is single, you have one qualifying child who has a valid SSN, and the amount you are looking up from your EIC Worksheet is $2,455, you would enter $842.

If the amount you are looking up from the worksheet is–		And your filing status is– Single, head of household, or qualifying surviving spouse and the number of children you have is–			
		0	1	2	3
At least	But less than	Your credit is–			
2,400	2,450	186	825	970	1,091
2,450	2,500	189	842	990	1,114

If the amount you are looking up from the worksheet is–		And your filing status is– Single, head of household, or qualifying surviving spouse★ and you have–				Married filing jointly and you have–			
		0	1	2	3	0	1	2	3
At least	But less than	Your credit is–				Your credit is–			
1	50	2	9	10	11	2	9	10	11
50	100	6	26	30	34	6	26	30	34
100	150	10	43	50	56	10	43	50	56
[illegible]	[illegible]	13	60	[illegible]	[illegible]	13	60	70	[illegible]
31,900	31,950	[illegible]	[illegible]	[illegible]	[illegible]	[illegible]	[illegible]	[illegible]	5,741
31,950	32,000	0	1,840	3,669	4,440	0	2,820	4,960	5,731
32,000	32,050	0	1,832	3,659	4,429	0	2,812	4,950	5,720
32,050	32,100	0	1,824	3,648	4,419	0	2,804	4,939	5,710
32,100	32,150	0	1,816	3,638	4,408	0	2,796	4,929	5,699
32,150	32,200	0	1,808	3,627	4,398	0	2,788	4,918	5,689
[illegible]	32,250	0	1,800	3,617	4,387	0	2,780	4,908	[illegible]

If the amount you are looking up from the worksheet is–		And your filing status is– Single, head of household, or qualifying surviving spouse★ and you have–				Married filing jointly and you have–			
		0	1	2	3	0	1	2	3
At least	But less than	Your credit is–				Your credit is–			
2,800	2,850	216	961	1,130	1,271	216	961	1,130	1,271
2,850	2,900	220	978	1,150	1,294	220	978	1,150	1,294
2,900	2,950	224	995	1,170	1,316	224	995	1,170	1,316
[illegible]	3,000	[illegible]	[illegible]	[illegible]	[illegible]	[illegible]	[illegible]	[illegible]	[illegible]
[illegible]	[illegible]	[illegible]	[illegible]	[illegible]	[illegible]	0	2,317	[illegible]	[illegible]
35,150	[illegible]	0	1,329	2,996	3,766	0	2,309	4,287	5,057
35,200	35,250	0	1,321	2,985	3,755	0	2,301	4,276	5,046
35,250	35,300	0	1,313	2,974	3,745	0	2,293	4,265	5,036
35,300	35,350	0	1,305	2,964	3,734	0	2,285	4,255	5,025
35,350	35,400	0	1,297	2,953	3,724	0	2,277	4,244	5,015
35,400	35,450	0	1,289	2,943	3,713	[illegible]	[illegible]	4,234	[illegible]

[115] IRC §32(b)(2).

[116] IRC §32(j).

[117] Rev. Proc. 2022-38, 2022-45 IRB 1. See §3.06 for 2023 information.

Example 21. Use the same facts as **Example 19.** Samantha's goal is to maximize her EIC in 2022, so she elects out of bonus depreciation (which is an all or nothing election) and needs to elect the appropriate amount of §179 deduction so that the sum of §179 plus regular depreciation on the remaining basis reduces her earned income to an ideal amount.

Samantha looks up the maximum EIC for a single taxpayer with no dependents ($560). According to the EIC table, earned income between $7,300 and $9,200 qualifies her for an EIC of $560.

Samantha works backwards to end up with earned income between $7,300 and $9,200. Her tax software calculates that if she elects §179 of $37,500, the depreciation on the remaining $22,500 of the asset's basis ($60,000 cost – $37,500 §179 deduction) is $4,500. This results in business income of $8,000 ($50,000 income – $37,500 §179 deduction – $4,500 regular depreciation). After taking a deduction for her 50% of SE tax (calculated as $565 for the year), Samantha has total earned income of $7,435 ($8,000 business income – $565 SE tax deduction).

Samantha looks up earned income of $7,435 for a single taxpayer with no dependents on the EIC Table, and is entitled to an EIC of $560.

2022 Earned Income Credit (EIC) Table

Caution. This is **not** a tax table.

1. To find your credit, read down the "At least - But less than" columns and find the line that includes the amount you were told to look up from your EIC Worksheet.

2. Then, go to the column that includes your filing status and the number of qualifying children you have who have valid SSNs as defined earlier. Enter the credit from that column on your EIC Worksheet.

Example. If your filing status is single, you have one qualifying child who has a valid SSN, and the amount you are looking up from your EIC Worksheet is $2,455, you would enter $842.

If the amount you are looking up from the worksheet is–		And your filing status is– Single, head of household, or qualifying surviving spouse and the number of children you have is–			
		0	1	2	3
At least	But less than	Your credit is–			
2,400	2,450	186	825	970	1,091
2,450	2,500	189	842	990	1,114

If the amount you are looking up from the worksheet is–		And your filing status is– Single, head of household, or qualifying surviving spouse★ and you have–				Married filing jointly and you have–			
		0	1	2	3	0	1	2	3
At least	But less than	Your credit is–				Your credit is–			
1	50	2	9	10	11	2	9	10	11
50	100	6	26	30	34	6	26	30	34
[illegible]	150	10	43	50	56	10	43	50	56
[illegible]	[illegible]	13	60	[illegible]	[illegible]	13	60	70	[illegible]
7,200	[illegible]	[illegible]	[illegible]	[illegible]	[illegible]	[illegible]	[illegible]	[illegible]	[illegible]
7,250	7,300	[illegible]	[illegible]	2,910	3,274	[illegible]	[illegible]	2,910	3,274
7,300	7,350	560	2,491	2,930	3,296	560	2,491	2,930	3,296
7,350	7,400	560	2,508	2,950	3,319	560	2,508	2,950	3,319
7,400	7,450	560	2,525	2,970	3,341	560	2,525	2,970	3,341
7,450	7,500	560	2,542	2,990	3,364	560	2,542	2,990	3,364
7,500	7,550	560	2,559	3,010	3,386	560	2,559	3,010	3,386
[illegible]	7,600	560	2,576	3,030	3,409	560	2,576	3,030	3,409

If the amount you are looking up from the worksheet is–		And your filing status is– Single, head of household, or qualifying surviving spouse★ and you have–				Married filing jointly and you have–			
		0	1	2	3	0	1	2	3
At least	But less than	Your credit is–				Your credit is–			
2,800	2,850	216	961	1,130	1,271	216	961	1,130	1,271
2,850	2,900	220	978	1,150	1,294	220	978	1,150	1,294
2,900	2,950	224	995	1,170	1,316	224	995	1,170	1,316
[illegible]	3,000	[illegible]	[illegible]	[illegible]	[illegible]	[illegible]	[illegible]	[illegible]	[illegible]
[illegible]	[illegible]	[illegible]	[illegible]	[illegible]	[illegible]	560	3,545	[illegible]	[illegible]
10,450	[illegible]	459	3,562	4,190	4,714	560	3,562	4,190	4,714
10,500	10,550	456	3,579	4,210	4,736	560	3,579	4,210	4,736
10,550	10,600	452	3,596	4,230	4,759	560	3,596	4,230	4,759
10,600	10,650	448	3,613	4,250	4,781	560	3,613	4,250	4,781
10,650	10,700	444	3,630	4,270	4,804	560	3,630	4,270	4,804
10,700	10,750	440	3,647	4,290	4,826	560	3,647	4,290	4,826
10,750	10,800	436	3,664	4,310	4,849	[illegible]	[illegible]	4,310	4,849

Observation. In **Example 20** and **Example 21,** Samantha's net earned income is subject to SE tax. Any further reduction in earned income reduces the EIC more than it reduces SE tax. Therefore, the ideal depreciation deduction for the remaining basis is the lowest current-year deduction for these purposes. (These options are discussed in detail later in the chapter.) Maximizing the current-year refund may not be the most prudent long-term strategy. However, the timing of the options matter for EIC purposes due to the phase-in and phase-out ranges applicable each year.

STEP 6 — DECIDE WHICH DEPRECIATION SYSTEM AND METHOD TO USE

Any basis remaining after a taxpayer makes the elections for §179 and bonus depreciation is depreciated under the depreciation system known as MACRS. This system modified the previous system in effect in 1986, which was known as the accelerated cost recovery system (ACRS).

As discussed previously, there are two primary sets of rules for calculating the depreciation deduction under MACRS: the GDS and the ADS.[118]

Under MACRS, there are four depreciation methods available.

1. The 200% declining balance method over a GDS recovery period
2. The 150% declining balance method over a GDS recovery period
3. The straight-line method over a GDS recovery period
4. The straight-line method over an ADS recovery period

Note. See IRS Pub. 946, Table 4-1 (shown in the appendix to this chapter), for a list of the types of property that can be depreciated under each method. It also gives a brief explanation of how the method affects the deduction.

The primary difference between the GDS and ADS is that ADS has a longer recovery life for most depreciable assets. GDS is the default system, except in some specific circumstances where ADS is required, as discussed later.

An asset's **salvage value** is the amount that a taxpayer expects to realize when they dispose of it.[119] Under all methods, the salvage value of assets is treated as $0.[120]

Taxpayers may elect to use any of the four methods **for any class** of property placed in service each year, so long as the taxpayer is electing a method that produces a lower current-year deduction than the default.[121] An election may be made on a **property-by-property** basis for non-residential real estate and residential rental property. Under all methods, such an election must be made by the due date of the return (including extensions) for the year the property is placed in service. On amended returns, the election is only available if the original return was filed timely and the amended return is filed by the extended due date. Once an election is made to use a method other than default, **it is irrevocable.**[122]

200% DECLINING BALANCE METHOD UNDER GDS

The 200% declining balance method is generally used to depreciate 3-, 5-, 7-, or 10-year property under MACRS.[123] It is the default in most cases for assets in these classes.[124] Under this method, the deduction is higher in earlier years than in later years. The applicable percentage tables are found in Appendix A of IRS Pub. 946. Most tax preparation software performs the actual computation of the allowable depreciation using this method.

118. IRC §168(g).

119. Treas. Reg. §1.167(a)-1(c)(1).

120. IRC §168(b)(4).

121. IRS Pub. 946, *How to Depreciate Property*.

122. IRC §168(b)(5).

123. IRC §168(b), noting how these recovery periods are excluded from §§168(b)(2) and (3).

124. IRC §168(b)(1). For exceptions see IRC §§168(b)(2)(B), (b)(3), and (e)(6).

150% DECLINING BALANCE METHOD UNDER GDS

The 150% declining balance method is the default method for most assets belonging to the 15- and 20-year classes. In addition, taxpayers may elect this method instead of the 200% method for 3-, 5-, 7-, and 10-year properties. Taxpayers might make this election if they want to claim less depreciation in earlier years and more in later years than the default allows.

The following are common examples of assets that default to this method and their recovery periods.[125]

Land improvements, including shrubbery, fences, and roads	15 years
Retail motor fuels outlets, including convenience stores	15 years
Certain general-purpose farm buildings	20 years

> **Note**. Prior to 2018, general-purpose farm assets were **required** to be depreciated under this method. However, this requirement was eliminated for farm assets placed in service after 2017.[126]

STRAIGHT-LINE METHOD UNDER GDS

The use of straight-line depreciation provides a steady annual depreciation deduction over the asset's recovery period. This method is required for the following types of assets, which must be depreciated over the stated recovery period.[127]

Nonresidential real property	39 years
Residential real property	27.5 years
QIP[127]	15 years
Certain general-purpose farm buildings	20 years
Fruit-or nut-bearing trees or vines[128]	10 years
Water utility property	25 years

STRAIGHT-LINE METHOD UNDER ADS

The difference between straight-line under GDS and under ADS is that the recovery periods for most properties are longer under ADS, as shown in the following table.[130]

	Recovery Period	
Description of Property	**GDS**	**ADS**
Personal property with no class life	7 years	12 years
Residential rental property	27.5 years	30 years
Nonresidential real estate	39 years	40 years
Railroad grading, tunnel bore, or water utility property	50 years	50 years
All other property	The class life	The class life

125. IRS Pub. 946, *How to Depreciate Property*; Rev. Proc. 87-56, 1987-2 CB 687.

126. IRC §168(b)(2) as amended by *Tax Cuts and Jobs Act,* PL 115-97, §13203(b).

127. IRC §168(b)(3).

128. IRC §§168(b)(3)(G) and 168(e)(6).

129. IRC §§168(b)(3)(E) and 168(e)(3)(D)(ii).

130. IRC §168(g)(2)(C).

7

Property required to be depreciated using ADS includes the following.[131]

1. Tangible property used predominantly outside the United States
2. Tax-exempt use property
3. Tax-exempt bond-financed property
4. Property imported from a foreign country identified by U.S. presidential executive order
5. Property for which an alternative MACRS election has been made
6. Residential rental property, nonresidential real property, and QIP owned by a real property trade or business that elects out of the rules in IRC §163(j)
7. Any property with a recovery period of 10 years or greater which is held by an electing farming business that elects out of the 30% interest deduction limitation (50% in tax years beginning in 2019 and 2020)
8. Farmers electing to deduct preproductive period expenses

Note. Bonus depreciation is **not** allowed for property required to be depreciated using ADS.[132]

Electing Real Property Trade or Business and Electing Farm Business[133]

Taxpayers with over $25 million in gross receipts may be subject to business interest deduction limits imposed by IRC §163(j). Certain types of real property businesses[134] and farming businesses[135] may elect out of these limitations even if their gross income exceeds the gross receipts threshold. Taxpayers who elect out **must use the slower ADS depreciation system** for the following types of property.[136]

- Nonresidential real property
- Residential rental property
- QIP owned by an electing real property trade or business
- Assets with recovery periods of 10 years or more used in farming operations[137]

Note. For more information on the business interest deduction limits, see the 2020 *University of Illinois Federal Tax Workbook,* Volume A, Chapter 1: New Developments. This can be found at **uofi.tax/arc** [taxschool.illinois.edu/taxbookarchive].

131. IRC §168(g)(1).
132. IRC §168(k)(2)(D).
133. IRC §168(g)(1).
134. IRC §168(g)(1)(F) referencing IRC §168(g)(8) referencing §163(j)(7)(B) defined by IRC §469(c)(7)(C).
135. IRC §168(g)(1)(G) referencing IRC §163(j)(7)(C).
136. IRC §168(g)(8).
137. IRC §168(g)(1)(G) referencing IRC §163(j)(7)(C) defined by IRC §263A(e)(4).

STEP 7 — DETERMINE THE PROPER RECOVERY PERIOD FOR ANY REMAINING BASIS

Once a tax practitioner decides on the depreciation system and the method of depreciation, they must determine the asset's class life and consider the asset's recovery period. This determination is governed not just by the nature of the **asset** but also by the nature of the **business activity** to which it is being used.

GDS PROPERTY CLASSES

The following table of class lives is excerpted from IRS Pub. 946. Not all property has been assigned a class life. Under GDS, personal property that has not specifically been assigned a class life qualifies as **7-year** property.[138] Under ADS, such property has a **12-year** recovery period.[139]

Property Classification	Examples of Property Types
3-year property	a) Tractor units for over-the-road use b) Any race horse over two years old when placed in service c) Any other horse (other than a race horse) over 12 years old when placed in service d) Qualified rent-to-own property
5-year property	a) Automobiles, taxis, buses, and trucks b) Any qualified technological equipment c) Office machinery (such as typewriters, calculators, and copiers) d) Any property used in research and experimentation e) Breeding cattle and dairy cattle f) Appliances, carpets, furniture, etc., used in a residential rental real estate activity g) Certain geothermal, solar, and wind energy property h) Any machinery equipment (other than any grain bin, cotton ginning asset, fence, or other land improvement) used in a farming business and placed in service after 2017, in tax years ending after 2017. The original use of the property must begin with the taxpayer after 2017
7-year property	a) Office furniture and fixtures (such as desks, files, and safes) b) Used agricultural machinery and equipment placed in service after 2017, grain bins, cotton ginning assets, or fences used in a farming business (but no other land improvements) c) Railroad track d) Any property that does not have a class life and has not been designated by law as being in any other class e) Certain motorsports entertainment property f) Any natural gas gathering line placed in service after April 11, 2005
10-year property	a) Vessels, barges, tugs, and similar water transportation equipment b) Any single purpose agricultural or horticultural structure c) Any tree or vine bearing fruits or nuts d) Qualified small electric meter and qualified smart electric grid system placed in service after October 2, 2008

7

138. Rev. Proc. 87-56, 1987-2 CB 674. See Table in §6, following asset class 80.0. See also IRS Pub. 946, *How to Depreciate Property*, p. 106 (2022).

139. IRC §168(g)(2).

Property Classification	Examples of Property Types
15-year property	a) Certain improvements made directly to land or added to it, such as shrubbery, fences, roads, and bridges b) Any retail motor fuels outlet, such as a convenience store c) Any municipal wastewater treatment plant d) Initial clearing and grading land improvements for gas utility property e) Electric transmission property that is §1245 property used in the transmission of 69 or more kilovolts of electricity placed in service after April 11, 2005. f) Any natural gas distribution line placed in service after April 11, 2005, and before January 1, 2011 g) Any telephone distribution plant and comparable equipment used for 2-way exchange of voice and data communications h) QIP placed in service after 2017
20-year property	a) Farm buildings (other than single purpose agricultural or horticultural structures) b) Municipal sewers not classified as 25-year property c) Initial clearing and grading land improvements for electric utility transmission and distribution plants
25-year property	Limited to water utility property
Residential rental property	Any building or structure, such as a rental home (including a mobile home), if 80% or more of its gross rental income for the tax year is from dwelling units. It does not include a unit in a hotel, motel, or other establishment in which more than half the units are used on a transient basis.
Nonresidential real property	Real estate such as an office building, store, or warehouse that is neither residential rental property nor property with a class life of less than 27.5 years.

At first glance, many assets may seem to belong to a particular class, but because of the type of activity in which the property is used, the property is in a different class.

- **Table B-2** of IRS Pub. 946 includes an exhaustive list of activities and related property that have classes and recovery periods specified by law.
- **Table B-1** lists class lives and recovery periods for assets not used in covered industries based on general categories, such as office furniture or vehicles.

Tables B-1 and B-2 must be used in conjunction with one another in determining the proper class life. The table most applicable to each situation must be used. Both tables are provided in their entirety as an appendix to this chapter.

The following examples demonstrate the proper use of these tables.

Example 22. LTD Papers, Inc. is a small paper manufacturer that, in 2023, makes improvements to the land on which its U.S. paper plant is located.[140] Table B-1 states that land improvements belong to asset class 00.3, which has a class life of 20 years, a GDS recovery period of 15 years, and an ADS recovery period of 20 years.

However, Table B-2 shows that because LTD is involved in paper manufacturing, the land improvements are asset class 26.1, which has a class life of 13 years, a GDS recovery period of 7 years, and an ADS recovery period of 13 years.

Had the tax preparer consulted only Table B-1, they would have depreciated the land improvements using the straight-line method over 15 years, an incorrect and unnecessarily long recovery period for these land improvements. Instead, LTD depreciated the land improvements using straight-line depreciation over 7 years. If LTD wanted to recover the costs of the improvements over a longer period, they could elect to use the straight-line depreciation with an ADS recovery period of 13 years.

Table B-1. **Table of Class Lives and Recovery Periods**

Asset class	Description of assets included	Class Life (in years)	Recovery Periods (in years) GDS (MACRS)	ADS
	SPECIFIC DEPRECIABLE ASSETS USED IN ALL BUSINESS ACTIVITIES, EXCEPT AS NOTED:			
	[illegible]niture, Fixtures [illegible] Equipment:			
[illegible]	in marine [illegible]			
00.3	**Land Improvements:** Includes improvements directly to or added to land, whether such improvements are section 1245 property or section 1250 property, provided such improvements are depreciable. Examples of such assets might include sidewalks, roads, canals, waterways, drainage facilities, sewers (not including municipal sewers in class 51), wharves and docks, bridges, fences, landscaping shrubbery, or radio and television transmitting towers. Does not include land improvements that are explicitly included in any other class, and buildings and structural components as defined in section 1.48-1(e) of the regulations. Excludes public utility initial clearing and grading land improvements as specified in Rev. Rul. 72-403, 1972-2 C.B. 102.	20	15	20
	[illegible] Steam and [illegible] Generation and/[illegible] Dist[illegible] S[illegible]s:			

Table B-2. **Table of Class Lives and Recovery Periods**

Asset class	Description of assets included	Class Life (in years)	Recovery Periods (in years) GDS (MACRS)	ADS
	DEPRECIABLE ASSETS USED IN THE FOLLOWING ACTIVITIES:			
	[illegible]ure:			
	other wood [illegible], including the [illegible] of poles and timber.			
26.1	**Manufacture of Pulp and Paper:** Includes assets for pulp materials handling and storage, pulp mill processing, bleach processing, paper and paperboard manufacturing, and on-line finishing. Includes pollution control assets and all land improvements associated with the factory site or production process such as effluent ponds and canals, provided such improvements are depreciable but does not include buildings and structural components as defined in section 1.48-1(e)(1) of the regulations. Includes steam and chemical recovery boiler systems, with any rated capacity, used for the recovery and regeneration of chemicals used in manufacturing. Does not include assets used either in pulpwood logging, or in the manufacture of hardboard.	13	7	13

140. Example based on Example 1 appearing in IRS Pub. 946, *How to Depreciate Property*, p. 96 (2022).

Example 23. FITS, LLC, is a tax-preparation service. It purchases a hydraulic hand dolly for $2,600, which it uses to distribute boxes of printer paper to each preparer's office. Hand dollies are not specifically listed in Table B-1. By default, the appropriate class appears to be *Office Furniture, Fixtures, and Equipment*. This asset class has a 7-year recovery period under the GDS.

However, professional services are specifically included under *Distributive Trades and Services* in Table B-2. Assets used in this *Distributive Trades and Services* classification have a 5-year recovery period. Consequently, the dolly qualifies to be depreciated over five years under GDS.

Table B-2. **Table of Class Lives and Recovery Periods**

Asset class	Description of assets included	Class Life (in years)	Recovery Periods (in years) GDS (MACRS)	ADS
	DEPRECIABLE ASSETS USED IN THE FOLLOWING ACTIVITIES:			
	Agriculture:			
50.0				
51.0	**Municipal Sewer**	50	20***	50
57.0	**Distributive Trades and Services:** Includes assets used in wholesale and retail trade, and personal and professional services. Includes section 1245 assets used in marketing petroleum and petroleum products.	9	5	9*
57.1	**Distributive Trades and Services—Billboard, Service Station Buildings, and Petroleum Land Improvements:**			

Note. The IRS has provided no guidance defining distributive trades and services. Wholesale and retail trade involves supplying goods without any intermediate physical transformation of the products.

Example 24. Steve's small business provides charter passenger flights. Table B-1 includes airplanes but excludes those used in carrying passengers. Therefore, he must use Table B-2, which lists airplanes used to carry passengers as 7-year assets. (Asset Class 45.0, not shown)

Steve also owns a helicopter. Table B-1 specifically mentions "all helicopters." Steve can depreciate the helicopter over five years, even though it is used to carry passengers.

The following table lists recovery periods and class lives for some industries and assets used in those industries that are covered by Table B-2.

Observation. This list is intended to alert practitioners to some of the less obvious classifications; the actual table should be reviewed for detailed information on the assets specifically included within each category.

Excerpts from Table B-2

Asset Class		GDS Recovery Period and Property Class
Agriculture Property		
01.1	Grain bins	7
01.1	Fences used in agricultural activities	7
01.221	Breeding/work horse age ≤ 12 yrs when placed in service	7
Construction		
15.0	Assets used by construction businesses (except railroad construction)	5
24.1	Cutting of timber	5
Distributive Trades and Services		
57.0	Assets used in wholesale and resale trade, and personal and professional services	5
Manufacturing of:		
20.1	Grain and grain mill products	10
20.2	Sugar and sugar products	10
20.3	Vegetable oils and related products	10
20.5	Food and beverage special handling devices	3
22.1	Knitted and netted fabrics and lace	5
22.2	Yarn, thread, and woven fabrics	7
22.3	Carpets	5
22.3	Textile products	5
22.3	Medical and dental supplies	5
22.5	Textile yarns — certain assets	5
25.0	Apparel and other finished products	5
28.0	Chemicals and allied products	5
30.11	Rubber products — special tools only	3
30.21	Finished plastic products — special tools only	3
32.11	Glass products — special tools only	3
32.3	Cement (not concrete)	15
33.21	Nonferrous metals — special tools only	5
34.01	Fabricated metals — special tools only	3
36.0	Electronic components, products, and systems	5
36.1	Semiconductors	5
37.12	Motor vehicles — special tools only	3
Sawmills		
24.2	Machinery and equipment installed in permanent sawmills	7
24.3	Machinery and equipment installed in temporary sawmills	5
Ship and Boat Building and Repairs		
37.31	Machinery and equipment	7
37.32	Dry docks and land improvements	10
37.33	Special tools only	5
Transportation		
44.0	Assets used to ferry freight or passengers on water	15
45.0	Assets used to carry freight or passengers by air, except helicopters	7

Even within this step, taxpayers may make decisions on multiple levels that they may later wish to change. These modifications may require changes in accounting method to be filed with the IRS, as discussed later.

STEP 8 — APPLY CORRECT CONVENTION

The tax practitioner's final determination when calculating depreciation for a return is if the taxpayer must use the mid-month convention for certain assets placed in service in the current year. Under MACRS, the conventions establish when the recovery period begins and ends. The conventions also determine the depreciation percentages applied each year during the recovery period. There are three conventions used for calculating depreciation deductions for tax purposes which are applied in the following order.

1. **Mid-month convention** — Required to be used for **nonresidential real property**, **residential rental property**, and any railroad grading or tunnel bore[141]
2. **Mid-quarter convention** — Used if the mid-month convention does not apply and the total depreciable bases of MACRS property placed in service during the last three months of the tax year are more than 40% of the total depreciable bases of all MACRS property placed in service during the entire year[142]
3. **Half-year convention** — Used for all other assets placed in service during the year[143]

Assets subject to the mid-month convention are **not** included in the test to determine if the mid-quarter convention must be used. Assets for which neither the mid-month nor the mid-quarter conventions must be used are subject to the half-year convention.

MID-MONTH CONVENTION

Under the mid-month convention, all property placed in service during a month is treated as placed in service at the midpoint of the month. Later, when the property is removed from service, the mid-month convention provides for a half-month of depreciation in the final month.[144]

Consequently, each asset subject to the mid-month convention is allowed one-half month of depreciation in its first and last months and a flat amount of depreciation for the intervening months. The mid-month convention is only applicable when required.

Although assets depreciated under the mid-month convention are required to use longer periods to recover their costs, the mid-month convention permits them to have a steady amount of depreciation over the life of the asset. This convention also matches the beginning of cost recovery more closely to an asset's placement into service. Depreciation under this method may also more closely match the taxpayer's cash flow if the property was purchased with debt financing.

On Form 4562, *Depreciation and Amortization,* the mid-month convention is identified as "MM" under column E in part III.[145]

MID-QUARTER CONVENTION[146]

Congress added a requirement to apply the mid-quarter convention to discourage taxpayers from delaying the tax impact of their purchases until the end of the year. This requirement applies when over 40% of the cost of applicable property is associated with assets placed in service during the final three months of the tax year.

---

141. IRC §168(d)(2).

142. IRC §168(d)(4)(C); Treas. Reg. §1.168(d)-1(b).

143. IRC §168(d)(4)(A); Treas. Reg. §1.168(d)-1(a).

144. IRC §168(d)(4).

145. See Instructions for Form 4562.

146. IRC §168(d)(3); Treas. Regs. §§1.168(d)-1(a) and (b).

Applicable property includes all assets not subject to the mid-month convention which are placed in service during the tax year. The percentage placed in service during the last 3 months is calculated by dividing the depreciable basis of assets placed in service during the final quarter of the year by the total depreciable basis of assets placed in service during the entire year.

When the 40% threshold is crossed, **all assets** placed in service during the year are treated as having been put in service at the midpoint of the quarter in which they were first used. Thus, an asset first used in the first quarter applies the mid-quarter convention beginning within the first quarter.

When it comes time to dispose of the property, depreciation is considered to stop at the mid-point of the quarter in which it is disposed of.[147]

Caution. For purposes of determining whether the mid-quarter convention applies, the depreciable basis of property placed in service during the tax year reflects the reduction in basis for amounts expensed under §179 and the part of the basis of property attributable to personal use.[148] However, it does not reflect any reduction in the basis for any special depreciation allowance.

Example 25. TUV Corporation, a C corporation with a tax year ending on December 31, puts the following purchases into service in 2023.

Date	Purchase	Cost	Percentage of Total Costs
Jan. 15	Laser printers	$20,000	33%
Oct. 6	Office furniture	40,000	67%

TUV does not elect §179 expense deduction for these purchases, and elects out of bonus depreciation for all classes of property. Because 67% of TUV's assets are put in service during the last 3 months of 2023, it must use the mid-quarter convention for both assets.

Depreciation under the mid-quarter convention for the two assets totals $8,428 calculated as follows.

Property	Recovery Period	Applicable Percentage[a]	Depreciation
Laser printers	5-year	35.00%	$7,000
Office furniture	7-year	3.57%	1,428
Total			$8,428

[a] The applicable percentage for depreciation is found in IRS Pub. 946.

Example 26. Use the same facts as **Example 25.** TUV sells the laser printers in July 2025. Because of the rule covering the disposition of mid-quarter property, TUV will be allowed to calculate the depreciation deduction for the printers as if the property were held through the middle of the third quarter of 2025, or on August 15.

147. IRC §168(d)(4)(C).

148. IRC §168(d)(3)(A). IRC §179 property is not included in the calculation because the language of §168(d)(3)(A) restricts it to property covered by that section, thereby excluding §179 property and personal use property.

Short-Year Considerations[149]

Taxpayers must apply the mid quarter **test** even if they have a short tax year. In such cases, the last three months[150] of the year are still used to perform the 40% mid-quarter test, regardless of the length of the tax year.[151]

Example 27. EFG Restaurants, Inc. is formed on September 1, 2023, and immediately elects to be taxed as an S corporation with a calendar tax year. During the same month, it places in service two laptop computers having a total basis of $5,000. It also issues purchase orders for $200,000 of restaurant equipment, which is placed in service when it is installed on October 25. Because more than 40% of EFG's purchases are made in the last three months of its tax year, the computers and the restaurant equipment are subject to the mid-quarter convention.

Note. If a short year consists of three months or less, the mid-quarter **convention** applies regardless of when the depreciable property is place in service during the taxable year.

Although the last three months are used to determine **if** the convention applies, **when applying** the convention, the length of each quarter is ¼ of the short year. The result is then prorated over 12 months based on the number of months in the short year.

Strategy for Using §179 to Avoid the Mid-Quarter Convention

Electing the §179 deduction for property placed in service during the last three months removes the amount of the election from the basis used for the 40% mid-quarter test.[152]

Example 28. HIJ Testing, Inc. uses expensive electronic equipment in its customer service business. HIJ is an S corporation with a calendar tax year. In 2023, HIJ purchases and places into service three pieces of business equipment.

Date	Purchase Cost	Percentage of Total Costs
Feb. 15	$ 50,000	42%
Oct. 15	20,000	16%
Dec. 15	50,000	42%
Total	$120,000	100%

In 2023, 58% (16% + 42%) of HIJ's property is placed in service during the last 3 months of the year. HIJ wants to use §179 to write off $45,000 of the costs. It also wants to maximize its remaining depreciation deduction without using bonus depreciation.

To avoid the requirement to use the mid-quarter convention, it applies the §179 election to the asset purchased in December. As shown below, after the §179 election, only 33% (27% + 6%) of the property is considered placed in service during the last three months.

Date	Purchase Cost	§179	Remaining Basis	Percentage of Total Basis
Feb. 15	$ 50,000	$ 0	$50,000	67%
Oct. 15	20,000	0	20,000	27%
Dec. 15	50,000	(45,000)	5,000	6%
Total	$120,000		$75,000	100%

149. Rev. Proc. 89-15, 1989-1 CB 816.

150. IRC §168(d)(3).

151. Rev. Proc. 89-15, 1989-1 CB 816.

152. IRC §168(d)(3)(A)(ii).

HALF-YEAR CONVENTION

All property not subject to mid-month or mid-quarter conventions is subject to the half-year convention.[153] As such, depreciation is calculated as if the property is placed in service or disposed of at the year's midpoint. Properties subject to the half-year convention when placed in service are treated as having been disposed of mid-year during their last year in service.

The half-year convention creates a small disincentive to acquire depreciable property during the first half of the year, assuming the property belongs to a class requiring the use of the half-year convention. Property acquired in January is effectively not depreciated for 5.5 months. Instead, property acquired late in the year is treated more favorably, as it is effectively depreciated before it was placed in service.

> **Example 29.** On September 29, 2023, the PQR Corporation, a C corporation with a calendar tax year, puts into service new office furniture having a delivered price of $40,000. It does not elect the §179 expense deduction for this property, and it elects out of bonus depreciation for the applicable property class. Under the half-year convention, PQR is entitled to a depreciation deduction of $5,716 ($40,000 × 14.29%[154]). This is the same amount of depreciation to which it would have been entitled if it had put the new office furniture into service on January 1, even though the payment is presumably made nine months later.

CHANGES IN BUSINESS USE OF ASSETS

7

After a taxpayer makes the initial determination of how to depreciate the asset, they may change the business use of the asset. Depending on whether the change is from business use to personal use, from personal use to business use, or from one business use to another, the taxpayer must account for the change on their depreciation schedule.

ASSETS SHIFTING FROM BUSINESS USE TO PERSONAL USE

It is not uncommon for owners of closely held businesses to start using business property for personal purposes. Depending on the depreciation decisions made when the property was initially placed in service, there can be significant adverse consequences when business use drops below 50%. If the taxpayer previously elected §179 for the property **or** if the property is listed property for which bonus depreciation was taken, some of the previous depreciation must be recaptured using Form 4797, *Sales of Business Property*, part IV, as discussed later. If neither situation applies, no depreciation recapture occurs until the taxpayer disposes of the property.[155]

At that time, the recapture amount is calculated and reported differently than the recapture amount applicable to changes in use. For example, consider the disposition of §179 property that would have been fully depreciated by the time it is sold. If the amount realized is equal to or less than the original basis of the asset, the entire amount is realized as ordinary income on Form 4797, part II.[156] If the asset is sold for more than its original basis, the amount greater than the basis is §1245 capital gain, which is reported on Form 4797, part I.[157]

---

153. IRC §168(d)(1).

154. IRS Pub. 946, *How to Depreciate Property,* Table A-1.

155. IRC §§1245(a) and 1250(a)(1).

156. Treas. Reg. §1.179-1(e)(1).

157. Treas. Reg. §1.179-1(e)(3).

IRC §179 Property

As mentioned previously, if the business usage of §179 property drops below 50% at any time before the end of the property's recovery period, the taxpayer must recapture any benefit derived from the §179 deduction.[158] This recapture is calculated on Form 4797, in part IV, in the tax year in which the usage of the property drops below 50%. The recapture amount is then included in "other income" on the same form or schedule on which the taxpayer took the depreciation deduction. The basis of the asset is increased by the recapture amount.[159]

If the property is **not listed** property, the recapture amount is calculated using the following two steps.[160]

Step 1. Calculate the depreciation that would have been allowable on the §179 expense deduction claimed. The calculation begins with the year the property was placed in service and ends with the year of recapture.

Step 2. Subtract the depreciation calculated in **Step 1** from the §179 expense deduction claimed. The result is the recapture amount.

Example 30. In January 2020, Alec bought and placed in service a copier costing $5,000. The copier is 5-year property and is used in his accounting practice, a sole proprietorship. Alec elected to expense the entire purchase price under §179. He used the copier solely for business purposes in 2020 and 2021. In 2022, Alec's wife uses the copier in her volunteer activities, which reduces Alec's business use of the copier to 40%. He calculates his recapture amount as follows.

§179 expense deduction claimed in 2020		$5,000
Allowable depreciation under MACRS for 2020	$1,000	
Allowable depreciation under MACRS for 2021	1,600	
Allowable depreciation under MACRS for 2022 ($960 full MACRS depreciation × 40% business use)	384	
Total allowed depreciation	$2,984	(2,984)
2022 recapture amount		$2,016

Alec reports the recapture on part IV of his business's Form 4797, which follows.

32 Su[...] other than casualty or theft on Form 4797, line [...] 32

Part IV Recapture Amounts Under Sections 179 and 280F(b)(2) When Business Use Drops to 50% or Less (see instructions)

			(a) Section 179	(b) Section 280F(b)(2)
33	Section 179 expense deduction or depreciation allowable in prior years	33	5,000	
34	Recomputed depreciation. See instructions	34	2,984	
35	Recapture amount. Subtract line 34 from line 33. See the instructions for where to report	35	2,016	

Form **4797** (2022)

Alec reports the $2,016 recapture as ordinary income on his 2022 **Schedule C.** His **basis** in the copier is **increased** by the $2,016 recapture.

158. IRC §179(d)(10).

159. Treas. Reg. §1.179-1(e); Instructions for Form 4797.

160. IRS Pub. 946, *How to Depreciate Property*.

Listed Property[161]

Like §179 property, depreciation on listed property must be recaptured when its business use falls to 50% or less. The recapture amount on listed property is the excess, if any, of the following two amounts.

1. The depreciation allowable for the property, including any §179 expense deduction and bonus depreciation deduction claimed for the years prior to the year the business usage of the property fell to less than 50%; **less**

2. The depreciation that would have been allowable for those years if the property had not been used predominantly for qualified business purposes in the year it was placed in service. This amount is determined by calculating the depreciation using the straight-line method and the **ADS recovery period**.

Example 31. In June 2018, Brandon Wax, owner of Candlestick Makers, purchased and placed in service a new SUV that cost $28,000. During the 2018–2021 tax years, he used it **exclusively** for qualified business purposes.

In 2018, Brandon claimed a $10,000 §179 deduction on the SUV and $8,000 of bonus depreciation. He began depreciating the balance of the purchase price using the 200% declining balance method over a 5-year GDS recovery period. The SUV's GVW is under 6,000 pounds, so it is subject to the annual limits for depreciation of passenger vehicles.[162] The depreciation limit for trucks and vans placed in service during 2018 was $18,000.[163]

During 2022, Brandon's business use of the vehicle drops to 50%. He must calculate the excess depreciation and include it in his 2022 gross income. The excess depreciation is calculated as follows.

Depreciation claimed:		
§179 expense	$10,000	
Bonus depreciation	8,000	
MACRS depreciation:		
2018 (($28,000 − $10,000 − $8,000) × 20.00%)	2,000	
2019 (($28,000 − $10,000 − $8,000) × 32.00%)	3,200	
2020 (($28,000 − $10,000 − $8,000) × 19.20%)	1,920	
2021 (($28,000 − $10,000 − $8,000) × 11.52%)	1,152	
Total depreciation claimed 2018–2021	$26,272	$26,272
Depreciation allowed (straight-line method and ADS recovery life of five years):		
2018 (10% × $28,000)	$ 2,800	
2019 (20% × $28,000)	5,600	
2020 (20% × $28,000)	5,600	
2021 (20% × $28,000)	5,600	
Total depreciation allowable 2018–2021	$19,600	(19,600)
Excess depreciation		$ 6,672

This $6,672 is shown in part IV of Form 4797 and carried to Brandon's 2022 Schedule C. It is subject to both **ordinary income tax** and **SE tax.**

32 Subtract line ... other than casualty or theft on Form 4797, line ... 32

Part IV Recapture Amounts Under Sections 179 and 280F(b)(2) When Business Use Drops to 50% or Less (see instructions)

			(a) Section 179	(b) Section 280F(b)(2)
33	Section 179 expense deduction or depreciation allowable in prior years	33		26,272
34	Recomputed depreciation. See instructions	34		19,600
35	Recapture amount. Subtract line 34 from line 33. See the instructions for where to report	35		6,672

Form **4797** (2022)

161. IRC §280F(b)(2)(B).

162. Rev. Proc. 2018-25, 2018-18 IRB 543. See Table 2.

163. Ibid.

Note. Excess depreciation that is recaptured under these rules is added back to the basis of the property. However, for property depreciated using the straight-line method and ADS property life, the amount of depreciation allowable in the year that business use drops to 50% or less is not changed by this adjustment. In **Example 29,** the 2022 depreciation is still 20% of $28,000 ($5,600) before it is allocated to business and nonbusiness use.

Practitioner Planning Tip

When business use of listed property or §179 property drops to 50% or less during the recovery period, the taxpayer may have reportable income that was not caused by disposing of the property. It is important to verify the taxpayer's business use of the property each year during its depreciable life.

Real Estate

Generally, if the qualified use of real estate drops below 50%, there are no tax consequences until the year the asset is sold.[164] Taxpayers who sell their home may be taxed on a portion of any gain realized depending on the timing and amount of the sale.[165] However, it is still necessary to determine the adjusted basis at the time the use changes.

Example 32. Stanley and Anne purchased a rental home in Arizona in 1995 for $65,000 with the intention of leasing it to unrelated persons until they were ready to retire. After purchasing the home, they made improvements totaling $75,000 to the home through the end of 2022.

Stanley and Anne had no personal use of the home until 2023, after they retired. They move into the rental home in April after the seasonal lease expired. Their adjusted basis in the real estate when it was taken out of service is equal to $140,000 ($65,000 + $75,000) less the total of all the depreciation allowed or allowable for the property while it was in service. Their accumulated depreciation on the property is $90,000, comprised of straight-line depreciation of the original structure and improvements since 1995.

Their adjusted basis at the time of the conversion to personal use is $50,000 ($140,000 – $90,000). They are not required to recapture any of the depreciation in the year of the change in use.

In certain circumstances, converting commercial rentals to personal use may trigger **§179 recapture** if the commercial property includes assets for which the taxpayer claimed the §179 expense deduction.[166] Types of improvements to **nonresidential** properties that may qualify for the §179 deduction include QIP, roofs, HVAC property, and safety and security systems.[167] Such real estate improvements first became eligible for §179 after December 31, 2017.

---

164. Treas. Reg. §1.168(i)-4(c).

165. IRC §121; See also IRS Pub. 523, *Selling Your Home.*

166. IRC §179(d)(10).

167. IRC §179(e).

> **Caution.** Although the §179 deduction was not available for most real estate investments until after 2017, the relevant provisions have been altered several times.[168] QIP[169] has undergone many transformations, and practitioners must be on alert for numerous phrases and acronyms that have been used to identify qualified improvements on depreciation schedules. Examples include qualified leasehold property,[170] qualified restaurant property,[171] and qualified retail improvement property.[172]

ASSETS SHIFTING FROM PERSONAL USE TO BUSINESS USE

If a taxpayer acquires property for personal use and converts it to business or income-producing use, they must apply the appropriate depreciation rules in effect on the date of the change, which is considered the placed-in-service date. This date determines the method, recovery period, convention, and applicability of bonus depreciation for the property.[173]

The depreciable basis of the property is the lesser of its FMV or its adjusted depreciable basis[174] at the time of the change to business or income-producing use.[175]

Example 33. Alethia bought her principal residence in Illinois in 1995.[176] In 2023, she retires to a warmer part of the country, but she does not want to sell the home because of her personal attachment to it.

In February, she engages a real estate agent to rent it, and the first tenant, an unrelated party, moves in late in the month. Alethia's tax practitioner advises her that she can begin depreciation of the home in mid-February, but she needs more information to determine the appropriate basis to use. After some research, they determine the following.

Alethia's original basis was the $159,000 she paid for the land and the house. Over the years, she added various improvements that probably cost at least $131,000. Thus, her **cost basis is $290,000** ($159,000 original cost + $131,000 improvements) when she starts using it as rental property.

A real estate agent estimates that the homestead is currently worth **$371,000.** To determine the lesser of the FMV or adjusted basis for depreciation purposes, these values must be separated between depreciable property and nondepreciable land. They make the following allocations after appropriate consultations.

	Total	Land	Depreciable
Cost basis	$290,000	$ 47,000	$243,000
FMV	371,000	118,000	253,000

Alethia's depreciable basis is $243,000 for the house and improvements (the lesser of cost or FMV.)

7

168. First added as IRC §179(f) by *Tax Cuts and Jobs Act,* PL 115-97, amended to (e) by *Tax Technical Corrections Act of 2018*, PL 115-141, Div. U.

169. IRC §168(e)(6).

170. IRC §§168(b)(3)(G) and (e)(6) before being struck out by *Tax Cuts and Jobs Act,* PL 115-97, §13204(a)(2).

171. IRC §§168(b)(3)(H) and (e)(7) before being struck out by *Tax Cuts and Jobs Act,* PL 115-97, §13204(a)(2).

172. IRC §§168(b)(3)(I) and (e)(8) before being struck out by *Tax Cuts and Jobs Act,* PL 115-97, §13204(a)(2).

173. Treas. Reg. §1.168(i)-4(b).

174. Treas. Reg. §1.168(b)–1 (a)(4).

175. Treas. Reg. §1.168(i)-4(b)(1).

176. Based on Treas. Reg. §1.168(i)-4(b)(2).

ASSETS SHIFTING FROM ONE BUSINESS USE TO ANOTHER[177]

Business and income-producing property may also change in use without being converted to personal use property. Examples include converting property from business use to farm use or from residential rental to commercial rental. The change is typically deemed to occur on the first day of the tax year.

The depreciation options available for such an asset vary depending on if the new **use** qualifies for a faster or slower recovery period than the old use. Taxpayers are not required to change the depreciation method for a property that now qualifies for faster recovery.[178]

Shifting to a Slower Depreciation Rate[179]

If the new use is slower than the old use, depreciation must be calculated using a specific formula provided in the regulations.[180] In this case, the depreciation is applied as though it had originally been placed in service at the slower depreciation rate. Starting with January 1 of the year of change, the asset should be depreciated using the original adjusted basis **on that date**. The lesser depreciation amount in the year of change is applied to the asset's remaining basis. If a change in the asset's use takes place, the convention used for depreciation does not change.

If a change in business use causes an asset's basis to be recovered over a shorter period, the taxpayer may elect to disregard the change in use.[181] This election can be revoked, but this requires a change in accounting method, as discussed later.[182]

> **Caution.** Depreciation elections, such as bonus depreciation, that are made for the tax year in which the property changes use may apply to the converted property as well as newly purchased property.[183]

CORRECTING ERRORS IN PRIOR YEAR DEPRECIATION

Given the complexities surrounding depreciation, it is not unusual to discover errors after tax returns have been filed. There are two methods for correcting depreciation errors.[184]

1. Filing an amended return for the year of the mistake
2. Filing Form 3115, *Application for Change in Accounting Method,* with the current year return

Not all depreciation errors can be corrected by filing an amended return. If the option to amend is not available, taxpayers must file Form 3115 to correct the calculations.

FILING AN AMENDED RETURN

A taxpayer can file an amended return to correct depreciation when the correction affects **only** the return being amended, such as when correcting **mathematical and posting errors.**[185]

177. Treas. Reg. §1.168(i)-4(d).
178. Treas. Reg. §1.168(i)-4(d)(3)(ii).
179. Treas. Reg. §1.168(i)-4(d)(4).
180. Treas. Regs. §§1.168(i)-4(d)(3)(ii) and (4).
181. Treas. Reg. §1.168(i)-4(d)(3)(ii).
182. Treas. Reg. §1.168(i)-4(d)(g)(3)(i).
183. IRC §168(b)(5).
184. Rev. Proc. 2015-13, 2015-05 IRB 419.
185. Ibid.

A taxpayer may change permissible methods of depreciation on an amended return if the amended return is filed before the original return is filed for the following tax year.[186]

Example 34. Jeremy elected to use straight-line depreciation for the 7-year property he placed in service in 2022 when he filed his 2022 return instead of the 200% declining balance method. He regrets that choice when working on his 2023 return. Because he has not filed his 2023 return yet, he may amend his 2022 return to change depreciation methods. Alternately, he may elect to file Form 3115 and claim the difference on his 2023 return.

Impermissible methods, such as failing to calculate depreciation, must be corrected by filing an amended return if the depreciation for that asset affects **only one** previous return.[187] If the impermissible method affects more than one previous return, the taxpayer must use Form 3115 to change to a permissible method.[188]

Example 35. Use the same facts as **Example 34,** except Jeremy omitted the asset from the 2022 return. Because he discovers the error before the lack of depreciation of the asset affects his 2023 return, he must amend the 2022 tax return. If Jeremy had discovered the error after his 2023 return was filed, the omission would be treated as affecting two returns, and his only option would have been to file Form 3115 with the next return he files.

FILING A CHANGE IN ACCOUNTING METHOD[189]

If a taxpayer does not qualify to correct their depreciation by filing an amended return, the IRS has provided taxpayers with an alternative method for correcting depreciation. Despite the general rule that mistakes cannot be corrected after the statute of limitations expires, missed depreciation can be corrected after the asset should have been fully depreciated. Filing Form 3115 to claim previously unclaimed depreciation allows the taxpayer to deduct in the current year the entire amount of depreciation not previously deducted.

Form 3115 is designed to cover hundreds of different situations that result in a change in accounting methods. Tax practitioners using the form should pay careful attention to the detailed instructions provided by the IRS and should review the revenue procedures applicable to the requested change.

Correcting depreciation is generally covered under the **automatic change procedures,** which do not require the taxpayer to obtain IRS consent before making the change.[190] Under the automatic change procedures, no application fee is required. The 2022 version of Form 3115 appears with the next example.

Note. For more information about changes in accounting methods, see IRM 4.11.6.2. Additionally, Form 3115 is covered in detail in the 2023 *University of Illinois Federal Tax Workbook,* Chapter 2: Capitalization vs. Repair Review.

A taxpayer who did not claim any of the allowable depreciation for certain assets on prior years' returns and is claiming the missed depreciation on the current year's return is changing from an **impermissible** method to a **permissible** method.[191] The total amount of missed depreciation includes the depreciation that should have been taken in both open and closed years. This total is reported as an "other expense" on the appropriate schedule of the taxpayer's return for the year of the change.

186. Rev. Proc. 2022-14, 2022-07 IRB 502, §6.01(1)(b).

187. Treas. Reg. §1.446-1(e)(2)(ii)(a).

188. Rev. Proc. 2015-13, 2015-05 IRB 419.

189. Ibid.

190. Ibid; Rev. Proc. 2022-14, 2022-07 IRB 502.

191. Rev. Proc. 2022-14, 2022-07 IRB 502, §6.01; Instructions for Form 3115.

Small Business Taxpayers[192]

Some small taxpayers qualify for a reduced filing requirement for Form 3115. A **qualified small taxpayer** is a taxpayer whose average annual gross receipts, as determined under Treas. Reg. §1.263(a)-3(h)(3), for the three preceding taxable years is less than or equal to $10 million. These small taxpayers must file only one of the following designated automatic accounting method change numbers (DCNs).[193]

DCN	Change
7	Depreciation or amortization (impermissible to permissible)
8	Depreciation (permissible to permissible)
21	Removal costs (IRC §263)
88	Change in method of accounting for depreciation due to a change in use
89	Depreciation of qualified non-personal-use vans and light trucks
107	Impermissible to permissible method of accounting for depreciation or amortization for disposed property
121	Repairable and reuseable spare parts (§263(a))
145	Tenant construction allowances
157	Classification of wireless telecommunications assets used by carriers
184–193	These DCNs generally deal with capitalization and repair accounting
198	Partial dispositions of tangible depreciable assets
199	Depreciation of leasehold improvements
200	Depreciation of §168 MACRS property (permissible to permissible)
205	Dispositions of a building or structural component
206	Dispositions of tangible depreciable assets in a general asset accounting
207	Dispositions of tangible depreciable assets in a general asset account (§168)
222	Remodel-refresh safe harbor method (§263)

Qualifying small taxpayers complete only the following information on Form 3115.[194]

- The identification section of page 1 (above part I)
- The signature section appearing on the first page
- Part I
- Part II, all lines except 13, 15, 17, and 19
- Part IV, all lines except line 25
- Schedule E, *Changes in Depreciation or Amortization*

Applicants requesting approval to change their method of accounting for depreciation or amortization must complete Schedule E of Form 3115. Per line 4a, the applicant must attach a statement to Form 3115 with the following information.[195]

- Description of the property subject to the change, which includes a description, type, placed-in-service year, and use in the applicant's trade or business or income-producing activity
- Type and amount of any federal tax credit claimed or grant received
- Any necessary adjustments to basis required per the Code

192. Rev. Proc. 2022-14, 2022-07 IRB 502, §6.07(4).

193. Instructions for Form 3115.

194. Rev. Proc. 2022-14, 2022-07 IRB 502, §6.07(4); Instructions for Form 3115.

195. See Form 3115.

Example 36. Toni is excited when she hears that Jack and Jill Hill made an appointment for help in preparing their 2023 income tax returns. When she first meets with them, she is surprised to learn that they have never taken a depreciation deduction for any of their five rental properties. The Hills purchased these rental properties between 2010 and 2022.

After attending a tax seminar, Toni learns that she could prepare Form 3115 to claim all the depreciation deductions the Hills had missed when they were preparing their own returns and the total of all the missed depreciation can be deducted on the Hill's 2023 Form 1040, Schedule E, *Supplemental Income and Loss*.

Toni calculates that the total prior years' depreciation was $63,091. She completes Form 3115 to document the adjustment and notify the IRS about the change. The missed depreciation for each property is deducted as other expenses on Schedule E, and the description "Form 3115 §481(a) adjustment" is entered on the description line.

The following pages show the Hill's 2023 Form 3115 and associated attachment, completed to take advantage of reduced filing requirements.

7

For Example 36

Form **3115**
(Rev. December 2022)
Department of the Treasury
Internal Revenue Service

Application for Change in Accounting Method

Go to *www.irs.gov/Form3115* for instructions and the latest information.

OMB No. 1545-2070
Attachment Sequence No. **315**

Name of filer (name of parent corporation if a consolidated group) (see instructions) **Jack and Jill Hill**	**Identification number** (see instructions) *****-**-3115 ***-**-4887**
	Principal business activity code number (see instructions) **531120**
Number, street, and room or suite no. If a P.O. box, see the instructions. **6900 Maple St**	Tax year of change begins (MM/DD/YYYY) **01/01/2023** Tax year of change ends (MM/DD/YYYY) **12/31/2023**
City or town, state, and ZIP code **Urbana, IL 61801**	Name of contact person (see instructions) **Toni Smith**
Name of applicant(s) (if different than filer) and identification number(s) (see instructions)	Contact person's telephone number **217-555-2443**

Does the filer want to receive a copy of the change in method of accounting letter ruling or other correspondence related to this Form 3115 by fax or encrypted email attachment? If "Yes," see instructions . . . . ☐ Yes ☒ No

If the applicant is a member of a consolidated group, check this box . . . . . ☐

If **Form 2848**, Power of Attorney and Declaration of Representative, is attached (see instructions for when Form 2848 is required), check this box . . . . . ☒

Check the box to indicate the type of applicant.

- ☒ Individual
- ☐ Corporation
- ☐ Controlled foreign corporation (Sec. 957)
- ☐ 10/50 corporation (Sec. 904(d)(2)(E))
- ☐ Qualified personal service corporation (Sec. 448(d)(2))
- ☐ Exempt organization. Enter Code section:
- ☐ Cooperative (Sec. 1381)
- ☐ Partnership
- ☐ S corporation
- ☐ Insurance co. (Sec. 816(a))
- ☐ Insurance co. (Sec. 831)
- ☐ Other (specify):

Check the appropriate box to indicate the type of accounting method change being requested. See instructions.

- ☒ Depreciation or Amortization
- ☐ Financial Products and/or Financial Activities of Financial Institutions
- ☐ Other (specify):

Caution: To be eligible for approval of the requested change in method of accounting, the taxpayer must provide all information that is relevant to the taxpayer or to the taxpayer's requested change in method of accounting. This includes (**1**) all relevant information requested on this Form 3115 (including its instructions), and (**2**) any other relevant information, even if not specifically requested on Form 3115.
The taxpayer must attach all applicable statements requested throughout this form.

Part I — Information for Automatic Change Request

		Yes	No
1	Enter the applicable designated automatic accounting method change number ("DCN") for the requested automatic change. Enter only one DCN, except as provided for in guidance published by the IRS. If the requested change has no DCN, check "Other," and provide both a description of the change and a citation of the IRS guidance providing the automatic change. See instructions.		
a	(1) DCN: 7 (2) DCN: ___ (3) DCN: ___ (4) DCN: ___ (5) DCN: ___ (6) DCN: ___ (7) DCN: ___ (8) DCN: ___ (9) DCN: ___ (10) DCN: ___ (11) DCN: ___ (12) DCN: ___		
b	Other ☐ Description:		
2	Do any of the eligibility rules restrict the applicant from filing the requested change using the automatic change procedures (see instructions)? If "Yes," attach an explanation . . .		×
3	Has the filer provided all the information and statements required (**a**) on this form and (**b**) by the List of Automatic Changes under which the applicant is requesting a change? See instructions . . . **Note:** Complete Part II and Part IV of this form, and, Schedules A through E, if applicable.		

Part II — Information for All Requests

		Yes	No
4	During the tax year of change, did or will the applicant (**a**) cease to engage in the trade or business to which the requested change relates, or (**b**) terminate its existence? See instructions . . .		×
5	Is the applicant requesting to change to the principal method in the tax year of change under Regulations section 1.381(c)(4)-1(d)(1) or 1.381(c)(5)-1(d)(1)? . . . If "No," go to line 6a. If "Yes," the applicant cannot file a Form 3115 for this change. See instructions.		×

Sign Here

Under penalties of perjury, I declare that I have examined this application, including accompanying schedules and statements, and to the best of my knowledge and belief, the application contains all the relevant facts relating to the application, and it is true, correct, and complete. Declaration of preparer (other than applicant) is based on all information of which preparer has any knowledge.

Signature of filer (and spouse, if joint return)	Date	Name and title (print or type)
		Jack and Jill Hill, Taxpayers

Preparer (other than filer/applicant)

Print/Type preparer's name	Preparer's signature	Date
Toni Smith		
Firm's name **Smith Tax Service**		

For Privacy Act and Paperwork Reduction Act Notice, see the instructions. Cat. No. 19280E Form **3115** (Rev. 12-2022)

For Example 36

Form 3115 (Rev. 12-2022) Page **2**

Part II	**Information for All Requests** *(continued)*	**Yes**	**No**
6a	Does the applicant (or any present or former consolidated group in which the applicant was a member during the applicable tax year(s)) have any federal income tax return(s) under examination (see instructions)? . . . . . If "No," go to line 7a.		×
b	Is the method of accounting the applicant is requesting to change an issue under consideration (with respect to either the applicant or any present or former consolidated group in which the applicant was a member during the applicable tax year(s))? See instructions		
c	Enter the name and telephone number of the examining agent and the tax year(s) under examination. Name ______ Telephone number ______ Tax year(s) ______		
d	Has a copy of this Form 3115 been provided to the examining agent identified on line 6c?		
7a	Does audit protection apply to the applicant's requested change in method of accounting? See instructions . . If "No," attach an explanation.		×
b	If "Yes," check the applicable box and attach the required statement. ☐ Not under exam ☐ 3-month window ☐ 120 day: Date examination ended ______ ☐ Method not before director ☐ Negative adjustment ☐ CAP: Date member joined group ______ ☐ Audit protection at end of exam ☐ Other		
8a	Does the applicant (or any present or former consolidated group in which the applicant was a member during the applicable tax year(s)) have any federal income tax return(s) before Appeals and/or a federal court? . . . . . If "No," go to line 9.		×
b	Is the method of accounting the applicant is requesting to change an issue under consideration by Appeals and/or a federal court (for either the applicant or any present or former consolidated group in which the applicant was a member for the tax year(s) the applicant was a member)? See instructions . . . . If "Yes," attach an explanation.		
c	If "Yes," enter the name of the (check the box) ☐ Appeals officer and/or ☐ counsel for the government, telephone number, and the tax year(s) before Appeals and/or a federal court. Name ______ Telephone number ______ Tax year(s) ______		
d	Has a copy of this Form 3115 been provided to the Appeals officer and/or counsel for the government identified on line 8c?		
9	If the applicant answered "Yes" to line 6a and/or 8a with respect to any present or former consolidated group, attach a statement that provides each parent corporation's (**a**) name, (**b**) identification number, (**c**) address, and (**d**) tax year(s) during which the applicant was a member that is under examination, before an Appeals office, and/or before a federal court.		
10	If for federal income tax purposes, the applicant is either an entity (including a limited liability company) treated as a partnership or an S corporation, is it requesting a change from a method of accounting that is an issue under consideration in an examination, before Appeals, or before a federal court, with respect to a federal income tax return of a partner, member, or shareholder of that entity?		×
11a	Has the applicant, its predecessor, or a related party requested or made (under either an automatic or non-automatic change procedure) a change in method of accounting within any of the 5 tax years ending with the tax year of change? . . . . If "No," go to line 12.		×
b	If "Yes," for each trade or business, attach a description of each requested change in method of accounting (including the tax year of change) and state whether the applicant received consent.		
c	If any application was withdrawn, not perfected, or denied, or if a Consent Agreement granting a change was not signed and returned to the IRS, or the change was not made or not made in the requested year of change, attach an explanation.		
12	Does the applicant, its predecessor, or a related party currently have pending any request (including any concurrently filed request) for a private letter ruling, change in method of accounting, or technical advice? . . . If "Yes," for each request attach a statement providing (**a**) the name(s) of the taxpayer, (**b**) identification number(s), (**c**) the type of request (private letter ruling, change in method of accounting, or technical advice), and (**d**) the specific issue(s) in the request(s).		×
13	Is the applicant requesting to change its **overall** method of accounting? . . . . If "Yes," complete Schedule A on page 4 of the form.		

Form **3115** (Rev. 12-2022)

7

For Example 36

Form 3115 (Rev. 12-2022) Page **3**

Part II	**Information for All Requests** *(continued)*	**Yes**	**No**
14	If the applicant is either **(i) not** changing its overall method of accounting, or **(ii)** changing its overall method of accounting **and** changing to a special method of accounting for one or more items, attach a detailed and complete description for each of the following (see instructions):		
a	The item(s) being changed.		
b	The applicant's present method for the item(s) being changed.		
c	The applicant's proposed method for the item(s) being changed.		
d	The applicant's present overall method of accounting (cash, accrual, or hybrid).		
15a	Attach a detailed and complete description of the applicant's trade(s) or business(es). See section 446(d).		
b	If the applicant has more than one trade or business, as defined in Regulations section 1.446-1(d), describe **(i)** whether each trade or business is accounted for separately; **(ii)** the goods and services provided by each trade or business and any other types of activities engaged in that generate gross income; **(iii)** the overall method of accounting for each trade or business; and **(iv)** which trade or business is requesting to change its accounting method as part of this application or a separate application.		
	Note: If you are requesting an automatic method change, see the instructions to see if you are required to complete lines 16a–16c.		
16a	Attach a full explanation of the legal basis supporting the proposed method for the item being changed. Include a detailed and complete description of the facts that explains how the law specifically applies to the applicant's situation and that demonstrates that the applicant is authorized to use the proposed method.		
b	Include all authority (statutes, regulations, published rulings, court cases, etc.) supporting the proposed method.		
c	Include either a discussion of the contrary authorities or a statement that no contrary authority exists.		
17	Will the proposed method of accounting be used for the applicant's books and records and financial statements? For insurance companies, see the instructions		
	If "No," attach an explanation.		
18	Does the applicant request a conference with the IRS National Office if the IRS National Office proposes an adverse response?		×
19a	If the applicant is changing to either the overall cash method, an overall accrual method, or is changing its method of accounting for any property subject to section 263A, any long-term contract subject to section 460 (see 19b), or inventories subject to section 471 or 474, enter the applicant's gross receipts for the 3 tax years preceding the tax year of change.		

1st preceding year ended: mo. yr.	2nd preceding year ended: mo. yr.	3rd preceding year ended: mo. yr.
$	$	$

b	If the applicant is changing its method of accounting for any long-term contract subject to section 460, in addition to completing 19a, enter the applicant's gross receipts for the 4th tax year preceding the tax year of change: 4th preceding year ended: mo. ______ yr. ____ $ __________		

Part III	**Information for Non-Automatic Change Request**	**Yes**	**No**
20	Is the applicant's requested change described in any revenue procedure, revenue ruling, notice, regulation, or other published guidance as an automatic change request?		
	If "Yes," attach an explanation describing why the applicant is submitting its request under the non-automatic change procedures.		
21	Attach a copy of all documents related to the proposed change (see instructions).		
22	Attach a statement of the applicant's reasons for the proposed change.		
23	If the applicant is a member of a consolidated group for the year of change, do all other members of the consolidated group use the proposed method of accounting for the item being changed?		
	If "No," attach an explanation.		
24a	Enter the amount of **user fee** attached to this application (see instructions) . . . . . . $ __________		
b	If the applicant qualifies for a reduced user fee, attach the required information or certification (see instructions).		

Form **3115** (Rev. 12-2022)

For Example 36

Part IV	**Section 481(a) Adjustment**	**Yes**	**No**
25	Does published guidance require the applicant (or permit the applicant and the applicant is electing) to implement the requested change in method of accounting on a cut-off basis? . . . . If "Yes," attach an explanation and do not complete lines 26, 27, 28, and 29 below.		
26	Enter the section 481(a) adjustment. Indicate whether the adjustment is an increase (+) or a decrease (-) in income. $ **(63,091)** Attach a summary of the computation and an explanation of the methodology used to determine the section 481(a) adjustment. If it is based on more than one component, show the computation for each component. If the applicant waived any deductions with respect to the method of accounting pursuant to Regulations section 1.59A-3(c)(6)(i), include a summary of the waived deductions. If more than one applicant is applying for the method change on the application, attach a list of the (**a**) name, (**b**) identification number, and (**c**) the amount of the section 481(a) adjustment attributable to each applicant.		
27	Is the applicant required to take into account in the year of change any remaining portion of a section 481(a) adjustment from a prior change (see instructions)? If "Yes," enter the amount. $ ______		
28	Is the applicant making an election to take the entire amount of the adjustment into account in the tax year of change? If "Yes," check the box for the applicable elective provision used to make the election (see instructions). ☐ $50,000 de minimis election ☐ Eligible acquisition transaction election		
29	Is any part of the section 481(a) adjustment attributable to transactions between members of an affiliated group, a consolidated group, a controlled group, or other related parties? . . . . If "Yes," attach an explanation.		

...le A—Change in Overall Method of Accounting (If Schedule A applies, Part I below must be completed.)

11 Other costs ...

Schedule E—Change in Depreciation or Amortization (see instructions)

Applicants requesting approval to change their method of accounting for depreciation or amortization complete this section. Applicants ***must*** provide this information for each item or class of property for which a change is requested.

Note: See the ***Summary of the List of Automatic Accounting Method Changes*** in the instructions for information regarding automatic changes under sections 56, 167, 168, or 197, or former sections 168, 1400I, or 1400L. **Do not** file Form 3115 with respect to certain late elections and election revocations. See instructions.

1 Is depreciation for the property determined under Regulations section 1.167(a)-11 (CLADR)? . . . . ☐ **Yes** ☒ **No**
If "Yes," the only changes permitted are under Regulations section 1.167(a)-11(c)(1)(iii).

2 Is any of the depreciation or amortization required to be capitalized under any Code section, such as section 263A? . . . . ☐ **Yes** ☒ **No**
If "Yes," enter the applicable section ______

3 Has a depreciation, amortization, expense, or disposition election been made for the property, such as the election under sections 168(f)(1), 168(i)(4), 179, 179C, or Regulations section 1.168(i)-8(d)? . . . . ☐ **Yes** ☒ **No**
If "Yes," state the election made ______

4a Attach a statement describing the property subject to the change. Include the property's description, type, placed-in-service year, and use in the applicant's trade or business or income-producing activity. Also include the type and amount of any federal tax credit claimed or grant received, along with any necessary adjustments to basis required under the Internal Revenue Code, with respect to the property.

b If the property is residential rental property, did the applicant live in the property before renting it? . . ☐ **Yes** ☒ **No**

c Is the property public utility property? . . . . ☐ **Yes** ☒ **No**

5 To the extent not already provided in the applicant's description of its present method, attach a statement explaining how the ...

7

For Example 36

Jack and Jill Hill SS# ***-**-3115 & ***-**-4887

FORM 3115 ATTACHMENT

This Form 3115 is filed for the following properties:

E1	A	4200 Elm St Urbana, IL 61801
E1	B	4000 Elm St Urbana, IL 61801
E2	A	8000 Beech St Urbana, IL 61801
E2	B	8200 Maple St Urbana, IL 61801

Note: No change is being made for property C (6900 Aspen Point) on Schedule E, Copy 1 because this property was placed in service in 2023.

Part II

Q14 a. **Items being changed:** Depreciation of residential real estate used in rental activity

b. **Present method:** No depreciation was taken

c. **Proposed method:** Calculate depreciation using 27.5-year life starting when properties purchased.

d. **Present overall accounting method:** Cash

Part IV

Q26 The correct amount of depreciation for each property is calculated using straight-line, mid-month convention over 27.5 years.

Property E1A: 4200 Elm St Urbana, IL 61801

The cost of the real estate including improvements was $46,000. The amount of the cost allocated to land is $7,360 based on the county assessor records.

		Improper Depr.	Per Year	Proper Depr.	IRC §481 Adj.
1	2010	$0	$ 293	$ 293	($ 293)
2	2011 through 2022	0	1,405	16,860	(16,860)
					($17,153)

Property E1B: 4000 Elm St Urbana, IL 61801

The cost of the real estate including improvements was $44,500. The amount of the cost allocated to land is $6,120 based on the county assessor records.

		Improper Depr.	Per Year	Proper Depr.	IRC §481 Adj.
1	2022	$0	$291	$291	($291)
					($291)

For Example 36

Property E2A: 8000 Beech St Urbana, IL 61801

The cost of the real estate including improvements was $65,000. The amount of the cost allocated to land is $2,922 based on the county assessor records.

		Improper Depr.	Per Year	Proper Depr.	IRC §481 Adj.
1	2011	$0	$1,223	$ 1,223	($ 1,223)
2	2012 through 2022	0	2,257	24,829	(24,829)
					($26,052)

Property E2B: 8200 Maple St Urbana, IL 61801

The cost of the real estate including improvements was $80,000. The amount of the cost allocated to land is $2,556 based on the county assessor records.

		Improper Depr.	Per Year	Proper Depr.	IRC §481 Adj.
1	2015	$0	$2,699	$ 2,699	($ 2,699)
2	2016 through 2021	0	2,816	16,896	(16,896)
					($19,595)

Schedule E - Change in Depreciation or Amortization

5	See Q14b above	
7a	Code section under which the property is depreciated:	IRC §167
7b	Asset class:	Residential real estate
7c	Facts in support of method:	See above
7d	Depr method:	§168(b)(3)(B)— Straight line
7e	Recovery period:	27.5 years
7f	Convention:	Mid-month convention
7g	First-year special depreciation allowance not claimed for any of the properties because the properties were not eligible.	

7

Table B-1. **Table of Class Lives and Recovery Periods**

Asset class	Description of assets included	Class Life (in years)	Recovery Periods (in years) GDS (MACRS)	ADS
	SPECIFIC DEPRECIABLE ASSETS USED IN ALL BUSINESS ACTIVITIES, EXCEPT AS NOTED:			
00.11	**Office Furniture, Fixtures, and Equipment:** Includes furniture and fixtures that are not a structural component of a building. Includes such assets as desks, files, safes, and communications equipment. Does not include communications equipment that is included in other classes.	10	7	10
00.12	**Information Systems:** Includes computers and their peripheral equipment used in administering normal business transactions and the maintenance of business records, their retrieval and analysis. Information systems are defined as: 1) Computers: A computer is a programmable electronically activated device capable of accepting information, applying prescribed processes to the information, and supplying the results of these processes with or without human intervention. It usually consists of a central processing unit containing extensive storage, logic, arithmetic, and control capabilities. Excluded from this category are adding machines, electronic desk calculators, etc., and other equipment described in class 00.13. 2) Peripheral equipment consists of the auxiliary machines which are designed to be placed under control of the central processing unit. Nonlimiting examples are: Card readers, card punches, magnetic tape feeds, high speed printers, optical character readers, tape cassettes, mass storage units, paper tape equipment, keypunches, data entry devices, teleprinters, terminals, tape drives, disc drives, disc files, disc packs, visual image projector tubes, card sorters, plotters, and collators. Peripheral equipment may be used online or offline. Does not incude equipment that is an integral part of other capital equipment that is included in other classes of economic activity, that is, computers used primarily for process or production control, switching, channeling, and automating distributive trades and services such as point of sale (POS) computer systems. Also, does not include equipment of a kind used primarily for amusement or entertainment of the user.	6	5	5
00.13	**Data Handling Equipment; except Computers:** Includes only typewriters, calculators, adding and accounting machines, copiers, and duplicating equipment.	6	5	6
00.21	**Airplanes (airframes and engines), except those used in commercial or contract carrying of passengers or freight, and all helicopters (airframes and engines)**	6	5	6
00.22	**Automobiles, Taxis**	3	5	5
00.23	**Buses**	9	5	9
00.241	**Light General Purpose Trucks:** Includes trucks for use over the road (actual weight less than 13,000 pounds)	4	5	5
00.242	**Heavy General Purpose Trucks:** Includes heavy general purpose trucks, concrete ready mix-trucks, and ore trucks, for use over the road (actual unloaded weight 13,000 pounds or more)	6	5	6
00.25	**Railroad Cars and Locomotives, except those owned by railroad transportation companies**	15	7	15
00.26	**Tractor Units for Use Over-the-Road**	4	3	4
00.27	**Trailers and Trailer-Mounted Containers**	6	5	6
00.28	**Vessels, Barges, Tugs, and Similar Water Transportation Equipment, except those used in marine construction**	18	10	18
00.3	**Land Improvements:** Includes improvements directly to or added to land, whether such improvements are section 1245 property or section 1250 property, provided such improvements are depreciable. Examples of such assets might include sidewalks, roads, canals, waterways, drainage facilities, sewers (not including municipal sewers in class 51), wharves and docks, bridges, fences, landscaping shrubbery, or radio and television transmitting towers. Does not include land improvements that are explicitly included in any other class, and buildings and structural components as defined in section 1.48-1(e) of the regulations. Excludes public utility initial clearing and grading land improvements as specified in Rev. Rul. 72-403, 1972-2 C.B. 102.	20	15	20
00.4	**Industrial Steam and Electric Generation and/or Distribution Systems:** Includes assets, whether such assets are section 1245 property or 1250 property, providing such assets are depreciable, used in the production and/or distribution of electricity with rated total capacity in excess of 500 Kilowatts and/or assets used in the production and/or distribution of steam with rated total capacity in excess of 12,500 pounds per hour for use by the taxpayer in its industrial manufacturing process or plant activity and not ordinarily available for sale to others. Does not include buildings and structural components as defined in section 1.48-1(e) of the regulations. Assets used to generate and/or distribute electricity or steam of the type described above, but of lesser rated capacity, are not included, but are included in the appropriate manufacturing equipment classes elsewhere specified. Also includes electric generating and steam distribution assets, which may utilize steam produced by a waste reduction and resource recovery plant, used by the taxpayer in its industrial manufacturing process or plant activity. Steam and chemical recovery boiler systems used for the recovery and regeneration of chemicals used in manufacturing, with rated capacity in excess of that described above, with specifically related distribution and return systems are not included but are included in appropriate manufacturing equipment classes elsewhere specified. An example of an excluded steam and chemical recovery boiler system is that used in the pulp and paper manufacturing equipment classes elsewhere specified. An example of an excluded steam and chemical recovery boiler system is that used in the pulp and paper manufacturing industry.	22	15	22

Table B-2. **Table of Class Lives and Recovery Periods**

Asset class	Description of assets included	Class Life (in years)	Recovery Periods (in years)	
			GDS (MACRS)	ADS
	DEPRECIABLE ASSETS USED IN THE FOLLOWING ACTIVITIES:			
01.1	**Agriculture:** Includes machinery and equipment, grain bins, and fences but no other land improvements, that are used in the production of crops or plants, vines, and trees; livestock; the operation of farm dairies, nurseries, greenhouses, sod farms, mushroom cellars, cranberry bogs, apiaries, and fur farms; the performance of agriculture, animal husbandry, and horticultural services.	10	7****	10
01.11	**Cotton Ginning Assets**	12	7	12
01.21	**Cattle, Breeding or Dairy**	7	5	7
01.221	**Any breeding or work horse that is 12 years old or less at the time it is placed in service****	10	7	10
01.222	**Any breeding or work horse that is more than 12 years old at the time it is placed in service****	10	3	10
01.223	**Any race horse that is more than 2 years old at the time it is placed in service****	*	3	12
01.224	**Any horse that is more than 12 years old at the time it is placed in service and that is neither a race horse nor a horse described in class 01.222****	*	3	12
01.225	**Any horse not described in class 01.221, 01.222, 01.223, or 01.224**	*	7	12
01.23	**Hogs, Breeding**	3	3	3
01.24	**Sheep and Goats, Breeding**	5	5	5
01.3	**Farm buildings except structures included in class 01.4**	25	20	25
01.4	**Single purpose agricultural or horticultural structures (within the meaning of section 168(i)(13) of the Code)**	15	10***	15
10.0	**Mining:** Includes assets used in the mining and quarrying of metallic and nonmetallic minerals (including sand, gravel, stone, and clay) and the milling, beneficiation, and other primary preparation of such materials.	10	7	10
13.0	**Offshore Drilling:** Includes assets used in offshore drilling for oil and gas such as floating, self-propelled and other drilling vessels, barges, platforms, and drilling equipment and support vessels such as tenders, barges, towboats, and crewboats. Excludes oil and gas production assets.	7.5	5	7.5
13.1	**Drilling of Oil and Gas Wells:** Includes assets used in the drilling of onshore oil and gas wells and the provision of geophysical and other exploration services; and the provision of such oil and gas field services as chemical treatment, plugging and abandoning of wells, and cementing or perforating well casings. Does not include assets used in the performance of any of these activities and services by integrated petroleum and natural gas producers for their own account.	6	5	6
13.2	**Exploration for and Production of Petroleum and Natural Gas Deposits:** Includes assets used by petroleum and natural gas producers for drilling of wells and production of petroleum and natural gas, including gathering pipelines and related storage facilities. Also includes petroleum and natural gas offshore transportation facilities used by producers and others consisting of platforms (other than drilling platforms classified in class 13.0), compression or pumping equipment, and gathering and transmission lines to the first onshore transshipment facility. The assets used in the first onshore transshipment facility are also included and consist of separation equipment (used for separation of natural gas, liquids, and in class 49.23), and liquid holding or storage facilities (other than those classified in class 49.25). Does not include support vessels.	14	7	14
13.3	**Petroleum Refining:** Includes assets used for the distillation, fractionation, and catalytic cracking of crude petroleum into gasoline and its other components.	16	10	16
15.0	**Construction:** Includes assets used in construction by general building, special trade, heavy, and marine construction contractors; operative and investment builders; real estate subdividers and developers; and others except railroads.	6	5	6
20.1	**Manufacture of Grain and Grain Mill Products:** Includes assets used in the production of flours, cereals, livestock feeds, and other grain and grain mill products.	17	10	17
20.2	**Manufacture of Sugar and Sugar Products:** Includes assets used in the production of raw sugar, syrup, or finished sugar from sugar cane or sugar beets.	18	10	18
20.3	**Manufacture of Vegetable Oils and Vegetable Oil Products:** Includes assets used in the production of oil from vegetable materials and the manufacture of related vegetable oil products.	18	10	18
20.4	**Manufacture of Other Food and Kindred Products:** Includes assets used in the production of foods and beverages not included in classes 20.1, 20.2, and 20.3.	12	7	12
20.5	**Manufacture of Food and Beverages—Special Handling Devices:** Includes assets defined as specialized materials handling devices such as returnable pallets, palletized containers, and fish processing equipment including boxes, baskets, carts, and flaking trays used in activities as defined in classes 20.1, 20.2, 20.3, and 20.4. Does not include general purpose small tools such as wrenches and drills, both hand and power-driven, and other general purpose equipment such as conveyors, transfer equipment, and materials handling devices.	4	3	4

* Property described in asset classes 01.223, 01.224, and 01.225 are assigned recovery periods but have no class lives.

** A horse is more than 2 (or 12) years old after the day that is 24 (or 144) months after its actual birthdate.

*** 7 if property was placed in service before 1989.

**** 5 if machinery and equipment used in a farming business (other than any grain bin, cotton ginning asset, fence, or other land improvement) placed in service after 2017, in tax years ending after 2017.

Table B-2. **Table of Class Lives and Recovery Periods**

Asset class	Description of assets included	Class Life (in years)	Recovery Periods (in years) GDS (MACRS)	ADS
21.0	**Manufacture of Tobacco and Tobacco Products:** Includes assets used in the production of cigarettes, cigars, smoking and chewing tobacco, snuff, and other tobacco products.	15	7	15
22.1	**Manufacture of Knitted Goods:** Includes assets used in the production of knitted and netted fabrics and lace. Assets used in yarn preparation, bleaching, dyeing, printing, and other similar finishing processes, texturing, and packaging are elsewhere classified.	7.5	5	7.5
22.2	**Manufacture of Yarn, Thread, and Woven Fabric:** Includes assets used in the production of spun yarns including the preparing, blending, spinning, and twisting of fibers into yarns and threads, the preparation of yarns such as twisting, warping, and winding, the production of covered elastic yarn and thread, cordage, woven fabric, tire fabric, braided fabric, twisted jute for packaging, mattresses, pads, sheets, and industrial belts, and the processing of textile mill waste to recover fibers, flocks, and shoddies. Assets used to manufacture carpets, man-made fibers, and nonwovens, and assets used in texturing, bleaching, dyeing, printing, and other similar finishing processes, are elsewhere classified.	11	7	11
22.3	**Manufacture of Carpets and Dyeing, Finishing, and Packaging of Textile Products and Manufacture of Medical and Dental Supplies:** Includes assets used in the production of carpets, rugs, mats, woven carpet backing, chenille, and other tufted products, and assets used in the joining together of backing with carpet yarn or fabric. Includes assets used in washing, scouring, bleaching, dyeing, printing, drying, and similar finishing processes applied to textile fabrics, yarns, threads, and other textile goods. Includes assets used in the production and packaging of textile products, other than apparel, by creasing, forming, trimming, cutting, and sewing, such as the preparation of carpet and fabric samples, or similar joining together processes (other than the production of scrim reinforced paper products and laminated paper products) such as the sewing and folding of hosiery and panty hose, and the creasing, folding, trimming, and cutting of fabrics to produce nonwoven products, such as disposable diapers and sanitary products. Also includes assets used in the production of medical and dental supplies other than drugs and medicines. Assets used in the manufacture of nonwoven carpet backing, and hard surface floor covering such as tile, rubber, and cork, are elsewhere classified.	9	5	9
22.4	**Manufacture of Textile Yarns:** Includes assets used in the processing of yarns to impart bulk and/or stretch properties to the yarn. The principal machines involved are falsetwist, draw, beam-to-beam, and stuffer box texturing equipment and related highspeed twisters and winders. Assets, as described above, which are used to further process man-made fibers are elsewhere classified when located in the same plant in an integrated operation with man-made fiber producing assets. Assets used to manufacture man-made fibers and assets used in bleaching, dyeing, printing, and other similar finishing processes are elsewhere classified.	8	5	8
22.5	**Manufacture of Nonwoven Fabrics:** Includes assets used in the production of nonwoven fabrics, felt goods including felt hats, padding, batting, wadding, oakum, and fillings, from new materials and from textile mill waste. Nonwoven fabrics are defined as fabrics (other than reinforced and laminated composites consisting of nonwovens and other products) manufactured by bonding natural and/or synthetic fibers and/or filaments by means of induced mechanical interlocking, fluid entanglement, chemical adhesion, thermal or solvent reaction, or by combination thereof other than natural hydration bonding as occurs with natural cellulose fibers. Such means include resin bonding, web bonding, and melt bonding. Specifically includes assets used to make flocked and needle punched products other than carpets and rugs. Assets, as described above, which are used to manufacture nonwovens are elsewhere classified when located in the same plant in an integrated operation with man-made fiber producing assets. Assets used to manufacture man-made fibers and assets used in bleaching, dyeing, printing, and other similar finishing processes are elsewhere classified.	10	7	10
23.0	**Manufacture of Apparel and Other Finished Products:** Includes assets used in the production of clothing and fabricated textile products by the cutting and sewing of woven fabrics, other textile products, and furs; but does not include assets used in the manufacture of apparel from rubber and leather.	9	5	9
24.1	**Cutting of Timber:** Includes logging machinery and equipment and roadbuilding equipment used by logging and sawmill operators and pulp manufacturers for their own account.	6	5	6
24.2	**Sawing of Dimensional Stock From Logs:** Includes machinery and equipment installed in permanent or well-established sawmills.	10	7	10
24.3	**Sawing of Dimensional Stock From Logs:** Includes machinery and equipment in sawmills characterized by temporary foundations and a lack, or minimum amount, of lumberhandling, drying, and residue disposal equipment and facilities.	6	5	6
24.4	**Manufacture of Wood Products, and Furniture:** Includes assets used in the production of plywood, hardboard, flooring, veneers, furniture, and other wood products, including the treatment of poles and timber.	10	7	10
26.1	**Manufacture of Pulp and Paper:** Includes assets for pulp materials handling and storage, pulp mill processing, bleach processing, paper and paperboard manufacturing, and on-line finishing. Includes pollution control assets and all land improvements associated with the factory site or production process such as effluent ponds and canals, provided such improvements are depreciable but does not include buildings and structural components as defined in section 1.48-1(e)(1) of the regulations. Includes steam and chemical recovery boiler systems, with any rated capacity, used for the recovery and regeneration of chemicals used in manufacturing. Does not include assets used either in pulpwood logging, or in the manufacture of hardboard.	13	7	13

Table B-2. **Table of Class Lives and Recovery Periods**

Asset class	Description of assets included	Class Life (in years)	Recovery Periods (in years)	
			GDS (MACRS)	ADS
26.2	**Manufacture of Converted Paper, Paperboard, and Pulp Products:** Includes assets used for modification, or remanufacture of paper and pulp into converted products, such as paper coated off the paper machine, paper bags, paper boxes, cartons, and envelopes. Does not include assets used for manufacture of nonwovens that are elsewhere classified.	10	7	10
27.0	**Printing, Publishing, and Allied Industries:** Includes assets used in printing by one or more processes, such as letter-press, lithography, gravure, or screen; the performance of services for the printing trade, such as bookbinding, typesetting, engraving, photo-engraving, and electrotyping; and the publication of newspapers, books, and periodicals.	11	7	11
28.0	**Manufacture of Chemicals and Allied Products:** Includes assets used to manufacture basic organic and inorganic chemicals; chemical products to be used in further manufacture, such as synthetic fibers and plastics materials; and finished chemical products. Includes assets used to further process man-made fibers, to manufacture plastic film, and to manufacture nonwoven fabrics, when such assets are located in the same plant in an integrated operation with chemical products producing assets. Also includes assets used to manufacture photographic supplies, such as film, photographic paper, sensitized photographic paper, and developing chemicals. Includes all land improvements associated with plant site or production processes, such as effluent ponds and canals, provided such land improvements are depreciable but does not include buildings and structural components as defined in section 1.48-1(e) of the regulations. Does not include assets used in the manufacture of finished rubber and plastic products or in the production of natural gas products, butane, propane, and by-products of natural gas production plants.	9.5	5	9.5
30.1	**Manufacture of Rubber Products:** Includes assets used for the production of products from natural, synthetic, or reclaimed rubber, gutta percha, balata, or gutta siak, such as tires, tubes, rubber footwear, mechanical rubber goods, heels and soles, flooring, and rubber sundries; and in the recapping, retreading, and rebuilding of tires.	14	7	14
30.11	**Manufacture of Rubber Products—Special Tools and Devices:** Includes assets defined as special tools, such as jigs, dies, mandrels, molds, lasts, patterns, specialty containers, pallets, shells; and tire molds, and accessory parts such as rings and insert plates used in activities as defined in class 30.1. Does not include tire building drums and accessory parts and general purpose small tools such as wrenches and drills, both power and hand-driven, and other general purpose equipment such as conveyors and transfer equipment.	4	3	4
30.2	**Manufacture of Finished Plastic Products:** Includes assets used in the manufacture of plastics products and the molding of primary plastics for the trade. Does not include assets used in the manufacture of basic plastics materials nor the manufacture of phonograph records.	11	7	11
30.21	**Manufacture of Finished Plastic Products—Special Tools:** Includes assets defined as special tools, such as jigs, dies, fixtures, molds, patterns, gauges, and specialty transfer and shipping devices, used in activities as defined in class 30.2. Special tools are specifically designed for the production or processing of particular parts and have no significant utilitarian value and cannot be adapted to further or different use after changes or improvements are made in the model design of the particular part produced by the special tools. Does not include general purpose small tools such as wrenches and drills, both hand and power-driven, and other general purpose equipment such as conveyors, transfer equipment, and materials handling devices.	3.5	3	3.5
31.0	**Manufacture of Leather and Leather Products:** Includes assets used in the tanning, currying, and finishing of hides and skins; the processing of fur pelts; and the manufacture of finished leather products, such as footwear, belting, apparel, and luggage.	11	7	11
32.1	**Manufacture of Glass Products:** Includes assets used in the production of flat, blown, or pressed products of glass, such as float and window glass, glass containers, glassware, and fiberglass. Does not include assets used in the manufacture of lenses.	14	7	14
32.11	**Manufacture of Glass Products—Special Tools:** Includes assets defined as special tools such as molds, patterns, pallets, and specialty transfer and shipping devices such as steel racks to transport automotive glass, used in activities as defined in class 32.1. Special tools are specifically designed for the production or processing of particular parts and have no significant utilitarian value and cannot be adapted to further or different use after changes or improvements are made in the model design of the particular part produced by the special tools. Does not include general purpose small tools such as wrenches and drills, both hand and power-driven, and other general purpose equipment such as conveyors, transfer equipment, and materials handling devices.	2.5	3	2.5
32.2	**Manufacture of Cement:** Includes assets used in the production of cement, but does not include assets used in the manufacture of concrete and concrete products nor in any mining or extraction process.	20	15	20
32.3	**Manufacture of Other Stone and Clay Products:** Includes assets used in the manufacture of products from materials in the form of clay and stone, such as brick, tile, and pipe; pottery and related products, such as vitreous-china, plumbing fixtures, earthenware, and ceramic insulating materials; and also includes assets used in manufacture of concrete and concrete products. Does not include assets used in any mining or extraction processes.	15	7	15

Table B-2. **Table of Class Lives and Recovery Periods**

Asset class	Description of assets included	Class Life (in years)	Recovery Periods (in years) GDS (MACRS)	ADS
33.2	**Manufacture of Primary Nonferrous Metals:** Includes assets used in the smelting, refining, and electrolysis of nonferrous metals from ore, pig, or scrap, the rolling, drawing, and alloying of nonferrous metals; the manufacture of castings, forgings, and other basic products of nonferrous metals; and the manufacture of nails, spikes, structural shapes, tubing, wire, and cable.	14	7	14
33.21	**Manufacture of Primary Nonferrous Metals—Special Tools:** Includes assets defined as special tools such as dies, jigs, molds, patterns, fixtures, gauges, and drawings concerning such special tools used in the activities as defined in class 33.2, Manufacture of Primary Nonferrous Metals. Special tools are specifically designed for the production or processing of particular products or parts and have no significant utilitarian value and cannot be adapted to further or different use after changes or improvements are made in the model design of the particular part produced by the special tools. Does not include general purpose small tools such as wrenches and drills, both hand and power-driven, and other general purpose equipment such as conveyors, transfer equipment, and materials handling devices. Rolls, mandrels, and refractories are not included in class 33.21 but are included in class 33.2.	6.5	5	6.5
33.3	**Manufacture of Foundry Products:** Includes assets used in the casting of iron and steel, including related operations such as molding and coremaking. Also includes assets used in the finishing of castings and patternmaking when performed at the foundry, all special tools, and related land improvements.	14	7	14
33.4	**Manufacture of Primary Steel Mill Products:** Includes assets used in the smelting, reduction, and refining of iron and steel from ore, pig, or scrap; the rolling, drawing, and alloying of steel; the manufacture of nails, spikes, structural shapes, tubing, wire, and cable. Includes assets used by steel service centers and ferrous metal forges, and assets used in coke production, regardless of ownership. Also includes related land improvements and all special tools used in the above activities.	15	7	15
34.0	**Manufacture of Fabricated Metal Products:** Includes assets used in the production of metal cans, tinware, fabricated structural metal products, metal stampings, and other ferrous and nonferrous metal and wire products not elsewhere classified. Does not include assets used to manufacture non-electric heating apparatus.	12	7	12
34.01	**Manufacture of Fabricated Metal Products—Special Tools:** Includes assets defined as special tools such as dies, jigs, molds, patterns, fixtures, gauges, and returnable containers and drawings concerning such special tools used in the activities as defined in class 34.0. Special tools are specifically designed for the production or processing of particular machine components, products, or parts, and have no significant utilitarian value and cannot be adapted to further or different use after changes or improvements are made in the model design of the particular part produced by the special tools. Does not include general small tools such as wrenches and drills, both hand and power-driven, and other general purpose equipment such as conveyors, transfer equipment, and materials handling devices.	3	3	3
35.0	**Manufacture of Electrical and Non-Electrical Machinery and Other Mechanical Products:** Includes assets used to manufacture or rebuild finished machinery and equipment and replacement parts thereof such as machine tools, general industrial and special industry machinery, electrical power generation, transmission, and distribution systems, space heating, cooling, and refrigeration systems, commercial and home appliances, farm and garden machinery, construction machinery, mining and oil field machinery, internal combustion engines (except those elsewhere classified), turbines (except those that power airborne vehicles), batteries, lamps and lighting fixtures, carbon and graphite products, and electromechanical and mechanical products including business machines, instruments, watches and clocks, vending and amusement machines, photographic equipment, medical and dental equipment and appliances, and ophthalmic goods. Includes assets used by manufacturers or rebuilders of such finished machinery and equipment in activities elsewhere classified such as the manufacture of castings, forgings, rubber and plastic products, electronic subassemblies or other manufacturing activities if the interim products are used by the same manufacturer primarily in the manufacture, assembly, or rebuilding of such finished machinery and equipment. Does not include assets used in mining, assets used in the manufacture of primary ferrous and nonferrous metals, assets included in class 00.11 through 00.4, and assets elsewhere classified.	10	7	10
36.0	**Manufacture of Electronic Components, Products, and Systems:** Includes assets used in the manufacture of electronic communication, computation, instrumentation and control system, including airborne applications; also includes assets used in the manufacture of electronic products such as frequency and amplitude modulated transmitters and receivers, electronic switching stations, television cameras, video recorders, record players and tape recorders, computers and computer peripheral machines, and electronic instruments, watches, and clocks; also includes assets used in the manufacture of components, provided their primary use is products and systems defined above such as electron tubes, capacitors, coils, resistors, printed circuit substrates, switches, harness cables, lasers, fiber optic devices, and magnetic media devices. Specifically excludes assets used to manufacture electronic products and components, photocopiers, typewriters, postage meters and other electromechanical and mechanical business machines and instruments that are elsewhere classified. Does not include semiconductor manufacturing equipment included in class 36.1.	6	5	6
36.1	**Any Semiconductor Manufacturing Equipment**	5	5	5

Table B-2. **Table of Class Lives and Recovery Periods**

Asset class	Description of assets included	Class Life (in years)	Recovery Periods (in years) GDS (MACRS)	ADS
37.11	**Manufacture of Motor Vehicles:** Includes assets used in the manufacture and assembly of finished automobiles, trucks, trailers, motor homes, and buses. Does not include assets used in mining, printing and publishing, production of primary metals, electricity, or steam, or the manufacture of glass, industrial chemicals, batteries, or rubber products, which are classified elsewhere. Includes assets used in manufacturing activities elsewhere classified other than those excluded above, where such activities are incidental to and an integral part of the manufacture and assembly of finished motor vehicles such as the manufacture of parts and subassemblies of fabricated metal products, electrical equipment, textiles, plastics, leather, and foundry and forging operations. Does not include any assets not classified in manufacturing activity classes, for example, does not include any assets classified in asset guideline classes 00.11 through 00.4. Activities will be considered incidental to the manufacture and assembly of finished motor vehicles only if 75% or more of the value of the products produced under one roof are used for the manufacture and assembly of finished motor vehicles. Parts that are produced as a normal replacement stock complement in connection with the manufacture and assembly of finished motor vehicles are considered used for the manufacture assembly of finished motor vehicles. Does not include assets used in the manufacture of component parts if these assets are used by taxpayers not engaged in the assembly of finished motor vehicles.	12	7	12
37.12	**Manufacture of Motor Vehicles—Special Tools:** Includes assets defined as special tools, such as jigs, dies, fixtures, molds, patterns, gauges, and specialty transfer and shipping devices, owned by manufacturers of finished motor vehicles and used in qualified activities as defined in class 37.11. Special tools are specifically designed for the production or processing of particular motor vehicle components and have no significant utilitarian value, and cannot be adapted to further or different use, after changes or improvements are made in the model design of the particular part produced by the special tools. Does not include general purpose small tools such as wrenches and drills, both hand and power-driven, and other general purpose equipment such as conveyors, transfer equipment, and materials handling devices.	3	3	3
37.2	**Manufacture of Aerospace Products:** Includes assets used in the manufacture and assembly of airborne vehicles and their component parts including hydraulic, pneumatic, electrical, and mechanical systems. Does not include assets used in the production of electronic airborne detection, guidance, control, radiation, computation, test, navigation, and communication equipment or the components thereof.	10	7	10
37.31	**Ship and Boat Building Machinery and Equipment:** Includes assets used in the manufacture and repair of ships, boats, caissons, marine drilling rigs, and special fabrications not included in asset classes 37.32 and 37.33. Specifically includes all manufacturing and repairing machinery and equipment, including machinery and equipment used in the operation of assets included in asset class 37.32. Excludes buildings and their structural components.	12	7	12
37.32	**Ship and Boat Building Dry Docks and Land Improvements:** Includes assets used in the manufacture and repair of ships, boats, caissons, marine drilling rigs, and special fabrications not included in asset classes 37.31 and 37.33. Specifically includes floating and fixed dry docks, ship basins, graving docks, shipways, piers, and all other land improvements such as water, sewer, and electric systems. Excludes buildings and their structural components.	16	10	16
37.33	**Ship and Boat Building—Special Tools:** Includes assets defined as special tools such as dies, jigs, molds, patterns, fixtures, gauges, and drawings concerning such special tools used in the activities defined in classes 37.31 and 37.32. Special tools are specifically designed for the production or processing of particular machine components, products, or parts, and have no significant utilitarian value and cannot be adapted to further or different use after changes or improvements are made in the model design of the particular part produced by the special tools. Does not include general purpose small tools such as wrenches and drills, both hand and power-driven, and other general purpose equipment such as conveyors, transfer equipment, and materials handling devices.	6.5	5	6.5
37.41	**Manufacture of Locomotives:** Includes assets used in building or rebuilding railroad locomotives (including mining and industrial locomotives). Does not include assets of railroad transportation companies or assets of companies which manufacture components of locomotives but do not manufacture finished locomotives.	11.5	7	11.5
37.42	**Manufacture of Railroad Cars:** Includes assets used in building or rebuilding railroad freight or passenger cars (including rail transit cars). Does not include assets of railroad transportation companies or assets of companies which manufacture components of railroad cars but do not manufacture finished railroad cars.	12	7	12
39.0	**Manufacture of Athletic, Jewelry, and Other Goods:** Includes assets used in the production of jewelry; musical instruments; toys and sporting goods; motion picture and television films and tapes; and pens, pencils, office and art supplies, brooms, brushes, caskets, etc. **Railroad Transportation:** Classes with the prefix 40 include the assets identified below that are used in the commercial and contract carrying of passengers and freight by rail. Assets of electrified railroads will be classified in a manner corresponding to that set forth below for railroads not independently operated as electric lines. Excludes the assets included in classes with the prefix beginning 00.1 and 00.2 above, and also excludes any non-depreciable assets included in Interstate Commerce Commission accounts enumerated for this class.	12	7	12

Table B-2. **Table of Class Lives and Recovery Periods**

Asset class	Description of assets included	Class Life (in years)	Recovery Periods (in years) GDS (MACRS)	ADS
40.1	**Railroad Machinery and Equipment:** Includes assets classified in the following Interstate Commerce Commission accounts: **Roadway accounts:** (16) Station and office buildings (freight handling machinery and equipment only) (25) TOFC/COFC terminals (freight handling machinery and equipment only) (26) Communication systems (27) Signals and interlockers (37) Roadway machines (44) Shop machinery **Equipment accounts:** (52) Locomotives (53) Freight train cars (54) Passenger train cars (57) Work equipment	14	7	14
40.2	**Railroad Structures and Similar Improvements:** Includes assets classified in the following Interstate Commerce Commission road accounts: (6) Bridges, trestles, and culverts (7) Elevated structures (13) Fences, snowsheds, and signs (16) Station and office buildings (stations and other operating structures only) (17) Roadway buildings (18) Water stations (19) Fuel stations (20) Shops and enginehouses (25) TOFC/COFC terminals (operating structures only) (31) Power transmission systems (35) Miscellaneous structures (39) Public improvements construction	30	20	30
40.3	**Railroad Wharves and Docks:** Includes assets classified in the following Interstate Commission Commerce accounts: (23) Wharves and docks (24) Coal and ore wharves	20	15	20
40.4	**Railroad Track**	10	7	10
40.51	**Railroad Hydraulic Electric Generating Equipment**	50	20	50
40.52	**Railroad Nuclear Electric Generating Equipment**	20	15	20
40.53	**Railroad Steam Electric Generating Equipment**	28	20	28
40.54	**Railroad Steam, Compressed Air, and Other Power Plan Equipment**	28	20	28
41.0	**Motor Transport—Passengers:** Includes assets used in the urban and interurban commercial and contract carrying of passengers by road, except the transportation assets included in classes with the prefix 00.2.	8	5	8
42.0	**Motor Transport—Freight:** Includes assets used in the commercial and contract carrying of freight by road, except the transportation assets included in classes with the prefix 00.2.	8	5	8
44.0	**Water Transportation:** Includes assets used in the commercial and contract carrying of freight and passengers by water except the transportation assets included in classes with the prefix 00.2. Includes all related land improvements.	20	15	20
45.0	**Air Transport:** Includes assets (except helicopters) used in commercial and contract carrying of passengers and freight by air. For purposes of section 1.167(a)-11(d)(2)(iv)(a) of the regulations, expenditures for "repair, maintenance, rehabilitation, or improvement" shall consist of direct maintenance expenses (irrespective of airworthiness provisions or charges) as defined by Civil Aeronautics Board uniform accounts 5200, maintenance burden (exclusive of expenses pertaining to maintenance buildings and improvements) as defined by Civil Aeronautics Board accounts 5300, and expenditures which are not "excluded additions" as defined in section 1.167(a)-11(d)(2)(vi) of the regulations and which would be charged to property and equipment accounts in the Civil Aeronautics Board uniform system of accounts.	12	7	12
45.1	**Air Transport (restricted):** Includes each asset described in the description of class 45.0 which was held by the taxpayer on April 15, 1976, or is acquired by the taxpayer pursuant to a contract which was, on April 15, 1976, and at all times thereafter, binding on the taxpayer. This criterion of classification based on binding contract concept is to be applied in the same manner as under the general rules expressed in sections 49(b)(1), (4), (5), and (8) of the Code (as in effect prior to its repeal by the Revenue Act of 1978, section 312(c)(1), (d), 1978-3 C.B. 1, 60).	6	5	6
46.0	**Pipeline Transportation:** Includes assets used in the private, commercial, and contract carrying of petroleum, gas, and other products by means of pipes and conveyors. The trunk lines and related storage facilities of integrated petroleum and natural gas producers are included in this class. Excludes initial clearing and grading land improvements as specified in Rev. Rul. 72-403, 1972-2 C.B. 102, but includes all other related land improvements.	22	15	22

Table B-2. **Table of Class Lives and Recovery Periods**

Asset class	Description of assets included	Class Life (in years)	Recovery Periods (in years) GDS (MACRS)	ADS
48.11	**Telephone Communications:** Includes the assets classified below and that are used in the provision of commercial and contract telephonic services such as: **Telephone Central Office Buildings:** Includes assets intended to house central office equipment, as defined in Federal Communications Commission Part 31 Account No. 212 whether section 1245 or section 1250 property.	45	20	45
48.12	**Telephone Central Office Equipment:** Includes central office switching and related equipment as defined in Federal Communications Commission Part 31 Account No. 221. Does not include computer-based telephone central office switching equipment included in class 48.121. Does not include private branch exchange (PBX) equipment.	18	10	18
48.121	**Computer-Based Telephone Central Office Switching Equipment:** Includes equipment whose functions are those of a computer or peripheral equipment (as defined in section 168(i)(2)(B) of the Code) used in its capacity as telephone central office equipment. Does not include private exchange (PBX) equipment.	9.5	5	9.5
48.13	**Telephone Station Equipment:** Includes such station apparatus and connections as teletypewriters, telephones, booths, private exchanges, and comparable equipment as defined in Federal Communications Commission Part 31 Account No. 231, 232, and 234.	10	7*	10*
48.14	**Telephone Distribution Plant:** Includes such assets as pole lines, cable, aerial wire, underground conduits, and comparable equipment, and related land improvements as defined in Federal Communications Commission Part 31 Account Nos. 241, 242.1, 242.2, 242.3, 242.4, 243, and 244.	24	15	24
48.2	**Radio and Television Broadcastings:** Includes assets used in radio and television broadcasting, except transmitting towers. **Telegraph, Ocean Cable, and Satellite Communications (TOCSC)** includes communications-related assets used to provide domestic and international radio-telegraph, wire-telegraph, ocean-cable, and satellite communications services; also includes related land improvements. If property described in classes 48.31–48.45 is comparable to telephone distribution plant described in class 48.14 and used for 2-way exchange of voice and data communication which is the equivalent of telephone communication, such property is assigned a class life of 24 years under this revenue procedure. Comparable equipment does not include cable television equipment used primarily for 1-way communication.	6	5	6
48.31	**TOCSC—Electric Power Generating and Distribution Systems:** Includes assets used in the provision of electric power by generation, modulation, rectification, channelization, control, and distribution. Does not include these assets when they are installed on customers' premises.	19	10	19
48.32	**TOCSC—High Frequency Radio and Microwave Systems:** Includes assets such as transmitters and receivers, antenna supporting structures, antennas, transmission lines from equipment to antenna, transmitter cooling systems, and control and amplification equipment. Does not include cable and long-line systems.	13	7	13
48.33	**TOCSC—Cable and Long-Line Systems:** Includes assets such as transmission lines, pole lines, ocean cables, buried cable and conduit, repeaters, repeater stations, and other related assets. Does not include high frequency radio or microwave systems.	26.5	20	26.5
48.34	**TOCSC—Central Office Control Equipment:** Includes assets for general control, switching, and monitoring of communications signals including electromechanical switching and channeling apparatus, multiplexing equipment patching and monitoring facilities, in-house cabling, teleprinter equipment, and associated site improvements.	16.5	10	16.5
48.35	**TOCSC—Computerized Switching, Channeling, and Associated Control Equipment:** Includes central office switching computers, interfacing computers, other associated specialized control equipment, and site improvements.	10.5	7	10.5
48.36	**TOCSC—Satellite Ground Segment Property:** Includes assets such as fixed earth station equipment, antennas, satellite communications equipment, and interface equipment used in satellite communications. Does not include general purpose equipment or equipment used in satellite space segment property.	10	7	10
48.37	**TOCSC—Satellite Space Segment Property:** Includes satellites and equipment used for telemetry, tracking, control, and monitoring when used in satellite communications.	8	5	8
48.38	**TOCSC—Equipment Installed on Customer's Premises:** Includes assets installed on customer's premises, such as computers, terminal equipment, power generation and distribution systems, private switching center, teleprinters, facsimile equipment, and other associated and related equipment.	10	7	10
48.39	**TOCSC—Support and Service Equipment:** Includes assets used to support but not engage in communications. Includes store, warehouse and shop tools, and test and laboratory assets. **Cable Television (CATV):** Includes communications-related assets used to provide cable television community antenna television services. Does not include assets used to provide subscribers with 2-way communications services.	13.5	7	13.5

* Property described in asset guideline class 48.13 which is qualified technological equipment as defined in section 168(i)(2) is assigned a 5-year recovery period.

Table B-2. **Table of Class Lives and Recovery Periods**

Asset class	Description of assets included	Class Life (in years)	Recovery Periods (in years) GDS (MACRS)	ADS
48.41	**CATV—Headend:** Includes assets such as towers, antennas, preamplifiers, converters, modulation equipment, and program non-duplication systems. Does not include headend buildings and program origination assets.	11	7	11
48.42	**CATV—Subscriber Connection and Distribution Systems:** Includes assets such as trunk and feeder cable, connecting hardware, amplifiers, power equipment, passive devices, directional taps, pedestals, pressure taps, drop cables, matching transformers, multiple set connector equipment, and convertors.	10	7	10
48.43	**CATV—Program Origination:** Includes assets such as cameras, film chains, videotape recorders, lighting, and remote location equipment excluding vehicles. Does not include buildings and their structural components.	9	5	9
48.44	**CATV—Service and Test:** Includes assets such as oscilloscopes, field strength meters, spectrum analyzers, and cable testing equipment, but does not include vehicles.	8.5	5	8.5
48.45	**CATV—Microwave Systems:** Includes assets such as towers, antennas, transmitting and receiving equipment, and broad band microwave assets used in the provision of cable television services. Does not include assets used in the provision of common carrier services.	9.5	5	9.5
49.11	**Electric, Gas, Water, and Steam Utility Services:** Includes assets used in the production, transmission and distribution of electricity, gas, steam, or water for sale including related land improvements. **Electric Utility Hydraulic Production Plant:** Includes assets used in the hydraulic power production of electricity for sale, including related land improvements, such as dams, flumes, canals, and waterways.	50	20	50
49.12	**Electric Utility Nuclear Production Plant:** Includes assets used in the nuclear power production and electricity for sale and related land improvements. Does not include nuclear fuel assemblies.	20	15	20
49.121	**Electric Utility Nuclear Fuel Assemblies:** Includes initial core and replacement core nuclear fuel assemblies (i.e., the composite of fabricated nuclear fuel and container) when used in a boiling water, pressurized water, or high temperature gas reactor used in the production of electricity. Does not include nuclear fuel assemblies used in breader reactors.	5	5	5
49.13	**Electric Utility Steam Production Plant:** Includes assets used in the steam power production of electricity for sale, combustion turbines operated in a combined cycle with a conventional steam unit and related land improvements. Also includes package boilers, electric generators, and related assets, such as, electricity and steam distribution systems as used by a waste reduction and resource recovery plant if the steam or electricity is normally for sale to others.	28	20	28
49.14	**Electric Utility Transmission and Distribution Plant:** Includes assets used in the transmission and distribution of electricity for sale and related land improvements. Excludes initial clearing and grading land improvements as specified in Rev. Rul. 72-403, 1972-2 C.B. 102.	30	20	30
49.15	**Electric Utility Combustion Turbine Production Plant:** Includes assets used in the production of electricity for sale by the use of such prime movers as jet engines, combustion turbines, diesel engines, gasoline engines, and other internal combustion engines, their associated power turbines and/or generators, and related land improvements. Does not include combustion turbines operated in a combined cycle with a conventional steam unit.	20	15	20
49.21	**Gas Utility Distribution Facilities:** Includes gas water heaters and gas conversion equipment installed by utility on customers' premises on a rental basis.	35	20	35
49.221	**Gas Utility Manufactured Gas Production Plants:** Includes assets used in the manufacture of gas having chemical and/or physical properties which do not permit complete interchangeability with domestic natural gas. Does not include gas-producing systems and related systems used in waste reduction and resource recovery plants which are elsewhere classified.	30	20	30
49.222	**Gas Utility Substitute Natural Gas (SNG) Production Plant (naphtha or lighter hydrocarbon feedstocks):** Includes assets used in the catalytic conversion of feedstocks or naphtha or lighter hydrocarbons to a gaseous fuel which is completely interchangeable with domestic natural gas.	14	7	14
49.223	**Substitute Natural Gas—Coal Gasification:** Includes assets used in the manufacture and production of pipeline quality gas from coal using the basic Lurgi process with advanced methanation. Includes all process plant equipment and structures used in this coal gasification process and all utility assets such as cooling systems, water supply and treatment facilities, and assets used in the production and distribution of electricity and steam for use by the taxpayer in a gasification plant and attendant coal mining site processes but not for assets used in the production and distribution of electricity and steam for sale to others. Also includes all other related land improvements. Does not include assets used in the direct mining and treatment of coal prior to the gasification process itself.	18	10	18
49.23	**Natural Gas Production Plant**	14	7	14
49.24	**Gas Utility Trunk Pipelines and Related Storage Facilities:** Excluding initial clearing and grading land improvements as specified in Rev. Rul. 72-40.	22	15	22
49.25	**Liquefied Natural Gas Plant:** Includes assets used in the liquefaction, storage, and regasification of natural gas including loading and unloading connections, instrumentation equipment and controls, pumps, vaporizers and odorizers, tanks, and related land improvements. Also includes pipeline interconnections with gas transmission lines and distribution systems and marine terminal facilities.	22	15	22

Table B-2. **Table of Class Lives and Recovery Periods**

Asset class	Description of assets included	Class Life (in years)	Recovery Periods (in years)	
			GDS (MACRS)	ADS
49.3	**Water Utilities:** Includes assets used in the gathering, treatment, and commercial distribution of water.	50	20***	50
49.4	**Central Steam Utility Production and Distribution:** Includes assets used in the production and distribution of steam for sale. Does not include assets used in waste reduction and resource recovery plants which are elsewhere classified.	28	20	28
49.5	**Waste Reduction and Resource Recovery Plants:** Includes assets used in the conversion of refuse or other solid waste or biomass to heat or to a solid, liquid, or gaseous fuel. Also includes all process plant equipment and structures at the site used to receive, handle, collect, and process refuse or other solid waste or biomass in a waterwall, combustion system, oil or gas pyrolysis system, or refuse-derived fuel system to create hot water, gas, steam, and electricity. Includes material recovery and support assets used in refuse or solid refuse or solid waste receiving, collecting, handling, sorting, shredding, classifying, and separation systems. Does not include any package boilers, or electric generators and related assets such as electricity, hot water, steam, and manufactured gas production plants classified in classes 00.4, 49.13, 49.221, and 49.4. Does include, however, all other utilities such as water supply and treatment facilities, ash handling, and other related land improvements of a waste reduction and resource recovery plant.	10	7	10
50.0	**Municipal Wastewater Treatment Plant**	24	15	24
51.0	**Municipal Sewer**	50	20***	50
57.0	**Distributive Trades and Services:** Includes assets used in wholesale and retail trade, and personal and professional services. Includes section 1245 assets used in marketing petroleum and petroleum products.	9	5	9*
57.1	**Distributive Trades and Services—Billboard, Service Station Buildings, and Petroleum Marketing Land Improvements:** Includes section 1250 assets, including service station buildings and depreciable land improvements, whether section 1245 property or section 1250 property, used in the marketing of petroleum and petroleum products, but not including any of these facilities related to petroleum and natural gas trunk pipelines. Includes car wash buildings and related land improvements. Includes billboards, whether such assets are section 1245 property or section 1250 property. Excludes all other land improvements, buildings, and structural components as defined in section 1.48-1(e) of the regulations.	20	15	20
79.0	**Recreation:** Includes assets used in the provision of entertainment services on payment of a fee or admission charge, as in the operation of bowling alleys, billiard and pool establishments, theaters, concert halls, and miniature golf courses. Does not include amusement and theme parks and assets which consist primarily of specialized land improvements or structures, such as golf courses, sports stadia, race tracks, ski slopes, and buildings which house the assets used in entertainment services.	10	7	10
80.0	**Theme and Amusement Parks:** Includes assets used in the provision of rides, attractions, and amusements in activities defined as theme and amusement parks, and includes appurtenances associated with a ride, attraction, amusement, or theme setting within the park such as ticket booths, facades, shop interiors, and props, special purpose structures, and buildings other than warehouses, administration buildings, hotels, and motels. Includes all land improvements for or in support of park activities (for example, parking lots, sidewalks, waterways, bridges, fences, landscaping, etc.), and support functions (for example, food and beverage retailing, souvenir vending, and other nonlodging accommodations) if owned by the park and provided exclusively for the benefit of park patrons. Theme and amusement parks are defined as combinations of amusements, rides, and attractions which are permanently situated on park land and open to the public for the price of admission. This guideline class is a composite of all assets used in this industry except transportation equipment (general purpose airplanes, etc., which are included in asset guideline classes with the prefix 00.2); assets used in the trucks, cars,provision of administrative services (asset classes with the prefix 00.1) and warehouses, administration buildings, hotels, and motels.	12.5	7	12.5
	Certain Property for Which Recovery Periods Assigned			
	A. Personal Property With No Class Life		7	12
	Section 1245 Real Property With No Class Life		7	40
	B. Qualified Technological Equipment, as defined in section 168(i)(2).	**	5	5
	C. Property Used in Connection with Research and Experimentation referred to in section 168(e)(3)(B).	**	5	class life if no class life—12
	D. Alternative energy property described in sections 48(l)(3)(A)(ix) (as in effect on the day before the date of enactment (11/5/90) of the Revenue Reconciliation Act of 1990).	**	5	class life if no class life—12
	E. Biomass property described in section 48(l)(15) (as in effect on the day before the date of enactment (11/5/90) of the Revenue Reconciliation Act of 1990) and is a qualifying small production facility within the meaning of section 3(17)(c) of the Federal Power Act (16 U.S.C. 796(17)(C)), as in effect on September 1, 1986.	**	5	class life if no class life—12
	F. Energy property described in section 48(a)(3)(A) (or would be described if "solar or wind energy" were substituted for "solar energy" in section 48(a)(3)(A)(i)).	**	5	class life if no class life—12

* Any high technology medical equipment as defined in section 168(i)(2)(C) which is described in asset guideline class 57.0 is assigned a 5-year recovery period for the alternate MACRS method.

** The class life (if any) of property described in class B, C, D, E, or F is determined by reference to the asset guideline classes. If an item of property described in paragraph B, C, D, E, or F is not described in any asset guideline class, such item of property has no class life.

*** Use straight line over 25 years if placed in service after June 12, 1996, unless placed in service under a binding contract in effect before June 10, 1996, and at all times until placed in service.

Table 4-1. **Depreciation Methods**

Note. The declining balance method is abbreviated as DB and the straight line method is abbreviated as SL.		
Method	**Type of Property**	**Benefit**
GDS using 200% DB	• Nonfarm 3-, 5-, 7-, and 10-year property • Farm 3-, 5-, 7-, and 10-year property placed in service after 2017, in tax years ending after 2017	• Provides a greater deduction during the earlier recovery years • Changes to SL when that method provides an equal or greater deduction
GDS using 150% DB	• Farm 3-, 5-, 7-, or 10-year property placed in service before 2018 • All 15- and 20-year property • Nonfarm 3-, 5-, 7-, or 10-year property[2] • Farm 3-, 5-, 7-, or 10-year property placed in service after 2017[2]	• Provides a greater deduction during the earlier recovery years • Changes to SL when that method provides an equal or greater deduction[1]
GDS using SL	• Nonresidential real property • Residential rental property • Trees or vines bearing fruits or nuts • Water utility property • All 3-, 5-, 7-, 10-, 15-, and 20-year property[2] • Property for which you elected section 168(k)(4) of the Internal Revenue Code for a tax year beginning before January 1, 2018 • Qualified improvement property (as defined in section 168(e)(6) of the Internal Revenue Code) placed in service after 2017	• Provides for equal yearly deductions (except for the first and last years)
ADS using SL	• Listed property used 50% or less for business • Property used predominantly outside the United States • Tax-exempt property • Tax-exempt bond-financed property • Farm property used when an election not to apply the uniform capitalization rules is in effect • Imported property[3] • Any property for which you elect to use this method[4] • Any nonresidential real property, residential rental property, or qualfied improvement property held by an electing real property trade or business (as defined in section 163(j)(7)(B) of the Internal Revenue Code) • Any property that has a recovery period of 10 years or more under GDS that is held by an electing farming business (as defined in section 163(j)(7)(C) of the Internal Revenue Code)	• Provides for equal yearly deductions (except for the first and last years)

[1] The MACRS percentage tables in Appendix A have the switch to the straight line method built into their rates.
[2] See section 168(b)(5) of the Internal Revenue Code.
[3] See section 168(g)(6) of the Internal Revenue Code.
[4] See section 168(g)(7) of the Internal Revenue Code.

Chapter 8: Retirement Plan Issues for Individuals

8

Note. Corrections for all of the chapters are available at **TaxSchool.illinois.edu.** For clarification about terms used throughout this chapter, see the **Acronyms and Abbreviations** section following the index.

For your convenience, in-text website links are also provided as short URLs. Anywhere you see **uofi.tax/xxx**, the link points to the address immediately following in brackets.

About the Authors

John W. Richmann, EA, is a Tax Materials Specialist at the University of Illinois Tax School. Prior to joining Tax School in 2021, he owned a tax practice in St. Charles, Illinois, and held positions in private industry and consulting firms. John earned a Masters Degree in Business Administration from the University of Texas and an electrical engineering degree from the Massachusetts Institute of Technology.

Rachel Szeklinski, CPA, has worked in public accounting for over six years and started writing for the University of Illinois Tax School in 2022. She graduated from Carroll University with honors in accounting in 2020 and passed the CPA exam in early 2021.

Other chapter contributors and reviewers are listed at the front of this book.

INHERITED RETIREMENT PLANS

The Setting Every Community Up for Retirement Enhancement (SECURE) Act[1] significantly changed the distribution rules related to inherited employer plans and individual retirement arrangements (IRAs) for many beneficiaries. The Act is effective for retirement plans and IRAs where the account owner dies after December 31, 2019. For taxpayers who inherited retirement plans and IRAs on or before December 31, 2019, the rules were not changed by SECURE. The Act established three tiers of beneficiaries: designated beneficiaries (DB), eligible designated beneficiaries (EDB), and nondesignated beneficiaries. EDBs include surviving spouses and certain other protected individuals, and EDBs are still able to use the prior rules relative to inherited plans during their lifetime.[2] This discussion focuses on the new rules that apply to DBs.

> **Note.** For more information about retirement plan distributions, see the 2020 *University of Illinois Federal Tax Workbook*, Volume B, Chapter 1: Retirement Plan Distributions. This can be found at **uofi.tax/arc** [taxschool.illinois.edu/taxbookarchive].

Prior to the SECURE Act, owners of retirement plans could use tax planning strategies such that the beneficiaries could extend taking distributions from an IRA over the longest period of time possible. These planning strategies were known as "stretch IRAs." The stretch IRA allowed family wealth to accumulate in inherited retirement accounts. The relatively small distributions permitted by the stretch IRA generally had a limited effect on DBs' tax planning unless their inherited IRAs were large.

The SECURE Act requires that DBs must take distributions of the entire interest in the inherited plan by the end of the 10th calendar year following the account owner's death.[3] Initially, many advisors were uncertain whether the new required minimum distribution (RMD) requirements applied during the nine calendar years following original owner's death. In February 2022, the IRS issued proposed regulations implementing the SECURE Act's RMD provisions. The proposed regulations caused additional confusion related to the RMD requirements. This led the IRS to issue Notice 2022-53[4] in August 2022 and then Notice 2023-54[5] in July 2023 (covered later.)

This section reviews the requirements of the proposed regulations as well as the implications of Notices 2022-53 and 2023-54.

> **Note.** This section uses the term "account owner" to refer to the deceased owner of a plan, regardless of whether the plan is an IRA, an annuity, or a qualified plan provided by the decedent's employer.

SECURE ACT CHANGES

The SECURE Act sharply curtailed the use of stretch IRAs in planning for inherited IRAs. For a DB, the period for distributions is reduced from their life expectancy to 10 years. Except for surviving spouses and other EDBs, the law requires DBs of IRAs to withdraw all remaining funds within 10 calendar years from the calendar year of the account owner's death.

---

1. *SECURE Act of 2019*, PL 116-94.
2. IRC §401(a)(9).
3. IRC §401(a)(9)(H)(i).
4. IRS Notice 2022-53, 2022-45 IRB 437.
5. IRS Notice 2023-54, 2023-31 IRB 382.

The revenue provisions of the SECURE Act made modifications to RMDs for DBs where the account owner dies before receiving the entire distribution of the account. Specifically, §401 of the Act amends IRC §401(a)(9) by adding a special rule, "that except in the case of a beneficiary who is not a designated beneficiary, subparagraph (B)(ii) shall be applied substituting '10 years' for '5 years.'" [6]

The Act did not change how the 5-year rule is applied to **nondesignated beneficiaries.** Under the 5-year rule, the entire remaining interest must be distributed within five years after the account owner's death without any requirement for RMDs.[7] Because Congress simply substituted 10 years for five years, many advisors interpreted the statute to mean that the remaining balance could be distributed at any time within the 10 years, even on the last day of the last calendar year.

Reflecting this interpretation, IRS Pub. 590-B, *Distributions from Individual Retirement Arrangements (IRAs)*, for 2020 and 2021 stated the following.

> *The 10-year rule requires the IRA beneficiaries who are not taking life expectancy payments to withdraw the entire balance of the IRA by December 31 of the year containing the 10th anniversary of the owner's death... The beneficiary is allowed, but* ***not required,*** *to take distributions prior to that date.* [emphasis added]

IRS Proposed Regulations[8]

In February 2022, the IRS issued proposed regulations that require DBs to receive **annual** distributions from inherited plans and IRAs. Waiting until the end of the 10-year period would not be adequate. In the proposed regulations, the IRS interpreted §401(a)(9)(B)(i) to require annual distributions be taken at least as rapidly as the account owner was taking distributions prior to death.

Following this logic, the IRS proposed that beneficiaries must start distributions during the calendar year following the original owner's death. For example, if an IRA owner aged 75 died in 2021, having already started RMDs, their beneficiaries must start distributions no later than December 31, 2022. The SECURE Act otherwise removed a provision distinguishing beneficiary RMDs if the account owner died before their required beginning date (RBD). With the SECURE Act, the rules for distributions apply regardless of whether the deceased account owner had begun taking distributions.[9]

In the explanation to the proposed regulations, the IRS states as an example that if an account owner dies **after their RBD**, then a DB that is not an EDB is responsible for taking distributions in the following years until the conclusion of the calendar year that includes the **9th anniversary** of the account owner's death. The remaining balance of the account owner's interest in the IRA or qualified plan must be distributed entirely in the following year.[10]

The proposed regulations apply to traditional IRAs, that are either individual retirement accounts or individual retirement annuities. They also apply to Roth IRAs, annuity contracts, custodial accounts, IRC §403(b) retirement accounts, and IRC §457(b) eligible deferred compensation plans.

6. IRC §401(a)(9)(H)(i).
7. IRC §401(a)(9)(B)(ii).
8. 87 Fed. Reg. 10504 (Feb. 24, 2022); Prop. Treas. Regs. §§1.401(a)(9)-1, 1.401(a)(9)-2, and 1.401(a)(9)-5.
9. IRC §401(a)(9)(H)(i)(II).
10. 87 Fed. Reg. 10504, 10514 (Feb. 24, 2022).

Scope of Proposed Regulations. The SECURE Act's new RMD requirement affected a wide range of retirement accounts.[11] By referencing §401(a)(9)(B)(ii), the 10-year RMD requirement affects the following types of retirement accounts.[12]

- Traditional IRAs[13]
- Roth IRAs[14]
- Qualified pensions
- Qualified profit-sharing plans
- Stock bonus plans
- Annuity contracts[15]
- Retirement income accounts (§403(b) plans)
- Eligible deferred compensation plans[16]
- Governmental plans
- Collective bargaining agreements
- Other custodial accounts

Simplified employee pensions (SEPs) and savings incentive match plans for employees (SIMPLE) IRAs are mentioned in a proposed regulation that also ties them to the new 10-year distribution rules.[17] The proposed regulations also apply to collective bargaining agreements and governmental plans, although the SECURE Act provisions for these plans have varying effective dates.

RMDs

Under the proposed regulations, RMDs for DBs must begin in the calendar year following the account owner's death.[18] For example, the DBs of an IRA owner who died on January 2, 2023, would have until December 31, 2024, to receive the first IRA distribution. Further, the proposed regulations provide that all funds must be distributed by the end of the 10th year following the death of the account owner. The IRS uses the example that if the owner died in 2021 then the entire balance must be distributed by the end of 2031.

> **Caution.** The following examples in this section are based on the **proposed** regulations for DBs inheriting IRAs after December 31, 2019. **Finalization** of the regulations is not likely to occur until 2024. The final regulations may change the rules from the proposed regulations that are reflected in the following examples.

---

11. IRC §401(a)(9)(H).
12. IRC §401(a)(9).
13. IRC §§408(a)(6) and (b)(3), referencing §401(a)(9).
14. IRC §408A(c)(5).
15. IRC §403(b)(10).
16. IRC §457(b).
17. Prop. Treas. Reg. §1.408-8(a)(4).
18. Prop. Treas. Reg. §1.401(a)(9)-3(c)(3).

Example 1. Faith, age 91, died in May 2021 after receiving her RMD from her traditional IRA for 2021. Her daughter, Hope, is the only beneficiary of her IRA. She was born in March 1956 and celebrated her 65th birthday in 2021 before her mother passed away.

Based on the proposed regulations, Hope is required to take the first RMD from this inherited IRA on or before December 31, 2022. However, Hope's tax preparer advised her that based on IRS Notice 2023-55 (discussed later), Hope can wait until **2024** to take the first RMD. Hope is still required to withdraw any remaining balance in the account by the end of 2031.

Designated Beneficiaries[19]

A DB is any individual whom the account owner has named as a beneficiary of the account. Individuals need not be specifically named as beneficiaries, but they must be identifiable by class, even if the class of individuals may increase or decrease in size. For example, if a person names "my children" as their beneficiary on the account and it is possible to determine who the oldest child is, the beneficiaries will be treated as DBs.

Under Proposed Treas. Reg. §1.401(a)(9)-4(b), **any beneficiary that is not an individual** will not be a DB. The beneficiary must be a DB to benefit from a 10-year distribution period. If the only beneficiary is the owner's estate, then the distribution period would be five years. If there are multiple beneficiaries and **all beneficiaries are considered DBs**, then the assets of the inherited retirement plan can be distributed over 10 years. However, if **even one beneficiary** does not qualify as a DB, the entire retirement plan balance must be distributed within five years.[20]

Practitioner Planning Tip

The DBs can avoid this result by distributing the balance due to the nondesignated beneficiary by the end of the calendar year following the account owner's death. The remaining balance is then due to only DBs and the 10-year rule applies.[21]

If a retirement account has no DBs or EDBs, it must be distributed according to the 5-year rule, requiring the account to be distributed by the end of the 5th calendar year after the account owner's death. Tax practitioners should suggest their clients regularly review their retirement account beneficiaries.

8

Calculating RMD for DBs

To calculate an RMD, a DB must consider factors such as life expectancy, the value of the retirement plan, and whether there are multiple beneficiaries. RMDs are determined using the following equation.

$$\text{RMD} = \frac{\text{Account value at the end of the valuation year}}{\text{Beneficiary's life expectancy}}$$

19. IRC §401(a)(9)(E)(i).

20. IRC §401(a)(9)(H)(i); Treas. Reg. §1.401(a)(9)-3. See A-4 (a)(2).

21. Prop. Treas. Reg. §1.401(a)(9)-8.

Life Expectancy. In the proposed regulations, the IRS did not make any changes to the life expectancy tables from IRS Pub. 590-B which are used in determining the amount of an RMD. If the account owner dies after the RBD, the denominator used to calculate the RMD of the DB is the greater of the DB's remaining life expectancy and the account owner's remaining life expectancy.[22] The DB's life expectancy is determined using the beneficiary's age in the year after the account owner's death,[23] generally referring to Appendix B in IRS Pub. 590-B. Each year after that, however, the denominator is reduced by one. The deceased account owner's life expectancy is determined using their age in the year of death. Unless the DB is older than the account owner, the DB's life expectancy should result in smaller distributions during the nine years.

Example 2. Use the same facts as **Example 1.** Because Hope had her 65th birthday in the year her mother died, she turns 66 in the year immediately after the year of her mother's death. Therefore, she determines that her life expectancy, for RMD purposes, is 22.0 years, as shown in the following table, excerpted from IRS Pub. 590-B. Presumably, 22.0 is greater than Faith's life expectancy, so Hope uses 22.0 as the denominator for computing her RMD in 2022 should she choose to take an RMD in 2022.

Table I
(Single Life Expectancy)
(For Use by Beneficiaries)

Age	Life Expectancy	Age	Life Expectancy
60	27.1	91	5.3
61	26.2	92	4.9
62	25.4	93	4.6
63	24.5	94	4.3
64	23.7	95	4.0
65	22.9	96	3.7
66	22.0	97	3.4
67	21.2	98	3.2
68	20.4	99	3.0

The life expectancy is significant even after Hope receives the first RMD. The denominator she uses in 2023 is **not** the value corresponding to age 67, her age in 2023, but one less than the value in the year after her mother's death (i.e., 21.0 years.) Thus, if Hope did not receive an RMD in 2022, she cannot use her life expectancy based on her age of 67 in the year of her first RMD (21.2 years).

If the account owner dies before the RBD, then the DB determines the RMDs for the first nine years using the same method previously described but the **DB's life expectancy is used.**[24] This number is referred to in the section as the "beneficiary's life expectancy."

In each subsequent year, the denominator is reduced by one.

22. Prop. Treas. Reg. §1.401(a)(9)-5(d)(1)(ii).

23. Treas. Reg. §1.401(a)(9)-5. See A-5(c)(1).

24. Prop. Treas. Reg. §1.401(a)(9)-5(d)(2).

Account Value. To calculate the RMD amount, the value of the retirement plan must also be known. The key information for the value of the retirement plan is its value at the end of the previous year, which the regulations refer to as the "valuation year."[25] The account's balance is decreased for any distributions for the valuation calendar year occurring after the valuation date.[26]

For example, if a taxpayer missed their RMD in the prior year, in calculating the current year RMD, they should reduce the prior year account value by the missed RMD amount.

Two more unusual situations can affect the value of the retirement plan.[27]

- Qualified longevity annuity contracts[28]
- Retirement plans rolled over into another plan, particularly when these plans are merged or consolidated

Example 3. Use the same facts as **Example 2.** Hope did not calculate an RMD during 2021, as Faith already received the RMD for that year. The retirement account's value on December 31, 2021, was $100,000. At the end of each year, the account is credited with 4% interest based on the year-end value of the account. Because Hope did not receive a distribution during 2022, the value of the account on December 31, 2022, is $104,000.

Hope may choose to receive an RMD in 2023 of $4,953 ($104,000 value of account ÷ 21.0 years). The denominator of 21.0 is based on Hope's deemed life expectancy of 22.0 in 2022 reduced by 1. Although Hope could choose to receive a larger distribution, she does not.

At the end of 2023, the value of the retirement account that Hope has inherited is $103,009 (($104,000 value at the end of 2022 – $4,953 distribution for 2023) + ($104,000 – $4,953 distribution) × 4% interest). Her distribution during 2024 must be at least $5,151 ($103,009 ÷ 20.0 years).

Note. This example simplifies calculations for illustrative purposes. It shows how RMDs may increase annually because the denominator decreases each year. Although this process reduces the retirement plan balance, beneficiaries should still plan for a significant distribution in the 10th year following the death of a retirement plan owner who designated them as a beneficiary.

Practitioner Planning Tip

Knowing that the money must all come out by the end of the 10th year, taxpayers may prefer to take larger distributions if they have lower tax years. Tax practitioners should consider multiple year projections for taxpayers with inherited IRA accounts.

25. Treas. Reg. §1.401(a)(9)-5, A-3(a); Prop. Treas. Reg. §1.401(a)(9)-5(b)(2).
26. Ibid, A-3(c).
27. Ibid, A-3(d) and (e).
28. Qualified longevity annuity contracts are annuity contracts purchased from an insurance company. Requirements for qualified longevity annuity contracts are listed in Treas. Reg. §1.401(a)(9)-6, A-17.

The same timeline applies to Roth IRAs.[29] Even though the retirement plan owner of a Roth IRA is not required to receive RMDs during their lifetimes,[30] the DB of a Roth IRA must receive distributions following the rules to withdraw funds from an inherited Roth plan within 10 calendar years of the account owner's death. However, if the account owner had the Roth IRA for at least five years prior to death, the distributions from the Roth IRA will not be taxable. Consequently, DBs may prefer to withdraw as little as possible from an inherited Roth IRA.

Multiple Beneficiaries. When an account owner designates multiple beneficiaries, the oldest DB's life expectancy applies for all beneficiaries.[31] For example, if two siblings were both beneficiaries of a parent's IRA but were born 15 years apart, the younger sibling must compute RMDs using their older sibling's life expectancy. Thus, the younger sibling has distributions in the years immediately following the parent's death that are greater than they would have been. In either case, the entire account must be distributed within 10 years.

However, DBs can instead create separate accounts no later than December 31 of the year following the year of the account owner's death.[32] Once they establish separate accounts, the RMD for each DB is determined by their own life expectancy, not that of the oldest beneficiary.

> **Example 4.** Use the same facts as **Example 2,** except that Hope has a brother, Justin, who is also a beneficiary. Justin was born in 1962 and turned 60 in **2022**, the year following their mother's death. Justin and Hope are 50% beneficiaries of their mother's retirement plan.
>
> Because Hope and Justin divide their mother's retirement account into separate accounts, Justin can use his life expectancy to calculate his RMDs, rather than that of his older sister. Both Justin's and Hope's inherited IRA accounts have $52,000 at the end of 2022. Assuming that Justin also waits until 2023 to receive the first distribution, his RMD for that year is $1,992 ($52,000 value of account ÷ 26.1 years Justin's life expectancy in 2023), while Hope's RMD is $2,477 ($52,000 value of account ÷ 21.0 years Hope's life expectancy in 2023).
>
> Although Justin can receive distributions at a slower rate than Hope in the nine years following their mother's passing, both Justin and Hope must completely distribute any remaining balances during the 10th year, 2031. If both Justin and Hope receive only the RMDs during the first nine years, Justin can expect a larger distribution in 2031 than Hope because his account balance has a larger expected balance.

Calculating RMDs for EDBs

The SECURE Act's changes **did not affect all beneficiaries** in the same way. Congress chose to establish a new class of beneficiaries with special rules related to inherited retirement accounts. These beneficiaries are known as EDBs.

- The surviving spouse of the retirement plan owner
- Minor children of the retirement plan owner
- Disabled individuals[33]
- A chronically ill individual provided that a doctor has certified that the illness is expected to be lengthy[34]
- Another individual who does not meet any of the previous four conditions and is not more than 10 years younger than the deceased retirement plan owner[35]

---

29. IRC §408A.
30. IRC §408A(c)(4).
31. Prop. Treas. Reg. §1.401(a)(9)-5(f)(1)(i).
32. Treas. Reg. §§1.401(a)(9)-8(a) and (b).
33. IRC §72(m)(7).
34. IRC §7702B(c)(2).
35. IRC §401(a)(9)(E)(ii)(v).

In general, these individuals are not subject to the requirement that all retirement plan funds be distributed by the end of the 10th year following the original owner's passing.[36] However, a minor child is exempt from the rules only for as long as they are minors. A proposed regulation puts the age of majority at 21 years.[37]

Surviving Spouses. Treatment for surviving spouses has undergone changes both under the SECURE Act and the SECURE 2.0 Act (covered extensively in the next section of the chapter).

From the SECURE Act. Surviving spouses can elect to treat their deceased spouse's IRA as their own assuming that the surviving spouse is the sole beneficiary.[38] By doing so, the surviving spouse becomes the account owner, and RMDs are determined based on the surviving spouse's age. They can accomplish this by either of the following.[39]

- Retitling the account as their own rather than as a beneficiary
- **Not** receiving a distribution from the inherited IRA within the required time, generally the end of the next year, if the deceased had received their RMD prior to, but in the year of, their death
- Making a contribution of their own to the inherited IRA

They may only make this election if there are no other beneficiaries of the IRA and there are no restrictions on their ability to receive distributions from the IRA.[40] If the surviving spouse does not treat themselves as the owner of their deceased spouse's retirement account, they must receive RMDs no later than the first year following their spouse's passing.[41]

Although they are not subject to the rule requiring total distribution of the retirement account by the end of 10 years following their spouse's passing, the amount must be distributed according to the surviving spouse's life expectancy.

From the SECURE 2.0 Act.[42] Taking effect in 2024, this legislation gives surviving spouses more flexibility to treat the inherited IRA as their own. They do not need to receive RMDs until the date the deceased spouse would have been required to receive RMDs had they lived to that age. The legislation directs the IRS to amend regulations to permit surviving spouses to use the uniform lifetime table.[43]

8

This limit is significant if the spouse who died was younger than the surviving spouse.

Example 5. Henry, age 66, and Wendy, age 61, married, both have IRAs that names the other spouse as the sole beneficiary. Wendy was born in December 1962. Sadly, Wendy passes away suddenly in January 2024. Henry can delay receipt of his first RMD until Wendy would have reached her RBD. Because Wendy would have turned 73 in 2035, her applicable age is 74. Thus, were it not for her premature death, Wendy would have reached her applicable age in 2036. This provision allows Henry to delay the receipt of RMDs from Wendy's IRA until April 1, 2037, after he reaches the beginning date for his own RMDs.

Note. Before this provision of the SECURE 2.0 Act goes into effect on January 1, 2024, surviving spouses can treat IRAs inherited from their spouses as their own, using their own RBD. This provision of the SECURE 2.0 Act requires them to start using their deceased spouses' RBD, likely requiring earlier RMDs if the deceased spouse was older.

---

36. IRC §401(a)(9)(H)(ii), which exempts EDBs from the requirement to distribute the inherited retirement account completely.
37. Prop. Treas. Reg. §1.401(a)(9)-4(e)(3).
38. Treas. Reg. §1.408-8, A-5; Prop. Treas. Reg. §1.408-8(c).
39. Prop. Treas. Reg. §1.408-8(c)(2).
40. Treas. Reg. §1.408-8, A-5 (a).
41. Prop. Treas. Reg. §1.408-8(c)(3).
42. *SECURE 2.0 Act of 2022,* PL 117-328, §327.
43. IRS Pub. 590-B, *Distributions from Individual Retirement Arrangements (IRAs)*, p. 65 (2022).

Minor Children.[44] Children are minors until they attain the age of 21. At that time, the 10-year mandatory distribution rule begins.

Disabled Individuals.[45] Provided the beneficiary was disabled when the retirement plan owner died, an individual is considered an EDB, and thereby exempt from the 10-year mandatory distribution rule. For a person who is at least 18 years old, disabled is defined as a condition preventing an individual from partaking in "substantial gainful activity" because of a physical or mental condition.[46] This judgment must be supported by a doctor's opinion that the impairment is of indefinite duration or result in the individual's death.

An individual younger than 18 is considered disabled if they have a physical or mental impairment that results in "marked and severe functional limitations." This must be supported by a doctor's opinion that the condition is of indefinite duration or result in the individual's death.

Chronically Ill Individuals.[47] Chronically ill individuals are also exempt from the 10-year distribution requirement. The designation must be supported by a certification of a licensed health care practitioner that the individual cannot perform two activities of daily living.[48] This illness should be indefinite and explicitly longer than 90 days.

Multi-Beneficiary Trusts.[49] Trusts may be established for individuals who are either disabled or chronically ill under the definitions provided by the SECURE Act. If **at least one** beneficiary of a trust is either disabled or chronically ill, then the provisions for EDBs apply to any disabled or chronically ill beneficiary.[50] This treatment is contingent on the trust containing terms that:[51]

- Provide for its immediate separation into separate trusts for each beneficiary as soon as the retirement plan owner dies,
- No beneficiary who is not disabled or chronically ill can receive a benefit under the trust until the death of the last disabled or chronically ill individual, and
- Any individual who is not disabled or chronically ill is a DB of the trust.

Individuals Younger than the Retirement Plan Owner by 10 Years or Less.[52] Unless there is impairment or chronic illness, an individual who is within 10 years of the retirement plan owner's age is also exempt from the 10-year distribution requirement.

---

44. Prop. Treas. Reg. §1.401(a)(9)-3.
45. Prop. Treas. Reg. §1.401(a)(9)-4(e)(4).
46. IRC §72(m)(7).
47. Prop. Treas. Reg. §1.401(a)(9)-4(e)(5).
48. IRC §7702B(c)(2).
49. IRC §401(a)(9)(H)(iv); 87 Fed. Reg. 10504, 10505 (Feb. 24, 2022).
50. IRC §§401(a)(9)(H)(iv) and (v).
51. IRC §401(a)(9)(H)(iv).
52. *Beneficiary IRAs: A guide to the RMD maze.* Roane, Dayna E. Mar. 30, 2023. Journal of Accountancy. [www.journalofaccountancy.com/issues/2023/apr/beneficiary-iras-a-guide-to-the-rmd-maze.html] Accessed on Jun. 19, 2023.

IRS Notice 2022-53[53]

In response to comments the IRS received related to the RMD provisions in the proposed regulations, the IRS issued Notice 2022-53 stating that they intend to issue final regulations with respect to RMDs that will apply no earlier than 2023. Further, the IRS provided guidance related to RMDs for 2021 and 2022. They announced that the IRS would not assert any **excise** tax assessments for persons not receiving RMDs during those years.[54]

> **Note.** When the SECURE Act was passed, the excise tax on missed RMDs was 50%. The SECURE 2.0 Act reduced the penalty on these missed distributions. If the taxpayer corrects the oversight within a correction window, the penalty is only 10%. Otherwise, the penalty is halved to 25%.[55]

The notice reiterated the language from the proposed regulations in support of RMDs for DBs. For DBs who inherited IRAs from account owners who died in 2020 or 2021, the notice provides relief from penalties if no RMDs were taken in 2021 or 2022. However, this notice does not provide any relief for 2023.

IRS Notice 2023-54[56]

In July 2023, the IRS announced that it would again suspend enforcement of the RMD requirements it announced during 2022. Accordingly, the IRS has stated that it will not assess excise tax against DBs who do not receive withdrawals from inherited IRAs during 2023.[57] The earliest these penalties would apply is 2024.

SECURE 2.0 ACT

8

President Biden signed the SECURE 2.0 Act into law on December 29, 2022, as part of the Consolidated Appropriations Act of 2023.[58] Congress designed the Act to help taxpayers save for retirement by changing retirement provisions at the taxpayer, plan, and business levels. The Act aims to incentivize retirement savings at the taxpayer level while making it easier for employers to offer retirement savings benefits.

Taxpayers and employers should evaluate the expanding retirement planning opportunities to leverage additional tax savings and reach retirement goals quicker than before. Some provisions of the SECURE 2.0 Act went into effect as of January 1, 2023. As such, developing an understanding of the changes and concepts within the Act is critical in implementing timely strategies for retirement. This section covers important topics within the SECURE 2.0 Act to assist in adapting to the changes and new opportunities that the Act introduced.

RMD AGE DELAY

An RMD is the least amount of withdrawal a taxpayer must take from their retirement account each year once they have reached a certain age. The SECURE Act increased the age for RMDs from 70½ to 72.[59] The SECURE 2.0 Act further increases the age (discussed later). This section covers the concepts behind RMDs and the implications of the changes that SECURE 2.0 Act establishes.

---

53. IRS Notice 2022-53, 2022-45 IRB 437.

54. IRC §4974(a).

55. *SECURE 2.0 Act of 2022*, PL 117-328, §302, amending IRC §4974(a).

56. IRS Notice 2023-54, 2023-31 IRB 382.

57. IRC §4974(c).

58. *Consolidated Appropriations Act of 2023,* PL 117-328, Division T.

59. *SECURE Act of 2019,* PL 116-94, §114.

History Behind RMDs

The Employee Retirement Income Security Act of 1974 legalized RMD rules.[60] Throughout the years, there have been instances where the government halted RMDs. These notable events include the Housing Market Crisis of 2008 and the recent COVID-19 pandemic. In each instance, Congress passed emergency legislation to provide temporary relief for taxpayers.[61]

These periods of temporary relief only lasted one year, prompting the question of why Congress is eager to enforce RMDs. Many retirement accounts operate under tax-deferred contributions, meaning taxpayers are only taxed when they withdraw funds. If taxpayers avoid taking withdrawals, their funds may move to an estate after death, which could free large balances from estate tax under the lifetime exemption.[62] Consequently, taxing authorities enforce RMDs to prevent taxpayers from completely avoiding tax by accumulating wealth in an IRA for beneficiaries to inherit.

Additionally, RMDs provide another income stream for the IRS through penalties associated with noncompliance with RMD rules. While the SECURE 2.0 Act decreased these penalties from 50% to 25% starting January 1, 2023, RMD penalties have the potential to provide a steady stream of revenue.[63] For example, on a $50,000 RMD, the IRS may impose $12,500 in penalties ($50,000 x 25%). However, if the offending taxpayer remedies the RMD distribution within a 2-year period, the penalty drops to 10%.[64] As mentioned previously, the IRS will not assess penalties until 2024.

Note. There has been speculation that the decrease in penalty for correcting missed RMD payments would result in the IRS no longer waiving missed RMD penalties as it had in the past. Before the enactment of the SECURE 2.0 Act, when taxpayers could establish that they missed their RMD due to a reasonable error and they took reasonable steps to remedy the error, the IRS could waive the penalty.[65] Although the penalty has been reduced, the IRS's ability to waive the penalties appears to remain intact. Taxpayers should emphasize that the error for missing the RMD was due to reasonable cause, as simply correcting the error appears to decrease the penalty instead of resulting in a waiver.

New Applicable Age for RMDs

The following are the new applicable ages for RMDs.[66]

- For the **2022** tax year, the RMD age is **72**.
- For tax years **2023** through **2032**, the RMD age is **73**.
- For tax years **2033** and on, the RMD age is **75**.

Taxpayers over 73 years old will not see any impact on their current RMDs. The SECURE 2.0 Act most profoundly affects taxpayers who are planning for retirement or are nearing the RMD age. Some taxpayers will delay RMDs, while others may perceive the time difference as immaterial.

---

60. *Employee Retirement Income Security Act of 1974,* PL 93-406, §408.

61. *Coronavirus Relief for Retirement Plans and IRAs.* May 31, 2022. IRS. [www.irs.gov/newsroom/coronavirus-relief-for-retirement-plans-and-iras] Accessed on Mar. 6, 2023; IRS News Rel. 2009-85 (Sep. 24, 2009).

62. IRS Pub. 590-B, *Distributions from Individual Retirement Arrangements (IRAs)*; IRC §2010(a).

63. *SECURE 2.0 Act of 2022,* PL 117-328, §302.

64. Ibid.

65. *Retirement Plan and IRA Required Minimum Distributions FAQs.* Mar. 14, 2023. IRS. [www.irs.gov/retirement-plans/retirement-plan-and-ira-required-minimum-distributions-faqs] Accessed on Apr. 25, 2023.

66. *SECURE 2.0 Act of 2022,* PL 117-328, §107.

Considerations of Starting RMDs Later in Life

Taxpayers should consider the consequences of starting RMDs later in life. For some taxpayers, the RMD age delay provides an incentive to work later in life. In doing so, they can continue making retirement contributions if they have earned income. If the retirement accounts are Roth or traditional IRA accounts, taxpayers can contribute to them regardless of their age.[67] Delaying RMDs an additional year can have a significant impact on accumulated income.[68] By delaying the RMDs, taxpayers are able to have funds remain in their retirement accounts and continue to accumulate earnings tax free.

However, additional wealth accumulation subjects taxpayers to an increase in the annual RMD once the taxpayer reaches the applicable age. With larger distributions and potentially higher tax rates, it is more likely they will be subject to a higher income tax. Furthermore, starting RMDs later in life increases the potential of leaving assets within one's estate. Taxpayers should consider the trade-off between wealth accumulation and desired retirement lifestyle, asking themselves if delaying RMDs for one year is worth working another 12 months or limiting current retirement expenses.

For taxpayers with large portfolios and other avenues of income, starting RMDs later in life can make sense from a financial and tax standpoint. These taxpayers can defer taxable RMDs, resulting in lower income to report on their tax returns compared to if they had taken their RMDs. These factors are positive considerations for high-net-worth taxpayers who wish to maximize funds to pass down to their beneficiaries while minimizing income taxes at the same time.

Example 6. John and Sally are siblings born one year apart in 1959 and 1960, respectively. John will reach age 73 in 2032, while Sally will be 73 in 2033. Because the RMD age delay will increase to 75 in 2033, the first year in which Sally is required to take an RMD is 2035, when she turns 75. Assume both John and Sally have $1 million in their retirement accounts at age 72, and their accounts are earning an annualized 10% return. The table below outlines the differences in RMD withdrawals and average account balances based on the additional two years Sally can delay RMDs.

	Age				
	72	73	74	75	76
John RMD	$ 0	$ 37,736	$ 41,509	$ 45,475	$ 49,811
John account balance	1,000,000	1,058,490	1,118,680	1,180,525	1,243,785
Sally RMD	0	0	0	49,187	53,877
Sally account balance	1,000,000	1,100,000	1,210,000	1,276,894	1,345,319

Note. The calculation of RMD distributions and account balances includes compounding interest annually.[69]

As the table illustrates, Sally's account balance earns higher growth despite the larger RMD when looking at the variance in account balances during ages 75 and 76 between John and Sally. The additional two years that Sally was able to retain funds in her account from ages 73 to 74 and accumulate earnings results in her RMD being higher than John's, but she is still able to maintain a higher ending account balance. Additionally, Sally did not have to pay income tax on RMDs when she was 73 and 74 years of age.

8

---

67. *Roth IRAs.* Oct. 26, 2022. IRS. [www.irs.gov/retirement-plans/roth-iras] Accessed on Mar. 6, 2023.

68. *What Is The Average Return Of The Stock Market?* Thune, Kent. Jan. 2, 2023. Seeking Alpha. [seekingalpha.com/article/4502739-average-stock-market-return] Accessed on Mar. 6, 2023.

69. *Required Minimum Distribution Calculator.* Jan. 1, 2022. Investor.gov. [www.investor.gov/financial-tools-calculators/calculators/required-minimum-distribution-calculator] Accessed on Mar. 6, 2023.

ADDITIONAL CATCH-UP CONTRIBUTIONS

Catch-up contributions allow taxpayers nearing retirement to make additional contributions to their retirement accounts. This provision intends to help taxpayers make up for prior years when they could not contribute as much and may currently be in a financial position to bolster their retirement accounts.

Prior to the enactment of the SECURE 2.0 Act, taxpayers over 50 years old could make catch-up contributions of up to $7,500 to their retirement plans. Section 109 of the SECURE 2.0 Act extends higher catch-up contributions to taxpayers, age 60 through 63. This provision gives them the ability to save extra money during what is likely their peak earning years. Most taxpayers in this age range have lower expenses and higher incomes. This age range is possibly the best time to put away extra money toward retirement. The following are specifics taxpayers should know.[70]

- Possible contributions are increased to either $10,000 or 50% of the regular catch-up amount, whichever is greater.
- Contributions depend on inflation (indexed after 2025) but will at least be **$10,000.**
- Only taxpayers between the age of 60 and 63 can leverage the additional catch-up contributions. For taxpayers who have reached age 50 but not 60, the existing catch-up provisions remain in effect.
- Individuals with wages exceeding $145,000 may only make additional catch-up contributions to Roth accounts.[71]
- Additional catch-up contributions do not go into effect until January 1, 2025.

Note. The SIMPLE plan limit for catch-up contributions is $3,500 for 2023.[72] Section 108 of the SECURE 2.0 Act allows adjustments for inflation to IRA catch-up contributions beginning on January 1, 2024. Section 109 applies to all other retirement plans.[73]

Caution. Currently, there is a drafting error in the SECURE 2.0 Act regarding catch-up contributions, resulting in individuals being unable to make catch-up contributions to pre-tax or Roth accounts after December 31, 2023. This appears to be an oversight and unintended by Congress. It is unknown whether Congress must amend the legislation or if the Treasury is able to ignore the drafting error. Practitioners should watch for guidance on the issue as the end of 2023 approaches.[74]

70. *SECURE 2.0 Act of 2022*, PL 117-328, §109.

71. Ibid, §603.

72. IRS Notice 2022-55, 2022-45 IRB 443.

73. *SECURE 2.0 Act of 2022*, PL 117-328, §108.

74. See *Major SECURE 2.0 Error Puts Catch-Ups in Jeopardy: ARAs Graff*. Sullivan, John. Jan. 24, 2023. National Association of Plan Advisors. [www.napa-net.org/news-info/daily-news/major-secure-20-error-puts-catch-ups-jeopardy-ara's-graff] Accessed on Jul. 20, 2023.

STUDENT LOAN PAYMENTS AS ELECTIVE DEFERRALS[75]

Many taxpayers might be unable to save for retirement because they have extensive student loan debt. In instances where employees make repayments on qualified student loans, employers can pay matching contributions to the employees' retirement accounts. The employees must be otherwise eligible for matching contributions.

Employers may rely on an employee's verbal payment confirmation for qualifying student loans. However, documentation should substantiate the match for qualification testing purposes. Plans can test student loan payments as a part of general discrimination testing or as a separate group. Student loan payments do not receive treatment as contributions to the plan outside of qualification testing.

Employer Treatment

Employers that offer a §401(k), §403(b), §457(b), or SIMPLE IRA can modify their plan terms to include student loan payments as elective deferrals to the employer plan. This allows an employee to at least qualify for matching contributions from the employer and create some retirement savings while still paying down student loans. Employers will need to follow the same matching provisions for qualifying student loan payments as are provided for all employee deferrals.

Practitioner Planning Tip

If an employer does not offer a qualifying retirement program, they cannot use the provisions under SECURE 2.0 Act, §110. Instead, these employers should consider offering a student loan repayment program as part of an Educational Assistance Program, which allows employers to allocate up to $5,250 of employee compensation to student loans without incurring payroll taxes.[76] The inclusion of student loan repayments as a part of this program currently will expire at the end of 2025. Practitioners should review the requirements for a qualified eligible education assistance program.

The match, submittal, and vesting schedules remain the same as regular plan participants. Some employers may choose to remit contributions annually instead of with each payroll cycle for administrative purposes.

Effective Date

Section 110 of the SECURE 2.0 Act is not effective until January 1, 2024, providing employers additional time to change plan documents and roll out a program.

Example 7. Sam is an employee at XYZ, Inc. Sam borrowed $10,000 from a private lender to help pay for his college education. Sam has been paying the loan back $200 per month. XYZ offers a §401(k) plan with a 3% employer match on elective deferrals. Sam does not currently contribute to the plan. XYZ amends its plan documents to provide that student loan repayments will be treated as elective deferrals beginning in 2024. Because Sam is making payments on a qualifying student loan, XYZ must establish a §401(k) account for Sam and make a matching contribution to his account for 2024. XYZ would contribute 3% of Sam's monthly $200 loan payments, or $6 a month totaling $72 for the year. In this case, maintaining Sam's §401(k) account may be burdensome for XYZ.

---

75. *SECURE 2.0 Act of 2022,* PL 117-328, §110.

76. IRC §127.

NEW RMD RULES FOR SPECIAL NEEDS TRUSTS

It is not unusual for family members to establish a special needs trust as part of their estate planning when there are children with disabilities. The intention is to provide benefits to the children without compromising access to various government benefits. The SECURE Act provided special rules for disabled beneficiaries which required that a trust document satisfy certain requirements to avoid the 10-year rule.[77] The modification provided by the SECURE 2.0 Act provides some flexibility in the types of trust beneficiaries permitted.

Clarification to the Original SECURE Act

Section 337 of the SECURE 2.0 Act changes the language surrounding certain trust beneficiaries of IRAs. Special needs trusts with a disabled person as an income beneficiary can now designate a charitable organization as a remainder beneficiary and have the remainder beneficiary treated as a DB. Absent this correction, the special needs trust would have a non-designated beneficiary and be subject to the 5-year rule. Section 337 goes into effect for the **2023 tax year.**

> **Example 8.** Brad was born physically disabled and was 18 years old when his parents passed away. Before their passing, Brad's parents set up and funded a special needs trust to provide for his needs in the event of their deaths. Both parents had IRAs that designated Brad's special needs trust as the beneficiary of the accounts. Additionally, the special needs trust provided that a charitable organization specializing in Brad's illness would be the remainder beneficiary of the trust.
>
> Brad's parents passed away in a tragic car accident in January 2023, just a week after the SECURE 2.0 Act clarified that charitable organizations named as remainder beneficiaries in special needs trusts would be considered DBs. If the special needs trust inherited the IRA accounts prior to the effective date of §337 of the SECURE 2.0 Act, the results would have been quite different. Although Brad would be an EDB under the SECURE Act and not subject to a shortened distribution period, the charity as a remainder beneficiary is a DB.

CHANGES TO SIMPLE RETIREMENT PLANS

The SECURE 2.0 Act introduced changes for employers offering SIMPLE plans. This section discusses two of these changes; additional nonelective contributions and changes to elective deferral limits.

Additional Nonelective Contributions to SIMPLE Plans

Section 116 of the SECURE 2.0 Act allows employers to make an additional nonelective contribution to SIMPLE plans for tax years beginning after December 31, 2023. This option supplements the existing requirement for employers to make contributions equal to a 2% nonelective contribution based on employee compensation or a 3% matching contribution of employee deferrals. There are limitations associated with the additional contributions. The additional contribution cannot exceed 10% of the employee's compensation or $5,000 (indexed for inflation), whichever is lower, on a per-employee basis. Furthermore, the employer must apply the additional contributions uniformly with no discrimination between employees.

---

77. IRS Pub. 590-B, *Distributions from Individual Retirement Arrangements (IRAs).*

Changes to SIMPLE Plan Elective Deferral Limits

Section 117 of the SECURE 2.0 Act increases the SIMPLE plan elective deferral limits. Currently, the limit for elective deferrals is $15,500 annually with an additional catch-up contribution of $3,500 for individuals who are 50 or older. For employers with 25 or fewer employees who received at least $5,000 of compensation in the prior year, the contribution limit, including the catch-up contribution, is increased by 10% above any usual cost of living increase. Employers with 26 to 100 employees can increase the employee deferral limit only if the employer match is also increased. The required employer match would be a 4% matching contribution or a 3% nonelective contribution.

> **Note.** SIMPLE plans are only available for small employers with 100 or fewer employees.

Example 9. A company with 15 employees switches from making 3% matching contributions to making a larger, nonelective contribution. They already have an existing SIMPLE plan in which 10 employees participate.

Assume all employees make $50,000 per year. If each employee makes $50,000 per year, 10% of compensation would be $5,000, which does not exceed the maximum limit. The maximum nonelective contribution is $75,000 ($5,000 per employee ×15 employees).

IRC §529 PLAN ROLLOVERS TO ROTH IRAS[78]

Taxpayers may hesitate to contribute to §529 plans because of the stiff penalties for funds that a taxpayer does not use for educational purposes. To incentivize investment in §529 plans, Congress added §126 to the SECURE 2.0 Act. This section allows tax-free rollovers from long-term §529 accounts to Roth accounts. The beneficiary of the Roth account must be the same as the beneficiary of the §529 plan. Taxpayers whose children have graduated from college without using all the §529 funds can use this option rather than paying income taxes and a 10% penalty on earnings. **Section 126 goes into effect for distributions after December 31, 2023.**

8

Rules for Rollover Distributions

There are specific rules that taxpayers must follow to have a qualifying rollover.

15-Year Holding Period. To qualify for the rollover, taxpayers must have maintained the §529 account for at least 15 years. This prevents taxpayers from taking advantage of the new provision by setting up new §529 plans that are never intended to be used for college. In addition, the qualifying distribution cannot exceed the aggregate amount contributed before the five years immediately preceding the distribution, including earnings on those contributions. This will prevent any back-end funding to maximize Roth IRA rollovers.

Trustee-to-Trustee Distribution. Congress specifically requires that §529 funds are paid to the Roth account in a trustee-to-trustee transfer. Therefore, taxpayers should not receive the funds personally, such as by check in the mail. The funds should move directly from the §529 account to the Roth IRA.

Annual Limitation. IRC §529 plan rollovers cannot exceed the annual limits of Roth IRA contributions. These amounts are adjusted each year for inflation. For the 2023 tax year, the Roth IRA limit is $6,500, or $7,500 for taxpayers 50 years of age or older.[79] This provision does not increase the amount that could otherwise be contributed on an annual basis.

Aggregate Limitation. Section 126 of the SECURE 2.0 Act provides a lifetime limit for rollovers from §529 accounts to Roth IRAs of $35,000 per DB. Any excess funds withdrawn are subject to regular taxes and penalties.

---

78. *SECURE 2.0 Act of 2022,* §126.

79. *Retirement Topics — IRA Contribution Limits.* Dec. 21, 2022. IRS. [www.irs.gov/retirement-plans/plan-participant-employee/retirement-topics-ira-contribution-limits] Accessed on Mar. 31, 2023.

Recipient of the Rollover

Only the named beneficiary of a §529 plan is entitled to have the balance rolled into a Roth IRA. Parents can open a §529 account for their child with one of the parents named as the beneficiary. This designation makes the parents eligible to roll over the funds to their Roth IRAs if their child does not use the money. If the child intends to use the funds, the parents can switch the beneficiary to the student to pay for educational expenses.[80]

Example 10. Sarah and Rick are married and have one daughter, Marie. Marie's wealthy grandparents fully fund a §529 account at Marie's birth. Rather than naming Marie as the account beneficiary, the grandparents listed Sarah and Rick as the beneficiaries. Marie is getting ready to attend college and receives a scholarship that covers all educational expenses. This means that she will not use her account for educational purposes. The account has been in place for 18 years. Rick and Sarah are both 50 years old, so their maximum annual Roth IRA contribution is $7,500 per year. If Marie was the beneficiary, then the funds could only be rolled into a Roth IRA for her, and the rollover would be limited by her earned income.

Note. If the account beneficiary is changed, commentators have questioned whether this would restart the 15-year holding period.

RMDS AND ROTH §401(K) PLANS[81]

Many employers have a Roth §401(k) option in their existing §401(k) plans. Employees who are not able to make Roth IRA contributions because of the income limitations find this to be a substantial benefit. However, unlike traditional Roth IRAs, the Roth §401(k)s were subject to RMD rules. Because the contributions to the accounts were made with after-tax dollars, the distributions were not taxable but the distributions stopped the income from growing tax-free.

Section 325 of the SECURE 2.0 Act changed the RMD requirement on Roth §401(k) accounts such that there are no RMD requirements until the death of the account owner. The change is effective to distributions starting on January 1, 2024. Any taxpayer distributions from employer-sponsored Roth plans in years before 2024 are subject to the old RMD rules.

This provision benefits employees, as they can put away more money than with Roth IRAs. Employer-sponsored Roth plans have higher contribution limits which include expanded contributions starting in 2025 once employees reach the age of 60 under §109. For 2023, the Roth §401(k) contribution limit is $22,500, while Roth IRAs have a contribution limit of $6,500.[82] Additionally, these plan participants are no longer required to start taking money out when they reach their RBD, leading to more potential growth and tax planning strategies.

Example 11. Jim and Gemma are a married couple who both have Roth accounts. Jim has a Roth IRA, and Gemma has a Roth §401(k). They were both born in 1951 and turn age 72 in 2023 before the SECURE 2.0 Act, §325 goes into effect. They both established their Roth accounts in 2007. The 5-year rule is satisfied for both Roth accounts. Jim is not required to take an RMD in 2023, but Gemma is because the plan is employer-sponsored. In 2024, neither of them is required to take RMDs from their accounts.

NEW EARLY WITHDRAWAL EXCEPTION FOR DOMESTIC ABUSE SURVIVORS[83]

Many survivors of domestic abuse face dire situations, such as finding alternative housing in emergency situations. To reduce the financial burden associated with these emergencies, the SECURE 2.0 Act enables penalty-free distributions from eligible retirement accounts for victims of domestic abuse, even those under the age of 59½.

---

80. *SECURE 2.0 Act of 2022,* PL 117-328, §126.

81. Ibid, §325.

82. IRS News Rel. IR-2022-188 (Oct. 21, 2022).

83. *SECURE 2.0 Act of 2022,* PL 117-328, §314.

Participants can take penalty-free withdrawals to ease the financial burden of escaping an unsafe situation. Domestic abuse survivors can withdraw the lesser of $10,000 or 50% of the vested account value. The distribution must be taken within 12 months from the date of abuse. The distribution is still taxable but is not subject to the 10% early withdrawal penalty. Taxpayers can repay the amount of the distribution over a 3-year period and then request a refund of the income tax paid.

> **Note.** The $10,000 withdrawal limit will be indexed for inflation.

A trustee does not need any formal legal complaint to distribute funds from retirement accounts. Instead, the taxpayer can self-certify that they have been a victim of domestic abuse. **Section 314 goes into effect beginning on January 1, 2024.**

EMPLOYER CONTRIBUTIONS[84]

Section 604 of the SECURE 2.0 Act allows employers to treat matching or nonelective contributions as Roth contributions at the employee's election in some cases. These contributions are not excludable from income. Previously, employers were unable to provide matching Roth contributions to §401(k), §403(b), and §457(b) plans. Employers can now contribute Roth matches to these accounts under the provisions of §604.

Tax-Free Withdrawals During Retirement

Before the enactment of the SECURE 2.0 Act, if an employee made contributions to their Roth §401(k), the employer matches were deposited in a traditional §401(k) account. When an employee retired or reached their RBD, distributions from their Roth account were not subject to tax, but distributions from their traditional §401(k) were taxable.

The employee must be fully vested in the Roth §401(k) so that the funds cannot be forfeited. If employers make Roth contributions to an employee's retirement account, the contributions must be included in that employee's wages and reported on their Form W-2, *Wage and Tax Statement,* for the tax year of the contribution. When the employee receives a distribution from their Roth account, the matching Roth contributions from the employer and the employee contributions will **both** be nontaxable.

ROTH PLANS FOR SIMPLE AND SEP IRAS[85]

The SECURE 2.0 Act also enabled Roth plans for SIMPLE and SEP IRA plans, although the taxpayer must make an affirmative election to do so in both cases.[86] Until this provision of the SECURE 2.0 Act went into effect, business owners sometimes used contributions to SIMPLE and SEP plans to reduce taxable income. This calculation changes when making contributions to Roth SIMPLE or SEP IRA plans.

Taxpayers cannot exclude contributions to individual retirement plans designated as Roth IRAs under SEPs or SIMPLEs.[87] In addition, employees receiving employer contributions into their plans may expect an increase in income, as their employers' contributions are included in their taxable income. This is especially true if an election is made to treat the employer's matching or non-elective contributions as Roth contributions.[88]

---

84. Ibid, §604.

85. Ibid, §601, amending IRC §§402(h)(1), 402(h)(3), 408(k), 408(p), and 408A.

86. IRC §§408(k)(7) and 408(p)(12).

87. IRC §§402(h)(1)(C), 408(k)(7), and 408(p)(12).

88. *SECURE 2.0 Act of 2022*, PL 117-328, §601, amending IRC §402A(a).

The SECURE 2.0 Act changes do not explicitly exclude the application of the income limitation for Roth contributions.[89] Unless the IRS issues guidance to the contrary, if a client makes a Roth IRA contribution to an IRA that is not a Roth SEP or SIMPLE, and their income exceeds the contribution threshold, they may be assessed an **excess contribution penalty.**[90]

Contributions made in excess of the general or Roth IRA contribution limits are considered excess contributions and are subject to a 6% penalty,[91] which is reported on Form 5329, *Additional Taxes on Qualified Plans (Including IRAs) and Other Tax-Favored Accounts.* This penalty cannot exceed 6% of the combined yearend value of all the taxpayer's IRAs. This penalty continues to apply each year to these excess contributions until the year they are withdrawn.[92]

The excess contribution to Roth IRAs is calculated as follows.

1. Current year contributions to Roth IRAs that are more than the Roth contribution limit for the year, plus
2. Any excess contributions for the preceding year, reduced by the total of:
   a. Any Roth IRA distributions for the year, plus
   b. The general contribution limit for the year less all IRA contributions for the year.

> **Note.** More information on the excess contribution penalty and examples are in the 2018 *University of Illinois Federal Tax Workbook,* Volume B, Chapter 5: Retirement Plans for Small Businesses. This can be found at **uofi.tax/arc** [taxschool.illinois.edu/taxbookarchive].

SAVER'S MATCH

Section 103 of the SECURE 2.0 Act helps taxpayers save for retirement by introducing a matching contribution to the taxpayer's retirement account. Section 104 outlines that the promotion of the saver's match primarily focuses on low and moderate-income taxpayers. The American Retirement Association estimates nearly 108 million Americans will be eligible for this new initiative.[93]

Changes Under SECURE 2.0 Act

Section 103 replaces the current nonrefundable **saver's credit** claimed on the individual tax return. Instead of reducing the taxpayer's tax liability like the saver's credit, the **saver's match** directs the Treasury to deposit funds directly into the taxpayer's IRA or retirement plan. The saver's match is equal to 50% of the first $2,000 that a taxpayer contributes to an eligible plan and is subject to phase out, with the maximum benefit remaining the same as the saver's credit at $1,000 per taxpayer.[94]

Eligible plans are all non-Roth retirement plans and includes employer deferred compensation plans under §§457(b), 401(k) plans, and 403(b) plans if they do not consist of a qualified Roth contribution program under IRC §402A(b).[95]

The following table compares the differences between the saver's credit and saver's match.

---

89. Ibid, §601.
90. IRC §§4973(a) and (f).
91. IRC §4973(a).
92. IRC §4973(b).
93. *ARA Applauds Sweeping New Retirement Security Legislation.* Dec. 20, 2022. American Retirement Association. [www.usaretirement.org/ara-applauds-sweeping-new-retirement-security-legislation] Accessed on Mar. 6, 2023.
94. *SECURE 2.0 Act of 2022,* PL 117-328, §103.
95. Ibid.

Change	Saver's Credit (Old)	Saver's Match (New)
Eligible accounts	Employer and IRAs	Non-Roth IRAs
Payment method	Nonrefundable credit on the individual tax return	Deposited directly into the IRA
Maximum credit	$1,000 per taxpayer	$1,000 per taxpayer
Early withdrawal penalties	Standard early retirement penalties	Standard early retirement penalties and possible repayment of match
Calculating the credit	10%, 20%, or 50% of the first $2,000 contributed to a retirement account (based on income)	50% of the first $2,000 contributed to a retirement account subject to phaseout for income thresholds

Year of Implementation

Unlike many of the provisions in the SECURE 2.0 Act, §103 does not go into effect until **2027.**[96] The phase-out thresholds and specifics of the credit can change by 2026. Section 104 mandates that the Treasury Secretary must outline the promotion efforts and specifics to Congress by July 1, 2026, six months before §103 goes into effect.[97]

Limitations of the Saver's Match

The match has a low phase-out threshold, excluding a sizable portion of taxpayers. The modified adjusted gross income (MAGI) phase-out thresholds for years after December 31, 2026, are as follows.[98]

- Single: $20,500–$35,500
- Married filing separately (MFS): $20,500–$35,500
- Head of household (HoH): $30,750–$53,250
- Married filing jointly (MFJ): $41,000–$71,000

Withdrawing funds early can result in the required repayment of the saver's match and early withdrawal penalties. These consequences make this program a less viable option for taxpayers that frequently take IRA loans and distributions before reaching the eligible age.

Despite superseding the saver's credit, many of the same qualification criteria are present in the saver's match. This criterion includes the exclusion of taxpayers claimed as a dependent on another return, taxpayers that are students, and taxpayers under 18 years of age.[99] This makes it difficult for college students to develop good retirement habits while still in school.

> **Example 12.** Jason is 21 years old and graduates from college in the spring of 2027. Jason is a single filer, and no other taxpayer claims him as a dependent. He works part-time at the coffee shop on his college campus and makes $15,000 annually. Jason has recently learned the importance of planning for retirement early and has opened a traditional IRA, to which he plans on contributing $2,000 per year.
>
> Jason cannot take the saver's match in 2027. He was a full-time student for half the year and therefore does not qualify for the match.

---

96. Ibid.

97. Ibid, §104.

98. Ibid, §103; IRC §6433(b)(2).

99. *Retirement Savings Contributions Credit (Saver's Credit).* Dec. 21, 2022. IRS. [www.irs.gov/retirement-plans/plan-participant-employee/retirement-savings-contributions-savers-credit] Accessed on Mar. 6, 2023.

Example 13. Use the same facts as **Example 12,** except that Jason takes the next year off from school for travel. Jason takes the saver's match in 2028, assuming he has earned income and contributes $2,000 to a traditional IRA. Because Jason is no longer a full-time student, is over 18 years old, and is under the MAGI threshold, he can receive a $1,000 saver's match contribution.

ROTH IRA UPDATE

Although taxpayers do not get a current tax deduction for contributions to Roth IRAs, the qualified distributions from Roth IRAs are not included in income. Taxpayers may contribute to Roth IRAs regardless of age, but the taxpayer must have earned income. High-income taxpayers (as defined by statute) are prohibited from contributing to Roth IRAs.[100]

Because qualified distributions from Roth IRAs are excluded from tax, they are attractive retirement planning vehicles for many taxpayers. This section examines methods for contributing funds into Roth IRA accounts either through new contributions, Roth conversions, backdoor conversions, or mega-backdoor conversions.

CONTRIBUTIONS

The general contribution limit applies to all IRAs (traditional or Roth).[101] However, the Roth IRA contribution limit requires that a taxpayer first reduce the general contribution limit by any traditional IRA contributions made.[102] For 2023, the general contribution limit applicable to all of a taxpayer's traditional and Roth IRA contributions is the lesser of:

- $6,500 ($7,500 for taxpayers 50 or older before the end of the year),[103] or
- The taxpayer's taxable compensation for the year.

IRC §408A(c)(3) limits annual Roth IRA contributions based on a taxpayer's MAGI. Annually, the IRS issues a notice containing the cost-of-living adjustment[104] to the Roth IRA MAGI limit for all taxpayers. Taxpayers with incomes over the following phaseout ranges[105] cannot make Roth IRA contributions.

Filing Status	2023 MAGI Phaseout Ranges
Single, HoH	$138,000–153,000
MFJ, Qualifying surviving spouse[106]	218,000–228,000
MFS (lived with spouse)	0– 10,000
MFS (lived apart from spouse)	138,000–153,000

100. IRC §408A(c)(3).

101. IRC §408A(c)(2).

102. Ibid.

103. IRS Notice 2022-55, 2022-45 IRB 443.

104. Ibid.

105. Ibid.

106. The filing status qualifying widow(er) is now called qualifying surviving spouse per IRS Pub. 17, *Your Federal Income Tax For Individuals* (2022). The rules for the filing status have not changed. The same rules that applied for qualifying widow(er) apply to qualifying surviving spouse.

For purposes of a Roth IRA, MAGI is defined as follows.[107]

	Adjusted gross income (AGI)
−	Income resulting from the conversion of a traditional IRA to a Roth IRA
−	Income resulting from the rollover of a qualified retirement plan to a Roth IRA
+	Traditional IRA deduction
+	Student loan interest deduction
+	Foreign-earned income exclusion and housing exclusion
+	Foreign housing deduction
+	Excludable qualified savings bond interest
+	Excluded employer-provided adoption benefits
	MAGI

Taxpayers with MAGI exceeding the phaseout ranges cannot make Roth IRA contributions. However, the age limit after which taxpayers can no longer contribute to IRAs no longer exists.[108]

Example 14. Shelly, a 49-year-old single filer with $5,500 of 2023 taxable wages, would like to make a $5,000 traditional IRA contribution and a $2,000 Roth IRA contribution for 2023. Shelly's general contribution limit is $5,500 (the lesser of compensation or $6,500). If Shelly makes a $5,000 traditional IRA contribution, her Roth IRA contribution limit is $500 ($5,500 general contribution limit – $5,000 traditional IRA contribution). Therefore, Shelly can make only a $500 Roth IRA contribution for 2023.

Spousal Roth IRA

Married couples filing joint returns may facilitate a spouse's Roth IRA contribution by using the working spouse's compensation.[109] This requires that the couple file jointly and that MAGI is not over the phaseout range.[110] For 2023, the general contribution limit for a spousal IRA, either Roth or traditional, is the lesser of:[111]

- $6,500 ($7,500 for spouses ages 50 or over before the end of the year),[112] or
- The combined compensation of both spouses includable in gross income for the year, reduced by any IRA contributions (traditional or Roth) made by the other spouse for the year.

Example 15. On December 31, 2023, Tom and Betty are married taxpayers aged 73 and 69, respectively. During 2023, Tom receives only retirement income. Betty has $5,000 taxable compensation. Tom makes a timely 2023 contribution to Betty's Roth IRA. Although Tom is over age 72, there is no maximum age for IRA contributions. However, the maximum contribution cannot exceed $5,000 (Betty's taxable compensation).

Example 16. On December 31, 2023, Elena and Kevin Simpson are married taxpayers aged 46 and 49, respectively. Elena and Kevin have $10,000 and $5,000 of 2023 taxable compensation, respectively. Elena makes a $6,500 timely 2023 contribution to her Roth IRA. Kevin would like to make the maximum 2023 contribution to his Roth IRA. Although the general contribution limit for Kevin is $6,500, he only has $5,000 of taxable 2023 compensation. Fortunately, Elena has $3,500 ($10,000 − $6,500) of available taxable compensation that Kevin can use to facilitate the remaining $1,500 of his $6,500 Roth IRA contribution for 2023.

---

107. IRS Pub. 590-A, *Contributions to Individual Retirement Arrangements (IRAs).*

108. *SECURE Act of 2019,* PL 116-94, §107, repealing IRC §§219(d)(1) and 408A(c)(4).

109. IRC §219(f)(2) defines compensation to include earned income and net earnings from self-employment in IRC §401(c)(2).

110. IRC §219(c)(2).

111. IRC §219(b)(1).

112. IRS Notice 2022-55, 2022-45 IRB 443.

Excess Contributions

As mentioned previously, if a taxpayer makes a Roth IRA **contribution** that exceeds their contribution limit, the taxpayer may be subject to a 6% excess contribution penalty unless steps are taken to correct the excess.[113] A taxpayer has several options for correcting the excess contribution.

Withdrawal of Excess Contribution. If a taxpayer withdraws the excess contribution plus any earnings on the contribution prior to the due date (including extensions) of the individual income tax return, then the taxpayer is deemed to have not made a contribution at all for that tax year. The pitfall to this option is that the earnings that are withdrawn are taxable in the year the excess contribution was made not in the year received.[114] This means that the earnings should be reported on Form 1040, *U.S. Individual Income Tax Return*, for the deemed contribution year.

When a tax return with an IRA contribution is timely filed (excluding extensions), the IRA contribution can still be returned penalty-free within six months of the original due date.[115] In this case, the taxpayer should file an amended return with "Filed pursuant to section 301.9100-2" written at the top. Any related earnings should be reported on the amended return and an explanation of the withdrawal should be included.[116]

> **Example 17.** Jan is in her early 30s and makes the maximum Roth IRA contribution of $6,500 in June 2023 after receiving a big bonus. She is single with no children and only has one Form W-2 and a small dividend. Her Form W-2 reports taxable wages of $150,000.
>
> Jan makes an appointment with Keith, a local practitioner. His first available appointment is on April 1, 2024. Keith advises Jan about the income limitation associated with Roth IRA contributions and to withdraw the funds together with any earnings on the $6,500. He explains that this needs to be done before the return is filed and that the earnings must be reported on the 2023 tax return. He also tells Jan that because she is under 59½, the earnings are subject to the 10% early withdrawal penalty tax. He recommends that Jan files an extension to have time to make the withdrawal. Once withdrawn, Jan lets Keith know the amount of earnings on the Roth IRA, and Keith reports the earnings on Jan's Form 1040 for 2023.
>
> **Example 18.** Use the same facts as **Example 17.** Jan files her 2023 tax return without making the withdrawal of the excess contribution. Jan still has until the extended due date for an individual tax return to withdraw the excess contribution with the earnings. However, now Jan must file an amended return for 2023 to report the earnings.

Carry Forward the Excess Contribution.[117] If a taxpayer has an excess contribution for a year, they have the option of applying the excess contribution to the next tax year. This presumes that the taxpayer knows that they have less than the maximum contributed for the carryforward year.

> **Example 19.** Use the same facts as **Example 17,** except that Jan knows that the bonus she receives in 2023 is the result of a special project and has already been told not to expect such a large bonus in 2024. Without a bonus, Jan's income is $100,000. Based on that amount of MAGI, Jan can make a $6,500 Roth IRA contribution for 2024 (lesser of $6,500 maximum contribution and $100,000 MAGI). Because she has not yet made a 2024 contribution, she elects to treat the 2023 contribution as a 2024 contribution.

---

113. IRC §7701(a)(37), referring to IRC §408(a) for IRAs and IRC §408(b) for individual retirement annuities.

114. IRC §408(d)(4).

115. Treas. Reg. §301.9100-2.

116. IRS Pub. 590-A, *Contributions to Individual Retirement Arrangements (IRAs).*

117. Ibid.

Recharacterize the Excess Contribution.[118] The most efficient tax option is to recharacterize the contribution as a traditional IRA contribution. The contribution is nondeductible but recharacterization prevents the taxpayer from having to withdraw the contribution altogether. Recharacterization involves undoing the original contribution and moving the funds to a traditional IRA. Taxpayers have until the due date of their return, including any extensions filed, to recharacterize a Roth contribution.[119] This is done in a trustee-to-trustee transfer and includes any earnings on the excess contribution. Although there would be no taxable income with the recharacterization, Form 8606, *Nondeductible IRAs*, is required to report the nondeductible IRA contribution.

Do Nothing. The 6% excess contribution penalty discussed previously applies each year that the excess contribution remains in the Roth IRA. Therefore, a taxpayer incurs additional penalties if they choose to do nothing to correct the excess contribution.

Practitioner Planning Tip

It is important that practitioners ask whether a taxpayer has made excess contributions to a Roth account as it may be necessary to extend the due date of the return in order to complete the recharacterization and correctly prepare the return.

DISTRIBUTIONS[120]

Amounts that taxpayers distribute from their Roth IRA accounts follow a defined order.

1. Roth IRA contributions, excluding conversion contributions
2. Conversion contributions on a first-in, first-out basis
3. Earnings on contributions

Note. The reason the distribution order is important is if the taxpayer takes a distribution before the 5-year period ends, the earnings are taxable and subject to a penalty.[121]

This sequence has the fortunate consequence of classifying premature distributions as coming from regular contributions. Because the contributions already have a basis, the first distribution amounts are considered a return of the taxpayer's contributions[122] and are not included in gross income. Distributions deplete each category before they deplete the next in the order listed previously.

Taxpayers must aggregate all Roth distributions during the year as one distribution. Thus, any one distribution is considered to have been made from all of a taxpayer's Roth accounts collectively.[123]

---

118. Treas. Reg. §1.408A-5.

119. Ibid.

120. Treas. Reg. §1.408A-6, A-8.

121. IRC §408A (d)(B).

122. Treas. Reg. §1.408A-6, A-1(b), referencing A-8.

123. Treas. Reg. §1.408A-6, A-9.

ROTH CONVERSIONS

A Roth IRA is an attractive retirement planning strategy for many taxpayers because there are no RMD requirements during the life of the account owner. If qualified withdrawals are made, they are completely tax-free.[124] Converting traditional IRAs into Roth IRAs makes it possible to shield more of a taxpayer's retirement account from future tax. This can be a complex process, and tax professionals must be able to navigate the confusing rules regarding conversions to advise their clients properly.

Taxpayers Benefiting from Roth Conversions

Not all taxpayers benefit from Roth conversions, regardless of their popularity. For most taxpayers, the strategy is converting a traditional IRA to a Roth IRA while realizing as little taxable income as possible. Having settled this, getting money out of the Roth IRA with as little tax as possible becomes paramount.

Taxpayers Not Needing Distributions for Five Years After Conversion.[125] Contributions to Roth IRAs must remain in place for at least five years until they can be withdrawn tax-free as a qualified distribution.[126] Known as the nonexclusion period, it begins on January 1, the first year the taxpayer makes a Roth contribution. When the taxpayer makes contributions in subsequent years, the nonexclusion period does not change.

The rule for **conversions** works differently. **Each** conversion has its own 5-year period that must expire before the money associated with that conversion can be withdrawn, regardless of the owner's age. Consequently, taxpayers approaching age 59½ years may have an unpleasant surprise if a need arises for converted money within five years. They may incur the 10% additional tax of IRC §72(t) even if they have reached the age at which withdrawals normally can be made tax-free.

However, there are exceptions to the nonexclusion period, which enable the taxpayer to receive a **qualified special purpose distribution.**[127] These exceptions include the taxpayer becoming disabled, separating from their employer, receiving distributions that are part of a series of substantially equal periodic payments, among others.[128]

Practitioner Planning Tip

While custodians should report these amounts with distribution code 2 on Form 1099-R, *Distributions From Pensions, Annuities, Retirement or Profit-Sharing Plans, IRAs, Insurance Contracts, etc.*, they may report it with code 1 because they are unaware that an exception exists.[129] Practitioners should follow up with their clients to ensure that no exclusions apply.

124. The provision for tax-free withdrawals is subject to the 5-year nonexclusion period in IRC §408A(d)(2)(B).

125. Treas. Reg. §1.480A-6, A-5.

126. IRC §408A(d)(2)(B).

127. IRC §§408A(d)(2)(A)(iv) and (t)(5), referring to IRC §72(t)(2).

128. IRC §72(t)(2).

129. Instructions for Forms 1099-R and 5498.

Example 20. Jeff is the account owner of a Roth IRA that had a value of $76,000 on December 31, 2022. The funds in this Roth IRA were converted from a traditional IRA with a $0 basis in 2020. Jeff turned 59 in January 2023.

Jeff needs money from his Roth IRA in November 2023, and none of the exceptions that could result in a qualified special purpose distribution apply. Although his 59th birthday occurred more than six months earlier, Jeff is still liable for tax on any portion of the Roth IRA conversion that he withdraws that year. The 5-year nonexclusion period during which he is still liable for the 10% penalty began on January 1, 2020, but does not expire until the last day of 2024.

Taxpayers With Traditional IRAs Having Basis. Ownership of a traditional IRA can trigger significant tax, even if the funds from an IRA with a 100% basis are used for the conversion. The rules for conversions assume that distributions are taken proportionately from each IRA an individual owns, regardless of the IRA from which the funds for the conversion come.[130]

No Income Limit on Roth IRA Conversions

One of the advantages of converting traditional IRA accounts to Roth IRAs is that there is no income limit on **conversions.**[131] This is true even if a taxpayer's MAGI precludes a current-year contribution to a Roth IRA.

Aggregate All IRAs

When determining the tax consequences of an IRA distribution, the IRS requires a pro rata distribution from **all** traditional IRA accounts.[132] This provision has the effect of requiring a taxpayer to aggregate the value of all IRA accounts. This can create unexpected tax consequences when a taxpayer has made both deductible and nondeductible contributions to an IRA. Because the IRAs are treated on an aggregate basis, each distribution includes only a partial basis recovery until all the basis has been recovered. If a taxpayer has multiple IRA accounts with a varying amount of basis, a conversion to a Roth IRA may be subject to additional taxes and possibly penalties.

Custodians or trustees of IRAs, including traditional, SIMPLE, SEP, and Roth IRA plans, report year-end values of accounts, as well as contributions, on Form 5498, *IRA Contribution Information.*[133] This information is valuable in determining the existence of accounts and their values as used to determine RMDs, if any. Custodians or trustees of IRAs are required to report this information on an annual basis to the IRS, which reports this information on wage and income transcripts.[134]

Example 21. Howard's income has increased substantially over his career. Although he started at one employer many years earlier at minimum wage, his income in 2023 at his second employer was too high for a single taxpayer to make deductible IRA contributions. Howard has actively contributed to a traditional IRA for the last five years, even though he was not able to deduct the contributions. By September 2023, Howard has built a traditional IRA with a significant basis and market value.

Shirley, Howard's new financial planner, knows the benefits of Roth IRAs and the tax ramifications of converting traditional IRAs to Roth IRAs. She also knows that converting a traditional IRA with a substantial basis can result in less tax. Reviewing Howard's tax returns for those five years, she confirms that Howard's basis in the IRA is $29,500, while the market's rise puts the value of the IRA at $40,000. Howard has forgotten about the SEP IRA from his first employer.

130. IRC §408(d)(2)(A).

131. IRC §408A(d)(3) provides for conversion but is not subject to the income limits of IRC §480A(d)(2), which apply only to contributions.

132. IRC §408(d)(2)(A).

133. Instructions for Forms 1099-R and 5498.

134. IRM 21.2.3.2.3 (2013).

In October 2023, Howard converts his entire traditional IRA into a Roth IRA, thinking he added only $10,500 to his total income ($40,000 total market value – $29,500 basis). Norma, Howard's new tax practitioner, obtains his 2022 wage and income transcript from the IRS in November in preparation for the upcoming tax season. The appearance of a SEP IRA with a $50,000 market value catches her attention, and she asks Howard about it. The custodian of the SEP IRA has reported its December 31, 2022, value on Form 5498, which the IRS records on Howard's annual wage and income transcript. Her phone call reminds Howard about the account, which has not crossed his mind in a decade. Unfortunately, Norma has to tell Howard that his Roth conversion generates more taxable income than he had been anticipating. Even though the conversion itself only touches the traditional IRA account with a substantial basis, the conversion must also consider the SEP that Howard had forgotten about, which had a zero basis.

Practitioner Planning Tip

If the taxpayer has SIMPLE or SEP IRAs without any basis as well as traditional IRAs with basis, a strategy might be to roll those SIMPLE or SEP IRAs into qualified employer plans **before** the Roth conversion. This will limit the taxability of the Roth conversion. However, the strategy will only be viable if the taxpayer is an active participant in such a plan, and the plan documents permit such transactions.

Reporting Roth Conversions[135]

IRA trustees and custodians are required to report contributions in box 1 of Form 5498. This form denotes these as contributions to a Roth IRA by marking the appropriate checkbox in line 7. The account's fair market value as of the last day of the prior year should appear in box 5. If the taxpayer makes any of the contributions for 2023 between January 1 and April 15, 2024, this amount should appear in box 10.

Form 5498 can also serve as a useful source of information about IRA conversions, as well, because box 3 reports the amount of Roth IRA conversions.

Practitioner Planning Tip

Tax practitioners should consider reviewing at least five years of IRS wage and income transcripts for **new clients**. This information may provide important information regarding the 5-year nonexclusion periods for the clients' Roth IRA contributions and the separate 5-year periods for their Roth conversions. This review may require new clients to execute Form 8821, *Tax Information Authorization*, or Form 2848, *Power of Attorney and Declaration of Representative*, so that the records can be obtained directly from the IRS.

135. Instructions for Forms 1099-R and 5498 (2023).

Consequences of Conversions

Roth conversions have consequences that affect taxpayers' tax and financial positions. Some of those consequences are discussed next.

Higher Taxes in Year of Conversion. As mentioned previously, the amount converted to a Roth IRA in excess of any basis in the IRA is subject to income tax in the year of the conversion. The increased income can result in higher taxes for the taxpayer.

Smaller Medical Deductions. If a taxpayer itemizes, a Roth conversion likely increases their AGI, decreasing their itemized medical deductions.[136]

Adjustments to Medicare Premiums in Future Years.[137] The income generated from a Roth IRA conversion can also result in higher Medicare premiums in future years. This unwelcome premium increase has an official name: the income-related monthly adjustment amount (IRMAA).

Practitioner Planning Tip

Tax practitioners with clients turning age 63 in the next year may choose to discuss with them the possibility that a Roth conversion may push the client into a higher Medicare premium bracket. For more information on IRMAA planning, see the 2022 *University of Illinois Federal Tax Workbook*, Volume B, Chapter 1: Elder Issues.

8

Net Investment Income Tax (NIIT). If a taxpayer converts a traditional IRA to a Roth IRA and the conversion increases their MAGI over the net investment income threshold, they may be subject to NIIT on their dividends, interest, and other net investment income.[138]

In the case of an individual, the NIIT is 3.8% on the lesser of:[139]

- Net investment income, or
- The excess of MAGI over the following threshold amounts:
  - $250,000 for MFJ or qualifying surviving spouse
  - $125,000 for MFS
  - $200,000 for single or HoH

---

136. See IRC §213.

137. *Premiums: Rules for Higher-Income Beneficiaries.* 2023. SSA. [www.ssa.gov/benefits/medicare/medicare-premiums.html] Accessed on Jun. 22, 2023.

138. IRC §1411.

139. *Topic No. 559, Net Investment Income Tax*. Apr. 6, 2023.IRS. [www.irs.gov/taxtopics/tc559] Accessed on Jul. 20, 2023.

Example 22. Alex is a junior manager for a large manufacturing firm, which pays him a taxable salary of $110,000 annually. As a single taxpayer, Alex has accumulated a significant traditional IRA from his early days with the firm in 2003. He has no basis in the IRA, as he made only tax-deductible contributions.

In 2022, Alex's Aunt Martha passes away, leaving him with a substantial inheritance consisting of dividend-paying stocks. In early January 2023, Aunt Martha's executor transfers the stock into Alex's name. Stella is Alex's financial planner, and she tells him to anticipate dividend income for 2023 of $80,000 from his inheritance. Alex's projected MAGI for 2023 is $190,000 ($110,000 salary + $80,000 dividend income). Stella informs Alex that although he can expect his tax to increase, he can be thankful that it is unlikely to cause an NIIT problem.

Stella is also aware of Alex's IRA and for the last several years has been discussing with him the possibility of converting it to a Roth IRA. At their yearend meeting in December 2022, Stella advises Alex that if he waits until 2023 to make the Roth IRA conversion, he may have NIIT because a Roth conversion would leave him with 2023 projected income exceeding the NIIT threshold.

Alex has a tax planning opportunity. He can convert some portion of his traditional IRA into a Roth IRA in the waning days of 2022 and be less likely to have a NIIT liability. Alternatively, he can wait until 2023 when the conversion likely creates a larger tax burden because of the combined effect of the dividend income and the NIIT. The threshold for the NIIT is not indexed, so Alex is unlikely to see his income drop below the threshold until he retires.

Recharacterization of Roth Conversions[140]

Before December 31, 2017, a taxpayer could convert from a Roth account back to a traditional IRA. After the Tax Cuts and Jobs Act[141] (TCJA), undoing a conversion is no longer permitted. The Code also prohibits recharacterizing amounts a taxpayer has converted from one of the following types of qualified retirement plans.

- Traditional, SEP, or SIMPLE IRAs
- IRC §401(k) plans
- IRC §§403(b) or 457 plans

If a taxpayer ends the year with a higher-than-expected taxable income, reversing the situation is impossible.

BACKDOOR ROTH CONVERSIONS

The Code contains MAGI limitations on contributions to Roth IRAs,[142] but it does not limit conversions and rollovers based on MAGI. This provision allows individuals to contribute to nondeductible traditional IRAs and convert the traditional IRA to a Roth IRA. This maneuver, often called a "backdoor Roth," only works well if the taxpayer does not have any other traditional IRAs because the portion of IRA distributions treated as a return of nondeductible contributions is prorated based on the total balance of the IRAs per the aggregation rule discussed previously.[143]

> **Note**. The total balance of the IRAs must be modified for amounts distributed and outstanding rollovers. Complete instructions for calculating the nontaxable portion of traditional IRA distributions when the taxpayer has basis are found in the instructions for Form 8606.

---

140. IRC §408A(d)(6)(B)(iii). See also *IRA FAQS - Recharacterization of IRA Contributions*. Jan. 15, 2020. IRS. [www.irs.gov/retirement-plans/retirement-plans-faqs-regarding-iras] Accessed on Jun. 22, 2023.

141. *Tax Cuts and Jobs Act,* PL 115-97.

142. IRC §408A(c)(3).

143. IRS Notice 87-16, 1987-1 CB 446.

Example 23. Ethan is a senior manager at a manufacturing company but did not have any traditional or Roth IRAs in 2021, the year he turned 56 years old. In 2022, his MAGI was $230,000, which was over the applicable Roth IRA contribution limit. Accordingly, he is not permitted to contribute directly to a Roth IRA.

Instead, Ethan contributes $6,000 to a traditional IRA for 2022 in early December of that year. Because Ethan is covered by a retirement plan with his employer, his MAGI is too high to deduct the traditional IRA contribution. On his 2022 return, he completes Form 8606 to establish a $6,000 basis in his traditional IRA.

After contributing the $6,000, Ethan converts the traditional IRA to a Roth IRA in mid-December 2022. The financial institution holding the funds issues a Form 1099-R for 2022, showing that Ethan received a $6,000 distribution from his traditional IRA. Ethan reports the distribution on his return and includes the distribution on Form 8606 to reduce the taxable portion of the $6,000 distribution by his $6,000 basis. The result is that Ethan could add $6,000 to a Roth IRA for 2022 without tax consequences despite his income being over the applicable limits.

The strategy loses its appeal if the taxpayer has a traditional IRA with little or no basis. In this event, a substantial portion of the backdoor IRA becomes taxable.

Example 24. Use the same facts as **Example 23,** except Ethan has $76,000 in traditional IRAs as of December 31, 2022, funded when his MAGI was low enough to make deductible contributions. Starting in 2003, Ethan made these contributions with no basis in his traditional IRAs and stopped in 2013 when his income increased to the point he could no longer make contributions.

When Ethan makes the contribution of $6,000 in 2022, he sets up a new traditional IRA for his nondeductible contribution. Ethan is thinking that he can specifically identify that account as the account that he is converting to a Roth IRA. However, this is not effective because the basis created by the 2022 contribution is applied to his aggregated traditional IRAs. Accordingly, $5,561 of the distribution is taxable, as shown on the following Worksheet 1-1 from IRS Pub. 590-B. Ethan's 2022 Form 8606 follows the worksheet.

1. Enter the basis in your traditional IRAs as of December 31, 2021	1.	0
2. Enter the total of all contributions made to your traditional IRAs during 2022 and all contributions made during 2023 that were for 2022, ***whether or not deductible***. Don't include rollover contributions properly rolled over into IRAs. Also, don't include certain returned contributions described in the instructions for line 7 of Form 8606	2.	6,000
3. Add lines 1 and 2	3.	6,000
4. Enter the value of all your traditional IRAs as of December 31, 2022 (include any outstanding rollovers from traditional IRAs to other traditional IRAs). Subtract any repayments of qualified disaster distributions	4.	76,000
5. Enter the total distributions from traditional IRAs (including amounts converted to Roth IRAs that will be shown on line 16 of Form 8606) received in 2022. Also, include repayments of qualified disaster distributions, qualified charitable distributions (QCDs), and a one-time distribution to fund a health savings account (HSA). (Don't include outstanding rollovers included on line 4 or any rollovers between traditional IRAs completed by December 31, 2022. Also, don't include certain returned contributions described in the instructions for line 7 of Form 8606.)	5.	6,000
6. Add lines 4 and 5	6.	82,000
7. Divide line 3 by line 6. Enter the result as a decimal (rounded to at least three places). If the result is 1.000 or more, enter 1.000	7.	0.07317
8. Nontaxable portion of the distribution. Multiply line 5 by line 7. Enter the result here and on lines 13 and 17 of Form 8606	8.	439
9. Taxable portion of the distribution (before adjustment for conversions). Subtract line 8 from line 5. Enter the result here, and if there are no amounts converted to Roth IRAs, **stop here** and enter the result on line 15a of Form 8606	9.	5,561
10. Enter the amount included on line 9 that is allocable to amounts converted to Roth IRAs by December 31, 2022. (See ***Note*** at the end of this worksheet.) Enter here and on line 18 of Form 8606	10.	5,561
11. Taxable portion of the distribution (after adjustments for conversions). Subtract line 10 from line 9. Enter the result here and on line 15a of Form 8606	11.	

Note. If the amount on line 5 of this worksheet includes an amount converted to a Roth IRA by December 31, 2022, you must determine the percentage of the distribution allocable to the conversion. To figure the percentage, divide the amount converted (from line 16 of Form 8606) by the total distributions shown on line 5. To figure the amounts to include on line 10 of this worksheet and on line 18 of Form 8606, multiply line 9 of the worksheet by the percentage you figured.

For Example 24

Form **8606**

Department of the Treasury
Internal Revenue Service

Nondeductible IRAs

Go to *www.irs.gov/Form8606* for instructions and the latest information.
Attach to 2022 Form 1040, 1040-SR, or 1040-NR.

OMB No. 1545-0074
2022
Attachment Sequence No. **48**

Name. If married, file a separate form for each spouse required to file 2022 Form 8606. See instructions.
Ethan Miller

Your social security number
*****-**-9999**

Fill in Your Address Only if You Are Filing This Form by Itself and Not With Your Tax Return

Home address (number and street, or P.O. box if mail is not delivered to your home): **101 S. Vermont St**
Apt. no.:

City, town or post office, state, and ZIP code. If you have a foreign address, also complete the spaces below (see instructions).
Burlington, IL 60109

Foreign country name | Foreign province/state/county | Foreign postal code

Part I **Nondeductible Contributions to Traditional IRAs and Distributions From Traditional, SEP, and SIMPLE IRAs**
Complete this part only if one or more of the following apply.

- You made nondeductible contributions to a traditional IRA for 2022.
- You took distributions from a traditional, SEP, or SIMPLE IRA in 2022 **and** you made nondeductible contributions to a traditional IRA in 2022 or an earlier year. For this purpose, a distribution does not include a rollover (other than a repayment of a qualified disaster distribution, if any, from 2022 Form(s) 8915-F (see instructions)), qualified charitable distribution, one-time distribution to fund an HSA, conversion, recharacterization, or return of certain contributions.
- You converted part, but not all, of your traditional, SEP, and SIMPLE IRAs to Roth IRAs in 2022 **and** you made nondeductible contributions to a traditional IRA in 2022 or an earlier year.

Line	Description	Inner line	Inner amount	Line	Amount
1	Enter your nondeductible contributions to traditional IRAs for 2022, including those made for 2022 from January 1, 2023, through April 18, 2023. See instructions			1	6,000
2	Enter your total basis in traditional IRAs. See instructions			2	
3	Add lines 1 and 2			3	6,000
	In 2022, did you take a distribution from traditional, SEP, or SIMPLE IRAs, or make a Roth IRA conversion? **No** — Enter the amount from line 3 on line 14. Do not complete the rest of Part I. **Yes** — Go to line 4.				
4	Enter those contributions included on line 1 that were made from January 1, 2023, through April 18, 2023			4	
5	Subtract line 4 from line 3			5	6,000
6	Enter the value of **all** your traditional, SEP, and SIMPLE IRAs as of December 31, 2022, plus any outstanding rollovers. Subtract certain repayments of qualified disaster distributions, if any, from 2022 Form(s) 8915-F (see instructions)	6	76,000		
7	Enter your distributions from traditional, SEP, and SIMPLE IRAs in 2022. **Do not** include rollovers (other than repayments of qualified disaster distributions, if any, from 2022 Form(s) 8915-F (see instructions)), qualified charitable distributions, a one-time distribution to fund an HSA, conversions to a Roth IRA, certain returned contributions, or recharacterizations of traditional IRA contributions (see instructions)	7			
8	Enter the net amount you converted from traditional, SEP, and SIMPLE IRAs to Roth IRAs in 2022. Also, enter this amount on line 16	8	6,000		
9	Add lines 6, 7, and 8 — 9: 82,000				
10	Divide line 5 by line 9. Enter the result as a decimal rounded to at least 3 places. If the result is 1.000 or more, enter "1.000"	10	× 0 . 0732		
11	Multiply line 8 by line 10. This is the nontaxable portion of the amount you converted to Roth IRAs. Also, enter this amount on line 17	11	439		
12	Multiply line 7 by line 10. This is the nontaxable portion of your distributions that you did not convert to a Roth IRA	12			
13	Add lines 11 and 12. This is the nontaxable portion of all your distributions			13	439
14	Subtract line 13 from line 3. This is **your total basis in traditional IRAs for 2022 and earlier years**			14	5,561
15a	Subtract line 12 from line 7			15a	
b	Enter the amount on line 15a attributable to qualified disaster distributions, if any, from 2022 Form(s) 8915-F (see instructions). Also, enter this amount on 2022 Form(s) 8915-F, line 18, as applicable (see instructions)			15b	
c	**Taxable amount.** Subtract line 15b from line 15a. If more than zero, also include this amount on 2022 Form 1040, 1040-SR, **or** 1040-NR, line 4b			15c	
	Note: You may be subject to an additional 10% tax on the amount on line 15c if you were under age 59½ at the time of the distribution. See instructions.				

For Privacy Act and Paperwork Reduction Act Notice, see separate instructions. Cat. No. 63966F Form **8606** (2022)

For Example 24

Form 8606 (2022) Page **2**

Part II **2022 Conversions From Traditional, SEP, or SIMPLE IRAs to Roth IRAs**
Complete this part if you converted part or all of your traditional, SEP, and SIMPLE IRAs to a Roth IRA in 2022.

16	If you completed Part I, enter the amount from line 8. Otherwise, enter the net amount you converted from traditional, SEP, and SIMPLE IRAs to Roth IRAs in 2022	16	6,000
17	If you completed Part I, enter the amount from line 11. Otherwise, enter your basis in the amount on line 16 (see instructions)	17	439
18	**Taxable amount.** Subtract line 17 from line 16. If more than zero, also include this amount on 2022 Form 1040, 1040-SR, or 1040-NR, line 4b	18	5,561

Distributions From Roth IRAs

As a result, very little of the basis from Ethan's 2022 nondeductible traditional IRA contribution is included in the basis of the Roth conversion. If Ethan realizes this after he has made the conversion and has second thoughts, he cannot undo the conversion.

Other Concerns

The IRS has not explicitly sanctioned any form of backdoor Roth conversion. Some speculate that the step transaction doctrine could be used to conclude that an attempted Roth conversion is not legitimate for an individual otherwise ineligible to make a Roth **contribution** because of their income.[144] The step transaction doctrine combines a series of actions into a single transaction if the series of actions seem to be directed to accomplish a particular result.[145]

In a 1987 case, the Tax Court used the step transaction doctrine to decide that a corporate reorganization was tax-deferred in light of its acquisition. The court offered the following logic.[146]

> *The step transaction doctrine is in effect another rule of substance over form; it treats a series of formally separate "steps" as a single transaction if such steps are in substance integrated, interdependent, and focused toward a particular result... There is no universally accepted test as to when and how the step transaction doctrine should be applied to a given set of facts.*

8

The House Conference Report on TCJA discusses Roth conversions, acknowledging in a footnote that taxpayers with incomes exceeding the Roth IRA contribution threshold may convert funds from traditional IRAs into Roth accounts.[147] A footnote in a report may indicate Congressional intent, but it does not carry the same weight as the enacted statute.

Caution. Absent any guidance from the IRS on this point, taxpayers and their tax practitioners must understand the risk associated with backdoor Roth IRA conversions. Although not enacted, legislation has been suggested that could restrict Roth conversions by income.[148]

Note. Although Treas. Reg. §1.408A-4, answer 2, still states that a conversion is not permitted for individuals with MAGI exceeding $100,000, this is no longer correct. It was overturned by the *Tax Increase Prevention and Reconciliation Act of 2005,* PL 109-222, §512(a). Although this law was enacted in 2006, the IRS has not removed this from the regulation.

144. *Backdoor Roth IRA Contributions — Strategy or Step Transaction Abuse?* Kitces, Michael. Jan. 24, 2012. Kitces.com. [www.kitces.com/blog/dodging-the-income-limits-on-roth-contributions-strategy-or-abuse] Accessed on Jun. 28, 2023.

145. *A walk through the step-transaction doctrine.* Knight, Ray and Knight, Lee. May 1, 2021. The Tax Adviser. [www.thetaxadviser.com/issues/2021/may/step-transaction-doctrine.html] Accessed on Jun. 27, 2023.

146. *Penrod, et al. v. Comm'r*, 88 TC 1415 (1987).

147. H.R. Rep. No. 115-466, at 289 (2017).

148. *Fact Sheet: The President's Budget Cuts Wasteful Spending on Big Pharma, Big Oil, and Other Special Interests, Cracks Down on Systemic Fraud, and Makes Programs More Cost Effective.* Mar. 9, 2023. The White House. [www.whitehouse.gov/briefing-room/statements-releases/2023/03/09/fact-sheet-the-presidents-budget-cuts-wasteful-spending-on-big-pharma-big-oil-and-other-special-interests-cracks-down-on-systemic-fraud-and-makes-programs-more-cost-effective] Accessed on Jun. 27, 2023.

MEGA-BACKDOOR ROTH CONVERSIONS[149]

Some taxpayers may wish to accumulate retirement funds in Roth accounts even faster. The "mega-backdoor" Roth conversion strategy allows high-income taxpayers to accumulate more wealth in Roth IRAs despite the MAGI limitations discussed previously.

This special mega-backdoor Roth conversion requires several factors to work.

- The taxpayer must have a §401(k) or §403(b) plan to which they can contribute, and the plan must offer a Roth contribution option. The conversion works even better if the plan allows additional after-tax contributions.
- The plan documents must permit the conversion of previously made contributions to Roth contributions; alternatively, the plan must allow participants to make withdrawals while still participating in the plan.

Contributions to §401(k) plans generally are subject to certain limits.[150]

1. IRC §402(g) limits an employee's salary deferrals ($22,500 in 2023), although this limit itself is increased under IRC §414(v) for individuals at least age 50. It is increased another $7,500 in 2023 to a $30,000 maximum elective deferral.[151] This is the **elective deferral** limit.
2. IRC §415(c) imposes an annual ceiling on total contributions, which is the lesser of the employee's compensation or an annual limit. In 2023, this limit is $66,000[152] for those under 50 ($73,500 for individuals over age 50).[153] This is the annual **additions limit.**[154]

> **Note.** The Code imposes a reduced limit on individuals whom it classifies as highly compensated employees or key employees,[155] as the organization needs the lower limit to meet a nondiscrimination test.[156] If an adjustment is needed under this test, then highly compensated individuals are refunded a portion of the money they set aside as elective deferrals in most cases.

Frequently, a §401(k) plan offers employees the option of contributing on an after-tax basis up to the maximum annual limitation. Because these additional contributions are made with after-tax dollars, these amounts are not taxable when withdrawn. If the employee is now able to convert these after-tax contributions into Roth contributions within the §401(k) plan, it may be possible for them to fund a Roth with a significant amount of money.

Example 25. Marcy is a single taxpayer. Her employer, Anatine Corporation, has §401(k) plans that allow elective deferrals as Roth contributions. In 2023, Marcy is 55 years old, qualifying her to make catch-up contributions to the retirement plan. Anatine matches her contributions at the rate of 8%. Marcy's salary and bonus for 2023 is $185,000 so her MAGI would prevent her from making a Roth contribution individually. However, Marcy can still participate in the Roth option allowed by Anatine's §401(k) plan.

Marcy's maximum §401(k) elective deferral is $30,000, consisting of a $22,500 maximum deferral for all covered employees plus a $7,500 catch-up contribution. If she makes her maximum elective deferral, Anatine contributes another $2,400 ($30,000 × 8%). Marcy can contribute up to $41,100 in after-tax contributions before reaching her annual limit. This is computed by reducing her annual limit of $73,500 by her $30,000 of elective deferrals and by the $2,400 employer's match. If all these funds are contributed to the Roth IRA, Marcy is able to put $73,500 into a Roth account, well beyond the $7,500 individual limit for a Roth IRA.

---

149. *How the mega-backdoor Roth works*. Long, Kelley. May 9, 2023. Journal of Accountancy. [www.journalofaccountancy.com/news/2023/may/how-mega-backdoor-roth-works.html] Accessed on Jun. 26, 2023.

150. *401(k) Contribution Limits — What You Need to Know*. Droblyen, Eric. Jun. 15, 2023. Employee Fiduciary. [www.employeefiduciary.com/blog/contribution-limits] Accessed on Jul. 19, 2023.

151. IRS Notice 2022-55, 2022-45 IRB 443.

152. Ibid. Any catch-up contributions are not included in the annual addition limit.

153. *Retirement Topics — 401(k) and Profit-Sharing Plan Contribution Limits*. Aug. 29, 2023. IRS. [www.irs.gov/retirement-plans/plan-participant-employee/retirement-topics-401k-and-profit-sharing-plan-contribution-limits] Accessed on Aug. 29, 2023.

154. IRC §415(c)(2).

155. IRC §414(q) or 416(i)(1).

156. IRC §401(m).

Chapter 9: Individual Taxpayer Issues

Note. Corrections for all of the chapters are available at **TaxSchool.illinois.edu**. For clarification about terms used throughout this chapter, see the **Acronyms and Abbreviations** section following the index.

For your convenience, in-text website links are also provided as short URLs. Anywhere you see **uofi.tax/xxx**, the link points to the address immediately following in brackets.

9

About the Authors

Kelly Golish, CPA, is the Assistant Director, Tax Materials, at the University of Illinois Tax School. She was previously a manager at Crowder, CPAs in Danville, IL and worked for both public and private accounting firms in Decatur, IL, Cleveland, OH, and San Jose, CA. Kelly earned a Masters in Accounting with an emphasis in Taxation and a Bachelors in Accounting at the University of Notre Dame.

Chris Korban, CPA, is a Tax Materials Specialist at the University of Illinois Tax School. He joined Tax School in 2023 with nine years of experience in public accounting. Chris earned both his Bachelor's Degree in Accounting and Master of Accounting Science from the University of Illinois.

Peg Phillips, CPA, is a writer and editor for the University of Illinois Tax School. She has been with the program since 2003. Peg graduated from the University of Illinois with high honors in accounting and passed the CPA exam in 1989. She currently owns and operates Phillips Tax Service in Pekin, IL.

Shane Smith, CPA, CMA, CFE, is a Tax Manager at AMG National Trust Bank and holds a Masters of Accountancy with an emphasis in Taxation from Gonzaga University.

Rachel Szeklinski, CPA, has worked in public accounting for over six years and started writing for the University of Illinois Tax School in 2022. She graduated from Carroll University with honors in accounting in 2020 and passed the CPA exam in early 2021.

Other chapter contributors and reviewers are listed at the front of this book.

ESTIMATED TAX PAYMENTS

BASICS

To avoid penalties, taxpayers should have sufficient withholding or make timely estimated tax payments. Income taxes are a pay-as-you-go system which means that either an employer or the taxpayer is required to withhold tax on income as earned or received. For taxpayers receiving income not associated with or in addition to a Form W-2, *Wage and Tax Statement,* this income may trigger the requirement to submit estimated tax payments separate from traditional wage withholding.[1] Income that is subject to tax but not typically subject to withholding includes, but is not limited to, the following.

- Self-employment (SE) income
- Interest
- Dividends
- Capital gains
- Prizes
- Rental income
- Gig economy income

Generally, taxpayers expecting to owe at least $1,000 in tax after subtracting withholding and credits are required to make estimated payments.[2] The general safe harbor is to timely pay either:

1. 90% of the tax to be shown on the current year return, or
2. 100% of the tax shown on the previous year tax return, which must cover all 12 months.

Taxpayers with adjusted gross income (AGI) in the prior year higher than $150,000 ($75,000 for individuals married filing separately (MFS)) must substitute 110% for the 100% withholding.[3]

Note. Individuals need to consider any liability for SE taxes,[4] the 3.8% net investment income tax (NIIT),[5] the 0.9% additional Medicare tax,[6] and any pass-through income from partnerships, trusts, estates, and S corporations, in addition to federal income tax liabilities when calculating their estimated tax liabilities.

Note. Certain taxpayers are subject to modified rules. For example, individuals who derive two-thirds of their annual gross income from fishing or farming qualify for special exceptions to the general requirements for estimated tax payments. Such taxpayers may avoid penalties by paying 66.67% of their liability in January or filing and paying 100% of the tax due by March 1 of the following year. Details on what is considered income is available in IRS Publication 505, *Tax Withholding and Estimated Tax.*

---

1. IRS Pub. 505, *Tax Withholding and Estimated Tax.*
2. IRC §6654.
3. Ibid.
4. IRC §7701(b)(1)(A).
5. IRC §1411.
6. IRC §1401(b)(2).

Married Individuals[7]

Married taxpayers can make joint estimated tax payments even if they are not living together. However, spouses cannot make joint estimated tax payments if they meet any of the following criteria.

- The couple is legally separated under a decree of divorce or separate maintenance
- The spouses have different tax years
- Either spouse is a nonresident alien

> **Note.** Couples who cannot make joint estimated tax payments apply the general rules to their separate estimated income.

Allocating Joint Estimated Payments on Separate Returns. Spouses who make joint estimated tax payments but subsequently file separate tax returns can claim their individual payments or divide the payments in any manner in which they both agree. If they cannot agree, each can only claim the estimated payment resulting from the following calculation.

$$\text{Individual's share of joint estimated payment} = \text{Joint estimated payment} \times \frac{\text{Individual tax liability on separate return}}{\text{Total tax liability of both individuals}}$$

> **Caution.** A difficult challenge occurs when one spouse is not willing to share their tax liability.

Taxpayers claiming any portion of a joint estimated tax payment should attach an explanation how they divided the payments and list the spouse's or ex-spouse's tax identification number (TIN) on the tax return. If divorced and remarried during the year, enter the current spouse's TIN on the return and the former spouse's tax TIN, followed by "DIV" on line 26 of Form 1040, *U.S. Individual Income Tax Return.*[8]

Prior Year Separate Returns and Current Year Joint Return. If a couple plans to file a joint return in the current year and filed separate returns in the prior year, for purposes of estimated tax, the prior year tax is the sum of the total tax shown on the separate returns.

Prior Year Joint Return and Current Year Separate Returns. If a couple plans to file separate returns in the current year and filed a joint return for the prior year, for purposes of estimated tax, the prior year tax is the amount of tax for the individual spouse.

The individual's share of tax on a joint return is calculated as follows, using the same filing status as the current year.

$$\text{Individual's share of tax on joint return} = \text{Tax on joint return} \times \frac{\text{Tax individual would have paid if filing separate returns}}{\text{Total tax spouses would have paid if filing separate returns}}$$

7. IRS Pub. 505, *Tax Withholding and Estimated Tax.*

8. IRS Pub. 504, *Divorced or Separated Individuals.*

Estates and Trusts

Estates and trusts generally must also pay estimated tax.[9] However, estates and certain grantor trusts that receive the residue of the decedent's estate under the decedent's will are exempt from making estimated tax payments for the first two years after the decedent's death.

Due Dates

For calendar year individual taxpayers, quarterly tax payment due dates are **typically** as follows.

- April 15
- June 15
- September 15
- January 15

> **Note.** A 1st quarter payment can be made with an extension payment to create an overpayment that carries over to the following tax year.

CALCULATING ESTIMATES ON FORM W-4

Taxpayers complete Form W-4, *Employee's Withholding Certificate,* to calculate the withholdings their employer should withdraw from their payments to cover the individual's income tax liability. Appropriately withheld tax helps individuals prevent underpayment penalties (covered later).

In 2020, the IRS redesigned the form to reduce the form's complexity and increase the transparency and accuracy of the withholding system. The worksheets on the previous form are replaced with questions in an attempt to simplify the process.[10] An example of a blank 2023 Form W-4 follows.

---

9. IRC §6654.

10. *FAQs on the 2020 Form W-4.* Jan. 24, 2023. IRS. [www.irs.gov/newsroom/faqs-on-the-2020-form-w-4] Accessed on Jun. 8, 2023.

Form **W-4**

Department of the Treasury
Internal Revenue Service

Employee's Withholding Certificate

Complete Form W-4 so that your employer can withhold the correct federal income tax from your pay.
Give Form W-4 to your employer.
Your withholding is subject to review by the IRS.

OMB No. 1545-0074

2023

Step 1: Enter Personal Information	(a) First name and middle initial	Last name	**(b) Social security number**
	Address		**Does your name match the name on your social security card?** If not, to ensure you get credit for your earnings, contact SSA at 800-772-1213 or go to *www.ssa.gov*.
	City or town, state, and ZIP code		
	(c) ☐ **Single** or **Married filing separately** ☐ **Married filing jointly** or **Qualifying surviving spouse** ☐ **Head of household** (Check only if you're unmarried and pay more than half the costs of keeping up a home for yourself and a qualifying individual.)		

Complete Steps 2–4 ONLY if they apply to you; otherwise, skip to Step 5. See page 2 for more information on each step, who can claim exemption from withholding, other details, and privacy.

Step 2: Multiple Jobs or Spouse Works

Complete this step if you (1) hold more than one job at a time, or (2) are married filing jointly and your spouse also works. The correct amount of withholding depends on income earned from all of these jobs.

Do **only one** of the following.

(a) Reserved for future use.

(b) Use the Multiple Jobs Worksheet on page 3 and enter the result in Step 4(c) below; **or**

(c) If there are only two jobs total, you may check this box. Do the same on Form W-4 for the other job. This option is generally more accurate than (b) if pay at the lower paying job is more than half of the pay at the higher paying job. Otherwise, (b) is more accurate . . . . ☐

TIP: If you have self-employment income, see page 2.

Complete Steps 3–4(b) on Form W-4 for only ONE of these jobs. Leave those steps blank for the other jobs. (Your withholding will be most accurate if you complete Steps 3–4(b) on the Form W-4 for the highest paying job.)

Step 3: Claim Dependent and Other Credits

If your total income will be $200,000 or less ($400,000 or less if married filing jointly):

Multiply the number of qualifying children under age 17 by $2,000 $ ______

Multiply the number of other dependents by $500 . . . . . $ ______

Add the amounts above for qualifying children and other dependents. You may add to this the amount of any other credits. Enter the total here . . . . | **3** | $

Step 4 (optional): Other Adjustments

(a) Other income (not from jobs). If you want tax withheld for other income you expect this year that won't have withholding, enter the amount of other income here. This may include interest, dividends, and retirement income . . . . | **4(a)** | $

(b) Deductions. If you expect to claim deductions other than the standard deduction and want to reduce your withholding, use the Deductions Worksheet on page 3 and enter the result here . . . . | **4(b)** | $

(c) Extra withholding. Enter any additional tax you want withheld each **pay period** . . | **4(c)** | $

Step 5: Sign Here

Under penalties of perjury, I declare that this certificate, to the best of my knowledge and belief, is true, correct, and complete.

Employee's signature (This form is not valid unless you sign it.) **Date**

Employers Only	Employer's name and address	First date of employment	Employer identification number (EIN)

For Privacy Act and Paperwork Reduction Act Notice, see page 3. Cat. No. 10220Q Form **W-4** (2023)

9

> **Note.** The IRS provides an online tool for calculating estimated tax withholding at **uofi.tax/23x9x8** [www.irs.gov/individuals/tax-withholding-estimator]. The tool estimates federal tax withholding, shows how a taxpayer's refund, take-home pay, or tax due are impacted by the withholding amount, and helps the taxpayer select an appropriate estimated withholding amount. See IRS Pub. 15-T, *Federal Income Tax Withholding Methods.*

Taxpayers should check their withholding amounts annually. Additionally, any time an individual has a **major life event,** such as a change in employment, major shift in income, a change in marital status or dependents, or alters their home ownership status, they should check their withholdings.[11]

PENALTIES

Penalties are based on the amount and timing of the underpayment. The IRS may also charge interest on the penalty itself.[12] The IRS publishes interest rates quarterly.[13]

Taxpayers can avoid penalties by making appropriate and timely payments. Withholding from Forms W-2, 1099s, and other forms applicable to line 25c of the Form 1040, as shown next, are considered to have been paid one-fourth on each payment due date.[14]

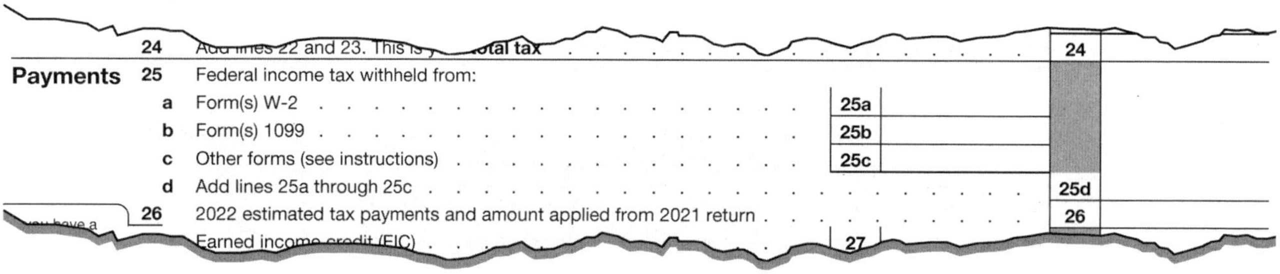

	24	Add lines 22 and 23. This is your total tax		24
Payments	25	Federal income tax withheld from:		
	a	Form(s) W-2	25a	
	b	Form(s) 1099	25b	
	c	Other forms (see instructions)	25c	
	d	Add lines 25a through 25c		25d
	26	2022 estimated tax payments and amount applied from 2021 return		26
	27	Earned income credit (EIC)	27	

There are limited circumstances in which the IRS may remove or reduce a penalty. The following are some circumstances where the IRS would consider abating a penalty.[15]

- The taxpayer, or their spouse if married filing jointly (MFJ), retired in the previous two years after turning age 62 or became disabled, **and** have **reasonable cause** for underpaying the estimated tax or paying late.
- Most of the taxpayer's income tax was withheld early in the year instead of spread evenly throughout the year.
- The taxpayer's income varies during the year.

---

11. *Tax Withholding Estimator.* Apr. 13, 2023. IRS. [www.irs.gov/individuals/tax-withholding-estimator] Accessed on Jun. 8, 2023.

12. *Underpayment of Estimated Tax by Individuals Penalty.* May 16, 2023. IRS. [www.irs.gov/payments/underpayment-of-estimated-tax-by-individuals-penalty] Accessed on Jun. 8, 2023.

13. For current year interest rates, see *Quarterly Interest Rates.* May 1, 2023. IRS. [www.irs.gov/payments/quarterly-interest-rates] Accessed on Jun. 9, 2023.

14. Instructions for Form 2210.

15. *Underpayment of Estimated Tax by Individuals Penalty.* May 16, 2023. IRS. [www.irs.gov/payments/underpayment-of-estimated-tax-by-individuals-penalty] Accessed on Jun. 8, 2023.

Figuring the Penalty[16]

Generally, the IRS figures any underpayment penalties and sends a bill to the taxpayer. However, taxpayers must compute their penalty for any of the following reasons.

- The taxpayer is requesting a waiver of part of their penalty.
- The taxpayer's income varied throughout the year and their penalty is reduced or eliminated when applying the annualized income installment method (explained later).
- The taxpayer's penalty is lower when treating the federal income tax withheld from their income as paid on the dates it was actually withheld, rather than in equal amounts on the payment due dates.

Taxpayers who file their return by the due date of the Form 1040, without extension, are not charged interest on the penalty if they pay the penalty by the date shown on the bill. If taxpayers would rather have the IRS figure the penalty, **they should not file Form 2210,** *Underpayment of Estimated Tax by Individuals, Estates, and Trusts,* and leave the penalty line on their return blank.

The required installment deficiencies are calculated using a daily penalty rate based on **the number of days** the balance is due, resulting in the net underpayment penalty. Taxpayers calculate the number of days their installment payment is delinquent and apply the applicable penalty rate of between 4% and 7%. The Worksheet for Form 2210, Part III, Section B — Figure the Penalty (Penalty Worksheet) guides taxpayers in calculating their quarterly penalties.

Practitioner Planning Tip

It is advisable to pay a late estimated payment as soon as possible to minimize penalties and interest.

9

There are two acceptable methods for calculating the estimated tax penalty: the regular method and the annualized income installment method.

Regular Method. Under the regular method, taxpayers must pay 25% of their required annual payment on each of the four installment payment due dates. If the taxpayer's estimated taxes and withholdings are equal to or more than their required annual payments for all payment periods, they do not owe a penalty. The withholding may consist of any prior year overpayments, specific payments, and withholdings. A taxpayer does not need to file a Form 2210 if their withholdings and estimated taxes exceed their required annual payment.

Note. Any prior year overpayment of tax is typically applied to the first quarterly installment.[17]

16. IRC §6654(d)(2) and Instructions for Form 2210.

17. See Instructions for Form 2210.

Example 1. Ricky and Julie are Florida residents who file MFJ. Their income consists of Form W-2 wages of $100,000 with $10,000 in withholdings. Their maximum required annual payment is $35,000 based on their prior year's tax.

In 2022, Julie became the beneficiary of a trust from her great uncle, Jim. The trust reported $500,000 in portfolio income which was paid to Julie in November. There were no additional withholdings, and the wage withholdings are assumed to have been paid evenly throughout the year.

Part I Required Annual Payment

1	Enter your 2022 tax after credits from Form 1040, 1040-SR, or 1040-NR, line 22. (See the instructions if not filing Form 1040.)	1	148,438
2	Other taxes, including self-employment tax and, if applicable, Additional Medicare Tax and/or Net Investment Income Tax (see instructions)	2	13,300
3	Other payments and refundable credits (see instructions)	3	( )
4	Current year tax. Combine lines 1, 2, and 3. If less than $1,000, **stop;** you don't owe a penalty. **Don't** file Form 2210	4	161,738
5	Multiply line 4 by 90% (0.90) — 5 — 145,564		
6	Withholding taxes. **Don't** include estimated tax payments. See instructions	6	10,000
7	Subtract line 6 from line 4. If less than $1,000, **stop**; you don't owe a penalty. **Don't** file Form 2210	7	151,738
8	Maximum required annual payment based on prior year's tax (see instructions)	8	35,000
9	**Required annual payment.** Enter the **smaller** of line 5 or line 8	9	35,000

Next: Is line 9 more than line 6?

☐ **No.** You **don't** owe a penalty. **Don't** file Form 2210 unless box **E** below applies.

☒ **Yes.** You may owe a penalty, but **don't** file Form 2210 unless one or more boxes in Part II below applies.

- If box **B**, **C**, or **D** applies, you must figure your penalty and file Form 2210.
- If box **A** or **E** applies (but not **B**, **C**, or **D**), file only page 1 of Form 2210. You **aren't** required to figure your penalty; the IRS will figure it and send you a bill for any unpaid amount. If you want to figure your penalty, you may use Part III as a worksheet and enter your penalty on your tax return, but **file only page 1 of Form 2210.**

…s for Filing. Check applicable boxes. If … **don't** file Form 2210

Line 5 shows the current year safe harbor is $145,564. The required annual payment is limited to the lesser of the safe harbor ($145,564) or the prior year maximum required annual payment based on prior year's tax ($35,000). For the regular method, the $35,000 will be divided equally over the four quarterly payment due dates, along with the wage withholdings of $10,000.

If Rick and Julie use the regular method, their net penalty due is $1,002, as shown on the following Form 2210.

Note. Interest of 0.5% (0.25% for months covered by an installment agreement) of the tax due for each month or part of a month a payment is late would likely be applied.[18] Interest has not been taken into account for this example.

18. *Notice 433-Interest and Penalty Information.* Jul. 2006. IRS. [www.irs.gov/pub/irs-pdf/n433.pdf] Accessed on Jul. 17, 2023.

For Example 1

Form 2210 (2022) Page **2**

Part III **Penalty Computation** (See the instructions if you're filing Form 1040-NR.)

Section A—Figure Your Underpayment		Payment Due Dates			
		(a) 4/15/22	**(b)** 6/15/22	**(c)** 9/15/22	**(d)** 1/15/23
10 **Required installments.** If box C in Part II applies, enter the amounts from Schedule AI, line 27. Otherwise, enter 25% (0.25) of line 9, Form 2210, in each column. For fiscal year filers, see instructions	10	8,750	8,750	8,750	8,750
11 Estimated tax paid and tax withheld (see the instructions). For column (a) only, also enter the amount from line 11 on line 15, column (a). If line 11 is equal to or more than line 10 for all payment periods, stop here; you don't owe a penalty. **Don't file Form 2210 unless you checked a box in Part II**	11	2,500	2,500	2,500	2,500
Complete lines 12 through 18 of one column before going to line 12 of the next column.					
12 Enter the amount, if any, from line 18 in the previous column	12				
13 Add lines 11 and 12	13		2,500	2,500	2,500
14 Add the amounts on lines 16 and 17 in the previous column	14		6,250	12,500	18,750
15 Subtract line 14 from line 13. If zero or less, enter -0-. For column (a) only, enter the amount from line 11	15	2,500	0	0	0
16 If line 15 is zero, subtract line 13 from line 14. Otherwise, enter -0-	16		3,750	10,000	
17 **Underpayment.** If line 10 is equal to or more than line 15, subtract line 15 from line 10. Then go to line 12 of the next column. Otherwise, go to line 18	17	6,250	8,750	8,750	8,750
18 Overpayment. If line 15 is more than line 10, subtract line 10 from line 15. Then go to line 12 of the next column	18				

Section B—Figure the Penalty (Use the Worksheet for Form 2210, Part III, Section B—Figure the Penalty in the instructions.)

19 **Penalty.** Enter the total penalty from line 14 of the Worksheet for Form 2210, Part III, Section B—Figure the Penalty. Also include this amount on Form 1040, 1040-SR, or 1040-NR, line 38; or Form 1041, line 27. **Don't file Form 2210 unless you checked a box in Part II**	19	1,002

Form **2210** (2022)

For Example 1

2022 Underpayment Penalty Worksheet

Client RICKY | **Ricky and Julie Star** | **123-12-1234**

Required Installment	Payment			Penalty				
	Date	Type *	Amount	Underpayment	Days Late	Rate	Amount of Penalty **	Penalty per Period
First Qtr								
8,750.	4/15/22	2	2,500.	6,250.	61	0.040	41.78	
	6/15/22	2	2,500.	3,750.	15	0.040	6.16	
Total								47.94
Rate Change	6/30/22			3,750.	77	0.050	39.55	
	9/15/22	2	2,500.	1,250.	15	0.050	2.57	
Total								42.12
Rate Change	9/30/22			1,250.	92	0.060	18.90	
Total								18.90
Rate Change	12/31/22			1,250.	15	0.070	3.60	
	1/15/23	2	1,250.					
Total								3.60
Second Qtr								
8,750.	6/15/22			8,750.	15	0.040	14.38	
Total								14.38
Rate Change	6/30/22			8,750.	92	0.050	110.27	
Total								110.27
Rate Change	9/30/22			8,750.	92	0.060	132.33	
Total								132.33
Rate Change	12/31/22			8,750.	15	0.070	25.17	
	1/15/23	2	1,250.	7,500.	90	0.070	129.45	
	4/15/23	5	7,500.					
Total								154.62
Third Qtr								
8,750.	9/15/22			8,750.	15	0.050	17.98	
Total								17.98
Rate Change	9/30/22			8,750.	92	0.060	132.33	
Total								132.33
Rate Change	12/31/22			8,750.	105	0.070	176.20	
	4/15/23	5	8,750.					
Total								176.20
Fourth Qtr								
8,750.	1/15/23			8,750.	90	0.070	151.03	
	4/15/23	5	8,750.					
Total								151.03

TOTAL UNDERPAYMENT PENALTY .... 1,002.

* **1** = Overpayment
2 = Withholding
3 = Estimate
4 = Extension
5 = Paid with return

** $\text{Underpayment} \times \frac{\text{Days Late}}{365} \times \text{Rate}$

FDIL1601L 01/06/23

Annualized Income Installment Method. For taxpayers with inconsistent yearly earnings (such as portfolio income, bonuses, capital dispositions, or seasonal business income), equal quarterly payments may not be sufficient to reduce or eliminate the underpayment penalty. Taxpayers who do not receive income evenly throughout the year are allowed to use **the annualized income installment method** to reflect the income earned in the period immediately before the installment due date. The annualized income installment method may result in estimated tax payments which differ from the traditional equal installments in an attempt to match prepayments to earnings.

Taxpayers using the annualized income installment method figure the required installments to enter on Form 2210 on Schedule AI, *Annualized Income Installment Method.* Schedule AI modifies a taxpayer's AGI and uses the annualization amounts to reflect the periods in which the income was earned. If a taxpayer uses Schedule AI for any payment due date, they must use it for all payment due dates. A taxpayer using the annualized income installment method must complete all the following steps.

1. Compute annualized income on part I of Schedule AI and part II if the taxpayer has SE income
2. Figure the penalty on part III of Form 2210
3. Select box C on part II of Form 2210, reflecting the taxpayer is using the annualized income installment method
4. Calculate income and deductions based on the taxpayer's method of accounting for each period on Schedule AI (cash method taxpayers must include all their income actually or constructively received and all deductions actually paid during the period)
5. Attach all parts of Form 2210 and Schedule AI to the taxpayer's return

Practitioner Planning Tip

If a taxpayer receives additional income later in the year, penalties can usually be reduced by using the annualized income installment method.

9

Example 2. Use the same facts as **Example 1,** except Ricky and Julie use the annualized income installment method. They allocate the $500,000 lump sum to the 4th quarter and allocate wage income evenly throughout the year.

The couple adjusts their penalty computation to reflect the tax withholding to be remitted during the period in which the income was earned. The total amount of tax to be withheld via the required installments does not change between **Example 1** and **Example 2,** just the timing on when the tax should have been remitted.

The net penalty due is $694 due as shown on the following Form 2210 and associated statement. This is a reduction in the penalty of $308 over the regular method ($1,002 – $694).

Note. No interest has been included in these calculations.

For Example 2

Form 2210 (2022) Page **3**

Schedule AI—Annualized Income Installment Method (See the instructions.)

Estates and trusts, **don't** use the period ending dates shown to the right. Instead, use the following: 2/28/22, 4/30/22, 7/31/22, and 11/30/22.		**(a)** 1/1/22–3/31/22	**(b)** 1/1/22–5/31/22	**(c)** 1/1/22–8/31/22	**(d)** 1/1/22–12/31/22
Part I **Annualized Income Installments**					
1 Enter your adjusted gross income for each period. See instructions. (Estates and trusts, enter your taxable income without your exemption for each period.)	1	**25,000**	**50,000**	**75,000**	**600,000**
2 Annualization amounts. (Estates and trusts, see instructions.)	2	4	2.4	1.5	1
3 Annualized income. Multiply line 1 by line 2	3	**100,000**	**120,000**	**112,500**	**600,000**
4 If you itemize, enter itemized deductions for the period shown in each column. All others, enter -0-, and skip to line 7. **Exception:** Estates and trusts, skip to line 9	4				
5 Annualization amounts	5	4	2.4	1.5	1
6 Multiply line 4 by line 5	6				
7 In each column, enter the sum of your standard deduction and line 12b from Form 1040 or 1040-SR. (Form 1040-NR filers, enter -0-. **Exception:** Indian students and business apprentices, see instructions.)	7	**25,900**	**25,900**	**25,900**	**25,900**
8 Enter the **larger** of line 6 or line 7	8	**25,900**	**25,900**	**25,900**	**25,900**
9 Deduction for qualified business income. **Estates and trusts:** Subtract this amount from the amount on line 3, skip line 10, and enter the result on line 11	9				
10 Add lines 8 and 9	10	**25,900**	**25,900**	**25,900**	**25,900**
11 Subtract line 10 from line 3	11	**74,100**	**94,100**	**86,600**	**574,100**
12 Form 1040, 1040-SR, or 1040-NR filers, enter -0- in each column. (Estates and trusts, see instructions.)	12	**0**	**0**	**0**	**0**
13 Subtract line 12 from line 11. If zero or less, enter -0-	13	**74,100**	**94,100**	**86,600**	**574,100**
14 Figure your tax on the amount on line 13. See instructions	14	**8,484**	**11,942**	**10,292**	**148,441**
15 Self-employment tax from line 36 (complete Part II below)	15				
16 Enter other taxes for each payment period including, if applicable, Additional Medicare Tax and/or Net Investment Income Tax. See instructions	16	**13,330**	**13,330**	**13,330**	**13,300**
17 Total tax. Add lines 14, 15, and 16	17	**21,784**	**25,242**	**23,592**	**161,741**
18 For each period, enter the same type of credits as allowed on Form 2210, Part I, lines 1 and 3. See instructions	18				
19 Subtract line 18 from line 17. If zero or less, enter -0-	19	**21,784**	**25,242**	**23,592**	**161,741**
20 Applicable percentage	20	22.5%	45%	67.5%	90%
21 Multiply line 19 by line 20	21	**4,901**	**11,359**	**15,925**	**145,567**
Complete lines 22–27 of one column before going to line 22 of the next column.					
22 Enter the total of the amounts in all previous columns of line 27	22		**4,901**	**11,359**	**15,925**
23 Subtract line 22 from line 21. If zero or less, enter -0-	23	**4,901**	**6,458**	**4,566**	**129,642**
24 Enter 25% (0.25) of line 9 on page 1 of Form 2210 in each column	24	**8,750**	**8,750**	**8,750**	**8,750**
25 Subtract line 27 of the previous column from line 26 of that column	25		**3,849**	**6,141**	**10,325**
26 Add lines 24 and 25	26	**8,750**	**12,599**	**14,891**	**19,075**
27 Enter the **smaller** of line 23 or line 26 here and on Form 2210, Part III, line 10	27	**4,901**	**6,458**	**4,566**	**19,075**
Part II **Annualized Self-Employment Tax** (Form 1040, 1040-SR, or 1040-NR filers only)					
28 Net earnings from self-employment for the period (see instructions)	28				
29 Prorated social security tax limit	29	$36,750	$61,250	$98,000	$147,000
30 Enter actual wages for the period subject to social security tax or the 6.2% portion of the 7.65% railroad retirement (tier 1) tax. **Exception:** If you filed Form 4137 or Form 8919, see instructions	30				
31 Subtract line 30 from line 29. If zero or less, enter -0-	31				
32 Annualization amounts	32	0.496	0.2976	0.186	0.124
33 Multiply line 32 by the **smaller** of line 28 or line 31	33				
34 Annualization amounts	34	0.116	0.0696	0.0435	0.029
35 Multiply line 28 by line 34	35				
36 Add lines 33 and 35. Enter here and on line 15 above	36				

Form **2210** (2022)

For Example 2

Form 2210 (2022) Page **2**

Part III **Penalty Computation** (See the instructions if you're filing Form 1040-NR.)

Section A—Figure Your Underpayment		**Payment Due Dates**			
		(a) 4/15/22	**(b)** 6/15/22	**(c)** 9/15/22	**(d)** 1/15/23
10 **Required installments.** If box C in Part II applies, enter the amounts from Schedule AI, line 27. Otherwise, enter 25% (0.25) of line 9, Form 2210, in each column. For fiscal year filers, see instructions	10	4,901	6,458	4,566	19,075
11 Estimated tax paid and tax withheld (see the instructions). For column (a) only, also enter the amount from line 11 on line 15, column (a). If line 11 is equal to or more than line 10 for all payment periods, stop here; you don't owe a penalty. **Don't file Form 2210 unless you checked a box in Part II**	11	2,500	2,500	2,500	2,500
Complete lines 12 through 18 of one column before going to line 12 of the next column.					
12 Enter the amount, if any, from line 18 in the previous column	12				
13 Add lines 11 and 12	13		2,500	2,500	2,500
14 Add the amounts on lines 16 and 17 in the previous column	14		2,401	6,359	8,425
15 Subtract line 14 from line 13. If zero or less, enter -0-. For column (a) only, enter the amount from line 11	15	2,500	99	0	0
16 If line 15 is zero, subtract line 13 from line 14. Otherwise, enter -0-	16		0	3,859	
17 **Underpayment.** If line 10 is equal to or more than line 15, subtract line 15 from line 10. Then go to line 12 of the next column. Otherwise, go to line 18	17	2,401	6,359	4,566	19,075
18 Overpayment. If line 15 is more than line 10, subtract line 10 from line 15. Then go to line 12 of the next column	18				

Section B—Figure the Penalty (Use the Worksheet for Form 2210, Part III, Section B—Figure the Penalty in the instructions.)

19 **Penalty.** Enter the total penalty from line 14 of the Worksheet for Form 2210, Part III, Section B—Figure the Penalty. Also include this amount on Form 1040, 1040-SR, or 1040-NR, line 38; or Form 1041, line 27. **Don't file Form 2210 unless you checked a box in Part II**	19	694

Form **2210** (2022)

9

For Example 2

2022 Underpayment Penalty Worksheet

Client RICKY | **Ricky and Julie Star** | **123-12-1234**

Required Installment	Payment			Penalty				
	Date	Type *	Amount	Underpayment	Days Late	Rate	Amount of Penalty **	Penalty per Period
First Qtr								
4,901.	4/15/22	2	2,500.	2,401.	61	0.040	16.05	
	6/15/22	2	2,401.					
Total								16.05
Second Qtr								
6,458.	6/15/22	2	99.	6,359.	15	0.040	10.45	
Total								10.45
Rate Change	6/30/22			6,359.	77	0.050	67.07	
	9/15/22	2	2,500.	3,859.	15	0.050	7.93	
Total								75.00
Rate Change	9/30/22			3,859.	92	0.060	58.36	
Total								58.36
Rate Change	12/31/22			3,859.	15	0.070	11.10	
	1/15/23	2	2,500.	1,359.	90	0.070	23.46	
	4/15/23	5	1,359.					
Total								34.56
Third Qtr								
4,566.	9/15/22			4,566.	15	0.050	9.38	
Total								9.38
Rate Change	9/30/22			4,566.	92	0.060	69.05	
Total								69.05
Rate Change	12/31/22			4,566.	105	0.070	91.95	
	4/15/23	5	4,566.					
Total								91.95
Fourth Qtr								
19,075.	1/15/23			19,075.	90	0.070	329.24	
	4/15/23	5	19,075.					
Total								329.24

TOTAL UNDERPAYMENT PENALTY .... 694.

* **1** = Overpayment
2 = Withholding
3 = Estimate
4 = Extension
5 = Paid with return

** $\text{Underpayment} \times \frac{\text{Days Late}}{365} \times \text{Rate}$

FDIL1601L 01/06/23

WITHHOLDING STRATEGIES

A taxpayer can implement a variety of withholding strategies to minimize or eliminate any estimated payment penalties. Available strategies depend on how the taxpayer is earning their money (a salaried job, a passthrough entity, etc.) and how much flexibility the taxpayer has in adjusting the timing of various payments.

Form W-4, Individual Estimates and Withholding Planning[19]

A carefully prepared Form W-4 is the first step to helping a wage-earning client plan for their payment of taxes because wage income and earnings are assumed to be evenly received throughout the year. As mentioned previously, taxpayers with wage withholding should regularly update their wage withholding via Form W-4 as income tax rates automatically change, as Congress enacts new legislation, or as their personal situations change. Form W-4 is typically submitted to an employee's payroll or human resources department.

Multiple Jobs. Taxpayers filing as MFJ or single taxpayers who hold at least two jobs should use the Multiple Jobs Worksheet (reproduced next) included with Form W-4 to project the proper withholding. For households with two or more jobs, the form guides taxpayers to an indexed worksheet where the sum of the higher paying and lower paying job withholdings are allocated throughout the number of pay periods. The calculated withholding amount is most accurate if the taxpayer inputs the data for the highest paying job on the Form W-4.

Form W-4 (2023) Page **3**

Step 2(b)—Multiple Jobs Worksheet *(Keep for your records.)*

If you choose the option in Step 2(b) on Form W-4, complete this worksheet (which calculates the total extra tax for all jobs) on **only ONE** Form W-4. Withholding will be most accurate if you complete the worksheet and enter the result on the Form W-4 for the highest paying job. To be accurate, submit a new Form W-4 for all other jobs if you have not updated your withholding since 2019.

Note: If more than one job has annual wages of more than $120,000 or there are more than three jobs, see Pub. 505 for additional tables.

1 **Two jobs.** If you have two jobs or you're married filing jointly and you and your spouse each have one job, find the amount from the appropriate table on page 4. Using the "Higher Paying Job" row and the "Lower Paying Job" column, find the value at the intersection of the two household salaries and enter that value on line 1. Then, **skip** to line 3 . . . . **1** $ ________

2 **Three jobs.** If you and/or your spouse have three jobs at the same time, complete lines 2a, 2b, and 2c below. Otherwise, skip to line 3.

a Find the amount from the appropriate table on page 4 using the annual wages from the highest paying job in the "Higher Paying Job" row and the annual wages for your next highest paying job in the "Lower Paying Job" column. Find the value at the intersection of the two household salaries and enter that value on line 2a . . . . **2a** $ ________

b Add the annual wages of the two highest paying jobs from line 2a together and use the total as the wages in the "Higher Paying Job" row and use the annual wages for your third job in the "Lower Paying Job" column to find the amount from the appropriate table on page 4 and enter this amount on line 2b . . . . **2b** $ ________

c Add the amounts from lines 2a and 2b and enter the result on line 2c . . . . **2c** $ ________

3 Enter the number of pay periods per year for the highest paying job. For example, if that job pays weekly, enter 52; if it pays every other week, enter 26; if it pays monthly, enter 12, etc. . . . . . . **3** ________

4 **Divide** the annual amount on line 1 or line 2c by the number of pay periods on line 3. Enter this amount here and in **Step 4(c)** of Form W-4 for the highest paying job (along with any other additional amount you want withheld) . . . . **4** $ ________

19. See Form W-4 and Instructions.

Practitioner Planning Tip

An employee may not wish to disclose other jobs to their current employer, in which case it would likely be in their best interest to use the tax withholding calculator discussed earlier.

Dependents and Other Credits. Taxpayers should consider any child tax or other dependent credits available if that may impact their estimated tax payments. Taxpayers with total income of $200,000 or less ($400,000 or less if MFJ) may be eligible for child and dependent care credits.[20]

In 2023, to qualify for the child tax credit, the taxpayer must have a child under age 17 as of December 31 who qualifies as a dependent. The child must live with the taxpayer for more than half of the year and must have a social security number (SSN).[21]

> **Note.** For more information on qualifications for the child tax credit, see IRC §24. Additionally, the IRS provides guidance at **uofi.tax/23x9x9** [www.irs.gov/credits-deductions/individuals/child-tax-credit].

When calculating withholding, taxpayers should also consider whether they are eligible to claim other dependents for whom they could claim a child tax credit. This would include an older child or a qualifying relative.[22]

> **Note.** For more information on the eligibility requirements for other dependents, see IRS Pub. 501, *Dependents, Standard Deduction, and Filing Information.*

Taxpayers should estimate any additional credits for which they are eligible when estimating their withholding amount. This may include the foreign tax credits and education tax credits.

Practitioner Planning Tip

Taxpayers who include these credits in their withholding calculation will increase their paycheck amounts, but this will likely reduce the amount of any refund they receive. Tax practitioners should have conversations with their clients and document answers as to whether their preference is higher paychecks throughout the year or a larger refund at the end of the year.

20. IRC §24.

21. Ibid.

22. Ibid.

Impact of Deductions. Currently, taxpayers are allowed either the standard or itemized deduction in computing taxable income and income tax. Unless the taxpayer expects to use the standard deduction on their income tax return, they should use the Form W-4 Deductions Worksheet under Step 4(b) to project the itemized deductions which would be reported on Form 1040, Schedule A, *Itemized Deductions*. This includes such itemized deductions as qualifying home mortgage interest, charitable deductions, state and local taxes (up to $10,000) and medical expenses (subject to limitations). Additionally, taxpayers should consider other deductions such as student loan interest and traditional individual retirement arrangement (IRA) contributions.

Step 4(b)—Deductions Worksheet *(Keep for your records.)*

1	Enter an estimate of your 2023 itemized deductions (from Schedule A (Form 1040)). Such deductions may include qualifying home mortgage interest, charitable contributions, state and local taxes (up to $10,000), and medical expenses in excess of 7.5% of your income	1	$
2	Enter: { • $27,700 if you're married filing jointly or a qualifying surviving spouse • $20,800 if you're head of household • $13,850 if you're single or married filing separately }	2	$
3	If line 1 is greater than line 2, subtract line 2 from line 1 and enter the result here. If line 2 is greater than line 1, enter "-0-"	3	$
4	Enter an estimate of your student loan interest, deductible IRA contributions, and certain other adjustments (from Part II of Schedule 1 (Form 1040)). See Pub. 505 for more information	4	$
5	**Add** lines 3 and 4. Enter the result here and in **Step 4(b)** of Form W-4	5	$

Shareholders and Partners[23]

Shareholders and partners include in their taxable income any share of the partnership or S corporation's income or loss for the months ending before the due date of the installment payment. This also includes distributive shares of partnership items, guaranteed payments, and gains/losses on partnership property distributions.

Tax withheld on Forms W-2, 1099s, and other forms as referenced on Form 1040, line 25c are assumed to have been paid evenly throughout the year.

Caution. If the taxpayer's year differs from the S corporation or partnership, the taxpayer's distributive share must be considered for the months in the entity's tax year ending within the tax year of the individual which precede the month in which the estimated tax installment date falls.

Withholding from Retirement Plan Withdrawals[24]

When taxpayers take a withdrawal from a retirement plan, including required minimum distributions (RMDs), they should calculate any estimated tax payments and appropriately withhold taxes from the distribution. Taxpayers must include the tax and any penalties from early withdrawals from an IRA or other retirement plan in their calculation of estimated tax payments.[25]

Taxpayers can choose not to withhold tax on a withdrawal unless they are **eligible rollover distributions.** Eligible rollover distributions are distributions eligible to be rolled over tax-free into a qualified retirement or annuity plan. Generally, 20% of an eligible rollover distribution is withheld for income tax. For example, an IRC §401(k) distribution paid directly to the taxpayer instead of a trustee-to-trustee transfer remains eligible for a taxfree rollover for 60 days.[26]

---

23. Treas. Reg. §1.6654-2.

24. IRS Pub. 505, *Tax Withholding and Estimated Tax;* IRS Pub. 575, *Pension and Annuity Income.*

25. See IRC §72(t).

26. *Rollovers of Retirement Plan and IRA Distributions.* Jun. 5, 2023. IRS. [www.irs.gov/retirement-plans/plan-participant-employee/rollovers-of-retirement-plan-and-ira-distributions] Accessed on Aug. 21, 2023.

There is no withholding on any part of a distribution if it is reasonable for a taxpayer to believe that the distribution will not be included in gross income. A taxpayer choosing not to have income tax withheld from retirement plan payments completes either Form W-4P, *Withholding Certificate for Periodic Pension or Annuity Payments,* or Form W-4R, *Withholding Certificate for Nonperiodic Payments and Eligible Rollover Distributions.* This determination remains in effect until the taxpayer revokes it.

Note. A payor may ignore a taxpayer's choice not to have tax withheld under specific situations that are described in IRS Pub. 575, *Pension and Annuity Income.* These include a taxpayer who does not give the payor their SSN or the IRS notifies the payor, prior to them making the payment, that the taxpayer provided an incorrect SSN.

Periodic payments (amounts paid at regular intervals (weekly, monthly, or yearly) for longer than one year) are treated as wages for withholding purposes. **Taxpayers who do not complete a Form W-4P or similar form will have tax withheld as if they are married and claiming three withholding allowances.**

Nonperiodic payments are all amounts a taxpayer receives that are not an annuity. This includes cash withdrawals, distributions of current earnings on investments, certain loans, etc. The withholding rate for nonperiodic distributions is **10%,** assuming it is not an eligible rollover distribution, and the taxpayer chooses to have no withholding. A taxpayer can request the payor withhold additional amounts on Form W-4R. Up to 100% can be withheld. Therefore, a taxpayer could take a withdrawal at the end of the year and withhold the entire amount to cover their estimated taxes during the year.

Form **W-4R**

Department of the Treasury
Internal Revenue Service

Withholding Certificate for Nonperiodic Payments and Eligible Rollover Distributions

Give Form W-4R to the payer of your retirement payments.

OMB No. 1545-0074

2023

1a First name and middle initial	Last name	**1b Social security number**
Address		
City or town, state, and ZIP code		

Your withholding rate is determined by the type of payment you will receive.

• For nonperiodic payments, the default withholding rate is 10%. You can choose to have a different rate by entering a rate between 0% and 100% on line 2. Generally, you can't choose less than 10% for payments to be delivered outside the United States and its territories.

• For an eligible rollover distribution, the default withholding rate is 20%. You can choose a rate greater than 20% by entering the rate on line 2. You may not choose a rate less than 20%.

See page 2 for more information.

2 Complete this line if you would like a rate of withholding that is different from the default withholding rate. See the instructions on page 2 and the Marginal Rate Tables below for additional information. Enter the rate as a whole number (no decimals) . . . . **2** %

Sign Here

Your signature (This form is not valid unless you sign it.) **Date**

Example 3. Jane calls her tax return preparer, Frank, in December of 2023 to inform him that she has just received an IRA distribution from her mother's estate. There were no taxes withheld on the distribution. Frank asks Jane about her other income, expenses, and life events for the year, and Jane tells him that "everything else is about the same as 2022."

Frank uses the information he has on hand to calculate a projection for 2023.

Total projected 2023 tax liability	$9,000
2023 tax withholding	(6,500)
Projected balance due	$2,500

Because Jane's projected balance due is over $1,000, she may need to make an estimated tax payment. In 2022, Jane's total tax liability was $6,000. Frank compares her actual 2022 and projected 2023 taxes to the amount of 2023 withholding to see if she meets one of the safe harbor exceptions.

	2022 Actual Taxes		2023 Projected
Total tax liability	$6,000		$9,000
Applicable percentage	× 100%		× 90%
Safe harbor threshold	$6,000		$8,100
Lower of two above thresholds		$6,000	
2023 withholding		$6,500	

Because Jane's 2023 withholding is greater than 100% of her 2022 taxes, she is not required to make an estimated tax payment for 2023.

RMDs. Retirement plan participants must begin taking RMDs starting at age 73 (if that individual reaches age 72 after December 31, 2022).[27] As a nonperiodic payment, RMDs are subject to the 10% withholding, as described previously. The IRS treats amounts withheld from IRA distributions, including RMDs, as paid evenly throughout the year, including lump-sum payments at the end of the year.[28]

Example 4. Phillip made wise investing decisions during his working career and does not require his RMDs to support himself. Based on his 2022 tax liability, Phillip must make estimated tax payments in 2023 of $15,000. His RMD for 2023 is also $15,000. Phillip waits until December to take his RMD and requests that 100% of the distribution be withheld to cover his tax estimate for the year. By using this strategy, Phillip avoids making quarterly estimates and avoids any underpayment penalties, while keeping his money in his IRA for most of the year.

Caution. Although the strategy of using withholding from an RMD works on federal tax liabilities, it may not work on state tax liabilities. Individuals should check with their IRA sponsors to ensure that their plan allows for state-tax withholding.

27. IRC §401(a)(9).

28. *The RMD Solution to the Hassle of Filing Estimated Taxes in Retirement.* McCormally, Kevin and Mengle, Rocky. Sep. 14, 2021. Kiplinger. [www.kiplinger.com/retirement/retirement-plans/required-minimum-distributions-rmds/603438/rmd-solution-for-estimated-taxes] Accessed on Jun. 26, 2023.

End-of-Year Bonuses

A bonus paid at the end of the year is considered supplemental wages.[29] Individuals can treat such payments as if paid evenly throughout the year.[30]

Generally, bonuses that are less than $1 million are subject to 22% withholding for income taxes.[31]

Withholding for Roth Conversions or High-Income Bonuses[32]

Generally, the conversion of a retirement plan into a Roth IRA is a taxable event. Therefore, a plan participant may need to increase their withholding or make an estimated tax payment to avoid an underpayment penalty. A taxpayer should also consider whether the taxable income from the Roth conversion puts them into a higher tax bracket. This may also require additional withholding or estimates.

Caution. Taxpayers who move into a higher tax bracket because of a Roth conversion or other bonus should also consider the impact of their higher modified adjusted gross income (MAGI) on Medicare premiums and NIIT. A taxpayer who is suddenly subjected to those additional taxes may require estimated tax payments to cover their increased liability.

Practitioner Planning Tip

It is essential for a practitioner to advise their client to appropriately tax plan and mitigate any potential penalties or interest assessments. While it may not be possible to know every detail about a client's current year tax situation, additional confidence could be found in setting up mid-summer tax planning appointments or requesting information from the client's investment advisor or attorney.

29. Treas. Reg. §31.3402(g)-1(a)(1)(i).

30. Treas. Reg. §31.3402(g)-1; IRS Pub. 15, *(Circular E), Employer's Tax Guide.*

31. IRS Pub. 15, (*Circular E), Employer's Tax Guide.*

32. *Retirement Plans FAQs on Designated Roth Accounts.* Nov. 1, 2022. IRS. [www.irs.gov/retirement-plans/retirement-plans-faqs-on-designated-roth-accounts] Accessed on Jun. 27, 2023.

COLLEGE COST PLANNING

Higher education costs can represent a significant expense, making it important to plan years in advance. The government and many state agencies have programs to subsidize a portion of higher education costs by leveraging tax-free growth within certain accounts designated for college savings.

Taxpayers should evaluate the different college cost-planning resources available to maximize earnings potential and tax-free growth. This section covers different college cost-planning strategies, associated potential tax implications, and ways to optimize education cost assistance through government and state-sponsored programs.

ACCOUNT OPTIONS

IRC §529 accounts are a common strategy for college planning. Other options also come with tax advantages, including standard brokerage accounts, educational savings accounts, retirement account funds, and insurance policies.

IRC §529 Accounts

IRC §529 accounts, also known as **qualified tuition plans** or **qualified savings plans,** are tax-advantaged accounts designed to encourage saving for education costs.[33] These accounts are commonly sponsored and run by state agencies and educational institutions.

IRC §529 accounts grow tax-free, and distributions from them are tax-free, provided the account holder uses the funds for qualifying education expenses. There may be situations where account holders withdraw funds from the account and do not use them for qualifying education expenses. In such cases, the portion of the withdrawal attributable to account growth is subject to ordinary income taxation and a 10% penalty.[34]

Qualifying education expenses include elementary, secondary, and higher education expenses. Common expenses include room and board, tuition and fees, books and supplies, special needs service expenses, and up to $10,000 of payments on qualified student loans.[35]

9

Caution. Not all states allow §529 funds to be used for elementary and secondary expenses. Allowed distributions may also vary by state.[36]

Contributions to §529 accounts are not deductible for federal tax purposes but may have state tax ramifications. Over 30 states, including the District of Columbia, offer a tax credit for qualifying contributions.[37]

Putting money into a §529 account may affect a college's judgment in awarding financial aid. The student **must disclose** the existence of any §529 accounts. Thus, it is important to consider the trade-off between potentially tax-free account growth and financial aid awards.[38]

---

33. *An Introduction to 529 Plans.* May 29, 2018. U.S. Securities and Exchange Commission. [www.sec.gov/about/reports-publications/investor-publications/introduction-529-plans] Accessed on May 31, 2023.

34. IRC §529(e); IRS Pub. 970, *Tax Benefits for Education.*

35. IRC §529(e)(3); IRS Pub. 970, *Tax Benefits for Education.*

36. *Using Your 529 Funds.* 2023. NEST 529 College Savings Plan. [nest529.com/use-of-funds] Accessed on Aug. 2, 2023.

37. *State Section 529 Deductions.* 2023. Finaid. [finaid.org/savings/state529deductions] Accessed on May 28, 2023.

38. *How do 529 plans Affect Financial Aid?* Jul. 28, 2022. Saving For College. [www.savingforcollege.com/intro-to-529s/does-a-529-plan-affect-financial-aid] Accessed on Jun. 13, 2023.

Brokerage Accounts

A brokerage account's design is to buy and sell investments. Funds in a brokerage account will continue to accumulate through interest, dividends, capital gain proceeds, and market appreciation.

Brokerage accounts under the name of a taxpayer's child may be subject to the **Kiddie Tax.** Under IRC §1(g), a child's unearned income is taxed at the parent's tax rate to avoid exploiting tax loopholes by placing assets and income in the child's name. Tax rates assessed on dependent returns can be significantly lower than those of the parents. The Kiddie Tax prohibits parents from taking advantage of the lower tax rates by requiring them to pay income tax at a rate equal to that of the parents. Dependents are subject to the Kiddie Tax when their situation meets the following criteria for 2023.[39]

- The child's unearned income is more than $2,500.
- The child is under the age of 18 and pays less than half of their support **or** was a full-time student between ages 19 and 24.
- The child has at least one parent alive at the end of the tax year.
- The child must file a tax return for the current tax year.
- The child does not file a joint return for the current tax year.

A child who meets these criteria must file an individual income tax return and attach Form 8615, *Tax for Certain Children Who Have Unearned Income*. Alternatively, parents can elect to report and pay taxes on the child's income by filing Form 8814, *Parents' Election to Report Child's Interest and Dividends*.[40]

Note. For 2023, parents can elect to pay taxes on the child's income that exceeds $2,500 but is less than $11,500. Income from interest, dividends, and capital gain distributions exceeding $11,500 will require the child to file an individual income tax return.[41] If the child has capital gains or losses from sales they will need to file their own return.[42]

Educational Savings Account

Educational savings accounts (ESAs), **also known as Coverdell Accounts,** work similarly to §529 accounts, where earnings within the account grow tax-free. However, ESAs have income phaseout thresholds and limit the contribution amount.[43]

Taxpayers can set up multiple accounts for the same beneficiary, but the total contribution to all accounts must aggregate to $2,000 or less.[44] Single taxpayers contributing to ESAs must have a MAGI under $110,000 or $220,000 if MFJ.[45]

39. IRC §1(g); *Topic Number 533 — Tax on a Child's Investment and Other Unearned Income (Kiddie Tax)*. Mar. 30, 2023. IRS. [www.irs.gov/taxtopics/tc553] Accessed on May 30, 2023.

40. Ibid.

41. Ibid.

42. *Topic Number 553 — Tax on a Child's Investment and Other Unearned Income (Kiddie Tax)*. Mar. 30, 2023. IRS. [www.irs.gov/taxtopics/tc553] Accessed on Aug. 21, 2023; Instructions for Form 8814.

43. IRC §530(c); IRS Pub. 970, *Tax Benefits for Education*.

44. IRC §530(b); IRS Pub. 970, *Tax Benefits for Education*.

45. IRS Pub. 970, *Tax Benefits for Education*, p. 38 (2022).

Similar to §529 accounts, account holders can use funds in ESAs for elementary and secondary education expenses. ESAs are also subject to a 10% penalty and ordinary income taxation on fund growth if the account beneficiary does not use the funds to pay for qualifying education expenses.[46] However, the additional 10% penalty **does not apply** in the following circumstances.[47]

- The distribution was a payment to a beneficiary or the designated beneficiary's estate following the death of a designated beneficiary.
- The purpose of the distribution was attributable to the designated beneficiary being disabled.
- The designated beneficiary received tax-free educational assistance. The distribution is exempt from the 10% penalty up to the amount of the aid.
- The designated beneficiary attends a military academy, including the United States Military Academy, the United States Naval Academy, the United States Air Force Academy, the United States Coast Guard Academy, and the United States Merchant Marine Academy. The distribution is exempt from the 10% penalty up to the amount of higher education costs for enrollment in such military academy.

Example 5. Barney and Betty anticipate sending their children to private elementary and secondary schools, even though their daughters are only a few months old. Their MAGI is under $200,000. Because Barney and Betty expect high educational costs, they establish an ESA for each child, listing them as beneficiaries. Because of a fortunate financial situation, their two daughters did not need to use these funds until college. As a result, the growth in their ESAs enables their children to attend college without incurring student loan debt.

Calculating the Taxable Portion of a Distribution. The taxable portion of a distribution is the amount of the excess distribution (distributions in excess of adjusted qualified education expenses (AQEE), discussed later) that represents earnings that have accumulated tax free in the account. The taxable portion is calculated as follows.[48]

Step 1. Multiply the total amount distributed by a fraction. The numerator is the basis (contributions not previously distributed) at the end of the prior year, plus total contributions for the current year, and the denominator is the value (balance) of the account at the end of the current year, plus the amount distributed during the current year.

Step 2. Subtract the amount in **step 1** from the total amount distributed during the current year. The result is the amount of earnings included in the distribution(s).

Step 3. Multiply the amount of earnings in **step 2** by a fraction: the numerator is the AQEE paid during the current year and the denominator is the total amount distributed during the current year.

Step 4. Subtract the amount determined in **step 3** from the amount determined in **step 2.** The result is the amount the beneficiary must include in income.

AQEE is calculated by reducing qualified education expenses by any tax-free educational assistance, including the following.[49]

- Tax-free part of any scholarship or fellowship grant (including Pell grants)
- Tax-free part of any employer-provided educational assistance
- Veterans' educational assistance
- Any other educational assistance that is excludable from gross income, other than as a gift, bequest, devise, or inheritance)

46. IRC §530(d); IRS Pub. 970, *Tax Benefits for Education.*

47. Ibid.

48. IRS Pub. 970, *Tax Benefits for Education.*

49. Instructions for Form 8863; IRS Pub. 970, *Tax Benefits for Education.*

9

Funds in Retirement Accounts or Insurance Policies

Taxpayers can withdraw funds penalty-free from an IRA or take a §401(k) loan to pay for higher education expenses.[50] Higher education expenses include tuition, books, supplies, and equipment necessary to attend an educational institution.[51] Special-needs equipment and expenses also constitute a qualified higher education expense.[52]

Insurance policies can also offer a flexible approach to higher education expenses. Funds from universal or whole life policies can pay for higher education expenses, including tuition.[53] Life insurance loans and proceeds generally do not have any tax implications on the individual income tax return.

Disclosure of retirement funds and insurance policies is generally not includable on the Free Application for Federal Student Aid (FAFSA) (explained later). However, they are includable on a student's College Scholarship Service (CSS) profile. The College Board maintains CSS profiles for students which includes information that extends beyond that required of the FAFSA. A CSS profile is a single common application that students and families can use to reduce the number of times they enter financial data to apply for scholarships. A student's ability to obtain nonfederal scholarships and other aid may be impacted by any funds in retirement or insurance accounts.[54] Thus, a deliberate shift to these accounts might not affect an applicant's FAFSA report and aid package, but can impact a potential student's CSS profile.

FEDERAL STUDENT AID TAX STRATEGIES

Federal Student Aid (FSA) helps students receive federal funding for higher education expenses through grants, scholarships, and loans. The U.S. Department of Education oversees the FSA, which manages the FAFSA under *Title IV* of the *Higher Education Act of 1965*. The FSA reviews applications, develops the FAFSA forms, reconciles federal student aid, monitors assistance, and manages the federal student loan portfolio.[55]

The FAFSA is a detailed form requesting financial information from students and parents. It was announced that a new FAFSA application will be launched in December 2023, for the 2024–2025 academic year.[56] It should have fewer questions and provide a more streamlined experience than the current form. A mandatory IRS Direct Data Exchange will replace the current IRS Data Retrieval Tool.

---

50. IRC §72(t)(2)(E); IRS Pub. 590-B, *Distributions from Individual Retirement Arrangements (IRAs).*

51. IRC §529(e)(3); IRS Pub. 590-B, *Distributions from Individual Retirement Arrangements (IRAs).*

52. Ibid.

53. *Using Your Life Insurance to Help Pay for a Child's College.* Sep. 18, 2018. Next Avenue. [www.nextavenue.org/life-insurance-pay-childs-college] Accessed on May 28, 2023.

54. *How to Complete the CSS Profile.* Sep. 27, 2022. U.S. News and World Report. [www.usnews.com/education/best-colleges/paying-for-college/articles/everything-you-need-to-know-to-complete-the-css-profile] Accessed on May 28, 2023.

55. *About Us.* May 13, 2023. Federal Student Aid. [www.studentaid.gov/about] Accessed on May 28, 2023.

56. *2024–2025 FAFSA Roadmap.* Apr. 12, 2023. U.S. Department of Education. [fsapartners.ed.gov/knowledge-center/topics/fafsa-simplification-information/2024-25-fafsa-roadmap]. Accessed on Aug. 2, 2023.

There are strategies students can use to obtain higher funds from FSA, including the following.

- **Filing Early.** The FAFSA generally opens in the fall and closes on June 30, before the end of the school year for which the student is seeking assistance. This window allows students to receive financial aid at any point in the school year. However, FAFSA works based on a first-come, first-serve model. Each state has its own priority deadline.[57]
- **Reduce Reportable Assets.** Because financial aid depends on an applicant's financial position, among other criteria, legally reducing reportable assets can result in higher scholarships, grants, and loans from the FSA. Strategies include using assets to pay down debt, leveraging reportable and non-reportable asset classes, and moving assets from the parent's name into the student's name. Larger assets reported on the FAFSA reduce a student's eligibility for need-based financial aid, regardless of whether their parents assist with higher education expenses.[58]
- **Reduce Income in the FAFSA Base Year.** For the 2023-2024 school year, the FAFSA uses income reported on the 2021 individual income tax return as the base year for calculating financial aid packages.[59] Reducing the base year income helps prospective students applying for financial aid in future years. Strategies to reduce the base year for the application include using capital losses to lower income and postponing bonuses and other large income payments until the following year.
- **Coordinate with the American Opportunity Tax Credit (AOC).** Taxpayers eligible for the AOC could allocate up to $4,000 of qualifying expenses to maximize this credit. The IRS prohibits double-dipping, where taxpayers cannot use the same qualifying expenses for tax-free distributions from §529 accounts and to claim the AOC.[60] The AOC is covered later in this section.

EARNINGS ON FORM 1099-Q[61]

Individuals receive a Form 1099-Q, *Payments From Qualified Education Programs (Under Sections 529 and 530),* when they receive distributions from a §529 account, which is a qualified tuition program (QTP). The form identifies the recipient's information, gross distribution, earnings within the account, and the individual's basis in those earnings.

☐ CORRECTED (if checked)

PAYER'S/TRUSTEE'S name, street address, city or town, state or province, country, ZIP or foreign postal code, and telephone no.		1 Gross distribution $	OMB No. 1545-1760 Form **1099-Q**	**Payments From Qualified Education Programs (Under Sections 529 and 530)**
		2 Earnings $	(Rev. November 2019) For calendar year 20____	
PAYER'S/TRUSTEE'S TIN	RECIPIENT'S TIN	3 Basis $	4 Trustee-to-trustee transfer ☐	**Copy B** **For Recipient**
RECIPIENT'S name Street address (including apt. no.) City or town, state or province, country, and ZIP or foreign postal code		5 Distribution is from: • Qualified tuition program— Private ☐ or State ☐ • Coverdell ESA ☐	6 If this box is checked, the recipient is not the designated beneficiary ☐	This is important tax information and is being furnished to the IRS. If you are required to file a return, a negligence penalty or other sanction may be imposed on you if this income is taxable and the IRS determines that it has not been reported.
		If the fair market value (FMV) is shown below, see **Pub. 970**, Tax Benefits for Education, for how to figure earnings.		
Account number (see instructions)				

Form **1099-Q** (Rev. 11-2019) (keep for your records) www.irs.gov/Form1099Q Department of the Treasury - Internal Revenue Service

57. *FAFSA Deadlines.* May 13, 2023. Federal Student Aid. [www.studentaid.gov/apply-for-aid/fafsa/fafsa-deadlines] Accessed on May 28, 2023.

58. *How to Shelter Assets on the FAFSA.* Kantrowitz, Mark. May 16, 2022. Saving for College. [www.savingforcollege.com/article/how-to-shelter-assets-on-the-fafsa] Accessed on May 28, 2023.

59. *Federal Student Aid Handbook.* 2023. Federal Student Aid. [fsapartners.ed.gov/sites/default/files/2023-2024/2023-2024_Federal_Student_Aid_Handbook/_knowledge-center_fsa-handbook_2023-2024_application-and-verification-guide.pdf] Accessed on Jun. 2, 2023.

60. *File the FAFSA to Get More Money In College.* Kantrowitz, Mark. Oct. 3, 2022. College Ave. Student Loans. [www.collegeavestudentloans.com/blog/file-the-fafsa-to-get-more-money-in-college] Accessed on Jan. 30, 2023.

61. Instructions for Form 1099-Q.

The reported gross distribution includes the portion of the earnings within the account. If the distribution equals or exceeds the qualified educational expenses incurred, taxpayers do not report the earnings as taxable income on their return.

However, if any portion of the distribution reported in box 1 is taxable, then the earnings in box 2 will be used to calculate the taxable portion of the distribution by applying an **earnings ratio.** The earnings ratio consists of earnings allocable in the account as of the distribution date multiplied by the percentage of the distribution the taxpayer used for noneducation expenditures.[62] Additionally, only accounts with the same tuition program, account holder, and designated beneficiary are aggregated to calculate earnings on distributions.[63]

Example 6. Noah and Alex are sending their daughter to college in the fall. They have not yet received an expected cost breakdown for the year, so they decided to pull out $50,000 from their daughter's §529 account. This distribution consists of $40,000 of contributions and $10,000 of earnings. Their daughter's actual qualifying expenses total only $45,000. Because they used 10% of the withdrawn funds for noneducational purposes (($50,000 – $45,000) ÷ $50,000), Noah and Alex are subject to income tax on $1,000 of earnings ($10,000 × 10%).

Caution. To eliminate any potential timing issues, taxpayers should take the distribution prior to making the payment in the same tax year.

Reporting Requirements

The responsible party for reporting Form 1099-Q earnings depends on the recipient's TIN, which is generally the beneficiary. Sometimes, Form 1099-Q lists a parent's TIN. Consequently, the parent would report the information from Form 1099-Q on their income tax return.[64] Usually, Form 1099-Q lists the designated beneficiary as the recipient for distributions made directly to the designated beneficiary or an educational institution on behalf of the designated beneficiary. If these two situations are not applicable, Form 1099-Q lists the account owner as the recipient of the distribution.

Note. If parents claim the AOC, but the student reports earnings from a Form 1099-Q on their income tax return, it is important to avoid double-dipping on qualified education expenses. The parents would not include the costs the Form 1099-Q covered on their return when calculating the AOC. Instead, the student should claim the expenses on their income tax return to offset the Form 1099-Q distribution or choose to include the taxable distribution in income.

PREPAID TUITION OR SAVINGS PLANS

IRC §529 accounts are segregated into two separate categories: prepaid tuition plans, and savings account plans. Contributors to either type of §529 accounts are not limited by AGI constraints as they would be for ESAs. This section highlights the nuances of each category.

---

62. IRS Notice 2001-81, 2001-52 IRB 617.

63. IRS Notice 2016-13, 2016-7 IRB 314.

64. Instructions for Form 1099-Q.

Prepaid Tuition Plans[65]

Prepaid tuition plans generally limit coverage to only tuition and fees in higher education. Many other expenses, such as room, board, and supplies, are not eligible. State-sponsored prepaid tuition plans provide credits for institutions within the states. Additionally, there are private tuition plans for participating college programs.

Prepaid tuition plans are limited to higher education institutions that participants may use the credits toward. For instance, specific prepaid plans apply to 2-year programs, while others only apply to 4-year programs. Depending on the specifics of the contract, certain graduate school tuition could be covered under the plan. Furthermore, the participant has no control over the funds' investments, as contributions go into the general fund to purchase future tuition credits. However, prepaid tuition plans can lock in tuition prices.

> **Caution.** Prepaid tuition plans generally require the taxpayer or their child to be a resident of the state sponsoring the plan.

> **Note.** If the beneficiary does not attend a college that is a part of the plan, the remaining prepaid tuition plan funds can be transferred to a new beneficiary, such as a sibling. Age restrictions might impact the transferability depending on the state sponsoring the plan. When the funds go unused for qualified tuition or the account holder cancels the plan, the account holder only receives the amount they contributed, less a potential cancellation fee.

Savings Account Plans[66]

A state or an agency of the state establishes savings account plans. IRC §529 savings plans are more flexible than prepaid tuition plans, applying to prospective students of all ages. Funds within savings account plans are available for a broader set of expenses, including textbooks, tuition, room, board, equipment, and computers. These plans also have provisions that apply to elementary and secondary education expenses.

9

Unlike prepaid tuition plans, savings account plans apply to universities across the country and some overseas programs. These provisions allow more flexibility in the use of the funds. Additionally, the investment mix within the account can be changed up to two times per year, giving taxpayers more control over how they invest their money.

Example 7. John and Carla are saving for their child, Joe, who wants to attend college in California. Their current home location is in Maine. However, John and Carla like a Montana §529 program. They decide to establish a §529 savings plan in Montana, even though they live in Maine and Joe wants to attend college in California. John and Carla can use these funds for tuition in California under a savings account plan, whereas they may face restrictions if they use a prepaid tuition plan.

> **Note.** Although individuals can contribute to plans outside their resident state, this can hinder state tax credits. Many states only offer credits for contributions to plans within that state. Therefore, state taxation laws are an important income tax consideration when deciding to contribute to out-of-state education savings programs.

---

65. *529 Plans*. 2023. FINRA. [www.finra.org/investors/investing/investment-accounts/college-savings-accounts/529-plans] Accessed on May 29, 2023.

66. Ibid.

SAVINGS BONDS[67]

Savings bonds are another method available to pay for higher education expenses. A qualified U.S. savings bond is one issued after December 31, 1989, to an individual who attained age 24 before the date of issuance at a discount under 31 USC §3105. To the extent that the holder uses proceeds from the savings bonds to pay qualifying higher education costs, the interest they receive from the bond is tax-free. Room and board and other recreational activities are **excluded** from qualifying education costs. However, students can use savings bonds for graduate or undergraduate studies.

This treatment is limited to individuals whose MAGI does not exceed an income threshold, despite being indexed for inflation. For 2023, the phaseouts are as follows.[68]

- $91,850 to $106,850 for single and head of household filers
- $137,800 to $167,800 for MFJ and qualifying surviving spouse filers

Individuals who exceed the phaseout amounts cannot exclude interest income from savings bonds. Individuals filing as MFS also cannot exclude savings bond interest, regardless of their AGI.

Example 8. Sarah's grandpa, Randy, buys a $15,000 savings bond in 2010 when he is 70 years old which he plans to use to pay for Sarah's eventual college expenses. When Sarah starts college in 2023, Randy cashes in the bond and uses the proceeds to pay her tuition. There is no tax liability on the bond proceeds because he meets the income and age requirements.

LOANS

Outside loans through public and private institutions can be used to pay for qualifying higher education expenses.[69] These loans are unsecured, recourse loans that require repayment. However, interest on loans tied to educational purposes can be taken as an adjustment on the federal tax return of up to $2,500 if certain circumstances apply.[70] The loan must solely pay higher education expenses on behalf of the taxpayer, the taxpayer's spouse, or a dependent. Additionally, the borrower must incur the educational costs within a reasonable timeframe from the loan date.[71]

Student loan interest is an above-the-line adjustment, altering a taxpayer's AGI, provided that the taxpayer does not exceed the MAGI limits. The MAGI limits for 2023 are as follows.[72]

- $90,000 for single, head of household, and qualifying surviving spouse filers
- $180,000 for MFJ filers

Taxpayers report their student loan interest deduction on part II of Schedule 1, *Additional Income and Adjustments to Income,* of the Form 1040. This deduction, along with taxpayers' other income and adjustments, flows through on the adjustments to the income line on Form 1040. Similar to savings bonds, taxpayers who file as MFS are excluded from taking the $2,500 adjustment.[73] Additionally, dependents may not take this deduction on their return.

---

67. IRC §135.
68. Rev. Proc. 2022-38, 2022-45 IRB 445.
69. IRC §221(d)(2).
70. IRC §221(b)(1).
71. IRC §221(d)(1).
72. IRC §221; Rev. Proc. 2022-38, 2022-45 IRB 445.
73. IRC §221(e)(2).

Example 9. Martha reports her total income of $50,000 on her 2022 Form 1040. She took out a loan to pay for her daughter's tuition. Interest on the loan totaled $2,000, and Martha used the entire amount toward tuition at an eligible institution. Martha enters $2,000 on line 21 of Schedule 1, which flows through to line 10 on Form 1040. Martha can thereby deduct $2,000 from her total income to generate an AGI of $48,000.

Schedule 1 (Form 1040) 2022 — Page 2

Part II Adjustments to Income

11	Educator expenses			11	
12	Certain business expenses of reservists, performing artists, and fee-basis government officials. Attach Form 2106			12	
13	Health savings account deduction. Attach Form 8889			13	
14	Moving expenses for members of the Armed Forces. Attach Form 3903			14	
15	Deductible part of self-employment tax. Attach Schedule SE			15	
16	Self-employed SEP, SIMPLE, and qualified plans			16	
17	Self-employed health insurance deduction			17	
18	Penalty on early withdrawal of savings			18	
19a	Alimony paid			19a	
b	Recipient's SSN				
c	Date of original divorce or separation agreement (see instructions):				
20	IRA deduction			20	
21	Student loan interest deduction			21	2,000
22	Reserved for future use			22	
23	Archer MSA deduction			23	
24	Other adjustments:				
a	Jury duty pay (see instructions)	24a			
b	Deductible expenses related to income reported on line 8l from the rental of personal property engaged in for profit	24b			
c	Nontaxable amount of the value of Olympic and Paralympic medals and USOC prize money reported on line 8m	24c			
d	Reforestation amortization and expenses	24d			
e	Repayment of supplemental unemployment benefits under the Trade Act of 1974	24e			
f	Contributions to section 501(c)(18)(D) pension plans	24f			
g	Contributions by certain chaplains to section 403(b) plans	24g			
h	Attorney fees and court costs for actions involving certain unlawful discrimination claims (see instructions)	24h			
i	Attorney fees and court costs you paid in connection with an award from the IRS for information you provided that helped the IRS detect tax law violations	24i			
j	Housing deduction from Form 2555	24j			
k	Excess deductions of section 67(e) expenses from Schedule K-1 (Form 1041)	24k			
z	Other adjustments. List type and amount:	24z			
25	Total other adjustments. Add lines 24a through 24z			25	
26	Add lines 11 through 23 and 25. These are your **adjustments to income**. Enter here and on Form 1040 or 1040-SR, line 10, or Form 1040-NR, line 10a			26	2,000

Schedule 1 (Form 1040) 2022

here

Income

Attach Form(s) W-2 here. Also attach Forms W-2G and 1099-R if tax was withheld.

If you did not get a Form W-2, see instructions.

1a	Total amount from Form(s) W-2, box 1 (see instructions)				1a	50,000
b	Household employee wages not reported on Form(s) W-2				1b	
c	Tip income not reported on line 1a (see instructions)				1c	
d	Medicaid waiver payments not reported on Form(s) W-2 (see instructions)				1d	
e	Taxable dependent care benefits from Form 2441, line 26				1e	
f	Employer-provided adoption benefits from Form 8839, line 29				1f	
g	Wages from Form 8919, line 6				1g	
h	Other earned income (see instructions)				1h	
i	Nontaxable combat pay election (see instructions)	1i				
z	Add lines 1a through 1h				1z	50,000
2a	Tax-exempt interest	2a		b Taxable interest	2b	
3a	Qualified dividends	3a		b Ordinary dividends	3b	
4a	IRA distributions	4a		b Taxable amount	4b	
5a	Pensions and annuities	5a		b Taxable amount	5b	
6a	Social security benefits	6a		b Taxable amount	6b	
c	If you elect to use the lump-sum election method, check here (see instructions) ☐					
7	Capital gain or (loss). Attach Schedule D if required. If not required, check here ☐				7	
8	Other income from Schedule 1, line 10				8	
9	Add lines 1z, 2b, 3b, 4b, 5b, 6b, 7, and 8. This is your **total income**				9	
10	Adjustments to income from Schedule 1, line 26				10	2,000
11	Subtract line 10 from line 9. This is your **adjusted gross income**				11	48,000

Attach Sch. B if required.

Standard Deduction for—
- Single or Married filing separately, $12,950
- Married filing jointly or Qualifying surviving spouse, $25,900
- Head of

Standard deduction or itemized deductions

9

EDUCATION CREDITS

Two credits are available to reduce the cost of higher education for taxpayers, their spouses, and their dependents: the AOC and the lifetime learning credit. The following table compares the two credits.

	American Opportunity Credit	Lifetime Learning Credit
Refundable	40% of the credit may be refundable (limited to $1,000 per student).	Nonrefundable
Annual limit	$2,500 credit per student (100% of the first $2,000 qualifying expenses, plus 25% of the next $2,000)	$2,000 credit per tax return
Qualified expenses	Tuition, books, supplies, equipment needed for a course of study, required enrollment or admission fees	Tuition and fees required for enrollment or admission
Qualifying expenses	Undergraduate	Undergraduate, graduate, and professional courses to acquire or improve job skills
Felony drug conviction restriction	Yes	No
Degree or certificate requirement	Yes: degree or other recognized credential	No requirement
Enrollment requirement	Yes, at least half-time for at least one academic period in tax year	One or more courses
MAGI phaseout for MFJ filers	$160,000–$180,000	$160,000–$180,000
MAGI phaseout for single, head of household, qualifying surviving spouse	$80,000–$90,000	$80,000–$90,000

In evaluating the two credit options, several factors warrant consideration.

- For each student, either the AOC or the lifetime learning credit may be claimed, but not both. If both credits are available, the AOC will always be greater than the lifetime learning credit.
- If qualified educational expenses are paid for more than one student, taxpayers can choose to claim the AOC for one student and the lifetime learning credit for another student in the same year. The AOC limitation is per student, not per tax return filed. The lifetime learning credit limit is per tax return, not per student.
- Unlike the AOC, there is no limit on the number of years the lifetime learning credit can be claimed for each student. The AOC is limited to four years.

Note. For more information on qualifications and calculations for the lifetime learning credit and the AOC, see the 2019 *University of Illinois Federal Tax Workbook,* Volume A, Chapter 1: Individual Taxpayer Issues. This can be found at **uofi.tax/arc** [taxschool.illinois.edu/taxbookarchive].

Practitioner Planning Tip

The AOC is more beneficial than a tax-free §529 distribution, but additional qualifying educational expenses can be allocated to other sources such as §529 plans.

Coordination of Credits and Deductions

An AOC can be claimed in the same year that a distribution is taken from a QTP or Coverdell, as long as the same expenses are not used for both benefits. This means that after the beneficiary reduces qualified education expenses by tax-free educational assistance, they must further reduce them by the expenses used in determining the credit. This calculation results in the AQEE (defined earlier).

Example 10. Tara incurs $8,500 of qualified education expenses, receives $3,500 in tax-free scholarships, and takes a $5,000 distribution from a §529 plan, of which $800 represents earnings.

Total qualified tuition expenses	$8,500
Less: tax-free educational assistance	(3,500)
AQEE	$5,000

$$\textbf{Tax-free earnings} = \textbf{\$800 earnings} \times \frac{\textbf{\$5,000 AQEE}}{\textbf{\$5,000 distribution}}$$

$$= \textbf{\$800}$$

No taxable distribution occurs in this situation, but no AQEE amount remains for potential education credits.

Example 11. Use the same facts as **Example 10,** except Tara's AQEE is reduced by $4,000 to claim the AOC (assuming she meets all requirements to claim this credit).

Total qualified tuition expenses	$8,500
Less: tax-free educational assistance	(3,500)
Less: expenses taken for the AOC	(4,000)
AQEE	$1,000

$$\textbf{Tax-free earnings} = \textbf{\$800 earnings} \times \frac{\textbf{\$1,000 AQEE}}{\textbf{\$5,000 distribution}}$$

$$= \textbf{\$160}$$

$800 earnings – $160 tax-free earnings = $640 taxable earnings (not subject to a 10% penalty).[74]

If Tara is in the 22% tax bracket, she incurs $141 of tax on the $640 of taxable earnings. However, if she qualifies, she can take a maximum $2,500 AOC.[75]

74. IRS Pub. 970, *Tax Benefits for Education.*

75. Ibid.

ALTERNATIVES

There are many alternatives for education cost-saving strategies, including those earned through military service and scholarships. The following are some alternative strategies for college cost planning.

GI Bill[76]

The GI Bill aims to help veterans and their families pay for higher education, including college, graduate school, and training programs. Recipients can use GI Bill funds to pay for tuition, supplies, and textbooks. Recipients may also use funds for monthly housing subject to certain criteria and limitations, such as how long the veteran served in active duty, how many credit hours the student is enrolled in, and the campus location. Funds are paid directly to the institution of attendance.

Employer Funding

Some employers are willing to invest in the education of employees if it results in more value for the company. Employers can take a qualifying business deduction on their tax return for payments made toward continuing education.[77] Although the employee has no income tax benefit, it can reduce the out-of-pocket costs associated with attending higher education institutions.

Scholarships

Scholarships are another option for funding higher education. Unlike loans, students are not required to repay funds from scholarships to the issuer. Instead, scholarship recipients obtain the award from community involvement, contests, applications, academic achievement, merit, or financial need. Both public and private institutions offer a variety of scholarship programs for current and prospective students.

> **Note.** Taxpayers can use scholarships in conjunction with other education savings programs. However, it is critical to offset education expenses with any awarded scholarships when calculating qualifying education expenses for tax credits to avoid inflated education credits and double-dipping expenses.

Scholarships are generally excluded from taxable income if a student actively participates in a degree program at an educational institution and spends the awarded funds on qualifying education expenses. These expenses include tuition, fees, supplies, books, and equipment.[78] In cases where services are furnished in exchange for a scholarship or the recipient uses the awarded funds for incidental expenses, such as travel or optional equipment, the taxpayer must include the funds as taxable gross income.[79]

ROTC

Army Reserve Officers' Training Corps (ROTC) programs also offer higher education benefits. ROTC members develop technical skills and receive a structured path to a career in the military after college. Additionally, ROTC members may apply for scholarships and monetary support from the United States Army. In addition to tuition, scholarship recipients receive a monthly stipend for housing expenses and an annual stipend for books.[80] Stipends are reported as pay excluded from gross income on Form W-2, similar to a reimbursement.[81] Accordingly, a recipient would not include the stipend as taxable income on their tax return.

---

76. *About GI Bill Benefits.* Feb.14, 2023. U.S. Department of Veteran Affairs. [www.va.gov/education/about-gi-bill-benefits] Accessed on May 29, 2023.

77. Treas. Reg. §1.162-5(a).

78. IRC §117(b).

79. *Topic Number 421 — Scholarships, Fellowships Grants, and Other Grants*. Apr. 4, 2023. IRS. [www.irs.gov/taxtopics/tc421] Accessed on Jun. 12, 2023.

80. *Army ROTC Scholarships*. May 30, 2023. U.S. Army. [www.goarmy.com/careers-and-jobs/find-your-path/army-officers/rotc/scholarships.html] Accessed on Jun. 5, 2023.

81. IRS Pub. 3, *Armed Forces' Tax Guide*, p. 8 (2022).

SETTLING A TAXPAYER'S ESTATE

Tax practitioners find themselves in a position of being sought for advice on a myriad of tax topics. It is not uncommon for a tax practitioner to have a client come to them and say, "I have recently had a passing in the family. Now what do I do?" In addition to mourning the passing of a loved one, surviving friends and family members are also often overwhelmed with settling the affairs of the decedent and are unfamiliar with or unsure of what steps they need to take in meeting their fiduciary responsibilities. Tax practitioners can provide an invaluable service to such clients by helping them navigate this process, but attorneys also need to be involved.

This section covers the processes and steps for settling the affairs of a deceased taxpayer. This section flows similarly to how a practitioner would walk through the steps with their client. Unless specifically stated, the client is assumed to be an executor of an estate for purposes of this section.

KEY DOCUMENTS FOR MAPPING THE SETTLEMENT PROCESS

When first discussing the issue of estates with clients, tax practitioners should request a copy of important documents that will direct the conversation and provide a roadmap of instructions on how to proceed with settling the decedent's affairs. The decedent may have a will, trust, both, or neither.

Last Will and Testament

A last will and testament (will) is a legal document providing instructions on what to do with a decedent's property upon death. The document names the executor charged with carrying out the stipulations listed in the will. Additionally, the will lists the estate beneficiaries who will inherit the property. As such, a decedent's will is often the primary document for settling an estate, as it details what to do with the property, who should receive the property, and who will distribute the property.[82]

Practitioner Planning Tip

As a first step, practitioners should begin any estate discussions with executors by **reading and developing an understanding** of the decedent's will. This step is critical in all cases, as each decedent's will differs from another's, and practitioners should not rely solely on an executor's interpretation or belief of a decedent's wishes. Legal advice should be sought to best understand these documents and the laws of applicable states.

Additionally, because individuals can amend their wills during their lifetime at any point, practitioners should request copies of any amendments or codicils to a will to ensure they are privy to the most current and complete provisions of a decedent's estate plan.

9

82. *Will.* ALM Global, LLC. [dictionary.law.com/Default.aspx?selected=2248] Accessed on Jul. 17, 2023.

Trust Instrument[83]

A common tool for estate planning, trusts are contractual arrangements under which an individual transfers legal property ownership to another party. Trusts are favored vehicles for managing and transferring property, as they offer flexibility in establishing criteria and timing provisions for handling assets and any income they generate.[84] When settling an estate, it is necessary to determine if the decedent established any trusts to ensure the assets placed in trust are distributed and handled in accordance with the trust provisions. Differentiating the assets by specific ownership will come into play when inventorying assets and assessing probate. This section discusses both topics later.

> **Note.** For an in-depth analysis of the fundamentals of trusts, see the 2020 *University of Illinois Federal Tax Workbook*, Volume B, Chapter 3: Trust Essentials. This can be found at **uofi.tax/arc** [taxschool.illinois.edu/taxbookarchive].

Like a will for an estate, a trust instrument governs what property is held in the trust and who the property will go to, known as **beneficiaries.** Additionally, the trust instrument identifies who will manage and distribute the property, known as the **trustee.**

Living Trusts. A living (or inter vivos) trust is an entity an individual (grantor) creates during their lifetime. The trust may be **revocable,** where the grantor retains the right to change or amend the trust. The trust instrument will contain language identifying whether the grantor has or maintains these rights. Alternatively, the trust can be **irrevocable,** where the grantor is unable to change or modify the trust. Upon the death of the grantor, any revocable trusts will become irrevocable by nature, as the grantor is no longer living and cannot exercise any right to change or modify the trust.[85]

For state law purposes, when a grantor transfers assets to a trust, they should title the assets in the name of the trust, a process known as **funding the trust.** Failure to transfer titled assets, such as real estate and brokerage accounts, to the trust may result in those assets being subject to probate,[86] discussed later, unless the grantor employs a different method, such as payable on death (POD) or transfer on death (TOD).[87]

Practitioner Planning Tip

Due to the complexity of the tax preparation process, it would be beneficial for practitioners to alert their clients to pay special attention to the titles of specific trust accounts.

83. See Treas. Reg. §301.7701-4.

84. *Trusts and estates: Uses and tax considerations*. Pippin, Sonja E. Feb. 2017. Journal of Accountancy. [www.journalofaccountancy.com/issues/2017/feb/trusts-and-estates-uses-tax-considerations.html] Accessed on Jul. 17, 2023.

85. *Trusts: Common Law and IRC 501(c)(3) and 4947*. Thomas, Ward L. and Henzke, Jr., Leonard J. 2003. IRS. [www.irs.gov/pub/irs-tege/eotopica03.pdf] Accessed on Jul. 17, 2023.

86. *The Probate Process*. American Bar Association. [www.americanbar.org/groups/real_property_trust_estate/resources/estate_planning/the_probate_process] Accessed on Jul. 18, 2023.

87. POD (bypasses the probate process and for the funds to go directly to the beneficiary) and TOD (automatically transfers assets to a named beneficiary when the holder dies) are defined at *Pros and Cons: Payable on Death (POD) Accounts*. Lake, Rebecca. May 27, 2023. SmartAsset. [smartasset.com/estate-planning/payable-on-death] Accessed on Jul. 18, 2023.

Testamentary Trusts. When a grantor creates a trust under the provisions of their will, the trust is known as a testamentary trust. Unlike living trusts, testamentary trusts can only be irrevocable, as the trust is established after the grantor's death. The trust instrument for a testamentary trust is not a separate document, but is rather created within the provisions of the grantor's will.[88]

Simple and Complex Trusts.[89] The status of a trust as a simple or complex trust is determined annually. A trust is designated as a simple trust if **all** the following are true for the tax year.

1. The trust instrument **requires** that all income must be distributed currently (regardless of whether or not the income is actually distributed);
2. The trust instrument does **not** provide that any amounts are to be paid, permanently set aside, or otherwise used for charitable purposes; and
3. The trust does not distribute amounts allocated to the corpus of the trust.

Any trust that does not qualify as a simple trust is a complex trust.

IDENTIFYING ESTATE BENEFICIARIES

A fundamental step in settling a taxpayer's estate is first identifying the beneficiaries and whether there is a surviving spouse. Additionally, practitioners should investigate the role that attorneys can play and consider executing a power of attorney (POA).

> **Caution.** Tax practitioners should exercise extreme caution before advising a client that they may not need an attorney.

Surviving Spouse as Sole Beneficiary

When reviewing the will and trust documents, the practitioner should identify if the surviving spouse is the sole beneficiary of the decedent's estate. If that is the case, settling the estate can be much simpler and less involved than estates with multiple beneficiaries. With fewer parties involved, the identification of assets and who the title should transfer to is one person compared to multiple people. As such, administrative time for tracking down beneficiaries and having them sign documents to transfer the title of assets is limited to one person. Additionally, if the decedent's assets were jointly owned with the surviving spouse, transferring those assets directly to the spouse is simpler, generally requiring notification of the decedent's death to the broker or account manager instead of obtaining signatures for signing documents and providing evidence to support the transfer of title of an asset to a non-joint owner.

9

No Surviving Spouse or Multiple Non-Spouse Beneficiaries

For estates with no surviving spouse or multiple non-spouse beneficiaries, it may behoove the executor to involve an attorney and grant a practitioner with powers of attorney to help facilitate the settlement of the estate due to higher complexity. When a surviving spouse inherits all or the majority of a decedent's assets, the administrative process of distributing assets primarily consists of transferring title of those assets to the spouse. When multiple parties are beneficiaries, there is more involvement in the administrative process of transferring assets. Additionally, there is a higher risk of conflicting interests among multiple beneficiaries which could potentially result in litigation. Involving an attorney to aid in the administration, legal interpretation, and beneficiary communication involved in settling an estate early in the process can help reduce the burden of stress arising from such fiduciary responsibilities.

---

88. *Trusts: Common Law and IRC 501(c)(3) and 4947.* Thomas, Ward L. and Henzke, Jr., Leonard J. 2003. [www.irs.gov/pub/irs-tege/eotopica03.pdf] Accessed on Jul. 17, 2023.

89. IRC §651; Treas. Reg. §§1.1471-1(b)(22) and (118); see also Instructions for Form 1041.

Role of an Attorney

Credentials and qualifications for tax return preparers **do not extend to the practice of law or legal interpretation.** Therefore, particularly in situations where a decedent's estate is complex, involves beneficiaries who disagree with each other, or the provisions of a will or trust instrument are difficult to interpret, an attorney may be needed to assist with the interpretation of the estate documents and the settlement of the estate. Tax practitioners can provide guidance on tax considerations for estate matters and serve as a translator between the executor and the attorney. There may be cases where the executor may feel more comfortable talking to their tax practitioner due to a longstanding and more familiar relationship with them compared to their attorney. Practitioners can provide value in multiple facets of these interactions with multiple parties. Practitioners and their clients should seek competent legal advice.

Authorization Forms

An executor may not have access to all pertinent tax documents and records needed while settling an estate. They must notify the IRS of their fiduciary relationship on behalf of the decedent, their estate, and any trusts. The executor can also grant the practitioner authorization to act as a representative on their behalf. In some cases, an executor may grant a practitioner with a POA, which authorizes the practitioner to perform "certain specified acts" on behalf of the taxpayer.[90] To initiate and establish these relationships and authorizations, the executor and practitioner must complete and submit the applicable forms.

Form 56.[91] Fiduciaries file Form 56, *Notice Concerning Fiduciary Relationship*, with the IRS to notify the agency of a fiduciary relationship for which the filer is engaged. A **fiduciary** is a person acting on behalf of another living person or entity to assume the person or entity's powers, rights, duties, and privileges. Therefore, an executor of an estate would file Form 56 with the IRS to notify the agency that the executor has the rights and duties of the estate. Form 56 does not grant any powers or rights to the fiduciary. Instead, the form informs the IRS of the established relationship.

If there is no surviving spouse, or if the executor instead of the surviving spouse is responsible for filing the decedent's final Form 1040, the executor would also file a separate Form 56 to notify the IRS that the executor has the rights and duties of the decedent.[92] These rights include receiving correspondence and obtaining information from the IRS. Duties include filing tax returns and paying any tax due on behalf of the taxpayer. A fiduciary also uses Form 56 to notify the IRS of the termination of their fiduciary relationship.

---

90. IRM 4.11.55.1.6 (2018).

91. Instructions for Form 56.

92. IRC §6903.

Example 12. Miranda passed away on June 12, 2023. She was widowed at the time of her passing, having been married to Stuart for 50 years before his passing on August 8, 2020. Miranda had two children living at the time of her death. In her will, she named Lydia, her eldest daughter, as the executor of her estate. In preparation for handling her mother's estate and expecting to have correspondence with the IRS, Lydia prepares and files the following Forms 56 with the IRS for both her mother and her mother's estate.

Form **56** (Rev. November 2022) Department of the Treasury Internal Revenue Service

Notice Concerning Fiduciary Relationship

(Internal Revenue Code Sections 6036 and 6903)

Go to *www.irs.gov/Form56* for instructions and the latest information.

OMB No. 1545-0013

Part I Identification

Name of person for whom you are acting (as shown on the tax return)	Identifying number	**Decedent's social security no.**
Miranda Dunmeyer		*****-**-6789**

Address of person for whom you are acting (number, street, and room or suite no.)
2640 Steiner St

City or town, state, and ZIP code (If a foreign address, see instructions.)
San Francisco, CA 94115

Fiduciary's name
Lydia Hillard

Address of fiduciary (number, street, and room or suite no.)
2640 Steiner St

City or town, state, and ZIP code	Telephone number (optional)
San Francisco, CA 94115	( )

Section A. Authority

1 Authority for fiduciary relationship. Check applicable box:
- a ☒ Court appointment of testate estate (valid will exists)
- b ☐ Court appointment of intestate estate (no valid will exists)
- c ☐ Court appointment as guardian or conservator
- d ☐ Fiduciary of intestate estate
- e ☐ Valid trust instrument and amendments
- f ☐ Bankruptcy or assignment for the benefit of creditors
- g ☐ Other. Describe:

2a If box 1a, 1b, or 1d is checked, enter the date of death: **6/12/2023**

b If box 1c, 1e, 1f, or 1g is checked, enter the date of appointment, taking office, or assignment or transfer of assets:

Section B. Nature of Liability and Tax Notices

3 Type of taxes (check all that apply): ☒ Income ☐ Gift ☒ Estate ☐ Generation-skipping transfer ☐ Employment ☐ Excise ☐ Other (describe):

4 Federal tax form number (check all that apply): **a** ☒ 706 series **b** ☐ 709 **c** ☐ 940 **d** ☐ 941, 943, 944 **e** ☒ 1040 or 1040-SR **f** ☐ 1041 **g** ☐ 1120 **h** ☐ Other (list):

5 If your authority as a fiduciary does not cover all years or tax periods, check here . . . . ☐ and list the specific years or periods within your authority:

For Paperwork Reduction Act and Privacy Act Notice, see separate instructions. Cat. No. 16375I Form **56** (Rev. 11-2022)

9

For Example 12

Form **56** (Rev. November 2022) Department of the Treasury Internal Revenue Service

Notice Concerning Fiduciary Relationship

(Internal Revenue Code Sections 6036 and 6903)

Go to *www.irs.gov/Form56* for instructions and the latest information.

OMB No. 1545-0013

Part I Identification

Name of person for whom you are acting (as shown on the tax return)	Identifying number	Decedent's social security no.
Miranda Dunmeyer Estate	**98-7654321**	

Address of person for whom you are acting (number, street, and room or suite no.)
2640 Steiner St

City or town, state, and ZIP code (If a foreign address, see instructions.)
San Francisco, CA 94115

Fiduciary's name
Lydia Hillard

Address of fiduciary (number, street, and room or suite no.)
2640 Steiner St

City or town, state, and ZIP code	Telephone number (optional)
San Francisco, CA 94115	( )

Section A. Authority

1 Authority for fiduciary relationship. Check applicable box:
- a ☒ Court appointment of testate estate (valid will exists)
- b ☐ Court appointment of intestate estate (no valid will exists)
- c ☐ Court appointment as guardian or conservator
- d ☐ Fiduciary of intestate estate
- e ☐ Valid trust instrument and amendments
- f ☐ Bankruptcy or assignment for the benefit of creditors
- g ☐ Other. Describe:

2a If box 1a, 1b, or 1d is checked, enter the date of death: **6/12/2023**

b If box 1c, 1e, 1f, or 1g is checked, enter the date of appointment, taking office, or assignment or transfer of assets:

Section B. Nature of Liability and Tax Notices

3 Type of taxes (check all that apply): ☒ Income ☐ Gift ☐ Estate ☐ Generation-skipping transfer ☐ Employment ☐ Excise ☐ Other (describe):

4 Federal tax form number (check all that apply): a ☒ 706 series b ☐ 709 c ☐ 940 d ☐ 941, 943, 944 e ☐ 1040 or 1040-SR f ☒ 1041 g ☐ 1120 h ☐ Other (list):

5 If your authority as a fiduciary does not cover all years or tax periods, check here . . . . ☐ and list the specific years or periods within your authority:

For Paperwork Reduction Act and Privacy Act Notice, see separate instructions. Cat. No. 16375I Form **56** (Rev. 11-2022)

Form 2848.[93] Taxpayers file Form 2848, *Power of Attorney and Declaration of Representative*, with the IRS to notify the agency that the taxpayer is authorizing an individual to represent them before the IRS. The taxpayer further uses the form to describe the specific matters, tax forms, and years or periods they authorize the individual to represent them. In the case of an estate, an executor, having filed Form 56 notifying the IRS of their fiduciary relationship to the estate, may file Form 2848, giving authority to their tax practitioner to represent the estate in income tax matters. This authorization would pertain to Form 1041, *U.S. Income Tax Return for Estates and Trusts*, and the executor would list the tax years for which they authorize the practitioner to represent the estate.

93. Instructions for Form 2848.

Example 13. Use the same facts as **Example 12.** Lydia, as executor, wishes to have her attorney, Juliette, and her accountant, Drew, represent her mother's estate before the IRS. She prepares and files the following Form 2848 with the IRS to grant this authorization.

Form **2848** (Rev. January 2021) Department of the Treasury Internal Revenue Service	**Power of Attorney and Declaration of Representative** ▶ Go to *www.irs.gov/Form2848* for instructions and the latest information.	OMB No. 1545-0150 **For IRS Use Only** Received by: Name ____ Telephone ____ Function ____ Date / /

Part I Power of Attorney

Caution: A separate Form 2848 must be completed for each taxpayer. Form 2848 will not be honored for any purpose other than representation before the IRS.

1 **Taxpayer information.** Taxpayer must sign and date this form on page 2, line 7.

Taxpayer name and address	Taxpayer identification number(s)	
Miranda Dunmeyer Estate **2640 Steiner St, San Francisco, CA 94115**		**98-7654321**
	Daytime telephone number **415-555-8268**	Plan number (if applicable)

hereby appoints the following representative(s) as attorney(s)-in-fact:

2 **Representative(s)** must sign and date this form on page 2, Part II.

Name and address	
Juliette Marshall **1200 Market St, San Francisco, CA 94115**	CAF No. **9007-16078R** PTIN ____ Telephone No. **415-555-7238** Fax No. ____
Check if to be sent copies of notices and communications ☐	Check if new: Address ☐ Telephone No. ☐ Fax No. ☐
Drew Letchworth **30 Pacific Ave Ste 203, San Francisco, CA 94115**	CAF No. **4006-16038R** PTIN **P03422666** Telephone No. **415-555-6496** Fax No. ____
Check if to be sent copies of notices and communications ☒	Check if new: Address ☐ Telephone No. ☐ Fax No. ☐
Name and address	CAF No. ____ PTIN ____ Telephone No. ____ Fax No. ____
(**Note:** IRS sends notices and communications to only two representatives.)	Check if new: Address ☐ Telephone No. ☐ Fax No. ☐
Name and address	CAF No. ____ PTIN ____ Telephone No. ____ Fax No. ____
(**Note:** IRS sends notices and communications to only two representatives.)	Check if new: Address ☐ Telephone No. ☐ Fax No. ☐

to represent the taxpayer before the Internal Revenue Service and perform the following acts:

3 **Acts authorized (you are required to complete line 3).** Except for the acts described in line 5b, I authorize my representative(s) to receive and inspect my confidential tax information and to perform acts I can perform with respect to the tax matters described below. For example, my representative(s) shall have the authority to sign any agreements, consents, or similar documents (see instructions for line 5a for authorizing a representative to sign a return).

Description of Matter (Income, Employment, Payroll, Excise, Estate, Gift, Whistleblower, Practitioner Discipline, PLR, FOIA, Civil Penalty, Sec. 4980H Shared Responsibility Payment, etc.) (see instructions)	Tax Form Number (1040, 941, 720, etc.) (if applicable)	Year(s) or Period(s) (if applicable) (see instructions)
Income	**1041**	**2023 - 2026**

Form 8821.[94] Taxpayers file Form 8821, *Tax Information Authorization,* with the IRS to notify the agency of an individual or entity the taxpayer authorizes to inspect and receive tax information. Like Form 2848, the taxpayer identifies the specific tax matter, form, and years or periods for which they authorize the designee to inspect and receive information. However, Form 8821 differs from Form 2848 in that the scope of the authorization is **substantially limited.** Form 8821 does not authorize a designee to represent the taxpayer before the IRS but provides authorization for the designee to obtain specific tax information. An executor may use Form 8821 to authorize their tax practitioner to receive tax information from the IRS if the executor does not want their practitioner to represent the estate before the IRS. Instead, the executor may wish to have their attorney or another tax specialist represent the estate before the IRS while authorizing their tax practitioner to obtain the estate's tax information from the IRS.

94. Instructions for Form 8821.

Example 14. Use the same facts as **Example 12.** Miranda's youngest daughter, Natalie, is a beneficiary of her mother's estate. Her accountant, Robert Lundy, would like access to Miranda's estate income tax returns to obtain detailed information regarding a net operating loss on Natalie's Schedule K-1 (Form 1041), *Beneficiary's Share of Income, Deductions, Credits, etc.* Believing it may be more convenient for him to obtain this information directly from the IRS, Robert suggests Lydia grant him authority to receive information regarding current and future Form 1041 filings. After discussing the matter with her attorney, Lydia agrees. She prepares and files the following Form 8821 to notify the IRS of this authorization.

Form **8821**

(Rev. January 2021)

Department of the Treasury
Internal Revenue Service

Tax Information Authorization

▶ Go to *www.irs.gov/Form8821* for instructions and the latest information.
▶ Don't sign this form unless all applicable lines have been completed.
▶ Don't use Form 8821 to request copies of your tax returns or to authorize someone to represent you. See instructions.

OMB No. 1545-1165
For IRS Use Only
Received by:
Name
Telephone
Function
Date

1 Taxpayer information. Taxpayer must sign and date this form on line 6.

Taxpayer name and address	Taxpayer identification number(s)	
Miranda Dunmeyer Estate **2640 Steiner St, San Francisco, CA 94115**	**98-7654321**	
	Daytime telephone number	Plan number (if applicable)

2 Designee(s). If you wish to name more than two designees, attach a list to this form. **Check here if a list of additional designees is attached ▶** ☐

Name and address	
Robert Lundy **44 Church St, Danville, CA 94526**	CAF No. **5007-16056R** PTIN **P01234567** Telephone No. **925-555-7200** Fax No.
Check if to be sent copies of notices and communications ☒	Check if new: Address ☐ Telephone No. ☐ Fax No. ☐
Name and address	CAF No. PTIN Telephone No. Fax No.
Check if to be sent copies of notices and communications ☐	Check if new: Address ☐ Telephone No. ☐ Fax No. ☐

3 Tax information. Each designee is authorized to inspect and/or receive confidential tax information for the type of tax, forms, periods, and specific matters you list below. See the line 3 instructions.

☐ By checking here, I authorize access to my IRS records via an Intermediate Service Provider.

(a) Type of Tax Information (Income, Employment, Payroll, Excise, Estate, Gift, Civil Penalty, Sec. 4980H Payments, etc.)	(b) Tax Form Number (1040, 941, 720, etc.)	(c) Year(s) or Period(s)	(d) Specific Tax Matters
Income	**1041**	**2023 - 2026**	

4 Specific use not recorded on the Centralized Authorization File (CAF). If the tax information authorization is for a specific use not recorded on CAF, check this box. See the instructions. If you check this box, skip line 5 . . . . . . ▶ ☐

5 Retention/revocation of prior tax information authorizations. If the line 4 box is checked, skip this line. If the line 4 box isn't checked, the IRS will automatically revoke all prior tax information authorizations on file unless you check the line 5 box and **attach a copy** of the tax information authorization(s) that you want to retain . . . . ▶ ☐

To revoke a prior tax information authorization(s) without submitting a new authorization, see the line 5 instructions.

6 Taxpayer signature. If signed by a corporate officer, partner, guardian, partnership representative (or designated individual, if applicable), executor, receiver, administrator, trustee, or individual other than the taxpayer, I certify that I have the legal authority to execute this form with respect to the tax matters and tax periods shown on line 3 above.

▶ IF NOT COMPLETED, SIGNED, AND DATED, THIS TAX INFORMATION AUTHORIZATION WILL BE RETURNED.

▶ DON'T SIGN THIS FORM IF IT IS BLANK OR INCOMPLETE.

Signature | Date

Print Name | Title (if applicable)

For Privacy Act and Paperwork Reduction Act Notice, see the instructions. Cat. No. 11596P Form **8821** (Rev. 01-2021)

Kovel Agreements[95]

Due to the nature of settling an estate, it is not uncommon for executors to work with both an attorney and an accountant. For example, an attorney may have sufficient knowledge of settling an estate but may not be knowledgeable regarding the associated accounting procedures and ramifications. Therefore, attorneys may work with an executor's accountant to consider and address the accounting aspects of settling the estate. However, while confidential communications between an attorney and a client have protection from disclosure under an attorney-client privilege, such protection does not generally extend between clients and their accountants. While IRC §7525 describes certain confidentiality privileges in taxpayer communications, they are limited in scope to noncriminal tax matters and proceedings brought before the IRS and United States Government. Furthermore, protection under §7525 relates to tax advice only, and does not cover compliance or business advice.

A **Kovel agreement,** coined after an appellate court decision,[96] is an agreement between a client's legal counsel and accountant, describing the services the accountant will provide at the attorney's discretion. The attorney will usually draft this letter for the accountant to sign. The client may also sign the draft letter, especially in cases where the client is responsible for paying the accountant's fees, which the agreement specifies. By establishing the relationship between the client's attorney and their accountant, the accountant's discussions, workpapers, and advice become protected under the attorney-client privilege. This extended privileged communication may be valuable when a tax controversy exists or occurs.

> **Note.** A Kovel agreement is similar to a tax practitioner's engagement letter with a client, where the document describes the scope of the work, responsibility, and payment terms. As with other binding agreements, it is important for an accountant and potentially their own legal counsel to review the agreement before signing it and retaining a copy for their records.

PROBATE PROCESS

Probate is a legal process requiring the court to ensure a decedent's will is valid, an executor is appointed, and all debts of the estate are paid. Potential issues associated with probate include the following.[97]

- Attorney's fees and other costs
- Delays in transferring property to the intended beneficiaries
- A less private process

Probate is a public process where documents such as the decedent's will and list of probate assets are filed with the court and become public records. Consequently, the public may view the documents in their entirety, perhaps virtually.

95. See *Kovel agreement basics for you and your client.* Nakamura, Karen. Jul. 1, 2022. Journal of Accountancy. [www.journalofaccountancy.com/issues/2022/jul/kovel-agreement-basics.html] Accessed on Jun. 20, 2023.

96. *U.S. v. Kovel*, 296 F.2d 918 (2nd Cir. 1961).

97. *The Probate Process.* American Bar Association. [www.americanbar.org/groups/real_property_trust_estate/resources/estate_planning/the_probate_process] Accessed on Jul. 18, 2023.

State law governs the probate process. As such, executors need to be conscientious about where the estate needs to enter probate and assess the specific requirements and adhere to the governing laws of the state. In instances where a decedent owned property in different states, multiple probate proceedings may be necessary, which increases expenses and further complicates the probate process. Other rules potentially differing among states include the claims period and process for the estate's debts.[98] Using the state of Illinois as an example, an executor must inform creditors of a probate case.[99] For creditors who are known to the executor, the executor must notify the creditors directly. For creditors unknown to the executor, the executor must publish a public notice of the probate case. Creditors have six months from the date the executor published a notice to submit any claim against the estate, otherwise any such claim would be barred.[100]

Probate Requirement

Not all estates are subject to probate. While most estates where a decedent did not create a will **must** go through probate, some exceptions may apply. Some states have applicable thresholds, where estates with total assets valued below a specified threshold are not subject to the state's probate. Using the state of Illinois as an example, executors may file a small estate affidavit exempting the estate from probate if the gross estate's probate assets are under $100,000.[101]

Additionally, not all assets of an estate are subject to probate. Assets are not subject to probate if they are scheduled to pass to a survivor under a contract or by operation of property law rather than through the decedent's will. Examples of nonprobate assets include the following.[102]

- Retirement plans, such as IRAs and §401(k) plans, with named beneficiaries that are not the estate
- Life insurance proceeds, with named beneficiaries that are not the estate
- Real estate owned by joint tenants with rights of survivorship
- Joint bank accounts with rights of survivorship
- Any assets that would pass to the surviving spouse under the statutory right of the surviving spouse
- Grantor trust assets
- Assets that are POD
- Assets that are TOD

Practitioner Planning Tip

While probate is often viewed as a process to avoid due to the cost and prolonged timing, there may be benefits for an estate going through probate. Using Illinois as an example, notifying creditors of a probate case results in a 6-month claims period from the date the executor provided notice, whereas the default claims period against estates is two years after the decedent's death.[103] Tax practitioners should work with attorneys familiar with the applicable state's probate rules.

98. See, *Ancillary Probate: Probate in Another State.* Randolph, Mary, JD. Nolo. [www.nolo.com/legal-encyclopedia/ancillary-probate-probate-another-state.html] Accessed on Jul. 18, 2023.

99. 755 ILCS 5/18-3.

100. Ibid.

101. 755 ILCS 5/24-22.

102. See, *Probate v. Non-Probate: What Is the Difference?* Dec. 9, 2022. ElderLawNet, Inc. [www.elderlawanswers.com/probate-v-non-probate-what-is-the-difference-14411] Accessed on Jul. 17, 2023.

103. 755 ILCS 5/18-12.

IDENTIFYING APPLICABLE TAX RETURNS

A critical step for an executor to settle an estate is determining which tax returns the estate will need to file. This concept can be difficult to explain due to the niche nature of fiduciary taxation and the multiple tax returns that may necessitate filing. Tax practitioners should discuss and explain the multiple tax returns an estate may need to file and assist the executor with identifying which returns apply to the estate.

Decedent's Final Form 1040[104]

Death does not exempt taxpayers from income tax filing and payment requirements for the year of death. Therefore, an executor may need to file a final Form 1040 for the deceased taxpayer to report and pay tax on income in the tax year of their death. There are not many differences in filing a final Form 1040 compared to a non-final return. For example, the due date of a final tax return is the same as all other Form 1040 calendar year filings (April 15). However, there are some considerations practitioners should discuss with the executor.

Requirements to File. A final Form 1040 is subject to the same filing requirements as a non-final Form 1040, where gross income and the filing status generally dictate when a filing requirement is present. There may be situations, particularly when the taxpayer's death occurred early in the tax year, where there is little to no income. Consequently, a final Form 1040 for the tax year of the taxpayer's death would not require filing.

If a final Form 1040 is required, the tax preparer must write "DECEASED," following the taxpayer's name and the date of their death at the top of the tax return. If there is a surviving spouse, they will sign the final return writing "Filing as surviving spouse" next to their signature. If the estate has an appointed personal representative, they will sign the tax return on behalf of the deceased taxpayer, while the surviving spouse will also sign their name on the return if filing jointly.

Income to Report. While the nature and type of income to report on a final Form 1040 is consistent with other Form 1040 requirements, the difference lies in when the income was earned and received. In general, income the decedent accounted for under the **cash method** is includable on their final Form 1040 if the decedent received it before their death. Accordingly, income the decedent accounted for under the **accrual method** is includable on the final Form 1040 if the decedent had earned it before their death.

9

While the general rule of income reporting appears simple, complexities can arise from the timing of receipt relative to the taxpayer's passing. **Constructive receipt of income** refers to taxpayers having income available for use without restriction. Using dividend income as an example, the following three dates are important when determining whether to report the dividend income on the decedent's final income tax return.

1. The declaration date when the dividend is declared
2. The record date where the issuer identifies the shareholders eligible to receive the dividend
3. The date when the issuer pays the dividend to the shareholders on record

If the taxpayer died after the declaration date, but before the record date, the final Form 1040 should not include the dividend income. If the taxpayer died after the record date, but before the payment date, the final Form 1040 should include the dividend as a constructive receipt of income.

Available Deductions. Final Form 1040 returns generally have the same deductions as non-final Form 1040 returns, including the full standard deduction if the taxpayer is not itemizing deductions. There are no special or unique deductions available to deceased taxpayers on their final income tax returns. For example, funeral and burial expenses are not deductible on the decedent's final Form 1040.

---

104. IRS Pub. 559, *Survivors, Executors, and Administrators.*

Medical expenses are one type of deduction where practitioners and executors have some discretion on which tax return to report them. Executors can elect to treat all medical expenses of the decedent that were not paid before the decedent's passing but were paid within a year after the decedent's passing as paid by the decedent when incurred. This treatment enables them to be deducted on the final Form 1040, if itemized, subject to the regular medical expense limitations. If the executor does not make this election or the expenses were paid after one year from the decedent's date of death, they could report these unpaid medical expenses on Form 706, *United States Estate (and Generation-Skipping Transfer) Tax Return*, discussed later.

Form 1310.[105] If a decedent's final Form 1040 results in a refund due for an overpayment of income tax, an executor may need to file Form 1310, *Statement of Person Claiming Refund Due a Deceased Taxpayer*. The form contains fields requesting information to identify the name, SSN, and address of the individual claiming the refund. When a Form 1310 must accompany the tax return, electronic filing may not be available.

Form 1041[106]

Because estates and trusts are separate entities from taxpayers, they have income tax return filing and payment requirements if there is reportable income. The income of an estate or trust is reported on Form 1041. While the nature and format of Form 1041 are similar to Form 1040, Form 1041 has unique attributes.

Income reported on Form 1041 may be either taxed at the entity level or passed through to beneficiaries and taxed at their level. Like partnerships and S corporations, trusts and estates may prepare a Schedule K-1 (Form 1041) for each beneficiary of the entity to report their share of income they will include on their tax return. The executor or trustee is responsible for filing Forms 1041 for the estate and the decedent's trusts if they meet the applicable filing requirements.

Requirements to File. Estates with gross income equaling or exceeding $600 during a tax year must file Form 1041. Simple trusts must file Form 1041 if gross income during a tax year exceeds $300.[107] Complex trusts must file Form 1041 if gross income during a tax year exceeds $100.[108]

Tax Year Determination. Estates can adopt either a fiscal or calendar year to report income and file income tax returns. If the estate adopts a **calendar year** and the initial filing is for the tax year of the decedent's death, the tax preparer files a short tax year return, with the beginning month being the month of the taxpayer's death and the ending month being December. Subsequent Form 1041 filings are full tax year returns unless the executor files the final Form 1041 early because they settled the estate before the end of a year. In that situation, the tax preparer would file a final short year Form 1041.

If the executor wishes to adopt a **fiscal year,** they may elect any yearend provided it ends on the last day of the month and the initial year does not exceed 12 months. The executor makes this election by **filing an initial Form 1041** (regardless of the yearend selected on the federal employer identification number (FEIN) application).

Caution. After an FEIN is assigned, the IRS issues the taxpayer a notice with the due dates for required returns based on the information provided on the application. The due date for Form 1041 may not be correct as shown because the yearend election is not made until the first return is filed.

The due date of Form 1041 is the 15th day of the 4th month following the close of the tax year. Filers can apply for an automatic 5½-month extension using Form 7004, *Application for Automatic Extension of Time to File Certain Business Income Tax, Information, and Other Returns.*[109]

---

105. Instructions for Form 1310.

106. IRS Pub. 559, *Survivors, Executors, and Administrators.*

107. Instructions for Form 1041.

108. Ibid.

109. Ibid.

Practitioner Planning Tip

Reasons an executor may wish to adopt a fiscal year for an estate may include the following.

- The estate's cash flow and ability to pay tax obligations, particularly if the estate will be open over a longer period, may be delayed by adopting a fiscal year that ends later than an initial calendar year.
- A fiscal year adoption may minimize the number of returns the executor must file if the estate is open for multiple calendar years but is expected to be closed within 12 months.

An executor may wish to adopt a calendar yearend in the following situation.

- Estates with income primarily from investment accounts may benefit from a calendar yearend so that income reported on the return matches the amounts reported on Forms 1099. Therefore, a breakout of income and associated reconciliation to Forms 1099 is not needed, and the tax return preparation time and accounting fees may be significantly reduced.

IRC §645 Election. A trust must generally use a December 31 yearend. However, a qualified revocable trust (QRT) can make an election per IRC §645, under which the trust is treated and taxed as if it were part of the estate. A QRT is any revocable trust owned by a deceased grantor that is includable in their taxable estate.[110] An executor may wish to make this election to simplify and reduce the number of filings they are responsible for, which generally results in reduced filing fees. Additionally, adopting a fiscal year generally allows the executor and tax practitioner more time to prepare and file the return, particularly when they use an extension. The due date is the 15th day of the 4th month following the close of the tax year.

9

Practitioner Planning Tip

Use of a fiscal year may defer income tax liability to a later year. It may allow beneficiaries more time to plan for the inclusion of taxable income allocated to them from an estate or trust. A trust with a calendar year ending December 31, 2022, results in the allocation of income to beneficiaries on their 2022 returns. Beneficiaries may not receive this unexpected Schedule K-1 until late in the filing season, which does not allow much time for planning. Conversely, a trust with a fiscal year ending March 31, 2023, results in the allocation of income to beneficiaries on their 2023 return, with beneficiaries receiving their Schedule K-1 well before the filing season.

110. IRC §645(b)(1).

To make the §645 election, filers use Form 8855, *Election to Treat a Qualified Revocable Trust as Part of an Estate.* By making the election, the estate and trust can file using a fiscal year if the fiscal yearend is not later than the end of the month before the month of death. For example, if the date of the decedent's death is June 12, 2023, the fiscal year must end by May 31, 2024. By filing a timely extension for the estate (or trust if no probate estate exists), Form 8855 receives an extended due date, thereby also extending the due date for the trust.[111] The fiscal yearend is established when the first Form 1041 is filed. The election period begins on the date of the decedent's death and ends two years after the decedent's death if Form 706 is not required. If Form 706 is required, the election period ends at the later of the following.[112]

- Two years after the date of the decedent's death, or
- Six months after the final determination of liability for estate tax.

Example 15. Use the same facts as **Example 12.** Because Miranda had established a QRT during her lifetime, Lydia thought it best to elect §645 treatment to reduce the number of tax return filings. Because Miranda's date of death was June 12, 2023, the fiscal yearend must end by May 31, 2024. Lydia chooses the May 31 yearend, resulting in a due date for the estate's first Form 1041 of September 15, 2024.

Income to Report. Form 1041 includes all items of income the estate or trust receives during the tax year, including dividends, interest, rents, capital gains, and business income. The income is reported on the respective Form 1099 under the estate or trust's TIN. Because Forms 1099 report income based on a calendar year, estates and §645 QRTs adopting a fiscal year need to reconcile the income they report on their Form 1041 filings to the issued Forms 1099.

In addition to reporting income the estate or trust receives, Form 1041 may need to include **income in respect of a decedent (IRD).** IRD is income for which a decedent would have received if they had not passed away and the income was not properly includable on the decedent's final Form 1040.[113] If the estate or trust has the right to receive this income, it must be included on the entity's Form 1041. However, if a beneficiary of the entity or other individual has the right to receive the income, they would report that income on their individual tax return instead of on the estate or trust Form 1041.

As mentioned previously, for cash basis income the decedent earned before their death but had not yet received at the time of their death, the income would not be properly includable on the final Form 1041. For accrual basis income the decedent earned before their death but did not receive at the time of their death, the income would be includable on the decedent's final Form 1041.

Example 16. Use the same facts as **Example 12.** Before her death, Miranda earned $1,400 of income from consulting services she provided. At the time of her death, Miranda had not yet received the payment from the client. Miranda historically reported income from consulting on her Schedule C, *Profit or Loss From Business*, using the cash accounting method. When preparing Miranda's final Form 1040 after her death, Lydia properly does not report the $1,400 on the return. Instead, Lydia reports the $1,400 on Form 1041 when Miranda's estate received the payment from the client.

Example 17. Assume the same facts as **Example 16,** except Miranda historically reported her consulting income using the accrual method of accounting. Lydia must include the $1,400 of consulting income on Schedule C for Miranda's final Form 1040.

Example 18. Assume the same facts as **Example 16,** except Lydia's sister, Natalie, has the right to receive the $1,400 of consulting income. Lydia would not include the consulting income on her mother's final Form 1040 or her estate tax return. When Natalie receives the $1,400 payment in 2024, she must include the income on her 2024 Form 1040.

---

111. Instructions for Form 8855.

112. IRC §645(b)(2).

113. IRC §691(a)(1).

Practitioner Planning Tip

These examples illustrate the importance of the executor providing current Forms W-9, *Request for Taxpayer Identification Number and Certification*, to payors so they can timely issue Forms 1099 to the estate.

Available Deductions.[114] Generally, estates and trusts may deduct the same expenses as individuals, including ordinary and necessary expenses paid or incurred in a trade or business[115] and expenses incurred in connection with the production or collection of income. Additionally, estates and trusts may deduct expenses incurred for the management, conservation, or maintenance of property used in producing income.[116] Business expenses are reported on the schedule corresponding to the reporting of that business's income, such as Schedule C.

The following are specific deductions the estate or trust may take on Form 1041.

- Investment interest, mortgage interest for qualified principal or secondary residence of a beneficiary, and interest on underpayment or nonpayment of tax
- State and local income or sales tax, real estate tax, and personal property tax
- Foreign or U.S. possession income taxes and generation-skipping transfer (GST) tax
- Fiduciary fees, such as probate court fees, legal publication costs of notices, printing costs for certified copies of the death certificate, and fiduciary accounts costs
- Attorney, accountant, and return preparer fees, including fees for filing a decedent's final Form 1040 (costs associated with preparing Form 709, *United States Gift (and Generation-Skipping Transfer) Tax Return*, are not deductible, as they are a common and customary expense for individuals and not necessitated by cause of death)
- Appraisal fees are deductible if they are not included on the estate's Form 706
- Investment advisory fees, but only for the portion above what an individual would normally incur because of the advice pertaining specifically to an estate or trust

Due to the ability for income to pass through to beneficiaries of an estate and trust for taxation at the beneficiary level, an **income distribution deduction** is available on Form 1041. For estates, when an executor distributes income to the estate beneficiaries, each beneficiary will receive a Schedule K-1 (Form 1041) reporting their share of the income. This form is prepared and filed with the estate's Form 1041. The income distribution deduction is calculated on Form 1041 Schedule B, *Income Distribution Deduction*. The deduction is then reported on page 1 of Form 1041, reducing the adjusted total income to reflect the amount the beneficiaries will report on their respective tax returns. Trusts operate similarly, except for simple trusts that have an income distribution deduction regardless of whether the trustee made distributions to the beneficiaries in the taxable year.

---

114. Instructions for Form 1041.
115. IRC §162.
116. IRC §212.

9

Form 706[117]

As discussed earlier, an estate is subject to taxation on its income, filing Form 1041 to report **income** and calculate federal income tax. However, estates may also be subject to taxation on the value of **assets** the estate holds.[118] Form 706 reports the estate's assets and calculates any associated federal estate tax.

Practitioner Planning Tip

In communication with clients regarding estate taxation, it may be helpful for practitioners to distinguish between the two types of estate tax returns by referring to Form 1041 as an estate's **income** tax return during a period of time after death (similar to the income statement) and Form 706 as an estate's **asset value** return at one moment in time (similar to the balance sheet) to avoid confusion.

Requirement to File. An executor for a U.S. citizen or resident's estate must file Form 706 for estates whose gross estate plus adjusted taxable gifts is more than the unified credit against the estate tax. A taxpayer's gross estate encompasses all property, both domestic and foreign, the decedent held an interest in at the time of their death. However, the gross estate also includes certain asset transfers the decedent made during their lifetime, certain life insurance proceeds, even if paid directly to estate beneficiaries, and digital assets.

When assessing whether Form 706 is required, it is critical to review the **unified credit against estate tax** and taxable gifts. The unified credit against estate tax, often referred to as a taxpayer's **lifetime exemption,** represents the tax credit every decedent is entitled to use in offsetting both estate value and gift taxation.[119] The amount of the basic exclusion for decedents who die between 2017 and 2025 is $10 million.[120] The basic exclusion is $5 million for tax years after 2025.[121] The exclusion is adjusted each year for inflation, with the resulting exclusion for decedents who die in 2023 being $12.92 million.[122]

A taxpayer's lifetime exemption is reduced by the amount of taxable gifts the taxpayer makes during their lifetime. When a taxpayer makes **taxable gifts** (gifts whose value exceeds the annual gift tax exclusion[123]) in a tax year, they report the taxable gifts on Form 709, which includes a schedule with the history of all taxable gifts the taxpayer made during their lifetime up until that tax year. Therefore, executors and tax practitioners must know all the taxable gifts a decedent made during their lifetime to determine how much of the decedent's lifetime exemption is available and to assess a filing requirement for Form 706.

Executors must file Form 706 within nine months after the decedent's date of death. However, executors may file for an extension using Form 4768, *Application for Extension of Time To File a Return and/or Pay U.S. Estate (and Generation-Skipping Transfer) Taxes*, which grants an automatic 6-month extension.

---

117. Instructions for Form 706.

118. IRC §2001(a).

119. IRC §2010(a).

120. IRC §2010(c)(3).

121. Ibid.

122. Rev. Proc. 2022-38, 2022-45 IRB 445.

123. For 2023, the annual gift exclusion is $17,000. This amount is adjusted annually. See, *What's New — Estate and Gift Tax*. Jun. 13, 2023. IRS. [www.irs.gov/businesses/small-businesses-self-employed/whats-new-estate-and-gift-tax] Accessed on Jul. 13, 2023.

Example 19. Use the same facts as **Example 12.** Form 706 is due March 12, 2024, which is nine months after Miranda's date of death (June 12, 2023). However, Lydia is unable to gather all the necessary records by March and files an extension. Lydia now has until September 12, 2024, to file the Form 706.

Benefits to Filing if Form 706 is Not Required. An executor may wish to file Form 706 in situations where the form would not otherwise require filing. Executors and their practitioners should explore these reasons to determine whether there is a benefit to filing the tax form.

Portability. An executor can make an election where the amount of a **deceased spouse's unused exclusion (DSUE)** is available for use by the surviving spouse's estate.[124] The process of "porting" this unused exclusion is known as "portability." The DSUE amount is available to the surviving spouse as of the date of the deceased spouse's death. The surviving spouse may apply it to gifts and their estate before using their own exemption. Accordingly, the surviving spouse may use the DSUE amount to shelter lifetime gifts from gift tax or to reduce their estate tax liability at the time of their death.[125]

A surviving spouse makes the portability election on a timely filed Form 706 for their spouse who preceded them in death.[126] However, the IRS allows estates to request late portability election relief by filing Form 706 up to five years after the first spouse's date of death.[127] This relief is available for decedents who were U.S. citizens or residents at the time of their death, whose date of death was after December 31, 2010, were survived by a spouse, and whose estate did not otherwise require filing Form 706.[128]

Part 6 of Form 706 is entirely dedicated to the portability election, the DSUE calculation, and the roll forward of the DSUE amount. Per the description of the section, "a decedent with a surviving spouse elects portability of the DSUE amount, if any, by completing and timely filing this return. No further action is required to elect portability..."[129] Therefore, the filer makes the election by default if there is a DSUE amount and they file Form 706. This is the case as long as the filer **does not check** the box in Form 706 part 6 section A. By checking the box, the filer **elects out** of portability.

> **Caution.** If a surviving spouse who elected portability on their deceased spouse's Form 706 remarries and their subsequent spouse predeceases them, the surviving spouse loses the amount of DSUE from their prior marriage.[130] To receive any DSUE, the surviving spouse would need to file Form 706 for their remarried spouse, if the remarried spouse has any of their exemption left to port over.

9

Establishing Stepped-Up Basis in Assets. A decedent's eligible assets receive a basis adjustment to their fair market value at the decedent's date of death.[131] A beneficiary may benefit from a step-up in basis when selling inherited assets which significantly appreciated in value from the time the decedent acquired the asset until their date of death. While this step-up in basis applies to estate assets regardless of whether an estate files Form 706, there may be a benefit in filing to have an easy reference for the estate's asset values. Having this information may be highly beneficial for future transactions, such as selling the assets and needing to determine the gain on the sale. If a dispute arises regarding the basis of inherited property, a beneficiary may use Form 706 to substantiate their claim of the basis amount, as the form clearly indicates its value the IRS accepted with its filing.

---

124. IRC §2010(c)(4); Treas. Reg. §20.2010-2.

125. Treas. Reg. §20.2010-3(b)(ii).

126. IRC §2010(c)(5)(A); Treas. Reg. §20.2010-2(a)(1).

127. Rev. Proc. 2022-32, 2022-30 IRB 101.

128. Ibid.

129. See Form 706.

130. Treas. Reg. §20.2010-3(a).

131. IRC §1014(a)(1).

Alternate Valuation.[132] The executor can make an election to value the estate within six months after the decedent's death if the value of the property in the gross estate and the estate's federal estate tax liability are both reduced by making the election.[133] This is known as an **alternate valuation election.** The election results in the estate's property being valued at six months after death or earlier if the property is disposed of before the end of the 6-month period.

Caution. Because the alternative valuation election is only permissible if it reduces both the gross estate and the federal estate tax liability, the election is only available to estates that must file Form 706. An estate that is not required to file Form 706 has zero federal estate tax liability, meaning an alternative valuation could not lower the estate tax liability.[134]

Need for an Appraisal. While determining the value of some assets is straightforward, such as cash or investment accounts, other asset values are not as easily determinable. For those assets, executors may need to hire an appraiser to assign a value to them. Real estate is a common asset an executor would normally need an appraisal to report the value on Form 706. If the executor uses any appraisals in determining the value of reported assets, they must include copies of those appraisals with the filed form.[135]

State Filings

Some states impose a tax on estates of decedents who were residents of or held property in those states. States may impose two types of taxes, consisting of an estate tax and an inheritance tax.

State Estate Tax. Similar to the federal estate tax, some states impose an estate tax based on the value of an estate's assets. The taxes, forms, and filing thresholds differ among the states. Therefore, it is important for executors and their practitioners to familiarize themselves with the requirements of the states the decedent was a resident of or in which they held property. The following table sets forth the various state estate tax exemptions and tax rates as of May 3, 2023.[136]

State	Exemption Amount	Maximum Tax Rate
CT	$12,920,000	12%
DC	4,528,800	16%
HI	5,490,000	20%
IL	4,000,000	16%
ME	6,410,000	12%
MD	5,000,000	16%
MA	1,000,000	16%
MN	3,000,000	16%
NY	6,580,000	16%
OR	1,000,000	16%
RI	1,733,264	16%
VT	5,000,000	16%
WA	2,193,000	20%

132. IRC §2032.

133. CCA 201926013 (May 30, 2019).

134. For more information regarding the alternative valuation election, see *Alternate Valuation — Useful Estate Tax Valuation Provision.* McEowen, Roger. Mar. 17, 2020. Law Professors Blog, LLC. [lawprofessors.typepad.com/agriculturallaw/2020/03/alternate-valuation-useful-estate-tax-valuation-provision.html] Accessed on Aug. 21, 2023.

135. Instructions for Form 706.

136. *State Death Tax Chart.* May 3, 2023. American College of Trust and Estate Counsel. [www.actec.org/resources/state-death-tax-chart] Accessed on Jun. 25, 2023; *Where Not To Die in 2022.* Ebeling, Ashlea. May 13, 2022. Forbes. [www.forbes.com/sites/ashleaebeling/2022/05/13/where-not-to-die-in-2022-the-greediest-death-tax-states] Accessed on Jun. 25, 2023.

Caution. While the federal estate tax exemption results in estates being subject to taxation for values above the exemption, some states treat their exemption as a filing threshold. For example, the Illinois exemption is $4 million, where estates with assets below the threshold are not required to file or pay estate tax. However, if an Illinois estate had $5 million of assets, the estate would be subject to estate taxation on the full amount, not just the $1 million over the exemption ($5 million – $4 million). The tax computation is only done via the online calculator provided by the Attorney General website and uses a graduated range of tax brackets from 0% to 16%.[137]

Connecticut is the only state to impose its own gift tax on its residents.[138] The Connecticut annual gift exemption is equal to the federal gift exemption, where taxpayers who make gifts in excess of this amount must file a Connecticut gift tax return. Therefore, executors of estates where the decedent was a resident of or held property in Connecticut must obtain copies of filed state gift tax returns to determine the amount of state estate tax exemption the decedent used to offset gift tax.

Inheritance Tax. Some states impose an inheritance tax on the beneficiaries of an estate. This differs from an estate tax, where the estate files a return and pays a tax on its assets. Instead, beneficiaries subject to this form of tax must file and pay tax on the amount of **assets they inherited.** The following table sets forth the various state inheritance tax exemptions and tax rates as of May 3, 2023.[139]

State	Exemption Amount	Maximum Tax Rate
IA	$ 0	15%
KY	500	16%
MD	0	10%
NE	25,000	15%
NJ	0	16%
PA	0	15%

9

Iowa began reducing its inheritance tax by 20% each year since 2021, which will result in repealing the tax beginning January 1, 2025.[140] Maryland is the only state imposing **both** an estate tax and an inheritance tax.

APPLYING FOR APPLICABLE FEINS

After determining which forms an estate or trust must file, executors and trustees are next responsible for applying for and obtaining an FEIN for each applicable entity. An FEIN is necessary to issue Forms 1099 and file tax returns. There are two ways a domestic applicant may apply for an FEIN, either mailing or faxing Form SS-4, *Application for Employer Identification Number,* or applying online at IRS.gov. Applying online via the proper IRS website (not a fake or pay-to-use site) is the preferred method.

---

137. *2013-2022 Decedents Estate Tax Calculator.* Aug. 2, 2022. Illinois Attorney General. [ag.state.il.us/publications/calculator/2013calc/calculator2013.html] Accessed on Jul. 7, 2023.

138. *Estate and Gift Tax Information.* 2023. Connecticut State Department of Revenue Services. [portal.ct.gov/DRS/Individuals/Individual-Income-Tax-Portal/Estate-and-Gift-Taxes/Tax-Information#overview] Accessed on Jun. 25, 2023.

139. *State Death Tax Chart.* May 3, 2023. American College of Trust and Estate Counsel. [www.actec.org/resources/state-death-tax-chart] Accessed on Jun. 25, 2023, *Where Not To Die in 2022.* Ebeling, Ashlea. May 13, 2022. Forbes. [www.forbes.com/sites/ashleaebeling/2022/05/13/where-not-to-die-in-2022-the-greediest-death-tax-states] Accessed on Jun. 25, 2023; Legislature of Nebraska 2022 LB310 §4(b).

140. *State Death Tax Chart.* May 3, 2023. American College of Trust and Estate Counsel. [www.actec.org/resources/state-death-tax-chart] Accessed on Jun. 25, 2023.

Applying for an FEIN Online

An applicant can obtain an FEIN immediately upon completing the online application and save a pdf copy of the confirmation page with the FEIN to distribute to their attorney and practitioner as needed. The online application mirrors the questions on Form SS-4.

> **Note.** The online FEIN application is only available Monday through Friday from 7AM to 10PM Eastern Standard Time.

Form SS-4[141]

Form SS-4 requests the entity's legal name that must match the one the IRS has on record. The form also requests the name and address of the responsible party (executor or trustee), the type of entity for which the responsible party applies, and the reason for the application.

Form SS-4 also asks for the date the entity started. For estates, this date is the decedent's date of death. For trusts, the date is when the trust began its taxable activity as its own entity. For disregarded grantor trusts, this date is the grantor's date of death, as any income-generating activity during the grantor's lifetime would be included in the grantor's tax return under their SSN. Non-grantor trusts should use the date the trust began earning income. The IRS will use this date with the closing month of the accounting year the applicant selects to initially determine what periods the entity should file.

If an applicant uses an incorrect starting date and the IRS notifies the applicant of the need to file tax returns for prior periods that are not applicable due to the entity not having taxable income, the applicant may notify the IRS of this situation and would not be bound to file the returns.

The responsible party may identify a third-party designee they would like the IRS to provide the FEIN to and direct any questions regarding the application. The applicant could list their tax preparer or other party who assisted them with preparing and mailing a Form SS-4. The IRS estimates it usually takes four weeks to mail the FEIN to the applicant or third-party designee. This timeframe differs significantly compared to the online option providing the FEIN immediately.

141. Instructions for Form SS-4.

Example 20. Use the same facts as **Example 12.** Lydia needed an FEIN for her mother's estate. Lydia completed the following Form SS-4 for the estate and used this information to file for the FEIN online.

Form **SS-4** (Rev. December 2019) Department of the Treasury Internal Revenue Service

Application for Employer Identification Number
(For use by employers, corporations, partnerships, trusts, estates, churches, government agencies, Indian tribal entities, certain individuals, and others.)
► Go to *www.irs.gov/FormSS4* for instructions and the latest information.
► See separate instructions for each line. ► Keep a copy for your records.

OMB No. 1545-0003

EIN

Type or print clearly.

1 Legal name of entity (or individual) for whom the EIN is being requested
Miranda Dunmeyer Estate

2 Trade name of business (if different from name on line 1)

3 Executor, administrator, trustee, "care of" name
Lydia Hillard

4a Mailing address (room, apt., suite no. and street, or P.O. box)
2640 Steiner St

5a Street address (if different) (Don't enter a P.O. box.)

4b City, state, and ZIP code (if foreign, see instructions)
San Francisco, CA 94115

5b City, state, and ZIP code (if foreign, see instructions)

6 County and state where principal business is located
San Francisco CA

7a Name of responsible party
Lydia Hillard

7b SSN, ITIN, or EIN
*****-**-3333**

8a Is this application for a limited liability company (LLC) (or a foreign equivalent)? . . . . ☐ Yes ☒ No

8b If 8a is "Yes," enter the number of LLC members . . . . . . ►

8c If 8a is "Yes," was the LLC organized in the United States? . . . . ☐ Yes ☐ No

9a **Type of entity** (check only one box). **Caution:** If 8a is "Yes," see the instructions for the correct box to check.

☐ Sole proprietor (SSN)
☐ Partnership
☐ Corporation (enter form number to be filed) ►
☐ Personal service corporation
☐ Church or church-controlled organization
☐ Other nonprofit organization (specify) ►
☐ Other (specify) ►
☒ Estate (SSN of decedent) *****-**-6789**
☐ Plan administrator (TIN)
☐ Trust (TIN of grantor)
☐ Military/National Guard ☐ State/local government
☐ Farmers' cooperative ☐ Federal government
☐ REMIC ☐ Indian tribal governments/enterprises
Group Exemption Number (GEN) if any ►

9b If a corporation, name the state or foreign country (if applicable) where incorporated | State | Foreign country

10 **Reason for applying** (check only one box)
☐ Started new business (specify type) ►
☐ Hired employees (Check the box and see line 13.)
☐ Compliance with IRS withholding regulations
☒ Other (specify) ► **Estate created due to taxpayer's death**
☐ Banking purpose (specify purpose) ►
☐ Changed type of organization (specify new type) ►
☐ Purchased going business
☐ Created a trust (specify type) ►
☐ Created a pension plan (specify type) ►

11 Date business started or acquired (month, day, year). See instructions.
06/12/2023

12 Closing month of accounting year **May**

13 Highest number of employees expected in the next 12 months (enter -0- if none). If no employees expected, skip line 14.

Agricultural	Household	Other

14 If you expect your employment tax liability to be $1,000 or less in a full calendar year **and** want to file Form 944 annually instead of Forms 941 quarterly, check here. (Your employment tax liability generally will be $1,000 or less if you expect to pay $5,000 or less in total wages.) If you don't check this box, you must file Form 941 for every quarter. ☐

15 First date wages or annuities were paid (month, day, year). **Note:** If applicant is a withholding agent, enter date income will first be paid to nonresident alien (month, day, year) . . . . ►

16 Check **one** box that best describes the principal activity of your business.
☐ Health care & social assistance ☐ Wholesale-agent/broker
☐ Construction ☐ Rental & leasing ☐ Transportation & warehousing ☐ Accommodation & food service ☐ Wholesale-other ☐ Retail
☐ Real estate ☐ Manufacturing ☐ Finance & insurance ☐ Other (specify) ►

17 Indicate principal line of merchandise sold, specific construction work done, products produced, or services provided.

18 Has the applicant entity shown on line 1 ever applied for and received an EIN? ☐ Yes ☒ No
If "Yes," write previous EIN here ►

Third Party Designee
Complete this section **only** if you want to authorize the named individual to receive the entity's EIN and answer questions about the completion of this form.
Designee's name | Designee's telephone number (include area code)
Address and ZIP code | Designee's fax number (include area code)

Under penalties of perjury, I declare that I have examined this application, and to the best of my knowledge and belief, it is true, correct, and complete.
Applicant's telephone number (include area code)
Name and title (type or print clearly) ►
Applicant's fax number (include area code)
Signature ► Date ►

For Privacy Act and Paperwork Reduction Act Notice, see separate instructions. Cat. No. 16055N Form **SS-4** (Rev. 12-2019)

FEINs For §645 Election[142]

When an executor elects the §645 election to treat a QRT as part of an estate, they normally must obtain an FEIN for both the electing QRT and the related estate. However, if an estate does not have an executor and one is not expected to be appointed, then the trustee only needs to obtain an FEIN for the QRT.

NOTIFICATION OF KEY PARTIES

Individuals who find themselves in the role of an executor of an estate must notify several parties of the decedent's death to facilitate the settlement of the estate. Some of this communication will come into play when preparing and filing necessary income and estate tax forms and assisting with the transfer or title of assets to beneficiaries.

Financial Advisors and Brokers

Executors should notify all financial advisors and brokers who worked with the decedent in handling their investments and accounts as soon as possible. The urgency of this communication is caused by the need for the advisors to assign the account in the name of the estate or joint owner with the right of survivorship. Additionally, the broker needs to know the date of death to begin separating investment activity between pre- and post-death. This communication should result in the brokerage firm issuing Forms 1099 to the correct party covering the correct reporting period. For example, brokers should issue Forms 1099 under the decedent's SSN for pre-death activity while issuing Forms 1099 under the estate's FEIN or joint owner's SSN for post-death activity.

Brokers also need to know the decedent's date of death so they may begin tracking basis accordingly. Because assets receive a step-up in basis at the time of the decedent's death, the broker **should** calculate the basis of each investment to report the correct basis on Forms 1099 for any investment sold within the reporting period.

Social Security Administration

If the decedent was receiving social security benefits at the time of their death, the Social Security Administration (SSA) will generally be automatically notified of the benefit holder's death. Individuals are no longer entitled to social security benefits once they die. However, surviving spouses or other family members may be eligible for the decedent's benefits based on the decedent's earnings and how long the decedent paid into social security.[143] Funeral directors may contact the SSA notifying them of the benefit holder's death, but executors should ensure this communication occurs. If a decedent receives social security benefits after their death they were not entitled to, the executor must pay back the excess benefits to the SSA.

Banks and Financial Institutions

Banks and financial institutions must know when an account holder dies to retitle any accounts to the estate or joint party. It may be best for the executor to wait until pending payments for the decedent go through processing before notifying the bank to prevent the transactions payable to the decedent from being rejected due to the name change on the account to the estate or other party.

Life Insurance Agents and Brokers

If a decedent held any life insurance policies, the agents and brokers of those policies should receive notification of the decedent's death to begin processing and fulfilling payments to the named beneficiaries. The life insurance agents will issue a Form 712, *Life Insurance Statement,* to the decedent, which provides information about a policy and its value. The executor will need this form to determine the values of the decedent's policies when compiling assets to determine if probate applies and if an estate tax form is necessary. If an estate with life insurance policies files Form 706, they must provide a copy of Form 712 for each policy with the filed return.[144]

---

142. Treas. Reg. §1.645-1(d).

143. *Survivors Benefits*. Nov. 25, 2019. Social Security Administration. [www.ssa.gov/benefits/survivors] Accessed on Jun. 25, 2023.

144. Instructions for Form 706.

DISTRIBUTION OF ASSETS TO BENEFICIARIES

Part of the fiduciary duties an executor is responsible for includes distributing estate assets to beneficiaries. Generally, it is beneficial for an executor to make these distributions as a final step in the settlement process after all expenses, creditor claims, and taxes have been paid. An executor may be held liable for an estate's unpaid debts, and in some cases, beneficiaries may be held liable as well.[145]

SCHEDULE H[146]

> **Note.** The majority of the information in this section is derived from IRS Pub. 926, *Household Employer's Tax Guide.*

People who hire individuals to provide services in their homes may be required to file Schedule H, *Household Employment Taxes,* with their Form 1040. Babysitters, butlers, caretakers, cleaning people, cooks, drivers, health aides, housekeepers, maids, nannies, private nurses, yard workers, and similar laborers are all potential household employees.

Taxpayers often ask their tax advisors what they should do when they are paying someone "on the side" to work in their homes. For 2020, nearly 180,000 Schedules H were filed reporting $1.2 million in employment taxes.[147] If everyone understood their obligations, the number of filings would be significantly higher. Fortunately, many common situations are **not subject to the household employer requirements.** Individuals do not have to report payments to the following.

- Their underage children (discussed later)
- Other people's underage children, except in rare circumstances
- Their parents, except in rare circumstances
- Businesses that are providing services in their home, including businesses operated as sole proprietorships (employees of such businesses are not employees of the payor.)

EMPLOYEE OR INDEPENDENT CONTRACTOR

When someone is providing a service regularly in the home **and** is being paid directly by the person receiving the service (or their agent,) the payments made to them might be considered wages. The payor must determine if they are paying a sole proprietor or an employee for the services.

If the recipient is an independent contractor, payments are not wages. The payor is not required to report the payments or assume any other employer obligations. Because the services are not being provided to a business, the payor is not required to file a Form 1099-NEC, *Nonemployee Compensation*, either.[148]

Example 21. Rosemary loves helping people with little tasks around their homes. She puts out the word at her favorite beauty shop and now spends a few hours every week with some of her favorite people for a little cash on the side. She charges each person $100 per week per visit.

Violet has agoraphobia. She does not mind paying Rosemary for her regular help. Because Rosemary offers her services to the public, Violet is not an employer.

---

145. *Estate of Kwang Lee v. Comm'r*, No. 21-2921 (3d Circ. 2022), aff'g TC No. 20531-18L.

146. IRS Pub. 926, *Household Employer's Tax Guide*; Schedule H Instructions; See also *Topic No. 756, Employment Taxes for Household Employees*. Apr. 7, 2023. IRS. [www.irs.gov/taxtopics/tc756] Accessed on Jun. 30, 2023.

147. IRS Pub. 4801, *Individual Income Tax Returns Line Item Estimates.*

148. *General Instructions for Certain Information Returns.* Mar. 27, 2023. IRS. [www.irs.gov/pub/irs-pdf/i1099gi.pdf] Accessed on Jul. 5, 2023.

Sometimes it is not obvious to the people involved if they are entering into a "business relationship" or an "employer-employee relationship." Questions they should ask include the following.

- Does the service provider have a bona fide trade or business? (A self-employed worker usually provides their own tools and offers services to the general public in an independent business.) If so, they are an independent contractor.
- Does the recipient of the services have the right to control the way the services are provided, such as the timing and other details? If so, the provider is an employee.

It is not necessary for the employer to actually exercise control as long as the employer has the **right to control.** It also does not matter whether the work is full-time or part-time or how the pay is structured.[149] The employee determination is made by looking at all the facts and circumstances of the situation.[150]

Example 22. Kendra's mother, Nan, is ailing. Rather than have Nan move into a private care facility, Kendra quits her job and starts caring for her mother in Nan's home. Kendra is an adult, and, therefore, not exempt from being treated as an employee, even though she is Nan's child. Nan plans to pay Kendra $500 a week for helping her.

Nan wants to know if she will have to report these payments as wages. It is clear that Kendra is not a sole proprietor, but Nan has the right to control how the services are provided. Nonetheless, because the payments are intended to compensate Kendra for services provided in the home, they are wages subject to reporting and tax requirements.

Note. For more information on factors indicating an employee or independent contractor relationship, see the 2023 *University of Illinois Federal Tax Workbook,* Chapter 3: Independent Contractors.

OTHER PAYMENT TRANSACTIONS

Some individuals might want to treat the payments as some other type of transaction to avoid these and other employment-related obligations. However, they must be careful that their circumstances match their claims about the nature of the payments. The different options have various factors that should be considered. A few are discussed next.

- **Gifts** — Under basic contract law, a gift is a voluntary and gratuitous transfer of property without obligation or expectation of favor. However, if the intent of a payment is to reward the recipient for performing as expected, the payment is compensation rather than a gift.
- **Virtual currencies** — Payments in virtual money, such as Bitcoin, are included as cash wages.[151]
- **Bequest for services** — Payment made from an estate as compensation for services provided while the decedent was alive is taxable income to the recipient.[152]
- **Benefits of being treated as an employee for the worker** — A person treated as an independent contractor instead of as an employee takes responsibility for all the related tax obligations. Failure to report earnings subject to the Federal Insurance Contributions Act (FICA) and the Self-Employed Contributions Act (SECA) might reduce the amount of retirement or disability benefits the laborer qualifies to receive in the future.

Note. SSA Pub. 05-10021, *Household Workers*, has information on how household work is credited to an employee's social security record. This can be found at **uofi.tax/23x9x1** [www.ssa.gov/pubs/EN-05-10021.pdf].

149. *Hiring Household Employees*. Feb. 7, 2023. IRS. [www.irs.gov/businesses/small-businesses-self-employed/hiring-household-employees] Accessed on Apr. 21, 2023.

150. Treas. Reg. §§31.3401(c)-1(b), (d), and (h).

151. IRS Pub. 525, *Taxable and Nontaxable Income;* See also IRS Notice 2014-21, 2014-16 IRB 938.

152. IRS Pub. 525, *Taxable and Nontaxable Income,* p. 35 (2022).

- **Exchange for rent** — FICA taxes are **only** due on **cash** wages paid to service providers. Cash wages typically do not include the value of food and lodging. However, if the agreement between the employer and the employee is such that there is a direct offset in pay relative to the fair market value of the food or lodgings, the arrangement might be a disguised cash transaction.
- **Clothing, transit passes, and other noncash items given to household employees** — These items are generally excluded from cash wages for employment tax purposes. However, the value of these types of items is not excludable if they are just money in disguise.

Example 23. Peg overhears another practitioner at a Tax Pro convention say, "And then my aunt said to me, I just buy all of her groceries and clothes, so we don't have to include her as an employee." Peg politely taps the other practitioner on the shoulder and explains that the groceries and clothes are just like money, and therefore, the aunt must report the income paid.

Caution. Although noncash wages are not subject to FICA taxes, they are typically included in wages subject to income tax withholding unless a specific exclusion applies. See IRS Pub. 15, *(Circular E), Employer's Tax Guide,* and IRS Pub. 15-B, *Employer's Tax Guide to Fringe Benefits,* for more information on cash and noncash wages and fringe benefits.

Caution. Although IRS Pub. 15 states that "Payments for the services of a child of any age who works for their parent are not subject to income tax withholding if paid for domestic work in the parent's home," this exception is actually very narrow. As explained in the publication and later in this section, under the Code, this **only** applies in very rare circumstances.[153]

EMPLOYER TAX RESPONSIBILITIES

Once a person determines that they are an employer, they must file for an FEIN. This is done by filing Form SS-4 on paper or by completing an interview-style online FEIN application, as discussed previously.[154] An individual's SSN can only be associated with one FEIN. Thus, a household employer should not file for a new FEIN if they previously were a household employer, operated a sole proprietorship, or applied for an FEIN for banking purposes.

If the payor and the person receiving the service are not the same person, it might be necessary to evaluate who in fact should file as the employer. This complication is covered later in this chapter under the heading "Rare Circumstances."

9

153. IRC §3121(b)(3)(B).

154. *Employer ID Numbers*. Jun. 12, 2023. IRS. [www.irs.gov/businesses/small-businesses-self-employed/employer-id-numbers] Accessed Jun. 26, 2023.

Each time a person hires someone to work as a household employee, they are required to obtain certain paperwork.[155]

1. Every household employee and their employer must complete the U.S. Citizenship and Immigration Services (USCIS) **Form I-9, *Employment Eligibility Verification.*** As part of this process, the employee must provide the employer with certain documents and proof of eligibility to work in the United States.

> **Note.** Form I-9 and the USCIS Handbook for Employers is available at **USCIS.gov/I-9-Central**. If the employer agrees to withhold federal income taxes, the employee must submit Form W-4 to their employer to request that federal income taxes be withheld. The Form W-4 is covered in more detail earlier in this chapter.

> **Note.** An in-home care service recipient may request that the IRS authorize their agent[156] to report, file, and pay **most** federal employment taxes on their behalf. See Form 2678, *Employer/Payer Appointment of Agent,* for more information. In addition, an individual who receives such home care services through a program administered by a federal, state, or local government agency may assign their federal unemployment taxes (FUTA) responsibilities to an agent.[157] Other individuals cannot assign their FUTA responsibilities.

2. It is advisable to have the employee sign appropriate paperwork documenting the terms of their employment.

Once the employee is hired, the payor **may be:**

- Allowed to withhold **federal income taxes** on behalf of the employee;
- Required to pay **FUTA** on the wages;
- Required to collect **social security and Medicare taxes** (FICA) on behalf of the employee and pay the employer's share of the taxes;
- Required to issue a **Form W-2** to the employee;
- Required to file **Schedule H and submit payments** to the IRS; and
- Required to withhold state and local taxes, pay state unemployment taxes, pay workers' compensation insurance, and/or be subject to **other rules** and regulations specific to their situation. (Links to common resources for these items are provided later in this material.)

> **Note.** Homeowners may also want to re-evaluate their homeowner liability insurance coverage in the event of an injury to a household employee on the premises.

Voluntary Withholding

Once the parties agree that they have an employment relationship, the payor is **allowed** to **withhold federal income taxes** at the employee's request upon receipt of Form W-4. However, the payor is **not required** to take on the liability of withholding income taxes. Once the payor withholds federal income taxes, they are obligated to file a Form W-2 and Schedule H.

---

155. *Hiring Employees.* May 17, 2023. IRS. [www.irs.gov/businesses/small-businesses-self-employed/hiring-employees] Accessed on Jun. 30, 2023.

156. Under IRC §3504.

157. See Rev. Proc. 2013-39, 2013-52 IRB 830, for more details.

FUTA

In 2023, the wage threshold is **$1,000** total in any calendar quarter paid to all employees of the household. Once this level is met, the payor is obligated to pay **federal unemployment tax** on covered employees.

Example 24. Skip enjoys helping people by paying them to help him around his house. In the 1st quarter of 2023, he pays the following amounts to individuals for their services as employees.

Howie	$ 300
Pat	400
Sidney	500
Total	$1,200

Skip is now obligated to pay FUTA on these payments. He must file a Schedule H to report the tax. The FUTA tax obligation does not require Skip to file Forms W-2 (explained in more detail later).

Note. The FUTA rate is based on the state in which the employee works and the unemployment tax liabilities of the employer in that state. Schedule H instructions provide guidance for determining the proper rate for the employer each year by state.

FICA

It is possible to be subject to FUTA tax and not be subject to the **FICA requirements.** FICA is activated when cash wages of **$2,600** or more are paid to **any one person** during the year.[158] This is a per person test, unlike the FUTA test, which is per quarter.

Example 25. Use the same facts as **Example 24.** Skip continues to pay his helpers throughout the year. For 2023, total payments to each person are as follows.

Howie	$1,200
Pat	1,600
Sidney	2,000
Total	$4,800

No one person was paid $2,600 or more, so Skip's only federal requirement is to pay FUTA tax by filing Schedule H for 2023.

Note. For more information on the definition of cash wages, see the instructions for Schedule H.

The $2,600 threshold sets in motion responsibility for FICA taxes and for filing Form W-2 and Schedule H (assuming the payor had not already volunteered for income tax withholding). With regard to the FICA taxes, payors have the option to:

- Withhold the employee's portion of FICA taxes (6.2% of social security and 1.45% of Medicare taxes for a total of 7.65%[159]); **or**
- Pay the employee portion on the employee's behalf, which becomes income subject to income tax withholding on the employee's Form W-2.

158. *Household Workers.* Jan. 2023. Social Security Administration. [www.ssa.gov/pubs/EN-05-10021.pdf] Accessed on Jul. 2, 2023.

159. *Topic No. 756, Employment Taxes for Household Employees.* Apr. 7, 2023. IRS. [www.irs.gov/taxtopics/tc756] Accessed on Jul. 18, 2023.

If the employer pays the employee portion from the employer's own funds, the FICA taxes paid to cover the employee's share must be included in the employee's wages for income tax purposes. However, they are not counted as FICA wages or as FUTA wages. The social security and Medicare taxes paid by the employer are reported in boxes 4 and 6 of the employee's Form W-2. The taxes are also added to the employee's wages reported in box 1 of Form W-2.[160]

Example 26. Bob pays Karry for help around the house. After the end of the year, he tells his accountant, Zach, that he paid Karry $3,000 "pretty evenly" over the course of the year. He mentions that Karry does not work for anyone else and that Karry asked him not to withhold any taxes. Bob agreed to pay any extra taxes due, and he asks Zach to make sure that all of the right taxes are paid and forms filed.

Zach determines that the employee portion of FICA taxes on $3,000 in wages is $229.50 (7.65% × $3,000). As the employer, Bob must match these taxes. In box 1 of Karry's Form W-2 (shown next), $3,229.50 reflects the total net pay ($3,000 wages + $229.50 FICA paid on her behalf). Boxes 3 and 5 reflect the net wages of $3,000. Boxes 4 and 6 reflect the allocation of the $229.50 withheld from her wages between her social security taxes (6.2%) and Medicare taxes (1.45%).

a Employee's social security number ***-**-0926	OMB No. 1545-0008	Safe, accurate, FAST! Use IRS e-file. Visit the IRS website at www.irs.gov/efile
b Employer identification number (EIN) 86-3229500	1 Wages, tips, other compensation 3229.50	2 Federal income tax withheld
c Employer's name, address, and ZIP code Bob Rainley 1500 Main St., Apt. 1 Your Town, WA 98052	3 Social security wages 3000.00	4 Social security tax withheld 186.00
	5 Medicare wages and tips 3000.00	6 Medicare tax withheld 43.50
	7 Social security tips	8 Allocated tips
d Control number	9	10 Dependent care benefits
e Employee's first name and initial / Last name / Suff. Karry Z. Betreuerin 1500 Main St., Apt. 1 Your Town, WA 98052	11 Nonqualified plans	12a See instructions for box 12 (Code)
	13 Statutory employee ☐ Retirement plan ☐ Third-party sick pay ☐	12b (Code)
	14 Other	12c (Code)
f Employee's address and ZIP code		12d (Code)

15 State / Employer's state ID number	16 State wages, tips, etc.	17 State income tax	18 Local wages, tips, etc.	19 Local income tax	20 Locality name

Form **W-2** **Wage and Tax Statement** 2023 Department of the Treasury—Internal Revenue Service

Copy B—To Be Filed With Employee's FEDERAL Tax Return.
This information is being furnished to the Internal Revenue Service.

---

160. IRS Pub. 926, *Household Employer's Tax Guide.*

Filing Forms W-2[161]

For tax year 2023 forms filed in 2024, any filers of 10 or more withholding tax returns[162] (e.g., Form W-2) in a calendar year are generally required to file the forms electronically. Employers with fewer than 10 Forms W-2 to file may still file printed copies by mail.[163]

Although the procedures for completing Form W-2 and its companion Form W-3, *Transmittal of Income and Tax Statements,* is beyond the scope of this material, filers may be interested to know that when tax software asks which type of payer a household employer is, the proper response is "941" if household employer is not an option.

The SSA offers employers the option of electronically filing Forms W-2 and W-3 via its Business Services Online (BSO) portal. The full-service online filing option is generally only available to taxpayers with Login.gov or ID.me credentials. Others may take advantage of limited online services.[164]

> **Note.** The BSO portal at **www.ssa.gov/bso** provides various types of information for employers, including forms and instructions. A brief online tutorial regarding BSO services may be found at **uofi.tax/23x9x2** [www.SSA.gov/employer/bsotut.htm].

Some standard rules apply to all Form W-2 filers, including household employers, such as the following.

- Employers must notify certain employees about the earned income credit (EIC). The notice must be given to all employees who have no income tax withheld even though they requested withholding. This notice must be similar to the one on the official IRS version of Form W-2, on the reverse side of Copy B.[165] Household employers who are not required to issue their employee a Form W-2 must nonetheless provide this EIC notice.[166]
- The due date for filing and mailing 2023 Forms W-2 is January 31, 2024.
- The IRS will only grant extensions of time to file Form W-2 with the SSA in extraordinary circumstances.
- Extensions of time to furnish Forms W-2 to employees are also not automatic and only granted in extenuating circumstances.

9

Filing Schedule H and Submitting Payments to the IRS

To encourage payors to participate in the system, household employers are allowed to forgo quarterly filing of employer wage activity on the usual business forms.[167] Instead, they are allowed to file Schedule H with their annual income tax return.[168] On this form, they report total wages, withholding, and employment taxes due as a result of paying any household employees.

---

161. *IRS General Instructions for Forms W-2 and W-3*. Dec. 29, 2022. IRS. [www.irs.gov/pub/irs-pdf/iw2w3.pdf] Accessed on Jul. 18, 2023.

162. TD 9972, 2023-31 IRB 530. Note that the 10-return threshold applies to the aggregate number of information return types covered by the regulation. Earlier regulations applied the 250-return threshold separately to each type of applicable information return.

163. The IRS provides printable copies at www.irs.gov, but the copies to submit to the SSA must be printed on machine readable paper approved by the SSA. Approved forms may be purchased from office supply stores.

164. *Business Services Online (BSO)*. 2023. Social Security Administration. [www.ssa.gov/bso/bsowelcome.htm] Accessed on Jul. 2, 2023.

165. Providing the employee with Notice 797, *Possible Federal Tax Refund Due to the Earned Income Credit (EIC),* is also an allowable way to inform them about EIC.

166. Instructions for Schedule H.

167. Such as Form 941, *Employer's QUARTERLY Federal Tax Return*; Form 940, *Employer's Annual Federal Unemployment (FUTA) Tax Return*; Form 943, *Employer's Annual Federal Tax Return for Agricultural Employees*; or Form 944, *Employer's ANNUAL Federal Tax Return.* Household employers who also have employees of their sole proprietorships may elect to include the household wages with the business wages on the employer filings instead of filing Schedule H.

168. Form 1040, *U.S. Individual Income Tax Return* or Form 1041, *U.S. Income Tax Return for Estates and Trusts*, as applicable.

Example 27. Use the same facts as **Example 26.** Bob files the following Schedule H with his 2023 Form 1040. The total taxes due from employing Karry are $459, as shown on line 8d. Because the $3,000 was spread evenly throughout the year, Bob did not pay more than $1,000 in any quarter to his household employee in 2023. Therefore, he does not owe any FUTA taxes. If he were subject to FUTA, the taxes would have been calculated on page 2 (not shown). The total of the taxes due calculated on this form are transferred to Schedule 2 (Form 1040), *Additional Taxes,* line 9, (not shown).

SCHEDULE H (Form 1040)

Department of the Treasury Internal Revenue Service

Household Employment Taxes

(For Social Security, Medicare, Withheld Income, and Federal Unemployment (FUTA) Taxes)

Attach to Form 1040, 1040-SR, 1040-NR, 1040-SS, or 1041.

Go to *www.irs.gov/ScheduleH* for instructions and the latest information.

OMB No. 1545-0074

2023

Attachment Sequence No. **44**

Name of employer: **Bob Rainley**

Social security number: ***-**-0607

Employer identification number: 8 6 3 2 2 9 5 0 0

Calendar year taxpayers having no household employees in 2023 don't have to complete this form for 2023.

A Did you pay **any one** household employee cash wages of $2,600 or more in 2023? (If any household employee was your spouse, your child under age 21, your parent, or anyone under age 18, see the line A instructions before you answer this question.)

☒ **Yes.** Skip lines B and C and go to line 1a.

☐ **No.** Go to line B.

B Did you withhold federal income tax during 2023 for any household employee?

☐ **Yes.** Skip line C and go to line 7.

☐ **No.** Go to line C.

C Did you pay **total** cash wages of $1,000 or more in **any** calendar **quarter** of 2022 or 2023 to **all** household employees? (**Don't** count cash wages paid in 2022 or 2023 to your spouse, your child under age 21, or your parent.)

☐ **No. Stop.** Don't file this schedule.

☐ **Yes.** Skip lines 1a–9 and go to line 10.

Part I Social Security, Medicare, and Federal Income Taxes

1a	Total cash wages subject to social security tax	1a	3,000		
b	Qualified sick and family leave wages paid in 2023 for leave taken after March 31, 2020, and before April 1, 2021, included on line 1a	1b			
2a	Social security tax. Multiply line 1a by 12.4% (0.124)			2a	372
b	Employer share of social security tax on qualified sick and family leave wages paid in 2023 for leave taken after March 31, 2020, and before April 1, 2021. Multiply line 1b by 6.2% (0.062)			2b	
c	Total social security tax. Subtract line 2b from line 2a			2c	372
3	Total cash wages subject to Medicare tax	3	3,000		
4	Medicare tax. Multiply line 3 by 2.9% (0.029)			4	87
5	Total cash wages subject to Additional Medicare Tax withholding	5			
6	Additional Medicare Tax withholding. Multiply line 5 by 0.9% (0.009)			6	
7	Federal income tax withheld, if any			7	
8a	Total social security, Medicare, and federal income taxes. Add lines 2c, 4, 6, and 7			8a	459
b	Nonrefundable portion of credit for qualified sick and family leave wages for leave taken before April 1, 2021			8b	
c	Nonrefundable portion of credit for qualified sick and family leave wages for leave taken after March 31, 2021, and before October 1, 2021			8c	
d	Total social security, Medicare, and federal income taxes after nonrefundable credits. Add lines 8b and 8c and then subtract that total from line 8a			8d	459
e	Refundable portion of credit for qualified sick and family leave wages for leave taken before April 1, 2021			8e	
f	Refundable portion of credit for qualified sick and family leave wages for leave taken after March 31, 2021, and before October 1, 2021			8f	
g	Qualified sick leave wages for leave taken before April 1, 2021			8g	
h	Qualified health plan expenses allocable to qualified sick leave wages reported on line 8g			8h	
i	Qualified family leave wages for leave taken before April 1, 2021			8i	
j	Qualified health plan expenses allocable to qualified family leave wages reported on line 8i			8j	
k	Qualified sick leave wages for leave taken after March 31, 2021, and before October 1, 2021			8k	
l	Qualified health plan expenses allocable to qualified sick leave wages reported on line 8k			8l	
m	Qualified family leave wages for leave taken after March 31, 2021, and before October 1, 2021			8m	
n	Qualified health plan expenses allocable to qualified family leave wages reported on line 8m			8n	

9 Did you pay **total** cash wages of $1,000 or more in **any** calendar **quarter** of 2022 or 2023 to **all** household employees? (**Don't** count cash wages paid in 2022 or 2023 to your spouse, your child under age 21, or your parent.)

☐ **No. Stop.** Include the amount from line 8d above on Schedule 2 (Form 1040), line 9. Include the amounts, if any, from lines 8e and 8f on Schedule 3 (Form 1040), line 13z. If you're not required to file Form 1040, see the line 9 instructions.

☐ **Yes.** Go to line 10.

For Privacy Act and Paperwork Reduction Act Notice, see the instructions. Cat. No. 12187K **Schedule H (Form 1040) 2023**

The total amount due shown on Schedule H is included as part of the taxpayer's total tax liability for the year. An individual who does not have an income tax filing obligation must file the Schedule H by itself. An extension for filing the income tax return also applies to Schedule H.

Generally, the employer must include the household taxes as part of **their total tax liability for estimated tax purposes.** To avoid estimated tax penalties, they may need to increase their federal income tax withholding from their wages, pension, annuity, etc., or increase their estimated tax payments.[169]

> **Note.** Estimated tax payments are covered in detail earlier in this chapter.

Example 28. Prior to 2022, Willie's normal income tax liability was around $2,000 each year. She covered this liability by withholding $200 a month from her social security benefits ($2,400 per year). In 2022, she also owed $3,000 in taxes because she paid her niece to work around the house. Thus, her total 2022 tax liability was $5,000 and she had to pay the balance of $2,600 ($5,000 total tax liability – $2,400 withholding from social security benefits) in April 2023.

Willie anticipates that her household employer taxes will increase to $4,000 in 2023. Her income tax will be the usual $2,000, which brings her total tax liability to $6,000 for the year.

The minimum amount she must pay in estimated taxes for 2023 is $5,000.[170] If she changes nothing, she will owe $3,600 in April 2024 ($6,000 total tax liability – $2,400 tax withheld from social security benefits) and she will be subject to estimated tax penalties. She may make up the shortfall by increasing her withholding, making estimated tax payments, or a combination of both.

> **Note.** If the amount of wages paid varies each month, it may be wise for household employers to make monthly estimated tax payments based on the prior month's pay **instead** of including the employer tax liability in the estimated payments that the taxpayer bases on income tax liability.

Household employers will not be penalized for failure to make estimated tax payments if **both** of the following apply for the year.

1. They will not have federal income tax withheld from wages, pensions, or any other payments they receive.
2. Their income taxes, excluding the household employment taxes, are not high enough to require payment of estimated taxes.

169. For more information, see IRS Pub. 505, *Tax Withholding and Estimated Tax.*

170. Per IRS Pub. 505, the minimum due is the lesser of 100% of prior year taxes ($5,000) or 90% of current year projected taxes ($6,000 x 90% = $5,400).

9

RARE CIRCUMSTANCES

There are a few exceptions and special rules that are important. For example, as shown in Table 1 from IRS Pub. 926 (2023), there are exceptions to the exclusions for FICA taxes.

Table 1. **Do You Need To Pay Employment Taxes?**

IF you ...		THEN you need to ...
A	Pay cash wages of $2,600 or more in 2023 to any one household employee. Don't count wages you pay to: • Your spouse, • Your child under the age of 21, • Your parent (see *Wages not counted*, later, for an exception), or • Any employee under the age of 18 at any time in 2023 (see *Wages not counted*, later, for an exception).	Withhold and pay social security and Medicare taxes. • The taxes are 15.3%[1] of cash wages. • Your employee's share is 7.65%.[1] (You can choose to pay it yourself and not withhold it.) • Your share is 7.65%.
B	Pay total cash wages of $1,000 or more in any calendar quarter of 2022 or 2023 to household employees. Don't count wages you pay to: • Your spouse, • Your child under the age of 21, or • Your parent.	Pay FUTA tax. • The tax is 6% of cash wages. • Wages over $7,000 a year per employee aren't taxed. • You may also owe state unemployment tax.
[1] In addition to withholding Medicare tax at 1.45%, you must withhold a 0.9% Additional Medicare Tax from wages you pay to an employee in excess of $200,000 in a calendar year. You're required to begin withholding Additional Medicare Tax in the pay period in which you pay wages in excess of $200,000 to an employee and continue to withhold it each pay period until the end of the calendar year. Additional Medicare Tax is only imposed on the employee. There is no employer share of Additional Medicare Tax. All wages that are subject to Medicare tax are subject to Additional Medicare Tax withholding if paid in excess of the $200,000 withholding threshold.		
Note. If neither A nor B above applies, you don't need to pay any federal employment taxes. But you may still need to pay state employment taxes.		

Wages paid to **unrelated children** are **taxable** if working for the payor is the child's **principal occupation.** Any employee who was under age 18 at any time during the year is considered a child for these purposes. If the child is a student, that is considered their principal occupation.

> **Example 29.** Chris, age 17, graduates from high school in the spring of 2023. In the fall, Chris becomes the full-time nanny for a neighborhood family. Even though she is under 18 years old, the wages the family pays Chris after she graduates are counted as FICA wages when the job becomes Chris's principal occupation.

According to the Code, a payor who has **never been married** is **not** required to report their **parent's** earnings in FICA wages. Only a person who was married, has not remarried, and who is without their spouse due to death or divorce is required to include their parent's earnings in FICA wages. Furthermore, only wages paid for services related to the grandparent's care of an underage or impaired child are included in FICA wages.[171]

> **Example 30.** Tobias and Rachel are married. In 2022, they welcome their first child. When Rachel and Tobias return to work, Rachel's mother watches the baby. They pay her $100 per week. Rachel and Tobias do not need to count the wages they pay to Rachel's mother in 2022 as FICA wages because they are married, and neither is incapacitated.

> **Example 31.** In 2023, Rachel and Tobias from **Example 30** divorce. Following their divorce, Rachel does not remarry, and her mother continues to care for the baby while Rachel works. The wages paid to Rachel's mother are included in FICA wages.

> **Example 32.** Use the same facts as **Example 31,** except Rachel and Tobias were never married. None of the wages paid to Rachel's mother in 2022 or 2023 must be treated as FICA wages.

> **Example 33.** Use the same facts as **Example 31,** except Rachel and Tobias paid Rachel's mother to watch their beloved pets. None of the wages paid to Rachel's mother in 2022 or 2023 must be treated as FICA wages.

---

171. IRC §3121(b)(3)(B).

Any person who is divorced, widowed, or whose spouse is incapacitated is without their spouse. In this context, incapacitations and impairments must last at least four continuous weeks during the calendar quarter in which the child's grandparent performs the services.

Identity of Employer Unclear

Generally, the employer is the person who receives the services **and** pays the employee.[172] However, if the service recipient does not control the payment of compensation to the household employee, then the employer is the person who controls compensation payments.[173] When it is unclear who the employer is, an examination of the facts and circumstances may be necessary to determine the identity of the employer.[174]

> **Observation.** Particularly in family situations, it is essential for the tax practitioner to clearly identify who the employer is, because it is the employer who has reporting and withholding obligations for the household employee.[175] Issuing a hiring letter that makes it clear who the employer is and making compensation payments consistently from an appropriate account belonging to the employer helps eliminate issues that could arise because of a lack of clarity regarding the identity of the employer.

Wages Paid to Employee but Form W-2 Reporting Not Required

A taxpayer may not know how to report income they receive from an employer when they do not receive a Form W-2. A household employee is more likely than other types of employees to legitimately receive wages and no Form W-2.

> **Example 34.** Skip's friends in **Example 25** are employees. However, because they earned less than $2,600 total from him for the year, they do not receive Forms W-2. As such, they incorrectly assume they have no filing obligation.

On the 2022 Form 1040, the IRS introduced **line 1b, "Household employee wages not reported on Form(s) W-2,"** for this situation. This line gives the employee a place to report their wages for income tax purposes and other potential issues, such as the EIC.

> **Note.** An employee who should have received a Form W-2, but has not, may file Form 4852, *Substitute for Form W-2, Wage and Tax Statement, or Form 1099-R, Distributions From Pensions, Annuities, Retirement or Profit-Sharing Plans, IRAs, Insurance Contracts, etc.*, if they do not receive the Form W-2 in time to timely file their income tax return.

POTENTIAL PENALTIES[176]

At one time, hiring undocumented workers and paying for household help off the books were commonplace practices. Then, in 1993, several political nominations were derailed when it became public that they had employed undocumented immigrants and/or not paid social security taxes on the wages.[177]

In addition to reputational consequences, there can be financial penalties imposed on taxpayers who fail to meet certain requirements related to their employees. Most of these penalty amounts have increased for returns required to be filed after December 31, 2023.

---

172. IRC §3401(d).

173. IRC §3401(d)(1); and Treas. Reg. §31.3401(d)-1(f).

174. Treas. Reg. §31.3401(c)-1(d).

175. Treas. Reg. §31.3401(d)-1(h).

176. *General Instructions for Certain Information Returns.* Mar. 27, 2023. IRS. [www.irs.gov/pub/irs-pdf/i1099gi.pdf] Accessed on Jul. 5, 2023.

177. See, e.g., *Nannygate.* Apr. 21, 2023. Wikipedia. [en.wikipedia.org/wiki/Nannygate] Accessed on Jul. 5, 2023.

Penalties for Failure to Timely File Correct Information Returns[178]

Penalties for not filing accurate and timely returns vary depending on when the correct Form W-2 is filed. Penalties currently range from $60 to $310 per Form W-2. Reasonable cause exceptions may apply, but the penalties for intentional disregard of the rules is $630 per Form W-2.[179]

The penalty may be assessed against employers who:

- Fail to timely file,
- Fail to include all information required to be shown on Form W-2,
- Include incorrect information on Form W-2,
- File on paper forms when required to file electronically,
- Report an incorrect TIN,
- Fail to report a TIN, or
- Fail to file paper Forms W-2 that are machine readable.

Penalties for Failure to Furnish Correct Payee Statements[180]

The employee's Form W-2 copies for 2023 must be mailed or provided by January 31, 2024. Penalties for failing to do so are similar to the penalties related to filing Form W-2 copies with the IRS as discussed previously, except that the penalties apply to the employee's copy rather than the government's copy.

Penalties for Failure to Withhold and Pay FICA, FUTA, and Federal Income Tax[181]

Failures involving withholding and reporting payroll taxes can result in both civil and criminal penalties, depending upon the circumstances. These penalties can potentially be as high as 100% of the tax due. However, for household employers, the penalties for late payments are under the rules applicable to estimated tax rules for the payor's Form 1040 or Form 1041 (as opposed to the rules for payments due with the Form 940 series.)

Failure to File Accurate Schedule H

There does not appear to be a specific penalty for filing an inaccurate Schedule H or failing to file one. However, penalties for accuracy and timeliness related to Form 1040 filings apply because the form is due as part of the Form 1040 filing.

If an employer files information with the IRS and the SSA that is not consistent between the agencies, they will likely receive correspondence from one or both asking for clarification and informing the taxpayer of the consequences for not providing the information.

---

178. IRC §6721.

179. *General Instructions for Certain Information Returns.* Mar. 27, 2023. IRS. [www.irs.gov/pub/irs-pdf/i1099gi.pdf] Accessed on Jul. 5, 2023.

180. IRC §6722.

181. IRS Pub. 15, *(Circular E), Employer's Tax Guide.*

TANGENTIAL OBSERVATIONS

Household Employees

Although the focus of this material is on the employer, tax practitioners may also have clients who are household workers. If a service provider receives a Form 1099-NEC for payments related to providing personal services in a home, it is more than likely someone has misunderstood the rules pertaining to their engagement.

In this situation, the practitioner should verify that their client **is or is not** in the business of providing services to the public such as those for which these payments were received. If the client received the funds in the course of their trade or business, the income is includable with the amounts for other gross receipts.

If the client is not operating a trade or business, the payor is probably skirting their duties as an employer. A person who is being misclassified for employment purposes may file Form SS-8, *Determination of Worker Status for Purposes of Federal Employment Taxes and Income Tax Withholding*. The worker files Form SS-8 if they want the IRS to make a determination of their status as an independent contractor or an employee. Filing Form SS-8 is the only way a person can initiate getting approval to file Form 8919, *Uncollected Social Security and Medicare Tax on Wages*, with their individual income tax return. This form is used to take responsibility for the unpaid employee portion of the FICA tax due on the wages received. It is typically used when a taxpayer is trying to document why they are not reporting income as subject to SE tax, which is twice the employee portion of FICA.

> **Note.** There are circumstances when a person gets paid for services that were neither in the course of a trade or business nor in the traditional sense of employment. For more information about reporting income from such activities, see the 2020 *University of Illinois Federal Tax Workbook,* Volume B, Chapter 5: Small Business Issues. This can be found at **uofi.tax/arc** [taxschool.illinois.edu/taxbookarchive].

Medical Deductions

Wages reported on Schedule H may be deductible on Schedule A if they were made for qualified medical purposes. A person who needs substantial supervision or help with at least two activities of daily living may be allowed to deduct up to 100% of the wages and related taxes they pay for household employees. See IRS Pub. 502, *Medical and Dental Expenses*, for more information on the deductibility of qualified long-term care services and nursing services.

9

ADDITIONAL RESOURCES

For additional information, the following links and recommendations may be helpful.

- Social Security Number Verification Service: **uofi.tax/23x9x3** [SSA.gov/employer/ssnv.htm]
- USCIS Central: **uofi.tax/23x9x4** [www.uscis.gov/i-9-central]
- USCIS online services for registered employers to confirm employment eligibility of newly hired employees: **E-Verify.gov**
- IRS webpage listing state government links: **uofi.tax/23x9x5** [www.irs.gov/businesses/small-businesses-self-employed/state-government-websites]
- U.S. Department of Labor list of state unemployment tax agencies: **uofi.tax/23x9x6** [oui.doleta.gov/unemploy/agencies.asp]
- U.S. Department of Labor list of labor laws applicable to **live-in** domestic workers: **uofi.tax/23x9x7** [www.dol.gov/agencies/whd/fact-sheets/79b-flsa-live-in-domestic-workers]
- For questions about the employment eligibility verification process or other immigration-related employment matters, contact the USCIS Office of Business Liaison at 800-357-2099

Chapter 10: Small Business Issues

Note. Corrections for all of the chapters are available at **TaxSchool.illinois.edu.** For clarification about terms used throughout this chapter, see the **Acronyms and Abbreviations** section following the index.

For your convenience, in-text website links are also provided as short URLs. Anywhere you see **uofi.tax/xxx**, the link points to the address immediately following in brackets.

10

About the Authors

Chris Korban, CPA, is a Tax Materials Specialist at the University of Illinois Tax School. He joined Tax School in 2023 with nine years of experience in public accounting. Chris earned both his Bachelor's Degree in Accounting and Master of Accounting Science from the University of Illinois.

John W. Richmann, EA, is a Tax Materials Specialist at the University of Illinois Tax School. Prior to joining Tax School in 2021, he owned a tax practice in St. Charles, Illinois, and held positions in private industry and consulting firms. John earned a Masters Degree in Business Administration from the University of Texas and an electrical engineering degree from the Massachusetts Institute of Technology.

Other chapter contributors and reviewers are listed at the front of this book.

PLANNING AND PITFALLS OF PASS-THROUGH ENTITY TAX

Among the many changes arising from the passage of the Tax Cuts and Jobs Act (TCJA)[1], taxpayers are subject to a limitation on the deductibility of itemized state and local taxes (SALT) of $10,000 ($5,000 if taxpayers are married filing a separate return).[2] Per IRC §164, taxpayers are generally allowed a deduction for certain taxes paid or accrued for the following taxes.

- State, local, and foreign real property taxes
- State and local personal property taxes
- State, local, and foreign income, war profits, and excess profits taxes

The SALT limitation is effective for tax years beginning after December 31, 2017, and before January 1, 2026.[3]

Some states implemented pass-through entity (PTE) tax legislation to allow a method to avoid the SALT limitation. These taxes shift the state income tax to the PTE and away from the PTE's owners. In this context, PTEs include partnerships and S corporations.[4]

> **Note.** Although the rules for PTE taxes apply to both shareholders in an S corporation and partners in a partnership, this section will use the term "shareholder" to encompass both groups of individuals.

Mechanically, the concept of PTE taxes works as an election a PTE makes on its state income tax return. Once a PTE makes this election, the state PTE tax is deductible as an expense on the entity's federal income tax return. When the PTE issues Schedule K-1 (1120-S), *Shareholder's Share of Income, Deductions, Credits, etc.*, or Schedule K-1 (1065), *Partner's Share of Income, Deductions, Credits, etc.,* to each shareholder, the Schedule K-1 reflects an additional deduction of the PTE tax paid by the entity. As a result, this deduction reduces the taxpayer's federal adjusted gross income (AGI), instead of producing a possible itemized state income tax deduction.[5]

> **Note.** The IRS issued Notice 2020-75[6] in 2020, stating that it intended to issue proposed regulations on PTE tax issues. However, in the three years since that notice was issued, there still are not any proposed regulations. This forces tax practitioners into the unenviable situation of having to take positions without substantial authority. The notice is not substantial authority, but it can be relied upon.

Because the PTE tax is a state income tax, the process, treatment, and allowability of the tax differ from state to state. This section contains an overview of the different state treatments of the PTE tax, a discussion of the benefits and costs of electing a PTE tax, and some planning considerations associated with the PTE tax.

PTE TAX APPROACH BY STATE

While each state has its own application and processes regarding the PTE tax, there are some similarities among state treatments. This section identifies the different types of treatments and which states have adopted them. The appendix to this chapter contains a list of states with PTE tax elections and associated tax rates.

1. *Tax Cuts and Jobs Act,* PL 115-97, §11042.
2. IRC §164(b)(6)(B).
3. *Tax Cuts and Jobs Act,* PL 115-97, §11042; IRC §164.
4. IRS Notice 2020-75, 2020-49 IRB 1453.
5. Ibid.
6. Ibid.

Requirement of Estimated Tax Payments

Most states require entities making the PTE tax election to pay the tax in estimated quarterly payments to avoid underpayment penalties. Using **Illinois** as an example, PTEs making the PTE tax election must pay estimated tax payments when the expected total tax due exceeds $500 or the PTE will incur late estimated payment penalties.[7] PTE estimated tax payments for most states are due by the 15th day of the 4th, 6th, 9th, and 12th month of the tax year. However, practitioners and taxpayers should be mindful of specific state due dates. For example, **Connecticut's** 4th quarter payment is due by the 15th day of the 1st month of the subsequent tax year.[8] These due dates are critical to avoid penalties, as PTEs must make the PTE estimated payments for the year they are seeking the PTE tax election in that tax year.

Practitioner Planning Tip

It is important to have the conversation about the PTE tax election early in the year with clients. This allows the taxpayer to make all the necessary estimated payments during the year.

PTEs make estimated tax payments periodically through the tax year and reconcile them with the amount of PTE tax they calculate after the tax year ends when preparing and filing their state tax returns. Most states have a safe harbor for estimated tax payments to avoid underpayment tax penalties. For example, **Illinois** PTEs must pay at least 90% of the filing tax year's liability or 100% of the preceding tax year's liability to avoid late payment penalties.[9]

Example 1. Veridian Innovations (Veridian) is an S corporation located in Illinois with a calendar yearend and uses the cash basis of accounting. In March 2022, the company's tax advisor, Monica, suggested making the PTE tax election for Illinois in 2022 after discovering all three shareholders could not deduct their total state income tax on their federal returns due to the SALT limitation. Veridian's state tax liability for 2021 was $7,000. Per Monica's instructions, Veridian paid estimated tax payments of $1,750 per quarter ($7,000 ÷ 4) to satisfy Illinois's estimated tax payment safe harbor (100% of the prior year tax liability of $7,000) to avoid underpayment penalties. Because Monica identified the benefit of the PTE tax election early in the year and communicated her suggestion to Veridian promptly, Veridian was able to pay the 1st quarter's $1,750 estimated tax payment by the April 15th deadline.

10

Note. If all Veridian shareholders were in the 22% federal tax bracket, excluding the qualified business income deduction, the potential PTE benefit is $1,540 ($7,000 × 22%).

7. 35 ILCS 5/201(p)(9).

8. *Pass-Through Entity Tax Information*. 2023. Connecticut State Department of Revenue Services. [portal.ct.gov/DRS/Taxes/Pass-Through-Entity/Tax-Information#estimated] Accessed on Jun. 29, 2023.

9. IDOR Pub. 129, *Pass-through Entity Information*.

Generally, electing PTEs that overpay the PTE tax receive a refund of the overpayment when preparing the state income tax return. Some states do not allow PTEs to apply the overpayment to the following tax year's estimated PTE tax payments.[10] Other states, such as **Illinois**, allow PTEs to apply the overpayment as a credit for the following tax year.[11] Regardless of the treatment of the overpayment, the amount of PTE tax on a shareholder's state Schedule K-1 reflects their share of the tax that the entity **elects,** not the amount of estimates that the entity made throughout the year. Therefore, the shareholder does not receive credit for an overpayment applied to a future tax return on their state Schedule K-1 for the current tax year.[12]

Annual Liability Payment

Not all states require PTEs to make estimated PTE tax payments. For example, **Missouri** does not require a PTE to make estimated tax payments regardless of the tax liability, where the PTE pays the liability by the 15th day of the 4th month after the PTE's yearend.[13] Some states, like **Missouri**, allow PTEs to make early payments via a voucher if they are so inclined.[14]

This may present an issue for PTEs using **cash basis accounting,**[15] where the PTE reports the PTE liability payment as an expense in the year it made the payment, as opposed to the tax year for which the payment was applicable.[16] The IRS proposed regulations clarifying such payments are deductible for the tax year the PTE made the payment.[17] Generally, **accrual-basis** taxpayers deduct the PTE payment in the year they make the payment, regardless of the tax year for which the payment is applied.[18] For example, a calendar-year, accrual-basis taxpayer that makes a 4th quarter estimate in January 2023 for the 2022 tax year could not deduct the 4th quarter payment for the 2022 tax year, rather deducting it on the 2023 tax return. The reasoning behind this treatment is attributable to the requirement of the liability being fixed and economic performance having occurred to deduct the accrued tax liability in 2022.[19] Because the election to have PTE tax be entity-based occurs when filing the income tax return after yearend, which proceeds the year for which the election is made, accrual-basis taxpayers do not meet the requirement of economic performance. Therefore, they cannot accrue the 4th quarter estimate as a deduction on the 2022 return.

---

10. *Help with pass-through entity elective tax*. Jun. 7, 2023. State of California Franchise Tax Board. [www.ftb.ca.gov/file/business/credits/pass-through-entity-elective-tax/help.html] Accessed on Jul. 5, 2023.
11. 2022 Instructions for IL-1120-ST.
12. IDOR Pub. 129, *Pass-through Entity Information*.
13. *Pass-Through Entity Tax FAQs*. 2023. Missouri Department of Revenue. [dor.mo.gov/faq/taxation/business/entity-tax.html] Accessed on Jul. 5, 2023.
14. Ibid.
15. IRC §446.
16. See Treas. Reg. §1.461-4(g)(6).
17. IRS Notice 2020-75, 2020-49 CB 1453.
18. See Treas. Reg. §1.461-4(g)(6).
19. Treas. Reg. §1.461-4.

Recurring Item Exception. There is an exception under Treas. Reg. §1.461-5 that accrual taxpayers may use to deduct an accrued tax payment in the year preceding the year in which the amount is paid known as the **recurring item exception.** This exception is a change in accounting method, where a taxpayer automatically adopts the method in treating a specific, recurring item in the 1st year the taxpayer incurs the item.[20] A taxpayer may implement this exception if the following criteria apply to the accrued item.[21]

1. At the end of the year, all events have occurred in establishing the liability, **and** the taxpayer can accurately determine its amount.
2. The taxpayer achieves **economic performance** on or before the 15th day of the 9th month following the tax yearend **or** the date that the taxpayer timely files their return (including extensions), whichever is earlier. Economic performance for tax payments occurs as the taxpayer **pays the tax** to the governmental authority.[22]
3. The liability is a recurring item, where the taxpayer expects to incur the liability from one tax year to the next, even if the taxpayer does not incur the liability in each tax year.
4. The liability is not material, **or** the accrued liability best matches the related income for the tax year that the taxpayer achieves economic performance. Materiality depends on the amount of the liability relating to the same activity's other income and expenses and includes, but is not limited to, materiality thresholds under generally accepted accounting principles (GAAP). For determining the matching requirement, GAAP may help substantiate the relationship, but it is not absolute.

Caution. Practitioners should note that authoritative guidance does not explicitly state that the recurring item exception may apply to PTE tax payments. While Treas. Reg. §1.461-4 states that taxpayers, if meeting the criteria, may use the exception for liabilities to pay a tax, it is silent as to which specific taxes apply. This omission contrasts with the regulations identifying the tax payments for which the general rules apply earlier in the same section.[23] Therefore, taxpayers should exercise caution if advising their accrual-basis clients making PTE tax payments to elect this accounting change for the exception.

PTE Tax Return

For some states, PTEs can make the PTE tax election on the state's tax return for partnerships and S corporations. For example, **Illinois** has a checkbox on page 1, line L of the IL-1120-ST, *Small Business Corporation Replacement Tax Return*, as shown next.

10

Note. Illinois partnerships and S corporations are subject to a replacement tax of 1.5% on entity income; this is treated like income tax.

20. Treas. Reg. §1.461-5(b)(1).

21. Treas. Reg. §1.461-5(b).

22. Treas. Reg. §1.461-4(g)(6).

23. Ibid.

Illinois Department of Revenue

2022 Form IL-1120-ST

Small Business Corporation Replacement Tax Return

Due on or before the 15th day of the 3rd month following the close of the tax year.

If this return is not for calendar year 2022, enter your fiscal tax year here. Tax year beginning ____ ____ 20____, ending ____ ____ 20____ (month day year, month day year) WARNING: This form is for tax years ending on or after December 31, 2022, and before December 31, 2023. For all other situations, see instructions to determine the correct form to use.	Enter the amount you are paying. $__________

Step 1: Identify your small business corporation

A Enter your complete legal business name. If you have a name change, check this box. ☐

Name: ____________

B Enter your mailing address. Check this box if either of the following apply: ☐

- this is your **first return**, or
- you have an **address change**.

C/O: ____________

Mailing address: ____________

City: ____________ State: ______ ZIP: ______

C If this is the first or final return, check the applicable box(es).

☐ First return

☐ Final return (Enter the date of termination. __ __ ____) (mm dd yyyy)

D If this is a final return because you sold this business, enter the date sold (mm dd yyyy) __ __ ____, and the new owner's FEIN __ __ - __ __ __ __ __ __ __.

E **Apportionment Formulas.** Check the appropriate box or boxes and see the Apportionment Formula instructions.

☐ Financial organizations ☐ Transportation companies

☐ Federally regulated exchanges ☐ Sales companies

F Check this box if you attached Form IL-4562. ☐

G Check this box if you attached Illinois Schedule M (for businesses). ☐

H Check this box if you attached Schedule 80/20. ☐

I Check this box if you attached Schedule 1299-A. ☐

J Check this box if you attached the Subgroup Schedule. ☐

K Check this box if you are a 52/53 week filer. ☐

L Check this box if you elected to file and pay Pass-through Entity Tax. See instructions. ☒

M If you are paying Pass-through Entity Tax and you annualized your income on Form IL-2220, check this box and **attach** Form IL-2220. ☐

N Enter your federal employer identification number (FEIN). __ __ - __ __ __ __ __ __ __

O ☐ Check this box if you are a member of a unitary business group and enter the FEIN of the member who prepared the Schedule UB, Combined Apportionment for Unitary Business Group. **Attach** Schedule UB to this return. __ __ - __ __ __ __ __ __ __

P Enter your North American Industry Classification System (NAICS) Code. See instructions. __ __ __ __ __ __

Q Enter your Illinois corporate file (charter) number issued by the Secretary of State. ____________

R Enter the city, state, and zip code where your accounting records are kept. (Use the two-letter postal abbreviation, ***e.g.***, IL, GA, etc.)

City ______ State ______ ZIP ______

S If you are making the business income election to treat all nonbusiness income as business income, check this box and enter zero on Lines 36 and 44. ☐

T If you have completed the following, check the box and **attach** the federal form(s) to this return.

☐ Federal Form 8886 ☐ Federal Sch. M-3, Part II, Line 10

U If you are making a discharge of indebtedness adjustment on Schedule NLD or Form IL-1120-ST, Line 48, check this box and **attach** federal Form 982. ☐

V Check this box if your business activity is protected under Public Law 86-272. ☐

However, other states have a unique tax return specifically for PTEs making the election. Using **Arkansas** as an example, a PTE making the election files Form AR1100PET, *Arkansas Pass-Through Entity Tax Return*, instead of Form AR1100S, *Arkansas S Corporation Income Tax Return*, or Form AR1050, *Arkansas Partnership Income Tax Return*. Alternatively, a PTE files Form AR1100S or AR1050 and includes Form AR362, *Arkansas Pass-Through Entity Income Tax Election Or Revocation Form*, to make a valid PTE tax election. Arkansas treats the PTE tax election as valid for each tax year until the PTE revokes it. Therefore, if a PTE decides to revoke the election for a given tax year, they must file Form AR362 with Form AR1100S or AR1050 for the tax year they are seeking revocation.[24]

24. Instructions for Form AR362.

Mandatory PTE Tax Treatment[25]

Connecticut is the only state to **require** PTEs doing business and filing in the state to adopt the PTE tax. PTEs doing business in Connecticut use the same tax form as in prior years to report income tax: Form CT-1065/CT-1120SI, *Connecticut Pass-Through Entity Tax Return*. The difference in procedure consists of the state assessing tax at the entity level instead of passing through to shareholders for taxation at their level. Connecticut does require quarterly estimated tax payments for PTEs with tax liabilities equaling or exceeding $1,000.

BENEFITS VS. COSTS OF THE ELECTION

The purpose of the PTE tax election is to allow taxpayers to deduct state income taxes that they may have otherwise not been able to deduct due to the SALT limitations. PTEs must consider the costs and hurdles associated with the election and weigh them against the tax benefits. In doing so, PTEs will be better equipped to decide whether to proceed with this potential tax-saving option. Because each state is different and does not conform to a unifying set of policies, procedures, and treatments, PTEs should consider the following issues to help them assess whether to elect PTE tax treatment for a given state.

Treatment of Out-of-State Income

One of the most complex areas practitioners face is multistate taxation. Unsurprisingly, PTEs with income in multiple states have additional complexity when assessing whether to make the PTE tax election. Most of this consideration revolves around how states treat out-of-state income. Some states use apportionment to differentiate between in-state and out-of-state income, where an entity determines the sourcing of its income based on property, payroll, sales, or a combination of the three. The method of determining income sourcing and how each state treats out-of-state income regarding PTE tax is a key consideration in estimating and calculating PTE tax under the election.

Some states calculate the PTE tax on income after apportioning global income to the state. For example, **Illinois** applies an apportionment percentage that results from dividing Illinois sales by global sales. This percentage is applied to the PTE's net business income to arrive at the amount of Illinois taxable pass-through income. Finally, this taxable pass-through income is multiplied by the state income tax rate to arrive at the amount of PTE tax. The PTE will pay this PTE tax in addition to the state replacement tax, and the shareholders will receive an Illinois tax credit for their share of the paid PTE tax (excludes the replacement tax). Through this methodology, the calculation of PTE tax is after the apportionment of Illinois income, resulting in a tax on the income sourced to Illinois based on a sales apportionment factor.[26]

10

Treatment of Nonbusiness Income

Some states use an allocation model in determining the taxability of nonbusiness income comprising investment and other passive activities. This method generally entails the allocation of nonbusiness income to a taxpayer's state of domicile or where the property resides.

25. *Pass-Through Entity Tax Information*. 2023. Connecticut State Department of Revenue Services. [portal.ct.gov/DRS/Taxes/Pass-Through-Entity/Tax-Information#whomustfile] Accessed on Jul. 5, 2023.

26. Form IL-1120-ST.

The PTE tax election and nonbusiness income revolves around the **source of the income.** States may differ on the treatment of nonbusiness income sourcing and a potential result is a portion of income may not have a source. This concept is often referred to as **"nowhere income."**[27] While this treatment may sometimes work favorably for the taxpayer where they do not pay any state tax on "nowhere income," some states have addressed this issue by imposing a throwback rule requiring taxpayers to include the "nowhere income" as taxable income to the state.[28] Thus, there may be instances where a taxpayer is taxed on the same income in multiple states. The PTE tax generally follows the state's treatment of nonbusiness income, where the election does not alter the treatment of nonbusiness income.[29] However, most states offering the PTE tax election assess the PTE tax at the highest personal income tax rate.[30] Considering this fact, double income taxation may result in a more unfavorable position than not making the PTE tax election. As such, PTEs with nonbusiness income should assess the states in which they have filing requirements and identify the respective states' treatment of nonbusiness income.

Source of Refunds

Generally, the overpayment of PTE tax results in a refund receivable by the PTE as opposed to shareholders directly. For example, if a PTE overpaid its **Illinois** PTE tax, the PTE would reflect the overpayment on the Illinois tax return and request a refund or apply it to next year's estimated tax. Because shareholders should only receive a state credit for the tax paid, the amount of the refund would reduce their credit by their ownership share.[31]

Example 2. Assume the same facts as **Example 1.** At the end of the year, Veridian's tax liability is $7,785, consisting of $1,845 replacement tax and $5,940 PTE tax. Therefore, Veridian records an underpayment of $785 ($7,785 total tax liability – $7,000 PTE estimated payments). While Veridian owes tax for 2022, Veridian in fact overpaid its PTE tax by $1,060 ($7,000 PTE estimated payments – $5,940 actual PTE tax), with the excess applied to the $1,845 replacement tax. Even though Veridian paid estimates of more than the $5,940 of PTE tax, Veridian's shareholders only collectively receive credit for the $5,940 of PTE tax. The balance is used to pay the replacement tax. Veridian's chief executive officer (CEO), Isaac Evers, who owns 50% shares in the company, receives a PTE tax credit of $2,970 ($5,940 × 50%) on his Illinois Schedule K-1-P, *Partner's or Shareholder's Share of Income, Deductions, Credits, and Recapture.*

Treatment of Out-Of-State Owners

The PTE tax election is entity-based in most states, where the electing PTE pays PTE tax on behalf of all its shareholders, regardless of their residency. Therefore, nonresidents of a state where a PTE elects the PTE tax will receive a state Schedule K-1 showing their share of the state income and the PTE tax credit. States have provided guidance and clarification stating the PTE election alone does not create a filing requirement for nonresidents in the state.[32] For most states, such as **Alabama,** if the nonresident shareholder would not otherwise be required to file a tax return in the state due to the source and amount of taxable income, then the shareholder is not obligated to file a tax return in the state.[33] Furthermore, some states, such as **Illinois,** have clarified that if the PTE tax credit satisfies the nonresident shareholder's state income tax liability, they need not file a tax return in the state.[34]

---

27. *Does Your State Have a Throwback or Throwout Rule?* Fritts, Janelle. Apr. 4, 2023. Tax Foundation. [taxfoundation.org/state-throwback-rule-state-throwout-rule-2023] Accessed on Jul. 28, 2023.

28. Ibid.

29. See, for example, IDOR Pub. 129, *Pass-through Entity Information.*

30. *Links to States' Pass-Through Entity (PTE) Tax Legislation and Tax Authorities' Information and Guidance.* Jun. 13, 2023. AICPA. [us.aicpa.org/content/dam/aicpa/advocacy/tax/downloadabledocuments/56175896-links-to-pass-through-entity-pte-taxes-states-legislation-and-tax-authorities-information-and-guidance.pdf] Accessed on Jul. 28, 2023.

31. IDOR Pub. 129, *Pass-through Entity Information.*

32. *Pass-Through Entity-Level Tax: Frequently Asked Questions.* May 5, 2023. Arkansas Department of Finance and Administration. [www.dfa.arkansas.gov/images/uploads/incomeTaxOffice/PET_TAX_FAQ_2023.pdf] Accessed on Jul. 28, 2023.

33. *FAQ for Electing Pass-Through Entities.* Jun. 30, 2022. Alabama Department of Revenue. [www.revenue.alabama.gov/individual-corporate/electing-pass-through-entities] Accessed on Jul. 5, 2023.

34. IDOR Pub. 129, *Pass-through Entity Information.*

The concept of a PTE tax credit alleviating a nonresident shareholder from a state filing requirement may sound familiar to multistate tax practitioners. This notion follows a similar framework to the concept of state composite tax returns. For states either allowing or requiring them, a PTE prepares and files a composite return on behalf of a consenting nonresident shareholder to report their share of state income tax and pay the corresponding tax liability on behalf of the shareholder.[35] The PTE treats the tax payment as a shareholder distribution and is not a deductible expense.[36] Therefore, a PTE tax election, which conceptually operates similarly, may prevent the need to file composite tax returns for nonresident shareholders. Some states conform to this reasoning, such as **Georgia,** where the PTE would not prepare a composite return if making the PTE tax election.[37] However, other states, such as **Oregon,** still require an entity to file composite tax returns on behalf of their nonresident shareholders when making the PTE tax election.[38] PTEs should be mindful of these filing requirements and how the PTE tax election creates any changes to these requirements.

Owner Approval Requirements

In the planning stages of assessing the benefits of making a PTE tax election, filers should consider the requirements surrounding owner approval of the election. This requirement may impact the feasibility of making the election if there are members who disagree on whether to do so in states that require unanimous or majority consent. The requirements for owner consent vary from state to state. **Arkansas** requires members collectively owning more than 50% of the PTE's voting rights to consent to make the election, but only requires one responsible party's signature indicating this consent.[39] Other states, such as **Illinois,** consider the election to be made by the entity, and does not require member signatures other than the signing party's signature for the tax return.[40]

Payment of Estimated Taxes

As discussed previously, states requiring PTEs to make estimated PTE tax payments generally require the 1st quarter payment by the 15th day of the 4th month following the PTE's yearend. This results in a relatively short period of time for a PTE to assess whether to plan on making a PTE tax election and pay the first installment on time to avoid late payment penalties. Therefore, PTEs should identify which states they are seeking the election for that require estimated tax payments and prioritize calculating and paying estimated taxes accordingly.

Revocability of Election

In some states, the PTE tax election is irrevocable for the tax year the PTE files the return making the election. For example, **New York** does not allow an amendment reversing the PTE tax election made on a filed tax return.[41] Taxpayers should be mindful of these states that generally consider the tax return filing event as making a valid election (i.e., making an estimated payment does not constitute making a valid election.) Other states, such as **Arkansas**, allow PTEs to revoke the election, usually by filing an amended return by an extended due date.[42] The flexibility of revocability may be a consideration for some PTEs whose tax situation changes from a necessitating or beneficial amendment.

---

35. *Considerations for Filing Composite Tax Returns*. Oppe, Ami and Zidik Jr., Donald. 2023. AICPA. [www.thetaxadviser.com/issues/2014/mar/tpm-mar2014.html] Accessed on Jul. 28, 2023.

36. Ibid.

37. *HB 149 Pass-Through Entity Tax FAQ*. 2023. Georgia Department of Revenue. [dor.georgia.gov/hb-149-pass-through-entity-tax-faq] Accessed on Jul. 6, 2023.

38. *Pass-Through Entity Elective (PTE-E) Tax*. 2023. Oregon Department of Revenue. [www.oregon.gov/dor/programs/businesses/pages/pass-through-entity-elective-tax.aspx] Accessed on Jul. 6, 2023.

39. *Pass-Through Entity-Level Tax: Frequently Asked Questions*. May 5, 2023. Arkansas Department of Finance and Administration. [www.dfa.arkansas.gov/images/uploads/incomeTaxOffice/PET_TAX_FAQ_2023.pdf] Accessed on Jul. 5, 2023.

40. IDOR Pub. 129, *Pass-through Entity Information*.

41. NYS Department of Taxation and Finance Technical Memorandum TSB-M-21(1)C, (1)I, *Pass-Through Entity Tax*.

42. *Pass-Through Entity-Level Tax: Frequently Asked Questions*. May 5, 2023. Arkansas Department of Finance and Administration. [www.dfa.arkansas.gov/images/uploads/incomeTaxOffice/PET_TAX_FAQ_2023.pdf] Accessed on Jul. 5, 2023.

Summary

A non-exhaustive list summarizing benefits and costs of adopting the PTE tax follows. Some items were previously discussed and others are simply items for consideration.

Benefits:

- Reduces federal AGI
- Transfers the payment of shareholder state tax to the entity
- Replaces pass-through withholding for out-of-state shareholders
- Ability to deduct state income tax without having to itemize
- May allow more utilization of other SALT deductions
- Reduces self-employment (SE) tax on partnerships
- May eliminate the requirement for an out-of-state shareholder to file a nonresident state income tax return
- May reduce or eliminate alternative minimum tax (AMT)

Costs:

- Additional professional fees
- Complexity of preparation, particularly for multistate returns
- Election may not benefit all shareholders
- May prompt additional estimated payment requirements
- A shareholder may fail to include their allocated PTE on their individual return
- May impact other tax credits on a shareholder's individual return
- Reduces the company's financial statement income
- Reducing federal AGI may decrease other benefits
- Lowering business income will reduce qualified business income (QBI)

Practitioner Planning Tip

If a PTE is uncertain whether to elect the PTE tax, it may be beneficial for them to pay estimated PTE tax payments regardless. When the PTE ultimately files its return, it can make a more informed decision on whether to make the election after reviewing the entity and shareholder tax situations, without penalty. Practitioners should be mindful of the state's overpayment refund processes before advising this approach to ensure the PTE can receive the funds without issue.

Practitioner Planning Tip

PTE owners must be mindful of the time needed in adopting the PTE tax and also the time of the tax practitioner. Due to the complexity involved, it is not unreasonable for a practitioner to charge a premium for the time spent researching and implementing PTE tax treatment for a client. Practitioners should be upfront about this extra cost with their clients so that they may better weigh the costs associated with making the PTE tax election against the benefits.

THE FLOW OF REPORTING THE PTE TAX

The PTE tax election likely encompasses several tax return forms and schedules. The flow of the reporting and how it impacts the different returns is important in understanding the nuances and functionality of adopting the PTE tax election. This section illustrates some of the forms, reporting, and the flow-through nature of the PTE tax election using the example of an Illinois company and shareholder.

Example 3. Use the same facts as **Example 2.** Based on Monica's suggestion, Veridian decided to elect the PTE tax in Illinois for the 2022 tax year. Veridian is owned by three shareholders, with CEO Isaac Evers owning 50% of the company.

During 2022, Veridian earned $300,000 gross income from its business and $3,000 nonbusiness interest income that is allocable to Illinois. Veridian incurred $160,000 in salary expenses and $20,000 in payroll tax expenses. Therefore, Veridian earned $123,000 of net income in 2022 before state income taxes ($300,000 gross income + $3,000 nonbusiness interest income – $160,000 salary expense – $20,000 payroll tax expenses). Veridian paid its estimated PTE tax payments totaling $7,000 on time for each quarter.

In preparing Form IL-1120-ST, Veridian makes the PTE tax election by checking box L on Step 1. Veridian then calculates its Illinois 1.5% replacement tax on its $123,000 net income as $1,845 ($123,000 × 1.5%). Veridian multiplied the $123,000 of income by the Illinois PTE tax rate of 4.95% to calculate its PTE tax of $6,089. Therefore, Veridian's total Illinois tax liability is $7,934 ($1,845 replacement tax + $6,089 PTE tax). Because Veridian paid $7,000 of estimated PTE tax for 2022, Veridian's unpaid Illinois tax liability is $934 ($7,934 – $7,000). Veridian is not subject to underpayment of tax penalties because the $7,000 of estimated tax payments were 100% of the prior year's Illinois tax. The following table summarizes the total federal Schedule K-1 income.

Gross income	$300,000
Salaries	(160,000)
Payroll taxes	(20,000)
PTE tax payments	(7,000)
Ordinary income	$113,000
Nonbusiness income	3,000
Total Schedule K-1 income	$116,000

Veridian takes the information from the table and completes Form IL-1120-ST, shown on the following pages.

Veridian prepares Form IL-1120-ST, Schedule B, *Partners' or Shareholders' Information*, which summarizes shareholders' information. In addition to reporting the names and addresses of its shareholders, Veridian reports each shareholder's share of income and PTE tax credit. The PTE tax credit for the shareholders totals the $6,089 PTE tax that Veridian calculated on Form IL-1120-ST. The shareholders do not receive a tax credit for the replacement tax, which has historically been an entity-level tax. Accordingly, Veridian prepares Schedules K-1-P for each shareholder, distributing a copy to each of them to assist with the preparation of their individual state income tax returns.

For Example 3

Illinois Department of Revenue

2022 Form IL-1120-ST

Small Business Corporation Replacement Tax Return

Due on or before the 15th day of the 3rd month following the close of the tax year.

If this return is not for calendar year 2022, enter your fiscal tax year here.
Tax year beginning ____ ____ 20____, ending ____ ____ 20____
month day year month day year

WARNING This form is for tax years ending on or after December 31, 2022, and before December 31, 2023. For all other situations, see instructions to determine the correct form to use.

Enter the amount you are paying. $ 934.00

Step 1: Identify your small business corporation

A Enter your complete legal business name. If you have a name change, check this box. ☐
Name: Veridian Innovations

B Enter your mailing address.
Check this box if either of the following apply: ☐
- this is your **first return**, or
- you have an **address change**.

C/O: ____
Mailing address: 2002 Warner Ave.
City: Champaign State: IL ZIP: 61822

C If this is the first or final return, check the applicable box(es).
☐ First return
☐ Final return (Enter the date of termination. ___ ___ ____) mm dd yyyy

D If this is a final return because you sold this business, enter the date sold (mm dd yyyy) ___ ___ ____, and the new owner's FEIN ___-________.

E **Apportionment Formulas**. Check the appropriate box or boxes and see the Apportionment Formula instructions.
☐ Financial organizations ☐ Transportation companies
☐ Federally regulated exchanges ☐ Sales companies

F Check this box if you attached Form IL-4562. ☐
G Check this box if you attached Illinois Schedule M (for businesses). ☐
H Check this box if you attached Schedule 80/20. ☐
I Check this box if you attached Schedule 1299-A. ☐
J Check this box if you attached the Subgroup Schedule. ☐
K Check this box if you are a 52/53 week filer. ☐
L Check this box if you elected to file and pay Pass-through Entity Tax. See instructions. ☒
M If you are paying Pass-through Entity Tax and you annualized your income on Form IL-2220, check this box and **attach** Form IL-2220. ☐

N Enter your federal employer identification number (FEIN).
9 9 - 9 9 9 9 9 9 9

O ☐ Check this box if you are a member of a unitary business group and enter the FEIN of the member who prepared the Schedule UB, Combined Apportionment for Unitary Business Group. **Attach** Schedule UB to this return.
___-________

P Enter your North American Industry Classification System (NAICS) Code. See instructions.
4 4 9 2 1 0

Q Enter your Illinois corporate file (charter) number issued by the Secretary of State.
____

R Enter the city, state, and zip code where your accounting records are kept. (Use the two-letter postal abbreviation, ***e.g.***, IL, GA, etc.)
Champaign (City) IL (State) 61822 (ZIP)

S If you are making the business income election to treat all nonbusiness income as business income, check this box and enter zero on Lines 36 and 44. ☐

T If you have completed the following, check the box and **attach** the federal form(s) to this return.
☐ Federal Form 8886 ☐ Federal Sch. M-3, Part II, Line 10

U If you are making a discharge of indebtedness adjustment on Schedule NLD or Form IL-1120-ST, Line 48, check this box and **attach** federal Form 982. ☐

V Check this box if your business activity is protected under Public Law 86-272. ☐

▼ Attach your payment and Form IL-1120-ST-V here. ▲

Step 2: Figure your ordinary income or loss

(Whole dollars only)

1	Ordinary income or loss, or equivalent from federal Schedule K.	1	113,000.00
2	Net income or loss from all rental real estate activities.	2	.00
3	Net income or loss from other rental activities.	3	0.00
4	Portfolio income or loss.	4	3,000.00
5	Net IRC Section 1231 gain or loss.	5	.00
6	All other items of income or loss that were not included in the computation of income or loss on Page 1 of U.S. Form 1120-S. See instructions. Identify: ________	6	.00
7	Add Lines 1 through 6. This is your ordinary income or loss.	7	116,000.00

Step 3: Figure your unmodified base income or loss

8	Charitable contributions.	8	.00
9	Expense deduction under IRC Section 179.	9	.00
10	Interest on investment indebtedness.	10	.00
11	All other items of expense that were not deducted in the computation of ordinary income or loss on Page 1 of U.S. Form 1120-S. See instructions. Identify: ________	11	.00
12	Add Lines 8 through 11.	12	.00
13	Subtract Line 12 from Line 7. This amount is your total unmodified base income or loss.	13	116,000.00

IR NS DR____

IL-1120-ST (R-12/22)

This form is authorized as outlined by the Illinois Income Tax Act. Disclosure of this information is REQUIRED. Failure to provide information could result in a penalty.

Page 1 of 5

For Example 3

Step 4: Figure your income or loss

Line	Description		Amount
14	Enter the amount from Line 13. **Unitary filers**, enter the amount from Schedule UB, Step 2, Col E, Line 30.	14	116,000 .00
15	State, municipal, and other interest income excluded from Line 14.	15	.00
16	Illinois taxes and surcharge deducted in arriving at Line 14. See instructions.	16	7,000 .00
17	Illinois Special Depreciation addition. **Attach** Form IL-4562.	17	.00
18	Related-Party Expenses addition. **Attach** Schedule 80/20.	18	.00
19	Distributive share of additions. **Attach** Schedule(s) K-1-P or K-1-T.	19	.00
20	The amount of loss distributable to a shareholder subject to replacement tax. **Attach** Schedule B.	20	.00
21	Other additions. **Attach** Illinois Schedule M (for businesses).	21	.00
22	Add Lines 14 through 21. This amount is your income or loss.	22	123,000 .00

Step 5: Figure your base income or loss

Line	Description		Amount		Amount
23	Interest income from U.S. Treasury or other exempt federal obligations.	23	.00		
24	Share of income distributable to a shareholder subject to replacement tax. **Attach** Schedule B.	24	.00		
25	River Edge Redevelopment Zone Dividend subtraction. **Attach** Schedule 1299-A.	25	.00		
26	River Edge Redevelopment Zone Interest subtraction. **Attach** Schedule 1299-A.	26	.00		
27	High Impact Business Dividend subtraction. **Attach** Schedule 1299-A.	27	.00		
28	High Impact Business Interest subtraction. **Attach** Schedule 1299-A.	28	.00		
29	Contribution subtraction. **Attach** Schedule 1299-A.	29	.00		
30	Illinois Special Depreciation subtraction. **Attach** Form IL-4562.	30	.00		
31	Related-Party Expenses subtraction. **Attach** Schedule 80/20.	31	.00		
32	Distributive share of subtractions. **Attach** Schedule(s) K-1-P or K-1-T.	32	.00		
33	Other subtractions. **Attach** Schedule M (for businesses).	33	.00		
34	Total subtractions. Add Lines 23 through 33.			34	.00
35	**Base income or loss**. Subtract Line 34 from Line 22.			35	123,000 .00

STOP

A If the amount on Line 35 is derived inside Illinois only, check this box and enter the amount from Step 5, Line 35 on Step 7, Line 47. You may not complete Step 6. (You must leave Step 6, Lines 36 through 46 blank.) ☒
Note→ If you are a unitary filer, do not check this box. Check the box on Line B and complete Step 6.

B If any portion of the amount on Line 35 is derived outside Illinois, or you are a unitary filer, check this box and complete all lines of Step 6. (Do not leave Lines 40 through 42 blank.) See instructions. ☐

Step 6: Figure your income allocable to Illinois (Complete only if you checked the box on Line B, above.)

Line	Description		Amount		Amount
36	Nonbusiness income or loss. **Attach** Schedule NB.			36	.00
37	Business income or loss included in Line 35 from non-unitary partnerships, partnerships included on a Schedule UB, S corporations, trusts, or estates. See instructions.			37	.00
38	Add Lines 36 and 37.			38	.00
39	Business income or loss. Subtract Line 38 from Line 35.			39	.00
40	Total sales everywhere. This amount cannot be negative.	40			
41	Total sales inside Illinois. This amount cannot be negative.	41			
42	Apportionment factor. Divide Line 41 by Line 40. Round to six decimal places.	42	.		
43	Business income or loss apportionable to Illinois. Multiply Line 39 by Line 42.			43	.00
44	Nonbusiness income or loss allocable to Illinois. **Attach** Schedule NB.			44	0 .00
45	Business income or loss apportionable to Illinois from non-unitary partnerships, partnerships included on a Schedule UB, S corporations, trusts, or estates. See instructions.			45	0 .00
46	**Base income or loss allocable to Illinois**. Add Lines 43 through 45.			46	.00

Page 2 of 5 IL-1120-ST (R-12/22)

10

Step 7: Figure your net income

47	Base income or net loss from Step 5, Line 35, or Step 6, Line 46.	47	123,000.00
48	Discharge of indebtedness adjustment. **Attach** federal Form 982. See instructions.	48	.00
49	Adjusted base income or net loss. Add Lines 47 and 48.	49	123,000.00
50	Illinois net loss deduction. If Line 49 is zero or a negative amount, enter zero. **Attach** Schedule NLD. Check this box and attach a detailed statement if you have merged losses. ◆☐◆	50	.00
51	**Net income**. Subtract Line 50 from Line 49.	51	123,000.00

Step 8: Figure the taxes, surcharges, pass-through withholding, and penalty you owe

52	Replacement tax. Multiply Line 51 by 1.5% (.015).	52	1,845.00
53	Recapture of investment credits. **Attach** Schedule 4255.	53	.00
54	Replacement tax before investment credits. Add Lines 52 and 53.	54	1,845.00
55	Investment credits. **Attach** Form IL-477.	55	.00
56	**Net replacement tax.** Subtract Line 55 from Line 54. If the amount is negative, enter zero.	56	1,845.00
57	Compassionate Use of Medical Cannabis Program Act surcharge. See instructions.	57	.00
58	Sale of assets by gaming licensee surcharge. See instructions.	58	.00
59	Pass-through withholding you owe on behalf of your members. Enter the amount from Schedule B, Section A, Line 5. See instructions. **Attach** Schedule B.	59	.00
60	Pass-through entity income. See instructions. ◆60 123,000.00 ◆		
61	**Pass-through entity tax**. Multiply Line 60 by 4.95% (.0495).	61	6,089.00
62	**Total net replacement tax, surcharges, pass-through withholding, and pass-through entity tax you owe.** Add Lines 56, 57, 58, 59, and 61.	62	7,934.00
63	Underpayment of estimated tax penalty from Form IL-2220. See instructions.	63	.00
64	**Total taxes, surcharges, pass-through withholding, and penalty**. Add Lines 62 and 63.	64	7,934.00

Step 9: Figure your refund or balance due

65	Payments. See instructions.				
	a Credit from previous overpayments.	65a	.00		
	b Total payments made before the date this return is filed.	65b	7,000.00		
	c Pass-through withholding reported to you. **Attach** Schedule(s) K-1-P or K-1-T.	65c	.00		
	d Illinois income tax withholding. **Attach** Form(s) W-2G.	65d	.00		
66	Total payments. Add Lines 65a through 65d.			66	7,000.00
67	Overpayment. If Line 66 is greater than Line 64, subtract Line 64 from Line 66.			67	.00
68	Amount to be **credited forward**. See instructions. Check this box and attach a detailed statement if this carryforward is going to a different FEIN. ◆☐◆			◆ 68	.00 ◆
69	**Refund.** Subtract Line 68 from Line 67. This is the amount to be refunded.			69	.00
70	Complete to direct deposit your refund Routing Number ☐☐☐☐☐☐☐☐☐ ☐ Checking or ☐ Savings Account Number ☐☐☐☐☐☐☐☐☐☐☐☐☐☐☐☐☐				
71	**Tax Due.** If Line 64 is greater than Line 66 subtract Line 66 from Line 64. This is the amount you owe.			71	934.00

Special Note Enter the amount of your payment on the top of Page 1 in the space provided.

Step 10: Sign below - Under penalties of perjury, I state that I have examined this return and, to the best of my knowledge, it is true, correct, and complete.

Sign Here	Signature of authorized officer	Date (mm/dd/yyyy)	Title	Phone ( )	☐ Check if the Department may discuss this return with the paid preparer shown in this step.
Paid Preparer Use Only	Print/Type paid preparer's name	Paid preparer's signature	Date (mm/dd/yyyy)	☐ Check if self-employed	Paid Preparer's PTIN
	Firm's name ▸			Firm's FEIN ▸	
	Firm's address ▸			Firm's phone ▸	( )

Refer to the 2022 IL-1120-ST Instructions for the address to mail your return.

IL-1120-ST (R-12/22) Printed by the authority of the state of Illinois. Electronic only, one copy. Page 3 of 5

For Example 3

Illinois Department of Revenue
2022 Schedule B

Veridian Innovations
Enter your name as shown on your Form IL-1065 or Form IL-1120-ST.

9 9 - 9 9 9 9 9 9 9
Enter your federal employer identification number (FEIN).

Section B: Members' information (See instructions before completing.)

	Member 1	Member 2	Member 3	Member 4
A Name	Isaac Evers	Mary Quinn	Victor Zimbalist	
C/O				
Address 1	2002 Warner Ave.	64 Harley Ln	4680 Fries Dr	
Address 2				
City	Champaign	Champaign	Champaign	
State, ZIP	IL 61822	IL 61822	IL 61822	
B Partner or Shareholder	I	I	I	
C SSN/FEIN	***-**-4567	***-**-5678	***-**-6789	
D Subject to Illinois replacement tax or an ESOP	☐	☐	☐	☐
E Member's distributable amount of base income or loss	61,500	30,750	30,750	
F Excluded from pass-through withholding	T	T	T	
G Share of Illinois income subject to pass-through withholding	0	0	0	
H Pass-through withholding before credits	0	0	0	
I Distributable share of credits	0	0	0	
J Pass-through withholding amount	0	0	0	
K PTE tax credit paid to members	3,045	1,522	1,522	
L PTE tax credit received and distributed to members	0	0	0	

Note If you have more members than space provided, attach additional copies of this page as necessary.

Schedule B Back (R-12/22) Printed by the authority of the state of Illinois. Electronic only, one copy. Page 5 of 5

10

For its federal return, Veridian prepares Form 1120-S, *U.S. Income Tax Return for an S Corporation,* reporting its income and expenses. Notably, the company deducts $27,000 of taxes on line 12 ($20,000 payroll tax + $7,000 state tax). If Veridian had not made the PTE tax election, the company would not have paid the $7,000 of estimated tax to Illinois. Instead, each shareholder would report the income on their Illinois tax return and pay the state income tax at their level. The Form 1120-S follows.

Form **1120-S** — Department of the Treasury, Internal Revenue Service

U.S. Income Tax Return for an S Corporation

Do not file this form unless the corporation has filed or is attaching Form 2553 to elect to be an S corporation.
Go to *www.irs.gov/Form1120S* for instructions and the latest information.

OMB No. 1545-0123 — **2022**

For calendar year 2022 or tax year beginning , 2022, ending , 20

A S election effective date: **1/01/2002**	TYPE OR PRINT	Name: **Veridian Innovations**	**D Employer identification number**: **99-9999999**
B Business activity code number (see instructions): **449210**		Number, street, and room or suite no. If a P.O. box, see instructions.: **2002 Warner Ave.**	**E** Date incorporated: **1/01/2002**
C Check if Sch. M-3 attached ☐		City or town, state or province, country, and ZIP or foreign postal code: **Champaign IL 61822**	**F** Total assets (see instructions): $ **238,700**

G Is the corporation electing to be an S corporation beginning with this tax year? See instructions. ☐ Yes ☒ No

H Check if: **(1)** ☐ Final return **(2)** ☐ Name change **(3)** ☐ Address change **(4)** ☐ Amended return **(5)** ☐ S election termination

I Enter the number of shareholders who were shareholders during any part of the tax year **3**

J Check if corporation: **(1)** ☐ Aggregated activities for section 465 at-risk purposes **(2)** ☐ Grouped activities for section 469 passive activity purposes

Caution: Include **only** trade or business income and expenses on lines 1a through 21. See the instructions for more information.

Income	1a	Gross receipts or sales	1a	300,000		
	b	Returns and allowances	1b			
	c	Balance. Subtract line 1b from line 1a			1c	300,000
	2	Cost of goods sold (attach Form 1125-A)			2	
	3	Gross profit. Subtract line 2 from line 1c			3	300,000
	4	Net gain (loss) from Form 4797, line 17 (attach Form 4797)			4	
	5	Other income (loss) (see instructions—attach statement)			5	
	6	**Total income (loss).** Add lines 3 through 5			6	300,000
Deductions (see instructions for limitations)	7	Compensation of officers (see instructions—attach Form 1125-E)			7	
	8	Salaries and wages (less employment credits)			8	160,000
	9	Repairs and maintenance			9	
	10	Bad debts			10	
	11	Rents			11	
	12	Taxes and licenses			12	27,000
	13	Interest (see instructions)			13	
	14	Depreciation from Form 4562 not claimed on Form 1125-A or elsewhere on return (attach Form 4562)			14	
	15	Depletion **(Do not deduct oil and gas depletion.)**			15	
	16	Advertising			16	
	17	Pension, profit-sharing, etc., plans			17	
	18	Employee benefit programs			18	
	19	Other deductions (attach statement)			19	
	20	**Total deductions.** Add lines 7 through 19			20	187,000
	21	**Ordinary business income (loss).** Subtract line 20 from line 6			21	113,000
		Ex... net passive income or LIFO recapture tax (see instructions)	22a			

For Example 3

Form 1120-S (2022) Page 3

Schedule B **Other Information** (see instructions) *(continued)*

		Yes	No
12	During the tax year, did the corporation have any non-shareholder debt that was canceled, was forgiven, or had the terms modified so as to reduce the principal amount of the debt?		
	If "Yes," enter the amount of principal reduction . . . $		
13	During the tax year, was a qualified subchapter S subsidiary election terminated or revoked? If "Yes," see instructions		
14a	Did the corporation make any payments in 2022 that would require it to file Form(s) 1099?		
b	If "Yes," did or will the corporation file required Form(s) 1099?		
15	Is the corporation attaching Form 8996 to certify as a Qualified Opportunity Fund?		
	If "Yes," enter the amount from Form 8996, line 15 . . . $		

Schedule K **Shareholders' Pro Rata Share Items**

					Line	Total amount
Income (Loss)	1	Ordinary business income (loss) (page 1, line 21)			1	113,000
	2	Net rental real estate income (loss) (attach Form 8825)			2	
	3a	Other gross rental income (loss)	3a			
	b	Expenses from other rental activities (attach statement)	3b			
	c	Other net rental income (loss). Subtract line 3b from line 3a			3c	
	4	Interest income			4	3,000
	5	Dividends: **a** Ordinary dividends			5a	
		b Qualified dividends	5b			
	6	Royalties			6	
	7	Net short-term capital gain (loss) (attach Schedule D (Form 1120-S))			7	
	8a	Net long-term capital gain (loss) (attach Schedule D (Form 1120-S))			8a	
	b	Collectibles (28%) gain (loss)	8b			
	c	Unrecaptured section 1250 gain (attach statement)	8c			
	9	Net section 1231 gain (loss) (attach Form 4797)			9	
	10	Other income (loss) (see instructions) . . . Type:			10	
	11	Section 179 deduction (attach Form 4562)				

Isaac, Veridian's CEO, is a single taxpayer with no other source of income. He uses Schedule K-1 to prepare his Form 1040, *U.S. Individual Income Tax Return*, where he reports the activity on part II of Schedule E, *Supplemental Income and Loss*. Isaac reports the $56,500 of ordinary business income ($113,000 ordinary income × 50% ownership) from Schedule K-1, line 1 on Schedule E, part II, line 28. This flows to Schedule 1, *Additional Income and Adjustments to Income*, on line 5 for income from S corporations. The $56,500 then flows to line 8 on Form 1040, which is added to Isaac's share of interest income of $1,500 he reports on line 2b, which was included on Schedule K-1, line 4. Isaac's total AGI is $58,000 ($1,500 interest + $56,500 ordinary business income). Isaac's federal forms follow.

Observation. Without the PTE election and estimates paid by Veridian, Isaac's amount on line 1 of Schedule K-1 would be $60,000 ($56,500 ordinary business income + 50% of $7,000 state tax).

For Example 3

671121

☐ Final K-1 ☐ Amended K-1 OMB No. 1545-0123

Schedule K-1 (Form 1120-S) **2022**

Department of the Treasury
Internal Revenue Service

For calendar year 2022, or tax year

beginning 1 / 1 / 2022 ending 12 / 31 / 2022

Shareholder's Share of Income, Deductions, Credits, etc. See separate instructions.

Part I Information About the Corporation

A Corporation's employer identification number
99-9999999

B Corporation's name, address, city, state, and ZIP code
Veridian Innovations
2002 Warner Ave
Champaign IL 61822

C IRS Center where corporation filed return
e-file

D Corporation's total number of shares
Beginning of tax year **100**
End of tax year **100**

Part II Information About the Shareholder

E Shareholder's identifying number
*****-**-4567**

F Shareholder's name, address, city, state, and ZIP code
Isaac Evers
2002 Warner Ave.
Champaign, IL 61822

Part III Shareholder's Share of Current Year Income, Deductions, Credits, and Other Items

1	Ordinary business income (loss) **56,500**	13	Credits	
2	Net rental real estate income (loss)			
3	Other net rental income (loss)			
4	Interest income **1,500**			
5a	Ordinary dividends			
5b	Qualified dividends	14	Schedule K-3 is attached if checked . . . . . ☐	
6	Royalties	15	Alternative minimum tax (AMT) items	
7	Net short-term capital gain (loss)			
8a	Net long-term capital gain (loss)			
8b	Collectibles (28%) gain (loss)			
8c	Unrecaptured section 1250 gain			
9	Net section 1231 gain (loss)	16	Items affecting shareholder basis	
10	Other income (loss)			

Schedule E (Form 1040) 2022 Attachment Sequence No. **13** Page **2**

Name(s) shown on return. Do not enter name and social security number if shown on other side. **Isaac Evers**

Your social security number *****-**-4567**

Caution: The IRS compares amounts reported on your tax return with amounts shown on Schedule(s) K-1.

Part II Income or Loss From Partnerships and S Corporations

Note: If you report a loss, receive a distribution, dispose of stock, or receive a loan repayment from an S corporation, you **must** check the box in column **(e)** on line 28 and attach the required basis computation. If you report a loss from an at-risk activity for which **any** amount is **not** at risk, you **must** check the box in column **(f)** on line 28 and attach **Form 6198**. See instructions.

27 Are you reporting any loss not allowed in a prior year due to the at-risk or basis limitations, a prior year unallowed loss from a passive activity (if that loss was not reported on Form 8582), or unreimbursed partnership expenses? If you answered "Yes," see instructions before completing this section . . . ☐ **Yes** ☒ **No**

28	(a) Name	(b) Enter P for partnership; S for S corporation	(c) Check if foreign partnership	(d) Employer identification number	(e) Check if basis computation is required	(f) Check if any amount is not at risk
A	Veridian Innovations	S	☐	99-9999999	☐	☐
B			☐		☐	☐
C			☐		☐	☐
D			☐		☐	☐

	Passive Income and Loss		Nonpassive Income and Loss		
	(g) Passive loss allowed (attach **Form 8582** if required)	(h) Passive income from **Schedule K-1**	(i) Nonpassive loss allowed (see **Schedule K-1**)	(j) Section 179 expense deduction from **Form 4562**	(k) Nonpassive income from **Schedule K-1**
A					56,500
B					
C					
D					
29a Totals					56,500
b Totals					

30	Add columns (h) and (k) of line 29a . . .	30	56,500
31	Add columns (g), (i), and (j) of line 29b. . . .	31	( )
32	**Total partnership and S corporation income or (loss).** Combine lines 30 and 31 . . .	32	56,500

Income or Loss From Estates and Trusts

For Example 3

Form 1040 Department of the Treasury—Internal Revenue Service
U.S. Individual Income Tax Return **2022** OMB No. 1545-0074 IRS Use Only—Do not write or staple in this space.

Filing Status Check only one box. ☒ Single ☐ Married filing jointly ☐ Married filing separately (MFS) ☐ Head of household (HOH) ☐ Qualifying surviving spouse (QSS)

If you checked the MFS box, enter the name of your spouse. If you checked the HOH or QSS box, enter the child's name if the qualifying person is a child but not your dependent:

Your first name and middle initial	Last name	Your social security number
Isaac Evers		*** ** 4567
If joint return, spouse's first name and middle initial	Last name	Spouse's social security number

Home address (number and street). If you have a P.O. box, see instructions.		Apt. no.
2002 Warner Ave.		
City, town, or post office. If you have a foreign address, also complete spaces below.	State	ZIP code
Champaign	IL	61822
Foreign country name	Foreign province/state/county	Foreign postal code

Presidential Election Campaign Check here if you, or your spouse if filing jointly, want $3 to go to this fund. Checking a box below will not change your tax or refund. ☐ You ☐ Spouse

Digital Assets At any time during 2022, did you: (a) receive (as a reward, award, or payment for property or services); or (b) sell, exchange, gift, or otherwise dispose of a digital asset (or a financial interest in a digital asset)? (See instructions.) ☐ Yes ☒ No

Standard Deduction **Someone can claim:** ☐ You as a dependent ☐ Your spouse as a dependent
☐ Spouse itemizes on a separate return or you were a dual-status alien

Age/Blindness **You:** ☐ Were born before January 2, 1958 ☐ Are blind **Spouse:** ☐ Was born before January 2, 1958 ☐ Is blind

Dependents (see instructions): If more than four dependents, see instructions and check here ☐

(1) First name	Last name	(2) Social security number	(3) Relationship to you	(4) Child tax credit	(4) Credit for other dependents
				☐	☐
				☐	☐
				☐	☐
				☐	☐

Income

Attach Form(s) W-2 here. Also attach Forms W-2G and 1099-R if tax was withheld. If you did not get a Form W-2, see instructions.

1a	Total amount from Form(s) W-2, box 1 (see instructions)	1a	
b	Household employee wages not reported on Form(s) W-2	1b	
c	Tip income not reported on line 1a (see instructions)	1c	
d	Medicaid waiver payments not reported on Form(s) W-2 (see instructions)	1d	
e	Taxable dependent care benefits from Form 2441, line 26	1e	
f	Employer-provided adoption benefits from Form 8839, line 29	1f	
g	Wages from Form 8919, line 6	1g	
h	Other earned income (see instructions)	1h	
i	Nontaxable combat pay election (see instructions) 1i		
z	Add lines 1a through 1h	1z	
2a	Tax-exempt interest 2a ; b Taxable interest	2b	1,500
3a	Qualified dividends 3a ; b Ordinary dividends	3b	
4a	IRA distributions 4a ; b Taxable amount	4b	
5a	Pensions and annuities 5a ; b Taxable amount	5b	
6a	Social security benefits 6a ; b Taxable amount	6b	
c	If you elect to use the lump-sum election method, check here (see instructions) ☐		
7	Capital gain or (loss). Attach Schedule D if required. If not required, check here ☐	7	
8	Other income from Schedule 1, line 10	8	56,500
9	Add lines 1z, 2b, 3b, 4b, 5b, 6b, 7, and 8. This is your **total income**	9	58,000
10	Adjustments to income from Schedule 1, line 26	10	
11	Subtract line 10 from line 9. This is your **adjusted gross income**	11	58,000
12	**Standard deduction or itemized deductions** (from Schedule A)	12	
13	Qualified business income deduction from Form 8995 or Form 8995-A	13	
14	Add lines 12 and 13	14	
15	Subtract line 14 from line 11. If zero or less, enter -0-. This is your **taxable income**	15	

Attach Sch. B if required.

Standard Deduction for—
- Single or Married filing separately, $12,950
- Married filing jointly or Qualifying surviving spouse, $25,900
- Head of household, $19,400
- If you checked any box under *Standard Deduction*, see instructions.

For Disclosure, Privacy Act, and Paperwork Reduction Act Notice, see separate instructions. Cat. No. 11320B Form **1040** (2022)

10

The $56,500 of pass-through income includes Isaac's share of the PTE tax that Veridian paid of $3,045 ($6,089 PTE tax × 50% ownership interest). Consequently, Isaac can deduct the Illinois income tax on his share of pass-through income from Veridian, regardless of whether he itemizes his expenses.

Isaac uses Schedule K-1-P to prepare his 2022 Form IL-1040, *Individual Income Tax Return.* He reports his federal AGI of $58,000 on line 1 but must add back $3,500 of Illinois tax (reported on Schedule K-1-P, line 33) to arrive at his Illinois base income of $61,500. After factoring in his Illinois exemption and property tax credit, Isaac calculates his Illinois income tax of $2,471. However, because Veridian paid PTE tax on his behalf, Isaac reports a PTE tax credit of $3,045 on line 28 of Form IL-1040. Isaac finds this amount on his Schedule K-1-P, line 53a. Because the refundable tax credit exceeds his tax liability, Isaac is due a refund of $574 ($3,045 PTE credit – $2,471 liability). Isaac's Illinois forms follow.

Illinois Department of Revenue

Schedule K-1-P

Partner's or Shareholder's Share of Income, Deductions, Credits, and Recapture

Year ending 12 2022 (Month / Year)

To be completed by partnerships filing Form IL-1065 or S corporations filing Form IL-1120-ST.

IL Attachment No. 12

Partners and Shareholders receiving Schedule K-1-P should attach this to their Illinois tax return.

Step 1: Identify your partnership or S corporation

1 Check your business type ☐ partnership ☒ S corporation

3 99-9999999 Enter your federal employer identification number (FEIN).

2 Veridian Innovations
Enter your name as shown on your Form IL-1065 or Form IL-1120-ST.

4 Enter the apportionment factor from Form IL-1065 or Form IL-1120-ST, Line 42. Otherwise, enter "1." 1

Step 2: Identify your partner or shareholder

5 Isaac Evers
Name

6 2002 Warner Ave.
Mailing address

Champaign IL 61822
City State ZIP

7 ***-**-4567
Social Security number or FEIN

8 50
Share (%)

9a Check the appropriate box. See instructions.
☒ individual ☐ corporation ☐ trust
☐ partnership ☐ S corporation ☐ estate

9b **To be completed by the recipient on Line 5 only.**
I am a: ☐ grantor trust ☐ disregarded entity
and the amounts on this schedule will be reported by:
Name: ______
SSN or FEIN: ______

Step 3: Figure your partner's or shareholder's share of your nonbusiness income or loss

			A Member's share (See instructions.)	B Member's share allocable to Illinois
10	Interest	10		
11	Dividends	11		
12	Rental income	12		
13	Patent royalties	13		
14	Copyright royalties	14		
15	Other royalty income	15		
16	Capital gain or loss from real property	16		
17	Capital gain or loss from tangible personal property	17		
18	Capital gain or loss from intangible personal property	18		
19	Other income and expense ______ Specify	19		

Step 4: Figure your partner's or shareholder's share of your business income or loss

			A Member's share from U.S. Schedule K-1, less nonbusiness income	B Member's share apportioned to Illinois
20	Ordinary income or loss from trade or business activity	20	56,500	56,500
21	Net income or loss from rental real estate activities	21		
22	Net income or loss from other rental activities	22		
23	Interest	23	1,500	1,500
24	Dividends	24		
25	Royalties	25		
26	Net short-term capital gain or loss	26		
27	Net long-term capital gain or loss. Total for year.	27		
28	Unrecaptured Section 1250 gain	28		
29	Guaranteed payments to partner (U.S. Form 1065 only)	29		
30	Net Section 1231 gain or loss (other than casualty or theft). Total for year.	30		
31	Other income and expense ______ Specify	31		

Schedule K-1-P Front (R-12/22)

This form is authorized as outlined by the Illinois Income Tax Act. Disclosure of this information is REQUIRED. Failure to provide this information could result in a penalty.

For Example 3

Enter identification number from Line 7.
***-**-4567

Step 5: Figure your partner's or shareholder's share of Illinois additions and subtractions

K-1-P Recipient: Before using the information provided in Step 5, you must read Schedule K-1-P(2) to correctly report the amounts listed in Columns A and B.

		A Member's share from Form IL-1065 or IL-1120-ST	B Member's share apportioned or allocated to Illinois
Additions			
32 Federally tax-exempt interest income	32		
33 Illinois taxes and surcharge deducted. See instructions.	33	3,500	3,500
34 Illinois Special Depreciation addition	34		
35 Related-Party Expenses addition	35		
36 Distributive share of additions	36		
37 Other additions (from Illinois Schedule M for businesses)	37		
Subtractions			
38 a Interest from U.S. Treasury obligations (business income)	38a		
b Interest from U.S. Treasury obligations (nonbusiness income)	38b		
39 River Edge Redevelopment Zone Dividend subtraction	39		
40 High Impact Business Dividend subtraction	40		
41 Contribution subtraction (Form IL-1120-ST filers only)	41		
42 River Edge Redevelopment Zone Interest subtraction (Form IL-1120-ST financial organizations only)	42		
43 High Impact Business within a Foreign Trade Zone Interest subtraction (Form IL-1120-ST financial organizations only)	43		
44 Illinois Special Depreciation subtraction	44		
45 Related-Party Expenses subtraction	45		
46 Distributive share of subtractions	46		
47 Other subtractions (from Illinois Schedule M for businesses)	47		

Step 6: Figure your partner's or shareholder's (except a corporate partner or shareholder) share of your Illinois August 1, 1969, appreciation amounts

		A Member's share from Illinois Schedule F (Form IL-1065 or IL-1120-ST)	B Member's share apportioned or allocated to Illinois
48 Section 1245 and 1250 gain	48		
49 Section 1231 gain	49		
50 Section 1231 gain less casualty and theft gain. See instructions.	50		
51 Capital gain	51		

Step 7: Figure your partner's or shareholder's share of your Illinois credits, recapture, pass-through withholding, pass-through entity tax credit, and federal income subject to surcharge

52 Illinois Income Tax Credits	Credit Code		Member's share from Illinois tax return
a Film Production Services	5000	52a	
b Enterprise Zone Investment	5080	52b	
c Enterprise Zone Construction Jobs	5120	52c	
d High Impact Business Construction Jobs	5160	52d	
e Affordable Housing Donations	5260	52e	
f EDGE	5300	52f	
g New Construction EDGE	5320	52g	
h Research and Development	5340	52h	
i Wages Paid to Ex-Felons	5380	52i	
j Student-Assistance Contributions	5420	52j	
k Angel Investment	5460	52k	
l New Markets Development	5500	52l	
m River Edge Historic Preservation	5540	52m	
n River Edge Construction Jobs	5560	52n	
o Live Theater Production	5580	52o	
p Hospital	5620	52p	
q Invest in Kids	5660	52q	
r Data Center Construction Employment	5820	52r	
s Apprenticeship Education Expense	0160	52s	
t Historic Preservation	1030	52t	
u REV Illinois Investment	5230	52u	
v Agritourism Liability Insurance	5440	52v	
w Recovery and Mental Health	0180	52w	
x Other income tax credits ______		52x	

		Member's share from Illinois tax return
53 Other credits		
a Pass-through Entity (PTE) Tax Credit See instructions.	53a	3,045
b Replacement Tax Investment Credits See instructions.	53b	
54 Recapture		
a Enterprise Zone or River Edge Redevelopment Zone Investment Credit recapture	54a	
b REV Illinois Investment Credit recapture	54b	
c Replacement Tax Investment Credit recapture	54c	
d Additional income tax credit recapture	54d	
55 Pass-through withholding See instructions.	55	
56 Federal income attributable to transactions subject to the Compassionate Use of Medical Cannabis Program Act surcharge. See instructions.	56	
57 Federal income attributable to the sale or exchange of assets by a gaming licensee surcharge. See instructions.	57	

Printed by the authority of the State of Illinois - web only - one copy.

Schedule K-1-P Back (R-12/22)

10

For Example 3

Illinois Department of Revenue
2022 Form IL-1040
Individual Income Tax Return

or for fiscal year ending __ __/__ __

Step 1: Personal Information Enter personal information and Social Security numbers (SSN). You must provide the entire SSN(s) - no partial SSN.

A Your first name and middle initial	Your last name	Year of birth	Your social security number
Isaac	Evers	1 9 8 7	***-**-4567
Spouse's first name and middle intial	Spouse's last name	Spouse's year of birth	Spouse's social security number

Mailing address (See inst. if foreign address)	Apartment number	City	State	Zip or postal code
2002 Warner Ave.		Champaign	IL	61822
Foreign nation if not US (do not abbreviate)	County (Illinois only)	Email address		

B Filing status: ☒ Single ☐ Married filing jointly ☐ Married filing separately ☐ Widowed ☐ Head of household

C Check If someone can claim you, or your spouse if filing jointly, as a dependent. See instructions. ☐ You ☐ Spouse

D Check the box if this applies to you during 2022: ☐ Nonresident - **Attach** Sch. NR ☐ Part-year resident - **Attach** Sch. NR

(Whole dollars only)

Step 2: Income

Line	Description		Amount
1	Federal adjusted gross income from your federal Form 1040 or 1040-SR, Line 11.	1	58,000 .00
2	Federally tax-exempt interest and dividend income from your federal Form 1040 or 1040-SR, Line 2a.	2	.00
3	Other additions. **Attach** Schedule M.	3	3,500 .00
4	**Total income**. Add Lines 1 through 3.	4	61,500 .00

Step 3: Base Income

Line	Description		Amount		Amount
5	Social Security benefits and certain retirement plan income received if included in Line 1. **Attach** Page 1 of federal return.	5	.00		
6	Illinois Income Tax overpayment included in federal Form 1040 or 1040-SR, Schedule 1, Ln. 1.	6	.00		
7	Other subtractions. **Attach** Schedule M.	7	.00		
8	Add Lines 5, 6, and 7. This is the total of your subtractions.			8	.00
9	**Illinois base income**. Subtract Line 8 from Line 4.			9	61,500 .00

Step 4: Exemptions

Line	Description		Amount		Amount
10	a Enter the exemption amount for yourself and your spouse. **See instructions.**	a	2,425 .00		
	b **Check** if 65 or older: ☐ You + ☐ Spouse **# of checkboxes X** $1,000 =	b	.00		
	c **Check** if legally blind: ☐ You + ☐ Spouse **# of checkboxes X** $1,000 =	c	.00		
	d If you are claiming dependents, enter the amount from Schedule IL-E/EIC, Step 2, Line 1. **Attach** Schedule IL-E/EIC.	d	.00		
	Exemption allowance. Add Lines 10a through 10d.			10	2,425 .00

Step 5: Net Income and Tax

Line	Description		Amount
11	***Residents:* Net income**. Subtract Line 10 from Line 9. ***Nonresidents and part-year residents:*** Enter the **Illinois net income** from Schedule NR. **Attach** Schedule NR.	11	59,075 .00
12	***Residents:*** Multiply Line 11 by 4.95% (.0495). Cannot be less than zero. ***Nonresidents and part-year residents:*** Enter the tax from Schedule NR.	12	2,924 .00
13	Recapture of investment tax credits. **Attach** Schedule 4255.	13	.00
14	**Income tax.** Add Lines 12 and 13. Cannot be less than zero.	14	2,924 .00

Step 6: Tax After Nonrefundable Credits

Line	Description		Amount		Amount
15	Income tax paid to another state while an Illinois resident. **Attach** Schedule CR.	15	.00		
16	Property tax and K-12 education expense credit amount from Schedule ICR. **Attach** Schedule ICR.	16	453 .00		
17	Credit amount from Schedule 1299-C. **Attach** Schedule 1299-C.	17	.00		
18	Add Lines 15, 16, and 17. This is the total of your credits. Cannot exceed the tax amount on Line 14.			18	453 .00
19	**Tax after nonrefundable credits.** Subtract Line 18 from Line 14.			19	2,471 .00

Step 7: Other Taxes

Line	Description		Amount
20	Household employment tax. See instructions.	20	.00
21	Use tax on internet, mail order, or other out-of-state purchases from UT Worksheet or UT Table in the instructions. **Do not** leave blank.	21	0 .00
22	Compassionate Use of Medical Cannabis Program Act and sale of assets by gaming licensee surcharges.	22	.00
23	**Total Tax**. Add Lines 19, 20, 21, and 22.	23	2,471 .00

Staple W-2 and 1099 forms here

Staple your check and IL-1040-V

IL-1040 Front (R-12/22) Printed by authority of the state of Illinois. Electronic only, one copy.

This form is authorized as outlined under the Illinois Income Tax Act. Disclosure of this information is required. Failure to provide information could result in a penalty.

For Example 3

24	Total tax from Page 1, Line 23.		24 2,471.00

Step 8: Payments and Refundable Credit

25	Illinois Income Tax withheld. **Attach** Schedule IL-WIT.	25 .00	
26	Estimated payments from Forms IL-1040-ES and IL-505-I, including any overpayment applied from a prior year return.	26 .00	
27	Pass-through withholding. **Attach** Schedule K-1-P or K-1-T.	27 .00	
28	Pass-through entity tax credit. **Attach** Schedule K-1-P or K-1-T.	28 3,045.00	
29	Earned Income Credit from Schedule IL-E/EIC, Step 4, Line 8. **Attach** Schedule IL-E/EIC.	29 .00	
30	**Total payments and refundable credit**. Add Lines 25 through 29.		30 3,045.00

Step 9: Total

31	If Line 30 is greater than Line 24, subtract Line 24 from Line 30.		31 574.00
32	If Line 24 is greater than Line 30, subtract Line 30 from Line 24.		32 .00

Step 10: Underpayment of Estimated Tax Penalty and Donations

33 Late-payment penalty for underpayment of estimated tax. 33 .00

- a ☐ Check if at least two-thirds of your federal gross income is from farming.
- b ☐ Check if you or your spouse are 65 or older and permanently living in a nursing home.
- c ☐ Check if your income was not received evenly during the year and you annualized your income on Form IL-2210. **Attach** Form IL-2210.
- d ☐ Check if you were not required to file an Illinois Individual Income Tax return in the previous tax year.

34 Voluntary charitable donations. **Attach** Schedule G. 34 .00

35 **Total penalty and donations**. Add Lines 33 and 34. 35 .00

Step 11: Refund or Amount you owe

36 If you have an amount on Line 31 and this amount is greater than Line 35, subtract Line 35 from Line 31. This is your **overpayment**. 36 574.00

37 Amount from Line 36 you want **refunded to you**. Check **one** box on Line 38. See instructions. 37 574.00

38 I choose to receive my refund by

a ☐ **direct deposit** - Complete the information below if you check this box.

You may also contribute to college savings funds here. See instructions!

Routing number ☐☐☐☐☐☐☐☐☐ ☐ Checking or ☐ Savings

Account number ☐☐☐☐☐☐☐☐☐☐☐☐☐☐☐☐☐

b ☒ **paper check.**

39 Amount to be **credited forward.** Subtract Line 37 from Line 36. See instructions. 39 .00

40 If you have an amount on Line 32, add Lines 32 and 35. **- or -** If you have an amount on Line 31 and this amount is less than Line 35, subtract Line 31 from Line 35. This is the **amount you owe**. See instructions. 40 .00

Step 12: Health Insurance Checkbox and Signature

41 ☐ Check this box if IDOR may share your income information with other Illinois state agencies in order to determine your eligibility for health insurance benefits. See instructions for more information.

Signature - Note: If this is a joint return, both you and your spouse must sign below.
Under penalties of perjury, I state that I have examined this return and, to the best of my knowledge, it is true, correct, and complete.

Sign Here	Your signature	Date (mm/dd/yyyy)	Spouse's signature	Date (mm/dd/yyyy)	Daytime phone number ( )
Paid Preparer Use Only	Print/Type paid preparer's name		Paid preparer's signature	Date (mm/dd/yyyy)	☐ Check if self-employed / Paid Preparer's PTIN
	Firm's name ▸ **University of Illinois Tax School**			Firm's FEIN ▸	
	Firm's address ▸ **1301 West Gregory Drive Urbana IL 61801**			Firm's phone ▸	( )
Third Party Designee	Designee's name (please print)		Designee's phone number ( )		☒ Check if the Department may discuss this return with the third party designee shown in this step.

Refer to the 2022 IL-1040 Instructions for the address to mail your return.

IL-1040 Back (R-12/22) DR______ AP______ RR DC IR ID

10

CONCLUSION

The PTE tax election is an avenue to obtain a tax benefit beyond the $10,000 SALT limit for state income tax on pass-through income. The appeal of this method is dependent on the benefit of the federal tax deduction in comparison to the nuances and hurdles of navigating through a state's laws and procedures regarding the PTE tax. The shareholders' tax situations also drive the decision-making process in evaluating the benefits of the PTE tax election. Another factor to consider is the time and effort to plan, implement, and execute the PTE tax election.

Practitioner Planning Tip

Each state's laws, procedures, and requirements regarding the PTE tax election are different, and the shareholders' tax positions can vary widely. PTEs and their tax practitioners should utilize the discussion points and considerations to assess whether adopting the PTE tax election is an optimal strategy for them to apply in their specific circumstances.

CORPORATE TRANSPARENCY ACT

In 2021, Congress passed the Corporate Transparency Act[43] that subjects certain companies operating in and from the United States to additional reporting requirements to the Financial Crimes Enforcement Network (FinCEN). Congress's goal is to curtail money laundering and terrorism financing through companies by providing law enforcement and security agencies with information on the owners of existing and new businesses.[44] With these requirements being effective on **January 1, 2024,** company owners and tax practitioners need to familiarize themselves with the provisions of the Corporate Transparency Act and plan accordingly.[45]

REPORTING COMPANIES

The entities subject to the new beneficial ownership information reporting requirements mandated by the Corporate Transparency Act are known as **reporting companies.** Reporting companies consist of any corporation, limited liability company (LLC), or other entity created by a filing with a secretary of state.[46] This definition also applies to foreign companies created under foreign law but registered to do business in the United States by filing with a secretary of state.[47] S corporations, C corporations, and partnerships more than likely have filed with a secretary of state to conduct business within that state. Depending on the state and facts and circumstances, sole proprietors may require filing with a secretary of state.[48]

---

43. The *Corporate Transparency Act* was enacted as part of the *Anti-Money Laundering Act of 2020*, which added new Section 31 USC 5336 to the Bank Secrecy Act.

44. *Corporate Transparency Act*, §6402.

45. *Beneficial Ownership Information Reporting Requirements*. Sep. 30, 2022. Financial Crimes Enforcement Network. [www.federalregister.gov/documents/2022/09/30/2022-21020/beneficial-ownership-information-reporting-requirements] Accessed on Jul. 27, 2023.

46. 31 USC §5336(a)(11)(A).

47. Ibid.

48. To look up the requirements by state, see *Business Formation Laws and Forms: 50-State Survey*. Oct. 2022. Justia. [www.justia.com/business-operations/business-forms-50-state-resources] Accessed on Jul. 27, 2023.

Practitioner Planning Tip

Practitioners should check with their clients to verify if they made such filings to determine whether they may be subject to the reporting requirements under the Corporate Transparency Act.

While the definition of a reporting company is broad, there are numerous exceptions that the law does not consider as reporting companies. The following **are not reporting companies** subject to additional disclosure requirements.[49]

- Publicly traded companies and entities filing reports with the Securities and Exchange Commission (SEC)
- Entities exercising governmental authority on behalf of the U.S. government
- Banks, credit unions, bank holding companies, and registered money-transmitting businesses
- Securities brokers and dealers
- Entities registered with the SEC
- Investment advisors
- Insurance companies
- Public accounting firms
- Public utility providers
- Non-profit organizations, including charities, political organizations, and trusts
- Entities employing **over 20 full-time employees** with **over $5 million in gross receipts** for the previous year (including receipts for entities for which it owns or is owned) that have an operating presence at a **physical office located in the United States**
- Entities existing for over one year not actively engaged in business, not directly or indirectly owned by a foreign person, did not change ownership, or send or receive over $1,000 in the last year, and do not hold any assets, including ownership in other entities
- Entities that the Secretary of the Treasury, the Attorney General, and the Secretary of Homeland Security have jointly determined are not subject to the reporting requirements due to such information not serving the public interest and not being useful to securities agencies or law enforcement in their efforts to prevent money laundering, financing terrorism, and other financial crimes

10

49. 31 USC §5336(a)(11)(B).

BENEFICIAL OWNERSHIP INFORMATION

As mentioned previously, the information disclosure mandated by the Corporate Transparency Act pertains to information about a reporting company's ownership. Specifically, reporting companies must submit information on all beneficial owners and the applicant, collectively known as **beneficial ownership information.** A **beneficial owner** is an individual or entity directly or indirectly exercising substantial control over the entity and owns or controls at least 25% of the entity's ownership interests.[50] An **applicant** is an individual who applies through a filing to form an entity under a state's laws or, in the case of a foreign entity, register with a secretary of state to do business in the United States.[51]

Required Beneficial Ownership Information[52]

Reporting companies required to submit beneficial ownership information must disclose the following information for each beneficial owner and applicant of the entity.

1. Name
2. Date of birth
3. Current residential or business address
4. Unique identification number or FinCEN identifier

Unique identification numbers must derive from a nonexpired U.S. passport, state identification card, or driver's license. A nonexpired foreign passport is acceptable if a beneficial owner or applicant does not have such documents.[53] A FinCEN identifier is an alternative identification number provided by FinCEN. An individual must provide FinCEN with the aforementioned required information to receive a FinCEN identifier for use in a beneficial ownership information report.[54]

Required Reporting Company Information

While the Corporate Transparency Act does not specify the information a reporting company must provide about the entity itself, FinCEN issued guidance identifying what information they require reporting companies to disclose. Reporting companies must include the following information about the reporting company in their report.[55]

1. Full name
2. Trade name or "doing business as" name
3. Business street address
4. State of formation
5. IRS taxpayer identification number (TIN)

---

50. 31 USC §5336(a)(3)(A).

51. 31 USC §5336(a)(2).

52. 31 USC §5336(b)(2)(A).

53. 31 USC §5336(a)(1).

54. 31 USC §5336(b)(3).

55. *Beneficial Ownership Information Reporting Requirements*. Sep. 30, 2022. Financial Crimes Enforcement Network. [www.federalregister.gov/documents/2022/09/30/2022-21020/beneficial-ownership-information-reporting-requirements] Accessed on Jul. 27, 2023.

Recipient of the Filed Information[56]

FinCEN will receive and process the information in the filed beneficial ownership reports. While FinCEN must maintain the confidentiality of the report's contents, they are authorized to provide the information contained therein to federal agencies in the intelligence, national security, and law enforcement fields. Additionally, state or local law enforcement may receive the information for use in a criminal or civil investigation as authorized by a court of competent jurisdiction. Financial institutions may receive the filed information to comply with customer due diligence requirements.

FILING REQUIREMENTS[57]

Reporting companies must submit a report containing beneficial ownership information to FinCEN electronically through its website, **www.fincen.gov**. FinCEN will accept reports beginning on January 1, 2024. Reporting companies created **before January 1, 2024,** must submit their beneficial ownership information report by **January 1, 2025.** Reporting companies created on or after January 1, 2024, must submit their initial report **within 30 days of their creation.** All reporting companies must file updated FinCEN reports within 30 days of any changes to required beneficial ownership information or reporting company information disclosed in a filed report. Consequently, filers must be aware of and track any changes in reporting information to maintain compliance with the Corporate Transparency Act. There is no fee for submitting the report to FinCEN.

FAILURE OF COMPLIANCE[58]

If reporting companies **willfully fail to file** a beneficial ownership information report or provide false or fraudulent information, they may be subject to criminal and civil penalties. The penalty is $500 per day the violation continues or has not been remedied, but shall not exceed $10,000 and not include imprisonment exceeding two years. The penalties for **unauthorized use or disclosure** of beneficial ownership information are more severe, with penalties not to exceed $250,000 and imprisonment not exceeding five years. However, if a filer believes a report contains inaccurate information and voluntarily submits a corrected report within 90 days of filing the erroneous report, the filer will not incur a penalty. This safe harbor against penalties does not apply to filers who, when filing, knew the report contained inaccuracies and purposefully acted to evade the reporting requirements.

Practitioner Planning Tip

As the penalty for noncompliance is high, entities must identify whether they are subject to reporting requirements. If they are required to file a report with FinCEN, reporting companies must accumulate the required information and submit it promptly. As this is a new rule that will begin in 2024, practitioners can provide value to their clients by alerting them to this new requirement and directing them to authoritative guidance to aid in their assessment, collecting, and submission of beneficial ownership information to avoid noncompliance with the Corporate Transparency Act.

56. 31 USC §5336(c)(2).

57. *Beneficial Ownership Information Reporting Frequently Asked Questions.* 2023. Financial Crimes Enforcement Network. [www.fincen.gov/boi-faqs] Accessed on Jul. 27, 2023.

58. 31 USC §5336(h).

FORM 7203

In recent years, the IRS has faced pressure to ensure that S corporation shareholders properly calculate their basis in S corporations,[59] and in December 2021, released Form 7203, *S Corporation Shareholder Stock and Debt Basis Limitations*. This section discusses how tax professionals can use Form 7203 to protect their clients' interests, properly report items on their tax return, and maintain their compliance with the Code and treasury regulations regarding basis.

The **shareholder** files Form 7203, not the S corporation. **It is the shareholder's responsibility to maintain their basis amounts.**

FORM 7203 OVERVIEW[60]

Accurately calculating basis is essential in gain or loss calculations because it affects the amount of taxable income or loss an individual or business reports on their tax return. Basis determines the amount of gain or loss on the sale or disposition of property, including stock of an S corporation.[61] If the basis is reported inaccurately, it can result in the underreporting or overreporting of income or losses.

The instructions for Form 7203 state that the IRS requires the form in the following circumstances.

- The shareholder is claiming a deduction for an aggregate loss from an S corporation that was not allowed in the previous year because they lacked basis
- The shareholder received a distribution from an S corporation
- The shareholder disposed of stock in an S corporation, even if no gain was recognized
- The shareholder received a loan repayment from an S corporation

In other words, anytime a taxable gain could be missed because a taxpayer's basis in an S corporation was miscalculated, they must file Form 7203 with their Form 1040. Although the dependence on accurate basis calculations is well established when a taxpayer disposes of stock, it is a less-established issue when a loan repayment is made, as discussed later.

Practitioner Planning Tip

Despite the requirement to file Form 7203 only for the individuals listed previously in the year required, tax practitioners should prepare Form 7203 each year because they will need the information in a future year.

---

59. *Tax Gap: Action Needed to Address Noncompliance with S Corporation Tax Rules.* Jan. 14, 2010. U.S. Government Accountability Office. [www.gao.gov/products/gao-10-195] Accessed on Jul. 11, 2023.

60. Instructions for Form 7203; See Form 7203.

61. IRC §1001(a).

Shareholder Identification

A shareholder enters their name on the first line of the form, and their social security number, if a natural person. If a taxpayer files a joint return and their spouse also receives a Schedule K-1 from the S corporation, the spouse must file a separate Form 7203. If the shareholder is an eligible estate,[62] an eligible trust,[63] or eligible charity,[64] their name should be entered on this line and their employer identification number (EIN) in the box labeled "Identifying number."

The S corporation itself is named on line A immediately beneath the shareholder's name. Its EIN is entered in the box B labeled "Employer identification number."

Tracking Stock Acquisition Block-by-Block (Item C)[65]

Form 7203, item C provides a space to enter a stock block's identification. If more than one block of stock exists, shareholders should expect to file multiple copies of Form 7203.

Note. Taxpayers may be required to file multiple Forms 7203 if during the year, there were capital contributions with different bases.[66] Each form is clearly distinguished by the indication of its stock block in item C near the top of the form's first page.

The form's instructions suggest that tracking different blocks is important when a partial stock sale or partial stock redemption occurs. Different stock blocks can have different bases.

Stock Acquisition Method (Item D)[67]

New for the 2022 version of Form 7203, a shareholder has five options to select as to how they acquired their stock.

1. Original shareholder
2. Purchased
3. Inherited
4. Gift
5. Other, which requires additional explanation by the shareholder

10

Practitioner Planning Tip

The presence of a gift option on Form 7203 suggests that shareholders who give their stock to another may wish to document the gift with a letter stating their basis in the stock and retain any copies of Form 709, *United States Gift (and Generation-Skipping Transfer) Tax Return*, that they may be required to file.

62. IRC §1361(c)(3).
63. IRC §1361(c)(2).
64. IRC §1361(c)(6).
65. Treas. Reg. §§1.1367-1(b)(2) and (c)(3).
66. Instructions for Form 7203 (2022).
67. Ibid.

Treas. Reg. §1.1367-1(g) Election (Item E)

New for the 2022 version of Form 7203 is an area for a shareholder to indicate they have elected to flip the order in which the following are deducted from their stock basis.

- Nondeductible and noncapital expenses,[68] as well as any oil and gas depletion deduction[69]
- Separately stated and non-separately stated items of loss and deduction[70]

Taxpayers may benefit from this election if their stock basis in an S corporation is less than their share of its nondeductible and noncapital expenses. This election allows the taxpayer to deduct separately stated expenses in the year they incur them instead of carrying them forward to the next year. A carryforward to the next year can occur if the nondeductible expenses have reduced basis before the separately stated expenses have reduced basis.

> **Note.** At first glance, making this election seems to be an easy decision. However, under the default method, the nondeductible losses **do not** carry forward to reduce basis in future years. Conversely, under the elective method, nondeductible losses in excess of basis **do** carry forward to reduce basis in future years. Accordingly, more basis is preserved over the long run when the default method is used rather than the elective method under Treas. Reg. §1.1367-1(g).

STOCK BASIS

Determining stock basis is the first step in calculating a shareholder's overall basis. Contributions to the S corporation's capital are added to the shareholder's stock basis.[71]

Ordering Rules

The sequence of **adjustments to stock** basis appears in four steps.[72]

1. Increase in basis attributable to income items (Form 7203, line 3)
2. Decrease in stock basis due to a distribution (Form 7203, line 6)
3. Decrease due to nondeductible expenses (Form 7203, line 8)
4. Decrease due to items of loss (Form 7203, line 11)

The treasury regulations apply these four items on the last day of the tax year, generally December 31 for an S corporation, unless the shareholder disposed of stock during the year.[73]

---

68. Treas. Reg. §1.1367-1(f)(3), referencing IRC §1367(a)(2)(D).

69. IRC §1367(a)(2)(E).

70. IRC §§1367(a)(2)(B) and (C).

71. *S Corporation Stock and Debt Basis.* Oct. 13, 2022. IRS. [www.irs.gov/businesses/small-businesses-self-employed/s-corporation-stock-and-debt-basis] Accessed on Jul. 26, 2023.

72. IRC §1367; Treas. Reg. §1.1367-1(f).

73. Treas. Reg. §1.1367-1(d)(1).

Income Items.[74] A shareholder's stock basis is increased by the following items of income.

- Ordinary business income
- Net rental real estate income
- Other net rental income
- Interest income
- Dividend income
- Royalties
- Capital gains
- Net IRC §1231 gain
- Other income
- Tax-exempt income

Distributions.[75] Distributions must be made from an S corporation's stock basis, not its debt basis. Only nondividend distributions reduce stock basis; dividend distributions generally do not.[76] The S corporation is responsible for informing the shareholder of the amount of nondividend and dividend distributions.[77] A nondividend distribution in excess of stock basis is taxed as a capital gain on the shareholder's personal return. It is a long-term capital gain (LTCG) if the S corporation stock has been held for longer than one year.[78]

Nondividend distributions generally decrease basis because they are not included in a shareholder's income. Under some circumstances, however, nondividend distributions may be included in income. This would result in the nondividend distribution **not** reducing basis. This could happen if a shareholder receives a nondividend distribution despite having $0 stock basis. Because these distributions are only taken from stock basis and not debt basis, basis is only decreased if they are **not** included in the shareholder's income. If they are included in income because the shareholder has an insufficient stock basis, some or all of the distribution may be included in the shareholder's net increase.[79] These are treated as gain from the sale or exchange of property.[80] In this case, the taxable portion of the distribution is reported on the shareholder's Schedule D, *Capital Gains and Losses*, and not on Form 7203, on which distributions are normally reported.[81]

Nondeductible Expenses. Nondeductible expenses reduce a shareholder's stock and/or debt basis before loss and deduction items. If nondeductible expenses exceed stock and/or debt basis, they are not considered suspended but are carried forward to be used in a future year.[82] The nondeductible portion of meals expense and the oil and gas depletion deduction under IRC §1367(a)(2)(E) also decrease basis.[83]

10

---

74. Instructions for Form 1120-S.

75. *S Corporation Stock and Debt Basis.* Oct. 13, 2022. IRS. [www.irs.gov/businesses/small-businesses-self-employed/s-corporation-stock-and-debt-basis] Accessed on Aug. 1, 2023.

76. IRC §1368(c).

77. 2022 Instructions for Form 1120-S, p. 24.

78. *S Corporation Stock and Debt Basis.* Oct. 13, 2022. IRS. [www.irs.gov/businesses/small-businesses-self-employed/s-corporation-stock-and-debt-basis] Accessed on Jul. 25, 2023.

79. IRC §1367(a)(2)(A).

80. IRC §§1368(b)(1) and (2).

81. Instructions for Form 7203.

82. Ibid.

83. Treas. Reg. §1.1367-1(f)(3).

Losses. A shareholder's stock basis is further reduced by losses and certain deductions. These include the following.[84]

- Ordinary business loss
- Net rental real estate loss
- Other net rental loss
- Capital losses
- Net §1231 loss
- Other losses
- IRC §179 expense deduction[85]

However, these items cannot reduce a shareholder's stock basis below $0.[86] If a loss is greater than remaining basis, it is carried forward subject to allocation with other loss limitations.[87]

Part I — Shareholder Stock Basis

Part I addresses adjustments to **stock basis.** The following section highlights some of the information reported on part I.

Capital Contributions (line 2). Any additional capital contributions are recorded on line 2 along with any stock purchases made during the year. The value of the basis recorded depends on how a taxpayer acquired the stock.

- **Purchased stock** is generally recorded at cost.[88]
- For **contributed property** in an IRC §351 exchange for stock, the stock basis is generally the carryover basis of assets transferred to the S corporation less the liabilities assumed by the S corporation.[89] This applies when the contributing shareholder controls at least 80% of the S corporation's stock.[90]
- **Inherited property** is generally fair market value (FMV) at the date of death or the alternate valuation date.[91]
- **Gifted stock** is generally the basis of the stock in the hands of the donor.[92]
- Stock received as **compensation** is recorded at FMV on the date the compensation is included in income.[93]
- **Noncash contributions** other than IRC §351 exchanges are valued at their basis in the hands of the shareholder. The shareholder increases their basis by the amount of any gain they recognize in making the transfer,[94] assuming no liabilities are transferred to the S corporation. However, the shareholder's basis is limited to the contributed property's FMV on the contribution date.[95]

---

84. See Instructions for Form 1120-S.
85. IRC §1366(a)(1).
86. IRC §1367(a)(2).
87. Treas. Reg. §1.1366-2(a)(3).
88. IRC §1012.
89. See IRC §358 for more information on the basis of stock received in a §351 transaction.
90. IRC §368(c).
91. See IRC §1014 and Treas. Reg. §1.1014-4 for more information.
92. See Treas. Regs. §§1.1015-1, 1.1366-2(a)(6), and 1.1366-2(a)(7).
93. See IRS Pub. 551, *Basis of Assets.*
94. IRC §362(a). See also IRC §1371 for the application of C corporation rules to S corporations.
95. IRC §362(d)(1).

Example 4. Sam incorporated Alpha Corporation on January 2, 2022, funding it with $2,000 of capital contributions, and immediately filed an S corporation election. In return, Sam acquired 200 shares of Alpha common stock.

After incorporation, Alpha has $2,000 in its bank account, and Sam has a $2,000 stock basis from his 2022 contributions. During 2022, Alpha loses $1,728, reducing Sam's stock basis at the end of the year to $272 ($2,000 – $1,728). Sam reports these transactions on the following Form 7203, part I.

Form **7203** (Rev. December 2022) Department of the Treasury Internal Revenue Service

S Corporation Shareholder Stock and Debt Basis Limitations

Attach to your tax return.
Go to *www.irs.gov/Form7203* for instructions and the latest information.

OMB No. 1545-2302
Attachment Sequence No. **203**

Name of shareholder	Identifying number
Sam Iam	*****-**-0987**
A Name of S corporation	**B** Employer identification number
Alpha Corporation	**12-3456789**

C Stock block (see instructions):

D Check applicable box(es) to indicate how stock was acquired:
(1) ☒ Original shareholder **(2)** ☐ Purchased **(3)** ☐ Inherited **(4)** ☐ Gift **(5)** ☐ Other:

E Check if you have a Regulations section 1.1367-1(g) election in effect during the tax year for this S corporation . . . . . . ☐

Part I Shareholder Stock Basis

1	Stock basis at the beginning of the corporation's tax year			1	0
2	Basis from any capital contributions made or additional stock acquired during the tax year			2	2,000
3a	Ordinary business income (enter losses in Part III)	3a			
b	Net rental real estate income (enter losses in Part III)	3b			
c	Other net rental income (enter losses in Part III)	3c			
d	Interest income	3d			
e	Ordinary dividends	3e			
f	Royalties	3f			
g	Net capital gains (enter losses in Part III)	3g			
h	Net section 1231 gain (enter losses in Part III)	3h			
i	Other income (enter losses in Part III)	3i			
j	Excess depletion adjustment	3j			
k	Tax-exempt income	3k			
l	Recapture of business credits	3l			
m	Other items that increase stock basis	3m			
4	Add lines 3a through 3m			4	
5	Stock basis before distributions. Add lines 1, 2, and 4			5	2,000
6	Distributions (excluding dividend distributions)			6	
	Note: If line 6 is larger than line 5, subtract line 5 from line 6 and report the result as a capital gain on Form 8949 and Schedule D. See instructions.				
7	Stock basis after distributions. Subtract line 6 from line 5. If the result is zero or less, enter -0-, skip lines 8 through 14, and enter -0- on line 15			7	2,000
8a	Nondeductible expenses	8a			
b	Depletion for oil and gas	8b			
c	Business credits (sections 50(c)(1) and (5))	8c			
9	Add lines 8a through 8c			9	
10	Stock basis before loss and deduction items. Subtract line 9 from line 7. If the result is zero or less, enter -0-, skip lines 11 through 14, and enter -0- on line 15			10	2,000
11	Allowable loss and deduction items. Enter the amount from line 47, column (c)			11	1,728
12	Debt basis restoration (see net increase in instructions for line 23)			12	
13	Other items that decrease stock basis			13	
14	Add lines 11, 12, and 13			14	1,728
15	**Stock basis at the end of the corporation's tax year.** Subtract line 14 from line 10. If the result is zero or less, enter -0-			15	272

Part II Shareholder Debt Basis

10

Separately and Nonseparately Stated Items (line 3). The series of separately and nonseparately stated items on line 3 reflect income information that appears on Schedule K-1 (Form 1120-S). Only positive amounts should appear on lines 3a through 3m, because negative amounts are reported in part III. The following items are listed on line 3.

- Ordinary business income (comes from Schedule K-1, box 1)
- Net rental real estate income (comes from Schedule K-1, box 2)
- Other net rental income (comes from Schedule K-1, box 3)
- Interest income (comes from Schedule K-1, box 4)
- Ordinary dividends (comes from Schedule K-1, box 5a)
- Royalties (comes from Schedule K-1, box 6)
- Net capital gains (comes from Schedule K-1, boxes 7 and 8a)
- Net §1231 gain (comes from Schedule K-1, box 9)
- Other income[96] (comes from Schedule K-1, box 10)
- Excess depletion adjustment (this is the amount by which the cumulative depletion deduction exceeds the proportionate share of basis in the property subject to depletion, **not** the actual depletion amount)[97] (comes from Schedule K-1, box 15, code C)
- Tax-exempt income (includes both tax-exempt interest income and other tax-exempt income) (comes from Schedule K-1, box 16, codes A and B)
- Recapture of business credits (see chart that follows)
- Other items that increase stock basis

S corporations may be required to recapture certain business credits, which can create taxable income, as well as increase basis. Line 31 includes recapture from the following credits, as denoted on Schedule K-1 with the following codes.[98]

Credit	Code for box 16 of Schedule K-1
Recapture of low-income housing credit through investments in partnerships subject to IRC §42(j)(5)	E
Recapture of low-income housing credit through investments in partnerships **not** subject to §42(j)(5)	F
Recapture of investment credit	G
Recapture of other credits, such as: • New markets credit • Indian employment credit • Credit for employer-provided childcare facilities and services • Alternative motor vehicle credit • Alternative fuel vehicle refueling property credit • Qualified plug-in electric motor vehicle credit	H

96. The instructions specifically refer to subpart F inclusion under IRC §959(a)(2), which relates to excluding previously taxed earnings. Discussion of subpart F is beyond the scope of this chapter.

97. See IRC §613.

98. 2022 Instructions for Schedule K-1 (Form 1120-S), p. 14.

Distributions (line 6). Generally, taxpayers report the distributions they receive from their S corporations on this line, as reported on Schedule K-1 (Form 1120-S) in box 16 with code D. Distributions that reduce basis are reported here because they are not included in the income of the shareholder; this is a specific requirement provided in the Code.[99] However, distributions from S corporations are included in a shareholder's income if they are made despite the shareholder's stock basis being $0.[100] In this event, the distribution is not reported on Form 7203, line 6. Instead, it is reported on the shareholder's Form 8949, *Sales and Other Dispositions of Capital Assets,* and then on Schedule D.[101] The amounts are not reported on line 6 because they are reported on Schedule D. They do not increase the stock basis for the amount of the capital gain distribution.

Example 5. Use the same facts as **Example 4,** except that Sam receives a $500 distribution on December 15, 2022, which reduces his stock basis to $1,500. The first $1,500 of the $1,728 loss reduces Sam's stock basis to $0. The remaining $228 ($1,728 loss – $1,500 remaining basis) is suspended and carried forward. This information is reported on the following Form 7203.

Form **7203** (Rev. December 2022) Department of the Treasury Internal Revenue Service

S Corporation Shareholder Stock and Debt Basis Limitations

Attach to your tax return.
Go to *www.irs.gov/Form7203* for instructions and the latest information.

OMB No. 1545-2302
Attachment Sequence No. **203**

Name of shareholder: **Sam Iam** — Identifying number: *****-**-0987**

A Name of S corporation: **Alpha Corporation** — B Employer identification number: **12-3456789**

C Stock block (see instructions):

D Check applicable box(es) to indicate how stock was acquired:
(1) ☒ Original shareholder **(2)** ☐ Purchased **(3)** ☐ Inherited **(4)** ☐ Gift **(5)** ☐ Other:

E Check if you have a Regulations section 1.1367-1(g) election in effect during the tax year for this S corporation ☐

Part I Shareholder Stock Basis

1	Stock basis at the beginning of the corporation's tax year			1	0
2	Basis from any capital contributions made or additional stock acquired during the tax year			2	2,000
3a	Ordinary business income (enter losses in Part III)	3a			
b	Net rental real estate income (enter losses in Part III)	3b			
c	Other net rental income (enter losses in Part III)	3c			
d	Interest income	3d			
e	Ordinary dividends	3e			
f	Royalties	3f			
g	Net capital gains (enter losses in Part III)	3g			
h	Net section 1231 gain (enter losses in Part III)	3h			
i	Other income (enter losses in Part III)	3i			
j	Excess depletion adjustment	3j			
k	Tax-exempt income	3k			
l	Recapture of business credits	3l			
m	Other items that increase stock basis	3m			
4	Add lines 3a through 3m			4	
5	Stock basis before distributions. Add lines 1, 2, and 4			5	2,000
6	Distributions (excluding dividend distributions)			6	500
	Note: If line 6 is larger than line 5, subtract line 5 from line 6 and report the result as a capital gain on Form 8949 and Schedule D. See instructions.				
7	Stock basis after distributions. Subtract line 6 from line 5. If the result is zero or less, enter -0-, skip lines 8 through 14, and enter -0- on line 15			7	1,500
8a	Nondeductible expenses	8a			
b	Depletion for oil and gas	8b			
c	Business credits (sections 50(c)(1) and (5))	8c			
9	Add lines 8a through 8c			9	
10	Stock basis before loss and deduction items. Subtract line 9 from line 7. If the result is zero or less, enter -0-, skip lines 11 through 14, and enter -0- on line 15			10	1,500
11	Allowable loss and deduction items. Enter the amount from line 47, column (c)			11	1,500
12	Debt basis restoration (see net increase in instructions for line 23)			12	
13	Other items that decrease stock basis			13	
14	Add lines 11, 12, and 13			14	1,500
15	**Stock basis at the end of the corporation's tax year.** Subtract line 14 from line 10. If the result is zero or less, enter -0-			15	0

Part II Shareholder Debt Basis

99. IRC §1367(a)(2)(A).

100. IRC §1368(b)(2).

101. 2022 Instructions for Form 7203, p. 3.

Example 6. Use the same facts as **Example 5,** except rather than a loss in 2022, Alpha has operating income of $2,500. It also has a capital gain of $1,000, and Sam takes a distribution of $6,200, of which $700 is taxable as a capital gain. Sam reports this on the following Form 7203.

Form **7203** (Rev. December 2022) Department of the Treasury Internal Revenue Service

S Corporation Shareholder Stock and Debt Basis Limitations

Attach to your tax return.
Go to *www.irs.gov/Form7203* for instructions and the latest information.

OMB No. 1545-2302
Attachment Sequence No. **203**

Name of shareholder: **Sam Iam** — Identifying number: *****-**-0987**

A Name of S corporation: **Alpha Corporation** — B Employer identification number: **12-3456789**

C Stock block (see instructions):

D Check applicable box(es) to indicate how stock was acquired:
(1) ☒ Original shareholder (2) ☐ Purchased (3) ☐ Inherited (4) ☐ Gift (5) ☐ Other:

E Check if you have a Regulations section 1.1367-1(g) election in effect during the tax year for this S corporation ☐

Part I Shareholder Stock Basis

1	Stock basis at the beginning of the corporation's tax year			1	0
2	Basis from any capital contributions made or additional stock acquired during the tax year			2	2,000
3a	Ordinary business income (enter losses in Part III)	3a	2,500		
b	Net rental real estate income (enter losses in Part III)	3b			
c	Other net rental income (enter losses in Part III)	3c			
d	Interest income	3d			
e	Ordinary dividends	3e			
f	Royalties	3f			
g	Net capital gains (enter losses in Part III)	3g	1,000		
h	Net section 1231 gain (enter losses in Part III)	3h			
i	Other income (enter losses in Part III)	3i			
j	Excess depletion adjustment	3j			
k	Tax-exempt income	3k			
l	Recapture of business credits	3l			
m	Other items that increase stock basis	3m			
4	Add lines 3a through 3m			4	3,500
5	Stock basis before distributions. Add lines 1, 2, and 4			5	5,500
6	Distributions (excluding dividend distributions)			6	6,200
	Note: If line 6 is larger than line 5, subtract line 5 from line 6 and report the result as a capital gain on Form 8949 and Schedule D. See instructions.				
7	Stock basis after distributions. Subtract line 6 from line 5. If the result is zero or less, enter -0-, skip lines 8 through 14, and enter -0- on line 15			7	0
8a	Nondeductible expenses	8a			
b	Depletion for oil and gas	8b			
c	Business credits (sections 50(c)(1) and (5))	8c			
9	Add lines 8a through 8c			9	
10	Stock basis before loss and deduction items. Subtract line 9 from line 7. If the result is zero or less, enter -0-, skip lines 11 through 14, and enter -0- on line 15			10	
11	Allowable loss and deduction items. Enter the amount from line 47, column (c)			11	
12	Debt basis restoration (see net increase in instructions for line 23)			12	
13	Other items that decrease stock basis			13	
14	Add lines 11, 12, and 13			14	
15	**Stock basis at the end of the corporation's tax year.** Subtract line 14 from line 10. If the result is zero or less, enter -0-			15	0

Part II Shareholder Debt Basis

Nondeductible Expenses (line 8a). Nondeductible expenses generally reduce stock basis. If a shareholder has insufficient stock basis to absorb these expenses, they reduce debt basis instead.[102] Common nondeductible expenses include meals and entertainment,[103] penalties such as parking tickets,[104] contributions to political campaigns,[105] and the portion of business gifts that exceed $25 per person.[106]

102. IRC §1367(b)(2)(A).

103. IRC §274(a).

104. IRC §162(f)(1).

105. IRC §162(e).

106. IRC §274(b).

Example 7. Use the same facts as **Example 6,** except Alpha Corporation also paid $800 in penalties in 2022. Because Sam had a basis of $0 before accounting for the nondeductible penalties, his Form 7203 looks the same as in **Example 6.**

DEBT BASIS

A shareholder's **debt basis** is increased by any loans made by a shareholder to the corporation, less the principal portion of any repayments. Debt basis restorations also increase debt basis, but only to the extent that they are taxable. Business operating losses that exceed stock basis reduce an S corporation's debt basis, and nondeductible expenses may also reduce debt basis.

Not all shareholder debt is treated the same way. If a loan is substantiated with a formal note or written instrument, repayment may be treated as capital gain.[107] If no documentation is associated with a loan, repayment may be treated as ordinary income.[108] Ideally, shareholders adequately document all loans they make to S corporations and all subsequent repayments on these loans.

If a shareholder provides money to an S corporation as a loan, they receive debt basis for the funds provided, assuming the lender and the shareholder are the same person.[109]

Losses may reduce a shareholder's debt basis.[110] This reduction in basis does not affect the amount the S corporation owes its shareholders.[111]

If the funds are loaned directly by a person or entity that does not own stock in the S corporation, generally the shareholder does not receive debt basis associated with that loan.[112] However, if the loan is made through a disregarded entity (such as an LLC) of which the S corporation shareholder is the sole member, the loan is assumed to have originated with the shareholder.[113]

Third-Party Debt

Extending a guarantee of the loan's repayment provides no debt basis until the shareholder makes a payment to the lender under the terms of the guarantee.[114] In that event, the shareholder's debt basis increases by the amount of the payment.

Example 8. Use the same facts as **Example 4.** In 2022, Sam loans Alpha $10,000. Alpha also obtains a $50,000 loan from First National Bank (First National) to expand its operations. First National requires Sam to guarantee the loan. Alpha has no other outstanding loans in 2022. Sam's stock basis is $2,000 at the beginning of the year. Alpha reports a $30,000 loss. Sam can deduct $12,000 of the 2022 loss on his individual tax return because he has $2,000 stock basis, plus he has debt basis for loaning Alpha $10,000. The loss reduces his basis in his note receivable from Alpha to $0. Sam carries the remaining $18,000 loss forward to 2023.

Sam reports his activity on the following Form 7203.

107. Instructions for Form 7203; Treas. Reg. §1.1367-2(a)(1).

108. Treas. Reg. §1.1367-2(a)(2).

109. Treas. Reg. §1.1366-2(a)(2)(i), referencing Treas. Reg. §1.1011-1.

110. IRC §1367(b)(2).

111. IRC §1361(c)(5)(B).

112. Rev. Rul. 70-50, 1970-1 CB 178, referencing *Perry v. Comm'r*, 47 TC 159 (1966), *aff'd* 392 F.2d 458 (8th Cir. 1968).

113. Treas. Reg. §1.1366-2(a)(2)(iii), Example 1.

114. Treas. Reg. §1.1366-2(a)(2)(ii).

For Example 8

Form **7203** (Rev. December 2022) Department of the Treasury Internal Revenue Service

S Corporation Shareholder Stock and Debt Basis Limitations

Attach to your tax return.
Go to *www.irs.gov/Form7203* for instructions and the latest information.

OMB No. 1545-2302
Attachment Sequence No. **203**

Name of shareholder	Identifying number
Sam Iam	***-**-0987
A Name of S corporation	B Employer identification number
Alpha Corporation	12-3456789

C Stock block (see instructions):

D Check applicable box(es) to indicate how stock was acquired:
(1) ☒ Original shareholder **(2)** ☐ Purchased **(3)** ☐ Inherited **(4)** ☐ Gift **(5)** ☐ Other:

E Check if you have a Regulations section 1.1367-1(g) election in effect during the tax year for this S corporation ☐

Part I Shareholder Stock Basis

1	Stock basis at the beginning of the corporation's tax year			1	0
2	Basis from any capital contributions made or additional stock acquired during the tax year			2	2,000
3a	Ordinary business income (enter losses in Part III)	3a			
b	Net rental real estate income (enter losses in Part III)	3b			
c	Other net rental income (enter losses in Part III)	3c			
d	Interest income	3d			
e	Ordinary dividends	3e			
f	Royalties	3f			
g	Net capital gains (enter losses in Part III)	3g			
h	Net section 1231 gain (enter losses in Part III)	3h			
i	Other income (enter losses in Part III)	3i			
j	Excess depletion adjustment	3j			
k	Tax-exempt income	3k			
l	Recapture of business credits	3l			
m	Other items that increase stock basis	3m			
4	Add lines 3a through 3m			4	
5	Stock basis before distributions. Add lines 1, 2, and 4			5	2,000
6	Distributions (excluding dividend distributions)			6	
	Note: If line 6 is larger than line 5, subtract line 5 from line 6 and report the result as a capital gain on Form 8949 and Schedule D. See instructions.				
7	Stock basis after distributions. Subtract line 6 from line 5. If the result is zero or less, enter -0-, skip lines 8 through 14, and enter -0- on line 15			7	2,000
8a	Nondeductible expenses	8a			
b	Depletion for oil and gas	8b			
c	Business credits (sections 50(c)(1) and (5))	8c			
9	Add lines 8a through 8c			9	
10	Stock basis before loss and deduction items. Subtract line 9 from line 7. If the result is zero or less, enter -0-, skip lines 11 through 14, and enter -0- on line 15			10	2,000
11	Allowable loss and deduction items. Enter the amount from line 47, column (c)			11	2,000
12	Debt basis restoration (see net increase in instructions for line 23)			12	
13	Other items that decrease stock basis			13	
14	Add lines 11, 12, and 13			14	2,000
15	**Stock basis at the end of the corporation's tax year.** Subtract line 14 from line 10. If the result is zero or less, enter -0-			15	0

Part II Shareholder Debt Basis

Section A—Amount of Debt (If more than three debts, see instructions.)

	Description	**(a)** Debt 1 ☒ Formal note ☐ Open account	**(b)** Debt 2 ☐ Formal note ☐ Open account	**(c)** Debt 3 ☐ Formal note ☐ Open account	**(d)** Total
16	Loan balance at the beginning of the corporation's tax year				
17	Additional loans (see instructions)	10,000			10,000
18	Loan balance before repayment. Add lines 16 and 17	10,000			10,000
19	Principal portion of debt repayment (this line doesn't include interest)				
20	Loan balance at the end of the corporation's tax year. Subtract line 19 from line 18	10,000			10,000

For Paperwork Reduction Act Notice, see separate instructions. Cat. No. 56396V Form **7203** (Rev. 12-2022)

For Example 8

Form 7203 (Rev. 12-2022) Page **2**

Part II **Shareholder Debt Basis** *(continued)*

Section B—Adjustments to Debt Basis

	Description	(a) Debt 1	(b) Debt 2	(c) Debt 3	(d) Total
21	Debt basis at the beginning of the corporation's tax year				
22	Enter the amount, if any, from line 17	10,000			10,000
23	Debt basis restoration (see instructions)				
24	Debt basis before repayment. Add lines 21, 22, and 23	10,000			10,000
25	Divide line 24 by line 18	1.0000			
26	Nontaxable debt repayment. Multiply line 25 by line 19				
27	Debt basis before nondeductible expenses and losses. Subtract line 26 from line 24	10,000			10,000
28	Nondeductible expenses and oil and gas depletion deductions in excess of stock basis				
29	Debt basis before losses and deductions. Subtract line 28 from line 27. If the result is zero or less, enter -0-	10,000			10,000
30	Allowable losses in excess of stock basis. Enter the amount from line 47, column (d)	10,000			10,000
31	**Debt basis at the end of the corporation's tax year.** Subtract line 30 from line 29. If the result is zero or less, enter -0-				

Section C—Gain on Loan Repayment

	Description	(a) Debt 1	(b) Debt 2	(c) Debt 3	(d) Total
32	Repayment. Enter the amount from line 19				
33	Nontaxable repayments. Enter the amount from line 26				
34	**Reportable gain.** Subtract line 33 from line 32				

Part III **Shareholder Allowable Loss and Deduction Items**

	Description	(a) Current year losses and deductions	(b) Carryover amounts (column (e)) from the previous year	(c) Allowable loss from stock basis	(d) Allowable loss from debt basis	(e) Carryover amounts
35	Ordinary business loss					
36	Net rental real estate loss					
37	Other net rental loss					
38	Net capital loss					
39	Net section 1231 loss					
40	Other loss					
41	Section 179 deductions					
42	Charitable contributions					
43	Investment interest expense					
44	Section 59(e)(2) expenditures					
45	Other deductions					
46	Foreign taxes paid or accrued					
47	**Total loss.** Add lines 35 through 46 for each column. Enter the total loss in column (c) on line 11 and enter the total loss in column (d) on line 30					

Form **7203** (Rev. 12-2022)

10

Example 9. Use the same facts as **Example 8,** except that First National requires Sam to personally pay $5,000 on the bank loan to keep it from going into default. This payment is treated as a loan from Sam to Alpha, increasing his debt basis by $5,000, which enables him to deduct a $17,000 loss in 2022 ($2,000 loss from stock basis + $15,000 loss from debt basis). Sam's activities are reported on the following Form 7203.

For Example 9

Form **7203** (Rev. December 2022) Department of the Treasury Internal Revenue Service

S Corporation Shareholder Stock and Debt Basis Limitations

Attach to your tax return.
Go to *www.irs.gov/Form7203* for instructions and the latest information.

OMB No. 1545-2302
Attachment Sequence No. **203**

Name of shareholder	Identifying number
Sam Iam	***-**-0987
A Name of S corporation	**B** Employer identification number
Alpha Corporation	12-3456789

C Stock block (see instructions): ____

D Check applicable box(es) to indicate how stock was acquired:
(1) ☐ Original shareholder **(2)** ☐ Purchased **(3)** ☐ Inherited **(4)** ☐ Gift **(5)** ☐ Other: ____

E Check if you have a Regulations section 1.1367-1(g) election in effect during the tax year for this S corporation ☐

Part I — Shareholder Stock Basis

1	Stock basis at the beginning of the corporation's tax year			1	0
2	Basis from any capital contributions made or additional stock acquired during the tax year			2	2,000
3a	Ordinary business income (enter losses in Part III)	3a			
b	Net rental real estate income (enter losses in Part III)	3b			
c	Other net rental income (enter losses in Part III)	3c			
d	Interest income	3d			
e	Ordinary dividends	3e			
f	Royalties	3f			
g	Net capital gains (enter losses in Part III)	3g			
h	Net section 1231 gain (enter losses in Part III)	3h			
i	Other income (enter losses in Part III)	3i			
j	Excess depletion adjustment	3j			
k	Tax-exempt income	3k			
l	Recapture of business credits	3l			
m	Other items that increase stock basis	3m			
4	Add lines 3a through 3m			4	
5	Stock basis before distributions. Add lines 1, 2, and 4			5	2,000
6	Distributions (excluding dividend distributions)			6	
	Note: If line 6 is larger than line 5, subtract line 5 from line 6 and report the result as a capital gain on Form 8949 and Schedule D. See instructions.				
7	Stock basis after distributions. Subtract line 6 from line 5. If the result is zero or less, enter -0-, skip lines 8 through 14, and enter -0- on line 15			7	2,000
8a	Nondeductible expenses	8a			
b	Depletion for oil and gas	8b			
c	Business credits (sections 50(c)(1) and (5))	8c			
9	Add lines 8a through 8c			9	
10	Stock basis before loss and deduction items. Subtract line 9 from line 7. If the result is zero or less, enter -0-, skip lines 11 through 14, and enter -0- on line 15			10	2,000
11	Allowable loss and deduction items. Enter the amount from line 47, column (c)			11	2,000
12	Debt basis restoration (see net increase in instructions for line 23)			12	
13	Other items that decrease stock basis			13	
14	Add lines 11, 12, and 13			14	2,000
15	**Stock basis at the end of the corporation's tax year.** Subtract line 14 from line 10. If the result is zero or less, enter -0-			15	0

Part II — Shareholder Debt Basis

Section A—Amount of Debt (If more than three debts, see instructions.)

	Description	**(a)** Debt 1 ☒ Formal note ☐ Open account	**(b)** Debt 2 ☒ Formal note ☐ Open account	**(c)** Debt 3 ☐ Formal note ☐ Open account	**(d)** Total
16	Loan balance at the beginning of the corporation's tax year				
17	Additional loans (see instructions)	10,000	5,000		15,000
18	Loan balance before repayment. Add lines 16 and 17	10,000	5,000		15,000
19	Principal portion of debt repayment (this line doesn't include interest)				
20	Loan balance at the end of the corporation's tax year. Subtract line 19 from line 18	10,000	5,000		15,000

For Paperwork Reduction Act Notice, see separate instructions. Cat. No. 56396V Form **7203** (Rev. 12-2022)

For Example 9

Form 7203 (Rev. 12-2022) Page **2**

Part II **Shareholder Debt Basis** *(continued)*

Section B—Adjustments to Debt Basis

	Description	(a) Debt 1	(b) Debt 2	(c) Debt 3	(d) Total
21	Debt basis at the beginning of the corporation's tax year				
22	Enter the amount, if any, from line 17	15,000			15,000
23	Debt basis restoration (see instructions)				
24	Debt basis before repayment. Add lines 21, 22, and 23	15,000			15,000
25	Divide line 24 by line 18	1.0000			
26	Nontaxable debt repayment. Multiply line 25 by line 19				
27	Debt basis before nondeductible expenses and losses. Subtract line 26 from line 24	15,000			15,000
28	Nondeductible expenses and oil and gas depletion deductions in excess of stock basis				
29	Debt basis before losses and deductions. Subtract line 28 from line 27. If the result is zero or less, enter -0-	15,000			15,000
30	Allowable losses in excess of stock basis. Enter the amount from line 47, column (d)	15,000			15,000
31	**Debt basis at the end of the corporation's tax year.** Subtract line 30 from line 29. If the result is zero or less, enter -0-				

Section C—Gain on Loan Repayment

	Description	(a) Debt 1	(b) Debt 2	(c) Debt 3	(d) Total
32	Repayment. Enter the amount from line 19				
33	Nontaxable repayments. Enter the amount from line 26				
34	**Reportable gain.** Subtract line 33 from line 32				

Part III **Shareholder Allowable Loss and Deduction Items**

	Description	(a) Current year losses and deductions	(b) Carryover amounts (column (e)) from the previous year	(c) Allowable loss from stock basis	(d) Allowable loss from debt basis	(e) Carryover amounts
35	Ordinary business loss					
36	Net rental real estate loss					
37	Other net rental loss					
38	Net capital loss					
39	Net section 1231 loss					
40	Other loss					
41	Section 179 deductions					
42	Charitable contributions					
43	Investment interest expense					
44	Section 59(e)(2) expenditures					
45	Other deductions					
46	Foreign taxes paid or accrued					
47	**Total loss.** Add lines 35 through 46 for each column. Enter the total loss in column (c) on line 11 and enter the total loss in column (d) on line 30					

Form **7203** (Rev. 12-2022)

10

Open Account Advances of $25,000 or Less[115]

Open account debt does not have any document associated with the loan. If the balance of open account debt owed to a single shareholder at the end of the S corporation's tax year is $25,000 or less, they are collectively treated as a single loan. If there are any repayments during the year, they are netted against advances made to the S corporation.[116] The reduction in the shareholder's debt basis is accordingly restored.[117] Loan repayments on reduced-basis open account debt create **ordinary income** for the shareholder.[118]

Open Account Advances of More than $25,000[119]

The situation changes when an S corporation closes a tax year with more than $25,000 of open account debt outstanding to a single shareholder. Beginning the next tax year, the ability to treat all open account debt as a single liability ceases for that shareholder. The $25,000 threshold that applies to each shareholder is not applied at the entity level. A debt that exceeds $25,000 at the end of the prior year is treated as a formal note for purposes of calculating the gain on loan repayment.

Indebtedness Evidenced by Written Instrument

When an S corporation's indebtedness to one of its shareholders is documented properly, the document makes the arrangement a security eligible for capital gain treatment.[120] If repayments result in a capital gain more than one year after the loan was taken out, the gain is considered a LTCG.[121]

Although the Code has not defined what qualifies as proper documentation for a written instrument, the **straight debt guidelines** of IRC §1361(c)(5) are a good rule for any S corporation indebtedness. By using the straight debt safe harbor provisions, it maximizes the likelihood that the IRS does not determine that the indebtedness is a second class of stock.[122] This determination would put the entity in violation of one of the requirements to be an S corporation,[123] thereby risking revocation of its S corporation status.

To qualify for the straight debt safe harbor, straight debt is any **written unconditional promise** to repay the loan if **all three** of the following conditions are met.[124]

- The interest rate (and interest payment dates) are not contingent on profits, the borrower's discretion, or similar factors. Fluctuations tied to the prime rate are acceptable.[125]
- There is no convertibility (directly or indirectly) into stock.
- The creditor is an individual, an estate, or a trust eligible to hold S corporation shares.[126]

---

115. Treas. Reg. §1.1367-2(a)(2).

116. Treas. Reg. §1.1367-2(d)(2)(i).

117. Ibid.

118. Rev. Rul. 68-537, 1968-2 CB 372.

119. Treas. Reg. §1.1367-2(a)(2)(ii).

120. IRC §1221(a). The note must arise from the shareholder's loan to the S corporation, not from their providing services to the S corporation.

121. IRC §1222(4).

122. IRC §1361(c)(5)(A).

123. IRC §1361(b)(D).

124. IRC §1361(c)(5).

125. Ltr. Rul. 9342019 (Jul. 21, 1993).

126. IRC §1361(c)(2). A trust meeting this qualification is identified as a qualified subchapter S trust or QSST.

Gift Loans and Imputed Interest

Some debt instruments may not have a stated rate of interest. If a loan incurs interest at a below-market rate, it is a **gift loan.**[127] When more than $10,000 has been loaned to an S corporation as a gift loan, the shareholder is responsible for reporting imputed interest as taxable income.[128] The minimum interest is based on the applicable federal rate (AFR) that the IRS publishes monthly.[129] In applying AFRs to a written instrument having no stated interest rate, taxpayers should look for the term most closely matching the repayment schedule on the written instrument.[130]

This provision may affect some situations in which a shareholder sells property to an S corporation. If the shareholder-seller takes a note, that note should carry an interest rate of at least as much as the AFR for the loan term.[131]

Multiple Debts[132]

When a shareholder has multiple debts to an S corporation at the end of the S corporation's tax year, the reduction in basis is applied to each debt in the same proportion that the debt basis has in relation to the aggregate bases of all the shareholder's debt.

Example 10. Use same facts as **Example 4.** Sam purchases $2,000 worth of Alpha's common stock on January 2, 2022. On the same day, he loans Alpha $10,000 under a promissory note that qualified as a written instrument (debt #1).

During 2022, Alpha incurs an ordinary business loss of $22,000, along with a $2,000 §179 expense deduction. As a result, Sam has a $0 basis in Alpha stock ($2,000 capital stock acquired – $2,000 maximum loss to be applied to the stock basis). Sam's basis in the debt he loans to Alpha is reduced to $0 ($10,000 loan – $10,000 ordinary business loss for 2022). Sam has a $10,000 suspended loss and $2,000 suspended §179 carryover to 2023.

On July 15, 2023, Sam loans Alpha $30,000 (debt #2). There is no separate loan document supporting debt #2, and, therefore, debt #2 is treated as open account indebtedness. During 2023, Alpha sustains another loss of $9,000. Sam's stock basis in the corporation is still $0. His basis in debt #1 is still $0, and his basis in debt #2 is $9,000 ($30,000 loan – $21,000 ($10,000 carryover + $2,000 §179 carryover + $9,000 current year loss)).

Even though Sam's loans have a combined principal amount of $40,000, Sam has $0 basis in debt #1 and $9,000 of debt basis in debt #2. Sam's 2023 Form 7203, part II, section A, follows.

15	zero or less, enter -0-				15	0

Part II Shareholder Debt Basis

Section A—Amount of Debt (If more than three debts, see instructions.)

	Description	**(a)** Debt 1 ☒ Formal note ☐ Open account	**(b)** Debt 2 ☐ Formal note ☒ Open account	**(c)** Debt 3 ☐ Formal note ☐ Open account	**(d)** Total
16	Loan balance at the beginning of the corporation's tax year	10,000	0		10,000
17	Additional loans (see instructions)	0	30,000		30,000
18	Loan balance before repayment. Add lines 16 and 17	10,000	30,000		40,000
19	Principal portion of debt repayment (this line doesn't include interest)		0		
20	Loan balance at the end of the corporation's tax year. Subtract line 19 from line 18	10,000	30,000		40,000

For Paperwork Reduction Act Notice, see separate instructions. Cat. No. 56396V Form **7203** (Rev. 12-2022)

127. IRC §7872(c)(1).

128. IRC §7872(c)(3).

129. For example, Rev. Rul. 2023-13, 2023-32 IRB 1, published the AFRs for August 2023.

130. IRC §1274(d)(1)(A).

131. IRC §483(b).

132. Treas. Reg. §1.1367-2(b)(3).

Order of Debt Basis Restoration[133]

After an S corporation shareholder incurs a debt basis reduction, their debt basis can be restored if there is a **net increase.**[134] A net increase is generally the amount that the income items collectively exceed losses, deductions, nondeductible expenses, some oil and gas depletion deductions, and certain nondividend distributions (discussed previously). These amounts are used to restore the taxpayer's debt basis in the S corporation before their stock basis.[135]

The net increase is figured as follows.[136]

	Sum of all increases to basis (line 4)
–	Distributions (line 6)
–	Sum of all nondeductible expenses (line 9)
–	Other items that decrease basis (line 13, as applicable)
–	Current year losses and deductions (line 47(a))
–	Carryover amounts from the previous year (line 47(b))
	Net increase

If the net increase exceeds the total reduction in debt basis (line 16 minus line 21), then the restoration is limited to the amount needed to restore debt basis to the face of the loan.

Repayment Restores Reduced Debt Basis First.[137] When a shareholder's basis in debt has been reduced, they apply any net increase first to restore their basis in any debt that was repaid during the tax year. Only after the basis of each outstanding shareholder debt is restored can the shareholder restore their stock basis.

Debt basis restoration may restore the basis of more than one debt. Treasury regulations give priority to any debt restoration that may result in a gain, which may benefit the shareholders.

Proportionate Restoration of Basis on Remaining Outstanding Debts.[138] If a shareholder has more than one debt, any net increase first restores the basis reduction associated with any loans that have been repaid. After restoring the debt basis of the repaid loans, the remaining net increase restores the shareholder's basis in each loan proportionately. The proportion is determined by the remaining basis reduction that each outstanding debt incurred at the beginning of the tax year. After considering the repayment of any debt, the remaining basis reduction is apportioned to all debts having reduced basis. The basis restoration allocated to each debt is based on the remaining reduction of debt basis.

Part II, Section A — Shareholder Debt Basis

A shareholder may extend multiple loans to an S corporation in which they have an interest, possibly with multiple written debt instruments. Generally, open account debt is consolidated into a single debt, while debts with separate formal notes are listed in separate columns in Form 7203, part II, section A.

Part II is divided into three sections, with section A determining the **amount of debt** the S corporation owes the shareholder at the end of the corporation's tax year.

---

133. Treas. Reg. §1.1367-2(c).

134. IRC §1367(b)(2)(B); Treas. Reg. §1.1367-2(c)(1).

135. IRC §1367(b)(2)(B).

136. Instructions for Form 7203.

137. Treas. Reg. §1.1367-2(c)(1).

138. Treas. Reg. §1.1367-2(c)(2).

A formal promissory note may document a shareholder's loan to an S corporation. In this circumstance, the shareholder should mark the "Formal note" checkbox above line 16. Taxpayers should mark "Formal note" if, at the end of the previous year, the S corporation owed the shareholder more than $25,000 on open account indebtedness. They should also mark this checkbox if the shareholder is owed $25,000 or less in current open account indebtedness, but was owed more than $25,000 at the end of **any** prior year.

Alternatively, the S corporation may owe open-account indebtedness to a single shareholder that nets out to $25,000 or less and has never been more than $25,000. In this circumstance, the shareholder should mark the "Open account" checkbox.

A shareholder with more than three debts at the beginning of the year should report any additional advances under a specific loan on line 17. Conversely, principal repayments to a shareholder under a specific loan should appear on line 19. Some or all of this amount may represent a capital gain to the shareholder, depending on the shareholder's debt basis, as discussed later with section B. Line 20, the final line of part II, includes the loan balance at the end of the corporation's tax year.

If a shareholder has extended more than three loans to the S corporation, they should file another Form 7203 with their return.

Part II, Section B — Adjustments to Debt Basis

As discussed previously, a shareholder's allocation of an S corporation's operating losses or deductions may reduce their basis in any debt owed to them. Its operating income or tax-exempt income may subsequently restore it. Part II, section B, of Form 7203 itemizes these adjustments.

Beginning Debt Basis (line 21). This amount is the end-of-year basis for the debt, as reported on line 31 of the prior year Form 7203. A shareholder who advances additional amounts under a loan reports these amounts on line 22, as they did on line 17 of section A. When line 16 exceeds line 21, debt basis has been used to allow losses.[139]

Current Year Debt Basis Restoration (line 23). If a shareholder reduced their debt basis in prior years, they report any current-year restoration on line 23. However, no restoration occurs unless one of the following has taken place.[140]

- The S corporation generates positive income.
- The S corporation has tax-exempt income.
- The S corporation has an excess depletion adjustment.

10

Debt Basis Restoration with Multiple Debts.[141] When an S corporation has multiple debt obligations to the shareholder, shareholders first apply the debt basis restoration to a debt repaid during the tax year.

> **Note.** The objective of the debt basis restoration is to minimize capital gains during the tax year associated with that debt repayment. However, it may not eliminate them, even if the debt basis restoration is greater than the principal repayment.

Fraction of Debt Basis Not Reduced (line 25). By dividing debt basis before repayment (line 24) by the loan balance before repayment (line 18), a shareholder calculates the fraction of the debt basis that has not been reduced.[142]

Nontaxable Debt Repayment (line 26). Line 26 reflects what amount of the repaid principal on the debt is a nontaxable principal repayment. A shareholder generally owes no tax on this amount, as it appears later on line 33. The nontaxable debt repayment amount reduces the shareholder's debt basis.

139. See Treas. Reg. §1.1367-2(c)(1), sentence that indicates the rules apply only to debt held by shareholder at the beginning of the tax year.

140. IRC §1367(b)(2); Treas. Reg. §1.1367-2(c).

141. Treas. Reg. §1.1367-2(c)(2).

142. Ibid.

Nondeductible Expenses (line 28). Line 28 reports a shareholder's portion of any expenses the S corporation cannot deduct from income. In general, these expenses reduce a shareholder's basis. However, they only reduce debt basis in specific circumstances.

If the shareholder has a **positive** stock basis after distributions are deducted, then nondeductible expenses are compared to line 7. If the nondeductible expenses exceed the stock basis reported on line 7, then the excess amount is reported on line 28. Any shareholder debt having a basis greater than $0 is reduced. If more than one debt has a basis greater than $0, the nondeductible expenses are apportioned.

If the shareholder reports a $0 stock basis on line 7, nondeductible expenses do not reduce the stockholder's debt basis unless they have made an election under Treas. Reg. §1.1367-1(g). This ordering rule was discussed previously.

> **Caution.** Nondeductible expenses are also grouped with excess oil and gas depletion expenses in certain circumstances. Discussion of excess oil and gas depletion is beyond the scope of this discussion.

The resulting difference is compared with the debt basis before nondeductible expenses, line 27 and the smaller of the two numbers is reported on line 28.

Line 28 is where the election under Treas. Reg. §1.1367-1(g), as discussed previously, makes a difference. If a shareholder skips this election, no nondeductible expenses **in excess of stock and debt basis** are carried forward to the next tax year. Alternatively, if they have made this election, the smaller of the following two amounts carries forward to the next year.

- Line 13 (other items that decrease basis that are attributable to the election)
- Line 27 debt basis before nondeductible expenses

Debt Basis at the End of the Corporation's Tax Year (line 31). If any loss is allowed over stock basis, it reduces the shareholder's debt basis as shown on line 31.

Part II, Section C — Gain on Loan Repayment

Shareholders with more than one loan to an S corporation must prorate any allocated reduction to the loans based on the ratio that each loan's basis bears to the aggregate bases of the loans.[143] The character of the gain on repayment depends on whether the debt is evidenced by a formal note or is an open account. Debt evidenced by a formal note results in **capital gain,** and is reported on Form 8949 and Schedule D. Any open account debt results in **ordinary gain** and is reported on Form 4797, *Sales of Business Property.*[144]

> **Observation.** Normally, debt repayment is not considered a taxable event.

Example 11. Use the same facts as **Example 10,** except that in 2024, Alpha has ordinary business income of $15,000, and Sam receives a repayment of $4,000 on debt #2 (formal note) to Alpha. Alpha has $100 of nondeductible expenses and also incurs a §1231 loss of $500 from the sale of equipment.

Not all of Alpha's ordinary business income is allocated to increase Sam's debt basis.

Alpha repays Sam $4,000 on debt #2 (formal note.) Alpha incurs nondeductible expenses that reduce the debt basis reduction available by $100, plus the §1231 loss of $500. Sam has $14,400 ($15,000 ordinary business income – $100 nondeductible expenses – $500 §1231 loss) available for debt basis restoration. This amount is split between debt #1 and debt #2 as shown on Sam's Form 7203 that appears next.

143. Treas. Reg. §1.1367-2(b)(3).

144. Instructions to Form 7203.

For Example 11

Form **7203** (Rev. December 2022) Department of the Treasury Internal Revenue Service

S Corporation Shareholder Stock and Debt Basis Limitations

Attach to your tax return.
Go to *www.irs.gov/Form7203* for instructions and the latest information.

OMB No. 1545-2302
Attachment Sequence No. **203**

Name of shareholder	Identifying number
Sam Iam	***-**-0987
A Name of S corporation	**B** Employer identification number
Alpha Corporation	12-3456789

C Stock block (see instructions):

D Check applicable box(es) to indicate how stock was acquired:
(1) ☐ Original shareholder **(2)** ☐ Purchased **(3)** ☐ Inherited **(4)** ☐ Gift **(5)** ☐ Other:

E Check if you have a Regulations section 1.1367-1(g) election in effect during the tax year for this S corporation ☐

Part I Shareholder Stock Basis

1	Stock basis at the beginning of the corporation's tax year			1	0
2	Basis from any capital contributions made or additional stock acquired during the tax year			2	
3a	Ordinary business income (enter losses in Part III)	3a	15,000		
b	Net rental real estate income (enter losses in Part III)	3b			
c	Other net rental income (enter losses in Part III)	3c			
d	Interest income	3d			
e	Ordinary dividends	3e			
f	Royalties	3f			
g	Net capital gains (enter losses in Part III)	3g			
h	Net section 1231 gain (enter losses in Part III)	3h			
i	Other income (enter losses in Part III)	3i			
j	Excess depletion adjustment	3j			
k	Tax-exempt income	3k			
l	Recapture of business credits	3l			
m	Other items that increase stock basis	3m			
4	Add lines 3a through 3m			4	15,000
5	Stock basis before distributions. Add lines 1, 2, and 4			5	15,000
6	Distributions (excluding dividend distributions)			6	
	Note: If line 6 is larger than line 5, subtract line 5 from line 6 and report the result as a capital gain on Form 8949 and Schedule D. See instructions.				
7	Stock basis after distributions. Subtract line 6 from line 5. If the result is zero or less, enter -0-, skip lines 8 through 14, and enter -0- on line 15			7	15,000
8a	Nondeductible expenses	8a	100		
b	Depletion for oil and gas	8b			
c	Business credits (sections 50(c)(1) and (5))	8c			
9	Add lines 8a through 8c			9	100
10	Stock basis before loss and deduction items. Subtract line 9 from line 7. If the result is zero or less, enter -0-, skip lines 11 through 14, and enter -0- on line 15			10	14,900
11	Allowable loss and deduction items. Enter the amount from line 47, column (c)			11	500
12	Debt basis restoration (see net increase in instructions for line 23)			12	14,400
13	Other items that decrease stock basis			13	
14	Add lines 11, 12, and 13			14	14,900
15	**Stock basis at the end of the corporation's tax year.** Subtract line 14 from line 10. If the result is zero or less, enter -0-			15	0

Part II Shareholder Debt Basis

Section A—Amount of Debt (If more than three debts, see instructions.)

	Description	**(a)** Debt 1 ☒ Formal note ☐ Open account	**(b)** Debt 2 ☒ Formal note ☐ Open account	**(c)** Debt 3 ☐ Formal note ☐ Open account	**(d)** Total
16	Loan balance at the beginning of the corporation's tax year	10,000	30,000		40,000
17	Additional loans (see instructions)	0			
18	Loan balance before repayment. Add lines 16 and 17	10,000	30,000		40,000
19	Principal portion of debt repayment (this line doesn't include interest)		4,000		4,000
20	Loan balance at the end of the corporation's tax year. Subtract line 19 from line 18	10,000	26,000		36,000

For Paperwork Reduction Act Notice, see separate instructions. Cat. No. 56396V Form **7203** (Rev. 12-2022)

10

For Example 11

Form 7203 (Rev. 12-2022) Page **2**

Part II **Shareholder Debt Basis** *(continued)*

Section B—Adjustments to Debt Basis

	Description	(a) Debt 1	(b) Debt 2	(c) Debt 3	(d) Total
21	Debt basis at the beginning of the corporation's tax year	0	9,000		9,000
22	Enter the amount, if any, from line 17				
23	Debt basis restoration (see instructions)	3,851	10,549		14,400
24	Debt basis before repayment. Add lines 21, 22, and 23	3,851	19,549		23,400
25	Divide line 24 by line 18	0.3851	0.6516		
26	Nontaxable debt repayment. Multiply line 25 by line 19		2,607		2,607
27	Debt basis before nondeductible expenses and losses. Subtract line 26 from line 24	3,851	16,942		20,793
28	Nondeductible expenses and oil and gas depletion deductions in excess of stock basis				
29	Debt basis before losses and deductions. Subtract line 28 from line 27. If the result is zero or less, enter -0-	3,851	16,942		20,793
30	Allowable losses in excess of stock basis. Enter the amount from line 47, column (d)				
31	**Debt basis at the end of the corporation's tax year.** Subtract line 30 from line 29. If the result is zero or less, enter -0-	3,851	16,942		20,793

Section C—Gain on Loan Repayment

	Description	(a) Debt 1	(b) Debt 2	(c) Debt 3	(d) Total
32	Repayment. Enter the amount from line 19		4,000		4,000
33	Nontaxable repayments. Enter the amount from line 26		2,607		2,607
34	**Reportable gain.** Subtract line 33 from line 32		1,393		1,393

Part III **Shareholder Allowable Loss and Deduction Items**

Of the $4,000 Sam received as repayment of open account debt, $2,607 is a nontaxable repayment. This amount appears on line 33 of Sam's Form 7203. The balance of the repayment, or $1,393, is taxed as capital gain because it now is classified as a formal debt. Sam reports the $1,393 gain on his Schedule D.

The following table shows Sam's allocation of debt basis restoration, as reported on line 23 of his Form 7203.

	Form 7203 Line No.	Formal Note	Open Account	Total
Loan balance before repayment	18	$10,000	$30,000	$40,000
Less: principal portion of debt repayment	19	(0)	(4,000)	(4,000)
Loan balance at yearend	20	$10,000	$26,000	$36,000
Less: debt basis at beginning of year	21	(0)	(9,000)	(9,000)
Difference		$10,000	$17,000	$27,000
		÷ $27,000	÷ $27,000	÷ $27,000
Proportion of total		37.037%	62.963%	100.000%
Total debt restoration amount after debt repayment		× $10,400	× $10,400	× $10,400
Allocation of debt basis restoration after debt repayment		$ 3,852	$ 6,548	$10,400
Debt repayment			4,000	4,000
Total allocation of debt basis restoration		$ 3,852	$10,548	$14,400

Thus, the net increase of $14,400 (line 23, column d) restores $3,852 (line 23, column a) of the basis of debt #1 and $10,548 (line 23, column b) of the basis of debt #2.

Observation. Although the first portion of the net increase restores debt basis, this does not mean that the repayment of the debt's principal is nontaxable. Line 23 presents the restoration of the debt basis, which is added to the debt basis at the beginning of the year to determine the debt basis before repayment.

Note. Even if an S corporation shareholder has a positive debt basis in loans they have extended to the corporation, distributions are still taxable if the stock basis is zero at the end of the year during which they are made.[145]

Practitioner Planning Tip

Tax practitioners should consider the possibility that any amount appearing on an S corporation shareholder's Schedule K-1 in box 16 with Code D (distributions) could cause a capital gain. The exception would be when the shareholder has a positive stock basis greater than the distribution.

Part III — Shareholder Allowable Loss and Deduction Items

Shareholders use Form 7203, part III, to determine which losses and deductions from Schedule K-1 they can use in the current year or carry over to the next year. While part II of Form 7203 is concerned with amounts associated with each debt owed to the shareholder, part III determines which losses are **allowed** and which are not.

If an S corporation sustains losses in more than one income category, the loss or deduction that exceeds the basis must be apportioned among stock basis, debt basis, and carryforward to next year.

Example 12. On December 31, 2022, George Gamma, the sole shareholder of Gamma Corporation, an established S corporation, has no stock basis in the corporation and $12,000 of debt basis. A promissory note documents the debt and meets the standards for a formal written instrument. During 2022, Gamma sustains an ordinary business loss of $11,000, a capital loss of $3,000, and a §179 expense deduction of $2,000. George's allowable losses are calculated as follows.

Debt basis		$12,000
Ordinary business loss	$11,000	
Capital loss	3,000	
§179 expense deduction	2,000	
Total losses and §179 deduction	$16,000	÷ 16,000
Allowable percentage		75%
Ordinary business loss ($11,000 × 75%)		$ 8,250
Capital loss ($3,000 × 75%)		2,250
§179 expense deduction ($2,000 × 75%)		1,500
Total allowable losses and deduction against debt basis		$12,000

145. IRC §1368(b)(2).

The losses and the §179 expense deduction eliminate George's remaining debt basis. The $4,000 balance of expenses ($16,000 total losses – $12,000 allowable losses) is carried forward to 2023 income. If Gamma reports nondeductible expenses on George's Schedule K-1, they cannot be carried forward unless George has an election under Treas. Reg. §1.1367-1(g), as discussed previously.

The following is an excerpt from George's 2022 Form 7203.

34 Reportable g... subtract line 33 fr... 32

Part III Shareholder Allowable Loss and Deduction Items

	Description	**(a)** Current year losses and deductions	**(b)** Carryover amounts (column (e)) from the previous year	**(c)** Allowable loss from stock basis	**(d)** Allowable loss from debt basis	**(e)** Carryover amounts
35	Ordinary business loss	11,000			8,250	2,750
36	Net rental real estate loss					
37	Other net rental loss					
38	Net capital loss	3,000			2,250	750
39	Net section 1231 loss					
40	Other loss					
41	Section 179 deductions	2,000			1,500	500
42	Charitable contributions					
43	Investment interest expense					
44	Section 59(e)(2) expenditures					
45	Other deductions					
46	Foreign taxes paid or accrued					
47	**Total loss.** Add lines 35 through 46 for each column. Enter the total loss in column (c) on line 11 and enter the total loss in column (d) on line 30	16,000	0	0	12,000	4,000

Form **7203** (Rev. 12-2022)

George may take $12,000 in losses, which offset his remaining debt basis. The 25% of losses George cannot use on his 2022 tax return are carried forward to 2023, as shown in column (e).

APPENDIX

QUESTIONS TO CONSIDER IN ELECTING THE PTE TAX

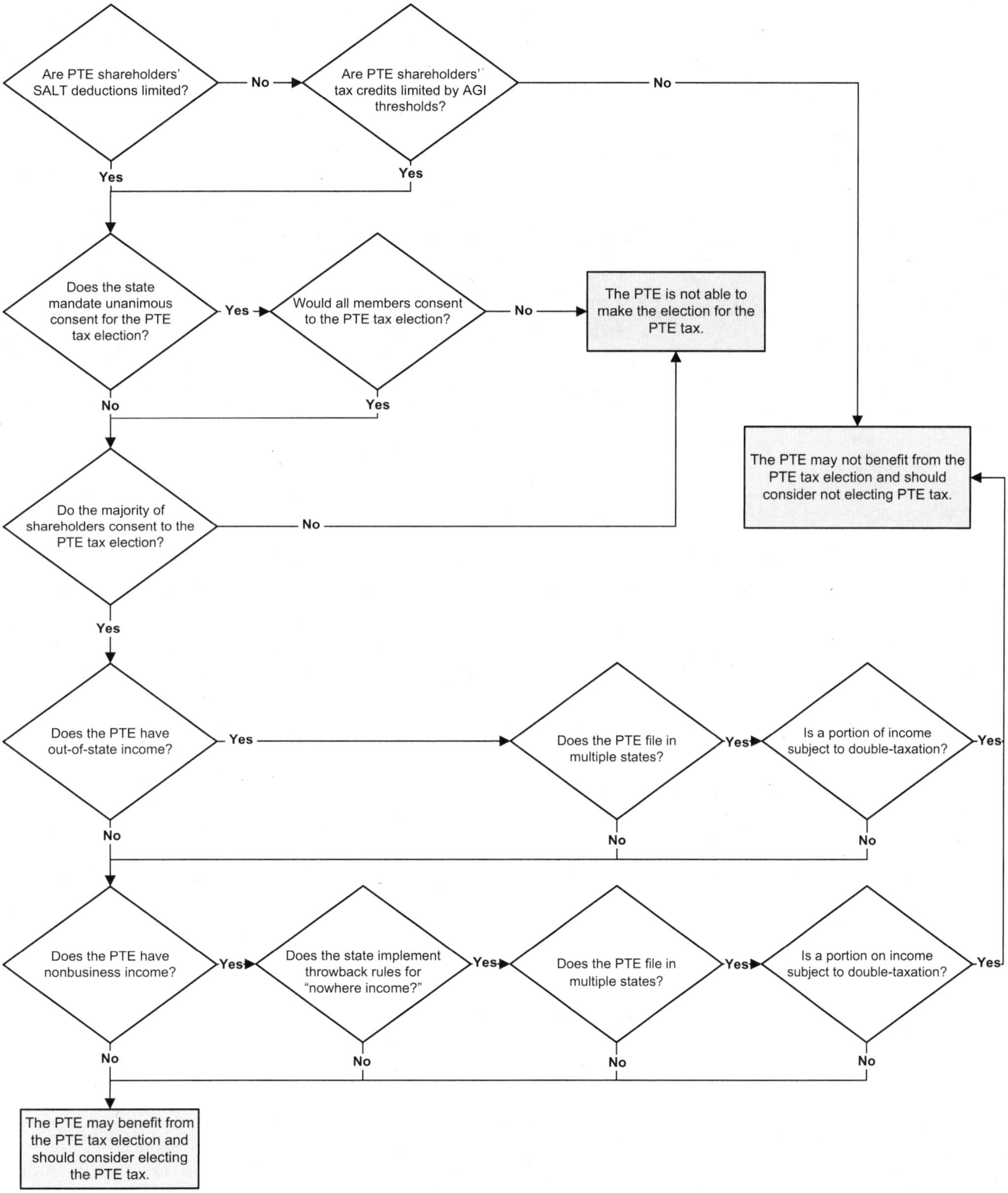

LIST OF STATES WITH PTE TAX ELECTIONS AND THEIR PTE TAX RATES[146]

State	PTE Tax Rate
AL	5.00%
AR	4.90%, 2.45% on cap gains
AZ	2.98%
CA	9.30%
CO	4.40%
CT	6.99%
GA	5.75%
HI	11.00%
IA	6.00%
ID	6.00%
IL	4.95%
IN	3.23%
KS	5.70%
KY	4.50%
LA	4.25%
MA	5.00%
MI	4.25%
MD	8.00%, 8.25% if there is an entity member
MN	9.85%
MO	5.40%
MS	5.00%
MT	6.75% before 2024, 5.9% after 2023
NC	4.99%
NE	6.84% before 2023, 6.64% for 2023
NJ	5.675%–10.900%
NM	5.90%
NY	6.85%–10.90%
NYC	3.876%
OH	5.00% through 2022, 3.00% in 2023 and later
OK	5.00%
OR	9.90%, 9.00% under $250,000
RI	5.99%
SC	3.00%
UT	4.85%
VA	5.75%
WI	7.90%
WV	6.50% for 2022, 5.12% for 2023

146. *Links to States' Pass-Through Entity (PTE) Tax Legislation and Tax Authorities' Information and Guidance.* Jun. 13, 2023. AICPA. [us.aicpa.org/content/dam/aicpa/advocacy/tax/downloadabledocuments/56175896-links-to-pass-through-entity-pte-taxes-states-legislation-and-tax-authorities-information-and-guidance.pdf] Accessed on Jul. 20, 2023.

Chapter 11: New Developments

Note. Corrections for all of the chapters are available at **TaxSchool.illinois.edu.** For clarification about terms used throughout this chapter, see the **Acronyms and Abbreviations** section following the index.

For your convenience, in-text website links are also provided as short URLs. Anywhere you see **uofi.tax/xxx**, the link points to the address immediately following in brackets.

11

About the Author

Kelly Golish, CPA, is the Assistant Director, Tax Materials, at the University of Illinois Tax School. She was previously a manager at Crowder, CPAs in Danville, IL and worked for both public and private accounting firms in Decatur, IL, Cleveland, OH, and San Jose, CA. Kelly earned a Masters in Accounting with an emphasis in Taxation and a Bachelors in Accounting at the University of Notre Dame.

Chris Korban, CPA, is a Tax Materials Specialist at the University of Illinois Tax School. He joined Tax School in 2023 with nine years of experience in public accounting. Chris earned both his Bachelor's Degree in Accounting and Master of Accounting Science from the University of Illinois.

Dwight Roberts is an advisor with FBFM and is president of the Tax Resolution Center of Illinois. He was employed by the Auditor General for the State of Illinois until 2005 and retired from the IRS as a revenue agent in 2020. He received his bachelor's and master's degrees in accountancy from the University of Illinois Springfield. Dwight resides in Springfield with his wife Sandra.

Rachel Szeklinski, CPA, has worked in public accounting for over six years and started writing for the University of Illinois Tax School in 2022. She graduated from Carroll University with honors in accounting in 2020 and passed the CPA exam in early 2021.

Other chapter contributors and reviewers are listed at the front of this book.

COVID-19 EMPLOYEE RETENTION CREDIT

The employee retention credit (ERC) was modified under the Coronavirus Aid, Relief, and Economic Security (CARES) Act,[1] and covered the period of March 13, 2020, through December 31, 2020.[2] Under the provisions of the CARES Act, employers who had received Payroll Protection Program (PPP) loans were not eligible for the ERC.[3]

This program was further expanded by Congress in 2021 through the Consolidated Appropriations Act of 2021.[4] This act permitted employers that received PPP loans to claim the ERC, and modified and extended the ERC from December 31, 2020, through June 30, 2021.[5] The American Rescue Plan Act (ARPA), provided an extended and modified ERC for wages paid after June 30, 2021, and before January 1, 2022.[6]

Although ARPA extended the ERC to employers even if those employers had received PPP loans, an employer could not claim ERC for wages that were used to receive forgiveness of their PPP loan. With the Infrastructure Investment and Jobs Act which was signed into law on November 15, 2021, the ERC was retroactively ended as of September 30, 2021, for all businesses except those that qualified as **recovery startup businesses.** Recovery startup businesses are businesses that began operations after February 15, 2020 and are only eligible for the ERC for 3rd and 4th quarters of 2021.[7]

---

1. *CARES Act,* PL 116-136, §2301.
2. *COVID-19-Related Employee Retention Credits: Overview.* Jan. 31, 2023. IRS. [www.irs.gov/newsroom/covid-19-related-employee-retention-credits-overview] Accessed on Aug. 22, 2023.
3. Ibid.
4. *Consolidated Appropriation Act of 2021,* PL 116-260, §276, Div. N.
5. Ibid, §§206 and 207.
6. IRS Notice 2021-23, 2021-16 IRB 1113.
7. *Frequently asked questions about the Employee Retention Credit.* Jul. 31, 2023. IRS. [www.irs.gov/coronavirus/frequently-asked-questions-about-the-employee-retention-credit] Accessed on Sep. 6, 2023.

Caution. Many practitioners do not prepare payroll tax returns and consequently, may not have been engaged by their clients to review and prepare ERC claims. However, as discussed later, some ERC claims may require the taxpayer to file amended income tax returns. Practitioners may have clients ask them to prepare the required amended returns. Practitioners will be well-advised to understand whether the client qualifies for the ERC and the professional responsibility that the practitioner has if the client does not qualify.

Note. For details on computing the ERC, see the 2021 *University of Illinois Federal Tax Workbook,* Volume A, Chapter 1: New Developments. This can be found at **uofi.tax/arc** [taxschool.illinois.edu/taxbookarchive].

Due to the perceived popularity of the ERC, a number of firms have popped up promoting the ERC. The **IRS issued an advisory warning** of third parties promoting improper ERC claims to employers who may or may not qualify.[8] Some of these promoters are claiming large refunds per employee and charging large fees for assisting in claiming the credit.

Note. The IRS also identified ERC fraud as one of its Dirty Dozen that represents the worst tax scams of the year. The Dirty Dozen, including ERC fraud, is covered in the 2023 *University of Illinois Federal Tax Workbook,* Chapter 12: Rulings and Cases.

The IRS identifies the following qualifications that an employer must meet to qualify for the ERC.[9]

1. Sustained a full or partial suspension of operations due to orders from an appropriate governmental authority limiting commerce, travel, or group meetings due to COVID-19 during 2020 or the first three quarters of 2021,
2. Experienced a significant decline in gross receipts during 2020, or a decline in gross receipts in the first three quarters of 2021, or
3. Qualified as a recovery start-up business for the 3rd or 4th quarters of 2021.

As the second qualification states, an employer must have a **significant decline** in gross receipts during 2020 or in the first three quarters of 2021. This is defined under the CARES Act as beginning in the quarter in which the gross receipts declined by more than 50% for the same calendar quarter in 2019.[10] The Taxpayer Certainty and Disaster Relief Act of 2020,[11] which expanded the ERC to 2021, defined the eligibility to include decreases in gross receipts in 2021 as **less than 80%** of the gross receipts in 2019 for the same calendar quarter. For businesses which were not in business in 2019, the comparison is made to the same quarter in 2020. Finally, the ARPA made the credit available to "recovery startup businesses" that do not otherwise meet the eligibility criteria.[12] The Infrastructure Investment and Jobs Act modified the ERC to end September 30, 2021, except for recovery start-up businesses which had limited availability and can include 4th quarter 2021.[13]

Note. For more information on the ERC rules and qualifications, see the 2020 *University of Illinois Federal Tax Workbook,* Volume A, Chapter 1: New Developments, and the 2021 *University of Illinois Federal Tax Workbook,* Volume A, Chapter 1: New Developments. These chapters can be found at **uofi.tax/arc** [taxschool.illinois.edu/taxbookarchive].

---

8. IRS News Rel. IR-2023-105 (May 25, 2023).

9. Ibid; IRC §3134(c)(2); *Frequently asked questions about the Employee Retention Credit* Jul. 31, 2023. IRS. [www.irs.gov/coronavirus/frequently-asked-questions-about-the-employee-retention-credit] Accessed on Aug. 4, 2023.

10. *CARES Act,* PL 116-136, §2301.

11. *Consolidated Appropriations Act of 2021,* PL 116-260, §§206 and 207.

12. *American Rescue Plan Act of 2021,* PL 117-2, §9651.

13. *Infrastructure Investment and Jobs Act,* PL 117-58.

SUPPLY CHAIN DISRUPTION[14]

The IRS is continuing to clarify terms of the ERC. On July 21, 2023, the IRS issued a General Legal Advice Memo (GLAM) that describes five scenarios involving supply chain disruptions where an employer's trade or business was fully or partially suspended in a calendar quarter because of a governmental order limiting commerce, travel, or group meetings due to COVID-19. As mentioned previously, an employer must have experienced a full or partial disruption of their business due to COVID-19 to qualify for the ERC. The general takeaway from these five scenarios is that the IRS is significantly reducing employers who qualify for ERC based on the full or partial disruption qualification.

1. Employer A was not eligible for the ERC because the employer was not subject to a government order that suspended their business. Even though the employer experienced delays from their supplier, the employer could not provide a government order suspending business from the supplier. Additionally, because the employer had a supply of critical goods, they were able to continue operating during the pandemic.

2. Similarly, Employer B also was not eligible for the ERC because they were not subject to any governmental orders suspending their business. Employer B's critical goods were stuck in port, which the employer assumed was due to COVID-19 but could not provide any specific order applicable to their supplier. There was speculation that the delay in supplies could have been attributed to increases in consumer spending, aging infrastructure, or a truck driver shortage (possibly due to COVID-19 illnesses but unconfirmed).

3. Employer C and their supplier **were subject to a government order** that suspended both of their business operations from April 2020 through May 2020. Employer C experienced delays in receiving goods from the supplier for the remainder of 2020 and 2021. The supplier did not provide a reason for the delay, but Employer C assumed the delay was due to COVID-19. Employer C is eligible for the ERC for the **2nd quarter of 2020** because there was a government order in place. However, Employer C is not eligible for the ERC for the remaining quarters of 2020 or any of 2021 because there was no government order in place. The existence of a government order in the 2nd quarter of 2020 does not extend to any future periods.

4. Employer D was not subject to any government orders due to the pandemic at any time. During 2020 and 2021, Employer D could not receive critical supplies from their supplier. However, they were able to obtain the goods from an alternate supplier, but at a 35% increase in costs. Employer D continued their operations, but with a lower profit than in 2019. Employer D is not considered an eligible employer because they continued to operate their business. An increase in the cost of supplies is not the same as having a full or partial suspension of operations.

5. Employer E, a retail business selling a variety of products, was not under a government order, but was unable to stock a limited number of products and had to raise prices on products that were in limited supply because of supply chain disruptions. Despite the product shortage, Employer E was able to continue full operations during 2021. Employer E does not qualify for the ERC because they cannot demonstrate a government order caused the supplier to not be able to provide supplies and that Employer E could not obtain critical goods that resulted in a full or partial suspension of their business.

> **Caution.** The GLAM may not be used or cited as precedent. However, it does show that the number of businesses that are eligible to claim to ERC is significantly limited.

14. Generic Legal Advice Memorandum (GLAM) AM 2023-005. Jul. 21, 2023. IRS. [www.irs.gov/pub/lanoa/am-2023-005-508v.pdf] Accessed on Aug. 23, 2023.

AMENDING PAYROLL TAX RETURNS

The window for amending payroll tax returns claiming COVID-19 ERC is beginning to close. For 2020 tax periods, the deadline to claim the ERC is April 15, 2024. For 2021 tax periods, the deadline to claim the ERC is April 15, 2025. The following table outlines the deadlines.[15]

Year	Quarter Ending	General Amended Due Date	Due Date for Amending ERC
2020	Jun. 30	Jul. 31, 2023	Apr. 15, 2024
2020	Sep. 30	Oct. 31, 2023	Apr. 15, 2024
2020	Dec. 31	Jan. 31, 2024	Apr. 15, 2024
2021	Mar. 31	Apr. 30, 2024	Apr. 15, 2025
2021	Jun. 30	Jul. 31, 2024	Apr. 15, 2025
2021	Sep. 30	Oct. 31, 2024	Apr. 15, 2025
2021	Dec. 31	Jan. 31, 2025	Apr. 15, 2025

Before a tax practitioner (in this case, CPA, attorney, or EA) claims an ERC for a client, they should be aware of their professional obligations under the Office of Professional Responsibility (OPR). Under Circular 230, practitioners are required to exercise due diligence in the accuracy of any written or oral representations to clients and the IRS. This includes preparing and filing tax returns (income, employment, or other) or other documents on behalf of a client. Therefore, practitioners must acquire sufficient details from their client to determine whether the client qualifies for the ERC and claim the accurate amount. A practitioner may rely in good faith on a client's responses to questions about eligibility if the responses appear to be **reasonable.** A practitioner who learns their client did not comply with the ERC requirements in a previous year must promptly inform the client of the noncompliance, error or omission, and any potential penalties.[16]

A practitioner who discovers that a client previously claimed an excessive ERC (including an ERC that they did not qualify for) must advise the client of the noncompliance as mentioned previously. **The practitioner is not required to prepare an amended ERC claim.** While it is considered a best practice to file an amended return, the client must request it and the practitioner must feel competent to prepare it.[17]

If a practitioner believes they meet their professional responsibilities as discussed previously, they may be requested to file the amended returns examined next.

Caution. The statute for assessment under the ERC is extended to five years after the filing of the amended returns. In addition, fraud penalties could be applied if fraud can be established in the claim.[18] Therefore, taxpayers that are in doubt about their eligibility for the credit should be cautious about claiming it.

15. *Frequently asked questions about the Employee Retention Credit.* Jul. 27, 2023. IRS. [www.irs.gov/coronavirus/frequently-asked-questions-about-the-employee-retention-credit] Accessed on Jul. 28, 2023.

16. *Professional Responsibility and the Employee Retention Credit.* Mar. 7, 2023. IRS. [www.irs.gov/pub/irs-utl/2023-02-professional-responsibility-and-the-employee-retention-credit-R2-508-compliant.pdf] Accessed on Jul. 28, 2023.

17. Ibid.

18. IRC §3134.

Taxpayer Qualified for ERC and Did Not Claim[19]

A taxpayer who is eligible to claim the ERC but did not claim the credit when they filed their original employment tax return may file an amended employment tax return to claim the credit. A business that files quarterly employment returns claims the credit for prior 2020 and 2021 quarters on Form 941-X, *Adjusted Employer's Quarterly Federal Tax Return or Claim for Refund.* A business that files annual employment returns use Form 944-X, *Adjusted Employer's ANNUAL Federal Tax Return or Claim for Refund,* to claim the ERC.[20]

A taxpayer must have filed an original employment tax return to claim the ERC on an amended return. Additionally, a taxpayer must have issued and filed Forms W-2, *Wage and Tax Statement,* to claim the credit.

> **Note.** An amended claim for the ERC will result in an employer also filing an amended income tax return to reduce the deduction for wages by the amount of the credit for the same period.

Taxpayer Claimed ERC and Did Not Qualify[21]

Anyone who claimed the ERC and did not qualify must return the funds (including interest received) to the IRS. In addition, they may be assessed additional penalties and interest. The steps to return an erroneous refund depends on the method the refund was issued.[22]

- **Refunds on paper Treasury checks that have not been cashed.** The taxpayer must write "void" in the endorsement section on the back of the check. They should submit the paper check immediately to the proper IRS location, which is based on the city listed on the refund check on the bottom text line in front of the words TAX REFUND. The IRS mailing address can be found at **www.irs.gov/taxtopics/tc161**.
- **Refunds on paper Treasury checks that have been cashed.** The taxpayer must submit a personal check, money order, etc. immediately, but no later than 21 days after cashing, to the appropriate IRS mailing address. As mentioned in the previous bullet point, the mailing address depends on the city listed on the check. Additionally, the taxpayer must write on the check/money order: Payment of Erroneous Refund, plus the tax period for which the refund was issued, and the taxpayer's identification number. Lastly, the taxpayer must include a brief explanation of why the taxpayer is returning the refund. Interest may also be due to the IRS.
- **Refund was direct deposited.** The taxpayer must contact the automated clearing house department of the bank or financial institution where the direct deposit was received and have them return the refund to the IRS. The taxpayer must also call the IRS (800-829-1040 for individual returns and 800-829-4933 for business returns) and provide an explanation of why the taxpayer is returning the refund. Interest may also be due to the IRS.

Taxpayers may receive a notice from the IRS if the IRS calculated an amount different than what was claimed on the return. Taxpayers should review the notice and call the number listed if they require additional assistance.[23]

---

19. *Frequently asked questions about the Employee Retention Credit.* Jul. 27, 2023. IRS. [www.irs.gov/coronavirus/frequently-asked-questions-about-the-employee-retention-credit] Accessed on Jul. 28, 2023.

20. *Employee Retention Credit.* Jul. 27, 2023. IRS. [www.irs.gov/coronavirus/employee-retention-credit] Accessed on Jul. 28, 2023.

21. *Frequently asked questions about the Employee Retention Credit.* Jul. 27, 2023. IRS. [www.irs.gov/coronavirus/frequently-asked-questions-about-the-employee-retention-credit] Accessed on Jul. 28, 2023.

22. *Topic No. 161, Returning an Erroneous Refund – Paper Check or Direct Deposit.* May 12, 2023. IRS. [www.irs.gov/taxtopics/tc161] Accessed on Jul. 28, 2023.

23. Ibid.

Fraudulently Filed Return. If the IRS determines that fraud exists, fraud penalties could be applied to the additional assessed tax. The fraud penalty is an additional tax of **75% of the portion of the underpayment attributable to fraud.**[24] Filing Forms 941-X or 944-X will not necessarily alleviate penalties; however, this action would be a positive step should the IRS pursue a fraud penalty. The employer may, however, still be subject to a **negligence penalty of 20% of the underpayment under IRC §6662.**

Example 1. Briar Company filed an amended Form 941-X for the 2nd quarter of 2021 in December 2022, knowing that they had not been affected by government shutdowns or experienced a decline in gross receipts. They received a refund check of $63,000 ($60,000 ERC and $3,000 interest) in June 2023. The IRS could impose a fraud penalty of $45,000 ($60,000 × 75%) in addition to repaying the $63,000 of tax.

Example 2. Use the same facts as **Example 1.** Briar decides the potential penalty of $45,000 is not worth the $60,000 credit. Briar files another amended Form 941-X (2nd quarter of 2021) return in 2023 and returns the $63,000 ($60,000 ERC + $3,000 interest). Briar may still be liable for interest and penalties on the erroneously filed Form 941-X, but it may avoid the $45,000 fraud penalty. It may also be liable for the 20% negligence penalty of $12,000 ($60,000 × 20%).

AMENDING AN ENTITY'S INCOME TAX RETURN

The ERC reduces wage expense for the tax year to which the payroll tax quarter relates. Thus, refunds received in later years require the previous income tax returns filed to be amended. This applies to both cash-basis and accrual-basis taxpayers. The following business entities are subject to amending their returns, including corporations, pass-through entities, sole proprietors, and exempt organizations that file Form 990-T, *Exempt Organization Business Income Tax Return (and proxy statement under section 6033(e))*.

S corporations, partnerships, and sole proprietorships must modify their taxable income. As their qualified business income (QBI) **increases** and the corresponding QBI-qualifying wages decrease, the QBI deduction (QBID) may be affected.

After pass-through entities amend their income tax returns, their shareholders or partners must amend their individual income tax returns. In many situations, income tax liabilities may increase, and as a result, shareholders and partners may incur interest and penalties because they paid income tax late.

Practitioner Planning Tip

Given the large number of amended returns this generates depending on the number of partners or shareholders in the entity, a practitioner may consider a cost-benefit analysis of claiming an ERC that was not claimed in the previous year. An incorrectly claimed ERC, however, likely requires amended returns, regardless of the cost-benefit.

24. IRC §6663.

STATUTE OF LIMITATIONS ISSUES

The following are three different statutes which apply to federal tax issues.

- Refund Statute Expiration Date (RSED)
- Assessment Statute Expiration Date (ASED)
- Collection Statute Expiration Date (CSED)

RSED[25]

The RSED is the date after which refunds are barred from being made by the IRS. Generally, the RSED is the later of three years from the date the return was filed, or two years from the date paid. There is usually no need to file an amended return once the RSED expires because the taxpayer is likely no longer entitled to the credit or refund.

> **Note.** Because the ERC requests a refund and/or a credit for the taxes paid in 2020 or 2021, the RSED has either already expired or is imminent.

ASED[26]

The ASED is the date the IRS is allowed to assess additional tax with respect to a tax year. Generally, the rule is within three years of the date the original return was received, or three years from the due date of the return, whichever is later.

Example 3. Alex files his 2020 Form 1040 before April 15th, 2021. The IRS has until April 15th, 2024, to assess additional tax.

Example 4. Bryson failed to file his 2020 Form 1040. The IRS assesses tax due based on information reported to the IRS by third-party reporters, (i.e., employers, banks, etc.). There is no ASED in effect because no tax return has been submitted by the taxpayer. Bryson should prepare and file these returns to start the ASED clock to prevent the IRS from making any further assessments.

Example 5. Carson and Sons, Co., timely filed Forms 941 for 2020 and 2021. Carson and Sons did not take the ERC. The normal ASED applies, and the IRS can assess additional payroll tax against Carson and Sons up to three years after the Forms 941 were filed or they were due, whichever is later.

The ARPA extended the statute of limitations for an IRS audit to five years for ERC claims for the second half of 2021.[27] However, the Infrastructure Investment and Jobs Act repealed the ERC as of the end of the 3rd quarter.[28] As such, the 5-year statute of limitations **only** applies to the 3rd quarter of 2021.

Example 6. Use the same facts as **Example 5,** except Carson and Sons took the ERC for the first three quarters of 2021. The statute of limitations for the first two quarters is the usual three years. However, the IRS has five years to audit Carson and Sons's 3rd quarter ERC.

---

25. *Time You Can Claim a Credit or a Refund.* Aug. 7, 2023. IRS. [www.irs.gov/filing/time-you-can-claim-a-credit-or-refund] Accessed on Aug. 28, 2023; *Taxpayer Claims Refund.* Taxpayer Advocate Service. [www.taxpayeradvocate.irs.gov/tax-terms/refund-statute-expiration-date-rsed] Accessed on Aug. 28, 2023.

26. *Time IRS Can Assess Tax.* Jun. 15, 2023. IRS. [www.irs.gov/filing/time-irs-can-assess-tax] Accessed on Aug. 28, 2023; *Assessment Statute Expiration Date (ASED).* Taxpayer Advocate Service. [www.taxpayeradvocate.irs.gov/tax-terms/assessment-statute-expiration-date-ased] Accessed on Aug. 28, 2023.

27. *American Rescue Plan Act of 2021,* PL 117-2, §6432(f).

28. *Infrastructure Investment and Jobs Act,* PL 117-58, §80604.

CSED[29]

The CSED establishes the length of time the IRS has to collect taxes. Generally, this is 10 years from the date of the assessment. There are certain circumstances when the IRS can suspend or extend the 10-year period, such as the following.

- The IRS is prohibited from collecting tax (suspended during the period the IRS cannot collect the tax, but the 10-year limit still applies).
- The IRS is legally authorized a specific amount of time to **extend** the initial 10-year period.

There are several common events that a taxpayer can do that can impact the CSED, such as the following.

- Requests an installment agreement
- Files for bankruptcy
- Submits an offer in compromise
- Requests a collection due process hearing
- Files an innocent spouse claim

Practitioner Planning Tip

Practitioners should research the statutes of limitations for the states in which their clients file to determine if the state has a different statute of limitations than the federal statute of limitations.

INFLATION REDUCTION ACT OF 2022

The Inflation Reduction Act of 2022 was signed into law on August 16, 2022.[30] This Act includes provisions that introduce new corporate taxes including the corporate alternative minimum tax (AMT), expand clean energy credits, and adjust healthcare and payroll tax provisions. Both individual and corporate taxpayers should understand the alterations made under the Inflation Reduction Act to maximize tax savings, with many of the provisions already in effect.

11

INDIVIDUAL ENERGY CREDITS

To motivate taxpayers to purchase energy-efficient home improvements and vehicles, numerous individual energy-efficient credits were passed in the Inflation Reduction Act. This section focuses on the energy efficient home improvement credit, the residential clean energy credit, the clean energy credit for new vehicles, and the clean energy credit for used vehicles.

---

29. *Time IRS Can Collect Tax.* Jun. 20, 2023. IRS. [www.irs.gov/filing/time-irs-can-collect-tax] Accessed on Aug. 28, 2023; *Collection Statute Expiration Date (CSED).* Taxpayer Advocate Service. [www.taxpayeradvocate.irs.gov/tax-terms/collection-statute-expiration-date-csed] Accessed on Aug. 28, 2023.

30. *Inflation Reduction Act of 2022*, PL 117-169.

Energy Efficient Home Improvement Credit[31]

The Inflation Reduction Act changed the name applied to IRC §25C from "nonbusiness energy property credit" to the "energy efficient home improvement credit."[32] Beginning with 2023, there is a $1,200 maximum aggregate yearly tax credit for all building envelope components, home energy audits, and energy property. Electric or natural gas heat pump water heaters, electric or natural gas heat pumps, and biomass stoves and biomass boilers have a separate aggregate yearly credit limit of $2,000. Thus, the maximum total yearly energy efficient home improvement credit amount may be up to $3,200. This replaces the old $500 lifetime limit for nonbusiness energy property.[33]

The energy efficient home improvement credit applies to the following types of improvements, which are classified into two groups.

Qualified Energy Efficient Improvements. For an improvement to be eligible for the energy efficient home improvement credit, it must be to a building envelope component that satisfies the energy efficiency requirements. Such improvements include the following.

- Exterior doors (30% of costs up to $250 per door, up to a total of $500)
- Exterior windows and skylights (30% of costs up to $600)
- Insulation materials or systems and air sealing materials or systems (30% of costs)
- Home energy audits (30% of costs up to $150)

The improvement must also satisfy the following requirements.

- Be installed in the United States
- Taxpayer must be the original user of the improvement
- Taxpayer must reasonably expect to use the improvement for at least five years, and the improvement must be to a principal residence as defined in IRC §121

Residential Energy Property Expenditures. The term "qualified energy property" means any of the following.

- Residential energy property (30% of costs, including labor, up to $600 for each item) that satisfy the energy efficiency requirements.
    - Natural gas, propane, or oil water heaters
    - Central air conditioners
    - Natural gas, propane, or oil furnaces and hot water boilers
- Improvements to or replacements of panelboards, sub-panelboards, branch circuits, or feeders that are installed along with building envelope components or other energy property and enable its installation and use.
- Heat pumps, biomass stoves, and biomass boilers (30% of costs, including labor) satisfying the energy efficiency requirements include the following.
    - Electric or natural gas heat pump water heaters
    - Electric or natural gas heat pumps
    - Biomass stoves and biomass boilers

---

31. IRC §25C as implemented by *Inflation Reduction Act of 2022,* PL 117-169, §13302.

32. *Inflation Reduction Act of 2022*, PL 117-169, §13301(h)(2).

33. IRC §25C(b) before amended by *Inflation Reduction Act of 2022,* PL 117-169.

In addition, the residential energy property expenditures must satisfy the following requirements.

- Installed in the United States
- Taxpayer is the original user of the property
- Installed on or in connection with a dwelling unit used as a residence (not necessarily a principal residence)

Rebates are subtracted from qualified expenses if **all** the following apply.[34]

- The rebate is based on the cost of the property
- The rebate comes from someone connected to the sale such as the manufacturer, distributor, seller, or installer
- The rebate is not given as payment for services the taxpayer provides

State energy efficiency incentives are generally **not** subtracted from qualified costs unless they qualify as a rebate or purchase-price adjustment under federal income tax law. Many states label energy efficiency incentives as rebates, even though they do not qualify under that definition. Those incentives could be included in the taxpayer's gross income for federal income tax purposes.[35]

Beginning after December 31, 2024, the taxpayer must meet the following qualifications to claim the residential energy property credit.[36]

1. The item is produced by a **qualified manufacturer**
2. The taxpayer includes the **qualified product identification number** of the item on their tax return for the tax year

For this purpose, the term **qualified product identification number** means the product identification number assigned to the item by the qualified manufacturer (e.g., a unique alphanumeric identification number).[37]

Home Energy Audits.[38] A home energy audit for a taxpayer's main home may qualify for a tax credit of up to $150. To qualify, the home energy audit must meet the following guidelines.

- Include a written report and inspection that identifies the most significant and cost-effective energy efficiency improvements with respect to the home, including an estimate of the energy and cost savings with respect to such improvement
- Be conducted and prepared by a home energy auditor

11

34. *Energy Efficient Home Improvement Credit.* Aug. 4, 2023. IRS. [www.irs.gov/credits-deductions/energy-efficient-home-improvement-credit] Accessed on Aug. 6, 2023.

35. Ibid; IRS Notice 2013-70, 2013-47 IRB 528.

36. IRS Notice 2022-48, 2022-43 IRB 316.

37. Ibid.

38. IRC §25C(e); *Energy Efficient Home Improvement Credit.* Aug. 4, 2023. IRS. [www.irs.gov/credits-deductions/energy-efficient-home-improvement-credit] Accessed on Aug. 6, 2023.

Starting in 2024, the following additional requirements must be met.

- The inspection must be conducted by a **qualified home energy auditor** (an individual certified by one of the qualified certification programs listed on the Department of Energy certification programs for the Energy Efficient Home Improvement Credit (Section 25C) at the time of the audit), or under the supervision of a qualified home energy auditor.
- The written report must be prepared and signed by a qualified home energy auditor, be consistent with industry best practices, and include the following.
  - The qualified home energy auditor's name and relevant employer identification number (EIN) or other type of appropriate taxpayer identifying number, if the auditor does not have an EIN
  - An attestation that the qualified home energy auditor is certified by a qualified certification program
  - The name of such qualified certification program

Residential Clean Energy Credit

Under IRC §25D, taxpayers who make clean energy improvements to their homes may be able to take the residential clean energy credit.[39] This credit replaces the residential energy efficient property credit for years prior to January 1, 2023. The residential clean energy credit is a 30% credit based on the cost of new, qualified clean energy property placed in service between January 1, 2023, and December 31, 2032. The credit extends into 2033 and 2034 but at a reduced rate. This credit is non-refundable but can be carried forward to future years.[40] This credit is different from the energy efficient home improvement credit (discussed previously),[41] formerly known as the nonbusiness energy property credit.

To qualify, the home must be located in the United States and the improvements must be made to the taxpayer's residence, whether owned or rented, but fuel cell property must be installed at the taxpayer's principal residence.[42] Landlords and other property owners who do not reside in the home are excluded from taking the credit. Qualifying expenses include the following.[43]

- Qualified solar electric property
- Qualified solar water heating property
- Qualified fuel cell property (only if installed at taxpayer's principal residence[44])
- Qualified small wind energy property expenditures
- Qualified geothermal heat pump property
- Qualified battery storage technology

Taxpayers who use their homes for business purposes face limitations on the credit. If business use in the home is up to 20%, taxpayers can claim the full credit. For taxpayers with business use greater than 20%, the credit is based on the share of expenses allocable to nonbusiness use.[45]

---

39. *Inflation Reduction Act of 2022*, PL 117-169, §13302, amending IRC §25D.
40. *Residential Clean Energy Credit*. Apr. 27, 2023. IRS. [www.irs.gov/credits-deductions/residential-clean-energy-credit] Accessed on Jun. 28, 2023.
41. IRC §25C. See *Inflation Reduction Act of 2022*, PL 117-169, §13301(h)(2) for the renaming of this credit.
42. IRC §25D(d).
43. IRC §25D(a).
44. IRC §25D(d)(3).
45. IRC §25D(e)(7).

Clean Energy Credit for New Vehicles[46]

This credit allows taxpayers to claim a $3,750 credit for purchasing vehicles that meet a mineral content requirement, and another $3,750 credit for vehicles with battery components manufactured or assembled in the United States, Canada, or Mexico, provided the vehicle was placed in service after April 17, 2023.[47]

> **Note.** Although there is a maximum credit of $7,500 per vehicle, the amount of the credit for each component was subject to a phase-in and was dependent on guidance from the IRS. On April 17, 2023, the IRS published proposed regulations related to the critical minerals and battery components requirements.[48] These proposed regulations are effective for vehicles placed in service on or after April 18, 2023. For vehicles placed in service from January 1 to April 17, 2023, the amount of the credit is determined without reference to the critical minerals and battery components test. Rather, IRC §30D(b) provides a base amount of credit of $2,500 which can be increased based on battery capacity up to a minimum of $3,751, up to a maximum credit of $7,500.

This credit is nonrefundable, and the excess cannot be carried forward to future years.[49] It applies to vehicles purchased through December 31, 2032.[50] After January 1, 2024, the purchaser may elect to transfer the credit to the dealer to reduce the purchase price under provisions of §30D(g), but not under the conditions of IRC §6418.[51] Taxpayers should consider the trade-off between claiming the credit on Form 8936, *Qualified Plug-in Electric Drive Motor Vehicle Credit*, or taking a reduction of the vehicle's purchase price.[52]

Qualifications. Qualifying vehicles must have a battery capacity of at least seven kilowatt-hours, have a gross weight under 14,000 pounds, be manufactured by a qualified company, have final assembly in North America, and meet the mineral and battery component tests, assuming they were placed in service after April 18, 2023.[53] Dealerships should provide taxpayers with information on eligible vehicles.

Practitioner Planning Tip

Practitioners are required to provide the vehicle identification number (VIN) for the qualified new or used vehicle to be entered on taxpayer's Form 8936. To see the potential credit amount, practitioner can search by year, make, and model at **uofi.tax/23x11x1** [www.fueleconomy.gov/feg/taxcenter.shtml].

Practitioners can verify the vehicle meets the manufacturing requirements for the clean energy credit by entering the VIN at **uofi.tax/23x11x2** [afdc.energy.gov/laws/electric-vehicles-for-tax-credit#vin-decoder].

These websites are just **tools** to assist the tax practitioner and are not definitive tax guidance.

46. *Inflation Reduction Act of 2022,* PL 117-169, §13401, amending IRC §30D.
47. Prop. Treas. Reg. §§1.30D-3(a)(2) and (b)(2).
48. Ibid.
49. IRC §30D(c)(2), referring to IRC subtitle A, part IV, subpart A, *Nonrefundable Personal Credits*.
50. *Inflation Reduction Act of 2022,* PL 117-169, §13401(a).
51. Ibid, §13401(g).
52. Form 8936, *Qualified Plug-in Electric Drive Motor Vehicle Credit.*
53. *Credits for New Clean Vehicles Purchased in 2023 or After.* Jun. 22, 2023. IRS. [www.irs.gov/credits-deductions/credits-for-new-clean-vehicles-purchased-in-2023-or-after] Accessed on Jun. 28, 2023.

In addition, the vehicle must be purchased new,[54] and the seller must furnish the information to the IRS at the time of purchase.[55] Vans, trucks, and sport utility vehicles with a manufacturer-suggested retail price (MSRP) over $80,000 do not qualify for the credit.[56] The MSRP of other vehicles, including passenger automobiles, must be $55,000 or less.[57]

The vehicle purchased must be for personal use. Taxpayers cannot purchase vehicles for business use and claim this credit on their individual tax returns.[58]

Modified Adjusted Gross Income (MAGI) Limitations. The MAGI limit is set at $300,000 for married filing jointly (MFJ) taxpayers, $225,000 for head of household (HoH) taxpayers, and $150,000 for all other filing statuses. Taxpayers can use MAGI either in the year of delivery or the prior year, whichever is less.[59]

Practitioner Planning Tip

Inquiring about the purchase of new vehicles is now an essential part of the tax preparation process. As many car manufacturers begin to implement green initiatives, the vehicle qualification range is expanded, and taxpayers may qualify without even knowing.

Additionally, because of the difference in MAGI limitations, practitioners should consider using the married filing separately filing status to maximize the clean energy credit.

Clean Energy Credit for Used Vehicles[60]

Beginning January 1, 2023, individual taxpayers who purchase used electric vehicles (EV) or fuel cell vehicles (FCV) from a **licensed dealer** may qualify for the used clean vehicle credit. This credit equates to 30% of the sale price, with a maximum non-refundable credit of $4,000.[61]

This credit is subject to MAGI limits of $150,000 for MFJ taxpayers, $112,500 for HoH taxpayers, and $75,000 for all other taxpayers. MAGI can either be applied to the year the vehicle was purchased or the preceding year.[62]

---

54. IRC §30D(a).

55. IRC §30D(g)(2); *Clean Vehicle Credit Seller or Dealer Requirements*. Jun. 22, 2023. IRS. [www.irs.gov/credits-deductions/clean-vehicle-credit-seller-or-dealer-requirements] Accessed on Jul. 20, 2023.

56. IRC §§30D(f)(11)(B)(i)–(iii).

57. IRC §30D(f)(11)(B)(iv).

58. IRC §30D(c)(1).

59. IRC §30D(f)(10).

60. *Inflation Reduction Act of 2022*, PL 117-169, §13402, creating IRC §25E.

61. IRC §25E(a).

62. *Inflation Reduction Act of 2022*, PL 117-169, §13402(b); IRC §25E(b)(1).

Previously Owned Clean Vehicles.[63] To qualify for the credit, the taxpayer must have acquired the used vehicle in a **qualified sale.** A qualified sale requires that the vehicle was purchased through a dealer, and the dealer furnishes sale information to the IRS. Additionally, the sale price must be less than $25,000, have a vehicle model year at least two years earlier than the purchase year, weigh less than 14,000 pounds, be eligible for FCV or plug-in EV with fewer than seven kilowatt-hours, and be used in the United States. The taxpayer is required to report the VIN with their tax return, and the dealer must report this VIN to the IRS. In addition, the vehicle is allowed only one clean energy credit during its existence.

Qualified Buyer.[64] A taxpayer may only claim this credit once every three years.[65] The taxpayer is ineligible for this credit if they purchase the vehicle from a spouse or a dependent.[66]

Taxpayers purchasing vehicles through avenues outside of dealerships are unable to take advantage of this tax incentive.[67] This credit only applies to vehicles purchased before the end of 2032.[68]

Practitioner Planning Tip

Tax practitioners will need to be aware of the specificities surrounding used vehicle purchases, especially the dealer requirements.

BUSINESS ENERGY INCENTIVES

One of the main components of the Inflation Reduction Act provides for business energy credits, deductions, and other incentives. The statutes provide incentives to use clean, renewable energy sources. Businesses that are looking to add improvements to existing structures or construct new premises should consider adopting energy-efficient equipment to leverage tax credits and deductions. This section focuses on the following incentives.

- Renewable electricity production credit
- Commercial clean vehicle credit
- Energy credit modifications
- Federal solar energy tax credit
- Commercial building energy deduction
- Contractor energy-efficient home credits
- Clean fuel credits
- Clean energy manufacturing and security investment incentives

63. IRC §25E.
64. IRC §25E(c).
65. IRC §25E(c)(3)(D).
66. IRC §25E(c)(3)(C).
67. IRC §25E(c)(2)(A), referring to IRC §30D(g)(8).
68. IRC §25E(g).

Renewable Electricity Production Credit[69]

Under IRC §45, businesses that **produce renewable energy** can claim a credit based on kilowatt-hours produced at a qualified facility or sold to an unrelated party.[70] Qualified facilities are those that are used for the generation of electricity, placed in service after December 31, 2024, and emit a greenhouse gas emission rate of less than zero. The credit covers facilities producing electricity using wind, closed-loop biomass, and landfill gas, among others.[71] Construction on the facility must have begun before January 1, 2025.[72]

Once the qualified facility is placed in service, the taxpayer can claim the **renewable electricity production tax credit for 10 years.**[73] The 2022 tax credit is calculated at a rate of 0.75 cents per kilowatt-hour for electricity generated from landfill gas, municipal solid waste, small irrigation power facilities, and open-loop biomass.[74] Wind and closed-loop biomass facilities can claim a 2.75 cents per kilowatt-hour credit if the facility was placed in service after 2021.[75] This credit is claimed on Form 8835, *Renewable Electricity Production Credit.* However, if wage and apprenticeship requirements are not met, the credit is 0.30 cents per kilowatt-hour.[76]

The Inflation Reduction Act modified many of the current provisions relating to renewable energy credits, including labor requirements. Facilities now must meet wage and apprenticeship requirements to qualify for the full tax credit. These requirements include paying all employees and contractors union wage rates, known as the **prevailing wage.** Additionally, qualified apprentices must complete 12.5% of the labor hours for facility construction in 2023 and 15% for construction beginning after 2023.[77]

Practitioner Planning Tip

The new labor requirements place a burden on business owners to ensure proper labor distribution between apprentices and prevailing market wages are present. The inability to meet these requirements can hinder credit-claiming ability and increase taxable income. Tax practitioners and business owners also have expanded tax planning opportunities based on the facility production dates. Credit computation and requirements vary, potentially resulting in tax advantages of speeding up or delaying tentative project start dates.

69. *Inflation Reduction Act of 2022*, PL 117-169, §13101(e), amending IRC §§45(b)(5), (d)(1), and 48(a)(5)(E).

70. IRC §45(a).

71. *Renewable Electricity Production Tax Credit Information.* Feb. 22, 2023. U.S. Environmental Protection Agency. [www.epa.gov/lmop/renewable-electricity-production-tax-credit-information] Accessed on Jul. 22, 2023.

72. IRC §45(d).

73. Instructions for Form 8835.

74. IRS Ann. 2022-23, 2022-48 IRB 499; Instructions for Form 8835.

75. Ibid.

76. Ibid.

77. Instructions for Form 8835.

Commercial Clean Vehicle Credit[78]

Businesses that purchase a qualified clean commercial vehicle may qualify for the commercial clean vehicle credit. This nonrefundable credit is calculated based on the lesser of 15% of the vehicle's basis or the incremental cost of the vehicle over a comparable vehicle that uses an internal combustion engine. Vehicles that are not powered by gas or diesel can increase the vehicle basis percentage to 30%.[79]

The credit is capped at $7,500 for vehicles under 14,000 pounds, and $40,000 for all other vehicles.[80] Qualifying vehicles must be made through a qualified manufacturer, be used primarily for business purposes in the United States, be classified as a motor vehicle under the Clean Air Act, have a qualifying fuel cell motor, and have a plug-in battery capacity of seven kilowatt-hours for vehicles under 14,000 pounds and 15 kilowatt-hours for all other vehicles.[81]

Note. IRC §45W(d)(3) precludes the commercial clean vehicle credit on any vehicle where the clean energy vehicle credit under §30D.

Businesses that frequently purchase vehicles should consider clean alternatives to leverage tax credits up to $40,000. However, business taxpayers claiming this credit must follow a number of requirements. Additionally, the statute specifically allows **tax-exempt organizations** to claim this credit, which may offset unrelated business income tax. The IRS is still in the process of finalizing forms and regulations.[82]

Energy Credit Modifications to Include Storage Technology[83]

The Inflation Reduction Act modifies the application of IRC §48 to include energy storage technology. Energy storage property is defined as thermal energy property or other property that receives, stores, or delivers energy for conversion to electricity, with a capacity of five kilowatt-hours or more.[84]

To qualify for the energy credit, construction on the facility must begin on or before December 31, 2024.[85]

Federal Solar Energy Tax Credit for Business

Before the enactment of the Inflation Reduction Act, the investment tax credit (ITC) under §48 applied to solar energy generation projects. Solar generation facilities were eligible for an ITC claim and subject to the standard phase-out of that credit. The Inflation Reduction Act retains the §48 credit for solar generation projects and reestablishes an opportunity to claim a 30% tax credit. There are two tax credits available for businesses, including not-for-profit entities, purchasing solar energy systems.

- The ITC[86] reduces the federal income tax liability based on a percentage of the cost of a solar system installed during the tax year.
- The production tax credit (PTC)[87] is a per kilowatt-hour tax credit for electricity generated by solar and other qualifying systems during the first 10 years of a system's operation. It reduces the federal income tax liability.

78. *Inflation Reduction Act of 2022*, PL 117-169, §13403, creating IRC §45W.
79. IRC §45W(b)(1)(A).
80. IRC §45W(b)(4).
81. IRC §45W(c)(3)(A).
82. *Commercial Clean Vehicle Credit*. Jun. 22, 2023. IRS. [www.irs.gov/credits-deductions/commercial-clean-vehicle-credit] Accessed on Jun. 28, 2023.
83. *Inflation Reduction Act of 2022,* PL 117-169, §13102(f), amending various paragraphs under IRC §48(a).
84. IRC §48(c)(6)(A).
85. IRC §48(c)(6)(D).
86. IRC §§48 and 48E.
87. IRC §§45 and 45Y.

Generally, business owners cannot claim both the ITC and the PTC for the same property, although they could claim different credits for co-located systems, like solar and storage, depending on further guidance issued by the IRS.

Solar systems that are placed in service in 2022 or later and begin construction before 2033 are eligible for a 30% ITC or a 2.75 cents per kilowatt-hour PTC if they meet labor requirements issued by the Treasury Department or are under one megawatt in size.

Note. For a summary of the ITC and PTC from 2006 through 2036, see **uofi.tax/23x11x3** [www.energy.gov/sites/default/files/2023-05/Summary-ITC-and-PTC-Values-Chart-2023.png].

Commercial Building Energy Deduction[88]

This provision of the Act provides for owners of qualified commercial buildings and designers of certain energy-efficient commercial building property to claim this deduction.[89] This deduction is also available for retrofit buildings.[90]

Qualified commercial buildings must be:

- Located in the United States;
- For commercial use (includes apartment buildings over three stories);[91]
- Built with qualified property;
- Certified to produce required minimum energy savings; and
- Subject to the American Society of Heating, Refrigerating and Air-Conditioning Engineers Standard 90.1.[92]

Interior lighting systems, heating, cooling, ventilation, and hot water systems are included in the qualified property. The deduction is calculated based on the lesser of the cost of the installed property or square footage. Buildings with 25% energy savings can claim $0.50 per square foot. An additional $0.02 deduction per square foot is added for each energy savings percentage point above 25. The deduction caps out at $1.00 per square foot.[93]

Note. Businesses can claim up to $5.00 per square foot if compliance with prevailing wage and apprenticeship requirements are met. The applicable deduction is calculated at a rate of $2.50 per square foot, with a cap of $5.00 per square foot.[94]

Prior to the Inflation Reduction Act, businesses needed to meet a 50% reduction in the baseline energy use intensity of the building. Lowering the credit threshold to 25% allows more architects and owners of commercial property to leverage additional deductions outside of depreciation. Additionally, exempt organizations can also take advantage of IRC §179D to reduce taxable income. Commercial business owners and architects may benefit from this deduction when planning energy-efficient additions and expansion projects.[95]

---

88. *Inflation Reduction Act of 2022*, PL 117-169, §13303, amending IRC §179D.

89. *Energy-efficient Commercial Building Deduction.* Jun. 30, 2023. IRS. [www.irs.gov/credits-deductions/energy-efficient-commercial-building-deduction] Accessed on Jun. 30, 2023.

90. IRC §179D(f).

91. *Energy Efficient Commercial Building Deduction.* Aug. 2, 2023. IRS. [www.irs.gov/credits-deductions/energy-efficient-commercial-building-deduction#building] Accessed on Aug. 3, 2023.

92. Ibid.

93. IRC §179D(b)(2).

94. IRC §§179D(b)(3) and (4).

95. Ibid.

Contractor Energy-Efficient Home Credits[96]

The energy-efficient home credit was set to expire on December 31, 2021; however, the Inflation Reduction Act extends this credit through 2032. This tax credit allows eligible contractors to claim a credit for qualified energy-efficient homes sold or leased to another person. An **eligible contractor** is a person that constructs a qualified energy-efficient home and has basis in the home.[97]

The credit is based on the energy efficiency of the home. Single-family homes that are **certified** under the Zero Energy Ready Home (ZERH) Program[98] requirements are eligible for a $5,000 per dwelling-unit credit. Single-family homes that do not meet the ZERH Program, but participate in the Energy Star Residential New Construction Program,[99] can receive a $2,500 credit per dwelling unit. The credit for multi-family homes is lower at $1,000 and $500 per dwelling unit, respectively.[100]

Note. The requirements for the ZERH Program depend on "the requirements of the applicable version based on building type, the builder/developer/plant must be registered as a ZERH program partner, and the project must be approved by an approved third-party verifier." For more information on the requirements by building type, see **uofi.tax/23x11x4** [www.energy.gov/eere/buildings/doe-zero-energy-ready-home-zerh-program-requirements].

A contractor set up as an S corporation or partnership claims this credit on Form 8908, *Energy Efficient Home Credit*. The credit then flows through to partners or shareholders, who in turn file Form 3800, *General Business Credit*.[101] The energy-efficient home credit is designed to motivate contractors to install energy-efficient equipment during the construction or remodeling process.

Practitioner Planning Tip

Contractors frequently install energy-efficient items in the normal course of their business that qualify for this credit, potentially creating a tax-saving opportunity. It is important to ask contractors about the products they use in the event the contractors do not know they qualify.

Caution. This credit does not reduce AMT.[102]

11

96. *Inflation Reduction Act of 2022*, PL 117-169, §13304, amending IRC §45L(a)(2), (c), and (g).

97. Instructions for Form 8908.

98. IRC §45L(c)(1)(B).

99. IRC §45L(c)(2)(A).

100. *Inflation Reduction Act of 2022,* PL 117-169, §13201(a); IRC §45L(c)(3)

101. Instructions for Form 8908; Partner's Instructions for Schedule K-1 (Form 1065); Shareholder's Instructions for Schedule K-1 (Form 1120-S).

102. See IRC §§45L, 38, and 55(c).

Clean Fuel Credits

Many fuel credits were extended and modified under the Inflation Reduction Act. These provisions affect fuel transportation, biodiesel, renewable diesel, aviation fuel, and alternative fuel industries.

Extension of Incentives to Biodiesel, Renewable Diesel, and Alternative Fuel Providers.[103] The clean fuel production credit now extends to biodiesel, renewable diesel, and alternative fuel providers. Inflation Reduction Act, §13201 also extends the end date to December 31, 2024.[104] This credit provides taxpayers with the ability to claim $1.00 for each gallon of biodiesel used and $0.10 for each gallon of qualified agro-biodiesel production.[105]

Many businesses in fuel transportation industries will now be able to reduce taxable income through this credit. This tax credit only applies to fuel used for transportation. Transportation can include aviation and other types of fuel.[106]

> **Note.** Inflation Reduction Act, §13701 creates IRC §45Y, the clean electricity production credit, while §13704 of the Inflation Reduction Act creates IRC §45Z, which establishes the clean fuel production credit. The clean **electricity** production credit provides a credit for producing electricity to limit production of carbon dioxide.[107] The clean energy **fuel** production credit provides a credit for fuel that is used for transportation. Use of the fuel must meet certain emissions requirements that are listed in §45Z(b).

Extension of Second-Generation Biofuel Incentives.[108] The Inflation Reduction Act, §13202, extends second-generation biofuel incentives until December 31, 2024.[109]

Sustainable Aviation Fuel Credits.[110] Aviation fuel producers are now eligible for a sustainable aviation fuel credit.[111] This credit is calculated at a rate of $1.25 plus the applicable supplementary amount multiplied by the gallons of sustainable aviation fuel sold.[112] The applicable supplementary amount equates to $0.01 for each percentage point that the lifecycle greenhouse gas emissions exceed 50%, with a max of $0.50.[113] This tax incentive helps alleviate the burden of rising material costs in the aviation fuel industry.

Alternative Fuel Credit Reinstatement.[114] The Inflation Reduction Act reinstates the IRC §6426 credit for alcohol, fuel, biodiesel, and alternative fuel mixtures for fuel sold, used, or removed, through December 31, 2024. Liquefied hydrogen is not considered an alternative fuel under the new legislation.[115] Taxpayers may need to file Form 720-X, *Amended Quarterly Federal Excise Tax Return*, to claim retrospective fuel credits.[116]

---

103. *Inflation Reduction Act of 2022,* PL 117-169, §13704(a), creating IRC §45Z.
104. Ibid, §13704(a).
105. IRC §40A(b).
106. Ibid.
107. IRC §45Y(b)(2).
108. IRC §40(b)(6).
109. *Inflation Reduction Act of 2022,* PL 117-169, §13202(a).
110. *Inflation Reduction Act of 2022,* PL 117-169, §13203; IRC §40B.
111. *Sustainable Aviation Fuel (SAF) Tax Credit.* U.S. Department of Energy, Alternative Fuels Data Center. [afdc.energy.gov/laws/13160] Accessed on Jul. 22, 2023.
112. *Inflation Reduction Act of 2022,* PL 117-169, §13203(a).
113. Ibid.
114. Ibid, §13201; IRC §§40A and 6426(c).
115. Ibid, §13201(a).
116. Instructions for Form 720-X.

Clean Energy Manufacturing and Security Investment Incentives

The Inflation Reduction Act establishes different incentives for qualified investments in energy programs. These programs prioritize qualified investments in advanced energy projects.

Advanced Energy Project Credit.[117] The advanced energy project credit was extended and adjusted under the Inflation Reduction Act, §13501. Total funds of $10 billion have been allocated, with at least $4 billion allocated to energy communities, which are environmentally and economically challenged areas.[118]

The credit equals 30% of the qualified investment costs that meet prevailing wage and apprenticeship requirements, and 6% for investments that do not.[119] A qualifying project creates or expands a facility that recycles specified advanced energy property, installs technology that reduces greenhouse gas emissions by 20%, or adds the recycling of critical materials. Costs for refining or blending non-renewable transportation fuels are specifically excluded.[120]

The project eligibility list has been expanded under the Inflation Reduction Act, §13501, providing more businesses with the opportunity to claim additional deductions for energy efficiency modifications to plants and premises.

Practitioner Planning Tip

The stark difference in credit amounts for complying with prevailing wage and apprenticeship requirements makes it important to consider the trade-off between paying higher rates for labor on energy-efficient projects and taking a lower credit. This may require businesses and their tax practitioner to spend more time in the project planning phase to make the most informed decision surrounding labor and tax saving opportunities.

Advanced Manufacturing Production Credit.[121] The advanced manufacturing production credit provides a tax incentive for producers of solar energy, wind components, alternating current, battery components, critical minerals, and invertors. The credit amount is dependent on the type of component being manufactured. Taxpayers can claim this credit on Form 7207, *Advanced Manufacturing Production Credit.*[122]

Clean Electricity Investment Tax Credit.[123] Investments in qualified electricity production facilities may also qualify for a tax credit. The credit is computed based on the **applicable percentage time** of the investment amount, which is 30% for facilities with a net output of less than one megawatt and was constructed within 60 days of the Secretary's published guidance. Investments in any other qualified facility warrant a 6% credit.[124]

Additionally, if the generating facilities are built on Indian tribal land, they qualify for a 10% bonus credit. An additional 20% is available for facilities built under housing programs that are federally subsidized, or companies that offer 50% or more of their power to low-income families.[125]

117. IRC §48C(e).

118. *Inflation Reduction Act of 2022,* PL 117-169, §13501(a); IRC §48C(e)(2), referring to IRC §45(b)(11)(B).

119. IRC §48C(e)(4).

120. Ibid.

121. *Inflation Reduction Act of 2022,* PL 117-169, §13502(a), creating IRC §45X.

122. Instructions for Form 7207.

123. IRC §48E.

124. *Inflation Reduction Act of 2022,* PL 117-169, §13702(a).

125. *Building a Clean Energy Economy,* p.16. Jan. 2023, Ver. 2. The White House. [www.whitehouse.gov/wp-content/uploads/2022/12/Inflation-Reduction-Act-Guidebook.pdf] Accessed on Jun. 30, 2023.

NEW CORPORATE TAXES

Embedded within the Inflation Reduction Act are two tax provisions that impact corporations: a new AMT and a tax on corporate share repurchases.[126]

15% Corporate AMT

IRC §55(b)(2)(a)(i) imposes a 15% AMT on corporate adjusted financial statement income.[127] This tax only applies to corporations with average **3-year adjusted financial statement income** that exceeds $1 billion, or corporations with foreign parents reporting adjusted financial statement income that exceeds $100 million.[128] Regulated investment companies, real estate investment trusts, and S corporations are specifically excluded from corporate AMT.[129] The 3-year adjusted financial statement income test looks at any three consecutive tax years that precede the tax year in which the taxpayer is computing the tax. This applies to 3-year periods beginning in which the 3rd year ends after December 31, 2021.[130]

> **Example 7.** Able Corporation is a calendar-year corporation. It is subject to the corporate AMT for 2023. When calculating the 3-year average, Able looks at the years ending December 31, 2020, December 31, 2021, and December 31, 2022.

Corporations that have not existed for three years substitute the number of years it has been in existence for the 3-year period. Tax years less than 12 months must be annualized.[131]

In addition, corporations that are members of foreign-parented multinational groups must also consider the adjusted financial statement income of U.S.-specific subsidiaries. U.S. subsidiaries that have an adjusted financial statement income above $100 million for the 3-year testing period are considered applicable corporations. The foreign-parented multinational groups must first satisfy the $1 billion test before the $100 million test is applied.[132]

The corporate AMT is designed to prevent large corporate taxpayers from leveraging current tax provisions to create a zero-tax liability. By assessing corporate AMT on adjusted financial statement income, corporations can no longer exploit book-to-tax differences to reduce their tax liability.

Calculating Adjusted Financial Statement Income. Adjusted financial statement income is the net income or loss of the corporation from **applicable financial statements,**[133] with certain adjustments. Applicable financial statements are those certified as being prepared in accordance with generally accepted accounting principles (GAAP), international statements equivalent to those filed with the U.S. Security and Exchange Commission (SEC), and statements filed with any U.S. federal agency for purposes other than federal income tax.[134] The following are some general adjustments for calculating adjusted financial statement income.[135]

- Removal of income not related to the current tax year
- Removal of income from certain related entities
- Inclusion of certain amounts from non-consolidated group corporations
- Inclusion of specific foreign income
- Adjustments for foreign taxes paid
- Adjustment for tax depreciation instead of book depreciation

---

126. *Inflation Reduction Act of 2022*, PL 117-169, §§10101 and 10201.

127. IRC §55(2)(a)(i).

128. *Inflation Reduction Act of 2022*, PL 117-169, §10101(a)(2), amending IRC §59 by adding subsection (k); IRC §§59(k)(1)(B)(i) and (B)(ii)(II).

129. Ibid, §10101(a)(2); IRC §59(k)(1)(A).

130. Ibid, §10101.

131. Ibid.

132. Ibid, §10101(d)(2).

133. IRC §56A(b), referencing IRC §451(b)(3).

134. IRC §451(b)(3).

135. IRC §56A(c).

Net Operating Loss (NOL).[136] An NOL is deductible from adjusted financial statement income. The deductible amount is the lesser of:

- The aggregate amount of financial statement NOL carryovers to the taxable year, or
- 80% of adjusted financial statement income computed without regard to the NOL.

Treatment of Credits.[137] The Act makes some modifications to the following three credits.

- **General business credit.**[138] General business credits are limited to 75% of the taxpayer's net income tax that exceeds $25,000. There is no limit on the first $25,000. Net income tax is the total of the taxpayer's U.S. federal income tax liability, including the **base erosion anti-abuse tax** under IRC §59A. The base erosion anti-abuse tax is a corporate minimum tax imposed on applicable taxpayers that make certain base erosion payments to foreign-related parties. Net income tax also includes AMT under §55 (including the corporate AMT).
- **Prior-year minimum tax credit.** The Act modified IRC §53, the net minimum tax imposed under §55, for all prior tax years beginning after 2022. Generally, the minimum tax credit can be carried forward and used as a credit against the taxpayer's regular tax liability, including any base erosion anti-abuse tax.
- **Foreign tax credit.** A taxpayer that chooses to apply its foreign tax credit against its regular U.S. federal tax reduces its corporate AMT. The foreign tax credit is the sum of:
    - The lesser of a corporation's (must be U.S. shareholder) pro rata share of income, war profits, and excess profits taxes that are paid or accrued by a controlled foreign corporation and included on the controlled foreign corporation's applicable financial statements, or 15% of the amount determined under IRC §56A(c)(3) (adjustments to certain items of foreign income), and
    - The amount of foreign income, war profits, and excess profits taxes the taxpayer pays or accrues and takes into account on their applicable financial statement.

Penalty Waiver. The IRS has not issued the promised proposed regulations clarifying the Act, although it has issued a notice[139] addressing some issues. Due to gray areas surrounding the corporate AMT calculation, the IRS has passed a temporary waiver on the underpayment of estimated taxes related to corporate AMT for tax years beginning after December 31, 2022, but before January 1, 2024.[140]

11

136. IRC §56A(d).

137. *Inflation Reduction Act of 2022,* PL 117-169, §10101.

138. IRC §38(c)(6)(E).

139. IRS Notice 2023-20, 2023-10 IRB 523.

140. IRS Notice 2023-42, 2023-26 IRB 1085.

1% Excise Tax on Corporate Stock Repurchases

The Inflation Reduction Act, §10201 imposes a 1% excise tax on corporations repurchasing their stock starting after December 31, 2022. The excise tax is non-deductible and cannot reduce the taxable income of the corporation.[141]

Corporations affected by this include any domestic corporation whose stock is traded on an established securities market, such as the New York Stock Exchange.[142] The excise tax is calculated as 1% of the fair market value (FMV) of any stock repurchases.[143] There are some exceptions.[144]

- The repurchased stock is part of a reorganization plan with no recognized gain or loss.
- The repurchased stock is contributed to an employee pension or stock ownership plan.
- The amount of repurchased stock is less than $1 million.
- The repurchase is made by a dealer in securities, a real estate investment company, or a regulated investment company.
- The repurchased stock is taxable as a dividend to shareholders.

Note. The IRS is still in the process of creating regulations surrounding value determination, employee stock repurchases, and privately negotiated transactions.

Practitioner Planning Tip

Corporations should consider the tax implications of stock buybacks and stock issuances following the passage of the Inflation Reduction Act. The application of the 1% excise tax is very broad, potentially applying in mergers, acquisitions, the use of derivatives, and preferred stock transactions.[145] As such, taxpayers must evaluate the full impact before engaging in transactions surrounding corporate stock.

HEALTHCARE AND PAYROLL TAX PROVISIONS

The Inflation Reduction Act also provides adjustments for research credits and healthcare provisions.

Research Credit Adjustments[146]

Inflation Reduction Act, §13902, increases the research credit against payroll tax to $250,000.[147] The credit is calculated at 20% of basic research payments, plus 20% of energy research consortium payments, plus 20% of the excess of qualified research expenses and the base amount.[148]

---

141. *Inflation Reduction Act of 2022,* PL 117-169, §10201(b), creating IRC §4501(b) and amending IRC §275(a)(6).

142. Ibid, §10201(a), creating IRC §4501(b).

143. IRC §4501(a).

144. IRC §4501(e).

145. IRC §4501(f)(2).

146. *Inflation Reduction Act of 2022,* PL 117-169, §13902, amending IRC §§41(h) and 3111(f).

147. Ibid, §13902(a).

148. IRC §41(a).

Qualified research expenses include contract research expenses and in-house research expenses, like wages, supplies, and qualified research.[149] The increase in available credit against payroll taxes allows small businesses to offset a portion of payroll taxes associated with research activities.

Part B and Part D Medicare Rebates[150]

The Inflation Reduction Act requires the federal government to negotiate prices with drug manufacturers. These drug companies are liable to pay rebates to Medicare when the prices of those drugs increase faster than the rate of inflation. The rebates are **not** paid to individuals. The law imposes requirements on the drug companies to report the total number of units sold, information on the average sale price, and the rebate amount within six months of the end of each calendar quarter. This regulation goes into effect for calendar quarters beginning in 2023. Companies will see rebate invoices beginning in September 2025.[151]

These provisions of the Inflation Reduction Act are intended to discourage unethical pricing by drug manufacturers and lower the out-of-pocket costs for Part B and Part D recipients. In addition, drug manufacturers that do not agree to fair prices are assessed an additional excise tax, further discouraging price gouging.[152]

> **Note.** As a result of this section of the Act, taxpayers should have expanded access to affordable drugs when utilizing Medicare Part B and Part D, as drug manufacturers will need to consider the tax implications of increasing prices faster than inflation.

Medicare Out-of-Pocket Caps[153]

The Inflation Reduction Act, §11201, imposes Medicare Part D out-of-pocket caps, potentially lowering medical and prescription costs for taxpayers. Beginning in 2025, Part B drugs will be 20% of the inflation-adjusted payment amount, while Part D drugs will be capped at 40% of the inflation-adjusted payment amount.[154] If provided through Medicare and not private insurance, insulin prices are limited to $35 per month through 2025.[155]

Affordable Care Act Subsidies[156]

Other healthcare-related provisions extend the refundable credit for qualified healthcare coverage through December 31, 2025. Taxpayers whose household income exceeds 400% of the poverty line can continue to claim a credit based on the percentage of income above the poverty line through 2025.[157]

11

149. Ibid.

150. *Inflation Reduction Act of 2022,* PL 117-169, §11101(a), amending 42 USC 1395w-3a, *Social Security Act,* §1847A. See also *Inflation Reduction Act and Medicare*, Jul. 5, 2023. U.S. Centers for Medicare & Medicaid Services. [www.cms.gov/inflation-reduction-act-and-medicare] Accessed on Aug. 23, 2023.

151. Ibid.

152. Ibid, §11103(a).

153. Ibid, §11101(a), amending 42 USC 1395w-102(b), *Social Security Act,* §1860D-2(b).

154. Ibid, §11201(b).

155. Ibid, §11406.

156. Ibid, §12001(b), amending IRC §36B.

157. IRC §36B(b).

FORM 1099-K CHANGES

For calendar years prior to 2022, the reporting threshold for a Form 1099-K, *Payment Card and Third Party Network Transactions,* was:

- Gross payments that exceed $20,000, and
- More than 200 transactions.

For calendar years beginning after December 31, 2021, the ARPA reduced the Form 1099-K reporting threshold to:[158]

- Gross payments for goods and services that exceed $600, and
- Any number of transactions.

On December 23, 2022, the IRS delayed the implementation of the reduced thresholds for Form 1099-K until the 2023 tax year.[159] The IRS attributed the delay to, "taxpayer confusion, lack of clear guidance, concerns about the existing backlog, and impact on the upcoming filing season."[160]

Form 1099-K reports payments and transactions from online platforms, apps, and processors.[161] Third-party networks include platforms like Uber, Amazon, eBay, PayPal, Venmo, Cash apps, and Facebook Marketplace.

Practitioner Planning Tip

Most businesses are already accustomed to Forms 1099-K for credit and debit cards. Many individual taxpayers will receive a Form 1099-K for the first time when the lower threshold is implemented. Prior to the upcoming filing season, practitioners should communicate the new law and educate their clients.

Form 1099-K identifies the type of transactions the taxpayer engaged in with the reporting entity. The following are examples of the types of transactions that may appear on a Form 1099-K.

- Error
- Personal items sold
- Hobby
- Business income
- Investment

158. *American Rescue Plan Act of 2021,* PL 117-2, §9674.

159. IRS News Rel. IR-2022-226 (Dec. 23, 2022).

160. *NTA Blog: Heard Loud and Clear: IRS Postpones Implementation of $600 Form 1099-K Reporting by a Year.* Dec. 27, 2022. Taxpayer Advocate Service. [www.taxpayeradvocate.irs.gov/news/nta-blog-heard-loud-and-clear-irs-postpones-implementation-of-600-form-1099-k-reporting-by-a-year] Accessed on Aug. 4, 2023.

161. *Understanding Your Form 1099-K.* Jul. 3, 2023. IRS. [www.irs.gov/businesses/understanding-your-form-1099-k] Accessed on Aug. 4, 2023.

Practitioner Planning Tip

Some issuers may not mail physical copies of a Form 1099-K, but rather the taxpayer can download their Form 1099-K from the appropriate website, app, etc. Practitioners should ask their clients to verify they have provided all the Forms 1099-K they received during the year.

ERRORS

The taxpayer should verify that the Form 1099-K they received is correct and accurate. There are a variety of errors that could arise, such as the following.[162]

- The individual is listed instead of their business
- The information on the Form 1099-K is incorrect (e.g., payee taxpayer identification number, gross amount of payment card/third party network transactions, number of payment transactions, merchant category code)
- The individual receives a Form 1099-K they should not have received (e.g., reports payments that were gifts or reimbursements from family or friends, does not belong to the taxpayer, or is a duplicate)

A taxpayer should request a corrected Form 1099-K from the issuer in the case of an error. If the taxpayer cannot get a corrected Form 1099-K, they should report the amount from the Form 1099-K on their Form 1040, *U.S. Individual Income Tax Return,* Schedule 1, *Additional Income and Adjustments to Income.* The taxpayer enters the incorrect amount on part I, line 8z, with the text, "Form 1099-K received in error" along with the amount. The erroneous amount is then adjusted out of income by entering the text "Form 1099-K received in error" along with the amount, on part II, line 24z. This results in net $0 effect on the taxpayer's adjusted gross income.

CHANGES TO SPECIFIED RESEARCH OR EXPERIMENTAL EXPENDITURES AND THE R&D CREDIT

The research and development (R&D) credit provides companies a credit for increasing their research activities, not just for undertaking them. Generally, companies use this credit to offset their income tax liability, acting as a general business credit.[163] There are two changes to R&D for 2023 and 2024, consisting of requiring the amortization of costs and creating an additional payroll credit.

Note. For information on the expanded reporting requirements for the R&D credit, as well as information on how to calculate the credit, see the 2022 *University of Illinois Federal Tax Workbook,* Volume A, Chapter 1: New Developments.

162. Ibid.

163. IRC §38(b)(3).

REQUIRED AMORTIZATION

One of the most notable provisions in the Tax Cuts and Jobs Act (TCJA) relating to deducting R&D costs is the elimination of immediate expenditure expensing. Prior to the enactment of the TCJA, taxpayers could deduct R&D expenditures as qualifying business expenses under IRC §174(a), reducing taxable income.[164] Under the TCJA rules, taxpayers must amortize expenditures over a 5-year period. However, specified R&D expenditures related to foreign research require taxpayers to amortize them over a 15-year period.[165] TCJA, §13206(d) states that alterations to the R&D expenditures are effective for tax years beginning after December 31, 2021.[166]

Practitioner Planning Tip

The 5-year amortization period can make it less advantageous for businesses to engage in R&D activities as they must spread the costs over a period of time instead of recognizing them all at once in the year incurred. Consequently, all other things being equal, taxable income would be higher each year for these taxpayers. Tax practitioners must effectively advise their clients on expected taxable income increases to remit proper estimated tax payments and remain in compliance with the IRS.

Note. Taxpayers must amortize research and experimentation expenditures regardless of claiming the credit for increasing research activities under IRC §41.[167]

Calculating the Deduction

R&D expenditures must be amortized over five years using the half-year convention, resulting in 10% of the cost being deductible in the first year.[168] If a qualifying taxpayer has $1 million in qualifying research expenditures for the year ended December 31, 2022, they can deduct $100,000 against taxable income ($1 million ÷ 5 years × ½ year). Over the next four years, the taxpayer can deduct $200,000 each year ($1 million ÷ 5 years). In the final year, the taxpayer can deduct the final $100,000 ($1 million ÷ 5 years × ½ year).[169] Tax practitioners should have detailed recordkeeping systems to calculate the proper amortization each year and maintain amortization tables.

Note. Even research projects that are abandoned continue to be amortized over the 5- or 15-year period.[170]

164. IRC §174(a)(1), prior to enactment of TCJA.

165. IRC §174(a)(2).

166. *Tax Cuts and Jobs Act,* PL 115-97, §13206(d)(b)(3).

167. Ibid, §13206(a).

168. Ibid; IRC §174(a)(2)(B).

169. Ibid.

170. IRC §174(d).

Accounting for Dispositions

Under §174(d), disposed of property included in R&D amortization cannot be immediately written off. Instead, taxpayers must continue amortizing the expense as they had been, disregarding the disposition.

Implementing the Change

Under §13206 of the TCJA, the alterations to §174 are considered a change in accounting method under IRC §481. This change will be treated as initiated by the taxpayer with the consent of the IRS on a cutoff basis with no §481(a) adjustment required.[171] Tax practitioners **will not** need to file Form 3115, *Application for Change in Accounting Method.* However, they must include a footnote or information statement outlining the taxpayer's name, EIN or social security number (SSN), and information regarding amortization adjustments.

CREDIT FOR INCREASING RESEARCH ACTIVITIES[172]

IRC §41 permits taxpayers a credit to the extent that research expenditures increase during the year over a base amount. The credit is better known as the R&D credit. The purpose of the credit is to incentivize research and experimentation by providing a tax credit for activities that develop a new component of a taxpayer's business or improve an existing component's performance, functionality, reliability, or quality. For a business with under $50 million in average annual gross receipts over the preceding three years, the credit offsets both regular tax and AMT.[173]

Eligible Recipient[174]

Taxpayers qualify for the R&D credit if they invest in developing new products, improving the performance of existing ones, or otherwise improve the quality or reliability of a product or business process. Because the credit is computed based on increased research expenditures, the taxpayer's research expenditures must grow over time to be eligible for the credit.

The research must focus on discovering information that is both technological and intended to aid in developing a new or improved business component for the taxpayer. Research must involve hard sciences (e.g., chemistry, physics, or biology) because research involving social sciences does not count for the credit. Research focusing on the style, taste, cosmetic, or seasonal design of products does not count as qualified research for the credit. Substantially all the activities undertaken under the umbrella of qualified research must be a part of a process of experimentation. The experimentation focuses on new or improved functions, improved performance or reliability, or quality. The qualified research expenditures must also satisfy the requirements of §174 (i.e., paid or incurred in connection with a trade or business and are reasonable[175]).

11

171. *Tax Cuts and Jobs Act,* PL 115-97, §13206(b); Rev. Proc. 2023-11, 2023-3 IRB 417.

172. IRC §41.

173. Instructions for Form 6765.

174. IRC §41(d).

175. IRC §§174(a)(1) and (e).

The following items are not eligible for the R&D credit.[176]

1. Research after the recipient has begun commercial production of a business component
2. Adaptation of an existing business component, especially if it adapts an existing business component to a customer's requirements
3. Duplicating an existing business component after examining the product itself, its plans, its specifications, or related public information
4. Surveys or studies
5. Computer software that is developed for internal use by the taxpayer unless it is used in an activity that itself constitutes qualified research
6. Foreign research that is conducted outside the United States, Puerto Rico, or any possession of the United States
7. Social sciences, as any research in social sciences, art, or humanities is specifically prohibited
8. Funded research, to the extent that it is funded by a grant, a contract, or by any other person, including grants from a government entity

Calculating the Credit

The R&D credit is claimed on Form 6765, *Credit for Increasing Research Activities*. The R&D credit is the sum of the following items.

- 20% of the amount that **qualified research expenses** exceed the base amount
- 20% of the **basic research payments**, consisting of the amount that basic research payments exceed the qualified organization base period amount
- 20% of the amount paid to an **energy research consortium** for energy research if paid while conducting a trade or business of the taxpayer

The credit for **qualified research expenses** (type 1) are incurred either through in-house research or through contract research. The **credit for basic research payments** (type 2) are payments for outsourced research, which a qualified organization must perform. Credits for research performed by an **energy research consortium** (type 3) are only available to a taxpayer who carries on a trade or a business, presumably in an energy-related business.

In addition to in-house expenses, the taxpayer can count 65% of contract research expenses paid to another person for research if the person is not an employee of the taxpayer. That percentage is increased to 75% if the payment is to a tax-exempt research consortium. The percentage further increases to 100% if the payment is to an eligible small business, a higher education institution, or a federal laboratory.[177]

Type 1: Qualified Research Expenses.[178] If the research occurs within the taxpayer's organization, the expense includes wages paid to an employee for services related to research, or the earned income of a sole proprietor. In addition, the expenditures may include supplies consumed in the process of qualified research, but the supplies cannot be improvements to land or depreciable items. Consequently, taxpayers who invest in improving their products, developing new ones, or improving processes are typically those who benefit from this credit.[179]

---

176. IRC §41(d)(4).

177. IRC §41(b)(3).

178. IRC §41(b).

179. IRC §41(d)(4)(F).

Example 8. The management of Reliable Pump Corporation (Reliable) anticipates a need in their agriculture market to offer an irrigation pump with better reliability. Two engineers based in Texas invested 40% of their time in 2022 to this task, and they were paid $60,000 in the year. To test the reliability of the pump with water having a higher-than-normal pH, they purchased $5,000 of sodium bicarbonate during 2022 and bought a vat to hold this water solution for $10,000. Reliable can count 40% of the wages of the two engineers, or $48,000 ($120,000 in total wages ($60,000 each) × 40%), toward the credit. The $5,000 of sodium bicarbonate counts as a supply, but the vat does not count toward the credit because it is depreciable property. Reliable thus has qualified research expenditures of $53,000 ($48,000 wages + $5,000 sodium bicarbonate supplies).

Alternative Simplified Credit.[180] Taxpayers may elect an alternative simplified credit to reduce the computational complexity of the credit. In this case, the credit is 14% of the amount by which qualified research expenses for the current tax year exceed 50% of the average qualified research expenses for the prior three tax years. Revocation of this election must be by consent of the Secretary of the Treasury.

Example 9. The 4N Fertilizer Corporation (4N), an Illinois C corporation incorporated in 2001, investigates new fertilizer products for corn production. It conducts this research in its facility in Mattoon, Illinois, rather than its office in Windsor, Ontario, so that the R&D credit is available. 4N experiments with using the new fertilizer on half of a 40-acre plot in Coles County while using a commercially available fertilizer on the other half of the plot. 4N elects the simplified method of computing the research expense credit. In 2022, its qualified research expenses consisted of $30,000 of wages and $10,000 of supplies. Its qualified research expenses in 2021 totaled $30,000, $25,000 in 2020, and $21,000 in 2019. Its average qualified research expense for the prior three years is $25,333. The 2022 alternative simplified credit is $3,827 (14% × ($40,000 qualified research expenses – (50% × $25,333 average qualified research expenses))). The Form 6765 for 4N follows.

11

180. IRC §41(c)(4).

For Example 9

Form **6765** (Rev. December 2020) Department of the Treasury Internal Revenue Service

Credit for Increasing Research Activities

► Attach to your tax return.
► Go to *www.irs.gov/Form6765* for instructions and the latest information.

OMB No. 1545-0619
Attachment Sequence No. **676**

Name(s) shown on return	Identifying number
4N Fertilizer Corporation	**12-3456789**

Section A—Regular Credit. Skip this section and go to Section B if you are electing or previously elected (and are not revoking) the alternative simplified credit.

1	Certain amounts paid or incurred to energy consortia (see instructions)			1	
2	Basic research payments to qualified organizations (see instructions)	2			
3	Qualified organization base period amount	3			
4	Subtract line 3 from line 2. If zero or less, enter -0-			4	
5	Wages for qualified services (do not include wages used in figuring the work opportunity credit)	5			
6	Cost of supplies	6			
7	Rental or lease costs of computers (see instructions)	7			
8	Enter the applicable percentage of contract research expenses. See instructions	8			
9	Total qualified research expenses. Add lines 5 through 8	9			
10	Enter fixed-base percentage, but not more than 16% (0.16) (see instructions)	10	%		
11	Enter average annual gross receipts. See instructions	11			
12	Multiply line 11 by the percentage on line 10	12			
13	Subtract line 12 from line 9. If zero or less, enter -0-	13			
14	Multiply line 9 by 50% (0.50)	14			
15	Enter the **smaller** of line 13 or line 14			15	
16	Add lines 1, 4, and 15			16	
17	Are you electing the reduced credit under section 280C? ► Yes ☐ No ☐ If "Yes," multiply line 16 by 15.8% (0.158). If "No," multiply line 16 by 20% (0.20) and see the instructions for the statement that must be attached. Members of controlled groups or businesses under common control, see instructions for the statement that must be attached			17	

Section B—Alternative Simplified Credit. Skip this section if you are completing Section A.

18	Certain amounts paid or incurred to energy consortia (see the line 1 instructions)			18	
19	Basic research payments to qualified organizations (see the line 2 instructions)	19			
20	Qualified organization base period amount (see the line 3 instructions)	20			
21	Subtract line 20 from line 19. If zero or less, enter -0-			21	
22	Add lines 18 and 21			22	
23	Multiply line 22 by 20% (0.20)			23	
24	Wages for qualified services (do not include wages used in figuring the work opportunity credit)	24	30,000		
25	Cost of supplies	25	10,000		
26	Rental or lease costs of computers (see the line 7 instructions)	26			
27	Enter the applicable percentage of contract research expenses. See the line 8 instructions	27			
28	Total qualified research expenses. Add lines 24 through 27	28	40,000		
29	Enter your total qualified research expenses for the prior 3 tax years. If you had no qualified research expenses in any one of those years, skip lines 30 and 31	29	76,000		
30	Divide line 29 by 6.0	30	12,667		
31	Subtract line 30 from line 28. If zero or less, enter -0-	31	27,333		
32	Multiply line 31 by 14% (0.14). If you skipped lines 30 and 31, multiply line 28 by 6% (0.06)			32	3,827
33	Add lines 23 and 32			33	3,827
34	Are you electing the reduced credit under section 280C? ► Yes ☐ No ☒ If "Yes," multiply line 33 by 79% (0.79). If "No," enter the amount from line 33 and see the line 17 instructions for the statement that must be attached. Members of controlled groups or businesses under common control, see instructions for the statement that must be attached			34	3,827

For Paperwork Reduction Act Notice, see separate instructions. Cat. No. 13700H Form **6765** (Rev. 12-2020)

For Example 9

Form 6765 (Rev. 12-2020) Page **2**

Section C—Current Year Credit

35	Enter the portion of the credit from Form 8932, line 2, that is attributable to wages that were also used to figure the credit on line 17 or line 34 (whichever applies)	35	
36	Subtract line 35 from line 17 or line 34 (whichever applies). If zero or less, enter -0-	36	3,827
37	Credit for increasing research activities from partnerships, S corporations, estates, and trusts . . .	37	
38	Add lines 36 and 37 . . . . • Estates and trusts, go to line 39. • Partnerships and S corporations not electing the payroll tax credit, stop here and report this amount on Schedule K. • Partnerships and S corporations electing the payroll tax credit, complete Section D and report on Schedule K the amount on this line reduced by the amount on line 44. • Eligible small businesses, stop here and report the credit on Form 3800, Part III, line 4i. See instructions for the definition of eligible small business. • Filers other than eligible small businesses, stop here and report the credit on Form 3800, Part III, line 1c. **Note:** Qualified small business filers, other than partnerships and S corporations, electing the payroll tax credit must complete Form 3800 before completing Section D.	38	3,827
39	Amount allocated to beneficiaries of the estate or trust (see instructions)	39	
40	Estates and trusts, subtract line 39 from line 38. For eligible small businesses, report the credit on Form 3800, Part III, line 4i. See instructions. For filers other than eligible small businesses, report the credit on Form 3800, Part III, line 1c	40	

Section D—Qualified Small Business Payroll Tax Election and Payroll Tax Credit. Skip this section if the payroll tax election does not apply. See instructions.

41	Check this box if you are a qualified small business electing the payroll tax credit. See instructions ☐		
42	Enter the portion of line 36 elected as a payroll tax credit (do not enter more than $250,000). See instructions	42	
43	General business credit carryforward from the current year (see instructions). Partnerships and S corporations, skip this line and go to line 44	43	
44	Partnerships and S corporations, enter the smaller of line 36 or line 42. All others, enter the smallest of line 36, line 42, or line 43. Enter here and on the applicable line of Form 8974, Part 1, column (e). Members of controlled groups or businesses under common control, see instructions for the statement that must be attached	44	

Form **6765** (Rev. 12-2020)

Example 10. The Smith family operates a 720-acre farm as a sole proprietorship in McLean County, Illinois. They typically grow soybeans in even years and corn in odd years. The soil at the Smith farm has a relatively high level of calcium, but a relatively low level of magnesium. Fred Smith is interested in the relationship between the temperature of irrigation water and the leaching of these nutrients, particularly magnesium, from the soil to levels at which it would not benefit the soybean plants. To test the effect of water temperature, Fred Smith set aside two 5-acre plots of soybeans in the southwest corner of the farm. The Smiths irrigated one plot with water heated to a temperature of 24°C, and they irrigated the other plot with unheated water. The water heater cost $5,500, and the propane to run it during April, May, June, and July 2022 cost an additional $350. The work for the experiment required two hired farmhands, who together worked 250 hours on the project and earned $12 per hour. They paid $200 to have the Illinois Farm Research Consortium[181] analyze the soil at the beginning of the study, and another $200 at the end of the growing season. The Illinois Farm Research Consortium is an IRC §501(c)(3) organization primarily organized to conduct research on behalf of family farms.

Because of the degree of experimentation involved, Fred Smith and his tax preparer believe that this qualifies for the R&D credit. The Smith family has never undertaken a research project of this nature and elects to use the alternative simplified credit.

The Form 6765 for Mr. and Mrs. Smith follows.

[181] This is a fictitious organization used only for the purposes of illustration.

11

For Example 10

Form **6765** (Rev. December 2020) Department of the Treasury Internal Revenue Service

Credit for Increasing Research Activities

▶ Attach to your tax return.
▶ Go to *www.irs.gov/Form6765* for instructions and the latest information.

OMB No. 1545-0619
Attachment Sequence No. **676**

Name(s) shown on return: **Fred and Gloria Smith**
Identifying number: ***-**-7891

Section A—Regular Credit. Skip this section and go to Section B if you are electing or previously elected (and are not revoking) the alternative simplified credit.

1	Certain amounts paid or incurred to energy consortia (see instructions)			1	
2	Basic research payments to qualified organizations (see instructions)	2			
3	Qualified organization base period amount	3			
4	Subtract line 3 from line 2. If zero or less, enter -0-			4	
5	Wages for qualified services (do not include wages used in figuring the work opportunity credit)	5			
6	Cost of supplies	6			
7	Rental or lease costs of computers (see instructions)	7			
8	Enter the applicable percentage of contract research expenses. See instructions	8			
9	Total qualified research expenses. Add lines 5 through 8	9			
10	Enter fixed-base percentage, but not more than 16% (0.16) (see instructions)	10	%		
11	Enter average annual gross receipts. See instructions	11			
12	Multiply line 11 by the percentage on line 10	12			
13	Subtract line 12 from line 9. If zero or less, enter -0-	13			
14	Multiply line 9 by 50% (0.50)	14			
15	Enter the **smaller** of line 13 or line 14			15	
16	Add lines 1, 4, and 15			16	
17	Are you electing the reduced credit under section 280C? ▶ Yes ☐ No ☐ If "Yes," multiply line 16 by 15.8% (0.158). If "No," multiply line 16 by 20% (0.20) and see the instructions for the statement that must be attached. Members of controlled groups or businesses under common control, see instructions for the statement that must be attached			17	

Section B—Alternative Simplified Credit. Skip this section if you are completing Section A.

18	Certain amounts paid or incurred to energy consortia (see the line 1 instructions)			18	
19	Basic research payments to qualified organizations (see the line 2 instructions)	19			
20	Qualified organization base period amount (see the line 3 instructions)	20			
21	Subtract line 20 from line 19. If zero or less, enter -0-			21	
22	Add lines 18 and 21			22	
23	Multiply line 22 by 20% (0.20)			23	
24	Wages for qualified services (do not include wages used in figuring the work opportunity credit)	24	3,000		
25	Cost of supplies	25	350		
26	Rental or lease costs of computers (see the line 7 instructions)	26			
27	Enter the applicable percentage of contract research expenses. See the line 8 instructions	27	300		
28	Total qualified research expenses. Add lines 24 through 27	28	3,650		
29	Enter your total qualified research expenses for the prior 3 tax years. If you had no qualified research expenses in any one of those years, skip lines 30 and 31	29			
30	Divide line 29 by 6.0	30			
31	Subtract line 30 from line 28. If zero or less, enter -0-	31			
32	Multiply line 31 by 14% (0.14). If you skipped lines 30 and 31, multiply line 28 by 6% (0.06)			32	219
33	Add lines 23 and 32			33	219
34	Are you electing the reduced credit under section 280C? ▶ Yes ☐ No ☒ If "Yes," multiply line 33 by 79% (0.79). If "No," enter the amount from line 33 and see the line 17 instructions for the statement that must be attached. Members of controlled groups or businesses under common control, see instructions for the statement that must be attached			34	219

For Paperwork Reduction Act Notice, see separate instructions. Cat. No. 13700H Form **6765** (Rev. 12-2020)

For Example 10

Form 6765 (Rev. 12-2020) Page **2**

Section C—Current Year Credit

35	Enter the portion of the credit from Form 8932, line 2, that is attributable to wages that were also used to figure the credit on line 17 or line 34 (whichever applies)	35	
36	Subtract line 35 from line 17 or line 34 (whichever applies). If zero or less, enter -0-	36	219
37	Credit for increasing research activities from partnerships, S corporations, estates, and trusts	37	
38	Add lines 36 and 37	38	219
	• Estates and trusts, go to line 39. • Partnerships and S corporations not electing the payroll tax credit, stop here and report this amount on Schedule K. • Partnerships and S corporations electing the payroll tax credit, complete Section D and report on Schedule K the amount on this line reduced by the amount on line 44. • Eligible small businesses, stop here and report the credit on Form 3800, Part III, line 4i. See instructions for the definition of eligible small business. • Filers other than eligible small businesses, stop here and report the credit on Form 3800, Part III, line 1c. **Note:** Qualified small business filers, other than partnerships and S corporations, electing the payroll tax credit must complete Form 3800 before completing Section D.		
39	Amount allocated to beneficiaries of the estate or trust (see instructions)	39	
40	Estates and trusts, subtract line 39 from line 38. For eligible small businesses, report the credit on Form 3800, Part III, line 4i. See instructions. For filers other than eligible small businesses, report the credit on Form 3800, Part III, line 1c	40	

Section D—Qualified Small Business Payroll Tax Election and Payroll Tax Credit. Skip this section if the payroll tax election does not apply. See instructions.

41	Check this box if you are a qualified small business electing the payroll tax credit. See instructions ☐		
42	Enter the portion of line 36 elected as a payroll tax credit (do not enter more than $250,000). See instructions	42	
43	General business credit carryforward from the current year (see instructions). Partnerships and S corporations, skip this line and go to line 44	43	
44	Partnerships and S corporations, enter the smaller of line 36 or line 42. All others, enter the smallest of line 36, line 42, or line 43. Enter here and on the applicable line of Form 8974, Part 1, column (e). Members of controlled groups or businesses under common control, see instructions for the statement that must be attached	44	

Form **6765** (Rev. 12-2020)

Information appears in Section B of Form 6765 because Mr. and Mrs. Smith elected to use the alternative simplified credit. The wages paid to farm laborers are shown on line 24, while 75%[182] of the $400 Mr. Smith paid to the research consortium to analyze soil appears on line 27. Mr. and Mrs. Smith file this form with their Form 1040.

Mr. and Mrs. Smith file the following applicable page of Form 3800 with their Form 1040.

11

182. IRC §41(b)(3)(C)(i).

Form 3800 (2022) Page **3**

Name(s) shown on return	Identifying number
Fred and Gloria Smith	***-**-7891

Part III **General Business Credits or Eligible Small Business Credits** (see instructions)

Complete a separate Part III for each box checked below. See instructions.

- **A** [X] General Business Credit From a Non-Passive Activity
- **B** [ ] General Business Credit From a Passive Activity
- **C** [ ] General Business Credit Carryforwards
- **D** [ ] General Business Credit Carrybacks
- **E** Reserved
- **F** Reserved
- **G** [ ] Eligible Small Business Credit Carryforwards
- **H** Reserved
- **I** If you are filing more than one Part III with box A or B checked, complete and attach first an additional Part III combining amounts from all Parts III with box A or B checked. Check here if this is the consolidated Part III . . . . [ ]

	(a) Description of credit **Note:** On any line where the credit is from more than one source, a separate Part III is needed for each pass-through entity.		**(b)** Enter EIN if claiming the credit from a pass-through entity.	**(c)** Enter the appropriate amount.
1a	Investment (Form 3468, Part II only) (attach Form 3468)	**1a**		
b	Advanced manufacturing production (Form 7207)	**1b**		
c	Increasing research activities (Form 6765)	**1c**		
d	Low-income housing (carryforward only) (see instructions)	**1d**		
e	Disabled access (Form 8826)*	**1e**		
f	Renewable electricity production (Form 8835)	**1f**		
g	Indian employment (Form 8845)	**1g**		
h	Orphan drug (Form 8820)	**1h**		
i	New markets (Form 8874)	**1i**		
j	Small employer pension plan startup costs and auto-enrollment (Form 8881)	**1j**		
k	Employer-provided child care facilities and services (Form 8882)*	**1k**		
l	Biodiesel, renewable diesel, or sustainable aviation fuel (attach Form 8864)	**1l**		
m	Low sulfur diesel fuel production (Form 8896)	**1m**		
n	Distilled spirits (Form 8906)	**1n**		
o	Nonconventional source fuel (carryforward only)	**1o**		
p	Energy efficient home (Form 8908)	**1p**		
q	Energy efficient appliance (carryforward only)	**1q**		
r	Alternative motor vehicle (Form 8910)	**1r**		
s	Alternative fuel vehicle refueling property (Form 8911)	**1s**		
t	Enhanced oil recovery credit (Form 8830)	**1t**		
u	Mine rescue team training (Form 8923)	**1u**		
v	Agricultural chemicals security (carryforward only)	**1v**		
w	Employer differential wage payments (Form 8932)	**1w**		
x	Carbon oxide sequestration (Form 8933)	**1x**		
y	Qualified plug-in electric drive motor vehicle (Form 8936)	**1y**		
z	Qualified plug-in electric vehicle (carryforward only)	**1z**		
aa	Employee retention (Form 5884-A)	**1aa**		
bb	General credits from an electing large partnership (carryforward only)	**1bb**		
zz	Other. Oil and gas production from marginal wells (Form 8904) and certain other credits (see instructions)	**1zz**		
2	Add lines 1a through 1zz and enter here and on the applicable line of Part I	**2**		0
3	Enter the amount from Form 8844 here and on the applicable line of Part II	**3**		
4a	Investment (Form 3468, Part III) (attach Form 3468)	**4a**		
b	Work opportunity (Form 5884)	**4b**		
c	Biofuel producer (Form 6478)	**4c**		
d	Low-income housing (Form 8586)	**4d**		
e	Renewable electricity production (Form 8835)	**4e**		
f	Employer social security and Medicare taxes paid on certain employee tips (Form 8846)	**4f**		
g	Qualified railroad track maintenance (Form 8900)	**4g**		
h	Small employer health insurance premiums (Form 8941)	**4h**		
i	Increasing research activities (Form 6765)	**4i**		219
j	Employer credit for paid family and medical leave (Form 8994)	**4j**		
z	Other	**4z**		
5	Add lines 4a through 4z and enter here and on the applicable line of Part II	**5**		219
6	Add lines 2, 3, and 5 and enter here and on the applicable line of Part II	**6**		219

* See instructions for limitation on this credit.

Form **3800** (2022)

The R&D credit flows from Form 3800 to Form 1040, Schedule 3, *Additional Credits and Payments.*[183]

Regular Credit.[184] Suppose the taxpayer does not elect to use the alternative simplified credit. The regular credit is calculated off a **base amount,** which is the product of the fixed-base percentage and the average annual gross receipts for the four preceding tax years prior to the year the taxpayer is calculating the credit. The base amount cannot be less than 50% of the qualified research expenses for the year. The **fixed-based percentage** is the ratio of the aggregate qualified research expenses for the taxpayer between 1984 and 1988 to the aggregate gross receipts for those years. There are exceptions to the fixed-base percentage for start-up companies when their first tax year with both gross receipts and qualified research expenses began after December 31, 1983, or had fewer than three tax years with both gross receipts and qualified research expenses between 1984 and 1988 inclusive. The fixed-base percentages for start-up companies are illustrated in the following table.

Taxable Year	Portion of Gross Receipts Eligible for Regular Credit
Each of the taxpayer's first five taxable years after 1993 during which it had qualified research expenses	3%
Sixth taxable year	0.16667 of the percentage that qualified research expenses bear to gross receipts for the fourth and five taxable years combined
Seventh taxable year	0.33333 of the percentage that qualified research expenses bear to gross receipts for the fifth and sixth taxable years combined
Eighth taxable year	0.5 of the percentage that qualified research expenses hear to gross receipts for the fifth, sixth, and seventh years combined
Ninth taxable year	0.66667 of the percentage that qualified research expenses bear to fifth, sixth, seventh, and eighth years combined
Tenth taxable year	0.83333 of the percentage that qualified research expenses bear to the fifth through tenth years combined
Subsequent taxable years	The percentage from any five years chosen by the taxpayer from among the fifth through the tenth years that qualified research expenses bear to gross receipts

The fixed-base percentage cap is 16%, and the number is rounded to the nearest 0.01%.

183. See instructions for Form 1040, Schedule 3.

184. IRC §41(c).

Type 2: Basic Research Payments.[185] Basic research is any original investigation for the advancement of scientific knowledge that does not have a specific commercial objective. It does not include research conducted outside of the United States or basic research in the social sciences, arts, or humanities.

There are a few hurdles associated with basic research payments. S corporations are not eligible for a credit arising from basic research payments; personal holding companies and service organizations are not eligible, either. IRC §41 imposes the following requirements on payments for basic research.

- The payments must be made in cash during the taxable year.
- The payments must be according to a written agreement.
- The written agreement must be between a corporation and a qualified organization. The qualified organization must perform the research. An exception to this requirement allows tax-exempt scientific organizations or certain grant organizations to perform research. The following requirements are placed on the grant organizations.
    - Qualified §501(c)(3) organizations
    - Established before July 10, 1981
    - Organized and operated exclusively to make grants to educational institutions
    - Make an election for treatment as a private foundation

Qualified organizations for conducting research include educational institutions and other tax-exempt organizations to perform scientific research, unless they are private foundations. A qualified organization can also be a corporation.

> **Example 11.** Use the same facts as **Example 9,** except that 4N contracts with the University of Illinois College of Agricultural, Consumer, and Environmental Sciences to research university land. The contract between 4N and the University stipulates that the University owns the intellectual property arising from the research, even though the results are to be shared with 4N under the terms of the contract. Payments under the contract are qualified as basic research payments for the R&D credit.

Type 2 payments are calculated as the amount that basic research payments exceed the qualified organization base period amount, which itself is equal to the sum of the following two items.

- Minimum basic research amount
- A maintenance-of-effort amount

The **minimum basic research amount** is the greater of the following.

- 1% of the average of any amounts paid or incurred during the base period for in-house research expenses and contract research expense, **or**
- Contract research expenses during the base period

The **maintenance-of-effort amount** reflects an increase in nondesignated university contributions made by a taxpayer in a current year over nondesignated contributions to a university in a base period, adjusted for inflation.

The base period is the three-year period ending with the tax year immediately before the taxpayer filed its first tax return. For example, the base period for a company formed in 2014 runs from January 1, 2014, to December 31, 2016.

---

185. IRC §41(e).

As a result, a portion of contributions to higher learning institutions become research credits under this provision of the R&D credit. They must exceed an inflation-adjusted amount of nondesignated contributions that were not used as a basic research payment but would have been allowable as a deduction under IRC §170. There is a floor under the minimum basic research amount of 50% of the basic research payments made.

Example 12. Use the same facts as **Example 9,** except that in 2022 4N also makes payments to the University of Illinois under a signed agreement for research. It pays $35,000 to the University because the University conducts technical research that is of interest to 4N but without immediate commercial application. In this case, the minimum research credit is $850 (1% × ($40,000 wages + $10,000 supplies + $35,000 contract research expenses)). The base period was 2001 through 2003, the first three years of 4N's existence, when it incurred no research expenses.

Type 3: Energy Research Consortium. The R&D credit for Type 3 payments to an energy consortium is beyond the scope of this chapter. For more information, see §41(f)(6).

ADDITIONAL PAYROLL CREDIT

Section §41 provides a special subsection that allows **qualified small businesses** to offset **payroll** tax liability with the R&D tax credit.[186] The Inflation Reduction Act of 2022 increases the maximum credit for small businesses from $250,000 to $500,000 starting in 2023.[187] A **qualified small business** is a corporation or partnership with gross receipts less than $5 million that did not have gross receipts for any tax year during the preceding 5-year period. This does not apply to tax-exempt organizations.[188]

The $500,000 is a combined credit; $250,000 applies against an employer's portion of social security tax, and $250,000 applies to an employer's portion of Medicare tax. Any remaining credit after reducing the employer's social security and Medicare taxes is carried forward to the next quarter. Taxpayers use Form 8974, *Qualified Small Business Payroll Tax Credit for Increasing Research Activities,* to determine the amount of payroll tax credit they can use in the current quarter.[189]

Employers making a new payroll tax election on Form 6765 for tax years beginning after December 31, 2022, a qualified small business can take the payroll tax credit against their social security and Medicare taxes starting with the first calendar quarter beginning after the date the taxpayer filed the income tax return including the election.[190]

Employers with a credit that carried forward from a previous year can apply that credit against the employer's portion of social security tax (up to $250,000), and then to the Medicare tax.[191]

11

186. IRC §41(h).

187. *Inflation Reduction Act of 2022,* PL 117-169, §13902(d); IRC §13902.

188. IRC §41(h)(3).

189. See *Inflation Reduction Act,* PL 117-179, §13902; IRC §3111(f); *Qualified Small Business Payroll Tax Credit for Increasing Research Activities.* Jun. 27, 2023. IRS. [www.irs.gov/businesses/small-businesses-self-employed/qualified-small-business-payroll-tax-credit-for-increasing-research-activities] Accessed on Jul. 31, 2023.

190. Ibid.

191. Ibid.

RECONTRIBUTED CARES ACT RETIREMENT PLAN DISTRIBUTIONS

The CARES Act, §2202 added special distribution options and rollover rules for retirement plans, individual retirement arrangements (IRA), and permissible loans.[192] Congress implemented many of these provisions to alleviate taxpayers' financial burdens during the COVID-19 pandemic. Tax practitioners must be aware of §2202 specifications to ensure taxpayers receive the most favorable tax treatment of distributions and remit timely repayments.

ALLOWABLE DISTRIBUTION AMOUNTS

Under §2202, taxpayers may take distributions up to $100,000 without triggering early-withdrawal penalties under IRC §72(t). Distributions may come from eligible retirement plans, including IRC §§401(k), 403(b), and IRAs between January 1, 2020, and December 31, 2020.[193]

TAXPAYER QUALIFICATIONS

Taxpayers qualifying for favorable treatment of retirement plan distributions must meet certain criteria.[194]

- The taxpayer was diagnosed with COVID-19 by an approved test by the Centers for Disease Control and Prevention (CDC).
- The taxpayer's spouse or dependent was diagnosed with COVID-19 by an approved test by the CDC.
- The taxpayer experienced adverse financial consequences from reduced work hours, layoffs, lack of childcare, or quarantine.

This criterion is a broad set of qualifications. However, if taxpayers cannot substantiate any of these factors, they will not qualify for distribution exclusions under §72(t) and §2202 of the CARES Act. Tax practitioners need to ensure that clients qualify before treating distributions as coronavirus-related. The taxpayer's employer can help furnish information surrounding work hours and layoffs.[195]

DISTRIBUTION TAX TREATMENT

Coronavirus-related distributions do not receive non-taxable treatment. Instead, §2202 only eliminates the 10% early withdrawal penalty.[196] 2023 marks the final year for repayment of a coronavirus-related distribution. Tax practitioners should advise their clients on the tax implications of previous taxable distributions.

Income Inclusion

Taxpayers may include qualifying distributions in income in the year of distribution or report them ratably over a 3-year period.[197] Before filing 2023 tax returns, tax practitioners should revisit prior year returns to determine the tax treatment of distributions. Form 8915-E, *Qualified 2020 Disaster Retirement Plan Distributions and Repayments,* should have been filed for 2020, and Form 8915-F, *Qualified 2021 Disaster Retirement Plan Distributions and Repayments,* should have been filed for 2021, to indicate distributions and repayments.[198] The information provided in the form should assist practitioners in assessing the tax treatment of 2023 distributions.

---

192. *CARES ACT,* PL 116-136, §2202(a)(3).

193. *Coronavirus-related relief for retirement plans and IRAs questions and answers.* Aug. 19, 2022. IRS. [www.irs.gov/newsroom/coronavirus-related-relief-for-retirement-plans-and-iras-questions-and-answers] Accessed on Jul. 17, 2023.

194. *CARES ACT,* PL 116-136, §2202(a)(4)(A)(ii).

195. Ibid, §2202(a)(4)(B).

196. *Coronavirus-related relief for retirement plans and IRAs questions and answers.* Aug. 19, 2022. IRS. [www.irs.gov/newsroom/coronavirus-related-relief-for-retirement-plans-and-iras-questions-and-answers] Accessed on Jul. 17, 2023.

197. *CARES ACT,* PL 116-136, §2202(a)(5).

198. Instructions for Form 8915-E.

Recontributions

Taxpayers can make repayments on qualifying distributions for three years, beginning on the distribution date. Any amounts taxpayers recontribute to the retirement account receive rollover contribution treatment.

An amended individual tax return is required to claim a refund of any taxable distributions that have been recontributed.

> **Example 13.** Elizabeth receives a distribution of $90,000 from her IRA on November 15, 2020. Elizabeth is a qualified individual and treats the distribution as a coronavirus distribution. She ratably includes the $90,000 distribution over a 3-year period.
>
> Without any recontribution, Elizabeth will include $30,000 in income with respect to the coronavirus distribution on each of the 2020, 2021, and 2022 tax returns. She then recontributes $45,000 to an IRA on November 10, 2023 (and made no other recontribution in the 3-year period).
>
> Pursuant to Notice 2005-92,[199] Elizabeth must amend a tax return. She can choose which return(s) to amend subject to statute of limitations.

REDUCED ESTATE TAX EXCLUSION CONSIDERATIONS

With many provisions of the TCJA[200] set to expire at the end of 2025, one impacted area is the increased estate tax exclusion. After the enactment of the TCJA, taxpayers could make larger taxable gifts without concern of exceeding their lifetime estate tax exclusion. With the decrease in the exclusion back to $5 million set to occur in 2026, taxpayers and practitioners should familiarize themselves with the treatment of taxable gifts made during the TCJA period and any of its impacts concerning future and uncompleted gifts. This section highlights these estate tax considerations and associated IRS guidance.

BASIC EXCLUSION AMOUNT

The **unified credit** against the estate tax is a tax credit every decedent is entitled to use in offsetting both estate value and gift taxation.[201] The credit comprises the estate tax on the **basic exclusion amount** that a taxpayer can reduce the value of their estate subject to the estate tax. The value of **taxable** gifts that a taxpayer makes over their lifetime reduces their basic exclusion amount. When a taxpayer makes taxable gifts (gifts valuing over $17,000 in 2023[202]) in a tax year, they report the amount of the taxable gifts on Form 709, *United States Gift Tax (and Generation-Skipping Transfer) Tax Return.* Form 709 includes a schedule with the history of taxable gifts the taxpayer made during their lifetime up until the current tax year. At the end of a taxpayer's life, executors, and tax practitioners must total the basic exclusion amount the taxpayer used for their lifetime taxable gifts to assess how much of the exclusion is available to offset the estate tax. The tax practitioner shows this amount on Form 706, *United States Estate (and Generation-Skipping Transfer) Tax Return.*

---

199. IRS Notice 2005-92, 2005-51 IRB 1165.

200. *Tax Cuts and Jobs Act,* PL 115-97.

201. IRC §2010(a).

202. Rev. Proc. 2022-38, 2022-45 IRB 445; *Frequently Asked Questions on Gift Taxes*. Jun. 16, 2023. IRS. [www.irs.gov/businesses/small-businesses-self-employed/frequently-asked-questions-on-gift-taxes] Accessed on Jul. 12, 2023.

Practitioner Planning Tip

The latest Form 709 should be kept in the taxpayer's permanent documents maintained by the practitioner and the taxpayer. A form could get lost in an annual tax return file which may eventually be purged.

The enactment of the TCJA resulted in the basic exclusion amount doubling from $5 million to $10 million for taxpayers who die between 2017 and 2026.[203] The exclusion is further adjusted each year for inflation, with the resulting exclusion for decedents who die in 2023 being $12,920,000.[204] However, when the provisions of the TCJA sunset at the end of 2025, the basic exclusion amount falls back down to $5 million[205] (this amount is projected to be $6.4 million adjusting for inflation).

SPECIAL RULE FOR THE BASIC EXCLUSION AMOUNT

Anticipating the basic exclusion amount reduction back down to the pre-TCJA amount, a question arises as to the impact on 2026 and future years' basic exclusion amount for gifts taxpayers made during 2017 through 2025. Historically, the basic exclusion amount increased over time, causing no issue when reconciling taxable gifts to the basic exclusion amount when an individual died. However, with a reduction in the basic exclusion amount after 2025, scenarios will arise where a taxpayer's lifetime taxable gifts exceed the basic exclusion amount at the time of their death post-2025 for gifts they made under the increased basic exclusion amount during 2017 through 2025.

The **clawback** concept refers to a taxpayer who is subject to estate tax because they used more than their basic exclusion amount available at death, even though they made taxable gifts **under** the annual basic exclusion amount at the time they gifted property. This treatment renders the benefits of the higher basic exclusion amount during the TCJA useless for taxpayers making gifts during that time who died after 2025.

To address the clawback issue, the IRS issued regulations providing a special rule for decedents whose basic exclusion amount for gifts in prior years exceeds the basic exclusion amount at the time of their death under Treas. Reg. §20.2010-1. This rule allows the basic exclusion amount at the decedent's date of death to consist of the sum of their allowed basic exclusion amount in calculating gift tax on their lifetime gifts. This special rule **only** applies to taxpayers whose allowable basic exclusion amount for lifetime gifts exceed the basic exclusion amount at their death. The special rule, therefore, prevents the estate being taxed on taxpayer gifts that were free from gift tax in the year the taxpayer made the gift.[206]

203. IRC §2010(c)(3).

204. IRC §2010(c)(3)(B); Rev. Proc. 2022-38, 2022-45 IRB 445.

205. Ibid.

206. TD 9884, 84 Fed. Reg. 64,995 (Nov. 26, 2019); Treas. Reg. §20.2010-1(c).

Example 14. Marcy, a single taxpayer, made a $7 million gift in 2019 to her nephew. The transaction was a complete gift when Marcy's nephew received the property title in 2019. In 2019, the basic exclusion amount was $11.4 million.[207] Marcy did not make any additional gifts during her lifetime before passing away in 2026. Assuming the basic exclusion amount for taxpayers dying in 2026 is $6.4 million, Marcy's basic exclusion amount for her lifetime taxable gifts exceeds the basic exclusion amount at the time of her passing. Therefore, the special rule under the basic exclusion amount applies to Marcy's estate.

Marcy's basic exclusion amount that she used for her 2019 gift was $6,985,000 ($7 million gift – $15,000 annual gift exclusion). Consequently, Marcy's basic exclusion amount for estate tax purposes is $6,985,000 instead of the standard $6.4 million. Her 2019 gift that was not taxable when she transferred the property to her nephew is still not taxable in 2026 when she died.

Deceased Spousal Unused Exclusion Considerations[208]

Relatively few individuals die leaving estates that use all the decedent's unified credit. In most cases, decedents have unused exclusions. The Code permits the transfer of a decedent's unused exclusion to pass to their surviving spouse. This process is referred to as **portability.** The amount available to be "ported" to the estate of the surviving spouse is the **deceased spouse's unused exclusion** (DSUE).[209]

Note. For additional information about portability and the DSUE, see the 2022 *University of Illinois Federal Tax Workbook*, Volume B, Chapter 4: Tax Considerations in the Distribution of Estate Assets.

The special rule for the basic exclusion amount under Treas. Reg. §20.2010-1 addresses decedents with a DSUE. For those taxpayers, the DSUE must be applied to their lifetime gifts before applying their basic exclusion amount in calculating the allowed basic exclusion amount on lifetime gifts. The sum of the basic exclusion amount and any DSUE is central to the computation of a surviving spouse's estate and gift tax. This sum is defined as the **applicable exclusion amount.**[210]

The applicable exclusion amount can offset a certain amount of tentative tax that would be imposed on a surviving spouse's estate and their prior gifts. This offset to this tentative tax is defined as the **applicable credit amount.**[211]

Example 15. Use the same facts as **Example 14,** except Marcy had a husband, Charlie, who predeceased her in 2018 and left her with a DSUE of $5 million. The exclusion amount for Marcy's taxable gift in 2019 is $7 million, consisting of the $5 million of DSUE that must apply first to the gift and $2 million of the basic exclusion amount. Therefore, 28.6% of the exclusion is attributable to the basic exclusion amount ($2 million ÷ $7 million). The 2019 estate and gift tax credit equivalent for the $7 million gift is $2,745,800 (using the 2019 estate tax table). The gift tax credit equivalent to the basic exclusion amount is $785,299 ($2,745,800 × 28.6% = $785,299).

The estate tax credit equivalent for the 2026 basic exclusion amount of $6.4 million is $2,505,800. Because the 2019 gift tax credit equivalent attributable to the basic exclusion amount ($785,299) is less than the 2026 estate tax credit equivalent attributable to the basic exclusion amount ($2,505,800), the special rule under Treas. Reg. §20.2010-1 does not apply to Marcy's estate. Therefore, Marcy's allowable applicable exclusion amount is $11.4 million ($5 million + $6.4 million).

11

207. Rev. Proc. 2018-57, 2018-49 IRB 827.

208. Treas. Reg. §20.2010-1(c).

209. IRC §2010(c)(4); Treas. Reg. §20.2010-2.

210. Treas. Reg. §20.2010-1(e)(2).

211. Treas. Reg. §20.2010-1(e)(1).

Treatment of Incomplete Gifts[212]

The IRS issued proposed regulations for treating incomplete gifts taxpayers made during 2017 through 2025, and who die after 2025. The regulations require these incomplete gifts to be included in the taxpayer's gross estate at the gifted property's FMV at the time of the taxpayer's death. Because incomplete gifts are not taxable and do not have the offsetting basic exclusion amount in the year of the gift, the special rule under Treas. Reg. §20.2010-1 would not apply to incomplete gifts. Consequently, taxpayers do not receive an adjustment to their basic exclusion amount at the time of their death for incomplete gifts that exceed the basic exclusion amount at the time of death but did not exceed the basic exclusion amount at the time the taxpayer initiated the gifts.

Example 16. Use the same facts as **Example 14,** except Marcy's 2019 gift to her nephew was incomplete because the property title did not transfer to her nephew until after Marcy's death. Marcy's basic exclusion amount for estate tax purposes is $6.4 million. If Marcy has no other assets at her death in 2026, $600,000 of her estate is subject to estate tax ($7 million – $6.4 million).

Practitioner Planning Tip

In considering estate tax matters, it may benefit taxpayers to complete taxable gifts that exceed the reduced basic exclusion amount before the end of 2025 to benefit from the increased basic exclusion amount provided by the TCJA.

DIGITAL ASSET TAXATION

Cryptocurrencies and other digital assets continue to rise in popularity among the public for business use, investing, and collecting. In response to this growing trend, the IRS has attempted to clarify the taxation impacts of involvement in digital asset activity and corresponding reporting compliance. As the population gravitates more towards participating in digital asset activity, the likelihood of a practitioner's client base holding digital assets increases. Therefore, practitioners need to follow up with clients and see if there are any changes in their behavior toward digital assets. This section highlights key developments in IRS communication regarding digital assets and how tax practitioners should proceed in aiding their clients in complying with these new developments.

DEFINING DIGITAL ASSETS[213]

Before 2022, the IRS required taxpayers to answer a question on Form 1040 regarding whether the taxpayer engaged in receiving, selling, exchanging, or disposing of any virtual currency financial interest.[214] The 2022 Form 1040 broadened the scope of this reporting requirement by replacing the term virtual currency with digital asset.[215] The IRS defines digital assets as "any digital representation of value which is recorded on a cryptographically secured distributed ledger or any similar technology as specified by the Secretary." In addition to virtual currency, the IRS mandates that taxpayers disclose their activity in other virtual assets. These assets can include the following.

1. Virtual currency and cryptocurrency, such as Bitcoin
2. Stablecoins, which are a type of cryptocurrency with values tied to a currency, commodity, or other financial instrument to achieve more value stability compared to traditional cryptocurrencies
3. Non-fungible tokens (NFTs), which comprise unique digital identifiers recorded in a blockchain

212. Prop. Treas. Reg. §20.2010-1.

213. *Digital Assets*. Jun. 15, 2023. IRS. [www.irs.gov/businesses/small-businesses-self-employed/digital-assets] Accessed on Jul. 10, 2023.

214. Form 1040, *U.S. Individual Income Tax Return* (2021).

215. Form 1040, *U.S. Individual Income Tax Return* (2022).

While this list is not comprehensive, the IRS specifically identified these items as examples that would meet the definition of digital assets. Therefore, practitioners and their clients must be mindful of participation in any of the above to adhere to reporting requirements while filing their tax returns.

> **Note.** For more information on digital assets, including terms, treatment, etc., see the 2022 *University of Illinois Federal Tax Workbook,* Volume A, Chapter 1: New Developments. This topic is also covered in the 2021 *University of Illinois Federal Tax Workbook,* Volume B, Chapter 2: Individual Taxpayer Issues.

TREATMENT OF SIGNIFICANT DECLINE IN VALUE[216]

Cryptocurrency market values experienced a significant decline in 2022, with the price of Bitcoin sharply falling and the collapse of the cryptocurrency exchange FTX. In response, the IRS advised taxpayers that they could not take a loss deduction for the decline of a digital asset's market value if they did not dispose of it or attempt to abandon it. While some could argue that a cryptocurrency whose value dropped to a fraction of a penny is worthless, the IRS took the position that as long as the cryptocurrency was traded on at least one exchange, the possibility existed that its value could increase in the future and, therefore, it was not worthless.

> **Caution.** The IRS memo is not an official ruling or position, and the IRS is not bound to its content and could be subject to change without notice. However, practitioners and their clients should exercise caution in this realm, as digital assets are relatively new territory, especially regarding taxation. There are several unprecedented scenarios in which taxpayers with digital assets may find themselves. Consequently, there is much uncertainty around positions one could take in reporting transactions involving digital assets. Therefore, following guidance issued by the IRS would be a conservative approach.

REPORTING DIGITAL ASSET ACTIVITY

In addition to broadening the subject matter for reporting digital assets, the IRS has further clarified reporting requirements pertaining to digital asset activity.

Form 1040 Disclosure

As mentioned previously, every individual filer must answer the question on the front of Form 1040 whether they received or sold a digital asset in the taxable year. The IRS modified the question and provided more specific instructions to help preparers correctly check the "Yes" or "No" boxes. The question on the draft 2023 Form 1040 (dated June 15, 2023) reads as follows.

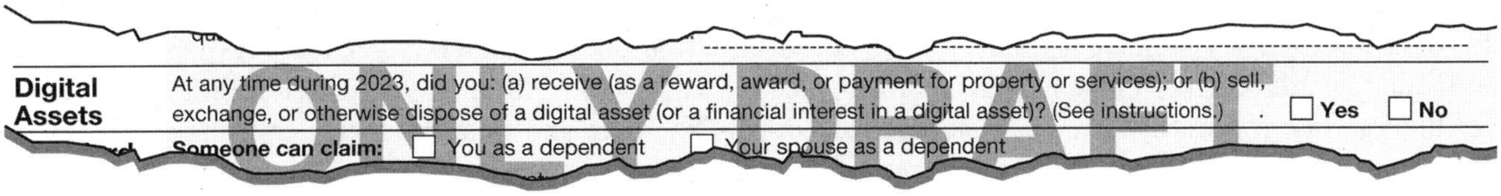
Digital Assets At any time during 2023, did you: (a) receive (as a reward, award, or payment for property or services); or (b) sell, exchange, or otherwise dispose of a digital asset (or a financial interest in a digital asset)? (See instructions.) . ☐ Yes ☐ No

Someone can claim: ☐ You as a dependent ☐ Your spouse as a dependent

DRAFT ONLY

216. CCA 202302011 (Jan. 13, 2023).

There are minor changes to the detailed list for Yes and No response to the preceding question. In general, a taxpayer should check "Yes" for the following activities.[217]

- Received digital assets as payment for property or services provided
- Transferred digital assets for free (without receiving any consideration) as a bona fide gift
- Received digital assets resulting from a reward or award
- Received new digital assets resulting from mining, **staking,** and similar activities
- Received digital assets resulting from a hard fork (a branching of a cryptocurrency's blockchain that splits a single cryptocurrency into two)
- Disposed of digital assets in exchange for property or services
- Disposed of a digital asset in exchange or trade for another digital asset
- Sold a digital asset
- Otherwise disposed of any other financial interest in a digital asset

In general, a taxpayer should check "No" if their activities were limited to one or more of the following.[218]

- Holding digital assets in a wallet or account
- Transferring digital assets from one wallet or account they own or control to another wallet or account they own or control
- Purchasing digital assets using U.S. or other real currency, including through electronic platforms such as PayPal and Venmo

Staking Income

The IRS provided guidance in Rev. Rul. 2023-14[219] on the taxability of income from staking. Staking is a way of earning rewards while holding onto certain cryptocurrencies. Staking is similar to mining; it is the method by which a network participant adds the latest batch of transactions to the blockchain and earns some digital assets in exchange. Stakers establish which blocks are valid through complex mathematical equations.[220] Although a comprehensive understanding of staking is beyond the scope of this chapter, it is important to understand the IRS' stance on reporting any income earned from stalking.

The takeaway from the Revenue Ruling is that if a cash-method taxpayer stakes cryptocurrency native to a **proof-of-stake blockchain** (cryptocurrency transactions that are validated by a consensus mechanism) and receives additional units of cryptocurrency as rewards when validation occurs, the taxpayer includes the FMV of the validation rewards received in their gross income in the tax year in which the taxpayer gains **dominion and control** over the validation rewards. The FMV is determined as of the date and time the taxpayer gains dominion and control over the validation rewards. Dominion and control in this Revenue Ruling was established when the taxpayer was able to sell, exchange, or otherwise dispose of the units of digital assets the taxpayer received as validation rewards.

---

217. IRS News Rel. IR-2023-12 (Jan. 24, 2023).

218. Ibid.

219. Rev. Rul. 2023-14, 2023-33 IRB 1.

220. *What is Staking?* Coinbase. [www.coinbase.com/learn/crypto-basics/what-is-staking] Accessed on Aug. 6, 2023.

Practitioner Planning Tip

With the cooling down of mining within the digital asset realm, it appears staking is the direction that digital asset activities are heading toward. Therefore, tax practitioners should have a basic understanding of the process and the reporting obligations.

Reporting Income and Losses

Generally, taxpayers report the receipt of income or realization of losses from digital asset activity based on the source and characteristics of the digital activity. Taxpayers may need to use different tax forms to report the activities correctly.

Wages on Form 1040. Taxpayers who receive wages from an employer that pays them in virtual currency or other digital assets must report the wages on Form 1040, line 1. The reporting requirements for the reporting and taxation of wages remain the same as taxpayers receiving wages in a nondigital currency.

Investments on Schedule D. A taxpayer selling digital assets as an investment activity reports income and losses on Form 1040, Schedule D, *Capital Gains and Losses*. Unless the taxpayer receives Form 1099-B, *Proceeds from Broker and Barter Exchange Transactions*, reporting digital asset activity with basis information reported to the IRS and no adjustments, the taxpayer must reconcile and report their activity on Form 8949, *Sales and Other Dispositions of Capital Assets*. The taxpayer receives capital gain and loss treatment for investment in digital asset activities. Accordingly, an individual taxpayer is limited to $3,000 of capital loss for a tax year.[221]

To calculate the gain or loss on the activity, the taxpayer must subtract their adjusted basis in the digital asset from the sales proceeds. The taxpayer's adjusted basis for digital assets follows the same principles as the basis of assets under IRC §1012.[222] If the taxpayer purchased the digital asset, their basis is the purchase cost. If the taxpayer received the digital asset as a payment for goods or services and holds the digital asset for investment purposes, their basis is the asset's FMV at the date of receipt.[223]

Example 17. William purchased one Bitcoin in June 2020 for $9,475. William intended to hold onto the Bitcoin over time and sell it as an investment. He sells the Bitcoin for $19,207 in October 2022. William does not receive a Form 1099-B reporting this transaction. While preparing his 2022 income tax return, he reports the sale of Bitcoin on Form 8949, calculating a long-term capital gain of $9,732. William's Schedule D, summarizing the transaction in part II, line 10, along with his Form 8949, are shown on the following pages.

11

221. IRC §1211(b).

222. Rev. Rul. 2019-24, 2019-44 IRB 1004.

223. IRS Notice 2014-21, 2014-16 IRB 938.

For Example 17

Form 8949 (2022) Attachment Sequence No. **12A** Page **2**

Name(s) shown on return. Name and SSN or taxpayer identification no. not required if shown on other side: **William Wonka**

Social security number or taxpayer identification number: ***-**-8842

Before you check Box D, E, or F below, see whether you received any Form(s) 1099-B or substitute statement(s) from your broker. A substitute statement will have the same information as Form 1099-B. Either will show whether your basis (usually your cost) was reported to the IRS by your broker and may even tell you which box to check.

Part II **Long-Term.** Transactions involving capital assets you held more than 1 year are generally long-term (see instructions). For short-term transactions, see page 1.

Note: You may aggregate all long-term transactions reported on Form(s) 1099-B showing basis was reported to the IRS and for which no adjustments or codes are required. Enter the totals directly on Schedule D, line 8a; you aren't required to report these transactions on Form 8949 (see instructions).

You *must* check Box D, E, *or* F below. Check only one box. If more than one box applies for your long-term transactions, complete a separate Form 8949, page 2, for each applicable box. If you have more long-term transactions than will fit on this page for one or more of the boxes, complete as many forms with the same box checked as you need.

☐ **(D)** Long-term transactions reported on Form(s) 1099-B showing basis was reported to the IRS (see **Note** above)
☐ **(E)** Long-term transactions reported on Form(s) 1099-B showing basis **wasn't** reported to the IRS
☒ **(F)** Long-term transactions not reported to you on Form 1099-B

1 (a) Description of property (Example: 100 sh. XYZ Co.)	(b) Date acquired (Mo., day, yr.)	(c) Date sold or disposed of (Mo., day, yr.)	(d) Proceeds (sales price) (see instructions)	(e) Cost or other basis See the **Note** below and see *Column (e)* in the separate instructions.	Adjustment, if any, to gain or loss. If you enter an amount in column (g), enter a code in column (f). **See the separate instructions.** (f) Code(s) from instructions	(g) Amount of adjustment	(h) **Gain or (loss)** Subtract column (e) from column (d) and combine the result with column (g).
1 Bitcoin	6/15/20	10/27/22	19,207	9,475			9,732
2 Totals. Add the amounts in columns (d), (e), (g), and (h) (subtract negative amounts). Enter each total here and include on your Schedule D, **line 8b** (if **Box D** above is checked), **line 9** (if **Box E** above is checked), or **line 10** (if **Box F** above is checked)			19,207	9,475			9,732

Note: If you checked Box D above but the basis reported to the IRS was incorrect, enter in column (e) the basis as reported to the IRS, and enter an adjustment in column (g) to correct the basis. See *Column (g)* in the separate instructions for how to figure the amount of the adjustment.

Form **8949** (2022)

For Example 17

SCHEDULE D
(Form 1040)

Department of the Treasury
Internal Revenue Service

Capital Gains and Losses

Attach to Form 1040, 1040-SR, or 1040-NR.
Go to *www.irs.gov/ScheduleD* for instructions and the latest information.
Use Form 8949 to list your transactions for lines 1b, 2, 3, 8b, 9, and 10.

OMB No. 1545-0074
2022
Attachment Sequence No. **12**

Name(s) shown on return: William Wonka | **Your social security number:** ***-**-8842

Did you dispose of any investment(s) in a qualified opportunity fund during the tax year? ☐ Yes ☒ No
If "Yes," attach Form 8949 and see its instructions for additional requirements for reporting your gain or loss.

Part I **Short-Term Capital Gains and Losses—Generally Assets Held One Year or Less** (see instructions)

See instructions for how to figure the amounts to enter on the lines below. This form may be easier to complete if you round off cents to whole dollars.	(d) Proceeds (sales price)	(e) Cost (or other basis)	(g) Adjustments to gain or loss from Form(s) 8949, Part I, line 2, column (g)	(h) Gain or (loss) Subtract column (e) from column (d) and combine the result with column (g)
1a Totals for all short-term transactions reported on Form 1099-B for which basis was reported to the IRS and for which you have no adjustments (see instructions). However, if you choose to report all these transactions on Form 8949, leave this line blank and go to line 1b				
1b Totals for all transactions reported on Form(s) 8949 with **Box A** checked				
2 Totals for all transactions reported on Form(s) 8949 with **Box B** checked				
3 Totals for all transactions reported on Form(s) 8949 with **Box C** checked				

4 Short-term gain from Form 6252 and short-term gain or (loss) from Forms 4684, 6781, and 8824	4	
5 Net short-term gain or (loss) from partnerships, S corporations, estates, and trusts from Schedule(s) K-1	5	
6 Short-term capital loss carryover. Enter the amount, if any, from line 8 of your **Capital Loss Carryover Worksheet** in the instructions	6	( )
7 **Net short-term capital gain or (loss).** Combine lines 1a through 6 in column (h). If you have any long-term capital gains or losses, go to Part II below. Otherwise, go to Part III on the back	7	

Part II **Long-Term Capital Gains and Losses—Generally Assets Held More Than One Year** (see instructions)

See instructions for how to figure the amounts to enter on the lines below. This form may be easier to complete if you round off cents to whole dollars.	(d) Proceeds (sales price)	(e) Cost (or other basis)	(g) Adjustments to gain or loss from Form(s) 8949, Part II, line 2, column (g)	(h) Gain or (loss) Subtract column (e) from column (d) and combine the result with column (g)
8a Totals for all long-term transactions reported on Form 1099-B for which basis was reported to the IRS and for which you have no adjustments (see instructions). However, if you choose to report all these transactions on Form 8949, leave this line blank and go to line 8b				
8b Totals for all transactions reported on Form(s) 8949 with **Box D** checked				
9 Totals for all transactions reported on Form(s) 8949 with **Box E** checked				
10 Totals for all transactions reported on Form(s) 8949 with **Box F** checked	19,207	9,475		9,732

11 Gain from Form 4797, Part I; long-term gain from Forms 2439 and 6252; and long-term gain or (loss) from Forms 4684, 6781, and 8824	11	
12 Net long-term gain or (loss) from partnerships, S corporations, estates, and trusts from Schedule(s) K-1	12	
13 Capital gain distributions. See the instructions	13	
14 Long-term capital loss carryover. Enter the amount, if any, from line 13 of your **Capital Loss Carryover Worksheet** in the instructions	14	( )
15 **Net long-term capital gain or (loss).** Combine lines 8a through 14 in column (h). Then, go to Part III on the back	15	9,732

For Paperwork Reduction Act Notice, see your tax return instructions. Cat. No. 11338H **Schedule D (Form 1040) 2022**

11

Business Income on Schedule C.[224] If the taxpayer receives payment for services they perform or other business activity, the taxpayer reports the income on Schedule C, *Profit or Loss From Business*. The amount of income for the taxpayer to report for this payment is the FMV of the digital assets on the date of receipt. This value also serves as the taxpayer's basis in the digital asset. If the taxpayer is in the business of selling, exchanging, or transferring digital assets to customers, income arising from this activity is also reported on Schedule C.[225] Income the taxpayer reports on Schedule C is subject to self-employment tax.

Ordinary Income on Schedule 1.[226] If a taxpayer sells or exchanges digital assets they are not holding for investment and would not otherwise meet the definition of a capital asset, the gain or loss on the sale is ordinary.[227] In some cases, this income is reported on Schedule 1, such as when the digital asset is not a capital asset or held in the course of a business.

Donating Digital Assets[228]

Taxpayers who donate digital assets to a qualified nonprofit organization can itemize the contribution as a charitable deduction. However, taxpayers must submit a qualified appraisal of the digital asset with their filed return to take the deduction for donations over $5,000.[229] Notably, taxpayers may not use values cryptocurrency exchanges report in lieu of qualified appraisals to support the deduction amount.

Note. Depending on the type of digital asset a taxpayer donates, appraising a digital asset may be more difficult than appraising traditional tangible assets. While cryptocurrencies are regularly traded, NFTs are more complex, as they are unique by nature. Until Congress passes legislation or the IRS issues different guidance, taxpayers should plan on obtaining an appraisal before donating digital assets to claim the deduction.

Digital Asset Treatment for Personal Use

Taxpayers may use digital assets, particularly cryptocurrencies, as a "checkbook" to purchase personal goods. This trend is evident in more businesses accepting cryptocurrencies as forms of payment from their customers. The facts and circumstances surrounding the use of the digital asset drive the classification and associated tax treatment for its associated activities.[230] While the IRS does not explicitly identify digital assets in this specific context, the agency explains that most personal use items are capital assets.[231] Therefore, if taxpayers use digital assets for the purchase of personal goods, the gain or loss from the change in the digital asset's value from the time of acquisition until the time of disbursement should receive the same tax treatment as a personal use asset. The IRS appeared to reinforce this concept by stating that virtual currency receives treatment as property instead of a currency for federal income tax purposes.[232] Consequently, digital asset transactions would not receive a $200 de minimis gain exclusion resulting from personal foreign currency transactions.[233]

224. Rev. Rul. 2019-24, 2019-44 IRB 1004.

225. IRS News Rel. IR-2023-12 (Jan. 24, 2023).

226. *Frequently Asked Questions on Virtual Currency Transactions*. Jun. 27, 2023. IRS. [www.irs.gov/individuals/international-taxpayers/frequently-asked-questions-on-virtual-currency-transactions] Accessed on Jul. 11, 2023.

227. IRS Notice 2014-21, 2014-16 IRB 938.

228. CCA 202302012 (Jan. 13, 2023).

229. IRC §170(f)(11).

230. IRS Notice 2014-21, 2014-16 IRB 938.

231. *Topic Number 409, Capital Gains and Losses*. Apr. 4, 2023. IRS. [www.irs.gov/taxtopics/tc409] Accessed on Jul. 11, 2023.

232. IRS Notice 2023-34, 2023-19 IRB 837.

233. IRC §988(e)(2).

When taxpayers realize a gain from the sale of personal property, the income receives capital gain treatment and is reported on Form 8949 and Schedule D.[234] Losses on the sale of personal-use property, however, are nondeductible.[235] Therefore, if digital asset transactions are considered in the context of personal-use property, taxpayers would recognize capital gains from the exchange of digital assets in a transaction, but would not recognize any losses.

Caution. Practitioners should monitor IRS communications regarding the treatment of digital assets, as this is a relatively new area in the realm of taxation, and the IRS continuously states that it intends to provide further guidance on associated topics at a future date.

Another consideration still requiring guidance is the classification of digital assets, particularly NFTs, as collectibles. The IRS has issued a notice stating that it intends to issue guidance regarding NFTs as IRC §408(m) collectibles subject to a higher tax rate.[236] As with personal-use assets, the facts and circumstances surrounding the nature of its actual and intended use determine the classification of the digital asset.

EXPIRING PROVISIONS

The following are some expiring provisions for which taxpayers may want to plan. Additionally, some provisions that expired in 2022 may impact a taxpayer's 2023 tax return.

DECEMBER 31, 2022

Code Sections	Description
45G(a)	Railroad track maintenance credit of 50%
274(n)(2)(D)	Allowance of full deduction for business meals

SEPTEMBER 30, 2023

Code Sections	Description
4043(d), 4081(d)(2)(B), 4083(b), 4261(j) and (k), 4271(d)	Various airport and airway trust fund excise taxes

11

234. Ibid.

235. Ibid.

236. IRS Notice 2023-27, 2023-15 IRB 634.

Code Sections	Description
40(b)(6)(J)	Second generation biofuel producer credit
40A(g)	Various income tax credits for biodiesel fuel, biodiesel used to produce a qualified mixture, and small agribiodiesel producers (also renewable diesel)
40B(h)	Credit for sustainable aviation fuel
45(d), 48(a)(5)	Beginning-of-construction date for renewable power facilities eligible to claim the renewable electricity production credit or investment credit in lieu of the production credit
48(a)(2)(A)(i)(II), 48(a)(3)(A)(ii) and (viii), 48(c)(1)(E), 48(c)(2)(D), 48(c)(3)(A)(iv), 48(c)(4)(C)	Beginning-of-construction date for increased credit for business solar energy property and credit for fiber optic solar lighting system property, qualified fuel cell and stationary microturbine power plant property, combined heat and power property, small wind property, and waste energy recovery property
48(a)(3)(A), 168(e)(3)(E)	Five-year recovery period for certain energy property
48(e)(4)(C)	Increase in energy credit for solar and wind facilities placed in service in connection with low-income communities
223(c)(2)(E)	Safe harbor for absence of deductible for telehealth
6426(c)(6)	Excise tax credits and outlay payments for (renewable) diesel fuel mixtures
6426(d)(5)	Excise tax credits and outlay payments for alternative fuel
6426(e)(3)	Excise tax credits for alternative fuel mixtures
6426(k)	Excise tax credits and outlay payments for sustainable aviation fuel
6427(e)(6)(B), (C), and (E)	Excise tax credits and outlay payments for (renewable) diesel fuel mixtures

DECEMBER 31, 2025

Code Sections	Description
1(j)	Modification of individual income tax rates
24(h)	Child tax credit amounts
25B(d)(1)(D), 529(c)(3)(C)(i)(III), 529A(b)(2)(B)	Achieving a Better Life Experience (ABLE) accounts: Contributions eligible for saver's credit; rollovers from qualified tuition plans permitted, and increased contribution amounts
36B	Premium assistance credit enhancements
45D(f)(1)	New markets tax credit
45S(i)	Employer credit for paid family and medical leave
51(c)(4)	Work opportunity tax credit
55	Modifications of exemption amount and phaseout threshold of individual AMT
59A(b)(2)	Rate on modified taxable income and treatment of credits in the calculation of base erosion minimum tax amount
63(c)(7)	Increase in standard deduction of individuals
67(g)	Suspension of miscellaneous itemized deduction
68(f)	Suspension of limitation on itemized deductions
108(a)(1)(E)	Exclusion from gross income of discharge of indebtedness on principal residence
108(f)(5)	Certain discharges of student loans
127(c)(1)(B)	Exclusion for certain employer payments of student loans
132(f)(8)	Suspension of exclusion for reimbursement of bicycle commuting
132(g)(2)	Suspension of exclusion for moving expense reimbursement
151(d)(5)	Suspension of deduction for personal exemptions
163(h)(3)(F)	Limitation on deduction for qualified residence interest, suspension of deduction for home equity interest
164(b)(6)	Limitation on deduction for state, local, etc., taxes
165(d)	Modification of rules relating to computation of wagering losses
165(h)(5)	Personal casualty losses limited to federally declared disaster areas
168(e)(3)(C)(ii), 168(i)(15)(D)	7-year recovery period for motorsports entertainment complexes
170(b)(1)(G)	Increase in percentage limitation on cash contributions to public charities
181(g)	Special expensing rules for certain film, television, and live theatrical productions
199A(i)	QBID
217(k)	Suspension of deduction for moving expenses
250(a)(3)	Deduction percentages for foreign-derived intangible income and global intangible low-taxed income

December 31, 2025 *(continued)*

Code Sections	Description
274(o)	Deductibility of employer de minimis meals and related eating facility, and meals for the convenience of the employer
420(b)(4)	Transfer of excess pension assets to retiree health and life insurance accounts
954(c)(6)(C)	Look-through treatment of payments between related controlled foreign corporations under the foreign personal holding company rules
1391(d), (h), 1394, 1396	Empowerment zones: Designation of an empowerment zone, tax-exempt bonds, employment credit
2010(c)(3)(C)	Increased estate and gift tax exemption
4611(f)(2)	Oil Spill Liability Trust Fund financing rate

DECEMBER 31, 2026

Code Sections	Description
25B	Elective deferrals and IRA contributions by certain individuals
48D(e)	Credit for advanced manufacturing investment
168(k) and 460(c)	Various additional first-year depreciation elections
1400Z-2(a)(2)(B)	Election to invest capital gains in an opportunity zone

DECEMBER 31, 2027

Code Sections	Description
45Z(g)	Credit for clean fuel production

Chapter 12: Rulings and Cases

Note. Corrections for all of the chapters are available at **TaxSchool.illinois.edu.** For clarification about terms used throughout this chapter, see the **Acronyms and Abbreviations** section following the index.

For your convenience, in-text website links are also provided as short URLs. Anywhere you see **uofi.tax/xxx**, the link points to the address immediately following in brackets.

Note. This chapter contains selected cases, revenue rulings, revenue procedures, Treasury regulations, announcements, and letter rulings issued during the past year, through approximately July 31, 2023. Each appears as a condensed version and should not be relied on as a substitute for the full document. A full citation appears for each item. This chapter is not intended to be a comprehensive coverage of all tax law changes. Rather, it reports the rulings and cases most likely to be of interest to tax professionals.

About the Authors

Kelly Golish, CPA, is the Assistant Director, Tax Materials, at the University of Illinois Tax School. She was previously a manager at Crowder, CPAs in Danville, IL and worked for both public and private accounting firms in Decatur, IL, Cleveland, OH, and San Jose, CA. Kelly earned a Masters in Accounting with an emphasis in Taxation and a Bachelors in Accounting at the University of Notre Dame.

Chris Korban, CPA, is a Tax Materials Specialist at the University of Illinois Tax School. He joined Tax School in 2023 with nine years of experience in public accounting. Chris earned both his Bachelor's Degree in Accounting and Master of Accounting Science from the University of Illinois.

John W. Richmann, EA, is a Tax Materials Specialist at the University of Illinois Tax School. Prior to joining Tax School in 2021, he owned a tax practice in St. Charles, Illinois, and held positions in private industry and consulting firms. John earned a Masters Degree in Business Administration from the University of Texas and an electrical engineering degree from the Massachusetts Institute of Technology.

Other chapter contributors and reviewers are listed at the front of this volume.

SUBSTANTIAL AUTHORITY

If there is substantial authority for a position taken on a tax return, neither the taxpayer nor the tax preparer will be subject to the penalty for underreporting income even if the IRS successfully challenges the position taken on the return. By contrast, if there is no substantial authority for a position taken on a tax return, the underreporting penalties may be imposed unless the position has been adequately disclosed and there is a reasonable basis for the position.

EVALUATION OF AUTHORITIES

There is substantial authority for the tax treatment of an item only if the weight of the authorities that support the treatment is substantial in relation to the weight of the authorities that support a contrary treatment.

- All the authorities relevant to the tax treatment of an item (including the authorities contrary to the treatment) are taken into account in determining whether substantial authority exists.
- The weight of the authorities is determined in light of the pertinent facts and circumstances. There may be substantial authority for more than one position with respect to the same item.
- Because the substantial authority standard is an objective one, the **taxpayer's belief** that there is substantial authority for the tax treatment of an item **is not relevant** in determining whether that is in fact true.

NATURE OF ANALYSIS

The weight accorded to an authority depends on its relevance and persuasiveness, as well as the type of document providing the authority. For example, a case or revenue ruling that has some facts in common with the tax treatment at issue is not particularly relevant if the authority is materially distinguishable on its facts or otherwise inapplicable to the tax treatment. An authority that merely states a conclusion ordinarily is less persuasive than one that reaches its conclusion by cogently relating the applicable law to pertinent facts. The weight of an authority from which information has been deleted (such as a private letter ruling) is diminished to the extent that the deleted information may have affected the authority's conclusions.

The type of document also must be considered. For example, a revenue ruling is accorded greater weight than a private letter ruling addressing the same issue. Private rulings, technical advice memoranda (TAM), general counsel memoranda (GCM), revenue procedures, and/or actions on decisions issued prior to the Internal Revenue Code (IRC) of 1986 generally must be accorded less weight than more recent ones.

There may be substantial authority for the tax treatment of an item despite the absence of certain types of authority. Thus, a taxpayer may have substantial authority for a position that is supported only by a well-reasoned construction of the applicable statutory provision.

AUTHORITY HIERARCHY

The following factors are considered in determining whether there is substantial authority for the tax treatment of an item.[1]

- Applicable provisions of the IRC and other statutory provisions
- Temporary and final Treasury regulations construing such statutes

> **Note.** A proposed regulation presents a **tentative** IRS position that may be changed when a temporary and/or final regulation is issued.

- Revenue rulings
- Revenue procedures
- Tax treaties and regulations thereunder, and Treasury Department and other official explanations of such treaties
- Federal court cases interpreting such statutes
- Congressional intent, as reflected in committee reports
- Joint explanatory statements of managers included in congressional conference committee reports, and floor statements made prior to enactment by one of a bill's managers
- General explanations of tax legislation prepared by the Joint Committee on Taxation
- Letter rulings and TAM issued after October 31, 1976
- Actions on decisions and GCM issued after March 12, 1981
- IRS information or press releases, and notices, announcements, and other administrative pronouncements published by the IRS in the Internal Revenue Bulletin (IRB)

Additional information on some of the preceding items follows.

IRC. Except where provisions violate the U.S. Constitution, IRC provisions are binding in all courts.

Treasury Regulations (Income Tax Regulations). The regulations are the Treasury Department's official interpretation and explanation of the IRC. Regulations have the force and effect of law unless they are in conflict with the statute they explain.

Revenue Rulings. The IRS is bound by the position taken in a revenue ruling. Revenue rulings that interpret Treasury regulations are entitled to substantial deference.

Letter Rulings and TAM. Private letter rulings and TAM are IRS rulings directed at particular taxpayers. A private letter ruling is issued for a fee. The IRS is bound to such a ruling only for the particular taxpayer who requested it. A TAM is issued in response to a request for a legal opinion.

Chief Counsel Advice (CCA). A CCA is an IRS ruling issued to IRS field operations by the Office of Chief Counsel. It may be directed at a particular taxpayer or a particular issue. Included in this category are various legal memoranda (e.g., Internal Legal Memoranda (ILM) and Litigation Guideline Memoranda (LGM)).

---

1. Treas. Reg. §1.6662-4(d)(3)(iii).

GCM. GCM detail the legal reasoning behind the issuance of a revenue ruling.

Service Center Advice (SCA). SCAs are issued by the IRS in response to a question coming from an IRS center. There are two types of SCAs: routine and significant. A **routine SCA** is answered by district counsel and not coordinated with the national office. A routine SCA is not issued to the public. A **significant SCA** (SSCA), on the other hand, is issued only with the approval of the national office. An SSCA is not legal advice and addresses only the interpretation or application of the Internal Revenue laws. SSCAs are made public, but any information identifying taxpayers is deleted.

Tax Court Summary Opinions. A case decided under the small-case procedures cannot be appealed by the taxpayer or the IRS. Without the appeals process, incorrect legal interpretations by the Tax Court cannot be challenged. Therefore, the Tax Court's decision is binding only on that particular case. However, reviewing the cases can still be useful; they explain the IRS's arguments, the taxpayer's arguments, and the Tax Court's reasoning.

JUDICIAL SYSTEM FOR TAX DISPUTES

Three levels of federal courts have jurisdiction to hear tax cases. The following diagram illustrates the three levels. The diagram is followed by a brief description of each court.

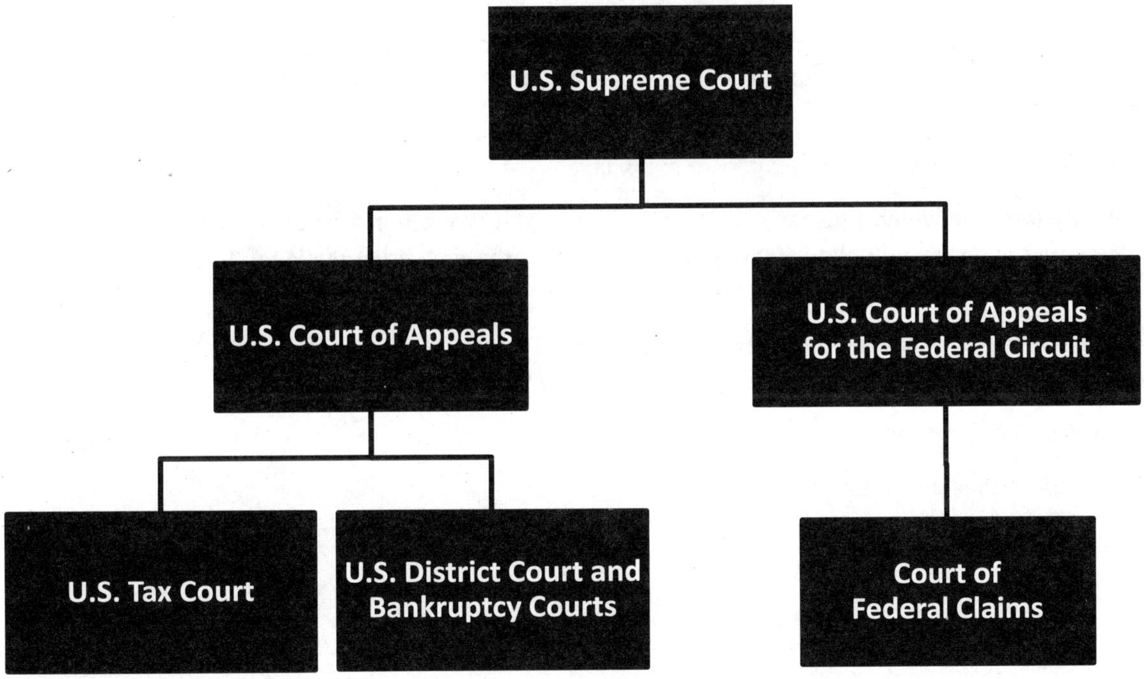

Note. Although tax liabilities are addressed by bankruptcy courts, they are generally addressed in a bankruptcy context under the terms of the Bankruptcy Code in a different manner than in the other courts noted in the above diagram.

12

CASE COMMENCEMENT

A taxpayer in a dispute with the IRS generally has two choices after they receive a statutory notice or notice of final determination (a 90-day letter).

1. File a petition in the Tax Court without paying the tax.
2. Pay the tax and file a claim of refund. If the IRS rejects the claim, the taxpayer can file suit in a U.S. District Court or the Court of Federal Claims.

> **Note.** U.S. District Courts also have jurisdiction to hear federal tax cases. However, these courts are generally used only for very substantial tax disputes because of the high costs and the complexities of using them to resolve tax issues. Consequently, these courts are rarely used by individual taxpayers to resolve tax disputes with the IRS.

THE U.S. TAX COURT

The U.S. Tax Court is a federal court of record that was established in 1942 by Congress under Article I of the Constitution. It replaced the Board of Tax Appeals. Congress created the Tax Court to provide a judicial forum in which taxpayers could dispute tax deficiencies determined by the Commissioner of Internal Revenue prior to the payment of the disputed amounts.

The Tax Court is located at 400 Second Street, N.W., Washington, DC 20217. Although the court is physically located in Washington, the judges travel nationwide to conduct trials in various designated cities.

As of July 2023, the Tax Court is composed of 19 judges (three currently vacant), 10 senior judges, and five special trial judges. The judges generally have expertise in tax law.

This is the only forum in which a taxpayer can contest a tax liability **without** first paying the tax. However, there is a $60 filing fee that may be paid online at **pay.gov**, or by check or money order made out to "Clerk, United States Tax Court."[2] Jury trials are not available in this forum.

The jurisdiction of the Tax Court was greatly expanded by the Revenue Reconciliation Act of 1998. The jurisdiction of the Tax Court includes the authority to hear tax disputes concerning the following.

- Notices of deficiency
- Notices of transferee liability
- Certain types of declaratory judgments
- Readjustment and adjustment of partnership items
- Review of the failure to abate interest
- Administrative costs
- Worker classification
- Relief from joint and several liability on joint returns
- Review of certain collection actions

The Tax Court also has limited jurisdiction under IRC §7428 to hear an appeal from an organization that is threatened with the loss of its tax-exempt status. Under IRC §7478, the Tax Court can also issue a declaratory judgment for a state or local government that has failed to get a tax exemption for a bond issue.

2. *How to Pay the Filing Fee.* United States Tax Court. [ustaxcourt.gov/pay_filing_fee.html] Accessed on Jul. 17, 2023.

The IRS issues a statutory notice of deficiency in tax disputes in which the IRS has determined a deficiency. In cases in which a deficiency is not at issue, the IRS issues a notice of final determination. A notice of final determination is issued in the following types of tax disputes.

- Employee versus independent contractor treatments
- Innocent spouse claim determinations
- Collection due process cases

To invoke the jurisdiction of the Tax Court, the taxpayer must file a petition in Tax Court within 90 days after the IRS notice of deficiency (or notice of final determination) is mailed.[3] **The 90-day date cannot be extended by the IRS.** Similarly, the Tax Court has no statutory authority to extend the 90-day period.[4] However, the Tax Court does have the discretion to accept a timely but nonconforming document as a petition and allow later amendments to that document that relate to the originally timely filed nonconforming petition.[5]

Observation. Taxpayers and practitioners should not rely on the Tax Court's discretion to extend the 90-day period by filing a nonconforming document that is not a valid Tax Court petition. There is no guarantee that the Tax Court will grant relief from the 90-day deadline.

Who May Practice in the U.S. Tax Court

A taxpayer may represent themselves in Tax Court, or they may be represented by a practitioner admitted to the bar of the Tax Court. Generally, an attorney who is a member of the bar of any state (or the District of Columbia) may be admitted to the bar of the U.S. Tax Court. The attorney must complete the required application for admission to practice (which must be notarized), attach the required proof of good standing in their state bar, and pay the required $50 fee.

A nonattorney may also be admitted to practice before the U.S. Tax Court. To do so, the nonattorney practitioner must pass a 4-hour examination consisting of the following four parts and pay the $150 examination fee.

- Tax Court rules of practice and procedure
- Federal taxation
- Federal rules of evidence
- Legal ethics

A score of at least 70% in each of the four parts is necessary to pass the examination. The examination is conducted at least once every two years. After passing the examination, the nonattorney practitioner must file the required application for admission.

The following resources for attorneys and nonattorneys provide information about admission to practice before the U.S. Tax Court (including the necessary forms, fee information, and mailing addresses).

- **Attorneys: uofi.tax/15b7x1** [www.ustaxcourt.gov/forms/Admission_Attorney_Form_30.pdf]
- **Nonattorneys: uofi.tax/15b7x2** [www.ustaxcourt.gov/resources/forms/Admission_Nonattorney_Info.pdf]

3. IRC §6213(a).
4. *R. S. Schoenfeld v. Comm'r*, TC Memo 1993-303 (Jul. 13, 1993); *Schake v. Comm'r,* TC Memo 2002-262 (Oct. 10, 2002).
5. *R. M. Crandall v. Comm'r*, 650 F.2d 659 (5th Cir. 1981); *N. E. Carstenson v. Comm'r,* 57 TC 542 (1972).

Tax Court Decisions

The Tax Court hears several types of cases and issues several types of opinions. Specifically, the court hears both regular cases and small tax cases (referred to as S cases).

An S case is generally one that involves less than $50,000 of unpaid tax. The $50,000 threshold includes penalties but does not include interest. S cases are heard using less formal procedures and do not provide the right of appeal to a higher court. For a case to be treated as an S case, the taxpayer must choose S case status and the Tax Court must agree that the case qualifies.

> **Note.** For more information about S cases, see IRC §7463 and **uofi.tax/15b7x3** [www.ustaxcourt.gov/petitioners_start.html].

A Tax Court **summary opinion** is an opinion rendered in an S case. It may **not** be relied on as precedent.

Regular opinions are opinions from cases that are not S cases, and a regular opinion may be a memorandum opinion or a Tax Court opinion. A **Tax Court opinion** is issued if the Tax Court believes the case involves a sufficiently important or novel legal or tax issue. All other regular cases result in **memorandum opinions.** Both memorandum opinions and Tax Court opinions may be appealed and may serve as precedents.

A **bench opinion** can be issued by the Tax Court in any regular or S case. A bench opinion occurs when the judge issues the opinion orally in court during the trial. The taxpayer receives a transcript of the bench opinion a few weeks after the trial. Bench opinions may **not** be relied on as precedents.

> **Observation.** Tax Court opinions may be viewed online. A search engine for finding cases is available at **uofi.tax/15b7x4** [www.dawson.ustaxcourt.gov].

> **Note.** Information about the Tax Court rules of practice and procedure are available at **uofi.tax/15b7x5** [www.ustaxcourt.gov/rules.html].

Tax Court Appeals

A Tax Court opinion or memorandum opinion may be appealed in a U.S. Court of Appeals. However, a taxpayer who commences their case in the U.S. Court of Federal Claims must appeal their case to the U.S. Court of Appeals for the Federal Circuit.

A final appeal can be made to the U.S. Supreme Court; but, because the Court's jurisdiction is discretionary, it hears relatively few tax cases. Many of the court transcripts from these cases can be accessed online at **uofi.tax/15b7x6** [www.uscourts.gov].

The taxpayer can file a refund suit in the Claims Court or the Federal District Court once they have paid the deficiency. In both of these courts, decisions of the Tax Court are not binding as precedents. A jury trial is available only in the Federal District Court. Many federal court opinions can be accessed online at **uofi.tax/15b7x6** [www.uscourts.gov].

The 13 judicial circuits of the United States are constituted as follows.

Circuits	Hears Appeals from Federal District Courts and U.S. Tax Court Cases Originating in:
D.C.	U.S. Tax Court cases originating in D.C., Federal Administrative agencies, and Federal District Court cases for the District of Columbia
1st	Maine, Massachusetts, New Hampshire, Puerto Rico, Rhode Island
2d	Connecticut, New York, Vermont
3d	Delaware, New Jersey, Pennsylvania, Virgin Islands
4th	Maryland, North Carolina, South Carolina, Virginia, West Virginia
5th	Louisiana, Mississippi, Texas
6th	Kentucky, Michigan, Ohio, Tennessee
7th	Illinois, Indiana, Wisconsin
8th	Arkansas, Iowa, Minnesota, Missouri, Nebraska, North Dakota, South Dakota
9th	Alaska, Arizona, California, Hawaii, Idaho, Montana, Nevada, Oregon, Washington, Guam
10th	Colorado, Kansas, New Mexico, Oklahoma, Utah, Wyoming
11th	Alabama, Florida, Georgia
Fed.	Any federal case involving subject matter within its jurisdiction; U.S. Court of Federal Claims; U.S. Court of International Trade

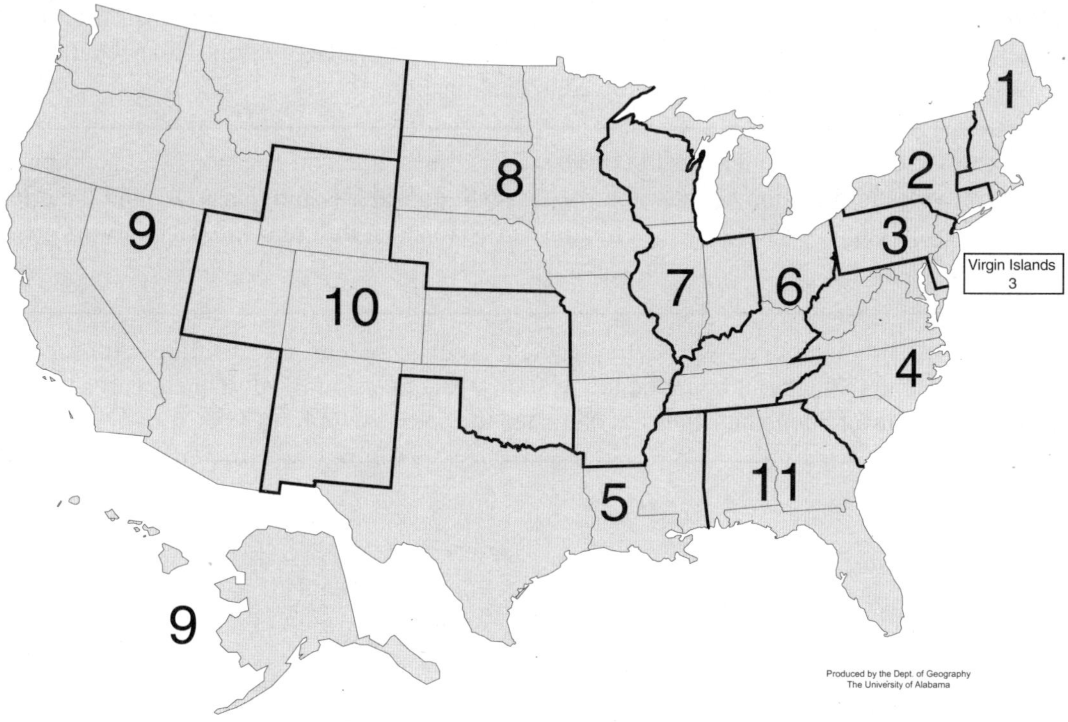

12

IRS ACTIONS ON DECISION[6]

The IRS has the ability to refuse to accept a court's legal reasoning in a tax case (unless the case was resolved by the U.S. Supreme Court). Generally, the IRS may issue an Action on Decision (AOD) for a case that it did not appeal but that decided issues that were adverse to it.

An AOD is a formal memorandum that alerts IRS officials and the public about the position the IRS will take in future litigation. An AOD is issued at the discretion of the IRS, and the IRS is not bound by it. An AOD does not have the force of a regulation or revenue ruling.

An AOD may take one of the following forms, depending on the position the IRS takes regarding the litigated case.

- **Acquiescence.** The IRS accepts the holding of a court in the case and will follow it in disposing of other cases in which the same facts are controlling.
- **Acquiescence in result only.** The IRS accepts the holding of a court in the case and will follow it in disposing of other cases in which the same facts are controlling. However, the IRS has general disagreement or concern with the court's reasoning in the case.
- **Nonacquiescence.** The IRS has decided against appealing the case but does not agree with the holding of the court and will not apply the court's decision in resolving similar cases with other taxpayers.

Observation. An AOD may provide a practitioner with insight on the stance the IRS will take on an issue that has been litigated. In this regard, an AOD may provide a useful source of information about taxpayers in the same or similar circumstances as those involved in the litigation.

The practitioner can view AODs online at **uofi.tax/15b7x7** [irs.gov/actions-on-decisions]. In addition, the Internal Revenue Manual provides information about when the IRS will consider issuing an AOD and the criteria used to determine when doing so is appropriate. This information can be found at **uofi.tax/15b7x8** [www.irs.gov/irm/part36/irm_36-003-001#d0e51].

Note. Although the IRS is bound by a particular Tax Court or federal court ruling with regard to the taxpayer(s) involved in that case, it is not bound to follow that decision in subsequent cases that have the same or similar facts. In addition, the IRS is not obligated to appeal a case from Tax Court or any other court.

6. *Actions on Decision (AOD).* IRS. [apps.irs.gov/app/picklist/list/actionsOnDecisions.html] Accessed on Aug. 21, 2023; IRM 36.3.1 (2013).

Interest Expense

***Alexander C. Deitch et al. v. Comm'r*, TC Memo 2022-86 (Aug. 25, 2022)**

IRC §163

☞ IRS Loses Interest Case

Facts. Alexander Deitch and Jonathan Barry formed West Town Square Investment Group, LLC (WTS) as a Georgia limited liability company (LLC) to acquire real estate for development as a local hospital's physical therapy facility. Both had experience in commercial real estate, giving them confidence that they could develop, manage, and eventually sell at a profit the shopping center, which a Walmart store had once anchored. Mr. Barry had access to loaned money from PLI, a subsidiary of Protective Life Corporation, an insurance company. WTS acquired the property with a $4.4 million loan from PLI, later borrowing additional sums to make needed renovations and provide the hospital with an allowance for moving costs.

The amounts loaned by PLI constituted almost 100% of the project's financing because Mr. Deitch and Mr. Barry formed WTS by contributing only $5 of capital each. Because borrowers could only secure conventional mortgages when the amount loaned was 75% or less of the property's value, acquiring the property required a special type of loan.

The special loan product turned out to be a **participating loan.** A participating loan is one in which a lender participates in the real estate's profits, either from the property's monthly cash flow or through a percentage of the profits when the borrower sells the property. WTS required both conventional and participating loans. Part of the additional interest was based on the appreciation of the property when sold, and the loan documents identified it as "appreciation interest."

These documents expressly provided that PLI and WTS would have a relationship of creditor and lender. The loan documents contained the following language.

> *Nothing contained in any Loan Document or instrument made in connection with the loan, shall be deemed or construed to create a partnership, tenancy-in-common, joint tenancy, joint venture, or co-ownership by or between Lender and Borrower, or any relationship other than that of creditor or debtor*

All loan documents consistently stated that PLI and WTS had a creditor-debtor relationship and only referred to the money WTS paid to PLI as interest.

Despite its thin capitalization, WTS made necessary payments and sold the property for $6.3 million. PLI benefitted from its assumption of risk with the payment of appreciation interest of $1,035,683, which was 50% of the net proceeds of the sale. WTS also fared well, as the transaction resulted in partner capital on its tax return for the year of $1,099,342.

This appreciation interest payment, however, caught the IRS's attention. The agency claimed that the participating loan made PLI effectively an equity partner in the project. WTS classified the transaction as interest on its tax return, but the IRS took the position that it was not interest but a guaranteed payment.

Therefore, the IRS adjusted Mr. Dietch's and Mr. Barry's tax returns by their shares of the appreciation interest payments made to PLI. After asserting changes of $517,842 in the taxable incomes of Mr. Dietch and the Barrys, the IRS issued statutory notices of deficiency to each. Mr. Dietch and Mr. Barry petitioned the Tax Court to redetermine the deficiency.

Issues. The issue in this case is whether WTS properly classified its payment of "appreciation interest" to PLI, its creditor, as deductible interest.

Analysis. The Tax Court decided it had jurisdiction in this case because of the small partner exception in IRC §6231(a)(1)(B). However, it could not decide issues at the **partnership** level because the IRS had failed to issue a final partnership administrative adjustment (FPAA) in the case, failing to even mention WTS in the statutory notice of deficiency.

The IRS said that it wanted the Tax Court to sustain its position that the relationship between WTS and PLI, the lender, constituted a partner. If it were successful in this contention, WTS could not treat payments of participatory interest as deductible.

Because PLI was a corporation and WTS was taxed as a partnership, the small partnership exception did not apply. Thus, the Tax Court lacked jurisdiction to decide whether a partnership existed between WTS and PLI.

The Tax Court turned to the central issue of whether the WTS's payment of "participation interest" actually satisfied the statutory definition of interest, concluding that it did. The following points led the court to this conclusion.

- The court observed that the parties had agreed that the agreements arose from an arm's length transaction.
- The court further observed that these agreements amounted to actual indebtedness by WTS to PLI.

The IRS was bound by its stipulation to these facts and disclaimed any allocation between debt and equity in the funds PLI extended to WTS. This stipulation forced the IRS to argue that the entire loan proceeds to WTS constituted an equity contribution, which it had disclaimed. Thus, the IRS's stipulations that the four loan agreements provided evidence of "genuine indebtedness" contradicted its argument that the payments to PLI were guaranteed payments. The court held that PLI did not have a "single equity interest" in WTS that would change the interest payments into guaranteed payments.

Holding. In view of the consistency between documents stipulating that the payments be considered interest, the Tax Court held that payments were indeed interest and were, therefore, deductible under IRC §163.

Substantiation of Business Expenses

***Nnabugwu C. Eze v. Comm'r,* TC Memo 2022-83 (Aug. 4, 2022)**
IRC §§162(a), 163(h), 274(d), and 280F

☞ Taxpayer Loses the Documentation Game

Facts. Nnabugwu Eze graduated from Rutgers University but had not established a clear career direction when the IRS audited his returns for 2015 and 2016. He filed two separate Schedules C, *Profit or Loss From Business*. One Schedule C was for his work as an information technology (IT) consultant, specifically in electronic healthcare. The other Schedule C was for his work in residential construction. This involved various home improvement tasks similar to handyman duties for individual customers. Mr. Eze's expenses for this endeavor greatly exceeded his income. No income was reported to Mr. Eze from his customers on a Form 1099-MISC, *Miscellaneous Income.* No records, even bank statements, supported the income or expenses appearing on Schedule C for the construction business. For his IT contracts, Mr. Eze worked as an independent contractor for Northrup Grumman, which paid him by direct deposit. His duties in the electronic healthcare field required him to visit medical clinics and doctors' offices.

He owned three vehicles to pursue these ventures: a 2008 luxury vehicle he used exclusively for IT consulting, a 2002 Ford SUV used exclusively for his residential construction business, and a 2004 Chrysler reserved exclusively for personal use. In conjunction with his IT consulting business, Mr. Eze claimed significant deductions for vehicle expenses, $21,490 in 2015 and $30,533 in 2016.

Mr. Eze timely filed his 2015 and 2016 federal income tax returns as head of household (HoH) with two dependents. His 2015 return reported taxable income of $3,314, with a refund of $774. His 2016 return reported taxable income of $0, with a refund of $744.

Upon examination, the IRS disallowed the following deductions.

- Itemized deduction for mortgage insurance of $2,847
- All vehicle expenses reported on both Schedules C
- Approximately 90% of the business expenses reported on the Schedule C for IT consulting
- All the business expenses associated with Mr. Eze's residential construction business

Not agreeing with the IRS, Mr. Eze engaged a California attorney to petition the Tax Court, who requested a Los Angeles, California, situs. Two months before the trial started, the attorney withdrew from representing Mr. Eze for the following reasons.

- Breakdown in the attorney-client relationship
- Mr. Eze's refusal to follow counsel's advice

The court granted this motion to withdraw and rescheduled the trial. The new attorney never appeared in court, and a second continuance due to COVID-19 postponed the trial again. Mr. Eze then informed the court he would represent himself, requesting a change in venue to Baltimore, Maryland. The court denied the request and tried the case via the Zoomgov computer network.

Issues. The issues in the case are the following.

- Whether Mr. Eze met the substantiation requirements for the mortgage insurance premium paid
- Whether Mr. Eze met the heightened requirements for substantiation associated with listed property used in his consulting business
- Whether Mr. Eze met the requirements for all deductions claimed, particularly those requirements for normal substantiation in the consulting business
- Whether Mr. Eze met the heightened requirements for vehicle expenses for his construction business
- Whether Mr. Eze purchased the building supplies, materials, and tools for use on building sites at which his construction business operated

Analysis. Mr. Eze produced a Form 1098, *Mortgage Interest Statement*, for the court, which substantiated the itemized deduction he had claimed on his tax return for 2016. He further established to the court's satisfaction the mortgage interest appearing on it was for his principal residence.

The court concluded that Mr. Eze "wholly failed to satisfy the requirements" in substantiating his vehicle expenses, finding the following three problems.

1. Mr. Eze did not document the vehicle expenses near the time they were made, rather waiting to reconstruct them in the face of the IRS audit. The court observed he could not explain how the details could have been recalled after so much time had passed.
2. Mr. Eze could neither identify a specific client nor provide evidence he had actually made trips to an address associated with the clients.
3. The court did not find plausible the entries Mr. Eze produced in his log, specifically visiting a client in Manhattan on January 1 in both years or a client in Brooklyn each year. The court's opinion stated, "[w]e did not find this plausible."

As a result of its audit, the IRS allowed only about $1,000 of expenses related to Mr. Eze's IT consulting business for both 2015 and 2016. Although Mr. Eze claimed a deduction for continuing education expenses, in court, he admitted the amounts on the return were for his daughter's tuition, not his own professional education. He could not provide any evidence his business incurred the computer expenses for business reasons. The court sustained the IRS's disallowance of most expenses Mr. Eze claimed for his IT business.

Mr. Eze's claims for deductions related to vehicle expenses were supported by the same calendar used for the IT business. The court used the term "annotated" to describe the calendars but attributed no credibility to them. Mr. Eze provided a mileage log for 2015 only, and it contained work descriptions the court found "repetitive." The court found that the documents submitted by Mr. Eze were missing "the indicia of reliability," noting explicitly that the **beginning** odometer reading was the same for **every** trip. The court determined Mr. Eze did not have any deductible mileage in 2015 for his construction business.

In the court's view, these flaws were compounded by Mr. Eze preparing the documents long after he incurred the expenses and likely in anticipation of the IRS's scrutiny. Given the more stringent substantiation requirements that Temp. Treas. Reg. §1.274-5T(c) impose, the court sustained the IRS's complete denial of vehicle deductions for Mr. Eze's construction business.

Mr. Eze presented a hodgepodge of paper receipts to support his claim of other deductions relative to his construction business. The IRS objected to admitting these receipts into evidence, an objection the court sustained. The court could not associate them with Mr. Eze, as he could furnish no contracts, bills, or invoices. The IRS claimed that the receipts originated with purchases made by other persons. The court agreed with this claim, particularly after Mr. Eze admitted the purchases were made by his spouse "and maybe somebody else."

Mr. Eze's claim of expenses for construction materials fared no better. The receipts often exceeded $5,000 but were all paid in cash. Mr. Eze stated he got the cash from ATMs or bank tellers but could not produce bank documentation to support this claim. Mr. Eze refused the court's request to include bank records with other evidence he provided.

The court stated it failed to see how Mr. Eze had the financial resources to sustain the purchases of materials and tools, given the total revenue reported. Based on Mr. Eze's tax return, the court concluded a claim of $175,000 deducted for materials and tools was unreasonable, given his financial circumstances.

The court thought the volume of materials Mr. Eze purchased was "implausibly large," considering where he purchased them and the relatively small vehicle in which Mr. Eze would have transported them. Noting the $21,000 spent on tools, Mr. Eze could not explain to the court's satisfaction what function the tools served.

Holding. Mr. Eze satisfied the statutory requirement to sustain the itemized deduction for mortgage insurance because the Form 1098 he retained satisfied the substantiation requirement. Only on this issue did he succeed.

For his consulting business, the court held Mr. Eze did not meet the heightened substantiation requirement for vehicle expenses because the records were not plausible. Similarly, the other expenses reported for this business were denied. The court sustained the IRS's denial of both types of expenses for the consulting business.

The court similarly sustained the IRS's denial of the vehicle expenses claimed for Mr. Eze's construction business. It also denied expenses for the purchase of construction supplies, materials, and tools.

Mr. Eze conceded the accuracy-related penalties as assessed by the IRS.

Note. This case provides a clear lesson on the importance of business records. Mileage logs should be constructed at the time of the trip, clearly showing accurate odometer readings and business purposes. Transactions that appear on bank statements are preferred over cash transactions. The involvement of a third-party provides credible evidence that a transaction took place. They also confirm the taxpayer made the expenditure. Lastly, noting the purpose of an expenditure near the time it was made substantiates the business purpose of the purchase.

Business Deduction Denied for Theft Loss

***Dennis and Suzanne Gomas v. U.S.*, No. 8:22-cv-01271 (M.D. Fla. Jul. 17, 2023)**
IRC §§162, 165, and 408

☞ No Tax Relief on Stolen Funds

Facts. Dennis and Suzanne Gomas retired in June 2016 after owning and operating their pet food business for several years. After closing the corporation's bank accounts, they turned the business over to Mrs. Gomas's daughter, Suzanne Anderson. Ms. Anderson had worked for the Gomas's business for a couple of years.

In May 2017, Ms. Anderson told Mr. and Mrs. Gomas that a former employee had opened sub-accounts under Mr. Gomas's identity to defraud customers. Per Ms. Anderson, this fraud had resulted in Merchant Services prosecuting the business and Mr. Gomas personally for the fraudulent transactions. She recommended hiring an attorney, Anthony Rickman, to represent Mr. Gomas to prevent his purported arrest.

Subsequently that year, the Gomas's withdrew funds from their individual retirement arrangements (IRAs) to pay for the legal services provided by Mr. Rickman, whom they had never met. Despite using $1,133,250 of IRA distributions to pay the attorney, they only corresponded with Ms. Anderson about the case. She supposedly facilitated all communication between the two parties.

In 2019, Mr. and Mrs. Gomas discovered that Ms. Anderson had lied to them when two of their friends reached out to Mr. Rickman directly. Mr. Rickman informed their friends that neither the Gomases nor Anderson were clients of his. As a result, the police were contacted and in due time, Ms. Anderson was arrested and sentenced to 25 years imprisonment for multiple theft and fraud charges.

In February 2020, Mr. and Mrs. Gomas filed an amended 2017 tax return to claim a business deduction for the amount of funds Ms. Anderson stole. To substantiate the deduction, they issued a Form 1096, *Annual Summary and Transmittal of U.S. Information Returns,* to Ms. Anderson showing income to her equal to the $1,174,020 in pension and IRA distributions they reported on their 2017 return. Per the documentation they submitted with the amended return, the payment of was for "fictitious invoices, fake attorneys' fees, and other fraudulent mechanisms used by…Anderson." The amended return showed a refund of income tax and penalties totaling $412,259.

In February 2021, the IRS disallowed the Gomases the deduction and rejected their claim for refund. In March 2021, the Gomases filed a protest and requested an appeal, stating the business nature of the deduction. In March 2022, the IRS rejected the appeal. In response, the Gomases sought summary judgement from the court.

Issues. The issue in this case is whether the IRA distributions are excludable from income.

Analysis. IRC §408(d)(1) requires retirement plan distributions to be included in the distributee's gross income. The distributee is generally the entitled participant or beneficiary[7], but some courts recognize an exception where the taxable distributee is a party other than the recipient.

However, the Gomases exercised their discretion over the fund payments from the retirement accounts. Although they distributed the funds to Ms. Anderson under false and fraudulent pretenses, they were the ones who requested and received the funds from their retirement account.

IRC §162 allows taxpayers to deduct ordinary and necessary expenses for engaging in a trade or business. For the business expense to be deductible, the expenditure must be intended to help realize a profit or to advance the business.[8] While the Gomases were under the impression that their retirement distributions were for legal services, the fact was that the funds were not actually used for attorney fees.

---

7. See *Roberts v. Comm'r*, 141 TC 569 (2013).

8. See *Brannen v. Comm'r,* 722 F.3d 695, 704 (11th Cir. 1984).

The presumption or belief that funds were used for business purposes does not change the nature or characteristic of the actual use of the funds. Furthermore, the legal fees in this situation would not be considered qualifying business expenses, because the Gomases had both been retired when they turned their business over to Ms. Anderson.

Holding. The court acknowledged that it was in fact Ms. Anderson who enjoyed the benefits of the funds. However, it held that the Gomases were the distributees of the IRA distributions. Consequently, the distributions must be included in Mr. and Mrs. Gomas's gross income. The court also held that the distributions did not qualify as ordinary and necessary business expenses and were therefore nondeductible as such.

> **Observation.** It is not clear from the summary judgement why the taxpayers did not claim a deduction for theft loss instead of trying to claim a business expense for the stolen funds. In the judgement, the court noted "It is highly unlikely that Congress, when it eliminated the theft loss deduction beginning in 2018, envisioned injustices like the case before this Court. Be that as it may, the law is clear here and it favors the IRS." However, because most of the funds were stolen in 2017, the court's observation would likely not apply to this case.

Home Office Deduction for Corporations

Greatest Common Factor v. Comm'r, **TC Memo 2023-39 (Mar. 23, 2023)**
IRC §§162, 167, 274, and 6662

☞ Expense Substantiation Not So Common for Greatest Common Factor

Facts. Greatest Common Factor (GCF) was taxed as a C corporation for the 2013 and 2014 tax years. During that time, Glenn Fyfe and his ex-wife Rhonda Fyfe were both 50% shareholders of GCF. Mr. Fyfe represented the company as an authorized officer.

As an employee of GCF, Mr. Fyfe provided technical consulting on classified projects at the Los Angeles Air Force Base as a subcontractor for Kinsey Technical Services. His duties required him to perform the services on site and adhere to restrictions on document removal. In 2013 and 2014, GCF reported $274,448 and $265,126 of income, all from Kinsey.

On GCF's returns, the company claimed deductions for home office costs and various car and truck expenses. GCF did not have a rental agreement with Mr. Fyfe to maintain a home office, and it did not pay for any such costs. GCF also claimed depreciation deductions for three vehicles but failed to provide supporting documents for the vehicles' purchase prices, ownership, or business use when requested by the IRS. The mileage logs provided by Mr. Fyfe included commuting between his home and the air force base he classified as business trips. None of the mileage logs or receipts for vehicle expenses substantiated a business purpose for the trips.

The IRS disallowed these deductions in a notice of deficiency issued on March 30, 2021. Per the notice, GCF owed $49,817 in tax deficiencies for 2013 and $12,454 for 2014, including accuracy-related penalties under IRC §6662(a).

Issues. The issues in this case are the following.

- Whether GCF is entitled to deduct expenses for a home office and vehicle expenses on its 2013 and 2014 income tax returns.
- Whether GCF is liable for accuracy-related penalties under §6662(a)

Analysis. A C corporation is allowed deductions to lease home office space from an employee or its owner as rent if the expense is ordinary and necessary, and directly connected with the corporation's trade or business. Mr. Fyfe did not provide evidence of a rental agreement with GCF. Therefore, the court determined that GCF could not deduct any home office expense.

Furthermore, if Mr. Fyfe were the taxpayer, rather than GCF, the court determined that he still would not be eligible to deduct a home office expense because the dwelling was not used exclusively as the principal place of business for his trade or business. Rather, Mr. Fyfe worked out of the Los Angeles Airforce Base and was prohibited from bringing any of his confidential work home.

Certain expenses specified in IRC §274, such as car and truck expenses, are subject to strict substantiation rules. To meet these rules, the taxpayer must substantiate the amount of the expense, the time and place of its occurrence, and the business purpose behind it. This can be achieved through adequate records and documentary evidence or by the taxpayer's statement corroborated by documentary or other direct evidence.

Although Mr. Fyfe provided mileage logs, those logs did not list a required business purpose for the trips. The logs included trips from his house to the airforce base, which are considered commuting expense and not deductible. As such, the court disallowed the car and truck expenses.

In addition, the depreciation deduction for property used in a trade or business requires substantiating the property's depreciable basis, including its cost, useful life, and previously allowable depreciation. Heightened substantiation requirements apply to listed property, which includes passenger automobiles. GCF did not provide evidence supporting the business purpose of the vehicles, the cost of the vehicles, nor any documents showing its ownership of the vehicles. The Court sustained the IRS's disallowance of GCF's depreciation deductions.

The accuracy-related penalty is imposed on an underpayment of tax due to negligence or disregard of rules and regulations. It encompasses any failure to comply with internal revenue laws or to keep adequate books and records. To avoid the penalty, a taxpayer must demonstrate reasonable cause and good faith. Because GCF did not show reasonable cause or good faith for their underpayment of tax, the court determined that GCF was liable for the 20% accuracy-related penalty attributable to negligence.

Holding. The court held that GCF was **not** entitled to deduct expenses for a home office or vehicle expenses on its 2013 and 2014 income tax returns because of the company's lack of proper substantiation. The court also held that the corporation was liable for 20% accuracy-related penalties under §6662(a).

12

CORPORATIONS

Corporate Alternative Minimum Tax

IRS Notice 2023-42 (Jun. 7, 2023)
IRC §§55, 59A, and 6655

☞ IRS Notice Waives Corporate AMT Estimated Tax Penalty

Purpose. IRS Notice 2023-42[9] provides relief for corporations from "penalties" for underpayment of estimated income taxes to the extent the underpayment is due to the new **corporate alternative minimum tax** (AMT) added to IRC §55 by the Inflation Reduction Act of 2022. This relief is only available for a corporation's tax year beginning in 2023.

> **Note.** IRC §6655(a) imposes an "addition to tax" rather than "penalty" on corporations that fail to make timely and sufficient payments of estimated taxes required by this provision. Thus, this IRS notice uses the phrase "relief from certain additions to tax" as opposed to "relief from penalty."

The corporate AMT is a minimum tax on large C corporations based on the corporations' **adjusted financial statement income (AFSI).**[10] It only applies to domestic C corporations with average AFSI greater than $1 billion.[11] Multinational corporations with foreign parents are subject to it if their average AFSI is greater than $100 million.[12] Corporations meeting these requirements are called applicable corporations.[13]

Analysis. The IRS issued this relief because of the uncertainties involved in calculating the corporate AMT for estimated tax purposes while the regulations are still under development. Section 3 of Notice 2023-42 makes three announcements for applicable corporations.

1. The IRS waives the addition to tax under IRC §6655 for 2023 for not making estimated tax payments.[14] This is because the IRS has had difficulty in determining which corporations are subject to the corporate AMT and in determining their corporate AMT liability. The addition to tax is often referred to as a penalty.
2. The IRS will modify the instructions for Form 2220, *Underpayment of Estimated Taxes by Corporations.*[15] Additional language is needed to explain that a failure to make payments for an estimated corporate AMT liability does not result in an addition to tax under §6655. However, this is expected to apply only for tax years that begin during 2023.
3. Affected corporations are still required to file Form 2220, even though they have no corporate AMT liability.[16] Form 2220 must be completed without reporting the corporate AMT liability that appears in Form 1120, *U.S. Corporation Income Tax Return,* Schedule J. They must show a number on Form 1120, line 34, the estimated tax penalty, even if they show $0. The IRS may send a penalty notice to corporations that do not follow the instructions. Although the corporation could request abatement of the penalty, they would have to send an abatement request.

> **Note.** This waiver applies to failure to make estimated tax payments only for the corporate AMT. It does not waive penalties for failure to pay other estimated income tax amounts.

---

9. IRS Notice 2023-42, 2023-26 IRB 1085.
10. *Inflation Reduction Act of 2022*, PL 117-169, §10101.
11. IRC §59(k)(1)(B).
12. IRC §59(k)(2).
13. IRC §59(k)(1).
14. IRS Notice 2023-42, 2023-26 IRB 1085, §3.01.
15. Ibid, §3.02.
16. Ibid, §3.03.

CREDITS

Education Credits

***John and Eliza Vassiliades v. Comm'r*, TC Summ. Op. 2023-1 (Jan. 9, 2023)**
IRC §25A, 6001; Treas. Reg. §1.6001-1(a)

☞ Taxpayers Lost the Opportunity for Education Credit

Facts. John and Eliza Vassiliades are married and reside in California. Mr. Vassiliades has a daughter (AM) from a previous relationship who attended the University College London (UCL). AM was a full-time student at UCL from 2017 until 2020, working on her bachelor's degree. Throughout 2017 and 2018, Mr. Vassiliades transferred money to his daughter's account in Europe to cover tuition, fees, and other expenses.

With the help of a paid preparer, Mr. and Mrs. Vassiliades filed their 2018 income tax return. The return claimed AM as a dependent and the American Opportunity Credit (AOC). Their Form 8863, *Education Credits (American Opportunity and Lifetime Learning Credits),* showed a refundable AOC of $1,000 for qualified education expenses and a nonrefundable education portion of $1,500. The couple did not receive a Form 1098-T, *Tuition Statement,* from UCL for 2018.

The IRS denied the $2,500 education credit because Mr. and Mrs. Vassiliades did not establish that they paid education expenses during the year in question.

Issues. The issue in this case is whether Mr. and Mrs. Vassiliades are entitled to the AOC.

Analysis. The AOC is a tax credit for qualified education expenses paid for an eligible student for the first four years of higher education. The maximum AOC per eligible student is $2,500, calculated as the sum of 100% of the first $2,000 of qualifying expenses and 25% of the next $2,000.[17] Qualified tuition and related expenses include fees paid to an eligible institution on behalf of a taxpayer, their spouse, or their dependents. Related expenses include amounts paid for course materials. The student must be enrolled at least half-time for at least one academic period beginning in the year. AM met all the qualifications for the AOC.

However, Mr. Vassiliades could not produce a tuition receipt due to the theft of many important documents during a burglary of his home in 2018. Mr. Vassiliades produced records of money transfers, currency conversion amounts, and a receipt for an online payment to UCL during the previous year to the one in question. Mr. Vassiliades claimed he was unable to acquire any supporting documents from UCL.

Holding. Although sympathetic to Mr. Vassiliades's inability to procure supporting documentation due to circumstances, the court held that Mr. and Mrs. Vassiliades were not entitled to the AOC because there was no support that they paid the qualified tuition and related expenses.

12

17. IRS Pub. 970, *Tax Benefits for Education.*

Filing Status, EIC, Business Deductions, and Fraud Repercussions

***Lakeisha Degourville v. Comm'r,* TC Memo 2022-93 (Sep. 12, 2022)**

IRC §§32, 6695(g), and 6663

☞ Troubleville for Degourville

Facts. Lakeisha and Kenneth Degourville were married on October 15, 1999. Together they share three children and lived together until mid-2016. Mrs. Degourville was a licensed cosmetologist and owned a tax preparation firm, TaxTime Service (TaxTime). She owned a hair salon, Xplosions Hair Design (Xplosions), and co-owned a restaurant with her husband. Mrs. Degourville worked as a tax preparer for the years prior to hosting her own tax preparation courses from 2011 to 2016.

On July 28, 2014, the IRS assessed a return preparer earned income credit (EIC) due diligence penalty against Mrs. Degourville of $45,000 for the 2012 tax year.

On June 10, 2016, the State of Georgia convicted Mrs. Degourville of state tax evasion for not reporting income on her Georgia return and theft by taking for improperly filing state income tax returns for her TaxTime clients. Consequently, the State of Georgia sentenced Mrs. Degourville to 15 years of probation and imposed a $31,300 fine. Additionally, the State of Georgia permanently barred Mrs. Degourville from preparing income tax returns for other people.

Mrs. Degourville testified that TaxTime earned fees in 2012 of $552,865, of which she reported $168,466 as profit on an amended 2012 state income tax return. Additionally, she testified that Xplosions had revenues of $150,000, and her restaurant had a substantial loss.

Mr. and Mrs. Degourville each filed a Form 1040, *U.S. Individual Income Tax Return,* for 2012. They both elected HoH filing status, despite living together during the entire year. The IRS adjusted Mrs. Degourville's filing status to married filing separately. Additionally, both spouses claimed the EIC on their respective tax returns from 2007 to 2012. The IRS disallowed the claim for 2012.

Mrs. Degourville attached a Schedule C for Xplosions reporting gross receipts of $20,316 and a second Schedule C for TaxTime that reported gross receipts of $15,811. The IRS rejected a rent/lease expense for Xplosions and commission expenses for TaxTime as there was no supporting documentation. Mrs. Degourville reported net profits of $980 and $9,088 for Xplosions and TaxTime, respectively.

Upon examination, Mrs. Degourville could not produce any business records. At trial, she claimed Georgia state officials were holding the records as part of their criminal investigation. The IRS conducted bank deposit analyses on the Degourville's seven bank accounts to determine the couple's adjusted gross income. The bank statements showed over a million dollars in deposits during 2012. The IRS calculated unreported gross receipts of $439,705.

Issues. The issues in this case are the following.

- Whether proceeds in Mrs. Degourville's accounts are taxable
- Whether Mrs. Degourville qualifies for HoH filing status
- Whether Mrs. Degourville is entitled to the EIC
- Whether Mrs. Degourville is entitled to the business deductions on her Schedules C
- Whether Mrs. Degourville is subject to a civil fraud penalty
- Whether Mrs. Degourville is subject to the EIC 10-year ban due to fraud

Analysis. The IRS used the bank deposits method to recreate the Degourvilles' income as the couple did not maintain records. Through this method, the IRS determined that the Degourvilles had taxable income exceeding $1 million, of which over $800,000 went unreported. The taxable income translated to $439,705 of gross receipts. Mrs. Degourville did not disagree with the IRS' methods or the amount. She disputed that she was solely responsible for the entire amount of gross receipts. Mrs. Degourville stated that other contractors at TaxTime earned gross receipts. However, Mrs. Degourville could not provide records supporting the amount, if any, that the other contractors earned. Similarly, she was unable to support the $250,000 loss on her restaurant.

Mrs. Degourville argued that she did not have records because they were in the custody of Georgia state authorities as part of her state criminal case. However, she did not request the documents. The court determined that because she could not prove otherwise, Mrs. Degourville was responsible for the $439,705 of gross receipts.

To qualify for HoH filing status if married, the taxpayer must:[18]

1. File a separate tax return,
2. Maintain a household for more than one-half of the taxable year as the principal place of abode of the taxpayer's child for whom the taxpayer would be entitled to claim a dependency exemption,
3. Furnish over one-half of the cost of maintaining such household during the taxable year, and
4. Not be a member of the household with their spouse during the last six months of the taxable year.

Mrs. Degourville admitted that although she and her husband listed separate addresses on their tax return, they lived together the entire year and were not legally separated. As such, they were ineligible to claim the HoH status.

The EIC is a credit based on a percentage of a taxpayer's earned income. To qualify for the credit under IRC §32(d), a married individual must file a joint return with their spouse. Because the Degourvilles filed separately as HoH, they did not qualify for the EIC. The court noted that they likely would not have qualified anyway because the additional gross receipts would have exceeded the phase-out limits for high-income earners.

The court denied Mrs. Degourville's expenses on her Schedules C due to a lack of records. Under certain circumstances, the court can estimate allowable expenses when the taxpayer can prove that they incurred the expenses but cannot substantiate the amount.[19] In this case, there were so few records that the court was unable to estimate the expenses.

The court determined that Mrs. Degourville was liable for civil fraud penalties. To be subject to the 75% of the underpayment of tax, the IRS must prove that there was an underpayment of tax during the year and that some part of the underpayment was because of fraud.[20] As illustrated in the previous discussion, there was an underpayment of taxes.

Proving fraudulent intent depends on the facts of the case. However, the following are some indicators of fraud.[21]

- Understating income
- Failing to maintain adequate records
- Offering implausible or inconsistent explanations
- Concealing income or assets
- Failing to cooperate with tax authorities

12

---

18. IRC §7703(b).

19. *Cohan v. Comm'r,* 39 F.2d 540, 543–44 (2nd Cir., 1930).

20. IRC §6663(a).

21. *Bradford v. Comm'r,* 796 F.2d 303, 307 (9th Cir., 1986), *aff'g* TC Memo 1984-601 (Nov. 19, 1984).

- Engaging in illegal activities
- Providing incomplete or misleading information to the taxpayer's tax return preparer
- Offering false or incredible testimony
- Filing false documents, including filing false income tax returns
- Failing to file tax returns
- Engaging in extensive dealings in cash

Generally, more than one indicator should be present to establish fraud. The court also considers the taxpayer's intelligence, education, and tax experience. The evidence in the case demonstrates that Mrs. Degourville acted with fraudulent intent by significantly underreporting her income and lying about her address and filing status in an attempt to claim the EIC, among other actions. As a tax preparer, the court determined that she had the required knowledge; therefore, her actions to evade taxes were deliberate and fraudulent. The court did not agree with her claim that she was merely negligent.

The court declined to address whether Mrs. Degourville is subject to the 10-year EIC ban. The IRS did not prove sufficient information to the court for it to make a judgement.

Holding. The court held that Mrs. Degourville underreported gross receipts and underpaid her taxes. She could not file as HoH because she was married and lived with her husband for the entire year. As a result of her HoH filing status and underreported income, she could not claim the EIC. Because she provided no records to support her Schedules C deductions, the court denied them. The court held that Mrs. Degourville was subject to the civil fraud penalty because her actions reflected fraudulent intent, and as a tax preparer, she would know her actions were incorrect. The court did not judge whether Mrs. Degourville was subject to the 10-year EIC ban.

Tax Forms and Instructions
Rev. Proc. 2023-23, 2023-22 IRB 883 (May 30, 2023)
IRC §223

☞ Inflation Adjusted Amounts for Health Savings Accounts

Purpose. The IRS is providing the inflation-adjusted amounts for health savings accounts (HSAs) and the maximum amount available for excepted benefit health reimbursement arrangements (HRAs) for 2024.

Analysis. For individuals with self-only coverage under a high deductible plan, the maximum deductible contribution allowed under IRC §223(b)(2)(A) is $4,150. For individuals with family coverage, the maximum deductible contribution under §223(b)(2)(B) is $8,300.

A **high deductible health plan** for 2024 is defined as a health plan with an annual deductible of at least $1,600 for self-only coverage or $3,200 for family coverage. Additionally, the annual out-of-pocket expenses, excluding premiums, must not exceed $8,050 for self-only coverage or $16,100 for family coverage.

Regarding HRAs, the inflation-adjusted item states that for plan years starting in 2024, the maximum amount available for an excepted benefit HRA under Treas. Reg. §54.8931-1(c)(3)(viii) is $2,100.

Effective Date. This revenue procedure applies to HSAs for the calendar year 2024 and excepted benefit HRAs for plan years beginning in 2024.

DIGITAL ASSETS

Digital Asset Reporting

IRS Ann. 2023-2, 2023-2 IRB 344
IRC §§6045 and 6045A

☞ Delay in Required Brokerage Reporting of Digital Assets

IRC §6045(a) requires all brokers to prepare a return that lists their customers' names, addresses, and details regarding gross proceeds and other such information. Brokers must also file information returns and provide payee statements to each customer to which the broker sold stocks, certain commodities, and other categories of assets for cash. Additionally, brokers must provide the payee statements to customers by February 15 of the year following the sale. Brokers must file Form 1099-B, *Proceeds From Broker and Barter Exchange Transactions,* with the IRS by February 28 (or March 31 if filing electronically) of the year following the sale. However, the current regulations do not specifically list digital assets as a specified security that requires basis reporting.

The Infrastructure Investment and Jobs Act[22] clarifies how brokers should report digital assets. The following amendments apply to returns requiring filing after **December 31, 2023.**

1. Revised §6045(c)(1) defines brokers to include any person who regularly provides any service transferring digital assets on behalf of another person for compensation.
2. Specified securities subject to basis reporting under §6045(g) specifically include digital assets treated as covered securities if acquired on or after January 1, 2023.
3. A digital asset is any digital representation of value recorded on a cryptographically secured distributed ledger (or similar technology).
4. Brokers must report transfers of digital assets that are covered securities, provided the transfer is not part of a sale or exchange, and not to someone the broker knows or should know is also a broker.

Until the issuance of the new final regulations, brokers may report gross proceeds, basis, and statements of transfers of covered securities per the existing law and regulations as of December 23, 2022. Similarly, the additional reporting of digital assets dispositions does not apply until the IRS issues new final regulations.

Tax on Crypto Currency Gains

***James H. Kim v. Comm'r,* TC Memo 2023-91 (Jul. 20, 2023)**
IRC §§61, 1001, 1212, and 1221

☞ Tax Court Washes Hands of Unclean Argument

12

Facts. During the periods from 2013 through 2017, James Kim traded Bitcoin, Litecoin, and Ethereum through an account he held with Coinbase, Inc. On his timely filed Forms 1040 for 2013 through 2016, Mr. Kim reported no gains or losses from these transactions. On his 2017 return, he reported a short-term capital gain of $42,069 from sales of $18,557,230 of virtual currencies with a basis of $18,515,161.

[22] *Infrastructure Investment and Jobs Act,* PL 117-58, §80603.

The IRS selected Mr. Kim's 2013 through 2017 tax returns for examination. When he failed to provide a computation of his cryptocurrency gains and losses, the IRS used records obtained from Coinbase to determine his gains and losses for the years at issue. The IRS applied a first-in, first-out (FIFO) method to match purchases and sales. Based on these calculations, the IRS concluded that Mr. Kim had a short-term capital gain of $75,400 for 2013, loss carryforwards for 2014-2016, and taxable gains of $4,115,177 for 2017.

On May 19, 2021, the IRS issued Mr. Kim a timely notice of deficiency, assessing tax deficiencies of $12,310 for 2013 and $1,572,391 for 2017, along with accuracy-related penalties. Mr. Kim did not dispute the amount or character of the net capital gains determined in the notice of deficiency.

Mr. Kim petitioned the court to prevent the IRS from collecting the tax due on the gains because the U.S. Government was purportedly to blame for the cryptocurrency losses he incurred in subsequent years. He had taken out a large loan to finance his cryptocurrency transactions. When the virtual currencies declined precipitously in a single day in 2020, he was unable to meet a margin call. As a result, his virtual currency positions were liquidated at a very substantial loss. Mr. Kim asserted that the actions (or inaction) of the U.S. Government in response to the COVID epidemic "directly caused [that] harm" and that, "under the Clean Hands doctrine of US law," the IRS should be estopped from collecting tax on his 2013 and 2017 gains.

Issues. The issue in this case is whether Mr. Kim owes capital gains tax for 2013 through 2017 on his cryptocurrency assets.

Analysis. Gross income encompasses all income from any source, including gains from property transactions under IRC §61(a)(3). Mr. Kim did not contest that the investments involved in his transactions from 2013 to 2017 were considered capital assets. Therefore, he was subject to taxation for 2013 and 2017 on the net capital gains resulting from these virtual currency transactions.

Rather, Mr. Kim asserts that under the Clean Hands doctrine, the IRS should be estopped from collecting tax on his gains. The "unclean hands" principle denies equitable relief to those who have acted improperly. For it to apply to this case, the IRS would have to be seeking equitable relief from Mr. Kim. Recovering taxes owed under the Code is not the same as seeking equitable relief.

Furthermore, the "unclean hands" defense only applies to conduct immediately related to the cause of the controversy. There was no evidence that any government agency, including the IRS, acted improperly regarding Mr. Kim's tax liabilities. The actions taken by the government in response to the COVID epidemic, which occurred in 2020, have no bearing on the determination of Mr. Kim's tax liabilities for 2013 and 2017.

Holding. The court concluded that Mr. Kim's arguments lacked a legal basis. The court affirmed the tax deficiencies for 2013 and 2017.

Claiming a Refund

***Richard J O'Neill Trust v. Comm'r,* TC Memo 2022-108 (Oct. 27, 2022)**
IRC §§1311 through 1314 and 1341

☞ Claim of Right Goes Wrong

Facts. Richard O'Neill established a revocable trust, the Richard J. O'Neill Trust, on April 18, 1968. Mr. O'Neill transferred his assets to the trust before his passing on April 4, 2009. The trust then became irrevocable. At the time, the trust held an 86.12% ownership interest in RMV Total Diversification, LLC (RMV).

In 2009 and 2010, RMV sold capital assets at a gain. The trust reported the passthrough income on its 2009 and 2010 Form 1041, *U.S. Income Tax Return for Estates and Trusts.* Additionally, at the time of Mr. O'Neill's passing, his estate borrowed money from RMV. The loan charged 9% interest, which the estate paid, and RMV reported as income. Consequently, the trust reported this flowthrough income on its tax returns.

After Mr. O'Neill's estate filed Form 706, *United States Estate (and Generation-Skipping Transfer) Tax Return,* on June 30, 2010, the IRS sent a notice with proposed adjustments to the return. The estate objected to these changes, and a settlement followed on February 3, 2015. The settlement included adjustments that reduced the estate's interest deduction of the RMV loan from 9% interest to 6% interest and increased the estate's RMV interest asset from $30,725,000 to $40,614,822. Accordingly, RMV rewrote the loan to reflect these changes, reducing the trust's accrued 2010 interest income by $500,538.

The trust filed Form 1045, *Application for Tentative Refund,* in October 2015 for the 2014 tax year to recover its overpayment of $1,537,780 in taxes for the 2009 and 2010 tax years. RMV did not amend its 2009, 2010, 2014, or 2015 partnership income tax returns. For those years in question, the trust did not file Form 8082, *Notice of Inconsistent Treatment or Administrative Adjustment Request (AAR),* pertaining to income treatment from RMV.

On July 17, 2017, the trust received a notice from the IRS stating a deficiency of $1,554,917 for the 2014 tax year, claiming the trust was not entitled to the refund requested on its filed Form 1045. As such, the IRS instructed that the trust return the refund proceeds in addition to penalties and interest. The trust disagreed, stating as support that the filed Form 1045 met the claim of right requirements under IRC §1341. Additionally, the trust asserted its entitlement to the refund met the provisions of IRC §§1311 through 1314. Finally, the trust defended its position under an equitable recoupment doctrine.

Issues. The issues in this case are the following.

- Whether the trust satisfies the claim of right requirements for the 2014 tax year refund under §1341
- Whether the trust meets the provisions of §§1311 through 1314 in claiming the refund
- Whether the trust is legally entitled to the refund under an equitable recoupment doctrine

Analysis. The trust argued that it was entitled to the refund under §1341. The code section allows a deduction in a tax year for income that a taxpayer claimed in a prior year that they had no unrestricted right to, and in retrospect, the taxpayer should not have claimed that income. The court found this argument invalid. Under IRC §6221, the partnership determines its treatment of income, whereas the individual partners do not make their own separate determination. Unless a partner files Form 8082, the partner must treat income consistently with the partnership's treatment. The partnership did not amend its 2009 and 2010 income tax returns regarding its capital gain and interest income treatment. Therefore, the trust's treatment of that income which served as the basis for claiming the refund on Form 1045 was inconsistent with the partnership. The trust, however, did not file Form 8082 to address this inconsistency.

Furthermore, the court explained that §1341 would not apply to the trust's argument regarding the unrestricted right to income concept. RMV, and the trust as its partner, had an unrestricted right to the proceeds from the sale of capital assets. Nothing changed the status of these rights, as RMV did not repay or otherwise restore the capital asset sale proceeds for any legal or contractual disputes revolving around RMV's claim to those proceeds. Therefore, the trust's right to the proceeds of the sale of capital assets remained unrestricted, contradicting the nature of §1341. Regarding the interest income, the court noted that RMV's negotiation with Mr. O'Neill's estate about reducing the interest terms from 9% to 6% did not retroactively change or restrict RMV's right to the interest income they reported in prior tax years. Consequently, the trust, as a partner of RMV, retained the trust's right to the interest income.

In addition to §1341, the trust claimed §§1311 through 1314 as support for its entitlement to the 2014 tax year refund. The Code sections grant a refund claim for a correction of an error. The court, however, stated that the trust did not follow the correct process to rely on these Code sections. The error occurred in the 2009 and 2010 tax years, which are the tax years that the trust should have filed a refund claim. However, the trust filed a refund claim for the 2014 tax year, invalidating its argument.

Lastly, the trust argued that its claim to the refund was valid through the doctrine of equitable recoupment. This doctrine provides relief in cases "where the Government has taxed a single transaction, item, or taxable event under two inconsistent theories."[23] The court found this argument to lack merit for two reasons. First, the deficiency serving as the basis for the trust's claim for recoupment pertains to Mr. O'Neill's estate taxes, not those of the trust. Second, the IRS did not apply two inconsistent theories in denying the refund. The IRS disallowed the refund based on the trust's claim for refund under §1341 specifically, which has no transactional connection to the trust's tax liabilities for tax years 2009 and 2010.

Holding. The court held that the trust did not satisfy the claim of right requirements for the 2014 tax year refund under §1341. Furthermore, the trust did not meet the provisions of §§1311 through 1314 in claiming the refund. Additionally, the court did not find that the trust was entitled to the refund through the doctrine of equitable recoupment. The court denied the trust's motion for partial summary judgment, instead granting the motion for partial summary judgment to the IRS.

Practitioner Planning Tip

This case highlights the importance of following correct procedures in claiming refunds, deductions, and any tax position in general. Distinguishing which parties are responsible in a multi-taxpayer situation is critical, especially in cases of passthrough entities and fiduciary relationships. The case illustrated instances where the argument's logic was sound, but the incorrect party performed some of the actions undertaken. Practitioners should also be mindful of which tax years pertain to the position under consideration and which of those years taxpayers should either amend, apply a change, or otherwise handle.

23. *U.S. v. Dalm*, 494 U.S. 596 (1990).

Assumption of Liability of Unpaid Estate Taxes

***Estate of Kwang Lee v. Comm'r*, No. 21-2921 (3d Circ. 2022), *aff'g* TC No. 20531-18L**

USC §3713(b) and IRC §7122

☞ Executor in (Un)Compromising Situation

Facts. Kwang Lee passed away testate on September 30, 2001. Anthony J. Frese, the successor executor of Mr. Lee's estate, filed an estate tax return but undercalculated the amount of estate tax liability. Consequently, the IRS issued a notice of deficiency to the estate for the remaining tax due in 2006. After challenging the IRS in the U.S. Tax Court, the estate received a formal assessment of tax liability in 2010.

The estate did not have the funds to pay the assessed tax due, as Mr. Frese had already disbursed over $1 million in distributions to its beneficiaries. Notably, of the total disbursements, the estate paid $640,000 to beneficiaries **after** receiving the notice of deficiency. Upon receiving a tax lien in 2013 for the remaining balance of tax due, Mr. Frese sought relief on behalf of the estate by making an offer in compromise (OIC) in the form of settling the liability with assets still held by the estate. These assets, which only included a checking account, reflected around one-third of the amount of the outstanding tax deficiency claim.

The IRS rejected the estate's OIC on the grounds that more funds were obtainable from all sources, including the estate beneficiaries and Mr. Frese as the executor. The estate challenged this decision in the U.S. Tax Court in 2021,[24] stating that the amount of reasonable collection probability (RCP) that the IRS used to reject the OIC was inflated by inappropriately including distributions to beneficiaries in its calculation. The Tax Court held that beneficiary distributions were correctly included in the RCP, stating that before the $640,000 distribution payout, the estate had sufficient funds to pay the deficiency claim, which takes precedence over other debt and claims.[25] Additionally, the Tax Court held that sufficient notice of the claim was provided to Mr. Frese through the issued notice deficiency that the estate received before making the distribution in question. In July 2022, the estate sought to appeal this decision before the U.S. Court of Appeals.

Issues. The issues in this case are the following.

- Whether the IRS abused its discretion in refusing the OIC
- Whether the time to collect from Mr. Frese has run out
- Whether Mr. Frese escapes liability under USC §3713 by distributions under operation of law
- Whether Mr. Frese avoids personal liability by relying on professional advice

Analysis. The estate argued that the time to collect funds from Mr. Frese to satisfy the outstanding tax deficiency claim had run out. An IRS Manual advises the inclusion of dissipated assets in RCP is generally appropriate using a 3-year time frame.[26] More than three years had passed since the $640,000 distribution and the IRS's assessment of RCP. The court determined that this argument was irrelevant, as the IRS was not alleging dissipation (intentionally disposing assets to avoid tax liability payment) of the beneficiary distribution. Moreover, even if the IRS alleged dissipation, the 3-year period described in the Manual is **guidance** and not mandatory criteria.

---

24. *Estate of Kwang Lee v. Comm'r,* TC Memo 2021-92 (Jul. 20, 2021).
25. 13 USC §3713.
26. IRM 5.8.5.18(2) (2021).

The estate made another point that the distributions to beneficiaries included non-probate stock options. The estate argued that the distribution of these assets constituted an act of operating under law and that Mr. Frese was fulfilling his legal obligation in making the distribution. Because he was bound by law and had no discretion in whether to make the distribution or not, the estate asserted Mr. Frese was free of personal liability under USC §3713. In response, the court clarified that its review was limited in scope and could only consider arguments raised before the Tax Court in the case under appeal. In the Tax Court case, the estate had only objected to the relevance of the distribution of the stock options, as opposed to whether Mr. Frese used discretion in making the distribution. Consequently, the court did not allow this new point under consideration for its review. Regardless, the court did note that the filed estate tax return listed the stock options as assets and the estate listed them incorrectly as probate assets, conflicting with the estate's argument.

Finally, the estate presented the argument that due to his reliance on professional advice, Mr. Frese could not be held personally liable for the outstanding tax deficiency claim. The court disagreed, illustrating that Mr. Frese's use of professional advice was for the preparation of the estate tax return as opposed to beneficiary distributions. The court further commented that when a tax deficiency is known to an executor, professional reliance is not a valid defense against personal liability. In this case, Mr. Frese had knowledge of the tax deficiency by receiving the tax lien notice issued to the estate.

Holding. The court held that the IRS did not abuse its discretion in refusing the estate's OIC and the Tax Court granted summary judgement appropriately. The time to collect the outstanding tax deficiency from Mr. Frese had not run out, and guidance from an IRS Manual did not reflect a binding timetable for the IRS. Mr. Frese did not avoid personal liability for the tax deficiency through professional reliance, as Mr. Frese was aware of the tax deficiency and could not use the advice of a practitioner as a defense for escaping liability. The court did not consider the argument of Mr. Frese avoiding liability under USC §3713 in the capacity of this appeal, as the estate did not argue before the Tax Court that the beneficiary distributions fell under operation of law instead of the discretion of the executor. The court affirmed the judgement of the Tax Court.

Practitioner Planning Tip

This case illustrates the magnitude of responsibility that falls upon estate executors and that mistakes made while undertaking this role can potentially have costly repercussions. Executors, as well as beneficiaries depending on the circumstances, could be personally liable for deficiencies in estate tax payment. Practitioners can add value to fiduciary engagements by simply communicating the need to exercise caution in navigating the settlement of an estate and alerting them to the potential personal risk. An option that could mitigate some of this risk is an executor waiting until receipt of an estate tax closing letter before making final distributions out of an estate to beneficiaries.

Basis Step-Up for Trusts Excluded From Taxpayer's Taxable Estate

Rev. Rul. 2023-2, 2023-16 IRB 658 (Apr. 17, 2023)

IRC §1014

☞ Step-Up Shuffle: When Trusts Skip the Party for Asset Basis Boosts

Purpose. This revenue ruling discusses whether there is a basis adjustment for assets held in a trust upon the death of the trust owner, but the trust assets are not includable in the owner's gross estate.

Under the scenario presented in the revenue ruling, Individual A is the owner of an **irrevocable trust.** While Individual A retains a power over the trust resulting in Individual A's ownership of the trust for income tax purposes, no power was held that would result in the inclusion of the trust assets in Individual A's taxable estate. Six years after creating and funding the trust, Individual A dies, and the assets held in the trust have appreciated in value since the trust's creation.

Analysis. IRC §1014(a) requires property receiving a basis adjustment be acquired or passed from a decedent. The Code identifies seven types of property that meet this criterion.

1. Property acquired by bequest, devise, or inheritance as described in §1014(b)(1)
2. Property transferred during the decedent's life in a revocable trust for paying income to the decedent or upon the decedent's direction as described in §1014(b)(2)
3. Property with the same attribute as #2, except that it applies to decedent's dying after December 31, 1951, and that the decedent had the power to alter, amend, or terminate the trust as described in §1014(b)(3)
4. Property is a transfer passing without consideration under a power of appointment that the decedent exercised by will as described in §1014(b)(4)
5. Property is the decedent's surviving spouse's one-half share of community property as described in §1014(b)(6)
6. Property is the transfer of property by reason of a decedent's death, form of ownership, or other reasons if the property is included in the decedent's gross estate as described in §1014(b)(9), except for annuities and foreign stock and securities
7. Property is includable in the decedent's gross estate under the marital deduction as described in §1014(b)(10)

The trust does not qualify as the first type, as the court in *Collins v. U.S.* clarified that a decedent could not transfer property by bequest, devise, or inheritance unless it was part of their probate estate under their resident state's laws.[27] Because Individual A did not retain the power to revoke or amend the trust, the assets in Individual A's trust do not qualify as the second, third, or fourth types of property. The assets held in Individual A's trust were not community property, and therefore fail to meet the fifth type of property. The assets in Individual A's trust fail both the sixth and seventh type of property tests, because the assets in the trust were not includable in Individual A's taxable estate.

Because the assets in Individual A's do not fall within any of the types of property under §1014, the assets in the trust do not receive a basis adjustment at the time of Individual A's death. Therefore, Individual A's death does not cause any change to the basis of the assets held in Individual A's trust, where the basis remains the same as it was before Individual A's death.

27. *Collins v. U.S.*, 318 F.Supp.382, 386 (C.D. Cal. 1970).

FBAR Failure to File Penalty

***Bittner v. U.S.*, 598 U.S. 85 (2023)**

31 USC §§5314 and 5321

☞ Biting Back Benefits Bittner

Facts. Alexandru Bittner, is a dual citizen of Romania and the United States. He emigrated to the United States in 1982, obtained American citizenship, and lived there until 1990 when he moved back to Romania. Between 1990 and 2011, Mr. Bittner invested in various assets in Romania, earning over $70 million. During this time, he maintained dozens of Romanian and other foreign accounts, each having high balances exceeding $10,000.

According to the Bank Secrecy Act of 1970 (BSA) and 31 CFR §1010.306, a U.S. citizen or resident[28] with foreign accounts exceeding $10,000 are required to report those accounts to the IRS. Under previous rules, they were required to file an FBAR, *Report of Foreign Bank and Financial Accounts*, form by June 30 of the following year. Under current rules, they are required to file Form FinCEN 114, *Report of Foreign Bank and Financial Accounts,* by the due date for federal tax returns.[29] Failure to disclose foreign accounts properly or in a timely manner can result in penalties.

Mr. Bittner was unaware of the FBAR filing requirement and failed to file FBARs for his foreign accounts until May 2012. These FBARs did not accurately report all of Mr. Bittner's foreign accounts, however, so another tax professional filed amended FBARs that properly reported in 2013 all of Mr. Bittner's foreign accounts. In 2017, the IRS calculated civil penalties of $2,720,000 against Mr. Bittner for his nonwillful violation of failing to timely disclose 272 instances of maintaining foreign accounts between 2007 and 2011. Mr. Bittner admitted to maintaining 177 of the undisclosed accounts from 2007 to 2010. The United States filed a motion for partial summary judgment, requesting $1,770,000 for those accounts.

Mr. Bittner disputed the penalties, claiming a reasonable-cause exception and denying liability. He argued that the penalty under §5321 of the BSA applies per failure to file an annual FBAR, not per account. The United States argued that Mr. Bittner's penalties should be based on the 177 separate violations. Both parties asked the district court to interpret BSA §5321.

The district court denied Mr. Bittner's defense of reasonable cause and found him liable for BSA violations. However, it held that the penalty for violating the BSA applies to each failure to file an annual FBAR, reducing Mr. Bittner's penalties to $50,000 for the five FBAR returns.

The United States appealed the district court's ruling to the Fifth Circuit Court of Appeals. The Fifth Circuit affirmed Mr. Bittner's liability but reversed the ruling on penalties, stating that failure to report each qualifying foreign account constitutes a separate violation of the BSA.

Mr. Bittner filed a petition for a writ of certiorari with the U.S. Supreme Court to challenge the Fifth Circuit's reversal ruling.

---

28. 31 USC §5314(a).

29. *Surface Transportation and Veterans Health Care Choice Improvement Act of 2015*, PL 114-41, §2006(b)(11).

Issues. The issues in this case are the following.

- Whether the nonwillful failure to report multiple foreign accounts during a single reporting period constitutes a single violation or multiple violations under the BSA
- Whether a violation under the BSA is defined as the failure to file an annual FBAR, regardless of the number of foreign accounts, or if there is a separate violation for each individual account that was not properly reported
- Whether the penalty for nonwillful failure to file applies on a per-account basis or per-form basis

Analysis. The Court began its interpretation of the law by distinguishing the differences between §§5314 and 5321 of the BSA. The Court stated that §5314 outlines an individual's legal responsibilities to file a report. Therefore, the Court interpreted that a violation of §5314 is that an individual failed to file a report, and that any omissions or errors contained in a filed report would constitute as one violation. BSA §5321, on the other hand, describes the penalties for violations of §5314, where the Secretary of the Treasury may impose a civil penalty of up to $10,000 for "any violation." Because the Court found that §5314 describes a violation as a failure to file a report subject to the BSA's requirements, one error or multiple errors constitute a single violation. Regarding the penalty, §5321 differentiates between willful and nonwillful violations, where willful violation penalties include a per-account stipulation, but nonwillful violation penalties make no such specification. In the eyes of the Court, this differentiation is proof that the intent of the law is that nonwillful violation penalties should be made on a per-report basis instead of a per-account basis.

Furthermore, the Court provided examples of communication to the public from the Department of Treasury and other government agencies that do not specify that the $10,000 penalty is on a per-account basis, including the instructions to the FBAR itself. While the Court acknowledged that such documents do not control or dictate the Court's interpretation of the law, courts in general may consider an agency's views and communications on the subject matter that it brings before a court.[30]

The Court also stated that when Congress amended the law for penalties for nonwillful violations in 2004,[31] it did not include language to mirror the penalties for willful violations specifying that such penalties were to have per-account stipulations. In addition to this argument of intent, the Court found that the purpose of the reports is to provide the government with information to aid in investigations, not to profit from penalties for every nonwillful mistake.[32] Reinforcing this interpretation was the Court's example showing that the government's interpretation of a per-account basis for nonwillful violations creating higher penalties compared to willful violations, which the Court argued did not make sense and would deviate from Congress's intent.

The Court asserted the rule of lenity[33] for doubt regarding the best interpretation of the law. This principle consists of a court applying law that is unclear or ambiguous in the most favorable way to a defendant. The Court stated that the Code and other federal statutory law does not impede the rule of lenity and described two reasons why it should apply to this case. First, under due process, individuals must receive fair warning in a way that is commonly understood. Not only do the BSA provisions not explicitly discuss per-account penalties for nonwillful violations, but accounting professionals were also confused as to the interpretation of those provisions, indicating that a "common understanding" would not be achieved if professionals specializing in the accounting field lacked an understanding. Second, if the government's interpretation is that nonwillful violation penalties should be on a per-account basis, the criminal sanctions associated with them would give rise to unintended severe criminal violations that would include prison time.

12

30. *Skidmore v. Swift & Co.*, 323 U.S. 134 (1944).

31. *American Jobs Creation Act of 2004*, PL 108-357, §821(a).

32. 31 USC §5311.

33. *Rule of lenity*. May 2022. Cornell Law School. [www.law.cornell.edu/wex/rule_of_lenity] Accessed on Jul. 26, 2023.

Holding. The Court held that nonwillful failure to report multiple foreign accounts during a single reporting period constitutes a single violation under the BSA. The Court further held that a violation under the BSA is a failure to file an annual report regardless of the number of foreign accounts described in said report. Finally, the Court held that penalties for nonwillfully failing to file FBARs are on a per-form basis instead of a per-account basis. Consequently, the Court reversed the Fifth Circuit's reversal ruling, concluding Bittner's penalties are $50,000 instead of $1,770,000.

> **Note.** The IRS has updated its procedures for FBAR examinations to incorporate the Supreme Court's decision in the *Bittner* case to provide clear language consistent with the Court's holding.[34]

GROSS INCOME

Wrongful Termination Settlement Payment

***Thomas J. and Peggy M. Dern v. Comm'r*, TC Memo 2022-90 (Aug. 30, 2022)**
IRC §§61(a) and 104

☞ Dern't Forget to Include Damages Received in Gross Income

Facts. Thomas J. Dern received a settlement payment of $327,416 from P.F.I., Inc. (PFI), Mr. Dern's former employer. This payment resulted from a lawsuit the Derns filed against PFI, alleging, among other things, wrongful termination, deliberate infliction of emotional distress, and violation of California's disability discrimination law. The lawsuit did not allege any physical injury or physical illness. PFI terminated Mr. Dern's employment in 2016 because of his inability to perform sales tasks following a heart attack and gastrointestinal bleeding he suffered in December 2015 and January 2016.

In the settlement agreement, PFI and its co-defendants agreed to pay Mr. Dern $550,000 to compensate him for "alleged personal injuries, costs, penalties, and all other damages and claims." The agreement also included a general release of claims which was "intended to include in its effect, without limitation, all claims known or unknown at the time of the execution" of the settlement agreement. However, it did not specifically cite physical injuries.

Mr. Dern reported none of the settlement as income on his 2017 tax return, where he only reported $6,000 of nonemployee income related to an appraisal business. The IRS determined that Mr. Dern had unreported nonemployee compensation of $324,000, based on a Form 1099-MISC, *Miscellaneous Income*, issued to him by his attorney for $330,000 ($550,000 gross settlement – $220,000 attorney fees).

Mr. Dern argued that the settlement payment was excludable from income under IRC §104(a)(2) because it arose from personal physical injuries or physical sickness.

Issues. The issue in the case is whether an amount received as a settlement of damages is includable as gross income without specifying that it arose from physical injury or sickness.

Analysis. IRC §61 states that gross income includes all income from whatever source derived unless it is specifically excluded. An exclusion exists under IRC §104(a)(2) for payments made on account of personal physical injuries or physical sickness. Emotional distress is not covered in the exclusion. Mr. Dern suffered some physical sickness, but this was not noted in either the lawsuit or the settlement.

Holding. The court found Mr. Dern failed to prove a "direct causal link" between his physical illness and the settlement payment. Therefore, the settlement payment was not excludable under §104(a)(2), and the Mr. Dern owed tax on the unreported income.

---

34. *Interim Guidance on FBAR Examination Case Procedures Due to Supreme Court Decision (Bittner v. US)* — SBSE-04-0723-0034. Lauer, Daniel. Jul. 6, 2023. IRS. [irs.gov/pub/foia/ig/sbse/sbse-04-0723-0034-redacted.pdf] Accessed on Jul. 26, 2023.

Settlement Payment

***U.S. and California Franchise Tax Board v. Levandowski*, No. 4:22-cv-02781 (N.D. Cal. Mar. 14, 2023)**
IRC §61(a) and 11 USC §505

☞ Bankruptcy Court Makes U-Turn for Self-Driving Vehicle Pioneer

Facts. Anthony Levandowski is a pioneer in self-driving cars and worked at a Google, LLC subsidiary at one time.[35] Mr. Levandowski left Google and formed his own company known as Ottomotto, LLC, which he subsequently sold to Uber Technologies, Inc. As part of the sale, Uber agreed to indemnify Mr. Levandowski for certain claims that could be brought against him by Google. Ultimately, Google did sue Mr. Levandowski in arbitration. After arduous and contentious litigation, Google obtained a judgment totaling over $179 million.

Mr. Levandowski filed for bankruptcy. Google, Uber, and Mr. Levandowski entered into a global settlement. Under the settlement, Uber would pay Google directly for damages Mr. Levandowski owed Google. Mr. Levandowski asked the bankruptcy court to approve the settlement and to deem these payments not subject to income tax on either a federal or state level.

The IRS and the California Franchise Tax Board (FTB) objected to Mr. Levandowski's motion that payments were not taxable. The bankruptcy court disagreed. The bankruptcy judge found that Uber's payment to Google was like an insurance transaction, which the judge believed was not taxable. Thus, the court concluded that the settlement payments on Mr. Levandowski's behalf were not income to him. The IRS and the FTB appealed the bankruptcy court's decision to a U.S. district court.

Issues. The issues in this case are the following.

- Whether the bankruptcy court has jurisdiction to approve the settlement with no tax reserve
- Whether the determination of future tax liabilities by the bankruptcy court is binding
- Whether the main payment Uber made to Google is gross income to Mr. Levandowski
- Whether the bankruptcy court's confirmation order of the settlement is proper, given the issues under consideration

Analysis. The appeals court found that the bankruptcy court had the authority to determine the tax issue. Although the Declaratory Judgment Act[36] generally does not permit federal courts jurisdiction over federal taxes, 11 USC §505(a)(1) authorizes the bankruptcy court to have jurisdiction in the determination of **any** tax.

However, the appeals court stated that the law is not clear on whether a bankruptcy court can make a forward-looking opinion on the future tax liabilities of Uber or Mr. Levandowski. It stated that the U.S. Constitution does not permit courts to decide abstract issues.[37] However, the appeals court noted that the Levandowski case did not have abstract issues, but rather actual facts at issue before the court. The appeals court found the fact that the IRS and FTB opposed the bankruptcy plan supported this point, even though they argued that only abstract matters were before the court. Further, the bankruptcy court realized that the amounts involved in the case were so large that without providing for tax consequences, the bankruptcy plan would not work.

The appeals court questioned the bankruptcy court's determination that the main payment was not subject to income tax. The bankruptcy court had relied on the claim that "all insurance is not deemed taxable." The appeals court found that the bankruptcy court did not consider the broad scope of gross income included by the Code. While Mr. Levandowski argued that the main payment was equivalent to insurance, the appeals court noted that insurance is **not always** excluded from taxation such as in IRC §61(a)(9), which includes life insurance in gross income.

---

35. *Anthony Levandowski*. May 23, 2023. Wikipedia [en.wikipedia.org/wiki/Anthony_Levandowski] Accessed on Jul. 15, 2023.

36. 28 USC §2201(a).

37. U.S. Const. art. III, §2.

All parties agreed that whether the confirmation order was appropriate depended on whether the tax order was appropriate. If the tax order was incorrect in its assumptions, the proposed debtor's plan to work out repayment should not have been confirmed by the bankruptcy court. The IRS claimed that the main reason for the bankruptcy plan was the avoidance of taxes. However, the bankruptcy court found that the main purpose for the bankruptcy was **not** the avoidance of taxes.

However, how the bankruptcy court handled set-off rights created a problem for the appeals court. Set-off in a bankruptcy proceeding is the right of a creditor to deduct a debt it owes to the debtor from the claim. The appeals court thought that the IRS's and the FTB's concerns were theoretical, yet expressed the view that the bankruptcy court had dismissed this issue with language that was too broad.

Holding. The appeals court found that the bankruptcy court had jurisdiction over the tax matters in Mr. Levandowski's bankruptcy case. Next, the appeals court found that the bankruptcy court was working within its limits when it concluded that the bankruptcy court issued an advisory opinion on the tax consequences of the settlement.

The appeals court found that the bankruptcy court used faulty logic when it concluded that the settlement payments were not subject to income tax. Thus, it reversed the bankruptcy court's tax order and remanded the case back to that court for further consideration due to legal error associated with the tax order.

Finally, the appeals court also found that the confirmation order did not properly consider legal precedent. It asked the bankruptcy court to reconsider the case in view of these precedents concerning set-off rights. However, it agreed with the bankruptcy court that Mr. Levandowski's main purpose in the agreement was not tax avoidance.[38]

Child Support Interest Taxable

***Susan D. Rodgers v. Comm'r,* TC Memo 2023-56 (May 9, 2023)**
IRC §§61 and 71

☞ Rodgers Attempts Dodging Tax on Interest Income

Facts. During 2011 and 2012, Susan Rodgers and her former spouse were involved in litigation in the Circuit Court of Mobile County, Alabama, over the termination of her former spouse's child support obligation. The state court entered an order in 2011 stating that Ms. Rodgers' former spouse was in arrears in the sum of $18,000, issuing a judgment against him in favor of Ms. Rodgers for the amount representing child support arrearages. In 2012, the state court amended its order, stating Ms. Rodgers was owed $16,044 from her former spouse, consisting of $5,362 in principal and $10,682 in interest. She received a series of payments from the State of Alabama from 2012 through 2014 that were identified with the code "CS NA AR" and collectively matched the $5,362 of the arrearage principal determined in the state court's order. During 2015 payments marked "CP INT" totaled $7,859.

Ms. Rodgers received a Form 1099-INT, *Interest Income*, from the State of Alabama showing $7,824 in interest income for 2015. When she filed her 2015 income tax return, she did not include this in her gross income, which led to the IRS issuing her a deficiency determination for $3,473 of unpaid tax.

Issues. The issue in this case is whether the $7,824 of income that Ms. Rodgers received should be characterized as interest that is includable in her gross income or instead as child support that is not includable in her gross income.

Analysis. The IRS's determinations in a notice of deficiency carry a presumption of correctness, and it is the taxpayer's responsibility to prove otherwise. In this case, Ms. Rodgers conceded that she received an unreported sum of $7,824, but contested whether it should be taxed as interest or classified as nontaxable child support. The evidence she provided was insufficient to challenge the deficiency determination made by the IRS.

---

38. This is stated in the court's conclusion as though the appeals court agreed with the bankruptcy court that Mr. Levandowski's principal purpose was tax avoidance, but this is an error, given the clear language in the court's discussion on this specific point.

According to federal tax law, a taxpayer's gross income includes all income sources, including interest under IRC §61(a)(4). Alimony and separate maintenance payments are also part of the recipient's gross income, except for child support payments fixed by the terms of a divorce or separation instrument, which are not taxable to the recipient under §71(a). However, interest paid on child support arrearages is considered taxable income under §61(a)(4).[39] In this case, Ms. Rodgers received interest on child support arrearages as reported by the State of Alabama.

The characterization of alimony, child support, or interest payments for federal tax purposes is determined by federal law. To establish whether a taxpayer received interest payments related to child support arrearages, the court considers various forms of evidence, including the taxpayer's admission, state court child support payment records, and the existence of a state court order directing interest payments on arrearages.[40]

In this particular case, the evidence supports Ms. Rodgers received interest income related to child support arrearages. Ms. Rodgers did not dispute receiving the reported amount on Form 1099-INT for a child support arrearage or her former spouse failing to make timely child support payments. Furthermore, the state court's order specifically directed payment of child support and interest in specific amounts, consistent with Alabama law that requires interest on past due child support obligations to be included in any judgment on arrearages.

Ms. Rodger's argument about a discrepancy in the arrearage principal from county payment records does not invalidate the interest classification. She failed to present evidence that the state court modified the judgment or took action based on her letter to the court regarding the discrepancy. The court explained that even if the arrearage principal was larger, it would only increase the interest due to Ms. Rodgers, not change the interest classification for tax purposes.

Holding. The court held that the $7,824 of income received by Ms. Rodgers from the State of Alabama during 2015 should be characterized as interest that is includable in her gross income pursuant to §61(a)(4). Therefore, the payment did not reflect nontaxable child support. As a result, the court sustained the IRS's deficiency determination.

Long-Term Contracts

Ltr. Rul. 202318008 (Feb. 7, 2023)
IRC §460

☞ Long-Term Contract Rules Apply Regardless of Whether Taxpayer Owns Property

Facts. A taxpayer provides services to a customer at specified facilities under a contract. The contract may last several years. Although the customer continues to own the land under the facilities, the taxpayer receives title to the facilities. The taxpayer also acquired an easement to access the facilities to perform the services. Under the easement's terms, its customer had the right to require the taxpayer to relocate facilities.

When the customer exercised this right, the taxpayer was required to perform specific construction work to relocate an item of property owned by its customer from one facility to another. The contract required the customer to reimburse the taxpayer only for the related costs. The taxpayer claimed it would not profit from the reimbursement payments but only maintain its financial position.

12

39. See *Fankhanel v. Comm'r*, TC Memo 1998-403 (Nov. 12, 1998).

40. Ibid.

Analysis. IRC §460(f)(1) defines "long-term contract" to mean any contract for the construction of property if the taxpayer does not complete the contract within the same tax year that it enters into the contract.[41] Treas. Reg. §1.460-1(b)(1) requires the use of the percentage-of-completion method (PCM) to account for its income under the contract. It is irrelevant if the taxpayer does not own the property or bear the risk of loss. It is also irrelevant if the taxpayer does not have to deliver the property to its customer.

Generally, a taxpayer must account for income under the PCM by determining the percentage of the contract completed.[42] This is done by comparing the allocated contract costs already incurred with the total estimated contract costs.[43]

In this case, the contract required the taxpayer to perform construction work that it did not complete within the same calendar year. Although there are exceptions that do not require the PCM method,[44] the taxpayer did not qualify for any of them.

Holding. The IRS concluded that the taxpayer must treat the contract as a long-term contract. The taxpayer must account for income using the PCM method. Using this method, it must recognize income as it incurs and deducts expenses.

INNOCENT SPOUSE

Relief From Joint and Several Liability

***Sydney Ann Chaney Thomas v. Comm'r*, 160 TC 4 (2023)**
IRC §§6013 and 6015

☞ Blogged Down With Evidence

Facts. Sydney Thomas and her husband Tracy filed joint tax returns for tax years 2012 through 2014. The couple still owed unpaid tax at the time of Mr. Thomas's death in 2016. Mrs. Thomas requested equitable relief from the amount of tax still due on those returns under IRC §6015(f). In 2020, the IRS denied the request, and Mrs. Thomas petitioned the Tax Court on the issue as a California resident.

The court tried the case in San Francisco in 2022 with Mrs. Thomas representing herself. Part of the evidence the IRS sought to enter for the case consisted of a series of Mrs. Thomas's personal blog posts dated from 2016 to 2022. The IRS wished to use this evidence to provide insight into Mrs. Thomas's financial position and her relationship with Mr. Thomas. While Mrs. Thomas objected, the court admitted the blog posts as evidence. The court held on proceeding the trial to give Mrs. Thomas the ability to file a motion to remove the blog posts as evidence, which she did a couple of months later after obtaining legal representation. The IRS in turn objected to Mrs. Thomas's motion for the evidence removal on the grounds that the blog posts represented newly discovered evidence pursuant to the scope as outlined in §6015(e)(7).

Issues. The issue in this case is whether the IRS may enter Mrs. Thomas's blog posts as evidence under §6015 as additional or newly discovered evidence.

---

41. See also Treas. Reg. §1.460-1(b)(1).

42. Treas. Reg. §1.460-4(b)(1).

43. Treas. Reg. §1.460-4(b)(4).

44. IRC §460(e)(3).

Analysis. The court began its interpretation of the §6015 phrase of "newly discovered evidence" by assessing its ordinary meaning. The court concluded that the ordinary meaning of the phrase was "recently obtained sight or knowledge of for the first time." Using this definition for the case, the court found that the blog posts met the criteria as newly discovered evidence. While Mrs. Thomas argued that the IRS had not conducted a reasonable search for this evidence to discover the blog posts during her administrative proceeding, the court found that §6015 does not impose a reasonable diligence standard. Congress not only excluded such language in the Code, but included an expanding qualifier in its language of "any additional" newly discovered evidence. This reinforced the court's interpretation of the intention of Congress in phrasing the Code as present.

Holding. The court held that Mrs. Thomas's blog posts were admissible as evidence under §6015 as newly discovered evidence. The court denied Mrs. Thomas's motion to strike the blog posts as evidence from the record.

IRS PROCEDURES — MISCELLANEOUS

IRS Notice Policy

***Hanna Polselli et al. v. IRS*, No. 21-1599 (2022)**

IRC §7609

☞ IRS Not Required to Alert Taxpayers of Summons

Facts. Remo Polselli was found to have underpaid his federal taxes by more than $2 million over a 10-year period. The IRS initiated an investigation to locate Mr. Polselli's assets and discovered that he had used various legal entities to evade asset collection. Evidence indicated that Mr. Polselli had paid a tax liability from an unrelated business entity's account instead of his own. IRS Revenue Officer Michael Bryant uncovered that Mr. Polselli had concealed his assets in bank accounts using Hanna, his wife's name. Mr. Bryant served summonses on Wells Fargo Bank and the law firm representing Mr. Polselli to obtain information useful for asset recovery. The IRS sought to determine the source of Mr. Polselli's funds, his connected bank accounts, the entities he owned or controlled, and the bank accounts linked to those entities. The law firm claimed attorney-client privilege and denied retaining the requested documents.

Mr. Bryant issued additional summonses to JPMorgan Chase and Bank of America to obtain financial information about Mr. Polselli and the law firm. Neither Mrs. Polselli nor the law firm were informed about the summonses. However, Wells Fargo notified Mrs. Polselli, and the other banks informed the law firm. Both the law firm and Mrs. Polselli filed motions to quash the summonses, arguing that proper notice was not given as required by IRC §7609. The IRS claimed lack of subject-matter jurisdiction and asserted that Mrs. Polselli and the banks were not entitled to notice. The IRS offered the law firm the opportunity to review the summoned records to ensure they were related to Mr. Polselli and the entities holding his assets. The District Court ruled in favor of the IRS, stating that notice was not necessary.[45]

12

Both the law firm and Mrs. Polselli appealed to the U.S. Court of Appeals for the Sixth Circuit. The Sixth Circuit upheld the district court's ruling, rejecting the petitioners' concerns about their ability to challenge third-party summonses and asserting that Congress has the authority to prioritize the IRS's asset collection over taxpayer privacy.[46]

Mr. Polselli filed a petition for certiorari to the U.S. Supreme Court, and the Court granted certiorari on December 9, 2022.

---

45. *Polselli v. U.S.,* 2020 WL 12688176 (ED Mich., Nov. 16, 2020).

46. *Polselli v. IRS,* 23 F.4d 616, 623 (6th Cir. 2022).

Issues. The issue in this case is whether a delinquent taxpayer must have legal interest in the accounts or records summoned by the IRS to meet the exception to the notice requirement in §7609(c)(2)(D)(i).

Analysis. Generally, the IRS must provide notice of summons to anyone identified in the summons to provide an opportunity for the named parties to quash the summons. There is an exception to this rule in §7609(c)(2)(D)(i). To satisfy this exception, the summons must meet the following conditions.

1. The summons must be issued in aid of collection.
2. The summons must aid the collection of an assessment made or judgement rendered.
3. The summons must aid the collection of assessments or judgements against the person with the liability to which the summons was issued.

> **Note.** None of the three conditions mention having a legal interest in the records that the IRS is requesting. There is especially no mention that a taxpayer must maintain such an interest for the notice exception to apply.

The Polsellis argued that "in the aid of collection" in the first condition means that the summons will only directly advance the IRS's collection efforts if the summons are targeted at an account that the IRS can collect assets from to satisfy the taxpayer's liability. As such, collectible assets can only be produced if the taxpayer has a legal interest in the account.

The Court countered that the term "aid" refers to helping or assisting. Therefore, even if a summons does not uncover taxpayer assets, it may help or assist the IRS in finding assets. In this case, the IRS issued summons to three banks. The summons may not result in the IRS identifying assets at those banks, but it could assist the IRS in uncovering entities that Mr. Polselli controlled, which could lead it to collectible assets to satisfy the $2 million liability.

The Polsellis next argued that there is no real distinction between conditions 1 and 2. Essentially, condition 1 covers every summons that the IRS would issue. There must therefore be an implied "legal interest" requirement to give condition 2 a reason to exist.

The Court disagreed. It interpreted the condition 1 as applicable upon an **assessment,** whereas the condition 2 is applicable upon the finding of a **liability.** A taxpayer's liability exists before the IRS makes an official assessment. However, a formal assessment is not required before the IRS begins collection efforts. The Court also asserted that the Polsellis overlooked that condition 1 addresses taxpayers, whereas condition 2 addresses a transferee or fiduciary. Therefore, the Court identified that the two conditions are distinct requirements.

Holding. The Court concluded that the plain language of the statute does not require a legal interest limitation for the exception and affirmed the judgment of the Court of Appeals for the Sixth Circuit.

Reasonable Cause for Abatement and Granting of Installment Agreement

***George Anton and Ellen Jones-Remisovsky v. Comm'r*, TC Memo 2022-89 (Aug. 30, 2022)**

IRC §§6320(c), 6330(d), and 6651(a)

☞ Blues and Booze Offer No Excuse

Facts. George Anton Remisovsky was a medical doctor in 2013, while his wife Ellen was a retail manager. The couple failed to file their joint federal income tax return for 2013 until May 25, 2016. The delinquent return reported a tax liability of $57,197 and a balance due of $19,690. The filed return did not include payment for the tax due. In response, the IRS assessed tax due of $19,690 and additions to tax totaling $7,845 under IRC §6651(a).

After receiving multiple notices of deficiency regarding their 2013 tax liability, Dr. and Mrs. Remisovsky timely submitted a request for a collection due process (CDP) hearing on March 22, 2019. Dr. and Mrs. Remisovsky sought to challenge the additions to their tax liability and discuss collection alternatives. The settlement officer (SO) from the IRS Office of Appeals overseeing the case communicated with Dr. and Mrs. Remisovsky that the tax liability and additions to tax assessments were correct and followed applicable law and procedure. When Dr. and Mrs. Remisovsky then requested first time abatement of the additions to tax, the SO explained that they did not qualify, as the couple had also been subject to additions to tax for the 2011 tax year.[47]

Subsequently, Dr. Remisovsky supplied alcoholism and depression as arguments for "reasonable cause" in failing to timely file their 2013 tax return. He explained that he had been hospitalized for alcoholism in 1990 and suffered a relapse in 2012, stating he could continue working due to being "a binge drinker while active." As additional support, Dr. Remisovsky supplied a letter from his psychiatrist dated July 23, 2019. The letter disclosed that Dr. Remisovsky had a history of alcoholism with periods of sobriety, and "his cognitive capacity to comply with his financial obligations and to pay his taxes in a timely fashion were severely diminished." The SO denied the penalty abatement under reasonable cause, explaining the argument did not adhere to the criteria in the Internal Revenue Manual.[48]

The SO offered the couple a $654 per month installment agreement, which included additions to tax. Dr. and Mrs. Remisovsky rejected this offer and did not provide any alternative or pursue other options. Consequently, the SO closed the case. Dr. and Mrs. Remisovsky then received a notice of determination dated September 2, 2020, sustaining the levy and lien notices for the 2013 tax year.

After receiving the notice, Dr. and Mrs. Remisovsky filed a petition with the U.S. Tax Court. They asserted that the SO erred in declining the reasonable cause abatement of 2013 additions to tax and refused to grant an installment agreement without merit.

Issues. The issues in this case are the following.

- Whether the SO erred in declining reasonable cause abatement of the additions to tax
- Whether the SO abused her discretion in sustaining an installment agreement

Analysis. A taxpayer can argue reasonable cause for a delay in filing if the taxpayer "exercised ordinary business care and prudence and was nevertheless unable to file the return within the prescribed time."[49] Similarly, a taxpayer could argue reasonable cause for a delay in payment if the taxpayer "exercised ordinary business care and prudence in providing for payment of his tax liability and nevertheless was either unable to pay the tax or would suffer undue hardship if he paid the tax on the due date."[50] Dr. and Mrs. Remisovsky did not state that **financial hardship** played any role in their failure to file and pay. Instead, they reasoned that their failure to file their tax return and pay their tax liability on time was attributable to Dr. Remisovsky's alcoholism and depression.

---

47. IRM 20.1.1.3.3.2.1 (2020).

48. IRM 20.1.1.3.2.2.1 (2011).

49. Treas. Reg §301.6551-1(c)(1).

50. *Hardin v. Comm'r,* TC Memo 2012-162 (Jun. 11, 2012).

The court noted that Dr. Remisovsky did not provide testimony or evidence that he suffered from depression and alcoholism at times pertaining to the filing and payment, including early in 2014 when the 2013 tax return was due, and in May 2016 when they filed the delinquent return but did not submit payment. The court further noted that the doctor's letter did not specify time periods or a timeframe when Dr. Remisovsky suffered from alcoholism. That omission would have been important in assessing the reasonableness for the lack of filing and payment, especially when the letter acknowledged Dr. Remisovsky experienced periods of sobriety. The court also found that Dr. Remisovsky failed to provide any evidence regarding the severity of his alcoholism and depression. For example, Dr. Remisovsky was neither admitted to a mental illness hospital nor an alcohol treatment center. The severity of his alcoholism and depression must be debilitating to meet the criteria for successfully arguing reasonable cause in performing financial obligations. That Dr. Remisovsky could practice medicine during this timeframe did not help his case. The court pointed out that it regularly rejects "reasonable cause" defenses based on similar illnesses where the taxpayer continued to work during the relevant time periods.

Additionally, the court explained that even if Dr. Remisovsky could prove he was too ill to file and pay on time, Mrs. Remisovsky provided no arguments or reasons as to why she could not file or pay. Mrs. Remisovsky received wages in 2013 for her retail manager position and had an independent filing obligation. Furthermore, Mrs. Remisovsky could not use her husband's illness as a per se excuse for failing to file their return.[51] The court also identified that Dr. and Mrs. Remisovsky had used an accountant to prepare and file their 2012 tax return, noting the couple did not explain why they could not reach out to that accountant for help in preparing and filing their 2013 return.

Dr. and Mrs. Remisovsky claimed that the SO handling their case arbitrarily refused to grant an installment agreement. The court's review of the record found that the SO fulfilled her statutory responsibilities in this matter by properly verifying the requirements of applicable law and administrative procedure were met, considering any relevant issues the taxpayers raised, and considering the balance between collecting the taxes and having the collection not exceeding a necessary level of intrusiveness concerning the taxpayers. When Dr. and Mrs. Remisovsky refused the SO's $654 per month offer and did not counter with an alternative proposal, the court stated that the SO was under no obligation to pursue a collection alternative.

Holding. The court held that the SO did not err in declining Dr. and Mrs. Remisovsky's request to abate additions to their 2013 tax liability through reasonable cause. Additionally, the court found that the SO did not abuse her discretion in sustaining collection actions as Dr. and Mrs. Remisovsky failed to offer and seek a collection alternative.

Practitioner Planning Tip

This case highlights the importance of following the criteria for arguing reasonable cause for failure to file a tax return and pay a tax liability. The burden of proof falls on the taxpayer to show that they reasonably made an effort to comply or that making a payment would cause undue hardship. This case also shows that spouses who file jointly are both equally responsible and that even if one is incapacitated, that fact alone does not preclude someone from filing a tax return or paying a tax liability in the eyes of the IRS.

51. *Fambrough v. Comm'r,* TC Memo 1990-104 (Feb. 28, 1990).

Tax Scams

IRS News Rel. IR-2023-71 (Apr. 5, 2023)

☞ IRS Releases "Dirty Dozen" List of Tax Scams

The IRS issued its "dirty dozen" list of tax scams and reminded taxpayers to remain vigilant to these schemes throughout the year. Such scams may peak during tax season, but taxpayers may encounter them at any time.

Following is a recap of this year's top scams.

1. **Employee retention credits (ERC).** Scammers promote large refunds related to the ERC, attempting to con ineligible individuals to claim the credit. Often the scammer's promotion is based on inaccurate information related to an individual's eligibility for the ERC and the computation of the credit. The scammers collect personally identifiable information and use that information to carry out identity theft.

2. **Phishing and smishing.** Scammers pose as legitimate organizations and send unsolicited text messages (smishing) or email (phishing), to entice unsuspecting victims to provide their personal and financial information. The thieves then use that information for identity theft. The IRS reminds everyone that it initiates most contact through regular mail, rather than email, text, or social media.

3. **Online account help from third-party scammers.** Taxpayers should not accept help from third parties who offer to help the taxpayer to set up an IRS Online Account. Once the taxpayer provides the third party with their personal information, the swindlers can use that valuable information for nefarious gains. Taxpayers should establish their own online accounts.

4. **False fuel tax credit claims.** The fuel tax credit is available for off-highway and farming use. Most taxpayers are not eligible for the credit. Unscrupulous practitioners and promoters entice taxpayers to incorrectly inflate their tax refunds by claiming the credit on Form 4136, *Credit for Federal Tax Paid on Fuels.*

5. **Fake charities.** Defrauders set up fake organizations whenever a crisis or natural disaster strikes to take advantage of the donor's generosity. The scammers acquire taxpayer's money and personal information, to ultimately exploit the donors. Individuals are only eligible to claim an itemized deduction if they donate to a qualified tax-exempt IRS-approved organization.

6. **Unscrupulous tax return preparers.** Common warning signs of a corrupt tax preparer include charging a contingency fee based on the size of a refund, refusing to sign the return as the preparer, or refusing to provide their preparer tax identification number.

7. **Social media: fraudulent form filing and bad advice.** A recent example of bad advice on social media the IRS has seen, is the recommendation to fraudulently file Forms W-2, *Wage and Tax Statement,* or Form 8944, *Preparer e-file Hardship Waiver Request.* The scheme encourages individuals to file these forms using false, inaccurate information to get a refund.

8. **Spearphishing and cybersecurity for tax professionals.** Spearphishing is a type of phishing (emails or text messages to entice individuals to provide personal information) that targets a specific business or organization. Tax professionals have a greater potential for harm if they are the victim of spearphishing because of all the client data they maintain. Scammers can use client data and the tax practitioner's identities to file fraudulent claims.

12

> **Note.** For more information on practitioners' responsibility to protect their client data from attacks, see the 2023 *University of Illinois Federal Tax Workbook,* Chapter 1: Written Information Security Plans and Protecting Client Data.

9. **OIC mills.** IRS OICs help individuals who are unable to pay their tax liability in full reach a settlement with the IRS. "Mills" aggressively promote OIC to individuals who do not meet the qualifications, often costing the taxpayer thousands of dollars.

10. **Schemes aimed at high-income filers.** The IRS identified two specific schemes that are aimed at high-income individuals.

    a. **Charitable remainder annuity trust (CRAT).** CRATs are irrevocable trusts that allow individuals to donate their assets to a charity and draw an annual income for life or a specific period. Some trusts are misused to eliminate ordinary income or capita gain on the sale of property.

    b. **Monetized installment sales.** Promoters focus on individuals who are attempting to defer the recognition of gain when they sell appreciated property. In exchange for a fee, these scammers facilitate an alleged monetized installment sale.

11. **Bogus tax avoidance strategies.** The IRS identified two specific tax avoidance strategies of which to be aware.

    a. **Micro-captive insurance arrangements.** Micro-captive insurance companies are insurance companies whose owners are taxed on the captive's investment income only. These schemes lack many of the characteristics of legitimate insurance and include improbable risks, failure to match legitimate business needs, and unnecessary duplication of insurance coverage for the taxpayer.

    b. **Syndicated conservation easements.** Conservation easements are restrictions on an individual's right to use real property. Generally, the taxpayer claims a charitable contribution for the fair market value of a conservation easement that they contribute to a qualified charity. The transfer must meet the requirements of IRC §170. Promoters abuse the system by grossly inflating the associated tax deduction.

12. **Schemes with international elements.** The IRS identified three specific international schemes of which to be aware.

    a. **Offshore accounts and digital assets.** The IRS continues to investigate individuals with offshore accounts. In recent years, it has increased scrutiny on accounts with digital assets, such as cryptocurrency. Individuals who attempt to conceal their assets in offshore banks, brokerage accounts, digital asset accounts, and nominee entities are subject to exposure by the IRS. The IRS can identify and track seemingly anonymous transactions involving foreign financial accounts and digital assets.

    b. **Maltese IRAs misusing treaty.** This scheme involves U.S. residents and citizens who contribute to IRAs in Malta (and other host countries also) but lack any local connection to the host country to avoid U.S. tax. The individuals claim the foreign arrangement is a pension fund and, based on the tax treaty, qualifies for an exemption from U.S. income tax on gains and earnings in and distributions from the foreign IRA.

    c. **Puerto Rican and foreign captive insurance.** This scheme involves U.S. business owners of closely held entities entering into an alleged insurance arrangement with a Puerto Rican or other foreign corporation in which the U.S. business owner maintains a financial interest. The U.S. business owner then claims a deduction for premiums paid for insurance coverage to a fronting carrier, which reinsures the coverage with the foreign corporation. However, the "insurance" arrangement typically lacks the characteristics of legitimate insurance.

> **Note.** More information on each of these scams can be found at **uofi.tax/23x12x1** [www.irs.gov/newsroom/dirty-dozen].

Amending Returns
IRS News Rel. IR-2023-77 (Apr. 11, 2023)

☞ Early Filers in 2023 Should Consider Amending Returns For Certain State 2022 Tax Refunds

The IRS instructed taxpayers who filed their federal income taxes early in 2023 and reported certain state 2022 tax refunds as taxable income to consider filing an amended return. During a review, the IRS determined that taxpayers in many states did not need to report these payments on their 2022 tax returns. Consequently, the IRS will not challenge the taxability of state payments related to **general welfare and disaster relief.** Taxpayers in the following states did not need to report these state payments on their 2022 return.

- Alaska[52]
- California
- Colorado
- Connecticut
- Delaware
- Florida
- Hawaii
- Idaho
- Illinois
- Indiana
- Maine
- New Jersey
- New Mexico
- New York
- Oregon
- Pennsylvania
- Rhode Island

Taxpayers in Georgia, Massachusetts, South Carolina, and Virginia will not include special state 2022 tax refunds as income for federal tax purposes if the payment is a refund of state taxes paid and the recipient either claimed the standard deduction for tax year 2022 or itemized their tax year 2022 deductions but did not receive a tax benefit.

Taxpayers who filed before February 10 in the states mentioned should check their tax return to ensure they paid tax on a state refund before filing an amended return. In addition, taxpayers who used a tax professional can consult with them to determine whether an amended return is necessary.

If taxpayers need to file an amended return and they submitted their original 2022 tax return electronically, they can also file their amended return electronically and may select direct deposit for any resulting refund. Taxpayers also have the option to submit a paper version of the Form 1040-X, *Amended U.S Individual Income Tax Return,* and receive a paper check. Direct deposit is not available on amended returns submitted on paper.

> **Caution.** Several states provided payments during 2023 that could be considered for general welfare and disaster relief. The IRS has not yet issued guidance on how those 2023 payments should be treated for federal purposes.

52. Applies only to the special supplemental Energy Relief Payment received.

Timely Filing Petitions with the IRS

Antawn Sanders v. Comm'r., 160 TC 16 (2023)

IRC §§6213, 7451 and 7502

☞ Less Than A Minute Didn't Win It

Facts. Antawn Jamal Sanders received a notice of deficiency from the IRS dated September 8, 2022. The notice instructed that Mr. Sanders could file a petition with the tax court for this matter no later than December 12, 2022. Prior to that date, Mr. Sanders created an account with the court's electronic filing system, DAWSON, to file a petition with the tax court regarding the deficiency notice.

Mr. Sanders did not attempt to file the petition until 11:03 p.m. on December 12, 2022, leaving him less than one hour to timely file the petition. For over 30 minutes, he attempted to file the petition through DAWSON via his smartphone but was unable to upload his documents through the system. After several failed attempts, Mr. Sanders switched to his Windows computer, where he had difficulty logging into DAWSON until 11:56 p.m. After referring to the instructions throughout the process and completing steps within the petition application, Mr. Dawson was able to file the petition 11 seconds after midnight.

On January 25, 2023, the IRS filed a motion to dismiss, citing a lack of jurisdiction due to Mr. Sanders's petition not being timely filed. The IRS noted that, per DAWSON logs, the system was accessible throughout December 12, 2022, and therefore was not inaccessible to the general public.

Mr. Sanders filed an objection to this motion on February 21, 2023, stating that he logged in and filed the petition on time. He explained that he made several attempts to file the petition well before midnight and was able to successfully upload the petition at exactly 12:00 a.m. The Center for Taxpayer Rights submitted an amicus brief arguing Mr. Sanders's petition was timely filed when he relinquished control of the submission through the lens of equitable tolling under IRC §7502.

Issues. The issues in this case are the following.

- Whether Mr. Sanders timely filed his petition under §7451
- Whether the filing location was inaccessible, resulting in an otherwise untimely filing being considered timely
- Whether equitable tolling applies to Mr. Sanders's case

Analysis. The court identified that IRC §6213(a) as the applicable prescription for the time for filing a petition for matters of tax deficiency. The Code mandates the timely filing of a petition as 90 days after the IRS mailed the notice of deficiency (excluding weekends and holidays as the last day). The petition is ordinarily deemed as filed when the Tax Court receives it.[53] Under Tax Court Rule 22(d), electronic submissions are considered timely filed at or before 11:59 PM Eastern Time on the last day of the filing period. Furthermore, electronic filing is considered accomplished when the server receives the transmission, not at the time when an applicant logs into the system or begins the filing process.[54] Per these criterion, Mr. Sanders did not timely file his petition on December 12, 2022, under §6213(a). While the court acknowledges that Mr. Sanders logged in and begin preparing his petition on December 12, 2022, the day that he filed his petition fell on December 13, 2022, 11 seconds after midnight.

---

53. See *Leventis v. Comm'r*, 49 TC 353, 354 (1968).

54. See *In re Sands*, 328 BR 614, 619 (Bankr. NDNY 2005).

Mr. Sanders argued that the filing location, in his case the DAWSON system, was inaccessible under §7451, thus rendering his submission as timely. The IRS disagreed, stating that logs proved that the system was accessible to the general public throughout December 12, 2022. In determining whether §7451 applied to Mr. Sanders's case, the court distinguished between the availability of DAWSON and user-specific errors. Because Mr. Sanders was able to log into the system using both his phone and his computer, DAWSON was accessible and available. The issues that Mr. Sanders's faced when filling out the forms on his phone did not pertain to the DAWSON filing system, because filling out the forms is completed separately and outside of the filing portal. Mr. Sanders's argument that he had to undertake multiple steps before filing his submission also did not have relevance to the DAWSON system being accessible. The court explained that the realities of filing, whether electronic or otherwise, involved multiple steps in the process, and was not a reflection of the availability of a filing location. Furthermore, the court's own records showed that DAWSON was operational and available at all relevant times on December 12, 2022. Because Mr. Sanders's difficulties were unique to him, §7451 does not apply to his case.

The court also assessed the argument of applying the doctrine of equitable tolling, where relief is provided to the litigant in cases where they diligently pursued their rights but extraordinary circumstances resulted in them failing to meet a deadline. The court identified that the petition filing deadline is jurisdictional under §6213(a) and therefore the court must enforce the deadline regardless of equitable considerations. Consequently, the court cannot apply the doctrine of equitable tolling to deadlines for filing a petition in a deficiency case.

Holding. The court held that Mr. Sanders did not timely file his petition under §6213(a). The court identified that §7451 does not apply to Mr. Sanders's case because the circumstances surrounding his inability to file on time pertained to user error instead of the accessibility and availability of the DAWSON system to the general public. The court also held that equitable tolling does not apply in the matter of an untimely petition in a deficiency case. The court dismissed Mr. Sander's petition for lack of jurisdiction.

> **Note.** This case is an example of the risks associated with last-minute filing, particularly through electronic means. The time it takes to go through the submission process and user-specific difficulties do not provide leniency in late submissions, even in matters where the submission was late by seconds.

Corporate President's Liability for Unpaid Taxes

***U.S. v. Isaac Neuberger*, No. 1:22-cv-02977 (Jul. 10, 2023)**

IRC §§6321 and 6323; 31 USC §3701

☞ Numerous Nuisances for Neuberger

Facts. On **November 20, 2019**, the IRS issued a notice of deficiency to Lehcim Holdings, Inc. (Lehcim), indicating that the company had tax liabilities arising from underreported taxes during the tax years 2010 through 2015. Consequently, Lehcim was liable for $2,091,455.16 in unpaid taxes.

The IRS sent the notice of deficiency to Lehcim's president, Isaac Neuberger at his law firm, Neuberger, Quinn, Gielen, Rubin & Gibber, P.A. The IRS informed Lehcim that it could contest the notice by submitting a petition to the U.S. Tax Court. However, Lehcim did not file a petition, and the tax liabilities were assessed against it on **July 13, 2020**.

During the period between the receipt of the notice of deficiency and the assessment of tax liability, Mr. Neuberger, acting as Lehcim's president, transferred the company's account balance to repay purported loans from third parties. After these payments Lehcim did not have sufficient assets to settle its tax liabilities.

On November 16, 2022, the United States filed a complaint in the U.S. District Court of Maryland, invoking the Priority Statute under 31 USC §3713, to assert that Mr. Neuberger bears personal liability for Lehcim's outstanding tax liability to the IRS. The United States contended that Mr. Neuberger became liable when he transferred the available funds to third parties with inferior claims while Lehcim was insolvent.

Subsequently, on January 25, 2023, Mr. Neuberger submitted a **motion to dismiss** the United States's complaint. He argued that the United States had not adequately alleged the existence of a claim in the relevant time period under the Federal Tax Lien Act (26 U.S.C. §6321 *et seq)*. Per his logic, because the claim was not perfected, the Priority Statute is not applicable. Additionally, Mr. Neuberger argued that even if it were applicable, the complaint lacked essential facts to constitute a valid cause of action under the Priority Statute.

In response, the United States contended that the Priority Statute is applicable in cases where the government does not seek priority for a tax lien against secured creditors and asserted that an unassessed tax liability qualifies as a claim under the statute. The United States maintained that the complaint included all necessary facts to support a claim pursuant to the Priority Statute.

Issues. The issues in this case are the following.

- Whether the United States adequately alleged the existence of a claim within the scope of the Tax Lien Act
- Whether a claim existed when Mr. Neuberger made the transfers to third party creditors
- Whether the United States's complaint fails to allege sufficient facts to state a claim under the Priority Statute

Analysis. In response to the United States's claim that the Priority Statute applies to the collection of unpaid tax debt, Mr. Neuberger argued that the Tax Lien Act should be the applicable law. According to him, in cases involving tax deficiencies, the government is required to obtain a tax lien against the taxpayer first before applying the priority rules established by the Tax Lien Act. To support this position, Mr. Neuberger cited the case of *U.S. v. Estate of Romani*, in which the Court emphasized the necessity of obtaining a tax lien before applying the rules of the Tax Lien Act. However, the United States countered this argument by asserting that the Priority Statute is not restricted to nontax claims and that Mr. Neuberger's creditors did not hold liens or debts superior to those of the United States, thereby warranting the application of the Tax Lien Act.

Mr. Neuberger contended that the Supreme Court's decision in *U.S. v. Estate of Romani* unequivocally supports their position. However, the United States refuted this interpretation, clarifying that in *Estate of Romani,* the Court specifically addressed priority concerning real property in the context of an unpaid tax liability of the deceased. The Court rejected the notion that the Priority Statute should grant priority to the United States over a judgment creditor's perfected and secured lien for real property. Contrary to Mr. Neuberger's broad assertion, the Court's analysis in *U.S. v. Russell* further illuminated the application of the Priority Statute following the *Estate of Romani* ruling. The Court in *Russell* explained that the *Estate of Romani* decision did not entirely exclude the application of the Priority Statute in all tax cases but necessitated that the government follows the correct procedures to secure and maintain its tax lien, ensuring priority over other secured creditors. In this case, the United States did not allege the existence of a tax lien at the time of Mr. Neuberger's purported transfers. Consequently, if any of Mr. Neuberger's creditors belonged to the specific categories outlined in the Tax Lien Act, it would be applicable. However, as the United States's complaint indicated that Mr. Neuberger transferred funds to repay purported loans from third parties, a category not explicitly addressed in the Tax Lien Act, the Priority Statute applies. Thus, the court rejected Mr. Neuberger's motion to dismiss based on the argument that any claim of priority related to a tax debt must be filed under the Tax Lien Act.

Next, Mr. Neuberger asserted that no claim existed within the scope of the Priority Statute at the time the transfers under consideration took place, and therefore, no personal liability could be attributed in the matter. Mr. Neuberger argues that only a lien, which the United States could not legally obtain until after the tax deficiency assessment on July 13, 2020, could qualify as a claim under the Priority Statute. In response, the United States contended that the Priority Statute's plain language defines "claim" more expansively, encompassing a tax liability even prior to the assessment of a tax deficiency and the establishment of a lien. The Priority Statute defines a claim as any amount of funds or property determined by an appropriate federal government official to be owed to the United States by an individual, organization, or entity other than another federal agency. Furthermore, the Supreme Court directed lower courts to interpret the Priority Statute liberally, and accordingly, courts have applied it to various types of government claims, including federal tax liabilities. Given the complaint alleged the issuance of a notice of deficiency to Mr. Neuberger before any of the alleged transfers occurred and his knowledge of Lehcim's unpaid tax liabilities, the United States maintained that it adequately alleged the existence of a claim within the meaning of the Priority Statute.

According to the United States, the notice of deficiency, issued on November 20, 2019, informed the Mr. Neuberger of the government's claim for unpaid tax liability before any transfers took place. The notice of deficiency specifically stated that the IRS determined additional tax or other amounts owed by Lehcim for the tax years 2010 through 2015, thereby providing the amount of debt determined by an appropriate government official (the IRS) as owed to the United States. Therefore, this information satisfied the definition of a "claim" under the Priority Statute, and courts should not unduly restrict the term "claim" within narrow or technical interpretations. Consequently, the United States's allegation that Mr. Neuberger received the notice of deficiency on November 20, 2019, disclosing the amount of Lehcim's tax liability and subsequently engaged in fund transfers with this knowledge sufficiently supported the presence of a claim within the meaning of the Priority Statute.

Finally, Mr. Neuberger asserted that even if the Priority Statute was applicable, the complaint fails to provide sufficient facts to support a claim under the Priority Statute. Specifically, the United States had not alleged the occurrence of an insolvency proceeding, a crucial element of the Priority Statute. In response, the United States contended that the statute does not explicitly mention the term "insolvency proceeding" and argued that such a proceeding is unnecessary for the Priority Statute to apply, as long as there is a voluntary assignment of property. The Priority Statute should then apply in cases where an insolvent debtor voluntarily assigns property, as demonstrated by the situation where Mr. Neuberger, as the corporate officer of Lehcim, transferred funds to repay purported loans while the corporation was insolvent.

The relevant section of the Priority Statute, 31 USC §3713, stipulates that a "Claim of the United States Government shall be paid first when" certain conditions are met, including when a person indebted to the government is insolvent and makes a voluntary assignment of property or when an act of bankruptcy is committed. Insolvency within the context of the Priority Statute refers to a situation where the liabilities of an entity exceed its assets. Furthermore, Section 3713(b) of the statute imposes personal liability on a representative, including corporate officers, who pays a non-federal debt on behalf of a corporation before satisfying a federal claim. To establish a cause of action under the Priority Statute, the plaintiff must allege that a corporate officer acting on behalf of the corporation paid a non-federal debt before the United States's claim, at a time when the corporation was insolvent, and with knowledge or notice of the federal claim. Mr. Neuberger did not dispute the United States's allegations that other creditors received payment before the United States while the corporation was insolvent, and after he had knowledge of the United States's claim. Therefore, the issue revolves around whether Mr. Neuberger's actions constitute a "voluntary assignment of property" within the meaning of the Priority Statute, as alleged by the United States.

Mr. Neuberger's argument centered on the contention that the United States's complaint lacked an essential requirement for the application of the Priority Statute, namely an insolvency proceeding. He insisted that to meet this requirement, the United States must allege the occurrence of an insolvency proceeding in which the debtor's property was transferred to a fiduciary. The United States, however, maintained that the Priority Statute does not specifically demand the allegation of an insolvency proceeding and emphasized that such a term is absent from the statute and its interpretations. Furthermore, the statute's language clearly focuses on the debtor's insolvency as a pivotal condition for its application. The complaint stated that at the time of Mr. Neuberger's transfer of Lehcim's assets to third parties, Lehcim was either insolvent or became insolvent, as its assets were insufficient to cover its expenses. As such, the United States contended it has adequately alleged Lechim's insolvency, thus fulfilling the requirement for invoking the Priority Statute.

Additionally, the Priority Statute necessitates an allegation that the debtor made a payment of a non-federal debt through a voluntary assignment of property, the provision in question in the case. Mr. Neuberger argued that a voluntary assignment denotes a specific legal concept where a debtor vests a receiver, trustee, or assignee with the authority to administer and distribute property to settle outstanding debts, and that liability can only attach if a corporate representative accepts the role of a receiver but fails to prioritize payment to the United States. The United States rebuted this argument by asserting that Mr. Neuberger's knowledge of Lehcim's insolvency and its debt to the United States, followed by transferring Lehcim's assets to other creditors instead of paying the United States, constituted a voluntary assignment of property under the Priority Statute.

Holding. The court held that the United States adequately alleged the existence of a claim, and that the Tax Lien Act was not required for claims of priority related to a tax debt. The court also held that Mr. Neuberger's knowledge and receipt of the notice of deficiency at the time he made the transfers to third parties resulted in the existence of a claim within the meaning of the Priority Statute. Finally, the court held that the United States adequately stated a claim for relief pursuant to the Priority Statue. Consequently, the court denied Mr. Neuberger's motion to dismiss.

IRS PROCEDURES — PENALTIES

Deadlines for Filing Claims for Credits or Refunds

IRS Notice 2023-21, 2023-11 IRB 563 (Mar. 13, 2023)
IRC §§6511, 6513, and 7508A

☞ Relief from Deadlines For Filing Claims for Refunds

Purpose. The IRS notice provides relief for taxpayers affected by the COVID-19 emergency. The IRS issued the notice in response to the emergency declaration made by the President on March 13, 2020. The notice grants relief under IRC §7508A to affected individuals and businesses that may file claims for credits or refunds.

Analysis. IRC §7508A grants the Secretary of the Treasury the authority to postpone deadlines for certain tax-related acts by taxpayers affected by a federally declared disaster. The notice clarifies that a postponement under §7508A is not an extension of the due date but allows for disregarding a certain period when determining the timeliness of acts, interest, penalties, taxes, credits, or refunds.

The notice explains that previous notices (Notices 2020-23[55] and 2021-21[56]) postponed certain tax return filing and payment obligations due to the COVID-19 pandemic. It did not extend them. Consequently, the 3-year lookback periods[57] for claiming credits or refunds were not affected. Taxpayers must submit claims for refunds or credits within three years of filing a return or two years of when they pay a tax, whichever expires later.[58] IRC §§6513(b)(1) and (2) deem a taxpayer to have paid taxes on the return's due date, generally April 15. This date applies to withheld and estimated taxes.

Section 3 of the notice grants relief to taxpayers filing series 1040 returns during the COVID-19 emergency. For these taxpayers, the IRS disregards the period between April 15, 2020, and July 15, 2020, or between April 15, 2021, and May 17, 2021, respectively, in determining the beginning of the lookback period for claiming credits or refunds under IRC §6511(b)(2)(A) of the Code. Without this notice, withheld or estimated taxes would not be eligible for a refund after April 15, 2023. This date is three years after the deemed date of deposit of the taxes.

The notice provides an example to illustrate the relief granted. If a taxpayer filed their 2019 federal income tax return on June 22, 2020, they would have until June 22, 2023, to file a claim for credit or refund. However, without the relief in the notice, the lookback period for claiming the refund would go back to only June 22, 2020. It would exclude the withheld income taxes deemed paid on April 15, 2020. The relief provides for the deemed paid taxes to be included. It disregards the period between April 15 and July 15, 2020, in the lookback period calculation.

Notably, the notice emphasizes that the relief granted in this notice is automatic. Affected taxpayers do not need to contact the IRS, file any forms, or submit additional documentation to receive relief.

RETIREMENT

IRC §401(k) Distribution for Medical Disability

***Robert B. Lucas v. Comm'r*, TC Memo 2023-9 (Jan. 17, 2023)**

IRC §§72(m)(7), 72(t), and 401(k); Treas. Reg. §1.72-17A(f)

☞ Taxpayer Cannot Use Disability to Avoid Early Withdrawal Penalties

Facts. In 2017, Robert B. Lucas lost his job at Life Cycle Engineering, where he worked as a software developer. To accommodate for his loss of income, Mr. Lucas received a $19,365 distribution that year from his IRC §401(k) plan. Matrix Trust Co. (Matrix) administered the §401(k) plan. Matrix issued a 2017 Form 1099-R, *Distributions From Pensions, Annuities, Retirement or Profit-Sharing Plans, IRAs, Insurance Contracts, etc.*, to Mr. Lucas, reporting the $19,365 as an early distribution with no known exception to the early withdrawal penalty.

Mr. Lucas's filed 2017 income tax return reported the §401(k) distribution but excluded it from taxable income. Upon review of the return, the IRS issued a notice of deficiency to Mr. Lucas for $4,899. The deficiency included an income tax assessment on the $19,365 distribution and a 10% early withdrawal penalty, as Mr. Lucas had not yet reached the age of 59½ at the time of the distribution.

12

55. IRS Notice 2020-23, 2020-18 IRB 742.

56. IRS Notice 2021-21, 2021-15 IRB 986.

57. IRC §6511(b)(2)(A).

58. IRC §6511(a).

Mr. Lucas contested the tax deficiency, explaining that the §401(k) distribution is not taxable income because he has a medical disability. Mr. Lucas was diagnosed with diabetes in 2015. Mr. Lucas used a website to defend his position that having diabetes allowed him to exclude the distribution from gross income reported on his tax return. Mr. Lucas believed this website was knowledgeable on medical disabilities and retirement account withdrawal issues.

Issues. The issues in this case are the following.

- Whether Mr. Lucas's §401(k) distribution is taxable income
- Whether Mr. Lucas is subject to the 10% early withdrawal penalty

Analysis. While Mr. Lucas acknowledged receipt of a §401(k) distribution that he made in 2017, he asserted that he correctly excluded the distribution from gross income, using a website to determine that the distribution was not taxable due to his diabetes constituting a medical disability exception. The court inspected the website and found that the information Mr. Lucas relied on pertained to the early withdrawal penalty and not the taxability of a §401(k) distribution. Moreover, the website did not constitute legal authority. The court noted that no authoritative guidance, such as the Code, Treasury Regulations, or relevant caselaw, supported Mr. Lucas's assertion. The court clarified that gross income includes distributions from employees' trusts, which include §401(k) plans.[59] Consequently, Mr. Lucas must include the §401(k) distribution as gross income on his 2017 tax return.

Regarding the 10% early withdrawal penalty, the court noted that such penalties are assessed on qualified retirement account distributions when the taxpayer is under the age of 59½ at the time of distribution.[60] There are exceptions to the penalty under certain circumstances, one of which is when the distribution is attributable to an individual's disability.[61] To qualify, the disability must result in the individual's inability "to engage in any substantial gainful activity by reason of any medically determinable physical or mental impairment which can be expected to result in death or to be of long-continued and indefinite duration."[62]

The court found that the facts and circumstances surrounding Mr. Lucas's diabetes did not meet the criteria for a disability exception to the early withdrawal penalty. The court acknowledged that Treas. Reg. §1.72-17A(f)(2) identifies diabetes as a cause of preventing an individual from engaging in substantial gainful activity. However, Treas. Reg. §1.72-17A(f)(2) further clarifies that the impairment must have factually caused the prevention of engagement. Mr. Lucas's diagnosis of diabetes occurred in 2015, but he continued to work for the same employer until he lost his job in 2017. Therefore, the court did not find that Mr. Lucas's diabetes prevented him from engaging in a customary substantial gainful activity and would not qualify as a disability for an exception to the early withdrawal penalty.

Holding. The court held that Mr. Lucas should have included his §401(k) distribution as taxable income on his 2017 tax return and that the IRS was correct in subjecting the distribution to the 10% early withdrawal penalty.

59. IRC §401(k).

60. IRC §72(t)(1).

61. IRC §72(t)(2)(A)(iii).

62. IRC §72(m)(7).

Practitioner Planning Tip

This case highlights the importance of considering the consequences of taking an early retirement account distribution and that facts surrounding it matter in determining whether they may be penalties that the taxpayer could face as a result. A disability in and of itself is not guaranteed to qualify as an exception to an early withdrawal penalty. Rather, the impact of the disability on a taxpayer's ability to engage in a substantial gainful activity is a key component in determining the qualification for an exception.

Another takeaway from this case is the importance of relying on authoritative guidance over nonauthoritative sources. Well-intentioned taxpayers may find themselves trying to research and resolve an issue on their own by using advice that is not factual or misinterpreting correct guidance. Practitioners can market their experience and resources to help taxpayers in avoiding similar situations to those found in this case.

S CORPORATION

Credit for Increasing Research Activities

***Jeffrey and Katherine Harper v. Comm'r*, TC Memo 2023-57 (May 10, 2023)**
IRC §41

☞ Military Design-Build Firm Qualifies for Credit for Increasing Research Activities

Facts. Jeffrey and Katherine Harper claimed the research and development (R&D) credit under IRC §41. The credit was connected with their S corporation, Harper Construction Co. (HCC), and was for $46,656 and $778,610 for the tax years 2012 and 2013, respectively. HCC specializes in military design-build projects. The IRS disallowed these credits and asserted deficiencies in federal income tax and accuracy-related penalties for 2012 and 2013. It also made lesser adjustments unrelated to the R&D credit. The IRS alleged that HCC's construction designs failed to meet the definition of "business components." The business components requirement is one of four threshold tests for qualified research that is required for the R&D credit.

The IRS requested that the court dismiss the Harpers' action in a motion for partial summary judgment.

Issues. The issue in this case is whether HCC's construction designs meet the definition of "business components" under §41(d)(1)(2)(B).

Analysis. The court analyzed whether HCC's construction designs meet the definition of "business components" under §41(d)(1)(2)(B). The court considered HCC's projects' unique aspects, such as a particular location, client need, and set of specifications, as well as regulatory and environmental constraints.

HCC argued that their construction designs qualified for the R&D credit because the company conducted extensive R&D activities. The company claimed that it engaged in a process of continuous improvement and used feedback from its clients and employees to enhance its designs and its construction processes. HCC also pointed out that it faced unique challenges in its work, such as environmental regulations and the need to comply with stringent military specifications.

The case ultimately came down to whether HCC's construction designs met the definition of "business components" under §41(d)(1)(2)(B). The court's analysis focused on the specifics of HCC's projects and the activities and services the company engaged in during preconstruction, construction, design/development, and postconstruction phases. The IRS contended that the HCC activities did not qualify for the R&D credit for the following four reasons.

1. HCC's designs were not "new or improved."
2. HCC did not produce a product.
3. HCC did not own the buildings it constructed for the U.S. military but instead built them on government land.
4. HCC did not use the designs in the way intended for the R&D credit.

Regarding the four points raised by the IRS, the tax court found the following.

1. HCC engaged in a long process of conceptual design that is useful for a new or improved business component.
2. The court agreed that HCC did not produce a product but found that its designs still were qualified processes, regardless.
3. HCC developed processes, techniques, and potential inventions that satisfied the business component requirement, even if it did not produce products.
4. The case record clearly contradicted the IRS's claim that HCC did not "use" the business components in a meaningful way.

The court ultimately concluded that HCC's construction designs meet the definition of "business components" under §41(d)(1)(2)(B).

Holding. The court denied the IRS's motion for partial summary judgment and supported the Harpers' claim that they were entitled to the R&D credit.

Index and Additional Information

The 2023 *University of Illinois Federal Tax Workbook* is a single volume, unlike prior years. Page numbers referenced in the index no longer have an A or B prefix.

If you need additional copies of workbooks, please visit our website at **TaxSchool.illinois.edu.**

Citation Index

COURT CASES

REGULATIONS

Treasury Regulations

Temporary Treasury Regulations

Proposed Treasury Regulations

REVENUE RULINGS

REVENUE PROCEDURES

OTHER IRS RELEASES

Chief Counsel Advice

IRS Letter Rulings

IRS News Releases

IRS Notices

Treasury Decisions

IRS Publications

IRS Forms

IRS Schedules

Alphabetical Index

NUMBERS

A

B

C

D

E

F

G

H

I

J

K

L

M

N

O

P

Q

R

S

T

U

V

W

Z

Acronyms and Abbreviations

2FA	Two-factor authentication
ACRS	Accelerated cost recovery system
ADS	Alternative depreciation system
AFR	Applicable federal rate
AFS	Applicable financial statement
AFSI	Adjusted financial statement income
AGI	Adjusted gross income
AICPA	American Institute of Certified Public Accountants
AMT	Alternative minimum tax
AMTI	Alternative minimum taxable income
AOC	American Opportunity Credit
AOD	Action on Decision
AOGI	Adjusted ordinary gross income
AQEE	Adjusted qualified education expense
ARPA	American Rescue Plan Act of 2021
ASC	Accounting Standards Codification
ASED	Assessment Statute Expiration Date
ATG	Audit Technique Guide
BAR	Betterment, adaptation, or restoration
BSA	Bank Secrecy Act
BSO	Business Services Online
CAF	Centralized Authorization File
CARES	Coronavirus Aid, Relief, and Economic Stimulus
CCA	Chief Counsel Advice
CCM	Completed contract method
CD	Certificate of deposit
CDC	Centers for Disease Control and Prevention
CDP	Collection due process
CEO	Chief executive officer
CFR	Code of Federal Regulations
CISA	Cybersecurity and Infrastructure Security Agency
COGS	Cost of goods sold
CPA	Certified public accountant
CRAT	Charitable remainder annuity trust
CRP	Conservation Reserve Program
CRUT	Charitable remainder unitrust
CSED	Collection Statute Expiration Date
CSS	College Scholarship Service
DB	Designated beneficiary
DCN	Designated change number
DISC	Domestic International Sales Corporation
DNI	Distributable net income
DRD	Deduction in respect of a decedent
DRO	Deficit restoration obligation
DSC	Data security coordinator
DSUE	Deceased spouse unused exclusion
EA	Enrolled agent
EDB	Eligible designated beneficiary
EFIN	Electronic filing identification number
EIC	Earned income credit
EIN	Employer identification number
EPCM	Exempt-contract percentage of completion method
ERC	Employee retention credit
ERISA	Employee Retirement Income Security Act
ERPA	Enrolled retirement plan agent
ESA	Educational savings account
ESBT	Electing small business trust
EV	Electric vehicle
FAI	Fiduciary accounting income
FASB	Financial Accounting Standards Board
FAFSA	Free Application for Federal Student Aid
FBAR	Report of Foreign Bank and Financial Accounts
FBFM	Illinois Farm Business Farm Management

FCV	Fuel cell vehicle
FEIN	Federal employer identification number
FICA	Federal Insurance Contributions Act
FIFO	First-in, first-out
FinCEN	Financial Crimes Enforcement Network
FLSA	Fair Labor Standards Act
FMV	Fair market value
FPAA	Final partnership administrative adjustment
FSA	Federal Student Aid
FSA	Field Service Advice
FTB	Franchise Tax Board
FTC	Federal Trade Commission
FUTA	Federal Unemployment Tax Act
GAA	General asset account
GAAP	Generally accepted accounting principles
GCM	General Counsel Memorandum
GDS	General depreciation system
GLAM	General Legal Advice Memo
GLBA	Gramm-Leach-Bliley Act
GST	Generation-skipping transfer
GVW	Gross vehicle weight
HoH	Head of household
HRA	Health reimbursements arrangement
HSA	Health savings account
HVAC	Heating, ventilating, and cooling system
IAF	Income apportionment formula
IDGT	Intentionally defective grantor trust
IDOR	Illinois Department of Revenue
ILM	Internal Legal Memorandum
IRA	Individual retirement arrangement
IRB	Internal Revenue Bulletin
IRC	Internal Revenue Code
IRD	Income in respect of a decedent
IRMAA	Income-related monthly adjustment amount
IRS	Internal Revenue Service
IT	Information technology
ITC	Investment tax credit
LGM	Litigation Guideline Memorandum
LIFO	Last-in, first-out
LLC	Limited liability company
LLP	Limited liability partnership
LTCG	Long-term capital gain
MACRS	Modified accelerated cost recovery system
MAGI	Modified adjusted gross income
MeF	Modernized e-File
MFJ	Married filing jointly
MFS	Married filing separately
MMLLC	Multi-member limited liability company
MSRP	Manufacturer-suggested retail price
MSSP	Market Segment Specialization Program
NAEA	National Association of Enrolled Agents
NATP	National Association of Tax Professionals
NFT	Non-fungible token
NII	Net investment income
NIIT	Net investment income tax
NIMS	Nonincidental materials and supplies
NOL	Net operating loss
NRCS	National Resources Conservation Service
OIC	Offer in compromise
OPR	Office of Professional Responsibility
OS	Operating system
PCI	Payment card industry
PCCM	Percentage-of-completion/capitalized-cost method
PCM	Percentage-of-completion method
PHC	Personal holding company
PII	Personally identifiable information
PIN	Personal identification number
PIO	Public information officer
POA	Power of attorney
POD	Payable on death

PPA	Power purchase agreement
PPP	Paycheck Protection Program
PTC	Production tax credit
PTE	Pass-through entity
PTIN	Preparer tax identification number
QBI	Qualified business income
QBID	Qualified business income deduction
QBL	Qualified business loss
QIO	Qualified income offset
QIP	Qualified improvement property
QRE	Qualified research expense
QRT	Qualified revocable trust
QTP	Qualified tuition program
R&D	Research and development
R&E	Research and experimentation
RA	Revenue agent
RBD	Required beginning date
RCP	Reasonable collection probability
RDP	Remote desktop protocol
RMD	Required minimum distribution
ROTC	Reserve Officers' Training Corps
RPO	Return preparer office
RSED	Refund Statute Expiration Date
RTRP	Registered tax return preparer
SAF	Sustainable aviation fuel
SALT	State and local taxes
SBA	Small Business Administration
SCA	Service Center Advice
SE	Self-employment
SEC	Securities and Exchange Commission
SECA	Self-Employment Contributions Act
SECURE	Setting Every Community Up for Retirement Enhancement Act
SEP	Simplified employee pension
SIMPLE	Savings incentive match plan for employees
SMS	Short message service
SO	Settlement officer
SPIA	Single premium immediate annuity
SSA	Social Security Administration
SSCA	Significant Service Center Advice
SSL	Secure sockets layer
SSN	Social security number
SSNVS	Social Security Number Verification Service
SUV	Sports utility vehicle
TAM	Technical Advice Memorandum
TCJA	Tax Cuts and Jobs Act of 2017
TD	Treasury Decision
TFA	Taxpayer First Act
TIA	Tax information authorization
TIN	Tax identification number
TOD	Transfer on death
UOP	Unit of property
URL	Uniform resource locator
UPS	United Postal Service
USB	Universal serial bus
USCIS	United States Citizenship and Immigration Services
USDA	United States Department of Agriculture
VCSP	Voluntary classification settlement program
VIN	Vehicle identification number
VPN	Virtual private network
WISP	Written information security plan
ZERH	Zero Energy Ready Home

Quick Tips for Deciphering Citations

When reading cases and other legal materials, you will often encounter citations to other materials. While it may look overwhelming, it is really quite simple with the help of these tips.

Some examples of the types of citations you might see:

- Statute: **7 USC 1308** or **7 USC §1308**
- Case: ***Bush v. Gore,*** **121 S.Ct. 525 (2000)**

Here are some tips for finding these types of citations:

- To determine what the abbreviation stands for, please reference the following table:

Abbreviation	Meaning
USC	United States Code
CFR	Code of Federal Regulations
AFTR	American Federal Tax Reporter
U.S. or **S.Ct.**	U.S. Supreme Court Reporter
F.2d or **F.3d**	Federal Reporter (Circuit Court of Appeals Opinions)
Fed.Appx.	Federal Appendix (Circuit Court Rulings)
F.Supp or **F.Supp.2d**	Federal Supplement (U.S. District Courts)
TC	U.S. Tax Court (Opinions)
TC Memo	U.S. Tax Court (Memorandum opinions)
TC Summ. Op.	U.S. Tax Court Summary Opinion
Fed.Cl. or **Cl.Ct.**	U.S. Court of Federal Claims
Bankr. or **B.R.**	Bankruptcy Court Reports
Aff'd	Decision affirmed by appellate court
Rev'd	Decision overturned by appellate court
Cert. denied	Appeal refused by U.S. Supreme Court

- The **number preceding** the abbreviation is:
  - Case: volume number
  - Statute: title number
- The **number following** the abbreviation is:
  - Case: page number where case or law review article starts
  - Statute: section number (may include a § symbol)
- Often, the **date** of the article or case decision is included in parentheses.

Using the examples above, they break down as follows:

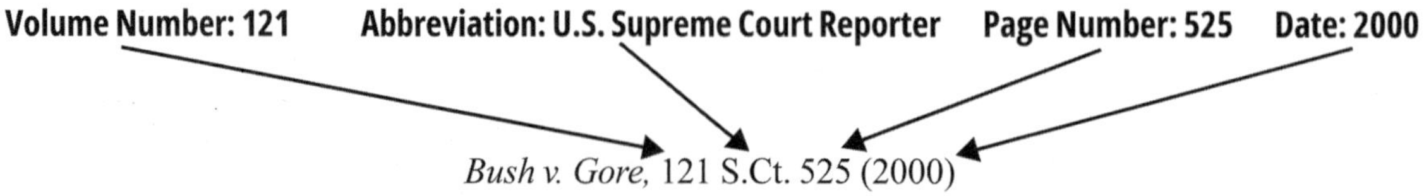